Juniper Networks® Routers:
The Complete Reference

About the Authors

Sean Christensen is a Professional Services Consultant with Juniper Networks. He has been working with various network technologies for the last 15 years and has a wide range of interests including electronics, programming, guitar, and hang gliding.

Avram Dorfman has a Master of Science in Computer Science from Tufts University. He began his internetworking career in 1994 in the U.S. Air Force, as a member of USAF headquarters' network configuration management branch. There he helped bring BGP to the Pentagon. He went on to conceive and build the Pentagon's Network Performance Management branch. He concluded his Air Force career with the rank of Captain, as chief of the Pentagon's Network Operations branch. Presently, Avram is a Professional Services Consultant with Juniper Networks. Avram lives in Newport, Rhode Island.

Jeff Doyle is a Professional Services Consultant with Juniper Networks and has assisted in the design and deployment of large-scale service provider networks throughout North America, Europe, and Japan. Jeff is the author of *CCIE Professional Development: Routing TCP/IP*, Volumes I and II.

Hannes Gredler is a Professional Services Engineer at Juniper Networks, where he deploys and advises for numerous carriers and ISPs running the IS-IS protocol in their core backbones including Deutsche Telekom, Vodafone/Arcor, Lambdanet, and others. He has been in the telecom industry for five years and holds a master's degree in Manufacturing & Automation from the Technical University of Graz (Austria). In addition to his engagement at Juniper Networks, Hannes is actively involved in open-source developments of the IS-IS protocol, where he contributed large parts of the IS-IS decoding engine for *tcpdump* **http://www.tcpdump.org/** and *Etherreal* **http://www.ethereal.com** as well as coding parts of *isisd* **http://sourceforge.net/projects/isisd/**, an open source implementation of the IS-IS routing protocol. Hannes currently lives near Innsbruck, Austria. He is married and has two daughters.

E. Gary Hauser Jr., JNCIE #12 and CCIE #4489, currently lives in Sunnyvale, California. He has been a Senior Education Engineer/JNCIE Examination Proctor/Course Developer for Juniper Networks for the past eleven and a half years, where he has specialized in the development of COS/QOS-related materials for instructional purposes. Previous to that, he was a Senior Instructor with Chesapeake Computer Consultants, Inc., where he was a primary Contract Instructor for the Cisco internal engineers in the San Jose headquarters of Cisco Systems, Inc. He specialized in Core Routing, Cable, DSL, and dial remote access platforms education. His ISP-related experience began with SURAnet, Inc., in College Park, Maryland, in 1991. He began his career in networking in 1986 installing enterprise Unix and Novell systems.

Tony Hill is a Professional Services Consultant for Juniper Networks. Tony consults directly with customers on the design and implementation of large-scale IP networks and has worked with implementing MPLS in commercial environments since 1998. Tony holds CCIE #3399.

Steven D. Holman, CCIE #3957, is a Professional Services Consultant for Juniper Networks, where he designs and implements large-scale ISP networks in the U.S. and Europe. Before he joined Juniper Networks, Steven was a Senior Network System Consultant for International Network Services, where he designed and implemented large scale networks in both the U.S. and Europe.

Matt Kolon is a Technical Marketing Manager for Juniper Networks, where he manages the Marketing Engineering group that produces technical and application notes on Juniper Networks technology. Prior to that, he was a Senior Member of Technical Staff with Hill Associates, a consulting and education firm. He is the author of numerous articles in networking magazines and coauthor of *IP Telephony* (McGraw-Hill, 1991).

Julian Lucek, JNCIE #21, graduated from Cambridge University with an M.A. in Physics. He joined the Photonics Research Department at BT where he co-built the world's first all-optical regenerator and gained a Ph.D. in ultrahigh-speed optical data transmission and processing. He then moved into the IP field and carried out detailed evaluations of new routing platforms from several vendors. In 1999, Julian joined the Professional Services group at Juniper Networks where he works with major service providers on the design and implementation of their networks, including large-scale MPLS rollouts.

Peter J Moyer, JNCIE #2, is a Professional Services Consulting Manager for Juniper Networks. Peter manages a team of IP consultants and also consults directly with customers on the design and implementation of large-scale IP networks. Peter holds a Bachelor of Science degree in Computer and Information Science from the University of Maryland and also holds CCIE #3286.

Galina Diker Pildush, JNCIE #18 and CCIE #3176, is the Education Services Engineer at Juniper Networks. After earning her M.Sc. in Computer Science, she worked for 13 years for major world-wide corporations in the areas of internetwork design, architecture, network optimization, implementation, and project management. She has been an academic teacher at York University, teaching computer science, data communications, and computer network courses. Prior to joining Juniper Networks, Galina was in charge of the Netgun Academy program for Global Knowledge, mentoring students for their CCIE preparations. Deploying her passion for teaching, Galina teaches a variety of Juniper courses. Her areas of interest and specialization are wireless, ATM, internetwork design and optimization, and Voice over IP. Galina's recent publications include *Cisco ATM Solutions* from Cisco Press. In addition to her demanding professional work, Galina, her husband, their two children, and their dog, who is a Canadian Champion, enjoy spending time together traveling, skiing, and cycling.

Harry Reynolds, JNCIE #3 and CCIE #4977, is a senior Education Services Engineer for Juniper Networks and has over 15 years of experience in data communication and networking technologies. Harry has developed and presented hands-on networking classes for companies such as Micom Systems, Hill Associates, and The American Institute, and has authored articles on T1 troubleshooting for *Business Communications Review.* Before entering into the realm of networking, Harry served in the U.S. Navy as an Anti-Submarine Warfare Technician (AX).

Scott F. Robohn is a JTAC Premier Account Engineer at Juniper Networks. He is JNCIE #25 and a Juniper Networks Authorized Trainer. In the past, Scott was a certified instructor for Cisco Systems and FORE Systems, and has enjoyed various roles in network design, analysis, and support.

Jason Rogan is a Senior Engineer with Juniper Networks in Sunnyvale, California. He is a Juniper Networks Certified Internet Expert (JNCIE #0008) and a Juniper Networks Authorized Trainer.

Joseph M. Soricelli is an Education Services Engineer at Juniper Networks. He is a Juniper Networks Certified Internet Engineer (#14), a Juniper Networks Authorized Trainer, and a Cisco Certified Internet Expert (#4803). He has worked with and trained numerous carriers and ISPs in the Internet. Having been in the networking industry for eight years, he has developed and taught a number of internetworking courses.

Thomas E. Van Meter is a trainer in the Education Services department for Juniper Networks. He has a B.S. from the U.S. Military Academy and an M.S. in Telecommunications and Computers from George Washington University. He was formerly a trainer and consultant with both Chesapeake Computer Consultants, Inc., and Automation Research Systems, Ltd. He served in the U.S. Army for 10 years, mostly in Infantry units, but his brief stint working as an automation officer and with Satellite Data Communications started him down the Internet routing path. He currently teaches as a member of the adjunct faculty in the George Mason University M.S. in Telecommunications program. He is JNCIE #34 and CCIE #1769.

Todd M. Warble is a senior instructor and regional manager for Juniper Networks Education Services and has been delivering courses on the M-series routers since July of 2000. Todd is JNCIE #7 and also performs grading of the practical exam, as well as development of the written test.

Juniper Networks® Routers:
The Complete Reference

Edited by Jeff Doyle and Matt Kolon

with Sean Christensen, Avram G. Dorfman, Jeff Doyle,
Hannes Gredler, E. Gary Hauser Jr., Tony Hill,
Steven D. Holman, Matt Kolon, Julian K. Lucek,
Peter J. Moyer, Galina Diker Pildush, Harry Reynolds,
Scott F. Robohn, Jason Rogan, Joseph M. Soricelli,
Thomas E. Van Meter, Todd M. Warble

McGraw-Hill/Osborne
New York   Chicago   San Francisco
Lisbon   London   Madrid   Mexico City
Milan   New Delhi   San Juan
Seoul   Singapore   Sydney   Toronto

McGraw-Hill/Osborne
2600 Tenth Street
Berkeley, California 94710
U.S.A.

To arrange bulk purchase discounts for sales promotions, premiums, or fund-raisers, please contact **McGraw-Hill/**Osborne at the above address. For information on translations or book distributors outside the U.S.A., please see the International Contact Information page immediately following the index of this book.

Juniper Networks® Routers: The Complete Reference

1234567890 DOC DOC 0198765432

ISBN 0-07-219481-2

Publisher
Brandon A. Nordin

Vice President & Associate Publisher
Scott Rogers

Editorial Director
Tracy Dunkelberger

Project Editor
LeeAnn Pickrell

Acquisitions Coordinator
Alexander Corona

Copy Editors
Lisa Theobald
Laura Ryan

Proofreaders
Marian Selig
Stefany Otis

Indexer
James Minkin

Computer Designers
Lauren McCarthy, Tabitha M. Cagan

Illustrators
Richard Coda, Michael Mueller, Lyssa Wald

Series Design
Peter F. Hancik

This book was composed with Corel VENTURA ™ Publisher.

I would like to dedicate my chapter to my family—my wife, Ginger and my son, Alex. Also to my Mom, Dad, and Sister. Thank you for your support and your love.
—*Sean Christensen*

My chapter is dedicated first to my mom, who wishes I never got involved with it, but is always there when I need her anyway. It is dedicated second to Stacy, who brought me into internetworking in the Pentagon and has stayed with me every step of the way. (And no, Stacy is a guy).
—*Avram Dorfman*

My chapter is dedicated to Caroline, Hannah, and Lena, the three most important women in my life.
—*Hannes Gredler*

I would like to dedicate my work on this book to my very patient and tolerant wife-to-be Aishah and our two dogs, who never let me forget when I was way too involved in this project and ignoring them too much!
—*E. Gary Hauser Jr.*

I would like to dedicate my chapter to my life's love and companion, my Little Happiness, my wife Lynn whose cheerful nature never ceased to encourage me. I would also like to dedicate my chapter to my Mom, whose influence in motivating me stems back many years to the first time she told me she was proud of me. I still remember.
—*Steven Holman*

It is to her parents, husband, and kids—David and Joseph—that Galina is grateful for their faithful patience, support, and understanding. Thank you for believing that everything is possible!
—*Galina Pildush*

To my wife, Stephanie, and my children, Holly, Kelsey, Benjamin, and Samantha. You make all the hard work worth the effort.
—*Scott Robohn*

My chapter is dedicated to my Mother.
—*Jason Rogan*

Contents at a Glance

Contents

Acknowledgments

Thanks to Chris Summers, Tom Schenkl, Gerold Arheilger, and Peter Lundqvist for proofreading and providing useful feedback. Special thanks to Dave Katz who stayed a friendly and approachable guy despite being *the* authority for the IS-IS protocol and took time answering questions in great detail.

—Hannes Gredler

I would like to thank Phil Shafer of Juniper Networks Engineering for his time, patience, and valuable input, without which my chapter (or gopher) would not have been possible. I would also like to thank Jeff Doyle of Juniper Networks Professional Services for his insightful, encouraging, and ever helpful editorial advice. Though incredibly busy editing other chapters of this book, in addition to writing one of his own, Jeff was ever supportive of the rest of us fledgling yet aspiring authors.

—Steven Holman

I want to thank the following people for taking the time to do technical editing, reviews, and provide technical advice for my chapter: Josef Buchsteiner, Harry Reynolds, Douglas Marschke, and Paul Goyette. Their feedback has contributed tremendously to its success.

—Jason Rogan

I would like to thank my wife, Christine, whose patience and love has allowed me to pursue those things in my life that excite me. In addition, my family and friends have provided encouragement beyond words that have helped me reach this point in my life. Finally, for the numerous peers in the industry who selflessly shared their knowledge with a young kid with too many questions, I would not have achieved all that I have without your assistance. A hearty thanks to all!

—Joe Soricelli

I would like to thank my parents, Lloyd and Jane, and my two brothers, Lloyd Jr. and Sandy, for all their support. I would like to thank Matt for giving me a break in this business, as well as Jason and Harry for keeping me somewhat focused. I would also like to thank my good friends Hazel, Chris, and Dan for their many proofreads, even if they had no idea what they were reading sometimes. Finally, I want to thank all my good friends and excellent co-workers at Juniper.

—Todd Warble

Preface

From the introduction of the M40 router in 1998, Juniper Networks has risen to a
position of considerable leadership in the Internet router marketplace, a position
it has maintained through the introduction of multiple succeeding router models
and software releases. That leadership has been acquired in large part by offering a
product with best-in-class forwarding and routing performance, but also by providing
an alternative to the incumbent router vendor for sources of information about the
challenges that Internet Service Providers and other users of high-speed routers face,
and by providing solutions to these challenges. We offer this book in that same spirit:
providing solutions to those who seek a better way.

This book is intended to serve as a reference for networking professionals who wish
to learn about the operation and configuration of Juniper Networks M-series routers.
As you can see by the cover and title page, writing it has been a collaborative effort
involving a large team of people. Our mission has been to produce—in a relatively
short period of time—a single volume that could be used by both novices and experienced
router jockeys as an aid in the operational aspects of using Juniper Networks routers.

Because router operation is so closely linked with the routing protocols they
implement, we have also addressed the protocols in detail. This should obviate your
need to combine this book with other "background" books on individual protocols.
You will find excellent introductions as well to some of the ancillary protocols and

techniques that are becoming important to the core of the Internet, such as traffic engineering with MPLS and packet filtering for security.

The chapters of the book are arranged to educate you in these topics as though you were studying in a hands-on classroom. Therefore, we begin with the hardware and software components of the router platform, and proceed through the syntax of the user interface and components of system management to give you a foundation in the tools of the platform and their control and operation. Building upon this foundation, we next explore the control of traffic interfaces, protocol-independent routing issues, and the central role of routing policy control in controlling the distribution of routing information.

Our routing protocol coverage extends to those protocols implemented by Juniper Networks that are in common use in today's Internet: RIP, OSPF, IS-IS, and BGP. We close the book with chapters on MPLS and firewall filters.

One note on the title: "The Complete Reference" is something of a misnomer. At this stage of the Internet's growth, and with the rapid pace of hardware, software, and protocol development, to write a truly complete reference to any modern platform or operating system is an impossible task. To address this point, we have concentrated on the features that are most likely to be used by the majority of router professionals as they complete their day-to-day tasks.

The Complete Reference

Chapter 1

Hardware and Architecture

by Todd M. Warble

In an industry accustomed to routers that utilize monolithic code bases and general purpose CPUs, the Juniper Networks design team built a router that is capable of handling the demands of Internet backbone traffic; yet it is also able to precisely control traffic to a degree sufficient for cutting-edge applications. An innovative design approach, backed by some of the best engineers in the business, has provided the Internet world with a stable, line-rate router. By segmenting the functions of a router and attacking each function with a purpose-built, high-performance piece of machinery, Juniper Networks has redefined how routing is accomplished on the Internet.

Fundamental to Juniper Networks' router design is the idea that the functions of a router can be split into two distinct parts: one portion for handling routing and control operations and another for forwarding packets. By separating these two operations, the router hardware can be designed and optimized to perform each function well. This chapter concentrates on this hardware design approach and the architectural characteristics of Juniper Networks routers.

System Evolution

The various models of the Juniper Networks router are built consistently with respect to system architecture and software. Each product builds upon the foundation that the previous products have supported and proven, allowing a single coherent product line to be enhanced with every new generation of code and hardware. From the release of the M40 router in August 1998, the architecture of the Juniper Networks router has remained essentially the same.

The value of such a consistent approach across all platforms is enormous. By enabling software compatibility across all platforms, software upgrades and bug fixes are immediately available across the entire product line. Commonality in system hardware architecture allows new systems to be built on a proven foundation. New hardware upgrades are also available to the entire line of routers with minimal individual system concerns.

Router Functionality

The functions of a router can be split into two distinct areas. In essence, a router is required to handle general routing operations and forward packets.

The portion of the Juniper Networks router that is designed to handle the general routing operations is referred to as the *Routing Engine (RE)*. The RE is designed to handle all the routing protocols (Open Shortest Path First, OSPF; Intermediate System to Intermediate System, ISIS; Border Gateway Protocol, BGP; and so on), user interaction, system management, and OAM&P (Operations, Administration, Maintenance & Provisioning).

The second portion of the Juniper Networks router is referred to as the *Packet Forwarding Engine (PFE)* and is specifically designed to handle the forwarding of packets across the router. A representation of how the router is split into two distinct areas is shown in Figure 1-1.

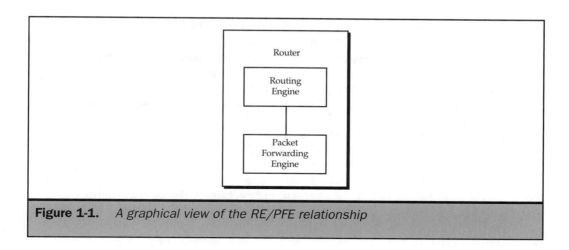

Figure 1-1.   *A graphical view of the RE/PFE relationship*

The fundamental philosophy of this "divide and conquer" architecture is prevalent throughout the Juniper Networks routers. Let's begin by taking a look at each portion of the router architecture.

Routing Engine

The RE is designed to be a robust, quick, PC-like host whose responsibility includes operation of routing protocols, troubleshooting and provisioning operations, and general management of the router. Its hardware consists of the following:

■ Intel Pentium-based compact Peripheral Component Interconnect (PCI) platform

■ Non-rotating compact flash drive (often called a RAM disk)

■ Standard rotating hard drive

■ Removable media drive

The JUNOS operating system software resides on the compact flash drive, with an alternate copy residing on the system hard drive. This is one of many reasons that Juniper Networks routers include a hard drive as part of the RE. As you will see in Chapter 2, the hard-drive copy serves as a backup copy of the operating system for disaster-recovery situations.

The RE is primarily responsible for the protocol intelligence of the router. It is therefore responsible for creating a *routing table*, which consists of all routes learned by all protocols running on the router. The RE parses the routing table to generate a subset of routes that will be used for all forwarding purposes, placing them in the *forwarding table*. The forwarding table is in turn fed to the PFE so that proper decisions can be made for packet handling. As route updates come into the RE via the routing protocols, the PFE's forwarding table is incrementally updated.

The incremental update of route changes is important. Rather than flushing the entire forwarding table and then replacing it with the new one, the RE sends a simple add, delete, or modify message to update the forwarding table. When routing on the Internet, it is common to see routing tables that consist of 100,000 routes or more. If a single route were to disappear, it is obviously more simple to remove the single route.

The remaining functions performed by the RE revolve around user interaction. The RE is responsible for the *command-line interface (CLI)*, Simple Network Management Protocol (SNMP) management, and *craft interface* interaction. The CLI is a user's primary method for performing OAM&P functions; it is accessed via a keyboard and a telnet device, secured shell (SSH), or direct-console connection. SNMP is used to provide a snapshot of the router's current status. It is often combined with network management software that can track the overall health of an entire network. The craft interface is a series of light-emitting diodes (LEDs) and buttons that assist field technicians in troubleshooting. The craft interface will be discussed in detail later in this chapter in the section "The Craft Interface." The remaining features will be discussed in detail in Chapter 3.

For comparison purposes, Table 1-1 is provided to show the hardware components of the different platforms.

In comparison to the M40s manufactured before mid-2001, the rest of the M-series routers have been upgraded to improve processor speed, available memory, and the external storage drive. Such upgrades are necessary because as time goes on, the RE components that formed the basis of the original design are being replaced in standard inventory by faster and larger components. For situations in which it is necessary, a hardware upgrade is available for "original" M40s that will provide identical RE hardware components to the rest of the M-series.

	Upgraded M40 and Other M-Series Routers	Original M40
Processor	Intel Pentium 333MHz	Intel Pentium, 233MHz
Memory	768MB	256MB
Solid State Flash Storage	80MB	80MB
Rotating Storage	6.4GB	6.4GB
External Storage	PCMCIA drive	LS-120 drive

Table 1-1.   *Comparison of M-Series RE Components*

Packet Forwarding Engine

The second half of a Juniper Networks router is the PFE, the portion of the router that is specifically designed to forward packets. Due to the specific job functions that are required of the PFE (such as packet encapsulation and route lookup), general-purpose processors are not necessary or desired. By designing microchips, or *application specific integrated circuits* (ASICs) specifically for these forwarding functions, the entire packet forwarding process can be implemented in hardware. This design technique allows for a more robust, consistent, and efficient packet forwarding implementation. The PFE is therefore highly efficient hardware that is responsible for forwarding packets as quickly as possible. It is also capable of delivering wire-rate packet filtering, rate limiting, and accounting services with minimal impact on packet forwarding.

The PFE consists of four separate hardware components: *Physical Interface Cards* (PICs), *Flexible PIC Concentrators* (FPCs), the *midplane*, and a control board. Each component has its own ASIC or several that account for a single piece of the forwarding puzzle. Only when all four components are brought together can a packet be received on one port and forwarded out another. Let's take a look at each component individually.

Physical Interface Card

The PIC port is the interface connecting the router to physical transmission facilities. In other words, the PIC is where the network cable is plugged in. Located on each PIC is an ASIC that is designed to handle media-specific functions, such as encapsulation, checksums, and media-specific signaling. Separate ASICs have been designed for each media type supported by Juniper Networks. For example, an ASIC has been designed for Synchronous Optical Network (SONET) functions, for ATM functionality, and to handle Fast Ethernet operations. Figure 1-2 shows the PIC and associated ASIC.

On some router models, PICs are equipped with an ejector lever. These PICs are *hot-swappable*, which means that insertion and removal is accomplished without significantly affecting the operation of the rest of the router.

PICs for some earlier router models do not have ejector levers and require that the FPC be removed prior to PIC removal. While removal of this PIC will disrupt the operation of any ports on that particular FPC, the rest of the router's ports will continue to operate without significant disruption.

Flexible PIC Concentrator

From the simplest viewpoint, the FPC is a chassis card that houses multiple PICs (see Figure 1-3). Each FPC can hold between one and four PICs of any type (with the exception of certain OC-192 and OC-48 PIC/FPC combinations that exist for certain router models). For most models, the FPC also houses 128MB of buffer memory that is utilized for storing data as it traverses the router, as well as a specially designed ASIC. This ASIC will be described in detail in the "Packet Flow" section.

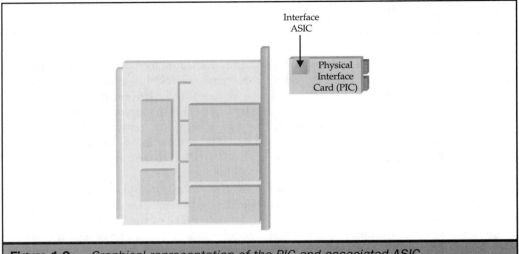

Figure 1-2. *Graphical representation of the PIC and associated ASIC*

A PowerPC 603e processor is located on every FPC. While this general-purpose processor has nothing to do with the forwarding of packets, the 603e is used for supervisory processes such as monitoring communication between the PFE ASICs and bringing up and taking down PFE components. It also monitors items such as the temperature sensors located on the FPC. This information is then relayed to the JUNOS software for proper processing.

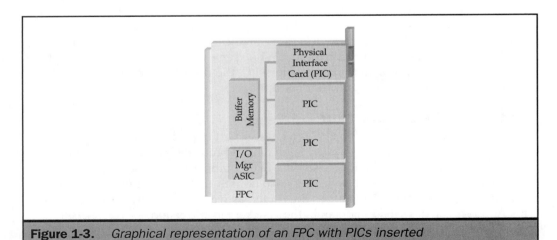

Figure 1-3. *Graphical representation of an FPC with PICs inserted*

FPCs are designed to be fully hot-swappable. To properly remove or insert an FPC from the system, the router must first be notified of this intention. On the craft-interface are online/offline buttons associated with each FPC. When a user wants to remove an FPC from an operational router, he/she simply presses the button for 3 seconds until the associated status light goes off. Once the status light goes off, it is safe to remove the FPC from the router.

To activate a currently installed FPC, the craft interface button must again be depressed for 3 seconds until the status light begins to flash green, indicating that the FPC is coming online. This procedure is necessary only in the case of an FPC that has been brought offline in the manner described in the preceding paragraphs; FPCs installed at boot time will come online automatically, as will newly installed FPCs. Again, the insertion or removal of any particular FPC will not significantly interrupt the operation of the router as a whole. The craft interface and all associated LEDs will be discussed in detail later in this chapter in the section "The Craft Interface."

Midplane

When the FPC is inserted into the router chassis, its electrical connectors make contact with mating connectors on the midplane. The midplane is nothing more than a passive connection between the FPCs and the control board that makes mechanical interconnection of the various components simple.

Control Board

The control board (which goes by different names, such as SCB, SSB, and SFM on the different router models) contains the central decision-maker for the PFE, the *Internet Processor II* ASIC (IP2). You will recall that the RE maintains a copy of the forwarding table on the PFE, which allows the IP2 to reference this information to properly route packets. The IP2, as well as some other important ASICs discussed in the "Packet Flow" section, is resident on the control board.

Having this centralized forwarding decision-maker has several inherent benefits. One key benefit is that all interfaces in the router will access the forwarding function in the same way, leading to consistent latency and jitter statistics.

The IP2 is also where firewall filtering operations are implemented. As you will see in Chapter 16, the IP2 contains a powerful filtering mechanism that allows the user to control IP traffic based on many characteristics. Since it is centrally located, a firewall filter can be implemented on any interface, flow, or traffic stream with the same level of performance.

In addition to the IP2 processor, the control board also contains a 603e PowerPC processor for supervisory functions. Again, this processor does not play any role in forwarding packets across the router. It is used for monitoring the environmental systems, maintaining communication between the RE and PFE, as well as managing the FPCs and all PFE ASICs. It is also responsible for loading and maintaining the forwarding table onto the IP2 and handling exception packets.

Now that you have examined all four components that comprise the PFE, you'll see how a packet traverses the router. This will also allow you to take a much closer look at the job responsibilities of the ASICs as well as how the components interact.

Packet Flow

Packet flow in the Juniper Networks M-series router is broken into components so that each stage of the router hardware has a specific job to do and is able to function efficiently. This section will discuss how the various router hardware components work together to provide the entire packet-forwarding picture. Here is an example in which we will follow a packet as it traverses a Juniper Networks router.

1. A packet arriving on a physical medium of some sort enters a PIC. That PIC contains a specially designed ASIC that will handle issues such as link layer errors and other physical layer issues. (See Figure 1-4.)

2. For this example, imagine that an L2 frame enters the router via a SONET link. The frame located in the media-specific header enters the PIC and has its SONET encapsulation removed. Then the stripped L2 frame is sent to the FPC.

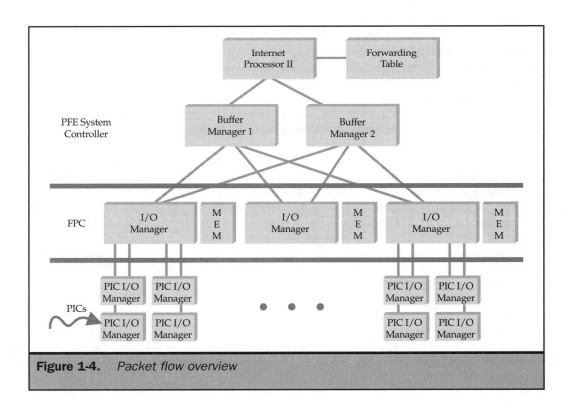

Figure 1-4.   *Packet flow overview*

3. When the packet leaves the PIC, it heads into the FPC as a Layer 2 PDU, such as a PPP or frame relay frame. The I/O Manager ASIC located on the FPC examines the L2 frame for errors and the CRC is recalculated. Any errors detected will be dealt with appropriately. Most likely, a packet with errors will be discarded and a notification will be sent to the JUNOS software to increment the interface's error counter.

4. After decapsulating the Layer 2 PDU and performing any necessary protocol functions for that layer, the I/O Manager ASIC chops the resulting packet (L3) into 64-byte chunks (called *jcells*) for efficient storage in memory. Memory for data storage is located on the router's installed FPCs, and all FPCs installed in the router contribute the greater part of their memory to a single pool that is used for this storage. This architecture insures that the router will never suffer from insufficient buffer memory to handle incoming packets.

5. The allotment of memory on each FPC has been chosen to be more than sufficient for any combination of four PICs inserted into the FPC. When more than four PICs are added to the router, a new FPC must be inserted, and hence additional memory is also added to handle the additional data load. The shared buffer memory located on each FPC is therefore mapped by the PFE to look like a single pool of memory.

6. Now that the I/O manager has divided up the incoming packet, the data is ready to be stored in the shared buffer memory until it is time to transmit. The 64-byte chunks coming from the I/O manager are passed to the buffer manager ASIC, which is located on the control board. The buffer manager is responsible for extracting the key information that is used for a proper forwarding decision. The buffer manager sends this "key cell" on to the IP2 for the route lookup. In the meantime, the buffer manager writes all the jcells (64-byte chunks) to the buffer memory slots in a round robin fashion, distributing the packet between the installed FPC's memory. (See Figure 1-5.)

7. Once the IP2 ASIC receives the key data, it references the forwarding table that it obtained from the RE. Based on this information, it determines the next-hop and outgoing interface information and stores this data in a result cell. The result cell is sent to the buffer manager ASIC. This ASIC then routes the notification to the appropriate FPC or, in the case of multicast, appropriate FPCs. (See Figure 1-6.)

8. A packet notification, a subset of the result cell, is then queued by the I/O manager ASIC until it is ready to be transmitted. When the packet notification reaches the front of the queue, the I/O manager notifies the buffer manager that the remainder of the packet is required. The buffer manager then reads the cells of the packet from the packet memory and assembles them. After the assembly, the L2/L3 header (re)write operation is done and the frame is streamed down to the outgoing PIC. (See Figure 1-7.)

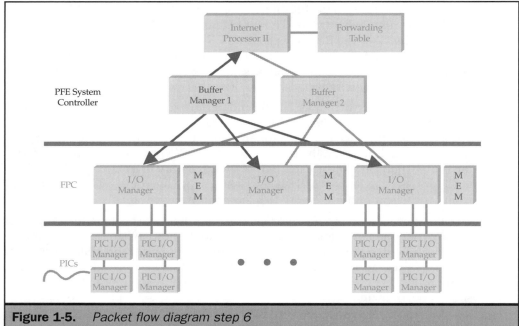

Figure 1-5. Packet flow diagram step 6

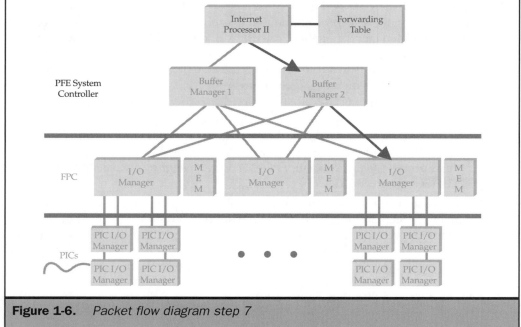

Figure 1-6. Packet flow diagram step 7

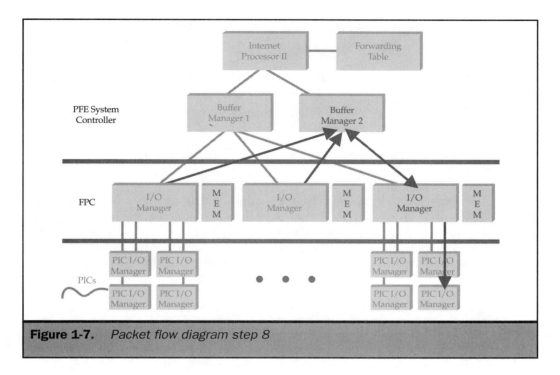

Figure 1-7.   *Packet flow diagram step 8*

9. In this fashion, the packet is reassembled on the fly as it is being transmitted onto the line. Given the shared memory architecture, the actual packet is written to and read from memory only once. This saves precious time by minimizing the number of memory reads and writes. Also, the ease with which the routers can now multicast traffic out of multiple ports at the same time is rather significant. When multiple ports are required to send a copy of the packet, multiple notifications are sent to the appropriate I/O manager ASIC(s), which can in turn send notification cells to each of the outgoing ports. When the packet is ready to be transmitted, the 64-byte chunks are simply read from the packet memory multiple times, once for each outgoing port.

Connecting the RE and PFE

The RE communicates with the PFE via a 100 Mbps Ethernet channel that is internally referenced as *fxp1*. Any data that requires a response or a logical decision outside the standard forwarding capability for the PFE is sent to the RE. These packets are referred to as *exception packets* and are flagged as such in the IP2. Once a packet is identified as an exception packet, it is sent to the PowerPC supervisory processor located on the control board for forwarding to the RE.

It is important that the fxp1 *interface never be manually configured on a production router. Any misconfiguration could cause the RE and the PFE to cease communicating.*

Two types of packets generally require attention by the RE: network control packets and local delivery packets. Some of the packets that would qualify as exception packets include these:

- Routing protocols
- Local delivery packets (such as a locally destined *ssh* session)
- Packets with IP options set, such as router alert

The *fxp1* connection is rate limited and uses flow control (queuing and per-protocol rate limits) to give priority to network control packets to ensure that the routing protocols receive priority over less important traffic. This is a form of built-in protection against denial of service (DoS) attacks, and at the same time it ensures that the router will attend to network control matters first. In other words, the router will attend to a BGP update message prior to answering a PING request if the two are in contention.

The Craft Interface

The craft interface lets you determine the status of the router by looking at the front of the box. The craft interface consists of status LEDs, online/offline buttons for FPCs, connectors for management communication with the router, and (on some models) an LCD display for system status messages. The following illustration shows the craft interface for the M160 router.

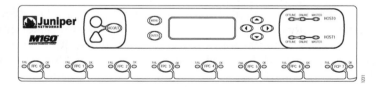

Maintaining Router Airflow

One of the most difficult challenges in high-performance electronic system design is keeping the device cool during operation. The components must maintain optimal operating temperature, even under the harshest of operating conditions.

The first step in controlling the operating environment is measuring its current state, which is accomplished via the numerous temperature sensors located on the router. These sensors provide data to the supervisory processors located on the

FPC, control board, and the Routing Engine. The current environmental status is reported to the JUNOS software so that the router can take any necessary actions.

Under normal operating conditions, recommended ambient room temperature of 32°F (0°C) through 104°F (40°C), the routers fans will operate at half speed. Once temperatures hit 129°F (54°C) all fans in the router are increased to full speed and a yellow alarm is generated. If the temperature should continue to increase to 167°F (75°C), the router will generate a red alarm and shut down the system.

To keep the system cool, the router chassis are equipped with high-powered fans and impellers. (The power supplies have their own dedicated fans.) Controlling the airflow for the rest of the chassis requires a push-and-pull system of fans working together. The half-rack routers (the M40 and M160) employ a bottom-to-top cooling method in which the air is sucked into the bottom front of the router and pushed out of the top back side of the router.

The air enters the router via an air filter that must be cleaned or replaced every 180 days. An associated yellow alarm condition will trigger by default every 180 days as a reminder to perform this action.

The smaller routers employ a side-to-side cooling system, employing either one or three sets of fans along the left side of the router.

Each of the field-replaceable units contains three high-powered fans that can direct air immediately across the entire PFE.

Using the Craft Interface

On the craft interface, two status LEDs are used for visual notification of red and yellow alarms. When a condition exists that triggers an alarm, the appropriate alarm notification is sent and the associated LED will glow. Each LED is also associated with a set of dry contact relays. These relays can trigger an external notification system, such as a siren or gong. To enable a sound event each time a red alarm occurs, hook the trigger leads for the gong to the dry contacts associated with the red alarm LED. POP technicians may hate the noise, but they will never miss a router alarm.

Also located on the craft interface are a series of buttons used to start or stop FPCs. Each FPC contains shared buffer memory. When a user wants to remove an FPC for maintenance, the system must be notified to gracefully remove the FPC memory from the system pool. This is accomplished by depressing the FPC's associated button on the craft interface for about 3 seconds.

The online/offline button is surrounded by two status LEDs of its own. A red LED to the left lights to indicate that the associated FPC is in failed status. This is a hardware error condition that indicates the router requires attention. On the right side of the FPC button is a green LED light that indicates the associated FPC is online and operating properly.

A set of three connectors is also located on the craft interface. These connectors allow out-of-band management for the router and provide a direct line into the Routing Engine. The connectors consist of a 10/100 Mbps RJ-45 Ethernet port, and two RS-232 connectors. One of the RS-232 connectors is designated as the console port and the second is the auxiliary console port. The console port is enabled by default with standard 9600-8-N-1 terminal settings, whereas the auxiliary console must be enabled via configuration to attach a modem or terminal device.

On the M160 and M40, you will find an LCD display that scrolls system status messages. The display shows items such as the router name and uptime. The LCD will also report the power supply status, fan speed, current temperature, and the current load on the router in packets per second.

Product Features

Each Juniper Networks router is built upon the same basic foundation. While the premise of using a dedicated PFE in conjunction with a physically separate RE for handling routing protocols remains consistent, each product is slightly different from its predecessors. This section examines the peculiarities of each box.

M40/M20

During initial product development, Juniper Networks' largest potential customers wanted a router that would provide line-rate performance on a stable platform, and they wanted it immediately. With this in mind, optional features such as redundancy and firewall capabilities were pushed aside to deliver the product to market in minimal time. The result was the half-rack sized M40.

The large carriers who wanted to deploy the M40 insisted that if they desired redundancy, they would deploy the routers in pairs. With this in mind, it is easy to understand why the M40 has no redundancy when it comes to hardware, with the exception of power supplies. Figure 1-8 shows the schematic of the M40 router.

The power supplies in an M40 can be either AC or DC (but not both simultaneously) and are fully redundant. While a single power supply can provide sufficient power for the entire router, if two are operating correctly, they will share the load. The DC power supplies have a maximum output of 1500W and an input current rating of 35A @ –48V. The input voltage can be in the range of –40 through –75VDC. The AC power supplies also run a maximum of 1500W and have an input current rating of 8A @ 208V. The acceptable input voltage range is from 180 to 264VAC.

The M40 has a single RE, a single board for PFE control, and can contain up to eight FPCs. The control board for the PFE is referred to as the *System Control Board (SCB)* and is located in the middle of the PFE. One significant difference between the M40 and the remaining product line is the fact that the distributed buffer manager ASIC's are located on the backplane of the M40 rather than on the control board as in the other router models.

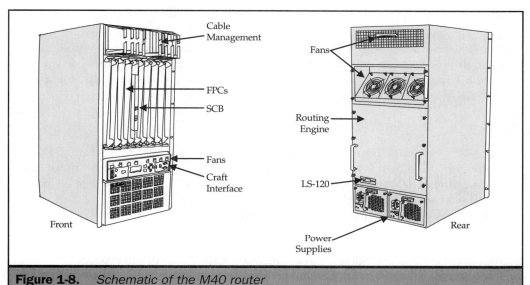

Figure 1-8. *Schematic of the M40 router*

The M20 platform was designed for greater port density and holds up to four FPCs in a chassis that is only 14-inches high. It also addresses concerns over redundancy. The router's schematic is shown in Figure 1-9.

The power supplies in an M20 can also be either AC or DC and are fully redundant. The DC power supplies have a maximum output of 750W and an input current rating of 24A @ –48V. The input voltage can be in the range of –40 through –72VDC. The AC power supplies also run a maximum of 750W and have an input current rating of 13A @ 90V. The acceptable input voltage range is from 90 to 264VAC.

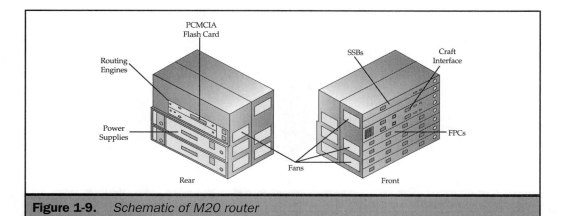

Figure 1-9. *Schematic of M20 router*

In the M20 platform the distributed buffer manager ASICs are moved from the backplane to the control board. This causes the control board to be renamed to the *System Switching Board (SSB)*. The M20 also implements full redundancy with dual REs and dual SSBs. Both the REs and the SSBs are redundant in that during normal operation, one is operational while the second is in standby mode. In the event of a failure, the second unit will assume control of the router.

M160

Like the M20, the M160 implements dual REs that provide failure redundancy. The PFE, however, is handled in a completely different manner. To quadruple the throughput of the M40, the M160 moved to a system that allows the forwarded traffic to be load balanced over several control boards.

The M160 implements four control boards that work in concert to handle the traffic transiting the router. The change in operation for the control board causes yet another name change to *Switching and Forwarding Module (SFM)*. In essence, each of the four SFM's does the job of a single SCB in an M40. Since the M160 FPCs have four times the throughput of the M40 platform, each SFM is effectively handling one quarter of the traffic on each FPC. Should one of the SFMs become inoperable, one quarter of the router's throughput would be lost, but it can still continue to forward packets at the reduced rate until the failed SFM is replaced. Figure 1-10 shows a block diagram of the M160 FPC.

When the serial stream of bits leaves the FPC, it must be directed to one of the four SFMs. To accomplish this, two *Packet Director (PD)* ASICs are utilized. The PD ASICs determine to which SFM to send the packet and direct the serial stream of bits to one of four I/O manager ASICs that have been installed on each FPC. Each I/O manager is assigned to a particular SFM and therefore directs packet chunks toward a designated control board.

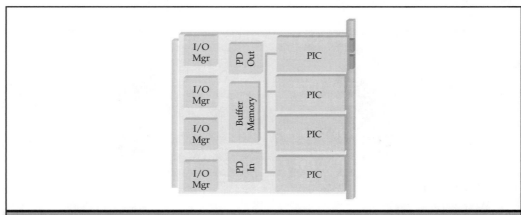

Figure 1-10.   *Block diagram of M160 FPC*

The M160 also improves on modularity in hardware, in part to make the replacement of failed parts easier, but mostly due to centralizing operation of common components found on the control board of other Juniper Networks routers. Because the M160 has four SFMs that work together, it is necessary to centralize operations such as internal clocking and system management. Figure 1-11 shows the schematic of the M160.

The *Miscellaneous Control System (MCS)* works in conjunction with the RE to monitor communications among the internal router components and to provide clocking for SONET interfaces. The MCS will monitor system components and sensors to gather information to send to the RE for processing. It will also handle the power-up cycle for components when the system is first started as well as the power-down sequence when the user requests that the unit be taken offline. The master MCS is hot-pluggable, and the backup MCS is hot swappable. In other words, the router does not need to be powered down when inserting/removing the master MCS, but the routing will be interrupted. The backup MCS can be inserted/removed without affecting the router operations.

The *PFE Clock Generator (PCG)* generates a clocking signal to synchronize the internal components. The PCG supplies a 125-MHz clock to modules of the PFE including the ASICs. The PCGs are also hot-pluggable.

Another key difference in the M160 architecture is the separation of the out-of-band management ports. The Ethernet and RS-232 connectors are located on a separate card on the left side of the FPCs.

This card is called the *Connector Interface Panel (CIP)*, shown in Figure 1-12, and is used for management connection to the M160s two REs. The upper set of connectors is

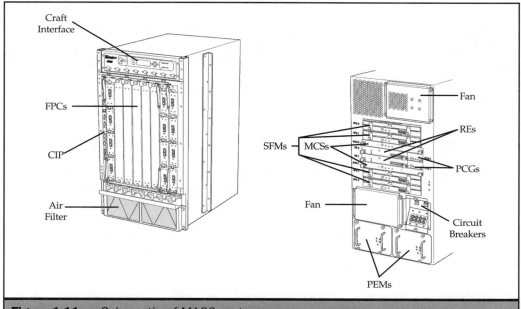

Figure 1-11. *Schematic of M160 router*

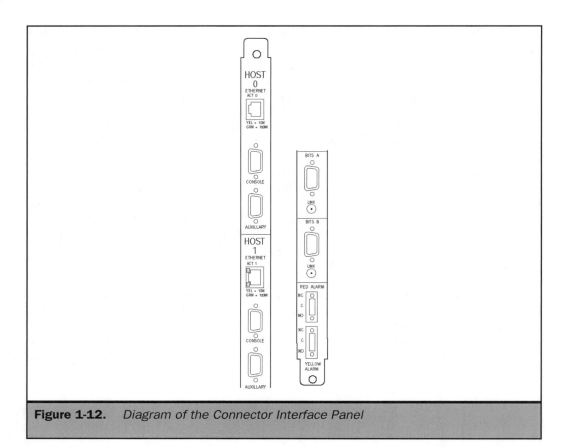

Figure 1-12.   *Diagram of the Connector Interface Panel*

labeled Host0 and connects directly to RE0. The second set of connectors labeled Host1 connect directly to RE1.

The final key differentiator for the M160 is the DC-only power supplies. Mostly due to the fact that AC power rectification produces a large amount of heat, the M160 does not offer AC power modules.

The DC power supplies are fully redundant, but in the case of the M160, two options exist for DC power. The original DC power supply provides a maximum output of 2600W with an input current rating of 65A @ –48V. The nominal DC input voltage should be in the range of –48 to –60VDC. The enhanced DC power supply provides slightly more power at 3200W max with a slightly higher input current rating of 80A @ –48V. The "enhanced" power supply is needed only in rare occasions when the M160 is loaded with numerous high draw cards.

M5/M10

Just as the M160 represents an increase in modularity and throughput, the M5 and M10 routers are reduced in size to increase port density. The loss of space causes the smaller routers to move, combine, and even remove certain components that exist in the other platforms.

When looking at the architecture of M5 and M10, the first thing that stands out is the lack of a distinguishable FPC. The FPC has been combined with the control board to form a single *Forwarding Engine Board (FEB)*, which allows for consolidation of the main PFE functions and saves valuable space. Figure 1-13 shows a diagram of the FEB.

The PICs used for an M5/10 router have their own ejector handle and can therefore be installed or removed without powering down the router. This is necessary since the PIC inserts directly into the router chassis. PIC offline/online buttons are located on the front of the router. Figure 1-14 shows a schematic of the M10.

Since the M5/10 have a single RE, only a single set of the Ethernet and RS-232 connectors are required for out-of-band management. The dry relay contacts are no longer present, and only the red and yellow alarm LEDs remain. Figure 1-15 shows a view of the craft interface.

The only aspect that externally differentiates the M5 from the M10 is the number of PICs that it can hold. The M5 router is capable of holding up to four PICs, while the M10 can consist of up to eight. Considering that both routers are only 5.25-inches high, this provides for outstanding port density.

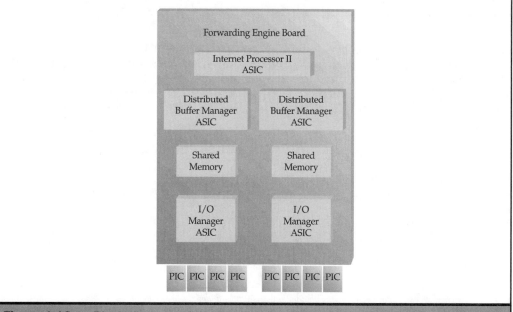

Figure 1-13.   *Block diagram of the Forwarding Engine Board*

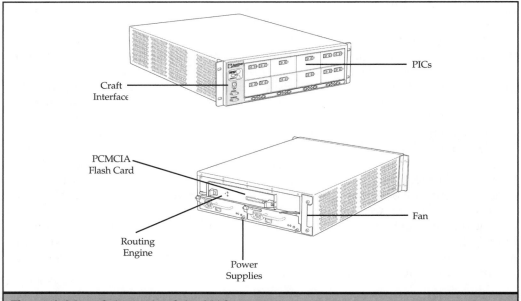

Figure 1-14. *Schematic of the M10 router*

Finally, the power supplies in the edge access routers are again available in both AC and DC and are fully redundant. The DC power supplies can provide up to 434W maximum output with an input current rating of 13.5A @ –48VDC. The acceptable input voltage range is from –42.5 through –72VDC. The AC power supplies also provide a maximum of 434W output with an input current rating of either 8A @ 100VAC, or 4A @ 240VAC.

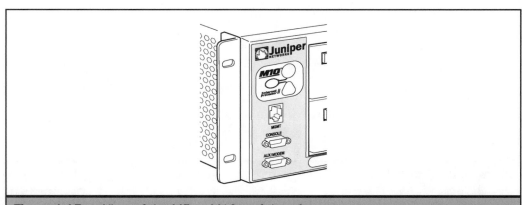

Figure 1-15. *View of the M5 or M10 craft interface*

Chapter 2

Juniper Software Design

by Scott F. Robohn

In Chapter 1, you learned about the specific hardware architecture of Juniper Networks routers. In this chapter, we'll examine some details regarding JUNOS software specifics, including

- JUNOS software architecture
- The JUNOS software file system
- Software mechanics (software components and upgrade procedures)

For readers familiar with UNIX, some details will look familiar. However, little or no knowledge of UNIX should not be a hindrance to understanding the information presented in this chapter.

Ensuring Performance with Juniper Networks Routers

It's clear that an operating system is needed to use a router. But what else does that router need, and what are the specific requirements of a router? These router requirements have resulted in *features* that are built into the *applications* that run on a router. These applications, their interactions, and their overall reliability are driven by how and where the router will be used and the characteristics of that operating environment. In this chapter, we'll focus on a substantial and challenging environment: the core of the Internet.

Divide and Conquer

We've seen that high system reliability and availability is crucial to a router that needs to operate continuously at consistently high loads. Juniper Networks routers use the concept of *divide-and-conquer* in several ways to achieve high performance and system availability. As discussed in Chapter 1, various pieces of hardware are dedicated to specific functions to achieve high packet-forwarding rates. Routing is performed by the Routing Engine (RE) and packet forwarding is performed by the Packet Forwarding Engine (PFE). In some router models, redundant hardware (for example, redundant REs and switching modules) is available to maintain operations in the event of a component failure.

A similar redundancy concept is used in the JUNOS software design. Certain RE software components can fail without bringing down the whole process and routing system. When a single process fails, the entire routing system does not necessarily fail (for example, if the routing process goes down, it can be brought back up without rebooting the entire system). In addition, a system management process in JUNOS software can attend to the crashed process and attempt to re-initialize the system, or start it back up.

The goal achieved by such redundancy is scalability, and increased reliability and availability.

At the Core: UNIX

UNIX serves as the base operating system (OS) for JUNOS software. The group of operating systems we know as UNIX has been developed from the beginning by a large community of software developers with diverse interests. The arrival of Linux in the 1990s captured a great deal of attention as a purely *open-source* effort, but the open-source approach goes back almost to the beginning of UNIX.

UNIX's community approach has fostered many desirable features, including the following:

- It has been ported to many different hardware platforms so as to impose fewer limitations on hardware selection. This assures flexibility in the selection of hardware platforms, allowing the development of code and hardware in parallel, and allowing the code and hardware to impact one another.

- A large development community is already familiar with UNIX variants, which means that even software developers without very specific experience can create robust operating systems.

Juniper Networks chose the FreeBSD (first Berkeley Standard Distribution; later Berkeley Software Design) implementation of UNIX for several reasons:

- It is *free* and does not involve complicated licensing or reselling agreements with multiple parties.

- It is *popular* (and therefore well-known) by many Internet Service Providers (ISPs) and people in the software development community.

- It leverages well-known features (such as file system structure, Transmission Control Protocol/Internet Protocol [TCP/IP], networking utilities, grep [UNIX's global regular expression print] and related functions, and piping output) and taps into the base of UNIX users.

- It runs on a standard PC platform, which makes code testing quick and relatively inexpensive, allowing testing and development of critical software components to commence before all (or any of) the hardware development was done.

- FreeBSD also allowed code and hardware to influence each other mutually and grow together. For example, as software was developed, it was easier to implement certain functions in the still-developing hardware.

Processes and Daemons

Most modern operating systems allow multiple user processes that accomplish specific functions and run concurrently. The same concepts apply to JUNOS software, which is a collection of smaller programs that are often referred to as *processes* or *daemons*. These processes are somewhat independent of one another, but certain processes may need to work together, depending on their respective functions. Interactions between these processes can occur—for example, interactions that prevent one process from failing when another goes down.

JUNOS Software Optimizations

Another important aspect of Juniper Networks routers' ability to offer scalability and high-performance routing are the optimizations found in JUNOS software. These optimizations involve the fact the UNIX operating system lies at the heart of JUNOS software. While the UNIX platform application is routing, other applications should not be running. Such installations may deem the router unsupported and can cause instability in the system. To avoid such problems, other hosts should be used to run nonrouting functions.

To ensure reliability of the routing system, modifications have been made to the base FreeBSD installation, including but not limited to the following:

- Nonessential TCP/IP services (such as server components) are turned off by default. File Transfer Protocol (FTP) (a hidden service), Telnet, finger, and secure shell (ssh) are configurable but are not active until configured.

- Some UNIX networking utilities, such as netstat, ifconfig, and traceroute, have been modified to handle issues such as interface naming conventions and other advanced protocol features (for example, Multi-Protocol Label Switching label values in traceroute).

- Many executables that are present in a standard distribution of FreeBSD are not present in JUNOS software's /bin and /usr/bin; for example, JUNOS software does not include Mail, banner, any C compiler, print utilities including lp/lpd/lpr, talk, and many other functions unrelated to routing.

- General de-emphasis on user, file system, and system management. JUNOS software contains mechanisms for performing all system management within the JUNOS software environment, rarely requiring that the user work at the UNIX prompt.

- Most important, new daemons, such as rpd, mgd, and chassisd, were added to accomplish the functions of first-class routers.

Juniper Networks Router Processes and Functions

Now it's time to discuss the details of the router processes. The processes running on the Juniper Networks RE implement all functions except packet forwarding.

Differentiation and distribution of functions across multiple software processes allow the system to recover from errors quickly—so, for example, if a process fails, it can be restarted without other processes (and their associated functionality) also being brought down (specifically, failure of the SNMP daemon does not impact the routing daemon or packet forwarding performance). Separate processes can also facilitate debugging, because as you debug, you can focus on a particular piece of the problem that appears to be the issue rather than having to debug the entire system. Figure 2-1 is a representation of the key processes supported by JUNOS software.

Table 2-1 lists several processes of JUNOS software and a summary of their functions.

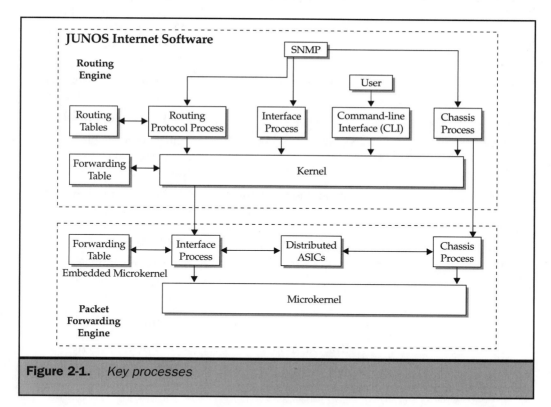

Figure 2-1.   *Key processes*

UNIX Process Name	Long Name	Functions
kernel	The Kernel	Process coordination and interface with hardware
init	Init Daemon	(Re)starts processes
watchdog	Watchdog Daemon	Manages RE failover
tnp processes	Trivial Network Protocol Daemon	Internal communications between RE, PFE, and other router components
dcd	Device Control Daemon	Physical interface management
chassid	Chassis Daemon	General chassis management (including PFE components, the chassis, and the environment)
alarmd	Alarm Daemon	Power, temperature, and other alarm management
craftd	Craft Daemon	Craft interface control
xntpd	Network Time Protocol Daemon	Time synchronization with external clock sources
mgd	Management Daemon	CLI implementation, sends commands from CLI to other JUNOS processes
snmpd	SNMP Daemon	External system management via the Simple Network Management Protocol (SNMP)
mib2d	MIB2 Daemon	MIB II management for SNMP

Table 2-1.   *Selected JUNOS Software Processes*

UNIX Process Name	Long Name	Functions
rpd	Routing Daemon	Implements routing protocols, MPLS, and routing policy; populates routing tables
apsd	APS Daemon	Manages SONET Automatic Protection Switching for link failover
vrrpd	VRRP Daemon	Implements the Virtual Router Redundancy Protocol
sampled	Sampling Daemon	Manages the collection and storage of transit traffic statistics
ilmid	ILMI Daemon	Implements the ATM Integrated Local Management Interface for PVC status info

Table 2-1.   *Selected JUNOS Software Processes* (continued)

The Kernel Process

The kernel is the base process that contains the modified FreeBSD kernel and selected JUNOS software enhancements. As in a UNIX system, the JUNOS kernel handles all basic system management functions and interacts with all other processes. These management functions include the following:

- **Memory management**   Protects software modules from each other and manages the memory space assigned to each process. To display memory and CPU usage, use the following script:

```
root@slippery> show task memory brief
Memory              Size (kB)  %Available  When
   Currently In Use:     1724         0%   now
   Maximum Ever Used:    1774         0%   01/10/28 22:45:32
   Available:          737223       100%   now
```

to show the buffer usage info/stats, you can type:

```
root@slippery> show system buffers
        658 mbufs in use:
        1 mbufs allocated to socket options
        1 mbufs allocated to socket send data
        400 mbufs allocated to pfe refill data
        256 mbufs allocated to fxp data (rx)
656/676 mbuf clusters in use
1516 Kbytes allocated to network (97% in use)
0 requests for memory denied
0 requests for memory delayed
0 calls to protocol drain routines
```

■ **Forwarding table**   Manages the forwarding table, including keeping the PFE's copy of the forwarding table synchronized with the master copy in the RE.

■ **Kernel Scheduler**   Causes the execution of processes in accordance with their relative priority. You can view the CPU load and the breakdown of process type by using the following script:

```
root@slippery> show chassis routing-engine
Routing Engine status:
  Slot 0:
    Current state                 Master
    Election priority             Master (default)
    Temperature                   30 degrees C / 86 degrees F
    DRAM                          768 Mbytes
    CPU utilization:
      User                         0 percent
      Background                   0 percent
      Kernel                       0 percent
      Interrupt                    0 percent
      Idle                        99 percent
    Serial ID                     70000004f8e98c01
    Start time                    2001-10-28 22:43:01 PST
    Uptime                        15 hours, 2 minutes, 28 seconds
    Load averages:                1 minute   5 minute  15 minute
                                    0.01        0.01       0.00
```

■ **Routing socket**   Provides a communication mechanism between the kernel and running processes.

■ **Various statistics**   Keeps track of various protocol statistics. For example, the following command shows the various system statistics that are tracked:

```
root@slippery> show system statistics ?
Possible completions:
   <[Enter]>            Execute this command
```

```
    arp                  Address Resolution Protocol
    clnl                 Connectionless Network Layer
    esis                 End System - Intermediate System
    icmp                 Internet Control Message Protocol
    icmp6                Internet Control Message Protocol version 6
    igmp                 Internet Gateway Management Protocol
    ip                   Internet Protocol
    ip6                  Internet Protocol version 6
    mpls                 MultiProtocol Label Switching
    rdp                  Reliable Datagram Protocol
    tcp                  Transmission Control Protocol
    tnp                  Trivial Network Protocol
    tudp                 Trivial User Datagram Protocol
    udp                  User Datagram Protocol
    |                    Pipe through a command
```

- **Device Drivers** Communicates with an external management network and the PFE using Ethernet device drivers, embedded in the kernel rather than being separate processes.

The init Process

The init process brings up all processes at boot time. It also restarts a process that terminates abnormally.

The following code listing shows how init automatically brings up a failed process. In this example, the sampling daemon is identified:

```
root@slippery> show system processes extensive |match sampled

  562 root       2  20  1872K  1148K select   0:00  0.00%  0.00% sampled
```

Then the sampling daemon is shut down by "brute force" with the restart command:

```
root@slippery> restart ?
Possible completions:
  class-of-service     Class of Service process
  gracefully           Gracefully restart the daemon
  immediately          Immediately restart (SIGKILL) the daemon
  interface-control    Interface process
  mib-process          SNMP MIB-II process
  remote-operations    Remote operations process
  routing              Routing protocol process
  sampling             Traffic sampling control process
```

```
snmp                    SNMP process
soft                    Soft reset (SIGHUP) the daemon




root@slippery> restart sampling
Traffic sampling control daemon started, pid 1019
```

Note *It is not recommended that you perform tasks such as restarting processes without the explicit direction of the Juniper Technical Assistance Center (JTAC).*

syslogd

The syslog Daemon reads and logs process messages into a set of files contained within the */var/log* directory. For example, if you create a syslog file and name it `catch-these-messages`, you can view the log file using the following command:

```
root@slippery> show log catch-these-messages
```

mgd and cli

The Management Daemon (mgd) is the user's primary tool for router configuration, operations, maintenance, administration, and provisioning. mgd spawns the command-line interface (CLI) process each time a user is logged in.

The cli daemon's job is to support the user interface and provide parsing ability and other user support.

rpd

The Routing Protocol Daemon (rpd) implements all the Juniper Networks–supported routing protocols, routing policy, MPLS forwarding, and many other routing-related functions. It is one of the most critical daemons in the system because it allows the system to function as a router. Other rpd functions include these:

- Initialization and operation of all configured routing protocols and handling of all routing messages.
- Maintenance of the routing tables that contain the routing information learned from all routing protocols.
- Maintenance of all other routes and MPLS tables.
- Determination of active routes from *inet.0* and installation of these routes into the RE's forwarding table. The PFE's forwarding table is automatically synchronized with the RE's forwarding table by the JUNOS software kernel.

■ Implementation of routing policy, which controls the distribution of routes between routing protocols and the modification of properties associated with routes.

The rpd subdivides its tasks and has its own scheduler to ensure that each protocol gets the amount of resources it needs and does not conflict with other routing processes. To see the task priorities within rpd, use the following:

```
root@slippery> show task summary
Pri Task Name                            Pro  Port So Flags
 10 IF
 13 RSVP                                  46 11
 15 INET6
 15 INET                                      9
 15 ISO
 15 Memory
 20 Aggregate
 20 RT
 30 ICMP                                   1 14
 30 Router-Advertisement
 30 ICMPv6                                58 10
 39 OSPF I/O                              89  8
 40 OSPF                                  89
 50 TED
 50 MPLS
 50 ASPaths
 60 KStat                                    13
 60 KRT Request                               5
 60 KRT                                  255  3
 60 Redirect
 60 Destination Class                         1
 70 MGMT.local                                       7
 70 MGMT_Listen./var/run/rpd_mgmt                   15 <Accept>
 70 SNMP Subagent./var/run/rpd_snmp               12
```

You can see how much memory each task uses with the following command:

```
root@slippery> show task memory detail
```

You can also view cumulative and maximum runtimes for each protocol with the JUNOS software task accounting function. Task accounting must be turned on with the following command:

```
root@slippery> set task accounting on/off
```

Accounting statistics may then be viewed:

```
root@slippery> show task accounting
Task accounting is enabled.

Task                        Started    User Time  System Time  Longest Run
Scheduler                        60      0.003        0.001        0.000
RSVP                             15      0.000        0.000        0.000
Memory                            1      0.000        0.000        0.000
OSPF I/O                          8      0.000        0.000        0.000
OSPF                             28      0.001        0.000        0.000
MPLS                              1      0.000        0.000        0.000
KRT                               2      0.000        0.000        0.000
MGMT_Listen./var/run/rpd_         1      0.000            0        0.000
```

dcd

The Device Control Daemon (dcd) is the interface control process. dcd handles configuration and control of the physical and logical interfaces. On the RE, dcd communicates with a "twin" dcd microkernel process on the PFE, giving the RE the correct status and condition of the router's interfaces.

snmpd

The Simple Network Management Protocol Daemon (snmpd) handles some optional network management functions on the router. JUNOS software supports Get, GetNext, GetBulk requests, and Traps but provides limited support for Set messages. You can view SNMP statistics with the following command:

```
root@slippery> show snmp statistics
SNMP statistics:
  Input:
    Packets: 497, Bad versions: 0, Bad community names: 0,
    Bad community uses: 0, ASN parse errors: 0,
    Too bigs: 0, No such names: 0, Bad values: 0,
    Read onlys: 0, General errors: 0,
    Total request varbinds: 497, Total set varbinds: 0,
    Get requests: 0, Get nexts: 497, Set requests: 0,
    Get responses: 0, Traps: 0,
    Silent drops: 0, Proxy drops 0
  Output:
    Packets: 501, Too bigs: 0, No such names: 0,
```

```
Bad values: 0, General errors: 0,
Get requests: 0, Get nexts: 0, Set requests: 0,
Get responses: 497, Traps: 4
```

mib2d

The Management Information Base (MIB) II Daemon (mib2d) manages access to MIB II objects. MIB II is specified in RFC 1213 and the "interfaces" group enhancements in RFC 1573, which define the objects that can be polled via SNMP when a network-attached device implements these RFCs.

ilmid

The Integrated Local Management Interface Daemon (ilmid) is used with Asynchronous Transfer Mode (ATM) interfaces. It is similar to frame relay's Local Management Interface (LMI) function, which is used to determine the up/down status of Permanent Virtual Connections (PVCs).

ilmi logs can be viewed by using the following command:

```
root@slippery> show log ilmid
```

vrrpd

The Virtual Router Redundancy Protocol Daemon (vrrpd) gives multiple Juniper routers on a single Ethernet and IP subnet the ability to listen and respond as a single IP address. VRRP is specified in RFC 2338.

vrrpd logs can be viewed by typing the following:

```
root@slippery> show log vrrpd
```

apsd

The Automatic Protection Switching Daemon (apsd) gives SONET interfaces the ability to fail over from one SONET port to another. You can use the following command to view the apsd log:

```
root@slippery> show log apsd
```

chassisd

The Chassis Daemon (chassisd) manages the router chassis' Flexible PIC Concentrators (FPCs) and environmental sensors. It also keeps track of the state of each chassis component by gathering that information from its twin process running on the PFE, giving the RE visibility into the status and condition of the router's chassis components. Restart of chassisd will cause restart of the PFE complex.

Chassis-related logs can been seen via the command

```
root@slippery> show log chassisd
```

Redundancy logs can be seen via the command

```
root@slippery> show log mastership
```

sampled

The Sampling Daemon (sampled) allows traffic sampling, which is used largely with firewall filters. It enables the collection of performance information about a network without examining every packet that passes through the router. Full use of the sampling capabilities of Juniper Networks routers is discussed in Chapter 16.

alarmd

The Alarm Daemon (alarmd) manages interface and chassis alarms. You can view current alarm conditions with the following command:

```
lab@hissy> show chassis alarms
1 alarm is currently active
Alarm time                Class Description
 2001-10-18 22:52:42 UTC Major PEM 0 Input Failure
```

Embedded JUNOS Software (PFE OS)

The *embedded OS* runs on the PFE components such as control boards and FPCs. The embedded OS was developed by Juniper Networks specifically for the hardware tasks it performs. It consists of a microkernel and threads.

The PFE microkernel is a small supervisory program comprising a simple thread scheduler and other basic OS functions. In addition, the microkernel receives the PFE forwarding table from the RE, converts it to a special format, and loads it on the Internet Processor II (IP2) so that the lookup engine can accomplish the packet-forwarding action and other value-added services, such as filtering, accounting, and rate-limiting, with a high performance.

Threads are similar to *processes* running on the RE. Threads have their own protected memory areas, and they are specialized on several functions. An example is the chassis manager thread, which is the peer of chassisd that specializes in chassis management.

Threads on the PFE communicate with the daemons or entities on RE with interprocess communication sockets.

The embedded OS is also responsible for the following:

- Generating certain messages: ICMP dest unreachable, TTL expired, and so on
- Rate limiting traffic destined to the router
- Sending the packets that pass rate limiting to the RE
- Exchanges control traffic with the RE

 Certain processes that are not configured may come up. For example, sampled, vrrpd, and apsd are up and active, even if sampling, VRRP, and SONET APS are not configured.

Routing Information Databases

As rpd is one of the most critical processes in JUNOS software, it needs to store routing information in several different databases on the RE. Link-state information from Open Shortest Path First (OSPF) and Intermediate System to Intermediate System (IS-IS) Protocol is stored in protocol-specific link-state databases. Route information produced from Shortest Path First (SPF) calculations and received via other routing protocols must be stored in the routing table. This table is called *inet.0.*

inet.0 holds all information about the next-hop addresses and/or interfaces for all reachable IP unicast prefixes learned by the active routing protocols on the router. This can include multiple next-hops for each prefix.

In most cases, there is one best way to reach each destination prefix. The Juniper Networks router architecture takes advantage of this by distilling from *inet.0* the least amount of routing information needed for packet-forwarding decisions and placing it in a separate database called the *Forwarding Table (FT)*. In the base case, the FT contains the single best next-hop for each reachable destination. The FT (not *inet.0*) is downloaded to the PFE for use by the Internet Processor application specific integrated circuit (ASIC). Because the FT is always smaller than *inet.0* (containing, as it does, only destination mappings to next-hops and little else), this allows the Internet Processor to sort through less routing information and make per-packet forwarding decisions more quickly.

Figure 2-2 shows the relationships between these databases and the processes and components that interact with them. The RE builds and maintains the FT (called the *master* FT) and then downloads a copy of the FT to the PFE. The kernel is responsible for copying the FT to the PFE. As routing updates insert new entries into *inet.0,* the kernel sends incremental updates to the PFE so as to not send too much information over the fxp1 interface. These update messages are `add`, `delete`, and `modify` commands containing the route and the next-hop.

Other routing and forwarding databases are maintained and will be discussed in later chapters.

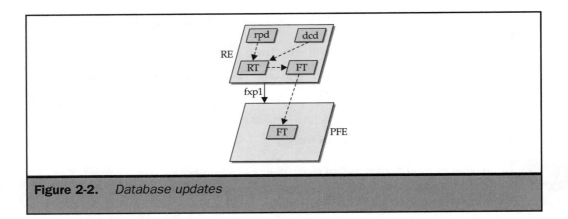

Figure 2-2.   *Database updates*

Boot Order and Process Interaction

The boot process can be thought of as a "rolling wave" of CPUs and ASICs coming on-line in a specific sequence. Component and process interaction is the key. In some models, more than 14 CPUs may boot in a specific order; they each get a copy of the jpfe package and need to interact with each other.

The general boot order of a Juniper Networks router follows:

1. The JUNOS kernel comes up first.

2. The kernel then downloads the PFE microkernel to the SCB/SSB/SFM, and so on.

3. Then various processes including dcd and chassisd come up.

4. The PFE initializes.

5. rpd comes up with all the locally configured routing protocols, which populates *inet.0*.

6. As *inet.0* is built, best routes are selected and placed in the master FT. The FT is downloaded to the PFE in the meantime.

Listing 2-1 shows the console output generated by a rebooting router. It shows the order in which hardware and software components are brought on-line. The listing contains comments regarding the events, listed after the output.

Listing 2-1
Boot
messages
seen by the
console

```
lab@Fiksdal> request system reboot
Reboot the system ? [yes,no] (no) yes


*** FINAL System shutdown message from root@Fiksdal ***
System going down IMMEDIATELY


shutdown: [pid 7813]
```

```
Shutdown NOW!

lab@Fiksdal> rdp retransmit error: Network is down (50)
rdp retransmit error: Network is down (50)
rdp retransmit error: Network is down (50)
rdp retransmit error: Network is down (50)
rdp retransmit error: Network is down (50)
rdp retransmit error: Network is down (50)
rdp retransmit error: Network is down (50)
rdp retransmit error: Network is down (50)
rdp retransmit error: Network is down (50)
rdp retransmit error: Network is down (50)
rdp retransmit error: Network is down (50)
rdp retransmit error: Network is down (50)
rdp retransmit error: Network is down (50)
rdp keepalive expired, connection dropped - src 0:1020 dest 2:48129
if_pfe_listener: soreceive() mute, error 64
Waiting (max 60 seconds) for system process `bufdaemon' to stop...stopped
Waiting (max 60 seconds) for system process `syncer' to stop...stopped

syncing disks...
done
Uptime: 8d6h11m24s
ata0: resetting devices .. done
Rebooting... ***1


Award Modular BIOS v4.51PG, An Energy Star Ally ***2
Copyright (C) 1984-98, Award Software, Inc.

TEKNOR APPLICOM INC. T1023 BIOS Version 0.9 'DWC'

03/14/2000-i440BX-SMC67X-2A69TU00C-00

PXE-M04: Initializing network boot device using interrupt 18h.....
PXE-M04: Initializing network boot device using interrupt 18h.....

Will try to boot from : ***3
PCMCIA ATA Flash Card...
Compact Flash...
Hard Disk...
Ethernet...

Trying to Boot from PCMCIA ATA Flash Card... ***4
Error: No Drive E...

Trying to Boot from Compact Flash... ***5
Console: serial port
BIOS drive A: is disk0
BIOS drive C: is disk1
BIOS drive D: is disk2
```

```
BIOS 639kB/785344kB available memory

FreeBSD/i386 bootstrap loader, Revision 0.8
(builder@fafnir.juniper.net, Tue Aug 14 23:05:22 GMT 2001)
Loading /boot/defaults/loader.conf
/kernel text=0x270c9a data=0x2b80c+0x2b5e8 syms=[0x4+0x33720+0x4+0x39ea0]

                    Loader Quick Help
                    -----------------
The boot order is PCMCIA or floppy -> Flash -> Disk -> Lan ->
back to PCMCIA or floppy. Typing reboot from the command prompt will
cycle through the boot devices. On some models, you can set the next
boot device using the nextboot command: nextboot compact-flash | disk

For more information, use the help command: help <topic> <subtopic>

Hit [Enter] to boot immediately, or any other key for command prompt.
Booting [kernel]...
Copyright (c) 1996-2001, Juniper Networks, Inc. ***6
All rights reserved.
Copyright (c) 1992-2001 The FreeBSD Project.
Copyright (c) 1979, 1980, 1983, 1986, 1988, 1989, 1991, 1992, 1993, 1994
        The Regents of the University of California. All rights reserved.
JUNOS 5.0R1.4 #0: 2001-08-14 23:14:13 UTC ***7
    builder@fafnir.juniper.net:/build/fafnir-b/5.0R1.4/src/sys/compile/JUNIPER
Timecounter "i8254"  frequency 1193182 Hz
CPU: Pentium II/Pentium II Xeon/Celeron (331.71-MHz 686-class CPU)
  Origin = "GenuineIntel"  Id = 0x66a  Stepping = 10
  Features=0x183f9ff<FPU,VME,DE,PSE,TSC,MSR,PAE,MCE,CX8,SEP,MTRR,PGE,MCA,CMOV,PA
T,PSE36,MMX,FXSR>
real memory  = 805240832 (786368K bytes)
sio0: gdb debugging port
avail memory = 779190272 (760928K bytes) ***8
Teknor CPU Card Recognized -- BIOS Version: 0.9
Preloaded elf kernel "kernel" at 0xc0438000.
DEVFS: ready for devices
Pentium Pro MTRR support enabled
md0: Malloc disk
npx0: <math processor> on motherboard
npx0: INT 16 interface
pcib0: <Intel 82443BX host to PCI bridge (AGP disabled)> on motherboard
pci0: <PCI bus> on pcib0 ***9
isab0: <Intel 82371AB PCI to ISA bridge> at device 7.0 on pci0
isa0: <ISA bus> on isab0
atapci0: <Intel PIIX4 ATA33 controller> port 0xf000-0xf00f at device 7.1 on pci0
ata0: at 0x1f0 irq 14 on atapci0
pci0: <Intel 82371AB/EB (PIIX4) USB controller> at 7.2 irq 11
smb0: <Intel 82371AB SMB controller> port 0x5000-0x500f at device 7.3 on pci0
pcic-pci0: <TI PCI-1251B PCI-CardBus Bridge> mem 0xe6205000-0xe6205fff irq 15 at
  device 13.0 on pci0
pcic-pci0: TI12XX PCI Config Reg: [pci only]
pcic-pci1: <TI PCI-1251B PCI-CardBus Bridge> mem 0xe6200000-0xe6200fff irq 7 at
  device 13.1 on pci0
```

```
pcic-pci1: TI12XX PCI Config Reg: [pci only]
fxp0: <Intel EtherExpress Pro 10/100B Ethernet> port 0xd800-0xd83f mem 0xe610000 ***10
0-0xe61fffff,0xe6204000-0xe6204fff irq 7 at device 16.0 on pci0
pcib1: <DEC 21150 PCI-PCI bridge> at device 17.0 on pci0
pci1: <PCI bus> on pcib1
fxp1: <Intel EtherExpress Pro 10/100B Ethernet> port 0xe000-0xe03f mem 0xe600000 ***11
0-0xe60fffff,0xe6207000-0xe6207fff irq 10 at device 19.0 on pci0
fdc0: direction bit not set
fdc0: cmd 3 failed at out byte 1 of 3
atkbdc0: <Keyboard controller (i8042)> at port 0x60,0x64 on isa0
vga0: <Generic ISA VGA> at port 0x3b0-0x3bb iomem 0xb0000-0xb7fff on isa0
sc0: <System console> at flags 0x100 on isa0
sc0: MDA <16 virtual consoles, flags=0x100>
pcic0: <VLSI 82C146> at port 0x3e0 iomem 0xd0000 irq 10 on isa0
pcic0: Polling mode
pccard0: <PC Card bus -- legacy version> on pcic0
pccard1: <PC Card bus -- legacy version> on pcic0
sio0 at port 0x3f8-0x3ff irq 4 flags 0x90 on isa0
sio0: type 16550A, console
sio1 at port 0x3e8-0x3ef irq 5 on isa0
sio1: type 16550A
sio2 at port 0x2f8-0x2ff irq 3 on isa0
sio2: type 16550A
sio3: configured irq 7 not in bitmap of probed irqs 0
fxp0: Ethernet address 00:a0:a5:12:27:d7
fxp1: Ethernet address 00:a0:a5:12:27:d6
DEVFS: ready to run
ad0: 91MB <SunDisk SDCFB-96> [734/8/32] at ata0-master using PIO1 ***12
ad1: 11513MB <IBM-DARA-212000> [23392/16/63] at ata0-slave using UDMA33
Mounting root from ufs:/dev/ad0s1a ***13
Mounted jbase package on /dev/vn1...
Mounted jcrypto package on /dev/vn2...
Mounted jdocs package on /dev/vn3...
Mounted jkernel package on /dev/vn4...
Mounted jpfe package on /dev/vn5...
Mounted jroute package on /dev/vn6...
swapon: adding /dev/ad1s1b as swap device
Automatic reboot in progress...
/dev/ad0s1a: FILESYSTEM CLEAN; SKIPPING CHECKS
/dev/ad0s1a: clean, 39200 free /dev/ad0s1e: FILESYSTEM CLEAN; SKIPPING CHECKS
/dev/ad0s1e: clean, 25256 free (16 frags, 4898 blocks, 0.0% fragmentation)
(8 frags, 3156 blocks, 0.0% fragmentation)
(16 frags, 4898 blocks, 0.0% fragmentation)
/dev/ad1s1f: FILESYSTEM CLEAN; SKIPPING CHECKS
/dev/ad1s1f: clean, 9670747 free (211 frags, 1208817 blocks, 0.0% fragmentation)
mgd: commit complete ***14
Setting initial options:  debugger_on_panic=NO debugger_on_break=NO.
Enable PC-card:PCCARD Memory address set to 0xd0000
.
Doing initial network setup:.
Initial interface configuration:
TNP: adding neighbor 4 to interface fxp1.
TNP: adding neighbor 4294967295 to interface fxp1.
```

```
additional daemons: syslogd.
checking for core dump...savecore: Router rebooting after a normal shutdown....
Additional routing options:.
Doing additional network setup:.
Starting final network daemons:. ***15
setting ldconfig path: /usr/lib
starting standard daemons: cron.
Initial rc.i386 initialization:.
rc.i386 configuring syscons:.
Local package initialization:.
starting local daemons:. ***16
Sun Sep 16 00:23:35 UTC 2001

Fiksdal (ttyd0) ***16

login:
```

Let's interpret the boot order (from the console output):

1. Request system reboot gracefully shuts down processes and filesystems.
2. Upon reboot, the machine basic input/output system (BIOS) must perform the most basic bootstrap functions.
3. Router displays the order in which it will try the boot sources.
4. If a PCMCIA card had been in the RE, it would have booted from there first. (Not true for warm reboot.)
5. It found the valid internal flash; the router boots from this source.
6. Kernel is booting up (FreeBSD and JUNOS copyright messages are displayed).
7. JUNOS version and compile information are displayed.
8. Memory (RAM) is made available to the RE for routing and other tables.
9. Discovers PCI bus and other devices.
10. The RE management port (fxp0) comes up.
11. The internal RE port to PFE (fxp1) comes up; other PFE interfaces don't come up until much later.
12. Discovers physical storage (disk and flash).
13. Discovers and mounts filesystems.
14. mgd has committed the last operational configuration file, making the configuration active.
15. rpd is up by now.
16. All remaining JUNOS processes are being brought up.
17. mgd prompts user to log in.

The default router configuration from the factory writes many of the boot messages to the file */var/log*/messages; this configuration information is listed below, and can be useful for troubleshooting when certain components of the router do not boot properly. The following section examines those messages in a slightly different manner. You can use the show system boot-messages command to view the boot log.

Process Boot Order

1. **Time 23:34**   The kernel comes up, issues boot messages (FreeBSD and JUNOS banners, CPU, memory, hardware discovery, and so on).

```
Sep 16 00:23:34 Fiksdal /kernel: Copyright (c) 1996-2001, Juniper Networks, Inc.
Sep 16 00:23:34 Fiksdal /kernel: All rights reserved.
Sep 16 00:23:34 Fiksdal /kernel: Copyright (c) 1992-2001 The FreeBSD Project.
Sep 16 00:23:34 Fiksdal /kernel: Copyright (c) 1979, 1980, 1983, 1986, 1988,
1989, 1991, 1992, 1993, 1994
Sep 16 00:23:34 Fiksdal /kernel: The Regents of the University of California. All rights reserved.
Sep 16 00:23:34 Fiksdal /kernel: JUNOS 5.0R1.4 #0: 2001-08-14 23:14:13 UTC
...
```

2. **Time 23:36**   The init process starts the following processes:

```
Sep 16 00:23:36 Fiksdal init: watchdog (PID 516) started
Sep 16 00:23:36 Fiksdal init: tnp-process (PID 517) started
Sep 16 00:23:36 Fiksdal init: interface-control (PID 518) started
Sep 16 00:23:36 Fiksdal init: chassis-control (PID 519) started
Sep 16 00:23:36 Fiksdal init: alarm-control (PID 521) started
Sep 16 00:23:36 Fiksdal init: craft-control (PID 522) started
Sep 16 00:23:36 Fiksdal init: ntp (PID 523) started
Sep 16 00:23:36 Fiksdal init: management (PID 524) started
Sep 16 00:23:36 Fiksdal init: snmp (PID 525) started
Sep 16 00:23:36 Fiksdal init: mib-process (PID 526) started
Sep 16 00:23:36 Fiksdal init: routing (PID 527) started
Sep 16 00:23:36 Fiksdal init: inet-process (PID 528) started
Sep 16 00:23:36 Fiksdal init: dhcp-relay (PID 529) started
Sep 16 00:23:36 Fiksdal init: sonet-aps (PID 530) started
Sep 16 00:23:36 Fiksdal init: vrrp (PID 531) started
Sep 16 00:23:36 Fiksdal init: sntp (PID 532) started
Sep 16 00:23:36 Fiksdal init: pfe (PID 533) started
Sep 16 00:23:36 Fiksdal init: sampling (PID 534) started
Sep 16 00:23:36 Fiksdal init: ilmi (PID 535) started
Sep 16 00:23:36 Fiksdal init: remote-operations (PID 536) started
```

Note that some processes come up even though they may not be explicitly configured (for example, snmp and vrrp).

3. **Time 23:38**   chassid starts to process internal interfaces.

```
Sep 16 00:23:38 Fiksdal chassisd[519]: CHASSISD_IFDEV_DETACH: ifdev_detach(0)
Sep 16 00:23:38 Fiksdal chassisd[519]: CHASSISD_IFDEV_DETACH: ifdev_detach(pseudodevices: all)
```

4. **Time 23:39**   snmpd sends a "cold start" message (for example, from a reboot).

```
Sep 16 00:23:39 Fiksdal snmpd[525]: SNMP_TRAP_COLD_START: SNMP trap: cold start
```

5. **Time 23:39**   rpd is prepared to process routing updates.

```
Sep 16 00:23:39 Fiksdal rpd[527]: RPD_TASK_BEGIN: commencing routing updates,
version 5.0R1.4, built 2001-08-14 22:49:56 UTC by builder
```

Note that because of the PFE components that are still booting (not shown here), rpd won't be receiving any routing updates yet. In fact, the internal fxp1 interface isn't even up yet. Once that interface comes up and dcd brings the external interfaces up, routing updates can be received.

6. **Time 23:51 through 24:05**   The kernel's interface drivers detect that the fxp1 interface is "flapping," which is a result of the PFE being not fully booted. fxp1 finally comes up, allowing the RE to communicate with the PFE.

```
Sep 16 00:23:51 Fiksdal /kernel: fxp1: link UP 100Mb / full-duplex
Sep 16 00:24:05 Fiksdal /kernel: fxp1: media DOWN 100Mb / full-duplex
Sep 16 00:24:05 Fiksdal /kernel: fxp1: link UP 100Mb / full-duplex
```

7. **Time 24:06 through 24:10**   The router is configured to peer with two BGP peers. However, since the external interfaces are still down and no routing updates have been received for these BGP peers' addresses, the BGP sessions cannot be brought up at this time.

```
Sep 16 00:24:06 Fiksdal rpd[527]: task_connect: task BGP_65412.192.168.24.1+179
addr 192.168.24.1+179: No route to host
Sep 16 00:24:06 Fiksdal rpd[527]: bgp_connect_start: connect 192.168.24.1
(Internal AS 65412): No route to host
Sep 16 00:24:10 Fiksdal rpd[527]: task_connect: task BGP_65412.192.168.5.1+179
addr 192.168.5.1+179: No route to host
Sep 16 00:24:10 Fiksdal rpd[527]: bgp_connect_start: connect 192.168.5.1
(Internal AS 65412): No route to host
```

Note that because this router is initiating the BGP sessions, it attempts to form a BGP session with each remote router using the well-known TCP port 179—the one used for BGP.

8. **Time 24:24**   chassid creates interfaces for all physically installed interfaces.

```
Sep 16 00:24:24 Fiksdal chassisd[519]: CHASSISD_IFDEV_CREATE: add ifd fe-0/0/0
Sep 16 00:24:24 Fiksdal chassisd[519]: CHASSISD_IFDEV_CREATE: add ifd fe-0/0/1
Sep 16 00:24:24 Fiksdal chassisd[519]: CHASSISD_IFDEV_CREATE: add ifd fe-0/0/2
Sep 16 00:24:24 Fiksdal chassisd[519]: CHASSISD_IFDEV_CREATE: add ifd fe-0/0/3
```

Keep in mind that the boot sequence displayed in Listing 2-1 and in this section is typical for a single router with a specific hardware and software configuration. While this is fairly representative of the boot sequence for many Juniper Networks routers, differences in the boot sequence will be present for different chassis-specific hardware features (for example, multiple switching controllers/SCBs/SFMs), multiple FPCs and PICs (for example, additional PIC types and generation of alarms for down interfaces), and software configuration (such as BGP and IGP configurations).

Note that the boot time shown here begins at 23:34 with the kernel coming up and ends at 24:24 with the first external physical interfaces coming on-line. This is a total of

50 seconds and does *not* include the time it took the RE to physically boot. In general, the more hardware components that are involved, the longer it will take the router to come up. With some complex configurations, this time (from power-on/reboot to the receipt of routing updates) can be on the order of 3 to 4 minutes.

Capturing Boot-Up Information

The output contained in the previous section comes from the router's syslog facility and is contained in a file called */var/log/messages*. The configuration that builds this file follows:

```
syslog {
    file messages {
        any notice;
        authorization info;
    }
}
```

These commands are included in the router's default configuration file. The configuration can be modified to capture more detailed information. Other facilities allow you to monitor in real-time the information written to this file.

Operational Processes after Boot-Up

After the router is operational, the state of all processes can be examined. Listing 2-2 shows an example of this.

Listing 2-2
Processes brought up after boot

```
lab@Fiksdal> show system processes | no-more
  PID  TT  STAT      TIME COMMAND
    0  ??  DLs    0:00.00  (swapper)
    1  ??  ILs    0:00.07  /sbin/init --
    2  ??  DL     0:00.00  (pagedaemon)
    3  ??  DL     0:00.00  (vmdaemon)
    4  ??  DL     0:00.00  (bufdaemon)
    5  ??  DL     0:00.01  (syncer)
    6  ??  DL     0:00.00  (netdaemon)
    7  ??  IL     0:00.00  (if_pfe_listen)
    8  ??  IL     0:00.00  (cb_poll)
    9  ??  SL     0:00.00  (if_pfe)
   10  ??  DL     0:00.00  (vmuncachedaemon)
  181  ??  ILs    0:00.62  mfs -o noauto /dev/ad1s1b /tmp (newfs)
  382  ??  Is     0:00.00  pccardd
```

```
403  ??  Ss    0:00.13 syslogd -s
489  ??  Is    0:00.02 cron
571  ??  S     0:00.00 /sbin/watchdog -t180
572  ??  I     0:00.08 /usr/sbin/tnetd -N
573  ??  S     0:00.18 /sbin/dcd -N
574  ??  S     0:00.56 /usr/sbin/chassisd -N
575  ??  S     0:00.09 /usr/sbin/alarmd -N
577  ??  I     0:00.08 /usr/sbin/craftd -N
578  ??  S<    0:00.17 /usr/sbin/xntpd -N (ntpd)
579  ??  I     0:00.07 /usr/sbin/mgd -N
580  ??  S     0:00.17 /usr/sbin/snmpd -N
581  ??  S     0:00.61 /usr/sbin/mib2d -N
582  ??  S     0:01.79 /usr/sbin/rpd -N
583  ??  I     0:00.11 /usr/sbin/inetd -N
584  ??  S     0:00.15 /usr/libexec/bprelayd -N
585  ??  I     0:00.14 /usr/sbin/apsd -N
586  ??  I     0:00.08 /usr/sbin/vrrpd -N
587  ??  I     0:00.01 /usr/sbin/tnp.sntpd -N
588  ??  S     0:00.10 /usr/sbin/pfed -N
589  ??  IN    0:00.10 /usr/sbin/sampled -N
590  ??  I     0:00.19 /usr/sbin/ilmid -N
591  ??  I     0:00.35 /usr/sbin/rmopd -N
666  ??  DL    0:00.00  (if_pfe_resync)
667  ??  Ss    0:00.15 mgd: (mgd) (lab)/dev/ttyd0 (mgd)
668  ??  R     0:00.01 /bin/ps -ax
593  v0  Is+   0:00.02 /usr/libexec/getty Pc ttyv0
594  v1  Is+   0:00.01 /usr/libexec/getty Pc ttyv1
595  v2  Is+   0:00.01 /usr/libexec/getty Pc ttyv2
596  v3  Is+   0:00.01 /usr/libexec/getty Pc ttyv3
597  d0  Ss+   0:01.23 -cli (cli)
598  d1  Is+   0:00.01 /usr/libexec/getty std.9600 ttyd1
```

When Processes Fail: The Core Dump

On occasion, processes and even entire routers do fail or crash. A *core dump* (also called a *panic file*) is a snapshot of the operational state of the router at the time of the crash. Core dumps are generated by the router for use by the JTAC and describe the exact state of the system when the error occurred. This information helps the JTAC re-create the conditions that caused the failure.

Core dumps show the program function calls, register values, and related state information that existed just before the crash. JTAC engineers then search several databases for similar chains of events and try to determine if this problem is related to an existing/known problem, tracked in the form of a Problem Report (PR). For new problems, PRs are created for bug fixes, and those fixes and their case histories are logged for future searches. With each release of JUNOS software, the release notes list the outstanding PRs for that release as well as the PRs that are fixed in that particular release, all identified by PR number. (And you thought you never needed to read those release notes.)

Three components of the JUNOS software can generate a core dump:

- The kernel running on the RE: stored in */var/crash*
- The PFE microkernel: stored in */var/crash*
- rpd and the other JUNOS software processes: stored in */var/tmp*

As of this writing, Juniper Networks routers do not generate and store RE kernel and PFE microkernel core dumps by default. However, having this information is useful to the JTAC, and it consumes few system resources, so it's a good idea to have the router do this in the event of a crash.

To generate and save kernel and JUNOS software process cores, issue the following command:

```
lab@Fiksdal# set system dump-on-panic
```

To generate and save PFE microkernel cores, issue this command:

```
lab@Fiksdal# set chassis dump-on-panic
```

These files need to be compressed with gzip and sent to the JTAC via FTP for analysis.

The File System

We've seen that the RE is based on a UNIX host. RAM on the RE is used to store routing databases and the working processes. But like most other hosts, some form of long-term storage is needed to store program executables, configuration files, and other information.

File System Components

Three basic components comprise an M-series router's filesystem: an internal flash drive (such as non-volatile RAM), a hard drive, and a removable media device (LS-120 disk or PCMCIA card). Each part of the filesystem plays a unique role in the operation of the router. Having multiple long-term storage devices provides redundancy, which promotes availability.

The Internal Flash Drive

The internal flash drive is the primary boot source for the router. It has the JUNOS software loaded on it from the factory. Compared to hard drives and removable media, flash memory has lower access times and no moving parts, making it less susceptible to failure. Flash memory also generates less heat and no noise. As a result, the internal flash is the primary storage location for the JUNOS software and configuration information.

The internal flash also contains the active configuration file and the three previous router configuration files. (More on configuration file management will be presented in upcoming chapters.)

The internal flash is also referred to as *compact flash* or *nonrotating media* in some Juniper Networks documentation.

The Hard Drive

Because the RE is based on a UNIX system, there is a hard drive. It contains a backup copy of the same system software loaded on the internal flash drive. Because the hard drive is much larger than the internal flash (6.4GB and greater, compared to 80MB), it is used to hold logging information, older configuration files (zipped and compressed using the tar-gzip/.tgz format), core dump files, swap filespace, and user home directories.

The Removable Media Device

The removable media device can be either an LS-120 SuperDisk or a PCMCIA flash card. Each M-series router has only one of these slot types, not both. Only the M40 ships with the LS-120 disk. All other models ship with PCMCIA flash cards.

LS-120 drives were used in the first Juniper Networks router, the M40, because it was an emerging technology and met the needs at the time the M40 was designed and developed. PCMCIA flash cards were later selected because of the technology's enhanced performance and increasing availability in the marketplace.

The removable media is used to recover from serious failures in the internal flash drive and/or hard drive. In most operating environments, the removable media slot is covered by an access plate and contains no LS-120 disk or PCMCIA card.

Each M-series router ships with the appropriate removable media device (for example, if it comes with an LS-120 drive, you get an LS-120 disk; if it comes with a PCMCIA slot, you get a PCMCIA card). In most cases, the device will have the same version of software that the router has installed. However, after three to six months, the router software may be upgraded, but the removable media is not. You can update the removable media to the latest version of JUNOS software by mounting it as a filesystem and copying the appropriate files to it.

Listing 2-3 shows the relative size of the internal flash and the hard drive.

The filesystems mounted on /dev/ad0s** are part of the internal flash.

The filesystem mounted on /dev/ad1s1f is the hard drive. Note its relatively large size (9,811,371, 1K blocks) compared to the internal flash (65,687 + 25,263 1K blocks). The additional /dev/vn* filesytems correspond to the JUNOS software package components, which will be discussed in the "Software Mechanics" section at the end of this chapter.

Note that no external media is installed in this router. You can tell this because it does not show up as a mounted filesystem in Listing 2-3.

Listing 2-3
Typical
M-series
router
filesystem
(JUNOS
software
version 5.0)

```
lab@Fiksdal> show system storage
Filesystem    1K-blocks    Used    Avail Capacity  Mounted on
/dev/ad0s1a      65687     26488    33945    44%    /
devfs               16        16        0   100%    /dev/
/dev/vn1          9270      9270        0   100%    /packages/mnt/jbase
/dev/vn2          1448      1448        0   100%    /packages/mnt/jcrypto-5.0R1.4
/dev/vn3           764       764        0   100%    /packages/mnt/jdocs-5.0R1.4
/dev/vn4          8392      8392        0   100%    /packages/mnt/jkernel-5.0R1.4
/dev/vn5         11400     11400        0   100%    /packages/mnt/jpfe-5.0R1.4
/dev/vn6          5698      5698        0   100%    /packages/mnt/jroute-5.0R1.4
mfs:181        1015815         3   934547     0%    /tmp
/dev/ad0s1e      25263         7    23235     0%    /config
procfs               4         4        0   100%    /proc
/dev/ad1s1f    9811371    140729  8885733     2%    /var
```

Note that in JUNOS software version 5.0 and later, the version of FreeBSD uses a different file structure compared to earlier FreeBSD versions. If you compare this output to that of earlier versions of JUNOS software, you will see a slightly different file structure.

Note   *As of the writing of this book, Juniper Networks routers ship with 80MB internal flash drives, 6GB (or larger) hard drives, and 110MB PCMCIA cards. However, the trend for all these technologies is to squeeze more memory into a smaller space. This drives the unit cost ($/MB) for memory down and displaces smaller devices. For example, the 20MB hard drive (yes, that does say megabyte) that seemed huge in 1991 is a museum piece today. So don't be surprised when you see future Juniper Networks routers with larger flash drives, hard drives, and PCMCIA cards.*

Important Directories

Several directories play key roles in the operation of the router:

Directory	Role
/config	Stores the active configuration file and previously active configuration files. This is mounted on the internal flash.
/var/tmp	Stores daemon core files when they fail. This is a popular place to store software upgrade files. This directory is mounted on the hard drive.
/var/log	Stores log and traceoptions (i.e., debugging) files. Mounted on the hard drive.

Directory	Role
/var/home	Contains user-specific home directories. A directory is created for each local user account. When a user logs in, all information the user stores locally (e.g., a copy of the configuration file) is saved in this directory.
/altroot and /altconfig	Special directories created by the command `request system snapshot`. Contain backup copies of the JUNOS software, which can be useful if a software upgrade does not complete successfully.

If you have root access to the router, you can start a UNIX shell and navigate and view the contents the directories and their contents via standard UNIX commands such as `pwd`, `ls`, and `cat`. However, since the router shouldn't typically be treated as a UNIX host, specific JUNOS commands provide similar functionality. These commands allow you to stay in JUNOS and, more importantly, are fully supported by the JTAC. If you start a shell and do your file work there, you may be entering unsupported territory.

The supported commands in JUNOS include these:

- `file list`   Similar to `ls` in UNIX
- `file show <filename>`   Similar to `more` in UNIX

Other file viewing and manipulation commands exist. They can be viewed using the command `file ?` on the router.

Boot Source Sequence

So far, we've discussed the boot process of the router with emphasis on the order in which the different components and processes come on-line. But what if a problem occurs with the most basic components, such that the JUNOS software cannot be loaded or even located? Redundancy of boot sources is a good feature for an Internet backbone router, and the router takes advantage of the presence of internal flash, hard drive, and removable media to provide this redundancy.

The boot sequence for Juniper Networks routers is deterministic (that is, the sequence is predefined) and is the same for all router models. Figure 2-3 shows the boot sequence.

First, the router will attempt to boot from the removable media slot. If an LS-120 disk or PCMCIA card is present at boot time, the router *will* boot from it and reformat the internal flash and hard drive, re-creating the default filesystems. This is useful for error and failure recovery, but it is probably not desirable for a production router. For this reason, the router is shipped with the removable media not present in the removable media slot. If you want to boot from the removable media, you must place the LS-120 or PCMCIA flash card in the slot yourself.

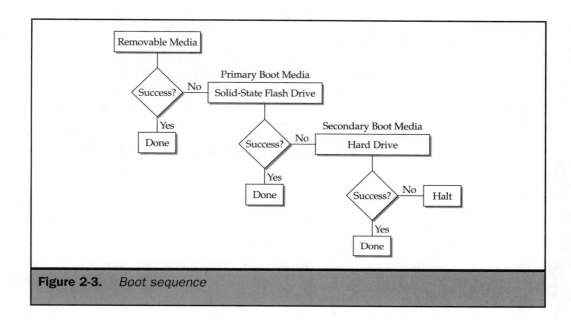

Figure 2-3.   *Boot sequence*

If no removable media card is present, the router will attempt to boot from the internal flash. If an image is there, the router will boot from it.

If no removable media card is present and the router is unable to boot from the internal flash, the router will attempt to boot from the hard drive. This can happen if the internal flash is damaged or if it contains a corrupted version of the JUNOS software. Once the router boots off the hard drive, it can continue to function normally; however, if unsolved problems are encountered with the internal flash, the router will boot off the hard drive again the next time a reboot is required.

You can see the media that the router booted from with the following command:

```
root@slippery> show system storage
Filesystem  1K-blocks     Used    Avail Capacity  Mounted on
/dev/ad0s1a     65687    32892    27541     54%   / << INTERNAL FLASH
devfs              16       16        0    100%   /dev/
/dev/vn1         9240     9240        0    100%   /packages/mnt/jbase
/dev/vn2         9900     9900        0    100%   /packages/mnt/jkernel-5.1-20011023-d67986
/dev/vn3        17290    17290        0    100%   /packages/mnt/jpfe-5.1-20011023-d67986
/dev/vn4         5904     5904        0    100%   /packages/mnt/jroute-5.1-20011023-d67986
/dev/vn5         1454     1454        0    100%   /packages/mnt/jcrypto-5.1-20011023-d67986
/dev/vn6          934      934        0    100%   /packages/mnt/jdocs-5.1-20011023-d67986
mfs:181        762223        3   701243      0%   /tmp
/dev/ad0s1e     10119       14     9296      0%   /config
procfs              4        4        0    100%   /proc
/dev/ad1s1f   7171668   875136  5722799     13%   /var
```

A Note on Rebooting Routers

As you can see, the filesystems for Juniper Networks routers provides a robust set of mechanisms for helping you ensure that the router comes up. The placement of these routers—key locations in the backbone of the Internet—necessitates this. Rebooting a core Internet router should not be done often, because doing so can induce extra overhead in routing protocols and force routing peers/neighbors to do path recalculation as a result of a reboot. As a result, you would not expect to reboot these routers often. If you must reboot, perform a "graceful" shutdown with the following command:

```
lab@Fiksdal> request system halt
Halt the system ? [yes,no] (no) yes
shutdown: [pid 2670]

*** FINAL System shutdown message from root@Fiksdal ***
System going down IMMEDIATELY

Shutdown NOW!
lab@Fiksdal>
Waiting (max 60 seconds) for system process `bufdaemon' to stop...stopped
Waiting (max 60 seconds) for system process `syncer' to stop...stopped
syncing disks...
done
Uptime: 5d12h55m11s
ata0: resetting devices .. done

The operating system has halted.
Please press any key to reboot.
```

At this point, the router may be powered off safely with no corruption to the internal flash or hard drive. Because a filesystem resides on a hard drive, problems can occur when the system is simply powered off.

Software Mechanics

Wouldn't it be nice if software never needed to be upgraded? But then you'd never get new functionality and features. All software eventually needs to be upgraded. This section describes the contents of a release of JUNOS software, what release numbers mean, and how to upgrade the software.

JUNOS Software Release Structure

It is common practice in the computer industry (and a helpful practice) for a software package to reflect version information. All JUNOS software images are named according to the following release numbering scheme,

jXXXXXX-m.nXa.b-EXPSTAT.tgz

where *jXXXXXX* is the package name, *m.n* is the software release number (*m* is the major release number and *n* is the minor release number), *X* is a single-character code for the type of release, *a.b* is the version number of the major software release, *EXPSTAT* is the legal software export status for the package, and *.tgz* is the file extension indicating that the file is a tar file compressed with gzip.

Package Name

A package is a UNIX term for an executable program or set of programs. When you install an application on a UNIX system, you install the corresponding package.

The JUNOS software package name reflects the actual contents of the file. The different package names contain the following components of JUNOS software:

- **jbundle**   All the program files required to install and run JUNOS software on the router. This package actually consists of all the following packages.
- **jkernel**   The operating system package, which contains the FreeBSD kernel and replacement support programs.
- **jbase**   Upgrades to the base OS that are not included in the kernel, routing, or PFE packages (can contain export-restricted software).
- **jpfe**   Software to be downloaded to the PFE (including code for the CPUs on the FPCs).
- **jroute**   The JUNOS software routing package, which contains rpd.
- **jdocs**   The online documentation package, which can be accessed from the CLI while operating the router, similar in concept to UNIX "man" pages.
- **jcrypto**   Cryptographic software.
- **jinstall**   A version of jbundle that includes FreeBSD updates that allow upgrade from versions 4.*x* and earlier to 5.*x*.

Many of these packages can be added individually, but most upgrades involve just jbundle or jinstall.

Release Numbers

The release number changes with the introduction of new features in the software release. The number is incremented when major sets of functionality are introduced; the major release number generally should not change more than once per year. For example, the first major releases of JUNOS software were 3.*x* in 1999/2000. Version 4.0 came out in 2000, and 5.0 was released in 2001.

The minor release number is incremented when smaller sets of functionality and important bug fixes are introduced. This number could change every 3 to 4 months due to Juniper Networks' desire to get out new features and bug fixes on a regular basis.

Software Release Code

This single-character code shows the intended use of the package. The values include the following:

- *I* for internal
- *A* for alpha
- *B* for beta
- *R* for released software—the only software you should be running in a production network!

Release Version Number

This number indicates releases with bug fixes for the version of the major software release, but generally it does not include new functionality or features. In some cases, the *.b* portion of the version number is not present. This number can change every 2 to 4 weeks, depending on the need. A given release may go through three or four version numbers over a period of 3 to 4 months.

Export Status

Software with certain encryption technology is restricted for export. Juniper Networks routers use encryption technology for use with secure shell (SSH). "Domestic" indicates that the software is for use in the United States or Canada. "Export" indicates that the software may be exported to other countries, but it contains weaker encryption technology.

A Note on Release Notes

Simply put, you should read those release notes. JUNOS software release notes contain important information that could affect your upgrade. Important release information can include the following:

- Version-specific upgrade and downgrade procedures.
- Bug fixes and enhancements for a particular version, listed by Problem Report (PR) and Enhancement Request (ER) numbers.
- Outstanding issues, such as known issues that have not been fixed yet. After all, honesty is the best policy.

Installing and Upgrading

One of the strengths of JUNOS software is its portability across router hardware platforms. As of this writing, JUNOS software packages are not hardware-specific; for a given version, the same code is loaded on any hardware platform, from the M5 to the M320 and beyond. This eliminates much of the guesswork involved with code upgrades and maintenance.

Each router comes with the version of JUNOS software that was the most recent release at the time the router was shipped. If you need to upgrade (or downgrade) to another version of software, follow these instructions:

1. Back up the current software and configuration information with the `request system snapshot` command.

2. Get the appropriate jbundle or jinstall file (or other package) from **http://www.juniper.net**; you will need login access to get the latest software.

3. Via FTP, copy the file (or other package) in binary mode to the router to be upgraded.

4. Use the `request system software add <path-and-name-for-package>` command to perform the upgrade.

5. Reboot the router when the installation is complete.

 The command `request system software add < path-and-name-for-package >` *effectively does a UNIX pkgadd.*

The software upgrade process looks like this at the console:

```
lab@Fiksdal> request system software add jbundle-5.0R1.4-domestic.tgz
Installing package '/var/home/lab/jbundle-5.0R1.4-domestic.tgz' ...
Auto-deleting old jroute...
Auto-deleting old jdocs...
Auto-deleting old jpfe...
Auto-deleting old jcrypto...
Unmounted /packages/mnt/jcrypto-5.0R1.4 package ...
/dev/vn2: cleared
Auto-deleting old jkernel...
Adding jkernel...
Restarting bootpd ...
Restarting xntpd ...
Restarting tnetd ...
Restarting tnp.sntpd ...
WARNING: Daemons will be restarted when the jroute package is installed
Restarting watchdog ...
Adding jcrypto...
```

```
Mounted jcrypto package on /dev/vn2...
Adding jpfe...
Adding jdocs...
Adding jroute...
Reloading /config/juniper.conf ...
Activating /config/juniper.conf ...
mgd: commit complete
Restarting mgd ...
Restarting rpd ...
Restarting aprobed ...
Saving package file in /var/sw/pkg/jbundle-5.0R1.4.tgz ...
Saving state for rollback ...

WARNING: cli has been replaced by an updated version:
CLI release 5.0R1.4 built by builder on 2001-08-14 22:47:59 UTC
Restart cli using the new version ? [yes,no] (yes) yes

Restarting cli ...
lab@Fiksdal>
```

You need to keep the following in mind regarding software upgrades:

- Once you type in the `request system software add <package-name>` command, no prompt confirms this action. When you press ENTER, the upgrade begins. You can still recover if you do this in error, but you can avoid such a problem by performing upgrades with caution.

- You are generally prompted to reboot the router when the upgrade requires it.

- It is a good practice to use the `request system snapshot` command before performing a software upgrade. If you have configuration maintenance procedures in your network, you might also consider backing up the configuration file to a remote server.

- When upgrading from 4.x to 5.x, use the jinstall file rather than the jbundle. Once upgraded to 5.x, you can use jbundle files to upgrade to new versions of the 5.x release.

- The software downgrade process is similar to the upgrade process: use `request system software add <package-name>`, where <package-name> is an older version of code. When moving from 5.x down to 4.x, you will also need to use the appropriate 4.x jinstall file.

- In general, you will upgrade all the packages using the jbundle file. You must upgrade the entire jbundle when moving to a new release. If the JTAC says you need to upgrade only a particular package, you may have to install individual packages in a particular order.

JUNOS Software Documentation

The JUNOS software configuration guides are available online. No password is needed. They can be viewed online with a Web browser at **http://www.juniper.net/techpubs**, or they can be downloaded as .pdf files.

Additionally, some documentation is available on the router, thanks to that large hard drive. You can access help via the help reference and help topic commands.

Here are some examples of how someone might look for information about the assignment of an ATM Virtual Circuit Identifier (VCI) to an interface:

```
lab@Fiksdal> help topic interfaces vci

  Configure a Point-to-Point ATM Connection

    To configure a VCI and a VPI on a point-to-point ATM interface,
    include the vci statement at the [edit interfaces interface-name unit
    logical-unit-number] hierarchy level:
    [edit interfaces interface-name unit logical-unit-number]
        vci vpi-identifier.vci-identifier;

    For each VCI, you configure the VCI and VPI identifiers. The default
    VPI identifier is 0. The VCI identifier cannot exceed the highest
    numbered VC configured for the interface with the vpi statement, as
    described in "Configure ATM Physical Interface Properties."

    When you are configuring point-to-point connections, the MTU sizes on
    both sides of the connections must be the same.

lab@Fiksdal> help reference interfaces vci

vci

    Syntax

  vci vpi-identifier.vci-identifier;

    Hierarchy Level

  [edit interfaces interface-name unit logical-unit-number],
  [edit interfaces interface-name unit logical-unit-number family family
  address address
```

```
multipoint-destination address]
```

Description

For ATM point-to-point logical interfaces only, configure the virtual
circuit identifier (VCI) and virtual path identifier (VPI).

To configure a VPI for a point-to-multipoint interface, specify the
VPI in the multipoint-destination statement.

Options

vci-identifier--ATM virtual circuit identifier. This value cannot
exceed the largest numbered VC configured for the interface with the
max-vcs option of the vpi statement.
Range: 0 through 4089

vpi-identifier--ATM virtual path identifier.
Range: 0 through 255
Default: 0

Usage Guidelines

See "Configure ATM Virtual Circuits" or page 139.

Required Privilege Level

interface--To view this statement in the configuration.
interface-control--To add this statement to the configuration.

See Also

encapsulation, multipoint-destination, vpi

Note the difference in the levels of detail. The help topic gives general
information about the subject, while help reference gives many more details,
especially configuration commands and valid values and ranges.

Chapter 3

JUNOS Software Command Line Interface

by Steven D. Holman

You might say that the CLI influences, either directly or indirectly, your perception of the usability of the router. The CLI becomes the personality of the router and helps to create a positive experience for the user. When the operation of CLI is relatively easy and the execution of various actions is straightforward, the operation of the router is a positive one.

To create a positive experience for you and increase your overall effectiveness, the CLI must possess a number of qualities. It must be user friendly, which is to say that it must be easy for you to operate. It must be intuitive and easy for the user to understand. You should not have to focus too much on the specific configuration syntax, so that you can focus on the issues of understanding the functionality of the technology or protocols. The CLI should guide you through the syntax, helping you locate and enter valid commands.

The JUNOS software CLI was created to address these requirements and to be the next generation CLI. It was created to provide a flexible and extensive method of operating Juniper Networks Internet routers while maintaining a consistent and easy-to-use command structure. In this chapter, you will learn about the features of the JUNOS software CLI, including

- A structural overview of the JUNOS software CLI addressing the architecture and CLI modes
- A description of the CLI functionality
- Instructions for navigating the JUNOS software CLI
- A list of features to enhance your effectiveness in using the JUNOS software CLI

Introduction to JUNOS Software CLI

Before discussing the architecture of the CLI, it is important to see an example of the CLI. In the following example, the current location is the login prompt:

```
iprouter (ttyd0)
login: _
```

From this location, you enter your username. You are then prompted for your password:

```
iprouter (ttyd0)
login: lynn
Password: _
Last login: Tue Jul 1 09:08:12 on ttyd0
--- JUNOS 4.4R1.5 built 2001-04-20 04:48:50 UTC
lynn@iprouter> _
```

Once you have entered your username and password, you are provided additional helpful information. First, the header above the prompt informs you of the day, date, time, and source of your previous logon. This information can be helpful in determining whether or not someone else has used your name and password. If the information indicates a more recent date than your last known login, it is possible someone else has used your account. The line following the date of your most recent login is the version of JUNOS software running on the router.

You are now logged in and your prompt provides you with two pieces of information. The first is the username currently logged into the router, in this case, `lynn`. The second is the name of the router, in this case, `iprouter`. This information serves as a valuable reference when logging onto a series of routers (a common occurrence while troubleshooting network problems) or when working with a number of terminal emulator windows.

Now that you have seen an example of a CLI, more in-depth topics such as CLI architecture, CLI keystrokes, and CLI modes can be explored.

CLI Architecture

Understanding the architecture of the CLI provides practical insight into the functionality of the operating system and will assist you in taking advantage of its capabilities.

A significant amount of research, planning, and design went into the development of the JUNOS software CLI. The primary focus of this effort was to evaluate the structure, capabilities, and features that would add to the functionality, ease of use, robustness, and flexibility of the CLI operation.

CLI-Related Processes

As mentioned in Chapter 2, JUNOS software is a modular operating system. It is composed of a core operating system kernel and a number of processes launched at the time of bootup. Of particular importance to the CLI is the master *management daemon* (MGD) process. Since the master MGD is launched by the init process early in the boot sequence, you can access the router before initialization is complete. It is important to note, however, that until all processes are launched, some functions or commands might be unavailable for execution.

Once the master MGD is launched, you can access the router via the CLI. There are a few client access methods available to you: the console or auxiliary port, Telnet, Secure Shell (SSH), and Extensible Markup Language (XML). XML requires extensive discussion beyond the scope of this book.

When the user initiates an access method, a CLI process is started, opening a connection to the master MGD. In turn, the master MGD opens a peer MGD process to handle all requests from that particular client. There is one CLI process and one peer MGD process opened for each user accessing the router via the CLI. When the user exits a connection, both the CLI process and peer MGD process for that connection exit as well. Instead of repeating the fact that it is a peer MGD process serving the CLI, from here on it will simply be referred to as *MGD*. *Master MGD* will be noted when it is discussed. Figure 3-1 illustrates the relationship between each of the processes.

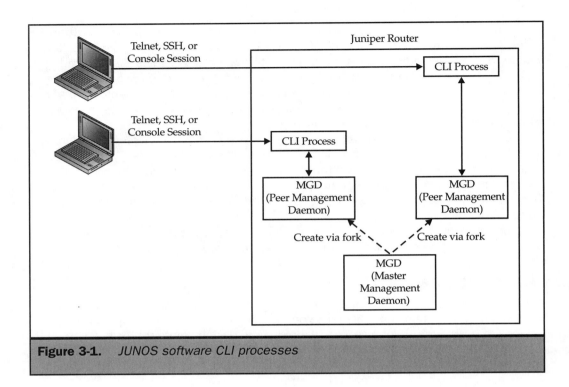

Figure 3-1. *JUNOS software CLI processes*

The CLI manages the terminal session, allowing the user's keystrokes to either build the text of the command line, invoke EMACS-style command-line editing functions, or pass the command along in a *remote procedure call* (RPC) to MGD for additional information. When MGD sends the results of the RPC, the CLI renders the output onto the user's terminal.

Command Structure Hierarchy

To understand how MGD evaluates commands received from the CLI, it is important to understand the command structure used by the operating system. JUNOS software commands are organized hierarchically. The hierarchy starts out general and becomes more specific as commands are entered at the command line. The command structure is stored in a schema, which is metadata detailing the command structure. The database contains each command in a tree structure, listing the options beneath each command. Figure 3-2 illustrates this command hierarchy.

The following example illustrates the hierarchy of the command structure. When an IP address is configured on an interface, the command starts out general and becomes increasing more specific, ending with the actual address:

```
set interface so-0/0/0 unit 0 family inet address 192.168.1.1/24
```

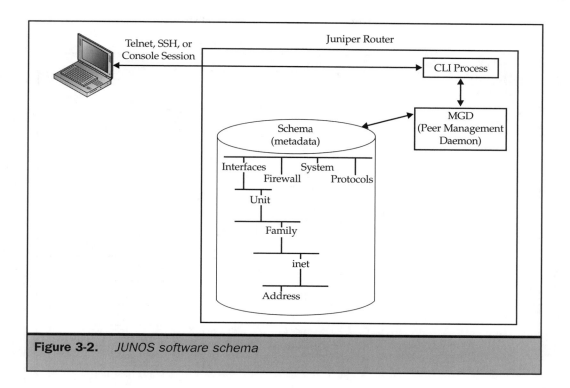

Figure 3-2.   *JUNOS software schema*

The previous example begins with the `set` command, requesting the user interface (UI) to create or assign the target statement or statements. This is followed by the target of the `set` command, the statement `interface`. A statement can be thought of as a category within the command structure hierarchy. In this example, the statement is the target of a command, therefore, the statement `interface` informs JUNOS software that an interface is the target of the `set` command. The next entry on the command line is the specific physical interface: `so-0/0/0`. This is referred to as an *identifier*. An identifier functions as a name uniquely identifying an instance of the statement. In other words, `so-0/0/0` is an identifier of the statement `interface`. Depending on the statement, it might have multiple instances, each represented by a different identifier or name. Identifiers allow the creation and manipulation of individual branches of the configuration hierarchy.

Because a physical interface might have more than one logical interface, the correct logical interface is identified: `unit 0`. `Unit` is a statement, whereas `0` is considered an identifier. Next, the protocol family `inet` (in this case, IP v4) is identified, and finally, the IP address is entered with its prefix length.

Once the command is received by MGD, a matching path is created in the configuration database hierarchy. Figure 3-3 provides an illustration of this operation.

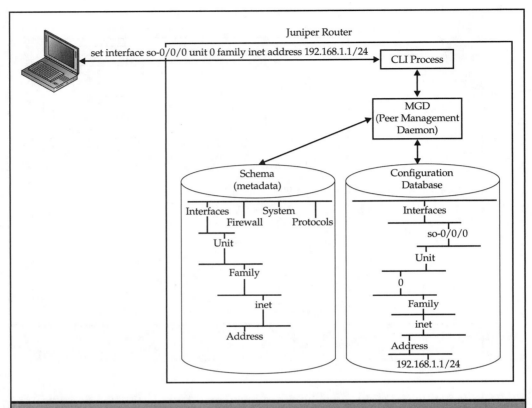

Figure 3-3. *JUNOS software configuration hierarchy database*

CLI Keystrokes

Once the command is entered at the CLI, it must be sent to the JUNOS software, or more specifically, to MGD assigned to the current CLI session, for processing. There are a number of keystrokes that cause the CLI to send the current command line to MGD for processing.

- SPACEBAR
- TAB
- ENTER (or RETURN)
- ?
- Additional JUNOS software CLI keystrokes

When one of these keystrokes is entered, the CLI sends an RPC with the current command line content to MGD for processing. In turn, MGD parses the entry to determine its content. As it parses the content received from the CLI, it evaluates the accuracy of each entry. Parsing the content also assists in determining the content of the command as well as the location of functional keystrokes. MGD also evaluates the type of functional keystroke entered to determine the response it must provide to the CLI. Once it does so, MGD returns the results to the CLI for display on the user's terminal. The following sections discuss the process taken by MGD when you enter one of these keystrokes.

SPACEBAR

Aside from the obvious task of separating words or commands, the SPACEBAR provides a real time evaluation of commands entered at the CLI. After each command or statement, you press the SPACEBAR to type the next entry. Pressing the SPACEBAR causes the CLI to send its content to MGD. As MGD parses the content it refers to the command structure contained in the schema to ensure the accuracy of each command, statement, or identifier. Look again at the previous example:

```
set <spacebar> interface <spacebar> so-0/0/0
```

You type in the command `set`, then press the SPACEBAR. This sends an RPC to MGD with the content, in this case, `set`. MGD evaluates the entry for its accuracy. Since it is accurate, it does nothing and allows you to continue typing. Next, you type in `interface`, then press SPACEBAR. An RPC is again generated from the CLI to MGD with its contents. MGD evaluates the entry to ensure that `interface` is a valid entry after the `set` command. Note in Figure 3-2 that `interface` is a valid entry after the `set` command, therefore, MGD does nothing and allows you to continue typing. This process continues until you press another functional keystroke.

If you typed an incorrect entry, MGD would warn you of the error and require a correction. For example, if you mistakenly excluded the statement `interface` and simply typed the actual interface after the `set` command, MGD would inform you immediately of this mistake. Furthermore, it would not allow you to continue until the error was corrected. The following example illustrates a situation when the command `show route` is typed incorrectly. The CLI returned a message indicating there is an error. It also includes an arrow pointing to the location of the error.

```
lynn@iprouter> show roue
                     ^
syntax error, expecting <command>.
lynn@iprouter> show roue
```

This feature ensures that, as you enter a command string, each entry is verified. This saves you the trouble of typing in an invalid command. It also saves you the trouble of retyping a command in the event of a mistake. All mistakes of a syntactical nature are addressed as you type. There are additional features provided by the SPACEBAR. These features are described later in the section "CLI Features."

TAB

The next functional keystroke is the TAB. Functionally, TAB is similar to the SPACEBAR. When pressed, TAB sends an RPC of the current contents of the CLI to MGD for processing. As with the SPACEBAR, this RPC includes the immediate command verification. TAB adds some additional features, which are discussed in the section "CLI Features."

ENTER

ENTER is the functional keystroke entered when you have completed typing a command. SPACEBAR and TAB cause the CLI to generate an RPC with the current contents and verify it for accuracy. ENTER causes the CLI to generate an RPC with the current contents and requests MGD to execute the command. Depending on the type of command entered, execution is made in one of two forms. If it is an operational type command such as displaying an interface or displaying the routing table, then it is executed by MGD and the results are presented immediately. If it is a configuration type command such as setting the IP address of an interface or the parameters of a protocol, it is entered in a temporary configuration database for execution later. The topic of the configuration database is explained in greater detail in the section "Configuration Commit Model."

In Chapter 2, you learned about various processes that run in the Juniper Networks router. If necessary, MGD might use one of these processes to execute the command. When MGD receives an RPC from the CLI, it parses the enclosed command line using the information contained in the schema. Once the command is deemed valid in syntax and content, MGD looks again at the schema to determine how to execute the command. If the UI is in configuration mode, all commands are handled internally by MGD by displaying or manipulating the information contained in the configuration database. In operational mode, MGD has three choices.

First, many commands are implemented as part of system processes called *daemons*. Daemons run as unattended processes, performing their work without human or system intervention. For example, the routing protocol daemon RPD handles all routing protocols, turning the information received from other routers into a table that directs all routing decisions. If a command needs information known only to a specific daemon, MGD passes the command to the daemon, and forwards the daemon's output to the CLI. If you abort the command using CTRL-C, MGD informs the daemon so that it can discontinue its operation or output.

Next, many other commands are implemented as traditional UNIX commands, launched by MGD when directed by you and exiting when your job is complete. MGD handles invoking the command and forwarding its output back to the CLI. If you abort the command, MGD interrupts and kills the command.

Finally, a small number of commands use information known only to MGD, and are implemented as functions inside MGD. MGD calls these functions when directed and sends the function's output to the CLI. If you abort the command, MGD discontinues the function.

Figure 3-4 illustrates the execution of a command. In this example, the command show route is entered by the user. The command is then forwarded by the CLI to MGD. MGD refers to the schema to ensure accuracy, determines the required process, and then enlists the service of the daemon RPD to execute the command.

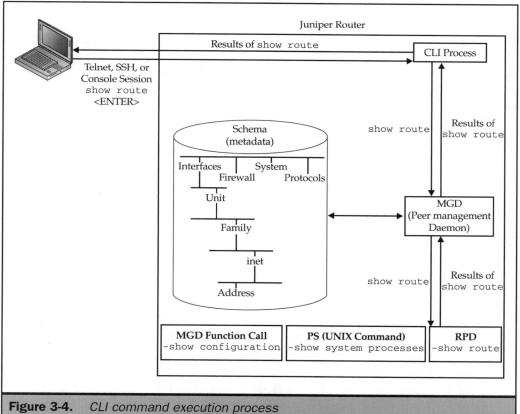

Figure 3-4.   *CLI command execution process*

Question Mark

The final functional keystroke is the question mark. As the saying goes, the question mark is your friend. The question mark provides you with context-sensitive help and can be used at any point while entering a command. It can be used prior to entering a command, in the middle of a command string, and even if only a portion of a command has been entered. The purpose of the question mark is to request information about the command string from the CLI.

When you type a question mark, the CLI takes the current contents of the command line and sends it in an RPC to MGD. MGD evaluates contents of the RPC against the schema and provides the requested information. There are two types of information provided in response to a question mark. The first is the command option. The command option displays a list of the available CLI commands. In the following example, a question mark is entered prior to any command string. The result is a list of available CLI commands.

```
lynn@iprouter> ?
Possible completions:
  clear              Clear information in the system
  configure          Manipulate software configuration information
  file               Perform file operations
  help               Provide help information
  monitor            Real-time debugging
  ping               Ping a remote target
  quit               Exit the management session
  request            Make system-level requests
  restart            Restart a software process
  set                Set CLI properties, date, time, craft display text
  show               Show information about the system
  ssh                Open a secure shell to another host
  start              Start a software process
  telnet             Telnet to another host
  test               Diagnostic debugging commands
  traceroute         Trace the route to a remote hos
lynn@iprouter> _
```

A variation of this type of information is the list of available CLI commands for a partial command-string entry. In the next example, part of a command string is entered, followed by a question mark. The CLI provides a list of the available CLI commands for the preceding partial command string. The command show interface is entered at the CLI. Entering a question mark sends a request to the CLI to provide a list of available CLI commands following the statement interface.

```
lynn@iprouter> show interface ?
Possible completions:
  <[Enter]>                Execute this command
  <interface-name>         Physical or logical interface
  descriptions             Show interface description strings
  destination-class        Display statistics for a specific destination class
  detail                   Display detailed info
  extensive                Display extensive info
  media                    Display media information
  queue                    Show queue statistics for this interface
  routing                  Display routing status
  snmp-index               Show interface with this SNMP index
  statistics               Display statistics and detailed info
  terse                    Display summary information
  | Pipe through a command
lynn@iprouter> show interface _
```

The second type of information provided by the CLI when you enter the question mark is command completion options. In the next example, part of a command string is entered at the command line and followed by the question mark. The CLI provides a list of the completion possibilities.

```
lynn@iprouter> show i?
Possible completions:
  igmp                 Show information about IGMP
  ilmi                 Show ILMI information
  interfaces           Show interface information
  isis                 Show information about IS-IS
lynn@iprouter> show i_
```

Additional JUNOS Software CLI Keystrokes

Finally, the JUNOS software CLI includes a rich set of keybindings, patterned after the EMACS editor. Depending on your terminal configuration, you might or might not be able to use certain keystrokes—for example, ARROW, DELETE, or BACKSPACE—to edit your commands. These allow you to move around within any command you are typing. It also allows you to edit or delete characters or words, repeat or scroll through previous commands, and insert previous words or commands into your command line. These features are applicable to both operational mode and configuration mode.

Table 3-1 lists and describes the various EMACS keybindings for editing your commands at the command line:

Category	Function	Keybinding
Move the Cursor	Move the cursor back one character.	CTRL-b
	Move the cursor back one word.	ESC-b or ALT-b
	Move the cursor forward one character.	CTRL-f
	Move the cursor forward one word.	ESC-f or ALT-f
	Move the cursor to the beginning of the command line.	CTRL-a
	Move the cursor to the end of the command line.	CTRL-e
Delete Characters	Delete the character before the cursor.	CTRL-h, DELETE, or BACKSPACE
	Delete the character at the cursor.	CTRL-d
	Delete all characters from the cursor to the end of the command line.	CTRL-k
	Delete all characters on the command line.	CTRL-u or CTRL-x
	Delete the word before the cursor.	CTRL-w, ESC-BACKSPACE, or ALT-BACKSPACE
	Delete the word after the cursor.	ESC-d or ALT-d
Insert Recently Deleted Text	Insert the most recently deleted text at the cursor.	CTRL-y

Table 3-1.   *CLI EMACS Keybindings*

Category	Function	Keybinding
Redraw the Screen	Redraw the current line.	CTRL-l
Display Previous Command Lines	Scroll backward through the list of recently executed commands.	CTRL-p
	Scroll forward through the list of recently executed commands.	CTRL-n
	Search the CLI history in reverse order for lines matching the search string.	CTRL-r
	Search the CLI history by typing some text at the prompt, followed by the keyboard sequence; the CLI attempts to expand the text into the most recent word in the history for which the text is a prefix.	ESC-/
Repeat Keyboard Sequences	Specify the number of times to execute a keyboard sequence; the number can be from 1 through 9.	ESC-*number sequence* or ALT-*number sequence*

Table 3-1.   *CLI EMACS Keybindings* (continued)

CLI Modes

The JUNOS software CLI offers two modes: operational mode and configuration mode. This model provides a distinct line between the ability to view operations on the router and the ability to change operations on the router. This section discusses these two modes and their capabilities.

Operational Mode

Operational mode allows you to monitor and troubleshoot the router's hardware and software, evaluate its performance, and view its routing protocols and network connectivity. Operational mode allows the interrogation and manipulation of the operational state of a router. These tasks include monitoring and troubleshooting hardware and software, system performance, routing protocols, and network connectivity. They also include such tasks as software upgrades, resetting faulty processes, and performing simple maintenance operations.

To access operational mode, you need a user account on the router. To view the various processes and components in the router, you need specific permissions or command access. The topics of user accounts, permissions, and command access are addressed in detail in Chapter 4. Operational mode access is used most frequently by the operations group responsible for monitoring and managing the routers in a network, therefore, it allows you to execute a number of operational type tasks. Most of these tasks focus on the ability of viewing events, processes, and status of various components. When you enter the CLI, you are placed into operational mode. Operational mode is easily determined by the prompt provided by CLI. The format includes the name of the current user, the @ sign, the host name of the router, and finally the > sign:

```
lynn@iprouter>
```

View into the Router

The CLI allows you to execute a number of show commands to view anything from the routing table created by the different routing protocols to the environmental temperature of different components in the router. From operational mode, the show command allows you to view traffic use of an interface or determine whether or not an interface is experiencing errors. This provides you the ability to evaluate the operations of a router or troubleshoot problems that might arise. From configuration mode, the show command allows you to view all or portions of the configuration database.

The list of options available with the show command is very extensive. To find out more about these options, please refer to the Juniper Networks documentation found on the Juniper Networks Web site at **www.juniper.net**.

CLI Environment

Operational mode allows you to control the CLI environment. You are able to configure such things as screen size and terminal type. Because this is a type of configuration, you might wonder why you are allowed to make these changes. The reason is that the changes affect only your session. They do not affect the CLI environment variables of any other user. Furthermore, operational mode allows you to define your specific session because it might be unique when compared with someone else's requirements.

To change your CLI environment, use the set command. The following displays the CLI environment variables you are able to change:

```
lynn@iprouter> set cli ?
Possible completions:
```

```
complete-on-space       Toggle word completion on space
idle-timeout            Set the cli maximum idle time
prompt                  Set the cli command prompt string
restart-on-upgrade      Set cli to prompt for restart after a software upgrade
screen-length           Set number of lines on screen
screen-width            Set number of characters on a line
terminal                Set terminal type
lynn@iprouter> set cli _
```

The following list defines the defaults settings for each of the preceding variables:

complete-on-space	on
idle-timeout	disabled
prompt	user@host>
restart-on-upgrade	on
screen-length	24 lines
screen-width	80 columns
terminal	unknown

To display your CLI settings, use the following command:

```
lynn@iprouter> show cli
CLI complete-on-space set to on
CLI idle-timeout disabled
CLI restart-on-upgrade set to on
CLI screen-length set to 24
CLI screen-width set to 80
CLI terminal is 'unknown'
CLI is operating in enhanced mode
lynn@iprouter> _
```

Access Other IP Devices

Operational mode also allows you to initiate access to other routers or IP devices by using Telnet or SSH. You can execute the command by identifying the destination device you wish to access. This can be done with either the destination device's IP address or host name. To reference the destination device's host name, a Domain Name Server (DNS) must first be configured on the router. The following example illustrates how to access another IP device:

```
lynn@iprouter> telnet 192.168.123.1 _
```

File Management

Operational mode provides some file management capabilities. You are able to view a list of files, view the contents of files, rename files, delete files, and copy files to other directories as well as other hosts or routers. This is done using the `file` command. The file management options available with the `file` command are as follows:

```
lynn@iprouter> file ?
Possible completions:
 copy                   Copy files (local or remote)
 delete                 Delete files from the system (local)
 list                   List file information (local)
 rename                 Rename files (local)
 show                   Display file contents (local)
lynn@iprouter> _
```

When executing the `file` command, remember that your current directory is normally your home directory under /var/home/. For a user named `lynn`, your home directory would be /var/home/lynn. You may use normal UNIX path constructs to refer to files in other directories. The following example illustrates how to list the contents of a directory other than the user's home directory:

```
lynn@iprouter> file list /var detail
total 46
drwxr-xr-x  21   root     wheel     512 Oct 17 01:28 ./
dr-xr-xr-x  18   root     wheel     512 Nov 1 19:27 ../
drwxr-xr-x  2    bin      bin       512 Mar 3 2001 account/
drwxr-xr-x  4    root     wheel     512 Oct 16 22:17 at/
drwxr-x---  2    root     wheel     512 Mar 3 2001 backups/
drwxr-x---  2    root     wheel     512 Nov 13 16:46 crash/
drwxr-x---  3    root     wheel     512 Oct 16 22:17 cron/
drwxr-xr-x  3    bin      bin       512 Nov 30 03:48 db/
drwxr-xr-x  3    root     wheel    2048 Nov 29 04:34 etc/
drwxrwxr-x  5    root     games     512 Oct 16 22:18 games/
drwxr-xr-x  5    root     wheel     512 Nov 16 13:54 home/
drwxr-xr-x  2    bin      bin      1024 Nov 29 04:34 log/
drwxrwxr-x  2    bin      mail      512 Mar 3 2001 mail/
drwxr-xr-x  2    daemon   bin       512 Mar 3 2001 msgs/
drwxr-xr-x  2    bin      bin       512 Mar 3 2001 preserve/
drwxr-xr-x  2    root     bin      1536 Nov 30 04:28 run/
drwxrwxr-x  2    bin      daemon    512 Mar 3 2001 rwho/
drwxr-xr-x  9    bin      bin       512 Oct 16 22:17 spool/
drwxr-xr-x  3    root     wheel     512 Oct 17 01:28 sw/
```

```
drwsrwxrwx   4   bin     field    512 Nov 13 16:48 tmp/
drwxr-xr-x   2   bin     bin      512 Oct 16 22:18 yp/
lynn@iprouter> _
```

Restarting Processes

In the course of troubleshooting, if you find that a daemon or process becomes unresponsive or is the cause of an operational issue, it can be killed and restarted with the restart command. As discussed in Chapter 2, the processes run in their own protected memory space. This enables you to restart a process without negatively affecting another process. Following is a list of the processes you are able to restart from the CLI:

```
lynn@iprouter> restart ?
Possible completions:
 class-of-service          Class of Service process
 interface-control         Interface process
 mib-process               SNMP MIB-II process
 remote-operations         Remote operations process
 routing                   Routing protocol process
 sampling                  Traffic sampling control process
 snmp                      SNMP process
lynn@iprouter> restart _
```

Restarting a process is executed from the CLI in operational mode. The following example illustrates restarting a process:

```
lynn@iprouter> restart routing
Routing protocol daemon started, pid 2929
lynn@iprouter> _
```

It should be noted, however, that restarting RPD will negatively affect the entire router, possibly including your terminal session.

System-Level Operations

Throughout the course of operating a Juniper Networks router, it will become necessary to perform various system-level operations. These operations include rebooting the router, upgrading the JUNOS software version, downing the router, stopping or restarting various components in the router, or creating a backup copy of the operating system and configuration. Following is a list of the system-level operations you are able to execute from the CLI.

```
lynn@iprouter> request ?
Possible completions:
 chassis                  Perform chassis specific operations
 message                  Send a text message to other users
 routing-engine           Login into routing engine
 support                  Perform JUNOS support tasks
 system                   Perform system-level operations
lynn@iprouter> request _
```

To perform these system-level operations, execute the command `request` from operational mode. Following is an example of executing a system-level operation. In this example, one of the physical interface cards is taken off line:

```
lynn@iprouter> request chassis pic pic-slot 0 offline fpc-slot 0
lynn@iprouter> _
```

Configuration Mode

The second mode is configuration mode. As the name implies, this mode is used to configure the router. Configuration mode requires a separate set of permissions to gain access. These permissions are described in Chapter 4. Configuration mode allows you to configure a wide variety of statements and, just like operational mode, is hierarchical. Configuration mode is organized in a tree structure. The base or root of the tree structure starts out general and becomes more specific the further into the branch you go. Table 3-2 lists and describes the root statements within configuration mode.

Statement	Description
[edit accounting-options]	This statement allows you to create profiles for accounting purposes.
[edit chassis]	This statement provides you the option of configuring chassis related alarms, FPC framing, and routing-engine redundancy.
[edit class-of-service]	In this statement, you configure class-of-service profiles and related parameters.

Table 3-2.   *Configuration Mode Statements*

Statement	Description
[edit firewall]	The firewall statement offers you the ability to create a variety of packet filters along with rate limiting.
[edit forwarding-options]	This statement allows you to configure cflowd along with other sampling related options.
[edit groups]	To reduce the number of redundant commands, you can create groups within this statement; these groups are then applied to the configuration.
[edit interfaces]	This statement provides you the ability to configure many different interface related parameters; this includes both logical commands (protocol addresses) and physical (encapsulation) modes.
[edit policy-options]	It is within this statement that you create routing policies, as-path regular expressions, BGP communities, and prefix lists.
[edit protocols]	Use this statement to configure the following protocols: BGP, DVMRP, IGMP, IS-IS, LDP, MPLS, MSDP, OSPF, PIM, RIP, Router Discovery, RSVP, and SDP/SAP.
[edit routing-instances]	The Juniper Networks router supports multiple routing instances. Use this statement to configure BGP/MPLS VPNs.
[edit routing-options]	This statement provides you the option of creating BGP confederations, injecting static and aggregate routes, assigning the router's BGP autonomous system number, creating a routing information base (RIB), assigning the router ID, altering the martian route list, and influencing the forwarding table.
[edit snmp]	This statement has the command necessary to configure SNMP support.
[edit system]	This statement contains the necessary fields to configure user accounts, host name, DNS assignment, router authentication methods, services such as telnet and ftp, and syslog parameters.

Table 3-2.   *Configuration Mode Statements* (continued)

You access configuration mode from operational mode using the `configure` command. This is illustrated in the following example. Once you execute the `configure` command, you see that the prompt changes to indicate that you are now in configuration mode. It uses the format that includes the name of the current user, the @ sign, and the host name of the router; however, it now uses a # sign instead of a > sign. Furthermore, there is a path listed above the prompt informing you of your current location in configuration mode hierarchy.

```
lynn@iprouter> configure _

[edit]
lynn@iprouter# _
```

Note that accessing configuration mode does not require an additional password. The user permissions assigned to your login account determine whether or not you can access configuration mode.

Navigating Configuration Mode Statements

JUNOS software provides command features to assist you in using the CLI. These commands help you navigate the command-line structure. In the last section, you explored the hierarchy of the configuration mode; in this section, you learn how to navigate this hierarchy. This categorical approach of statements assists you with configuring the Juniper Networks router. Along with the help of the question mark, this clearly defined hierarchical approach makes configuring the router more intuitive. Configuration statements are arranged in a natural hierarchy organized by subject matter. Viewing the configuration as a tree makes navigation and manipulation simpler by limiting the scope of operations to portions of the tree.

Within the list of statements there are substatements. These define your configuration more specifically. The following examples illustrate how you navigate the hierarchy of configuration mode.

Editing a Statement

To change your location in the statement hierarchy, use the `edit` command followed by the name of a destination statement.

```
[edit]
lynn@iprouter# edit interfaces

[edit interfaces]
lynn@iprouter# _
```

Notice that the change in location is reflected in the banner above the CLI prompt. This clearly defines the statement in which any command you execute will be entered. In this example, the banner informs you that you are in the `interfaces` statement, therefore, any configuration must be related to an interface.

You can now change into a specific interface by using the `edit` command. The following example illustrates two things. First, you are able to change into multiple levels using the same command. Second, you are in fact adding the physical interface and logical interface to your configuration database. These did not necessarily exist in the configuration database prior to your entering this command.

```
[edit interfaces]
lynn@iprouter# edit so-0/0/0 unit 0 _

[edit interfaces so-0/0/0 unit 0]
lynn@iprouter# _
```

Moving Up the Configuration Mode Hierarchy

Now that you are in a statement, as reflected by the banner above your prompt, you can enter the configuration by using the `set` command followed by the configuration parameters. You will encounter specific configuration statements in all of the subsequent chapters.

Once you have entered the configuration mode, there are three commands you can use to exit your current location: `exit`, `up`, or `top`. Exit returns you to the point of the previous `edit` command. The following example illustrates the use of the `exit` command.

```
[edit]
lynn@iprouter# edit interfaces so-0/0/0 unit 0 _

[edit interfaces so-0/0/0 unit 0]
lynn@iprouter# exit _

[edit]
lynn@iprouter# _
```

Up moves you up or back the number of levels you specify. The default is one level. The following example illustrates the use of the `up` command.

```
[edit interfaces so-0/0/0 unit 0]
lynn@iprouter# up _
```

```
[edit interfaces so-0/0/0]
lynn@iprouter# _

[edit interfaces so-0/0/0 unit 0]
lynn@iprouter# up 3 _

[edit]
lynn@iprouter# _
```

Top moves you up or back to the root level. The following example illustrates the use of the command top.

```
[edit interfaces so-0/0/0 unit 0]
lynn@iprouter# top _

[edit]
lynn@iprouter# _
```

This last option illustrates how you exit configuration mode. To return to operational mode, use the command exit at the root of configuration mode.

```
[edit]
lynn@iprouter# exit _
lynn@iprouter> _
```

If your prompt is a few levels in, however, the exit command alone requires you to enter it a few times. Alternatively, use the exit configuration mode command to return to operation mode from anywhere in the configuration hierarchy.

```
[edit interfaces so-0/0/0 unit 0]
lynn@iprouter# exit configuration-mode _
Exiting configuration mode

lynn@iprouter> _
```

CLI Features

There are several features performed by the JUNOS software CLI. This section describes some of the more notable ones, which add to the ease of using the JUNOS software CLI. Some of these features are automatic, while some can be employed when using the CLI.

Automatic Command Completion

To assist in your typing and reduce the number of characters you need to enter, the JUNOS software CLI includes automatic command completion.

SPACEBAR

The section "CLI Keystrokes" introduced the use of the SPACEBAR when typing in commands. The SPACEBAR sends an RPC to MGD requesting an evaluation of the current command-line content. Added to this feature is the ability of MGD to complete the command automatically, eliminating the need to type the full command. The following example illustrates the use of the SPACEBAR when entering a command:

```
lynn@iprouter> sh<spacebar>ow ch<spacebar>assis ha<spacebar>rdware
lynn@iprouter> show chassis hardware _
```

Once you have entered enough characters to distinguish the command from any other command, press the SPACEBAR, and the CLI will automatically complete the command.

TAB

Notice in the previous example that the commands that were automatically completed are statements. The SPACEBAR does not automatically complete identifiers. Remember, an identifier is a name that identifies a specific instance of a statement. To complete an identifier, you must use the TAB. The following example illustrates the use of TAB to automatically complete an identifier:

```
[edit]
lynn@iprouter# sh<spacebar>ow in<spacebar>terface so-<tab key>0/0/0 _
[edit]
lynn@iprouter# show interface so-0/0/0 _
```

Command Completion Error Message

It is important to note that when using either the SPACEBAR or TAB, you must enter enough characters to distinguish the entry from any other option. If you have not entered enough characters, the CLI returns an error message and, if possible, it provides you with options for completion. This is shown in the next example:

```
lynn@iprouter> show i
        ^
'i' is ambiguous.
Possible completions:
  igmp                    Show information about IGMP
```

```
 ilmi                    Show ILMI information
 interfaces              Show interface information
 isis                    Show information about IS-IS
lynn@iprouter> show i
```

The CLI returns with a message informing you that there are not enough characters for it to distinguish the statement you intend to enter. It also provides you with the possible completions it knows and returns you to the place where you pressed the SPACEBAR.

Simultaneous Multiple User Access

There are times when operating a Juniper Networks router that the need arises for multiple users to access the CLI. These users might be located in disparate locations and will, therefore, require remote access. This can be done via Telnet, SSH, or the console. The JUNOS software CLI allows multiple users to access the CLI. Only one user can access the CLI via the console port at a time, however, multiple users can access the CLI via Telnet or SSH. For each user accessing the router, a separate CLI and MGD process is launched. Both of these processes exit when the user exits the CLI.

Simultaneous Configuration

This brings up an important point. When multiple users access configuration mode, they are accessing the same configuration database, therefore, any changes made by any user are included in this configuration database. This could result in a user unknowingly saving some unintended configurations, however, this also provides a benefit. When multiple users need to collaborate on a configuration, they all can be in the same configuration database and see any changes to this database immediately. This is often useful when multiple users are coordinating the diagnosis and solution of a problem, but users need to be aware that others can be changing the configuration data in unrelated ways. To understand the concept of the configuration database in the JUNOS software architecture, refer to the section "Configuration Commit Model."

Restricting Multiple-User Configuration Access

Nevertheless, a situation might arise when you do not want multiple users to be able to configure the router at same time. For example, some operators write script files to automatically Telnet into the router, make configuration changes, save these changes, then log out. To prevent this automatic process from making changes to the router while you are making changes, use the `configure exclusive` command when entering configuration mode.

This does not prevent other users from accessing configuration mode, however, it does prevent them from making any configuration changes while you are in configuration mode. Once the user issuing the restriction exits configuration mode, other users are able to make changes.

In the following example, user `lynn` accesses configuration mode. The CLI informs her that user `ginger` is also in configuration mode and has set `configure exclusive`. When user `lynn` tries to make a configuration, however, the CLI informs her that it is not possible.

```
lynn@iprouter> configure
Entering configuration mode
Users currently editing the configuration:
  ginger terminal d0 (pid 3050) on since 2001-08-03 01:23:27 UTC
      exclusive [edit]

[edit]
lynn@iprouter# set interfaces so-0/0/0 unit 0
error: configuration database locked by:
  ginger terminal d0 (pid 3050) on since 2001-09-03 01:23:27 UTC
      exclusive [edit]

[edit]
lynn@iprouter#
```

Viewing Other Users

You are able to see whether or not other users are logged into the router. To do so, execute the `show system users` command. The following example illustrates the use of this command:

```
lynn@iprouter> show system users _
12:39AM  up 1 day, 12:41, 2 users, load averages: 0.04, 0.02, 0.00
USER      TTY    FROM                          LOGIN@   IDLE WHAT
lynn      d0     -                             12:36AM    - -cli (cl
ginger    p0     r3                            12:37AM    3 -cli (cl
lynn@iprouter> _
```

There are also situations when the CLI informs you that another user is currently logged into the router. This is done when you enter configuration mode and another user is already configuring the router. In this next example, the user "ginger" is logged in and configuring the router when user "lynn" enters configuration mode.

```
lynn@iprouter> configure
Entering configuration mode
Users currently editing the configuration:
```

```
   ginger terminal d0 (pid 3216) on since 2001-08-03 00:45:44 UTC
      [edit interfaces so-0/0/0 unit 0]
The configuration has been changed but not committed

[edit]
lynn@iprouter#
```

Note that the CLI informs the user `lynn` not only that user `ginger` is in configuration mode, it informs her where in configuration mode `ginger` is editing. The CLI also informs user `lynn` that there have been changes made to the configuration, but those changes have not been saved.

An additional command providing information of the activities of the users currently logged in is the `status` command. This command must be executed from the configuration mode. The following example illustrates the use of this command.

```
[edit]
lynn@iprouter# status _
Users currently editing the configuration:
milt terminal p1 (pid 1850) on since 2001-10-21 00:06:48 PST, idle 0:05:15
[edit interfaces so-0/0/0]
ginger terminal p3 (pid 2187) on since 2001-10-21 10:34:23 PST
exclusive [edit]
scott terminal p2 (pid 2189) on since 2001-10-21 13:34:33 EST
[edit]

[edit]
lynn@iprouter# _
```

Configuration Commit Model

Juniper Networks products are targeted for complex, high-performance networks. This complexity is manifest in the configuration data. In designing its UI for the next generation router, Juniper Networks incorporated several features into its configuration model. Central to the model is the concept of being commit-based, where changes can be aggregated, reviewed, and checked for correctness before affecting the operational state of the router. If configuration changes are deemed unacceptable, they can be corrected or discarded. If acceptable, they can be committed. Only when committed are the changes propagated throughout the system, where they are implemented by the various components of JUNOS software.

This section discusses these and other features of the configuration component that can help you maintain your network. You have seen a number of these features and functionalities in Chapters 1 and 2. This section addresses the concept of database and configuration management in greater detail.

Configuration Files

In addition to maintaining the most current configuration database, the Juniper Networks router also maintains previous configuration databases. When you are editing the configuration database, the data you are seeing is called the candidate configuration, and is stored in an internal binary form in the file /var/db/juniper.db. As you make changes, they appear only in the internal database.

When you perform a `commit`, the database is saved in ASCII form in the file /config/juniper.conf. The most current configuration database is juniper.conf and is located in the /config directory. As you learned in Chapter 2, there is flash memory in the Juniper Networks router. The directory /config is located on this flash memory.

The configuration database juniper.conf is considered the active configuration database and is referenced by JUNOS software each time the router is booted. Also included in the /config directory are the three most-recent configuration databases: juniper.conf.1.gz, juniper.conf.2.gz, and juniper.conf.3.gz. The number following the name indicates how recently it was the active configuration database, .1 being the most recent, followed by .2, then .3; however, these are not the only recent active configuration databases. There are six additional recently active configuration databases numbered .4 through .9 stored in the /var/db/config directory. This directory is located on the hard drive, therefore, the Juniper Networks router maintains the nine most-recent active configuration databases.

Active vs. Candidate Database

You learned in the previous section that the Juniper Networks router maintains a single currently active configuration database. In addition to this, the router also creates another database when new configurations are made. When you access configuration mode, JUNOS software creates another database called the candidate configuration database. This candidate configuration database is a copy of the active configuration database, therefore, any adds, changes, or deletions you make are done to the candidate configuration database and not to the active configuration database. This provides you the opportunity to make your configuration changes without these changes becoming effective immediately. Changes can be entered, reviewed, checked for errors, and committed only when you are satisfied with their accuracy.

Commit Command

To make these changes effective, you must execute the command `commit`. When you do this, a number of steps occur. First, the candidate configuration is saved in text form, then any secondary text files are generated based on data in the candidate configuration database. For example, the contents of the [system login user] configuration hierarchy are translated into the traditional UNIX /etc/master.passwd file format.

The UI uses a filenaming convention to mark these files are candidates. Files with a plus sign appended to the name are the incoming candidate files, and files with a minus sign appended are outgoing old files. For example, master.passwd+ contains data from the candidate database, and master.passwd- contains data from the old active database.

Configuration data is also propagated to several daemon configuration files, using the same filenaming configuration. MGD checks for several types of errors during this propagation processing and reports any errors as they are detected.

Once the configuration data is propagated, MGD requests each daemon or system component to inspect its portion of the candidate configuration database to see if any errors exist. These errors are reported back to you. If any errors are detected, the commit operation is halted and an error message is reported.

Following is an example of the `commit` command executed with an incomplete candidate configuration database:

```
[edit]
lynn@iprouter# commit _
Policy error: Policy route-filter referenced but not defined
error: configuration check-out failed

[edit]
lynn@iprouter# _
```

In this example, a policy filter, `route-filter`, was applied to the protocol OSPF. As the CLI error message indicates, a policy was not defined or created.

Once each configuration item in the candidate configuration database has successfully passed the evaluation, MGD turns the candidate files into active files and signals the daemons that a new active configuration database is available. The daemons then access the configuration database to retrieve their new configuration data. The most recently active configuration database is then renamed to juniper.conf.1.gz., then previous juniper.conf.1.gz database is renamed juniper.conf.2.gz, and so on. The previous juniper.conf.9.gz database is overwritten and, as a result, eliminated. Following is an example of a successful `commit` of the candidate configuration database:

```
[edit]
lynn@iprouter# commit
commit complete

[edit]
lynn@iprouter# _
```

Figure 3-5 illustrates the relationship between the active configuration database and the candidate configuration database. It also illustrates the process when either

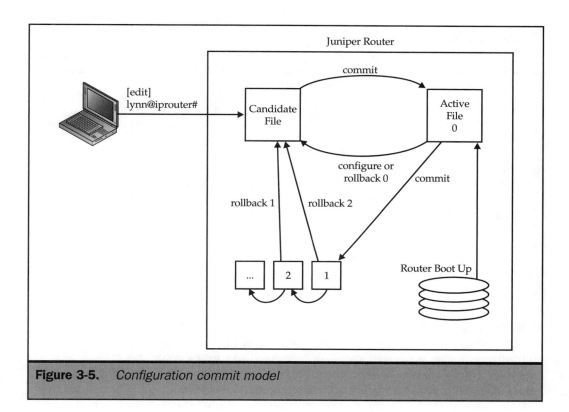

Figure 3-5.   *Configuration commit model*

the `configure`, `commit`, or `rollback` commands (addressed in the section, "Rollback a Configuration") are executed.

JUNOS software provides a few variations to the use of the command `commit`. The following example lists these variations:

```
[edit]
lynn@iprouter# commit ?
Possible completions:
  <[Enter]>            Execute this command
  and-quit             Quit configuration mode if commit succeeds
  check                Check only, do not apply changes
  confirmed            Automatically rollback if not confirmed
  |                    Pipe through a command
[edit]
lynn@iprouter# commit _
```

Commit and-quit

Commit and-quit is a convenience option that performs a commit and, if successful, exits configuration mode. This is useful when making quick changes to a configuration. The following example illustrates this feature.

```
lynn@iprouter> configure _
Entering configuration mode

[edit]
lynn@iprouter# deactivate interfaces so-0/0/0 _

[edit]
lynn@iprouter# commit and-quit _
commit complete
Exiting configuration mode

lynn@iprouter> _
```

Commit Check

JUNOS software also allows you to test the validity of the configuration before committing it. Use the commit check command to run the contents of the candidate configuration database through the commit tests without making it an active configuration. This feature allows incremental tests while building a large complex configuration, therefore, you are able to configure the router prior to a maintenance window and test the accuracy of the syntax. The following example illustrates this feature.

```
[edit]
lynn@iprouter# commit check _
configuration check succeeds

[edit]
lynn@iprouter# _
```

Commit Confirmed

Configuration changes in a complex network can result in an inability to reach the configured device. Traditionally this results in using out-of-band console access or forcing you to access the device via the front panel. JUNOS software incorporates a mechanism for reverting to the previous configuration if the router loses connectivity to the network.

The `commit confirmed` command will automatically perform a rollback if the commit operation is not confirmed within a small window of time. The default window is 10 minutes, and confirmation is performed simply by executing a second `commit` command. If the commit is successful, you simply type `commit` a second time and the commit is confirmed. If the commit is not successful and you cannot reach the router to type a second commit command within the confirmation period, the UI will rollback to the previous configuration and commit it, restoring connectivity.

In this example, the user deletes the wrong interface. Since the CLI session is using this interface for connectivity, the user can no longer type at the CLI or issue further commands. After the confirmation period expires, however, the automatic rollback restores connectivity and the user can again issue commands.

```
[edit]
lynn@iprouter# delete interfaces so-0/0/0

[edit]
lynn@iprouter# commit confirmed 2
commit complete
```

At this point, the user cannot type, but after 2 minutes, the session returns to normal and the deleted interface is again included in the configuration database. The user can then access the router again and proceed with deleting the correct interface.

```
[edit]
lynn@iprouter# show interfaces so-0/0/0 _
description "connection to fastnet";
unit 0 {
    family inet {
        address 192.168.1.1/24;
    }
}

[edit]
lynn@iprouter# _
```

Comparing the Active and Candidate Databases

In the event that you need to evaluate the difference between the active configuration database and the candidate configuration database, you can use the `show` command. Included with the `show` command, you pipe the command to `compare`. The UI displays the combined results of the candidate configuration database and the active configuration database. Differences are indicated by a plus or minus sign. In other words, if an entry was added to the candidate configuration database and is not in the active configuration database, it is indicated with a plus sign. If an entry was deleted from the candidate configuration database but is in the active configuration database, it is indicated with a minus sign. The following example illustrates this feature. The plus sign indicates the interface so-0/0/1 was added to the candidate configuration database, but does not exist in the active configuration database. The minus sign indicates the interface so-0/2/1 was deleted in the candidate configuration database, but still exists in the active configuration database:

```
[edit]
lynn@iprouter# show interfaces |compare rollback 0
+so-0/0/1 {
+    unit 0 {
+        family inet {
+            address 172.16.5.1/30;
+        }
+    }
+}
-so-0/2/1 {
-    unit 0 {
-        family inet {
-            address 172.16.1.6/30;
-        }
-    }
-}
 fxp0 {
     unit 0 {
         family inet {
             address 10.255.254.2/24;
         }
     }
 }
 lo0 {
     unit 0 {
         family inet {
             address 192.168.100.3/32;
         }
     }
 }
[edit]
lynn@iprouter# _
```

Rollback a Configuration

In the event that committing a candidate configuration database to become the new active configuration database causes some undesired effects, you have the option to return to the previous active configuration database. This is done with the command `rollback`. Rollback requests that the UI retrieve a previously active configuration database and make it the current candidate configuration database. Once this is done, you must execute the `commit` command to make it the new active configuration database.

For example, if you have just entered the `commit` command, the candidate configuration database is now your new active configuration database. Your previous active configuration database is no longer active. If you want to return to this previous active configuration database, enter the command `rollback 1` followed by the command `commit`. The number following the `rollback` command is the number of the previous active configuration database as noted in the name. Rollback 1 requests the CLI to retrieve the file juniper.conf.1.gz and make it the current candidate configuration database. When you execute the `commit` command, it makes this new candidate configuration database the new active configuration database. Refer to Figure 3-4 to see this feature illustrated.

It is important to note that not only does the `rollback` command need to be executed from configuration mode, it can be executed only from the top of configuration hierarchy. This is shown in the following example:

```
[edit]
lynn@iprouter# rollback 1
```

Hierarchical Save and Load

JUNOS software includes the ability to copy portions of the configuration to a separate file without using cut-and-paste. It also allows you to retrieve these configurations without using cut-and-paste.

Save Command

The `save` command allows you to copy all or selected portions of the configuration file to a text file. Execute the `save` command followed by the name of the file you want to create with the saved configuration. The CLI then evaluates your current location in the configuration hierarchy and saves it along with anything below it. If your current location is the top of the configuration hierarchy, then executing the `save` command saves the whole configuration file. If your current location is the `interfaces` statement, then the `save` command saves only the contents of the `interfaces` statement.

In the following example, the current location is in the `interfaces` statement. The command `save` is entered followed by the name of the file to save the configuration. This command saves only the contents of the `interfaces` statement.

```
[edit interfaces]
lynn@iprouter# save interfaces.conf _
Wrote 29 lines of configuration to 'interfaces.conf'

[edit interfaces]
lynn@iprouter# _
```

By default, the CLI saves the file in your home directory. The location of the home directory is /var/home/user_name; however, you can redirect the file and save it in another directory or on another system. To redirect the location for saving the file, enter a path prior to the name of the file. The following examples illustrate two ways to save the file in the directory of another user:

```
[edit]
lynn@iprouter# save /var/home/ginger/interface.conf _
Wrote 112 lines of configuration to '/var/home/ginger/interface.conf

[edit]
lynn@iprouter# _
```

Load Command

To retrieve a configuration file, use the load command. The load command retrieves the contents of the specified file and loads it into the candidate configuration database. There are three options when you execute the load command. You must specify one. The syntax for the load command is as follows:

```
[edit]
lynn@iprouter# load (merge|override|replace) <file> _
```

The first option is load merge. The option merge adds the contents of the specified configuration to the candidate configuration database. If there are any conflicts between the loaded file and the current candidate configuration database, the loaded file overrides those conflicts.

The second option is load override. The option override completely overrides the existing candidate configuration database by discarding its current contents and loading the new file in its place. In other words, it alone becomes the new candidate configuration database.

The third option is load replace. The option replace attempts to replace portions of the candidate configuration database with the content of the loaded file. For this to work properly, the loaded file must contain the tag replace: prior to the configuration entry.

In addition to using files to load into the JUNOS software candidate configuration file, the CLI also provides you a method to cut and paste all or portions of a configuration file. To cut or copy the configuration text from an external source, simply use the standard cut, copy, and paste methods available with your workstation operating system. Highlight the text using your mouse or cursor, then either right-click the mouse and select Copy, press the Copy button on the screen menu, or press the COPY key on the keyboard. To execute this feature, use the `load` command with the source file as "terminal." The following example illustrates the initiation of this method:

```
[edit]
lynn@iprouter# load merge terminal
[Type ^D to end input]
_
```

At this point the UI is waiting for input. To paste the copied text into the candidate configuration database, simply use the standard cut-n-paste method available with your workstation operating system. Highlight the text using your mouse or cursor, then either right-click the mouse and select Paste, press the Paste button on the screen menu, or press the PASTE key on the keyboard. The text is then pasted into the screen. As noted in the prompt to end the input, press CTRL-d.

It is important to ensure the correct information is copied into the candidate configuration database. This means that the copied text must follow the same hierarchical format used in the configuration database. The configuration text you copy into the router must include the primary root statement for the configuration, it must be in a hierarchical format with the substatements indented below the root statement, and it must include the open and close brackets and semicolon for the entries. Furthermore, you must be in configuration mode and your path location must be at the root of the statement hierarchy. The following example illustrates the correct method for entering a configuration text:

```
[edit]
lynn@iprouter# load merge terminal _
[Type ^D to end input]
interfaces {
    so-0/2/0 {
        unit 0 {
            family inet {
                address 150.200.1.1/24;
            }
        }
    }
}load complete
[edit]
lynn@iprouter# _
```

The portion pasted into the candidate configuration database includes everything from the statement `interface` to the last bracket. Once you have pasted it, press the keystroke CTRL-d. Keep in mind this configuration is still in the candidate configuration database and to activate the new configuration the `commit` command must be executed.

Save and Load Caution

It is important to ensure when using these commands that your path location in the statement hierarchy is set for the desired location. Saving the database when the path location is set incorrectly, then later loading the incomplete configuration can have an undesired affect. For example, if the path location of the statement hierarchy is mistakenly set to `[policy policy-statement filter1]` when you intend to save the complete configuration, the database created contains only the contents of this filter.

Later, if you execute the `load override` command to retrieve this database in an attempt to override the existing database with a new configuration database, the result is a configuration with only the policy filter defined. All other configurations are gone. Of course, you can use the `rollback` command to retrieve the previous configuration database. Whatever change you originally intended to make, however, you still need to reconfigure.

Using Operational Mode Commands in Configuration Mode

When configuring the Juniper Networks router, it is often necessary to evaluate the operational effects created by a configuration. The JUNOS software CLI provides a nice feature that allows you to execute operational mode commands from configuration mode. All operational mode commands are executable in this manner. These commands are executable regardless of your current location in configuration hierarchy. To execute an operational mode command from configuration mode, add the command `run` in front of any of these commands. The following example illustrates this capability:

```
[edit]
lynn@iprouter# run show interfaces terse _
Interface         Admin Link Proto Local                Remote
so-0/2/0          up    up
so-0/2/1          up    up
so-0/2/1.0        up    up    inet  172.16.1.6/30
so-0/2/2          up    up
so-0/2/3          up    down
fxp0              up    up
```

```
fxp0.0              up    up    inet   10.255.254.2/24
fxp1                up    up
fxp1.0              up    up    tnp    4
gre                 up    up
ipip                up    up
lo0                 up    up
lo0.0               up    up    inet   192.168.100.3      --> 0/0
pimd                up    up
pime                up    up
tap                 up    up

[edit]
lynn@iprouter# _
```

Online Documentation

To provide immediate and easily accessible assistance to help you with operating the Juniper Networks router, the documentation is included with JUNOS software. There might be times when accessing the manuals any other way is either difficult or impossible, therefore, you need only to log in to the router to access the documentation. To access the online documentation, use the command `help`. The documentation always matches the version of software running on the router.

Command Reference Example

There are three options available when using the online documentation. First, you can access reference material relating to the syntax of a particular command. This provides you with an example of using the command. To access an example configuration, use the command `help reference` followed by the command in question. The following example illustrates the use of accessing the online documentation for help in configuring a BGP peer type.

```
lynn@iprouter> help reference bgp type _
type
     Syntax
  type type;
     Hierarchy Level
  [edit protocols bgp group group-name],
  [edit routing-instances routing-instance-name protocols bgp group
  group-name]

     Description
  Type of BGP peer group.
```

```
    Options
type--Type of group:
  * internal--Internal group
  * external--External group

   Usage Guidelines
See "Define BGP Groups and Peers".

   Required Privilege Level
routing--To view this statement in the configuration.
routing-control--To add this statement to the configuration.
```

```
lynn@iprouter> _
```

Command Topic Explanation

The second option provides you with a more detailed explanation of the concepts behind the command. To access an explanation of a particular topic, use the command help topic followed by the topic in question. Using the preceding command, the following example provides you with the results when you use the help topic command:

```
lynn@iprouter> help topic bgp type _

  Define the Group Type

  When configuring a BGP group, you can indicate whether the group is an
  internal BGP (IBGP) group or an external BGP (EBGP) group. All peers
  in an IBGP group are in the same AS, while peers in an EBGP group are
  in different ASs and normally share a subnet.

  To configure an IBGP group, which allows intra-AS BGP routing, include
  the following form of the type statement at the [edit protocols bgp
  group group-name] hierarchy level (for routing instances, include the
  statement at the [edit routing-instances routing-instance-name
  protocols bgp group group-name] hierarchy level):
  [edit protocols bgp group group-name]
      type internal;

  To configure an EBGP group, which allows inter-AS BGP routing, include
  the following form of the type statement at the [edit protocols bgp
  group group-name] hierarchy level:
  [edit protocols bgp group group-name]
      type external;

lynn@iprouter> _
```

Command Apropos Explanation

The third option is available in configuration mode only. Help apropos provides sample configurations for the command, topic, or regular expression in question. The following example illustrates the use of the help apropos command in configuring a BGP. Note that it is shortened due to the length of options available.

```
[edit]
lynn@iprouter# help apropos bgp _
set routing-options rib <rib_name> static defaults community
    BGP community identifier
set routing-options rib <rib_name> static defaults community <value>
    BGP community identifier
set routing-options rib <rib_name> static defaults as-path <address>
    Address of BGP system that formed the route
set routing-options rib <rib_name> static route <destination> community
    BGP community identifier
---(more)---
```

The help apropos command provides output for your current location in the statement hierarchy. For example, the previous output provides information on BGP at the top of the statement hierarchy. The following example provides help for BGP while editing the BGP statement.

```
[edit protocols bgp]
lynn@iprouter# help apropos bgp _
set disable
    Disable BGP
set traceoptions flag packets
    Trace all BGP protocol packets
set traceoptions flag open
    Trace BGP open packets
set traceoptions flag update
    Trace BGP update packets
---(more)---
```

Scrolling Large Files Feature

There are times when you need to view files from the CLI. This might be when you are viewing a configuration database or the messages file, which contains the syslog messages, or some other type of log file. The JUNOS software CLI has added some features to assist you in this effort. When viewing the messages file, you will find that it can be very large, reaching thousands of bytes in size of text entries. Searching through this file line after line, looking for a particular entry, can be quite cumbersome. When the output of a JUNOS software command exceeds the number of lines on your terminal window, JUNOS software will automatically switch into *automore* mode, in which the output is stopped and buffered until you scroll forward. This mode is similar in function to the UNIX more or less programs, and uses consistent keybindings to those programs.

The CLI has added the ability to search forward and backward in the file, searching for a particular text string. It might also be necessary for you to move back and forth between the beginning and end of the file. With a large file, this too can be a lengthy process. The CLI has added a feature that allows you to jump back and forth between the beginning and end of the file immediately.

These are a couple of the features added to enhance your ability to view large text files quickly and efficiently. Table 3-3 provides the list of the features and their commands.

Category	Action	Keystrokes
Get Help	Display information about the keyboard sequences you can display at the -More- prompt.	h
Scroll Down	Scroll down one line.	ENTER, RETURN, k, CTRL-m, CTRL-n, or DOWN ARROW
	Scroll down one-half screen.	TAB, d, CTRL-d, or CTRL-x
	Scroll down one whole screen.	SPACEBAR or CTRL-f
	Scroll down to the bottom of the output.	CTRL-e or G
	Display the output all at once instead of one screen at a time (same as specifying the |no-more command).	N
Scroll Up	Display the previous line of output.	j, CTRL-h, CTRL-p, or UP ARROW
	Scroll up one-half screen.	u or CTRL-u
	Scroll up one whole screen.	b or CTRL-b
	Scroll up to the top of the output.	CTRL-a or g
Search	Search forward for a string.	/string
	Search backward for a string.	?string

Table 3-3. *CLI Keystrokes*

Category	Action	Keystrokes
	Repeat the previous search for a string.	n
	Search for a text string; you are prompted for the string to match (same as specifying the `|match string` command).	M or m
	Search, ignoring a text string; you are prompted for the string to not match (same as specifying the `|except string` command).	E or e
Interrupt or End Output, Redraw the Output, and Save the Output to a File	Interrupt the display of output.	CTRL-C, q, Q, or CTRL-k
	Do not redisplay the CLI prompt immediately after displaying the output, but remain at the -More- prompt (same as specifying the `|hold` command).	H
	Clear any match conditions and display the complete output.	C or c
	Redraw the output on the screen.	CTRL-I
	Save the command output to a file. You are prompted for a filename (same as specifying the `|save filename` command).	S or s

Table 3-3. *CLI Keystrokes* (continued)

Command Pipe Option

There are times when it becomes necessary to modify the output of a command. For example, you want to display the output of a command that is longer than the length of your computer screen. You might also find it necessary to search for some text string contained in large file. The JUNOS software CLI has added the pipe option to the command line. Similar to the UNIX pipe option, this allows you to modify the output of a command in many ways. For example, you might want to find a specific configuration in a saved configuration file. The following example illustrates how this is accomplished.

```
lynn@iprouter> file show test-L3VPN |find policy _
policy-options {
    policy-statement static {
        from protocol [ static direct ];
        then accept;
    }
}

[edit]
lynn@iprouter> _
```

Notice that the find variable is used and the object is listed after this variable. It is also possible to include multiple pipe options. In this next example, the output of the previous example is directed to be saved in a file.

```
lynn@iprouter> file show test-L3VPN | find policy | save policy_file _
Wrote 6 lines of output to 'policy_file'

lynn@iprouter> _
```

Table 3-4 provides a list of the options available for use with the pipe option.

Option	Description
Compare	Compare configuration changes with a prior version
Count	Count occurrences
Display	Display additional information
Except	Show only text that does not match a pattern
Find	Search for the first occurrence of a pattern
Hold	Hold text without exiting the -More- prompt
Match	Show only text that matches a pattern
no-more	Do not paginate output
Resolve	Resolve IP addresses
Save	Save output text to a file
Trim	Trim specified number of columns from start of line

Table 3-4.   *Pipe Options*

The Complete Reference

Chapter 4

System Management and Services

by Sean Christensen

This chapter touches on some of the more important management and operations features of JUNOS software. With all the available processes and mechanisms at your disposal, an elegant and scalable scheme can be set up for what many times is a thankless job. Also, with the battery of commands and features, the router can be used as a tool that can help in diagnosing network problems.

IP networks can become complex, and for some service providers, very complex. Such complex networks require mechanisms and procedures to securely control the network elements and provide the needed management of the network. JUNOS software was designed for the proper functioning of large service-provider networks, sporting a large array of management, monitoring, security, and diagnostic tools.

JUNOS software provides a wide range of features and functions to aid network administrators, including

- Root account
- Creating user accounts
- Security protocols
- Domain Name System (DNS) usage
- Telnet
- Secured shell (SSH)
- File Transfer Protocol (FTP)
- Finger
- Date/Time and Network Time Protocol (NTP)
- Simple Network Management Protocol (SNMP)
- PING and traceroute commands
- System event logging (syslog)
- Protocol event logging (traceoptions)

This chapter examines each of these functions.

Operating System and File Locations

With its lineage in FreeBSD UNIX, JUNOS software is designed to be a multi-user operating system. Juniper Networks took the FreeBSD operating system and rewrote major portions of it for use as the JUNOS software core. JUNOS software kept the multi-user facilities and further enhanced FreeBSD to provide a protected real-time environment. By using the rewritten portions of FreeBSD as a foundation, the designers of JUNOS software started from a clean slate to develop all the active protocols and services.

The following list of directories gives the organization of the files and where they are located. Although this list is not comprehensive, it represents the more important files and locations that you might have to deal with:

- /config is located on the primary boot device; that is, on the drive from which the router booted (generally the flash disk, device wd0). This directory contains the current operational router configuration and the last three committed configurations, in the files juniper.conf, juniper.conf.1, juniper.conf.2, and juniper.conf.3, respectively.

- The /var directory is located on the hard disk of the routing engine (device wd2). It contains the following subdirectories:

  - /var/home contains the users' home directories, which are created when you create user access accounts. For accounts using SSH authentication (more about this later), their .ssh file, which contains their SSH key, is placed in their home directory. When a user saves or loads a configuration file, unless the user specifies a full path name, that file is loaded from his or her home directory.

  - /var/db/config contains up to six previous versions of committed configurations, which are stored in the files juniper.conf.4 through juniper.conf.9.

  - /var/log contains system log and tracing files.

  - /var/tmp contains core files. The software saves the current core file (0) and the four previous core files, which are numbered 1 through 4 (from newest to oldest).

Although it is tempting to poke around the files of the core system with an editor such as *vi*, fight that temptation. Only under very special circumstances is it necessary to delve into the guts of the system. Just about any router-based feature is available in the *command-line interface* (CLI), and most tasks will always be performed there. Also, do not attempt to load any other UNIX programs or utilities into the router system. Doing so will void any warranty or service agreement and can result in a corrupted routing engine.

Being a multi-user operating system, there are a number of features to manage user accounts and access to the system. Users can be created and assigned permissions to selected portions of the system. These permissions can be quite granular. For example, you can allow one user of the system full access while curtailing some users to just a subset of commands, allowing upper-level administrators to delegate some of the management of the network while still maintaining control and security.

Root Account

When a new router is shipped to a customer, it has only one account: the all-important *root* account. The only access to a new router is through this account.

Root is always present in Juniper Networks routers and represents the *superuser* account. The superuser has control over all the functions of the router and is the highest level in the accounts hierarchy.

When the router is powered on, it is ready to be configured. Initially, you log into the router as the user `root` with no password. From here, you will see a prompt similar to the following:

```
login: root
Last login: Mon Mar 19 08:19:39 on ttyd0

--- JUNOS 4.3R2 built 2001-02-22 03:24:10 UTC

Terminal type? [vt100]

root@%
```

When the router asks for the terminal type, VT100 is the default. VT100 terminal emulation provides you the greatest compatibility and functionality for the console port.

The root account is special in that it always defaults to the *command shell* of the JUNOS software. The command shell is not the CLI that you use to configure the router. Essentially, it is a UNIX-style terminal interface that gives you direct control to the file system of JUNOS software and other low-level services. You might notice that the file system and directory structure are much like a UNIX system, a reminder that JUNOS software was derived from FreeBSD UNIX and shares many of the same features. Once you are logged in using the root account, you must enter the CLI. To do this, enter `cli` at the prompt.

```
root@% cli
root@>
```

The greater-than sign following the `root@` tells you that you are at the CLI. You should be aware that the root account is not accessible remotely. For instance, you cannot use the root account to Telnet into the router. The only place that you can directly use the root account is through the console port on the front panel of the router. Note that SSH under JUNOS software version 5 does permit root login.

To prevent any unwanted access to the router via the console port, you must add a root password. After you log in for the first time, you can configure the root password by including the `root-authentication` statement at the `[edit system]` hierarchy level. First enter the configuration mode, and then change the default root password:

```
root@> configure
root@# edit system
```

```
[edit system]
root# set root-authentication plain-text-password
root# New password: myrouter45
root# Retype new password: myrouter45
```

As you can see, you are prompted to enter the password (the password you type will not display; it is shown here only as an example). This is followed by a verification step to ensure that the password was typed correctly. Although the password is entered as plain text, the password is never displayed in an unencrypted form. For example, when the user account section is displayed using the show configuration command, the password field is a series of unreadable characters. JUNOS software uses an MD5 algorithm to encode the root and user account passwords:

```
root@> show configuration
root-authentication {
encrypted-password "$1$05d7t3h9n2r5df783dyg$df32f675"; # SECRET-DATA
}
```

The plain-text password is just one of the ways that a secure password can be entered. JUNOS software provides other security options to configure root and user account passwords. Another example of a password entry is the encrypted-password option. This option is used to enter a password character string that has already been encrypted by an MD5 algorithm:

```
[edit system]
root# set root-authentication encrypted-password "$1$05d7t3h9n2r5df783dyg$df32f675"
```

The top-level root account allows you to perform any function in the system; however, having a single account limits the auditing capabilities network administration.

Managing User Accounts and Access

JUNOS software can be configured to support any number of user accounts, each with its own access level, to distribute the administrative load and delegate authority.

User Accounts

For each account, you define the login name for the user and, optionally, information that identifies the user. After you create an account, the software creates a home directory in the file system for the user.

To create a user account, include the `login user` statement at the `[edit system]` hierarchy level:

```
[edit system]
root# set login user robert
```

This statement creates a new account that is identified by the username (`robert`, in this example). All account names must be unique within the router and cannot contain space, comma, or colon characters. A username by itself is not secure. There are a number of options, not the least of which is the password for the account. If a password is not associated with the account, the user cannot log in to the router. To configure the account password, enter the following statement into the configuration:

```
[edit system]
root# set login user robert authentication plain-text-password
```

This entry will be followed by prompts to type in a new password and verify it, as demonstrated in the previous section.

Now that an account and password have been created for a new user, it is necessary to identify the amount of access the user has to the router.

Security Classes

For all user accounts created on the system, there exists any number of security *classes*. Security classes define the limits of what an individual can do with the system. Users who can log into the router must be in a login class to accomplish any task. With login classes, you define the following:

- Access privileges that users have when they are logged into the router
- Commands and statements that users can and cannot specify
- Parts of the configuration that they can view and change
- How long a login session can be idle before it times out and the user is logged off

Each top-level CLI command and each configuration statement has an access privilege level associated with it. Users can execute only those commands and configure and view only those statements for which they have access privileges.

Associated with each class is a 32-bit field that can be set to any combination bit pattern. Each bit corresponds to a set of commands that the class is authorized to run. One or more *permission bits* define the access privileges for each login class. That is, with every login class definition, there exists a 32-bit *permissions field* that defines which commands can be entered by the associated user. Any combination of these permissions bits allows subsets of commands to be executed. Each permission bit in the 32-bit permission field has an associated keyword, so that you do not have to specify the bits themselves. Table 4-1 lists the keywords for each permission bit.

Permission Bit	Description
admin	Can view user account information in configuration mode and with the `show configuration` command
admin-control	Can view user accounts and configure them at the `[edit system login]` hierarchy level
all	Has all permissions
clear	Can clear (delete) information learned from the network that is stored in various network databases using the `clear` command
configure	Can enter configuration mode using the `configure` command, and commit configurations using the `commit` command
control	Can perform all control-level operations (all operations configured with the control-permission bits)
edit	Can edit all portions of a configuration, can load a configuration from an ASCII file, and can commit new and modified configurations using all the commands in configuration mode
field	Reserved for field (debugging) support
firewall	Can view the firewall filter configuration in configuration mode
firewall-control	Can view and configure firewall filter information at the `[edit firewall]` hierarchy level
floppy	Can read from and write to the removable media
interface	Can view the interface configuration in configuration mode and with the `show configuration operational mode` command
interface-control	Can view interface configuration information and configure interfaces at the `[edit interfaces]` hierarchy level

Table 4-1.   *Login Class Permission Bits*

Permission Bit	Description
maintenance	Can perform system maintenance, including starting a local shell on the router and becoming the superuser in the shell by issuing the `su root` command, and can halt and reboot the router using the `request system` commands
network	Can access the network by entering the `ping`, `ssh`, `telnet`, and `traceroute` commands
reset	Can restart software processes using the `restart` command and can configure whether software processes are enabled or disabled at the `[edit system processes]` hierarchy level
rollback	Can use the `rollback` command to return to a previously committed configuration other than the most recently committed one
routing	Can view general routing, routing protocol, and routing policy configuration information in configuration and operational modes
routing-control	Can view general routing, routing protocol, and routing policy configuration information and configure general routing at the `[edit routing-options]` hierarchy level, routing protocols at the `[edit protocols]` hierarchy level, and routing policy at the `[edit policy-options]` hierarchy level
secret	Can view passwords and other authentication keys in the configuration
secret-control	Can view passwords and other authentication keys in the configuration and can modify them in configuration mode
shell	Can start a local shell on the router by entering the `start shell` command
snmp	Can view SNMP configuration information in configuration and operational modes

Table 4-1.   *Login Class Permission Bits* (continued)

Permission Bit	Description
snmp-control	Can view SNMP configuration information and configure SNMP at the [edit snmp] hierarchy level
system	Can view system-level information in configuration and operational modes
system-control	Can view system-level configuration information and configure it at the [edit system] hierarchy level
trace	Can view trace file settings in configuration and operational modes
trace-control	Can view trace file settings and configure trace file properties
view	Can use various commands to display current system wide, routing table, and protocol-specific values and statistics

Table 4-1. *Login Class Permission Bits* (continued)

Predefined Classes

At first the permissions in Table 4-1 might appear cumbersome to work with, however, it is not necessary to define class access levels in this manner. JUNOS software has defined four very common access classes that can be used instead of these specific command subsets. Any of these four classes, shown in Table 4-2, can be used to define the access level of a user in the system.

Login Class	Permission Bits Set
operator	clear, network, reset, trace, view
read-only	view
superuser	all
unauthorized	none

Table 4-2. *Default System Login Classes*

For example, if you want to use the predefined superuser class, all you need to enter is

```
[edit system]
root# set login user robert class super user
```

Using this statement associates the predefined superuser class with the provided username. This results in the defined user gaining complete top-level control similar to that of the root account. The difference between the root and superuser account is that the superuser can log in remotely, whereas the root account can log in only to the console port. Like root, the superuser can perform any operation on the router.

If you want to limit a defined user to view access, you could associate the given username with the predefined read-only class:

```
[edit system]
root# set login user user-name class read-only
```

This account allows the user to access many of the show commands such as show interface and show route, but not to change any of the router's operational parameters or to see the router's configuration. Read-only is just that: you can look, but you cannot change anything.

The operator class is a little more powerful than the read-only class. The operator can clear ARP tables, reboot the router, issue PINGs and Telnets, and review the output from show commands, but still cannot view the configuration. For example, if the user issued the show configuration, he or she would see the following output:

```
root@>  show configuration
version /* ACCESS-DENIED */
system /* ACCESS-DENIED */
interfaces /* ACCESS-DENIED */
```

It is quite customary when using a new router for the first time to create a superuser account to perform the steps to bootstrap the router into the network. Create an account (superuser) that can perform all tasks, log out of the root account, and start working in the newly created account. Just as it is not a good idea to always work from the root account under UNIX, it is the same under JUNOS software. The action of forming a new account generates your home directory on the system where you can safely save files.

When you log in using a created account, a few things change when compared with using the root account. First, you always default to the CLI rather than having to manually start the CLI, as root requires:

```
Login: sean
Password:
Last login: Wed Apr 25 05:46:51 from 10.1.1.5
--- JUNOS 4.3R1.4 built 2001-01-19 07:26:27
sean@atl-core-r1>
```

After the standard banner is displayed, notice that the prompt is now changed to reflect the account name that logged in to the router. Also, the prompt reflects the host name (if the host name has been set) of the router you have logged into.

Custom Classes

The predefined classes discussed in the last section can come in handy when the needed access is not too granular. As you can see, giving someone just the `operator` class could result in an administrator that really cannot help in the area of provisioning new interfaces or performing other tasks.

JUNOS software allows you to create customized classes tailored to provide any amount of access you require. You define a specific class and its access privileges by using the `class` statement at the `[edit system login]` hierarchy level:

```
[edit system]
sean@atl-core-r1# set login class class-name permissions permissions
```

Specifying the correct permissions bits results in the respective access permissions listed in Table 4-1.

Network engineering and network operations are often two distinct organizations within a service provider. The operations group might be involved in the provisioning of interfaces for new customers, while engineering is busy building the network backbone. The top-level administrators in engineering might want to give the network operations group specific access to configure interfaces and perform other operational duties. Such an operational policy requires a customized class and can be configured this way:

```
[edit system]
sean@atl-core-r1# set login class provisioning permissions [clear network reset trace
view configure interface-control]
```

This statement creates a new class with the given class-name `provisioning`, and with the specified permissions. This newly created class can be associated with any number of user accounts to give the same access as the predefined `operator` class but with the added ability to configure and control interfaces.

After creating the new class, it must be associated with the accounts that are to receive the specified level of access. For example, to add user `tony` to the defined `provisioning` class, the statement is

```
[edit system]
sean@atl-core-r1# set login user tony class provisioning
```

Allow and Deny Commands

Instead of using permission bits, it may be easier to allow or deny specific commands to set the desired access. For example, you might want to give a specific user all the privileges of superuser access except for one or two commands. Instead of adding permission bits on top of permission bits to get the desired level of access, you can allow or deny specific commands. For each login class, you can explicitly deny or allow commands that would otherwise be permitted or disallowed by a privilege level specified in the permissions statement.

To explicitly deny a command that would otherwise be permitted, include the `deny-commands` statement at the `[edit system login class class-name]` hierarchy level:

```
[edit system]
sean@atl-core-r1# set login class class-name deny-commands regular-expression
```

The regular expression that follows the `deny-commands` is a text string that represents the commands that are to be denied. A regular expression is just a fancy name for a formula (set of operations) that performs comparisons on a string of characters. These regular expression operations are the extended set as defined in POSIX 1003.2[1] implementation. Table 4-3 shows the reserved operators and their meanings. An example of using regular expressions is shown later in this section.

Operator	Match
|	One of the two terms on either side of the pipe.
^	At the beginning of an expression, used to denote where the command begins, where there might be some ambiguity.

Table 4-3.   *Common Regular Expression Operators*

---

[1]   "IEEE Standard for Information Technology—Portable Operating System Interface: Shell and Utilities," POSIX 1003.2, 1992.

Operator	Match
$	Character at the end of a command used to denote a command that must be matched exactly up to that point, for example, `allow-commands "show interfaces $"` means that the user cannot issue show interfaces detail or show interfaces extensive.
[ ]	Range of letters or digits; to separate the start and end of a range, use a hyphen.
( )	A group of commands indicating an expression to be evaluated, with the result then evaluated as part of the overall expression.

Table 4-3.   *Common Regular Expression Operators* (continued)

Any of these operators can be applied to the text to identify the permitted and denied commands. For an example of using the `deny-commands`, suppose you have an otherwise very good network engineer who has a nasty habit of panicking and rebooting a production network router at the first signs of trouble (most engineers have had to resort to this "advanced technique" at one time or another). You would want to give this user all privileges, but take away the `system request reboot` command. This is how it can be done:

```
[system login]
sean@atl-core-r1# set class all-but-reboot permissions all deny-commands "request system reboot"
```

This statement gives the user `all-but-reboot` superuser permissions, but takes away the ability to reboot the router.

If the user entered a command that was denied for that user, the router would display a syntax error when it was typed. It would look as though the user entered a command that the router did not understand:

```
operations>request system reboot
     ^
syntax error, expecting <command>
```

To explicitly allow additional commands that would otherwise be denied, include the `allow-commands` statement at the `[system login]` hierarchy level:

```
[edit system]
sean@atl-core-r1# set login class class-name allow-commands regular-expression
```

You can, of course, use any combination of `allow-commands` and `deny-commands` to give any level of access that can be thought up. The last example of this section demonstrates a combination of `allow-commands` and `deny-commands`:

```
[edit system]
sean@atl-core-r1# set login class operations permissions [clear network reset trace
view configure interface-control] allow-commands "system request reboot" deny-commands
"(show system | show chassis | show version)"
```

This statement results in the `operations` class getting the ability to perform the tasks defined by the permissions bits, in addition to rebooting the router; however, members of the class cannot perform the specific commands `show system`, `show chassis`, or `show version`.

As you can see, JUNOS software can accommodate any set of access permissions you can think of. This flexibility has great value when the user community is specialized and custom permissions are desirable.

As a part of network maintenance, these login user accounts and permissions classes can be created and edited off line in a text editor. They can later be uploaded into other routers in the network to provide a consistent access policy.

Session Timeout

You can configure under the class definitions a timeout period for terminating an idle login session. An idle login session is one in which the CLI operational mode prompt is displayed but there is no input from the keyboard. By default, a login session remains established until a user logs out of the router, even if that session is idle.

To define the timeout value for idle login sessions, include the `idle-timeout` statement at the `[edit system]` hierarchy level and specify the number of minutes that a session can be idle before it is automatically closed:

```
[edit system]
sean@atl-core-r1# set login class class-name idle-timeout minutes;
```

If you configure a timeout value, the CLI displays messages similar to the following when timing out an idle user. It starts displaying these messages 5 minutes before timing out:

```
sean@atl-core-r1> Session will be closed in 5 minutes if there is no activity.
 Warning: session will be closed in 1 minute if there is no activity
 Warning: session will be closed in 10 seconds if there is no activity
 Idle timeout exceeded: closing session
```

The session closes after the specified time has elapsed, unless the user is running Telnet or monitoring interfaces using the monitor `interface` or `monitor traffic` command.

RADIUS and TACACS+

Things can start to get inconsistent when there are large numbers of routers in the network. You might want to make some changes in the permissions classes to open up new access, or take away some command that you feel could be a security risk. Making these changes in 10 routers might take only a few minutes to accomplish, assuming that you are sure you configured every router in your network. In a larger network with tens or hundreds of routers, the problem of changing access parameters becomes a bit more daunting. Given this, centralizing router access and security has some obvious advantages.

The original version of *Terminal Access Controller Access Control System* (TACACS), described in RFC 927,[2] has its origins in the early days of the Internet. The protocol was created for the ARPAnet community to centralize dial-in network access and to avoid double login issues between the hosts. The first version of TACACS focuses on authenticating Telnet users. TACACS has since been extended to support more functionality and is now commonly referred to as *TACACS plus* (TACACS+).

Remote Authentication Dial-In User Service (RADIUS) is a standards-based protocol that is part of the IETF's Authentication, Authorization, and Accounting (AAA) efforts. Like TACACS+, RADIUS (the latest version as of this writing is RFC 2865[3]) is focused on the authentication of network access servers, but is an extensible protocol that is able to support other features and accommodate vendor extensions.

Both RADIUS and TACACS+ work in the client/server model. The routers are the clients, and are authenticated by a central server. This scenario is shown in Figure 4-1.

JUNOS software can use RADIUS or TACACS+ or both to authenticate users instead of the individual accounts that you would have to maintain in a multitude of routers. This facility provides a greater amount of scalability and manageability that would otherwise be difficult to realize with discrete accounts.

TACACS+

Juniper Networks supports TACACS+ for authentication services, but not for authorization. User authentication is accomplished by specifying the address of TACACS+ server(s) that the router is to authenticate against. Configuring TACACS+ is straightforward:

```
[edit system]
sean@atl-core-r1# set tacplus-server server-address secret password
```

---

[2]   Brian A. Anderson, "TACACS User Identification Telnet Option," RFC 927, December 1984.

[3]   C. Rigney, S. Willens Livingston, A. Rubens Merit, W. Simpson Daydreamer, "Remote Authentication Dial-In User Service (RADIUS)," RFC 2865, June 2000.

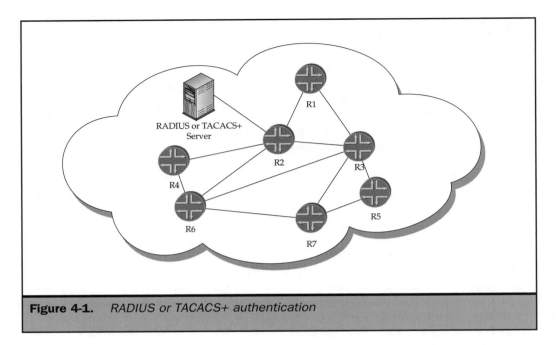

Figure 4-1. *RADIUS or TACACS+ authentication*

The `server-address` is the TACACS+ server itself. The *password* following the keyword `secret` is a password that the router uses to gain access to this server. This secret password can contain space characters. Note that this password is not the password that the user would enter, but is used by the local router to match the password used by the server.

Some optional parameters are associated with the TACACS+ server statement, such as the amount of time that the local router waits to receive a response from a TACACS+ server:

```
[edit system]
sean@atl-core-r1# set tacplus-server server-address timeout delay
```

By default, the router waits 3 seconds. You can configure `delay` to be a value from 1 to 90 seconds.

Optionally, you can configure the software to maintain one open TCP connection to the server for multiple requests, rather than opening a connection for each attempt, thus optimizing attempts to connect to a TACACS+ server. Using this configuration can lead to faster authentication times if the network is relatively stable. To do this, include the `single-connection` statement:

```
[edit system]
sean@atl-core-r1# set tacplus-server server-address single-connection
```

Unfortunately, we do not live in a perfect world. There is always the potential of a problem with a TACACS+ server or a network problem between the router and the server. The TACACS+ server cannot authenticate if the router cannot reach the server. Given this possibility, having redundant TACACS+ servers at different points in the network is prudent. Juniper Networks routers can be configured to use redundant servers. To configure multiple TACACS+ servers, just specify additional `tacplus-server` statements. If the first configured TACACS+ server exceeds the timeout delay, the next server configured is queried to authenticate the user. The user accounts and password files on these redundant servers must be maintained and synchronized for consistency.

Once the TACACS+ server is configured, a common user account must be created in each router that is shared by all the users. Again, when you are using local password authentication, you must create a local account for each user who wants to access the system. When you are using RADIUS or TACACS+ authentication, however, you can create a shared account for all users who do not have an individual account configured locally on the system. These accounts are sometimes called *template* accounts. Shared accounts share the same home directories, file ownership, and class access.

To configure a template account for TACACS+, specify a username of `remote`, just as you would create any other account:

```
[edit system]
sean@atl-core-r1# set login user remote class class
```

When the user attempts to log in to the router, the user specifies his or her login account name as configured on the TACACS+ server. The user does *not* use the username `remote`. This user, if authenticated, gains all the access of the configured class that is specified for this template. It is a requirement when using TACACS+ that the template username configured in the router is always the name `remote`. When using TACACS+, there can be only one template account.

RADIUS

RADIUS is more flexible and extensible compared with TACACS+. In addition to being a more open and maintained protocol standard than TACACS+, RADIUS has extensions built into the protocol that allow flexibility in the creation of customizable accounts. Because of this, you should seriously consider using RADIUS rather than TACACS+.

Configuration for RADIUS support is very similar to that of TACACS+. RADIUS service is configured by specifying the address of the RADIUS server(s) that the router uses to authenticate the user. For example:

```
[edit system]
sean@atl-core-r1# set radius-server server-address secret password
```

The `server-address` given in this example is the address of the RADIUS server. The password following the keyword `secret` is the password that the router uses to gain access to the server.

RADIUS also has some optional parameters. As with TACACS+, a timeout period can be specified for how long the router waits for an authentication acknowledgment:

```
[edit system]
sean@atl-core-r1# set radius-server server-address timeout delay
```

If there is no acknowledgement (accept or deny access) within the set time `delay`, the router attempts to retry the request. By default, the router waits 3 seconds before attempting another authentication request. You can configure this period to be a value from 1 to 90 seconds.

By default, the router retries connecting to the same server three times. You can change this default to a value from 1 to 10, using the `retry` option:

```
[edit system]
sean@atl-core-r1# set radius-server server-address retry number
```

Early versions of RADIUS use UDP port number 1645, which conflicts with the "datametrics" service. Subsequently, RADIUS was officially assigned port number 1812; however, you might want to change this default configuration to keep backward compatibility with older implementations. You can specify any legal port number to be used by the router to initiate an access query. Use the `port` option to change this port number:

```
[edit system]
sean@atl-core-r1# set radius-server server-address port number
```

A single RADIUS server has the same vulnerability as a single TACACS+ server. If the RADIUS server is down or the router cannot reach the server, authentication using this method fails. Again, it is a good idea to have redundant servers at different points of the network in anticipation of such a problem. JUNOS software can be configured to use redundant servers by specifying additional `server-address` pairs. You can specify any number of RADIUS servers the router is to use for authentication.

As with TACACS+, RADIUS supports template accounts; however, while TACACS+ can support only one template account and associated access class, RADIUS accommodates any number of template accounts. This is due to RADIUS support of vendor-specific attributes.

The JUNOS software supports the configuration of Juniper Networks–specific RADIUS attributes. These attributes are known as vendor-specific attributes and are described in an earlier RADIUS specification (RFC 2138[4]). The Juniper Networks–specific attributes are encapsulated in a RADIUS vendor-specific attribute with the vendor ID set to the Juniper Networks ID number, 2636. Table 4-4 lists the Juniper Networks–specific attributes you can configure.

All the attributes in this list are configured as ASCII text strings. It is up to the RADIUS server administrator to configure these additional details to handle the vendor-specific attributes. How this is done within RADIUS depends on the particular implementation and RADIUS product used.

As you can see from Table 4-4, the RADIUS server can be used to support more granular access, such as `named` template accounts (not just one called `remote`, as under TACACS+), each with its own access level. In addition, the RADIUS server can be configured with the regular expressions described in Table 4-3 earlier in this chapter, providing a more centralized, maintainable, and specialized-access scheme for users.

Name	Description	Type
Juniper-Local-User-Name	Indicates the name of the user template entered by this user when logging into a device. This attribute is used only in Access-Accept packets.	1
Juniper-Allow-Commands	Contains an extended regular expression that allows the user to run commands in addition to the commands authorized by the user's login class permission bits. This attribute is used only in Access-Accept packets.	2
Juniper-Deny-Commands	Contains an extended regular expression that denies the user permission to run commands authorized by the user's login class permission bits. This attribute is used only in Access-Accept packets.	3

Table 4-4. *Juniper Networks–Specific RADIUS Attributes*

---

[4] C. Rigney, S. Willens Livingston, A. Rubens Merit, W. Simpson Daydreamer, "Remote Authentication Dial-In User Service (RADIUS)," RFC 2138, April 1997.

When specifying a template account under RADIUS, you create a new user account just as you did before:

```
[edit system]
sean@atl-core-r1# set login user template-name class class
```

In this case, however, you have the flexibility to enter any `template-name` desired. Any RADIUS account (username) that matches this template name is associated with the access level of the defined class. On the RADIUS server, you set up a similar template name (username) and password that the user(s) enter to gain access. Users that do not have a matching account can be given access to a default template account on the router.

Authentication Order

With several methods of authentication, trying the preferred process first is important. Then, if the preferred method fails, you can try a different method to authenticate the user. If an adverse condition exists, such as a failed or inaccessible authentication server, you can maintain the needed security while allowing the user access to the system.

Using the `authentication-order` option, you can specify TACACS+, RADIUS, and local password authentication in any order.

To configure the authentication order, include the `authentication-order` statement at the `[edit system]` hierarchy level:

```
[edit system]
sean@atl-core-r1# set authentication-order [ authentication-methods ]
```

In *authentication-methods*, specify one or more of `radius`, `tacplus`, or `password`, from first tried to last tried. If you do not include the `authentication-order` statement, users are verified based on their configured password. Although it is not common to run different security protocols, you can configure both RADIUS and TACACS+ authentication and specify their order.

In the following example, the login section of a configuration is displayed:

```
[edit]
system {
      authentication-order [radius password];
      radius-server {
            10.1.1.10 {
                  port 1645;
                  secret "$9$kqfz3nCuBEk.0IRhrloJGimT"; # SECRET-DATA
                  timeout 5;
                  }
```

```
                }
login       {
        user alex {
                full-name "Alex the great";
                uid 2001;
                class superuser;
                authentication {
                        encrypted-password "$1$70E2.$wAfawecty6Z30aT48oq940"; # SECRET-DATA
                }
        }
        user operators {
                full-name "All operators";
                uid 2002;
                class read-only;
        }
        user remote {
                full-name "All other users";
                uid 2003;
                class read-only;
        }
    }
}
```

Assume that your RADIUS server is configured with the following account details:

- User `alex` with password `climber`
- User `ginger` with password `cruncher` and username `operators`
- User `george` with password `breaker` and username `operators`
- User `elaine` with password `all others`

The router first tries to authenticate user Alex (using the account name `alex`) on the RADIUS server at IP address 10.1.1.10. If this attempt fails for any reason, Alex is authenticated using his local password on the system. If his password does not match the one configured, he is denied access. If he succeeds, either by RADIUS or his local password, he is given access as a superuser because he has his own local user account.

The router first tries to authenticate Ginger and George (using the account name `operators`) on the RADIUS server. If this fails, they are denied access to the router. If the authentication attempts succeed, they gain read-only access to the router.

Elaine, logging in with the name `elaine`, has no template-user override, so she shares access with all the other remote users, getting read-only access.

Services and Processes

Once the user has gained access to the system, other useful (and in some cases necessary) features can be configured. This section explains the details of services and processes that are helpful in a large production network.

Host Names and DNS

Names are an important aspect to any kind of communication. If everyone or thing was not in some way uniquely named, it would be very difficult to maintain the references and relationships between people, places, things, and ideas. The same is true for a network and its elements.

Host Names

One of the first things that a network engineer should do when he or she gets a new piece of equipment is to give it a name. There should be a scheme for naming all devices in a network. The naming plan could be a cute system following your favorite Star Wars characters; however, you might find it more useful if the naming system were more meaningful. One example is to use a concatenation of the city the router is located in and some meaningful identifier. For the city part of the naming scheme, you could use the airport abbreviation. For example, "lax-core-j01," could be used to identify Los Angeles network-core Juniper Networks router 1, or "atl-access-M10-03" to indicate Atlanta network access layer M10 number 3. The system you use is up to you. The most important parts of the scheme are that it is consistent and it makes sense to those maintaining the network.

To give the local router a name, use the `host-name` statement under the `[edit system]` hierarchy:

```
[edit system]
sean@atl-core-r1# set host-name name
```

Name can be any ASCII character string, but it cannot contain spaces. Once a name is chosen and the configuration is committed, the prompt changes to reflect the new host name that you configured:

```
[edit system]
sean@atl-core-r1# set host-name lax-core-r1
sean@atl-core-r1# commit
commit complete

[edit system]
sean@lax-core-r1#
```

In a network with hundreds of IP addresses, keeping track of which router is configured with which address is difficult even when the numbering scheme is well organized. It makes a lot of sense to associate all the routers' IP loopback or other interface addresses to their assigned host names. The address-to-name associations can be configured either statically or by using DNS.

Static Host Tables

JUNOS software supports static host tables that associate host (router) names with IP addresses. The host table is not limited to routers; it can be populated with anything that has a name and an IP address. Configure the static mapping at the [system] subgroup:

```
[edit system]
sean@lax-core-r1# set static-host-mapping host-name inet address alias alias
```

This statement builds a static host mapping entry between the entered host name and IP address. The alias is just that: an optional informal name for the device. Note that more than one IP address can be associated with a particular host name. When the entries of the host table are set up, it is possible to refer to the host names in the table rather than just the IP address. For example, a PING using the host name issued from this router is resolved to the IP address. Given a host table of

```
system {
    static-host-mapping {
            atl-core-r1 inet 10.1.1.1 alias speeder1
            atl-core-r2 inet 10.1.1.2 alias speeder2
            lax-core-r1 inet 10.1.1.3 alias surfer1
            lax-core-r2 inet 10.1.1.4 alias surfer2
    }
}
```

issuing a PING from the command line using the host name results in the output

```
sean@lax-core-r1# ping atl-core-r2
PING atl-core-r2 (10.1.1.2): 56 data bytes
64 bytes from 10.1.1.2: icmp_seq=1 ttl=255 time=0.803
64 bytes from 10.1.1.2: icmp_seq=2 ttl=255 time=0.630
```

Notice that the IP address 10.1.1.2 is substituted for the host name atl-core-r2. There is no limit to the number of entries to the host table. Be aware that static host mappings work on the local router; you cannot use static host names on a router that does not have a table built. You must have a copy of the same table on all your routers for this scheme to be consistent, which is one of the big problems of using static host mappings.

With a separate table for every router, there is always the chance that one host table will be up to date while another is not. Updating these tables and copying them to every router when address changes occur or when additions are made to the network can be burdensome. For those who have a DNS, centralized control over host names and IP address mappings can be of great value.

DNS

A Domain Name Server (DNS) is a client/server application for host name to IP address bindings. The DNS system has gone through many revisions and updates. Many of these revisions add new functionality such as binding e-mail services and address families to the DNS. Domain concepts and facilities (RFC 1034[5]) cover the organization and conventions of the DNS, while RFC 1035[6] delves into some of the structures and protocol coding aspects.

DNS works on a hierarchical system of organizational entities (domains) and host names within those domains. The idea is simple: Host names are mapped by a local server for their respective domains. A client program called a *resolver* queries the DNS to associate the domain name with its IP address. If the host name is not resolvable by the local service, a server higher up the hierarchy is queried. This process continues until the correct mapping is found or an error has occurred (an error could be that there is no such host in the system). Figure 4-2 shows a simple example of a DNS system in action.

Juniper Networks routers can use a name-server to resolve IP addresses. To configure the address of a DNS, use the name-server statement at the [system] hierarchy:

```
[edit system]
sean@lax-core-r1# set name-server address
```

The address parameter is (you guessed it) the IP address of the name server. You can configure any number of name servers under the [system] level.

A fully qualified name includes the full hierarchy. For example, the name lax-core-r1.cloudbase.net is fully qualified because the entire name hierarchy is specified. It is not convenient to always use fully qualified names, especially if the hosts that you are dealing with the most reside in your domain. It is much easier to use just the host name lax-core-r1 if you are in the "cloudbase.net" domain; however, you need to give the DNS a place to start looking when you use only the host name. For each router, you should configure the name of the domain in which the router is located. This is the default domain name that is appended to host names that are not fully qualified. To configure the domain name, include the domain-name statement at the [edit system] hierarchy level:

```
[edit system]
set domain-name domain-name;
```

---

[5]   P. Mockapetris, "Domain Names—Concepts and Facilities," RFC 1034, November 1987.

[6]   P. Mockapetris, "Domain Names—Implementation and Specification," RFC 1035, November 1987.

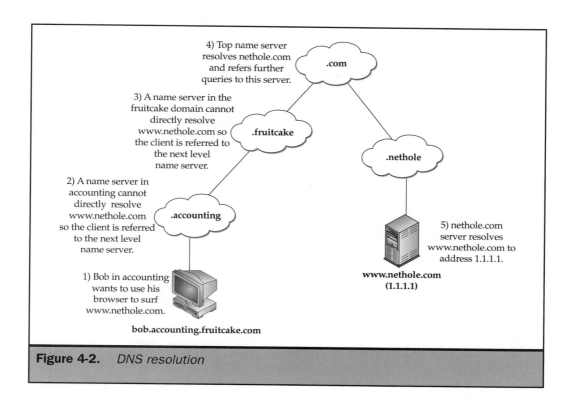

4) Top name server resolves nethole.com and refers further queries to this server.

3) A name server in the fruitcake domain cannot directly resolve www.nethole.com so the client is referred to the next level name server.

2) A name server in accounting cannot directly resolve www.nethole.com so the client is referred to the next level name server.

1) Bob in accounting wants to use his browser to surf www.nethole.com.

5) nethole.com server resolves www.nethole.com to address 1.1.1.1.

.com

.fruitcake

.nethole

.accounting

www.nethole.com (1.1.1.1)

bob.accounting.fruitcake.com

Figure 4-2.   *DNS resolution*

Note that sometimes the router might be located in more than one domain. In fact, the router could be located in several domain-name structures. You can configure a list of domains to which the router will try to resolve entered host names. To configure more than one domain to be searched, include the domain-search statement at the [edit system] hierarchy level:

```
[edit system]
domain-search [domain-list];
```

You can enter up to six domain names, with a total of 256 characters. For example, the configuration below will cause any host-name starting with domain-one.net and ending with domain-three.com to be queried against the DNS. As long as there is an entry for the host-name entered in one of the DNS systems, the IP address should be resolved.

```
[edit system]
set domain-search [domain-one.net domain-two.com domain-three.com]
```

Telnet

Telnet was invented to fill the need to connect large numbers of people to a central host computer. Until the mid-1980s, computers were extremely expensive; not everyone could afford to have a high-powered CPU on their desk, lap, or palm (that is, if it could even fit in the room with you). In those days, computer users were connected to the timesharing host via dedicated terminal servers running over serial (RS232 or similar) links. The access to the host computer was a "dumb terminal" that was really nothing more than a very simple, low power computer, keyboard, and CRT screen. This paradigm was extended to UNIX as those platforms and networking technologies such as Ethernet became popular. Telnet became prevalent as the UNIX operating system gained predominance, and represented a nonproprietary way to gain access to a remote host.

The Telnet process represents a virtual terminal server by which any number of users can access the host computer. Telnet is really two parts: a terminal serving process (daemon) running on the host system, and the Telnet client application.

The client program is the part that most people deal with. It is common to launch Telnet by typing the command `telnet` followed by the IP address or host name of the system you wish to communicate with. From there, you control the host through your interaction with the Telnet client. The Telnet client packs each of your keystrokes into tiny (usually 2-byte) TCP packets and ships them across the network to the server daemon on the host.

By default, Juniper Networks routers do not run a Telnet server process; you must explicitly turn it on. In fact, no remote access to the router is enabled by default. This was done for a good reason: Some might not want to run Telnet or other services in their networks because of security concerns.

If you do want to use Telnet, you can turn on the server process by entering the following statement under the `[edit system services]` section of the configuration:

```
[edit system]
set services telnet connection-limit connections rate-limit limit
```

The `connection-limit` parameter is used to specify how many concurrent Telnet sessions the router is to maintain. The `rate-limit` is used to set the number of connections that can be initiated in 1 minute. These parameters are useful for controlling the remote access a user community has to a given router's CLI.

Also, the router has a Telnet client that can be used to access other systems. In the CLI, type `telnet`, and the host you want to access:

```
sean@lax-core-r1> telnet 10.1.1.1
```

The glaring issue with Telnet is that it is unsecure. Each of the keystrokes generated by Telnet is sent "in the clear." Telnet has no facility for encrypting the information and, therefore, is susceptible to being intercepted by a packet capture/decode device. Anyone being authenticated by a host could have his or her passwords compromised by such a scheme. To address these security shortcomings, Juniper Networks routers support a more secure method to gain remote access to the CLI.

SSH

Originally written by Tatu Ylönen at Helsinki University of Technology Finland, SSH is a program similar to Telnet that is used to log into another computer over a network, to execute commands in a remote system. In fact, it was intended as an outright replacement for Telnet, rlogin, rsh, and rcp UNIX remote shells. SSH has been adopted by the Internet community and is now a maintained standard.

The SSH mission statement calls for strong authentication and secure communications over unsecure networks. It uses the popular RSA key system to authenticate and identify the hosts on both sides of the terminal session. SSH then uses DES, 3DES, or the Blowfish encryption algorithm to encode the resulting data stream of the session. Because of this series of secure processes, you are less likely to have your communications compromised.

For JUNOS software below version 5, the SSH protocol is 1 (SSH 1), and for JUNOS software version 5 and above, you have a choice of running either SSH version 1 or 2. Note that these two versions are incompatible with each other. You must use matching versions of SSH on both sides of the terminal session.

Like Telnet, SSH has two parts: the SSH client application and the background daemon process. The first step to using SSH is to enable the service on the router. You do this at the [edit system] level:

```
[edit system]
set services ssh connection-limit connections rate-limit limit
```

The options following the ssh statement are the same as those described in the setup for telnet service. The connection-limit parameter specifies how many concurrent SSH sessions the router is to maintain, and the rate-limit sets the number of connections that can be initiated in 1 minute.

Once the router is setup to accept SSH connections, you must provide a public key for the router to use to encrypt the data that is sent back to your host system. This public key is generated by your host system using a "key gen" program included with the SSH system. This program will usually generate two files. The first file will be a private-key file that your system uses to decrypt the authentication request and a second public-key file that the router uses to encrypt and carry out the authentication. There is usually an option to encrypt your private key (on your host) with a *pass phrase*. It is generally recommended that a pass phrase be used to secure your private key. The public-key file will contain a large sequence of numbers similar to:

```
1024 65537 14606923203252826605866260964102069072265621522064361885142149050684983498285202512837580
113794290512776502350173234765451487802282729186311120905213076410719586759432771374614673489870617282220302218512886903249692977635537897209558050093700369560290473747441832617340286714323272174105482212317080155520559 tester@bubba.net
```

For SSH to correctly authenticate the session, you must configure the public key sequence on the login account that is to use SSH:

```
[edit system]
sean@lax-core-r1# set login user tester authentication ssh-rsa "1024 65537
46069232032528266058662609641020690722656215220643618851421490506849834982852025128375801137942905127765023501732347654514878022827291863111209052130764107195867594327713746146673489870617282220302218512886903249692977635537897209558050093700369560290473747441832617340286714323272174105482212317080155520559 tester@bubba.net"
```

This statement loads the public key into the router for the user `tester`. Because the public key is quite long to type in, it might be best to copy and paste the entry to your terminal. Also, do not forget to use double quotation marks at the start and end of the public key.

Whenever the user `tester` uses the SSH program to log in to the router, the RSA exchange takes place. The router sends its public key to the SSH client, and the router in turn uses the preconfigured public key for user `tester`. These keys, using the RSA algorithm, are used to transmit a *session key* that the `tester` account uses to connect to the router. The resulting session, if the authentication passes, is then encrypted using DES, 3DES, or Blowfish. The client program defines which one is used based on its configuration.

As stated earlier, under JUNOS software version 5 and above, you can run either SSH version 1 or 2; however, you can specify that all SSH sessions are forced to a particular version. You can also specify that either version be supported. You can do this by using the `protocol-version` statement under the `[edit system services]` level:

```
[edit system services]
lab@smyrna-re0# set ssh protocol-version v2
```

This statement forces all SSH sessions to use version 2. If the client tries to use the SSH protocol version 1, the service will fail. To allow either SSH protocol to be used, specify both versions in the `protocol-version` command. The router can distinguish between the two protocols.

Due to a known vulnerability in the version 1 specification, SSH version 2 should be used if you have the choice. Also, version 2 is currently being maintained, while version 1 is considered obsolete.

Earlier in the chapter, it is stated that root account access is provided only through the physical console port and SSH. If JUNOS software version 5 or above is used, you can allow root account access over the network. To allow an SSH protocol to log in using the root account, use the `root-login allow` statement.

```
[edit system services]
lab@smyrna-re0# set ssh root-login allow
```

To disable the root account login (the default), use the `root-login deny` command:

```
[edit system services]
lab@smyrna-re0# set ssh root-login deny
```

SSH has only a few more configuration details than Telnet; however, SSH affords the network administrator greater security in a potentially hostile Internet. It is a good idea to consider using SSH instead of Telnet.

Finger

Finger (RFC 1288[7]) is an optional informational protocol/process supported under JUNOS software. Finger gives a user community a way to retrieve information about other members of the community. For example, a user can send a finger request to an e-mail address and the returned information can be (depending on the options) the full first and last name of the user or even the home directory the user is working from. Enable the finger daemon process from the `[edit system]` level of the configuration:

```
[edit system]
set services finger connection-limit connections rate-limit limit
```

The `connection-limit` parameter specifies how many concurrent finger requests the router allows. The `rate-limit` sets the number of connections that can be initiated in 1 minute.

---

[7] D. Zimmerman, "The Finger User Information Protocol," RFC 1288, December 1991.

Once the finger daemon is running, you can issue a finger query targeted at the router. One of the parameters of a finger query is the name (either a login or full name) of the account of interest. As an example of using a finger program, a query of a router that has a username of `Sam Smith` returns:

```
Finger command issued.
Waiting for reply...
Login: sam                              Name: Sam Smith
Directory: /var/home/ssmith             Shell: /usr/sbin/cli
On since Sun Aug 26 15:36 (EST) on ttyp0, idle 0:01, from 172.16.1.3
No Mail.
No Plan.
Finger command completed.
```

As you can see, finger returns the account information for `Sam Smith`. Also note that finger returns the home directory, the shell environment, login time/date, and even the IP address of the host that Sam is using to access the router.

Finger can be used to gather information on the users of the system, but be aware that finger can be exploited by anyone in the Internet. There is no built-in control over who can finger the system. It is for this reason that the use of finger is restricted.

File Transfer Protocol

The *File Transfer Protocol* (FTP) is the one of the oldest and widely used protocols on the Internet. FTP is used to send and receive files between any two hosts. You can define the router to be an FTP server by configuring the [edit system] section:

```
[edit system]
set services ftp connection-limit connections rate-limit limit
```

Again, the `connection-limit` parameter specifies how many concurrent FTP sessions the router maintains and `rate-limit` sets the number of connections that can be initiated in 1 minute.

The accounts that are used when connecting to a router that has been set up as a FTP server are the ones set up in the login accounts. The home directory of the server is also that of the login accounts. While you might find it convenient to use the router as a place to copy and store files, the FTP service must be used only for router-based operations. The router does incorporate a hard drive for mass storage, but the drive is limited. Files FTP'ed into the router can take up space needed by the router's log files. Also, having another process (daemon) exposed to the Internet represents a possible security risk. For these reasons, FTP should be enabled only when it is needed.

Setting Time and Location

When troubleshooting, you need to know when a particular event, problem, or error occurred. The JUNOS software system has a real-time clock that is used to populate system logs (syslogs) and provide an accurate local time. To set the local time, use the `set date` command from the operations (not edit) mode:

```
set date YYYYMMDDhhmm.ss
```

YYYY is the four-digit year, *MM* is the two-digit month, *DD* is the two-digit date, *hh* is the two-digit hour, *mm* is the two-digit minute, and *ss* is the two-digit second. At a minimum, you must specify the two-digit minute. All other parts of the date and time are optional. Once set, the router uses this date and time in all subsequent log entries. To display the current date and time, use the `show system uptime` command:

```
sean@lax-core-r1> show system uptime
Current time:       2001-07-12 12:36:41 UTC
System booted:      2001-07-12 12:13:32 UTC (00:23:09 ago)
Protocols started:  2001-07-12 12:14:38 UTC (00:22:03 ago)
Last configured:    2001-07-12 12:26:48 UTC (00:09:53 ago) by ssimmons
12:36PM up 23 mins, 1 user, load averages: 0.00, 0.02, 0.07
```

Show system uptime displays a number of fields in addition to the current time. The date of the last reboot of the router is shown, along with the amount of time the router has been in operation. Also, there is a field that displays the last time the router was configured (committed) and by whom.

After you set the correct local time, you should set the correct time zone the router resides in. Notice in the previous example that the time is in *Universal Coordinated Time* (UTC). UTC is the same as *Greenwich Mean Time* (GMT) and *Zulu* (Z) time, which are based at the prime meridian (0° longitude) of the Earth. Figure 4-3 shows the 24 time zones of the Earth and the areas that they cover.

With systems that can reside in almost any place on the planet, it is important to set the time of each system in relation to where it is located. Alternatively, you might want to set the times of all your worldwide routers to that of your network operations center for easier coordination. To modify the correct time zone, use the `time-zone` statement at the [edit system] hierarchy level:

```
[edit system]
set time-zone time-zone
```

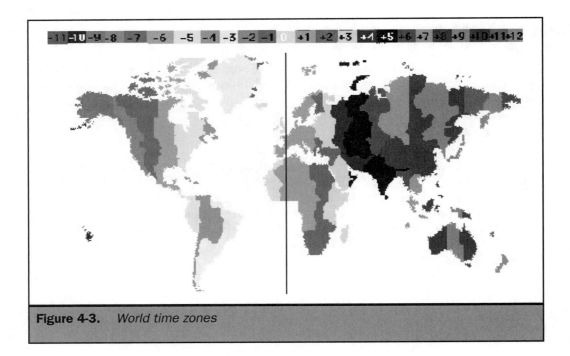

Figure 4-3.   *World time zones*

Specify the *time-zone* using the continent/country/zone primary name. For example, if the router resides in Shanghai, China, set the time zone with the following statement:

```
[edit system]
jnpr@q-net-r1# set time-zone Asia/Shanghai
```

For the time zone change to take effect for all processes running on the router, you must reboot the router.

NTP

Setting the time manually is sufficient in many situations; however, if you want to make the process of time synchronization automatic, you can configure the Network Time Protocol (NTP) (RFC 1305[8] covers version 3) to set the correct time for you. Also, NTP can be used to provide synchronization services to other hosts via unicast request or even broadcast the time on to a local subnet, enabling the hosts to set their clocks to

---

[8]   David L. Mills, "Network Time Protocol (Version 3) Specification, Implementation and Analysis," RFC 1305, March 1992.

that of the router. NTP provides an accuracy of around 1 to 50 milliseconds, depending on the characteristics of the synchronization source and network makeup. Note that the *Simple Network Time Protocol* (SNTP) (RFC 1769[9]) is a variant of NTP that has reduced overhead at the sacrifice of robustness, but should in most cases work with NTP. As of this writing, Juniper Networks provides only NTP services.

Stratum Clocks

There is a saying, "A person with a watch always knows what time it is; a person with two is never sure." This illustrates the problem of which clock to believe when there are multiple sources for time synchronization, and the motivation behind a stratum clock designation. A stratum is a definition of how far away (how accurate) a clock is from a definitive UTC time.

Atomic clocks are hyper-accurate and have been used in laboratories for many years to provide timing for experiments that required such accuracy. Usually, these clocks are based on a process of obtaining the resonance frequency of the element cesium. This frequency is used to correct a quartz crystal oscillator that generates the actual time reference. Atomic clocks are considered "primary" or stratum 1 time sources; there are none more accurate than this.

A stratum 2 clock is one that synchronizes to a stratum 1 source and is considered more accurate than stratum 3. A stratum 3 clock synchronizes to a stratum 2 source and is considered more accurate than stratum 4. This hierarchy is continued until stratum 16 is reached, the furthest away from external UTC. In NTP, a server is not believed unless it is synchronized to another NTP server, which itself must be synchronized to something up stream, eventually terminating in a high-precision stratum 1 clock.

NTP attempts to synchronize to the best external source of UTC. Its success depends on several factors such as propagation delays, availability, and general temporal agreement among all other sources. NTP uses integer math to calculate the time stamp and a 64-bit value to present the time figure. Using integers avoids using more "CPU expensive" floating-point calculations. If a real-time clock in a host is running fast, and is more than 128 milliseconds, but less than 128 seconds, the clocks are slowly stepped into synchronization.

NTP Considerations

NTP servers operate in one of two modes: as a peer or as a server. In peer mode, the NTP process is willing to receive, as well as provide, time information. The peer processes are symmetric with each other, and are sometimes referred to as *symmetric active mode*. This is the mode to select when there are a number of redundant time servers in a network. Within your own network, you might want to fully mesh each of your time servers to guarantee that there are no discrepancies between them. In turn, these time servers would be synchronized to higher stratum (lower numbered) clocks.

---

[9]   David L. Mills, "Simple Network Time Protocol (SNTP)," RFC 1769, March 1995.

The NTP process can also be run in server mode, in which the time server(s) are willing to synchronize only to other sources and not send their own time figures. This is the mode most likely appropriate for the majority of the routers in a typical network. From these lower-level servers, many client hosts can be synchronized to that of the network.

Figure 4-4 shows an example of an NTP design that can be used for most networks. In this diagram, notice that several stratum 1 and 2 servers external to the autonomous system feed peer-configured NTP routers. These routers are further peered with each other to provide redundancy and diversity in the network. The three peers feed server-configured time servers. Further beyond these NTP servers, there are clients that synchronize their clocks to that of the network. This system of coordinated time servers can be extended to scale to any size desirable.

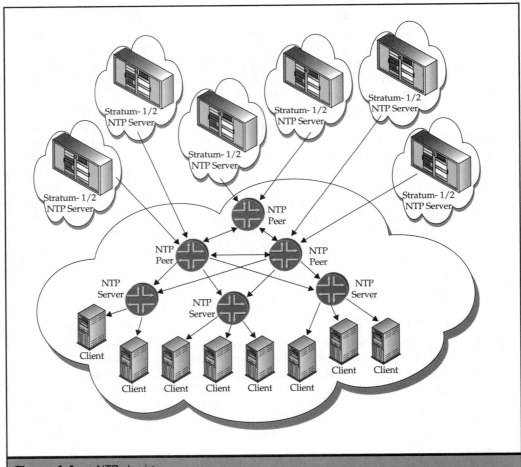

Figure 4-4. *NTP design*

Configuring NTP Peers and Servers

To use NTP, you must first select the NTP role that the router is to provide. If you want to use the public NTP servers in the Internet, it might make sense to use routers that are generally more WAN-connected and represent well-connected exit points for your network as peer NTP time servers. To configure the router for peer NTP operation, use the following statement at the [edit system] level:

```
[edit system]
set ntp peer address key key-number version version-value prefer
```

The *address* is the NTP process that you wish to peer with. You must specify an IP address, not a host name. The other parameters following the address are optional. The key keyword and following 32-bit *key-number* value are used to secure the NTP session by encrypting the authentication fields in the NTP packets. The configured key must match the authentication values on the other side. There are further steps that are needed to use authenticated NTP, and are covered later in this section. The optional version keyword is used to provide backward compatibility to lower-version NTP servers. The default is the current version 3 of the standard. Finally, the prefer keyword is used to specify that the remote NTP server is the preferred source of UTC time.

To designate the local router to run in server mode, (also known as *client* mode) use this statement at the [edit system] hierarchy:

```
[edit system]
set ntp server address key key-number version version-value prefer
```

The optional parameters following the IP address are the same as that in the peer statement above.

If the difference between the configured NTP servers is more than 128 seconds, the clocks are not synchronized. You must set the time on the local router so that the difference is less than 128 seconds to start the synchronization process. NTP will not synchronize to a time server if the server's time appears to be very far off from local time. You can synchronize the clocks using the set date command.

The configuration process can be somewhat automated by specifying a boot-server pointing to a reliable NTP server. When you boot the router, it issues an *ntpdate* request, which polls the network server to determine the local date and time. You must configure a central server that the router uses to determine the time when the router boots by specifying a boot-server from the [edit system] level:

```
[edit system]
set ntp boot-server address
```

The IP address is the NTP server that you want the router to set its clock to when booting.

When selecting router-NTP roles, routers that are LAN-connected can be set up to announce NTP messages. Juniper Networks routers can be configured to broadcast or multicast NTP time information onto these subnets. In addition, NTP can be configured to listen to a LAN subnet for other sources of synchronization. To configure the router to broadcast or multicast NTP messages, specify the broadcast address on one of the local networks or a multicast address assigned to NTP:

```
[edit system]
set ntp broadcast address key key-number version version-value ttl ttl-value
```

You must specify an IP broadcast address, not a host name. For example, if you have a subnet that is using 172.16.1.0/24 for its address, the broadcast for this segment is 172.16.1.255. For multicasting support, the multicast address must be 224.0.1.1. The other optional parameters are similar to those of the server and peer statements. The last ttl parameter is useful if you are running a multicast supported network. You can configure the *Time-to-Live* (TTL) value of the NTP packets to be bounded to the requested NTP multicast service diameter.

Junipers Networks routers can also be configured to listen to broadcast or multicast NTP messages. To configure the router to be a broadcast client on a segment, use the broadcast-client statement:

```
[edit system]
set ntp broadcast-client
```

When the router hears a broadcast message for the first time, it measures the nominal network delay using a brief client/server exchange with the remote server. It then enters broadcast client mode, in which it listens for, and synchronizes to, succeeding broadcast messages.

To set up the router to listen to multicast NTP announcements, use the multicast-client statement:

```
[edit system]
set ntp multicast-client
```

You can specify one or more IP addresses. If you do, the router joins those multicast groups. If you do not specify any addresses, the software uses 224.0.1.1.

Authenticated NTP Services

By default, network time synchronization is unauthenticated. The system will synchronize to whatever system appears to have the highest-quality time. Authentication of network time services is recommended to ensure that no spoofing of service is successful. When an NTP time server runs in authenticated mode, for each packet transmitted, there is a 32-bit key value and a cryptographic checksum for the packet's contents. The receiving peer computes the checksum and compares it with the one included in the packet. Only time servers transmitting network time packets that contain one of the specified key numbers and with keys that match the value configured for that key number are eligible to be synchronized to. Other systems can synchronize to the local router without being authenticated.

The first step to using authentication is to define the authentication keys by including the `authentication-key` statement at the `[edit system]` hierarchy level:

```
[edit system]
set ntp authentication-key key-number type encryption-type value password
```

The specified `key-number` is used to decrypt the NTP packets received and sent to this local router. The `type` is either MD5 or DES and specifies the encryption/decryption algorithm that is used. The `password` is the secret character string that is used for this key. You can enter multiple authentication keys for each of the different peers or servers used. The key number, type, and password must match on all systems using that particular key for authentication.

In addition to setting up the authentication keys, you must specify the trusted keys that the system uses to authenticate the other peers. Trusted keys are a set of keys that are configured for the trusted remote peers communicating with this NTP server. Set up the trusted key set in the `[edit system]` section:

```
[edit system]
set ntp trusted-key [ key-numbers ]
```

You can specify any number of trusted keys that will be associated with the remote time servers. For example, suppose you want to set up NTP authentication between two routers A and B. For router A (IP address 73.236.128.252), the following configuration is used:

```
ntp {
    authentication-key 1234 type md5 value "$9$pjN.uRSvMX-b2Lxb2oaHk"; # SECRET-DATA
    peer 73.236.128.253 key 1234;
    trusted-key 1234;
}
```

For router B (IP address 73.236.128.253), the following NTP configuration is used:

```
ntp {
    authentication-key 1234 type md5 value "$9$Vab4ZHkPQ39mf39tpEh"; # SECRET-DATA
    peer 73.236.128.252 key 1234;
    server 172.17.27.46;
    trusted-key 1234;
}
```

Whenever router A sends an NTP time message, router B uses the authentication key and password value specified in its configuration. Note that only a matching key `1234` and the password will correctly decrypt on the other NTP peer. Also note that when the NTP configuration is displayed that the authentication-key values are encrypted.

Displaying NTP Operation

Once NTP has been configured, there are a number of ways that its operation can be monitored. One check of operation is to view the NTP protocol status. This can be accomplished with the `show ntp status` command:

```
lab@smyrna-re0> show ntp status
status=06a4 leap_none, sync_ntp, 10 events, event_peer/strat_chg,
processor="i386", system="JUNOS5.1B1.2", leap=00, stratum=2,
precision=-20, rootdelay=76.389, rootdispersion=60.119, peer=64669,
refid=coetanian.juniper.net,  reftime=bf3a87af.5873eee5  Fri, Aug 31 2001 18:01:19.345, poll=6,
clock=bf3a87ed.64a63305  Fri, Aug 31 2001 18:02:21.393, state=4,
phase=52.401, frequency=-17.439, jitter=56.929, stability=98.365
```

The first line is the status flag showing that this NTP server is synchronized (sync_ntp). Had this displayed a condition of `sync_alarm`, it would indicate that this NTP server had not stepped its clock to an external source (remember that NTP will not synchronize clocks that are not within at least 128 seconds of each other). In addition, there is a 2-bit code that warns of an impending leap second to be inserted in the NTP timescale. In this case, a leap second will not be inserted. A leap-second code is set before midnight of the present day.

Another field that is important to notice is the stratum designation of this server. The second line of the output denotes this server as a stratum 2 source. The `refid` shows that the primary source of synchronization is the server at coetanian.juniper.net. If the `refid` had been 0.0.0.0, it would be another indication that this server was not synchronized to an external source.

The other parameters of this output correspond to the functioning of the NTP server. These parameters are feedback from the algorithms that guarantee synchronization between NTP servers.

In addition to displaying the status of NTP, you can show a list of peer and server sources using the `show ntp associations` command.

```
lab@smyrna-re0> show ntp associations
     remote           refid      st t when poll reach   delay   offset  jitter
==============================================================================
+host253.staffbr coetanian.junip  2 u   21   64  377   0.687   62.185   1.530
*coetanian.junip .GPS.            1 -    5   64  377  75.879   72.195   1.004
```

This output shows the two servers peered with the router and their relationship with the local router. At the start of the line is a status character that denotes the preference of the NTP peer selection. Table 4-5 shows the possible status characters.

Status Character	Meaning
(space)	Discarded because of a high stratum value or failed sanity checks (also means that the clocks are not synchronized).
X	Designated "falsticker" by the intersection algorithm; this is an indication that the time sent by this peer is not trusted.
.	Culled from the end of the candidate list; this peer will not be considered for selection.
–	Discarded by the clustering algorithm; a time-server that is considered least preferred candidate.
+	Included in the final selection set; a server that is considered a good source for synchronization.
#	Selected for synchronization, but selection parameters exceeds maximum "distance" parameters.
*	Selected for synchronization, this peer is considered to be the best source of external UTC time.
o	Selected for synchronization, but pulse per seconds signal is in use.

Table 4-5.   *NTP Association Status Character*

In addition to the remote server name (or IP address), a reference ID is associated with the peer. The *st* field tells the stratum designation of the peer.

The *t* field is the type of server the peer is. A *b* indicates that broadcast facilities are being used. An *m* means that multicast time messages are in use. A *u* indicates that time synchronization supports unicast operation. If the minus sign is used, it indicates that the server supports more than one method of synchronization.

The When field shows the last time, in seconds, an NTP time message was received. The Poll field is an indication of how often the local NTP server will poll the respective server. Note that poll times will generally increase (get longer) as the NTP clocks become closer to being synchronized with each other.

The rest of the output indicates the accuracy of the clocks as it relates to network performance. NTP uses these parameters to make corrections to the messages received.

There are a number of ways to obtain a good synchronization source through NTP. As previously cited, one method is to use one or more higher-level public NTP servers on the Internet to synchronize your clocks. There are literally hundreds of stratum 2 and even stratum 1 servers on the Internet. Many of these servers might require that you register your interest for use beforehand by sending an e-mail to the administrator. The U.S. Navy operates a number of public NTP servers, and their addresses can be found at: http://tycho.usno.navy.mil/ntp.html.

If you feel that you need even more accuracy for your devices or clients in your network, you can use a radio or GPS receiver/NTP server instead of relying on others in the Internet. There are several radio services that broadcast time information over the airwaves. Also, *Global Positioning System* (GPS) units receive time information. These too can be interfaced to an NTP server to provide an accurate time base.

SNMP

A network represents a complex organization of nodes and processes that must operate reliably and efficiently. Having a single node or link failure in a network can undermine the network's performance and result in loss of service; therefore, determining where and when a network failure is occurring is an absolute necessity.

In addition, gathering statistics can give you insight into how well the network is running. This statistic insight can help you find bottlenecks in a network, help in the justification of more bandwidth, and aid in traffic engineering tasks. SNMP can be used for both troubleshooting and monitoring.

SNMP is a popular and open client/server standard that has been implemented on countless platforms. The original purpose of SNMP was to provide a simple way to monitor and in some cases control network elements in the Internet.

The first version, standardized in RFC 1157,[10] was meant to be a tactical short-term answer to the problem of managing the Internet. It was hoped that the long-term solution of an International Standards Organization (ISO)-based protocol would be realized. That protocol, *Common Management Information Services/Common Management Information Protocol* (CMIS/CMIP), was developed and was considered to be superior to SNMP at the expense of more complexity; however, with the failure of the ISO-based protocols to catch on in the Internet, the popularity of SNMP prevailed.

Being a client/server protocol, SNMP-enabled nodes can be broken down into two categories: SNMP managers and SNMP agents.

SNMP managers are the central points that collect, interpret, and present the status and performance of the network elements. These management stations run applications that actively poll or listen to messages produced by the SNMP agents in the network.

An SNMP agent represents a server (daemon) process that gathers and stores the status and performance of the respective element. The SNMP agent then facilitates the transfer of the information to the manager.

SNMP uses UDP-based, structured *protocol data units* (PDUs) to transfer the status and performance information. These packets are generally the result of SNMP commands that are sourced from the agent or manager. With the gathering and collection of this information from all the nodes in the network, the manager can form a composite view, while presenting the status and performance of the network. An example of this interaction between SNMP agents and managers is shown in Figure 4-5.

---

[10]   J. Case, M. Fedor, M. Schoffstall, J. Davin, "A Simple Network Management Protocol," RFC 1157, May 1990.

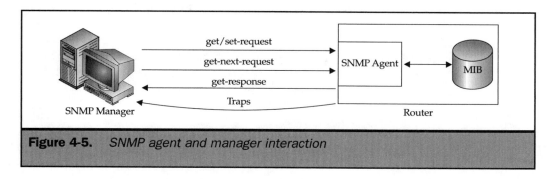

Figure 4-5.   *SNMP agent and manager interaction*

SMI, MIBs, and OIDs

The SNMP agent uses a hierarchical database called the *Structure of Management Information* (SMI) that is similar to a file system directory (SMI for TCP/IP is covered in RFC 1155[11]). This structure is assembled from various files called *Management Information Bases* (MIBs) to store information, status, and performance statistics (RFC 1213[12] covers the standard MIB-II structure). These MIB structures can be viewed as a tree that starts at a root with many branches and leaves. At each branch there is a new entry that might have more entries further down. Eventually, the branches will end in a leaf that contains the information that is of interest. Of course, this all assumes that you know where the information is stored in the tree. Figure 4-6 shows a section of a MIB tree.

Notice that there is a namespace that is associated with the entries of the MIB tree. This namespace is used for navigating the MIB. For example, if you wanted to get the "sysDescr" of the respective system, you would specify the notation

```
"iso.org.dod.internet.mgmt.mib-2.system.sysDescr"
```

However, names are used for your benefit. They generally do not have meaning to a computer, so a numeric notation is used in the encoding of the SNMP message. The numeric notation for the same example of sysDescr is 1.3.6.1.2.1.1.1. These numbers correspond to the index numbers of the entries in the MIB. This scheme of specifying a particular node in a MIB is called the *Object ID* (OID). MIB objects can be defined as being READ-ONLY or READ-WRITE, and are referred to as the object's access mode. A SNMP manager can issue a `set` command to MIB objects that have the READ-WRITE attribute.

The MIB structure is used as a way to access the operational status of the network element. The SNMP agent process is used as a way for a remote machine to get or set the MIB information. The SNMP manager can then target a specific node in a network to gather the status or statistic of interest.

---

[11]   M. Rose, K. McCloghrie, "Structure and Identification of Management Information for TCP/IP-based Internets," RFC 1155, May 1990.

[12]   K. McCloghrie, M. Rose, "Management Information Base for Network Management of TCP/IP-based Internets: MIB-II," March 1991.

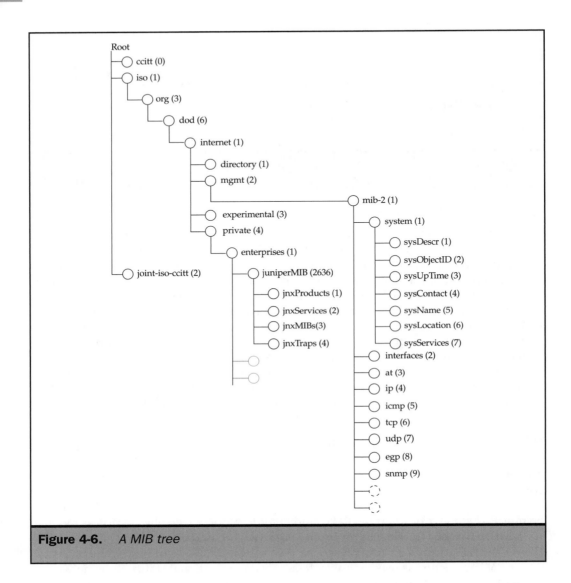

Figure 4-6. *A MIB tree*

It was realized that there needed to be a way to secure only authorized access to the nodes of the network. For this reason, SNMP uses a simple security scheme to restrict only those systems that should have access. A *community string* represents a simple password that an SNMP manager uses to gain access to the SNMP agent and OID. This password is in no way secure, in fact it is sent "in the clear" with no encryption. Because of this problem Juniper Networks' implementation of its SNMP agent does not support READ-WRITE MIB objects. Version 2 of the specification was intended to add a more secure mechanism to SNMP; however, general disagreement on how it should be done has left secure implementations unrealized.

MIBs are defined using a language called Abstract Syntax Notation 1 (ASN.1), which specifies where in the tree the information is stored and what kind of data it is. SNMP uses only a subset of the ASN.1 definition language. The following is a small selection of the start of the MIB-II definition:

```
RFC1213-MIB DEFINITIONS ::= BEGIN
        IMPORTS
                mgmt, NetworkAddress, IpAddress, Counter, Gauge, TimeTicks
                    FROM RFC1155-SMI
                        OBJECT-TYPE
                    FROM RFC-1212;
        --   This MIB module uses the extended OBJECT-TYPE macro as
        --   defined in [14];
        --   MIB-II (same prefix as MIB-I)
        mib-2       OBJECT IDENTIFIER ::= { mgmt 1 }
        -- textual conventions
        DisplayString ::= OCTET STRING
        -- This data type is used to model textual information taken
        -- from the NVT ASCII character set.  By convention, objects
        -- with this syntax are declared as having
        --
        --      SIZE (0..255)
        PhysAddress ::= OCTET STRING
        -- This data type is used to model media addresses.  For many
        -- types of media, this will be in a binary representation.
        -- For example, an ethernet address would be represented as
        -- a string of 6 octets.
        -- groups in MIB-II
        system      OBJECT IDENTIFIER ::= { mib-2 1 }
        interfaces  OBJECT IDENTIFIER ::= { mib-2 2 }
        at          OBJECT IDENTIFIER ::= { mib-2 3 }
        ip          OBJECT IDENTIFIER ::= { mib-2 4 }
        icmp        OBJECT IDENTIFIER ::= { mib-2 5 }
        tcp         OBJECT IDENTIFIER ::= { mib-2 6 }
        udp         OBJECT IDENTIFIER ::= { mib-2 7 }
        egp         OBJECT IDENTIFIER ::= { mib-2 8 }
```

Proprietary MIBs

As you can see from the listing at the end of the last section, the MIB tree structure is quite extensible. It is quite easy to enumerate a new MIB index, to add information to the MIB tree that can represent other parameters of interest. In fact, the MIB is designed to support extensions in a standard way. In Figure 4-6, you can see that under the hierarchy "iso.org.dod.internet.private.enterprises" is an entry named "juniperMIB." This object ID represents the top-level proprietary MIB for all Juniper Networks equipment. While it is beyond the scope of this book to go into detail about the contents of the Juniper Networks MIBs, you should note that there are a number of statistics that can be of interest to a network administrator. For example, as Chapter 1 discusses, there are a great number of temperature sensors in a router. In fact nearly every subsystem has at least one. MIB information can be used to get the readings of these temperature sensors.

To facilitate the access of such information, the proprietary MIBs must be loaded into the network management system (NMS). Consult the JUNOS software SNMP documentation to find where the Juniper Networks proprietary MIB files can be obtained.

Configuring the SNMP Agent

The JUNOS software supports SNMP version 1 and version 2 (also known as version 2c, or v2c) of the specification. The first step to configuring the SNMP agent is enabling and authorizing the network management system access to the router. This is done in the top-level portion of the configuration:

```
[edit]
set snmp community tester authorization read-only clients 172.16.1.1/32
```

In this example, the NMS station at 172.16.1.1 is given access to the router's SNMP MIB when it uses the community string of *tester*. This statement gives only the machine with the address 172.16.1.1 access to the router, and you must specify an address, not a host name. If you do not specify any addresses, all SNMP clients have access to the router. Also, the station has only READ-ONLY authorization to the contents of the MIB. JUNOS software allows you to put in READ-WRITE, but because of the security concerns of SNMP the agent supports only READ-ONLY operations.

You can allow more than one station to access the SNMP agent by listing any number of clients:

```
[edit]
set snmp community "bobs nms" authorization read-only clients 172.16.2.1/32
set snmp community "erics nms" authorization read-only clients 172.16.3.1/32
```

These statements permit the clients 172.16.2.1 and 172.16.3.1 access to the SNMP agent. These two stations would have to use the community strings "bobs nms" and "erics nms," respectively. You must use quotation marks around a community string that uses space characters.

In addition to listing the NMS stations individually, you can authorize access to an entire range of IP addresses by specifying a smaller mask:

```
[edit]
set snmp community "tester" authorization read-only clients 172.16.0.0/16
```

This statement permits any station in the range of 172.16.0.0–172.16.255.255 access to the router's SNMP agent; however, this configuration might represent a security issue. You can also exclude a specific station or range:

```
[edit]
set snmp community "tester" authorization read-only clients 172.16.5.0/24 restrict
```

This statement disallows any client NMS in the range 172.16.5.0–172.16.5.255 from access to the router.

There are a number of interesting objects that are part of the standard MIB specification such as "system description" (sysDescr), "system contact" (sysContact), and "system location" (sysLocation). These fields can be configured in the router to provide this information about the specific node. For example, the `location` statement can be set to give a street address for a router:

```
[edit]
set snmp location "4th floor, 1234 Anywhere Lan, Olympus-mons, Mars"
```

Whenever a network administrator performs an SNMP "get" on the *location* OID (1.3.6.1.2.1.1.6), the returned data can be used to dispatch help to the address where the router is located (although it is unlikely a field service call to Mars will be viable for sometime because of the cost involved). Be sure to use the quotation marks to enter any string that contains space characters.

The `contact` and the `description` fields can also be set:

```
[edit]
set snmp description "This router is a core router"
set snmp contact "Contact Alex in the IS dept. at: 770-555-1234 before doing any work"
```

These commands have the same effect for any NMS stations that do a "get" on these OIDs.

Traps

SNMP traps are a little different from the `get` and `set` commands used in SNMP network management. Usually a network management system polls for the status and statistics that it has interest in. Polling can be untimely for real-time events such as an over-temperature warning. The trap message is an unsolicited form of notification that can be used to track critical events in a network. For example, if a problem such as an over-temperature warning occurs, the router sends a trap message to the network management system to notify it of the event. There are a great number of trap messages that can be sent to a network management system, each with different meanings. The NMS must be configured to interpret these messages by loading the appropriate MIBs.

Configuring Trap Targets

To specify the traps to be sent to the SNMP manager, use the `trap-group` command:

```
[edit]
set snmp trap-group critical-events targets 172.16.1.1
```

This statement specifies that the trap messages generated by the router are to be sent to the `critical-events` group target 172.16.1.1. Any number of trap groups or targets can be set up in the router. Networks that have more than one network management system require `targets` addresses for each system.

JUNOS software supports trap versions 1 and 2, and by default, JUNOS software sends both versions of the traps to the network management system. Trap messages are interpreted based on how each NMS station is set up. Stations that are interpreting version 1 traps see the messages listed in Table 4-6. Stations that are interpreting version 2 traps see the messages listed in Table 4-7.

Trap Type	Trap Name	Enterprise ID	Generic Trap Number	Specific Trap Number
Standard Traps	Cold start	1.3.6.1.4.1.2636	0	0
	Warm start	1.3.6.1.4.1.2636	1	0
	Link down	1.3.6.1.4.1.2636	2	0
	Link up	1.3.6.1.4.1.2636	3	0
	Authentication failure	1.3.6.1.4.1.2636	4	0
Enterprise-Specific Traps	BGP established	1.3.6.1.2.1.15.7	6	1
	BGP backward transition	1.3.6.1.2.1.15.7	6	2
	Power failure	1.3.6.1.4.1.2636.4.1	6	1
	Fan failure	1.3.6.1.4.1.2636.4.1	6	2
	Over temperature	1.3.6.1.4.1.2636.4.1	6	3

Table 4-6.   *Version 1 Traps*

Trap Type	Trap Name	Enterprise ID	Generic Trap Number	Specific Trap Number
Enterprise-Specific Traps	MPLS LSP up	1.3.6.1.4.1.2636.3.2.4	6	1
	MPLS LSP down	1.3.6.1.4.1.2636.3.2.4	6	2
	MPLS LSP change	1.3.6.1.4.1.2636.3.2.4	6	3
	OSPF virtual interface state change	1.3.6.1.2.1.14.16.2	6	1
	OSPF neighbor state change	1.3.6.1.2.1.14.16.2	6	2
	OSPF virtual neighbor state change	1.3.6.1.2.1.14.16.2	6	3
	OSPF interface configuration error	1.3.6.1.2.1.14.16.2	6	4
	OSPF virtual interface configuration error	1.3.6.1.2.1.14.16.2	6	5
	OSPF interface authentication error	1.3.6.1.2.1.14.16.2	6	6
	OSPF virtual interface authentication error	1.3.6.1.2.1.14.16.2	6	7
	OSPF interface receiving bad packet	1.3.6.1.2.1.14.16.2	6	8

Table 4-6.   *Version 1 Traps* (continued)

Trap Type	Trap Name	Enterprise ID	Generic Trap Number	Specific Trap Number
Enterprise-Specific Traps	OSPF virtual interface receiving bad packet	1.3.6.1.2.1.14.16.2	6	9
	OSPF transmit packet retransmitted	1.3.6.1.2.1.14.16.2	6	10
	OSPF virtual interface transmit packet retransmitted	1.3.6.1.2.1.14.16.2	6	11
	OSPF originating LSA (currently not supported)	1.3.6.1.2.1.14.16.2	6	12
	OSPF maximum aged LSA	1.3.6.1.2.1.14.16.2	6	13
	OSPF LSDB overflow (currently not supported)	1.3.6.1.2.1.14.16.2	6	14
	OSPF LSDB approaching overflow (currently not supported)	1.3.6.1.2.1.14.16.2	6	15
	OSPF interface state change	1.3.6.1.2.1.14.16.2	6	16

Table 4-6.   *Version 1 Traps* (continued)

Trap Type	Trap Name	snmpTrapOID	Literal Meaning
Standard Traps	Cold start	1.3.6.1.6.3.1.1.5.1	coldStart
	Warm start	1.3.6.1.6.3.1.1.5.2	warmStart
	Link down	1.3.6.1.6.3.1.1.5.3	linkDown
	Link up	1.3.6.1.6.3.1.1.5.4	linkUp
	Authentication failure	1.3.6.1.6.3.1.1.5.5	authenticationFailure
	BGP established	1.3.6.1.2.1.15.7.1	bgpEstablished
	BGP backward transition	1.3.6.1.2.1.15.7.2	bgpBackwardTransition
	OSPF virtual interface state change	1.3.6.1.2.1.14.16.2.1	ospfVirtIfStateChange
	OSPF neighbor state change	1.3.6.1.2.1.14.16.2.2	ospfNbrStateChange
	OSPF virtual neighbor state change	1.3.6.1.2.1.14.16.2.3	ospfVirtNbrStateChange
	OSPF interface configuration error	1.3.6.1.2.1.14.16.2.4	ospfIfConfigError
	OSPF virtual interface configuration error	1.3.6.1.2.1.14.16.2.5	ospfVirtIfConfigError
	OSPF interface authentication failure	1.3.6.1.2.1.14.16.2.6	ospfIfAuthFailure
	OSPF virtual interface authentication failure	1.3.6.1.2.1.14.16.2.7	ospfVirtIfAuthFailure
	OSPF interface receiving bad packet	1.3.6.1.2.1.14.16.2.8	ospfIfRxBadPacket
	OSPF virtual interface receiving bad packet	1.3.6.1.2.1.14.16.2.9	ospfVirtIfRxBadPacket
	OSPF transmit packet retransmitted	1.3.6.1.2.1.14.16.2.10	ospfTxRetransmit
	OSPF virtual interface transmit packet retransmitted	1.3.6.1.2.1.14.16.2.11	ospfVirtIfTxRetransmit
	OSPF originating LSA (currently not supported)	1.3.6.1.2.1.14.16.2.12	ospfOriginateLsa
	OSPF maximum aged LSA	1.3.6.1.2.1.14.16.2.13	ospfMaxAgeLsa

Table 4-7.   *Version 2 Traps*

Trap Type	Trap Name	snmpTrapOID	Literal Meaning
Standard Traps	OSPF LSDB overflow (currently not supported)	1.3.6.1.2.1.14.16.2.14	ospfLsdbOverflow
	OSPF LSDB approaching overflow (currently not supported)	1.3.6.1.2.1.14.16.2.15	ospfLsdbApproachingOverflow
	OSPF interface state change	1.3.6.1.2.1.14.16.2.16	ospfIfStateChange
Enterprise-Specific Traps	Power failure	1.3.6.1.4.1.2636.4.1.1	jnxPowerSupplyFailure
	Fan failure	1.3.6.1.4.1.2636.4.1.2	jnxFanFailure
	Over temperature	1.3.6.1.4.1.2636.4.1.3	jnxOverTemperature
	MPLS LSP up	1.3.6.1.4.1.2636.3.2.4.1	mplsLspUp
	MPLS LSP down	1.3.6.1.4.1.2636.3.2.4.2	mplsLspDown
	MPLS LSP change	1.3.6.1.4.1.2636.3.2.4.3	mplsLspChange

Table 4-7.   *Version 2 Traps* (continued)

Using the `version` keyword, you can specify that the SNMP agent send messages of only one version rather than the default of both versions:

```
[edit]
set snmp trap-group critical-events version v2
```

This statement informs JUNOS software to send traps in the version 2 format only. The options for the `version` keyword are `v1`, `v2`, and `all`.

As you might have noticed in Tables 4.5 and 4.6, there are several categories for trap notifications. For example, there are routing protocol-based traps that cover status changes such as "OSPF neighbor state change." Also, there is a group of traps that indicates the change of status in the interfaces of the router such as "link up/down." Many of these trap messages will be of interest, but not all of them. JUNOS software allows you to select only those traps that are of interest. You can use the `categories` statement to select which traps the router will send to its targets:

```
[edit]
set snmp trap-group critical-events categories authentication startup chassis
```

This statement enables the traps in the categories `authentication`, `startup`, and `chassis` to be sent to the configured NMS stations for the `trap-group` `critical-events`. The other options for this command are `routing` and `link`. If you omit the `categories` statement, then all trap types are sent.

The SNMP agent running on the router keeps track of the statistics for the SNMP process itself. To view these statistics, use the `show snmp statistics` command from the operation mode:

```
jnpr@q-net-r1> show snmp statistics
SNMP statistics:
  Input:
    Packets: 306, Bad versions: 0, Bad community names: 5,
    Bad community uses: 0, ASN parse errors: 0,
    Too bigs: 0, No such names: 0, Bad values: 0,
    Read onlys: 0, General errors: 0,
    Total request varbinds: 0, Total set varbinds: 0,
    Get requests: 204, Get nexts: 2056, Set requests: 0,
    Get responses: 0, Traps: 0,
    Silent drops: 0, Proxy drops 0
  Output:
    Packets: 16,452, Too bigs: 0, No such names: 0,
    Bad values: 0, General errors: 0,
    Get requests: 0, Get nexts: 0, Set requests: 0,
    Get responses: 2260, Traps: 409
```

These statistics can be helpful in diagnosing problems with a network management station. A common problem with using SNMP is using the wrong community string to access the agent. A check of the "Bad community names" could indicate a problem. If this number is increasing with the number of SNMP "get" queries, it is a good chance that the community string is incorrect.

Diagnostic Tools

Network problems are an unfortunate consequence of running a complex system. With so many interconnected systems and subsystems, spanning great distances, things invariably go wrong. Hopefully the problem will not be critical, and some form of backup or redundancy allows the network to continue running. Once a problem is identified, the network administrator must use all the available resources to find the source of the problem. The problem is then eliminated and a strategy on how to keep the problem from occurring again is developed.

Problems of an unsubtle nature are easy to identify. For instance, consider a problem where a heavily loaded WAN link fails. Any practical *Network Operations*

Center (NOC) has network management systems actively monitoring the network. The instant that the problem occurs, alarm bells and warning lights are activated to indicate the fault; however, the majority of problems tend to be much less obvious. There are a number of tools for the investigation of such problems.

PING

Usually a PING is the first test of operational status. Inspired by the sound of a sonar, the PING application sends an IP packet that mimics an ICMP message. In the IP/ICMP packet is an "echo request" message that is sent through a network. PING expects the target system to repeat the same packet contents to the originator as an "echo reply" message. If the originator receives the PING responses, the test is generally considered a success. The simple form of using the `ping` command is from the operation mode of the CLI.

```
alex@Juniper1> ping 172.16.255.2
PING 172.16.255.2 (172.16.255.2): 56 data bytes
64 bytes from 172.16.255.2: icmp_seq=0 ttl=254 time=0.649 ms
64 bytes from 172.16.255.2: icmp_seq=1 ttl=254 time=0.597 ms
64 bytes from 172.16.255.2: icmp_seq=2 ttl=254 time=0.599 ms
64 bytes from 172.16.255.2: icmp_seq=3 ttl=254 time=0.599 ms
--- 172.16.255.2 ping statistics ---
4 packets transmitted, 4 packets received, 0% packet loss
round-trip min/avg/max/stddev = 0.597/0.611/0.649/0.022 ms
alex@Juniper1>
```

The host (router) at IP address 172.16.255.2 in this example answered to the PING. The PING application continues indefinitely until the CTRL-C key sequence is issued. You can also use host names in place of an IP address if the router is configured to use DNS or has the appropriate static host mappings configured.

A successful PING returns several fields. The `icmp_seq` indicates the current outstanding PING packet. Had there been a problem with a link, or congestion somewhere in the network, you might see missing ICMP sequences. In addition to the sequence number, the TTL value of the packet is displayed. The TTL value of a packet is decremented by 1 for every router the packet passes through. PING uses a default TTL value of 255. So this example shows a returned TTL of 254, indicating that the PING'ed host is only one router hop away from the PING source. The round-trip time it took the packet to transverse the network is also displayed. In this example, the average round-trip time as listed on the last line of the PING output is 611 microseconds. PING can be used to get an idea of the network latency (delay of the transmission path), but its report should not be taken as completely accurate. The PING application represents a relatively low-priority process; other processes in the router take precedence, therefore, PING round-trip figures reflect only the general case and are not to be completely relied on.

   Suppose that the PING'ed IP address is on a subnet that does not exist in the router table. In the following example, the router cannot match address 162.10.0.1 to any router table entry:

```
alex@Juniper1> ping 162.10.0.1
PING 162.10.0.1 (162.10.0.1): 56 data bytes
36 bytes from 172.16.32.2: Destination Host Unreachable
Vr HL TOS  Len    ID Flg  off TTL Pro  cks       Src       Dst
 4  5  00 0054 998c   0 0000   fe  01 b4ff 172.16.32.1  162.10.0.1

36 bytes from 172.16.32.2: Destination Host Unreachable
Vr HL TOS  Len    ID Flg  off TTL Pro  cks       Src       Dst
 4  5  00 0054 9993   0 0000   fe  01 b4f8 172.16.32.1  162.10.0.1

36 bytes from 172.16.32.2: Destination Host Unreachable
Vr HL TOS  Len    ID Flg  off TTL Pro  cks       Src       Dst
 4  5  00 0054 999b   0 0000   fe  01 b4f0 172.16.32.1  162.10.0.1

36 bytes from 172.16.32.2: Destination Host Unreachable
Vr HL TOS  Len    ID Flg  off TTL Pro  cks       Src       Dst
 4  5  00 0054 99a0   0 0000   fe  01 b4eb 172.16.32.1  162.10.0.1

--- 162.10.0.1 ping statistics ---
4 packets transmitted, 0 packets received, 100% packet loss
```

   Clearly something is amiss with this kind of output. The error "Destination Host Unreachable" is an indication that the host 162.10.0.1 does not exist. In fact, the subnet route does not exist in the network. Had the subnet and host existed, the host would have returned the PING and this error would not have occurred. The source address 172.16.32.1 is the outgoing interface of the router that issued this PING. The other fields that are reported in the output correspond to the IP packets contents. Notice that the source of the ICMP error message is the router at address 172.16.32.2. The ICMP echo requests made their way to this router, but there was no route to the subnet 162.10.0.1. An ICMP error was then generated at the point where the problem occurred.

   What do you suppose would be the output from a subnet that existed, but for which its host was not on? The output from such a scenario is shown:

```
sean@Juniper1> ping 10.64.1.2
PING 10.64.1.2 (10.64.1.2): 56 data bytes
--- 10.64.1.2 ping statistics ---
7 packets transmitted, 0 packets received, 100% packet loss
```

A control-C key sequence was needed to return back to the CLI, after issuing this PING. This output (or lack of) indicates that the targeted host has not returned the ICMP replies that the issuing router was expecting. If the subnet route had not existed, the result would have been similar to previous "Destination Host Unreachable" error. The IP address 10.64.1.2 is not currently active. More importantly, no other errors were returned from the intervening routers to indicate that you have targeted a subnet (network) that does not exist.

PING has a number of options that can help with the diagnosis of problems or other network issues. The following sections explain how some of these options can help you troubleshoot your network.

PING Options: Do-Not-Fragment and Size

The `do-not-fragment` option allows you to discover the *Maximum Transmission Unit* (MTU) the network path can support. Look at the output using the `do-not-fragment` option:

```
sean@Juniper1> ping 172.16.255.3 do-not-fragment size 1500
PING 172.16.255.3 (172.16.255.3): 1500 data bytes
ping: sendto: Message too long
ping: sendto: Message too long
ping: sendto: Message too long
ping: sendto: Message too long
ping: sendto: Message too long
--- 172.16.255.3 ping statistics ---
5 packets transmitted, 0 packets received, 100% packet loss
```

Also introduced in this command is the use of the `size` option. Notice that the PING packet has been issued with the size set to 1500 bytes. It is apparent from this output that a packet of 1500 bytes or greater can not be transmitted without being fragmented. A quick check of the outgoing interface verifies this:

```
sean@Juniper1> show interfaces
Physical interface: fxp0, Enabled, Physical link is Up
  Interface index: 1, SNMP ifIndex: 1
  Type: Ethernet, Link-level type: Ethernet, MTU: 1514, Speed: 100mbps
  Flags: Present Running Recv-All-Multicasts SNMP-Traps
  Link type: Full-Duplex, Link flags: None
  Current  MAC 00:d0:b7:60:8e:5d
  Hardware MAC 00:d0:b7:60:8e:5d
  Input packets: 22201 Output packets: 8040
  Logical interface fxp0.0 (Index 1) (SNMP ifIndex 12)
    Flags: SNMP-Traps, Encapsulation: ENET2
    Protocol inet, MTU: 1500, Flags: Is-Primary
      Addresses, Flags: Is-Preferred Is-Primary
```

```
           Destination: 172.16.64.8/30, Local: 172.16.64.9, Broadcast: 172.16.64.11
        Protocol iso, MTU: 1497, Flags: Is-Primary
        Protocol mpls, MTU: 1500, Flags: Is-Primary
```

PING Options: Record Route

Another useful option of PING is `record-route`. `Record-route` collects the router subnets that the ICMP echo request and echo reply have traversed. The routers in the path of the packet store their interface IP addresses in the IP Options field of the IP packet. The following example shows the output from the `record-route` option:

```
sean@Juniper3> ping 10.64.1.1 record-route
PING 10.64.1.1 (10.64.1.1): 56 data bytes
64 bytes from 10.64.1.1: icmp_seq=0 ttl=253 time=7.280 ms
RR:      172.16.32.1
         192.168.32.5
         10.64.1.1
         192.168.32.6
         172.16.32.2
         172.16.1.2
         172.16.1.3
64 bytes from 10.64.1.1: icmp_seq=1 ttl=253 time=7.719 ms (same route)
64 bytes from 10.64.1.1: icmp_seq=2 ttl=253 time=7.385 ms (same route)
64 bytes from 10.64.1.1: icmp_seq=3 ttl=253 time=7.249 ms (same route)
--- 10.64.1.1 ping statistics ---
4 packets transmitted, 4 packets received, 0% packet loss
round-trip min/avg/max/stddev = 7.249/7.408/7.719/0.186 ms
```

The recorded route is the round trip of the packet. After the packet gets to the destination 10.64.1.1, the return path is concatenated with the outgoing path. In this example, four subnets and two routers were traversed, as evident by the returned routes and TTL value.

Also notice that the PING continues and denotes that the same route is used. If an active PING using the record-route option encounters a change in the path, a new route is returned:

```
sean@Juniper3> ping 10.64.1.1 record-route
PING 10.64.1.1 (10.64.1.1): 56 data bytes
64 bytes from 10.64.1.1: icmp_seq=0 ttl=253 time=7.562 ms
RR:      172.16.32.1
         192.168.32.5
         10.64.1.1
         192.168.32.6
         172.16.32.2
         172.16.1.2
         172.16.1.3
64 bytes from 10.64.1.1: icmp_seq=1 ttl=253 time=7.473 ms (same route)
```

```
64 bytes from 10.64.1.1: icmp_seq=2 ttl=253 time=7.539 ms (same route)
ping: sendto: Network is down
64 bytes from 10.64.1.1: icmp_seq=14 ttl=252 time=7.207 ms
RR:     172.16.64.10
        172.16.32.1
        192.168.32.5
        10.64.1.1
        192.168.32.6
        172.16.32.2
        172.16.64.9
        172.16.64.13
        172.16.64.14
64 bytes from 10.64.1.1: icmp_seq=15 ttl=252 time=7.585 ms (same route)
64 bytes from 10.64.1.1: icmp_seq=16 ttl=252 time=7.246 ms (same route)
--- 10.64.1.1 ping statistics ---
23 packets transmitted, 13 packets received, 43% packet loss
round-trip min/avg/max/stddev = 7.201/7.442/7.585/0.142 ms
```

The display shows that the recorded route changed from the original path to a different one. Also note that the new path includes an extra router hop, because TTL=252. PING would continue to report the same path until there was yet another change. This option is useful for problems related to unstable routing. Keeping an active PING with the record-route option going can be useful to discover where the instability exists.

PING Options: Detail

The detail PING option can be used to discover the direction (interface) from which a PING reply is received. For example, the following display, using the detail option, shows that the PING reply from the remote host 10.64.1.1 is coming in on the so-1/1/0 interface:

```
sean@Juniper1> ping 10.64.1.1 detail
PING 10.64.1.1 (10.64.1.1): 56 data bytes
64 bytes from 10.64.1.1 via so-1/1/0.0: icmp_seq=0 ttl=254 time=3.333 ms
64 bytes from 10.64.1.1 via so-1/1/0.0: icmp_seq=1 ttl=254 time=3.349 ms
--- 10.64.1.1 ping statistics ---
4 packets transmitted, 4 packets received, 0% packet loss
round-trip min/avg/max/stddev = 3.298/3.321/3.349/0.021 ms
```

Detail comes in handy when the external routing (outside the router) is unknown. Finding the return path back to the router can be of use in diagnosing network issues. For example, it is possible that the outgoing path taken by a PING is not the same as the incoming path. The detail option can be used to find those cases where the routing is not symmetric in a network.

These are not all the options available under PING. Table 4-8 is a summary of those that have not been in included earlier.

Option	Description
bypass-routing	Bypass the normal routing tables and send PING requests directly to a system on an attached network. If the system is not on a directly attached network, an error is returned. Use this option to PING a local system through an interface that has no route through it.
count	Number of PING requests to send. This can range from 0 through 10,000. The default is no limit to the number of requests sent. You must type the CTRL-C key sequence to interrupt a PING command.
interval	This is how fast the PING packets are sent. This interval can be specified to be 0.1 to 10,000 seconds. The default is 1 second.
interface	This is the interface of the router where the packets will be issued from. This is not the source IP address of the PING packets.
local	This is the source address to use for outgoing packets. By default, PING leaves the choice of local address up to the kernel, which usually chooses the local address based on the interface the packet uses to leave the router.
pattern	This is a bit pattern that is placed into the payload of the PING packet. This pattern can be any value of 0 through 65535.
rapid	The PING requests are sent rapidly. The results are reported in a single message, not in individual messages for each PING request. By default, five PING requests are sent before the results are reported.
tos	The Type of Service (ToS) bits of the IP packet are set to the pattern specified. This can be used to test Class of Service (CoS) operations.
via	Specify the intermediate router through which the packet should traverse on its way to the system being PING'ed. Configuring an intermediate router address sets the loose source route field (IP options) in the IP header.

Table 4-8.   *Additional PING Options*

Traceroute

Traceroute is very similar to PING with the record-route option. The difference between PING and `traceroute` is both in the packets used and in the way that it works. Where PING uses an IP/ICMP packet, `traceroute` uses a UDP packet. Traceroute starts by sending a set of three UDP packets pointing to the destination and sets the TTL value to 1. As each packet arrives at the first router, that router decrements the TTL to zero, discards the packet, and sends an ICMP "Time-To-Live (TTL) exceeded" error message back to the source of the packet. The router originating the traceroute displays the source of the ICMP error messages as the first hop. Next, traceroute sends another set of UDP packets with the TTL set to 2. The TTL of these packets is decremented to zero by the second router in the path, which then sends the "TTL exceeded" error messages to the originator. These ICMP messages reveal the second hop of the packet's path, which is displayed in the output. This process continues until the final destination is reached. An example of the traceroute process is shown in Figure 4-7.

The output from this traceroute is

```
sean@Juniper2> traceroute r4.lax.netflyers.net
traceroute to r4.lax.netflyers.net (172.16.255.4), 30 hops max, 40 byte packets
 1  r2.atl.netflyers.net (172.16.1.2)  0.367 ms  0.458 ms  0.231 ms
 2  r3.nyc.netflyers.net (172.16.2.2)  2.187 ms  2.460 ms  2.131 ms
 3  r4.lax.netflyers.net (172.16.3.2)  3.250 ms  3.550 ms 3.461 ms
```

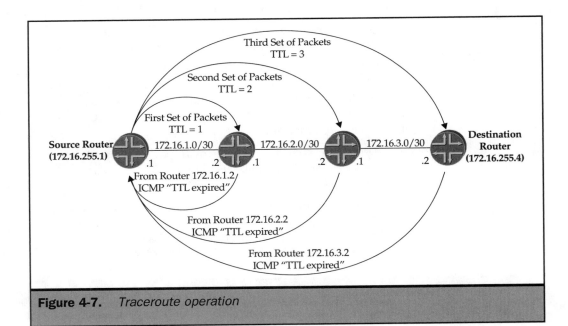

Figure 4-7.   *Traceroute operation*

The output from this command shows the maximum number of hops for this traceroute is 30, which is the default. The packet size for this traceroute is 40 bytes, also the default. The first field in the list of routers traversed shows the distance of each router in hops. The routers interface IP address and the resolved name are then shown. The three columns of time figures are the average, maximum, and minimum round-trip times of the UDP packets. For each packet sent, traceroute waits 5 seconds (by default) for a response back. If there is no response, traceroute displays an asterisk for those packets that timed out.

As with PING, traceroute has a number of options. The following sections examine the use of some of these options.

Traceroute Options: noresolve

By default, traceroute resolves and reports the names of any routers the packet traverses. The `noresolve` option overrides the name resolution:

```
sean@Juniper2> traceroute r4.lax.netflyers.net noresolve
traceroute to r4.lax.netflyers.net (172.16.255.4), 30 hops max, 40 byte packets
1  172.16.1.2   0.367 ms  0.458 ms  0.231 ms
2  172.16.2.2   2.187 ms  2.460 ms  2.131 ms
3  172.16.3.2   3.250 ms  3.550 ms 3.461 ms
```

The output here indicates only the IP addresses, not the host names, in the DNS. This option might be helpful to make the traceroute more readable for those that are familiar with the network addressing. In addition, using the `noresolve` option speeds up the output of the display by eliminating the resolution delay associated with DNS queries.

Traceroute Options: source

By default, traceroute uses the outgoing IP interface address toward the destination. You can specify a different source address of the traceroute using the `source` option:

```
sean@Juniper3> traceroute 10.64.1.1 source 172.16.64.14
traceroute to 10.64.1.1 (10.64.1.1) from 172.16.64.14, 30 hops max, 40 byte packets
1  172.16.1.2 (172.16.1.2)   0.549 ms  0.369 ms  0.351 ms
2  172.16.32.2 (172.16.32.2)  2.417 ms  2.399 ms  2.469 ms
3  192.168.32.6 (192.168.32.6)  5.727 ms *  3.440 ms
```

The source of the traceroute packets is now the interface with the address 172.16.64.14. A decode of the traceroute session, shown in Figure 4-8, verifies that the packets are being sourced from the IP address of 172.16.64.14.

Notice in the summary field of the decode that TTL is exceeded. This is the result of the traceroute setting the TTL to 1 for the first set of sent packets.

The source IP address that you provide must exist on the router. The consequence of using an address that does not exist on the local router, or that is not in the router

Source Address	Dest Address	Summary	Len
[172.16.64.14]	[10.64.1.1]	Expert: Time-to-live expiring UDP: D=33435 S=33117 LEN=20	60
[172.16.1.2]	[172.16.64.14]	Expert: Time-to-live exceeded in transmit ICMP: Time exceeded (Time to live exceeded in transit)	70
[172.16.64.14]	[10.64.1.1]	Expert: Time-to-live expiring UDP: D=33436 S=33117 LEN=20	60
[172.16.1.2]	[172.16.64.14]	Expert: Time-to-live exceeded in transmit ICMP: Time exceeded (Time to live exceeded in transit)	70
[172.16.64.14]	[10.64.1.1]	Expert: Time-to-live expiring UDP: D=33437 S=33117 LEN=20	60
[172.16.1.2]	[172.16.64.14]	Expert: Time-to-live exceeded in transmit ICMP: Time exceeded (Time to live exceeded in transit)	70

Figure 4-8. *Decoded traceroute session*

tables of the remote routers, is that the packets will never find their way back to the source. This is the value of using the source option. You can use the source option to locate "holes" in the router tables of the network. If you are able to successfully traceroute from one local IP address, but not from another, you can probably conclude that the nonworking address is not in the router tables of the transit routers.

Traceroute Options: TTL

As explained, the TTL field of a traceroute packet is set to 1 for the first set of packets, 2 for the second set of packets, and so on, until a maximum of 30 hops has been reached (TTL=30). Although 30 hops does represent a great number, the size of the Internet might require you to change this default to some larger number. To do this, use the ttl option in the traceroute command:

```
sean@Juniper3> traceroute www.farawaynetwork.com ttl 50
```

This command allows the traceroute to extend up to 50 hops from the source (you might find it difficult to find a case for having to set the TTL to anything greater than 30, but it is sure to exist somewhere).

Although all the traceroute options are not covered, the others are listed in Table 4-9 for your reference.

Syslog

With the tasks of maintaining routing tables, forwarding of packets, monitoring of subsystems, and administration processes, it is easy to see that routers can be complicated things. With the torrent of information flowing through and inside the router there must be a way to intercept and store messages that are of interest to you.

Option	Description
gateway	This is the IP address of the router the traceroute packet is to pass through. This option sets the source route field of the IP packet options.
tos	The Type of Service(ToS) bits of the IP packet are set to the pattern specified. This can be used to test Class of Service (CoS) operations.
wait	This is the amount of time that the traceroute process waits for a response before it is timed out. By default, this time is 5 seconds.

Table 4-9.   *Additional Traceroute Options*

For example, you might find it necessary to log all the commands that have been performed on the router, and you probably want to log critical system messages that represent an abnormal condition.

If you are familiar with UNIX or Linux systems, syslog is a familiar construct. As with those operating systems, syslog is the central error and information logging system of a Juniper Networks router. Syslog can be configured to log a great amount of information, all of which is under your control.

Facilities and Severity Levels

Messages that are created by the system can come from a variety of places. One source of messages is from the kernel of the JUNOS software operating system. Another source could be from one of the daemon processes of the system. All these message sources send their messages to the syslog process. Because only some of these messages will be of interest to you, syslog has a filtering mechanism. Filtering can help you select those messages and subsequently display and/or store them.

System messages can be broken down into several categories called *facilities*. These facilities represent the sources of system messages. Table 4-10 shows all the available facilities for the JUNOS software syslog implementation.

Not all these messages might be important to you. Some of the messages generated are informational. For this reason, you can be even more granular in your selection of logging information. In addition to being able to filter on the facility of system messages, you can specify the severity level. Table 4-11 lists the severity levels thata message might have.

Facility	Description
any	Messages from any facility
authorization	Any authorization attempt
change-log	Any change to the configuration
cron	Messages generated by the Cron daemon
daemon	Messages from various system daemons
interactive-commands	Messages denoting commands executed in the CLI
kernel	Messages generated by the JUNOS software kernel
user	Messages from random user processes

Table 4-10. *System Logging Facilities*

The *emergency* level is the highest level, while *debug* is the lowest level of any message. You can assume that messages of an emergency nature are things that need your immediate attention while debug information will tend to be much less critical.

Severity Level	Description
emergency	Panic or other conditions that cause the system to become unusable
alert	Conditions that should be corrected immediately, such as a corrupted system database
critical	Critical conditions, such as hard-drive errors
error	Standard error conditions
warning	System warning messages
notice	Conditions that are not error conditions, but that might warrant special handling
info	Informational messages; this is the default
debug	Software debugging messages

Table 4-11. *System Logging Severity Levels*

Logging messages have a format of time stamp, host name, and messages. The following list shows a number of syslog messages that have been displayed:

```
Aug 29 13:51:52 Juniper1 login: login from 172.16.1.3 on ttyp0 as jack

Aug 29 15:25:57 Juniper1 /kernel: fxp2: link DOWN 10Mb / half-duplex

Aug 29 15:25:57 Juniper1 rpd[312]: RPD_ISIS_ADJDOWN: IS-IS lost L1 adjacency to Juniper3
on fxp2.0, reason: Interface Down

Aug 29 15:25:57 Juniper1 mib2d[311]: SNMP_TRAP_LINK_DOWN: ifIndex 3, ifAdminStatus
up(1), ifOperStatus down(2), ifName fxp2

Aug 29 15:26:22 Juniper1 /kernel: fxp2: link UP 10Mb / half-duplex

Aug 29 15:30:34 Juniper1 login: login from 172.16.1.10 on ttyp1 as jack

Aug 29 15:54:04 Juniper1 mgd[347]: UI_REBOOT_EVENT: system rebooted by 'jack'

Aug 29 15:54:06 Juniper1 rpd[312]: RPD_ISIS_ADJDOWN: IS-IS lost L2 adjacency to Juniper2
on fxp0.0, reason: Interface Down

Aug 29 15:54:06 Juniper1 rpd[312]: RPD_ISIS_ADJDOWN: IS-IS lost L1 adjacency to Juniper2
on fxp0.0, reason: Interface Down

Aug 29 15:54:06 Juniper1 rpd[312]: RPD_ISIS_ADJDOWN: IS-IS lost L1 adjacency to Juniper3
on fxp2.0, reason: Interface Down
```

Notice that the time stamps increase the further down in the syslog file. The oldest entries are located at the top of a log file. As you can see, quite a large number of messages can be captured and stored by the system. The next section shows how system messages can be filtered, stored, and displayed.

Syslog Files

When a syslog message is generated and has passed through the filtering mechanism, which is the specification of facility and priority, you must specify an action to take place. One option is to have the message stored in a syslog file. Under this option, you can specify the name, size, and number (archive) of log files. The following configuration is an example of logging messages to a file. The syslog section of a configuration is located in the [edit system] hierarchy:

```
[edit system]
set syslog file messages any notice
```

This statement tells the router to log any message that is of a severity level of notice to the file messages.

With the great number of messages that are generated, syslog files can grow quickly. When the syslog file reaches its limit, the file is renamed (archived) to a new file. The file rename format is *file.x*.gz, in which *file* is the name of the syslog file and *x* is the generation of the log file. For example, if you have a syslog file called `messages`, and that file reaches its size limit, it is renamed `messages.0.gz`. When `messages` reaches its limit again, `messages.0.gz` is renamed `messages.1.gz`, `messages` is renamed `messages.0.gz`, and the logging action continues with the `messages` file. When the default limit of 10 files has been reached, the oldest file is discarded. Figure 4-9 shows this progression.

The default for syslog file size is 128k and the number of generations is 10. If you want to change the file size or the number of files that are to be kept, you can configure this using the `archive` option:

```
[edit system]
set syslog archive size 1m files 20
```

In the preceding example, the `archive` option is used to specify a syslog file size of 1 megabyte and 20 generations. You can specify a file size that is 64 kilobytes through 1 gigabyte. The number of generations that you can specify for syslog files is 1 through 1000. Also, you can use *k, m,* or *g* to denote kilobytes, megabytes, and gigabytes for the file size. You should be careful that you do not oversize the amount of files kept. Remember the hard drive is of a finite size. Syslog files that total tens of megabytes are a good size to use.

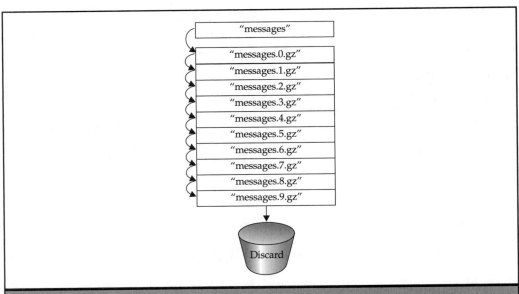

Figure 4-9.   *Syslog file archive*

You can add any number of facilities and severity levels to a syslog file. You can also configure the router to log messages to different file names. In the following example `authorization` and `interactive-commands` are logged to the `authorization` file:

```
[edit system]
set syslog file authorization authorization any
set syslog file authorization interactive-commands any
```

Once a log file has been created, you can view the contents of the file with the `show log` command from the operations mode of the CLI. In this output, the syslog file `authorization` shows the login, and subsequent commands typed in by the user `sean`:

```
show log authorization
Aug 29 18:58:08 Juniper2 login: login from 172.16.1.10 on ttyp0 as sean
Aug 29 18:58:08 Juniper2 mgd[721]: UI_CMDLINE_READ_LINE: user '(unauthenticated user)',
command 'set auth environment user sean logname sean host Juniper2 agent "JUNOS CLI" tty
dev/ttyp0 current-directory /var/home/sean pid 720'

Aug 29 18:58:08 Juniper2 mgd[721]: UI_AUTH_EVENT: authenticated user 'sean' at level 'j-superuser'
Aug 29 18:58:08 Juniper2 mgd[721]: UI_LOGIN_EVENT: user 'sean' login, class 'j-superuser' [255841]
Aug 29 18:58:11 Juniper2 mgd[721]: UI_CMDLINE_READ_LINE: user 'sean', command 'show configuration '
Aug 29 18:58:16 Juniper2 mgd[721]: UI_CMDLINE_READ_LINE: user 'sean', command 'show interfaces '
Aug 29 18:58:30 Juniper2 mgd[721]: UI_CMDLINE_READ_LINE: user 'sean', command 'show isis database '
```

Sometimes syslog messages are so critical that they must be displayed as they are happening. Another option under syslog is to display messages to any or all users logged into the router by using the `user` command option:

```
[edit system]
set syslog user jack any emergency
```

With this configuration, if the user `jack` is logged in, he will see any emergency message generated by the system. The message is printed at the command prompt (Jack's appropriate response would be to jump up and down like a crazy man). You could also use an asterisk in place of any username in the configuration, which allows everyone that is logged in to join in the hysteria.

Just as you can configure the router to send syslog messages to users, you can configure the router to send syslog messages to the console. The console is any terminal, telnet or ssh session that is connected to the system, regardless of username. To set this mode of operation, use the `console` command. In the following example, syslog is configured to direct messages of any emergency to the console:

```
[edit system]
set syslog console any emergency
```

Remote Logging

In addition to displaying and storing files on the local router, you can configure JUNOS software to send syslog messages across the network to another host. These messages are transferred on the network using UDP. The remote host (usually UNIX or Linux) must be running a syslog process that is open to network logging (a syslog daemon running at UDP port 514).

When the remote host receives a syslog message, a script or program can be coded to parse, process, and/or trigger other events. For example, any critical network problems might trigger a program that e-mails or pages the administrators of the network. This could greatly cut down on the response time of fixing network problems.

To setup syslog to send messages to a remote host use the `host` option:

```
[edit system]
set syslog host 172.16.1.12 any emergency
set syslog host 172.16.1.12 any alert
```

These statements cause syslog messages with a severity level of *emergency* and *alert* to be sent to the remote host at IP address 172.16.1.12. How those messages are treated depends on the syslog configuration on the remote host.

When sending messages to a remote host, you can override the message facility. For example, you can configure all messages from a single router to go to a single log file on the remote host. You can also configure different routers to send messages to different log files on the same remote host, to keep the files organized by a particular network region or area. When `facility-override` is used, the remote host must be configured to act on the new message facility. Here is an example of using the `facility-override` option:

```
[edit system]
set syslog host 172.16.1.12 facility-override local0
```

This command option causes all the messages sent to the remote host 172.16.1.12 to be flagged with the facility of `local0`. Local0 is a standard syslog facility designation. Table 4-12 lists the facility-override designations that are available.

Traceoptions

When configuring a new feature, service, protocol, or interface, you might find it difficult to get it to work the first time. When something does not work as expected, you need to have visibility into the root cause to correct the issue. *Traceoptions* provides that visibility. Traceoptions is a debug facility that can be turned on to diagnose a number of protocol and service-related problems.

Authorization	local2
Cron	local3
Daemon	local4
Kernal	local5
User	local6
local0	local7
local1	

Table 4-12. *Syslog Facility-Overrides*

Traceoptions also can give you insight into the health of a network from a link/protocol standpoint. Having traceoptions log network events that signify instability or suboptimal performance has great value. When traceoptions are configured, you can view the output by viewing the log file that traceoptions generates.

Traceoptions can be enabled in many locations in a router's configuration. For instance, all the active protocols such as OSPF, IS-IS, RIP, and BGP have traceoptions. In addition, interfaces have traceoptions that can aid in the diagnosis of Layer 2 point-to-point protocol issues.

Table 4-13 shows the sections of a configuration that have traceoptions.

[edit snmp]	[edit protocols ospf]
[edit interface]	[edit protocols pim]
[edit forwarding-options sampling]	[edit protocols rip]
[edit protocols vrrp]	[edit protocols router-discovery]
[edit protocols bgp]	[edit protocols ldp]
[edit protocols dvmrp]	[edit protocols mpls]
[edit protocols igmp]	[edit protocol rsvp]
[edit protocols isis]	[edit routing options]
[edit protocols msdp]	

Table 4-13. *Traceoptions Configuration Locations*

Because there are so many applications of traceoptions, and because they are protocol- or interface-dependent, only a few introductory examples are provided in this chapter; however, the configuration of traceoptions for all sections is implemented consistently. Protocol-specific examples of traceoptions are provided as the protocols are introduced in subsequent chapters.

Traceoptions file setup is similar to that of syslog. The first step is to define the file names, sizes, and file archive scheme using the `traceoptions file` statement. In the following example, the trace options are enabled under the `[edit protocols isis]` section of a configuration:

```
[edit protocols isis]
sean@Juniper1# set traceoptions file isis-log size 1m files 10
```

This statement configures the traceoptions file `isis-log` to a size of 1 megabyte and specifies 10 archive files.

Traceoptions archives files the same as syslog. When the file `isis-log` grows to be 1 megabyte, the file is renamed `isis-log.0`. When the file again grows to 1 megabyte, the file `isis-log.0` is renamed `isis-log.1`, and `isis-log` is renamed `isis-log.0`. Further traceoptions logging action is sent to `isis-log`. This scheme continues until a total of 10 files is produced. The oldest file is then discarded as new files are produced.

Once traceoptions file logging options are set, you can choose the parts of the protocols operations that are to be monitored, using the `flag` statement. The `flag` statement is where you specify protocol dependent options. To use traceoptions effectively, you must know something about how the protocol works. Without this knowledge you might find it difficult to target where the problem is occurring. The specifics of the routing protocols are covered in subsequent chapters.

The following `flag` statement enables the logging of IS-IS `hello` packets:

```
[edit protocols isis]
sean@Juniper1# set traceoptions flag hello
```

This traceoptions statement instructs the IS-IS routing process to store all Hello protocol-based messages to the isis-log file configured earlier. To view the traceoptions log, use the `show log` command:

```
sean@Juniper1> show log isis-log
Sep  4 17:12:42 trace_on: Tracing to "/var/log/isis-log" started
Sep  4 17:12:44 Received L1 LAN IIH, source id Juniper3 on fxp2.0
Sep  4 17:12:46 Received L1 LAN IIH, source id Juniper3 on fxp2.0
Sep  4 17:12:47 Received L2 LAN IIH, source id Juniper2 on fxp0.0
```

```
Sep  4 17:12:47 Received L1 LAN IIH, source id Juniper2 on fxp0.0
Sep  4 17:12:48 Sending L1 LAN IIH on fxp0.0
Sep  4 17:12:48 Sending L2 LAN IIH on fxp0.0
Sep  4 17:12:49 Received L1 LAN IIH, source id Juniper3 on fxp2.0
Sep  4 17:12:49 Received L1 LAN IIH, source id Juniper2 on fxp0.0
Sep  4 17:12:49 Received L2 LAN IIH, source id Juniper2 on fxp0.0
```

Here you can see a number of Hello protocol messages sent and received by the router. Note that the log has a timestamp indicating when the event took place. Timestamps help you track issues that happened hours or even days ago.

Traceoptions as a Debugging Tool

In a network running the IS-IS routing protocol, an administrator is having difficulty bringing up an adjacency between two routers. After conducting numerous tests to ensure that the link integrity between the two routers is good, the administrator decides to turn on traceoptions. Because the problem is related to the routers becoming adjacent, the administrator wants to flag any error messages. Here is the traceoptions configuration:

```
[edit protocols isis]
sean@Juniper1# set traceoptions file isis-log size 1m files 10
sean@Juniper1# set traceoptions flag error detail
```

The statement `flag error detail` tells the router to log any IS-IS protocol errors to the isis-log file. The `detail` option permits more detail than what is normally logged. After the traceoptions are set and the configuration committed, the administrator can view all errors generated with the `show log` command:

```
sean@Juniper1> show log isis-log
Sep  4 20:31:30 trace_on: Tracing to "/var/log/isis-log" started
Sep  4 20:31:35 ERROR: IIH authentication failure
Sep  4 20:31:35 ERROR: previous error from L1, source Juniper3 on so-1/1/0.0
Sep  4 20:31:42 ERROR: IIH authentication failure
```

These log entries show that the IS-IS routing protocol is experiencing authentication failures on the interface `so-1/1/0.0`. It is a sure bet that the routers are not configured correctly for protocol authentication. Without the traceoptions command it might be difficult to find the root cause of this problem; particularly if one of the routers is outside of your administrative domain, and you cannot view the router's configuration file.

In addition to being able to flag IS-IS errors, there are other parts of the protocol that can be monitored. Table 4-14 shows the traceoptions available for the IS-IS protocol.

The list of traceoption flags is different for each protocol. For example, you will not find an `spf` flag under BGP traceoptions. Because BGP is a distance-vector protocol, it has no *Shortest Path First* (SPF) algorithm. Although the flag options vary, traceoptions files and archiving schemes are set up identically under all other configuration sections.

Monitoring Network Operations with Traceoptions

Frequently, network events must be investigated after they have occurred; these events might have happened minutes or even days earlier. Traceoptions can be configured ahead of time to log critical protocol error conditions that affect network operations. This section demonstrates how traceoptions can be used to track network events.

Flag Option	Description
normal	All normal operations, including adjacency changes
general	A combination of the normal and route trace operations
all	All tracing operations
error	Errored IS-IS packets
hello	Hello packets
lsp	Link-state PDU packets
lsp-generation	Link-state PDU generation packets
packets	All IS-IS protocol packets
psn	Partial Sequence Number PDU (PSNP) packets
spf	Shortest-path-first calculations
csn	Complete Sequence Number PDU (CSNP) packets
policy	Policy operations and actions
route	Routing table changes
state	State transitions
task	Interface transactions and processing
timer	Timer usage

Table 4-14.   *IS-IS Traceoptions Flag Options*

In this example, the administrator of a service provider network receives complaints from customers that the Internet is inaccessible. The customers note that many hosts had a problem that occurred around 5:50 P.M. the previous day. The administrator asks for some of the problematic IP addresses, and receives "30.40.0.12" as one of the failed hosts.

Before the problem was reported, the administrator had set up a traceoptions log for the *Border Gateway Protocol* (BGP) on all peering (external connection to the Internet) routers:

```
bgp {
        traceoptions {
                file bgp-log size 1m files 10 world-readable;
                flag route;
                flag state;
        }
}
```

This traceoptions setup tells the router to log any change in routes, and to log any change in the state of the BGP session between routers to the file bgp-log.

The network administrator had no error to indicate a link failure in the network, so decides to check the bgp-log.

```
sean@Juniper1> show log bgp-log | find "30.40.0"
Sep  5 17:51:33 CHANGE   30.40.0.0        255.255.0.0      gw 172.16.32.2      BGP        pref 170/-
1001 metric  fxp1.0 <Delete Ext>  as 65524

Sep  5 17:51:33 CHANGE   30.42.0.0        255.255.0.0      gw 172.16.32.2      BGP        pref 170/-
1001 metric  fxp1.0 <Delete Ext>  as 65524

Sep  5 17:51:33 CHANGE   30.44.0.0        255.255.0.0      gw 172.16.32.2      BGP        pref 170/-
1001 metric  fxp1.0 <Delete Ext>  as 65524

Sep  5 17:51:33 CHANGE   40.128.0.0       255.255.0.0      gw 172.16.32.2      BGP        pref 170/-
1001 metric  fxp1.0 <Delete Ext>  as 65524

Sep  5 17:51:33 CHANGE   40.192.0.0       255.255.0.0      gw 172.16.32.2      BGP        pref 170/-
1001 metric  fxp1.0 <Delete Ext>  as 65524

Sep  5 17:51:33 CHANGE   50.50.0.0        255.255.0.0      gw 172.16.32.2      BGP        pref 170/-
1001 metric  fxp1.0 <Delete Ext>  as 65524
```

These entries confirm the administrator's suspicions that the problem was caused by a failure elsewhere in the Internet. The BGP protocol withdrew the route 30.42.0.0/16 (along with many others from the same AS number) from the local router table. The fact that the update was learned from a router outside the network (the router at address 172.16.32.2) reinforces this assumption.

This `show log` command demonstrates how to find a text string in a log file. In this use, the `show log bgp-log` is piped to the `find` command. The `find` command then searches for the text "30.42.0." Once this text is found, the associated log entries are displayed. The log display is then continued from that point.

The Complete Reference

Chapter 5

Interface Configuration and Control

by Thomas E. Van Meter

Juniper Networks routers support a wide variety of interfaces. This chapter will discuss configuration issues and some theoretical aspects of various interface features. The chapter breaks down this large subject into smaller sections—each focusing on one of a variety of topics: general interface properties, logical interface properties, Synchronous Optical Network/Synchronous Digital Hierarchy (SONET/SDH) interfaces, Asynchronous Transfer Mode (ATM) interfaces, plesiochronous interfaces (T/E-series), and Ethernet interfaces. A brief section on troubleshooting highlights some commands that can be used for determining link and interface status.

Different interfaces sometimes share the same type of configuration parameter, such as line buildout for T-1 and T-3 interfaces. You have different options for the same type of parameter in these different interfaces. In such cases, only the information relevant to that particular interface will be discussed.

Permanent vs. Transient Interfaces

When you configure a router, two types of interfaces are used: *permanent* and *transient*. Permanent interfaces are always displayed when issuing a `show interfaces` command. These interfaces are used for internal processes, and for the most part, you will not need to concern yourself with them.

Permanent interfaces may be *logical* interfaces, in that you physically cannot touch them; or they may represent *physical* interfaces that are installed in the router for intra-router communication. Transient interfaces represent ports on Physical Interface Cards (PICs). They show up in the configuration output only after you have configured them. The TAP interface, for the Trivial Access Protocol, is an example of a permanent interface; it is used internally by Juniper routers to exchange information between different parts of the router. You do not need to (and should not) configure most permanent interfaces because they are internal to the router. They will show up when you issue a `show interface` command, but they will not show up in the configuration output when you issue a `show configuration` command.

You should configure *only one* permanent interface: *fxp0*, which provides out-of-band management to your routers. Juniper routers do not route traffic from other (transient) interfaces over *fxp0*; consequently, you cannot use *fxp0* as a routable port. You must use transient interfaces for transit network traffic—although be aware that routing protocol adjacencies can form over the *fxp0* interface, so be cautious about configuring `all` interfaces under routing protocols such as Open Shortest Path First (OSPF). These adjacencies are not considered transit routing traffic because the updates *terminate* at the routing engine.

You can configure interfaces not currently installed in the router and then enable the configuration when you do install the PICs. This feature is very useful when you're staging routers prior to deployment. You may come across an interesting troubleshooting issue, however: if you make a typographic error and misconfigure an interface by typing the wrong keys, the router will not generate an error message as long as the syntax is valid. For example, if you type interface so-0/3/0 when you really meant to type so-3/0/0, the router accepts the command as long as it's valid syntax for the router. When you commit the configuration, you will probably discover the error when the interface you thought you were configuring does not work. The good news is that you can easily fix this error by renaming the interface to the correct interface name with the configuration rename command.

Use the following naming convention when configuring an interface:

interface type-FPC # / PIC Slot # / Port #

A valid example is *at-0/0/0*.

Slot and Port Numbering on Juniper Networks Routers

Identifying the PIC slots and port numbers on the PICs can be challenging if you do not understand the origin of the numbering structure. Juniper Networks first router was called the M40. Connections to the backplane/midplane from the Flexible PIC Concentrator (FPC) were vertically oriented. On M40s, the PIC slot positions started with slot 0 at the top of the FPC, with slot numbers increasing down the FPC. Juniper Networks called the second router the M20. The backplane FPC connections for the M40 were reduced from eight to four, and the orientation turned 90 degrees clockwise. You can think of the M20 as horizontally oriented. In terms of identifying PIC slots, you count PIC slots on the M20 from right to left, starting with 0. These first two routers set the groundwork for the naming convention used for the entire family of Juniper Networks routers. The taller routers, like the M40 and M160, use vertical PIC conventions. The shorter routers, like the M5/10 and the M20, use horizontal PIC conventions.

The actual port identification for the PIC varies, depending upon the type of router in use. Vertically oriented routers identify ports from top to bottom, and right to left. Port 0 is at the upper right, port 1 is lower right, port 2 is upper left, and port 3 is lower left (see Figure 5-1).

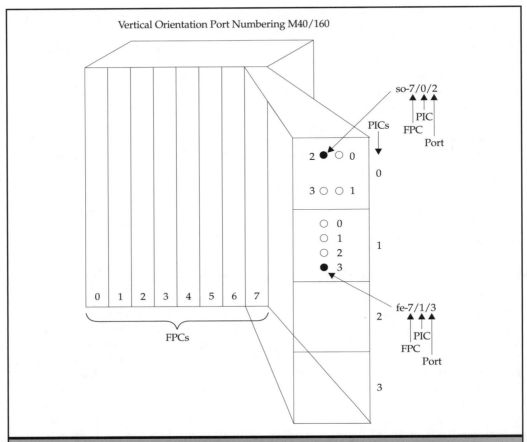

Figure 5-1. *Vertical orientation port numbering for the M40 and M160*

Horizontally oriented routers start port identification bottom to top, right to left (see Figure 5-2). Port 0 is at the lower right, port 1 is lower left, port 2 is upper right, and port 3 is upper left.

Some PICs have only a single row of ports, like the Fast Ethernet modules; these ports start at port 0 and increase to port 3 from top to bottom (for vertical orientation) or right to left (for horizontal orientation).

Some PICs support *channelized* interfaces. For example, the channelized OC-12 consists of 12 T-3 channels. The channelized DS-3 consists of 28 DS-1 channels. To identify the logical channel, add a colon (:) after the port number—*t3-0/0/0:0* for channelized OC-12 or *t1-0/0/0:26* for a channelized DS-3.

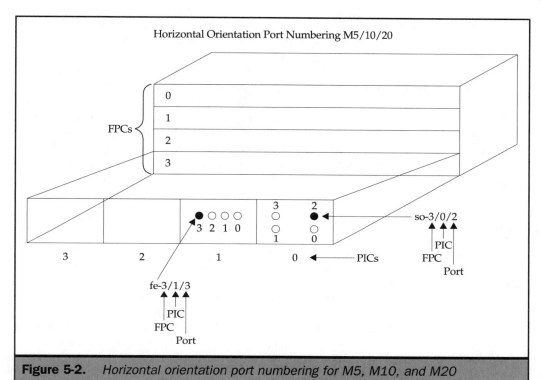

Figure 5-2. *Horizontal orientation port numbering for M5, M10, and M20*

Interface and Address Categories

Juniper Networks routers use a *default* address and a *primary* interface. On any given interface, a *preferred* address and a *primary* address can exist. The router's default address is used to source packets on unnumbered interfaces, and it is used as the source address any time the destination address of the packet does not imply a specific interface, such as a destination address of 224.0.0.1. The default address also serves as the default router-id for routing protocols. The default address is the primary address configured on the loopback interface that is a non-127 address. You can specify the router's default address with the `[edit system]` set `default-address-selection` command.

The preferred address on an interface is used when there are multiple addresses configured on the same interface in the same subnet and the router needs to pick one of them as the source address for traffic. By default, it picks the lowest one; however, you can override this default behavior by specifying the keyword `preferred`. The primary address for an interface is the numerically lowest address, regardless of subnet. It is used to source broadcast traffic and unnumbered traffic on that interface.

The primary interface and the primary address are two separate things. The primary interface for the router is typically *fxp0* (the lowest index number broadcast interface; if there are no broadcast interfaces, it is the lowest index number for Point-to-Point links). The primary interface is the address that packets go out if there is no interface specified or if the destination address does not imply any outgoing interface (like PING to 224.0.0.1). Add the keyword `primary` after the address if you wish to make the primary address on the interface different than the normal primary address (numerically lowest on the interface). If you want to specify a different interface as the primary interface for the router, use the `primary` keyword after the protocol family on that interface. The default address is derived from the router's primary address on the primary interface if there are no non-127 addresses on *lo0*; the default address is used to source packets for unnumbered interfaces.

Clocking

When configuring the router, you can configure the transmit clock on each interface; the transmit clock aligns each outgoing packet transmitted over the router's interfaces. Juniper routers have an onboard stratum 3 clock.

You cannot take loop timing from one interface and redistribute it to drive clocking to other interfaces on the router. If you need a common clocking source, you can use the onboard stratum 3 clock or use loop timing on all interfaces connected to a network driven by the same network clock source. The default clocking is internal. You can set the clocking to loop timing with the following command:

```
lab@hongkong# set interfaces so-0/0/0 clocking external
```

or back to internal timing with:

```
lab@hongkong# set interfaces so-0/0/0 clocking internal
```

Configuring the Juniper Networks Interface

Each Juniper Networks interface supports physical and logical properties. Physical properties include physical media maximum transmission units (MTUs), linecodes, framing methods, encapsulation types, and vlan/IEEE 802.1Q virtual LAN tagging information. Using logical units, you can break a single physical interface into up to 65,535 logical interfaces. Each logical unit supports Layer 2 and Layer 3 protocol addressing plus interface-specific configuration features such as Virtual Router Redundancy Protocol (VRRP).

Physical Layer Parameters

Many options allow parameter modification at the physical layer. These options resolve issues such as sufficient clock transitions for timing synchronization and payload scrambling for SONET.

Encapsulations

Juniper Networks routers can support many logical interfaces per physical interface, depending upon the encapsulation type employed. Encapsulations that are inherently Point-To-Point protocols, such as the Point-to-Point Protocol (PPP) and Cisco high-level data link control (HDLC), support only a single logical unit, *unit 0*. Other protocols such as frame relay support many logical interfaces. When you configure an interface for frame relay, for example, you can configure a non-zero unit. Frame relay logical configurations can either be Point-to-Point (P2P) configurations or Point-to-Multipoint (P2MP) configurations.

The interfaces with a "CCC" encapsulation permit circuit cross-connect on that interface. If you do configure a physical interface for some form of CCC encapsulation, you cannot configure a protocol family on the logical unit(s) that uses the CCC encapsulation (which is an additional encapsulation statement at the unit level). Do not worry about remembering this fact, as the router will bark at you if you try to commit the configuration with a family on a logical unit configured for CCC.

Logical Interface Configuration

Configure each logical interface as a *unit* under a physical interface. You can configure Layer 3 protocol families and addressing information and Layer 2 protocol-related parameters, like frame relay data-link connection identifier (DLCI) values, under the unit level of the hierarchy.

Protocol Families

Juniper Networks routers support four protocol families on logical interfaces: family *iso* for IS-IS (Intermediate System to Intermediate System), family *inet* for IP (Internet Protocol), family *inet6* for IPv6, and family *mpls* for MPLS (Multi-Protocol Label Switching).

It is imperative that you configure the family type for each interface. Each interface uses the configured protocol families to verify valid packet types. If you do not configure the protocol family on an interface, the router discards any valid packets in that protocol family as unrecognized packets. For example, the router discards MPLS packets that arrive on an interface without the protocol family mpls configured; even though the interface may be defined under the [edit protocols mpls] hierarchy.

The following configurations show various families configured on different logical interfaces. They also illustrate encapsulations configured at the physical interface level. These examples show Point-to-Point interface configurations. The other common configuration for the frame relay encapsulation includes a P2MP configuration.

PPP Encapsulation   Interface *so-0/1/0* illustrates the default PPP encapsulation. The interface has an IP address configured under the protocol family *inet*. Additionally, the interface recognizes the IS-IS packets because of the `family iso` statement. The IS-IS protocol typically uses a single address to represent the router; in this case, the iso address appears on the *lo0* interface so is not shown here.

```
so-0/1/0 {
    unit 0 {
        family inet {
            address 10.1.2.1/30;
        }
        family iso;
    }
}
```

Cisco-HDLC Encapsulation   Interface *so-0/1/1* illustrates the Cisco-HDLC encapsulation. Although HDLC is standards based, each vendor has the opportunity to implement a particular field in its own way. Juniper Networks' implementation of HDLC works with Cisco System's implementation.

The default encapsulation for Juniper Networks routers is PPP, and Cisco System's default is HDLC. You must configure one side of the circuit to match the other for the circuit to come up into an up state. Notice that while interface *so-0/1/0* (described in the previous section) does not permit MPLS packets, interface *so-0/1/1* does:

```
so-0/1/1 {
    encapsulation cisco-hdlc;
    unit 0 {
        family inet {
            address 10.1.1.1/30;
        }
        family iso;
        family mpls;
    }
}
```

Frame Relay Encapsulation   Interface *so-0/1/2* shows a P2P link using frame relay encapsulation. Notice that this side of the connection is the data circuit-terminating equipment (DCE). If you have a back-to-back router connection (as you would in a lab), one side of the link must specify DCE for the connection to become active. Enabling DCE disables sending keepalives. Alternatively, you can manually disable keepalives on both sides of the frame relay connection. Either way will allow a back-to-back configuration to come up.

Frame relay encapsulation requires that a DLCI value appear on the logical unit. Legal DLCI values are 1 through 1022; however, different frame relay standards reserve different DLCI values. As a general rule, use DLCI values between 16 and 992. JUNOS software supports ANSI T1.617 Annex D (the default) and ITU Q933a Annex A LMI formats. Set the Local Management Interface (LMI) type with the `set interfaces in-#/#/# encapsulation frame-relay lmi lmi-type [ ansi | itu ]` configuration command.

Note *Notice the logical unit number—and notice that the DLCI value mirrors the logical unit number. Whenever possible, pick the logical unit value to mirror the DLCI value; it makes troubleshooting much easier.*

```
so-0/1/2 {
    dce;
    encapsulation frame-relay;
    unit 75 {
        dlci 75;
        family inet {
            address 172.16.1.1/24;
        }
    }
}
```

When keepalives are enabled on the router, it affects the maximum number of configurable DLCI values for multipoint/multicast interfaces. The maximum configurable DLCI values are determined by the formula *(MTU-12)/5*. Disable keepalives to increase the number of configurable DLCI values with the `[edit interfaces in-#/#/#]` `no-keepalive` command. Additionally, on channelized T-3 interfaces, the router imposes a DLCI range limit of 1 through 63. The DLCI value is locally significant, so this should not impose any significant technical hurdle.

By default, the router sends only unicast frame relay traffic. If the frame relay switch to which the router is connected supports multicast replication, you can configure that DLCI to send multicast traffic with this command:

```
[edit interfaces in-#/#/# unit #] multicast-dlci
```

You can configure this command on multipoint interfaces only. The following listing shows DLCI 600 configured for multicast traffic:

```
so-0/1/0 {
    description "to Montreal";
    encapsulation frame-relay;
    unit 100 {
        multipoint;
        multicast-dlci 600;
        family inet {
            address 10.100.1.1/24 {
                multipoint-destination 10.100.1.2 dlci 100;
                multipoint-destination 10.100.1.3 dlci 600;
            }
        }
    }
}
```

The `show interface terse` command, illustrated next, is a great way to determine which protocol families are enabled on particular interfaces. Notice in this case that although the family *iso* is enabled on all interfaces, only *lo0* actually has an *iso* address. This is the simplest case scenario. It is possible to specify additional *iso* addresses on different interfaces (one per interface); but this is not the normal situation. This occurs only when you must have a different ISO address advertised out a particular interface. Notice that several permanent interfaces, such as pime, pimd, tap, fxp0, and fxp1 show up in this command output.

```
lab@Montreal> show interfaces terse
Interface       Admin Link Proto Local                Remote
fe-0/0/0        up    up
fe-0/0/1        up    up
fe-0/0/1.0      up    up   inet  10.1.0.17/30
fe-0/0/2        up    down
fe-0/0/3        up    up
fe-0/0/3.0      up    up   inet  10.1.87.1/24
so-0/1/0        up    up
so-0/1/0.0      up    up   inet  10.1.2.1/30
                               iso
so-0/1/1        up    up
so-0/1/1.0      up    up   inet  10.1.1.1/30
                               iso
                               mpls
```

```
so-0/1/2          up     up
so-0/1/2.75       up     up    inet   172.16.1.1/24
so-0/1/3          up     down
gr-0/2/0          up     up
ip-0/2/0          up     up
pd-0/2/0          up     up
pe-0/2/0          up     up
fxp0              up     down
fxp0.0            up     down  inet   172.29.1.4/24
fxp1              up     up
fxp1.0            up     up    tnp    4
gre               up     up
ipip              up     up
lo0               up     up
lo0.0             up     up    inet   10.1.255.1          --> 0/0
                               iso    49.0001.0192.0168.0001.00
pimd              up     up
pime              up     up
tap               up     up
```

Configuring Unnumbered Interfaces

You can configure an unnumbered interface to preserve IP addresses. Unnumbered interfaces use the address of another configured interface as the default source address for packets sent out via the unnumbered interface.

Here's how you configure a unit without an address for an unnumbered configuration:

```
so-0/1/0 {
    unit 0 {
        family inet;
        family iso;
    }
}
```

By default, the router uses the *loopback 0* interface address as the source address for packets sourced by unnumbered interfaces, as long as you have not configured the interface with a martian address. Martian addresses are not routable addresses. View the martian table with the `show route martians` command. You can also use the `[edit system] default-address-selection` command to set the default address, which will be the source address for the packets sent out via the unnumbered interface.

Configuring SONET Interfaces

Synchronous Optical Network (SONET) was developed at Bellcore (Bell Communications Research) in the 1980s. It uses high-speed fiber optic transmissions to send information at data rates in multiples of 51.84 Mbps. This value is referred to as the *optical carrier value*.

The SONET stream reflects the amount of traffic as a multiple of the optical carrier, or OC, value. For example, OC-3 is 155.520 Mbps (3 × 51.84 Mbps). OC-12 is 622.08 Mbps (12 × 51.84 Mbps). Frequently, the letter *c*, for concatenation, follows the SONET designation. This reflects whether or not the SONET stream uses the redundant path overhead bytes to carry overhead information or data. There are three types of SONET overhead: Section, Line, and Path. Each OC-1 stream of data has all three types of overhead. When SONET combines multiple OC-1s to make a higher data rate, it only requires one set of path overhead values. The remaining path overhead values can be used to carry data. The SONET stream is concatenated when it carries path overhead information in only the first OC-1 and uses the other path overhead bits for data transmission.

Each interface has a set of common physical parameters and different logical parameters. The physical parameters affect all the logical interfaces.

Physical Interface Card Properties

Juniper Networks routers support SONET interfaces at the following data rates: OC-3c, OC-12c, OC-48c, and OC-192c. All interfaces on the PIC share the same properties for framing mode and concatenation method.

SONET framing and Synchronous Digital Hierarchy (SDH) framing affect the organization and order of bit transmission. Outside of North America, SDH is the standard framing method used for optical carrier streams. You configure the framing mode with this command:

```
[edit chassis fpc # pic #] framing
```

Specify either the *sonet* or *sdh* framing mode, for example,

```
[edit]
lab@hongkong# set chassis fpc 0 pic 0 framing sdh
```

The OC-12 and OC-48 interfaces support nonconcatenated configuration. This means that subrates can be configured as separate logical interfaces, where the subrate is some portion of the OC-12 or OC-48. The OC-12 breaks down into four separate OC-3s, while the OC-48 breaks down into four separate OC-12s.

Note *The Channelized OC-12 interface automatically breaks down into 12 separate DS-3 values. You do not configure concatenation for the Channelized OC-12 interface.*

Configure interfaces for nonconcatenated mode with the following command:

```
[edit chassis fpc 0 pic 1]
set no-concatenate
```

The `show interface` output displays the framing method. The output also shows the different MTUs for media type, and the INET (Internet), ISO (International Organization for Standardization), and MPLS protocols.

```
lab@hongkong> show interfaces so-0/0/0
Physical interface: so-0/0/0, Enabled, Physical link is Up
  Interface index: 19, SNMP ifIndex: 21
  Link-level type: PPP, MTU: 4474, Clocking: Internal, SDH mode, Speed: OC3,
  Loopback: None, CRC: 16, Payload scrambler: Enabled
  Device flags   : Present Running
  Interface flags: Point-To-Point SNMP-Traps
  Link flags     : Keepalives
  Keepalive settings: Interval 10 seconds, Up-count 1, Down-count 3
  Keepalive Input: 41 (00:00:01 ago), Output: 40 (00:00:05 ago)
  LCP state: Opened
  NCP state: inet: Opened, iso: Opened, mpls: Opened
  Input rate     : 654176 bps (288 pps), Output rate: 74028608 bps (32583 pps)
  SONET alarms   : None
  SONET defects  : None
  Logical interface so-0/0/0.0 (Index 9) (SNMP ifIndex 28)
    Flags: Point-To-Point SNMP-Traps Encapsulation: PPP
    Protocol inet, MTU: 4470, Flags: None
      Addresses, Flags: Is-Preferred Is-Primary
        Destination: 10.0.21/24, Local: 10.0.21.1
    Protocol iso, MTU: 4470, Flags: Is-Primary
    Protocol mpls, MTU: 4458, Flags: Is-Primary
```

SONET Options

You configure parameters affecting physical layer properties in the `[edit interfaces so-#/#/# sonet-options]` hierarchy. The parameters include automatic protection switching, frame check sequence capability, loopback capability, SONET path-trace designation, payload scrambling, and RFC 2615 capability.

Automatic Protection Switching

SONET (and ATM SONET) interfaces support Automatic Protection Switching (APS). This means the carrier can have a protection (or backup) circuit to provide physical layer failover for either an entire router or a port/fpc on a router. The Juniper Networks implementation works like *1+1 APS*. It can be *revertive* or *nonrevertive*, although the default behavior is nonrevertive—once the protect circuit activates, it stays active, even if the working circuit that failed returns to a good state. Network operators may not like the revertive capability because it means that the link will recognize two failures: the first when the link fails, and the second when it moves back from the protect circuit to the working circuit. Juniper Networks' implementation only supports bidirectional configuration. The K2 byte in the SONET header indicates protection status. These are the significant bits in the K2 byte, counting from the left:

- Bit 4 set to 1 indicates the (1+1) working channel.
- Bit 4 set to 0 indicates channel 0.
- Bit 5 set to 0 indicates 1+1 APS.
- Bits 6–8 set to 101 indicate bidirectional configuration.

This means that the valid K2 byte patterns are 0x05 or 0x15.

Note *If you are configuring APS on a SONET Channelized OC-12, you can configure only channel 0 for APS; the router ignores APS configurations on the other channels.*

You must configure two circuits in APS: a *working* circuit and a *protect* circuit. The working circuit becomes the primary physical path. The protect circuit becomes the backup physical path. Either path can become active based on link failures. The protect router determines link failure through state information transmitted once per second via IP, with a 3 second hold time. Change the default 1 second advertisement interval for state information with the [edit interfaces interface-name sonet-options aps] advertise-interval command, where you specify the time in milliseconds. If three status messages are missed, the link fails and the protect circuit becomes active. Change the default 3 second hold-time with the [edit interfaces interface-name sonet-options aps] hold-time command, again with the time in milliseconds. If you want to specify revertive behavior, meaning the working circuit becomes active again after the specified number of seconds, use the [edit interfaces interface-name sonet-options aps] revert-time command. The default setting is 0 seconds, which means do not revert. If you specify revertive behavior, the working circuit will be the active path whenever it is up.

When you specify working and protect circuits, you group the interfaces together in the router with a common group name. Additionally, you must specify a password common to both the protect and the working circuit configurations. These minimal requirements allow you to provide protection between two routers on two different physical circuits. This provides protection either for a port or for an FPC. Figure 5-3 depicts this scenario.

The minimal configuration does not provide protection in case of router failure, because if the router fails, the protect circuit also fails. To protect against router failure, the protect circuit must connect to a different router. Because the protect and working circuits terminate on different routers when protecting the entire router, they need to communicate state information (that the router knew automatically when protect and

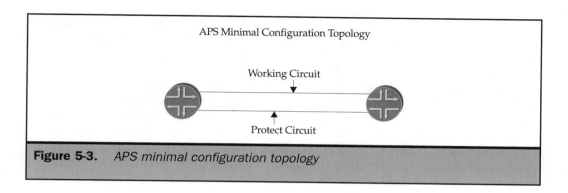

Figure 5-3. *APS minimal configuration topology*

working circuits both terminated on the same system). Consequently, you add an IP address as a neighbor under each circuit. This address specifies the IP address where the other circuit is located. Because the router transmits the state information via IP, it is possible that the state information could be routed out the working circuit interface. To prevent the situation where APS state information is routed out the working circuit it is *highly recommended* that the routers providing backup be directly connected. Furthermore, the neighbor address should be the address of the next-hop of the directly connected interface. Because the network is directly connected, no reachability problems should occur because the state information went out the interface that just failed.

Consider the following example shown in Figure 5-4, in which two routers, San Jose and Denver, provide protection for a circuit to Montreal. The working circuit connects Denver and Montreal. The protect circuit connects San Jose and Montreal. Both San Jose and Denver are directly connected via the 10.1.3.x network. The same addressing information is configured on the logical units for both the protect and working circuit. The inactive circuit does not propagate duplicate address information.

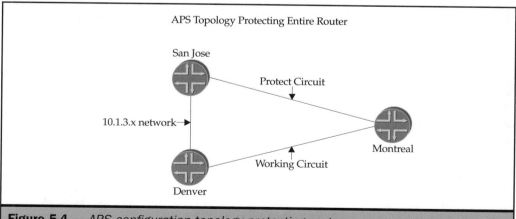

Figure 5-4. *APS configuration topology protecting router*

Once it becomes active, the other circuit has already failed, so there is still no duplicate address propagation. There is a potential convergence issue however. Link-state protocols must issue link-state updates when they either lose or gain a link.

In the following code examples, notice that routers Denver and San Jose both list the other router as a neighbor on a directly connected interface. Router Montreal does not list any neighbor, because it is home to both protect and working circuits. As a matter of fact, if you tried to configure a neighbor statement on Montreal, the router will give you a parsing error because the neighbor statement implies that the same group name cannot exist as working and protect on the same router. The working and protect neighbors must be on different routers; otherwise you don't need a neighbor statement to get to the other circuit.

Here's the Denver configuration:

```
[edit]
lab@Denver# show interfaces so-0/1/1
sonet-options {
    aps {
        working-circuit tom1;
        neighbor 10.1.3.2;
        authentication-key "$9$X5fxb2mPQ/Cuf5"; # SECRET-DATA
    }
}
unit 0 {
    family inet {
        address 10.1.1.2/30;
    }
}
```

Here's the San Jose configuration:

```
[edit]
lab@SanJose# show interfaces so-0/1/2
sonet-options {
    aps {
        protect-circuit tom1;
        neighbor 10.1.3.1;
        authentication-key "$9$c41SvLaJD.PQZG"; # SECRET-DATA
    }
}
unit 0 {
    family inet {
        address 10.1.1.2/30;
    }
}
```

Here's the Montreal configuration:

```
[edit]
lab@Montreal# show interfaces so-0/1/2
sonet-options {
    aps {
        protect-circuit tom1;
        authentication-key "$9$5T6AleWNdsKv";  # SECRET-DATA
    }
}
unit 0 {
    family inet {
        address 10.1.1.1/30;
    }
}


[edit]
lab@Montreal# show interfaces so-0/1/1
sonet-options {
    aps {
        working-circuit tom1;
        authentication-key "$9$f5nCrlM7-weK";  # SECRET-DATA
    }
}
unit 0 {
    family inet {
        address 10.1.1.1/30;
    }
}
```

APS operational mode commands help you identify state. The following output shows useful information about current APS status. Notice the bolding on several different fields. The `Circuit`, `Interface`, and `State` fields indicate the status and type of circuit; in this case the working circuit is an `up` state. The `Channel` state indicates the working channel.

```
lab@Denver> show aps detail
Interface  Group                              Circuit  Intf State
so-0/1/1   tom1                               Working enabled, up
  Neighbor 10.1.3.2, adj up, neighbor interface disabled, dead 2.520
  Channel state Working
```

The `detail` and `extensive` flag offer similar information, with the `extensive` flag showing K1 byte status information. The routers use the K1 byte to signal requests and acknowledgements related to protection switch actions. The routers on opposite ends of the physical link essentially do a three-way handshake, similar to a TCP/IP session establishment, using the K1 byte to indicate desired actions. The first four bits, counting from the left, indicate the desired switch action. The final four bits indicate which channel requests the switch action. The channel indication can either be 0000 for channel 0 or 0001 for channel 1.

There are three general types of switch action: *automatically initiated* requests (such as link failure or degradation), *external* requests (lockout, force, and request), and *state* requests (which indicate current state when no other requests are indicated). There are 16 possible bit combinations, ranked in descending priority order 1111 to 0000. The three general types of switch action are spread throughout the range of possible values.

The three-way handshake determines which router's switch action request has the highest priority. Both routers then take that action. The process requires each router to determine its highest local switch action request by comparing the highest desired local request with the current local request. If the desired local request has a higher priority, it becomes the current priority. The router then compares the current local request with the remote request from the other side of the physical link. Unless the received request has a higher priority than the current local request, the router transmits its current local request to the far side of the link. If the received request does have a higher priority, the local router transmits an acknowledgement of the other router's higher priority switch action request by signaling one of the state requests (for example, K1-0×21). This handshake process serves to synchronize both routers on the highest priority switch action request. Once three successive receipts of identical request information are made indicating the desired switch action, the action can occur.

Of the external requests, lockout (meaning working channels cannot switch to the protection line) is the highest priority (1111), followed by force (1110), and request—called Manual in GR-253-CORE—(1000). Typically, lockout is used in a maintenance mode. Both force and request explicitly switch the working channel to the protect line (or vice versa), just at different priority levels. The automatically initiated requests (1100 and 1010) are between force and request in terms of priority. The state switch action requests occupy the bottom part of the priority range and include the ability to signal nonreversion (0001) and acknowledgment that the far-side router has a higher request priority (0010). The request, receive, and transmit K1 byte values are displayed with the extensive flag output, as shown here, aiding the troubleshooting process:

```
lab@Denver> show aps extensive
Interface   Group                      Circuit  Intf State
```

```
so-0/1/1   tom1                              Working  enabled, up
  Neighbor 10.1.3.2, adj up, neighbor interface disabled, dead 2.740
  Channel state Working
  Req K1 0x00, rcv K1 0x00, xmit K1 0x00, nbr K1 0x00, nbr paired req 0
  Revert time 0, neighbor revert time 0
  Hello due in 0.555
```

Remember to remove explicit lockout, force, or request configurations from the APS configuration once they are no longer needed. Set lockout with the `set interfaces so-0/0/0 sonet-options aps lockout` command. You set either force or request with the `set interfaces so-0/0/0 sonet-options aps (force | request) (protect | working )` command. The protect option allows you to force or request for the protect circuit. The working option lets you force or request for the working circuit.

Frame Check Sequence

The default Frame Check Sequence (FCS) value is CRC-16. Change it to CRC-32 at the `[edit interfaces so-#/#/# sonet-options]` hierarchy. Be aware that older SONET equipment may not support CRC-32.

The following example shows how to see the current FCS, change it to FCS 32, and verify the correct configuration.

```
lab@hongkong> show interfaces so-0/0/0
Physical interface: so-0/0/0, Enabled, Physical link is Up
  Interface index: 19, SNMP ifIndex: 21
  Link-level type: PPP, MTU: 4474, Clocking: Internal, SONET mode, Speed: OC3,
  Loopback: None, CRC: 16, Payload scrambler: Disabled
lab@hongkong# configure
Entering configuration mode
[edit]
lab@hongkong# set interfaces so-0/0/0 sonet-options fcs 32
[edit]
lab@hongkong# show interfaces
so-0/0/0 {
    sonet-options {
        fcs 32;
    }
}
```

Loopback

You can configure a SONET interface to loop traffic back either at the remote end or the local end of the circuit using this syntax:

[edit interfaces so-#/#/# sonet-options] loopback (local | remote)

See the "Troubleshooting" section later in this chapter for a more detailed discussion of how to use the `loopback` command. The following shows the configured local loopback:

```
lab@hongkong> show interfaces so-0/0/0
Physical interface: so-0/0/0, Enabled, Physical link is Up
   Interface index: 19, SNMP ifIndex: 21
   Link-level type: PPP, MTU: 4474, Clocking: External, SONET mode, Speed: OC3,
   Loopback: Local, CRC: 16, Payload scrambler: Enabled
   Device flags    : Present Running Loop-Detected
   Interface flags: Point-To-Point SNMP-Traps
```

The following example shows the router configuration for routes between hongkong and Tokyo routers. Here, if you configure the `remote` loopback option, the local router will display a "remote" value in the loopback field of `show interfaces` but will indicate normal operation. The remote router (Tokyo, in this instance) will display no indication of a loopback setting in the loopback field, but it will display the loop detected on the link.

```
lab@hongkong> show interfaces so-0/0/0
Physical interface: so-0/0/0, Enabled, Physical link is Up
   Interface index: 19, SNMP ifIndex: 21
   Link-level type: PPP, MTU: 4474, Clocking: Internal, SONET mode, Speed: OC3,
   Loopback: Remote, CRC: 16, Payload scrambler: Enabled
Device flags    : Present Running

lab@Tokyo> show interfaces so-0/0/0
Physical interface: so-0/0/0, Enabled, Physical link is Up
   Interface index: 19, SNMP ifIndex: 21
   Link-level type: PPP, MTU: 4474, Clocking: Internal, SONET mode, Speed: OC3,
   Loopback: None, CRC: 16, Payload scrambler: Enabled
   Device flags    : Present Running Loop-Detected
   Interface flags: Point-To-Point SNMP-Traps
```

SONET Path-Trace

The SONET path-trace feature allows you to specify what character string you want transmitted in the SONET overhead. Use this syntax to set a specific trace:

[edit interfaces so-#/#/# sonet-options] set path-trace

The router transmits the router name and interface identifier as the default path-trace:

```
[edit]
lab@hongkong# set interfaces so-0/0/0 sonet-options path-trace JUNIPER_ROCKS
```

Payload Scrambling

Payload scrambling is enabled by default. You can verify the current scrambling status by looking for the *Payload scrambler* field in the output of `show interfaces`. Payload scrambling helps prevent long strings of ones and zeros, which could cause a DC component and a resultant loss of synchronization.

```
[edit]
lab@hongkong# set interfaces so-0/0/0 sonet-options no-payload-scrambler
lab@hongkong> show interfaces so-0/0/0
Physical interface: so-0/0/0, Enabled, Physical link is Up
  Interface index: 19, SNMP ifIndex: 21
  Link-level type: PPP, MTU: 4474, Clocking: Internal, SONET mode, Speed: OC3,
  Loopback: None, CRC: 16, Payload scrambler: Disabled
```

RFC 2615

RFC 2615 specifies use of the self-synchronizing polynomial $X^{43} + 1$ and FCS 32. Without the RFC 2615 optimizations, it is possible that a string of bad data can be generated that would be interpreted incorrectly by the SONET/SDH equipment, such as a bit pattern that caused SONET/SDH-layer low transition density synchronization problems or emulated the SDH set-reset scrambler pattern. This pattern then would prevent the link from operating properly. Using the self-synchronizing polynomial, the probability that someone could randomly generate a bit stream that could cause a bad transmission is $9e^{-16}$. When you set RFC 2615, you automatically set the FCS to CRC-32. Look in the output of the SONET overhead byte C2 to determine whether or not the self-synchronizing polynomial is used. A value of *0xCF* means it is not in use, while a *0x16* value means that it is in use. Juniper Networks routers default to the C2 byte with a *0xCF* value. The following example sets the *so-0/0/0* interface to use the RFC 2615 options and displays the output that indicates that the these options are in effect. Notice that the CRC is set to 32 and the C2 byte is set to 0x16, indicating a successful RFC 2615 setting.

```
[edit]
lab@hongkong# set interfaces so-0/0/0 sonet-options rfc-2615
lab@hongkong> show interfaces so-0/0/0 extensive
Physical interface: so-0/0/0, Enabled, Physical link is Up
  Interface index: 19, SNMP ifIndex: 21, Generation: 22
  Link-level type: PPP, MTU: 4474, Clocking: Internal, SONET mode, Speed: OC3,
  Loopback: None, CRC: 32, Payload scrambler: Enabled
  .
  .
  .
Transmitted SONET overhead:
```

```
F1    : 0x00, J0    : 0x01, K1    : 0x00, K2    : 0x00
S1    : 0x00, C2    : 0x16, F2    : 0x00, Z3    : 0x00
Z4    : 0x00, V5    : 0x00
```

Maximum Transmission Unit

The physical interface MTU value must always exceed the logical family MTU values. For example, the following table shows the SONET default MTU values for the physical interface and the INET, ISO, and MPLS protocol families on an M5 router. Notice that in all cases, the physical MTU exceeds the logical MTU. The router automatically configures the protocol MTU when you configure the interface initially. If you later change the media MTU, the protocol MTU does not automatically adjust. In addition, the router adds a CRC value when it transmits Ethernet frames. The router does not include the CRC in the MTU calculation.

Do not forget to consider the Ethernet FCS bits when calculating MTUs with other vendors for interoperability.

Interface/Protocol	PPP	Cisco-HDLC	Frame Relay
Physical Interface	4474	4474	4474
INET	4470	4470	4470
ISO	4470	4470	4470
MPLS	4458	4458	4458

Interoperability

A brief statement on setting up SONET interfaces to interoperate with other routers is worthwhile, because overlooked default values can cause much consternation. JUNOS software defaults to payload scrambling, no self-synchronizing polynomial, and PPP encapsulation. Other manufacturers may have different default configurations. You must make sure that both sides of the link share the same parameters for the link to work properly.

Configuring the ATM Interface

Juniper Networks ATM interfaces support DS-3/E-3, OC-3, and OC-12 rates. Interfaces can be configured either as P2P or as P2MP permanent virtual circuits. Various physical and logical properties can be configured, some of which are mandatory.

Physical Interface Properties

Physical interface properties can be configured in a variety of different areas within the interface section of code: atm-options, sonet-options, t3-options, e3-options, and directly under the physical interface for clocking, encapsulation, and MTU.

Configuring the *atm-options* Section

You can configure only a few ATM properties under the *atm-options* section at the physical interface level: Virtual Path Identifiers (VPIs) and maximum Virtual Circuit Identifier (VCI) values per virtual path and Integrated Local Management Interface (ILMI) capability.

To configure the ATM interface correctly, you must define the VPI values you wish to use on the interface. For each VPI you define, you must define the maximum VCI value for that virtual path. This value specifies the number of virtual channel values in the interface table, starting at zero, that can be used for that path. For example, if you want to use VCI value 201, you must define a maximum VCI value of at least 202. This allocates space in the data structure for the maximum VCI value; it does not mandate that you must use all 201 VCIs. You can define multiple paths on a physical interface, as long as you define the maximum VCI value for each path. Between all VPI values on an interface, the total of the maximum VCI values can be 4090. The ATM Forum reserves VCI values 0–31; therefore, you should start actual VCI assignment at VCI 32.

Optionally, you can configure the ability to communicate with the ATM switch via ILMI by configuring the *ilmi* option under the *atm-options* section. ILMI stands for Integrated Local Management Interface (although in earlier ATM specifications it was called Interim Local Management Interface). ILMI uses a reserved VCI, channel 16, to communicate information using SNMP formatted messages between ATM devices. Information such as IP addresses and link status can be learned from directly connected devices via ILMI. Some service providers use ILMI to verify which router is connected to specific ATM switches; enabling ILMI on the ATM router interface helps the switch query the router for identification purposes.

The following output shows ILMI capability enabled and the *maximum-vcs* set to 200 for VPI 0. In this case, the largest numerical VPI, VCI combination that can be used is 0,199, where the VPI is 0 and the VCI is 199.

```
at-0/1/0 {
    encapsulation atm-pvc;
    atm-options {
        vpi 0 maximum-vcs 200;
        ilmi;
    }
    unit 100 {
        point-to-point;
```

```
        vci 0.100;
        family inet {
            address 10.0.11.2/24;
        }
        family iso;
        family mpls;
    }
}
```

Configuring the *sonet-options* Section

You can also configure various SONET options such as APS for ATM OC-3 and OC-12 interfaces. See the *sonet-options* parameters in the "Configuring SONET Interfaces" earlier in this chapter for an explanation of these features.

Configuring *t3-options* and *e3-options* Sections

For DS-3 or E-3 ATM interfaces, you may configure specific parameters under the *t3-options* or *e3-options* section. Specific T-3 and E-3 ATM parameters not explained in the T-3 and/or E-3 section are ATM encapsulation, E-3 framing, and payload scrambling.

Configuring ATM Encapsulation

You can configure ATM encapsulation in two ways: by direct mapping and via the Physical Layer Convergence Procedure (PLCP). Both direct mapping and PLCP are methods of cell delineation, or more simply, of determining where in a stream of bits the ATM cell begins.

Direct ATM encapsulation means that the ATM cells are mapped directly into the payload portion of the DS-3/E-3 frame. Basically, the payload portion of the DS-3/E-3 frame starts with an ATM cell, followed immediately by another ATM cell. This continues as long as the cells can fit into the payload of the DS-3/E-3. This is the most efficient way to pack ATM cells.

Upon receiving a stream of bits, equipment configured for direct mapping takes the first 4 bytes and computes a Header Error Check (HEC) value. If that HEC value matches the fifth byte—the theoretical HEC—you can (potentially) say that you have found the beginning of an ATM cell. If the fifth byte does not match the HEC computed over the first 4 bytes, the system shifts 1 bit and runs the computation again. Eventually you get a match, and then you can assume that you have found the cell header for an ATM cell. Therefore, you can offset by 53 bytes and check the HEC pattern again. If you can successfully offset several times in a row, you can be sure that you have found the beginning of the ATM cell boundary.

PLCP adds an extra 4 bytes of overhead to the ATM cell when it is carried within the DS-3/E-3 frame. The extra 4 bytes of overhead provide 2 bytes for frame alignment (meaning the first 2 bytes are a specific A1/A2 pattern (11110110 00101000). Practically speaking, the 2 bytes behind the frame alignment bytes are overhead, followed by 53 bytes of ATM cell. After the first 2 frame alignment bytes, the third byte indicates which overhead byte follows, while the last byte is the overhead byte itself. Because each overhead byte indicator has a specific bit pattern, the third overhead byte also serves to identify which ATM cell follows the four overhead bytes. Many carriers like the PLCP format because it happens to multiplex nicely into the plesiochronous digital hierarchy.

Consider the following example. A DS-3 frame configured for PLCP carries 12 ATM cells. Each ATM cell is preceded by 4 extra overhead bytes. The third overhead byte identifies which ATM cell in the logical stack of 12 ATM cells that particular cell happens to be. The fourth byte is typical overhead information, like BIP-8 or stuffing indication. The actual ATM cell begins at the fifth byte after the start of the special A1/A2 frame alignment pattern.

Configure ATM encapsulation at the `[edit interfaces at-#/#/# t3-options]` hierarchy level by using the `atm-encapsulation` command with either the *direct* or *PLCP* option.

Configuring ATM E-3 Framing

For E-3 interfaces, if you specify G.832 framing, you can only use direct mapping as the ATM encapsulation. If framing is unspecified, you will get G.751 framing with PLCP cell delineation. Specify ATM E-3 framing with the following command:

```
set interfaces at-0/2/0 e3-options framing (g.751 | g.832)
```

Note that you must be on an ATM interface to be able to specify an E-3 framing method. Framing methods are not configurable for normal E-3 interfaces. In any case, opposite ends of the same link must agree on the framing method for the link to come up.

Payload Scrambling

Payload scrambling serves to prevent a false positive when checking HEC values. For example, a random pattern of payload bits may happen to simulate a valid HEC pattern for the fifth byte of an ATM cell header. Without scrambling, the ATM receiver may indicate a false positive and think that the ATM cell begins in the middle of what is actually the cell payload. With scrambling enabled, you basically reduce the possibility of getting a false positive.

The following example shows the *t3-options* setting, but is equally valid for *e3-options*.

```
lab@hongkong# set edit interfaces at-0/1/0 t3-options ?
Possible completions:
  no-payload-scrambler  Don't enable payload scrambling
  payload-scrambler     Enable payload scrambling
```

The key factor to remember when configuring *t3-options* or *e3-options* is that both parameters on opposite ends of the link must match for the link to work. One parameter setting may be more efficient for your network, but both ends of the link must still match.

So if you set one side for *no-payload-scrambler*, you also need to set the other side to *no-payload-scrambler*.

In addition to specifying options specific to the media type, like *sonet-options*, *t3-options*, or *e3-options*, you can specify the clocking source with the [edit interface at-#/#/#] clocking command, the interface MTU with a value ranging from 256 to 9192, and the type of ATM encapsulation available on the interface.

MTU   The valid MTU sizes are from 256 to 9192 bytes, with a default size of 4482. Protocol family INET has a default MTU of 4470. If you use the RFC 1483 SNAP encapsulation, the protocol family ISO also uses an MTU of 4470, while MPLS uses an MTU of 4458.

Encapsulation

At the physical interface level, you can configure the interface for CCC or for normal ATM Permanent Virtual Connections (PVCs). (See Chapter 15 for CCC explanations.)

The default encapsulation type is ATM PVC encapsulation. If you wish to set it explicitly, use the [edit interfaces at-0/1/0] atm-pvc command. This encapsulation allows you to specify logical families on the interface. Verify the encapsulation setting with the show interfaces command:

```
lab@hongkong> show interfaces at-0/1/0
Physical interface: at-0/1/0, Enabled, Physical link is Up
  Interface index: 13, SNMP ifIndex: 25
  Link-level type: ATM-PVC, MTU: 4482, Clocking: Internal, SONET mode,
  Speed: OC3, Loopback: None, Payload scrambler: Enabled
  Device flags   : Present Running
  Link flags     : None
  Input rate     : 552 bps (0 pps), Output rate: 312 bps (0 pps)
  SONET alarms   : None
  SONET defects  : None

[edit]
lab@hongkong# show interfaces at-0/1/0
encapsulation atm-pvc;
atm-options {
    vpi 0 maximum-vcs 200;
}
unit 100 {
    encapsulation atm-snap;
    point-to-point;
    vci 0.100;
    family inet {
        address 10.0.15.2/24;
    }
}
```

Logical Interface Properties

You can configure a variety of ATM interface logical properties to include ATM encapsulation types and protocol families; VPI, VCI values; traffic shaping; OAM (Operations, Administration, and Maintenance) cells for keepalive status; inverse ARP; multicast and multipoint capability.

ATM Encapsulation Types

Juniper Networks routers implement different routed encapsulations defined in RFC 1483: Sub Network Point Attachment (SNPA), VC-based multiplexing (VC-MUX), and two flavors of Network Layer Protocol Identification (NLPID). The most common interface encapsulation is the SNAP encapsulation, which takes the IEEE SNAP pattern (*0xaa-aa-03*) using an organizational unique identifier (OUI) of 0x00-00-00 with the protocol ID representing the protocol being carried on the PVC. For example, IP traffic has the pattern 0xaa-aa-03-00-00-00-08-00, with 0x0800 being the protocol code for IP. The SNAP encapsulation supports all protocol families (INET, ISO, MPLS) over a single VPI, VCI combination. Additionally, the inverse *arp* feature (described in the "Inverse ARP" section later in the chapter) works only with the SNAP encapsulation. All the other encapsulation types support only the INET protocol family.

VC-MUX encapsulation does not add a header that indicates a protocol type; instead, it assumes that the protocol carried is IP traffic. Using this encapsulation makes it possible for a TCP ACK to fit into a single ATM cell payload, enhancing transmission efficiency. The NLPID encapsulation adds the header *0xfe-fe-03* followed by an Organizational Unique Identifier and protocol ID. *There is also a proprietary* Cisco NLPID for use when communicating with a Cisco router configured for NLPID. As a general rule, RFC 1483 discourages the use of NLPID, preferring SNAP or VC-MUX instead. There are two CCC encapsulations. See Chapter 15 for an explanation of their use.

Configure the ATM encapsulation within the logical interface. Verify the configured encapsulation with the show interfaces command:

```
lab@Tokyo# set interfaces at-0/1/0 unit 100 encapsulation ?
Possible completions:
  atm-ccc-cell-relay    ATM Cell Relay for CCC
  atm-ccc-vc-mux        ATM VC for CCC
  atm-cisco-nlpid       Cisco-compatible ATM NLPID encapsulation
  atm-nlpid             ATM NLPID encapsulation
  atm-snap              ATM LLC/SNAP encapsulation
  atm-vc-mux            ATM VC multiplexing

lab@hongkong# show interfaces at-0/1/0
encapsulation atm-pvc;
atm-options {
    vpi 0 maximum-vcs 200;
```

```
    }
unit 100 {
    encapsulation atm-snap;
    point-to-point;
    vci 0.100;
    family inet {
        address 10.0.15.2/24;
    }
}
lab@hongkong> show interfaces at-0/1/0
Physical interface: at-0/1/0, Enabled, Physical link is Up
  .
  .
  .
Logical interface at-0/1/0.100 (Index 21) (SNMP ifIndex 29)
    Flags: Point-To-Point SNMP-Traps Encapsulation: ATM-SNAP
  Input packets: 10 Output packets: 13
    Protocol inet, MTU: 4470, Flags: None
      Addresses, Flags: Is-Preferred Is-Primary
        Destination: 10.0.15/24, Local: 10.0.15.2
    VCI 0.100
      Flags: Active
      Total down time: 0 sec, Last down: Never
      Traffic statistics:
       Input  packets:                    10
       Output packets:                    13
```

VPI and VCI Values

Within the P2P ATM PVC, you configure a single VPI and VCI value. You only need to specify only the VPI value if you have more than one VPI value configured at the *atm-options* level; otherwise, the VPI parameter is optional. For multicast interfaces, you specify a VPI, VCI combination for each multicast destination.

Traffic Shaping Parameters

You can configure traffic shaping for ATM connections to limit the router's cell transmission rate so that ATM switches do not police the traffic. Typically, service providers configure ATM switches to either tag or drop ATM cells that exceed a traffic contract. Common traffic contracts specify either Constant Bit Rate (CBR) or Variable Bit Rate (VBR) traffic parameters, which specify the transmission rates that cells cannot exceed. A CBR traffic contract establishes a peak cell rate. A VBR traffic specifies a peak rate, a sustained rate, and a maximum burst size. The ATM switch checks the rate on a cell-by-cell basis.

For example, a cell rate of 10,000 cells per second means that an individual cell arrives every 1/10,000 second, or every 100 microseconds (called the *cell inter-arrival time*). The ATM switch compares the expected, or theoretical, arrival time against the actual inter-arrival time. A specific traffic contract peak cell rate may be set for 10,000 cells per second. If the cells actually arrive every 97 microseconds instead of every 100 microseconds, each cell arrives 3 microseconds too soon. 97 microseconds equates to a 10,300 cells per second rate (invert 10,300 and you get approximately 97 microseconds). This means that the traffic arrives faster than the traffic contract allows. At this point, the ATM switch can tag or drop the traffic. Tagging allows the ATM cell to transmit but gives it a higher cell loss priority, which may mean it can be discarded downstream by other ATM switches sooner than other cells. Dropping means the ATM switch discards the cell immediately.

The traffic contract makes cell-by-cell policing decisions (pass/tag/drop) using an implementation of the Generic Cell Rate Algorithm (GCRA). The GCRA recognizes that actual transmission rates are not perfect and provides for a tolerance value, a limit or early arrival window that cells can arrive within, without being tagged or dropped. The tolerance for the CBR connection is called the Cell Delay Variation Tolerance (CDVT). The tolerance for the VBR connection is called the Burst Tolerance (BT), which is defined by this equation:

$$BT = [(1/scr) - (1/pcr)] [MBS - 1]$$

where scr = sustained cell rate, pcr = peak cell rate, and MBS = Maximum Burst Size.

For VBR connections, the GCRA algorithm adds the CDVT and the BT together to determine the total early arrival tolerance. For CBR connections, the GCRA just uses the CDVT value as the total early arrival tolerance. Without going through the agony of the actual GCRA calculation, you can think of the total early arrival tolerance as a limit, like a checking overdraft account. As long as the sum of the early arrival tolerances do not exceed the limit, the cells pass. Just like the sum of the checking overdrafts cannot exceed the overdraft limit, otherwise the checks bounce. The minor difference is that as soon as a cell arrives without using any of the early arrival tolerance, the limit is reset.

Because ATM switches check arrival times on a cell-by-cell basis, the routers that connect to the switches need to rate limit their cell transmissions so that the ATM switches do not drop cells unnecessarily. A common problem, for example, might be an IP packet that arrives on *fe-0/0/0.0*. The router converts this packet, say 1500 bytes, to ATM cells using ATM adaptation layer 5 (AAL 5) with a SNAP header, which adds another 36 bytes to the IP packet prior to slicing the data into cells. Each cell can carry 48 bytes of payload, so the 1500-byte IP packet requires 32 ATM cells. An OC-3 link transmits an ATM cell every 2.72 microseconds (at line rate). It will transmit all the cells as soon as it can. So all 32 cells can actually transmit in about 87 microseconds. If the traffic contract were set for 10,000 cells per seconds as the peak rate (which is admittedly a low value), all the cells would arrive within the time window for a single cell—and would probably be tagged or dropped. So you configure shaping on your ATM router interface to slow the router's cell transmissions to a rate that corresponds to the ATM switch's policing rate.

You can actually specify the transmission rates in either cells per seconds (a pain—although the most accurate method) or in bits per second. Identifiers like *k,m,g* identify rates as thousands, millions, or billions (gigabit rates). The *c* identifier identifies a value of cells. The router converts a bit rate to cells per second by dividing the number of bits of payload in an ATM cell by 384. The maximum rate you can configure for OC-3 interfaces is 138 Mbps for OC-3, which is the maximum effective payload. The maximum OC-12 rate is half of the effective line rate and is 276 Mbps. The burst size is specified as a cell value in the range of 1–255 cells.

The rate may not display exactly as you typed it. The router accepts only specific rate values; it rounds up to the next available valid rate when you enter a value. Depending on the interface speed, thousands of different rates are available, so the fact that you are limited to predefined rate values should not greatly affect your performance.

Configure shaping within the logical unit, which is at the same hierarchy level as the VCI value. So if you configure a P2P connection, the shaping parameters are located immediately below the unit hierarchy, as illustrated next. If you configure a P2MP connection, the shaping values are listed after each destination when you list the VCI values. Note that the VBR shaping parameter requires another hierarchy level, because there are three shaping parameters, instead of the single peak rate for CBR shaping.

```
Shaping options:
lab@Tokyo# set interfaces at-0/1/0 unit 100 shaping ?
Possible completions:
+ apply-groups         Groups from which to inherit configuration data
  cbr                  Continuous bandwidth utilization (33000..271000000)
  queue-length         Queue length (1..16383)
> vbr                  Variable bandwidth utilization
[edit]

VBR Shaping options:
lab@Tokyo# set interfaces at-0/1/0 unit 100 shaping vbr ?
Possible completions:
  burst                Burst size (1..255)
  peak                 Peak rate (33000..271000000)
  sustained            Sustained rate (33000..271000000)
```

The following example shows VBR shaping parameters configured on a P2MP interface:

```
at-0/1/0 {
    atm-options {
        vpi 0 maximum-vcs 200;
    }
    unit 100 {
        multipoint;
        family inet {
```

```
address 1.1.1.1/24 {
    multipoint-destination 1.1.1.2 vci 0.107;
    multipoint-destination 1.1.1.3 {
        vci 0.108;
        shaping {
            vbr peak 1m sustained 700k burst 200;
            queue-length 256;
        }
        oam-liveness {
            up-count 3;
            down-count 3;
        }
        inverse-arp;
    }
}
}
}
}
```

The values displayed in the help screens are in bits per second. You can also configure a queue length, in case the traffic is particularly slow. By default, there is no limit to the queue size. If the cells are slow, it is possible that other traffic could be delayed by slow cells. Putting a maximum queue size in place limits the maximum amount of time that passes between the arrival of two cells from the same connection.

Caution *Be cautious when configuring shaping rates that match the ATM switch's policing rate exactly. ATM switch policing parameters may be denominated in bits per second (bps) instead of cells per second (cps). The ATM switch vendor may have specified a translation rate between cps and bps that includes the 5-byte cell header. Juniper Networks routers do not include the 5-byte cell header when translating between cps and bps. Suppose, for example, that you contact the carrier and ask its policing rate. If the rate comes back as 10,000 bps, you cannot be sure whether that number should be divided by 384 or 424 (the number of bits in a cell, including the five byte cell header) to determine the number of cells it represents. If you want to match the policing rate, the best choice is to ask what the policing rate is in cps. Then let the router convert the value to bps for you. Do not forget to include the c to indicate cps when you use this value—otherwise the router thinks you are configuring bps.*

Operations, Administration, and Maintenance (OAM) Capability

You can configure keepalive capability on a connection by enabling OAM. ITU specifications I.361 and I.310 define special ATM cells, called OAM cells, that are used for overhead functions. Enabling OAM transmits these special overhead cells.

The router keeps track of the number of OAM cells sent and received. Failure to receive enough OAM cells means the connection is down. You can specify the number of OAM cells received or not received to indicate an up or down PVC status with the *oam-liveness* parameter. The default for both the up-count and down-count is 5 OAM cells. You specify the time interval to send/receive OAM cells with the `oam-period` command. OAM capability is disabled by default.

The following code shows the possible values for both the *oam-liveness* and the *oam-period* parameters.

```
[edit]
lab@Tokyo# set interfaces at-0/1/0 unit 100 oam-liveness ?
Possible completions:
+ apply-groups         Groups from which to inherit configuration data
  down-count           Number of OAM cells to consider VC down (1..255)
  up-count             Number of OAM cells to consider VC up (1..255)
[edit]
lab@Tokyo# set interfaces at-0/1/0 unit 100 oam-period ?
Possible completions:
  <oam_period>         OAM cell period (1..900 seconds)
  disable              Disable OAM loopback
```

Inverse ARP

You can enable the router to respond to inverse ATM ARP requests (InATMARP) issued by other routers. RFC 2225, Classical IP and ARP over ATM, defines the InATMARP request and reply capability for the ATMARP server to determine what IP address is at the other end of the (in this case) PVC. Basically, the ATMARP server issues a command down the PVC that asks, "Who are you?" The IP host at the other end of the PVC—the Juniper router—responds back with "I'm IP Address <X>." Now the ATMARP server knows which destination IP address to map to the specific PVC.

You can configure this on both P2P and P2MP interfaces; however, you must use the SNAP encapsulation. If you specify inverse ARP, you can respond to inverse ARP requests initiated by other routers; you cannot initiate inverse ARP requests. Inverse ARP does not work with other encapsulations besides SNAP. Remember that the SNAP encapsulation allows multiple protocols to use the same PVC. In this case, the InATMARP message uses protocol ID 0x0806, while the IP packet uses protocol ID 0x0800.

Point-to-Multipoint and Multicast ATM Connections

When using P2MP connections, you are listing multiple VPI, VCI values within the same logical interface. As shown in the following output, you need to specify the destination address for each VPI, VCI value listed. You can configure Inverse ARP on multipoint interfaces. For each VCI value listed, you can list shaping parameters and OAM liveness parameters. Additionally, if the ATM switch is capable of multicast replication, you can specify a specific VPI, VCI combination to use for multicast traffic. Note that you cannot use the multicast VPI, VCI combination anywhere else within the logical interface. This behavior is different from frame relay multicast replication, which allows specifying the same DLCI value for both the multipoint destination and multicast replication.

```
[edit]
lab@SanJose# show interfaces at-0/1/0
at-0/1/0 {
    atm-options {
        vpi 0 maximum-vcs 200;
    }
    unit 0 {
        vci 0.100;
        family inet {
            address 10.0.15.2/24;
        }
    }
    unit 100 {
        multipoint;
        family inet {
            address 1.1.1.1/24 {
                multipoint-destination 1.1.1.2 vci 0.107;
                multipoint-destination 1.1.1.3 {
                    vci 0.108;
                    shaping {
                        vbr peak 1m sustained 700k burst 200;
                        queue-length 256;
                    }
                    oam-liveness {
                        up-count 3;
                        down-count 3;
                    }
                    inverse-arp;
                }
            }
        }
    }
}
```

Configuring the Plesiochronous Digital Hierarchy: T-1/E-1

The plesiochronous digital hierarchy (PDH) represents communications systems that are nearly synchronous in terms of network clocking. The PDH forms the basis of the telephone network. At its base level, the PDH carries voice traffic encoded with pulse code modulation (PCM). Because the PDH network exists nearly everywhere, you may have to configure the router to use a PDH network interface to carry data if higher speed interfaces are not available or feasible.

You can configure Juniper Networks routers with PDH interfaces to carry any valid protocol—IP, MPLS, and ISO. Your effective data rate becomes the payload rate that was originally designed for the voice signals. For example, a T-1 line rate is 1.544 Mbps; the effective data rate is 1.536 Mbps because of overhead (1 bit out of every 193 is an overhead bit used to delineate frame boundaries).

This section discusses many properties you can configure for T-1 and E-1 interfaces, including line coding (how ones and zeros are transmitted), line buildout (how much signal strength to apply based upon distance from the router interface), the framing mechanisms (how to represent large blocks of ones and zeros logically), payload scrambler, idle-cycle flag (0xFF versus 0x07), and idle-cycle/efficiency (two idle-cycle patterns or not between subsequent frames).

Framing Methods

The T-carrier (*T* stands for *Terrestrial*) system was developed in the early 1960s to digitize analog voice traffic. After a network digitizes a phone call, the information can be rerouted based on the individual phone call's destination. The T-carrier network carries individual digital stream (DS) signals. Technically, a T-1 carrier network consists of DS-1 signals. Today, the data networking community uses the terms T-1 and DS-1 interchangeably. A T-1 carries 24 voice channels, each at 64 Kbps for a data rate of 1.544 Mbps. The bits transmit serially, but different logical representations, called Superframe and Extended Superframe, permit viewing the serial stream as a logical block of data. The framing bits in the T-1 frames define the boundaries of the Superframe and Extended Superframe data blocks.

Superframe Data Blocks

A (logical) stack of 12 T-1 frames is called a *Superframe*. The 12 framing bits from the constituent T-1 frames form a precise pattern (100011011100). A buffer capable of containing $12 \times 193 = 2316$ bits checks every one hundred ninety-third bit. When the expected pattern of ones and zeros show up in the bit positions designated as framing bit positions, the network equipment knows the Superframe boundary. Each byte—also called a timeslot, channel, or DS-0 (DS zero)—represents a different phone call. Multiplexing equipment can break a phone call out of a T-1 and redirect it to another T-1. Since the framing bit indicates the start of the T-1 frame, each voice channel becomes an offset from the start of the T-1 frame.

A precise pattern of ones and zeros indicates the Superframe structure. Once the Superframe structure syncs up, the individual T-1 frames become identifiable within a serial bit stream. Pretty neat stuff. If the framing bit pattern does not match when checked, the network just slips a bit and checks the pattern, a bit at a time, until the pattern does match. The network cannot transmit valid information until a pattern match occurs.

Extended Superframe Data Blocks

The Extended Superframe is a logical stack of 24 T-1 frames. The network uses the framing bits from the constituent T-1 frames for framing, error detection, and as an in-band facilities data link. The framing bits used as a facilities data link provide a 4 Kbps data channel with the capability to send up to 64 distinct messages.

Section 2.1.3.1.3, ITU specification G.704, defines the use of the facilities data link. The network uses six of the T-1 framing bits for Extended Superframe framing. The framing bit pattern *001011* in frames 4, 8, 12, 16, 20, and 24 indicate the Extended Superframe boundary. Six of the framing bits form a cyclic redundancy checksum, CRC-6. G.704 specifies the generator polynomial as $X^6 + x + 1$. The CRC covers the previous Extended Superframe. Because of this, the CRC value from the very first Extended Superframe is meaningless.

Configure T-1 lines either for Superframe or Extended Superframe within the *t1-options* hierarchy:

```
[edit]
lab@Tokyo# set interfaces t1-0/3/3 t1-options framing ?
Possible completions:
  esf                  Extended super frame
  sf                   Super frame
```

E-1 Framing (G.704 Multiframe and Unframed)

You can configure E-1 lines either as unframed or G.704 (with or without CRC-4 error checking). E-1 transmissions use 32 instead of 24 timeslots to make up the E-1 frame. The first timeslot, timeslot 0, and the seventeenth timeslot, timeslot 16, provide signaling and framing information, respectively, leaving 30 timeslots available to carry data. All framing options use timeslot 0 for channel associated signaling (CAS); the unframed option uses the remaining 31 timeslots for data.

The G.704 option uses two sets of 16 frames, each frame consisting of 32 timeslots, to carry information. Each set of 16 frames is called a *multiframe*. Timeslot 0 carries CAS, while timeslot 16 provides framing information, such as a Multiframe Alignment Signal (0000) in the first frame to help delineate the beginning of each 16-frame multiframe and ABCD-robbed bit telephone signaling patterns in the remaining 15 frames. Depending on whether or not you desire error checking in the 16-frame multiframe, you can select a CRC-4 option, which interleaves two 4-bit CRC values in with the Frame Alignment Signaling pattern of even frames in timeslot 0. The Frame Alignment Signaling value is 001011. The interleaved error-checking pattern is

c1 0 c2 0 c3 1 c4 0 c1 1 c2 1 c3 R c4 R

where R is a reserved bit, and the C bits represent the Xth CRC bit—so c1 is the first CRC bit, for example. The following code shows the different framing options for E-1 lines. Remember that both ends of a link must be configured the same for framing.

```
[edit interfaces e1-0/1/0 e1-options]
lab@Tokyo# set framing ?
Possible completions:
  g704                    G704 mode with CRC4
  g704-no-crc4            G704 mode without CRC4
  unframed                Unframed mode
```

Linecodes and Ones Density

Physical transmission rates require some guidelines on how to transmit ones and zeros. This issue is called *ones density*—too many zeros transmitted in a row could lead to clocking instability. Basically, the sending and receiving clock disagree on the clock signal. The receiver samples the signal at what it thinks is the correct time but is really the incorrect time, and consequently the receiver may interpret the value incorrectly. Transmit and receive clocks require signal transitions to maintain synchronization.

The Bellcore standards specify that a signal transition must occur once in every 16 bits, with the additional requirement for three transitions in a floating window of 24 bits. Without a transition within the specified window, the transmit and receive clocks on opposite sides of a link can become unsynchronized. T-1/E-1 links use Alternate Mark Inversion (AMI) to transmit signals. This means that zeros are transmitted as no signal and successive ones alternate polarity between positive and negative. So two successive ones, both either positive or negative, indicate a problem. This problem even has a special name—*bipolar violation* (BPV). Because AMI has no signal (0 volts) for binary zeros, it is possible that 2 bytes of all zeros would generate a transitionless signal 16-bit time periods in length. Binary eight zeros substitution (B8ZS) intentionally inserts two bipolar violations in a string of eight zeros to generate four signal transitions, which keep the clocks synchronized. E-1 interfaces use a similar strategy of forcing bipolar violations to self-synchronize clocking, but instead of using 8 bits like B8ZS, E-1 uses High-Density Bipolar 3, or HDB3, which forces a bipolar violation (BPV) in the fourth bit position, based upon whether or not transitions appear in the preceding 3 bits and in a manner that maintains DC balance.

Configure B8ZS or AMI in pairs. So ports 0 and 1 must share the same value; likewise, ports 2 and 3 share the same value. The first pair can use a different line coding than the second pair. Here's an example:

```
lab@HongKong# set interfaces t1-0/3/3 t1-options line-encoding ?
Possible completions:
  ami                     Automatic mark inversion
  b8zs                    8 bit zero suppression
```

You can view the current setting with the `show interfaces extensive` command—look near the bottom of the following listing:

```
lab@Tokyo> show interfaces t1-0/3/3 extensive
Physical interface: t1-0/3/3, Enabled, Physical link is Up
  Interface index: 18, SNMP ifIndex: 43, Generation: 25
  Link-level type: PPP, MTU: 1504, Clocking: Internal, Speed: T1,
  Loopback: None, CRC: 16, Framing: ESF
  Device flags   : Present Running
  Interface flags: Point-To-Point SNMP-Traps
  Link flags     : Keepalives
  Statistics last cleared: Never
  Traffic statistics:
   Input  bytes  :                     0                     0 bps
   Output bytes  :                     0                     0 bps
   Input  packets:                     0                     0 pps
   Output packets:                     0                     0 pps
  Input errors:
    Errors: 0, Drops: 0, Framing errors: 0, Policed discards: 0,
    L3 incompletes: 0, L2 channel errors: 0, L2 mismatch timeouts: 0,
    HS link CRC errors: 0, SRAM errors: 0
  Output errors:
    Carrier transitions: 1, Errors: 0, Drops: 0, Aged packets: 0
  DS1   alarms  : None
  DS1   defects : None
  T1  media:          Seconds       Count  State
     SEF               1               1   OK
     BEE               0               0   OK
     AIS               0               0   OK
     LOF               1               1   OK
     LOS               0               0   OK
     YELLOW            2               3   OK
     BPV               1               1
     EXZ               1               1
     LCV               1              36
     PCV               1             112
     CS                0               0
     LES               1
     ES                1
     SES               1
     SEFS              1
     BES               1
     UAS               0
  HDLC configuration:
    Policing bucket: Disabled
    Shaping bucket : Disabled
    Giant threshold: 1514, Runt threshold: 3
    Timeslots      : All active
```

```
   Line encoding: B8ZS, Byte encoding: Nx64K, Data inversion: Disabled
   Buildout        : 0 to 132 feet
 DS1 BERT configuration:
   BERT time period: 10 seconds, Elapsed: 0 seconds
   Induced Error rate: 10e-0, Algorithm: Unknown (0)
 PFE configuration:
   Destination slot: 0, PLP byte: 1 (0x00)
   CoS transmit queue bandwidth:
     Queue0: 95, Queue1: 0, Queue2: 0, Queue3: 5
   CoS weighted round-robin:
     Queue0: 95, Queue1: 0, Queue2: 0, Queue3: 5
```

Since HDB3 is the only option available for E-1, you cannot set the value. You can verify the setting using the show interfaces extensive command. The line encoding displays near the bottom of the following output:

```
lab@Tokyo# run show interfaces e1-0/1/0 extensive
Physical interface: e1-0/1/0, Enabled, Physical link is Up
   Interface index: 21, SNMP ifIndex: 36, Generation: 20
   Link-level type: PPP, MTU: 1504, Clocking: Internal, Speed: E1,
   Loopback: None, FCS: 16, Framing: G704
   Device flags   : Present Running
   Interface flags: Point-To-Point SNMP-Traps
   Link flags     : Keepalives
 .
[output lines deleted]
 .
   HDLC configuration:
     Policing bucket: Disabled
     Shaping bucket : Disabled
     Giant threshold: 1514, Runt threshold: 3
     Timeslots      : All active
     Line encoding: HDB3
 DS1 BERT configuration:
     BERT time period: 10 seconds, Elapsed: 0 seconds
     Induced Error rate: 10e-0, Algorithm: Unknown (0)
 PFE configuration:
     Destination slot: 0, PLP byte: 1 (0x00)
     CoS transmit queue bandwidth:
       Queue0: 95, Queue1: 0, Queue2: 0, Queue3: 5
     CoS weighted round-robin:
       Queue0: 95, Queue1: 0, Queue2: 0, Queue3: 5
```

Data Inversion

If you transmit long strings of zeros, you could cause clock synchronization problems if you use plain AMI encoding. You can configure data inversion, which inverts all the bits, so that the long string of zeros becomes a long string of ones. This prevents clock synchronization problems. Data inversion is generally used only when you set the linecode to AMI. You should try to use HDB3 or B8ZS for your line encoding scheme whenever possible. The previous display shows whether data inversion is enabled or not on the same line as the B8ZS or AMI setting. You can set data inversion with the following command:

```
[edit]
lab@HongKong# set interfaces t1-0/3/3 t1-options invert-data
```

Simple Test Patterns

When you are testing the transmission line to verify that it will transmit data without problems, you should run specific bit patterns to see whether problems arise. These patterns should try to mimic patterns that could cause problems if that bit pattern actually shows up in the data stream. You can use pseudo-random test patterns to generate these bit patterns.

You can also use a quick and dirty PING with a specified payload pattern to generate some testing bit patterns. Several different bit patterns can stress test the line to verify its stability. Use very large payloads when testing these bit patterns, just to give the transmission line the maximum opportunity to fail—remember, you want it to fail in testing, not in production.

- **All zeros (0000)**   If this pattern is successful, it means that the transmission line probably can recover timing correctly.
- **All ones (1111)**   If this pattern fails, it could mean that line transmission equipment is set to invert the data and an AMI encoding scheme is used. Remember that some older equipment cannot support B8ZS encoding, so it may have to use AMI.
- **All As (1010)**   This pattern stresses the line by sending alternating patterns of ones and zeros.
- **All 5s (0101)**   This pattern stresses the line by sending alternating patterns of ones and zeros.
- **7E (01111110)**   This is the serial communications line flag pattern that indicates start or end of frame. PPP and HDLC both use this pattern. If this pattern fails, it means that something in the transmission system is not doing bit stuffing properly (placing an extra zero after the fifth one before transmission so that the receiving side never receives a string of six ones unless it truly is the start or end of the frame).

Line Buildout

Line buildout indicates how much electrical power the port must apply to drive the signal to the demarcation point. T-1 lines provide several different distances to drive the signal:

```
[edit]
lab@HongKong# set interfaces t1-0/3/3 t1-options buildout ?
Possible completions:
    0-132              Line buildout is between 0-132 feet
  133-265              Line buildout is between 133-265 feet
  266-398              Line buildout is between 266-398 feet
  399-531              Line buildout is between 399-531 feet
  532-655              Line buildout is between 532-655 feet
```

Idle-Cycle Flag and Transmission Efficiency

Normally, the router sends two idle-cycle bit patterns between each frame. You can force the router to use the end pattern of one frame as the start pattern of the next frame by specifying the *shared* option in the [edit interfaces t1-#/#/# t1-options] or [edit interfaces e1-#/#/# e1-options] hierarchy, like so:

```
lab@HongKong# set interfaces t1-0/3/3 t1-options start-end-flag ?
Possible completions:
  filler              Send two idle cycles between start/end flags
  shared              Share start/end flags on transmit
```

The default frame delimiter is *0x7E*, which is also the default idle-cycle bit pattern. You can change the idle-cycle pattern to be *0xFF* with the *idle-cycle* option:

```
[edit]
lab@HongKong# set interfaces t1-0/3/3 t1-options idle-cycle-flag ?
Possible completions:
  flags               Transmit 0x7E in idle cycles
  ones                Transmit 0xFF (all ones) in idle cycles
```

Subrate and Timeslot Configuration

You can configure either T-1 or E-1 interfaces to support subrate capability. In other words, you can configure the T-1 or E-1 interfaces to use only some of the timeslots for data transmission. Many CSU/DSUs allow you to use specific timeslots within the PDH. Set up to 24 timeslots for T-1 lines and up to 32 timeslots for E-1 lines. Separate contiguous timeslots with a hyphen. Separate noncontiguous timeslots with a comma. Group together combinations of timeslots using either hyphens or commas—but don't use any spaces!

```
lab@HongKong# set interfaces t1-0/3/3 t1-options timeslots ?
Possible completions:
  <timeslots>          1..24 eg. 1-3,4,9,22-24 (no space)
```

Frame Check Sequence

Both T-1 and E-1 lines let you set the FCS value to either 16 or 32, with the default being 16. Use the *fcs* option at the [edit interfaces T1-#/#/# t1-options] or the [edit interfaces E1-#/#/# e1-options] hierarchy.

Encapsulations

T-1 and E-1 interfaces support CCC, PPP, Cisco-HDLC, and frame relay encapsulations, as illustrated here. See Chapter 15 for information on CCC.

```
lab@Tokyo# set interfaces t1-0/3/3 encapsulation ?
Possible completions:
  cisco-hdlc           Cisco-compatible HDLC framing
  cisco-hdlc-ccc       Cisco-compatible HDLC framing for a cross connection
  frame-relay          Frame Relay encapsulation
  frame-relay-ccc      Frame Relay encapsulation for cross connection
  ppp                  Serial PPP device
  ppp-ccc              Serial PPP device for a cross connection
```

Configuring the Plesiochronous Digital Hierarchy: T-3/E-3 Interfaces

The PDH extends to T-3 and E-3 rate traffic. The 3 means the level of multiplexing, so a T-3 has three levels of multiplexing. The T-1 circuit, for example, multiplexed constituent DS-0s into DS-1s. Likewise, the T-3 will multiplex T-1s into T-2s and those T-2s into T-3s. The T-2 conversion is transparent to the user; you will only see the T-1s and the T-3s.

This section discusses many properties you can configure for T-3 and E-3 interfaces, including framing mode (how the T-1 framing bit positions inside the T-3 frame are used), FCS, idle cycle flag (0xFF versus 0x07), and idle cycle efficiency (two idle-cycle patterns or not between subsequent frames), line buildout (how much signal strength to apply based on distance from the router interface), CSU compatibility modes, and different encapsulation types.

Framing Mode

You can configure M13 or C-bit parity for T-3 framing. C-bit parity, the default, uses the stuffing bits intended to align components of the T-2 (called M-frames) during the T-2 to T-3 multiplexing stage for additional overhead. M13 framing mode actually uses the stuff bits for their intended purpose, instead of for additional overhead. C-bit parity uses stuff bits whenever possible instead of in specific bit positions, so it can use the designated stuff bit positions for overhead. Set M13 framing mode by using the *no-cbit-parity* option in the [edit interfaces t3-#/#/# t3-options] hierarchy level.

Framing specified in G.751, *General Aspects of Digital Transmission Systems: Terminal Equipment*, applies to E-3 interfaces. You cannot explicitly set E-3 framing, although, as mentioned in "Configuring the ATM Interface," setting an ATM cell-delineation method, like direct mapping or PLCP, requires specific E-3 framing methods that can be configured for ATM E-3 interfaces.

FCS

Both T-3 and E-3 lines let you set the FCS value to either 16 or 32, with the default being 16. Use the *fcs* option at the [edit interfaces T3-#/#/# t3-options] or the [edit interfaces E3-#/#/# e3-options] hierarchy.

Idle-Cycle Flag and Transmission Efficiency

Normally, the router sends two idle-cycle bit patterns between each frame. You can force the router to use the end pattern of one frame as the start pattern of the next frame by specifying the *shared* option in the [edit interfaces t3-#/#/# t3-options] or [edit interfaces e3-#/#/# e3-options] hierarchy:

```
lab@HongKong# set interfaces t3-0/3/3 t3-options start-end-flag ?
Possible completions:
   filler              Send two idle cycles between start/end flags
   shared              Share start/end flags on transmit
```

The default frame delimiter is *0x7E*, which is also the default idle-cycle bit pattern. You can change the idle-cycle pattern to be *0xFF* with the *idle-cycle* option.

Line Buildout

Unlike T-1 transmission lines, you can set only a single option for T-3 transmission power—either the line is shorter or longer than 255 feet. Use the *long-buildout* flag at the [edit interfaces t3-#/#/# t3-options] hierarchy to set the length longer.

You can set line buildout only for copper DS-3 lines; you cannot set the value for DS-3s that are part of a Channelized OC-12.

CSU Compatibility Mode/Subrate

You can specify three different compatibility modes, based upon the vendor of the CSU: Digital Link, Larscom, and Kentrox. For T-3, both the Digital Link and Larscom options support subrate values, but the Kentrox option does not. For E-3 lines, only the Digital Link option supports subrate. The default compatibility mode is Digital Link. Set the compatibility mode under either the [edit t3-#/#/# t3-options] or the [edit e3-#/#/# e3-options] hierarchy.

```
lab@Tokyo# set e3-options compatibility-mode ?
Possible completions:
> digital-link          Compatible with Digital Link CSU
  kentrox               Compatible with Kentrox CSU
  larscom               Compatible with Larscom CSU
```

For Digital Link, set the subrate by specifying a subrate value in the format *xKb* or *x.xMb*. For Larscom, set the subrate with the number of 3.158 Mbps partitons, from 1 to 14, that matches your CSU configuration.

Encapsulations

T-3 and E-3 interfaces support encapsulations for PPP, Cisco-HDLC, and frame relay, as well as those for CCC, as illustrated by the following example.

```
lab@Tokyo# set interfaces t1-0/3/3 encapsulation ?
Possible completions:
  cisco-hdlc          Cisco-compatible HDLC framing
  cisco-hdlc-ccc      Cisco-compatible HDLC framing for a cross connection
  frame-relay         Frame Relay encapsulation
  frame-relay-ccc     Frame Relay encapsulation for cross connection
  ppp                 Serial PPP device
  ppp-ccc             Serial PPP device for a cross connection
```

Configuring Ethernet Interfaces: Gigabit Ethernet and Fast Ethernet

Juniper routers support both Gigabit Ethernet and Fast Ethernet interfaces. Within the physical interface, you can hard code a MAC address to override the default MAC address, enable virtual LAN (VLAN) tagging, set the MTU and encapsulation, and configure a variety of link-specific parameters in either the Fast Ethernet options or Gigabit Ethernet options section.

MAC Address Setting

Each router provides a block of 1024 MAC addresses that can be used by the various interfaces on the router. Sixteen of these are reserved for internal use, while the remaining 1008 can be assigned to logical interfaces. Two other MAC addresses exist on the router—one each for the *fxp0* and *fxp1* interfaces. They both use the MAC addresses provided with the Intel chipset. Use the `show chassis mac` command to see the MAC address pool assigned to the router.

You may find a need to hard code a specific MAC address—possibly for security reasons. You can assign a specific MAC address and override the default assigned MAC address with the `set mac` statement at the [`edit interfaces fe/ge-#/#/#`] hierarchy.

You can verify that the current MAC address is different from the hardware MAC address using the `show interfaces` command:

```
lab@SaoPaulo> show interfaces fe-0/0/0
Physical interface: fe-0/0/0, Enabled, Physical link is Up
  Interface index: 9, SNMP ifIndex: 34
  Link-level type: Ethernet, MTU: 1514, Speed: 100mbps, Loopback: Disabled,
  Source filtering: Enabled, Flow control: Enabled
  Device flags   : Present Running
  Interface flags: SNMP-Traps
  Link flags     : None
  Current address: aa:bb:cc:11:22:33, Hardware address: 00:90:69:67:0c:00
  Input rate     : 0 bps (0 pps), Output rate: 0 bps (0 pps)
  Active alarms  : None
  Active defects : None
[output truncated]
```

VLAN Tagging

Juniper Networks routers support IEEE 802.1Q VLAN tagging. The IEEE 802.1Q specification provides for an additional 4 bytes of header information to be placed between the source MAC address field and the Ethernet Type/Length field. Twelve of the bits in the extra header identify the VLAN ID. The VLAN IDs 0 and 4095 are reserved values. The VLAN ID serves to identify the specific VLAN to which that frame belongs. Basically, it is a tag field. When configured, only interfaces with the specified tag, or *vlan-id*, will receive that Ethernet frame. IEEE 802.1Q is a standards based method of using an Ethernet link as a trunk link—in other words, using the Ethernet link to carry multiple different Ethernet segments' worth of traffic over a single physical link. First, you enable the VLAN tagging capability on the physical interface, and then you configure each different logical interface to support a different *vlan-id* value. Because each different logical Ethernet segment has a different *vlan-id* value, the traffic does not cross between the different logical segments.

You specify that you want to enable VLAN tagging for a physical interface with the `vlan-tagging` statement. Once you enable VLAN tagging at the physical interface, you must specify a *vlan-id* within each logical unit on that interface. In the following example, two different Ethernet segments have been defined. Normally, you can configure only one logical family and address on an Ethernet interface, but enabling IEEE 802.1Q allows you to specify separate logical Ethernet segments.

```
fe-0/0/1 {
    vlan-tagging;
    unit 1 {
        vlan-id 1;
        family inet {
            address 10.32.1.1/24;
        }
        family iso;
    }
    unit 2 {
        vlan-id 2;
        family inet {
        vlan-id 2;
        family inet {
            address 10.32.2.1/24;
        }
        family iso;
    }
```

Fast Ethernet/Gigabit Ethernet Options

Both Fast Ethernet and Gigabit Ethernet allow you to specify a variety of capabilities such as flow control, source MAC filtering, and link aggregation (IEEE 802.3ad). Ethernet interfaces default to full duplex. Notice in the following output that the options parameters under both the Fast Ethernet and Gigabit Ethernet options hierarchies are identical.

```
[edit]
lab@HongKong# set interfaces fe-0/0/0 fastether-options ?
Possible completions:
  802.3ad               join an aggregated ethernet interface
+ apply-groups          Groups from which to inherit configuration data
  flow-control          Enable flow control
  loopback              Enable loopback
  no-flow-control       Don't enable flow control
  no-loopback           Don't enable loopback
  no-source-filtering   Don't enable source address filtering
> source-address-filter  Source address filters
  source-filtering      Enable source address filtering
```

Here are the Gigabit Ethernet options:

```
lab@Montreal# set interfaces ge-0/2/0 gigether-options ?
Possible completions:
  802.3ad              join an aggregated ethernet interface
+ apply-groups         Groups from which to inherit configuration data
  flow-control         Enable flow control
  loopback             Enable loopback
  no-flow-control      Don't enable flow control
  no-loopback          Don't enable loopback
  no-source-filtering  Don't enable source address filtering
> source-address-filter  Source address filters
  source-filtering     Enable source address filtering
```

Source Filtering

An extremely important security capability on Juniper Networks routers is the ability to configure a source filter based on a MAC address. You can specify a unicast MAC address from which you want the router to accept traffic; all other MAC addresses are denied.

Source filtering is a two-step process. You configure the source-filtering capability, and then you specify the specific MAC address(es) you want to enable. If you specify any MAC address with the group address set, the configuration will not pass the parsing process.

The following example shows how to enable source filtering and specify the only acceptable source MAC address on interface *ge-0/2/0*.

```
interfaces {
    ge-0/2/0 {
        gigether-options {
            source-filtering;
            source-address-filter {
                0090696eb801;
            }
        }
    }
    unit 0 {
        family inet {
            address 10.0.1.2/24;
        }
    }
}
```

The next example shows multiple MAC addresses configured. It also highlights which bit is the group bit. Remember that Ethernet uses the *little-endian* format, which means that the router transmits the least significant bit first. The multicast group bit is the most significant bit and is therefore transmitted last on a per-byte basis. So a MAC starting with *0b* is illegal, but *b0* is not illegal. Hexadecimal *b* equals *1011*. If the MAC starts with *0x0b*, the eighth bit in the first octet is a *1* (from the pattern 00001011). The eighth bit is the most significant bit (MSB) in Ethernet and therefore represents a group address.

```
[edit]
lab@SaoPaulo# show interfaces
fe-0/0/0 {
    mac aa:bb:cc:11:22:33;
    fastether-options {
        source-filtering;
        source-address-filter {
            00bb.1111.cccc;
            b0bb.1111.cccc;
        }
    }
    unit 0 {
        family inet {
            address 10.16.0.34/30;
        }
    }
}
```

Logical Interface Parameters

Several features can be configured within a logical unit: Virtual Router Redundancy Protocol (VRRP), DHCP relay capability, interface encapsulations, the ability to disable ICMP redirects, and the previously mentioned VLAN ID.

Virtual Router Redundancy Protocol

VRRP allows two routers to share the same virtual MAC address and IP address, which lets you configure all your hosts to use the same virtual IP/MAC address combination as the default gateway. Only one of the two routers sharing the virtual address combination stays active at any one time. The active router functions as your default gateway. If that router dies, the other router takes over as the default router, still advertising the same virtual MAC/IP address combination. The virtual MAC/IP resides on the routing engine because it is a logical—not physical—entity. Because the same virtual address combination is advertised, all the routers configured for that IP default gateway (and with the virtual MAC in their ARP cache) do not have to be reconfigured. Juniper Networks Fast Ethernet and Gigabit Ethernet interfaces support VRRP.

Examine the following configuration example. Notice that two VRRP interfaces are configured on different VLANs. The VLAN tagging configuration at the physical configuration level indicates that this interface supports 802.1Q VLAN tags. Within each logical unit, the *vlan-id* identifies which tag is prepended to the Ethernet frame.

Notice that both logical interfaces configure VRRP as part of the IP address. Each VRRP group number must have a virtual address—the address that users configure as their default gateway. You specify a priority value only if you do not want the interface to use the default priority of 100. The tracking option gives you the ability to adjust the current priority value based on the status of one or more interfaces. If the tracked interface goes down, the priority-cost value listed is subtracted from the current priority value.

This example shows tracking a single interface. Multiple interfaces may be tracked, as long as the sum of the priority costs does not exceed the configured priority value. Multiple interface tracking allows for a sliding scale. Whichever system has the higher priority value is the master virtual router. Consider a scenario, for example, in which a master router is tracking two interfaces. If a single tracked interface fails, you might not want the virtual router to change. However, if both tracked interfaces fail, you might want the virtual router to change. So you would set the priority cost for each tracked interface to *one-half plus one* of the difference between the master and backup virtual router. In the following example, the other router is configured with a priority value of 25 for *vlan-id* 100. If the master interface, with a value of 95, drops to 20 because the tracked interface fails, the other router becomes the master.

This example shows VRRP and VLAN tagging together. You can configure VRRP without VLAN tagging; you just configure VRRP on unit 0 in that case.

```
lab@SaoPaulo# show interfaces fe-0/0/1
vlan-tagging;
unit 100 {
    vlan-id 100;
    family inet {
        address 172.17.1.1/24 {
            vrrp-group 0 {
                virtual-address 172.17.1.5;
                priority 95;
                track {
                    interface fe-0/0/1.0 priority-cost 75;
                }
            }
        }
    }
}
unit 200 {
    vlan-id 200;
    family inet {
        address 172.18.1.1/24 {
            vrrp-group 0 {
```

```
                    virtual-address 172.18.1.5;
                    priority 25;
                    track {
                        interface fe-0/0/1.0 priority-cost 4;
                    }
                }
            }
        }
    }
```

Use the `show vrrp detail` command to verify VRRP information. The detail flag provides concise status information for relevant information. The *extensive* flag provides information proving that hello information exchange is occurring. The `vrrp detail` output is good for viewing normal status information, while the `vrrp extensive` output may prove useful in troubleshooting scenarios. For example, you can verify the current interface address, whether or not the interface is the master or the backup, the virtual IP address (VIP), and what the master router address and virtual MAC are. Additionally, an entire section of the output for each interface highlights tracking status.

```
lab@SaoPaulo> show vrrp detail
Physical interface: fe-0/0/1, Unit: 100, Vlan-id: 100, Address:
172.17.1.1/24
  Interface state: up, Group: 0, State: master
  Priority: 95, Advertisement interval: 1, Authentication type: none
  Preempt: yes, Accept-data mode: no, VIP count: 1, VIP: 172.17.1.5
  Advertisement timer: 0.400s, Master router: 172.17.1.1
  Virtual MAC: 00:00:5e:00:01:00
  Tracking: enabled
    Current priority: 95, Configured priority: 95
    Interface tracking: enabled, Interface count: 1
      Interface           Int state       Priority cost
      fe-0/0/1.0          up              75

Physical interface: fe-0/0/1, Unit: 200, Vlan-id: 200, Address:
172.18.1.1/24
  Interface state: up, Group: 0, State: backup
  Priority: 25, Advertisement interval: 1, Authentication type: none
  Preempt: yes, Accept-data mode: no, VIP count: 1, VIP: 172.18.1.5
  Dead timer: 2.952s, Master priority: 95, Master router: 172.18.1.2
  Tracking: enabled
    Current priority: 25, Configured priority: 25
    Interface tracking: enabled, Interface count: 1
      Interface           Int state       Priority cost
      fe-0/0/1.0          up              4
```

Configuring DHCP Relay Capability for BOOTP and DHCP

You can configure a relay capability for the Boot Protocol (BOOTP) and Dynamic Host Configuration Protocol (DHCP). You configure the address of the DHCP/BOOTP server under the family *inet*. In later revisions of code, the commands are available, but they will move to the *[edit system]* hierarchy. The router will accept the command under the interface hierarchy in later versions, but it will not display the options with the ? key.

```
lab@Montreal# show interfaces
fe-0/0/1 {
    description "To Amsterdam";
    unit 0 {
        family inet {
            dhcp-relay server 1.1.1.1;
            address 10.1.0.17/30;
        }
        family iso;
    }
}
```

No ICMP Redirects

Disabling ICMP redirects helps minimize the ability for hackers to send false traffic to destinations, expecting to receive traffic that identifies specific routers (as the source of the ICMP redirect). Use the *no-redirects* option under the logical unit to configure this ability, like so:

```
fe-0/0/0 {
    unit 0 {
        family inet {
            no-redirects;
            address 10.32.0.2/30;
        }
        family iso;
    }
}
```

Configuring Encapsulations

You can configure several different encapsulations on a logical interface. See Chapter 15 for an explanation of the VLAN-CCC encapsulation. Other encapsulations allow you to use 802.3-LLC, 802.3-SNAP, or Ethernet Type II encapsulation (*dix* encapsulation—for Digital, Intel, and Xerox). Both LLC and SNAP encapsulations use a Length field in place of the Type field that Ethernet Type II uses. The 802.3 flavors specify the protocol carried within the Layer 2 frame via a protocol code carried in a DSAP/SSAP field (for LLC) or within the Protocol ID field of the SNAP header (for the SNAP encapsulation).

Set the encapsulation at the logical unit level. The default encapsulation is Ethernet Type II. You can verify the encapsulation with the `show interfaces` command—look in the logical unit for the setting. The next example shows an interface set for 802.3-LLC.

> **Note**   *The physical MTU for all encapsulation types is 1514. Note that this value does not include the Ethernet FCS. You should remember this fact if interoperating with other vendors that include the FCS within their physical MTU encapsulation.*

```
[edit]
lab@HongKong# set interfaces fe-0/0/0 unit 0 encapsulation ?
Possible completions:
  802.3-llc             Ethernet IEEE 802.3 LLC (RFC 1042)
  802.3-snap            Ethernet IEEE 802.3 SNAP (RFC 1042)
  dix                   Ethernet DIXv2 (RFC 894)
  vlan-ccc              802.1Q tagging for a cross connection
  [edit]
lab@SaoPaulo# run show interfaces fe-0/0/0
Physical interface: fe-0/0/0, Enabled, Physical link is Up
  .
  .

  Logical interface fe-0/0/0.0 (Index 13) (SNMP ifIndex 12)
    Flags: SNMP-Traps Encapsulation: IEEE802.3-LLC
    Protocol inet, MTU: 1500, Flags: Is-Primary
      Addresses, Flags: Is-Preferred Is-Primary
        Destination: 10.16.0.32/30, Local: 10.16.0.34, Broadcast: 10.16.0.35
    Protocol iso, MTU: 1497, Flags: Is-Primary
    Protocol mpls, MTU: 1500, Flags: Is-Primary
```

Configuring Tunnel Interfaces

Tunnel Services PICs are required for many multicasting applications and must be used any time you wish to encapsulate traffic within IP. A tunnel interface enables a private path through an otherwise public network.

Multicasting and Tunnel PICs

Tunnel Services PICs are required any time the sparse mode Protocol Independent Multicast (PIM) first-hop router connected to the multicast source and the rendezvous point (RP) are not colocated. PIM sparse mode traffic destined for the RP must be encapsulated within unicast IP packets for forwarding across the IP backbone. The tunnel PIC creates a PD or PE interface (for PIM decapsulation or PIM encapsulation) to accomplish this task. When the multicast traffic must cross the IP backbone, the PE interface encapsulates it. When the PIM sparse mode multicast traffic reaches the RP, the PD interface decapsulates the multicast traffic for the RP to transmit through its multicast tree. You simply install the PIC and the PIM encapsulation and decapsulation process will work. You need a tunnel services PIC on both the RP and the first-hop router connected to the multicast source.

Generic Route Encapsulation/IP-IP and Tunnel PICs

If you want to configure Generic Route Encapsulation (GRE) or IP Encapsulation within IP (IP-IP), you also need to install tunnel services PICs. You must configure these tunneling capabilities—they are not automatic like the multicast encapsulation. Because encapsulated traffic loops around once within the router, you are limited to a percent of the interface speed as a *maximum encapsulation speed*. You use GRE or IP-IP encapsulation when you want the IP traffic to follow a different path than would normally be used, or if you want to hide the networks on the endpoints of the tunnels from the middle of the IP network.

GRE/IP-IP configuration is fairly tame. You should specify your interface address; then you specify the tunnel source and destination; and then you commit. As long as the tunnel destination is reachable via IP, the encapsulated traffic will reach the destination. The GRE encapsulation, defined in RFCs 1701 and 1702, adds 24 bytes of overhead to each IP packet. The IP-IP encapsulation, defined in RFC 2003, adds 20 bytes of overhead.

The following example shows a basic GRE configuration. In this case, the tunnel source is the loopback address of the local router and the destination address is the loopback of the far router. Traffic that has a next-hop of the tunnel destination will use the tunnel—not all the traffic uses the tunnel automatically; only that traffic that normally goes to the tunnel destination as next-hop uses the tunnel. Just because you establish a tunnel does not mean traffic will transit the tunnel.

```
[edit]
lab@London# show interfaces
gr-0/2/0 {
    unit 0 {
        tunnel {
            source 192.168.36.1;
            destination 192.168.16.1;
        }
        family inet {
            address 172.25.1.1/24;
        }
    }
}
lo0 {
    unit 0 {
```

```
        family inet {
          address 192.168.36.1/32;
        }
        family iso {
          address 49.2020.0202.2222.1921.6803.6001.00;
        }
      }
    }
}
```

In terms of viewable output, the tunnel interface displays provide the same useful information that other show commands provide. The following output highlights the maximum speed through the tunnel, the encapsulation type and header, packets through the interface, and the logical address:

```
lab@London>show interfaces gr-0/2/0
Physical interface: gr-0/2/0, Enabled, Physical link is Up
  Interface index: 17, SNMP ifIndex: 32
  Type: GRE, Link-level type: GRE, MTU: Unlimited, Speed: 800mbps
  Device flags   : Present Running
  Interface flags: Point-To-Point SNMP-Traps
  Input rate     : 0 bps (0 pps)
  Output rate    : 0 bps (0 pps)

  Logical interface gr-0/2/0.0 (Index 6) (SNMP ifIndex 34)
    Flags: Point-To-Point SNMP-Traps
    IP-Header 192.168.16.1:192.168.36.1:47:df:64:00000000
    Encapsulation: GRE-NULL
  Input packets : 8
  Output packets: 8
    Protocol inet, MTU: Unlimited, Flags: None
      Addresses, Flags: Is-Preferred Is-Primary
        Destination: 172.25.1/24, Local: 172.25.1.1
```

Management Interface Configuration

The *fxp0* interface supports auto-sensing the interface speed at either 10 or 100 Mbps. You should be aware, as stated previously, that routing protocol adjacencies will form over the *fxp0* interface, even though the router will not route transit traffic over that interface. So if you specify `all` interfaces under the OSPF protocols hierarchy, for example, you could end up with OSPF neighbor relationships that you did not want. You can hard code the link speed only on the management interface. All other Ethernet interfaces operate at either Fast or Gigabit Ethernet speeds. You can configure all Fast Ethernet properties on the management interface.

Troubleshooting

You can troubleshoot an interface a variety of ways. Some of the most common methods include the `monitor interface` and `show interfaces extensive` commands and PINGing using loopback configurations.

The monitor interface Command

The `monitor interface` command is an operational mode command. It enables you to see bytes transmitted and received on a particular interface. By default, it refreshes every second. A variety of screen commands enable you to view the next interface, freeze the output, and unfreeze the output. They are displayed at the bottom of the output that follows. The delta column in the output shows the change in the total number since the last refresh:

```
SaoPaulo                          Seconds: 8                  Time: 15:58:15
                                                              Delay: 1/1/1

Interface: fe-0/0/0, Enabled, Link is Up
Encapsulation: Ethernet, Speed: 100mbps
Traffic statistics:                                           Current delta
  Input bytes:                     4189 (0 bps)                       [0]
  Output bytes:                    5252 (0 bps)                       [0]
  Input packets:                     64 (0 pps)                       [0]
  Output packets:                    75 (0 pps)                       [0]
Error statistics:
  Input errors:                       0                               [0]
  Input drops:                        0                               [0]
  Input framing errors:               0                               [0]
  Policed discards:                   0                               [0]
  L3 incompletes:                     0                               [0]
  L2 channel errors:                  0                               [0]
  Packet error count                  0                               [0]
Next='n', Quit='q' or ESC, Freeze='f', Thaw='t', Clear='c', Interface='i'
```

The show interfaces extensive Command

The next output shows a `show interfaces extensive` command for a frame relay SONET interface (the pipe to `no-more` prevents pagination on commands with significant amounts of output, like this one). At the bottom of the output, you can even see what system is being advertised in the SONET path trace information, so you can tell what router you are connected to. The path trace information does not show when the command displays an ATM SONET interface. When working with Automatic Protection Switching, you can examine the K1/2 byte information on a particular interface. Many different parameters discussed earlier in the text are shown in boldface.

```
lab@Montreal> show interfaces so-0/1/2 extensive | no-more
Physical interface: so-0/1/2, Enabled, Physical link is Up
  Interface index: 15, SNMP ifIndex: 24, Generation: 14
  Link-level type: Frame-Relay, MTU: 4474, Clocking: Internal, SONET mode,
  Speed: OC3, Loopback: None, FCS: 16, Payload scrambler: Enabled
  Device flags   : Present Running
  Interface flags: Point-To-Point SNMP-Traps
  Link flags     : No-Keepalives DCE
  Hold-times     : Up 0 ms, Down 0 ms
  ANSI LMI settings: n392dce 3, n393dce 4, t392dce 15 seconds
  LMI statistics:
    Input : 229 (last seen 00:00:09 ago)
    Output: 229 (last sent 00:00:09 ago)
  Statistics last cleared: Never
  Traffic statistics:
   Input  bytes  :              3206                 0 bps
   Output bytes  :              3625                 0 bps
   Input  packets:               229                 0 pps
   Output packets:               229                 0 pps
  Input errors:
    Errors: 0, Drops: 0, Framing errors: 0, Runts: 0, Giants: 0,
    Bucket drops: 0, Policed discards: 0, L3 incompletes: 0,
    L2 channel errors: 0, L2 mismatch timeouts: 0, HS link CRC errors: 0,
    HS link FIFO overflows: 0
  Output errors:
    Carrier transitions: 1, Errors: 0, Drops: 0, Aged packets: 0,
    HS link FIFO underflows: 0
  SONET alarms    : None
  SONET defects   : None
  SONET PHY:             Seconds        Count   State
    PLL Lock                0              0     OK
    PHY Light               0              0     OK
  SONET section:
    BIP-B1                  0              0
    SEF                    16              1     OK
    LOS                    16              1     OK
    LOF                    16              1     OK
    ES-S                   16
    SES-S                  16
    SEFS-S                 16
  SONET line:
    BIP-B2                  0              0
    REI-L                   0              0
    RDI-L                   1              1     OK
    AIS-L                  16              1     OK
    BERR-SF                 0              0     OK
```

```
    BERR-SD                      0              0  OK
    ES-L                        16
    SES-L                       16
    UAS-L                        6
    ES-LFE                       1
    SES-LFE                      1
    UAS-LFE                      0
SONET path:
    BIP-B3                       0              0
    REI-P                        0              0
    LOP-P                        0              0  OK
    AIS-P                       16              1  OK
    RDI-P                        0              0  OK
    UNEQ-P                       0              0  OK
    PLM-P                        0              0  OK
    ES-P                        16
    SES-P                       16
    UAS-P                        6
    ES-PFE                       0
    SES-PFE                      0
    UAS-PFE                      0
Received SONET overhead:
    F1      : 0x00, J0      : 0x00, K1      : 0x00, K2      : 0x00
    S1      : 0x00, C2      : 0xcf, C2(cmp) : 0xcf, F2      : 0x00
    Z3      : 0x00, Z4      : 0x00, S1(cmp) : 0x00, V5      : 0x00
    V5(cmp) : 0x00
Transmitted SONET overhead:
    F1      : 0x00, J0      : 0x01, K1      : 0x00, K2      : 0x00
    S1      : 0x00, C2      : 0xcf, F2      : 0x00, Z3      : 0x00
    Z4      : 0x00, V5      : 0x00
Received path trace: SanJose so-0/1/2
    53 61 6e 4a 6f 73 65 20 73 6f 2d 30 2f 31 2f 32   SanJose so-0/1/2
    00 00 00 00 00 00 00 00 00 00 00 00 00 00 00 00   ................
    00 00 00 00 00 00 00 00 00 00 00 00 00 00 00 00   ................
    00 00 00 00 00 00 00 00 00 00 00 00 00 00 0d 0a   ................
Transmitted path trace: Montreal so-0/1/2
    4d 6f 6e 74 72 65 61 6c 20 73 6f 2d 30 2f 31 2f   Montreal so-0/1/
    32 00 00 00 00 00 00 00 00 00 00 00 00 00 00 00   2...............
    00 00 00 00 00 00 00 00 00 00 00 00 00 00 00 00   ................
    00 00 00 00 00 00 00 00 00 00 00 00 00 00 00 00   ................
HDLC configuration:
    Policing bucket: Disabled
    Shaping bucket : Disabled
    Giant threshold: 4484, Runt threshold: 3
PFE configuration:
    Destination slot: 0, PLP byte: 1 (0x00)
    CoS transmit queue bandwidth:
       Queue0: 95, Queue1: 0, Queue2: 0, Queue3: 5
```

```
    CoS weighted round-robin:
       Queue0: 95, Queue1: 0, Queue2: 0, Queue3: 5

Logical interface so-0/1/2.75 (Index 7) (SNMP ifIndex 38) (Generation 6)
   Flags: Point-To-Point SNMP-Traps Encapsulation: FR-NLPID
   Traffic statistics:
    Input  bytes  :                        0
    Output bytes  :                        0
    Input  packets:                        0
    Output packets:                        0
   Local statistics:
    Input  bytes  :                        0
    Output bytes  :                        0
    Input  packets:                        0
    Output packets:                        0
   Transit statistics:
    Input  bytes  :                        0                        0 bps
    Output bytes  :                        0                        0 bps
    Input  packets:                        0                        0 pps
    Output packets:                        0                        0 pps
   Protocol inet, MTU: 4470, Flags: None, Generation: 14 Route table: 0
     Addresses, Flags: Is-Preferred Is-Primary
        Destination: 172.16.1/24, Local: 172.16.1.1, Broadcast: Unspecified,
        Generation: 14
   DLCI 75
     Flags: Active
     Total down time: 0 sec, Last down: Never
     Traffic statistics:
      Input  bytes  :                      0
      Output bytes  :                      0
      Input  packets:                      0
      Output packets:                      0
```

Loopback

You can configure the router to place the local interface or the interface into response mode for a remote loopback. Set the loopback parameter under the [edit interfaces *interface-type*-#/#/#] hierarchy. Loopback is available for T-1, E-1, T-3, E-3, and SONET interfaces. Local loopback transmits to the CSU and receives its own pattern. Remote loopback receives from the CSU and immediately retransmits what it receives back to the CSU:

```
lab@Tokyo# set loopback ?
Possible completions:
   local                    Local loopback
   remote                   Remote loopback
```

To PING your own interface when you have placed the interface in loopback, you must disable keepalives. By default, the router marks the route for the interface with the *reject* flag whenever you place an interface in loopback. By disabling keepalives, you disable the ability for the router to recognize the interface is looped, and it consequently will not mark the route as rejected.

Additionally, the default PPP encapsulation must be changed to something like `cisco-hdlc` because the PPP NCP negotiation will not be successful if one of the interfaces is placed in loopback.

Chapter 6

Protocol-Independent Routing

by Joseph M. Soricelli

The routing table on a Juniper Networks router contains all route information known to the router at any particular point in time. Information can be placed into the routing table in a number of ways, including routing protocols, static routes, and aggregate routes. Within the JUNOS software, static and aggregate routes are considered protocol-independent information and are configured within the [edit routing-options] configuration hierarchy. Other protocol-independent features within this configuration directory include martian addresses, additional routing tables, router identification, and forwarding table options.

Route Types

Route prefixes in a network can be learned from multiple sources, including both interior and exterior routing protocols. Locally configured information in the routing table is also available to be advertised via these routing protocols. One of the most basic forms of locally configured information is the *static route*.

Static Routes

Once configured and activated, static routes are always available. They do not respond to dynamic network changes (unless those changes are local to the router). Static routes have multiple uses in a networking environment. For an enterprise network, a static route can be as simple as a default route pointing to the Internet Service Provider (ISP) connecting that enterprise to the Internet. In the case of a specific ISP, static routes are often used to represent enterprise customers within the ISP's own network. The ISP will configure a static route for each customer on the router that connects that particular customer to the ISP network. These routes are then injected into the ISP's Interior Gateway Protocol (IGP) and perhaps their Border Gateway Protocol (BGP) network to provide reachability for that customer.

The situation described here is typical of most Internet connections. The ISP and the enterprise customer each have static routes pointing at each other for connectivity. While it may seem odd to have such critical information not responsive to dynamic changes, recall that local changes to an individual router can affect the availability of static routes configured on that router. For example, take a scenario in which both the ISP and the customer are sharing a point-to-point link. If that link becomes unavailable for any reason, both of the routers on either side of the link will notice this change and make those static routes unusable. In such a case, a static routing solution is perfectly acceptable.

On a Juniper Networks router, static routes are installed into the routing table *inet.0* when they are considered to be active. To achieve this active state in the routing table, a static route must have a valid next-hop configured.

Next-Hop Options

Valid next-hop options in a Juniper Networks router typically fall into one of two categories: an IP address or a configured null value.

In the majority of situations in which a static route will be used, the next-hop is specified as an IP address. Typically, this IP address is the address of the neighboring router directly connected across a local interface. For example, the static route that connects Customer 1 to the *Daytona* router looks like this:

```
routing-options {
    static {
        route 172.16.100.0/24 next-hop 172.31.1.2;
```

The ability for the local router to know that the specified next-hop address is directly connected is quite important, because the JUNOS software will not perform a recursive lookup to validate that address.

The router must have explicit knowledge that a next-hop is directly connected. Typically, the IP address on an interface allows the router to verify connectivity. For example, an IP address of 192.168.1.1/24 on an interface tells the router that any address in the range 192.168.1.2 through 192.168.1.254 is directly connected. In some cases, this subnet address does not provide enough information to the router to determine whether a host is directly connected. This is often the case when a /32 IP address is configured on a router's interface.

For example, the *Daytona* router is connected to Customer 2 via a point-to-point Asynchronous Transfer Mode (ATM) connection. To use the IP address of the customer router (172.31.1.6) as a next-hop for a static route, the interface on *Daytona* would use the following syntax:

```
interfaces {
    at-0/3/0 {
        atm-options {
            vpi 0 maximum-vcs 200;
        }
        unit 150 {
            vci 150;
            family inet {
                address 172.31.1.5/32 {
                    destination 172.31.1.6;
```

This type of interface configuration is sometimes seen on a point-tp-point link. Often, however, these types of links are configured with an IP address that uses a 30-bit subnet mask (such as 172.16.100.4/30), and the router can verify the enxt-hop as previously described. In the case of the Daytona router, an option fo rhte next-hop value on a static route is to use the name of the interface. This will also allow the router to verify that the next-hop is directly connected.

For Customer 2, *Daytona* has a configuration like so:

```
routing-options {
    static {
        route 172.16.101.0/24 next-hop at-2/2/0.100;
```

If an IP address or interface name is not specified for a static route's next-hop, a keyword that represents a null value must be configured. When a packet matches a route that has a next-hop value of a configured null, it is dropped off of the network. In a typical environment, this option is used when you want to inject routing information into your network for routes that are not actually reachable via that router. This type of configuration is valuable in a lab or classroom environment, where you need to simulate routes that would actually go someplace in a real network.

Within the JUNOS software are two keywords that represent a configured null value: `reject` and `discard`. While both of these options will remove packets from the network, the difference between them is in the router's response to that drop action. The `reject` option returns an Internet Control Message Protocol (ICMP) message of "administratively prohibited" from the router back to the source of the IP packet. The `discard` option does not return an ICMP message and silently removes the packet from the network.

Daytona has two routes (10.10.10/24 and 10.10.11/24) that it would like to inject into the ISP network. The configuration for those two routes is shown here:

```
routing-options {
    static {
        route 10.10.10.0/24 discard;
        route 10.10.11.0/24 reject;
```

The last possible option for a next-hop value on a static route is `receive`. This option informs the router that all packets matching that route should be sent to the Routing Engine (RE). The RE will process and interpret only packets with a destination address that matches one of the router's configured IP addresses. In essence, by using this option you are creating a host static route (32-bit subnet mask) on the router. This can be useful in a network environment where routing information must be shared among several different routing tables on a router, such as in a virtual private network (VPN) environment.

Consider, for example, that the *Darlington* router is participating in a VPN network and is connected to Site 1 of VPN A. *Richmond* requires reachability to the *Darlington* interface connected to the VPN site. *Darlington* can configure a static route such as:

```
routing-options {
    static {
        route 172.30.30.1/32 receive;
```

Associating Metrics

When a Juniper Networks router is presented with identical routes to the same destination, it must make a decision as to which route to install in the forwarding table. If the routes were installed into the routing table *inet.0* by different protocols, for example, the default JUNOS software preference values typically decide which protocol is more "believable" and hence which route to use. Should the same protocol install multiple copies of the same route (or if multiple protocols share the same preference value), the "tiebreaker" becomes the metric associated with those routes.

Static routes in the JUNOS software can be assigned a metric value between 1 and 65,535. As with most metrics, a lower value is preferred. Since static routes are local to the router, this metric value is also local to the router and is not advertised. Generally speaking, this value does not factor into routing decisions because the JUNOS software preference values favor static routes over routing protocols and most other route information. If the default protocol preference values have been altered, however, both a static route and a protocol route might have the same value. In this case, any metric values associated with those routes (including those that you have configured) will be evaluated to determine which route to use.

In this example, *Daytona* would like to add a metric to its static route for Customer 1. This configuration would now appear like so:

```
routing-options {
    static {
        route 172.16.100.0/24 metric 25;
            next-hop 172.31.1.2 metric 25;
```

Assigning Community Values

In an ISP environment in which BGP is being used to route transit traffic, it might be valuable to "tag" certain routes with an administrative value. These tags are then associated with the routes and are transmitted across the network within BGP. Other routers within the ISP's network can then use the tags to make routing decisions. Within BGP, such tags are known as *communities*. If your network is using communities to make routing decisions and you are representing your customer networks with the use of static routes, you would most likely assign community values to your static routes.

BGP communities are 32-bit values with the first 16 bits assigned to your Autonomous System (AS) number and the last 16 bits left aside as an open value for each AS to decide upon. While many applications are available for them, communities are commonly expressed in the format of *AS#:Value*—where the *value* is determined by the policies of the service provider. For example, an AS of 65001 could assign a value of 100 and the resulting community would be 65001:100.

After the AS has decided upon community values, the values can then be assigned to static routes. Within the JUNOS software, an individual static route can be configured with a single community value or with multiple community values.

In the example network, the *Daytona* router would like to assign a community value of 100 to the route to Customer 2. This configuration now appears as this:

```
routing-options {
    static {
        route 172.16.101.0/24
            next-hop at-0/3/0.150;
            community 65001:100;
```

Defaults Section

Within the configuration hierarchy for static routes is a section called *defaults*. This portion of the configuration can be used to set any of the static route options (metric, community, and so on) that have been discussed. The function of this section of the configuration is to allow a network administrator to assign a value to all the static routes in the configuration. For example, if all the static routes on a router represent customers and all customer routes should have a community value of 65001:1111, that value can be placed in the *defaults* section of the configuration. All static routes on the router would then inherit that value.

Should some of the routes require a different community value, that new value can be configured within the hierarchy of the actual static route. When a route has a value assigned in this manner, no inheritance from the *defaults* section occurs and the more specific value takes precedence. All of the static routes on *Daytona* should have a value of 65001:1111. The exception is the route to Customer 1, which should retain its earlier value of 65001:100.

The defaults section can be used on *Daytona* to accomplish this goal as follows:

```
routing-options {
    static {
        defaults {
            community 65001:1111;
        }
        route 172.16.100.0/24 {
            next-hop 172.31.1.2;
            metric 25;
        }
        route 172.16.101.0/24 {
            next-hop at-0/3/0.150;
            community 65001:100;
        }
```

Aggregate Routes

Aggregate routes are a second method for injecting routing information into a network. Like static routes, aggregate routes are locally defined and configured on a single router. Once considered active in the *inet.0* routing table, aggregate routes are always available. One of the most compelling reasons for the use of aggregates in a network is *route summarization*.

In the world of Internet routing there are always two competing interests: the need for detailed routing knowledge versus the need for reasonable routing table size. When a router has detailed knowledge of the network, it can make the best routing decision possible. For example, if an ISP has four possible paths through the Internet to reach a host destination, it can choose the best path if it knows about all the /24 networks in the Internet. The down side of this is that all of those /24 networks could total hundreds of thousands of routes. A routing table of that size can place an enormous load on a router. To ease that load, detailed routing knowledge can be summarized. For example, the customer networks 172.16.16/24, 172.16.20/24, 172.16.24/24, and 172.16.28/24 can be summarized into one routing entry of 172.16.16/20.

Another way of looking at a summarized route is to say that it is made up of smaller pieces that add up to a single larger route. In technical terms, an aggregate route represents multiple *contributing routes*.

Contributing Routes

Not only are contributing routes the routes that comprise the aggregate, they are also what make the aggregate route active and available in the *inet.0* routing table. A contributing route can be from any viable protocol in *inet.0*. Possibilities include Local, Direct, Static, Open Shortest Path First (OSPF), Intermediate System to Intermediate System (IS-IS), and BGP. To be considered a contributing route, a route must itself be active and reside within the network range specified by the aggregate.

To view what routes are contributing to an individual aggregate, use the show route extensive command. On the *Charlotte* router, this command results in the following:

```
user@Charlotte> show route extensive
inet.0: 5 destinations, 5 routes (5 active, 0 holddown, 0 hidden)
+ = Active Route, - = Last Active, * = Both
172.16.16.0/20 (1 entry, 1 announced)
        *Aggregate      Preference: 130
                Next hop type: Reject
                State: <Active Int Ext>
                Age: 21:40
                Task: Aggregate
                Announcement bits (1): 0-KRT
                AS path: I
                Flags: Depth: 0        Active
                AS path list:
                        AS path: I Refcount: 4
                Contributing Routes (4):
                        172.16.16.0/24          proto Static
                        172.16.20.0/24          proto Static
                        172.16.24.0/24          proto Static
                        172.16.28.0/24          proto Static
```

An individual route in *inet.0* can only contribute to one aggregate route. If four aggregate routes are configured on your router, there must be four separate contributors available to activate all the aggregates.

Next-Hop Options

In the aggregate route on *Charlotte*, the next-hop value is listed as `reject`. Since this is the default next-hop assigned to all aggregate routes, the configuration on *Charlotte* is simply this:

```
routing-options {
    aggregate {
        route 172.16.16.0/20;
```

The other valid next-hop option for an aggregate route is `discard`. Recall from earlier in the chapter that both `reject` and `discard` represent the dropping of a packet. This apparent contradiction makes sense if you remember that a router performs a longest match lookup to route any packet. In addition, an aggregate can be active in *inet.0* only if it has at least one active contributing route. When a packet arrives at the router and the destination is within the aggregate, it is hoped that one of the contributing routes will better match the destination address. If not, the longest match lookup will in fact match the aggregate prefix and the packet will be dropped. In addition, any packet explicitly addressed to the aggregate will also be dropped. Remember that the longest prefix match always wins.

Associating Metrics

Aggregate routes can be assigned metrics. Much like static routes, the metric value can be between 1 and 65,535. These configured metrics often are not consulted in the determination of an active route because the default JUNOS software preference values typically decide which route to use. In a case for which the preference values have been changed, it is possible that an aggregate might have the same preference value as a route from another protocol. In such a case, the configured metric value would then be used to determine which route to make active in *inet.0*.

To assign a metric value of *50* to the aggregate route on *Charlotte*, the configuration is changed to the following:

```
routing-options {
    aggregate {
        route 172.16.16.0/20 {
            metric 50;
```

Assigning Community Values

BGP community values can also be assigned to aggregate routes. The function of communities in relation to aggregates is the same as for static routes, so an in-depth discussion here will be skipped. As before, an individual aggregate route can be configured with a single community value or with multiple community values.

The *Charlotte* configuration has been changed to add a community value of 65001:333 to the aggregate route:

```
routing-options {
    aggregate {
        route 172.16.16.0/20 {
            metric 50;
            community 65001:333;
```

Policies

As discussed, an aggregate route becomes active in the *inet.0* routing table only when one or more of the aggregate's contributing routes are also active. By default, all possible contributing routes are used to activate the aggregate route. You can control which routes get used to contribute through the use of a JUNOS software policy.

One application for this type of policy would be when a network provider wants to use and/or advertise an aggregate route only when the contributing routes are learned from a dynamic routing protocol. A policy would be configured that rejects all Local, Direct, and Static routes that would typically contribute to the aggregate. The policy would then be applied to the configuration of the aggregate route.

For example, the *Atlanta* router would like to send a single route of 172.16.0.0/16 to its ISP peer only when customer routes from *Daytona* or *Charlotte* are active. The configuration would become this:

```
routing-options {
    aggregate {
        route 172.16.16.0/20 {
            policy only-dynamic-protocols;
            metric 50;
            community 65001:333;
```

The aggregate route would then be active in *inet.0* and would be eligible for advertisement. Should the customer routes become inactive, the aggregate route would also become inactive. In this way, you can create a "dynamic" aggregate route.

Defaults Section

Within the configuration hierarchy for aggregate routes is a *defaults* section. This area of the configuration can be used to set route properties for all aggregate routes. The inheritance functions of the *defaults* section as well as the ability to define a parameter within a specific aggregate route are the same in form and function as static routes, so a more in-depth discussion will be skipped.

Generated Routes

Generated routes are identical to aggregate routes in their operation. In fact, when a generated route is active in *inet.0*, it is listed as protocol *Aggregate*. Only the differences between a generated route and an aggregate route will be discussed here.

The primary difference between the two types of routes is the default next-hop value. For generated routes, the next-hop is an IP address instead of the `reject` keyword used for aggregate routes. This next-hop IP address is inherited from the primary contributing route of the generated route. This primary contributing route is the one with the smallest numerical prefix value.

The *Bristol* router is configured for a generated route of 172.16.64/20. From the output of the `show route extensive` command, we find that 172.16.64/24 is considered to be the primary contributing route:

```
user@Bristol> show route extensive
inet.0: 14 destinations, 14 routes (14 active, 0 holddown, 0 hidden)
+ = Active Route, - = Last Active, * = Both
172.16.64.0/20 (1 entry, 1 announced)
        *Aggregate       Preference: 130
                Nexthop: 172.31.1.34 via so-0/0/0.100, selected
                State: <Active Int Ext>
                Age: 2:53
                Task: Aggregate
                Announcement bits (1): 0-KRT
                AS path: I
                Flags: Generate Depth: 0         Active
                Contributing Routes (3):
                        172.16.64.0/24        proto Static
                        172.16.68.0/24        proto Static
                        172.16.72.0/24        proto Static
```

A comparison between this output and the network map reveals that *Bristol* has more static routes than those contributing to the summary. Because the default next-hop value for a generated route is an IP address, only active routes with a next-hop value of an IP address are eligible to contribute.

The other valid next-hop option for a generated route is the `discard` keyword. This configuration option does not, however, alter the fact that only IP address next-hop routes can contribute to a generated route. The *Bristol* configuration is changed to `discard`. Notice in the `show route extensive` output that the same contributing routes are listed:

```
user@Bristol> show route extensive
inet.0: 14 destinations, 14 routes (14 active, 0 holddown, 0 hidden)
+ = Active Route, - = Last Active, * = Both
172.16.64.0/20 (1 entry, 1 announced)
        *Aggregate       Preference: 130
                Next hop type: Discard
                State: <Active Int Ext>
                Age: 8:29
                Task: Aggregate
```

```
Announcement bits (1): 0-KRT
AS path: I
Flags: Generate Discard Depth: 0          Active
Contributing Routes (3):
          172.16.64.0/24        proto Static
          172.16.68.0/24        proto Static
          172.16.72.0/24        proto Static
```

Martian Routes

Martian routes should never be used to route user traffic. These routes often contradict common sense or best usage in public networks. For example, the 127.0.0.0/8 network is reserved for loopback addresses. Juniper Networks routers have seven predefined martian routes. The format of the martians follows the JUNOS software policy framework notation of a *route-filter*. For a complete examination of the policy framework, please see Chapter 7.

The default martian routes are listed here:

- 0.0.0.0/8 orlonger

- 127.0.0.0/8 orlonger

- 128.0.0.0/16 orlonger

- 191.255.0.0/16 orlonger

- 192.0.0.0/24 orlonger

- 223.255.255.0/24 orlonger

- 224.0.0.0/4 orlonger

At first glance, this list may appear quite short. Other addresses do exist that many ISPs never route in the global Internet. The default route of 0.0.0.0/0 is not included. Certain Internet Assigned Numbers Authority (IANA)-reserved networks are not included. The RFC 1918 private address networks of 10.0.0.0/8, 172.16.0.0/12, and 192.168.0.0/16 are not included.

Within the JUNOS software, any network included in the martian route list can never be placed into the *inet.0* routing table. Even though the RFC 1918 private address should not be routed in the Internet, many ISPs use those addresses within their autonomous systems. If they were included in the default martian list, they would never be installed as an active route in the router. Therefore, these types of reserved but usable networks are not included by default in the martian route list simply because they might be used in a network.

As an example, the route 172.16.24/24 is currently in the *inet.0* routing table on the *Charlotte* router. This route can be defined as a martian network within `routing-options`:

```
routing-options {
    martians {
        172.16.24.0/24 orlonger;
```

After the configuration has been committed, the route is no longer in the routing table:

```
user@Charlotte> show route 172.16.24/24
inet.0: 5 destinations, 5 routes (4 active, 0 holddown, 1 hidden)
+ = Active Route, - = Last Active, * = Both
```

Routing Tables

The routing table within the JUNOS software is composed of several smaller route tables. Thus far, only the *inet.0* route table used for IPv4 unicast routes has been discussed.

The default route tables on a Juniper Networks route include the following:

- *inet.0*   IPpv4 unicast routes
- *inet6.0*   IPpv6 unicast routes
- *inet.1*   IP multicast cache
- *inet.2*   Unicast routes used for multicast Reverse Path Forwarding (RPF) checks
- *inet.3*   IP routes reachable via Multi-Protocol Label Switching (MPLS) engineered tunnels
- *inet.4*   Source Active (SA) information from Multicast Source Discovery Protocol (MSDP)
- *mpls.0*   MPLS label-swapping table
- *bgp.l3vpn.0*   VPN BGP routes used for 2547bis VPNs
- *bgp.l2vpn.0*   VPN routes used for Layer 2 VPNs
- *iso.0*   IS-IS NSAP addresses

Technically speaking, the *mpls.0* table is actually a switching table and not a route table. It is included here because it is displayed in the output of a show route command. It also shares some characteristics with the other routing tables in its format and operation.

The tables listed are created within the JUNOS software when they are needed. For example, if no IP addresses are configured on the router, no *inet.0* route table will exist.

In the following output from the *Atlanta* router, there is neither an *inet.1* nor an *inet.2* route table shown because multicast protocols are not currently operational on the router:

```
user@Atlanta> show route
inet.0: 14 destinations, 14 routes (14 active, 0 holddown, 0 hidden)
+ = Active Route, - = Last Active, * = Both
172.31.200.0/24    *[IS-IS/18] 00:08:35, metric 30, tag 2
                    > to 172.31.202.1 via so-0/0/0.0
```

```
172.31.202.0/24      *[Direct/0] 00:09:09
                        > via so-0/0/0.0
172.31.202.2/32      *[Local/0] 00:09:09
                         Local
172.31.203.0/24      *[IS-IS/18] 00:08:53, metric 30, tag 2
                        > to 172.31.205.1 via so-0/0/2.0
172.31.255.9/32      *[IS-IS/18] 00:08:53, metric 10, tag 2
                        > to 172.31.205.1 via so-0/0/2.0
172.31.255.10/32     *[Direct/0] 00:09:09
                        > via lo0.0

inet.3: 1 destinations, 1 routes (1 active, 0 holddown, 0 hidden)
+ = Active Route, - = Last Active, * = Both
172.31.255.6/32      *[RSVP/7] 00:00:38, metric 30, metric2 0
                        > via so-0/0/0.0, label-switched-path LSP1

mpls.0: 2 destinations, 2 routes (2 active, 0 holddown, 0 hidden)
+ = Active Route, - = Last Active, * = Both
0                    *[MPLS/0] 00:02:06, metric 1
                         Receive
1                    *[MPLS/0] 00:02:06, metric 1
                         Receive
```

Interpreting the Output

When examining the route table, several aspects are worth noting. First, each table is listed separately in the output and is identified by its name, such as *inet.0*. Second, a listing of the total number of routes in the table appears. This listing is further divided into the total number of destinations, the number of active routes, and the number of hidden routes. The concept of active routes is quite important within the JUNOS software. Only active routes get exported to the forwarding table on the Packet Forwarding Engine (PFE). Only active routes are eligible to be exported by routing protocols to neighboring routers. Only active routes can be evaluated by routing policies. The opposite of an active route is a *hidden route*. A route can be hidden within *inet.0* for a number of reasons including route filtering, an unusable next-hop value, or BGP damping.

Last, each route will typically be marked with both an asterisk (*) and a pointer (>). The pointer is used to designate the next-hop router for the route. If multiple equal cost paths exist for a single prefix, one of the paths gets randomly chosen as the next-hop for that route. This one next-hop value gets installed into the forwarding table on the PFE. As an example, the *Bristol* router has two equal cost paths via IS-IS for the Lo0 address of *Atlanta*:

```
user@Bristol> show route 172.31.255.10
inet.0: 27 destinations, 27 routes (27 active, 0 holddown, 0 hidden)
```

```
+ = Active Route, - = Last Active, * = Both
172.31.255.10/32   *[IS-IS/18] 00:04:46, metric 30, tag 2
                       to 172.31.200.2 via so-0/0/0.0
                     > to 172.31.203.2 via so-0/0/2.0
```

The default selection of the single next-hop value can be altered such that multiple paths for a single route are installed in the forwarding table. Information on modifying this default will be discussed in the "Load Balancing" section later in this chapter.

The asterisk is used to designate the active route for any individual prefix. When a prefix is learned from multiple sources, only one of the sources is chosen as the best. It is the next-hop for this route that gets included in the forwarding table. The decision about which of the route sources is the best is the topic of the next section.

Protocols and Preferences

Every route in the routing table on a Juniper Networks router is placed there by a *protocol*. This term encompasses more than just routing protocols and generally means *a source of information*. For example, a static route is not generated from a dynamic routing protocol, but the routing table lists these routes as protocol *Static*. In short, the term means, *"Who placed the route into the table?"*

The following list details some of the protocols that place information into the routing table:

- Direct
- Local
- Static
- RSVP (Resource Reservation Protocol)
- LDP (Label Distribution Protocol)
- OSPF (Open Shortest Path First)
- IS-IS (Intermediate System to Intermediate System)
- RIP (Routing Information Protocol)
- PIM (Protocol Independent Multicast)
- Aggregate
- BGP (Border Gateway Protocol)

Associated with each protocol is a value known as the *preference*. The protocol preference is a number in the range of 0–255, inclusive, with lower values being preferred. Some of the protocol preference values within the JUNOS software are listed here:

- Direct = 0
- Local = 0
- Static = 5
- RSVP = 7
- LDP = 9
- OSPF Internal = 10
- IS-IS Level 1 Internal = 15
- IS-IS Level 2 Internal = 18
- RIP = 100
- PIM = 105
- Aggregate = 130
- OSPF External = 150
- IS-IS Level 1 External = 160
- IS-IS Level 2 External = 165
- BGP = 170

Using this guide reveals that the protocols with the best route preference value of 0 are Direct and Local. Both of these protocols represent directly connected networks, but there is an important distinction between them. A Local route is the IP address configured on the router interfaces. Any subnet information assigned to that interface is conveyed via a Direct route. As the name implies, Local routes are local to the router and only Direct routes can be exported from the routing table.

The output of a show route command on the *Daytona* router shows the distinction between these two protocols:

```
user@Daytona> show route
inet.0: 16 destinations, 16 routes (16 active, 0 holddown, 0 hidden)
+ = Active Route, - = Last Active, * = Both
172.31.203.0/24    *[Direct/0] 00:19:06
                    > via so-0/0/0.0
172.31.203.2/32    *[Local/0] 00:19:08
                     Local
172.31.204.0/24    *[Direct/0] 00:14:37
                    > via so-0/0/2.0
172.31.204.1/32    *[Local/0] 00:19:08
                     Local
```

Additional Route Tables

By default, the *inet.0* route table is used as the primary source of routing information for the router. All routing protocols use this table to store and exchange information. In addition, all locally configured routes are placed into *inet.0* by default. Additional route tables might be required when routing information needs to be kept separate on the router.

The reasons for keeping separate routing information are wide and varied and most are outside the scope of this chapter. One possibility might be for multicast routing information. The router might be participating in a Layer 3 VPN in which multiple VPN Routing and Forwarding (VRF) tables are needed. Another possibility includes having multiple routing instances for packet forwarding by policy, known as *Filter Based Forwarding* (FBF).

FBF allows network administrators to alter the "normal" forwarding actions of the router based on some set of criteria. For example, instead of routing all packets based solely on the destination address, the source of the user packet might also be examined. Different IP source addresses could cause different route tables to be examined prior to packet forwarding. These alternate tables often contain static default (0.0.0.0/0) routes.

Locally configured routes that can be placed into additional route tables include static routes, aggregate routes, generated routes, and martian routes. The configuration of these routes and the options associated with them are identical to those discussed previously in this chapter. The default action was to place these routes into *inet.0*. To populate other route tables with locally configured routes, include the `rib` keyword.

In this example, the *Charlotte* router has been configured with additional tables:

```
routing-options {
    rib fbf-north.inet.0 {
        static {
            route 0.0.0.0/0 next-hop 172.31.205.2
        }
    }
    rib fbf-south.inet.0 {
        static {
            route 0.0.0.0/0 next-hop 172.31.204.1
        }
    }
}
```

In certain situations, routing information from all protocols might be needed for both *inet.0* and an additional route table. To accomplish this, JUNOS software uses a concept known as a *rib-group*.

Rib-Groups

A rib-group is a way to have a routing protocol, in most cases, place information in multiple route tables. Within the JUNOS software configuration language, rib-groups must first be defined before they are applied. Each rib-group is named and told where to place and retrieve route information. An example of a rib-group definition is shown here:

```
routing-options {
    rib-groups {
        interface-rib {
            import-rib [ inet.0 inet.2 ];
        }
        multicast-rib {
            export-rib inet.2;
            import-rib inet.2;
        }
    }
}
```

The `export-rib` and `import-rib` statements tell the rib-group what to do with the route information. As these statements imply, some directionality is at work here. To properly interpret the commands, place yourself in the position of the route table. The `export-rib` command tells the router which tables to take information from. For any individual rib-group, only one table can be specified in the `export-rib` statement. Conversely, the `import-rib` command tells the router which tables to place information into. Unlike its counterpart, the `import-rib` statement can specify multiple route tables.

Once defined, the rib-groups can then be associated with a particular routing protocol. In the case of the example above, the rib-group multicast-rib can be assigned to a multicast protocol such as PIM. This will allow PIM to use the *inet.2* routing table for its RPF check.

Thus far, routes in the network will not be included in *inet.2* since PIM does not actually send or receive routing information. The routes are currently in the *inet.0* table via an IGP such as IS-IS. The behavior of IS-IS needs to be modified so that its routes are placed into both *inet.0* and *inet.2*. Here, a rib-group called *isis-rib* is created and applied to the IS-IS configuration:

```
routing-options {
    rib-groups {
        isis-rib {
            import-rib [ inet.0 inet.2 ];
        }
    }
}
```

```
protocols {
    isis {
        rib-group isis-rib;
        interface all {
```

The final pieces of information needed in *inet.2* to replicate *inet.0* are the directly connected interface routes on the router. This is again accomplished through the use of a rib-group. The difference in this case is the application of the group. It will be applied within the *routing-options* configuration hierarchy within the *interface-routes* directory.

Currently a rib-group called *interface-rib* is defined. Its only specification is to place information in both *inet.0* and *inet.2* via the import-rib statement. Here, the rib-group is then applied to the *interface-routes*:

```
routing-options {
    interface-routes {
        rib-group inet interface-rib;
    }
    rib-groups {
        interface-rib {
            import-rib [ inet.0 inet.2 ];
        }
    }
}
```

Other Features

Thus far, only features specific to routes in the routing tables have been discussed. Other features in the JUNOS software are considered to be protocol-independent functions. Some of these include the router's Router ID (RID), Autonomous System (AS) number, BGP AS Confederation information, and load balancing.

Router ID

A Router ID (RID) is an IP address that identifies the router in the network when operating routing protocols such as OSPF and BGP. The JUNOS software default for the selection of a RID is to use the address configured on the Loopback 0 (Lo0) interface. If multiple IP addresses are configured on Lo0, the primary interface address is used. The primary interface address is defined as the lowest numerical IP address configured. If Lo0 does not contain any IP addresses, the first available IP address currently configured on the router becomes the RID.

In most environments, the default action of using the loopback address is sufficient. Some network administrators, however, may wish to ensure that a particular IP address becomes the RID. To accommodate such a situation, the JUNOS software allows for a RID to be configured for the router.

As an example, the administrators of the *Atlanta* router wish to make the Lo0 address of 172.31.255.10 the RID. Although this address would most likely be chosen by default as the RID, future IP addresses configured on Lo0 might alter this default. To ensure its use, the *Atlanta* router has been configured with the following:

```
routing-options
    router-id 172.31.255.10
```

Autonomous System Number

BGP is the routing protocol most often associated with an Autonomous System (AS) number. In a BGP environment, a router is configured to be within a single AS only. This AS information needs to be transmitted to every BGP peer with whom the local router wishes to communicate. The configuration specifics of BGP make it difficult to have a single location within [edit protocols bgp] to place the AS number. Therefore, this information is configured within the [edit routing-options] directory where BGP (and other protocols) can access the information. Within our example network, each router is communicating via BGP within AS 65001. Each router will have the following configuration:

```
routing-options
    autonomous-system 65001
```

Autonomous System Confederations

The requirements of Internal BGP communications cause the protocol to have an inherent scalability problem for large-scale AS networks. One possible solution to this issue is to use a BGP *confederation*. A confederation segments a large AS into smaller AS networks. Since this solution requires changes to the router's AS configuration, confederation information is also placed within the [edit routing-options] directory.

The sample network that we have been investigating throughout this chapter is quite small. If 500 routers were added to the network, a BGP confederation might be needed. If this situation occurred, AS 65001 could be split up into four smaller AS networks numbered 65400, 65401, 65402, and 65403. The *Darlington* router might be within the 65400 AS.

```
routing-options
    autonomous-system 65400
    confederation 65001 members [ 65400 65401 65402 65403 ]
```

Load Balancing

In the previous investigation of the routing tables, the topic of load balancing was briefly mentioned and bears a more detailed look. The load balancing of routing information in the JUNOS software is either accomplished in a per-prefix or a per-packet manner. Per-prefix load balancing interacts with BGP routes and how that information is handled within the routing tables. Per-packet load balancing interacts with all routing information as it is exported into the forwarding table on the router's PFE.

Forwarding Table

When *inet.0* receives multiple equal-cost paths for any single IP prefix, the default action is to choose one of the paths randomly and install it into the forwarding table. Examining the network map reveals that the *Bristol* router has two network paths to 172.31.255.10, the Lo0 address of *Atlanta*. The routing table shows

```
user@Bristol> show route 172.31.255.10
inet.0: 27 destinations, 27 routes (27 active, 0 holddown, 0 hidden)
+ = Active Route, - = Last Active, * = Both
172.31.255.10/32   *[IS-IS/18] 00:22:26, metric 30, tag 2
                      to 172.31.200.2 via so-0/0/0.0
                    > to 172.31.203.2 via so-0/0/2.0
user@Bristol> show route forwarding-table destination 172.31.255.10
Routing table:: inet
Internet:
Destination          Type RtRef Nexthop        Type Index NhRef Netif
172.31.255.10/32     user    0 172.31.203.0    ucst    61     6 so-0/0/2.0
```

The path through 172.31.203.2 is marked with a pointer ">." It is this next-hop that is placed in the forwarding table.

To use all the available next-hops and network paths to a specific destination, a policy can be applied to the forwarding table. This policy performs a load balancing action on all routes in *inet.0* or a subset of routes. A policy named *load-balance* has been configured and is applied on *Bristol*:

```
routing-options {
    forwarding-table {
        export load-balance;
user@Bristol> show route forwarding-table destination 172.31.255.10
Routing table:: inet
Internet:
Destination          Type RtRef Nexthop        Type Index NhRef Netif
172.31.255.10/32     user    0                 ulst    18     1
                                172.31.200.0    ucst    59     6 so-0/0/0.0
                                172.31.203.0    ucst    61     6 so-0/0/2.0
```

After the application of the policy, the forwarding table on Bristol contains multiple next-hop values for 172.31.255.10.

Within the JUNOS software, the actual form of the load balancing action will be based on the type of Internet Processor in the router. With early M40s and M20s with the Internet Processor I, the load balancing is a per-packet function with each separate IP packet headed towards a destination sent down a different path.

This behavior changes with the second-generation (and much more common) Internet Processor II, where load balancing is flow-based and each individual micro-flow follows a different path that remains consistent for packets within that flow.

Packets that share the IP Layer 3 characteristics of source IP address, destination IP address, and incoming interface on the router are considered to belong to an individual micro-flow. Additionally, the IP Layer 4 characteristics of source port, destination port, and protocol can be used.

These same per-packet load balancing actions also apply to network paths formed by MPLS protocols. These paths are defined as *label switched paths* (LSPs) and are stored in the *inet.3* routing table.

In the following example, *Bristol* has two LSPs to 172.31.255.9:

```
user@Atlanta> show route table inet.3
inet.3: 1 destinations, 1 routes (1 active, 0 holddown, 0 hidden)
+ = Active Route, - = Last Active, * = Both
172.31.255.6/32    *[RSVP/7] 00:01:17, metric 30, metric2 0
                      via so-0/0/2.0, label-switched-path LSP1
                    > via so-0/0/0.0, label-switched-path LSP2
```

As before, only one of the paths is marked with a pointer (>) and is installed into the forwarding table. To place the next-hops for all the LSPs into the forwarding table, a load balancing policy can be applied as shown.

Border Gateway Protocol

The second load-balancing behavior in the JUNOS software is *per-prefix balancing*. This type of load balancing is exclusively for BGP routes. Per-prefix load balancing applies when multiple equal cost paths exist to the BGP next-hop IP address. The total number of routes that share that same next-hop are distributed across the available paths. In this fashion, an AS has BGP transit traffic spread evenly across the network.

Autonomous System 65001 is supporting transit BGP traffic between *Bristol* and *Atlanta*. These two routers are IBGP peers and are exchanging routes with the BGP next-hop set to 172.31.255.10. Prior to *Bristol* placing any received BGP routes into *inet.0*, it must first ensure that the BGP next-hop attribute is reachable. The current routing table on *Bristol* shows this:

```
user@Atlanta> show route 172.31.255.6
inet.0: 20 destinations, 20 routes (20 active, 0 holddown, 0 hidden)
+ = Active Route, - = Last Active, * = Both
```

```
172.31.255.6/32    *[IS-IS/18] 00:01:16, metric 30, tag 2
                   > to 172.31.205.1 via so-0/0/2.0
                     to 172.31.202.1 via so-0/0/0.0
```

Although only one of ISIS paths is placed in the forwarding table, BGP is able to recognize that, in fact, two possible paths exist to 172.31.255.10. *Bristol* will then evenly distribute the BGP routes across the two paths.

As with the ISIS route, each of the individual BGP routes has a single next-hop placed into *inet.0*. To have multiple next-hop values installed in the forwarding table for a single BGP prefix, a load-balancing policy should be applied to the forwarding table.

The Complete Reference

Chapter 7

Routing Policy

by Avram G. Dorfman

Once you correctly configure routers with addressing plans and protocols, the routers step up to the task of providing data connectivity pretty much on their own. They make decisions on which paths to take to get traffic from its various sources to its different destinations; they make decisions on which sources and destinations to honor versus deny. However, they will take no notice of any wishes or preferences you may have when making these decisions.

When you develop a network architecture, you often want to influence the decisions the routers make for business, performance or security reasons. In many cases, the business reasons are fundamental to the foundation of your company; sending traffic one way may *cost* you money, while sending it another way may *make* you money. For these reasons you to need to develop a *routing policy*. A routing policy starts out as a figment of your imagination—a group of interrelated wishes that your network will make a certain set of decisions that may be very different from the decisions it would make on its own.

A routing policy is not real unless your network obeys it. Unless you have an RJ-45 jack in your brain, your imagination is not going to do any good; you have to somehow make it real—you have to *implement* it. The policy framework is the JUNOS software's mechanism that enables you to manipulate and override the router's default decision-making process. It is how you realize your routing policy. This chapter discusses the basic concepts of defining routing policy and shows you how to use Juniper Networks' policy framework to implement your routing policy.

The JUNOS software policy framework makes sense at a basic level. This chapter starts out drawing the analogy between the word *policy* and the JUNOS software concept of policy. It then gives you an overview of what you can do with the policy framework. Next is the real nuts, bolts, and gears of exactly how it works. Finally, the chapter covers some techniques for designing and troubleshooting your policy. By this point, you should understand the components of the policy framework, and how they interact.

Basic Routing Policy

The concept of routing policy is not specific to Juniper Networks routers. Routing policy has been around since long before Juniper Networks. In fact, making routing policy more powerful and easier to operate is fundamental to the IP focus for which Juniper was founded.

This section breaks down the basic concepts behind general routing policy. The concepts covered here are what it means to define policies and specify parameters, apply a policy, and what it means for the router to evaluate a policy.

An Example Policy Scenario

To help you relate them to real world needs, the numerous policy examples throughout this chapter are based on a network scenario. Here is that scenario, followed by a simple example of a routing policy to govern the scenario. Keep this in mind as you come across the examples in the following sections.

Suppose you are the IP architect responsible for all Internet access to a secret military installation called the Hexagon. You control redundant connections to two different Internet service providers: Tenth Millennium (Ten-M), and Internet Gas & Electric (IG&E).

As with many large installations, your current network is the result of an evolutionary process. Several customers reside within this installation. They have their own networks (and their own agendas). Although numerous customers access your system and address spaces, for simplicity, the examples here will focus on just three customers (the Chair Force, the Tub Club, and the Army) and two address ranges. You administer the 205.134/16 supernet, and the Tub Club owns its own supernet, 185.140/16.

Figure 7-1 shows a simplified depiction of your core network, the connections to your two providers, and connections to two of your customers. Tub Club has its own address space, and Chair Force is using addresses assigned by you.

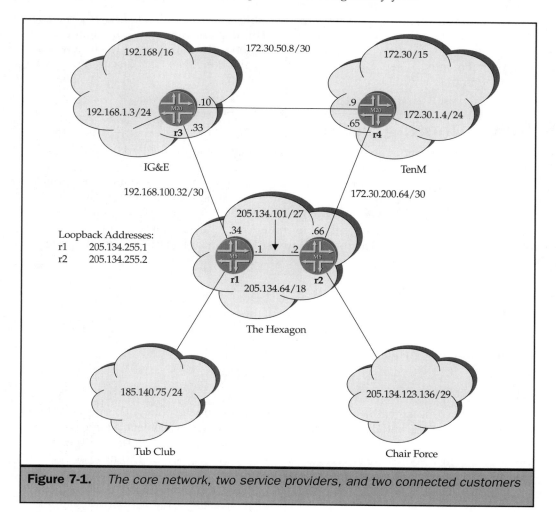

Figure 7-1. *The core network, two service providers, and two connected customers*

Creating a Routing Policy

Your customers have sensitive unclassified data that you must not let out of your network. You also have connections to a global military network that is a little out of date in its network architecture, the result being that it (unintentionally) announces your routes to the Internet as originating from itself. This creates the possibility of your internal data traversing the public Internet. Normally, because the Internet is not the best path, it would not be used. However, in certain failure scenarios, if your network becomes split, the Internet could be the only available path. Your Hexagon customers would rather lose service than risk having their secrets exposed to the world. As a result, you need to make sure that neither of your service providers ever advertise your routes to you. You could call this policy "Ignore my routes."

Thus, your first routing policy is "Ignore routes starting with 205.134, or 185.140, if they are learned from either IG&E or Ten-M." This demonstrates how a thought process can result in a need for a routing policy in your network. At this point, your new policy is not implemented—it's "a figment of your imagination." Next is a discussion of what you do to implement it.

Basic Routing Policy

To get a network to enforce a policy, you need to understand the network tools that are available to allow you to do so.

Nearly every router has some sort of mechanism for implementing routing policy. These concepts are valid with respect to all of them. If you are familiar with other policy mechanisms, and have never thought about some of these concepts, it is probably because those mechanisms are inflexible enough that they do not warrant discussion of some of these concepts. The following five major concepts describe routing policy:

- **Definition**   Define the policy.
- **Parameters**   Set criteria for the policy.
- **Application**   Specify where and how the router uses your policy.
- **Results**   The decision the policy makes.
- **Evaluation**   How the router interprets the results.

Definition

The first task in implementing a routing policy is to define the policy. This involves two steps: defining criteria and defining effect. With many routes available in a large network, a given policy is usually relevant for only a subset of them. The criteria you specify establishes which routes are affected by the policy. The "Ignore my routes" policy that you created affects only routes for your own prefixes, and furthermore, if affects only announcements of those routes that come from your providers. Such a policy specifies the events that occur to the routes that meet the policy's criteria. The effect of "Ignore my routes" is to ensure that you never use those routes to direct traffic in your network.

You must tell the router about a policy you've created before the router can enforce it, by writing something like this:

```
Inbound Internet Policy:

    for any routes which
        have a destination of 205.134.xx.yy
            or of 180.145.xx.yy
        and come from IG&E
            or Ten-M
    do the following:
            ignore them
```

This simple set of statements is the *policy definition*.

Note   *You need to think carefully about how you define policy. Routers do exactly what you tell them to do, even if it is not what you meant.*

Parameters

Most criteria require *parameters*, which are the bounds within which the route's attribute must fall. For example, you may specify criteria for a route's next-hop. If so, the parameters for that criteria are a list of acceptable next-hop IP addresses. Criteria can be relatively simple or lengthy and complex, such as some of the parameters required by certain policy match criteria. In some cases, several different policies may need to specify some identical parameters. You can define some parameters outside the policy and name them. Then policies can refer to those parameters by name—these are called *named parameters*. Named parameter names can be reused in multiple policies, even though you defined the parameters only once.

In our network example, defining what constitutes "from IG&E" and "from Ten-M" independent of the policy itself is useful, because these are the types of parameter concepts that you are likely to need to reuse, and they could be based on criteria that might change, such as the IP address of a provider's router.

Application

Application refers to where and how you apply your policies. You can apply policy to OSPF, so it will announce routes that come from other protocols. You can apply it to BGP and other protocols. There are other places, which are not protocols, where you can apply policy as well, such as to an aggregate route, to the forwarding table, or in another policy. These are all examples of *where* you apply policy; this is the application *context*.

How you apply policies is an example of a concept that is a nonissue with less flexible policy mechanisms. Many other vendors do not give you choices of how to apply policies. JUNOS software does; you can apply just a single policy (for example, My_Routes); you can apply a list of policies (for example, [My_Routes Your_Routes]; and you can apply policies using expressions (for example, (My_routes | | Your_Routes)). This is the application *method*. When you apply a policy inside another policy, it is called a policy *subroutine*; this is really both an application method and context.

Most of these tools can be combined. Doing so can involve as little or as much complexity as you want (or need). This means that there can be more than one context and method in effect at a time. A policy can be within another policy—and that policy may be applied to a specific protocol, such as BGP. Thus, there are two contexts: the fact that the policy is in another policy, and the fact that the pair are working on the BGP protocol. You can also have multiple methods because you can put an expression in a chain (for example, [(My_Routes | | Your_Routes) Other_Routes]. Although some other vendor implementations may only give one way to use policy, the concept is still generic.

This is all important because context and method have a significant effect on how the router will evaluate your policies—how it will process them, and what it will do with the results.

Results

Every policy produces a result for every route. You can think of the policy as a function $f(x)$ and a route as x. You determine how $f(x)$ behaves for all possible values of x. If you remember your algebra, you might recognize a function like this: $f(x) = 2x$. If x is 2, then $f(x)$ is 4. If x is -6, then $f(x)$ is -12. With a policy, the input is a route, and the output is an opinion on the route. The typical possible results for most routers are either an affirmative, such as *yes* or a negative, such as *no*. JUNOS software also has a neutral or *don't care* result. So, for policy MyPolicy and route x, MyPolicy(x) is a function with these kinds of results:

If x = RIP route to 10/8 via 1.1.1.1, metric 10, MyPolicy(x) = *yes*.
If x = BGP route to 172.16/16 via 2.2.2.2, local preference 100, MyPolicy(x) = *no*.
If x = OSPF route to 192.168/16 via 3.3.3.3, cost 25, MyPolicy(x) = *don't care*.

The JUNOS cli uses the term *accept, reject,* and *next policy,* to mean *yes, no,* and *don't care,* respectively.

Don't care? That's right. Many policies will turn out not to have anything to say about a given route. This might seem unusual seeing as the general purpose of all of this is to either announce or learn a route, or avoid doing so. How can there be any middle ground? In fact, a policy can say *yes* or *no* for routes coming from IG&E or Ten-M, but *don't care* for routes that are not from either provider. It is this ability that enables the policy framework to be so flexible. The policy framework has its own default policies in place to catch any routes that your policies *don't care* about (see the

"Policy Framework Mechanics" section for details). As you continue reading, you will see how these policy framework characteristics are not ambiguous and work together to give you incredible power.

Policies can modify various attributes of routes while making decisions on those routes. This happens independently from the policy's result. For example, suppose that one of your providers is the target of a newly discovered Denial of Service (DoS) attack. But because the attack is not impacting the entire network, you decide not to shut off the network completely (and lose redundancy). While the providers are adapting their systems to this new vulnerability, you might want to prefer another provider that is not being impacted by the DoS attack. You could add a policy to the affected provider that changes the metrics on the routes learned from it to be less preferable. In such a case, you aren't changing the policy's decision on these routes, but your policy now has *side effects* that can affect network routing.

Evaluation

With any routing policy mechanism, your understanding of how the OS will interpret your instructions is critical. In many cases, interpretation may be obvious. However, "interesting" situations can arise when you provide seemingly conflicting or incomplete instructions. It is quite normal to want the router to do one thing in one case and a different thing in a different but similar case. Likewise, you do not want to have to specify every single possibility. It would be best if the OS had some reasonable defaults in place.

JUNOS software is unique in that you have a choice of ways that it can interpret your policies. The policy framework interprets the results of a policy differently, depending on the context and method with which you applied it. Policy *chains* interpret the results differently from policy *expressions*. Policy *subroutines* use a policy's results in a different way than a protocol uses them. Such a framework gives you more power to write your policies in alternative ways and to tailor them to solve specific problems within your network.

The following sections discuss the syntax of these policy constructs.

The JUNOS Software Policy Framework

The JUNOS software policy framework is a toolbox. It is equipped with a policy language for you to use in defining your policies, numerous match criteria and effects for you to specify, evaluation methods from which you can choose when telling a Juniper Networks router to use your policies, and a carefully designed default policy architecture within which all of your policies will operate. This section provides an overview of the *components* of the policy framework. It shows you how these components fit together. Specifics of how each component behaves is covered later in the "Policy Framework Mechanics" section.

Policy Components

The fundamental component of the policy framework is the policy. A policy is a series of instructions telling the software what action to perform and on which routes. You define policies with the *policy-statement* configuration directive, which is found at the *[edit policy-options]* level.

Here are the beginnings of a policy:

```
[edit]
user@r1# show policy-options
policy-statement BGP_Import {
    term From_IGnE {
        from neighbor 192.168.101.33;
        then accept;
    }
    term From_Ten-M {
        from neighbor 192.168.205.129;
        then accept;
    }
}

[edit]
user@r1#
```

This policy is called "BGP_Import." If you apply this policy to routes being received by your router's BGP process, it will cause all routes from either of the neighbor IP addresses 192.168.101.33 or 192.168.205.129 to be installed in your routing table. This policy is actually unnecessary, however, as you will soon see that the default is to accept all BGP routes from all BGP neighbors, but it suffices to show you the components of policy.

Although the router might not use all of the routes learned, it will learn them all. For more on selection of the active route for a destination, see Chapter 6.

Terms

Policies contain a series of one or more *term* statements, or *terms* for short. Terms are the basic building blocks of policy definition. Although policies can include varying numbers and types of components, those components are always grouped into terms. Thus, syntactically, the only thing policies can contain is terms, and the terms contain all of the policy's relevant elements.

Terms usually have names, which follow the same rules used by policy names. The policy shown in the previous section contains two terms, called From_IGnE and From_Ten-M. JUNOS software does not limit the number of terms a policy can contain.

It is possible for a term to have no name, however, and every policy can have one such term—which is always the last term in a policy. Including a term that is guaranteed to be last can have several benefits; for example, it can enable you to define your own default behavior for a policy. However, some caveats with respect to editing the policy are discussed in detail in the "Policy Framework Mechanics" section.

Terms can have two types of components, called *match conditions* and *actions*.

Match Conditions   Initially, terms affect all routes that pass through them, but a term can contain criteria that limit which routes it will affect. These criteria are called *match conditions*. Many match conditions are associated with the source of routing information. For example, a route can be learned from the BGP, or it can be learned from a neighbor with a specific IP address. A few match conditions relate to where the router will announce the routing information. Some match conditions have nothing to do with a route's source or where it will be sent, such as whether it matches specific IP prefix or has various other attributes.

To match routes based on their source, you use a *from* clause. To match on where a route will be sent, you use a *to* clause. To match on other characteristics of a route, you can put the characteristics in either the *from* or the *to* clause. The "Policy Framework Mechanics" section later in this chapter covers the differences between *to* and *from* clauses. When in doubt, though, use a *from* clause.

Both types of clauses are optional. If you omit both of them, you simply are not limiting the routes your term will affect. Thus, all routes will match and will be processed by the *then* clause. The following term, excerpted from the example in the previous section, contains a *from* clause:

```
term From_Ten-M {
    from neighbor 192.168.205.129;
    then accept;
}
```

This *from* clause matches a route if the route announcement packets containing it came from the specified neighbor. In the case of BGP, matching routes come in announcement packets with a source address of 192.168.205.129.

Actions   Match conditions identify routes, but they do not modify the routes. You specify actions with a *then* clause. All of the terms you have seen so far have contained *then* clauses.

| Note | *One match condition does affect a route indirectly. The policy match condition refers to another policy, which could do something to the route. This is covered in the "Policy Framework Mechanics" section later in the chapter.* |

You can specify many different actions in a *then* clause. So far, you have seen *accept* and *reject*. In some examples, these actions have controlled whether routes would be installed in the routing table. In others, they have controlled whether routes would be announced to a protocol. Although these results appear similar, installing a route and announcing it are not the same thing.

When a route passes through a policy, the policy can either accept it, reject it, or do neither. The impact of the policy's result is entirely up to the function of the router that applied the policy. Protocols have an *import* function that uses policies to decide whether to install routes in the routing table. They also have an *export* function that uses policies to decide whether to announce routes. Aggregate routes use policies to decide whether or not a given route should activate the route. The accepting, rejecting, or ignoring of a route by a policy is a generic result that is meant to be used in any number of ways, many of which may have not even been conceived yet.

You can specify many different actions in addition to accept or reject, which along with two other actions, *next term* and *next policy*, are called *flow control* actions—they affect how the route flows through the policy. The rest of the actions cause the policy to have some sort of side effect, such as changing the route's attributes.

Many actions can change a route's attributes. Some of these actions can change values that affect how preferable the route is, thereby influencing how the router chooses between that route and other routes to the same destination. Other actions add, change, or remove nonmetric attributes such as community strings or autonomous system paths. Community strings are marks that you can add to a route so that another policy or another router notices them and behaves according to some sort of instruction (which is generally up to the network administrators to define and implement, although some are standard). Another action logs the flow control actions for routes that satisfy the term's match conditions.

You specify actions in a term's *then* clause. The software applies all actions in the *then* clause to any routes that match all of the conditions in the associated *from* and *to* clauses.

A term can involve several actions. Here is an example term used to change a route's metric information:

```
user@r1# set term From_IGnE then local-preference add 50

[edit policy-options policy-statement BGP_Import]
user@r1# show
term From_IGnE {
    from neighbor 192.168.101.33;
    then {
        local-preference add 50;
        accept;
    }
}
```

```
}
term From_Ten-M {
    from neighbor 192.168.205.129;
    then accept;
}
```

The router now prefers routes coming from IG&E. For more information on BGP route selection and the local-preference attribute, see Chapter 12.

Setting Parameters

All match conditions, and nearly all actions, require parameters. In the example shown in the previous section, the *neighbor* match condition requires a neighbor's IP address as a parameter. The *local-preference add* action requires an integer to add to the existing local preference.

Some match conditions and actions require complex parameters. In many cases, you define these parameters outside the policy. This makes the policy easier to read and allows you to define the parameters only once, yet reuse them many times.

One example of a complex parameter is the *prefix list*, which is a list of explicit destinations in network/mask notation. Recall our "Ignore my routes" policy, which prevents your router from learning any of your networks from your service providers. You can use a prefix list to identify your networks. Prefix lists are defined at the *[edit policy-options]* level:

```
[edit policy-options]
user@r1# set prefix-list My_Nets 205.134.0.0/16
user@r1# set prefix-list My_Nets 185.180.0.0/16
user@r1# show
prefix-list My_Nets {
    205.134.0.0/16;
    185.180.0.0/16;
}
```

You can now use this prefix list in a policy:

```
[edit policy-options]
user@r1# edit policy-statement BGP_Import

[edit policy-options policy-statement BGP_Import]
user@r1# set term Block_Mine from prefix-list My_Nets
user@r1# set term Block_Mine then reject
```

```
user@r1#
user@r1# show

term Block_Mine {
    from prefix-list My_Nets;
    then reject;
}
```

You can use this policy in conjunction with the other policies to achieve the desired result. Once you have defined your policies, you must apply them.

Applying Policies

It's important that you pay attention to the context in which you apply policies—including where you apply them and how you apply them. These are the specific methods and contexts in which you can apply policies:

- Protocol and direction (methods and contexts)
- Application method (context)
- Subroutine (method)

A policy's effect and the manner in which it is evaluated can differ based on all the contexts and methods that are active when the policy is being evaluated.

Protocol and Direction

If a policy is being evaluated, it is because it has been applied to a protocol or a *pseudo-protocol*. All routing information comes from the various routing protocols you have enabled in your network or from routes configured on the router, such as the networks configured on directly connected interfaces or static routes. These are sometimes called pseudo-protocols, because while they are a valid source of routing information, they do not involve interaction between multiple entities (and thus no actual protocol is required).

When you build a policy, it has no effect until you apply it. The protocols are like different channels feeding information into and removing information from the routing table. The combination of a protocol and a direction is part of the context that determines how the policy behaves. So when you apply policies to the protocols, the result is a modification of the behavior of that channel. This is depicted in Figure 7-2.

When you apply a policy to a protocol, you also specify whether it is affecting information coming into the routing table or information being sent out from the routing table. Juniper Networks policy takes place from the perspective of the routing table. As you read and write policy configuration statements, think of them from the perspective of the routing table. Receiving routing information from a protocol is called *importing*. Announcing information from the routing table into a protocol is called *exporting*. The software does not permit you to announce information into a protocol

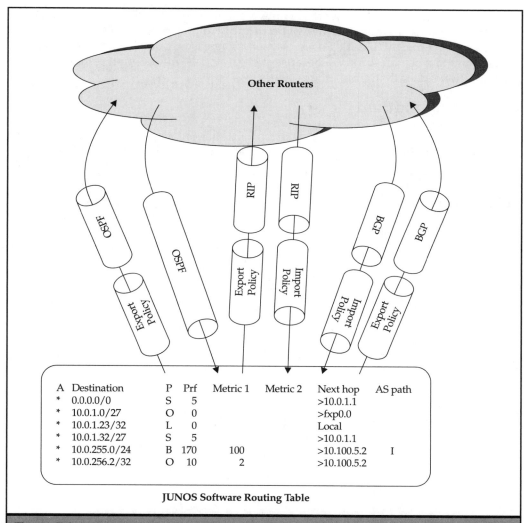

Figure 7-2.   *Protocols feed routes through policies into the routing table, and the routing table feeds routes through policies back into the protocols.*

from anywhere else but the routing table. So before you can export it, you must first somehow get the information into the routing table.

Note   *When using multiple routing tables, as with IP-based virtual private networks (VPNs), each routing table is its own policy world. Multiple routing protocols contributing to a single routing table is a single policy world.*

Some protocols would not work if you were to modify what they learn. In those cases, JUNOS software does not allow you to apply import policies to them (for more detail, see the "Protocol Specific Policy" section). There is no point in exporting routing information to a pseudo-protocol because such protocols' information comes from configuration rather than from other routers.

Application Method

You can apply policies in two ways:

- **Policy chain**   A list of policies that will be evaluated in order from left to right.
- **Policy expression**   A logical formula that compares two policies.

Policy Chains   Perhaps you built policies to identify each of your customers' networks. They might look like this:

```
[edit policy-options]
user@r1# show

policy-statement Army
    term Match_Army {
        from route-filter 185.140.0.0/17 orlonger;
        then accept;
    }
}
policy-statement Tub_Club
    term Match_Tub_Club {
        from route-filter 185.140.128.0/17 orlonger;
        then accept;
    }
}
policy-statement Chair_Force
    term Match_Chair_Force {
        from route-filter 205.134.0.0/16 orlonger;
        then accept;
    }
}
```

You can apply these policies to BGP as an export policy chain. It is called a *policy chain* because JUNOS software "chains" the multiple policies together into a single policy. Each route goes into the first policy, and if that policy does not accept or reject it, the route goes into the next one, and so on.

In JUNOS software policy language, a policy chain looks like this:

```
user@r1# set protocols bgp export [Chair_Force Tub_Club Army]
user@r1# show protocols
bgp {
    export [Chair_Force Tub_Club Army];
}
```

The brackets can be omitted with only one policy. If you apply just one policy, and then later apply more policies, JUNOS software turns the application into a chain for you, chaining the later policies after the first one:

```
[edit protocols]
user@r1# set bgp export Chair_Force
user@r1# show protocols

bgp {
    export Chair_Force;
}

user@r1# set bgp export Tub_Club
user@r1# set bgp export Army
user@r1# show

bgp {
    export [Chair_Force Tub_Club Army];
}
```

Expressions   A policy expression uses the rules of classical logic, wherein a logical operator considers two truth values and returns a new truth value. Take the *and* operator for example: The expression "a and b" is true if both *a* and *b* are true, and false otherwise. Likewise, the policy expression equivalent to "PolicyA and PolicyB" would accept a route if both PolicyA and PolicyB would accept it, and it would reject the route otherwise.

Imagine that you want to announce all Chair Force OSPF routes to IG&E, but you want to announce only aggregated Chair Force routes to Ten-M. You can do this by combining your Chair_Force policy with a policy to identify OSPF routes in one case and aggregate routes in the other:

```
policy-statement Chair_Force
    term Match_Chair_Force {
        from route-filter 205.134.0.0/16 orlonger;
        then accept;
    }
```

```
    }
policy-statement OSPF {
    term Match_OSPF {
        from protocol ospf;
        then accept;
    }
}
policy-statement Aggregate {
    term Match_Aggregate {
        from protocol aggregate;
        then accept;
    }
}
```

JUNOS software lets you apply different import or export policies to different BGP neighbors. In this way, you can accomplish the desired result by exporting to IG&E routes that satisfy both the Chair_Force policy and the OSPF policy. Likewise, for Ten-M, you want to export routes that satisfy Chair_Force and Aggregate.

Policy expressions treat "accept" as true, and "reject" as false. So the expression "Chair_Force or Tub_Club," in theory, runs a route through both policies. If either returns *accept*, the expression's result is *accept*. If they both return *reject*, the expression's result is *reject*. In reality, the expression stops as soon as it knows the result, so if Chair_Force returns *accept* for a route, the expression stops and immediately returns *accept* for that route.

You would then combine the Chair_Force policy with the Match_Aggregate policy like this:

```
protocols {
    bgp {
        export (Match_Aggregate && Chair_Force)
    }
}
```

This is a simple *export* statement containing an expression. This expression uses only the *&&* ("and") operator.

Subroutines

In addition to applying policies directly to protocols, you can apply policies within other policies as additional match conditions. This effectively turns a policy into a subroutine or function call:

```
policy_options {
    policy_statement to_peers {
        term match_peers {
            from policy [ AS_548 AS_686 AS_745 ];
            then accept;
        }
        term otherwise {
            then reject;
        }
    }
}
```

Evaluation

As discussed, multiple contexts can be in effect at once. You will soon see that you can apply a policy in a policy expression that is a subroutine in a BGP import policy. This policy is simultaneously in subroutine context, expression context, and BGP import context.

Policies can be applied in three ways: serially, logically, or as subroutines. How policies are evaluated is determined by how they are applied. Policy chains are evaluated serially, one after the other until the process is complete (until the route is accepted or rejected). Policy expressions are evaluated logically, until a complete result is certain (what it means to be certain for a policy expression is discussed in the "Mechanics" section).

Single policies are not really a separate case, because default policies are always in place. When you apply a single policy, the policy framework chains it in front of a default policy and the chain is evaluated serially.

Policy chains result in the immediate acceptance or rejection of a route at the instant specified. Conversely, expressions use logical (Boolean) evaluation. Logical evaluation treats policies as having values of true or false. They contribute to the final acceptance or rejection of a route, but an individual policy does not exclusively control it.

Policy Framework Mechanics

Now we'll discuss the nuts and bolts of how the policy framework works. It will show you how the different syntactical constructs are evaluated and where and how results differ depending on context. Although this is primarily a discussion of what policies do with routes, you first need to know what routes will be seen by a policy. This is determined by where you apply your policy. An export policy will process all active routes in the routing table that are not marked "no-readvertise." Local routes (a router's own interface addresses) are marked this way by default, and other routes can be configured in this way. The protocol code for the protocol doing the exporting, not the policy framework code, determines which routes to process via a policy. Typically, a protocol has its own rules governing what to advertise. Thus, the protocol's code will skip any active routes that the protocol requires the router not advertise, and the export policy will never see them. For example, a BGP router is normally required not to announce routes from one internal peer to another. Similarly, OSPF will not export OSPF routes back into the same OSPF domain from which they came.

An import policy will process all routes that the router learns via the importing protocol. In some cases, you can place the policy at more specific levels of a protocol, such as at a specific neighbor's or group's configuration level. In this case, the policy sees only routes learned through the relevant subset of the router's neighbors using that protocol. As with exporting, the protocol code has rules to consider regarding which routes it should be willing to receive. If the router hears a route that the protocol requires it to ignore, the code will not bother sending that route through the import policy.

When you configure an aggregate (or generate) route, you can apply a policy to dictate which routes will activate the aggregate. These policies will see only routes that are more specific examples of the aggregate. For example, if you create an aggregate 205.134/16, you can write a policy so that only 205.134.123.144/29 will activate it. However, if you try to write a policy so that only 1.1.1/24 will activate the aggregate, the policy will never be activated; the policy will never see 1.1.1/24 because it is not a subset of the aggregate. Aggregate policies do not have the same directions associated with them as import or export policies; they have only one direction, which is essentially that routes contribute "to the aggregate."

Note	*Aggregate and generated routes are single prefixes, also called* supernets, *that encompass a contiguous range of subnets. In JUNOS software, you configure these explicitly and can export them into a protocol, as though they came from another protocol. Typically you do this in conjunction with a policy somewhere that blocks the announcement of the more specific subnets. Together, these tasks help you decrease the size of the Internet's routing tables without causing gaps in connectivity.*

The forwarding table policy will see all active routes in the routing table. Forwarding table polices allow you to modify how the router uses routes to forward traffic. You apply these types of policies between the routing engine and the forwarding engine. These policies have only one direction associated with them, which is "to the forwarding table." (For more information on the functions of the routing and forwarding engines, see Chapter 1.)

Flow Control Actions

When a policy evaluates a route, the result is a *flow control action*. A policy can result in four flow control actions:

- *accept*
- *reject*
- *next term*
- *next policy*

All other actions produce side effects and do not directly contribute to the evaluation of a route. Of course, side effects can change a route's attributes and can therefore have an indirect effect by affecting how future terms evaluate the route.

When you apply policies, you do so using policy chains. What happens to a route as it is evaluated by a policy chain is determined by which of the flow control actions the policies in the chain specify for the route.

> *The* next *action has two versions,* next term *and* next policy. *These both equate to* next policy *if they are a policy's result for a route. The distinction between them is relevant during the evaluation inside a policy. This is discussed in the upcoming "Terms" section.*

Default Policies

Each routing protocol has a default import policy and a default export policy, which are in place before you apply policies. All protocols share the same default import policy to accept all routes.

Following are descriptions of the default import and export policies for each protocol:

Protocol	Import	Export
BGP	accept all	accept BGP reject others
OSPF	n/a	reject all
IS-IS	n/a	reject all
RIP	accept all	reject all
DVMRP	accept all	accept DVMRP as well as direct routes for interfaces running DVMRP
PIM-SM	accept all	accept all
PIM-DM	accept all	accept all

The concept of import policies does not make sense for link-state protocols, because such protocols do not actually announce routes; instead, they "flood" link-state information. Because link-state protocols rely on having identical information everywhere, they would not work properly if you interfered with that process. Thus, OSPF and IS-IS do not allow import policies, and therefore do not require a default import policy. They do allow export policies, but the link-state information that they normally share is not affected by these policies. Export policies are used only for the purpose of introducing routes from other protocols. So, in fact, the default export policy for link-state protocols is to reject everything.

The default export policy for RIP is also to reject everything. This may be surprising, because it means that simply enabling RIP on your interfaces does not result in protocol activity. See Chapter 8 for further discussion.

The following pseudo-protocols allow policies for certain tasks that are not exactly importing or exporting. Their default policies accept all routes they are fed.

Pseudo-Protocol	Default Policy
Aggregate (and generate)	accept all
Forwarding table	accept all
Test policy	accept all

Aggregate routes and forwarding table policies are discussed in Chapter 6. The test policy `cli` command is discussed in the "Troubleshooting Policy" section later in this chapter.

Keep in mind that protocols usually have their own rules about what is acceptable to announce in various conditions. If a protocol isn't allowed to announce a route in a certain case, the protocol will not send that route through the policy framework in the first place; it will not matter what policies you establish.

Policy Chains

The policy framework evaluates routes using an import policy chain and an export policy chain for each running protocol. Routes flow from the routing protocol, through an import policy chain, and into the routing table. Then they flow from the routing table, through an export policy chain, to the protocols. Each route goes through one "link" of the chain at a time, until the policy chain determines a final route—either the policy chain accepts or rejects the route. Figure 7-3 shows a sample routing table and a sample policy chain. The routing table has four routes. The policy chain has two policies, one of which is the protocol's default export policy.

In the figure, the entire routing table is input into the policy chain, one route at a time. The top of the figure shows the routes before evaluation. Each route goes through the chain. If the first policy accepts (or rejects) it, the route comes out of the policy and skips the remaining policies in the chain. If the first policy in the chain does not express an opinion on the route, the route flows on to the remaining policies. The bottom of the figure shows what occurs after evaluation. If a route flows through all the policies in the chain and none of them express an opinion, it then flows onto the default policy. Every protocol has default import and export policies that it implicitly attaches to the end of any policy chains it encounters, based on whether they are applied as import or export chains.

You do not have to specify a policy chain to configure a protocol. Each protocol's default policies will decide whether to accept or reject any route that has not been

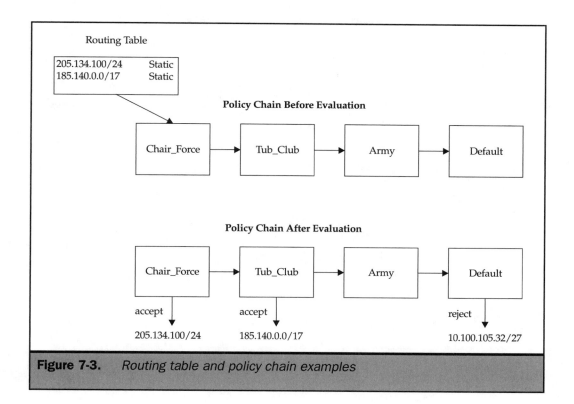

Figure 7-3.   *Routing table and policy chain examples*

controlled by a user-defined policy. You need only specify your own policy chain if you want to modify the router's default behavior. If no user configured policies are present in a chain, the default policy takes over. If user-configured chains are present, each protocol's default import and export policies are appended to the user-configured import and export chains, respectively.

After the chain has made a final decision for one route, the next route goes through the chain, starting at the beginning. The chain's evaluation of the current route is unaffected by the fact that the chain may have evaluated other routes.

A policy within a chain may result in any of the flow-control actions mentioned previously. A policy *chain* must either accept or reject all routes, or the protocol would not know what to do with the route, so *next policy* is not a valid result for a chain. To satisfy this requirement, the policy framework's default policies were all intentionally designed to specify either accept or reject for all possible routes—so *they always have an opinion.* That is why it is acceptable not to apply your own policies to a protocol, and it is OK for a policy to not express an opinion on a route by returning *next policy* for the route. The default policy becomes the *next* policy. Figure 7-4 depicts each route and how it is evaluated by a simple policy chain.

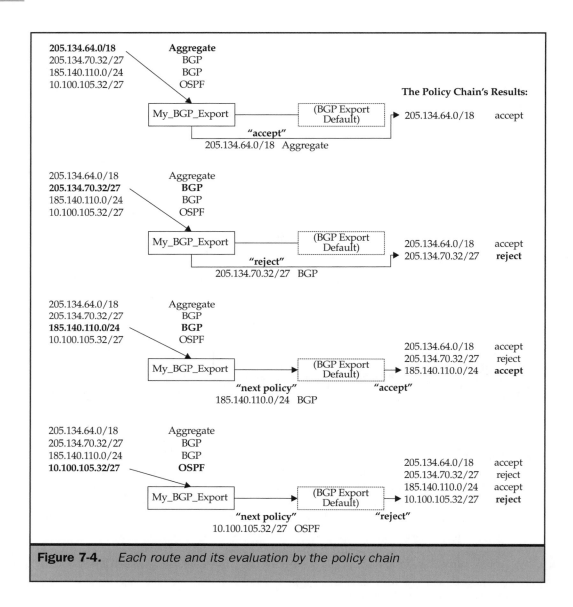

Figure 7-4.   *Each route and its evaluation by the policy chain*

As routes are evaluated, a policy can avoid expressing an opinion by specifying an action of *next policy* or by specifying no flow control action for that route, since *next policy* is the default. In this case, the route is then evaluated by the next policy in the chain.

Because a route goes through the chain until a policy specifies accept or reject, the order of the policies in the chain is significant. An earlier policy may reject a route that a later policy might have accepted.

You would create the policy chain shown in Figure 7-4 by using BGP's *export* statement:

```
user@r1# set protocols bgp export My_BGP_Export
user@r1# show protocols
bgp {
    export My_BGP_Export;
}
```

Note that the BGP default export policy is not seen.

User-Defined Policies

As you know, policies consist of terms, and everything that happens in a policy is specified in its terms. Thus, the policy results *accept*, *reject*, *next term*, and *next policy*, are specified in a policy's terms. Every term results in one of these flow control actions for every route.

The terms in a policy are evaluated one at a time, in the order in which they appear in the configuration. When a term specifies *accept*, *reject*, or *next policy* for a route, the policy is finished with that route. Any remaining terms or policies are skipped. When a term specifies *next term*, the policy continues to the next term. If a term does not specify a flow control action, *next term* is used. If a policy's last term results in *next term* for a route, the policy framework treats that result the same as *next policy*.

Figure 7-5 shows the same routing table shown in Figure 7-4, with the evaluation details of the My_BGP_Export policy shown. Each term has a result for each route, and together they determine the results of the policy itself.

Each term has a result for each route. Together they determine the results of the policy for all possible routes. When a policy results in *next policy* for a route, that route is evaluated by the next policy. For completeness, Figure 7-6 depicts the default BGP export policy indicated in the previous examples. Note that these are multiple terms in one policy, whereas Figure 7-3 depicted a chain of policies. The only routes that will be accepted by this default policy are those accepted by its first term; it accepts all BGP routes. Its final term is designed so that it will reject all routes, thus ensuring that a policy chain will specify an opinion on all routes. This policy, then, will accept all BGP routes and reject all others.

If you were to configure it, here is what this policy would look like:

```
ps@r9# show policy-statement bgp-default
term Accept_BGP {
    from protocol bgp;
    then accept;
}
term Reject_Everything {
    then reject;
}
```

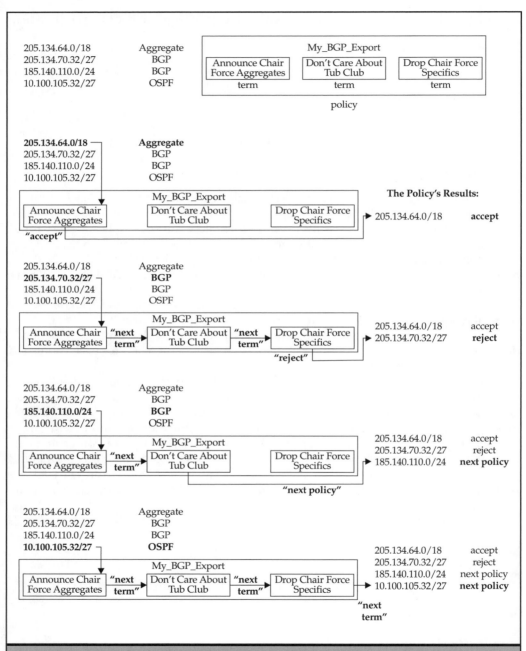

Figure 7-5. *Details of the My_BGP_Export policy's evaluation*

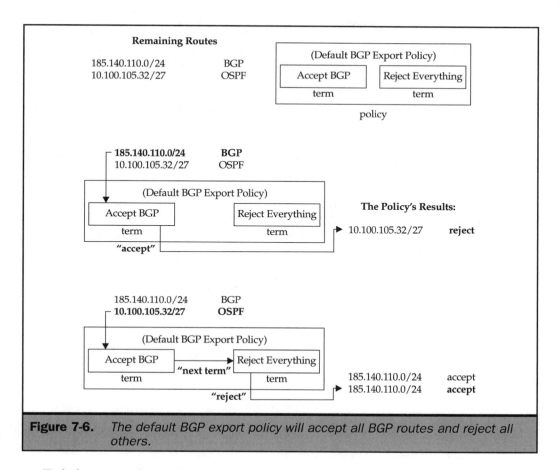

Figure 7-6. *The default BGP export policy will accept all BGP routes and reject all others.*

To help you understand and build a policy, you need to understand the purpose and contents of terms.

Terms

A term's job is to specify one of the flow-control actions for a route. To accomplish this, the term first decides whether it will apply to the route. If it does apply, it acts on the route according to the actions specified. If it does not apply, the policy will continue to the next term, and so on until the end of the policy.

A term has two optional match condition clauses, the *from* clause and the *to* clause. Together, these clauses specify all the criteria a route must match for the term to apply to the route. A term also contains an optional *then* clause, which specifies the actions to take if the term applies to the route.

If a route matches all the criteria, the term's actions are applied to the route. If a route fails to match just one of the term's criteria, the actions in the *then* clause are ignored. All actions are optional—both flow-control actions and side effects. If a term does not specify a flow-control action for a route, the default flow-control action is *next term*. This could be due to the term omitting the *then* clause or omitting a flow control action from the *then* clause. It could also be due to the *then* clause being ignored when the match conditions are not all satisfied.

In Figure 7-7, the first two routes are being evaluated by the terms in the policy from Figure 7-5. The first route is from protocol aggregate, and it matches the route filter. All conditions in the first term match, so the first term's actions are applied. They specify that the policy should accept the route. The second route is not from protocol aggregate, so it does not satisfy all the match conditions in the first term. That term's actions are ignored, and the default action of *next term* is applied. The remaining terms are evaluated, and the third term accepts the route.

In Figure 7-8, the second and third routes are being evaluated by the terms of the policy. The third route's evaluation is similar to the first two evaluations, but the action specified is *next policy*; thus, the remaining terms are skipped. The fourth route does not satisfy the match conditions of any of the terms. The final term's default action of *next term* becomes the policy's result for this route.

You could configure the terms in Figures 7-7 and 7-8 as follows:

```
ps@R10# show
policy-statement My_BGP_Export {
    term Annc_Chair_Force_Aggs {
        from {
            protocol aggregate;
            route-filter 205.134.0.0/16 orlonger;
        }
        then accept;
    }
    term Dont_Care_Re_Tub_Club {
        from {
            route-filter 185.150.0.0/16 orlonger;
        }
        then next policy;
    }
    term Drop_Chair_Force_Specs {
        from {
            protocol bgp;
            route-filter 205.134.0.0/16 orlonger;
        }
        then reject;
    }
}

[edit policy-options]
ps@R10#
```

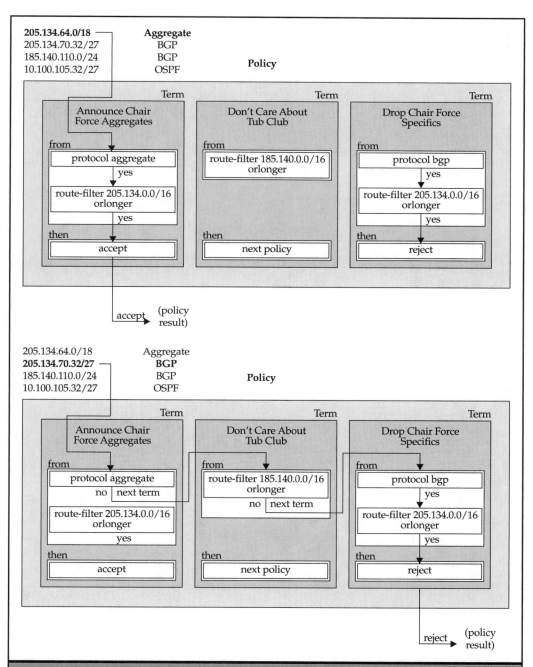

Figure 7-7. *The first two routes being evaluated by the terms in the policy*

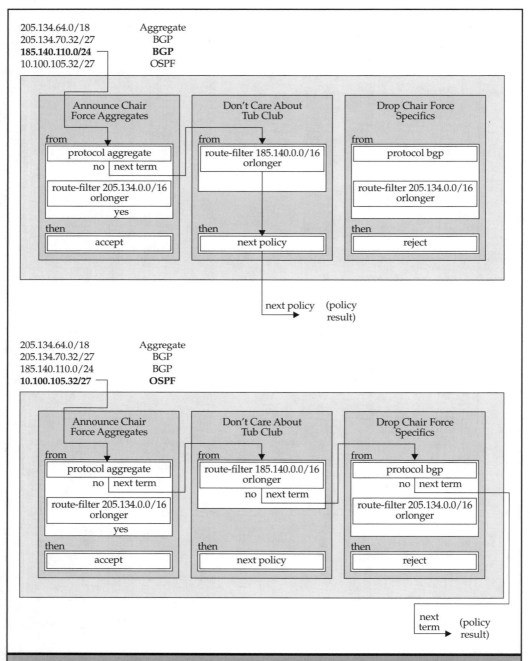

Figure 7-8. *The second and third routes being evaluated by the terms of the policy*

When a term specifies *next policy* as its action, the remainder of the policy is skipped. Any remaining polices are then evaluated, including the appropriate default policy. The second term in the policy in Figure 7-8 would pass certain routes, such as 185.140.20.0/24, onto the next policy rather than let them go through the third term.

Term Order

The order of terms is significant. As mentioned, in the default BGP export policy, you can place a term that accepts certain routes before one that rejects all routes. The resulting policy will accept the specified routes. If you reversed these terms, the policy would reject all routes. Depending on the terms themselves, order may not matter, however. The My_BGP_Export policy in the preceding code example would have the same effect if the terms were arranged in any order.

Sometimes, though, you may define a few terms in a policy and then later define another term that you want to be evaluated before some of the earlier terms. To accommodate this, the JUNOS software cli allows you to change the order of terms that you have already defined. New terms always start out at the end of the policy. The one exception is the *unnamed* term, which is always last (see "The Unnamed Term," later in this section).

You reorder terms using the `insert` configuration mode command. The following moves the Dont_Care_Re_Tub_Club to be the first term of the policy:

```
[edit policy-options policy-statement My_BGP_Export]
ps@R10# insert term Dont_Care_Re_Tub_Club before term Annc_Chair_Force_Aggs
```

Compare the previous form of this policy to its current form:

```
[edit policy-options policy-statement My_BGP_Export]
ps@R10# show
term Dont_Care_Re_Tub_Club {
    from {
        route-filter 185.150.0.0/16 orlonger;
    }
    then next policy;
}
term Annc_Chair_Force_Aggs {
    from {
        protocol aggregate;
        route-filter 205.134.0.0/16 orlonger;
    }
    then accept;
}
term Drop_Chair_Force_Specs {
```

```
    from {
        protocol bgp;
        route-filter 205.134.0.0/16 orlonger;
    }
    then reject;
}

[edit policy-options policy-statement My_BGP_Export]
ps@R10#
```

You can also use `insert ... after...`, which can make a term appear last, since there is no other term to place it "before."

The Unnamed Term

Using the unnamed term has a couple of specific uses. One use is to force a term always to be last so that it acts like a default term. Another use is to make single-term policies shorter and easier to read. However, because the unnamed term can be difficult to operate, you are better off always naming your terms, except in these circumstances.

There are also some notes of caution regarding unnamed terms, with which you must be aware even if you do not intend to use them.

Creating Default Terms

If you want a specific term always to appear last, you can save yourself some trouble by making it an unnamed term. Normally, when you add new terms to a policy, they appear after any existing terms—except for the unnamed term, which always appears last. This means that when you add new terms to the policy, your default unnamed term will stay last. Aesthetically, it can be appealing to name your default term something like "default" or "otherwise." Leaving terms unnamed, however, will save you from having to do an *insert* to move newer terms to appear before your intended default term.

You create the unnamed term in a policy by omitting the *term <name>* component of the term's configuration statements:

```
[edit policy-options]
ps@R10# show
policy-statement Misc_Exceptions {
    term Annc_SekDef {
        from {
            route-filter 110.131.0.0/16 orlonger;
        }
        then accept;
    }
    from protocol bgp;
    then reject;
```

```
    }

[edit policy-options policy-statement Misc_Exceptions]
ps@R10# set term Annc_RootShell_Com from route-filter 110.207.115.0/24 orlonger
ps@R10# set term Annc_RootShell_Com then accept
ps@R10# up

[edit policy-options]
ps@R10# show
policy-statement Misc_Exceptions {
    term Annc_SekDef {
        from {
            route-filter 110.131.0.0/16 orlonger;
        }
        then accept;
    }
    term Annc_RootShell_Com {
        from {
            route-filter 110.207.115.0/24 orlonger;
        }
        then accept;
    }
    from protocol bgp;
    then reject;
}

[edit policy-options]
ps@R10#
```

Creating Single-Term Policies   Unnamed terms are also useful in extremely simple policies that will have only one term. Configuring a single term policy without a term name saves you two lines of configuration length, making the policy a little easier to read. You could have configured the My_BGP_Export policy as two separate policies (to chain together)—one for Chair_Force and one for Tub_Club. In this configuration, the Tub_Club policy would contain only one term. Naming this single term would provide no benefit, so you could write it like this:

```
[edit]
ps@R10# show policy-options
policy-statement Tub_Club {
    from {
        route-filter 185.140.0.0/16 orlonger;
    }
    then accept;
```

```
}

[edit]
ps@R10#
```

Compare that to this:

```
[edit policy-options]
ps@R10# show
policy-statement Tub_Club {
    term Annc_Tub_Club {
        from {
            route-filter 185.140.0.0/16 orlonger;
        }
        then accept;
    }
}

[edit policy-options]
ps@R10#
```

This might not seem like much of a big deal, but when you have a thousand lines of policies, writing code in this way can shorten a configuration file by a screen or two. By reordering your policy definitions to put the short ones next to each other, you can also see more policies on the screen at a time.

Unnamed Term Cautions   As hinted, using the unnamed term can be dangerous. One problem is simple—deleting an unnamed term can be annoying, and renaming it is impossible. Since the term is not surrounded by a distinct configuration level, you have to delete it one piece at a time. So if the term includes a *from* clause, a *to* clause, and a *then* clause, you would have to delete each clause separately, or delete the entire policy.

Another problem is the fact that it is always last. It is common for someone to "whip up a quick policy" and forget to name the first term. If a second term is added that needs to be evaluated second, it will have to be fixed. Terms (and policies) can be renamed using the configuration mode `rename` command. However, the unnamed term *cannot* be renamed, so you would have to delete it piecemeal and rebuild it from scratch as a named term.

Another problem deals with unintended use of the unnamed term. Sometimes users accidentally leave out the term name from one of the configuration statements, but not others. The following configuration commands, for example, will result in a policy that does not do what the user appears to intend:

```
ps@R10# edit policy-options policy-statement Block_Private

[edit policy-options policy-statement Block_Private]
ps@R10# set term Match_Private from route-filter 10.0.0.0/8 orlonger
ps@R10# set then reject
ps@R10# up

[edit policy-options]
ps@R10# show
policy-statement Block_Private {
    term Match_Private {
        from {
            route-filter 10.0.0.0/8 orlonger;
        }
    }
    then reject;
}

[edit policy-options]
ps@R10#
```

At first glance, this policy looks fine. But it will not do anything special to 10/8, and it will reject everything. Notice that the *then* statement is not aligned with the word *from*, and that the *then* statement is not inside of the *Match_Private* term. This *then* statement is actually part of an unnamed term, one that has no *from* conditions. Therefore, it applies to all routes. Furthermore, the term *Match_Private* has no *then* statement, so it does nothing at all.

Note   *Keep in mind that these types of mistakes occur when you have no intention of using the unnamed term, so always keep your eye out for it.*

You have seen a few simple match conditions so far, but the discussion of how they are evaluated and what they do has been limited to the fact that they all have to match a route before the term's actions are applied. Because a term's match conditions can become quite complex, and certain types of matches require their own discussion of how they are evaluated, the next section covers match conditions in detail.

Match Conditions

You just learned about how a route is evaluated against multiple match conditions. The important points are

- A route is compared against each condition
- It must satisfy all of the conditions, or the *then* clause is skipped

The conditions are tested in the order they appear in the configuration file, which becomes relevant with subroutines.

That is about all there is to say generically about match conditions—if a single condition doesn't match a specific route, the term basically doesn't exist, with respect to that route. Individual available match conditions themselves warrant much more discussion, however. Many of them are straightforward, but others have subtleties regarding how match success or failure is determined.

Here are a few issues to note regarding how a match condition behaves compared to other matches:

- How (or if) it allows multiple values
- Whether its parameters are extended (require extra definition to match multiple values)
- Whether it behaves differently when used in a *to* clause (versus a *from* clause)
- Whether it behaves differently when matching routes from different protocols
- For which protocols' routes it is valid

The different types of extended parameters will be discussed shortly. Table 7-1 details the match conditions and provides an indication of which issues apply to particular conditions. This table shows which match conditions involve special evaluation. [*x*] indicates that multiple versions of that condition exist; for example, metric[234] represents four conditions: metric, metric2, metric3, and metric4. (Some match conditions have been omitted because they are beyond the scope of this book.)

Condition	Multiple Values?	Extended Parameters ?	*to* Differs	Source Protocol Specific**	Valid Protocols
area	–	–	–	–	OSPF
as-path	list	*regex, named*	–	–	BGP, static, aggregate
color[2]	–	–	–	–	–
community	list	*regex, named*	–	–	–
external	–	–	–	–	OSPF

Table 7-1.   *Match Conditions That Involve Special Evaluation*

Condition	Multiple Values?	Extended Parameters ?	to Differs	Source Protocol Specific**	Valid Protocols
interface	list	–	–	–	RIP, direct, local
level	–	–	Yes	–	IS-IS
local-preference	–	–	–	BGP	BGP
metric[234]	–	–	–	BGP	–
neighbor	list	–	–	–	BGP
next-hop	list	–	–	–	–
origin	–	–	–	–	BGP
policy	chain	*named*	Yes[*]	–	–
preference[2]	–	–	–	BGP	–
prefix-list	separate statements	*named*	n/a	–	–
protocol	list	–	Yes	–	–
route-filter	separate statements	*mask spec, action*	n/a	–	–
source-address-filter	separate statements	*mask spec, action*	n/a	–	Multicast protocols
tag[2]	–	–	–	OSPF, IS-IS	–

[*] Indirectly; this is discussed in the "Subroutines" section later in this chapter.

** The Source Protocol Specific column indicates which conditions treat their parameters differently, depending on the protocol from which the route being evaluated was learned. These are discussed in the "Protocol Specific Policy" section.

Table 7-1. *Match Conditions That Involve Special Evaluation* (continued)

Where there is a blank cell, what you can do and how the policy framework will evaluate it should be straightforward. Blank cells in the Multiple Values column indicate conditions that allow only one value. Blanks in Extended Parameters cells indicate that the parameters represent discrete values. Blanks in *to* Differs cells indicate that the condition behaves the same when used in either a *from* or *to* clause. In the Source Protocol Specific column, blank cells indicate the condition will act the same regardless of what route the protocol was learned through. Blank cells in Valid Protocols indicate the condition can be used with routes from any protocol.

Following are the types of extended parameters that various match conditions accept, along with discussions of how they are evaluated.

Lists

The simplest extended parameter format is the *list*. Several match conditions allow you to include a list of parameters, enclosed in brackets ([ ]) as an alternative to including just a single parameter. The contents of the list must all be the appropriate type of parameter for the match condition. For example, you can say from neighbor 1.1.1.1 or you can say from neighbor [1.1.1.1 2.2.2.2]. Conversely, you couldn't configure from neighbor [1.1.1.1 3561:400] or from neighbor [3561:200 3561:400] because neighbor expects a list of IP addresses, not communities.

Lists are treated the same way when used with AS paths, communities, interfaces, neighbors, next-hops, and protocols. Specifically, only one member of a list need match a route for the condition to be considered a successful match on that route. The following example shows a policy with the next-hop match condition and a list of two next-hops. Note that the route that it accepts actually has two next-hops, but only one of them is in the match condition's list.

```
[edit policy-options]
user@r1# show
policy-statement Has_Bad_Next_Hop {
    term Next_Hops {
        from {
            protocol static;
            next-hop [ 205.134.101.20 205.134.101.30 ];
        }
        then accept;
    }
    term Otherwise {
        then reject;
    }
}

user@r1# run show route terse protocol static

inet.0: 10 destinations, 10 routes (10 active, 0 holddown, 0 hidden)
+ = Active Route, - = Last Active, * = Both
```

```
A Destination           P Prf Metric 1   Metric 2     Next hop        AS path
* 185.140.75.0/24       S   5                         >205.134.101.10
* 205.134.123.136/29 S   5                             205.134.101.12
                                                       >205.134.101.20

user@r1# run test policy Has_Bad_Next_Hop 0.0.0.0/0

inet.0: 10 destinations, 10 routes (10 active, 0 holddown, 0 hidden)
Prefixes passing policy:

205.134.123.136/29 *[Static/5] 00:07:23
                        to 205.134.101.12 via fxp0.0
                    > to 205.134.101.20 via fxp0.0

Policy Has_Bad_Next_Hop: 1 prefix accepted, 9 prefixes rejected

user@r1#
```

This example uses the test policy `cli` command to show what routes the policy accepts. It takes a policy name and a prefix. Any active routes that match the prefix are tested against the policy. Those which it accepts are listed. (For more information, see the "Troubleshooting Policy" section later in this chapter.)

If you set a list-capable match condition more than once within a term, the successive parameters you give are appended to the end of the list. The brackets are added if the list previously had only one member. You can delete individual members from the list, and you can rearrange the list using the `insert ... before/after` configuration command. Order does not effect evaluation, but you may use it to make the configuration easier to read.

AS paths and communities have two differences: their parameters are named, and the parameter definitions allow regular expression syntax.

Regular expressions allow you to describe a pattern, such as "everything that starts with 6," instead of enumerating all possibilities. (See Chapter 12 for further discussion. In this chapter, techniques employing regular expressions are demonstrated in the "Policy Design" section, and an example is presented in the "Protocol Specific Policy" section later.)

One point is worth noting here: You can define a community (or an AS path) that contains multiple explicit values. If you do so, the values all must match a route for that community (or AS-path) to match the route. A community match condition listing several named communities will succeed as long as just one of the named communities matches a route. A named community that itself contains several community expressions will match a route only if all of the expressions match the route.

Named Parameters

Some match conditions, including communities, AS paths, prefix lists, and policy subroutines, require that you define their parameters separately and name them. You then specify the name when configuring the match condition. This is the same concept as defining an entire policy and giving it a name; you can then apply the policy to a protocol *export* statement by specifying its name.

Named parameters are defined in the *policy-options* configuration level, along with the policies themselves. Rather than discuss this as a unique concept, you can see the use of this technique in the sections that follow, for the conditions that use it.

Repeated Statements

Prefix lists, route filters, and source address filters also allow multiple values. However, rather than appear as lists, you see multiple configuration lines containing the *prefix-list*, *route-filter*, or *source-address-filter* statement. Here is a policy that uses multiple prefix lists:

```
policy-statement Multi_Prefix_Lists {
    from {
        prefix-list Chair_Force;
        prefix-list Tub_Club;
        prefix-list Army;
    }
    then accept;
}
```

Prefix Lists   Here is an example of a prefix list:

```
[edit]
ps@R10# show policy-options
prefix-list All_Hexagon_Routes {
    185.140.0.0/16;
    205.134.0.0/16;
}

[edit]
ps@R10#
```

For a route to match a prefix list, it must have exactly the same network number and the same length mask as one of the prefixes in the list. To match routes with varying masks, you use the *route-filter* match condition.

Note that it is possible for you to include overlapping prefixes in your list. Since the mask must match exactly, this does not result in any conflict. Thus, the order of prefixes in a list is unimportant.

Route Filters   Route filters are similar to prefix lists in that they test the destination prefix (address and mask) in the route. They are also similar to lists allowed by other conditions, in that you can have more than one value in the policy, and a route needs to match only one of your values for the *route-filter* condition to be considered a successful match.

Two key differences exist between route filters and prefix lists:

- A single route filter can match routes with several different addresses or masks.

- Each route filter in the list can specify alternative actions to take immediately on routes matching just that filter.

You define route filters inside a term. As with prefix lists, you use the *route-filter* configuration directive multiple times. When you define a route filter, you give it a destination prefix in address/mask-length notation and a description of how a route's mask must compare to the destination prefix's mask.

Following are the different ways you can compare a route to the destination prefix you specify. These descriptions are extracted directly from configuration mode context-sensitive help. This table is followed by a discussion of exactly how each type of route filter behaves.

`route-filter` Type	CLI Description
exact	Exactly match the prefix length
longer	Mask is greater than the prefix length
orlonger	Mask is greater than or equal to the prefix length
prefix-length-range	Mask falls between two prefix lengths
upto	Mask falls between two prefix lengths
through	Route falls between two prefixes

- *exact*, *longer*, and *orlonger* do just what the cli says they do. So, for example, *10/8 exact* matches only 10.0.0.0/8. *10/8 longer* does not match 10/8, but it matches 10.0/9, 10.128/9 10.64/10, and so on. *10/8 orlonger* matches all of these prefixes.

- *prefix-length-range* takes an additional parameter, which specifies a range of masks. It matches any routes with a network number that falls under the specified prefix and a mask falling in the range. For example, *10/8 prefix-length-range /16-/24* will match *10.x.x.x*, but only if the mask is between /16 and /24. 10.28.0.0/18 will match, but 10.28.0.0/15 will not.

- *upto* is almost identical to prefix-length-range. The difference is that you provide it only one more mask instead of a range. It matches masks between the prefix's mask and the additional mask. For example, *10/8 upto /24* will match both 10.28.0.0/18 and 10.28.0.0/15; both mask lengths are between /8 and /24.

■ *through* takes two prefixes. It matches every prefix which is overlapped by the first prefix and overlaps the second prefix. (Note that for the purposes of this discussion, a prefix is considered to "overlap" itself.) For example, 10.0/12 through 10.15/16 matches exactly these prefixes (and no others):

10.0.0.0/12
10.8.0.0/13
10.12.0.0/14
10.14.0.0/15
10.15.0.0/16

10.12/12 overlaps 10.12.0.0/14, which in turn overlaps 10.15.0.0/16. Note that 10.12.0.0/14 is the *only* 14-bit long prefix that overlaps 10.15/16. 10.13/14, 10.14/14, and 10.15/14 theoretically also overlap 10.15/16, but they are not valid prefixes—they all compute to 10.12/14 after mask processing (it is generally incorrect behavior to announce routes with host bits set; however, if you did encounter these, they would also match).

Furthermore, 10.16/14 is an example of another valid /14 prefix—it does not match because it does not overlap 10.15/16. For a given mask length, at most one (valid) prefix overlaps a given more specific prefix. Note also that if the first prefix configured in the route filter does not overlap the second, no routes will match.

The most common use of through is to block prefixes with all zero bits in their network numbers. You can specify this as *route-filter 0/0 through 0/32*. This will match 0/0, 0/1, 0/2, and so on, to 0/32. In other words, this matches all prefixes which overlap 0/32. If you do not wish to block the default route itself, use *route-filter 0/1 through 0/32*.

The diagrams shown in Figure 7-9 and Figure 7-10 may be helpful. Visualize the space of IP numbers as an inverted tree (with its root at the top), where the root of the tree does not specify any bits of the address. At the first level below the root is a split, specifying a 0 to the left and a 1 to the right; this is the value of the first bit of the address, which gives you two possibilities. The next level specifies the value of the second bit, so there are four possibilities—two for each value of the first bit, times two for each value of the second bit. If you continue down to 32 levels below the root, this last level will enumerate every possible IP address. The tree itself enumerates every possible IP prefix, and shows what actual addresses each prefix contains. Figure 7-9 shows a piece of that tree, starting at the 16th level below the root, with bits thus far corresponding to the addresses starting with 192.168.

Figure 7-10 depicts which of these prefixes will match an example of each route-filter match type. The highlighted prefixes match the indicated route-filter type. The first one, for example, would be configured as

```
route-filter 192.168/16 exact
```

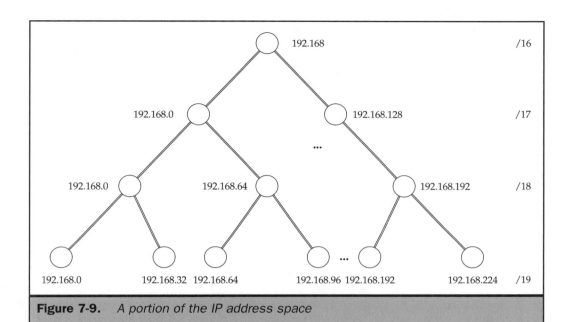

Figure 7-9.   *A portion of the IP address space*

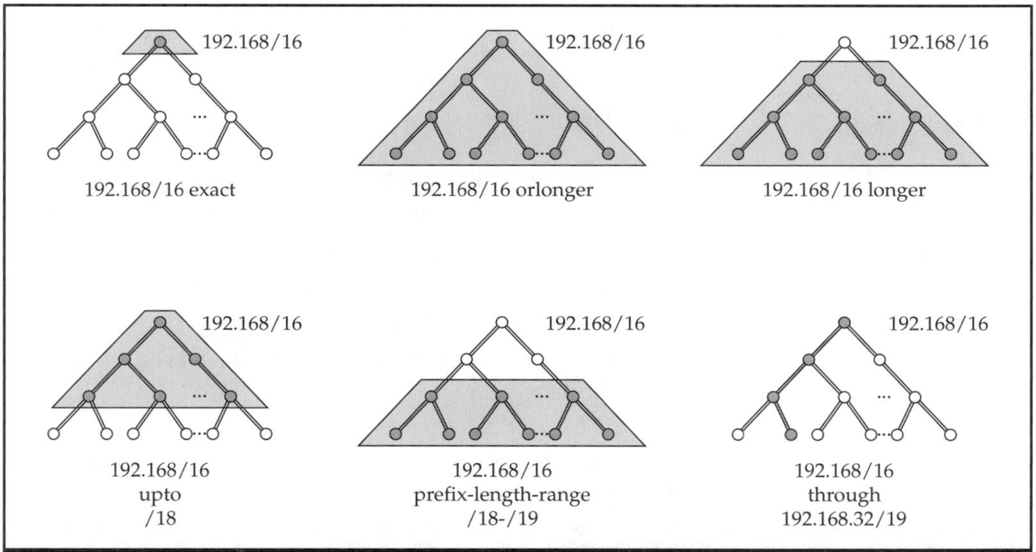

Figure 7-10.   *Prefixes matching example route-filter match types*

Here is a sample policy using route filters:

```
[edit]
ps@R10# edit policy-options policy-statement Accept_All_Hex

[edit policy-options policy-statement Accept_All_Hex]
ps@R10# set from route-filter 205.134/16 orlonger
ps@R10# set from route-filter 185.140/16 prefix-length-range /18-/27
ps@R10# set from route-filter 185.140/16 upto /17 reject
ps@R10# set then accept
ps@R10# up

[edit policy-options]
ps@R10# show
policy-statement Accept_All_Hex {
    from {
        route-filter 205.134.0.0/16 orlonger;
        route-filter 185.140.0.0/16 prefix-length-range /18-/27;
        route-filter 185.140.0.0/16 upto /17 reject;
    }
    then accept;
}
```

Following are some sample routes and what will happen to them with the aforementioned route filters.

Destination	Result
205.134.10.0/23	Matches first route filter; matches 205.134.0.0/16, and mask matches "/16 or longer." Route is accepted by *then* clause.
185.140.0.0/16	Does not match second route filter (mask is not in range). Matches third route filter's prefix and mask criteria. The route is rejected immediately by the route filter's action.
185.140.100.0/24	Matches second route filter's prefix and mask criteria. Route is accepted by *then* clause.

Each *route-filter* statement allows you to specify actions as an alternative to the term's *then* clause. The policy framework will substitute these actions for the *then* clause only for routes that match this specific route filter. You can use any actions that are valid in a *then* clause. You can even put multiple actions in a route filter's *action* clause. Thus, you can have a single term that applies different actions to different routes by choosing different action statements for each route filter. Other than the route filter actions you define, a term can have only one outcome: the set of actions in its *then* clause. The route filter action is the only way to make a term do one thing to one route and another thing to a different route. If the actions you choose for the route filter actions include a flow-control action, it becomes the term's flow-control action for that route.

When you define route filter actions, routes matching that filter will skip the term's *then* clause. Thus, if the *route-filter* actions do not include a flow-control action, the route will take the default flow-control action *next term*, regardless of what appears in the *then* clause. Furthermore, if a term includes *route-filter* conditions, and they *all* have actions, the term's *then* clause cannot possibly be applied to any routes; routes matching a filter will get the *filter's* actions instead of those of the *then* clause. Routes that do not match any filters will fail to match the term and will skip its *then* clause, as normal.

Here is an example policy with a useless *then* clause:

```
[edit policy-options]
ps@R7# show
policy-statement Catch_All_Filters {
    from {
        protocol ospf;
        route-filter 185.140.0.0/16 orlonger {
            metric add 10;
        }
        route-filter 205.134.0.0/16 orlonger {
            local-preference 200;
        }
    }
    then {
        local-preference 150;
    }
}
```

The JUNOS software policy framework evaluates route-filters from longest mask to shortest, based on the mask length of the first prefix (the one that appears before the route filter type). It uses the first route filter with a prefix that overlaps the route being tested. If the route fails to pass that route filter's specifications (for example, the route filter type is "exact" and the route's mask is longer), the entire series of route filters is considered a failure, and therefore the term is finished with the route. The route continues with the next term, as with any failed match condition. The important point here is that even though another route-filter might appear in the same term that would have matched the route, it is never evaluated because of the failure of the first route filter.

Consider the following example:

```
[edit policy-options]
ps@R6# show policy-statement rf
term rf {
    from {
        route-filter 10.1.0.0/23 exact accept;
        route-filter 10.1.0.0/16 orlonger accept;
    }
}
/* default unnamed term */
then reject;
```

(Note: the comment enclosed in /* and */ is an annotation, which is discussed in the "Policy Design" section later in this chapter.)

```
[edit policy-options]
ps@R6# run show route terse protocol static

inet.0: 5 destinations, 5 routes (4 active, 0 holddown, 1 hidden)
+ = Active Route, - = Last Active, * = Both

A Destination       P Prf Metric 1   Metric 2    Next hop        AS path
* 10.1.0.0/16       S   5            0           Reject
* 10.1.1.0/24       S   5            0           Reject

[edit policy-options]
ps@R6# run test policy rf 0/0

inet.0: 5 destinations, 5 routes (4 active, 0 holddown, 1 hidden)
Prefixes passing policy:

10.1.0.0/16          *[Static/5] 00:10:05, metric 0
                      Reject

Policy rf: 1 prefix accepted, 3 prefixes rejected


[edit policy-options]
ps@R6#
```

If you compare the results of the *test policy* output to the routes matching the *show route* output, you will see that 10.1.1.0/24 is missing, even though it matches the second route filter. This is because it is in the first route filter's prefix (10.1.0.0/23). As soon as the conditions of the first route filter are met, that route filter becomes the one that the term will test the route against. Success or failure is determined immediately, and remaining route filters will not be considered for that route.

It is also possible to configure multiple route filters in a term to look for the same prefix but use different types of route filter—or the same type of route filter, but with different parameters. In the following policy, three route filters specify a first mask of /23:

```
[edit policy-options]
ps@R6# show policy-statement rf
term rf {
    from {
        route-filter 10.2.0.0/24 exact accept;
        route-filter 10.1.0.0/23 exact accept;
        route-filter 10.1.0.0/23 upto /26 metric add 10;
        route-filter 10.1.0.0/23 upto /29 metric add 20;
        route-filter 10.1.0.0/16 orlonger accept;
    }
}
/* default unnamed term */
then reject; /* this is the unnamed term */
```

You already know that route filters are evaluated longest-mask first, and that they stop evaluating a route as soon as a route filter's first prefix overlaps the route's prefix. In this case, the several route filters with a mask of /23 could all match a given route. All the /23 route filters are evaluated against the route, in the order in which they appear in the configuration, until one of them matches completely. If none of them match, the route filter and, therefore, the term fail to match.

In this last case, consider routes with the following prefixes:

- **10.1.0.0/23**   The policy framework tests this against the route filters in order of longest prefix first (only the first prefix in each route-filter is considered in determining order). It fails to match the /24 route filter. There are three /23 route-filters, and the JUNOS software tests the route against them in the order in which they are listed in the configuration. It matches the first route filter's criterion, which is *exact*. The route is accepted.

- **10.1.1.64/27**   This fails to match the /24. It matches /23, so it is tested against the first /23 route filter. It does not match that filter's criteria, so it is tested against the second. It fails again, and is tested against the third. It does satisfy both the first prefix, 10.1.1.0/23, and the criteria "upto /29." It receives this route filter's specific action, which is to add 20 to its metric. There is no *then* clause in this term, which would not matter because it would be skipped due to the specific action. The route receives a default flow-control action for this term of *next term* because no other action was specified. The next term is the unnamed term, and it rejects everything. The route is rejected.

- **10.1.1.40/30**   This also does not match the /24. It does match the first prefix 10.1.0/23, but it does not match "exact." It also does not match "upto /26" or "upto /29." It has failed to match the route filter type and criteria for all of the /23 route filters. However, since it did match their initial mask, it is finished with being processed by route filters. It is not tested by the /16 route filter at all; it simply fails to match the first term's match conditions. It receives the default term action *next term* and flows to the unnamed term, which rejects it.

Chains   The *policy* match condition allows a list, which appears in bracket notation. This is called a *policy subroutine*. Although a policy chain looks like a list syntactically, it is evaluated in the same way as other policy chains, rather than as a list. Policy subroutines are discussed in the "Subroutines" section later.

Communities

A *community* is a number that you attach to a route as an attribute—just a tag that becomes part of the route. Communities exist so that you can use policies with them.

The choice of the word *community* has its roots in the original intended use for the attribute, which was to identify common groups of people or organizations such as a "customer community" or "service provider community." The concept has since outgrown its original intent in the sense that community implies a personal or organizational connection, while a community on a route could imply something quite impersonal such as "this is a backup route."

In JUNOS software, a community is a generic match condition. Communities deserve special discussion here, specifically with regard to JUNOS software. While other router vendors let you use communities only with BGP, with JUNOS software, you can *announce* communities only on BGP routes, but you can *use* them locally on any type of route.

Using a community, you can label a route so that you can refer to it later; therefore, the community's meaning is determined by the people who configure it. Later on, you can recognize and use the community to make routing decisions. The router ignores a community unless you specifically tell it to do otherwise.

Note   *Three globally significant communities exist, and community-aware implementations are expected to understand and obey them. See RFC 1997 for details.*

You can infer a lot of information from where and how a route enters your network, but once it is *inside* your network, that information is lost. By adding a community at the point of entry, you can preserve that information and then reference it anywhere. For example, your network might include a router that peers with a provider's router. You may learn a given route from one of your customers, but that may occur on a different router over a certain connection that you know is a customer connection. When the route arrives at the peering router, normally it is impossible to distinguish it as a customer route. But if you use a policy to add a specific tag to all routes you learn from the customer connection, the peering router can look for that tag and know the routes that have it are from customer routers.

Of course, it is up to the network designers and operators to make sure that each router treats each tag in an appropriate manner. The tags themselves are arbitrary values; therefore, you should use them consistently for them to be effective.

The community concept is most valuable in BGP, because BGP announces this attribute to other routers. For example, a route can originate in Dallas and show up in Moscow, and a Moscow router will "know" whether it is a management route or a customer route just by looking for the appropriate community. Of course, a router does not really know the difference between a management network and a customer network, nor would it "care" if it did know. You can make your network "care" by configuring the Dallas router to stick the tag *1:50*, for example, on a management route. Then you could configure the Moscow router not to announce anything with a *1:50* tag on it to customers.

With JUNOS software, you can attach community values to all routes, not just BGP routes. You can do this explicitly for static and aggregate routes, and you can also do it with policies on any routes. Because protocols other than BGP do not know how to deal with communities, JUNOS software will not insert communities when it announces routes into those protocols. But the community will stay attached to the route for as long as the route is known to the local router.

You can combine the community feature with the policy framework's flexibility and extensibility in powerful ways. You can mark a route with several communities in a policy and chain that policy together with other policies. Then later policies can match on communities and take action.

If you have programming experience, you can also think of a policy chain as a program and a community as a variable that you set in one part of the program and reference in another part. In this sense, communities are like Boolean variables—that is, they are either on or off, by being there or not there—but you cannot assign them values.

When you use communities for local router purposes on BGP routes, the communities will be included with the routes when BGP announces them. You should remove these locally significant communities explicitly so they do not confuse other routers. This is discussed in more detail in the "Policy Design" section later in the chapter.

 You can determine whether a policy had an effect on a route by adding a community in the policy and then looking to see whether the community appears.

Community Structure   In JUNOS software, a community is displayed as a pair of numbers in the range of 0 to 65,535, separated by a colon. For example, 1:1, 1:2, and 65535:1 are three different communities. You can add a large number of communities to a route, up to a limit that is determined by the maximum size of the packet announcing the route, minus the space taken up by any other information necessary.

You can theoretically put over 1000 communities on a route. Communities are defined by RFC 1997, which does not specify any bounds on the number of communities an implementation can support.

Here is a static route before communities are added:

```
[edit]
user@r1# edit routing-options static route 185.140.75/24

[edit routing-options static route 185.140.75.0/24]
user@r1# set next-hop 205.134.101.10
user@r1# commit
commit complete

user@r1# run show route detail protocol static

inet.0: 10 destinations, 10 routes (10 active, 0 holddown, 0 hidden)
+ = Active Route, - = Last Active, * = Both

185.140.75.0/24 (2 entries, 0 announced)
        Static Preference:    5
                Nexthop: 205.134.101.10 via fxp0.0, selected
                State: <Int Ext>
                Inactive reason: Route Preference
                Age: 2:35
                Task: RT
                AS path: I
```

Here is the same static route after communities are added:

```
user@r1# set community [ 1:1 1:2 65535:1 ]
user@r1# commit
commit complete

user@r1# up 2

[edit routing-options]
user@r1# show
static {
    route 185.140.75.0/24 {
        next-hop 205.134.101.10;
        community [ 1:1 1:2 65535:1 ];
```

```
    }
}

user@r1# run show route detail protocol static

inet.0: 10 destinations, 10 routes (10 active, 0 holddown, 0 hidden)
+ = Active Route, - = Last Active, * = Both

185.140.75.0/24 (2 entries, 0 announced)
        Static Preference:    5
                Nexthop: 205.134.101.10 via fxp0.0, selected
                State: <Int Ext>
                Inactive reason: Route Preference
                Age: 3:18
                Task: RT
                AS path: I
                Communities: 1:1 1:2 65535:1

[edit routing-options]
user@r1#
```

Following is a policy that will accept only routes that have a community value of 65535:1:

```
[edit]
user@r1# show policy-options
policy-statement Allow_Comm_1 {
    term Accept_Comm_1 {
        from community Comm_1;
        then accept;
    }
    term Otherwise {
        then reject;
    }
}
community Comm_1 members 65535:1;

user@r1# run show route terse

inet.0: 9 destinations, 9 routes (9 active, 0 holddown, 0 hidden)
+ = Active Route, - = Last Active, * = Both
```

```
A Destination          P Prf Metric 1    Metric 2    Next hop          AS path
* 185.140.75.0/24      S   5                          >205.134.101.10
* 192.168.100.32/30    D   0                          >fxp1.110
* 192.168.100.33/32    L   0                          Local
* 205.134.1.0/24       D   0                          >fxp1.1
* 205.134.1.1/32       L   0                          Local
* 205.134.101.0/27     D   0                          >fxp0.0
* 205.134.101.1/32     L   0                          Local
* 205.134.255.1/32     D   0                          >lo0.0
* 224.0.0.5/32         O  10           1              MultiRecv

user@r1# run test policy Allow_Comm_1 0/0

inet.0: 9 destinations, 9 routes (9 active, 0 holddown, 0 hidden)
Prefixes passing policy:

185.140.75.0/24      *[Static/5] 00:23:27
                      > to 205.134.101.10 via fxp0.0

Policy Allow_Comm_1: 1 prefix accepted, 8 prefixes rejected

user@r1#
```

Note   *The "Policy Design" section later in this chapter demonstrates some powerful ways that you can simplify your policies using communities. The "Policy Framework Mechanics" section also uses communities to demonstrate some of the basic concepts.*

The Match Condition   The community match condition will succeed on any route that has the specified community. As with other parameter lists, when a list of named communities is provided, only one needs to match. However, as indicated, a specific named community must match *completely*. The same is true for named AS paths.

For example, *from community [comm1 comm2]* will match a route if only *comm1* matches the route. However, if *comm1* is specified as *community comm1 members [100:1 100:2 100:3]*, a route must have all three of these communities to match *comm1*.

To vs. From

For the most part, the *to* match conditions are simply copies of the *from* match conditions; for import policies, and BGP and RIP export policies, these conditions are exactly the same. For example, the same match behavior will result whether you use *to metric 5* or *from metric 5*. For most OSPF and IS-IS conditions, *to* and *from* are also the same. Notable exceptions are *protocol* and *level*: *to protocol* will match *ospf* in a policy applied as an OSPF *export*. It will match *isis* in a policy applied as IS-IS *export*. In other words, for these protocols, *to protocol* matches the protocol that is doing the exporting. On the other hand, *to level* is used specifically for IS-IS, and it allows you to control how IS-IS announces routes between level 1 and level 2. You should not use *to level* in policies that are referenced by any protocol other than IS-IS.

The *policy* match condition uses other policies as parameters. In an indirect sense, this condition can behave differently in a *from* clause than in a *to* clause. (See the "Subroutines" section below for more information.)

Side-Effects

You can use the following actions to manipulate routes. These do not directly affect the policy framework's evaluation of a route; thus, when you include them in a policy, the policy has "side effects"—some change a route attribute and others affect the behavior of the routing or forwarding engines for a route.

Action	Affects
as-path-prepend	Route attribute
color[2]	Route attribute
community	Route attribute
damping	Routing engine
external	Route attribute
install-nexthop	Forwarding engine
load-balance	Forwarding engine
local-preference	Route attribute
metric[234]	Route attribute
next-hop	Route attribute
origin	Route attribute
preference[2]	Route attribute
tag[2]	Route attribute
trace	Routing engine

Note   *Some actions have been omitted from this table because they are beyond the scope of this book.*

Although the meaning of most of these side-effect actions is beyond the scope of this chapter, they are as much a part of why policy exists as are the flow-control actions. These actions let you influence how the router makes its routing decisions.

Side-effect actions are always applied immediately, as soon as they are encountered. This all happens to a copy of the route. Specifically, a protocol (or other policy using function of the router) makes a copy of a route before it hands it to the policy framework. The framework works on that copy, modifying it as necessary, until it is done. It then hands it back to the protocol. Along the way, each modification takes effect immediately, so the rest of the policy chain can act on the results of those changes if necessary.

The *trace* action is specific to the policy framework, and it does not affect a route. If you have defined a log file with the *routing-options traceoptions file* configuration directive, you can log when policy terms match. If you include the *trace* action in the *then* clause of any term, whenever a route matches that term, the term's name, the destination prefix and the term's flow-control action will be logged to that file. (In JUNOS software versions prior to 5.0, if the term does not contain any flow-control actions, the term's name will show up as *<default>* instead of the actual term name.)

Expressions

Within a policy chain, each policy in order has a chance to have an opinion on a route. As soon as one policy has an opinion—*accept* or *reject*—the chain is done with that route.

Policy expressions allow you to run routes through multiple policies. You can make the policy framework consider the results of all these policies before making its final decision on the route. You can create instructions such as, "if any of these policies accepts a route, accept it," or "accept the route only if all of these policies accept the route." You can build an expression that will skip a few policies based on the result of one policy and then continue with the rest of the chain.

Policy expressions use the Boolean operators *&&*, *||*, and *!* (*and*, *or*, and *not*, respectively). They take policies as arguments. As usual, the policies result in the flow-control actions *accept*, *next policy*, or *reject* for each route. Expressions defer the application of these actions, treating them at first as true/false values. They return the appropriate result according to the standard rules of Boolean arithmetic.

If you have a programming background, you may appreciate this interesting bonus: Because of the nature of logical operators, you can theoretically build any function you want out of policy expressions. Perhaps the most feasible and useful example is that you can get policy expressions to simulate an *if... then... else...* clause. Admittedly, fabricating anything much more advanced than this would likely be unfeasible, but if you really need to, you can encapsulate it in a subroutine to spare others the complexity.

Note   *You may already be aware that all computer chips, at the most basic level, are essentially collections of nothing more than true/false calculators called* gates, *which have one of three functions:* and, or, *or* not. *That is why binary numbers are so fundamental in computer science: 1 is true and 0 is false. Ultimately, all actions a computer takes come down to 1's and 0's going into these gates, with the results going through more gates.*

Boolean Arithmetic

Boolean, or logical, arithmetic lets you build functions that take multiple inputs and produce a result. With logical functions, the values you put into and get out of your functions can be only true or false—so, for example, you might see a function like this: *f(true,false) = false*. These functions use logical operators (*and*, written *&&*; *or*, written | |; and *not*, written *!*) instead of arithmetic operators (such as + or –).

Here is how it works: *x && y* is true if both *x* and *y* are true; it is false if either *x* or *y*, or both, are false. *x | | y* is true if at least one of *x* or *y* is true, and it's false if neither are true. *!x* is true if *x* is false, and it's false if *x* is true, so really it just reverses *x*. Table 7-2 shows results for each operator to help you visualize this.

An operator can take another expression as an argument. It computes the result of the expression first, which becomes the value of the expression. So, for example, you can say *x && (y | | z)*, which is a more complex, or *compound*, expression. Table 7-3 shows the results of this operation.

Results of x && y		
x	*y*	*x && y*
True	True	True
True	False	False
False	True	False
False	False	False
Results of x // y		
x	*y*	*x		y*
True	True	True
True	False	True
False	True	True
False	False	False
Results of ! x		
x	*! x*	
True	False	
False	True	

Table 7-2.   *Results of Operators for All Possible Inputs*

x	*y*	*z*	*x && (y || z)*
True	True	True	True
True	True	False	True
True	False	True	True
True	False	False	False
False	True	True	False
False	True	False	False
False	False	True	False
False	False	False	False

Table 7-3. *The Results of x && (y || z) for All Possible Inputs*

Policy Arithmetic

Policy expressions treat *accept* and *next policy* as true and *reject* as false. They run a route through each policy in the expression and calculate the result the same way the Boolean operators do. Recall that *next policy* is the default action for a policy when no action is explicitly specified. Thus, when a policy does not match a route at all, its result for that route is *next policy*.

Policy expressions use a technique called *shortcut evaluation*; as soon the result of an expression is certain, the router stops and skips evaluation of any remaining policies in the expression. In Table 7-3, notice the fifth row: The expression is *False && (True || True)*. As soon as you see *False &&...* you know the expression is going to be false—because **False && <anything>** is false. Thus, there is no point in computing the remaining (*y || z*) part of the equation. This is significant because if a policy is skipped due to shortcut evaluation, its side-effect actions are also not executed.

With the same example, imagine that *x*, *y*, and *z* are policies, and 205.134.0.0/16 is the route. Assume that *x* would reject it, *y* would accept it, and *z* would have no opinion. Thus

reject && (*y || z*)

Policy expressions treat *reject* as false, so *reject && <anything>* is rejected. Here, policies *y* and *z* are not evaluated due to a short-cut evaluation. The expression is done, and its action is *reject*.

Now imagine a different route, say 185.140.0.0/16. Assume that *x* would have no opinion on this route (i.e. *next policy*), *y* would reject it, and *z* would accept it. This is equivalent to the seventh row in Table 7-3. At first, the expression is

next policy && (*y || z*)

Here, *next policy* is treated as true, so the expression must continue because *next policy && <unknown>* could go either way. So then the expression becomes this:

next policy && (reject | | z)

Here, *reject | | z* could still come out either way. So the expression evaluates *z*, and gets this:

next policy && (reject | | accept)

Here, *(reject | | accept)* is accepted, just like *(false | | true)* is true. So the expression reduces to this:

next policy && accept

This is interesting. You know that *true && true* is true. You know that *next policy* and accept are both treated like true. So you know that this expression is going to have some sort of true result, but which one? The answer is "the last one." If multiple *accept/next policy* results are found in an expression, and the expression results in *accept/next* policy, it uses the last *accept* or *next* policy result that it evaluated. If the expression results in a reject, it doesn't matter what it saw for accepts or next policies—the result is still reject.

Here is a more algorithmic way to think of this: The action of the last policy evaluated determines the expression's action. This is because of shortcut evaluation. It is like that silly old adage: "You always find something in the last place you look." At one point or another, you probably realized "Well yeah…. once you find it, you stop looking." In fact, the last action found always works out to be the expression's result, except when the last operator evaluated was *!*.

Note *There is probably a proof to this effect, but rather than go down that road, consider this: The policy framework never has to remember what was the result of a previous policy. It has to know only what any current operators are and what the current policy's result is. For example, if the current operator is &&, the previous policy must have been* accept/next *policy, or it would have already stopped with a* reject*. Whether it was* accept *or* reject *does not matter, because the* next policy *will determine the result of the &&.*

So with two different values of true, you might wonder exactly how *!* works. You might ask "What is *! next policy*?" Or you might ask "What determines whether *! reject* becomes *accept* or *next policy*? Well, *accept* and *next policy* both become *reject* when you negate them, and *reject* simply becomes *accept* when you negate it. If you happen to want *! My_Policy* to produce *next policy* instead of *accept*, you can define a policy called *next*, and then say *(! My_Policy && next)* like this:

```
[edit policy-options]
ps@R10# show
policy-statement Next {
```

```
        then next policy;
    }
ps@R10# show protocols
bgp {
    group One_Half {
        export ( ! My_Policy && Next );
    }
}
```

If My_Policy is true (either *accept* or *next policy*), this will become a *reject*. If it is false (*reject*), this will become *next policy*. If you somehow come up with a scenario where you need *reject* to negate to *accept* in one case and *next policy* in another case, you can modify My_Policy to put a community on the route that indicates this, and then build a smarter *next* that looks for that community and does what is appropriate. It is perfectly acceptable for a policy to reject a route, but first cause side effects—the side effects will carry through. This is another local use for community, and it should also be "cleaned up" before announcing to other routers with BGP.

Expressions and Chains

You can place a policy expression anywhere that you can place a policy. Thus, you can insert expressions into chains, and expressions can include other expressions (to arbitrary complexity). You create an expression by surrounding policy names and operators with parentheses. (Parentheses are optional when the expression is part of a larger expression.)

Recall that you create a chain by surrounding policy names with brackets. So, the following are all legal:

```
ps@R10# show protocols
bgp {
    group One_Half {
        export ( Is_IGnE && Make_Better ); /* a simple expression */
or...

        export [ Block_Privates (Is_IGnE && Make_Better ) ]; /* a chain with an expression */
or...
        export [ (Is_TenM && Make_Much_Better) (Is_IGnE && Make_Better ) ];
                /* a chain of two expressions */
or...
        export [ ( (Is_TenM && Make_Much_Better) || (Is_IGnE && Make_Better ) ) ];
                /* an expression containing two expressions */
    }
}
```

Keep in mind that since an expression is just part of a chain, the resulting chain has a default policy implicitly linked to the end of it. Thus, whenever an expression results in *next policy* for a route, it is up to the rest of the chain to decide whether to *accept* or *reject* that route—and if the explicitly configured chain does not make a decision, the default policy will.

Parentheses can be used to group expressions together. This controls the order of evaluation in nested expressions. Take the following example:

(*a && ! b | | c*)

The subexpressions in this compound expression are evaluated from left to right. The *!* is associated with the argument immediately to its right. So, it is equivalent to this:

((*a && ! b*) | | *c*)

if *a* is reject, *! b* is skipped, and *c* is evaluated. Conversely, you could explicitly say this:

(*a && (! b | | c)*)

Then, if *a* is reject, (*! b | | c*) is all skipped. You can also force a compound expression to be negated like this:

(*a && !(b | | c)*)

Now if *a* is *accept* or *next policy*, (*b | | c*) is evaluated, and its entire result is negated. Let's assume that *b* is also *reject*, and *c* is *next policy*. Then *reject | | next policy* is *next policy*, and *!next policy* is *reject*. Only then is the result fed to the *&&* operator to decide the expression's result. Whether *a* is *accept* or *next policy*, that *&& reject* is *reject*.

Note | *The expression (My_Policy) is also legal, and its result is the same as the policy My_Policy.*

Examples of Policy Expressions

Here are some examples of policy expressions in action.

```
[edit policy-options]
ps@R7# show
policy-statement Reject_10-10 {
    from {
        route-filter 10.10.0.0/16 orlonger;
    }
    then {
        community add 90-1;
        reject;
    }
}
policy-statement Accept_10-20 {
    from {
        route-filter 10.20.0.0/16 orlonger;
    }
```

```
    then {
        community add 100-1;
        accept;
    }
}
community 100-1 members 100:1;
community 90-1 members 90:1;
```

Notice that neither of these policies specifies the *next policy* action. Keep in mind that *next policy* can still be a result of one of these policies; that is what happens if a route does not match a policy (it is also what happens if a route matches, but the matching term does not specifically *accept* or *reject* the route).

Here are a few policy applications using expressions:

```
[edit protocols bgp group Expression_Examples]
ps@R7# set neighbor 172.16.201.2 export (Reject_10-10 && Accept_10-20)
ps@R7# set neighbor 172.16.202.2 export (Reject_10-10 || Accept_10-20)
ps@R7# set neighbor 172.16.203.2 export (Accept_10-20 || Reject_10-10)
ps@R7# set neighbor 172.16.204.2 export (! Reject_10-10)
ps@R7# set neighbor 172.16.205.2 export (! Accept_10-20)
```

Here is a sample routing table:

```
ps@R7# run show route terse 10/9

inet.0: 15 destinations, 15 routes (14 active, 0 holddown, 1 hidden)
+ = Active Route, - = Last Active, * = Both

A Destination        P Prf Metric 1   Metric 2    Next hop           AS path
* 10.10.1.0/24       B 170      100          0 >172.16.100.2         1 I
* 10.10.2.0/24       O  10        2            >at-0/1/1.10
* 10.20.1.0/24       B 170      100          0 >172.16.100.2         1 I
* 10.20.2.0/24       O  10        2            >at-0/1/1.10
* 10.99.30.0/24      B 170      100          0 >172.16.100.2         1 I
* 10.99.40.0/24      O  10        2            >at-0/1/1.10
```

Following are the results of each route, for each expression, including discussion.

export (Reject_10-10 && Accept_10-20)

- **10.10.1.0/24** *Reject_10-10* returns *reject* which is false. *false && <anything>* is false, so that's it. *&&Accept_10-20* is never evaluated. The expression returns *false* and rejects the route. You can see this indirectly because the route does not appear when you list the routes you are advertising to your neighbor:

```
ps@R7> show route advertising-protocol bgp 172.16.201.2 detail 10.10.1.0/24

ps@R7>
```

- **10.10.2.0/24** Same as 10.10.1.0/24.

- **10.20.1.0/24** *Reject_10-10* does not match, and returns a default *next policy*. *accept_10-20* returns *accept* and adds community 100:1. *next policy* and *accept* are both true, and *true && true* is true, so the expression result is true and its action is *accept*. The expression accepts the route, so the router announces it, including the community:

```
ps@R7> show route 10.20.1.0/24 advertising-protocol bgp 172.16.201.2 detail

inet.0: 23 destinations, 23 routes (22 active, 0 holddown, 1 hidden)
Prefix              Nexthop              MED     Lclpref AS path
10.20.1.0/24 (1 entry, 1 announced)
 BGP group Expression_Examples type External
     Nexthop: Self
     AS path: 1 I
     Communities: 100:1

ps@R7>
```

- **10.20.2.0/24** Same as 10.20.1.0/24.

- **10.99.30.0/24** Neither policies match, so both return a default *next policy*. *next policy && next policy* is true, with an action of *next policy*. There are no more policies in the chain, so the default policy is used. BGP's default policy accepts BGP routes, so this route is accepted. No communities are added:

```
ps@R7> show route advertising-protocol bgp 172.16.201.2 detail 10.99.30.0/24

inet.0: 23 destinations, 23 routes (22 active, 0 holddown, 1 hidden)
Prefix              Nexthop              MED     Lclpref AS path
10.99.30.0/24 (1 entry, 1 announced)
 BGP group Expression_Examples type External
     Nexthop: Self
     AS path: 1 I
     Communities:

ps@R7>
```

■ **10.99.40.0/24** The expression's result is identical with 10.99.30.0/24. However, this is an OSPF route. OSPF routes are rejected by BGP's default policy, so this route is not announced:

```
ps@R7> show route advertising-protocol bgp 172.16.201.2 detail 10.99.40.0/24

ps@R7>
```

export (Reject_10-10 II Accept_10-20)

■ **10.10.1.0/24** *Reject_10-10* matches, sets community 90:1, and returns *reject*, which is *false*. *Accept_10-20* does not match and returns *next policy*, which is true. The result of the expression is *false || true*, which is true, with the action *next policy*. The default policy accepts this route because it is BGP. The route is announced, with community 90:1 added:

```
ps@R7> show route advertising-protocol bgp 172.16.202.2 detail 10.10.1.0/24

inet.0: 23 destinations, 23 routes (22 active, 0 holddown, 1 hidden)
Prefix              Nexthop            MED    Lclpref AS path
10.10.1.0/24 (1 entry, 1 announced)
 BGP group Expression_Examples type External
     Nexthop: Self
     AS path: 1 I
     Communities: 90:1

ps@R7>
```

■ **10.10.2.0/24** The expression result is the same as with 10.10.1.0/24; however, the default action for OSPF routes under BGP export is *reject*. So although the community was added, the route is rejected:

```
ps@R7> show route advertising-protocol bgp 172.16.202.2 detail 10.10.2.0/24

ps@R7>
```

■ **10.20.1.0/24** *Reject_10-10* does not match and returns *next policy*. *true ||* *<anything>* is true, so *Accept_10-20* is never evaluated. The expression returns true, with an action of *next policy*. The BGP default policy accepts the route. The router announces the route with no communities:

```
ps@R7> show route advertising-protocol bgp 172.16.202.2 detail 10.20.1.0/24

inet.0: 23 destinations, 23 routes (22 active, 0 holddown, 1 hidden)
Prefix              Nexthop            MED    Lclpref AS path
10.20.1.0/24 (1 entry, 1 announced)
 BGP group Expression_Examples type External
     Nexthop: Self
     AS path: 1 I
```

```
              Communities:

 ps@R7>
```

- **10.20.2.0/24**   The expression result is the same as for 10.20.1.0/24. However, since this is an OSPF route, the BGP default policy rejects it:

```
 ps@R7> show route advertising-protocol bgp 172.16.202.2 detail 10.20.2.0/24

 ps@R7>
```

- **10.99.30.0/24**   *Reject_10-10* returns *next policy. Accept_10-20* is not evaluated. *true || <anything>* is true. The expression returns true, with a *next policy* action. The BGP default policy accepts the route. It is announced with no communities:

```
 ps@R7> show route advertising-protocol bgp 172.16.202.2 detail 10.99.30.0/24

 inet.0: 23 destinations, 23 routes (22 active, 0 holddown, 1 hidden)
 Prefix              Nexthop              MED    Lclpref AS path
 10.99.30.0/24 (1 entry, 1 announced)
  BGP group Expression_Examples type External
       Nexthop: Self
       AS path: 1 I
       Communities:

 ps@R7>
```

- **10.99.40.0/24**   The expression result and action are identical to 10.99.30/24. However, this is an OSPF route, and is rejected by the BGP default:

```
 ps@R7> show route advertising-protocol bgp 172.16.202.2 detail 10.99.40.0/24

 ps@R7>
```

export (Accept_10-20 || Reject_10-10)

- **10.10.1.0/24**   Does not match *Accept_10-20*, and defaults to *next policy. Reject_10-10* is skipped, accepted by BGP default policy, and announced with no communities added:

```
 ps@R7> show route advertising-protocol bgp 172.16.203.2 detail 10.10.1.0/24

 inet.0: 23 destinations, 23 routes (22 active, 0 holddown, 1 hidden)
 Prefix              Nexthop              MED    Lclpref AS path
 10.10.1.0/24 (1 entry, 1 announced)
  BGP group Expression_Examples type External
       Nexthop: Self
       AS path: 1 I
       Communities:

 ps@R7>
```

■ **10.10.2.0/24**   Same expression result as 10.10.1.0/24, but OSPF routes are rejected by BGP's default policy:

```
ps@R7> show route advertising-protocol bgp 172.16.203.2 detail 10.10.2.0/24

ps@R7>
```

■ **10.20.1.0/24**   Matches *Accept_10-20*, which adds community 100:1 and accepts route. *true || <anything>* is true, so expression results is true, with action of *accept*. Route is announced with community 100:1:

```
ps@R7> show route advertising-protocol bgp 172.16.203.2 detail 10.20.1.0/24

inet.0: 23 destinations, 23 routes (22 active, 0 holddown, 1 hidden)
Prefix              Nexthop              MED    Lclpref AS path
10.20.1.0/24 (1 entry, 1 announced)
 BGP group Expression_Examples type External
     Nexthop: Self
     AS path: 1 I
     Communities: 100:1

ps@R7>
```

■ **10.20.2.0/24**   Same result as 10.20.1.0/24.

■ **10.99.30.0/24**   Does not match *Accept_10-20*, and receives default action of *next policy*, with no community added. Accepted by BGP default policy, and announced with no community:

```
ps@R7> show route advertising-protocol bgp 172.16.203.2 detail 10.99.30.0/24

inet.0: 23 destinations, 23 routes (22 active, 0 holddown, 1 hidden)
Prefix              Nexthop              MED    Lclpref AS path
10.99.30.0/24 (1 entry, 1 announced)
 BGP group Expression_Examples type External
     Nexthop: Self
     AS path: 1 I
     Communities:

ps@R7>
```

■ **10.99.40.0/24**   Same expression result as 10.99.30.0/24, but OSPF route is rejected by BGP default policy:

```
ps@R7> show route advertising-protocol bgp 172.16.203.2 detail 10.99.40.0/24

ps@R7>
```

export (! Reject_10-10)

- **10.10.1.0/24**   *Reject_10-10* matches the route, adds community 90:1, and rejects it. *! false* is true, so the expression result is true, with an action of *accept*. The router announces the route with community 90:1:

```
ps@R7> show route advertising-protocol bgp 172.16.204.2 detail 10.10.1.0/24

inet.0: 23 destinations, 23 routes (22 active, 0 holddown, 1 hidden)
Prefix              Nexthop              MED    Lclpref AS path
10.10.1.0/24 (1 entry, 1 announced)
 BGP group Expression_Examples type External
     Nexthop: Self
     AS path: 1 I
     Communities: 90:1

ps@R7>
```

- **10.10.2.0/24**   Same as previous example.
- **10.20.1.0/24**   *Reject_10-10* doesn't match, and returns *next policy*. *! true* is false, and reverses *next policy* to reject. The route is rejected:

```
ps@R7> show route advertising-protocol bgp 172.16.204.2 detail 10.20.1.0/24

ps@R7>
```

- **10.20.2.0/24**   Same as previous example.
- **10.99.30.0/24**   Same as previous example.
- **10.99.40.0/24**   Same as previous example.

export (! Accept_10-20)

- **10.10.1.0/24**   Does not match *Accept_10-20*, so result is true, with an action of *next policy*. *!* reverses true to false, and *next policy* to reject. Route is not announced:

```
ps@R7> show route advertising-protocol bgp 172.16.205.2 detail 10.10.1.0/24

ps@R7>
```

- **10.10.2.0/24**   Same result as previous example.
- **10.20.1.0/2**   Matches *Accept_10-20*, with result of true, and action of *accept*. *! true* is false, and reverses *accept* to *reject*. Route is not announced:

```
ps@R7> show route advertising-protocol bgp 172.16.205.2 detail 10.20.1.0/24

ps@R7>
```

- **10.20.2.0/24**   Same result as previous example.
- **10.99.30.0/24**   Same result as 10.10.1.0/24.
- **10.99.40.0/24**   Same result as 10.10.1.0/24.

Subroutines

You can use one policy as a match condition in another policy. In fact, you can apply an entire policy chain as a match condition. This is called a *policy subroutine.*

Policy subroutines serve two functions: they enable you to define complex match conditions or complex side-effect actions. This works by writing a policy, which tests the conditions you wish or has the side effects you wish (or both), and then using that policy as a *policy* match condition in another policy. In either case, you apply them as a match condition. If they have side effects, the side effects occur immediately at the point where you specify the subroutine as a match condition.

Here's an example:

```
[edit policy-options]
ps@R7# show
policy-statement Example_Policy {
    term Call_Subroutine {
        from policy [ subA subB ];
        then {
            metric 101;
            accept;
        }
    }
}
```

In this example, the chain [subA subB] is the policy subroutine. Do not think of it as two policy subroutines. The entire chain is evaluated to determine the subroutine's result. This uses the same evaluation method as *import* and *export* statements. The *from* policy and *to* policy match conditions take each route and use the result of the subroutine chain to determine the success or failure of the policy match condition. *Accept* is a successful match, and *reject* is an unsuccessful match (this is the case even if the result comes from the default policy instead of your configured policies).

How the subroutine comes to these results is not relevant. In particular, it does not really matter whether the subroutine's terms matched the route or not; it only matters whether the subroutine chain as a whole returned *accept* or *reject* for the route. It is possible for a term in the subroutine policy to match a route, but specify neither *accept* nor *reject*—thus, that term's match success has no affect on whether the *from* policy match condition succeeds or fails.

Furthermore, here is an important caveat regarding the fact that policy subroutines employ policy chains. Recall that policy chains have a default policy at the end, whose behavior depends on how the chain was applied. In the case of a policy subroutine, the policy has not actually been applied to any specific protocol or other routing function, so its default policy has not yet been determined. A calling policy is always part of a chain, and a chain always has a default policy. The calling policy chain's default policy is used as the called chain's default policy.

This means that if your subroutine chain does not produce an explicit *accept* or *reject* for all possible routes, there may be some routes for which your subroutine will behave differently when used under different applications. For example, it may accept certain BGP routes when applied under BGP, but not when applied under OSPF. Conversely, when applied to the forwarding table, the subroutine chain would accept everything. You can use several strategies to deal with this; they are discussed in the "Techniques" section later in this chapter. To make a long story short, you probably want to make sure any policies you use as subroutines have a catch-all term at the end that provides an answer for all possible routes.

Recall that *accept* and *reject* are generic policy results. How the policy match condition evaluates *accept* or *reject* is unrelated to how import and export statements evaluate them. Sometimes people confuse *accept* with "announce a route" and *reject* with "discard a route." When a policy subroutine accepts a route, that affects only the success of that particular policy match condition. That result is not seen by any import or export statements that happened to reference the calling policy. A policy subroutine cannot directly communicate *accept* or *reject* to an import or export statement, and therefore it cannot directly cause a route to be announced, installed, ignored, or discarded (it does, however, apply side effects directly).

As discussed earlier, the purpose of *from* and *to* clauses in a term is to specify match criteria that a route must meet before that term's actions will be applied to the route. Since a policy subroutine is a match condition, its ultimate purpose is to say "it matches" or "it doesn't match" to the term. The policy match condition may well be just one of many match conditions in a term. Any conditions before the policy must already have succeeded before the policy will be called. Any remaining match conditions will be tested for a given route only if the policy match condition (and all previous conditions) were successful. Since side effects in policy subroutines occur immediately, the order of match conditions becomes significant.

JUNOS software stores match conditions in a specific order. The policy condition falls toward the end of this order, but it is not last. This is significant when a policy subroutine has side effects. There are two implications:

- Side-effect actions can be applied to a route even if it fails to match the term.

- Side effects may not be applied even though you specified a subroutine that would *definitely* apply them.

This first point may seem counterintuitive. In all other cases, a route must completely satisfy all of a term's match conditions before its actions are applied. With subroutines, the subroutine's actions are applied by the subroutine policy, which is done with its job (including side effects) before the calling policy is finished evaluating match conditions. Also, the subroutines' actions are applied even if the route fails to match the `policy` condition itself—as you have seen, a policy can apply side effects and still reject a route. When a subroutine does this, the route is still "alive"—a later term may still accept it.

The second point is more intuitive, but it can still catch you off guard. It is common to write terms that have *only* the policy condition. In this case, you are accustomed to the subroutine's effects always being applied. If you then add another condition, which happens to come before the policy condition, the subroutine's effects will not be applied to routes that fail the first condition. Here's an example:

```
policy-statement Surprise {
    from {
        policy Side_Effects;
        route-filter 192.168.0.0/16 orlonger;
    }
    then {
        metric add 10;
    }
}
policy-statement Side_Effects {
    then {
        community add My_Community;
    }
}

[edit policy-options]
```

In the Surprise policy, the side effects in the Side_Effects subroutine will be applied to all routes, even though some routes will fail to match the *from* clause. Here's what happens if you then add a condition that comes before *policy*, such as *as-path*:

```
policy-statement Surprise {
    from {
        as-path My_Friend;
        policy Side_Effects;
        route-filter 192.168.0.0/16 orlonger;
    }
    then {
        metric add 10;
    }
}
```

The side effects in the subroutine will be applied only to routes that match the *as-path*. Thus, a route may not go through the subroutine at all, or it could go through the subroutine but still not go through the same term's *then* clause. Or it could go through all three.

The *policy* match condition behaves the same in both *from* and *to* clauses. The policies in the subroutine may of course contain both *from* and *to* clauses. The evaluation of those clauses is unaffected by which type of clause contains the subroutine.

Protocol-Specific Policy

This section highlights some policy behavior that is specific to certain protocols. By necessity, then, it discusses several topics that have not yet been covered in this book and with which you may not yet be familiar. Much of this will still probably make perfect sense to you from past experience. If some of it does not, you are probably not using those protocols and may not "need to know" these issues. Just remember that this information is here if you find yourself needing it.

Protocol-Specific Match Conditions

As indicated, some match conditions work only on routes from certain protocols. Others work on all routes but behave differently depending on the protocol from which the route was learned (the *source* protocol).

Here are excerpts from the match conditions table that indicate which match conditions are unique to a specific protocol and which behave differently depending on the protocol routes they are matching against.

Condition	Source Protocol Specific	Valid Protocols
area		OSPF
as-path		BGP, static, aggregate
external		OSPF
interface		RIP, BGP, direct, local
level		IS-IS
local-preference		BGP
metric[234]	BGP	
neighbor		BGP
origin		BGP
preference[2]	BGP	
tag[2]	OSPF, IS-IS	

Conditions listed under "Valid Protocols" test for attributes that are specific to those protocols. For example, *area* is an attribute that is valid only for OSPF routes.

Internal to JUNOS software, all routes are capable of having all attributes. However, the values for irrelevant attributes are officially undefined and generally set to *null* (the "nonexistent" value—this is different than zero, which is a valid value for many attributes). These values generally will not match anything you specify, but you should always qualify matches on protocol-specific attributes with the *protocol* match condition.

Attributes above listed as "Source Protocol Specific" are used differently by the various protocols when they build a route's data structure. This also means you must qualify which protocol's routes you are looking for, because another protocol's routes could possibly match one of these conditions for reasons unrelated to what you are testing.

These cases are discussed in detail in the following sections.

Interface

`Interface` matches the interface that will be used to forward packets to the route. This is not protocol specific. However, you should avoid using this with routes that involve recursive next-hops (for example, internal BGP or multihop external BGP routes).

Policies are evaluated as needed by the protocols and other router functions. Those needs are not directly coupled to next-hop resolution. If a protocol has computed a specific forwarding interface by means of a recursive lookup, that information could change after a policy is evaluated. If the recursive route later changes resulting in a different forwarding interface, then the policy's results will become invalid after the fact. The result of that policy will remain incorrect until some other event causes that policy to be reevaluated.

This is not an issue for the `next-hop` match condition, because it is tested against the route's actual next-hop, whether it is local or remote. Only `interface` requires a recursive lookup for remote next-hops because without that lookup, it would have no value. You should specify additional criteria to avoid the possibility of matching on `interface` for recursive routes.

Level

This is specific to IS-IS and is discussed in Chapter 11. Routes from other protocols will not match it.

Metric[234]

Metric is a protocol's primary measure of how preferable a route is. For most protocols, metric[2-4] are protocol-independent values that are local to the router. They are undefined unless you set them yourself. (See "Side-Effect Actions" earlier in this chapter.)

For BGP, the metric is MED (for multiexit discriminator), and metric2 represents the IGP cost to the BGP next-hop of the route.

Neighbor

This is only defined for BGP. It is the IP address from which the announcing router sourced the packet containing the route. It corresponds to the `_neighbor_bgp` configuration statement that created the peering session over which the route was learned.

Preference2

Preference and preference2 are protocol-independent metrics. However, the current implementation of JUNOS software uses the preference2 field of a route's data structure internally to store the BGP local-preference attribute.

Thus, you should neither match against, nor set preference2 for BGP routes via policy. It is best to limit policies using preference2 to a specific protocol using the *protocol* match condition. If you truly need to match "every protocol other than BGP," your best bet is to make a policy subroutine that rejects *protocol bgp*, and accepts everything else.

Protocol

from protocol behaves as you might expect, and *to protocol* comes close. The details of *to protocol* are discussed in the "To vs. From" section earlier in the chapter. *from protocol* matches the protocol through which the router learned the route.

Tag[2]

Tag and tag2 are similar to communities; they are arbitrary 32-bit values you can attach to a route and reference later. They are protocol independent and local to the router, with two exceptions.

Tag corresponds to the OSPF and RIP2 tag field. If you set this field on a route and then export that route into OSPF or RIP2, the tag field will be set to that value during export. Other routers will see it and can match on it in their policies. If you do not set it, JUNOS software initializes it to zero. Note that some other vendors implement RFC 1850, which specifies rules for auto-generating this field. Thus, you cannot count on this field having a zero value. However, RFC 1850 requires routers auto-generating tag values to set the highest order bit (0x80000000 or 128.0.0.0). Thus, you should be able to trust that there will be no nonzero tags in your network without that bit set, unless someone in your network sets them manually.

Tag2 is used internally by IS-IS for leaking routes between levels. You should not set or match on tag2 for IS-IS routes, and you should configure any policies that use this attribute to ignore IS-IS routes. See Chapter 11 for more detail.

Regular Expressions

Regular expressions define patterns. A pattern may match more than one attribute's value. In some cases, it may be better to define the distinct communities or AS paths separately and just list them all. In other cases, it may make sense to define a pattern that matches everything you want, and then just list it.

Here is an example of a community regular expression:

```
[edit policy-options]
user@r1# show
```

```
policy-statement match-com {
    term com {
        from community private;
        then accept;
    }
    then reject;
}
community private members "(65(4((1[2-9])|([2-9][0-9])))|(5..)):*";
```

This rather nasty regular expression will match any community that starts with a private ASN. Following is a routing table containing some routes with the community attribute and a test policy run showing the routes it accepts.

Note *Although beyond the scope of this chapter, this regex matches 6541 followed by 2-9, 6542-9 followed by 0-9, and 655 followed by any two digits.*

```
user@r1# run show route detail protocol static | match "(Com|entry)"
185.140.75.0/24 (1 entry, 1 announced)
                    Communities: 1:1 1:2 65412:1
185.140.76.0/24 (1 entry, 1 announced)
                    Communities: 65410:1
185.140.77.0/24 (1 entry, 1 announced)
                    Communities: 65510:1
185.140.78.0/24 (1 entry, 1 announced)
                    Communities: 65432:1
205.134.123.136/29 (1 entry, 1 announced)

[edit policy-options]
user@r1# run test policy match-com 0/0

inet.0: 14 destinations, 14 routes (14 active, 0 holddown, 0 hidden)
Prefixes passing policy:

185.140.75.0/24     *[Static/5] 1d 02:20:10
                     > to 205.134.101.10 via fxp0.0
185.140.77.0/24     *[Static/5] 00:30:58
                      Reject
185.140.78.0/24     *[Static/5] 00:18:30
                      Reject

Policy match-com: 3 prefixes accepted, 11 prefixes rejected
```

Notice that 185.140.76.0/24 does not pass the policy. Its community's first part, 65410, is not in the private ASN space (64512-65535).

Troubleshooting Policy

As you can see, JUNOS software offers you an extensive array of tools to implement your routing policy. This chapter has kept policy examples simple to avoid confusion. The examples in the "Policy Design" section later in this chapter are more involved. However, they will still pale in comparison to the complexity of policy in a significant network.

You can solve problems in simple policies like those in this chapter just by looking at them. Sometimes you may still find a usage that does not behave as you expect. It is likely, though, that as your policies get longer and more complicated, you'll find it more difficult to spot these problems. JUNOS software offers you two valuable tools, and some additional techniques, for troubleshooting your policy.

The two tools are the CLI *test policy* command and the JUNOS software's policy flag under *routing-options traceoptions*. If you run into policies that you are unable to troubleshoot with these tools, you can combine a few powerful aspects of JUNOS software that are not specific to policy into a troubleshooting technique that should fill in the gaps. However, this technique is slightly more intrusive to your network than the use of the tools alone.

Test Policy

You have already seen the *test policy* CLI command in action. It takes a policy name and a prefix, and then processes all active routes matching the prefix, or with longer masks, with the policy you specified. This is absolutely the quickest way to test a policy; it requires no setup work or reconfiguration.

One caveat with *test policy* is that only routes currently in the routing table are tested by the command. Therefore, it cannot see routes that were learned but rejected or otherwise not installed in the routing table.

Another caveat is that its default policy accepts all routes. This is no problem if you are testing policies applied by any of the protocols whose default policy is the same (all import policies, aggregates, and forwarding table export). However, you need to be careful when using *test policy* with the remaining protocols. Following is a case in which *test policy* does not provide accurate results. Consider the following policy, BGP configuration, routing information displays, and policy test results:

```
user@r1# show protocols
bgp {
    group IGnE {
        type external;
```

```
        export All_Supernets;
        peer-as 3;
        neighbor 192.168.100.33;
    }
}
user@r1# show
policy-statement All_Supernets {
    term Chair_Force {
        from {
            route-filter 205.134.0.0/16 prefix-length-range /18-/18;
        }
        then accept;
    }
    term Tub_Club {
        from {
            route-filter 185.140.0.0/16 upto /24;
        }
        then accept;
    }
}

user@r1# run show route terse 205.134/16

inet.0: 19 destinations, 19 routes (19 active, 0 holddown, 0 hidden)
+ = Active Route, - = Last Active, * = Both

A Destination          P Prf Metric 1    Metric 2     Next hop           AS path
* 205.134.0.0/18       A 130                           Reject
* 205.134.1.0/24       D   0                          >fxp1.1
* 205.134.1.1/32       L   0                           Local
* 205.134.64.0/18      A 130                           Reject
* 205.134.101.0/27     D   0                          >fxp0.0
* 205.134.101.1/32     L   0                           Local
* 205.134.123.136/29   S   5                           205.134.101.12
                                                      >205.134.101.20

* 205.134.255.1/32     D   0                          >lo0.0

user@r1# run show route advertising-protocol bgp 192.168.100.33 205.134/16

inet.0: 19 destinations, 19 routes (19 active, 0 holddown, 0 hidden)
```

```
Prefix                Nexthop                MED    Lclpref AS path
205.134.0.0/18        Self                                  I
205.134.64.0/18       Self                                  I


user@r1# run test policy All_Supernets 205.134/16


inet.0: 19 destinations, 19 routes (19 active, 0 holddown, 0 hidden)
Prefixes passing policy:

205.134.0.0/18       *[Aggregate/130] 02:21:19
                        Reject
205.134.1.0/24       *[Direct/0] 2d 02:21:12
                        > via fxp1.1
205.134.1.1/32       *[Local/0] 2d 02:21:12
                        Local
205.134.64.0/18      *[Aggregate/130] 02:21:19
                        Reject
205.134.101.0/27     *[Direct/0] 2d 03:57:14
                        > via fxp0.0
205.134.101.1/32     *[Local/0] 2d 03:57:14
                        Local
205.134.123.136/29   *[Static/5] 2d 01:24:21
                           to 205.134.101.12 via fxp0.0
                        > to 205.134.101.20 via fxp0.0
205.134.255.1/32     *[Direct/0] 2d 03:57:14
                        > via lo0.0


Policy All_Supernets: 8 prefixes accepted, 0 prefixes rejected


[edit policy-options]
user@r1#
```

The `show route advertising protocol` CLI command shows that the router is announcing exactly two routes from the 205.134/16 supernet to the BGP neighbor. You can see many more routes in the router's own routing table from the `show route` command. However, `test policy` reports that all the 205.134/16 routes pass the policy. This is because `test policy`'s default policy accepts everything. Although you could correct this by adding an unconditional *reject* at the end of the policy, you would probably not want to do so, because that would also block any BGP routes you may have learned. Normally, you want to re-announce these routes.

One way around this is to make a copy of the policy and then make a small modification to the copy so that it emulates the default policy you desire, like so:

```
[edit]
user@r1# show policy-options
policy-statement All_Supernets {
    term Chair_Force {
        from {
            route-filter 205.134.0.0/16 prefix-length-range /18-/18;
        }
        then accept;
    }
    term Tub_Club {
        from {
            route-filter 185.140.0.0/16 upto /24;
        }
        then accept;
    }
}

user@r1# copy policy-options policy-statement All_Supernets to policy-statement All_Supernets_test
user@r1# edit policy-options policy-statement All_Supernets_test

[edit policy-options policy-statement All_Supernets_test]
user@r1# set term BGP_Default_1 from protocol bgp
user@r1# set term BGP_Default_1 then accept
user@r1# set term BGP_Default_2 then reject
user@r1# up

[edit policy-options]
user@r1# show policy-statement All_Supernets_test
term Chair_Force {
    from {
        route-filter 205.134.0.0/16 prefix-length-range /18-/18;
    }
    then accept;
}
term Tub_Club {
    from {
        route-filter 185.140.0.0/16 upto /24;
    }
    then accept;
}
term BGP_Default_1 {
    from protocol bgp;
    then accept;
}
term BGP_Default_2 {
    then reject;
}

[edit policy-options]
user@r1# commit
commit complete

user@r1# run test policy All_Supernets_test 205.134/16
```

```
inet.0: 19 destinations, 19 routes (19 active, 0 holddown, 0 hidden)
Prefixes passing policy:

205.134.0.0/18     *[Aggregate/130] 02:33:05
                       Reject
205.134.64.0/18    *[Aggregate/130] 02:33:05
                       Reject

Policy All_Supernets_test: 2 prefixes accepted, 6 prefixes rejected
```

Now *test policy* is showing you how the policy behaves under BGP export.

This is even easier with RIP and OSPF; their default policy is just *then reject;*. Note that this is slightly intrusive in that you *do* have to reconfigure the router. However, you are not changing the configuration of any active statements; you are only adding a new policy that is not applied anywhere.

test policy has the following benefits over the techniques described in the next section:

- No preparation is necessary.
- No reconfiguration (and no need for configuration permissions) is needed.
- It does not impact running protocols.
- No sifting through log files is required.
- It's easy to test a subset of routes.

Alas, this ease of use and lack of undesirable side effects comes with limitations in effectiveness:

- It will test routes even if they are marked *no-readvertise*.
- It will ignore the *to* clause if a policy has one.
- You cannot currently test a chain or expression.
- The default policy, which accepts all routes, can make it difficult to discern how a route will behave under applications that use a different default.

As indicated, many of these problems can be overcome by working with a copy of the policy and modifying it to reflect your application's defaults. The only cost of this is that the user must have configuration permission and must change the configuration.

test policy is a fairly simple tool; while it is quick, it does not tell you much information about policy. Policy tracing can give you much more insight, and combining the two can give you even more powerful results.

Policy Tracing

As you work your way through this book, you will learn that the amount of debugging information available to you on a Juniper Networks router is staggering. Much of this is available via the various *traceoptions* clauses. Many components of the configuration include this clause, which contains flags in each place that are relevant to the section.

The "magic" flag for policy is the *policy* flag in the *routing-options traceoptions* configuration section. You need to specify the name of a log file and turn on the flag:

```
user@r1# show routing-options
traceoptions {
    file route.log;
    flag policy;
}
```

This will cause the following information to be logged in *route.log*:

- The destination address of every route that is processed by the policy framework (even default policies)
- Whether it is an import, export, or subroutine policy
- The type of match condition it is being tested against (excluding route filters and prefix lists)
- Whether it succeeded (1) or failed (0) that match
- Optionally, the flow-control action that a given term imposed on the route, and the term's name

The flow-control action and term's name are logged only for terms that include the *trace* action in their *then* clauses. This action has absolutely no effect on how the policy framework processes a route or on a route's attributes. This continues to be true even if the term had no *then* clause before you added the trace action.

With the trace action in place, any route that matches the term's *from* and *to* clauses will trigger an entry in the trace file indicating the route's prefix, the name of the term, and the flow-control action that was executed. These trace file entries will be prefixed with the string *policy_actions_export* (even if it is not an export policy). Any prefix that triggers such a message matched all the conditions of the term that contained the trace action. Note that if a route matches a route filter that has an action, that term's *then* clause will be skipped, including a trace action if there is one. In this case, you can add the *trace* action to that specific route filter's actions.

No log message tells you that a route failed to match a term's *from* or *to* clause. However, if a route failed any condition other than route-filter, source-address-filter, or prefix-list, you will see that it failed that specific condition. You can deduce that it failed a term by the lack of a *policy_actions_export* entry if the term in question had a trace action.

You can put trace actions in as many or as few terms as you like. Keep in mind that actions are logged only for terms with trace actions. You need to choose your trace terms appropriately so that you can tell the difference between "it didn't match," "it matched, but not the term I'm tracing," and "the route I'm questioning was never even processed." Other messages that the software adds to the file can indicate which neighbor's import or export statements it is processing.

A Sample Trace File

Here is a partial configuration and a single route going through the indicated export chain:

```
protocols {
    bgp {
        group IGnE {
            export [ Tub_Club Chair_Force Send ];
        }
    }
}
routing-options {
    traceoptions {
        file route.log;
        flag policy;
    }
}
policy-options {
    prefix-list Chair_Force {
        205.134.64.0/18;
        205.134.128.0/18;
        205.134.192.0/18;
    }
    policy-statement Chair_Force {
        term Trace_Chair_Force {
            then {
                trace;
                next term;
            }
        }
        from {
            protocol aggregate;
            route-filter 205.134.0.0/16 prefix-length-range /18-/18;
            prefix-list Chair_Force;
        }
        then {
            community add Advertise;
        }
    }
    policy-statement Tub_Club {
        term Trace_Tub_Club {
            then {
                trace;
                next term;
            }
        }
        from {
            origin igp;
            policy ( ! is_Host );
            route-filter 185.140.0.0/16 orlonger;
        }
        then {
```

```
                community add Advertise;
            }
        }
    policy-statement is_Host {
        term Trace_is_Host {
            then {
                trace;
                next term;
            }
        }
        from {
            route-filter 0.0.0.0/0 prefix-length-range /32-/32 accept;
            route-filter 0.0.0.0/0 orlonger reject;
        }
    }
    policy-statement Send {
        term Trace_Send {
            then {
                trace;
                next term;
            }
        }
        from community Advertise;
        then accept;
    }
    community Advertise members 1:99;
}

[edit]
user@r1# run show log route.log
1. Sep 15 17:44:18 export: Dest 10.250.0.0 proto BGP
2. Sep 15 17:44:18 policy_actions_export: Prefix 10.250.0.0/16 term Trace_Tub_Club --> next term
3. Sep 15 17:44:18 policy_match_qual_or: Qualifier origin Sense: 1
4. Sep 15 17:44:18 subroutine: Dest 10.250.0.0 proto BGP
5. Sep 15 17:44:18 policy_actions_export: Prefix 10.250.0.0/16 term Trace_is_Host --> next term
6. Sep 15 17:44:18 policy_match_qual_or: Qualifier policy Sense: 1
7. Sep 15 17:44:18 policy_actions_export: Prefix 10.250.0.0/16 term Trace_Chair_Force --> next term
8. Sep 15 17:44:18 policy_match_qual_or: Qualifier proto Sense: 0
9. Sep 15 17:44:18 policy_actions_export: Prefix 10.250.0.0/16 term Trace_Send --> next term
10. Sep 15 17:44:18 policy_match_qual_or: Qualifier community Sense: 0
```

The policies here have a term at the beginning that deliberately does nothing but indicate the name of the policy. The only action is *trace*, and the term's name is chosen to reflect the policy that is starting to process the route.

Here is a discussion of each line of the log file. (The line numbers have been added for discussion.)

1. JUNOS software is exporting 10.250.0.0, which was learned from BGP.

2. Policy Tub_Club is processing this route (see comment about including the policy name in the first term's name; without using this technique, you would not be able to identify to which policy the log file entry refers).

3. This route passes the origin condition. *policy_match_qual_or* means that the software is considering a list of possible values (or *qualifiers*), and that any of them matching is sufficient for the condition to match (in the minds of

the engineers, they are like a *logical or*). (Note that the same message is used even for conditions in which you are not allowed to configure a list. These are treated as though you had a list with exactly one entry.) The entry *Sense: 1* indicates that the condition was a success.

4. A policy subroutine is about to process 10.250.0.0.

5. Policy is_Host is processing the route. (Note that this is the policy subroutine.)

6. The policy subroutine match condition was a success. The lack of other *qual_match_or* messages indicates that the subroutine used only route-filter, source-address-filter, or prefix-list, or possibly none of them.

Note | *At this point, the route is tested against the route-filter. It fails to match, but route-filters are not logged. Furthermore, this term's then clause contains no trace action, so the silence is not related to the fact that the term failed to match. This is strictly deduction without that trace action.*

7. Policy Chair_Force is processing the route.

8. The protocol match condition was checked and failed.

9. Policy Send is processing the route.

10. The route failed the community match condition.

Navigating Trace Files

JUNOS software does the tracing in real time whenever the policy framework processes a route. That includes whenever a route is imported or exported, even if you did not have any user-configured policies controlling it.

If you already have your traceoptions set, and you want to know about a route that was processed recently, you can use `show log route.log`. This command shows the entire log file through a pager that is like the UNIX `more` command.

Tips on Searching the Log File

While this is really beyond the scope of this chapter, here are a couple of tips: Your log file may well be days, and megabytes, long. Type **G** and it will transport you immediately to the end of the file—that is, the most recent log message. Then type **?** and enter a search string. This will search backward until it locates the string in your log file. Try the network number of the prefix you are researching, or just type **policy** or **port** (for export or import). A tremendous amount of information is located in the log file—possibly much of it having nothing to do with policy, if you have other flags set. These tips should help you sift through it. The pager search functions do accept UNIX regular expressions, so typing **?Sep 10 16:40.*policy** will take you to a policy entry from that time, if there is one. Note that if there is still too much information, you can pipe your output through *except* to weed out things you know do not matter to you. For example, you can say

```
user@r1> show log route.log | except "cats|dogs"
```

and your output will be sure not to include lines that contain either the string cats or the string dogs (| is a special character to except and match).

Real-Time Tracing

If you did not already have *traceoptions* set, or you did not already carefully place *then trace* actions, the existing log file will not help you. You will be starting from scratch once you set them up. In this case, you are looking for new log information. The *show log* CLI tool is not appropriate for this because it shows only what was in the file when you typed the command. If you want to see what is happening as it happens, you can monitor new entries in a log file with monitor start route.log. Your session will now blurt out new log file entries right on top of whatever you were doing, whenever they are generated. This is extremely rude, so you probably want to do it only when you are not typing or reading anything else. However, you can "shush" the router by typing ESC-Q. Typing it again will "un-shush." You could also just use a second Telnet session for the monitoring.

If you have other trace flags set, or if you just have a lot of routes, you may find yourself inundated with more information than you can process—much of it being irrelevant to your particular cause. Fortunately, you can filter the log monitoring. First, cancel it with monitor stop route.log (omit the filename to cancel all log monitoring). Then reissue the command, but pipe it through match like this:

```
user@r1> monitor start route.log | match "policy|port"
```

Now, the software will interrupt you only with messages that contain the strings policy, or port (such as import or export). Match also accepts regular expressions if you put them in double quotation marks (").

You might still have a problem using the real-time technique because the route you are researching may not need to be announced for a long time. In particular, BGP announces a route only when something about it changes. If your network is for production, you probably do not want to reset your BGP session just to force reannouncement, because you will disrupt traffic for seconds or even minutes.

Fortunately, you already know a completely noninvasive way to force routes through a policy—with *test policy*. When you use this, the policy framework dutifully logs match conditions, subroutine usage, and any *then trace* actions, just as when a protocol processes a route. One thing that is great about combining monitoring, tracing, and *test policy* versus plain *test policy* is that the combination tells you the exact flow-control action for each route, not just the *accept* or *reject* results. If you combine this with the policy copying technique, you can put a final term at the end of the policy, with no match conditions, that just says *then trace*. *Test policy* will tell you if the policy rejects or accepts the route, and the trace file will tell you if the accept was really a *next policy*.

When you use policy tracing with *test policy*, no protocol is actually announcing the routes. Thus, nothing logs the fact that it is sending the route through a policy. If you have too many routes, this may be a blessing. Or, you may wish that you could see that a route is about to be processed, just in case it does not match any terms that have trace actions. You can insert a term that has no conditions before the first term, and then add a trace action. Now you are guaranteed to see every route as it goes through the policy, and you can make that happen whenever you like without disrupting your network. Remember that you can limit the routes that *test policy* processes if this is still giving you too much information. You can also always filter which routes get logged by adding a route-filter condition in any of these "for tracing only" terms.

More Trace Tips

Following are a handful of miscellaneous techniques you may find useful.

- When setting the trace action to terms that do not have *accept*, *reject*, or *next policy*, explicitly set the *next term* action. If you do not, in older versions the trace action logs a term name of *<default>* instead of the actual term name when the *next term* action is defaulted rather than explicit.

- When you combine *test policy* with trace file monitoring, the output from the two tools will intersperse, becoming difficult to read. Run *test policy* with | *no-more*. This will generally cause all the *test policy* output to come out before any of the trace file monitoring.

- If your policy is sufficiently well laden with trace actions such that you do not want to see the output of *test policy* at all, get rid of it by adding | *save /dev/null*. This pipes the output into the UNIX equivalent of oblivion. You will see only the trace monitoring output.

- Use *groups* and *apply-groups* to apply the trace action invisibly to every term in every policy. Leave it in place at all times. Keep the *policy* trace flag under routing-options turned off normally so it will have no effect. Combine this with putting a *trace only* term at the beginning of any complex policies.

Then, if you have policy concerns, you can set the *policy* trace flag. Between the match condition log messages and the trace actions, you should be able to see just about everything that is going on with policy. This technique lets you avoid having to reconfigure any policies. Thus, committing this configuration will not trigger any route churn. Also, you may choose to restrict many of your network operators from editing the policy configuration—even so, these people will still be able to do meaningful policy debugging.

Large-Scale Tracing

If you use a lot of policies or they are long, and inserting trace actions all over the place is impractical, you can have the JUNOS software CLI do it for you using configuration groups. The following code shows you how you use groups to put the *then trace* action in all your terms. This can save you a lot of time and shorten a configuration, because it has a global effect on the configuration with only a few lines of actual directives.

```
user@r3# show
version 4.4R2.3;
groups {
    Policy_Trace {
        policy-options {
            policy-statement <*> {
                term <*> {
                    then trace;
                }
                then trace;
            }
        }
    }
}
policy-options {
    apply-groups Policy_Trace;
    policy-statement Customers {
        from community Customer;
        then {
            community add Advertise;
        }
    }
    policy-statement Others {
        from community [ Transit Peer ];
        then {
            community add Advertise;
        }
    }
    policy-statement Send {
        from community Advertise;
        then accept;
    }
    policy-statement set_Customer {
        then {
            community add Customer;
```

```
            }
        }
    policy-statement set_Peer {
        then {
            community add Peer;
        }
    }
    policy-statement Ours {
        from community Our_Net;
        then {
            community add Advertise;
        }
    }
    community Advertise members 3:99;
    community Customer members 3:1;
    community Our_Net members 3:4;
    community Peer members 3:2;
    community Transit members 3:3;
}
```

Configuration groups are configuration patterns that you can define. You give them a name and a subset of any configuration directives you like. Then you can apply them to select sections of your configuration and they are merged with the actual configuration. In the preceding code, the group Policy_Trace is defined. Then, under policy-options, Policy_Trace is applied. You can see the result of the merge by piping *show* through *display inheritance* like this:

```
ps@r10# show policy-options | display inheritance
policy-statement Customers {
    from community Customer;
    then {
        community add Advertise;
        ##
        ## 'trace' was inherited from group 'Policy_Trace'
        ##
        trace;
    }
}
policy-statement Others {
    from community [ Transit Peer ];
    then {
```

```
                community add Advertise;
                ##
                ## 'trace' was inherited from group 'Policy_Trace'
                ##
                trace;
        }
}
policy-statement Send {
    from community Advertise;
    then {
        ##
        ## 'trace' was inherited from group 'Policy_Trace'
        ##
        trace;
        accept;
    }
}
policy-statement set_Customer {
    then {
        community add Customer;
        ##
        ## 'trace' was inherited from group 'Policy_Trace'
        ##
        trace;
    }
}
policy-statement set_Peer {
    then {
        community add Peer;
        ##
        ## 'trace' was inherited from group 'Policy_Trace'
        ##
        trace;
    }
}
policy-statement Ours {
    from community Our_Net;
    then {
        community add Advertise;
        ##
        ## 'trace' was inherited from group 'Policy_Trace'
        ##
```

```
        trace;
    }
}
community Advertise members 3:99;
community Customer members 3:1;
community Our_Net members 3:4;
community Peer members 3:2;
community Transit members 3:3;

[edit]
ps@r10#
```

You can apply a group within a subset of a configuration as well. For example, instead of applying the group at the policy-options level, you could apply it at the policy-statement level. Then it would affect only the policy where you applied it.

As stated earlier, terms with a trace action and no flow control action are logged with the name *<default>* instead of their real name. This is true up through JUNOS software version 4.4. As of version 5.0, you see the actual term name in all cases. This makes the configuration group technique even more valuable. By combining this with the trace-only first term, you can see every route go through every policy, almost every match condition (except route-filter, and prefix-list), and the resulting action, right in the trace file.

Keep in mind that when you configure the recommended *apply-groups* statement, it does in fact modify the policies to which you apply it. Therefore, when you commit the configuration, the JUNOS software will reevaluate every policy application. Since the *trace* flag has no effect on the results of policy evaluation, everything should come out the same as before. If there are no changes in the local routing table, there will be no reason for any protocol to announce anything it would not otherwise have announced. Thus, there should be no route churn, but the processing may still be significant.

Policy Tracing Strengths and Weaknesses

Policy tracing is extremely comprehensive. It can tell you pretty much everything you could possibly want to know about what is happening as routes go through your policies.

Combining tracing, working with copies of policies, and *test policy* gives you the maximum amount of information with the minimum impact on your network. Reconfiguring a policy that you have not applied anywhere (a copy that you have made for testing) will not cause any reevaluation.

However, policy tracing can be a little, or a lot, of extra trouble to configure. Being prepared in advance with the techniques indicated in this chapter, can help significantly.

It is easy to get too much information—100,000 answers you do not need with 1 that you do need is worth little more than no answers at all. If your network is substantial and the slightest risk of impact during operation is unacceptable, it is worth practicing with these monitoring, searching, and filtering techniques during a maintenance window in which nothing is actually broken, so it will come more naturally when there is a real emergency and so you are aware of any impact from the extra processing.

Sometimes, you do not really need to know every detail about how the JUNOS software evaluated the policies—you just need to have a little more insight into the result. The next technique may be a better fit in such a case.

Debug Communities

Communities can also serve as useful debugging tools. You can use communities on import policies in any protocol that allows import, or on BGP export policies. If you have concerns about whether or not a term is acting on a certain route, add an *add community* to the term. If you have concerns about whether the JUNOS software is pushing a given route through a certain policy, insert a new first term in the policy, with no conditions, that adds a community.

Then, by looking at the routes in the routing table, you can see which terms end up with the new communities. That will tell you which terms acted on which routes. You can see the communities on a route using the `show route` command's *detail* option.

In your network numbering plan, you may find it useful to reserve a large block of private communities for debugging purposes. A range that is easy to match helps, such as 65420-65499:0-65535, which you can match with the regular expression *654[2-9].:**. If you can do this, then multiple-router policy debugging is even easier. Assign each router a number between 20 and 99. Assign the terms on that router a community starting with the router's number. The first term on the first router would get 65420:1, and the second term 65420:2. The first term on the second router would get 65421:1, and so on. This way, you know which router put it there, just by looking at the community.

Weaknesses and Strengths

The trace action techniques can tell you anything that debug communities can tell you. Furthermore, the communities technique is significantly more intrusive. Adding communities is a nontrivial change to your policies that will absolutely cause route churn. You are also more likely to make an unintentional—and unfortunately meaningful—change to a policy.

The concept of troubleshooting a copy of the policy still applies. However, in this case, it is better to make a backup copy and edit the original. This way, you do not have to rewrite your import and export chains. Then when you are done, you can overwrite the original with the backup.

You can use debug communities only with BGP, and it should work with import policies on any protocol that allows them, because the communities can exist on the routes in JUNOS software even if the protocol does not support them. However, RIP2 is the only unicast routing protocol other than BGP that currently allows import.

Despite all the restrictions, caveats, and warnings, however, this technique has some strengths. It saves you from having to sift through truckloads of trace file output. It saves you from the worry of missing the moment a route went through the policy (perhaps before you turned on tracing, or before the last trace file rolled over). All you have to do is look at the route. If the term acted on the route, the community will appear.

Finally, with BGP, using debug communities is an easier way to troubleshoot policy across multiple routers. If you use unique communities across all terms and all routers, you can look at one router to see the effect of all policies affecting the route on its way to that router. Of course, this requires a comprehensive understanding of what path the route announcement is taking through your network. Unless you are specifically testing how a route leaves your network, you should delete these communities from routes that are announced to external peers.

Policy Design

Your routing policy may be relatively simple, but even in a moderately complex network, the configuration that enforces that policy can grow to become a considerable maintenance concern. If somebody makes a mistake somewhere, and 500 lines of policy configuration are stored on 100 routers enforcing your policy, that can be quite a lot of troubleshooting. Even worse, if you need to make a change to your routing policy, it can be a nightmare to implement even the simplest change ("use a metric of 200 instead of 150 for all backup routes") when 50,000 lines of configuration are spread across your network.

Most IP routers offer some mechanism to enforce your routing policy. Juniper Networks actually calls its mechanism "policy," while other vendors use their own names for similar mechanisms. Most of the other mechanisms out there suffer from monumental inflexibility, however. This tends to cause two major problems that make enforcing policy about an order of magnitude more difficult and error prone than it could otherwise be.

First, other policy mechanisms are not modular. They generally require that you apply exactly one policy in a given location. While many of them do let you reuse a policy in more than one place, the policy's behavior will be identical in both places. Thus, if you have two locations that need five identical tasks, and one different task, you need to write two completely different policies. This makes your configuration longer and creates a lot more code to troubleshoot. It also doubles the amount of work you need to do (and the number of places you could make a mistake) if you ever decide to change the like part of the two policies.

While the amount of work required to write a few policies is trivial, with larger networks, you may have to write a huge number of policies, possibly in proportion to the number of unique types of neighbors you have—so 500 neighbor routers could result in 500 unique polices.

Second, many other policy mechanisms cannot execute multiple sets of actions on a single route. Frequently, their evaluation strategy is "first match," meaning that for a given route, they find the first set of match criteria that it satisfies, execute a set of actions associated with that match set, and stop. If you want to execute five actions on a certain group of routes, and a sixth on some subset of those routes, you would need to duplicate the match/action configuration for the subset. Furthermore, you need to do careful organization of the pairs to ensure that the OS does not execute the superset first, thus causing it to eclipse the subset. The result, then is that you have many terms (or the equivalent of terms in the other vendor's policy mechanism) that are near duplicates. You end up with policy configuration that fails to scale because it grows proportionally to (*neighbors × number of routes*).

These are extremes, because in most networks, many neighbors and routes are identical from a policy perspective. In the end, however, it is normal in today's networks to have 10 to 100 times as much policy configuration as you have policy needs. It is also common, therefore, to see large networks with home-grown tools for automating policy configuration. Making such systems stable and easy to understand, use, and modify is rarely a priority. Thus, you not only have an unnecessarily painful amount of policy configuration to face, but a similarly painful piece of software to face as well.

With JUNOS software, you should find that duplication of configuration is never necessary. Because it allows you to apply a chain of policies anywhere you need to, you can modularize your policies so that you use just the functions you need in the appropriate places. Furthermore, since multiple terms can act on a route, you can organize the contents of individual policies so that you never need to repeat the conditions and actions within them.

If you find yourself thinking that you need a tool to automate the generation of your policies, by the nature of automation, you must be doing the same thing in many different places. You will probably find that by using the tactics and strategies in the following sections, you can actually put that would-be automation tool's intelligence right into your policy implementation. This will result in drastically fewer and shorter policies. As a bonus, you will save yourself from having to build and maintain the automation tool.

Tactics for Improving Policies

Here you will find several techniques to help you make better policies. You can write a policy in many different ways, and each will still do exactly the same thing. As long as there are no doubts about the intent of the policy and nobody needs its result to change, differences will not matter. But in many networks, that "as long as" will end somewhere between 5 minutes and a month after you write your policies; then it will matter how you constructed them.

Note	*All the following examples serve to show techniques for designing the implementation of your routing policy. Do not take them in any way to indicate what your routing policy should actually be. Many examples involve some amount of absurdity in the decisions being made, because they do not reflect a real-world routing policy. Telling you what your routing policy should be is beyond the scope of this, and perhaps any, book, because policy is always tied to both physical environment and business decisions, which are invariably unique to every organization.*

Subroutine Matches

One of the easiest ways to simplify policy is to use subroutines. If you use a set of match conditions in multiple locations, you can define a policy with just those conditions and use that policy as a *from policy* condition in other policies. You can use this technique to make a complex route-filter series reusable, but other uses are many. Note that you usually cannot use a named prefix list to replace a route-filter, because prefix lists do not allow mask criteria or actions; they are only exact matches.

Imagine that you frequently need to check to determine whether routes are from your most difficult customer, the Department of Aggravation & Tomfoolery (A&T for short). A&T's routes come from a common AS path. However, due to the politics of your environment, A&T has negotiated to provide network service to a few other organizations. You need to take special actions on A&T's routes in several cases, but you don't need to bother with the other organizations to whom they provide network services. Thus, an AS path condition is insufficient. A&T has many subnets, and it tends to change those frequently, so a route-filter describing these subnets is undesirable. However, the exceptions constitute only a few subnets. Thus, a route-filter will work fine to weed out the exceptions. You might have several policies that use an identical *from* block. Here are two such policies:

```
[edit policy-options]
user@r1# show
policy-statement AnT_Backup {
    from {
        as-path AnT;
        route-filter 205.134.105.192/27 exact next term;
        route-filter 205.134.212.128/26 exact next term;
        route-filter 0.0.0.0/0 orlonger;
    }
    then {
```

```
            local-preference 50;
            community add Customer;
            community add PITA;
            community add AnT;
            community add Backup;
        }
    }
policy-statement AnT {
    from {
        as-path AnT;
        route-filter 205.134.105.192/27 exact next term;
        route-filter 205.134.212.128/26 exact next term;
        route-filter 0.0.0.0/0 orlonger;
    }
    then {
        community add Customer;
        community add PITA;
        community add AnT;
    }
}
community AnT members 1:666;
community Backup members 1:100;
community Customer members 1:1;
community PITA members 1:13;
as-path AnT 65501;

[edit policy-options]
user@r1#
```

These are reasonable policies to see on your peering sessions with A&T's primary and backup connections. The differences between them are the less desirable local-preference and the additional "Backup" community.

A route must first have a matching AS path. (See "Interdomain Routing" for details.) The exception routes will match one of the first two route filters, and their optional action *next term* will skip the *then* clause. Remaining routes will match the final route filter (all routes match 0/0 *orlonger*), which has no optional action, so the *then* clause will act on these routes.

Note that in this case, *next policy* would have had the same effect as *next term* because there are no more terms. However, *next term* is more future-proof—that is, you might someday add more terms to this policy, and you wouldn't want them to be ignored.

You can simplify this by capturing the A&T match conditions into a subroutine policy:

```
user@r1# show |no-more
policy-statement is_AnT {
    term match_AnT {
        from {
            as-path AnT;
            route-filter 205.134.105.192/27 exact next term;
            route-filter 205.134.212.128/26 exact next term;
            route-filter 0.0.0.0/0 orlonger;
        }
        then accept;
    }
    then reject;
}
policy-statement AnT_Backup {
    from policy is_AnT;
    then {
        local-preference 50;
        community add Customer;
        community add PITA;
        community add AnT;
        community add Backup;
    }
}
policy-statement AnT {
    from policy is_AnT;
    then {
        community add Customer;
        community add PITA;
        community add AnT;
    }
}
community AnT members 1:666;
community Backup members 1:100;
community Customer members 1:1;
community PITA members 1:13;

[edit policy-options]
user@r1#
```

The *from* clause in this new policy *is_AnT* is identical to the ones used in the original policies, so it will act on and ignore the same routes. However, this policy is designed to be used as a match condition, rather than an import policy. Instead of manipulating the matching routes, it simply accepts them. Nonmatching routes will flow to the next term (the unnamed term in this case) and get rejected.

Now you have a one-line match condition that does everything the old *from* clauses did. It will succeed for A&T routes and fail anything else. You have shortened your configuration and removed some duplication. If you ever need to change how you identify A&T routes, you will have to fix it in only one place. And if you need to match them again in another policy, it will be a simple, rather than complicated, match condition.

Collapsing Terms

If you have a series of different conditions, and routes meeting any of those conditions will receive the same actions, you can write the policy so that you specify the actions only once. In other words, you may be able to *collapse* terms together so that a common action block acts on more of your routes.

If the series of conditions use only one type of match, that match condition may allow a parameter list. Suppose you have five different AS paths defined, and you want to put a local preference of 200 on all of them. You could make a term for each condition, like this:

```
term Friends {
    from as-path Friends;
    then {
        local-preference 200;
        accept;
    }
}
term Acquaintences {
    from as-path Acquaintances;
    then {
        local-preference 200;
        accept;
    }
}
[etc...]
```

However, because match condition parameter lists treat the parameters as alternatives, you can simplify like this:

```
term Local_Pref_200 {
    from as-path [ Friends Acquaintences Strangers Customers Partners ];
    then {
        local-preference 200;
        accept;
    }
}
```

Note that if you needed to test additional conditions for each term, this technique would work only if the criteria for the remaining conditions were the same in each case.

If you wanted to specify that all of the above terms also require that the route is learned from neighbor 1.1.1.1, that would be fine. However, suppose you wanted a route matching an AS path to receive these actions, but only if the route came from a certain neighbor, and you want a different AS path to come from a different neighbor. You could not convert this

```
term Friends {
    from {
        neighbor 1.1.1.1;
        as-path Friends;
    }
    then {
        local-preference 200;
        accept;
    }
}
term Acquaintences {
    from {
        neighbor 2.2.2.2;
        as-path Acquaintences;
    }
    then {
        local-preference 200;
        accept;
    }
}
[etc...]
```

to this:

```
term Local_Pref_200 {
    from {
        neighbor [ 1.1.1.1 2.2.2.2 ];
        as-path [ Friends Acquaintences Strangers Customers Partners ];
    }
    then {
        local-preference 200;
        accept;
    }
}
```

The second form is not the equivalent of the original policy. This will act on any route from any of the AS paths as long as they come from either neighbor. So a route with an AS path of Friends that came from neighbor 2.2.2.2 will also have its local-preference set to 200, which is not the desired effect.

Shoot First, Ask Questions Later

Another opportunity to collapse terms together arises when you have an "all or nothing" policy. Often, you may find that your policies reject some routes and perform several of the same actions to the rest.

It is OK to set an attribute on a route, and then later reject the whole route. Sometimes you may find yourself thinking, "I'm not going to announce that route. I had better get rid of it before I add this community." Attributes do not cost much—only a few bytes of memory each. You can often set several attributes up front and unconditionally, and do your rejecting later. Rejecting a route before you change an attribute does not buy you any significant time, but worrying about it can complicate your policies.

Here is a policy that sets up routes from a few different peers:

```
[edit policy-options policy-statement From_Transit]
user@r1# show | no-more
term IGnE {
    from as-path IGnE;
    then {
        local-preference 90;
        community add Transit;
        next-hop self;
        accept;
    }
}
term Ten-M {
    from as-path Ten-M;
    then {
        local-preference 70;
        community add Transit;
        community add Backup;
        next-hop self;
        accept;
    }
}
term Special_Case_Transit {
    from {
        route-filter 64.252.0.0/16 orlonger;
    }
```

```
    then {
        local-preference 90;
        community add Transit;
        next-hop self;
        accept;
    }
}
then reject;
```

Notice that this policy acts like these terms have nothing in common. It does some things to one type of route, and then accepts them (so it is done with those). It then moves on to two other types of routes that it has not touched yet (because if it had, they would have been accepted by now). After that, it throws everything else away, with a condition-free unnamed term.

But these terms do have something in common. They all add the Transit community, and they all set next-hop self. You could also say that "most of them" set local-preference to 90. Since this policy rejects everything that it does not accept, you can move the common actions to a conditionless term at the beginning of the policy. Let them act on everything—the remaining terms will accept the good ones, and it won't matter that you made those changes to the ones you threw away:

```
[edit policy-options policy-statement From_Transit]
user@r1# show | no-more
term Set_Transit {
    then {
        local-preference 90;
        community add Transit;
        next-hop self;
    }
}
term IGnE {
    from as-path IGnE;
    then accept;
}
term Ten-M {
    from as-path Ten-M;
    then {
        local-preference 70;
        community add Backup;
        accept;
    }
```

```
    }
    term Special_Case_Transit {
        from {
            route-filter 64.252.0.0/16 orlonger;
        }
        then accept;
    }
    then reject;
```

This even sets local-preference to 90, despite the fact that this action is not ubiquitous. It is in the majority, so it is just as well to set it and let the one different case override it. It appears to be something of a default, so if you add more terms for new special cases, they will also benefit from it.

You can generalize this technique beyond just "all or none" as well. If, for example, you do not want some routes to receive the common actions, you can match them first and either *accept* or *next policy* them. *Accept* will prevent them from receiving actions from other policies. *Next policy* will cause them to slip past the *reject* and the end of this policy, unscathed. However, with this much variety going on in a policy, it is quite possible that it would warrant being divided into multiple policies, as discussed in the "Strategies" section later on.

Collapsing with Expressions

Yet another way to simplify a policy comes when you have a series of terms with identical *then* clauses, if their criteria consist solely of policy subroutines. In this case, rather than have a series of terms like this:

```
policy-statement Many_Subroutines {
    term one {
        from policy is_Ant;
        then {
            metric add 50;
            community add PITA;
            next policy;
        }
    }
    term two {
        from policy is_Customer_B;
        then {
            metric add 50;
            community add PITA;
            next policy;
```

```
            }
        }
    }
```

You can join the terms together with the expression | | (or) operator:

```
[edit policy-options]
user@r1# show
policy-statement Many_Subroutines {
    term one {
        from policy ( is_Ant || is_Customer_B );
        then {
            metric add 50;
            community add PITA;
            next policy;
        }
    }
}
```

Subroutine Actions

Ending a policy with an unconditional *reject* works well for subroutine matches. However, doing so eclipses the rest of the policy, which may well be useful to you. Subroutines give you an even more flexible way to avoid redundancy in your actions, much like they do with match conditions.

You can build a policy for use as an action-only subroutine. Recall that although subroutines are available as a match condition, they do reference other policies, and side-effect actions in those policies do take place. The earlier example could also be written like this:

```
[edit policy-options]
user@r1# show | no-more
policy-statement set_Transit {
    then {
        local-preference 90;
        community add Transit;
        next-hop self;
        accept;
    }
}
policy-statement From_Transit {
```

```
term IGnE {
    from {
        as-path IGnE;
        policy set_Transit;
    }
    then accept;
}
term Ten-M {
    from {
        as-path Ten-M;
        policy set_Transit;
    }
    then {
        local-preference 70;
        community add Backup;
        accept;
    }
}
term Special_Case_Transit {
    from {
        policy set_Transit;
        route-filter 17.0.0.0/8 orlonger;
    }
    then accept;
}
then reject;
}
```

The set_Transit policy was intentionally designed to accept all routes. All terms process match conditions until they encounter a failure. By making this policy always succeed, its result will not alter the accumulated results of conditions preceding it, nor will it eclipse testing of conditions that follow it. This is discussed in more detail later in the "Designing Subroutine Policies" section.

The policy framework tests almost all other match conditions before the policy match condition. A failure in any of these matches will prevent the *from policy* from being executed. Thus, the actions in an action-only subroutine will not be executed. However, there are three exceptions to this: The policy framework tests the route-filter, source-address-filter, and prefix-list conditions *after* the policy condition. Thus, if your *from* clause uses these conditions, the subroutine's actions may be executed on a route even if these conditions fail to match that route. There are two ways around this:

- You can move the necessary conditions into another policy and join the two together in a subroutine expression.

- You can put the policy subroutine in the *to* clause rather than the *from* clause. The *to* conditions are not considered until all of the *from* conditions have succeeded. Normally, you would have to be careful that the conditions in your policy subroutine are not ones that would behave differently in a *to* clause than in a *from* clause. In this case, however, you are safe because your subroutine policy is action-only. It has no conditions.

As a side note, if you specified the optional action to a route-filter condition, the *to* clause is still evaluated. Any failed matches in the *to* clause will cause the route-filter's action to be skipped just as they would cause a *then* clause to be skipped. Furthermore, any side-effect actions in a *to policy* statement will be executed even if a *from route-filter* action specifies *accept* (or any other action).

Here is what happens if you use an action-only subroutine in a *from* clause along with a route-filter:

```
[edit policy-options]
user@r1# show | no-more
policy-statement Demo_Sub_Actions {
    from {
        as-path Upto2;
        policy set_Backup;
        route-filter 172.0.0.0/8 orlonger;
    }
}
policy-statement set_Backup {
    then {
        community add Backup;
    }
}
community Backup members 1:2;
community Customers members 1:1;
community Transit members 1:95;
as-path Upto2 ".{0,2}";
```

This policy is applied as a BGP import policy to neighbor 192.168.100.33.

Here are the results (| *match* is used simply to strip out irrelevant output):

```
user@r1# run show route next-hop 192.168.100.33 detail | match "^[0-9]|com|as p"
10.250.0.0/16 (2 entries, 1 announced)
                AS path: 3 5 10 I
```

```
                  Communities: 3:3 3:99
172.30.0.0/15 (2 entries, 1 announced)
                  Inactive reason: AS path
                  AS path: 3 4 I
                  Communities: 1:2 3:2 3:99 4:4 4:99
192.168.0.0/16 (1 entry, 1 announced)
                  AS path: 3 I
                  Communities: 1:2 3:4 3:99
```

Note that the 192.168 route gets the 1:2 community even though it does not match the 172/8 route-filter.

Conversely, here's how it looks if you move the action subroutine to the *to* clause:

```
[edit policy-options policy-statement Demo_Sub_Actions]
user@r1# show
from {
    as-path Upto2;
    route-filter 172.0.0.0/8 orlonger {
        community add Transit;
        community add Customer;
        accept;
    }
}
to policy set_Backup;

user@r1# run show route next-hop 192.168.100.33 detail | match "^[0-9]|com|as p"
10.250.0.0/16 (2 entries, 1 announced)
                  AS path: 3 5 10 I
                  Communities: 3:3 3:99
172.30.0.0/15 (2 entries, 1 announced)
                  Inactive reason: AS path
                  AS path: 3 4 I
                  Communities: 1:1 1:2 1:95 3:2 3:99 4:4 4:99
192.168.0.0/16 (1 entry, 1 announced)
                  AS path: 3 I
                  Communities: 3:4 3:99
```

You can see that now the policy subroutine's actions are applied only to the one route that actually matches both the route-filter and the AS path regular expression. Note that there are route-filter actions in the second version—although they appear visually "before" the *to* clause, they are in fact dependent on it. They will not be executed if the *to* clause fails to match a route.

Annotate

Policies are a staggeringly appropriate application for JUNOS software's annotation capability. Although it is not policy specific, *annotate* has its roots in software engineering, from the "comment" concept. The JUNOS software policy framework is more like software engineering than any other router configuration mechanism you are likely to see. You may find that methods that are obvious to you when you create them are not obvious to people who read them later. And if, for example, you go six months without reading your own policy, you may wonder "what on earth was he thinking?"

Consider the first version of the Demo_Sub_Actions policy in the "Subroutine Actions" section earlier in this chapter. It applied a policy action subroutine before the route-filter. Someone might see this as a technique to kill two birds with one stone, and leverage the fact that the actions occur despite the fact that the total match conditions are as yet uncertain. It would be wiser to annotate the configuration to indicate that this is intentional, like so:

```
user@r1# edit policy-statement Demo_Sub_Actions

[edit policy-options policy-statement Demo_Sub_Actions]
user@r1# annotate from "Note: policy below tags routes as Backup even if they fail the route-filter"
user@r1# up

[edit policy-options]
user@r1# show | no-more
policy-statement Demo_Sub_Actions {
    /* Note: policy below tags routes even if they fail the route-filter */
    from {
        as-path Upto2;
        policy set_Backup;
        route-filter 172.0.0.0/8 orlonger community add Customers;
    }
}
```

Now you have an extremely dynamic policy, and it can have three different outcomes: nothing, just the actions in set_Backup, or those plus the added community. It's best to describe the intended usage of any policy that has restrictions, such as a subroutine-only policy, or a policy that is intended to be chained after certain other policies.

Strategies for Implementing Routing Policies

Strategies are general ways of thinking about and organizing problems. When you employ a strategy in implementing your routing policy—whatever the strategy—you increase your chances of maintaining control of that implementation. It is not too hard to start out with a simple implementation. With a good strategy though, you might actually be able to *keep* it simple when your network is 100 times larger than when you started.

The main strategies you should employ when implementing your routing policy is to

- Make your policies as reusable as possible.
- Make single-use policies as short as possible.

Try to make your policies accomplish a specific task rather than all tasks associated with a given neighbor. If you have a few policies that share some identical terms, ask yourself what those terms do. If the logic behind those terms really is the same, then move them into their own policy and apply both policies. The policy being modified should not use the *accept* action, because it would prevent routes from being modified by the backup policy. Instead, it should either let routes flow to the end of the default *next policy*, or use an explicit *next policy* if it needs to force certain routes to bypass remaining terms.

Modifier Policies

Frequently, you may find yourself with a need for two nearly identical policies. In such a case, you can create a *modifier policy* that is intended to be used in conjunction with the other policy, rather than create a near duplicate of it. Take the example in the "Subroutine Matches" section. There, you created two policies for your A&T customer—one for their backup connection and one for their primary connection. Recall that A&T was an exceptional case, so it is reasonable to assume that you would also have a generic pair of policies in most similar situations. They might look like this:

```
policy-statement Customer {
    then {
        community add Customer;
    }
}
policy-statement Customer_Backup {
    then {
        local-preference 50;
        community add Customer;
        community add Backup;
    }
}
```

Note that no match conditions appear in these policies. Their intelligence comes from where you apply them. Rather than have the policy figure out whether a route is from a customer, you as the administrator make a point to apply these policies only as *import* statements on customer links.

You probably noticed that these two policies have something in common—the Customer community. The second policy here also has something in common with the A&T backup policy—the local-preference and the Backup community. Here is an example protocol bgp section where you might see these policies in action:

```
show |no-more
group Customer_1 {
    peer-as 101;
    neighbor 205.134.199.2 {
        import Customer;
    }
    neighbor 205.134.199.6 {
        import Customer_Backup;
    }
}
group Ant {
    peer-as 103;
    neighbor 205.134.197.2 {
        import AnT;
    }
    neighbor 205.134.197.6 {
        import AnT_Backup;
    }
}
```

This concept of a backup version of a policy is starting to look like something that might be reusable. You can extract it from the two "_Backup" policies, into a new policy, like this:

```
policy-statement Backup {
    then {
        local-preference 50;
        community add Backup;
    }
}
```

You can chain this to the end of the non–"_Backup" policies to produce the same results, so the "_Backup" policies are now completely unnecessary. Here is the resulting policy section:

```
policy-statement AnT {
    from policy is_AnT;
    then {
```

```
            community add Customer;
            community add PITA;
            community add AnT;
        }
    }
    policy-statement Customer {
        then {
            community add Customer;
        }
    }
    policy-statement Backup {
        then {
            local-preference 50;
            community add Backup;
        }
    }
```

Here is how you would rebuild the *protocol bgp* section to use the new policy strategy:

```
    [edit protocols bgp]
    user@r1# show
    group Customer_1 {
        peer-as 101;
        neighbor 205.134.199.2 {
            import Customer;
        }
        neighbor 205.134.199.6 {
            import [ Customer Backup ];
        }
    }
    group Ant {
        peer-as 103;
        neighbor 205.134.197.2 {
            import AnT;
        }
        neighbor 205.134.197.6 {
            import [ AnT Backup ];
        }
    }
```

Now the mere existence of the "Backup" policy converts the primary policy into a backup policy. Note that the backup policy does not specify flow-control actions. In general, a modifier policy should use only the *next policy* or *next term* flow-control actions. It is intended to be "stuck in the middle" of an existing chain with little concern for where it goes—it generally just needs to go before any *accept* statements. Letting it accept or reject would deny this flexibility.

Minimize Specific Policies

You will inevitably have customers, or peers, like A&T, who demand special treatment. In the end, you will not be able to make every single policy reusable; some tasks will happen only at one place in your network. In these cases, it is still critical that you minimize the use of one-shot policies. Although you cannot reuse these policies, you will still benefit from keeping as much logic as you can in the generic policies and putting just the necessary logic into the one-shot policies.

At this point, you may also have noticed redundancy between the A&T policy and the generic customer policy. A&T is, after all, a customer. For the moment, the Customer policy is about as simple as it could be—a one-liner. But you can still remove the redundancy from the A&T policy and get the same effect by adding the generic Customer policy to A&T's import chain.

The differences strictly pertaining to A&T now look like this:

```
protocols {
    bgp {
        group Ant {
            peer-as 103;
            neighbor 205.134.197.2 {
                import [ Customer AnT ];
            }
            neighbor 205.134.197.6 {
                import [ Customer AnT Backup ];
            }
        }
    }
}
policy-options {
    policy-statement AnT {
        from policy is_AnT;
        then {
            community add PITA;
            community add AnT;
        }
    }
}
```

This difference may seem minor, visually. However, imagine having thousands of customers, and realize that some day, you might need to do something new or different to your customer routes. Perhaps you will want to modify *their* local preference. If you had left the "Customer" functionality embedded in the AnT policy, you would almost certainly have overlooked it when you modified your Customer policy with the new action. The rest of your thousands of customers would all be fine, and your one biggest nightmare customer would not get the change.

Deferred Actions

Another way to simplify policies is by using local communities. You can set communities at the beginning of a policy, or policy chain, and match and act on them later. These communities will have no meaning outside of the local router, and in fact it is best to delete them before the execution of the policy chain is done, to ensure that they do not confuse another policy chain elsewhere. Likewise, to be safe, you should delete them at the beginning of the policy, in case another peer or policy accidentally left them there.

You reserve a block of communities for local-policy use only. You should expect never to see these communities on an installed or announced route; they will exist only for the duration of a policy chain. The way this works is to divide a policy chain into three phases:

- Initialize
- Check
- Execute

You surround this system with a Begin and an End policy. These clean up the policy-local communities. Begin makes sure that no policies are coming from an external neighbor or left over by an import policy. End gets rid of them all, and it also does the actual accepting and rejecting of the routes.

The initialization phase allows you to set some communities that assert facts to the rest of the policy chain. For example, you can assign a community to mean "import policy" and one to mean "route reflector client." Then, terms and policies later on in the chain can consider these assertions when they make their routing decisions.

Showing how to set and check communities is beyond the scope of this section. However, here are a couple of example policy chains and a discussion of what would be going on inside the policies.

```
[edit protocols]
user@r1# show
bgp {
    group Internal {
        export [ Begin I_Int I_Exp C_Private X_Self X_Backup End ];
    }
    group External {
        import [ Begin I_Ext I_Imp C_Private X_Backup End];
    }
}
```

The three prefixes used above have the following meanings:

I_ = initialize
C_ = check
X_ = execute

I_Int asserts to the rest of the chain that this is an internal peer. I_Exp asserts that this is an export policy Normally, there is no easy way for a policy to conclude information about how it was applied. This is a new capability that does not exist outside this strategy. To take different actions based on how a policy is applied, you would normally either try to deduce it with match conditions or have duplicate policies with minor differences, and then differentiate based on which policy you choose to apply. With this technique, you can simply *tell* a policy anything you wish about how or where you called it. This phase is optional, so if you do not need this capability, you can omit it.

With the last of the I_... policies, your chain is "initialized." It is ready for the real work. Now you divide your chain into a "questions" phase and a "results" phase. You relegate the questions phase to *check*ing various conditions about the routes. The only actions you should see in a C_ policy should be *community add, next policy,* and *next term.* Whenever a C_ policy concludes something about a route, it attaches a policy-local community indicating as much. This is the "smart part" of the policy chain—the part that figures everything out. All these communities either directly or indirectly communicate actions that need to happen to the remainder of the policy chain. These could be side effects or information on whether to accept or reject a route.

Once your chain is done checking everything, it can *execute* all of those decisions. The X_ policies consist of nothing more than *from community* conditions and *then* actions—only side-effects actions though—manipulating route attributes. These policies execute the decisions that the C_ policies made. They do not accept or reject routes.

Finally, when you are done processing your routes, it is time for them to "stay or go." One of the decisions you presumably made in the check phase was whether to announce the route. This decision needs to be saved for the last policy for two reasons: First, it allows you to concentrate cleanup of all of the policy-local communities you used into a single term of one policy; otherwise, that would become a burden. More importantly, by delaying acceptance until the last policy, you may be able to make the order of the X_ policies, as well as that of the C_ policies, independent. You would have to ensure that different policies do not make conflicting decisions, of course. If your policies are solving specific unrelated problems, such independence tends to happen naturally. Policy order independence is one of the primary strengths of this strategy. All you have to do is make sure the policies move from I_, to C_, and then to X_. This saves you and your operators from having to know which other policies have to be applied before or after a particular policy.

You might find it easier to read the policy chain if you use longer prefixes, such as "Init_" and "Chk_." However, this strategy can lead to long chains, and that can make readability harder. Also, you may choose to do the rejecting during the check or execute phases, which may introduce some amount of order dependence, depending on how you do it. If you do all of your rejecting in the execute phase, you should make sure that you design your policies so that order does not matter. If you do it all in the End policy, you may not have to worry about the order.

Designing Subroutine Policies

Following is a discussion of the behavior of an entire subroutine chain—not the individual policies or expressions within that chain, because they behave exactly as in a direct import/export statement. The differences center around how default policies affect subroutines.

Syntactically, you can design policy chains with respect to default policies, in five ways:

1. Let the protocol decide.
2. Default does not matter (result is ignored).
3. Catch-all match conditions (with explicit results).
4. Explicitly default to *accept*.
5. Explicitly default to *reject*.

Using the first two options, some routes can slip through your subroutine without being accepted or rejected. In these cases, the applying protocol will determine the default policy (which is always terminal).

In the third, you design your conditions and actions such that all routes will match either a term with an *accept* or a term with a *reject*. In the last two options, you configure your own default action by putting in a final unconditional term with an *accept* or *reject*.

All five of these subroutine chain designs have different implications and, therefore, applications. The following cases describe general usage. Certainly after you understand the flow-control implications, you are free to disregard these generalities. You have all the rope you need. Juniper Networks hopes you will build just the right net, rather than just the wrong noose. Until then, following is a discussion of each case.

Default Doesn't Matter

If you are using a policy subroutine solely for the purposes of its side effects, you can apply it in such a way that it does not matter what flow-control action it returns. Previously, in the "Tactics for Improving Policies" section, it was suggested that you should terminate action-only subroutines with a default *accept*. That is safer, because you will always know what you will get. However, you could choose to leave it open ended.

Specifically, if the term containing the "from policy" condition that is calling the subroutine in question does not itself have any meaningful *then* clause (that is, it contains nothing but *trace* or *next term*), the subroutine's result is irrelevant. The only effect it could possibly have had would be to determine whether or not the *then* clause is executed. If there is no *then* clause, the route will flow to the next term. Thus it is safe to use any of the default styles—protocol default, accept, or reject—since they will be ignored.

Here's an example that takes advantage of this technique:

```
[edit policy-options]
ps@r10# show | no-more
policy-statement sub_Adjust_Local_Pref {
    term Preferred_Customers {
        from community Preferred_Customers;
        then {
            local-preference add 100;
        }
    }
    term Economy_Customers {
        from community Economy_Customers;
        then {
            local-preference subtract 20;
        }
    }
}
policy-statement Adjust_Gold_Link {
    term Adjust_Local_Pref {
        from policy sub_Adjust_Local_Pref;
    }
    term Other_Issues {
        from protocol rip;
        then {
            metric add 0;
        }
    }
}
```

This will generate the desired side effects, without impacting flow control. It is important that no *then* clause is used in term `Adjust_Local_Pref`—it is not enough that there is simply no *accept* or *reject*. If you include a *then* statement, even just for side effects, you are letting the protocol default impact the execution of those actions.

The risk of using this strategy does bring with it a reward: This type of policy can be used both as an action-only subroutine *and* as a modifier policy in an import or export statement. It returns an action of *next policy* for all routes, so all it does is change something along the way.

Catch-All Match Conditions

You can design a policy chain whose match conditions together capture everything, although it takes special care and analysis to be certain that you have not left any holes in your subroutine. If you do this, it is unnecessary to provide a conditionless *accept* or *reject*.

The following example is overly simple, but it illustrates the concept:

```
[edit policy-options]
ps@r10# show | no-more
policy-statement Modify_Half_Of_Internet {
    from {
        route-filter 0.0.0.0/2 orlonger;
        route-filter 64.0.0.0/2 orlonger;
    }
    then {
        metric add 1;
        accept;
    }
}
policy-statement Modify_Other_Half {
    from {
        route-filter 128.0.0.0/2 orlonger;
        route-filter 192.0.0.0/2 orlonger;
    }
    then {
        metric subtract 1;
        accept;
    }
}
policy-statement Modify_The_Net {
    from policy [ Modify_Half_Of_Internet Modify_Other_Half ];
    then accept;
}
```

The policy subroutine chain in the last policy has no default action; neither of the policies in it have an unconditional *accept* or *reject*. However, between the two policies in the subroutine, they will return an *accept* for any possible route. If this statement were applied as an export policy under a protocol, it would then accept the routes and you could be certain that no routes slipped through.

With more complex situations, you might find yourself mixing different match types. For example, one policy might match on AS path, and another might match on route-filter. Keep in mind that it may not be obvious whether or not every route is caught by at least one of your conditions. If one is not caught, your subroutine will have effects that you did not consider.

Default Is Desired

The key to all of this, and the reason so much explanation is necessary are the policy framework's default policy statements. Under protocol import and export, the default policy statements perform about how you would expect; let the protocol run unhindered, and do not add information from other protocols (RIP being the notable exception). Their impact on policy subroutines is much subtler, though. They give you a power that you otherwise would not have, but they come with a responsibility that you might not have expected.

You may wish to design a policy subroutine that intentionally relies on the default policies for its final decision. Since these policies are different for different protocols, this subroutine's behavior will depend on where you apply the policy that calls it. Although there may be some value to this specifically with BGP, it is difficult to imagine a policy subroutine that uses the framework default, yet is actually useful under multiple protocols. If you go with the BGP case, it again becomes the user's responsibility to make sure she uses the policy as intended. Annotations and well-chosen policy names should help here. It is surprisingly easy to look at a policy you have written for a specific case and think "Hey, I can use that over here too."

Default Reject

This is the "standard" case of a policy subroutine as subroutine match condition. By virtue of *policy* appearing as a *from* or *to* match condition option, it is safe to say that the engineers designed it to be used this way; a policy subroutine designed in this way most closely resembles the other match conditions—that is, it succeeds for certain routes that satisfy specified criteria, and it fails for the rest.

With that in mind, the normal use of a policy subroutine is to capture a complex series of match conditions and give it a name so you can easily use and reuse it.

All you do is move the conditions into a term in their own policy and give them an action of *accept*. Then create a default action of *reject*, and you have a new match condition that will succeed and fail the same way as the original block.

Default Accept

As discussed, this is the more obvious way of designing an action-only subroutine. The logic is more predictable and easier to follow. In short, you can say the following: "A term executes its *then* clause unless there is a failed match condition." By making a subroutine accept everything, it thus has no impact on a term's *then* clause. It's side effects, therefore, pose no risk to the completion of the term. (As it turns out, you can use policy expressions to convert a next policy into an accept, and vice versa.)

The other obvious use for this style of default is simply as the opposite of a default *reject*. Sometimes, you may find that you want to match "just about everything" and omit only a few cases. You may notice that while it is easy to pick out specific characteristics, it can be more difficult to say "everything but" a couple of specific characteristics. With a default *accept* policy, you build the opposite of a default *reject*: Specify your conditions and give them a *then reject*. Then give a default *accept*, and you have a new "everything else but" condition.

If you already have a policy subroutine and you want a condition that gives you the opposite result, you do not need to go to these lengths. You can simply use the ! expression operator. This is discussed next in "Subroutines and Expressions."

Classify Your Policies

In the "Designing Subroutine Policies" section earlier in the chapter, you saw that you need to design policy subroutines with a different thought process than you use to design import and export policies. This thought process is different enough that with limited exceptions, policy subroutines are not useful as import or export policies, and vice versa.

The convention used in this chapter has been this: For policies designed to be used as match condition subroutines, prefix the policy name with *is_*. For those to be used as action-only subroutines, prefix the name with *set_*. You may have also noticed that all other policy names here start with uppercase letters. This is so you can immediately recognize *any* policy starting with a lowercase letter as a subroutine-only policy. In other words, do not use these policies in an import or export statement, because they will not do what you intended. If you consider this too subtle a flag, consider prefixing all subroutine policies with *sub-* or something similar. Ultimately, your naming convention is up to you. However, you will find that since you have to design subroutine policies differently than import/export policies, it is helpful to name them so that they stand out.

The benefits of using *is_* and *set_* will become apparent in the next section. Expressions, among other things, allow you to convert a policy designed as a subroutine to serve the same function directly in an import or export statement. You will find that the *is_* and *set_* prefixes makes sense in that case; the policy chain, when read, will sound like a description of what the chain is doing.

Either way, keep in mind that many other people may have to understand your policies and will need to be able to figure out how to use them. A naming standard like this can save somebody a lot of effort in troubleshooting an existing import/export statement or configuring a new one. Annotating your policies right in the configuration will also go a long way toward making sure you and others use them as intended.

Subroutines and Expressions

All but the simplest policy expressions are probably too visually alarming to place in a protocol import or export statement. Import and export statements tend to change with more frequency than policy definitions, so using complex expressions creates a lot of opportunity for a typo or a logic oversight. However, policy expressions are a great way to do powerful things in the safety of another policy—namely as part of a policy subroutine.

With this in mind, following are a couple of techniques that you can use with policy expressions. Do not forget, however, that as with any other policy subroutine, you must be deliberate about how you design the default behavior of your subroutine.

Reversing a Policy

Perhaps the following is obvious, or perhaps it is worth pointing out: As indicated earlier in this chapter, if a policy tells you something, and you want a match condition that tells you when that something is not true, you can easily get this information. Just negate the policy subroutine using the expression *!* (not) operator.

Interestingly, the whole default policy versus policy subroutines issue goes away when you negate a policy. This is because *!* reverses both *accept* and *next policy* to *reject*, but it only reverses *reject* to *accept*. You cannot get a *next policy* out of a *!* expression.

Earlier, you saw a policy that would match successfully on routes that belonged to your A&T customer. If, for any reason, you need to do something to all routes that are *not* A&T routes, you can do so like this:

```
[edit policy-options]
user@r1# show | no-more
policy-statement Prefer_Friends {
    from policy ( ! AnT );
    then {
        metric subtract 20;
    }
}
```

Converting Between Next Policy and Accept

The characteristic of policy expressions that *accept* and *next policy* are both treated similarly to the Boolean value "true," creates an interesting capability. You have seen a possible advantage in creating an action-only subroutine that defaults to *accept*, and you have seen the benefits of creating one that defaults to *next policy*.

Expressions enable you to convert either one to the other. Suppose you create two policies like this:

```
user@r1# show policy-options
policy-statement next {
    then next policy;
}
policy-statement accept {
    then accept;
}
```

You can now take any action subroutine, regardless of how it defaults, and specify a different "default." Take the policy Set_Transit. This policy accepts everything, so you cannot use it as a modifier policy:

```
policy-statement set_Transit {
    then {
        local-preference 90;
        community add Transit;
        next-hop self;
        accept;
    }
}
```

With the "next" policy, you can use set_Transit as a modifier policy:

```
user@r1# show protocols
bgp {
    import [ AnT Customer ( set_Transit && next ) Backup ];
}
```

This is similar to the policy import chain used with these policies previously. However, you have converted the action-only subroutine set_Transit into a modifier policy. set_Transit always returns *accept*. Accept is true, so the policy framework sees the *&&* and continues to determine whether the expression is true. Policy *next* always returns *next policy*, so the expression is true and returns the last value computed, which is *next policy*. Thus, the set_Transit side effects have been executed, and the chain continues.

You can use the reverse of this technique to convert a modifier policy into an action-only subroutine that is safe to use in a term with a *then* clause. That is, it avoids the issue of letting the subroutine flow through to the default policy. You do this by adding *&& accept* to your modifier policy. Modifier policies, by definition, result in *next policy* for all routes. Thus, *(Modifier && accept)* will match all routes, and therefore has no impact on the match status of a given term. You may find that the name *continue* reads better than *accept*, like this: *(Modifier && continue)*.

The key to this technique is that the policies you are using with it have fixed results. It is not just the *&&* operator that creates this magic, but the conjunction of *&&* and policies that have only one possible result.

Using Match and Action Subroutines Together

You've learned that you can simplify policies using subroutine matches or action-only subroutines. But how do you use them both in the same term? Pushing the action subroutine to the *to* clause is one option. Another is to join them with expressions.

Here is one version of the policy AnT_Backup.

```
policy-statement AnT_Backup {
    from policy is_AnT;
    then {
        local-preference 50;
        community add Customer;
        community add PITA;
        community add AnT;
        community add Backup;
    }
}
```

You can simplify this using the set_Backup policy using *&&* (again). In this case, the *&&* is relying on the fact the policy to the left is making a decision, *and* that the policy on the right will always result in an accept. The latter fact is necessary to be sure that it does not fail, and it causes the *then* clause to be skipped. It would look like this:

```
[edit policy-options]
user@r1# show
policy-statement AnT_Backup {
    from policy ( is_AnT && set_Backup );
    then {
        community add Customer;
        community add PITA;
        community add AnT;
    }
}
```

If, Then, Else

If shortcut evaluation causes a policy not to be evaluated, that policy's side effects do not happen. This has a powerful, if unexpected, benefit—you can effectively say *if... then... else...* with JUNOS software policy. (If you are familiar with programming languages such as Perl or C, you may have already seen this technique.)

Imagine a policy tells you whether a route is from Internet Gas & Electric—that is, it accepts IG&E routes and rejects others. Call it Is_IGnE. Say you have another that identifies Ten-M routes, Is_TenM. Perhaps you want IG&E to be the preferred provider in part of your network and Ten-M to be preferred in another part. One option is to build two more policies that do exactly these tasks for you. But you could also build one more policy that makes any route more preferable—call it Make_Better.

Then, in one part of your network, you would say:

"If the route is from IG&E, make it more preferable, otherwise, leave it alone."

In another part, you would say:

"If the route is from Ten-M, make it more preferable, otherwise, leave it alone."

You could do so like this:

```
[edit protocols bgp]
 ps@R10# show protocols
bgp {
    group One_Half {
        export ( Is_IGnE && Make_Better || next);
        neighbor 205.134.50.45;
        neighbor 205.134.50.50;
        neighbor 205.134.50.55;
    }
    group Other_Half {
        export ( Is_TenM && Make_Better || next);
        neighbor 140.185.101.5;
        neighbor 140.185.101.10;
        neighbor 140.185.101.20;
    }
}
ps@r9# show policy-options
policy-statement Is_IGnE {
    term IGnE {
        from as-path IGnE;
        then accept;
    }
    then reject;
}
policy-statement Is_TenM {
    term TenM {
        from as-path TenM;
        then accept;
    }
    then reject;
}
policy-statement Make_Better {
    then {
```

```
          metric subtract 10;
      }
  }
}
policy-statement next {
    then next policy;
}
as-path TenM ".* 1234";
as-path IGnE ".* 10";
```

The *&&* ... *||* ... becomes an *if... then....* Due to shortcut evaluation, if Is_IGnE rejects a route, Make_Better will not be evaluated. If it accepts a route, Make_Better will be evaluated (to determine whether the expression is true). Make_Better returns *next policy*, so matching routes will flow on to the rest of the policy chain. *next* also returns *next policy*, so nonmatching routes will also flow on to the rest of the chain. You could not do this with a policy chain, because as soon as Is_IGnE accepts a route, the chain would stop processing that route. If you wanted to do an *if... then... else...* you would replace the *next* policy in the expression with your *else* case, making sure that it also specified a flow control action of *next policy* for all routes.

In this case, this technique saves you from having to write one policy (three versus four total to solve this problem—or perhaps there is no savings if you did not already have a *next* policy). Imagine that you have 50 peers, though, and that you have two levels of preference. You could define Make_Better and Make_Much_Better. You may want to explicitly control which peer is better or much better in different parts of your network. To do this by building a separate policy for each peer (Make_X_Better, Make_Y_Better, Make_X_Much_Better, and so on) would take 100 policies. Conversely, using *if...then...else*, you would need only 52 policies—an Is_X for each peer and then Make_Better and Make_Much_Better. Furthermore, you may already have Is_<*peer*> policies for each peer, in which case, it really only takes two new policies to satisfy all 100 cases.

This concept becomes even more powerful if you have other side effects you would like to apply selectively. If you want to add a community in some places but not others, you could make a policy called Add_Community_X. Then you would *&&* it to the neighbors you want and not to those you do not.

```
ps@R10# show protocols
bgp {
    group One_Half {
        export ( Is_IGnE && Make_Better && Add_Community_X || next);
        neighbor 205.134.50.45;
        neighbor 205.134.50.50;
        neighbor 205.134.50.55;
```

```
    }
    group Other_Half {
        export ( Is_TenM && Make_Better || next);
        neighbor 140.185.101.5;
        neighbor 140.185.101.10;
        neighbor 140.185.101.20;
    }
}
ps@r9# show policy-options |no-more
/* previous policies omitted */
policy-statement Add_Community_X {
    then {
        community add X;
    }
}
community X members 65500:1;
```

Again, if you had 50 peers that you may or may not want to mark with a community, independently of whether you want to mark them better, you just saved yourself *another* 150 policies (50 to add the community without making them better; 50 to add it and make them better; and 50 to add it and make them much better).

Here is how *if... then... else...* would look,

```
    import (Is_IGnE && Make_Better || Make_Worse)
```

Remember that an expression is simply one element of a policy chain. If you want to apply this logic to a peer, but *unconditionally* apply the Add_Community_X policy, you can do so like this:

```
    import [ ( Is_IGnE && Make_Better || Make_Worse ) Add_Community_X ]
```

This equates to "If it is from IGnE, make it better, otherwise, make it worse. Add community X to all routes. Use defaults for accept and reject."

Summary

Here is an auctioneer's version of the entire policy framework behavior. Because this chapter is huge and intense, this list is intended for you to use as a quick reference memory jogger.

- A policy's purpose is to accept or reject a route.
  - The user of the policy decides what significance that result has.

- A policy can also change a route's attributes.
  - This has no direct effect on *accept* or *reject*.
- Policies are made of terms.
- Terms have match conditions and actions.
- As long as none of the match conditions fail on a route, the actions are applied to it.
- Many match conditions allow a list of parameters.
  - One matching list member makes the condition succeed.
- Every term in a policy evaluates every route, unless...

  a term specifies accept

  or reject

  or next policy.

  - *Accept* terminates the policy, with that as result.
  - *Reject* terminates the policy, with that as result.
  - *Next policy* skips the rest of the current policy and continues with the next one in the chain, or the default policy if no other policy is configured.
- Policies can be chained together.
  - The result is effectively one big long policy.
  - Except that a policy can use the next policy action to skip its remainder and move on to the next policy in the chain.
- There is always at least one policy in any chain: the policy framework's default.
  - Each protocol and direction has its own default.
  - All import default policies accept everything.
  - BGP default export accepts BGP and rejects others.
  - RIP and OSPF defaults reject all.
- Chains can contain logical expressions, using &&, | |, and !.
  - These take policy results as input.
  - They produce the respective output according to classical logic, treating accept and next policy as true and reject as false.
    - When the result is true, the resulting action is next policy or accept—which ever was last.
    - ! negates reject to accept always.

- You can use a policy as a match condition in another policy; this is called a *policy subroutine*.
  - If it accepts, the condition is a success.
  - If it rejects, the condition is a failure.
  - If it returns *next policy*, the default policy of the calling policy is also the subroutine's default.
  - Because of this, you should design subroutine policies to have an explicit default.
  - Any side-effect actions are executed immediately.

The Complete Reference

Juniper Networks

Chapter 8

Routing Information Protocol

by Jeff Doyle

Y ou have learned how the routing and forwarding tables are organized and managed in Juniper Networks routers. In Chapter 6 you learned how to make manual— that is, static—entries into the routing table. *Routing Information Protocol* (RIP) is the first and simplest of the *dynamic* routing protocols to be discussed in this book.

A dynamic routing protocol is a language spoken between routers for determining the best path to a given destination or set of destinations. Using the term "language" to describe routing protocols carries several implications. As with languages,

- there is more than one routing protocol;
- nothing is understood if two neighbors are not speaking the same protocol to each other; and
- there are advantages and disadvantages to each routing protocol.

The obvious advantage of a dynamic routing protocol over manual configuration of a routing table is improved administrative scalability. Automatic discovery of new prefixes and new routes, and automatic adaptation to topology changes, mean that as the complexity of a network increases, the advantage of a dynamic routing protocol increases.

Most, although not all, dynamic routing protocols increase their usefulness by not only automatically exchanging route information with neighbors and deriving route table entries from that information, but also by automatically discovering their neighbors. When a dynamic routing protocol is enabled on a router, the interfaces on which the protocol should run are designated. The protocol then sends some sort of signaling data on those interfaces and listens for signals from other routers on those interfaces.

 BGP is a notable exception to the rule of automatic neighbor discovery. With this protocol, neighbors are manually designated. This is no shortcoming; BGP is designed to be more restrictive both in who it peers with and what information it shares with its neighbors. BGP is covered thoroughly in Chapters 12 and 13.

This chapter introduces you to the operation of RIP Version 2 (RIPv2), and demonstrates how to configure and troubleshoot RIPv2 with JUNOS software. Before getting to RIP, you first learn the basics of distance vector routing protocols. Chapter 9 introduces you to the basics of link-state routing protocols.

Distance Vector Routing Protocols

Presently, all dynamic IP routing protocols fall into one of two classes: *distance vector* and *link state*. Although there are many distance vector protocols (Novell's IPX, Apple's AppleTalk, and Cisco's IGRP and EIGRP, for example), RIP is one of only two distance vector routing protocols supported by JUNOS software. The other, BGP, is commonly called *path vector* rather than distance vector, due to BGP's different path structure (autonomous system hops rather than router hops), but functionally BGP is still a distance vector protocol.

What Is Distance Vector?

Every dynamic routing protocol has two core functions:

- **Information distribution**   How routers share information about the network
- **Route calculation**   How routers use the distributed information to determine the best path to a destination

Distance vector routing protocols share information locally and use a distributed route calculation, that is, information necessary for the calculation of best paths is sent only to neighbors sharing a common subnet, and those neighbors must perform their best-path calculation before sending information to their own neighbors. This is in contrast to link-state protocols, in which information is distributed unchanged to all routers in a domain or area and then each router performs a local best-path calculation.

A Distance Vector Calculation Example

A few illustrations will help to clarify this concept of a distributed calculation of local information. R1 in Figure 8-1 has a directly connected subnet, 10.1.1.0/24. The router is, of course, aware of the subnet because its connecting interface is configured as a member of the subnet. The subnet address is entered into the router's routing table, with an indication that the subnet is directly connected. The router is also aware of two neighbors, R2 and R3, which speak the same "routing language." R1 sends packets to these neighbors containing *updates*—information notifying the neighbors about the existence of R1's connected subnet. The update information will contain, at a minimum, the address of the subnet and some indicator of the distance of the subnet from the originator of the update. In the example of Figure 8-1, the distance indicator is the number of router hops from the destination. Because the subnet in question is directly connected, R1 tells its neighbors that the subnet is zero hops away.

When R2 and R3 receive the updates from R1, they run a very simple calculation. The algorithm for the calculation states that if a neighboring router claims a destination prefix is some number of hops away from itself, the destination is obviously one more hop away from the router receiving the neighbor's update; therefore, the advertised hop-count is incremented by one and the resulting route is entered into the routing table along with the address of the router advertising the route. The address of the advertising router is known from the source address of the update packet. R2 and R3 now know that subnet 10.1.1.0/24 is reachable via their respective shared links with R1, one hop away.

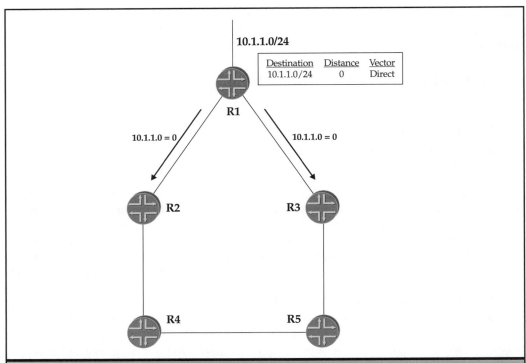

Destination	Distance	Vector
10.1.1.0/24	0	Direct

Figure 8-1. *A distance vector routing protocol informs its neighbors of all known and valid routes.*

Both R2 and R3 then advertise 10.1.1.0/24 in updates to their own neighbors (Figure 8-2). The advertised hop-count is again incremented and the results are entered into the routing tables of R4 and R5.

R4 and R5 might then want to advertise the route information to their own neighbors. Interestingly, in this example, R4's neighbor is R5 and R5's neighbor is R4. Suppose both routers send updates, as shown in Figure 8-3. On receipt of the update, each router increments the hop-count. R4 determines that the route to 10.1.1.0/24 is 2 hops away via R2, but 3 hops away—a longer distance—via R5; therefore, the best route to 10.1.1.0/24 is via R2, and R4 discards the route advertised by R5. R5 performs the same operation, determining that the best route to the subnet is via R3, and discards the route information from R4.

You can now easily see that R4 and R5 cannot calculate the best route to subnet 10.1.1.0/24 until R2 and R3 have first performed their calculations. Likewise, R2 and R3 cannot perform their calculations until R1 has performed its own. Hence, a distance vector is a distributed calculation; a router is dependent on every router upstream

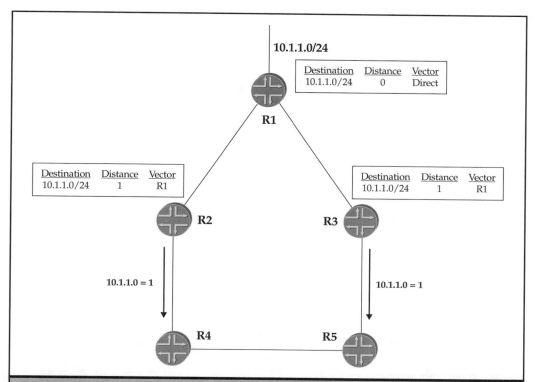

Figure 8-2.   *When R2 and R3 have calculated their distance to subnet 10.1.1.0/24 and entered the route into their routing table, they advertise the results to their own neighbors.*

along a route to correctly perform its own calculation first. Stated differently, a route is processed hop by hop in a downstream direction—that is, away from the destination.

At the same time, the information that is advertised between neighbors is local. All any router knows of the network, aside from what it knows about its own connected subnets, is what its neighbors tell it. R3 in Figure 8-2, for example, knows only that 10.1.1.0/24 is one router hop away (the distance) via R1 (the vector).

Periodic Updates

What happens if a distance vector router quietly ceases to function, or through some accident loses a route? What happens if an entry in a routing table somehow becomes corrupted? A mechanism is required for detecting failed neighbors, missing routes, and stale or corrupted routing table entries.

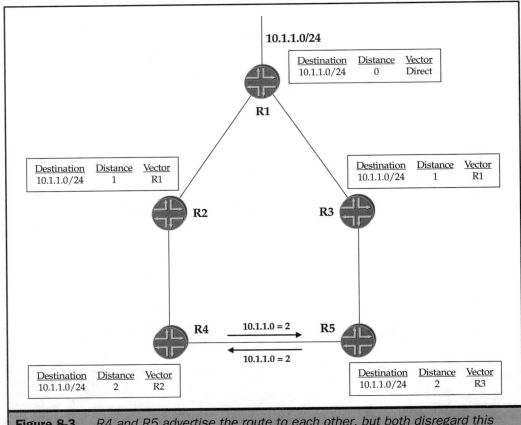

Figure 8-3. *R4 and R5 advertise the route to each other, but both disregard this route because they each have a closer route to 10.1.1.0/24.*

This mechanism, for most distance vector protocols, is *periodic updates*. After a router has sent updates to its neighbors, it sets an update timer for some period (30 seconds, for example). When the timer expires, the router resends its updates and resets the timer.

When an update is received, a *dead timer* is set for some period (three times the update period, for example). Updates are expected from all neighbors for all routes within that period. When an update is received, the dead timer is reset. If a dead timer for a route expires before an update is received, the neighbor that originated the route is determined to be dead for that route, and the route is declared invalid. In this way periodic updates serve as keepalives both for neighbors and for individual routes.

Distance Vector Problems and Solutions

The simple example presented in the "Distance Vector Calculation Example" section raises some interesting questions, and the questions in turn introduce some of the difficulties of distance vector protocols. This section examines the two most common problems with distance vector protocols—slow convergence and vulnerability to routing loops—and the solutions used to avoid or reduce those problems.

Slow Convergence

The hop-by-hop processing of route information, as described in the "Distance Vector Calculation Example" section, is inherently slow. Each router, having received an update, cannot send an update to its own neighbors until it has processed the update and performed its route calculation; but given the simplicity of distance vector protocols, and the high processing speed of many modern routers, the negative effects of hop-by-hop processing are minimized.

A larger problem is the periodic updates. If, for example, a distance vector protocol uses an update period of 30 seconds, a route change might take 300 seconds to be communicated across 10 router hops. During those 5 minutes, the network has incomplete and, therefore, unreliable routing information.

The solution to these slow updates is *triggered* (also called *flash*) updates. Updates are still sent at some regular period, but if there is a change—either a new route is added, an existing route becomes invalid, or a distance changes—that change is immediately communicated. With flash updates, the periodic delay is eliminated and the slow convergence properties are reduced to the hop-by-hop processing delays.

Note   *Whether the flash update contains just the change or the entire routing table depends on the particular distance vector protocol implementation. The relative efficiency of including just the changed information, rather than the entire routing table, is readily apparent.*

Routing Loops

The description of a distributed route calculation in the "Distance Vector Calculation Example" section left an important factor unstated: If a router's only knowledge of remote (that is, nonconnected) subnets is from what its neighbors tell it, the router depends on that neighbor to give it accurate knowledge. In fact, it depends on all routers along the path between it and the destination subnet to perform their route calculations correctly. A router has no first-hand knowledge of any destination prefixes that are not directly connected.

If some router along a path makes a mistake in its route calculation, under the rules of distance vector it will pass the mistake along to its neighbors. Those neighbors incorporate the mistake into their own calculations, compounding the resulting routing inaccuracy. One potential result of this inaccuracy is that a router might choose some path to the destination other than the shortest one—an undesirable condition, but not necessarily a disastrous one. Another result is that the router could mistakenly forward packets on an entirely invalid path, causing the packets to eventually be dropped or *black holed*.

Note   *Black holes are not always a bad thing. Many network administrators intentionally configure some of their routers to black-hole certain traffic—that is, to quietly drop certain packets—as part of a security policy.*

The most insidious result of inaccurate routing is a *routing loop*. A routing loop results in packets being passed repeatedly among a set of two or more routers. If a route describes a path that passes through the same router more than once, that route contains a loop. In some cases, such as during very short-lived routing instabilities, a packet caught in a loop might eventually be forwarded out of the loop and on to its destination; but a packet is far more likely to continue looping until its *Time to Live* (TTL) expires and it is dropped. Aside from the obvious problem of lost packets, loops deplete network bandwidth and router resources. Applications detecting the lost packets will retransmit, compounding the problem.

Routing loops can be either transient or permanent. A transient loop usually occurs when the network topology changes in some way, and the routers have not completed their calculations of the new topology—that is, the protocol has not converged on the new topology. Designers of modern routing protocols invest much thought into developing algorithms that avoid looping during convergence. Permanent loops are the result either of some calculation error or of a human intervention that has overridden the calculation. Permanent loops are, by their permanency, far more destructive.

In addition to the two core functions of information distribution and route calculation, modern routing protocols all implement various functions to prevent routing loops. It is commonly argued, in fact, that *Exterior Gateway Protocol* (EGP), the predecessor to BGP, is not a routing protocol at all because it possesses neither an algorithm for determining a best path from among multiple paths to a single destination, nor any mechanism for detecting avoiding loops.

The two most common mechanisms for avoiding routing loops are *split horizon* and *infinite distance*.

Split Horizon   Revisiting the simple distance vector example, suppose subnet 10.1.1.0/24 becomes unreachable for some reason. Its directly connected router advertises this information to the router's directly connected neighbors, as shown in Figure 8-4.

Note   *The reasons for the subnet becoming unreachable can range from a physical failure (in which case the Layer 1 or 2 processes of R1's interface detect that failure) to some sort of configuration error, such as an operator inadvertently changing the address of R1's interface to the subnet.*

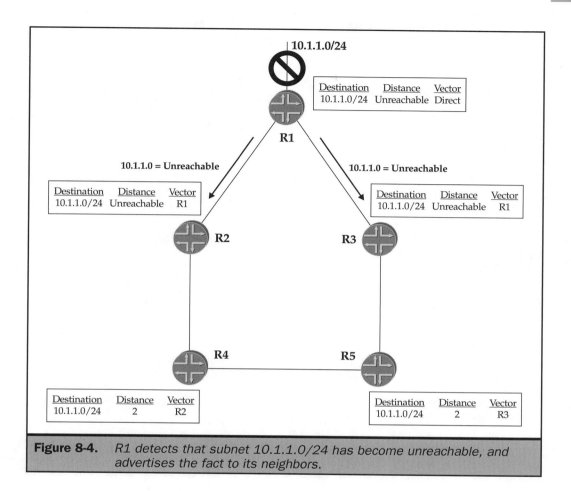

Figure 8-4.   *R1 detects that subnet 10.1.1.0/24 has become unreachable, and advertises the fact to its neighbors.*

In Figure 8-5, R2 passes the information learned from R1 on to its own neighbors, as expected. At the same time, however, something interesting happens between R3 and R5. Before R3 can convey to R5 the information it has learned from R1, R3 sends its regularly scheduled periodic update, stating that it can reach subnet 10.1.1.0/24, 2 hops away.

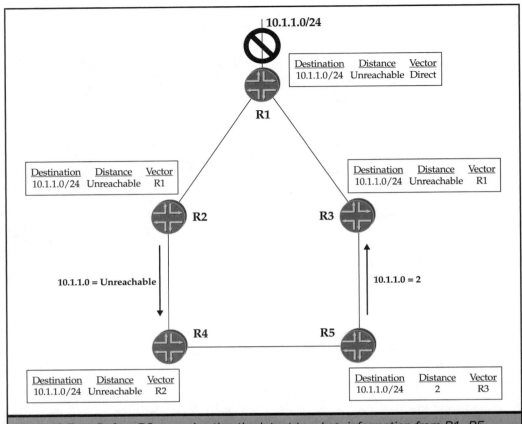

Destination	Distance	Vector
10.1.1.0/24	Unreachable	Direct

Destination	Distance	Vector
10.1.1.0/24	Unreachable	R1

Destination	Distance	Vector
10.1.1.0/24	Unreachable	R1

10.1.1.0 = Unreachable

10.1.1.0 = 2

Destination	Distance	Vector
10.1.1.0/24	Unreachable	R2

Destination	Distance	Vector
10.1.1.0/24	2	R3

Figure 8-5. *Before R3 can advertise the latest topology information from R1, R5 advertises its own topology information, based on what it currently knows.*

The result is both interesting and destructive. R3 knows that 10.1.1.0/24 is no longer reachable via R1, but now has a claim from R5 that it can reach the subnet 2 hops away. R3 has no way of knowing that this claim is based on information that R3 itself originated. So, the router makes an entry in its routing table, indicating that subnet 10.1.1.0/24 is reachable via R5, 3 hops away.

The result is a single-hop routing loop, shown in Figure 8-6. R3 forwards packets to R5, and R5 forwards packets to R3.

This behavior conforms to the simple distance vector algorithm as described so far, in which a router periodically tells all its neighbors everything it knows about the network topology. The example here is simply a case of unfortunate timing, in which R5 shares its information before it receives the latest update from R1 via R3.

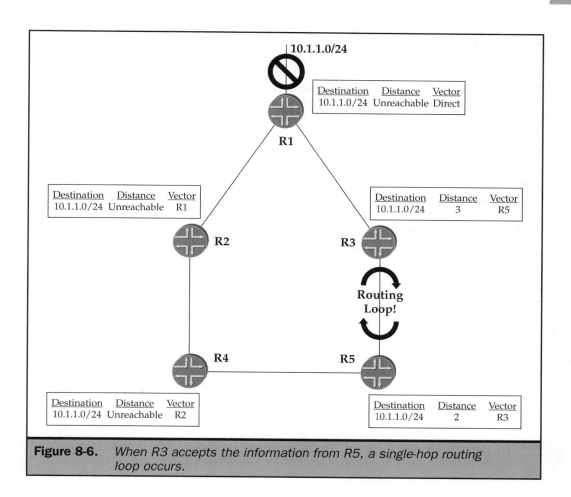

Destination	Distance	Vector
10.1.1.0/24	Unreachable	Direct

Destination	Distance	Vector
10.1.1.0/24	Unreachable	R1

Destination	Distance	Vector
10.1.1.0/24	3	R5

Destination	Distance	Vector
10.1.1.0/24	Unreachable	R2

Destination	Distance	Vector
10.1.1.0/24	2	R3

Figure 8-6.   *When R3 accepts the information from R5, a single-hop routing loop occurs.*

It does not make much sense for a distance vector router to advertise reachability information back to the neighbor from which it learned the information. If the neighbor is advertising the information, it obviously already knows the information. More importantly, if a router does not echo information to the neighbor from which it received the information, single-hop routing loops can be avoided. This issue is addressed with an addendum to the basic rules of distance vector, called *split horizon.*

With split horizon, when a router sends reachability information to a neighbor, it does not include information learned from that neighbor. So, for example, R5 in Figure 8-5 advertises to R3 information it has learned from R4, but not information it learned from R3—including subnet 10.1.1.0/24. Likewise, R5 advertises to R4 information it learned from R3—including subnet 10.1.1.0/24—but nothing it learned from R4.

Infinite Distance Split horizon is effective against single-hop routing loops, but is limited in preventing routing loops when the physical topology itself contains loops. Figure 8-7 shows how a routing loop might occur in the presence of a physical loop. The same subnet failure occurs, and the same unreachable messages are sent by R1. The messages are received and processed by R2 and R3, which subsequently send their own updates.

Before the update from R3 is completely received and processed by R5, R5 sends its regularly scheduled update to R4. R4, having just learned that 10.1.1/24 is no longer reachable via R2, has now received a claim from R5 that that router can reach the subnet at a distance of 2 hops.

In Figure 8-8, R4 acts on the information received from R5 and adjusts its routing table accordingly. It then sends an update to R2, which updates R1, which updates R3. Looking at the topology in the illustration, you can easily see that the information

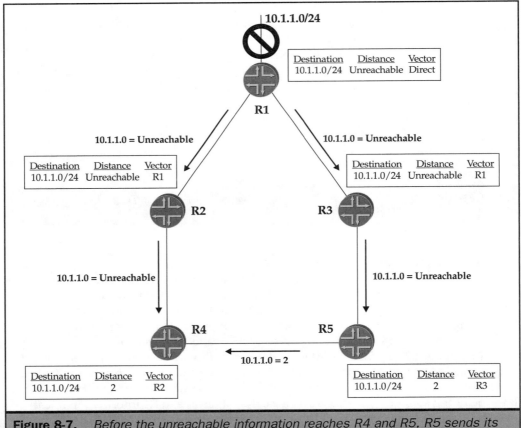

Figure 8-7. *Before the unreachable information reaches R4 and R5, R5 sends its periodic update to R4.*

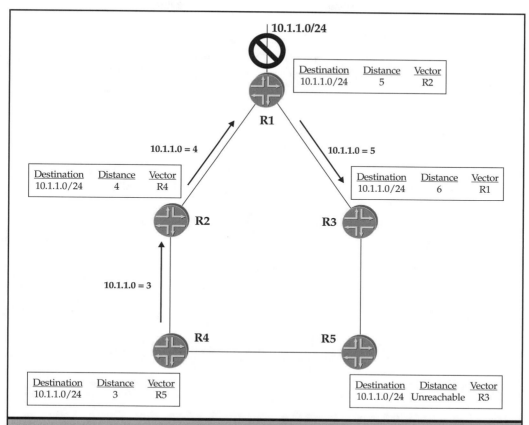

10.1.1.0/24

Destination	Distance	Vector
10.1.1.0/24	5	R2

R1

10.1.1.0 = 4

10.1.1.0 = 5

Destination	Distance	Vector
10.1.1.0/24	4	R4

Destination	Distance	Vector
10.1.1.0/24	6	R1

R2

R3

10.1.1.0 = 3

Destination	Distance	Vector
10.1.1.0/24	3	R5

R4

R5

Destination	Distance	Vector
10.1.1.0/24	Unreachable	R3

Figure 8-8.   *R4 incorrectly determines that R5 has a path to subnet 10.1.1/24, and passes this information to R2; a series of incorrect route calculations results as R2 updates its own neighbor.*

being passed around is incorrect; but the routers along the path, which know only what their immediate neighbors tell them, have no way of seeing the bigger picture.

After sending an update to R4 in Figure 8-7, R5 received the update from R3 and marked the path to 10.1.1/24 as unreachable; but now, in Figure 8-9, R3 sends a new update with a distance of 6. R5 processes this update, and sends an update to R4. From the perspective of R4, the distance of the path has increased. R4 then updates R2, which updates R1, and so on. You can see the routing loop form as each router passes on the update to its neighbor, adding 1 to the distance at each hop.

Such a loop would theoretically continue, with the distance increasing at each hop, to an infinite distance. Such a problem is called *counting to infinity*.

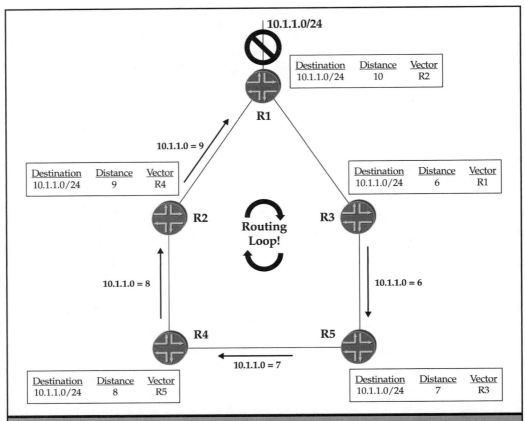

Destination	Distance	Vector
10.1.1.0/24	10	R2

Destination	Distance	Vector
10.1.1.0/24	9	R4

Destination	Distance	Vector
10.1.1.0/24	6	R1

Destination	Distance	Vector
10.1.1.0/24	8	R5

Destination	Distance	Vector
10.1.1.0/24	7	R3

Figure 8-9. *As the looped routing update reaches R5, it updates its table and sends a new update to R4; the hop-by-hop increase in distance around this topological loop will continue to infinity.*

The solution to the counting to infinity problem is to define just what infinity is—to make infinity finite, in other words. For example, infinity can be defined as 16 router hops. So in this example, the updates will continue until each router increments to 16. At that point the route is determined to be unreachable. In fact, the "unreachable" routes that are advertised in Figure 8-7 are shown as such by setting the distance to 16.

Defining infinity as 16 hops does not prevent the type of looping update depicted here; it merely adds a reasonable boundary. Any packet that is forwarded to destination 10.1.1/24 before the distance reaches 16 will be caught in this transient loop. Flash updates certainly help reduce the negative impact of counting to infinity by sharply reducing the time it takes for the updates to count to 16.

A tool for preventing most instances of counting to infinity is a *holddown timer*. When an update is received from a downstream neighbor increasing the distance to a destination (including increasing the distance to infinity to advertise unreachability), the receiving router starts a holddown timer. Until that timer expires, the router will not accept an update from any other neighbor unless the distance is less than or equal to the distance of the original path. As a result, in most cases the original unreachable route is correctly communicated throughout the network before any other information is accepted. Holddown timers trade some reconvergence speed for reduced susceptibility to routing loops.

Split Horizon with Poisoned Reverse   Defining infinity with a finite number such as 16 hops, and accepting that number as signifying an unreachable destination, enables a modification of the basic split horizon rule called *split horizon with poisoned reverse*. Rather than suppressing the advertisement of routes back to the neighbors from which the routes were learned, split horizon with poisoned reverse sends the routes but sets the metric to infinity. Because positive information is advertised ("this destination is not reachable in this direction"), rather than hiding information, this approach can speed reconvergence. In some cases single-hop routing loops are more likely to be immediately broken rather than waiting for a timer to expire.

The price for this somewhat safer mechanism is an increase in the amount of bandwidth required to advertise these poisoned routes. In some cases, this increased bandwidth might be significant. Take the example of an Ethernet backbone with 10 attached routers. Suppose one of these routers advertises 100 routes to its neighbors. Each of the nine neighbors must then send poisoned reverse updates to the originator, adding 900 routes to the normal update traffic carried on the link. Now suppose that each of the 10 routers advertises 100 routes to its neighbors. The result is 9000 poisoned updates on the link.

Introduction to RIP

RIP is almost universally thought of as the classic distance vector protocol, but it certainly is not the first. RIP has its heritage in a routing protocol developed by Xerox, called *Gateway Information Protocol* (GWINFO). When the Xerox Network Systems (XNS) architecture was introduced, GWINFO was updated and given the name Routing Information Protocol. RIP was first adapted for IP in the Berkeley distribution of UNIX. Although that adaptation was called *routed*, the open standard of that routing protocol continues to be called RIP.

There are currently two versions of RIP. Version 1, or RIPv1, is specified in RFC 1058.[1] RIPv2, described in RFC 2453,[2] adds several significant enhancements but is fully backward compatible with RIPv1.

[1]   C. Hedrick, "Routing Informaiton Protocol," RFC 1058, June 1988.

[2]   G. Malkin, "RIP Version 2," RFC 2453, November 1998.

The sections that follow discuss RIPv1, and then examine the enhancements introduced by RIPv2. You then learn how to configure and troubleshoot RIP using JUNOS software.

RIPv1

RIPv1 is the simplest IP routing protocol in use today, unless you consider static routing a type of routing protocol, a fact reflected by the very short (32-page) RFC 1058. It uses a single message format, containing the following information:

- A command, which signifies either a request to a neighbor to send all or part of its routing table, or a response, which is either a response to a request or a normal routing update. Requests are an infrequently used diagnostic function; most RIP messages are responses in the form of regular or triggered updates.

- A version number, which for RIPv1 is of course 1.

- One or more *Address Family Identifiers* (AFI), which are always the numerical value 2, specifying the IPv4 address family. RIPv1 and RIPv2 carry no other AFIs, but you will encounter them again, when you study IS-IS and multi protocol BGP in Chapters 11 and 12.

- One or more IP addresses, representing an advertised destination. Each address can represent a major class (A, B, or C) IP prefix or the default address 0.0.0.0.

- One or more metrics, describing the distance in router hops to the associated destination address. The metric range is 1–16, with 16 representing an unreachable destination. There is one metric for each IP address carried.

A single RIP message can carry a maximum of 25 AFI/address/metric triples. Stated more simply, a single RIP message can advertise 25 destinations. So if a RIP-speaking router must send an update for 200 destinations, it must send 8 messages every update period.

The RIP update period is 30 seconds, but in most implementations updates are not sent exactly every 30 seconds. Each time an update is sent, a small random number is generated. This *update jitter* is added to or subtracted from the update interval, and the update timer is set to the resulting time. When the timer expires, another update is sent. By randomly offsetting each 30-second update interval, RIP avoids a phenomenon known as *update synchronization,* in which a large number of routers attached to a common broadcast network can all begin attempting to send their updates at the same time.

Note	*Ensuring that the RIP update timer is not affected by the router's system load is also important in avoiding update synchronization. For more information on update synchronization, see Sally Floyd and Van Jacobson, "The Synchronisation of Periodic Routing Messages," ACM Sigcomm 1993 Symposium, September 1993.*

When RIP sends an update, it applies the rule of split horizon with poison reverse. All known routes are included in the update, but if the vector of the route points out the interface on which the update is to be sent, the metric of the route is set to 16.

RIP also uses triggered updates. To avoid excessive update loads in times of network fluctuation, a timer is set to a random value of between 1 and 5 seconds after a triggered update is sent. If another event occurs that would trigger an update, that update cannot be sent until the timer expires. To further reduce load, RFC 1058 recommends (but does not require) that RIP implementations include only the changed routes, not all known routes.

RIP updates are sent to UDP port 520, and RIP routers listen for updates on that port. Typical RIP implementations automatically send IP packets containing RIP updates to the broadcast address 255.255.255.255, but RFC 1058 does not require this address to be used.

When a route is learned from a RIP update and added to the routing table, a timer is set to a value of 180 seconds—the *timeout* period. Every time an update is received for that route, the timer is reset. If the timer expires before another update is received for the route, the route is declared invalid.

Note that the timeout period is six times the update period. This multiple insures that routes are not mistakenly declared invalid if a few updates are lost or delayed. The interval also reflects the age of RIP, which was designed in an era of relatively unreliable networks and routers. More recently-developed protocols also employ a "wait period" for their updates and keepalives, but the period is typically 3× or 4× rather than 6×.

When a route is declared invalid, it is not immediately expunged from the routing table. Instead, the route's metric is changed to 16 and an update is triggered. A timer called the *garbage-collection* timer is set to 120 seconds (four update periods). The invalid route is held in the routing table and included in all updates until the garbage-collection timer expires, to ensure that the status of the changed route is learned by the rest of the network. When the garbage collection timer expires, the route is deleted.

RIPv2 Extensions

Its simplicity made RIPv1 an efficient protocol when networks themselves were small and simple, but as both network architectures and network architects became more sophisticated, RIPv1 became increasingly deficient in supporting newer network requirements. The most important of these requirements include

- Network diameters larger than 16 router hops
- Variable length subnet masking (VLSM)
- Secure communication of routing information

Support for network diameters larger than 16 hops remains a deficiency of RIP. The protocol fundamentally depends on a low maximum hop-count to counter the effects of counting to infinity. Expanding the maximum hop-count significantly, say to 64 or 128 hops, introduces a corresponding increase in the time it takes to count to infinity and hence for the network to converge; therefore, RIP remains a "small network" protocol.

Even small networks, however, require VLSM and secure updates. RIPv2 is a backward-compatible extension of RIPv1 that introduces VLSM and authenticated messages, plus a few more useful features.

VLSM Support

RIPv1 is often called a "classful" routing protocol, because what it can deduct from advertised address prefixes is essentially limited to the prefixes' class A, B, or C membership.

Take, for example, a RIPv1 advertisement containing the prefix 172.16.128.0. What is the prefix length of this address? Is it 17 bits? 18 bits? 24 bits? No other information is included in the RIPv1 message to hint at the answer. The only way RIPv1 can interpret the prefix is to look at the interfaces of the router on which it is running. Suppose the router has an interface with an address of 172.16.212.5/24. Because that address belongs to the same class B prefix 172.16.0.0, the router concluded that the advertised prefix 172.16.128.0 was a 24-bit prefix.

Because RIPv1 makes such deductions, it is up to the network architects to ensure that all such deductions are accurate. To make that guarantee, every subnet address within the RIPv1 domain taken from a major-class address must have the same subnet mask. In this case, if one subnet taken from the class B address 172.16.0.0 is given a 24-bit mask, every subnet derived from that address must have a 24-bit mask. Address assignment under such restrictions is inefficient, because all subnets must use the same mask as the subnet with the largest number of hosts.

Suppose the prefix 172.16.128.0 is advertised to a router that has no interface addresses belonging to 172.16.0.0. How does the router interpret this prefix length? It cannot; therefore, a RIPv1 router never advertises a subnetted prefix to a neighbor with an interface that does not belong to that subnet's major class address. Instead, the router advertises only the major-class address.

This rule is illustrated in Figure 8-10. The router RIPv1 is connected to three neighbors, N1, N2, and N3. RIPv1's interface addresses to those neighbors are 172.16.1.1, 172.16.2.1, and 172.17.1.1, respectively. N1 advertises prefix 172.16.128.0. RIPv1, receiving the update, must make some assumptions. Because the address of the interface to N2 is 172.16.2.1, RIPv1 knows that N2 has an interface address belonging to 172.16.0.0, and assumes that that neighbor can correctly deduce the subnet mask; therefore, it advertises the prefix 172.16.128.0 to N2 unchanged.

The address of RIPv1's interface to N3, however, is 172.17.1.1. Because the subnet address does not belong to the class B address 172.16.0.0, RIPv1 must assume that N3 does not know how to derive the mask for 172.16.128.0; therefore, RIPv1 advertises the major-class prefix 172.16.0.0 to N3. This summarization can, in some topologies, reduce optimum path selection.

Because of this automatic summarization, N3 cannot have any other interfaces connecting to a subnet belonging to 172.16.0.0. Stated another way, the domain of subnets derived from 172.16.0.0 must be *contiguous*—the address domain cannot be

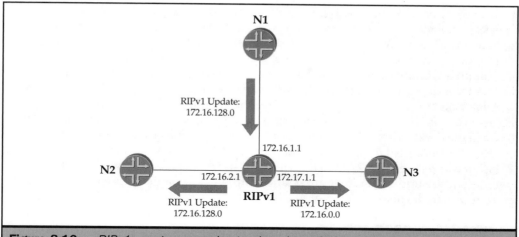

Figure 8-10. *RIPv1 must summarize to class boundaries when advertising outside a major address boundary.*

divided by any one or more subnets belonging to another major-class address. Doing so causes indistinct routing and misdelivered packets.

All these troublesome RIPv1 restrictions—"one size fits all" subnet masks, inability to advertise subnets across major-class address boundaries, and contiguous address domains—can be solved by adding a single piece of information to each advertised prefix. That one piece of information is a prefix length.

RIPv2 includes the subnet mask with each advertised IP address in its updates. As a result, VLSM can be used to size individual subnets efficiently. Class A, B, and C are no longer important; in other words, RIPv2 is *classless*. Subnets can be advertised directly into other address domains, increasing routing accuracy in some topologies. Address domains can be discontiguous, increasing the options available for address designs.

Authentication

An important element in modern network design is ensuring that each router accepts updates only from trusted neighbors. By authenticating route updates, the chance of bad routing information being introduced into the network either maliciously or inadvertently is reduced.

RIPv2 provides an authentication option. Although RFC 2453 specifies only plain-text passwords, JUNOS software allows you the option of using plain-text passwords or MD5 encrypted keys.

Next Hop Address

When RIPv1 learns a destination from a neighbor, it assumes that that neighbor is the next hop to the destination. In most cases this is true, but not always. Take, for example, the three routers in Figure 8-11 sharing the same subnet. R1 speaks RIPv1, and R3 speaks some other routing protocol. For this example BGP is chosen. R2 speaks BGP to R3, and RIP to R1. When R2 learns a destination from R3 via BGP, it advertises the destination to R1 via RIP. In other words, R2 redistributes BGP routes into RIP.

Suppose R2 learns a destination address 10.1.2/24 from R3, and advertises it to R1. R1 installs the address in its routing table, with R2 as the next hop. When a packet is sent to that destination, it is forwarded to R2 over the shared link. R2 then forwards the packet to R3 over the same link. It would obviously be more efficient if R1 were programmed to forward the packet directly to R3, the true next hop router toward the destination.

RIPv2 adds a field in its updates for the next hop address. If R1 and R2 are speaking RIPv2, R2 advertises 10.1.2/24 to R1 with R3's address in the next hop field. R1 can then install this address in its routing table with the destination address, and forward packets to that destination directly to R3.

Multicast Messages

RIPv1 broadcasts its messages. It is efficient to send a single message on a broadcast link such as Ethernet if all or most of the devices attached to the link are RIP speakers; however, the procedure becomes inefficient as more non-RIP devices are added to the link. Each device must receive a copy of the broadcast message and forward it internally to its UDP process. Only at that point do the non-RIP devices see that UDP port 520 (the RIP port) is not for them, and drop the packet.

RIPv2 retains the efficiency of sending a single message to all RIPv2 speakers on a shared link, while eliminating the inefficiency of broadcasting to every device on the link, by using a dedicated multicast address. All RIPv2 messages are sent to 224.0.0.9, and all RIPv2 routers listen for this address. Non-RIPv2 devices ignore packets with this address.

IP multicast addresses with a first octet of 224 belong to a special class called *link-local* addresses. Such addresses are never forwarded off the link on which they originated. So when a RIPv2 router sends its updates on an Ethernet link with a destination address of 224.0.0.9, other RIPv2 routers receive the updates but do not forward the messages to any other neighbor.

Route Tags

RIPv2 messages include a 16-bit field called a *route tag*. Route tags can be thought of as "pouches" for carrying external route attributes across a routing domain. Take, for

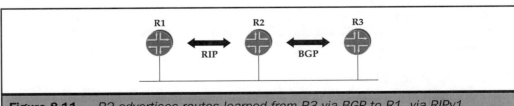

Figure 8-11. *R2 advertises routes learned from R3 via BGP to R1, via RIPv1.*

example, a network in which BGP routes are redistributed into RIP, carried across the RIP domain, and then redistributed back into BGP. The BGP domains on each side of the RIP domain might need to communicate information to each other such as autonomous system numbers. The information can be written into the route tag field of the RIPv2 message and carried transparently across the RIP domain. The information has no relevance to RIP itself, and RIP ignores the field.

Route tags are supported not only by RIPv2, but also by OSPF and IS-IS; however, they are rarely used in modern networks for the simple reason that BGP is rarely redistributed into an IGP. Furthermore, because the semantics of the tag field are not specified, use of the field would constrain the network implementer to a single vendor's products, where the interpretation of the tag field can be reliably defined.

Backward Compatibility with RIPv1

RIPv2 is designed to be backward-compatible with RIPv1. As much as this compatibility is designed into RIPv2, it also reflects the forethought that went into RIPv1. Figure 8-12 compares the RIPv1 and RIPv2 message formats. You can see that all the extra information necessary to implement the RIPv2 extensions is placed into fields that in RIPv1 are labeled "must be zero."

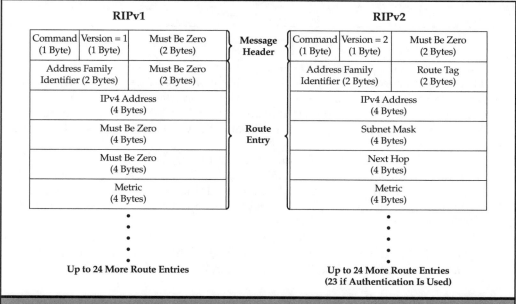

Figure 8-12.   *The RIPv1 and RIPv2 message formats; when RIPv2 uses authentication, the necessary authentication information is carried in place of the first route entry.*

Version Value	Processing Procedure*
0	Datagrams with a version number of zero are to be ignored. These are from a previous version of the protocol, in which the packet format was machine-specific.
1	Datagrams with a version number of 1 are to be processed as described in RFC 1058. All fields that are described above as "must be zero" are to be checked. If any such field contains a nonzero value, the entire message is to be ignored.
>1	Datagrams with a version number greater than 1 are to be processed as described in RFC 1058. All fields that are described above as "must be zero" are to be ignored. Future versions of the protocol might put data into these fields. Version 1 implementations are to ignore this extra data and process only the fields specified in this document.

* C. Hedrick, "Routing Information Protocol," RFC 1058, June 1988.

Table 8-1.   *RIPv1 Procedures for Processing Messages*

Table 8-1 shows the procedure RFC 1058 sets for processing messages, according to the value of the version field. What is interesting is the way messages with version numbers greater than 1 are to be processed. While the "must be zero" fields are checked if the version number is 1, for version numbers greater than 1 the fields are ignored. So, if a RIPv2 router sends a message to a RIPv1 router, RIPv1 reads only the fields it would normally expect to see.

Of course, if RIPv2 multicasts the message, a RIPv1 router cannot receive it because the router does not listen for 224.0.0.9; therefore, RIPv2 includes a *compatibility switch*, which specifies how RIPv2 routers send messages. Table 8-2 shows the four possible settings of the compatibility switch, along with the keywords used when setting the compatibility switch in JUNOS software.

RIPv2 also provides a *receive control switch*, that specifies how a RIPv2 router receives messages. Table 8-3 shows the four possible settings of the receive control switch, along with the keywords used when setting the switch in JUNOS software.

Configuring RIPv2

Now that you have read about how RIP works in both its versions, it is time to see how to configure the protocol using JUNOS software. This section explains the most common

Compatibility Switch	JUNOS Keyword	Processing Procedure
RIP-1	version-1	Only RIPv1 messages are sent. Broadcast addresses are used.
RIP-2	multicast	Only RIPv2 messages are sent. Multicast addresses are used.
RIP-1 Compatibility	broadcast	RIPv2 messages are sent, but broadcast addresses are used. This is the JUNOS software default.
None	none	No RIP messages are sent.

Table 8-2.   *RIPv2 Compatibility Switch Settings*

configuration options, and provides everything you need to know for the great majority of RIP applications; however, it does not cover every available command. See the *JUNOS Internetwork Software Configuration Guide* for a comprehensive listing of RIP commands.

Basic RIPv2 Configuration

Begin your RIP configuration by going to the `protocols rip` level of the JUNOS software configuration hierarchy. Set one or more groups with some arbitrary name, whatever is meaningful to you. Under the group, specify one or more RIP neighbors by specifying the interface connected to each neighbor.

Receive Control Switch	JUNOS Keyword	Processing Procedure
RIP-1 only	version-1	Accept only RIPv1 messages.
RIP-2 only	version-2	Accept only RIPv2 messages.
Both	both	Accept both RIPv1 and RIPv2 messages. This is the JUNOS default.
None	none	Do not accept any RIP messages.

Table 8-3.   *RIPv2 Receive Control Switch Settings*

For example, if you want to create a group called "Demogroup" with a single neighbor connected to interface so-1/1/0, the configuration steps are

```
[edit]
jeff@Juniper7# edit protocols rip

[edit protocols rip]
jeff@Juniper7# set group Demogroup neighbor so-1/1/0

[edit protocols rip]
jeff@Juniper7# commit
commit complete
```

The resulting configuration is

```
[edit protocols]
jeff@Juniper7# show
rip {
    group Demogroup {
        neighbor so-1/1/0.0;
    }
}
```

The use of groups might strike you as odd. BGP uses them, but OSPF and IS-IS do not. Yet this slight similarity to BGP is easily understood when you consider the environment for which Juniper Networks routers are primarily built: large-scale service-provider backbones.

Because of its limitations, RIP is highly unlikely to be used as the IGP in such large networks. Where you are more likely to find RIP in these networks is as an "edge" protocol, speaking to devices external to the primary IGP domain. The wise network architect carefully regulates the routes that are accepted into and advertised out of the core domain. By assigning external neighbors to groups, the policies necessary for controlling the exchange of route information with these neighbors become more flexible. You have the option of setting policies for the entire routing protocol, for a group of neighbors, or for an individual neighbor.

Unlike more traditional IGP-oriented RIP implementations, JUNOS requires you to configure policies that specify exactly what routes RIP advertises. The following sections demonstrate a few basic RIP policies.

RIP Export Policies

Figure 8-13 shows a simple network with two Juniper Networks routers, one of which has a connection to an external network. An assumption of this example is that the

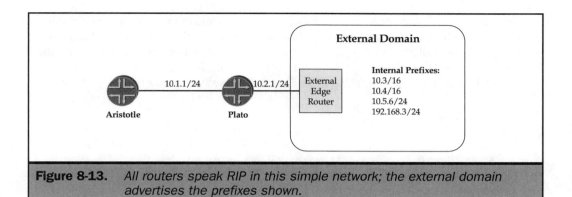

Figure 8-13.   *All routers speak RIP in this simple network; the external domain advertises the prefixes shown.*

external domain is under a different administrative authority—a customer network, for instance. The domain's edge router could be any vendor's router; all you know is that it speaks RIP and advertises the prefixes shown in the illustration. RIP is also spoken between the two Juniper Networks routers.

The preliminary configurations of the two routers in Figure 8-13 are

```
[edit]
jeff@Plato# show protocols
rip {
    group external_domain {
        neighbor so-3/2/1.0;
    }
    group Aristotle {
        neighbor ge-0/1/0.0;
    }
}
```

and

```
[edit]
jeff@Aristotle# show protocols
rip {
    group Plato {
        neighbor ge-0/0/1.0;
    }
}
```

You can observe the routes entered into the inet.0 routing table with the command show route. There are a number of options you can use with this command to narrow the output to the routes you are interested in. One of these options is to display only the routes entered into the table by a specific routing protocol. Using show route protocol rip, the RIP-learned routes in router Plato's routing table are shown:

```
jeff@Plato> show route protocol rip

inet.0: 11 destinations, 11 routes (11 active, 0 holddown, 0 hidden)
+ = Active Route, - = Last Active, * = Both

10.3.0.0/16         *[RIP/100] 01:40:20, metric 2
                     > to 10.2.1.2 via so-3/2/1.0
10.4.0.0/16         *[RIP/100] 01:40:20, metric 3
                     > to 10.2.1.2 via so-3/2/1.0
10.5.6.0/24         *[RIP/100] 00:00:49, metric 3
                     > to 10.2.1.2 via so-3/2/1.0
192.168.3.0/24      *[RIP/100] 00:00:12, metric 6
                     > to 10.2.1.2 via so-3/2/1.0
224.0.0.9/32        *[RIP/100] 01:26:07, metric 1
```

All the prefixes advertised by the external edge router appear in the table, as does the RIPv2 multicast address, but Aristotle's routing table shows that none of the external prefixes have been entered:

```
jeff@Aristotle> show route protocol rip

inet.0: 5 destinations, 5 routes (5 active, 0 holddown, 0 hidden)
+ = Active Route, - = Last Active, * = Both

224.0.0.9/32         *[RIP/100] 01:51:00, metric 1
```

A policy must be configured that specifies what routes are to be exported to what neighbors. At Plato, a policy named "externals" is created, which accepts all RIP routes:

```
[edit]
jeff@Plato# show policy-options
policy-statement externals {
    from protocol rip;
    then accept;
}
```

The policy is then applied as an export policy to the group Aristotle:

```
[edit]
jeff@Plato# show protocols
rip {
    group external_domain {
        neighbor so-3/2/1.0;
    }
    group Aristotle {
        export externals;
        neighbor ge-0/1/0.0;
    }
}
```

With this policy in place, the routes learned from the external domain are now advertised to Aristotle:

```
jeff@Aristotle> show route protocol rip

inet.0: 9 destinations, 9 routes (9 active, 0 holddown, 0 hidden)
+ = Active Route, - = Last Active, * = Both

10.3.0.0/16         *[RIP/100] 00:39:22, metric 3
                     > to 10.1.1.1 via ge-0/0/1.0
10.4.0.0/16         *[RIP/100] 00:39:22, metric 4
                     > to 10.1.1.1 via ge-0/0/1.0
10.5.6.0/24         *[RIP/100] 00:39:22, metric 4
                     > to 10.1.1.1 via ge-0/0/1.0
192.168.3.0/24      *[RIP/100] 00:39:22, metric 7
                     > to 10.1.1.1 via ge-0/0/1.0
224.0.0.9/32        *[RIP/100] 02:37:38, metric 1
```

Notice, however, that there is one subnet missing: 10.2.1/24, the subnet connecting Plato to the external edge router. This might be fine, if you do not want Aristotle to know about that subnet. Aristotle certainly does not need it for sending packets to the prefixes of the external domain, but you might want Aristotle to be able to send packets to the subnet for maintenance purposes—to PING the external edge router's interface, for example.

Subnet 10.2.1/24 is listed in Plato's routing table as a directly connected subnet, not a RIP route, so the policy "externals" does not pick it up; therefore, another policy is required:

```
[edit]
jeff@Plato# show policy-options
policy-statement externals {
    from protocol rip;
    then accept;
}
policy-statement ext_interface {
    from protocol direct;
    then accept;
}
```

The new policy, "ext_interface," is then added as an additional export policy for group Aristotle:

```
[edit]
jeff@Plato# show protocols
rip {
    group external_domain {
        neighbor so-3/2/1.0;
    }
    group Aristotle {
        export [ externals ext_interface ];
        neighbor ge-0/1/0.0;
    }
}
```

An alternative configuration is to make "ext_interface" a second term under the policy "externals," rather than a separate policy, so that a single export policy is cited for group Aristotle. They work the same; your choice is driven partly by personal preference, and partly by whether any of the policy conditions are used in more than one place in the configuration.

With the new export policy applied, subnet 10.2.1/24 now appears in Aristotle's routing table:

```
jeff@Aristotle> show route protocol rip

inet.0: 11 destinations, 11 routes (11 active, 0 holddown, 0 hidden)
```

```
+ = Active Route,  - = Last Active,  * = Both

10.2.1.0/24          *[RIP/100] 00:17:30, metric 2
                     > to 10.1.1.1 via ge-0/0/1.0
10.3.0.0/16          *[RIP/100] 01:12:27, metric 3
                     > to 10.1.1.1 via ge-0/0/1.0
10.4.0.0/16          *[RIP/100] 01:12:27, metric 4
                     > to 10.1.1.1 via ge-0/0/1.0
10.5.6.0/24          *[RIP/100] 01:12:27, metric 4
                     > to 10.1.1.1 via ge-0/0/1.0
10.200.255.254/32    *[RIP/100] 00:14:51, metric 2
                     > to 10.1.1.1 via ge-0/0/1.0
172.16.1.0/24         [RIP/100] 00:17:30, metric 2
                     > to 10.1.1.1 via ge-0/0/1.0
192.168.3.0/24       *[RIP/100] 01:12:27, metric 7
                     > to 10.1.1.1 via ge-0/0/1.0
224.0.0.9/32         *[RIP/100] 03:10:43, metric 1
```

But there is a problem. Not only has 10.2.1/24 shown up, so have two more prefixes: 10.200.255.254/32 and 172.16.1.0/24. Where did those prefixes come from?

The answer is that they are subnets directly connected to router Plato, but not shown in Figure 8-13. The policy "ext_interface" has a match condition of `protocol direct`, meaning it matches all directly-connected subnets. This is not, however, the desired result. 10.2.1/24 is the only directly connected subnet that Plato should advertise to Aristotle via RIP.

Rather than using a broad statement such as `protocol direct`, you can use a route filter to specify exactly the prefix you want:

```
[edit]
jeff@Plato# show policy-options
policy-statement externals {
    from protocol rip;
    then accept;
}
policy-statement ext_interface {
    from {
        route-filter 10.2.1.0/24 exact;
    }
    then accept;
}
```

With this correction to the policy "ext_interface," Aristotle's routing table now contains only the desired prefixes:

```
jeff@Aristotle> show route protocol rip

inet.0: 10 destinations, 10 routes (10 active, 0 holddown, 0 hidden)
+ = Active Route, - = Last Active, * = Both

10.2.1.0/24        *[RIP/100] 01:33:02, metric 2
                    > to 10.1.1.1 via ge-0/0/1.0
10.3.0.0/16        *[RIP/100] 02:27:59, metric 3
                    > to 10.1.1.1 via ge-0/0/1.0
10.4.0.0/16        *[RIP/100] 02:27:59, metric 4
                    > to 10.1.1.1 via ge-0/0/1.0
10.5.6.0/24        *[RIP/100] 02:27:59, metric 4
                    > to 10.1.1.1 via ge-0/0/1.0
192.168.3.0/24     *[RIP/100] 02:27:59, metric 7
                    > to 10.1.1.1 via ge-0/0/1.0
224.0.0.9/32       *[RIP/100] 04:26:15, metric 1
```

So far the policies apply to the routes advertised to Aristotle. As a last example, suppose you want Plato to advertise a default route to the external domain. The first step is to configure a static default route:

```
[edit]
jeff@Plato# show routing-options
static {
    route 0.0.0.0/0 {
        reject;
        retain;
    }
}
```

The `reject` option means that packets that do not find a better match are rejected and an ICMP error message is sent to the originator. The `retain` option means that the route is always held in the forwarding table.

Next, a new policy is added to the configuration. This new policy is named "default_route," and accepts static routes that match 0.0.0.0/0 exactly:

```
[edit]
jeff@Plato# show policy-options
policy-statement externals {
    from protocol rip;
```

```
        then accept;
    }
policy-statement ext_interface {
    from {
        route-filter 10.2.1.0/24 exact;
    }
    then accept;
}
policy-statement default_route {
    from {
        protocol static;
        route-filter 0.0.0.0/0 exact;
    }
    then accept;
}
```

Last, the new policy is added as an export policy for group "external_domain":

```
[edit]
jeff@Plato# show protocols rip
group external_domain {
    export default_route;
    neighbor so-3/2/1.0;
}
group Aristotle {
    export [ externals ext_interface ];
    neighbor ge-0/1/0.0;
}
```

RIP Import Policies

You saw in the "RIP Export Policies" section several examples of implementing export policies. Returning to the network in Figure 8-13, suppose you want to accept only prefixes 10.4/16 and 192.168.3/24. An import policy is called for here, which will block undesired routes before they are entered into Plato's routing table. The policy is named "external_routes":

```
[edit]
jeff@Plato# show policy-options policy-statement external_routes
from {
    route-filter 10.4.0.0/16 exact accept;
```

```
        route-filter 192.168.3.0/24 exact accept;
        route-filter 0.0.0.0/0 orlonger;
}
then reject;
```

The desired routes match one of the first two lines of the route filter and are accepted. All other routes match the third line, and are rejected. The filter is then applied to the RIP configuration:

```
[edit]
jeff@Plato# show protocols
rip {
    group external_domain {
        export default_route;
        neighbor so-3/2/1.0 {
            import external_routes;
        }
    }
    group Aristotle {
        export [ externals ext_interface ];
        neighbor ge-0/1/0.0;
    }
}
```

The import policy can be placed either globally for the entire RIP process, or under a specific neighbor as shown here. The choice depends on your network. If you are sure you will never need to accept the rejected addresses from any RIP neighbor, place it globally. Placing the import policy under the specific neighbor means you can apply different policies to other neighbors. Usually the more specific policy application is the better application.

With the import policy in place, Plato's routing table reflects the result:

```
[edit]
jeff@Plato# run show route protocol rip

inet.0: 11 destinations, 11 routes (11 active, 0 holddown, 0 hidden)
+ = Active Route, - = Last Active, * = Both

10.4.0.0/16         *[RIP/100] 01:55:41, metric 3
                     > to 10.2.1.2 via so-3/2/1
192.168.3.0/24      *[RIP/100] 00:20:21, metric 6
```

```
                             > to 10.2.1.2 via so-3/2/1
      224.0.0.9/32           *[RIP/100] 00:13:44, metric 1
```

The logic of policies is not always easy to follow. In the policy "external_routes," if the last line of the route filter list were not included, the policy would not work. Any routes that did not match either the 10.4/16 or the 192.168.3/24 statements would not match anything at all. As a result they would go to the default action rather than the `then reject` action. The default action for a RIP import policy is to accept, so all routes would be accepted into Plato's routing table.

An alternative policy configuration, which provides the same results, is

```
[edit]
jeff@Plato# show policy-options policy-statement external_routes
term good_routes {
    from {
        route-filter 10.4.0.0/16 exact;
        route-filter 192.168.3.0/24 exact;
    }
    then accept;
}
term bad_routes {
    then reject;
}
```

This policy uses two terms. The desired routes match the first term and are accepted into the routing table. All other routes pass to the second term, where they are rejected.

Authentication

As mentioned in the previous "Authentication" section, authentication of routing protocol messages is an important part of securing any network. The costs in administration, CPU processing, and bandwidth are negligible compared to the added protection. Failure to authenticate leaves your routers open to the introduction of incorrect routing information, either inadvertent or malicious.

JUNOS software gives you the choice of using either plain-text passwords or MD5 encryption when authenticating RIPv2 messages. With either method, the same password must be configured on directly connected neighbors. Plain-text authentication includes this password in all messages sent to the neighbor. The neighbor accepts the message only if the password matches its own. MD5 never sends the password. Instead, it creates a cryptographic checksum from the combination of the message and the password. This checksum is then transmitted with the message. The receiving router runs the same algorithm, using the received message and its own password. If the resulting checksum does not match the checksum in the message, the message is rejected.

Plain-text passwords are less secure because they can be easily read from captured RIP messages. Use MD5 encryption whenever possible and plain-text passwords only when you must, such as when peering with a router that supports only plain-text passwords.

JUNOS software allows you to set RIPv2 authentication at either the global level or per neighbor. If you intend to use the same password for all neighbors, use global authentication so that you have to configure the password only once per router. Using unique passwords for each neighbor affords better security, but at the expense of more configuration and a higher chance of configuration error.

Configuring authentication is a simple matter of specifying:

- Which level the authentication is used (global or per-neighbor)
- The password, using the `authentication-key` command
- The authentication mode, using the `authentication-type` command

Continuing with the network in Figure 8-13, suppose the network policy is to use MD5 authentication. All internal neighbors are authenticated with the single password "Democritus," but each external neighbor must have a unique password. For the external neighbor shown in the illustration, "Parmenides" has been assigned. Assume that the administrator of the external domain has configured the external edge router correctly.

Plato is configured as follows:

```
[edit protocols rip]
jeff@Plato# set group external_domain neighbor so-3/2/1 authentication-key Parmenides
[edit protocols rip]
jeff@Plato# set group external_domain neighbor so-3/2/1 authentication-type md5
[edit protocols rip]
jeff@Plato# set group Aristotle neighbor ge-0/1/0 authentication-key Democritus
[edit protocols rip]
jeff@Plato# set group Aristotle neighbor ge-0/1/0 authentication-type md5
```

Plain text passwords are configured exactly the same, except that `authentication-type simple` rather than `authentication-type md5` is used.

The resulting configuration is

```
[edit protocols rip]
jeff@Plato# show
group external_domain {
    export default_route;
    neighbor so-3/2/1.0 {
        import external_routes;
        authentication-type md5;
        authentication-key "$9$nuLb6t0B1hyeWp0EyeW-daZUDi.Qz6Au1"; #
SECRET-DATA
```

```
        }
    }
    group Aristotle {
        export [ externals ext_interface ];
        neighbor ge-0/1/0.0 {
            authentication-type md5;
            authentication-key "$9$ED/hSl8LNs2a8X-w2gDjTz3ntOhSeWX-"; #
    SECRET-DATA
        }
    }
```

Notice that although the passwords were typed in plain text, they are automatically encrypted in the configuration.

Assuming that all router Aristotle's neighbors are internal to the network, it is not necessary to configure the single internal password on every neighbor. Aristotle's configuration, with authentication configured globally, is

```
[edit protocols rip]
jeff@Aristotle# show
authentication-type md5;
authentication-key "$9$SN7ylvx7VgoGxNb2oaHkFn/90IylMXNb"; # SECRET-DATA
group Plato {
    neighbor ge-0/0/1.0;
}
```

Global and neighbor-specific authentication can also be used together. For example, if router Plato has many external neighbors and also many internal neighbors, the internal password can be configured globally. The unique passwords for the external neighbors can be configured for those neighbors. If a neighbor has authentication configured, that password is used. If the neighbor does not have authentication configured, the global authentication is used.

Configuring for Backward Compatibility

When you configure RIP on a Juniper Networks router, the default is to listen for both RIPv1 and RIPv2 messages, and to send only RIPv2 messages but using broadcast rather than multicast. That is, the default receive control switch setting is "Both," and the default compatibility switch setting is "RIP-1 Compatibility." Tables 8-2 and 8-3 show the possible options for setting these two switches, and the JUNOS software keywords for each option.

The default receive control switch is changed with the command `receive`, and the default compatibility switch setting is changed with the command `send`. For example, suppose a second external neighbor is added to router Plato in Figure 8-13, and this neighbor is a RIPv1 router. Depending on the specifics of that router's RIP process, Plato's default settings will probably work. In this example, though, a pure RIPv1 relationship is required. Putting the new neighbor under the group "OldRouter," Plato's RIP configuration becomes

```
[edit]
jeff@Plato# show protocols rip
group external_domain {
    export default_route;
    neighbor so-3/2/1.0 {
        import external_routes;
        authentication-type md5;
        authentication-key "$9$nuLb6t0B1hyeWp0EyeW-daZUDi.Qz6Au1"; #
SECRET-DATA
    }
}
group Aristotle {
    export [ externals ext_interface ];
    neighbor ge-0/1/0.0 {
        authentication-type md5;
        authentication-key "$9$ED/hSl8LNs2a8X-w2gDjTz3ntOhSeWX-"; #
SECRET-DATA
    }
}
group OldRouter {
    neighbor so-3/2/2.0 {
        send version-1;
        receive version-1;
    }
}
```

Authentication is not configured for the new neighbor, of course, because RIPv1 does not support it.

The receive control and compatibility switches can also be set at the global level. If router Aristotle in Figure 8-13 is an internal router that will never be connected to a RIPv1 router, you might want to set it so that it receives only RIPv2 messages, and uses the reserved multicast address 224.0.0.9 when sending RIPv2 messages. The router's configuration is

```
[edit]
jeff@Aristotle# show protocols rip
send multicast;
receive version-2;
authentication-type md5;
authentication-key "$9$SN7ylvx7VgoGxNb2oaHkFn/90IylMXNb"; # SECRET-DATA
group Plato {
    neighbor ge-0/1/0;
}
```

Troubleshooting RIPv2

RIP is such a simple protocol, troubleshooting it is usually no more difficult than verifying neighbor reachability and correct configuration. If the problem is that a particular destination is unreachable, the routing table is the first place to look. Using `show route protocol rip`, as demonstrated several times in this chapter, displays all the entries RIP has made in the routing table along with the metric, the age of the entry, and the next hop. There are many other options for narrowing or broadening your examination of the entire routing table or of a single route. You can see the available options with `show route ?`:

```
jeff@Aristotle> show route ?
Possible completions:
  <[Enter]>             Execute this command
  <destination>         Destination prefix and prefix length information
  advertising-protocol  Information transmitted by a particular routing protocol
  all                   All entries including hidden entries
  aspath-regex          Entries learned via a specific AS path
  best                  Show longest match
  brief                 Brief view
+ community             A community to match, possibly including wildcards
  damping               Entries that have been subjected to route damping
  detail                Detailed view
  exact                 Show exact match
  extensive             Extensive view
  forwarding-table      Entries in all forwarding tables
  hidden                Hidden entries
  inactive              Inactive entries
  instance              Show information about Routing-instances
  label-switched-path   Entries associated with a particular LSP tunnel
  martians              Show martian networks
  next-hop              Entries pointing to a particular next hop
  output                Entries sending packets out a particular interface
  protocol              Information learned from a particular routing protocol
  range                 Show entire prefix range
  receive-protocol      Information learned from a particular routing protocol
  source-gateway        Entries learned from a particular router
  summary               Routing table statistics
  table                 Entries in a particular routing table
  terse                 Terse view
  |                     Pipe through a command
```

For the few occasions you need to see what is going on in the background, traceoptions are called for. RIP traceoptions are configured globally; to see what you can monitor, use the question mark:

```
[edit protocols rip]
jeff@Plato# set traceoptions flag ?
Possible completions:
  all                   Trace everything
  auth                  Trace RIP authentication
  error                 Trace RIP errors
  expiration            Trace RIP route expiration processing
  general               Trace general events
  holddown              Trace RIP holddown processing
  normal                Trace normal events
  packets               Trace all RIP packets
  policy                Trace policy processing
  request               Trace RIP information packets
  route                 Trace routing information
  state                 Trace state transitions
  task                  Trace routing protocol task processing
  timer                 Trace routing protocol timer processing
  trigger               Trace RIP triggered updates
  update                Trace RIP update packets
```

Broad options such as all are usually not useful because they give you too much information. Instead, try to focus on the problem at hand and your educated suspicions of the cause. For example, if you want to look at the updates sent and received by router Aristotle in Figure 8-13, the configuration is

```
[edit protocols rip]
jeff@Aristotle# show
traceoptions {
    file rip-updates;
    flag update;
}
send multicast;
receive version-2;
authentication-type md5;
authentication-key "$9$EsPhS18LNs2a8X-w2gDjTz3ntOhSeWX-"; # SECRET-DATA
group Plato {
    neighbor fxp1.0;
}
```

This configuration sends all update information to a file called "rip-updates." To view the contents of the file, use show log rip-updates:

```
jeff@Aristotle> show log rip-updates
Aug 25 21:47:20 trace_on: Tracing to "/var/log/rip-updates" started
Aug 25 21:47:24 Creating job to send RIP updates.
Aug 25 21:47:24 Update job: sending 100 msgs; group: Plato.
Aug 25 21:47:24          nbr ge-0/0/1.0; msgp: 0x0.
Aug 25 21:47:24          nbr ge-0/0/1.0 done.
Aug 25 21:47:24       Group Plato done.
Aug 25 21:47:24 Update job done!
Aug 25 21:47:26 received response: command 2, version 2, mbz: 0; 5 routes.
Aug 25 21:47:26             10.2.1.0/0xffffff00: tag 0, nh       10.1.1.1, met 1.
Aug 25 21:47:26             10.4.0.0/0xffff0000: tag 0, nh       10.1.1.1, met 3.
Aug 25 21:47:26             192.168.3.0/0xffffff00: tag 0, nh    10.1.1.1, met 6.
Aug 25 21:47:51 Creating job to send RIP updates.
Aug 25 21:47:51 Update job: sending 100 msgs; group: Plato.
Aug 25 21:47:51          nbr ge-0/0/1.0; msgp: 0x0.
Aug 25 21:47:51          nbr ge-0/0/1.0 done.
Aug 25 21:47:51       Group Plato done.
Aug 25 21:47:51 Update job done!
Aug 25 21:47:53 received response: command 2, version 2, mbz: 0; 5 routes.
Aug 25 21:47:53             10.2.1.0/0xffffff00: tag 0, nh       10.1.1.1, met 1.
```

Chapter 9

OSPF Theory

by Galina Diker Pildush

In the mid-1980s, the Internet Engineering Task Force (IETF) was looking for a fast, scalable, efficient interior routing protocol that could scale better than Routing Information Protocol Version 1 (RIPv1). As a result, the OSPF Working Group was formed in 1987 and the work began, resulting in the Open Shortest Path First (OSPF) version 1 release in 1989 as RFC 1131. OSPF version 2 was defined in 1991, with further enhancements released in 1997 as RFC 2178, which was replaced by RFC 2328 in 1998.

This chapter focuses on OSPF, including its link-state nature, and the depth and complexities of its state machine, adjacency formation, exchange of information, path computations, and hierarchical architecture.

OSPF: A Link-State Routing Protocol

In contrast to distance vector routing protocols, link-state routing protocols are based on the router's full knowledge of the entire network—that is, each router has a complete understanding of the network topology. Each router must keep track of its own link conditions, or *states*, and must immediately notify all the other routers of changes.

> **Note**   *My favorite comparison between distance vector and link-state protocols is as follows: Distance vector protocols learn by rumor—one router tells its neighbor routers the entire story from its own perspective; link-state protocols learn by propaganda—each router screams to all the other routers about its own links.*

Link-state routing enables each router on the network to see the entire network topology, thus allowing a router to compute the most efficient path to a specific destination from its own perspective. Link-state routing protocols typically use the *Dijkstra algorithm* (also known as *Shortest Path First*, or *SPF*). The Dijkstra algorithm, invented by a Dutch scientist Edsger Dijkstra, has been in existence since 1959. It is interesting to note that scientist Whiting and Hillier independently discovered the SPF algorithm in 1960.

The Dijkstra algorithm determines only the distances from a specific network node (router) to all other nodes (routers), not the actual shortest path. The SPF algorithm extends the Dijkstra algorithm through a simple idea of keeping track of the predecessors nodes (routers) in the SPF tree.

The fact that a link-state router sees the entire network topology allows the implementation of traffic engineering extensions. Some of these concepts have already been implemented in ATM's PNNI, where the computation of a path for a specific traffic flow, constrained by requested QoS parameters, takes place at the ingress point of the network and is carried within a signal request throughout the network.

OSPF packets are encapsulated directly in the Internet Protocol (IP) using protocol number 89, which has five packet types that are identified uniquely by the packet type number, as itemized in Table 9-1.

Prior to identifying details and specifics of OSPF, let's examine a sample network and SPF decisions that must take place for determining the best route for any given network.

Value	Meaning
1	Hello protocol packets
2	Database Description packets
3	Link-State Request packets
4	Link-State Update packets
5	Link-State Acknowledgement packets

Table 9-1. *OSPF Protocol Packet Type Values*

Shortest Path First Computation

SPF is a fairly involved and complex algorithm. Picture several hundreds of nodes in a given network. According to link-state rules, every router on that network must know about every other single link, must include each link in its link-state database, and must include each link in its SPF computations.

To reduce the database size, the link-state noise on the networks, and the SPF algorithm time, OSPF networks can be grouped into logical *areas*. Each area is an independent entity. With introduction of areas, the routers within an area must have identical link-state databases. Between the areas, though, the databases could differ. Inter-area OSPF routing is not truly SPF, but is much more similar to distance vector routing. The "OSPF Hierarchy" section, later in this chapter, covers this concept in depth.

A sample network topology is illustrated in Figure 9-1, with the SPF calculations for Router A reaching all the other routers on the network.

Router A builds a topological link-state database consisting of the entries shown here:

Link	Cost
A-B	2
A-E	10
B-C	3
B-E	7
C-E	6
C-D	4
D-E	5

Note *The cost of the links does not need to be identical from both sides of the link. That is, an AB link can have a cost of 2, but a BA link can have a different cost. This exercise assumes the cost of the links to be the same on both sides.*

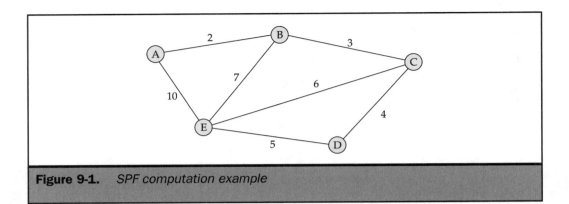

Figure 9-1.   *SPF computation example*

Step 1: Destination—Router B

Router B can be reached in more than one way. SPF examines all the possible paths and enters them into a tentative table, illustrated in Figure 9-2, from which it derives the shortest path to reach Router B.

 The shortest path to reach Router B is to use the direct link A-B, with a cost of 2. SPF creates a tree structure from the source Router A to the destination Router B.

Step 2: Destination—Router C

SPF examines the database and enters possible routes into the tentative database, from which it derives the shortest path to reach destination Router C, as illustrated in Figure 9-3.

 The shortest path to reach Router C is A-B-C. At the same time, SPF creates a loop-free tree from the source Router A to the destination Router C.

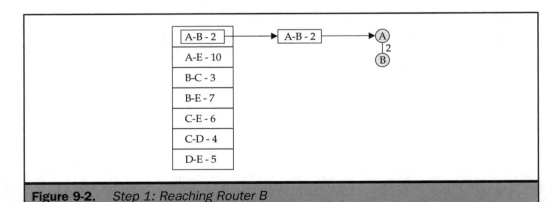

Figure 9-2.   *Step 1: Reaching Router B*

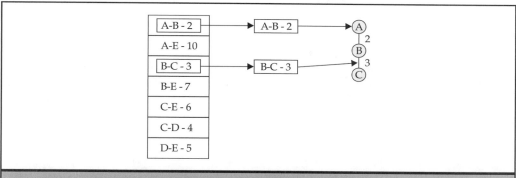

Figure 9-3.   *Step 2: Reaching Router C*

Step 3: Destination—Router D

To get to destination Router D, SPF examines various possibilities, using the link-state database and already computed paths to reach destination Routers B and C. Eliminating various possibilities, SPF derives the shortest path to reach Router D to be A-B-C-D, with a cost of 9, as illustrated in Figure 9-4.

At the same time, SPF creates a loop-free tree from Router A to Router D destination.

Step 4: Destination—Router E

Again, going through the same steps of using the topological database and already computed paths to reach other destinations (B, C, and D), SPF selects the path A-B-E with the cost of 9 to reach destination Router E. This is illustrated in Figure 9-5.

At the same time, SPF creates a loop-free tree from Router A to Router E.

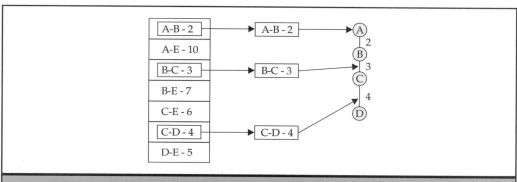

Figure 9-4.   *Step 3: Reaching Router D*

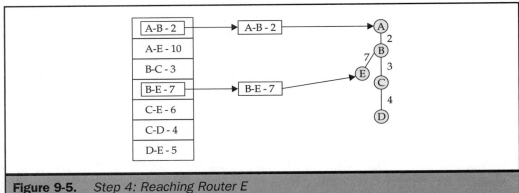

Figure 9-5.   *Step 4: Reaching Router E*

OSPF Network Types

OSPF's behavior varies on different network types. Overall, we distinguish between four different types of network:

- Point-to-Point (P2P)
- Broadcast Multiaccess (BMA)
- Non-Broadcast Multiaccess (NBMA)
- Point-to-Multipoint (P2MP)

One could also argue that virtual links, discussed in "Virtually Attached OSPF Areas," constitute an additional type of network, but because they are usually a temporary measure for contingency use, we will concentrate on the four more intentional types of network.
    Let's examine each network type.

Point-to-Point Network

A P2P network is the simplest of all the network types. As illustrated in Figure 9-6, only two routers are connected to each other, which implies that each router has only one neighbor on a P2P network.

Broadcast Multi-access Network

Broadcast networks include any local area network (LAN)-type connection between your routers that is capable of broadcasting. The most common examples of this are Ethernet and Token Ring.
    Broadcast networks are one type of multi-access network, and therefore there is a need for a designated router function (explained later in "Considerations for Multi-access Networks").

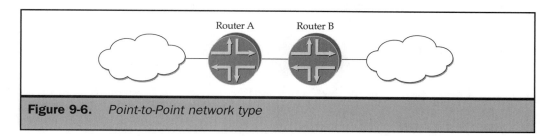

Figure 9-6.   *Point-to-Point network type*

Non-Broadcast Multi-access Network

NBMA is the type of multi-access network that connects multiple routers across a non-broadcast domain, similar to X.25, frame relay, and Asynchronous Transfer Mode (ATM). These networks are characterized by the existence of intermediate switches that are responsible for virtual circuit (VC) setup, and do not support broadcasting.

The default behavior of OSPF networks over NBMA requires a designated router (explained later in "Considerations for Multi-access Networks") and requires manual establishment of neighbor relationships between routers. Your NBMA networks could be fully meshed or partially meshed, as illustrated in Figure 9-7. In a fully-meshed NBMA network, redundant connectivity allows the designated router to be located anywhere. If, however, your NBMA network is partially meshed, as shown in Figure 9-7B, you should be careful in allowing or disallowing certain routers to carry or not to carry designated router responsibilities. In partially-meshed topologies, you need to set the router priorities to 0 for the routers that are not directly connected to all the routers. Using Figure 9-7B as illustration, priorities of Routers B, C, and D would have to be to 0.

OSPF allows you to change the network type on an NBMA-type interface, so that NBMA networks can be declared to be P2P, BMA, NBMA, or P2MP networks. Of course, OSPF will treat the networks according to how they are declared, regardless of which physical network the routers are connected to. If the NBMA network is declared to be P2MP, no Designated Router (DR) and Backup Designated Router (BDR) routers are used and the behavior is identical to that of multiple P2P networks. (For more on DR and BDR, see the section "Multi-access Network Rules," shortly.) If you leave the NBMA network to its default, NBMA, you must ensure that OSPF elects properly positioned routers to become DR/BDR (these would be routers that have connections to all the other routers across the NBMA network), and you will be required to perform some initial configurations for neighbor discovery.

Point-to-Multipoint Network

OSPF treats the P2MP network type as a collection of P2P networks. A P2MP network can be used as a replacement of the NBMA network types. P2MP does not require DR/BDR, and, although P2MP results in all directly attached routers peering with each other, it is a useful and simplified model to use across partially-meshed NBMA networks. A good example of P2MP applicability is illustrated in Figure 9-7B. The four routers on the network are partially meshed. By declaring the P2MP network type, you no longer have to worry about proper DR/BDR election.

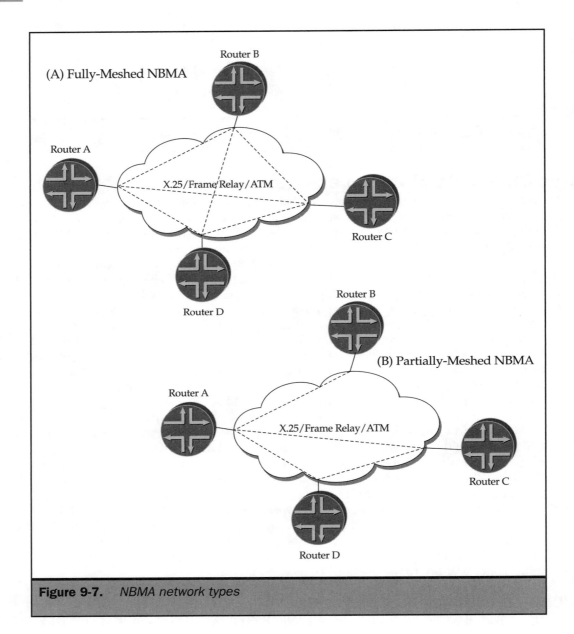

Figure 9-7.   *NBMA network types*

Considerations for Multi-access Networks

Consider the sample network topology illustrated in Figure 9-8. Routers A, B, C, and D are attached via an Ethernet link, which makes them neighbors.

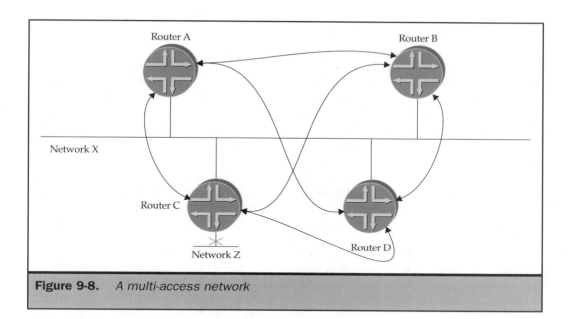

Figure 9-8. *A multi-access network*

Upon activating the OSPF on the routers, they all share their OSPF links information with other OSPF-speaking routers within their autonomous system (or area, should it exist). Before information exchange can take place, though, each OSPF-speaking router must understand and establish a neighbor relationship with all neighboring routers on immediately connected networks. How this neighbor relationship is established will be discussed later in the chapter in the section "Adjacency Establishment" For now, assume that the routers shown in Figure 9-8 have established adjacencies with each other.

Now assume that Network Z loses direct connectivity to Router C through some physical problem. Router C must notify all its neighbors of this change. C's neighbors, in turn, must notify their neighbors about the link-state change. But which routers are C's neighbors? In this instance, they are Routers A, B, and D. Assume that each router receives a link-state change about Network Z from Router C. Router A, in turn, will propagate this link-state change to its neighbors, Routers B and D. Finally, Router B will propagate this link-state change to Router D. You have just witnessed six unnecessary conversations about the same story on that Ethernet link. For multi-access networks having N immediately attached routers, the number of conversations would be $Nx(N-1)/2$. Not very pleasant, is it?

To reduce the number of conversations on multi-access links, multi-access network rules were created, which are discussed next.

Multi-access Network Rules

Each router on a multi-access network has *N-1* neighbors, where *N* is the total number of routers on the network. Examine Figure 9-8, and you'll see that Network X has four routers attached, which means that each router has three neighbors. To reduce the amount of conversations that must take place between the neighbors, OSPF elects a "CEO—Chief Executive Officer" of the multi-access network, called the *Designated Router* (DR), and its "secretary," the *Backup Designated Router* (BDR). The DR and BDR election takes place during the adjacency formation, which is addressed later in the chapter (see the "Adjacency Establishment" section).

The job of the DR is to spread the news about topological changes to all the neighbors on the BMA network. All the routers on the multi-access network form adjacencies with DR and BDR routers only, resulting in *2N-3* adjacencies.

Now let's assume that Router B, illustrated in Figure 9-9 has been elected to be a DR, and Router A has been elected to be a BDR.

When Network Z dies, Router C sends a link-state update packet to the *AllDRouters* multicast address 224.0.0.6, which includes DR and BDR only. When DR receives the packet, it propagates the news to other SPF-speaking routers *AllSPFRouters* on a multicast address 224.0.0.5. The BDR is sitting in a hot stand-by mode, waiting to hear from a DR on a 224.0.0.5 address about the change. Should the BDR not hear from the DR within the link-state advertisement retransmission interval, which is typically 5 seconds, it will take on DR's responsibilities and flood the link-state change into the multi-access Network X. At the same time, a new BDR is elected.

This intelligent use of DR/BDR greatly reduces the amount of conversations that must take place between the neighbors over multi-access networks. Instead of *N*(N-1)/2* number of adjacencies, you now have *2N-3*.

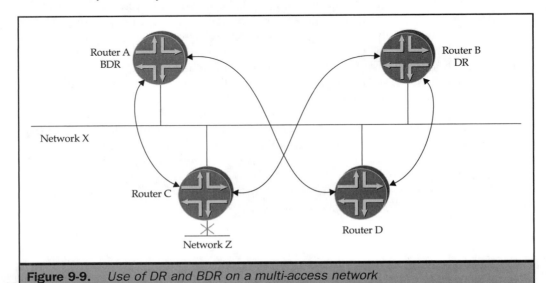

Figure 9-9.   *Use of DR and BDR on a multi-access network*

Designated Router/Backup Designated Router Election

DR/BDR election happens during the initial adjacency establishment between the routers over a multi-access network. If only one router exists on a multi-access network, this router is the DR. When you add another router to the network, that router becomes a BDR. That is all—no new elections take place until a DR and/or BDR becomes dysfunctional.

When a multi-access network has more than one router, or when the BDR must be re-elected (in case of a DR failure, the BDR is now a DR), OSPF uses strict rules for choosing the DR or a BDR candidate. OSPF uses a router priority value, which is in the range of 0 to 127, inclusive. The higher the priority, the better the chances of a router becoming a DR or a BDR. Should the routers' priorities be the same (in most implementations they are by default), OSPF uses Router ID (RID) to make the final election.

A priority of 0 has a special meaning. When a router has its priority equal to 0, it cannot become a DR or a BDR. This is a useful technique in NBMA partially-meshed topologies, where partially-meshed routers cannot have DR/BDR functionality because they are not immediately connected to all the routers on that NBMA network. Figure 9-10 illustrates an example network in which it is highly undesirable for Routers B and C to be DR and/or BDR. A 0 priority can also be used when you want to offload some routers from being DRs/BDRs for multiple BMA/NBMA networks, as shown in Figure 9-10.

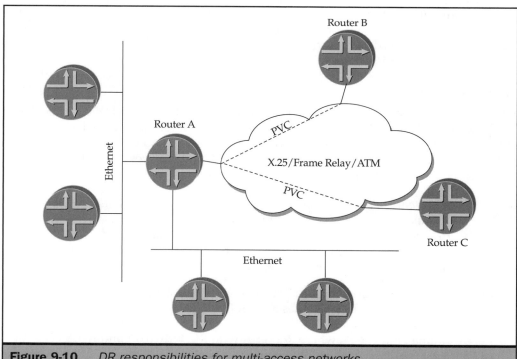

Figure 9-10.   *DR responsibilities for multi-access networks*

Router A is connected to two Ethernet networks and one X.25/Frame Relay/ATM network. If the router priorities are equal, Router A might be elected as a DR or a BDR. If you want to ensure that Router A participates in DR/BDR election only for one of these three networks, you must ensure that Router A's priority is set to 0 for the other two networks.

Adjacency Establishment

When you enable OSPF on the routers, you typically must specify which interfaces are participating in the OSPF process. By doing this, you are declaring that an interface X is now an OSPF interface, which is the connection between a router and a network. In addition, each router is identified uniquely with its RID. The RID is often taken from the loopback address of the router for convenience's sake, but may in fact be any legal and unique IP address. Upon the selection of a RID, OSPF is ready to talk to other SPF-speaking routers on directly connected networks. The goal of these conversations is to create adjacencies among neighboring routers so that OSPF can exchange routing information. OSPF uses a "Hello protocol" as its method of announcing a router on the network and as its heartbeat. The rules of OSPF adjacency formation are rigid—not every two neighboring OSPF routers can become adjacent. For example, if the Hello intervals are different between the two neighbor routers, adjacency is not formed. All routers connected to a common network must agree on such parameters as *HelloInterval*, *RouterDeadInterval*, network mask, AreaID, and Authentication. (See the section "OSPF Adjacency State Machine" later in the chapter for more information.)

Hello Protocol

OSPF uses Hello for more than just adjacency formation. It uses the Hello protocol for maintaining neighbor relationship via neighbor failure detection—should a router miss hearing a Hello from its established neighbor for a period of RouterDeadInterval, which is 40 seconds by default, it considers that neighbor *dead* and removes its link to that router from subsequent advertisements.

> **Tip** *It is important to differentiate between a "link state" nature of link-state routing protocols and the fact that link state protocols use "Hello" for various purposes. The Hello protocol does not make a routing protocol link state. A good example is Enhanced Interior Gateway Routing Protocol (EIGRP), Cisco's proprietary distance vector routing protocol, which uses a Hello protocol.*

On multi-access networks, such as BMA and NBMA, the Hello protocol elects a DeR. The Hello protocol has additional duties for OSPF extensions, which are discussed in the section titled "OSPF Extensions."

Let's examine Figure 9-11, where Router A with RID = 20.0.0.1 and Router B with RID = 20.0.0.2 have OSPF enabled on the interfaces between them.

In Figure 9-11, Routers A and B send the Hello packets periodically, by default every 10 seconds, to each other, ensuring that the communication between them is bidirectional.

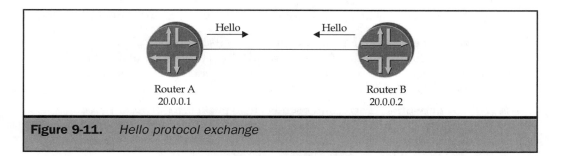

Figure 9-11. *Hello protocol exchange*

Bidirectional communication, used to prevent "black holes" in the network, is indicated when the router sees itself listed in a neighbor's Hello packet.

Let's look at the ingredients of a Hello packet that is sent from Router A to Router B in Figure 9-11. The Hello packet, like all OSPF packets, resides on top of IP, using Protocol 89. Figure 9-12 illustrates the Hello packet ingredients between Routers A and B.

The Hello packet type field is 1, as indicated earlier in Table 9-1.

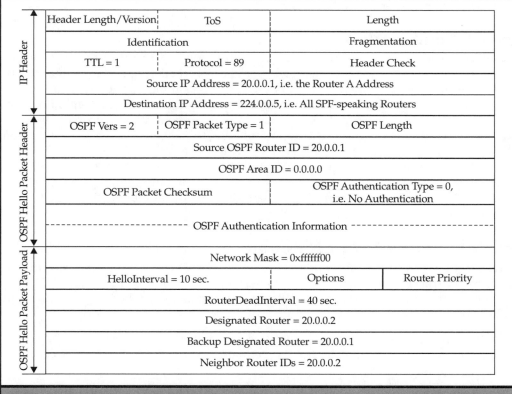

Figure 9-12. *Hello packet in detail*

The Hello protocol's behavior varies for different network segment types, as follows:

■ **Broadcast networks** Each router advertises itself periodically, allowing all its neighbors to be discovered dynamically. The periodical interval, the *HelloInterval*, is 10 seconds by default. Routers send the Hello on a multicast address *AllSPFRouters*, which is 224.0.0.5.

■ **NBMA networks** Each router sends Hello packets to all other potential DR routers. If a router itself is a DR, it begins sending the Hello protocol to all other routers attached to the network. The Hellos are sent on a unicast address to a router's predefined neighbors.

■ **Point-to-Multipoint networks** A router sends separate Hello packets to each attached neighbor with which it communicates directly every *HelloInterval*.

■ **Point-to-Point networks** A router sends Hello packets to its directly attached neighbor on a multicast address *AllSPFRouters*.

Upon the discovery of a neighbor, establishment of bidirectional communication, and a DR/BDR election for multi-access networks, OSPF is ready to decide whether or not the routers can form an adjacency among each other.

OSPF Authentication

OSPF allows routers to use authentication. As illustrated in Figure 9-12, the OSPF header includes an authentication type field, which indicates whether or not authentication is used. The authentication type field equals to 0 when no authentication is used.

Authentication is interface-specific—that is, a single router can use authentication with another OSPF router via one interface, and yet use no authentication with another OSPF router via a different interface. The important thing to remember is that authentication between OSPF routers on a single network *must be the same*.

RFC 2328 specifies two types of authentication schemes: *simple password* and *cryptographic*. When the simple password is used, the authentication type field has a value of 1; when the cryptographic password is used, the authentication type field has a value of 2.

OSPF Adjacency State Machine

You can view an OSPF adjacency as a "highly developed conversation between the two routers." Not every two neighbor OSPF routers form an adjacency, however. OSPF uses a rigid set of rules for adjacency formation between neighbors. These rules include the following:

■ Agreement on *HelloInterval*, *RouterDeadInterval*, network mask, AreaID, authentication parameters, and potentially other network-type-dependent capability information.

■ Successful bidirectional communication establishment.

■ A valid network type and, if applicable, designated router identity.

The OSPF adjacency formation follows the neighbor state machine, shown in Figure 9-13.

The initial state of an OSPF neighbor connection is *Down*. Should a router be attached to an NBMA network, and if no recent information is received from the neighbor(s), the router enters an *Attempt* state. When a router receives a Hello and if it is in either the *Attempt* or *Down* state, OSPF changes the state to *Init*. At this stage, the communication between the neighbors is unidirectional.

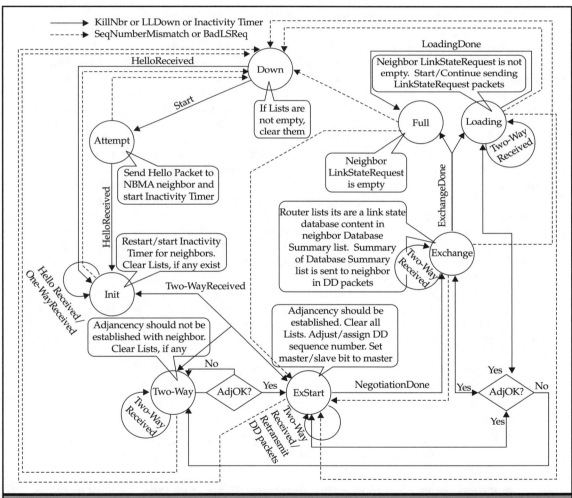

Figure 9-13.   *OSPF neighbor state machine*

The *Two-WayReceived* event indicates that Hellos have been received by two neighbors, and the communication becomes bidirectional as routers enter either the *Two-Way* state or the *ExStart* state. The *Two-Way* state indicates that something is wrong within the adjacency establishment that is preventing the adjacency formation. For example, Hello timers could be different, or Area Ids could be different between the neighbors. The *Two-Way* state can change to the *ExStart* state should the status of the adjacency formation change to positive checking.

The *ExStart* state indicates that the OSPF protocol is now "assured" that the adjacency formation between the neighbors should be established. Within this state, the decisions on the master router and the initial database description (DD) sequence number are made. At this point negotiation between the two neighbors is complete, and routing information may be exchanged.

Upon processing the *NegotiationDone* event, the router's state is changed to *Exchange*. In this state, the neighbors send the content of their DD packets to each other. The DD packets are general descriptions of the links that also indicate how recent the information is using the sequence number. Should a receiving neighbor have no details associated with certain link-state acknowledgments (LSAs), or should it have old information about some LSAs, it will send link-state request (LSR) packets asking for more recent LSAs. Upon receiving LSR packets, routers send link-state update (LSU) packets containing LSAs.

Upon receiving *ExchangeDone* event, routers enter either *Loading* or *Full* states. When routers enter the *Loading* state, the link-state requests are not empty, meaning that more information is still required to send to/from neighbor(s). At the *LoadingDone* event, routers enter the *Full* state, indicating that the link-state request is empty. The *Full* state is an optimal state that indicates that neighbor adjacency is formed successfully.

Figure 9-13 illustrates that neighbor adjacency states can deteriorate back to the *Down* state or *ExStart* state. The return to the *Down* state could be triggered by either *KillNbr*, or *LLDown*, or *InactivityTimer* events. The return to the *ExStart* state is triggered by either *SeqNumberMismatch* or *BadLSReq* events.

Figure 9-14 illustrates an example of the adjacency formation between Router1 and Router2. The Ethernet segment has four routers attached. Router4 and Router3 have already formed their adjacencies with the designated Router2, which was elected based on its higher priority. Now a new router joins in—Router1.

1. When Router1's interface becomes part of OSPF, Router1 starts sending Hello packets.

2. Router2 hears this Hello and moves its neighbor state with Router1 from *Down* to *Init*.

3. Router2 sends its Hello packet, indicating that it is the DR for this network and that it has heard Hello packet from Router1. This causes Router1 to change the state to *ExStart*.

4. Router1 starts claiming that it is the master. When it sees that Router2 is the master, because of its higher RID (192.168.10.1 is larger than 192.168.9.1), it does not argue and becomes the slave and its neighbor's DD sequence number. The relationship between the routers moves to the *Exchange* state.

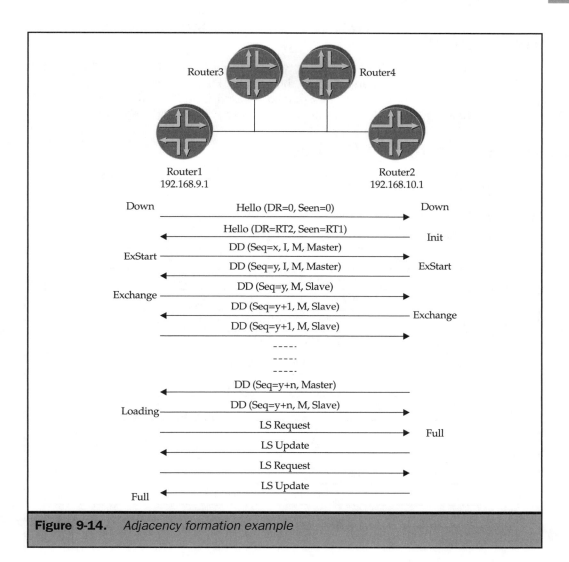

Figure 9-14. *Adjacency formation example*

5. Now the master, Router2, begins to poll DD packets from the slave, Router1. This exchange ends when both poll and the responses have the M-bit turned off.

6. The relationship between Router1 and Router2 moves to *Loading* state. At this stage, Router2 has a completely up-to-date database, but Router1, being a new kid on the block, doesn't.

7. So, Router1 sends LSR packets to Router2, asking for more details on the DD information that it had received from Router2.

8. Router2 replies with LSU packets.

9. Upon the completion of the exchange, the relationship enters the *Full* state.

OSPF Packets

Recall that OSPF has five different packet types, as identified in Table 9-1. The type 1 Hello packet was elaborated on earlier in the section "Hello Protocol." This section presents details of the other four types: database description (DD), link-state request (LSR), link-state update (LSU), and link-state acknowledgement (LSA) packets.

Database Description Packet

Figure 9-15 illustrates the DD packet details for the Router1 (shown in Figure 9-14). The DD packet is a type 2 packet.

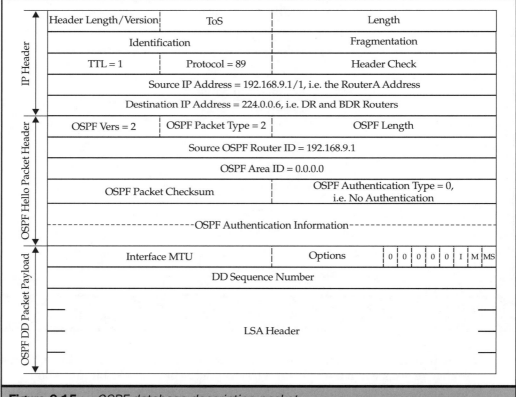

Figure 9-15. *OSPF database description packet*

Field	Meaning
Interface MTU	The size in bytes (maximum transfer unit) of the largest IP packet that can be sent from the interfaces without fragmentation
Options	Optional capabilities supported by the router
I-bit	The Init bit; I=1 indicates that this is the first packet in the sequence of DD packets
M-bit	The More bit; M=1 indicates that there are more DD packets to follow
MS-bit	The Master/Slave bit; MS=1 indicates that the router is a master during the exchange state
DD Sequence Number	Used to sequence the collection of DD packets, it increments until the entire database description has been sent
LSA Header	A list of LSA headers containing all the information required to uniquely identify each LSA

Table 9-2. *Database Description Packet Fields and Definitions*

Table 9-2 lists the definitions for all the fields in the DD packet. The IP and the OSPF headers are identical for all OSPF packets, with the exception of the OSPF Packet Type field, which is equal to a corresponding value as identified in Table 9-1.

Link-State Request Packet

Figure 9-16 illustrates the LSR packet details for the Router1 shown in Figure 9-14. The LSR packet is a type 3.

Table 9-3 lists the definitions for all the fields in the LSR packet. The IP and the OSPF headers are identical for all OSPF packets, with the exception of the OSPF Packet Type field, which is equal to a corresponding value as identified in Table 9-1.

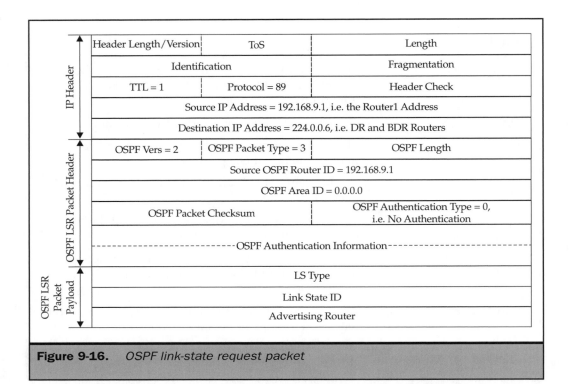

Figure 9-16. OSPF link-state request packet

Field	Meaning
LS Type	Link-state type to uniquely identify the LSA
Link-State ID	Link-state identifier
Advertising Router	Advertising router ID

Table 9-3. Link-State Request Packet Fields and Definitions

Link-State Update Packet

Figure 9-17 illustrates the LSU packet details for Router1 shown in Figure 9-14. The LSU packet is a type 4. Each LSU packet carries a collection of LSAs.

Table 9-4 lists the definitions for all the fields in the LSU packet. The IP and the OSPF headers are identical for all OSPF packets, with the exception of the OSPF Packet Type field, which is equal to the corresponding value as identified in Table 9-1.

Multiple LSAs appear in the list of LSAs, each beginning with a common 20-byte header.

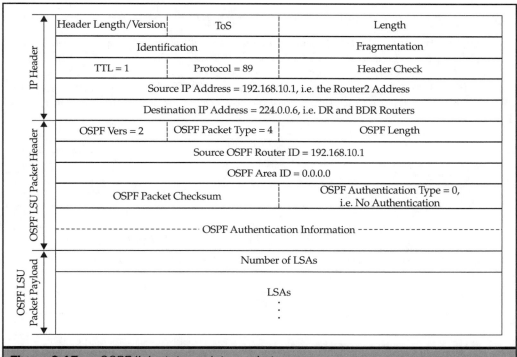

Figure 9-17. *OSPF link-state update packet*

Field	Meaning
Number of LSAs	The number of LSAs included in this update
LSAs	List of LSAs

Table 9-4.   *Link-State Update Packet Fields and Definitions*

Link-State Acknowledgement Packet

Figure 9-18 illustrates the LSA packet details for Router1 shown in Figure 9-14. the LSA packet is a type 5. It is used to make flooding reliable (see the next section). Multiple LSAs can be acknowledged in a single LSA packet.

The IP and the OSPF headers are identical for all OSPF packets, with the exception of the OSPF Packet Type field, which is equal to a corresponding value as identified in Table 9-1.

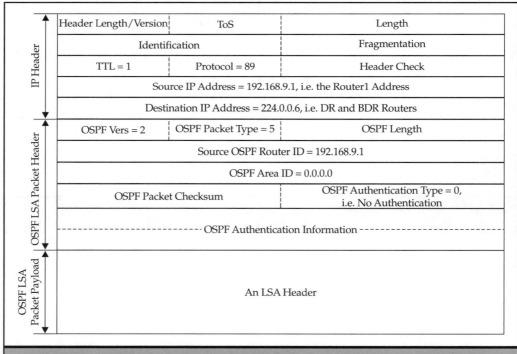

Figure 9-18.   *OSPF link-state acknowledgement packet*

Flooding

The network flooding procedure takes effect during adjacency formation and topology maintenance. Remember the "propaganda" comparison of a link-state protocol mentioned at the beginning of the chapter? Every router on the network must completely understand the network topology as it is, without anybody's interpretation. This implies that every router must notify all its SPF neighbors about its links. In turn, the neighbors must propagate this information to their own SPF neighbors, and so on. Notice, that the routers are sending the information in a totally unchanged format, so that every single SPF-speaking router receives this information in its original state and is capable of building the topological map of the network. This process of propagating link-state information to all SPF-speaking routers is called *flooding*.

Flooding Procedure

You can imagine the flooding procedure as a chain reaction process. The flooding procedure starts when a router receives an LSU packet. Remember that an LSU packet is transmitted when a router notices a topological change, or as a response to an LSR packet. An LSU packet may contain multiple LSAs that are destined to go to all the established adjacencies of a router. In turn, the receiving routers' job is to propagate these LSAs further to their own adjacencies, and so on, until the entire OSPF area is flooded.

OSPF applies rigid procedural rules to flooding. Prior to accepting an LSA as valid, its checksum, type, and validity are checked. Should one of those be invalid, the LSA is discarded. Furthermore, for an LSA to be valid, the sending neighbor must be in at least the Exchange state. If the LSA's age has reached its maximum, the adjacency state is Full, and it is a new LSA, this LSA is first acknowledged and then discarded. Otherwise, if it is a new LSA (meaning it does not exist in the database) or if the received LSA is more recent than the existing one, the router notes the length of time between the arrival of this LSA and the prior one. If the time period is below a predefined minimum arrival interval, this newly received LSA is ignored.

Next, the LSA is flooded out of the router's interfaces to all other adjacencies. At the same time, the LSA entry in the database is replaced by the newer, just received copy. Then, it is timestamped and the LSA packet is sent back to the sender. Should the received LSA be of the same age as an existing LSA within a router's database, the router might treat this LSA as an acknowledgement to the previously sent LSA. Should the received LSA be older than the existing LSA within a router's database, and the LSA's age has reached its maximum, the router discards the received LSA without acknowledging it. Otherwise, if the LSA has not reached its maximum age, the router sends it back to the sending neighbor as an LSU packet.

The Link-State Database

The OSPF link-state database is a collection of various representations of the entire network's link types that allow each router to understand the complete network topology. OSPF determines the routing table entries using the database. The link-state database is maintained in every OSPF router. Upon successful adjacency formation and exchange of LSAs, all router databases are identical

Using the link-state database, each router computes a shortest path tree with the router itself as a root of that tree. The tree provides the router with the entire path to any destination. The tree is also used for determining the entries in the routing table for specific destinations. Traditional IP routing (without traffic engineering extensions) is a hop-by-hop paradigm. Thus, routers use only the next-hop information in the forwarding process to a specific destination.

The database consists of various LSA types, including these:

- Router-LSAs
- Network-LSAs
- Summary-LSAs
- AS-external-LSAs

Table 9-5 summarizes types of LSAs identified in the RFC 2328, which excludes the OSPF extensions LSAs, which are specified later in this chapter in the section "OSPF Extensions."

LSA Type	Name	Purpose
1	router-LSA	Describes the states of the router's interfaces
2	network-LSA	Describes the set of routers attached to the network; originated by the DR
3	network-summary-LSA	Describes the inter-area routes to the networks; originated by the area border routers at the area borders
4	ASBR-summary-LSA	Describes the inter-area routes to the AS boundary routers (ASBRs); originated by the area border routers at the area borders
5	AS-external-LSA	Describes routes to the destinations external to the OSPF routing domain; originated by the AS boundary routers

Table 9-5.   *LSA Types Based on RFC 2328*

All routers originate router-LSAs. A router also originates the network-LSAs for those networks for which it is the Designated Router. Area border routers, which are discussed later in the section "OSPF Hierarchy," originate a summary-LSA for each inter-area destination. AS boundary routers originate an external LSA for each external destination.

Let's look closer at each LSA type.

Router-LSA

A router originates a router-LSA for all its links within each area to which it belongs. These LSAs are flooded to all the routers within a single area only. The format of the router-LSA, which is a type 1 LSA, is depicted in Figure 9-19.

Each LSA begins with a standard 20-byte LSA header, which identifies the LSA type, link-state ID, who the advertising router is, length of LSA, the time of LSA origination, and a few other fields identified in Table 9-6. This table describes not only the standard LSA header but also information pertaining specifically to the router-LSA. The router-LSA carries the additional information about the LSA, including the number of router links described in the LSA, router link description, link ID, metric, and so on.

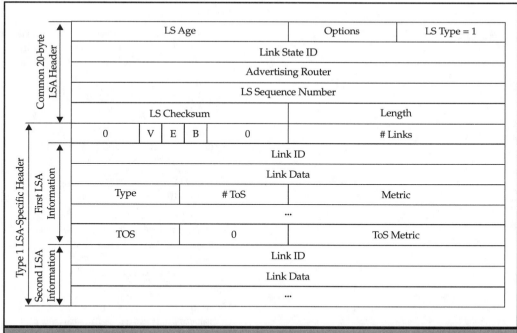

Figure 9-19.   *Router-LSA format*

	Router-LSA Field	Meaning
Common LSA Header	LS age	Time since the LSA was originated (in seconds)
	Options	Optional capabilities, including the flooding of external-LSAs, ability to handle type 7 LSAs, etc.
	LS type	LSA type equal to 1 for router-LSA
	Link-State ID	In the router-LSA, this field is the router's OSPF RID
	Advertising Router	The RID of the router that originated the LSA
	LS sequence number	The LSA sequence number used to detect old or duplicate LSAs
	LS checksum	The checksum of the complete content of the LSA
	Length	The length of LSA in bytes, including the 20-byte LSA header
Router-LSA Fields	Bit V	Indicates whether a router is an endpoint of one or more virtual links (described in the "OSPF Hierarchy" section)
	Bit E	Indicates that the router is an AS boundary router (described in the "OSPF Hierarchy" section)
	Bit B	Indicates that the router is the area border router (described in the "OSPF Hierarchy" section)
	# links	The total number of router links described in this LSA
	Link ID	Identifies the object the router link connects to; depending on the link's type value it can be equal to the RID of the neighbor router, IP address of the designated router, or the IP subnet number
	Link Data	Value depends on the link's type; can be network's IP address mask, router interface's IP address, and so on

Table 9-6.   *Description of the Router-LSA Content*

Router-LSA Fields	Router-LSA Field	Meaning
	Type	A link description that can be either P2P, P2MP, stub transit, or virtual link
	# ToS	The number of different ToS metrics given to this link, excluding the required ToS 0 metric
	Metric	Cost of using this router link
	ToS and ToS metric	ToS-specific metric information, if ToS is used

Table 9-6. *Description of the Router-LSA Content* (continued)

Network-LSA

NBMA and BMA type networks use the DR to spread the news about network topological changes within the network. When the DR is elected, it originates a network-LSA for that network, which is a type 2 LSA. The format of the network-LSA is illustrated in Figure 9-20.

The network-LSA describes all routers attached to the network, including the DR itself. Note that the distance from the network to all attached routers is 0. This is why the metric field does not need to be specified for this LSA. Table 9-7 describes the information carried within the network-LSA.

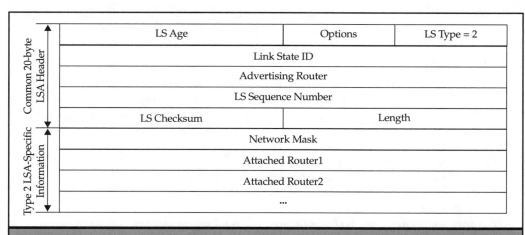

Figure 9-20. *Network-LSA format*

	Router-LSA Field	Meaning
Common LSA Header	LS age	Time since the LSA was originated (in seconds)
	Options	Optional capabilities, including flooding of external-LSAs, ability to handle type 7 LSAs, etc.
	LS type	LSA type; equal to 2 for network-LSA
	Link-State ID	In the network-LSA this field is the IP address of the DR
	Advertising Router	The RID of the router that originated the LSA
	LS sequence number	The sequence number of LSA; used to detect old or duplicate LSAs
	LS checksum	The checksum of the complete content of the LSA
	Length	The length of LSA in bytes, including the 20-byte LSA header
Network-LSA Fields	Network Mask	The IP address mask for the network
	Attached Router	The RIDs of all fully adjacent routers to the designated router

Table 9-7. *Description of the Network-LSA Content*

Summary-LSA

OSPF does not perform route summarization by default. The only place where you can summarize routes is at an area border router (ABR), which is discussed in the "OSPF Hierarchy" section later in this chapter. The ABR sends the summarized routes as summary-LSAs to other routers. It is interesting to note that ABRs send summary-LSAs whether or not the route summarization took place. This means that all router and network LSAs are converted to summary-LSAs. Summary-LSAs are types 3 and 4. Type 3 summary-LSAs describe summaries of the internal OSPF networks, while type 4 summary-LSAs describe inter-area paths to an ABSR. The only field that differentiates the two types is the Link-State ID, as denoted in Table 9-8.

The format of summary-LSAs is illustrated in Figure 9-21.

Table 9-8 provides the description of all summary-LSA fields.

	Router-LSA Field	Meaning
Common LSA Header	LS age	Time since the LSA was originated (in seconds)
	Options	Optional capabilities, including the flooding of external-LSAs, ability to handle type 7 LSAs, etc.
	LS type	LSA type; equal to 3 or 4 for summary-LSA
	Link-State ID	In the summary-LSA type 3, this field is the IP network number; in the summary-LSA type 4 this field is the AS boundary router's OSPF RID
	Advertising Router	The RID of the router that originated the LSA
	LS sequence number	The sequence number of LSA used to detect old or duplicate LSAs
	LS checksum	The checksum of the complete content of the LSA
	Length	The length of LSA in bytes, including the 20-byte LSA header
Summary-LSA Fields	Network Mask	For type 3 summary-LSAs, the destination network's IP address mask; for type 4 summary-LSAs this field must be 0
	Metric	The cost of this route
	ToS/ToS metric	Type of Service and ToS-specific metric information

Table 9-8.   *Description of the Summary-LSA Content*

AS-External-LSA

An AS-external-LSA is generated by the ASBR (discussed in the "OSPF Hierarchy" section) within the OSPF architecture. The AS-external-LSAs include all LSAs that are external to the OSPF process, which can include static, Routing Information Protocol,

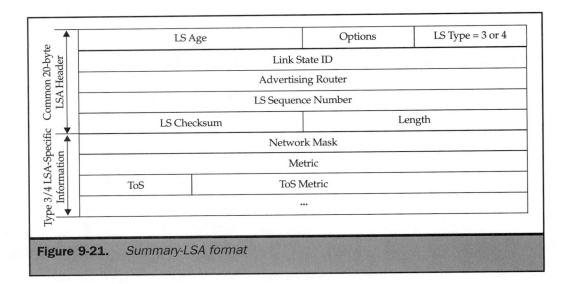

Figure 9-21.   *Summary-LSA format*

Intermediate System to Intermediate System Protocol, and Border Gateway Protocol routes. AS-external-LSAs, which are type 5 LSAs, can either describe a particular external destination or a default route.

The format of the AS-external-LSA is illustrated in Figure 9-22.

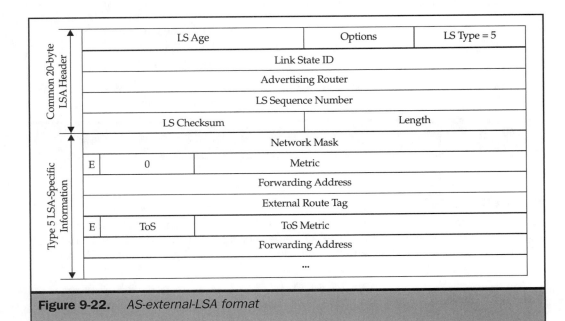

Figure 9-22.   *AS-external-LSA format*

Table 9-9 presents the detailed description of the AS-external-LSA fields.

	Router-LSA Field	Meaning
Common LSA Header	LS age	Time since the LSA was originated (in seconds)
	Options	Optional capabilities, including the flooding of external-LSAs, ability to handle type 7 LSAs, etc.
	LS type	LSA type; equal to 5 for AS-external-LSA
	Link-State ID	In the AS-external-LSA, this field is the IP network number, unless the AS-external-LSA describes a default route, in which case the Link-State ID is set to 0 and the Network Mask is set to 0
	Advertising Router	The RID of the router that originated the LSA
	LS sequence number	The sequence number of LSA; used to detect old or duplicate LSAs
	LS checksum	The checksum of the complete content of the LSA
	Length	The length of LSA in bytes, including the 20-byte LSA header
AS-external-LSA Fields	Network Mask	The IP address mask for the advertised destination
	Bit E	The type of external metric, identifying a type 2 or type 1 of external metric
	Metric	The cost of this route: if the metric is type 2, the cost = internal + external costs; if the metric is type 1, the cost = external cost only
	Forwarding address	Address of the advertised destination to which the data traffic will be forwarded

Table 9-9. *Description of the AS-External-LSA Content*

	Router-LSA Field	**Meaning**
AS-external-LSA Fields	External Route Tag	This field is attached to each external route and used to communicate information between AS boundary routers, and is opaque to OSPF itself
	ToS/ToS metric	Type of Service and ToS-specific metric information

Table 9-9.   *Description of the AS-External-LSA Content* (continued)

Topology Maintenance

Up-to-date topology maintenance is absolutely crucial for the link-state routing protocol. Link-state routing protocols have an absolute need for the most current topology information. (Imagine yourself driving in Los Angeles with a 10-year-old city map. I doubt very much that you will be getting where you want to go!) Should a router or a network die, all routers must know about it and adjust their topological databases accordingly. Fast convergence is the key!

OSPF maintains the network topology using both the Hello protocol and flooding of link-state information. The Hello protocol provides the heartbeat between the adjacent routers.

Looking at the example in Figure 9-23, Routers A and D established adjacencies with a DR and BDR, Routers B and C. Should Router B, which is a DR, disappear, Routers A,

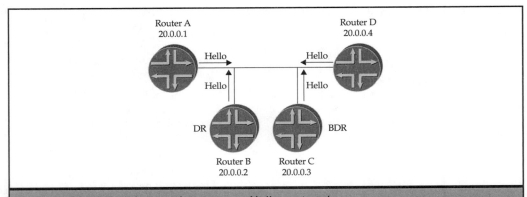

Figure 9-23.   *Topology maintenance—Hello protocol*

C, and D will miss hearing the Router B's Hello. Upon reaching the *RouterDeadInterval*, which is 40 seconds by default, Router C (who is a BDR) will consider Router B dead and originate a new network LSA for the LAN, not listing Router B. Router C will assume the responsibility of the DR and the new BDR gets elected.

Database synchronization takes place during the adjacency formation and during the continuous communication between the routers. Each LSA must be flooded at least every refresh time, which is 30 minutes.

OSPF Hierarchy

The link-state algorithm has its own disadvantages. For example, every network change must be propagated to every other router on the network. Every router receiving the change must insert the change into the topological database and run the Dijkstra algorithm, which is not a simple algorithm. This might not be a big task for 50 or even 100 routers, but imagine the case of 1000 routers or more. The database size as well as the complexity of Dijkstra computation increases greatly with the increase in the number of networks that you might have within your infrastructure.

As a result, the OSPF Working Group decided to create a two-layer architecture of the OSPF model—the *backbone* and the *other*. The OSPF architecture combines the link-state and the distance vector ideas into a blended design, which provides a more scalable architecture. You can think of an ideal OSPF architecture as a daisy flower (see Figure 9-24). Every area must connect to the backbone area, period. The other areas, or the white petals of the daisy, surround the backbone area, or the yellow center of the daisy, as illustrated in the figure.

OSPF has one strict rule: All areas must connect to a single, contiguous, backbone area. The method of connection to the backbone can be physical or logical. Why is the rule of area attachment so rigid? The answer lies within the realization that the OSPF inter-area connectivity has a distance vector flavor. The routers' knowledge of the *intra*-area destinations is a link-state type, where routers are fully aware of their own area topology. The routers' knowledge of the *inter*-area destinations is of a distance vector type, where the topology of other areas is invisible from the routers within a specific area. Examining Figure 9-25, you can see that the routers in area 1 are fully aware of the complete topology within area 1. Yet routers in area 1 know nothing of the detailed topology of areas 3, 5, and 0 (the backbone area).

Because a router can belong to multiple areas, each router must have a separate link-state database for each area it is connected to. Databases must be identical for the routers belonging to the same area.

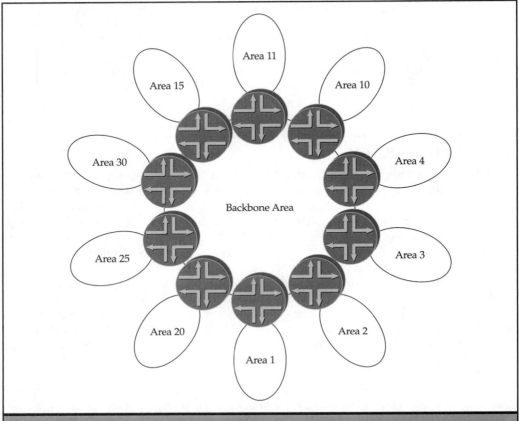

Figure 9-24. *The two-layer OSPF architecture—the daisy*

OSPF Router Classification

OSPF's hierarchical nature allows the differentiation between various types of routers and assignment of various types of responsibilities.

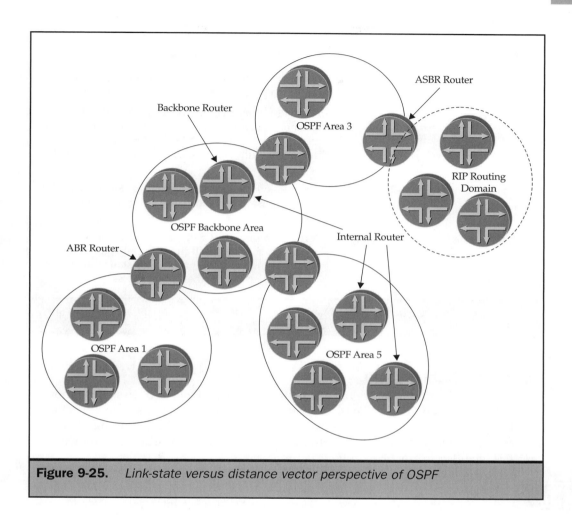

Figure 9-25. *Link-state versus distance vector perspective of OSPF*

Table 9-10 presents OSPF router classification and the description/responsibilities for each router type.

Router Type	Description and Responsibilities
Backbone	A router within the backbone. Often responsible for inter-area packet transfer.
Internal	A router within an area, which can be either the backbone or another area. Responsible for intra-area packet transfer. By default it has knowledge of all the routes within its area, other areas, and external networks.
Area border router (ABR)	A router joining more than one area. Responsible for packet transfer from/to an area to/from the backbone area.
Autonomous System Boundary Router (ASBR)	A router joining the OSPF process to other processes. In addition to running OSPF, it runs other routing protocols and/or has static routes that could be injected into the OSPF process.

Table 9-10. *OSPF Router Classification and Responsibilities*

OSPF Backbone Area

Should the OSPF infrastructure have more than one area, OSPF requires one of those areas to be *area 0*, also called the *backbone area*. Inter-area packet transfer requires that area 0 be involved—all inter-area packets must go through the backbone area. The backbone area must be contiguous, physically or logically. This means that only one area 0 is included in any OSPF infrastructure.

 You cannot have redundant backbone areas. An OSPF routing domain has only one area 0. In fact, when multiple backbone areas, separated by other areas, are created, they must be virtually joined together into one area 0. (This is discussed in the "Virtually Attached OSPF Areas" section later in the chapter.)

OSPF Regular Area

An area that is not area 0 is called a *regular* OSPF area. All regular OSPF areas must be attached to area 0. If your topology has only one OSPF area, it does not have to be an area 0; it can be any number.

 The maximum number of routers that you can place within an area depends on the types of routers that have been deployed, including memory, processing power, and architecture. It also depends on the stability of the networks involved. Unstable networks utilize more resources, including bandwidth and routers' CPU.

Intra-area routing is straightforward—all routers within an area are aware of area topology and the SPF algorithm is used. Inter-area routing is a little bit more involved, however. You can break up the inter-area routing into three pieces—intra-area routing within the origination area + backbone routing + intra-area routing within the destination area. OSPF inter-area routing imposes a star architecture with the backbone area being a *hub* and any other area being a *spoke*.

OSPF Stub Area

A regular OSPF area is *promiscuous*—that is, by default, ABR routers allow all LSAs to be propagated into all the areas. This behavior can be detrimental to the OSPF scalability, especially in cases of an excessive number of AS-external-LSAs. Consequently RFC 2328 specifies a *stub* area, which is a regular area that is not flooded with AS-external-LSAs. Routing to AS-external destinations in these areas is accomplished with help of default routes. Stub areas reduce the link-state database size and hence memory requirements.

Stub areas have a couple of restrictions:

- A stub area cannot have an AS boundary router.
- Virtual links (discussed in the next section of this chapter) cannot be configured through stub areas.

Some vendors extend the stub capability further by allowing you to suppress type 3 LSAs at ABRs. Theoretically, this feature allows OSPF to scale even further. In fact, the knowledge base of the routers in such areas is similar to the IS-IS level 1 routers, where the routers' database is restricted only to the area links.

Virtually Attached OSPF Areas

OSPF uses virtual links for two purposes: to virtually connect a physically discontiguous backbone area 0, and to virtually connect a physically detached area to the backbone area.

Discontiguous Backbone Area 0

Well-designed networks have one continuous area 0. Sometimes, however, various company mergers result in a network topology with multiple backbone areas. Although you could have best intentions to create a single physically continuous area 0, such a change cannot happen overnight. As an intermediate step you must think of a *migration path*, in which you come up with a temporary solution. Just make sure it does not stay as a permanent solution! Virtual links add complexity to the network, which should be avoided.

Figure 9-26 illustrates the example of discontiguous backbone areas. The area 1 through which a virtual link is set is called a *transit* area. The two endpoints of a virtual link, Routers A and B, are ABRs. The virtual-link configuration must take place in both routers.

The virtual link is treated as a P2P network belonging to the backbone area and joining the two ABRs.

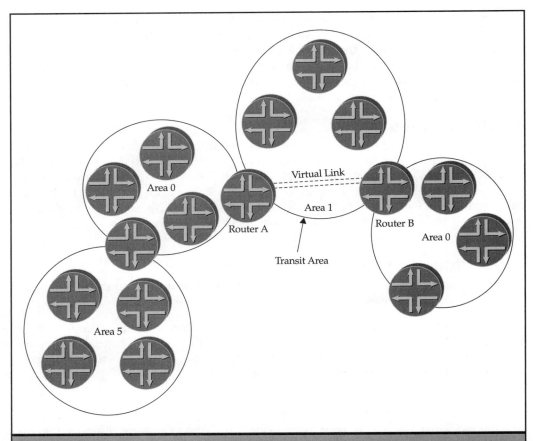

Figure 9-26. *Example of discontiguous backbone area*

Physically Detached Area from the Backbone Area

Ideally, all OSPF areas must be physically attached to the backbone area (in a form of a daisy, as mentioned earlier in the chapter). RFC 2328 allows virtual attachment of other areas (I call these "mutated daisy flowers"), as illustrated in Figure 9-27.

Area 50 is virtually attached to the backbone area through the transit area 3. You can "mutate" the flower as much as your heart desires. That is, you can daisy-chain

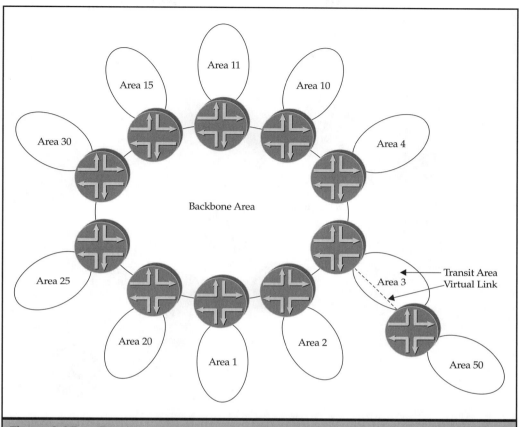

Figure 9-27. *Example of physically detached area from the backbone area*

areas infinitely, so long as the transit area is attached to the backbone—physically or logically. This is illustrated in Figure 9-28.

Area 50 is physically attached to area 3 and logically attached to area 0 through the virtual link going through transit area 3. In turn, area 51 is physically attached to area 50, while logically attached to area 0 through the virtual link going through the transit area 50. Note that should the virtual link going through area 3 die, areas 50 and 51 will become nonreachable from the physical area 0.

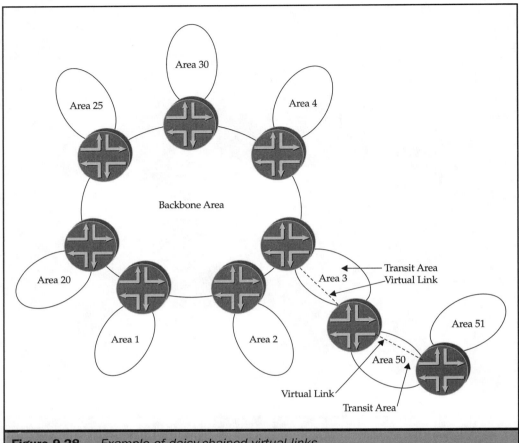

Figure 9-28. *Example of daisy-chained virtual links*

OSPF Extensions

In parallel with the major OSPF RFC releases, the IETF OSPF Routing Working Group is continuously modifying OSPF protocol. As a result, various OSPF extensions have been finalized into the RFCs:

RFC	Title and Date
1587	The OSPF NSSA Option, March 1994
2370	The OSPF Opaque LSA Option, July 1998

RFC	Title and Date
1584	Multicast Extensions to OSPF, March 1994
2740	OSPF for IPv6, December 1999

Furthermore, the OSPF Working Group has posted various Internet drafts, including "Extensions to OSPF for Support of Diff-Serv-Aware MPLS Traffic Engineering." RFCs 1587, 2370, 1584, and 2740 extend OSPF to other LSAs, as illustrated in Table 9-11.

LSA Type	Name	Purpose
1	router-LSA	Describes the states of a router's interfaces
2	network-LSA	Describes the set of routers attached to the network; originated by the DR
3	network-summary-LSA	Describes the inter-area routes to the networks; originated by the area border routers at the area borders
4	ASBR-summary-LSA	Describes the inter-area routes to the AS boundary routers; originated by the area border routers at the area borders
5	AS-external-LSA	Describes routes to the destinations external to the OSPF routing domain; originated by the AS boundary routers
6	Group Membership	Indicates the directly attached networks belonging to an area that contain members of a particular multicast group
7	Not-So-Stubby area (NSSA) LSA	Describes external routes information through the NSSA area
8	Link LSA	Provides the router's link-local address to other routers attached to the link; informs the other routers of IPv6 prefixes to be associated with the link
9, 10, 11	Opaque LSAs	Provides a mechanism for future extensibility of OSPF

Table 9-11.   *LSA Types Based on RFC 2328 and OSPF Extensions*

LSA type 8 was first used as an external-attributes-LSA, specified by Dennis Ferguson in "The OSPF External Attributes LSA." It used the LSA to move external attributes associated with the exterior routing protocols routes, such as BGP and IDRP, between AS border routers, providing route re-advertisement using OSPF link-state flooding. RFC 2740 uses the type 8 LSA, calling it Link-LSA, *for IPv6 OSPF implementation.*

Let's examine some highlights of the OSPF extensions.

Multicast OSPF

RFC 1584 defines specifications and extensions for OSPF for providing multicast routing ability. The extensions are built on top of OSPF version 2. The specification allows for coexistence of both multicast and unicast routers within a routing domain, thus providing for backward compatibility. Multicast enhancements to OSPF resulted in creation on MOSPF, which uses a group-membership-LSA, type 6, to locate all multicast group members in the database. Similar to unicast OSPF, MOSPF uses an SPF algorithm to compute the path of a multicast packet.

NSSA

RFC 1587 specifies the OSPF Not-So-Stubby Area (NSSA) option, which is similar to the stub option, in that no external routes are allowed into the stub area. Because of this, stub areas cannot have ASBRs. NSSA areas, however, allow ASBRs, and they allow their routers to import AS-external routes; they do not allow external-route LSAs to be propagated through the ABR. You can say that NSSA is an exceptional stub area that allows ASBRs but does not allow any other external routes in from area 0. Figure 9-29 illustrates a stub and NSSA areas.

Area 4 is a regular area, area 5 is stub, and area 1 is NSSA. ABR Router C does not allow any AS-external-LSA type 5 and summary-LSA type 4 packets into area 5. ABR Router A does not allow any AS-external-LSA type 5 and summary-LSA type 4 packets (about RIP routing domain 1) into area 1 as well. However, Router A accepts the NSSA LSAs from ASBR Router B, which it then converts into type 5 LSAs. The job of the ABR Router A is to flood area 0 with the type 5 LSAs of the RIP routing domain 2. Regular area 4 has all the external LSAs from both RIP routing domains.

Type 7 LSA was defined to support NSSA, and the option bit N is used to ensure that routers belonging to an NSSA and neighbors agree on the N bit setting for the OSPF adjacency to be formed.

RFC 2740 defines OPSF extensions to handle IPv6. The document signifies that the OSPF IPv4 fundamental mechanisms remain unchanged. These include flooding, DR election, area support, SPF calculation, and so on. In addition, the support of on-demand circuits, multicasting, and NSSA areas is maintained.

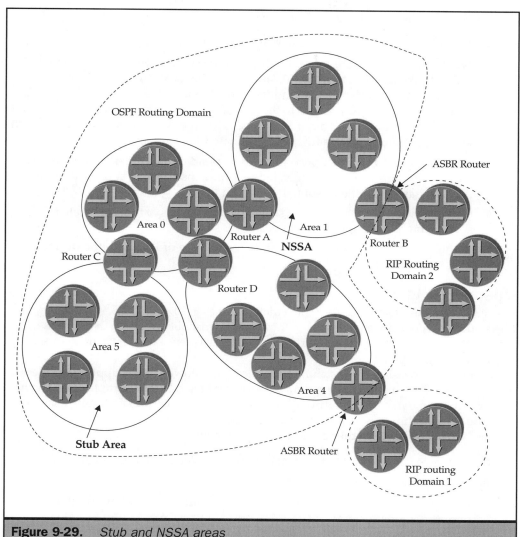

Figure 9-29. *Stub and NSSA areas*

The new additions to the OSPF IPv6 include

■ The removal of addressing from OSPF packets and basic LSAs.

■ The creation of new LSAs to carry IPv6 addresses and prefixes. The new LSA, called Link-LSA, is a type 8 LSA, and it has the local-link flooding scope. It provides the router's link-local address to all other routers attached to the link, informs other routers attached to the link of IPv6 prefixes that are associated with the link, and allows the router to change Option bits to indicate the association with the Network-LSA that will be originated for the link.

■ OSPF's ability to run on a per-link basis, instead of on a per-IP-subnet basis. Now OSPF interfaces are connected to a link, instead of a subnet. A single link can have multiple IP subnets assigned to it.

■ Generalization of LSAs flooding scope, which consists of three separate flooding scopes: link-local scope, area scope, and AS scope.

■ Removal of OSPF authentication and, instead, use of IPv6's Authentication Header for OSPF.

Opaque LSAs

RFC 2370 specifies Opaque LSAs, which include types 9, 10, and 11 LSAs. These LSAs provide a generalized mechanism for future extensibility of OSPF. One of these extensibilities, for example, includes traffic engineering extensions, which are discussed in the following section.

Opaque LSA consists of the standard LSA header, followed by the application-specific 32-bit header. This implies that Opaque LSAs can be used by some applications trying to distribute some information throughout the OSPF routing domain. OSPF uses the same flooding techniques to flood Opaque LSAs.

RFC 2370 clearly states the scope of the Opaque LSAs:

■ LSA type 9 is allowed to be flooded within the local network/subnetwork.

■ LSA type 10 is allowed to be flooded within an area.

■ LSA type 11 is allowed to be flooded throughout the OSPF routing domain or autonomous system.

The OSPF Options field, which is present in OSPF Hello, database description, and all link-state advertisements, enables OSPF to support additional capabilities. Routers can choose not to forward certain link-state advertisements to a neighbor should the neighbor have reduced functionality.

Traffic Engineering Extensions

Several drafts on OSPF traffic engineering extensions have been submitted to the IETF. The discussion in this section is based on these drafts, which are really works in progress.

The drafts include "Traffic Engineering Extensions to OSPF," "OSPF Extensions to Support Inter-Area Traffic Engineering," "TE LSAs to extend OSPF for Traffic

Engineering," and "Extensions to OSPF for support of Diff-Serv-aware MPLS Traffic Engineering."

Table 9-12 summarizes the proposed drafts and the highlights the types of extensions discussed in each.

Draft	Highlights
draft-katz-yeung-ospf-traffic-05.txt	Identifies the method of adding traffic engineering extensions to OSPF. The extension uses Opaque LSA type 10, which has an area flooding scope. The LSA payload consists of one or more nested type/length/value (TLV) triplets for extensibility.
draft-bitar-rao-ospf-diffserv-mpls-01.txt	Describes extensions to Opaque LSA to support Diffserv and MPLS. The specified extensions include additional Link sub-TLV to the ones defined in draft-katz-yeung-ospf-traffic-os.txt: * Diffserv available bandwidth * Oversubscription * Diffserv capability * Diffserv max delay * Link propagation delay * Priority reserved bandwidth * Link capability/resources
draft-venkatachalam-ospf-traffic-01.txt	Describes the OSPF Traffic Engineering Summary LSAs and its support across the area boundaries. It proposes the use of new LSA, called Traffic Engineering Summary LSA. This new LSA would be generated by an ABR and be a type 10 Opaque LSA.
draft-srisuresh-ospf-te-01.txt	Specifies traffic engineering extensions to OSPF by using new TE LSAs, modeled after existing LSAs, without the use of Opaque LSAs. The document defines a use of TLVs, Tag-Length-Values, which refer to a Traffic Engineering attribute of TE-node or TE-link.
draft-ietf-ospf-diff-te-00.txt	Proposes extensions to OSPF for support of Diffserv Traffic Engineering on a per-Class-Type basis. These extensions are additional to the ones defined in draft-katz-yeung-ospf-traffic-os.txt.

Table 9-12.   *Traffic Engineering Extensions Draft Summary*

The Complete Reference

Chapter 10

OSPF Configuration

by Jason Rogan

Once you understand the theoretical aspects of the OSPF routing protocol, the next topic of interest is the configuration of OSPF on Juniper Networks routers. The purpose of this chapter is to introduce you to various OSPF configuration options and commands you can use to monitor and troubleshoot the protocol. The chapter presents several case-study networks of increasing complexity. For each case study, you learn the necessary configuration commands and use OSPF monitoring and troubleshooting commands to verify and investigate OSPF operation.

The following OSPF case studies are presented in this chapter:

- Point-to-Point network with unnumbered interfaces
- Point-to-Point network with numbered interfaces
- Broadcast Multiaccess (BMA) network
- Hierarchical routing—multiple-area configuration
- Route redistribution into OSPF
- Stub Area configuration
- OSPF Route summarization
- NSSA configuration
- Virtual Link configuration
- Metrics and Shortest Path calculation

The configurations illustrated in this chapter use from two to nine routers, which have been named R1 through R9. All these routers have been given a basic starting configuration with no routing protocols configured.

As you have seen in previous chapters, there are multiple ways to navigate within configuration mode. In this chapter, most configuration modifications are done from the root of the configuration hierarchy, and most operational mode commands are executed from within configuration mode using the `run` configuration mode option. This is the most convenient approach when viewing router operation while in the process of router configuration.

OSPF Minimum Configuration Requirements

There are two mandatory steps needed to configure and run OSPF on a router.

1. Define which interfaces will run OSPF.
2. Define the areas to which these interfaces will be attached.

A minimal OSPF configuration is illustrated here; all other OSPF configuration statements are optional:

```
[edit]
protocols {
    ospf {
        area area-number {
            interface interface-name;
        }
    }
}
```

In addition to the above conditions, a router must have a Router ID. The Router ID is used by both the OSPF and BGP protocols to identify the router from which a packet originated. There are several ways to configure a Router ID.

- The Router ID can be explicitly configured using the `router-id` statement:

```
[edit]
routing-options {
        router-id address;
}
```

- If a unicast IP address is configured on interface lo0 (loopback 0), then that interface will be the first one detected on the router and be used as the Router ID.

- If no Router ID is explicitly configured and no unicast IP address is applied to interface lo0, the IP address of the first interface detected by the router when the *routing protocol daemon* (rpd) is starting up is used as the Router ID.

The need for a Router ID is illustrated in the following case study.

Case Study 1: Point-to-Point Network with Unnumbered Interfaces

A Point-to-Point network is used to connect exactly two routers together. T1, E1, and SONET links (using PPP or HDLC encapsulation) are all examples of Point-to-Point links.

Unnumbered interfaces are used to conserve address space on Point-to-Point links. As the name implies, unnumbered interfaces have no IP address assigned to them. The link between the interfaces has no subnet number assigned, and so address space is conserved.

In Figure 10-1, you see R1 and R2 connected by a SONET oc3 link. R1 uses interface so-0/0/0 and R2 uses interface so-0/1/0. Both interfaces are attached to Area 0 (backbone), and no other interfaces are configured on these routers. At this point in the example, there are no IP addresses configured on R1 or R2.

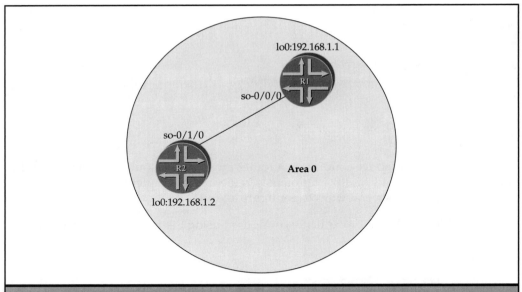

Figure 10-1.   *R1 and R2 connected via a Point-to-Point, unnumbered link*

The pertinent portions of R1's configuration are

```
[edit]
lab@R1# show interfaces
so-0/0/0 {
    unit 0 {
        family inet;
    }
}
[edit]
lab@R1# show protocols
ospf {
    area 0.0.0.0 {
        interface so-0/0/0.0;
    }
}
```

Interface so-0/0/0 is configured with family *inet* but with no IP address. Under protocols OSPF, interface so-0/0/0 is specified as being attached to Area 0. Aside from the interface name, the configuration for R2 is the same as R1 and is, therefore, not shown.

Viewing OSPF Interfaces

The command `show ospf interface` is used to view the status of all interfaces running OSPF.

```
[edit]
lab@R2# run show ospf interface
OSPF instance is not running
```

Notice that when you execute this command on R2, the message "OSPF instance is not running" is displayed. This is because an OSPF router needs a Router ID with which to tag *link-state advertisements* (LSAs) that it generates.

Since no interface on either router has yet been assigned an IP address, no Router ID has been chosen by the router. As stated previously, your options for assigning a Router ID to a router with no physical interface IP addresses are to either assign an IP address to interface lo0, or to use the `router-id` command. Here you see the assignment of the IP address 192.168.1.2 to R2's loopback 0 interface:

```
[edit]
lab@R2# set interfaces lo0 unit 0 family inet address 192.168.1.2
[edit]
lab@R2# commit
commit complete
```

Even after the application of this configuration, the router still has no OSPF instance running. When the `router-id` command is not used, routers choose a Router ID from the first detected interface with an IP address while starting the rpd. In the case of R2, the rpd has already been started, and so a change in interface IP address on interface lo0 has no effect on R2's Router ID until the rpd is restarted.

```
[edit]
lab@R2# run show ospf interface
OSPF instance is not running
```

The `restart routing` command shown here restarts the rpd.

```
[edit]
lab@R2# run restart routing
Routing protocol daemon started, pid 1656
```

On R2, this will cause the router to select the address assigned to interface lo0 as its Router ID. Issuing the `show ospf interface` command on R2 now will provide information about its interfaces running OSPF—in this case, only interface so-0/1/0 unit 0.

```
[edit]
lab@R2# run show ospf interface
Interface         State   Area          DR ID         BDR ID        Nbrs
so-0/1/0.0        PtToPt  0.0.0.0       0.0.0.0       0.0.0.0          0
```

Since only R2 has been configured with a Router ID, this command shows R2 with no neighbors (`Nbrs = 0`). R1 is still alone in the world. Once R1 is also configured with a Router ID (configuration not shown), the two routers form an adjacency, shown here.

```
[edit]
lab@R1# run show ospf interface
Interface         State   Area          DR ID         BDR ID        Nbrs
so-0/0/0.0        PtToPt  0.0.0.0       0.0.0.0       0.0.0.0          1
```

In general, the command `show ospf interface` is used to view the status of all interfaces running OSPF on the local router. In this case, R1 is configured to run OSPF on interface so-0/0/0, logical unit 0. The state of this interface is Point-to-Point and it is attached to Area 0.0.0.0. As expected on a Point-to-Point link, there is no designated or backup designated router and, therefore, the designated router (DR) and backup designated router (BDR) identifiers are set to 0.0.0.0. In cases in which there is a DR (and BDR), these fields show the IP address of the DR's (BDR's) interface that is attached to the network held in common with the local router. R1 has a single neighbor, which you know to be R2.

The state of an interface indicates the interface's progress on the way to becoming fully functional as dictated by the OSPF interface state machine (RFC 2328, Sections 9.1–9.3). The various states that a router interface can attain are

- **Down**   Initial interface state; no protocol traffic is sent or received.
- **Loop**   The router's interface to the network is looped back in hardware or software.
- **Waiting**   The router is "waiting" to learn, via received Hello packets, if a DR and BDR exist on the network.
- **PtToPt**   Interface is operational and connected to a network of type Point-to-Point, Point-to-Multipoint, or virtual link.
- **DRother**   Interface it operational, but not the DR or BDR for the attached network.
- **BDR**   Interface is operational and is the BDR for the attached network.
- **DR**   Interface is operational and is the DR for the attached network.

The command `show ospf interface detail` is used to display more detailed information about the OSPF interfaces than the brief version of the command provides.

```
[edit]
lab@R1# run show ospf interface detail
Interface          State    Area          DR ID          BDR ID          Nbrs
so-0/0/0.0         PtToPt   0.0.0.0       0.0.0.0        0.0.0.0           1
Type P2P, address 0.0.0.0, mask 0.0.0.0, MTU 4470, cost 1
DR addr 0.0.0.0, BDR addr 0.0.0.0, adj count 1
Hello 10, Dead 40, ReXmit 5, Not Stub
```

The above illustrates the `show ospf interface detail` command executed on R1. From that output, you can see that R1's interface so-0/0/0 is attached to a link of type Point-to-Point. The interface `Type` field is used to indicate the type of network that the interface is attached to. The possible values for this field correspond the five link types defined for OSPF:

- **LAN**   Broadcast networks, such as Ethernet, Token Ring, and FDDI, also known as BMA networks.
- **NBMA**   Non-BMA networks, such as ATM, frame relay, and X.25.
- **P2MP**   Point-to-Multipoint networks; these are NBMA networks configured as a collection of Point-to-Point links.
- **P2P**   Point-to-Point networks, such as T1 or E1 links used to connect a single pair of routers
- **Virtual**   Virtual links; routers treat virtual links as unnumbered P2P networks.

Since we have assigned no IP address or subnet mask, the `address` and `mask` fields are both set to 0.0.0.0. The interface's *maximum transmission unit* (MTU) is 4470 bytes, which is the default MTU for Packet Over SONET (POS) interfaces.

For the purpose of OSPF show commands, cost and metric are synonymous. The cost of this interface is 1, which is the default. OSPF metrics are discussed in a later case study.

The `adj count` field indicates how many adjacencies the router has formed on the particular interface. In this case, so-0/0/0, unit 0 has a single adjacency formed. Recall that a router can have fewer adjacencies than neighbors.

The configurable OSPF timers Hello Interval, Router Dead Interval, and LSA Retransmission Interval for the local interface are shown as being set at their default values of 10, 40, and 5 seconds, respectively. The Hello and Router Dead Intervals are sent to neighbors via Hello packets to inform neighbors of how often to expect Hello packets from the local router, and how long to wait after not receiving a Hello packet to declare the local router "dead." Neighbors must agree on these two parameters. The LSA Retransmission Interval is the time a router will wait after sending an LSA to a neighbor for an acknowledgement to that LSA.

OSPF Timer Configuration

The Hello Interval, Router Dead Interval, and LSA Retransmission Interval timers can be modified. You might wish to change these timers from their default values, for instance, to cut down on bandwidth use. For example, the Hello Interval can be increased to reduce the amount of Hello packets exchanged between a set of neighbors.

The default Hello Interval is 10 seconds. To modify how often a router sends Hello packets out of an interface, use the following command:

```
[edit protocols ospf area area-id interface interface-name] or
[edit protocols ospf area area-id virtual-link]
set hello-interval seconds;
```

The default Router Dead Interval is 40 seconds. To modify the router dead interval for a particular interface, use the following command:

```
[edit protocols ospf area area-id interface interface-name] or
[edit protocols ospf area area-id virtual-link]
set dead-interval seconds;
```

The default LSA Retransmission Interval is 5 seconds. To modify the LSA Retransmission Interval for a particular interface, use the following command:

```
[edit protocols ospf area area-id interface interface-name] or
[edit protocols ospf area area-id virtual-link]
set retransmit-interval seconds;
```

Finally, the output shows the OSPF area type to be "Not Stub." Other possible area types are "Stub" and "Stub NSSA." Stub Areas and NSSA are discussed in later case studies.

Viewing OSPF Neighbors

The command show ospf neighbor is used to display information about a router's OSPF neighbors. Here you can see that R1 has a single neighbor, R2, on the network that its so-0/0/0 interface is attached. The address field contains the IP address to use as the destination of packets sent to this neighbor. In this example, the address field contains R2's Router ID since its interface has not yet been assigned an IP address. The ID field is used to display the neighbor's Router ID.

```
[edit]
lab@R1# run show ospf neighbor
  Address         Interface        State      ID           Pri  Dead
192.168.1.2      so-0/0/0.0       Full       192.168.1.2   128   33
```

The `State` field displays the state of the conversation between the local router and the neighbor. Here you can see that the R1-R2 conversation is in the `Full` state, meaning that R1 and R2 are fully adjacent and that each router lists the adjacency in its LSA.

The various neighbor states that can be displayed in this field (RFC 2328, Section 10.1) are

- **Down**   The initial state of a neighbor conversation; no recent information has been received from the neighbor.
- **Attempt**   Similar to the Down state, but applies to neighbors attached to NBMA networks
- **Init**   Hello packets have been received from the neighbor, but bidirectional communication has not yet been established.
- **2Way**   Bidirectional communication has been established. Remember that since not all router pairs form adjacencies with each other, it is normal to see some neighbors remain in this state.
- **ExStart**   In this state, the master of the two routers is decided, as well as the initial Database Description packet sequence number.
- **Exchange**   The router is sending the neighbor Database Description packets describing its entire link-state database.
- **Loading**   Link-state request packets are sent to the neighbor asking for newer LSAs if needed.
- **Full**   The router is fully adjacent with its neighbor.

The `show ospf neighbor` command also displays the neighbor's configured interface priority for designated router election in the `Pri` field. A router's interface priority is advertised in its Hello packets transmitted on that interface.

Interface Priority Configuration

For all multiaccess networks, a DR is elected based on the priorities advertised via the OSPF Hello protocol. The higher the priority assigned to an interface, the greater the chance that router has to become the designated router for the network the interface attaches to. In practice, the first router to come up on a network becomes the DR, and the second one becomes the BDR. OSPF DR election is nonpreemptive, meaning that a new router with a higher priority will not preempt an existing DR and take over as the new DR. Typically, an election will occur only when the existing DR leaves the network, the BDR becomes the new DR, and a new BDR is elected from the remaining routers on the network.

The default OSPF interface priority value is 128 and can be modified in the range 0 to 255. A priority of 0 prevents the router from becoming the DR for the attached network. To modify the router's interface priority value, use the following command:

```
[edit protocols ospf area area-id interface interface-name]
set priority number;
```

The show ospf neighbor detail displays more detailed information about a router's OSPF neighbors than the brief version of the command. The additional fields of this command can be seen here. The area field shows the area that the neighbor and the local router share. The opt field shows the option bits received from the neighbor in its Hello packets.

```
[edit]
lab@R1# run show ospf neighbor detail
  Address          Interface        State      ID          Pri  Dead
10.10.1.2          so-0/0/0.0       Full       192.168.1.2  128  36
    area 0.0.0.0, opt 0x42, DR 0.0.0.0, BDR 0.0.0.0
    Up 00:00:04, adjacent 00:00:03
```

In cases in which there is a DR (and BDR) elected, the DR (and BDR) fields contain the IP address of the DR's (BDR's) interface, which is attached to the network that the local router and the neighbor have in common. Since the network illustrated is a P2P network, the DR and BDR fields contain 0.0.0.0, indicating that no DR or BDR is present.

The Up and adjacent fields show the time since the neighbor came up and the time since the adjacency with the neighbor was established, respectively.

Viewing the OSPF Link-State Database

Recall that all routers in an OSPF routing domain generate one or more LSAs. These LSAs describe the router's portion of the routing domain, and are collected in the link-state database of each router. The link-state database can be thought of as a map of an individual area, containing all entries for the routers and links that connect them. All routers in an OSPF area must have identical link-state databases for the particular area that they share. The SPF algorithm is run on a router's link-state database to find the router's shortest path to each destination. This is how a router's OSPF routing table is derived.

The show ospf database command is used to view the contents of the local router's link-state database. The show ospf database and show ospf database brief commands are equivalent to each other. Both display a listing of the LSAs in the router's link-state database. The output of these commands shows only the contents of eight of the fields in the LSA headers, not the information stored in each LSA. The three fields in the LSA header used to identify an LSA uniquely are the LSA Type (Type), LSA ID (ID), and Advertising Router (Adv Rtr). The LS Checksum (Cksum), LS Sequence Number (Seq), and the LS Age (Age) fields identify the particular instance of the LSA.

The LSA Type field is used to identify the portion of the OSPF routing domain that the LSA describes. The information stored in the LS ID field varies depending on the type of LSA. Table 10-1 illustrates the relationship between the LSA Type and the contents of the LSA ID field for the most commonly seen LSAs.

Router LSAs describe the states of each of the local router's links to an area. They have area-flooding scope. A router will generate a type 1 LSA for each of the areas it is attached to.

In the output shown next, you see that the P2P network has two LSAs, both of type router. Consistent with the rules listed above, for Router LSAs (type 1), the ID field and the Adv Rtr field both contain the Router ID of the LSA's originating router. The asterisk in the ID field is used to indicate which LSAs have been originated by the local router, R1 in this case. The Seq field displays the sequence number of the LSA. The value (0x80000002) indicates that this is the second instance of the LSA. The Age field shows the age of the LSA in the link-state database. LSAs are generated with an age of zero. The LSA age is incremented by routers as the LSA is flooded throughout the network, and as it resides in the link-state database. An LSA is removed from the link-state database when its age reaches the MaxAge value, which is 3600 seconds (1 hour). To

LSA Type	LSA ID
1 Router LSA	Router ID of the originating router
2 Network LSA	Interface's IP address of the DR for the network described by the LSA
3 Network Summary LSA	IP address of the destination network described by the LSA
4 ASBR Summary LSA	Router ID of the AS boundary router described by the LSA
5 AS External LSA	IP address of the destination network described by the LSA
7 NSSA External LSA	IP address of the destination network described by the LSA

Table 10-1. *Common LSA Types and LSA IDs*

prevent LSAs from timing out, originating routers regenerate their LSAs every 50 minutes in the JUNOS software implementation of OSPF. This is a departure from the standard RFC 2328 value of 30 minutes.

```
[edit]
lab@R1# run show ospf database

    OSPF link state database, area 0.0.0.0
  Type       ID                Adv Rtr          Seq        Age  Opt  Cksum   Len
  Router   *192.168.1.1      192.168.1.1      0x80000002    58  0x2  0x2ee6  60
  Router    192.168.1.2      192.168.1.2      0x80000002    62  0x2  0x20f3  60
```

Within a Router LSA, each link is categorized by the type of network it attaches to. Links are assigned a link type and labeled with a link ID that is used to identify the entity on the other end of the link. Link type should not be confused with LSA type. Table 10-2 describes the relationship between link type number and link ID contents.

Each link also has a 32-bit Link Data field associated with it. Like the Link ID field, the value of the Link Data field varies depending on the type of link. For links to transit networks, virtual links, and numbered P2P links, this field is set to the IP interface address of the associated router interface. For links to Stub networks, this field is set to the Stub network's subnet mask. Finally, for unnumbered P2P links, this field is set to the unnumbered interface's MIB-II ifIndex value.

The show `ospf database detail` command allows us to see the information contained within the LSAs themselves. The output of this command on R1 is shown next. For Area 0, three links or connections are reported in each of the two Router LSAs.

Each router generates two link descriptions for its P2P interfaces. The first link is of type PointToPoint (1) representing the P2P connection to the neighboring router. For link type 1, the value of the Link ID field is set to the Router ID of the neighboring router. So for example, the first LSA is generated by R1, and for the PointToPoint (1) link in this LSA, the LSA ID field is set to R2's Router ID. Since the link is unnumbered, the

Description	Link Type Number	Link ID Field
P2P link	1	Router ID of neighbor
Link-to-Transit network	2	Interface address of DR
Link-to-Stub network	3	IP network number
Virtual link	4	Router ID of neighbor

Table 10-2.   *Link Types and the Contents of the Link ID Field*

Link Data field (data 0.0.0.2) is set to the MIB-II ifIndex value (Index 2) for the corresponding router interface. This can be seen by comparing the output of the two commands shown next. The cost or metric for this link is set to the configured output cost of the P2P interface, which is 1 in the following example.

The second link is of type Stub (3). Because no subnet has been assigned to the P2P link, this link description's link ID is set to the neighbor's address (192.168.1.2), and its Link Data field is set to a /32 mask, indicating a host route. So both the first and second links in the LSA from R1 and R2 are used to describe each router's P2P interface. The cost for this link is also set to the configured output cost of the P2P interface, which is 1 in this example.

```
[edit]
lab@R1# run show ospf database detail

    OSPF link state database, area 0.0.0.0
 Type       ID              Adv Rtr         Seq        Age  Opt  Cksum  Len
Router *192.168.1.1     192.168.1.1     0x80000002   187  0x2  0x2ee6  60
  bits 0x0, link count 3
  id 192.168.1.2, data 0.0.0.2, type PointToPoint (1)
  TOS count 0, TOS 0 metric 1
  id 192.168.1.2, data 255.255.255.255, type Stub (3)
  TOS count 0, TOS 0 metric 1
  id 192.168.1.1, data 255.255.255.255, type Stub (3)
  TOS count 0, TOS 0 metric 0
Router  192.168.1.2     192.168.1.2     0x80000002   191  0x2  0x20f3  60
  bits 0x0, link count 3
  id 192.168.1.1, data 0.0.0.2, type PointToPoint (1)
  TOS count 0, TOS 0 metric 1
  id 192.168.1.1, data 255.255.255.255, type Stub (3)
  TOS count 0, TOS 0 metric 1
  id 192.168.1.2, data 255.255.255.255, type Stub (3)
  TOS count 0, TOS 0 metric 0
```

The third link is also of type Stub (3), this one represents the host's (R1's) loopback interface. The link ID is set to the IP interface address, 192.168.1.1 in the case of R1, and the Link Data field is set to a /32 mask, indicating a host route. Since this link represents the local router's loopback interface, the cost is set to zero. The three links described in the Router LSA generated by R2 can be interpreted in the same way as those in the Router LSA generated by R1.

```
[edit]
lab@R1# run show interfaces so-0/0/0
Physical interface: so-0/0/0, Enabled, Physical link is Up
  Interface index: 9, SNMP ifIndex: 13
```

```
     Link-level type: PPP, MTU: 4474, Clocking: Internal, SONET mode
     Speed: OC3, Loopback: None, CRC: 16, Payload scrambler: Enabled
     Device flags   : Present Running
     Interface flags: Point-To-Point SNMP-Traps
     Link flags     : Keepalives
     Keepalive settings: Interval 10 seconds, Up-count 1, Down-count 3
     Keepalive Input: 182142 (00:00:09 ago), Output: 182144 (00:00:03 ago)
     LCP state: Opened
     NCP state: inet: Opened, iso: Not-configured, mpls: Not-configured
     Input rate     : 264 bps (0 pps), Output rate: 0 bps (0 pps)
     Active alarms  : None
     Active defects : None
     Logical interface so-0/0/0.0 (Index 2) (SNMP ifIndex 23)
       Flags: Point-To-Point SNMP-Traps, Encapsulation: PPP
       Protocol inet, MTU: 4470, Flags: Is-Primary
```

For an abbreviated view of the link-state database contents, the `show ospf database summary` command is useful. This command lists the number of each type of LSA in each area in the link-state database. AS External LSAs are also listed. For the P2P two-router network, you have already seen that the link-state database contains two router (type 1) LSAs. This is confirmed here.

```
[edit]
lab@R1# run show ospf database summary
Area 0.0.0.0:
   2 Router LSAs
Externals:
```

Viewing OSPF Routes

As you know, the whole purpose of building a link-state database and running the shortest-path-first algorithm on it is to find the shortest path to each destination in the network from the local router. These paths or routes are then placed in the OSPF routing table. After comparing routing protocol preferences, allowing for better paths to the same destinations learned via other protocols, the remaining OSPF routes are placed in the *inet.0* routing table.

Here you see the output of the `show route` command on R1. From R1's perspective there are three destinations, its own loopback interface and the loopback interface of R2. The multicast address 224.0.0.5, AllSPF Routers (which is received by all OSPF routers), is automatically placed in *inet.0* when the router is configured with a running OSPF instance.

```
[edit]
lab@R1# run show route

inet.0: 3 destinations, 3 routes (3 active, 0 holddown, 0 hidden)
+ = Active Route, - = Last Active, * = Both

192.168.1.1/32     *[Direct/0] 00:07:53
                    > via lo0.0
192.168.1.2/32     *[OSPF/10] 00:05:43, metric 1
                    > via so-0/0/0.0
224.0.0.5/32       *[OSPF/10] 00:07:53, metric 1
```

Executing the command show route protocol ospf reveals the routes in *inet.0* that have been learned from the OSPF routing protocol. R1 chooses the route to 192.168.1.1/32 (its own loopback interface) learned from protocol Direct with a route preference of 0 rather than from protocol OSPF with a route preference of 10.

```
[edit]
lab@R1# run show route protocol ospf

inet.0: 3 destinations, 3 routes (3 active, 0 holddown, 0 hidden)
+ = Active Route, - = Last Active, * = Both

192.168.1.2/32     *[OSPF/10] 00:09:18, metric 1
                    > via so-0/0/0.0
224.0.0.5/32       *[OSPF/10] 00:53:32, metric 1
```

Case Study 2: P2P Network with Numbered Interfaces

While unnumbered interfaces are useful to conserve address space, they have the disadvantage of being harder to troubleshoot. Interfaces with IP addresses can be PING'ed, traced to, and managed with management software such as SNMP.

In Figure 10-2, we have taken the network from the previous example and added an IP subnet, 10.10.1/30, to the P2P link by assigning IP addresses to the two interfaces connecting R1 and R2. The changed portion of the configuration on R1 is shown here:

```
[edit]
lab@R1# set interfaces so-0/0/0 unit 0 family inet address 10.10.1.1/30

[edit]
```

```
lab@R1# commit
commit complete

[edit]
lab@R1# show interfaces
so-0/0/0 {
    unit 0 {
        family inet {
            address 10.10.1.1/30;
        }
    }
}
lo0 {
    unit 0 {
        family inet {
            address 192.168.1.1/32;
        }
    }
}
```

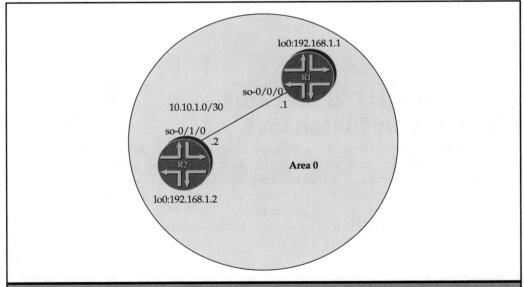

Figure 10-2.   *R1 and R2 connected via a P2P, numbered link*

P2P interfaces are treated as inherently unnumbered. When one or more IP addresses are assigned to the interface, the system generates an additional interface for each address and marks all the numbered interfaces as implicitly passive. It is actually only the unnumbered interface that is used to send packets and form adjacencies. The `show ospf interface` command displays only active and explicitly passive interfaces. The output illustrated next shows R1's unnumbered, active so-0/0/0.0 interface with one adjacency established to R2. You also see the output of `show ospf interface detail`, which displays the numbered, implicitly passive interface with IP address 10.10.1.1. The additional interface is marked as passive and has zero adjacencies established across it.

```
[edit]
lab@R1# run show ospf interface
Interface          State     Area           DR ID          BDR ID        Nbrs
so-0/0/0.0         PtToPt    0.0.0.0        0.0.0.0        0.0.0.0         1
  [edit]
lab@R1# run show ospf interface detail
Interface          State     Area           DR ID          BDR ID        Nbrs
so-0/0/0.0         PtToPt    0.0.0.0        0.0.0.0        0.0.0.0         1
Type P2P, address 0.0.0.0, mask 0.0.0.0, MTU 4470, cost 1
DR addr 0.0.0.0, BDR addr 0.0.0.0, adj count 1
Hello 10, Dead 40, ReXmit 5, Not Stub
so-0/0/0.0         PtToPt    0.0.0.0        0.0.0.0        0.0.0.0         0
Type P2P, address 10.10.1.1, mask 255.255.255.252, MTU 4470, cost 1
DR addr 0.0.0.0, BDR addr 0.0.0.0, adj count 0 , passive
Hello 10, Dead 40, ReXmit 5, Not Stub
```

The link-state database for the numbered P2P example is very similar to the unnumbered one in the previous case. The difference is in the Link Data fields of the type PointToPoint (1) link descriptions. When a P2P link is assigned a subnet, this field is set to the interface IP address of the associated link.

```
[edit]
lab@R1# run show ospf database detail

    OSPF link state database, area 0.0.0.0
 Type        ID              Adv Rtr            Seq      Age  Opt  Cksum  Len
Router   *192.168.1.1      192.168.1.1       0x80000006  183  0x2  0x9db9  60
  bits 0x0, link count 3
  id 192.168.1.2, data 10.10.1.1, type PointToPoint (1)
  TOS count 0, TOS 0 metric 1
  id 10.10.1.0, data 255.255.255.252, type Stub (3)
  TOS count 0, TOS 0 metric 1
  id 192.168.1.1, data 255.255.255.255, type Stub (3)
  TOS count 0, TOS 0 metric 0
```

```
Router   192.168.1.2      192.168.1.2      0x80000006  185  0x2  0xb3a0  60
  bits 0x0, link count 3
  id 192.168.1.1, data 10.10.1.2, type PointToPoint (1)
  TOS count 0, TOS 0 metric 1
  id 10.10.1.0, data 255.255.255.252, type Stub (3)
  TOS count 0, TOS 0 metric 1
  id 192.168.1.2, data 255.255.255.255, type Stub (3)
  TOS count 0, TOS 0 metric 0
```

Comparing the current routing table shown next with the one from the previous example, you can see that two additional routes have been added. The subnetwork 10.10.1/30 is learned via protocol Direct, that is, R1 is directly connected to the P2P link. Note that R1 also learns of this destination from protocol OSPF, but rejects it as the active route due to its higher protocol preference. The host address 10.10.1.1/32 is learned via protocol Local, since this is the address of the interface owned by R1.

```
[edit]
lab@R1# run show route

inet.0: 5 destinations, 5 routes (5 active, 0 holddown, 0 hidden)
+ = Active Route, - = Last Active, * = Both

10.10.1.0/30          *[Direct/0] 00:02:18
                       > via so-0/0/0.0
                       [OSPF/10] 00:02:17, metric 1
                       > via so-0/0/0.0
10.10.1.1/32          *[Local/0] 00:02:18
                        Local
192.168.1.1/32        *[Direct/0] 00:35:39
                       > via lo0.0
192.168.1.2/32        *[OSPF/10] 00:02:17, metric 1
                       > via so-0/0/0.0
224.0.0.5/32          *[OSPF/10] 00:35:40, metric 1
```

Case Study 3: BMA Network

As discussed in Chapter 9, OSPF behaves differently on BMA networks than on P2P links. The characteristics of OSPF on BMA networks include:

- Multiple router adjacencies on a single logical unit
- Election of a DR and a BDR for each BMA network
- Generation of a Network LSA for each transit BMA network

Figure 10-3 illustrates a new OSPF area consisting of four routers, named R3 through R6, and two Ethernet networks, numbered 10.10.2.32/28 and 10.10.2.16/28. The network 10.10.2.32/28 is called a Stub network because packets can enter or leave it only via R4. Stub networks can be only the source or destination of a packet. In contrast, network 10.10.2.16/28 is a transit network, since packets can travel through it from one router to another. A transit network can carry packets generated by and destined to networks other than itself.

In this example, the area has been given the name Area 1. This is done to illustrate the fact that an Area 0 is necessary only when connecting two or more areas. A single area existing alone can be named any 32-bit number. In the next case study, we will join Area 1 with the Area 0 from previous examples by making R3 an *area border router* (ABR).

Executing the command `show ospf interface detail` on R6 (seen next), you can observe the following facts. R6 is not the DR or BDR for 10.10.2.16/28. You can tell this because its fe-0/0/2.0 interface's state is DRother, and also by looking at the `DR ID` and `BDR ID` fields, which indicate that the DR is R5 and the BDR is R4.

For broadcast network connections such as Ethernet, the `Type` field is LAN. The Address field shows the IP address assigned to fe-0/0/2.0 attached to the LAN. The `DR addr` and `BDR addr` fields show the IP addresses assigned to interfaces of the DR

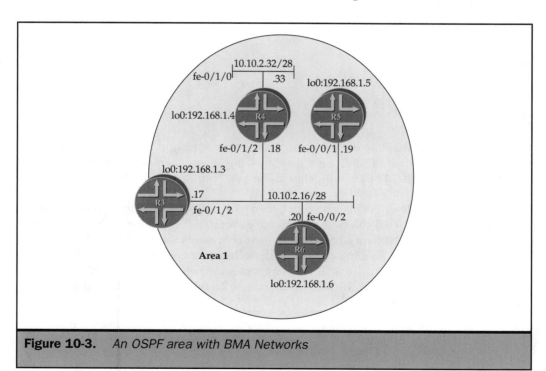

Figure 10-3. *An OSPF area with BMA Networks*

and BDR, respectively, that connect R5 and R6 to the LAN, and the MTU is shown to be 1500 bytes, the default for Ethernet.

```
[edit]
lab@R6# run show ospf interface detail
Interface          State    Area        DR ID         BDR ID        Nbrs
fe-0/0/2.0         DRother  0.0.0.1     192.168.1.5   192.168.1.4   3
Type LAN, address 10.10.2.20, mask 255.255.255.240, MTU 1500, cost 1
DR addr 10.10.2.19, BDR addr 10.10.2.18, adj count 2
Hello 10, Dead 40, ReXmit 5, Not Stub
```

Note that while the `Nbrs` field shows R6 as having three neighbors, the `adj Count` is only two. This is because routers in the DRother state become adjacent only with the DR and BDR. By the process of elimination, you can determine that R3 is also in the DRother state for this LAN, and so forms no adjacency with R6, even though they are neighbors. This can also be seen using the `show ospf neighbors` command, shown next. There you see R6 fully adjacent to R4 and R5, the BDR and DR, respectively, and in the 2Way state with R3, since both R3 and R6 are in the state DRother for the common network 10.10.2.16/28.

```
[edit]
lab@R6# run show ospf neighbor
  Address          Interface         State     ID             Pri   Dead
  10.10.2.17       fe-0/0/2.0        2Way      192.168.1.3    128   35
  10.10.2.18       fe-0/0/2.0        Full      192.168.1.4    128   35
  10.10.2.19       fe-0/0/2.0        Full      192.168.1.5    128   35
```

Analysis of the link-state database can provide more insight into the operation of OSPF on a BMA network. Using the `show ospf database` command shown next, you see that Area 1 has 5 LSAs in its link-state database. Four are Router LSAs and one is a Network LSA.

A Network LSA describes all routers attached to a particular network and is generated by the DR for that network. Network LSAs are generated for every transit BMA (and NBMA) network. The Network LSA shown next represents the 10.10.2.16/28 network. The LS ID field contains R5's interface IP address for the network. Applying the mask /28 to the R5 interface IP address 10.10.2.19 reveals the network address 10.10.2.16. The other network attached to R4, 10.10.2.32/28, has no Network LSA generated for it since it is a Stub network (not transit).

```
[edit]
lab@R6# run show ospf database

    OSPF link state database, area 0.0.0.1
```

```
Type          ID                 Adv Rtr            Seq        Age   Opt   Cksum   Len
Router    192.168.1.3        192.168.1.3        0x80000003    414   0x2   0x6345   48
Router    192.168.1.4        192.168.1.4        0x8000002c    431   0x2   0xde64   60
Router    192.168.1.5        192.168.1.5        0x80000028    431   0x2   0x413a   48
Router   *192.168.1.6        192.168.1.6        0x80000003    924   0x2   0x9ffc   48
Network   10.10.2.19         192.168.1.5        0x80000008    431   0x2   0x9174   40
```

A detailed view of the database shown next indicates that the Network LSA lists all four routers connected to 10.10.2.16/28. These are the routers that are fully adjacent to the DR (R3, 4, and 6 in this case), plus the DR itself (R5).

Also, three of the four Router LSAs shown list two links each. These are generated by R3, R5, and R6. The first link in each is of type transit and describes the router's connection to the transit network 10.10.2.16/28, with the Link ID field set to the interface IP address of the DR, and the Link Data field set to the interface IP address of the router that generated the Router LSA. The second link in each of these three Router LSAs describes the router's connection to its own host or Router ID and are of type Stub. For Stub links, the Link ID field contains the IP network number. In the case of a router, this is the Router ID. The Link Data field contains the Stub network's IP address mask. As in previous examples, this link is of type Stub, with its Link ID and Link Data fields set to the host IP address and /32, respectively.

The Router LSA generated by R4 lists three links, the last two of which are similar to the links described in the other three Router LSAs. The first link in this LSA describes R4's connection to the Stub network 10.10.2.32/28. This link is of type Stub with its Link ID and Link Data fields set to the IP network number and Stub network's subnet mask, /28, respectively. Recall that no Network LSA is generated for this network. Being the only router on the LAN, R4 is the DR for 10.10.2.32/28. Network LSAs are generated only for transit broadcast or NBMA networks.

```
[edit]
lab@R6# run show ospf database detail

    OSPF link state database, area 0.0.0.1
  Type        ID                 Adv Rtr            Seq        Age   Opt   Cksum   Len
Router    192.168.1.3        192.168.1.3        0x80000003    438   0x2   0x6345   48
   bits 0x0, link count 2
   id 10.10.2.19, data 10.10.2.17, type Transit (2)
   TOS count 0, TOS 0 metric 1
   id 192.168.1.3, data 255.255.255.255, type Stub (3)
   TOS count 0, TOS 0 metric 0
Router    192.168.1.4        192.168.1.4        0x8000002c    455   0x2   0xde64   60
   bits 0x0, link count 3
   id 10.10.2.32, data 255.255.255.240, type Stub (3)
   TOS count 0, TOS 0 metric 1
   id 10.10.2.19, data 10.10.2.18, type Transit (2)
```

```
  TOS count 0, TOS 0 metric 1
  id 192.168.1.4, data 255.255.255.255, type Stub (3)
  TOS count 0, TOS 0 metric 0
Router   192.168.1.5      192.168.1.5       0x80000028   455  0x2  0x413a  48
  bits 0x0, link count 2
  id 10.10.2.19, data 10.10.2.19, type Transit (2)
  TOS count 0, TOS 0 metric 1
  id 192.168.1.5, data 255.255.255.255, type Stub (3)
  TOS count 0, TOS 0 metric 0
Router  *192.168.1.6      192.168.1.6       0x80000003   948  0x2  0x9ffc  48
  bits 0x0, link count 2
  id 10.10.2.19, data 10.10.2.20, type Transit (2)
  TOS count 0, TOS 0 metric 1
  id 192.168.1.6, data 255.255.255.255, type Stub (3)
  TOS count 0, TOS 0 metric 0
Network  10.10.2.19       192.168.1.5       0x80000008   455  0x2  0x9174  40
  mask 255.255.255.240
  attached router 192.168.1.5
  attached router 192.168.1.3
  attached router 192.168.1.6
  attached router 192.168.1.4
```

The OSPF routing table on R6, shown next, indicates that a route has been learned to each of the other routers attached to the transit network 10.10.2.16/28 and also to the Stub network 10.10.2.32/28 via R4. Recall that the route to the transit network is learned via protocol Direct, since R6 is directly attached to it.

```
[edit]
lab@R6# run show route protocol ospf

inet.0: 8 destinations, 8 routes (8 active, 0 holddown, 0 hidden)
+ = Active Route, - = Last Active, * = Both

10.10.2.32/28      *[OSPF/10] 00:17:24, metric 2
                    > to 10.10.2.18 via fe-0/0/2.0
192.168.1.3/32     *[OSPF/10] 00:09:08, metric 1
                    > to 10.10.2.17 via fe-0/0/2.0
192.168.1.4/32     *[OSPF/10] 00:17:24, metric 1
                    > to 10.10.2.18 via fe-0/0/2.0
192.168.1.5/32     *[OSPF/10] 00:17:24, metric 1
                    > to 10.10.2.19 via fe-0/0/2.0
224.0.0.5/32       *[OSPF/10] 00:17:39, metric 1
```

Case Study 4: Hierarchical Routing—Multiple-Area Configuration

OSPF is a hierarchical routing protocol allowing network designers to divide a network into separate areas for the purpose of conserving bandwidth, router CPU cycles, and router memory. The advantages of a multiple area OSPF routing domain are

- Smaller link-state databases maintained by interior routers—conserves router memory
- Fewer LSAs to process—conserves router CPU cycles
- Less LSA flooding—conserves bandwidth within an area
- Faster convergence within an area

Figure 10-4 illustrates the new network in which the two separate areas that were created in previous case studies are joined. Router R3 becomes an ABR connecting Area 0 to Area 1.

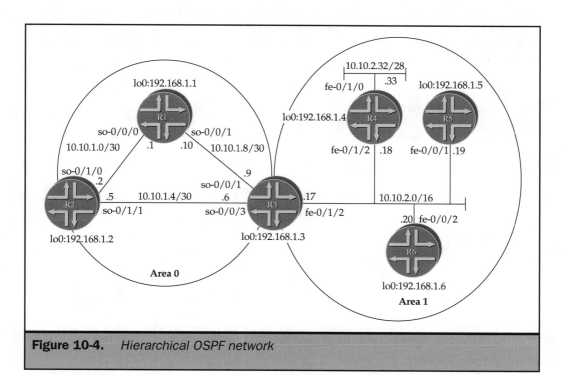

Figure 10-4. *Hierarchical OSPF network*

The configuration of an ABR is simple to implement. For each area that the router participates in, you must add the interfaces that are attached. The configuration of R3 is shown here:

```
[edit]
lab@R3# show protocols ospf
area 0.0.0.0 {
    interface so-0/0/1.0;
    interface so-0/0/3.0;
}
area 0.0.0.1 {
    interface fe-0/1/2.0;
}
```

Once committed, this configuration makes R3 an ABR with two interfaces attached to Area 0 and one interface attached to Area 1. Next you see that R3's interface fe-0/1/2.0 is attached to Area 1, is in state DRother, and has three neighbors (R4, R5, and R6). Interfaces so-0/0/1.0 and so-0/0/3.0 are both attached to Area 0, and connect R3 to R1 and R2, respectively. Similar information on R3's number of neighbors, as well as the interface IP addresses of those neighbors and the state of the neighbor relationships, is shown in the output of the show ospf neighbor command.

```
[edit]
lab@R3# run show ospf interface
Interface        State      Area         DR ID          BDR ID         Nbrs
fe-0/1/2.0       DRother    0.0.0.1      192.168.1.5    192.168.1.4    3
so-0/0/1.0       PtToPt     0.0.0.0      0.0.0.0        0.0.0.0        1
so-0/0/3.0       PtToPt     0.0.0.0      0.0.0.0        0.0.0.0        1
[edit]
lab@R3# run show ospf neighbor
  Address        Interface        State    ID            Pri  Dead
10.10.2.18       fe-0/1/2.0       Full     192.168.1.4   128  39
10.10.2.19       fe-0/1/2.0       Full     192.168.1.5   128  38
10.10.2.20       fe-0/1/2.0       2Way     192.168.1.6   128  31
10.10.1.10       so-0/0/1.0       Full     192.168.1.1   128  35
10.10.1.5        so-0/0/3.0       Full     192.168.1.2   128  31
```

ABRs maintain separate link-state databases for each area to which they are attached. Next you see the content of R3's link-state database for Area 0 and Area 1. For each area, the ABR generates a set of Summary LSAs, representing the Router and Network LSAs of the other attached networks. For example, R3 generates five Summary LSAs in Area 0, which represent the two LANs (10.10.2.16/28 and 10.10.2.32/28) and three attached routers (R4, R5, and R6) in Area 1. Likewise, Area 1 contains summary LSAs representing the three P2P links in Area 0, as well as the two routers, R1 and R2.

```
[edit]
lab@R3# run show ospf database

    OSPF link state database, area 0.0.0.1
 Type        ID              Adv Rtr          Seq          Age  Opt  Cksum   Len
Router   *192.168.1.3     192.168.1.3      0x80000008    85   0x2  0x5c46   48
Router    192.168.1.4     192.168.1.4      0x80000030    84   0x2  0xd668   60
Router    192.168.1.5     192.168.1.5      0x8000002c    84   0x2  0x393e   48
Router    192.168.1.6     192.168.1.6      0x80000007    85   0x2  0x9701   48
Network   10.10.2.19      192.168.1.5      0x8000000c    84   0x2  0x8978   40
Summary  *10.10.1.0       192.168.1.3      0x80000004    80   0x2  0x3c9c   28
Summary  *10.10.1.4       192.168.1.3      0x80000003    85   0x2  0xcca    28
Summary  *10.10.1.8       192.168.1.3      0x80000003    85   0x2  0xe3ee   28
Summary  *192.168.1.1     192.168.1.3      0x80000003    80   0x2  0x85fb   28
Summary  *192.168.1.2     192.168.1.3      0x80000003    80   0x2  0x7b05   28

    OSPF link state database, area 0.0.0.0
 Type        ID              Adv Rtr          Seq          Age  Opt  Cksum   Len
Router    192.168.1.1     192.168.1.1      0x800002d4    84   0x2  0x823d   84
Router    192.168.1.2     192.168.1.2      0x8000034b    85   0x2  0x4905   84
Router   *192.168.1.3     192.168.1.3      0x80000003    85   0x2  0x275f   84
Summary  *10.10.2.16      192.168.1.3      0x80000004    80   0x2  0x3e96   28
Summary  *10.10.2.32      192.168.1.3      0x80000004    80   0x2  0xa71c   28
Summary  *192.168.1.4     192.168.1.3      0x80000004    80   0x2  0x6518   28
Summary  *192.168.1.5     192.168.1.3      0x80000004    80   0x2  0x5b21   28
Summary  *192.168.1.6     192.168.1.3      0x80000004    80   0x2  0x512a   28
```

Here is a more detailed view of a type 3 LSA. Summary LSAs describe inter-area destinations. The Link-State ID field of type 3 LSAs contain the IP address of the destination.

```
[edit]
lab@R1# run show ospf database lsa-id 192.168.1.4 detail

    OSPF link state database, area 0.0.0.0
 Type        ID              Adv Rtr          Seq          Age  Opt  Cksum   Len
Summary   192.168.1.4     192.168.1.3      0x80000004    248  0x2  0x6518   28
  mask 255.255.255.255
  TOS 0x0, metric 1
```

Case Study 5: Route Redistribution into OSPF

External routes are injected into an OSPF network via route redistribution. As previously discussed, JUNOS software uses policy to accomplish route redistribution. The network in Figure 10-5 shows that a third area, Area 2, has been added and that R8 participates in Area 2 via interface fe-0/0/0. R8 is also connected to a RIP network via interface fe-0/0/2.

R9 connected to R8 advertises routes 172.100.20/24–172.100.23/24 via RIP. R8 is now an *Autonomous System Boundary Router* (ASBR). The configuration on R8 used to redistribute the incoming RIP routes into outgoing OSPF routes is

```
[edit]
lab@R8# show policy-options
policy-statement RIP {
    from protocol rip;
    then accept;
}

[edit]
lab@R8# show protocols ospf
export RIP;
area 0.0.0.2 {
    interface fe-0/0/0.0;
}
```

Viewing the RIP routing table on R8 shown next, you see the four 172.100/16 routes received from the RIP router. These routes are received with a metric of 2.

```
[edit]
lab@R8# run show route protocol rip

inet.0: 24 destinations, 24 routes (24 active, 0 holddown, 0 hidden)
+ = Active Route, - = Last Active, * = Both

172.100.20.0/24    *[RIP/100] 00:33:53, metric 2
                    > to 10.10.10.1 via fe-0/0/2.0
172.100.21.0/24    *[RIP/100] 00:33:53, metric 2
                    > to 10.10.10.1 via fe-0/0/2.0
172.100.22.0/24    *[RIP/100] 00:33:53, metric 2
                    > to 10.10.10.1 via fe-0/0/2.0
172.100.23.0/24    *[RIP/100] 00:33:53, metric 2
                    > to 10.10.10.1 via fe-0/0/2.0
224.0.0.9/32       *[RIP/100] 00:51:59, metric 1
```

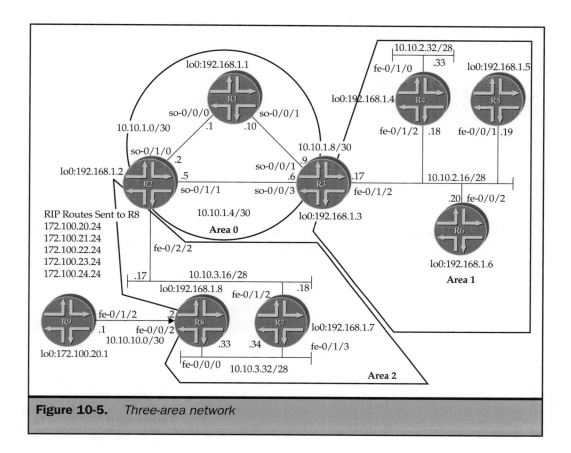

Figure 10-5.   *Three-area network*

R8 re-advertises these routes to R7 via OSPF AS External (type 5) LSAs. Type 5 LSAs have AS-flooding scope. Next you see the 172.100/16 routes in R7's OSPF routing table. By default, OSPF AS External routes are given a protocol preference of 150 by the local router, and are redistributed with type 2 metrics. Unlike type 1 metrics, type 2 metrics do not increase as they are advertised throughout the OSPF routing domain because they do not take into account the cost to reach the ASBR; therefore, the 172.100/16 routes maintain a metric of 2 across the OSPF routing domain.

The External Route Tag field is not actually used by the OSPF protocol. Using routing policy, this field can be modified by border routers importing a route, and then interpreted by other border routers when determining if the route should then be exported to another autonomous system.

```
[edit]
lab@R7# run show route 172.100/16
```

```
inet.0: 22 destinations, 22 routes (22 active, 0 holddown, 0 hidden)
+ = Active Route, - = Last Active, * = Both

172.100.20.0/24    *[OSPF/150] 00:36:39, metric 2, tag 0
                    > to 10.10.3.33 via fe-0/1/3.0
172.100.21.0/24    *[OSPF/150] 00:36:39, metric 2, tag 0
                    > to 10.10.3.33 via fe-0/1/3.0
172.100.22.0/24    *[OSPF/150] 00:36:39, metric 2, tag 0
                    > to 10.10.3.33 via fe-0/1/3.0
172.100.23.0/24    *[OSPF/150] 00:36:39, metric 2, tag 0
                    > to 10.10.3.33 via fe-0/1/3.0
```

Looking back at R8 for a moment, you can see next that its link-state database contains four AS External (type 5) LSAs. Like Network Summary (type 3) LSAs, type 5 LSAs use the Link ID field to carry the route being advertised.

```
[edit]
lab@R8# run show ospf database

    OSPF link state database, area 0.0.0.2
 Type       ID              Adv Rtr         Seq         Age   Opt  Cksum  Len
 Router     192.168.1.2     192.168.1.2     0x80000007  740   0x2  0x5a4c  48
 Router     192.168.1.7     192.168.1.7     0x80000006  1008  0x2  0xa76f  60
 Router    *192.168.1.8     192.168.1.8     0x80000006  1794  0x2  0x56f   48
 Network    10.10.3.17      192.168.1.2     0x80000004  1041  0x2  0x8271  32
 Network   *10.10.3.33      192.168.1.8     0x80000004  1494  0x2  0xf9dd  32
 Summary    10.10.1.0       192.168.1.2     0x80000005  599   0x2  0x36a3  28
 Summary    10.10.1.4       192.168.1.2     0x80000005  441   0x2  0xec7   28
 Summary    10.10.1.8       192.168.1.2     0x80000005  299   0x2  0xefe0  28
 Summary    10.10.2.16      192.168.1.2     0x80000006  1355  0x2  0x4a88  28
 Summary    10.10.2.32      192.168.1.2     0x80000001  1355  0x2  0xbd09  28
 Summary    192.168.1.1     192.168.1.2     0x80000004  1465  0x2  0x89f7  28
 Summary    192.168.1.3     192.168.1.2     0x80000004  1465  0x2  0x750a  28
 Summary    192.168.1.4     192.168.1.2     0x80000001  1355  0x2  0x7b05  28
 Summary    192.168.1.5     192.168.1.2     0x80000001  1355  0x2  0x710e  28
 Summary    192.168.1.6     192.168.1.2     0x80000001  1355  0x2  0x6717  28
    OSPF external link state database
 Type       ID              Adv Rtr         Seq         Age   Opt  Cksum  Len
 Extern    *172.100.20.0    192.168.1.8     0x80000002  1194  0x2  0x5bdc  36
 Extern    *172.100.21.0    192.168.1.8     0x80000002  894   0x2  0x50e6  36
 Extern    *172.100.22.0    192.168.1.8     0x80000002  594   0x2  0x45f0  36
 Extern    *172.100.23.0    192.168.1.8     0x80000002  294   0x2  0x3afa  36
```

Next you see a more detailed view of a single type 5 LSA, the one advertising 172.100.20/24. The additional fields shown reveal that the mask for this route is /24, the metric is 2 and is of type 2, and the Tag and TOS fields are set to 0 (default). The Forwarding Address field is set to 0, which means that packets addressed to the route should be sent to R8.

```
[edit]
lab@R8# run show ospf database lsa-id 172.100.20.0 detail

    OSPF link state database, area 0.0.0.2
  Type       ID                Adv Rtr           Seq       Age  Opt  Cksum  Len
    OSPF external link state database
  Type       ID                Adv Rtr           Seq       Age  Opt  Cksum  Len
Extern   *172.100.20.0    192.168.1.8       0x80000002 1283  0x2  0x5bdc  36
   mask 255.255.255.0
Type 2, TOS 0x0, metric 2, fwd addr 0.0.0.0, tag 0.0.0.0
```

With the exception of Stub and Not-So-Stubby Areas, type 5 LSAs are flooded throughout the entire OSPF routing domain. To make use of external routes, routers with type 5 LSAs in their link-state database also need to know the location of the LSA's originating router. To accomplish this, ABRs in areas containing an ASBR originate ASBR Summary LSAs (type 4) for each ASBR and flood them into the backbone area. Like type 1, 2, and 3 LSAs, type 4 LSAs have area-flooding scope.

This output shows R2's link-state database. R2, the ABR connecting Area 2 to the backbone area, generates a type 4 LSA for Area 0 describing R8.

```
[edit]
lab@r2# run show ospf database

    OSPF link state database, area 0.0.0.0
  Type       ID               Adv Rtr           Seq       Age  Opt  Cksum  Len
Router    192.168.1.1      192.168.1.1       0x80000007   431  0x2  0x246b  84
Router   *192.168.1.2      192.168.1.2       0x8000000b  1093  0x2  0xd5ba  84
Router    192.168.1.3      192.168.1.3       0x80000009  1228  0x2  0x1b65  84
Summary  10.10.2.16        192.168.1.3       0x80000008  1552  0x2  0x369a  28
Summary  10.10.2.32        192.168.1.3       0x80000001  1552  0x2  0xad19  28
Summary  *10.10.3.16       192.168.1.2       0x80000008   335  0x2  0x319f  28
Summary  *10.10.3.32       192.168.1.2       0x80000006   193  0x2  0x9e23  28
Summary  192.168.1.4       192.168.1.3       0x80000001  1552  0x2  0x6b15  28
Summary  192.168.1.5       192.168.1.3       0x80000001  1552  0x2  0x611e  28
Summary  192.168.1.6       192.168.1.3       0x80000001  1552  0x2  0x5727  28
Summary  *192.168.1.7      192.168.1.2       0x80000004  1659  0x2  0x4d2e  28
Summary  *192.168.1.8      192.168.1.2       0x80000004  1659  0x2  0x4d2c  28
ASBRSum  *192.168.1.8      192.168.1.2       0x80000004  1659  0x2  0x3f39  28

    OSPF link state database, area 0.0.0.2
  Type       ID               Adv Rtr           Seq       Age  Opt  Cksum  Len
```

```
Router   *192.168.1.2      192.168.1.2      0x80000007    935  0x2  0x5a4c  48
Router    192.168.1.7      192.168.1.7      0x80000006   1204  0x2  0xa76f  60
Router    192.168.1.8      192.168.1.8      0x80000007    192  0x2  0x370   48
Network  *10.10.3.17       192.168.1.8      0x80000004   1235  0x2  0x8271  32
Network   10.10.3.33       192.168.1.8      0x80000004   1692  0x2  0xf9dd  32
Summary  *10.10.1.0        192.168.1.2      0x80000005    793  0x2  0x36a3  28
Summary  *10.10.1.4        192.168.1.2      0x80000005    635  0x2  0xec7   28
Summary  *10.10.1.8        192.168.1.2      0x80000005    493  0x2  0xefe0  28
Summary  *10.10.2.16       192.168.1.2      0x80000006   1549  0x2  0x4a88  28
Summary  *10.10.2.32       192.168.1.2      0x80000001   1549  0x2  0xbd09  28
Summary  *192.168.1.1      192.168.1.2      0x80000005     35  0x2  0x87f8  28
Summary  *192.168.1.3      192.168.1.2      0x80000004   1659  0x2  0x750a  28
Summary  *192.168.1.4      192.168.1.2      0x80000001   1549  0x2  0x7b05  28
Summary  *192.168.1.5      192.168.1.2      0x80000001   1549  0x2  0x710e  28
Summary  *192.168.1.6      192.168.1.2      0x80000001   1549  0x2  0x6717  28
    OSPF external link state database
 Type      ID               Adv Rtr           Seq       Age  Opt  Cksum  Len
Extern    172.100.20.0     192.168.1.8      0x80000002   1392 0x2  0x5bdc  36
Extern    172.100.21.0     192.168.1.8      0x80000002   1092 0x2  0x50e6  36
Extern    172.100.22.0     192.168.1.8      0x80000002    792 0x2  0x45f0  36
Extern    172.100.23.0     192.168.1.8      0x80000002    492 0x2  0x3afa  36
```

Here is a more detailed view of the type 4 LSA. The Link-State ID field of type 4 LSAs contains the Router ID of the ASBR it advertises.

```
[edit]
lab@r2# run show ospf database asbrsummary detail

    OSPF link state database, area 0.0.0.0
 Type      ID               Adv Rtr           Seq       Age  Opt  Cksum  Len
ASBRSum *192.168.1.8        192.168.1.2      0x80000001   1037 0x2  0x4536  28
  mask 0.0.0.0
  TOS 0x0, metric 2
    OSPF link state database, area 0.0.0.2
```

The following output shows R6's link-state database and OSPF routing table, respectively. Note that in addition to the Area 1 Router and Network LSAs, R6's link-state database contains nine type 3 LSAs advertising destinations in Areas 0 and 2, one type 4 LSA advertising the ASBR (R8), and the four type 5 LSAs originated by R8.

R6's OSPF routing table contains routes to six of the seven networks in the OSPF routing domain. Since R6 is directly connected to network 10.10.2.16/28, it uses protocol Direct rather than protocol OSPF to reach it. This table also contains the four external routes and routes to the other seven OSPF routers.

The following case studies illustrate techniques to reduce the size of the link-state database and OSPF routing tables using Stub Areas, Stub Areas with no summaries, route summarization, and Not-So-Stubby Areas.

```
[edit]
lab@R6# run show ospf database

    OSPF link state database, area 0.0.0.1
  Type        ID                Adv Rtr         Seq          Age  Opt  Cksum   Len
  Router      192.168.1.3       192.168.1.3     0x80000004   1694 0x2  0x6e37  48
  Router      192.168.1.4       192.168.1.4     0x80000003   1693 0x2  0x4724  60
  Router      192.168.1.5       192.168.1.5     0x80000003   1694 0x2  0x950a  48
  Router     *192.168.1.6       192.168.1.6     0x80000002   1694 0x2  0xabf0  48
  Network    *10.10.2.20        192.168.1.6     0x80000001   1694 0x2  0x8b7f  40
  Summary     10.10.1.0         192.168.1.3     0x80000002   1233 0x2  0x409a  28
  Summary     10.10.1.4         192.168.1.3     0x80000002   1064 0x2  0xec9   28
  Summary     10.10.1.8         192.168.1.3     0x80000002    933 0x2  0xe5ed  28
  Summary     10.10.3.16        192.168.1.3     0x80000002    765 0x2  0x4193  28
  Summary     10.10.3.32        192.168.1.3     0x80000002    633 0x2  0xaa19  28
  Summary     192.168.1.1       192.168.1.3     0x80000002    465 0x2  0x87fa  28
  Summary     192.168.1.2       192.168.1.3     0x80000002    333 0x2  0x7d04  28
  Summary     192.168.1.7       192.168.1.3     0x80000002    165 0x2  0x5526  28
  Summary     192.168.1.8       192.168.1.3     0x80000002     33 0x2  0x5524  28
  ASBRSum     192.168.1.8       192.168.1.3     0x80000001   1776 0x2  0x4930  28
    OSPF external link state database
  Type        ID                Adv Rtr         Seq          Age  Opt  Cksum   Len
  Extern      172.100.20.0      192.168.1.8     0x80000002   1532 0x2  0x5bdc  36
  Extern      172.100.21.0      192.168.1.8     0x80000002   1231 0x2  0x50e6  36
  Extern      172.100.22.0      192.168.1.8     0x80000002    931 0x2  0x45f0  36
  Extern      172.100.23.0      192.168.1.8     0x80000002    631 0x2  0x3afa  36


[edit]
lab@R6# run show route protocol ospf terse

inet.0: 21 destinations, 21 routes (21 active, 0 holddown, 0 hidden)
+ = Active Route, - = Last Active, * = Both

A Destination       P Prf Metric 1   Metric 2    Next hop      AS path
* 10.10.1.0/30      O  10          3             >10.10.2.17
* 10.10.1.4/30      O  10          2             >10.10.2.17
* 10.10.1.8/30      O  10          2             >10.10.2.17
* 10.10.2.32/28     O  10          2             >10.10.2.18
* 10.10.3.16/28     O  10          3             >10.10.2.17
* 10.10.3.32/28     O  10          4             >10.10.2.17
* 172.100.20.0/24   O 150          2             >10.10.2.17
* 172.100.21.0/24   O 150          2             >10.10.2.17
* 172.100.22.0/24   O 150          2             >10.10.2.17
* 172.100.23.0/24   O 150          2             >10.10.2.17
* 192.168.1.1/32    O  10          2             >10.10.2.17
* 192.168.1.2/32    O  10          2             >10.10.2.17
* 192.168.1.3/32    O  10          1             >10.10.2.17
* 192.168.1.4/32    O  10          1             >10.10.2.18
* 192.168.1.5/32    O  10          1             >10.10.2.19
```

```
*  192.168.1.7/32      O  10           3             >10.10.2.17
*  192.168.1.8/32      O  10           4             >10.10.2.17
*  224.0.0.5/32        O  10           1              MultiRecv
```

Case Study 6: Stub Area Configuration

To reduce the size of an area's link-state database and reduce the size of router's OSPF routing tables within the area, the area can be configured as type Stub. Recall that only LSA types 1, 2, and 3 are permitted within a Stub Area and that, therefore, areas containing ASBRs cannot be configured as Stub. ABRs block LSAs of type 4 and 5 from flooding into a Stub Area.

In this case study, we take the three-area network in Figure 10-5 and turn Area 1 into a Stub Area. As shown next, routers are configured to participate in a Stub Area using the stub command in the area's configuration. Here only the configuration for R3 is shown, however, all routers in a Stub Area must be configured with the stub command. Routers participating in a Stub Area send their Hello packets into the Stub Area with the E bit in the Options field set to 0. Routers must agree on the value of the E bit to become neighbors.

```
[edit]
lab@R3# show protocols ospf
area 0.0.0.0 {
    interface so-0/0/1.0;
    interface so-0/0/3.0;
}
area 0.0.0.1 {
    stub;
    interface fe-0/1/2.0;
}
```

Using the show ospf interface detail command, you can see that the routers in Area 1 are now attached to a Stub Area. Next you see R6 attached to Area 1 (a Stub Area) on its fe-0/0/2.0 interface.

```
[edit]
lab@R6# run show ospf interface detail
Interface          State     Area            DR ID         BDR ID        Nbrs
fe-0/0/2.0         DR        0.0.0.1         192.168.1.6   192.168.1.5    3
Type LAN, address 10.10.2.20, mask 255.255.255.240, MTU 1500, cost 1
DR addr 10.10.2.20, BDR addr 10.10.2.19, adj count 3
Hello 10, Dead 40, ReXmit 5, Stub
```

Once configured as a Stub Area, all type 4 and 5 LSAs are removed from Area 1's link-state database. Before configured as a Stub Area, the link-state database for Area 1 contains 19 LSAs. Once configured as a Stub Area, the size of Area 1's link-state database is reduced to 14 LSAs. Here is a listing of the number of LSAs in R6's link-state database before the Stub Area configuration.

```
[edit]
lab@R6# run show ospf database summary
Area 0.0.0.1:
    4 Router LSAs
    1 Network LSAs
    9 Summary LSAs
    1 ASBRSum LSAs
Externals:
    4 Extern LSAs
```

The following is the database after the Stub configuration. Notice next that the one type 4 and four type 5 LSAs have been eliminated from Area 1 by configuring it as a Stub Area.

```
[edit]
lab@R6# run show ospf database summary
Area 0.0.0.1:
    4 Router LSAs
    1 Network LSAs
    9 Summary LSAs
Externals:
```

Since type 5 LSAs are not flooded through Stub Areas, Area 1 has no knowledge of AS External routes once configured as a Stub Area. You can confirm that there are no AS External (172.100/16) routes present after the Stub Area configuration.

```
lab@R6# run show route protocol ospf terse

inet.0: 21 destinations, 17 routes (17 active, 0 holddown, 0 hidden)
+ = Active Route, - = Last Active, * = Both

A Destination        P Prf Metric 1   Metric 2   Next hop        AS path
* 10.10.1.0/30       O  10      3                >10.10.2.17
* 10.10.1.4/30       O  10      2                >10.10.2.17
* 10.10.1.8/30       O  10      2                >10.10.2.17
```

```
*  10.10.2.32/28      O   10          2          >10.10.2.18
*  10.10.3.16/28      O   10          3          >10.10.2.17
*  10.10.3.32/28      O   10          4          >10.10.2.17
*  192.168.1.1/32     O   10          2          >10.10.2.17
*  192.168.1.2/32     O   10          2          >10.10.2.17
*  192.168.1.3/32     O   10          1          >10.10.2.17
*  192.168.1.4/32     O   10          1          >10.10.2.18
*  192.168.1.5/32     O   10          1          >10.10.2.19
*  192.168.1.7/32     O   10          3          >10.10.2.17
*  192.168.1.8/32     O   10          4          >10.10.2.17
*  224.0.0.5/32       O   10          1          MultiRecv
```

The link-state database of a Stub Area can be further reduced by preventing the flooding of type 3 LSAs into the area. This is accomplished using the `no-summaries` command in the Stub Area configuration. The `no-summaries` command is configured only on the ABRs of the Stub Area, thus preventing the ABRs from flooding the type 3 LSAs into the area. All routers in area must be configured for Stub. The configuration applied to router R3 is

```
[edit]
lab@R3# show protocols ospf
area 0.0.0.0 {
    interface so-0/0/1.0;
    interface so-0/0/3.0;
}
area 0.0.0.1 {
    stub no-summaries;
    interface fe-0/1/2.0;
}
```

Next you see that after R3 is configured with the `no-summaries` command, the Area 1 link-state database is further reduced by the elimination of the nine type 3 LSAs. At this point, R6's link-state database has been reduced from its original size of 19 LSAs to 5 LSAs.

```
[edit]
lab@R6# run show ospf database summary
Area 0.0.0.1:
```

```
    4 Router LSAs
    1 Network LSAs
Externals:
```

R6's routing table, shown next, now contains routes only to destinations within Area 1. In fact, at this stage in the configuration, routers in Area 1 have no default route (0/0) that would allow them to reach destinations external to Area 1.

```
[edit]
lab@R6# run show route protocol ospf terse

inet.0: 8 destinations, 8 routes (8 active, 0 holddown, 0 hidden)
+ = Active Route, - = Last Active, * = Both

A Destination       P Prf Metric 1    Metric 2    Next hop         AS path
* 10.10.2.32/28     O  10           2              >10.10.2.18
* 192.168.1.3/32    O  10           1              >10.10.2.17
* 192.168.1.4/32    O  10           1              >10.10.2.18
* 192.168.1.5/32    O  10           1              >10.10.2.19
* 224.0.0.5/32      O  10           1              MultiRecv
```

To allow a Stub Area to reach external destinations, one or more ABRs must advertise a default route into the area via type 3 LSAs. The `default-metric` command is used within the Stub Area configuration of the one or more ABRs to inject a default route into a Stub Area. The `default-metric` command requires that a metric value also be set for the ABR to advertise the route. The configuration on R3 used to advertise a default route with a metric of 10 into Area 1 is

```
[edit]
lab@R3# show protocols ospf
area 0.0.0.0 {
    interface so-0/0/1.0;
    interface so-0/0/3.0;
}
area 0.0.0.1 {
    stub default-metric 10 no-summaries;
    interface fe-0/1/2.0;
}
```

Next you see the single type 3 LSA generated by R3 to advertise the default route with a metric of 10 into Area 1:

```
[edit]
lab@R3# run show ospf database area 1 netsummary detail

    OSPF link state database, area 0.0.0.1
 Type       ID              Adv Rtr          Seq       Age  Opt  Cksum  Len
Summary *0.0.0.0           192.168.1.3     0x80000001   40  0x0  0xc81f  28
  mask 0.0.0.0
  TOS 0x0, metric 10
```

Now you can see a default route in R6's routing table. At this point, Area 1 can once again reach external destinations.

```
[edit]
lab@R6# run show route protocol ospf terse

inet.0: 9 destinations, 9 routes (9 active, 0 holddown, 0 hidden)
+ = Active Route, - = Last Active, * = Both

A Destination        P Prf Metric 1   Metric 2    Next hop        AS path
* 0.0.0.0/0          O  10         11              >10.10.2.17
* 10.10.2.32/28      O  10          2              >10.10.2.18
* 192.168.1.3/32     O  10          1              >10.10.2.17
* 192.168.1.4/32     O  10          1              >10.10.2.18
* 192.168.1.5/32     O  10          1              >10.10.2.19
* 224.0.0.5/32       O  10          1              MultiRec
```

Case Study 7: OSPF Route Summarization

Since the backbone area must be able to carry LSAs of type 4 and 5 from one attached area to another, Area 0 cannot be a Stub Area. Some of the advantages of a Stub Area can be realized in the backbone by summarizing or aggregating routes as they are flooded into Area 0. Doing so reduces the size of the Area 0 link-state database and routing tables, and hides flapping routes within a nonbackbone area from the backbone and, therefore, the rest of the network.

Referring back to Figure 10-5, in this case study, routes from Area 2 are summarized as they are flooding into the backbone. The networks 10.10.3.16/28 and 10.10.3.32/28 can be most easily summarized as 10.10.3/24. Summarization is configured on ABRs using the area-range command. The configuration of router R2 is shown next. Note that the area-range command is applied to the area where the routes originate from, Area 2 in this case.

```
[edit]
lab@r2# show protocols ospf
area 0.0.0.0 {
    interface so-0/1/0.0;
    interface so-0/1/1.0;
}
area 0.0.0.2 {
    area-range 10.10.3.0/24;
    interface fe-0/2/2.0;
}
```

Comparing the two following commands shows that the link-state database on router R1 is reduced by one LSA after summarization is configured on router R2. The two Summary LSAs that represented the two LANs in Area 2 are now advertised by a single Summary LSA. This is before the summarization takes place:

```
[edit]
lab@R1# run show ospf database summary
Area 0.0.0.0:
    3 Router LSAs
    9 Summary LSAs
    1 ASBRSum LSAs
Externals:
    4 Extern LSAs
```

This is after the summarization is configured on R2:

```
[edit]
lab@R1# run show ospf database summary
Area 0.0.0.0:
    3 Router LSAs
    8 Summary LSAs
    1 ASBRSum LSAs
Externals:
    4 Extern LSAs
```

The routing table on router R1 before summarization is configured on router R2 (shown next) contains routes to both network destinations in Area 2. Note that R1's cost to 10.10.3.16/28 is 2, and its cost to 10.10.3.32/28 is 3.

```
[edit]
lab@R1# run show route protocol ospf terse
```

```
inet.0: 22 destinations, 22 routes (22 active, 0 holddown, 0 hidden)
+ = Active Route, - = Last Active, * = Both

A Destination          P Prf Metric 1   Metric 2    Next hop         AS path
   10.10.1.0/30        O  10         1               >so-0/0/0.0
 * 10.10.1.4/30        O  10         2               >so-0/0/0.0
                                                      so-0/0/1.0
   10.10.1.8/30        O  10         1               >so-0/0/1.0
 * 10.10.2.16/28       O  10         2               >so-0/0/1.0
 * 10.10.2.32/28       O  10         3               >so-0/0/1.0
 * 10.10.3.16/28       O  10         2               >so-0/0/0.0
 * 10.10.3.32/28       O  10         3               >so-0/0/0.0
 * 192.168.1.2/32      O  10         1               >so-0/0/0.0
 * 192.168.1.3/32      O  10         1               >so-0/0/1.0
 * 192.168.1.4/32      O  10         2               >so-0/0/1.0
 * 192.168.1.5/32      O  10         2               >so-0/0/1.0
 * 192.168.1.6/32      O  10         2               >so-0/0/1.0
 * 192.168.1.7/32      O  10         2               >so-0/0/0.0
 * 192.168.1.8/32      O  10         3               >so-0/0/0.0
 * 224.0.0.5/32        O  10         1               MultiRecv
```

After summarization is configured on R2, the same routing table, shown next, now contains only a single route to the summarized destination 10.10.3.0/24. Summarized routes are advertised with a metric equal to the largest metric from the routes being summarized. In this example, R1's cost to the summarized destination is, therefore, 3.

```
[edit]
lab@R1# run show route protocol ospf terse

inet.0: 21 destinations, 21 routes (21 active, 0 holddown, 0 hidden)
+ = Active Route, - = Last Active, * = Both

A Destination          P Prf Metric 1   Metric 2    Next hop         AS path
   10.10.1.0/30        O  10         1               >so-0/0/0.0
 * 10.10.1.4/30        O  10         2               >so-0/0/0.0
                                                      so-0/0/1.0
   10.10.1.8/30        O  10         1               >so-0/0/1.0
 * 10.10.2.16/28       O  10         2               >so-0/0/1.0
 * 10.10.2.32/28       O  10         3               >so-0/0/1.0
 * 10.10.3.0/24        O  10         3               >so-0/0/0.0
 * 172.100.20.0/24     O 150         2               >so-0/0/0.0
```

```
*  172.100.21.0/24    O 150        2            >so-0/0/0.0
*  172.100.22.0/24    O 150        2            >so-0/0/0.0
*  172.100.23.0/24    O 150        2            >so-0/0/0.0
*  192.168.1.2/32     O  10        1            >so-0/0/0.0
*  192.168.1.3/32     O  10        1            >so-0/0/1.0
*  192.168.1.4/32     O  10        2            >so-0/0/1.0
*  192.168.1.5/32     O  10        2            >so-0/0/1.0
*  192.168.1.6/32     O  10        2            >so-0/0/1.0
*  192.168.1.7/32     O  10        2            >so-0/0/0.0
*  192.168.1.8/32     O  10        3            >so-0/0/0.0
*  224.0.0.5/32       O  10        1             MultiRecv
```

The two networks in Area 1 can also be summarized. The configuration on R3 is shown here:

```
lab@R3# show protocols ospf
area 0.0.0.0 {
    interface so-0/0/1.0;
    interface so-0/0/3.0;
}
area 0.0.0.1 {
    stub default-metric 10 no-summaries;
    area-range 10.10.2.0/24;
    interface fe-0/1/2.0;
}
```

Finally, here you can see that after the configuration change on R3, the routing table of R1 has been further reduced by one route.

```
[edit]
lab@R1# run show route protocol ospf terse

inet.0: 20 destinations, 20 routes (20 active, 0 holddown, 0 hidden)
+ = Active Route, - = Last Active, * = Both

A Destination       P Prf Metric 1   Metric 2    Next hop          AS path
  10.10.1.0/30      O  10        1              >so-0/0/0.0
* 10.10.1.4/30      O  10        2               so-0/0/0.0
                                                >so-0/0/1.0
  10.10.1.8/30      O  10        1              >so-0/0/1.0
* 10.10.2.0/24      O  10        3              >so-0/0/1.0
```

```
* 10.10.3.0/24        O  10        3           >so-0/0/0.0
* 172.100.20.0/24     O 150        2           >so-0/0/0.0
* 172.100.21.0/24     O 150        2           >so-0/0/0.0
* 172.100.22.0/24     O 150        2           >so-0/0/0.0
* 172.100.23.0/24     O 150        2           >so-0/0/0.0
* 192.168.1.2/32      O  10        1           >so-0/0/0.0
* 192.168.1.3/32      O  10        1           >so-0/0/1.0
* 192.168.1.4/32      O  10        2           >so-0/0/1.0
* 192.168.1.5/32      O  10        2           >so-0/0/1.0
* 192.168.1.6/32      O  10        2           >so-0/0/1.0
* 192.168.1.7/32      O  10        2           >so-0/0/0.0
* 192.168.1.8/32      O  10        3           >so-0/0/0.0
* 224.0.0.5/32        O  10        1            MultiRecv
```

Case Study 8: NSSA Configuration

Referring again to the network illustrated in Figure 10-5, since Area 2 contains an ASBR (R8), it is not eligible to be configured as a Stub Area. Stub Areas cannot carry AS External LSAs; however, since Area 2 sends AS External LSAs to the backbone but does not need to receive any from the backbone, Area 2 can be configured as an NSSA. Recall that an NSSA uses type 7 LSAs, rather than type 5, to describe external routes.

NSSA configuration is similar to Stub Area configuration. All routers in the area must be configured with the nssa configuration command, as shown here on R2:

```
[edit]
lab@R2# show protocols ospf
area 0.0.0.0 {
    interface so-0/1/0.0;
    interface so-0/1/1.0;
}
area 0.0.0.2 {
    nssa;
    area-range 10.10.3.0/24;
    interface fe-0/2/2.0;
```

Once this configuration is committed, R2 can be shown to be connected to an NSSA using the show ospf interface command:

```
[edit]
lab@R2# run show ospf interface fe-0/2/2.0 detail
Interface          State    Area        DR ID      BDR ID      Nbrs
```

```
fe-0/2/2.0          BDR      0.0.0.2        192.168.1.7    192.168.1.2      1
Type LAN, address 10.10.3.17, mask 255.255.255.240, MTU 1500, cost 1
DR addr 10.10.3.18, BDR addr 10.10.3.17, adj count 1
Hello 10, Dead 40, ReXmit 5, Stub NSSA
```

Before Area 2 is configured as an NSSA, its link-state database, shown next on R7, contains the four type 5 LSAs describing the external routes coming from the ASBR, R8. Once Area 2 is configured as an NSSA, R8 injects these routes into the area as type 7 LSAs.

```
[edit]
lab@R7# run show ospf database

    OSPF link state database, area 0.0.0.2
  Type        ID              Adv Rtr          Seq        Age   Opt   Cksum   Len
  Router    192.168.1.2      192.168.1.2      0x80000009  1881  0x2   0x6043   48
  Router   *192.168.1.7      192.168.1.7      0x80000007  2847  0x2   0xaf65   60
  Router    192.168.1.8      192.168.1.8      0x80000007  1484  0x2   0x370    48
  Network  *10.10.3.18       192.168.1.7      0x80000002  2849  0x2   0x4aa5   32
  Network   10.10.3.33       192.168.1.8      0x80000004  1184  0x2   0xf9dd   32
  Summary   10.10.1.0        192.168.1.2      0x80000004  1684  0x2   0x38a2   28
  Summary   10.10.1.4        192.168.1.2      0x80000004  1581  0x2   0x10c6   28
  Summary   10.10.1.8        192.168.1.2      0x80000005  1388  0x2   0xefe0   28
  Summary   10.10.2.0        192.168.1.2      0x80000001  1936  0x2   0x597e   28
  Summary   192.168.1.1      192.168.1.2      0x80000004  1281  0x2   0x89f7   28
  Summary   192.168.1.3      192.168.1.2      0x80000004  1088  0x2   0x750a   28
  Summary   192.168.1.4      192.168.1.2      0x80000003   981  0x2   0x7707   28
  Summary   192.168.1.5      192.168.1.2      0x80000003   788  0x2   0x6d10   28
  Summary   192.168.1.6      192.168.1.2      0x80000003   681  0x2   0x6319   28
    OSPF external link state database
  Type        ID              Adv Rtr          Seq        Age   Opt   Cksum   Len
  Extern    172.100.20.0     192.168.1.8      0x80000003  1784  0x2   0x59dd   36
  Extern    172.100.21.0     192.168.1.8      0x80000003   884  0x2   0x4ee7   36
  Extern    172.100.22.0     192.168.1.8      0x80000003   584  0x2   0x43f1   36
  Extern    172.100.23.0     192.168.1.8      0x80000003   284  0x2   0x38fb   36
```

Here you can see the link-state database on R7 after Area 2 is configured as an NSSA:

```
[edit]
lab@R7# run show ospf database

    OSPF link state database, area 0.0.0.2
  Type        ID              Adv Rtr          Seq        Age  Opt   Cksum   Len
  Router    192.168.1.2      192.168.1.2      0x80000007   46  0x0   0x881d   48
  Router   *192.168.1.7      192.168.1.7      0x80000009   47  0x0   0xc94b   60
  Router    192.168.1.8      192.168.1.8      0x80000007   60  0x0   0x2154   48
```

```
Network *10.10.3.18      192.168.1.7   0x80000004  50  0x0  0x648b  32
Network  10.10.3.33      192.168.1.8   0x80000005  61  0x0  0x16c2  32
Summary  10.10.1.0       192.168.1.2   0x80000004  51  0x0  0x5686  28
Summary  10.10.1.4       192.168.1.2   0x80000004  51  0x0  0x2eaa  28
Summary  10.10.1.8       192.168.1.2   0x80000002  34  0x0  0x14c1  28
Summary  10.10.2.0       192.168.1.2   0x80000001  39  0x0  0x7762  28
Summary  192.168.1.1     192.168.1.2   0x80000002  34  0x0  0xabd9  28
Summary  192.168.1.3     192.168.1.2   0x80000001  39  0x0  0x99ea  28
Summary  192.168.1.4     192.168.1.2   0x80000001  39  0x0  0x99e8  28
Summary  192.168.1.5     192.168.1.2   0x80000001  39  0x0  0x8ff1  28
Summary  192.168.1.6     192.168.1.2   0x80000001  39  0x0  0x85fa  28
NSSA     172.100.20.0    192.168.1.8   0x80000002  17  0x8  0xc235  36
NSSA     172.100.21.0    192.168.1.8   0x80000002  17  0x8  0xb73f  36
NSSA     172.100.22.0    192.168.1.8   0x80000002  17  0x8  0xac49  36
NSSA     172.100.23.0    192.168.1.8   0x80000002  17  0x8  0xa153  36
```

Next, you can see that type 7 LSAs are identical in content to type 5 LSAs. The difference between the two is in the `Type` field, which defines the flooding scope. Recall that type 5 LSAs have domain-wide flooding scope unless blocked by the ABR of a Stub or NSSA, while type 7 LSAs have only area-flooding scope.

```
[edit]
lab@R7# run show ospf database lsa-id 172.100.20.0 detail

    OSPF link state database, area 0.0.0.2
  Type       ID            Adv Rtr        Seq      Age  Opt  Cksum  Len
NSSA     172.100.20.0    192.168.1.8   0x80000002  52  0x8  0xc235  36
  mask 255.255.255.0
  Type 2, TOS 0x0, metric 2, fwd addr 10.10.3.33, tag 0.0.0.0
```

The following output shows the link-state database information on router R2. Router R2 receives type 7 LSAs from Area 2 and converts these into type 5 LSAs for flooding into the backbone and to the rest of the network. Note that the type 5 LSAs are shown with an asterisk, indicating that they were generated by the local router, R2. Also note that R2 continues to generate a type 4 ASBR Summary LSA for flooding into the backbone, indicating the location of the ASBR.

```
[edit]
lab@R2# run show ospf database

    OSPF link state database, area 0.0.0.0
  Type       ID            Adv Rtr        Seq      Age  Opt  Cksum  Len
Router   192.168.1.1     192.168.1.1   0x80000009  242  0x2  0x206d  84
Router  *192.168.1.2     192.168.1.2   0x8000000e  238  0x2  0xd5b5  84
```

Router	192.168.1.3	192.168.1.3	0x80000009	249	0x2	0x1b65	84
Summary	10.10.2.0	192.168.1.3	0x80000004	386	0x2	0x4391	28
Summary	*10.10.3.0	192.168.1.2	0x80000002	245	0x2	0x4294	28
Summary	192.168.1.4	192.168.1.3	0x80000006	386	0x2	0x611a	28
Summary	192.168.1.5	192.168.1.3	0x80000005	386	0x2	0x5922	28
Summary	192.168.1.6	192.168.1.3	0x80000005	386	0x2	0x4f2b	28
Summary	*192.168.1.7	192.168.1.2	0x80000004	240	0x2	0x4d2e	28
Summary	*192.168.1.8	192.168.1.2	0x80000005	240	0x2	0x4b2d	28
ASBRSum	*192.168.1.8	192.168.1.2	0x80000005	240	0x2	0x3d3a	28

```
    OSPF link state database, area 0.0.0.2
```

Type	ID	Adv Rtr	Seq	Age	Opt	Cksum	Len
Router	*192.168.1.2	192.168.1.2	0x80000007	247	0x0	0x881d	48
Router	192.168.1.7	192.168.1.7	0x80000009	250	0x0	0xc94b	60
Router	192.168.1.8	192.168.1.8	0x80000007	263	0x0	0x2154	48
Network	10.10.3.18	192.168.1.7	0x80000004	253	0x0	0x648b	32
Network	10.10.3.33	192.168.1.8	0x80000005	264	0x0	0x16c2	32
Summary	*10.10.1.0	192.168.1.2	0x80000004	252	0x0	0x5686	28
Summary	*10.10.1.4	192.168.1.2	0x80000004	252	0x0	0x2eaa	28
Summary	*10.10.1.8	192.168.1.2	0x80000002	235	0x0	0x14c1	28
Summary	*10.10.2.0	192.168.1.2	0x80000001	240	0x0	0x7762	28
Summary	*192.168.1.1	192.168.1.2	0x80000002	235	0x0	0xabd9	28
Summary	*192.168.1.3	192.168.1.2	0x80000001	240	0x0	0x99ea	28
Summary	*192.168.1.4	192.168.1.2	0x80000001	240	0x0	0x99e8	28
Summary	*192.168.1.5	192.168.1.2	0x80000001	240	0x0	0x8ff1	28
Summary	*192.168.1.6	192.168.1.2	0x80000001	240	0x0	0x85fa	28
NSSA	172.100.20.0	192.168.1.8	0x80000004	273	0x8	0xbe37	36
NSSA	172.100.21.0	192.168.1.8	0x80000004	273	0x8	0xb341	36
NSSA	172.100.22.0	192.168.1.8	0x80000004	273	0x8	0xa84b	36
NSSA	172.100.23.0	192.168.1.8	0x80000004	273	0x8	0x9d55	36

```
    OSPF external link state database
```

Type	ID	Adv Rtr	Seq	Age	Opt	Cksum	Len
Extern	*172.100.20.0	192.168.1.2	0x80000002	240	0x2	0x7fbe	36
Extern	*172.100.21.0	192.168.1.2	0x80000002	240	0x2	0x74c8	36
Extern	*172.100.22.0	192.168.1.2	0x80000002	240	0x2	0x69d2	36
Extern	*172.100.23.0	192.168.1.2	0x80000002	240	0x2	0x5edc	36

Like a Stub Area, the ABRs of an NSSA can be configured to block type 3 LSAs. This is accomplished using the no-summaries configuration command, as shown here on router R2:

```
[edit]
lab@R2# show protocols ospf
area 0.0.0.0 {
    interface so-0/1/0.0;
```

```
        interface so-0/1/1.0;
}
area 0.0.0.2 {
    nssa no-summaries;
    area-range 10.10.3.0/24;
    interface fe-0/2/2.0;
}
```

After committing the configuration change on R2, you can see that the Area 2 link-state database now has no type 3 LSAs:

```
[edit]
lab@R7# run show ospf database

    OSPF link state database, area 0.0.0.2
  Type        ID              Adv Rtr          Seq          Age  Opt  Cksum   Len
  Router      192.168.1.2     192.168.1.2      0x80000009     7  0x0  0x841f   48
  Router     *192.168.1.7     192.168.1.7      0x8000000b     7  0x0  0xc54d   60
  Router      192.168.1.8     192.168.1.8      0x80000009     7  0x0  0x1d56   48
  Network    *10.10.3.18      192.168.1.7      0x80000008     7  0x0  0x5c8f   32
  Network     10.10.3.33      192.168.1.8      0x80000006     7  0x0  0x14c3   32
  NSSA        172.100.20.0    192.168.1.8      0x80000006     7  0x8  0xba39   36
  NSSA        172.100.21.0    192.168.1.8      0x80000006     7  0x8  0xaf43   36
  NSSA        172.100.22.0    192.168.1.8      0x80000006     7  0x8  0xa44d   36
  NSSA        172.100.23.0    192.168.1.8      0x80000006     7  0x8  0x9957   36
```

As with Stub Area configuration, configuring an NSSA does not automatically create a default route for the area. Viewing the OSPF routing table on R7 shows that routers in Area 2 have no knowledge of destinations in Areas 0 or 1, making them unreachable.

```
[edit]
lab@R7# run show route protocol ospf terse

inet.0: 12 destinations, 12 routes (12 active, 0 holddown, 0 hidden)
+ = Active Route, - = Last Active, * = Both

A Destination         P Prf Metric 1   Metric 2   Next hop         AS path
* 172.100.20.0/24     O 150         2              >10.10.3.33
* 172.100.21.0/24     O 150         2              >10.10.3.33
* 172.100.22.0/24     O 150         2              >10.10.3.33
* 172.100.23.0/24     O 150         2              >10.10.3.33
* 192.168.1.2/32      O  10         1              >10.10.3.17
* 192.168.1.8/32      O  10         1              >10.10.3.33
* 224.0.0.5/32        O  10         1               MultiRecv
```

To inject a default route into Area 0, the ABR (R2) is configured with the `default-metric` configuration command. The default route is sent with a metric of 10.

```
[edit]
lab@R2# show protocols ospf
area 0.0.0.0 {
    interface so-0/1/0.0;
    interface so-0/1/1.0;
}
area 0.0.0.2 {
    nssa {
        default-metric 10;
        no-summaries;
    }
    area-range 10.10.3.0/24;
    interface fe-0/2/2.0;
}
```

Viewing the link-state database now shows the presence of an additional type 7 LSA, this one generated by R2, describing the default route. You can also see the OSPF routing table of R7, now containing a default route with a metric of 10.

```
[edit]
lab@R7# run show ospf database

    OSPF link state database, area 0.0.0.2
 Type       ID               Adv Rtr          Seq         Age  Opt  Cksum   Len
 Router     192.168.1.2      192.168.1.2      0x8000000b   3   0x0  0x8021  48
 Router    *192.168.1.7      192.168.1.7      0x8000000c   3   0x0  0xc34e  60
 Router     192.168.1.8      192.168.1.8      0x8000000a   3   0x0  0x1b57  48
 Network   *10.10.3.18       192.168.1.7      0x80000009   3   0x0  0x5a90  32
 Network    10.10.3.33       192.168.1.8      0x80000007   3   0x0  0x12c4  32
 NSSA       0.0.0.0          192.168.1.2      0x80000002   3   0x0  0x2833  36
 NSSA       172.100.20.0     192.168.1.8      0x80000007   3   0x8  0xb83a  36
 NSSA       172.100.21.0     192.168.1.8      0x80000007   3   0x8  0xad44  36
 NSSA       172.100.22.0     192.168.1.8      0x80000007   3   0x8  0xa24e  36
 NSSA       172.100.23.0     192.168.1.8      0x80000007   3   0x8  0x9758  36
```

```
[edit]
lab@R7# run show route protocol ospf terse

inet.0: 13 destinations, 13 routes (13 active, 0 holddown, 0 hidden)
+ = Active Route, - = Last Active, * = Both

A Destination        P Prf Metric 1   Metric 2    Next hop        AS path
* 0.0.0.0/0          O 150      10                >10.10.3.17
```

```
* 172.100.20.0/24    O 150        2           >10.10.3.33
* 172.100.21.0/24    O 150        2           >10.10.3.33
* 172.100.22.0/24    O 150        2           >10.10.3.33
* 172.100.23.0/24    O 150        2           >10.10.3.33
* 192.168.1.2/32     O  10        1           >10.10.3.17
* 192.168.1.8/32     O  10        1           >10.10.3.33
* 224.0.0.5/32       O  10        1           MultiRecv
```

In an NSSA, external routes can be summarized using the `nssa area-range` configuration command. In this example, the four external routes in Area 2 are summarized with the address 172.100.20/22 on router R2, as shown here:

```
[edit]
lab@R2# set protocols ospf area 2 nssa area-range 172.100.20/22

[edit]
lab@R2# show protocols ospf
area 0.0.0.0 {
    interface so-0/1/0.0;
    interface so-0/1/1.0;
}
area 0.0.0.2 {
    nssa {
        default-metric 10;
        no-summaries;
        area-range 172.100.20.0/22;
    }
    area-range 10.10.3.0/24;
    interface fe-0/2/2.0;
}
```

As is apparent from the output shown here, the four type 5 LSAs flooded into the backbone from Area 2 are now summarized by a single one representing the aggregate address. Here is the database before the `nssa area-range` command:

```
[edit]
lab@R1# run show ospf database

    OSPF link state database, area 0.0.0.0
 Type       ID              Adv Rtr          Seq       Age  Opt  Cksum  Len
 Router  *192.168.1.1      192.168.1.1    0x8000002d  2116  0x2  0xd791  84
 Router   192.168.1.2      192.168.1.2    0x80000047   246  0x2  0x63ee  84
```

```
Router     192.168.1.3      192.168.1.3       0x8000003e    967   0x2   0xb09a   84
Summary    10.10.2.0        192.168.1.3       0x80000007     96   0x2   0x3d94   28
Summary    10.10.3.0        192.168.1.2       0x80000005    966   0x2   0x3c97   28
Summary    192.168.1.4      192.168.1.3       0x8000002c     67   0x2   0x1540   28
Summary    192.168.1.5      192.168.1.3       0x8000002b   2118   0x2   0xd48    28
Summary    192.168.1.6      192.168.1.3       0x8000002a   2118   0x2   0x550    28
Summary    192.168.1.7      192.168.1.2       0x80000004    652   0x2   0x4d2e   28
Summary    192.168.1.8      192.168.1.2       0x80000006    652   0x2   0x492e   28
ASBRSum    192.168.1.8      192.168.1.2       0x80000006    652   0x2   0x3b3b   28
    OSPF external link state database
  Type       ID               Adv Rtr            Seq       Age   Opt   Cksum   Len
Extern     172.100.20.0     192.168.1.2       0x80000006    652   0x2   0x77c2   36
Extern     172.100.21.0     192.168.1.2       0x80000006    652   0x2   0x6ccc   36
Extern     172.100.22.0     192.168.1.2       0x80000006    652   0x2   0x61d6   36
Extern     172.100.23.0     192.168.1.2       0x80000006    652   0x2   0x56e0   36
```

Here is the database after summarization via the `nssa area-range` command:

```
[edit]
lab@R1# run show ospf database

    OSPF link state database, area 0.0.0.0
  Type       ID               Adv Rtr            Seq       Age   Opt   Cksum   Len
Router    *192.168.1.1      192.168.1.1       0x8000002e     34   0x2   0xd592   84
Router     192.168.1.2      192.168.1.2       0x80000049     34   0x2   0x5ff0   84
Router     192.168.1.3      192.168.1.3       0x8000003f     34   0x2   0xae9b   84
Summary    10.10.2.0        192.168.1.3       0x80000007     96   0x2   0x3d94   28
Summary    10.10.3.0        192.168.1.2       0x80000005    966   0x2   0x3c97   28
Summary    192.168.1.4      192.168.1.3       0x8000002d     34   0x2   0x1341   28
Summary    192.168.1.5      192.168.1.3       0x8000002c     34   0x2   0xb49    28
Summary    192.168.1.6      192.168.1.3       0x8000002b     34   0x2   0x351    28
Summary    192.168.1.7      192.168.1.2       0x80000006     34   0x2   0x4930   28
Summary    192.168.1.8      192.168.1.2       0x80000008     34   0x2   0x4530   28
ASBRSum    192.168.1.8      192.168.1.2       0x80000008     34   0x2   0x373d   28
    OSPF external link state database
  Type       ID               Adv Rtr            Seq       Age   Opt   Cksum   Len
Extern     172.100.20.0     192.168.1.2       0x80000008     34   0x2   0x6ecb   36
```

As you can see in this output of the `show route protocol ospf terse` command, after summarization, router R1 has a single route, 172.100.20/22, representing the four summarized /24 routes.

```
[edit]
lab@R1# run show route protocol ospf terse
```

```
inet.0: 19 destinations, 19 routes (19 active, 0 holddown, 0 hidden)
+ = Active Route, - = Last Active, * = Both

A Destination          P Prf Metric 1   Metric 2    Next hop        AS path
  10.10.1.0/30         O  10         1               >so-0/0/0.0
* 10.10.1.4/30         O  10         2                so-0/0/0.0
                                                     >so-0/0/1.0
  10.10.1.8/30         O  10         1               >so-0/0/1.0
* 10.10.2.0/24         O  10         3               >so-0/0/1.0
* 10.10.3.0/24         O  10         3               >so-0/0/0.0
* 172.100.20.0/22      O 150         3               >so-0/0/0.0
* 192.168.1.2/32       O  10         1               >so-0/0/0.0
* 192.168.1.3/32       O  10         1               >so-0/0/1.0
* 192.168.1.4/32       O  10         2               >so-0/0/1.0
```

Case Study 9: Virtual Link Configuration

In Figure 10-6, with the link between routers R1 and R9 broken, two separate Area 0's are created. This causes reachability problems between the two segments of the backbone.

The OSPF configuration on R2 is

```
[edit]
lab@R2# show protocols ospf
area 0.0.0.0 {
    interface so-0/1/0.0;
    interface so-0/1/1.0;
}
area 0.0.0.2 {
    area-range 10.10.3.0/24;
    interface fe-0/2/2.0;
}
```

The OSPF configuration on R8 is

```
[edit]
lab@R8# show protocols ospf
area 0.0.0.2 {
    area-range 10.10.3.0/24;
    interface fe-0/0/0.0;
}
area 0.0.0.0 {
    interface fe-0/0/2.0;
}
```

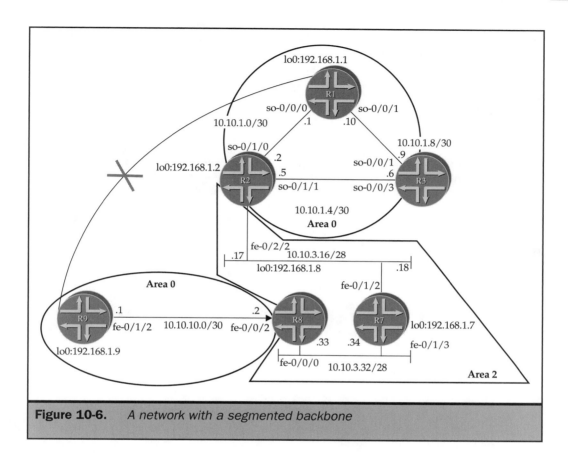

Figure 10-6. *A network with a segmented backbone*

Comparing the two databases shown next, you see that both R2 and R8 agree on the content of the Area 2 link-state database, but disagree on the content of the Area 0 link-state database. For Area 0, each router sees only LSAs for its own physically connected Area 0 routers and networks, and Summary LSAs describing destinations within Area 2. Since the backbone has been segmented, the backbone routers in the different segments will not have consistent link-state databases. Here is R2's view of things:

```
[edit]
lab@R2# run show ospf database

    OSPF link state database, area 0.0.0.0
  Type       ID                Adv Rtr            Seq       Age  Opt  Cksum  Len
  Router     192.168.1.1       192.168.1.1       0x80000025    6  0x2  0xe789  84
  Router    *192.168.1.2       192.168.1.2       0x80000034    7  0x2  0x83e3  84
```

```
Router    192.168.1.3      192.168.1.3      0x80000032   7   0x2   0xc592   84
Summary   *10.10.3.0       192.168.1.2      0x80000004   2   0x2   0x3e96   28
Summary   *192.168.1.7     192.168.1.2      0x80000003   2   0x2   0x4f2d   28
Summary   *192.168.1.8     192.168.1.2      0x80000003   2   0x2   0x4f2b   28

    OSPF link state database, area 0.0.0.2
  Type      ID               Adv Rtr          Seq         Age Opt   Cksum   Len
Router    *192.168.1.2      192.168.1.2      0x80000003   7   0x2   0x6c3d   48
Router    192.168.1.7      192.168.1.7      0x80000026   6   0x2   0x7184   60
Router    192.168.1.8      192.168.1.8      0x80000038   6   0x2   0x9da5   48
Network   10.10.3.18       192.168.1.7      0x80000002   6   0x2   0x4aa5   32
Network   10.10.3.33       192.168.1.8      0x8000002f   6   0x2   0xa309   32
Summary   *10.10.1.0       192.168.1.2      0x80000002   7   0x2   0x3ca0   28
Summary   *10.10.1.4       192.168.1.2      0x80000002   7   0x2   0x14c4   28
Summary   *10.10.1.8       192.168.1.2      0x80000004   2   0x2   0xf1df   28
Summary   10.10.10.0       192.168.1.8      0x80000033   6   0x2   0x524a   28
Summary   *192.168.1.1     192.168.1.2      0x80000004   2   0x2   0x89f7   28
Summary   *192.168.1.3     192.168.1.2      0x80000003   2   0x2   0x7709   28
Summary   192.168.1.9      192.168.1.8      0x80000031   6   0x2   0xba8b   28
```

Here is R8's view:

```
[edit]
lab@R8# run show ospf database

    OSPF link state database, area 0.0.0.0
  Type      ID               Adv Rtr          Seq         Age  Opt   Cksum   Len
Router    *192.168.1.8      192.168.1.8      0x8000003a   182  0x2   0x3f33   48
Router    192.168.1.9      192.168.1.9      0x8000001f   1416 0x2   0x6a22   48
Network   10.10.10.1       192.168.1.9      0x8000001e   1416 0x2   0x14b3   32
Summary   *10.10.3.0       192.168.1.8      0x8000002d   1840 0x2   0xc7dd   28
Summary   *192.168.1.2     192.168.1.8      0x80000002   182  0x2   0x6912   28
Summary   *192.168.1.7     192.168.1.8      0x80000030   182  0x2   0xd078   28

    OSPF link state database, area 0.0.0.2
  Type      ID               Adv Rtr          Seq         Age  Opt   Cksum   Len
Router    192.168.1.2      192.168.1.2      0x80000003   104  0x2   0x6c3d   48
Router    192.168.1.7      192.168.1.7      0x80000026   101  0x2   0x7184   60
Router    *192.168.1.8      192.168.1.8      0x80000038   99   0x2   0x9da5   48
Network   10.10.3.18       192.168.1.7      0x80000002   101  0x2   0x4aa5   32
Network   *10.10.3.33      192.168.1.8      0x8000002f   99   0x2   0xa309   32
Summary   10.10.1.0        192.168.1.2      0x80000002   104  0x2   0x3ca0   28
Summary   10.10.1.4        192.168.1.2      0x80000002   104  0x2   0x14c4   28
Summary   10.10.1.8        192.168.1.2      0x80000004   99   0x2   0xf1df   28
Summary   *10.10.10.0      192.168.1.8      0x80000033   99   0x2   0x524a   28
Summary   192.168.1.1      192.168.1.2      0x80000004   99   0x2   0x89f7   28
Summary   192.168.1.3      192.168.1.2      0x80000003   99   0x2   0x7709   28
Summary   *192.168.1.9     192.168.1.8      0x80000031   99   0x2   0xba8b   28
```

Routers in one backbone partition cannot reach routers in the other backbone partition. For example, even though a physical path exists from R2 to R9, R2 has no knowledge of R9, as you can see here.

Note that the aggregate route 10.10.3.0/24 is shown with an infinite metric and a next-hop of Discard. Recall that we had previously configured R2 to summarize the Area 2 routes. When R2 performs this summarization, it installs the route in its routing table in this fashion to indicate that packets destined to the aggregate should be discarded. Once you realize that the aggregate route is not an actual destination, but rather a collection of destinations, this process makes sense.

```
[edit]
lab@R2# run show route protocol ospf terse

inet.0: 15 destinations, 15 routes (15 active, 0 holddown, 0 hidden)
+ = Active Route, - = Last Active, * = Both

A Destination        P Prf Metric 1    Metric 2    Next hop         AS path
  10.10.1.0/30       O  10          1               >so-0/1/0.0
  10.10.1.4/30       O  10          1               >so-0/1/1.0
* 10.10.1.8/30       O  10          2               >so-0/1/0.0
                                                    so-0/1/1.0
* 10.10.3.0/24       O  10   16777215               Discard
* 10.10.3.32/28      O  10          2               >10.10.3.18
* 192.168.1.1/32     O  10          1               >so-0/1/0.0
* 192.168.1.3/32     O  10          1               >so-0/1/1.0
* 192.168.1.7/32     O  10          1               >10.10.3.18
* 192.168.1.8/32     O  10          2               >10.10.3.18
* 224.0.0.5/32       O  10          1               MultiRecv
```

To repair a partitioned backbone, a virtual link is established between two ABRs sharing a common transit area. In this example, the ABRs R2 and R8 are connected via the transit area, Area 2. The virtual link is established using the virtual-link configuration command, as shown here. On each ABR, the configuration information needed is the Router ID at the other end of the virtual link, and the area ID of the common transit area.

```
[edit]
lab@R2# show protocols ospf
area 0.0.0.0 {
    virtual-link neighbor-id 192.168.1.8 transit-area 0.0.0.2;
    interface so-0/1/0.0;
    interface so-0/1/1.0;
}
area 0.0.0.2 {
    area-range 10.10.3.0/24;
```

```
        interface fe-0/2/2.0;
}
[edit]
lab@R8# show protocols ospf
area 0.0.0.2 {
    area-range 10.10.3.0/24;
    interface fe-0/0/0.0;
}
area 0.0.0.0 {
    virtual-link neighbor-id 192.168.1.2 transit-area 0.0.0.2;
    interface fe-0/0/2.0;
}
```

Next you see the output of the show ospf interface and show ospf
interface detail commands on R2. Once the virtual link is established, a virtual
link interface of type "Virtual" is created, with a single neighbor present at the other
end of the link. The virtual link is treated like an unnumbered P2P network belonging
to Area 0. The cost of the link is the intra-area cost between the two ABRs, and is not a
configurable parameter.

```
[edit]
lab@R2# run show ospf interface
Interface         State    Area        DR ID         BDR ID        Nbrs
so-0/1/0.0        PtToPt   0.0.0.0     0.0.0.0       0.0.0.0       1
so-0/1/1.0        PtToPt   0.0.0.0     0.0.0.0       0.0.0.0       1
vl-192.168.1.8    PtToPt   0.0.0.0     0.0.0.0       0.0.0.0       1
fe-0/2/2.0        BDR      0.0.0.2     192.168.1.7   192.168.1.2   1
```

```
[edit]
lab@R2# run show ospf interface vl-192.168.1.8 detail
Interface         State    Area        DR ID         BDR ID
Nbrs
vl-192.168.1.8    PtToPt   0.0.0.0     0.0.0.0       0.0.0.0
1
Type Virtual, address 10.10.3.17, mask 0.0.0.0, MTU 0, cost 2
DR addr 0.0.0.0, BDR addr 0.0.0.0, adj count 1
Hello 10, Dead 40, ReXmit 5, Not Stub
```

Executing the show ospf neighbor command on R2 reveals that the neighbor
address is R8's IP interface address, 10.10.3.33, and that the designated router priority
is set to zero since the concept of a DR has no meaning on a virtual link.

```
[edit]
lab@R2# run show ospf neighbor
  Address         Interface         State        ID           Pri  Dead
```

```
10.10.1.1           so-0/1/0.0          Full        192.168.1.1     128   32
10.10.1.6           so-0/1/1.0          Full        192.168.1.3     128   35
10.10.3.33          vl-192.168.1.8      Full        192.168.1.8       0   37
10.10.3.18          fe-0/2/2.0          Full        192.168.1.7     128   33
```

The Router LSAs generated by each endpoint ABR contain a type 4 link representing the virtual link. The type 4 link has its link ID set to the virtual neighbor's Router ID and its link data set to the virtual interface's IP address, as you can see here:

```
[edit]
lab@R2# run show ospf database area 0 router lsa-id 192.168.1.2 detail

    OSPF link state database, area 0.0.0.0
 Type       ID               Adv Rtr           Seq       Age  Opt  Cksum  Len
 Router  *192.168.1.2       192.168.1.2       0x8000003d 1117 0x2  0x2888 96
   bits 0x1, link count 6
   id 192.168.1.1, data 10.10.1.2, type PointToPoint (1)
   TOS count 0, TOS 0 metric 1
   id 10.10.1.0, data 255.255.255.252, type Stub (3)
   TOS count 0, TOS 0 metric 1
   id 192.168.1.3, data 10.10.1.5, type PointToPoint (1)
   TOS count 0, TOS 0 metric 1
   id 10.10.1.4, data 255.255.255.252, type Stub (3)
   TOS count 0, TOS 0 metric 1
   id 192.168.1.8, data 10.10.3.17, type Virtual (4)
   TOS count 0, TOS 0 metric 2
   id 192.168.1.2, data 255.255.255.255, type Stub (3)
   TOS count 0, TOS 0 metric 0
```

Once established, the virtual link repairs the partitioned backbone, and so both R2 and R9 have consistent Area 0 link-state databases. Next you can see that R2 now has link-state information about R9 and the network between R8 and R9, 10.10.10/30. You can also see that R2 now has a route to R9, 192.168.1.9/32.

```
[edit]
lab@R2# run show ospf database

    OSPF link state database, area 0.0.0.0
 Type       ID               Adv Rtr           Seq       Age  Opt  Cksum  Len
 Router   192.168.1.1       192.168.1.1       0x8000001f 2213 0x2  0xf383 84
 Router  *192.168.1.2       192.168.1.2       0x8000002a  182 0x2  0x4e75 96
 Router   192.168.1.3       192.168.1.3       0x8000002d 1007 0x2  0xcf8d 84
 Router   192.168.1.8       192.168.1.8       0x80000035  181 0x2  0xcef0 60
```

```
Router    192.168.1.9    192.168.1.9    0x8000001e    90    0x2    0x6c21    48
Network   10.10.10.1     192.168.1.9    0x8000001d    90    0x2    0x16b2    32
Summary  *10.10.3.0      192.168.1.2    0x80000001   829    0x2    0x4493    28
Summary   10.10.3.0      192.168.1.8    0x8000002b   215    0x2    0xcbdb    28
Summary   192.168.1.2    192.168.1.8    0x80000003   187    0x2    0x6713    28
Summary  *192.168.1.7    192.168.1.2    0x80000002   241    0x2    0x512c    28
Summary   192.168.1.7    192.168.1.8    0x8000002d   187    0x2    0xd675    28
Summary  *192.168.1.8    192.168.1.2    0x80000002   241    0x2    0x512a    28

    OSPF link state database, area 0.0.0.2
 Type      ID              Adv Rtr          Seq        Age   Opt  Cksum   Len
Router   *192.168.1.2    192.168.1.2    0x80000004   182    0x2    0x762e    48
Router    192.168.1.7    192.168.1.7    0x80000022   832    0x2    0x7980    60
Router    192.168.1.8    192.168.1.8    0x80000033   182    0x2    0xb390    48
Network   10.10.3.18     192.168.1.7    0x80000001   832    0x2    0x4ca4    32
Network   10.10.3.33     192.168.1.8    0x8000002b  1415    0x2    0xab05    32
Summary  *10.10.1.0      192.168.1.2    0x80000003   241    0x2    0x3aa1    28
Summary  *10.10.1.4      192.168.1.2    0x80000002   241    0x2    0x14c4    28
Summary  *10.10.1.8      192.168.1.2    0x80000002   241    0x2    0xf5dd    28
Summary   10.10.10.0     192.168.1.8    0x8000002f   188    0x2    0x5a46    28
Summary  *192.168.1.1    192.168.1.2    0x80000002   241    0x2    0x8df5    28
Summary  *192.168.1.3    192.168.1.2    0x80000002   241    0x2    0x7908    28
Summary   192.168.1.9    192.168.1.8    0x8000002d   188    0x2    0xc287    28
```

```
[edit]
lab@R2# run show route protocol ospf terse

inet.0: 17 destinations, 17 routes (17 active, 0 holddown, 0 hidden)
+ = Active Route, - = Last Active, * = Both

A Destination         P Prf Metric 1  Metric 2   Next hop         AS path
  10.10.1.0/30        O  10         1             >so-0/1/0.0
  10.10.1.4/30        O  10         1             >so-0/1/1.0
* 10.10.1.8/30        O  10         2              so-0/1/0.0
                                                  >so-0/1/1.0

* 10.10.3.0/24        O  10  16777215             Discard
* 10.10.3.32/28       O  10         2             >10.10.3.18
* 10.10.10.0/30       O  10         3             >10.10.3.18
* 192.168.1.1/32      O  10         1             >so-0/1/0.0
* 192.168.1.3/32      O  10         1             >so-0/1/1.0
* 192.168.1.7/32      O  10         1             >10.10.3.18
* 192.168.1.8/32      O  10         2             >10.10.3.18
* 192.168.1.9/32      O  10         3             >10.10.3.18
* 224.0.0.5/32        O  10         1              MultiRecv
```

Case Study 10: OSPF Metrics and Shortest Path Calculation

This case study looks at how an OSPF router differentiates between intra-area and inter-area paths when calculating the shortest path to a destination and how assigned metrics affect this decision.

Figure 10-7 illustrates a network with three areas, numbered 0 through 2 and seven routers named R1–R5, X, and Y. The loopback interfaces of routers X and Y have been assigned the addresses 192.168.10.1 and 192.168.10.2, respectively. Note that routers R1, R2, and R3 are ABRs attached to two or, in the case of R2, three areas. This point is critical to understanding this case study.

Before continuing, ask yourself these questions: What path would a packet take to travel from X to Y, and what metric would this path have?

If the approach you used was to simply add all the metrics between X and Y, and then choose the path with the lowest metric, you may have arrived at the path:

X, R5, R1, R2, R3, R4, Y—with a metric of **1202** (1 + 500 + 400 + 100 + 200 + 1)

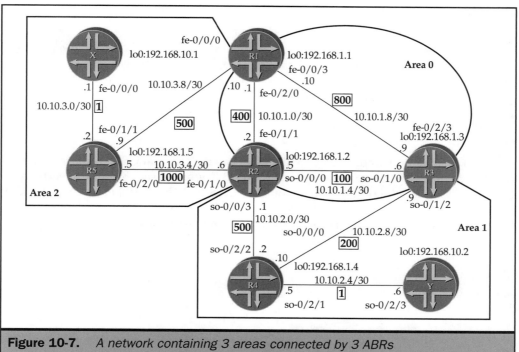

Figure 10-7.   *A network containing 3 areas connected by 3 ABRs*

Looking at X's routing table for route 192.168.10.2, it appears that this assumption is correct; the metric is indeed 1202, and this is the only path that yields this exact value.

```
[edit]
lab@X# run show route 192.168.10.2

inet.0: 18 destinations, 18 routes (18 active, 0 holddown, 0 hidden)
+ = Active Route, - = Last Active, * = Both

192.168.10.2/32    *[OSPF/10] 00:59:00, metric 1202
                    > to 10.10.3.2 via fe-0/0/0.0
```

However, performing a traceroute from X to 192.168.10.2 reveals that the path actually taken by packets from X to Y is

X, R5, R1, R2, R4, Y

R3 is skipped. The metric for this path is **1402** (1 + 500 + 400 + 500 +1).

```
[edit]
lab@X# run traceroute 192.168.10.2
traceroute to 192.168.10.2 (192.168.10.2), 30 hops max, 40 byte packets
 1  10.10.3.2 (10.10.3.2)  0.686 ms  0.507 ms  0.471 ms
 2  10.10.3.10 (10.10.3.10)  0.575 ms  0.560 ms  0.543 ms
 3  10.10.1.2 (10.10.1.2)  0.576 ms  0.544 ms  0.529 ms
 4  10.10.2.2 (10.10.2.2)  0.584 ms  0.567 ms  0.558 ms
192.168.10.2 (192.168.10.2)  0.770 ms  0.717 ms  0.699 ms
```

The key to understanding this result is to recall the fact that OSPF routers prefer intra-area routes to inter-area routes. In Figure 10-7, you can see this more clearly by analyzing the route each router holds for Y (192.168.10.2), by working backwards from Y to X.

As expected, R4 has a metric of 1 to Y, as shown here. R4 advertises this metric to R2 and R3.

```
[edit]
lab@R4# run show route 192.168.10.2

inet.0: 20 destinations, 20 routes (20 active, 0 holddown, 0 hidden)
+ = Active Route, - = Last Active, * = Both

192.168.10.2/32    *[OSPF/10] 00:58:32, metric 1
                    > via so-0/2/1.0
```

Router R2 is in a unique position because it is attached to all three areas. Because it has a lower cumulative metric, you might expect R2 would prefer the path via R3 (metric of 301) to the one directly to R4 (metric of 501). However, because R2 and Y are both in Area 1, R2 prefers the intra-area path via R4—even though it has a larger metric! R2 advertises a route to 192.168.10.2 with a metric of 501 into area 0.

```
[edit]
lab@R2# run show route 192.168.10.2

inet.0: 21 destinations, 21 routes (21 active, 0 holddown, 0 hidden)
+ = Active Route, - = Last Active, * = Both

192.168.10.2/32    *[OSPF/10] 00:58:16, metric 501
                    > via so-0/0/3.0
```

Remember, OSPF routers prefer intra-area routes to inter-area routes.

Continuing with the example, router R3 sees a metric of 201 to 192.168.10.2 and advertises this to Area 0, as shown here:

```
[edit]
lab@R3# run show route 192.168.10.2

inet.0: 20 destinations, 20 routes (20 active, 0 holddown, 0 hidden)
+ = Active Route, - = Last Active, * = Both

192.168.10.2/32    *[OSPF/10] 00:58:24, metric 201
                    > via so-0/1/2.0
```

Based on the metrics advertised into Area 0 by R2 and R3, router R1 has four intra-area routes to the ABRs leading to router Y:

- Via router R2 with metric 501 + 400 = 901
- Via router R3 with metric 201 + 800 = 1001
- Via routers R3 and R2 with metric 501 + 100 + 800 = 1401
- Via routers R2 and R3 with metric 201 + 100 + 400 = 701

Router R1 chooses the path with the lowest metric, **701,** as shown here:

```
[edit]
lab@R1# run show route 192.168.10.2
```

```
inet.0: 20 destinations, 20 routes (20 active, 0 holddown, 0 hidden)
+ = Active Route, - = Last Active, * = Both

192.168.10.2/32    *[OSPF/10] 00:55:42, metric 701
                    > to 10.10.1.2 via fe-0/2/0.0
```

The key observation is that although router R1 has chosen a path to Area 1 that goes through R2 and R3 (metric of 701), packets do not actually traverse this path. When packets arrive at R2, they are immediately forwarded to R4 in accordance with R2's routing table, shown previously.

Finally, R5 must choose between two paths to Area 0:

- Via router R1 with metric 701 + 500 = 1201
- Via router R2 with metric 501 + 1000 = 1501

Router R5 chooses the path with the lowest metric, **1201**, as shown here:

```
[edit]
lab@R5# run show route 192.168.10.2

inet.0: 20 destinations, 20 routes (20 active, 0 holddown, 0 hidden)
+ = Active Route, - = Last Active, * = Both

192.168.10.2/32    *[OSPF/10] 00:58:35, metric 1201
                    > to 10.10.3.10 via fe-0/1/0.0
```

To summarize, if the network in Figure 10-7 were a single area, the path

X, R5, R1, R2, R3, R4, Y—with a metric of **1202** (1 + 500 + 400 + 100 + 200 + 1)

would have been chosen. When implementing multiple areas, OSPF routers (R2 specifically) prefer intra-area routes to inter-area routes. This accounts for the path X, R5, R1, R2, R4, Y, with a metric of **1402** being chosen.

An interesting exercise would be to perform the previous calculations in the reverse order to prove the path taken from Y to X.

OSPF Metric Configuration

For the purpose of this discussion, the terms *metric* and *cost* are synonymous. The cost associated with an OSPF interface is described by a single dimensionless metric that is determined using the following formula:

cost = reference-bandwidth / bandwidth

with *bandwidth* being the actual interface bandwidth and *reference-bandwidth* being the system-wide reference bandwidth that affects the cost of all OSPF interfaces according to the formula. The *reference-bandwidth*'s default value is 100 Mbps, which you specify as 100000000. It gives a metric of 1 for any bandwidth that is 100 Mbps or greater.

To modify the metric for routes advertised from a particular interface:

```
[edit protocols ospf area area-id interface interface-name]
set metric metric ;
```

To modify the reference bandwidth:

```
[edit protocols ospf]
set reference-bandwidth reference-bandwidth;
```

By default, the loopback interface (lo0) metric is 0. No bandwidth is associated with the loopback interface.

The Complete Reference

Chapter 11

IS-IS

by Hannes Gredler

Accosrding to the ISO 10589[1] specification, "Intermediate system to Intermediate system intra-domain routeing information exchange protocol" is the correct naming for a protocol that people in the IP world simply call IS-IS.

When you first read this specification you might think that there is too much emphasis on the wording and not enough on technical content. Do not be misled. IS-IS is a fine protocol, and once you learn the art of *not* reading all paragraphs of the ISO specs, you will find it to be a lean, simple, but powerful protocol.

You do not need to grasp the sometimes arcane ISO speak of ISO standards on your own. In this chapter, you will acquire an understanding of the protocol, how it routes IP, and its implementation in JUNOS software.

Introduction and Historical Background

In Chapter 9 you learned about OSPF. Now you are about to learn IS-IS, another link-state IGP. Why bother having another link-state IGP for routing TCP/IP, especially if it is so similar to OSPF? On first sight, supporting both OSPF and IS-IS seems to be a double effort. Only by looking back in history can you understand why IS-IS has its place in today's Internet.

History of IS-IS

Using either the OSPF or IS-IS standards as a cookbook for implementations of those protocols produces a naïve implementation at best. For carrier-class implementations, such an approach leads to failure. Years of real-world engineering experience are required to create true carrier-class implementations of IGPs, as the following account illustrates.

In 1987 IS-IS, large parts of which are based on DECnet Phase V, was selected by ANSI as the Open Systems Interconnection (OSI) intradomain protocol. This first version of IS-IS was designed purely to route the *Connectionless Network Protocol* (CLNP), the network layer protocol of the OSI suite.

In 1988, when the NSFnet was commissioned and deployed, the first IGP was an IS-IS clone (see RFC 1074[2] for details) developed by Dr. Yakov Rekhter. This clone gave the operators of NSFnet their first experience with the sometimes-catastrophic dynamics of link-state protocols and the resulting network-wide meltdowns. Dr. Rekhter, now a Distinguished Engineer with Juniper Networks, relates the following story:

---

[1] ISO, "Intermediate system to Intermediate system routing information exchange protocol for use in conjunction with the Protocol for providing the Connectionless-mode Network Service (ISO 8473)," ISO/IEC 10589:1992

[2] Y. Rekhter, "The NSFnet Backbone SPF–Based Interior Gateway Protocol," RFC 1074, October 1988, http://www.ietf.org/rfc/rfc1074.txt.

"One thing that happened in the NSFnet backbone concerns the way my code handled IS-IS link-state updates. When a router received an IS-IS link-state update, the router would do some processing on that update, then flood the update to its neighbors, and then complete the rest of the processing on this update. Due to some bug in the code the last part ("the rest of the processing") caused router crash; but since the router crashed *after* it flooded the link-state update to its neighbors, the update also caused the neighbors to crash as well, resulting in the overall network meltdown."

Such bad experiences proved a good education for the early implementers, and their knowledge of how *not* to do things helped to create better implementations in the second run. Dave Katz, another Juniper Networks software engineer whose experience goes back to the infancy of link-state protocols, expresses that experience succinctly: "Link-state protocols are hard."

In 1988 the then-young IETF began work on a replacement for RIP, which was proving insufficient for large networks. The resulting protocol was OSPF, much of which was based on experience with IS-IS. In turn, some OSPF enhancements have been fed back into IS-IS.

By 1989 OSPFv1 was published; Proteon was the first vendor to ship OSPF in its routers. Controversy raged within the IETF concerning whether to adopt IS-IS or OSPF as the endorsed IGP. A fear that the working and deployed TCP/IP protocol suite would soon be replaced with the more complex OSI protocol suite aroused strong emotions in the discussions. At one IETF meeting there was bickering and shouting, and even a T-shirt distributed displaying the equation "IS-IS = 0."

It is typical for the decision process in the IETF that if no consensus on a debate can be reached, the mantra "let the market decide" is followed, so the IETF declared both OSPF and IS-IS to be equal. In fact this was not entirely true, as there was some soft pressure to give OSPF precedence. Hence people often say, "IS-IS and OSPF are equal, with OSPF being somewhat *more* equal."

In 1990 IS-IS became "IP-aware" with the publication of RFC 1195,[3] which describes extensions for *integrated* IS-IS, which can both transport CLNP and IP routes. OSPFv2 was published that same year. Cisco Systems began shipping routers with both OSPF and CLNP-only IS-IS, and soon after began supporting integrated IS-IS.

Novell published *Netware Link Services Protocol* (NLSP), an IS-IS clone with extensions to transport IPX reachability information, in 1993.

Both the IP and the NSLP extensions demonstrate the flexibility built into IS-IS from day one. Adding another protocol family such as IP or NLSP is just a matter of adding a few hundred lines of code, rather than having to rewrite the entire code base.

---

[3]   R. Callon, "Use of OSI IS-IS for Routing in TCP/IP and Dual Environments," RFC 1195, December 1990, http://www.ietf.org/rfc/rfc1195.txt.

Such extensibility is again showing its usefulness as demand for support of IPv6 grows. While making OSPF capable of transporting IPv6 means transitioning to a completely new and unproven code, IS-IS requires only extensions to the existing code.

Based on increasing demand from customers, Cisco Systems began shipping NLSP in 1994. Because NLSP and IS-IS are so similar, Cisco engineering decided to do some internal code housekeeping and to rewrite the IS-IS code.

ISPs as we know them today began springing up around the same time. Many of those early national backbones chose integrated IS-IS as their IGP. Some modern accounts attribute that choice to the United States government's Government Open Systems Interconnection Profile (GOSIP) initiative, which actively advocated the use of OSI. The true motive behind the decision, however, was Cisco's recent code rewrite that made IS-IS more stable than the implementations of OSPF available at the time. What was true then remains true: Stability is paramount when choosing protocols for large-scale networks.

From 1995 to 1998 the popularity of IS-IS within the ISP niche continued to grow, and some service providers switched to it from OSPF. Even in large link-state areas/levels (400-plus routers) IS-IS proved to be a stable protocol.

From 1999 to today most of the IP extensions are done within the IETF, not ITU-T committees. Most of the IS-IS base protocol is still maintained in ITU-T, but little has changed in the past decade. The IS-IS working group inside the IETF (see www.ietf.org/html.charters/isis-charter.html) maintains the further development of IS-IS. Most IETF work is typically carried out in the form of mailing lists. There is a small set of individuals from both vendors and ISPs interested in the further evolvement of IS-IS. Because the community is so small, consensus is reached very fast and the standardization process itself is often just a matter of documenting the existing behavior that has been deployed in the field.

Just as many early ISPs chose IS-IS because it was stable earlier than OSPF, IS-IS still tends to support new features earlier than OSPF. Within recent years extensions such as traffic engineering, IPv6, and multiple topology TLVs (Type/Length/Value) have been first specified and shipped for the more easily extended IS-IS. The OSPF extensions follow, if ever, usually several months later.

Sample Network

To better illustrate the sometimes complex explanations around the IS-IS routing protocol, the topology shown in Figure 11-1 is used throughout this chapter. The sample topology is a simple ISP network consisting of a set of core routers surrounded by regional access routers. The topology is segmented into areas, similar to the way OSPF topologies are segmented into areas. In IS-IS terminology, however, the areas are called *levels*. All the subsequent examples contain explanations, graphics, and code snippets based on the sample topology of Figure 11-1.

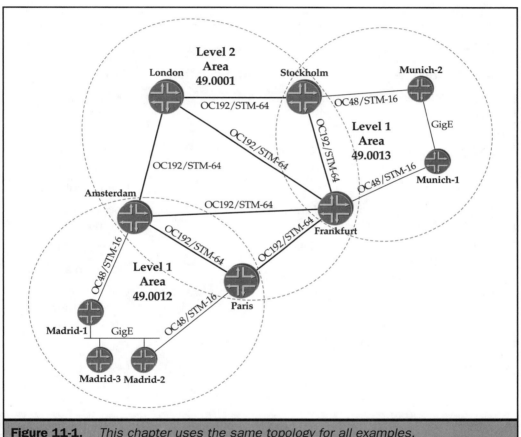

Figure 11-1.   *This chapter uses the same topology for all examples.*

IS-IS Terminology

IS-IS uses a different terminology than the IP world does. Table 11-1 provides a quick reference to make the subsequent paragraphs more readable, contrasting IS-IS terms with their functional equivalents in the IP and OSPF world. Note that some of these comparisons are not 100 percent accurate, but are there for better illustration purposes.

IS-IS/OSI		OSPF/IP	
Abbreviation	**Term**	**Abbreviation**	**Term**
DIS	Designated Intermediate System	DR	OSPF Designated Router
SNPA	Sub Network Point of Attachment		MAC Address
sys-ID	System ID		OSPF Router-ID
NET	Network Entity Title		Loopback IP Address
NSEL	Network Selector		IP Protocol ID
L2	Level 2		OSPF Area 0
L1	Level 1		OSPF Not-So-Stubby Area (NSSA)
PDU	Protocol Data Unit		Packet
CSNP	Complete Sequence Number PDU		OSPF DD exchange mechanism
PSNP	Partial Sequence Number PDU		OSPF DD exchange mechanism
TLV	Type/Length/ Value Triplet	LSA	Link-State Advertisement
	Hello Timer		Hello Timer

Table 11-1.   *IS-IS Terms and the OSPF Equivalents*

IS-IS/OSI		OSPF/IP	
Abbreviation	**Term**	**Abbreviation**	**Term**
	Hold Timer		Dead Timer
	Pseudonode		Type-2 LSA
LSP	Link-State PDU		The sum of all LSAs

Table 11-1.   *IS-IS Terms and the OSPF Equivalents* (continued)

Link-State Protocol Fundamentals and Introduction to IS-IS

Link-state routing protocols are very popular and are found in many technical disciplines. Among the network routing protocols, IS-IS, OSPF, and PNNI are the most popular ones. Many vendors' proprietary implementations of routing and signaling protocols found in such technologies as SONET/SDH, frame relay, and ATM products are based on link-state concepts.

Some similarities are shared within the family of link-state protocols. You have already read about link-state basics in Chapter 9. This section reviews those basics, but from the viewpoint of IS-IS.

IS-IS shares several similarities with OSPF, such as

- Distribution of information by flooding, aging, and reflooding link-state packets
- Hierarchical routing
- Pseudonodes and designated routers on broadcast LANs
- SPF-based route calculation

In the next four sections, all these similarities, as well as properties unique to the IS-IS protocol, are discussed.

Distribution by Flooding, Aging, and Reflooding

Link-state protocols use a number of techniques to send and receive topological information in a controlled way. This section briefly covers these mechanisms.

Distributed Databases and Local Computation

Link-state protocols are based on a simple principle called distributed databases and local computation. Distributed databases means that each node in a network has all the information it needs for computing optimal routes. Local computation means that one node independently computes the routes that it determines as best. This principle is in contrast to routing protocols such as RIP, BGP, and IEEE spanning tree, where the process to discover best routes has to go through various transient stages in the network.

You can imagine a distributed topological database as a collection of fragments of a big jigsaw puzzle, as shown in Figure 11-2. Every node in the topology contributes a small piece to the puzzle. It does so by announcing to all its directly connected neighbors that there is a bidirectional *possibility* for exchanging traffic, and the preference associated with the link between them for forwarding traffic. This preference is typically a dimensionless scalar, indirectly proportional to the delay or bandwidth of the respective link. In IS-IS the scalar is called the *metric*; in OSPF it is called *cost*. In other link-state protocols, such as ATM's PNNI, the term *administrative weight* is used as well.

Typically the metrics of a link are symmetrical, such as Paris-London=5, London-Paris=5. It might be, however, that for reducing the load on a congested link, the metric is set artificially higher, thus expressing a depreference for forwarding traffic. In Figure 11-2, for example, the metric of the Frankfurt-Stockholm link is 20. This early form of traffic engineering is almost obsolete due to the availability of much more powerful tools such as MPLS. Chapter 15 presents the basics of MPLS and traffic engineering.

The pieces of the entire puzzle are distributed and accumulated, so that each node has all the puzzle-pieces. The nodes store the distributed puzzle-pieces in a database.

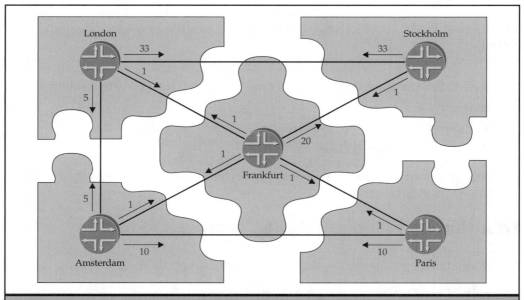

Figure 11-2.   *A distributed link-state database can be thought of as a jigsaw puzzle describing a network topology.*

Using this distributed database, each node independently and locally runs some sort of graph algorithm to compute a loop-free path to each node. In IS-IS, as in OSPF, that graph algorithm is called a *Dijkstra* or *SPF* algorithm. The IP routing paradigm is often described as *hop-by-hop routing*. This means that routes are calculated in such a way that each node on a path contributes to transporting a packet one router-hop closer to the final destination. Hop-by-hop routing requires each node to run the same route calculation process. In large link-state domains, other graph algorithms, such as the dual spanning trees discussed on the IETF IS-IS working group mailing list, can theoretically be used as well, as long as each node shares one common route-calculation algorithm. Today virtually all implementations of the IS-IS protocol use the SPF algorithm.

Sequence Numbers and LSP Aging

The previous section explained that the topological puzzle-pieces are distributed throughout the link-state network. In IS-IS, these puzzle-pieces of information are called *link-state PDUs* (LSPs). This section focuses on how LSPs are distributed. Given the sample topology, imagine that the link between London and Stockholm breaks (Figure 11-3).

The LSPs contain a version field, which tells the other nodes in the network that a more recent LSP is available, and to disregard previous ones. In IS-IS, as in OSPF, this version field is a 32-bit entity called the *sequence number*.

In the topology break example, both the London and the Stockholm nodes must reissue information about all their bidirectional links to their neighbors associated with

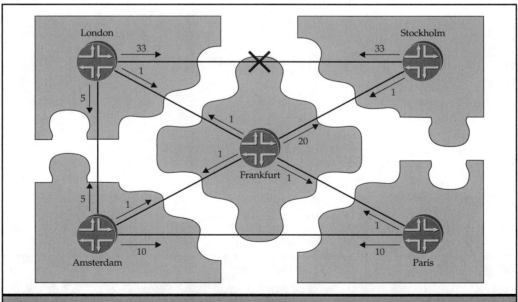

Figure 11-3. *A topology break occurs between London and Stockholm.*

some metric (or preference) and increment their sequence number by one. This causes all the other hops to disregard previous versions of the announcement.

IS-IS starts at a sequence number of 1 and stops at the sequence number 2^32-1, which is roughly above 4.2 billion. Because this space contains only positive numbers, in C-programming language it is called an *unsigned integer*. This is contrary to OSPF, which distributes its sequence numbers in a *signed integer* format in which half of the numbers are positive and half of the numbers are negative.

OSPF sequence numbers range from 0x80000001h in hex notation (this is –2.1 billion in decimal notation) for the oldest to 0x7FFFFFFFh (+2.1 billion) for the highest. Both sequence spaces are illustrated in Figure 11-4.

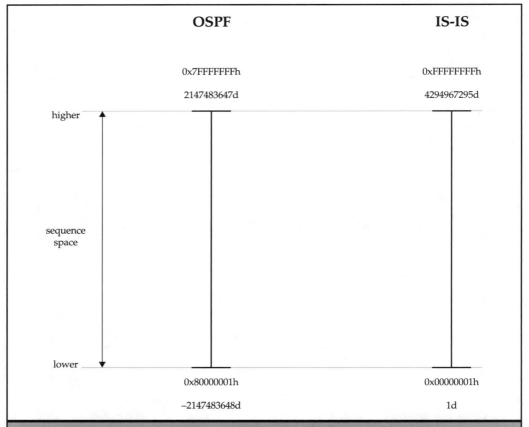

Figure 11-4.   *In this OSPF and IS-IS sequence number comparison, IS-IS is using an unsigned 32-bit space, and OSPF is using a signed 32-bit space.*

Understanding the unsigned integer issue is important because when you start debugging the LSPs in a link-state database you must know whether a lower number means *older* or *newer;* therefore, you need to know the structure of the sequence space.

Flooding

Link-state protocols such as OSPF and IS-IS distribute their information by a simple but robust algorithm called *flooding.* Flooding means that a packet is forwarded on all links except the one it was received from; however, unless the network knows when to stop flooding, a flooding storm can occur in which information loops endlessly. Sequence numbers are again useful here.

On receipt of a known LSP—that is, a copy of an LSP that is already in the link-state database—a router looks first at its sequence number. If the sequence number is higher than the sequence number of the LSP in the database, then this is an update LSP and hence the packet is reflooded on all interfaces of a given level, except the one on it has been received. The same procedure applies if the LSP is new; then the LSP is installed in the link-state database and reflooded as well.

Flooding Example   Using the sample topology shown in Figure 11-1, suppose that the link between Amsterdam and Paris is broken. Both Amsterdam and Paris re-advertise a new version of their LSP, both declaring their connection to the respective remote router being down. Figure 11-5 shows the chain of events that distributes the bad news.

As you can see there are plenty of lines where a router receiving an LSP already knows the updated LSP. This is one of the unwanted side effects of flooding. The denser the mesh between the routers gets the more excess LSP updates are flying around. The worst-case scenario is a full mesh, in which a single link failure can cause up to N^3 LSP updates. A single router failure can even cause N^4 LSP updates. Because link-state protocols scale badly in full mesh environments, dense-mesh and full-mesh topologies should generally be avoided. Sometimes, however, you cannot get around the full-mesh topology problem.

Think of an ISP that does not have its own infrastructure and has to buy transit service over a carrier's ATM or frame relay mesh. Figure 11-6 shows a typical such *overlay* network. There are ATM switches as core devices, which interconnect the carrier's six Points of Presence (POPs). There is a pair of core routers located on each POP.

Each POP is connected with every other POP forming a logical full-mesh topology. For a better visibility, in Figure 11-6 you can see only the logical connections from one of the Sunnyvale-based routers to the rest of the routers in the network.

Loosening the full-mesh and forming a partial mesh does not help, because optimal (shortest path) routing within the cloud is desired.

Fortunately there is a way out of this dilemma. All you need to do is tell the router about any links on which reflooding would be redundant because of the high likelihood the remote router will get the update from other sources. In fact several links from the flooding tree get pruned to avoid the excess LSP updates. In the sample topology of Figure 11-1, pruning the flooding on the links between Frankfurt and London and between Frankfurt and Amsterdam avoids all the unnecessary reflooding and still

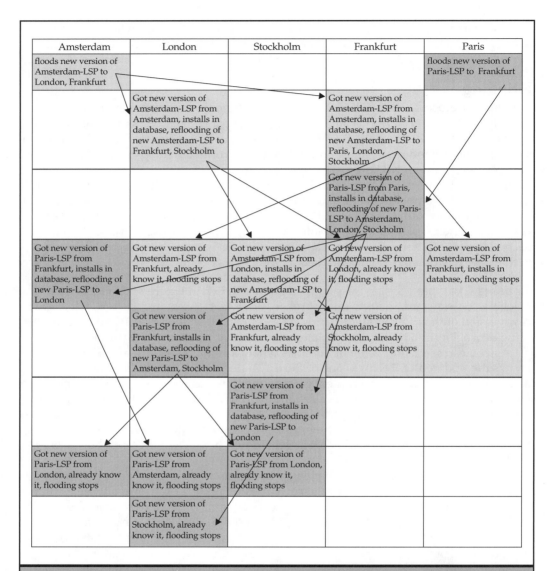

Figure 11-5. Amsterdam and Paris begin LSP flooding when the link between them breaks

provides enough robustness to overcome a single link failure. Note that the sample topology does not need this optimization because flooding is doing no harm; however, the closer you get to a full mesh and the bigger the number of routers gets, the more severe the flooding load becomes.

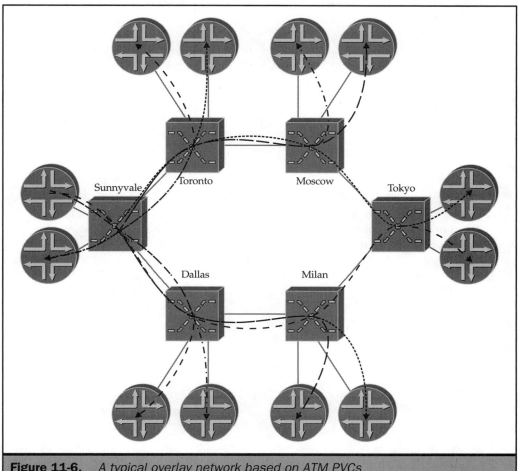

Figure 11-6. *A typical overlay network based on ATM PVCs*

The pruning of flooding links is done using *mesh groups*. You can configure mesh groups by setting the `mesh-group blocked` statement in the `protocols isis` interface section:

```
hannes@Frankfurt> show configuration
protocols {
    isis {
        interface so-7/0/0.0 {
            level 2 {
```

```
                    te-metric 2000;
          }
        interface so-7/0/0.0 {
            mesh-group blocked;
            level 2 {
                te-metric 3000;
            }
        }
     }
}
```

The designers of IS-IS were also very cautious about the pacing of LSPs. In Figure 11-5 you can see that even in simple topologies two or more LSPs have to be sent subsequently out a given interface. If an implementation does not carefully pace the flooding of its LSPs then there might be a risk of overrunning the receiver(s).

Consequently, JUNOS software has a configurable LSP *interval timer* that defaults to 100ms. This timer controls the interval between two consecutive LSP PDUs. You can modify the LSP interval under the `protocols isis interface` statement:

```
hannes@Paris> show configuration
[ ... ]
protocols {
    isis {
        interface so-7/0/0.0 {
            lsp-interval 200;
        }
    }
}
[ ... ]
```

Synchronizing Databases

Chapter 9 discusses link-state adjacencies, which are formed between two neighbors when their link-state databases are synchronized. Much of OSPF's complexity comes from its database synchronization, which uses a heavyweight database description (DD) exchange protocol to synchronize databases. The DD protocol maintains a lot of internal state, and is hence inherently complex. In contrast, IS-IS uses an almost stateless algorithm that maintains little overhead for each LSP transmitted on a given link.

IS-IS has two different mechanisms to synchronize databases. The mechanism used depends on the physical link, which falls into one of two categories:

- Point-to-Point (P2P) circuits
- Broadcast circuits

Synchronizing Databases on P2P Links   The IS-IS vehicle that makes updates to the link-state database reliable on P2P links is called *Partial Sequence Number PDUs* (PSNPs). A PSNP is an envelope for a *link-state-PDU-ID* (LSP-ID) augmented with the following information:

- Sequence number (version information)
- Checksum
- Remaining lifetime

Given the example topology, imagine one of Amsterdam's links goes down and Amsterdam has to send a new version of its LSP. It floods the new LSP containing its new link-states to all its neighbors once. These event-triggered PDUs are called *one-shot*. This is in contrast to periodic packets, which you will see later. Figure 11-7 shows what happens on the link between Amsterdam and Paris. Paris acknowledges the receipt of the LSP back to Amsterdam by sending a PSNP containing the new sequence number of Amsterdam's recently generated LSP. By reflecting the LSP-ID (not the LSP itself) back to where it came from, Amsterdam can clear the LSP from its retransmission list. In ISO speak, "clearing from the retransmission list" is termed "clearing the SRM flag."

If Paris does not acknowledge by sending a PSNP, Amsterdam will reflood the LSP toward Paris after 5 seconds.

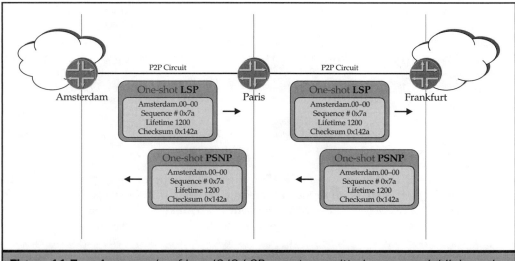

Figure 11-7.   *An example of how IS-IS LSPs are transmitted over a serial link, and how PSNPs help make the update reliable*

Once the LSP is received and checked by Paris, it is flooded to all circuits on which Paris has adjacencies in the same level. Now the same cycle starts again. Figure 11-6 shows the resulting flooding behavior between Paris and Frankfurt.

Synchronizing Databases on Broadcast LAN Links   On broadcast LANs there is no explicit acknowledgement of LSPs transmitted to that LAN. The designers of IS-IS feared the acknowledgement load generated by all receiving routers on the LAN could hurt the transmitter of that LSP. With advances of CPU processing power for modern route processors, this historical issue has become a nonissue nowadays.

So how does IS-IS ensure on broadcast links that every speaker on the LAN gets his copy of the updated LSP?

As described in Figure 11-8, IS-IS periodically transmits all the LSP-IDs (again, not the LSPs themselves), sequence numbers, remaining lifetimes, and checksums in *Complete Sequence Number PDUs* (CSNPs) at periodic intervals. In JUNOS the CSNP interval defaults to 10 seconds. Each speaker on the LAN compares its own link-state database against the information broadcasted by the router sending the CSNP. If in the CSNP a newer LSP version is detected, the router requests a "personal" copy of that LSP via a PSNP.

Imagine in this example that Madrid-3 gets disconnected, and is missing the update that Madrid-1 is getting from Amsterdam and transmitting to the LAN. Madrid-3 then becomes connected again. As Madrid-3 is receiving the CSNP it sees that the Amsterdam 00-00 LSP-ID has a higher sequence number (0x79) than its last copy, which is 0x78; therefore, Madrid-3 sends a PSNP back to Madrid-1, containing Amsterdam's LSP-ID, the old sequence number (0x78), plus its lifetime and checksums. Madrid-1 in turn refloods Amsterdam's most recent LSP to the LAN. The new LSP (sequence number 0x79) will not be flooded beyond one of the synchronized routers on that LAN. A router floods an LSP further only if the sequence number indicates a more recent version of that LSP. Once the LSP with sequence number 0x79 is flooded on the LAN the databases are again synchronized.

Note that CSNPs are not exclusively used on broadcast LANs. In two cases they are also used on P2P links:

- Initial database synchronization for a new adjacency
- Periodic synchronization for better robustness

ISO 10589 does mention to send a CSNP for synchronization on adjacency formation and it leaves it completely open to the implementer to send additional CSNPs for further synchronization if needed. The use of mesh groups can make the link-state database to become desynchronized if the "wrong" links of the flooding topology are pruned.

JUNOS software uses an interesting scheme for tackling desynchronized databases on P2P links. It first determines all P2P interfaces where it has an adjacency in the *up*

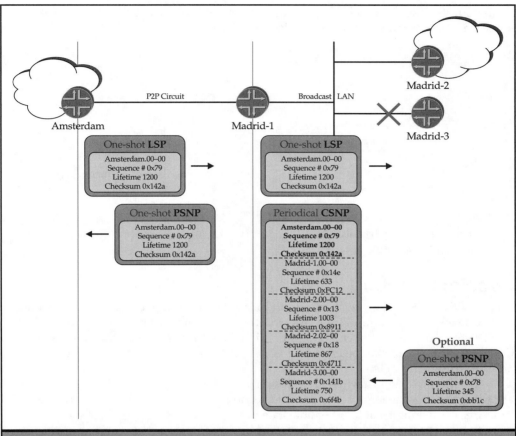

Figure 11-8. *Router Madrid-1 broadcasts a CSNP, which contains a description of all known LSPs, to the local LAN every 10 seconds.*

state and multiplies this number by 5 seconds. This timer is jittered by 25 percent and is used on all interfaces to send periodic CSNPs. The computational load for sending at average one CSNP each 5 seconds is eating up less than 0.1 percent of CPU cycles given link-state databases that hold hundreds of entries. Sending periodic CSNPs at a rate that decreases with the amount of interfaces IS-IS runs upon, provides good link-state database synchronization at almost zero cost. This behavior cannot be turned off and due to the open nature of ISO 10589 has no reported interoperability issues.

If your IS-IS domain is carrying a large number of LSPs you can lower the broadcast stress on a LAN by modifying the CSNP interval:

```
hannes@Madrid-1> show configuration
[ ... ]
protocols {
    isis {
        interface ge-4/3/0.0 {
            csnp-interval 30;
        }
    }
}
[ ... ]
```

You can also totally disable CSNP generation on a given interface by setting the csnp-interval to "disable."

Hierarchical Routing

Both OSPF and IS-IS use areas to support hierarchical routing. OSPF uses a backbone and nonbackbone areas, and IS-IS uses multiple *levels.* According to the base spec ISO 10589 there are two levels (Levels 1 and 2). Level 2 is the functional equivalent to OSPF area 0 (= the backbone area) and Level 1 is the functional equivalent to an OSPF *not-so-stubby-area* (NSSA).

The reason why link-state protocol designers decided to split the link-state domain in areas was the fear that large domains could consume too many CPU cycles during an SPF run. Areas also limit the amount of link-state propagation. For large parts of your network it might be uninteresting to know that a small access router is not available anymore.

In Figure 11-9 there are three areas. Area 49.0001 is at Level 2 and areas 49.0012 and 49.0013 are at Level 1. All the topological information stays within an area. It is, therefore, impossible for area 49.0012 or 49.0013 to "see" who is connected with whom in area 49.0001. The only information that is leaked through is prefix information, or as link-state protocol experts call it, *leaf information.* This terminology comes from the real-world analogy that links between nodes (routers) span a tree, and leaves (prefixes) are attached to these trees.

Figure 11-9 shows the prefix 172.16/16 is leaked from Level 1 up to Level 2. From the Level 2 router's perspective, the L1L2 router (ID 0000.0000.00005) becomes the new originator of the prefix.

Note that once prefix information is passed up to the backbone (Level 2 area), the prefix information always gets a different originator, because the routers in the backbone do not know how to reach the original originator.

The router between the Level 1 and the Level 2 is called an L1L2 router. This router makes the translation of the link-state information to the backbone by replacing the

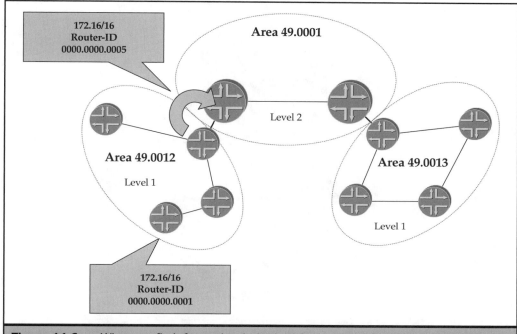

Figure 11-9.   When prefix information is leaked from L1 to L2, L2 routers see the
L1L2 router as the originator.

originating router's LSP-ID or router-ID with its own. In our example a router with the
IS-IS router-ID 0000.0000.0001 originates a prefix 172.16/16. The L1L2 router reoriginates
this information in its Level 2 link-state information and sets itself as the originator
(router-ID 0000.0000.0005) of the prefix.

Route Leakage

The process of passing Level 1 prefixes up to Level 2 is called *route-leakage*. By default
IS-IS passes all its Level 1 prefixes up to the Level 2. RFC 1195 strictly forbids leakage
of routes in the opposite direction, from Level 2 to Level 1. The reason for this is that
there is no way of marking a *passed-down* route as being *passed-down*. In Figure 11-10
you can see what can happen without that rule:

- London, which is at Level 2, generates prefix 10/8.
- Frankfurt leaks 10/8 down to Level 1.
- The prefix gets flooded inside the Level 1.
- Stockholm leaks 10/8 up to the Level 2.

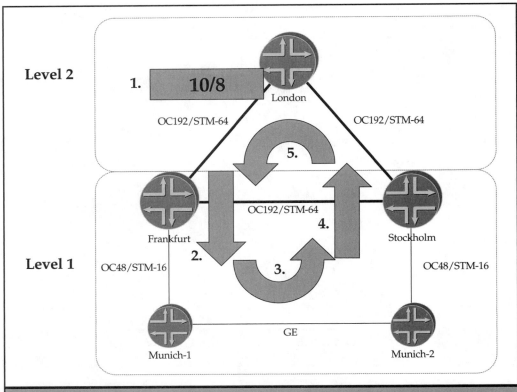

Figure 11-10. *A routing loop generated via unconditionally leaking prefixes between Level 1 and Level 2*

For some reason the link between Frankfurt and Stockholm has a lower IGP cost. The result is a persistent forwarding loop.

RFC 2966[4] defines an additional bit called the *up/down bit* to mark prefixes that have been passed down from the Level 2. It also permits *external* routes (routes from another routing protocol) to be injected at Level 1, overriding the explicit prohibition in RFC 1195 of the injection of external information at Level 1. By generating and honoring the up/down bit no routing loops can occur between levels.

A Level 1 area with a conformant RFC 2966 behavior shares properties that are similar to those of an OSPF NSSA area.

---

[4]   T. Li, T. Przygienda, H. Smit, "Domain-Wide Prefix Distribution with Two-Level IS-IS," RFC 2966, October 2000, http://www.ietf.org/rfc/rfc2966.txt.

Levels, Areas, and Demarcation Lines

In OSPF the most loaded routers in a network are typically the *area border routers* (ABRs). The reason for the heavy loads is that an ABR must maintain a copy of the link-state database of every area it is connected to. Together with the way OSPF leaks prefixes between areas, which is by default full leakage, these multiple databases are a major scalability liability. All the critical resources of a router such as CPU and memory are used N times, where N is the number of areas a router is connected to. IS-IS has only two link-state databases, one for the Level 1 and one for the Level 2. Although you can imagine the Level 2 area as OSPF area 0 and the Level 1 area as a nonzero OSPF area, there are small but significant differences between levels and areas.

On the left side of Figure 11-11 you can see an ABR that interconnects area 51 and area 52 to the backbone. This router has a dedicated link-state database for each of its three attached areas. The demarcation line between the areas is inside the router. The demarcation between the backbone and nonbackbone areas is inside the router as well.

On the right side of Figure 11-10 you can see an IS-IS L1L2 router, which connects the Level 1 area to the Level 2 area. In IS-IS speak, area 49.0012 is *attached*. The demarcation line between the areas is clearly outside the router; more precisely, the demarcation line is on the link. The L1L2 router is in area 49.0012, and the demarcation line between the Level 1 and the Level 2 is inside the router; therefore, it maintains only one link-state database for each level.

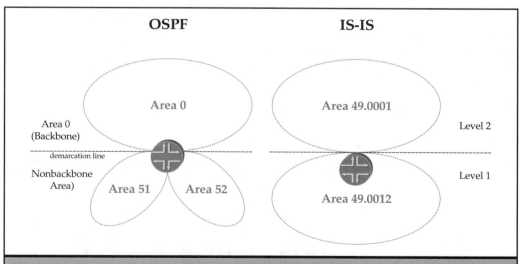

Figure 11-11. *The OSPF demarcation line between different areas is inside the router; the IS-IS demarcation line between levels is on the link.*

Repairing Partitioned Backbones

ISO 10589 states that IS-IS routers should support partitioning repair. Partition repair means that if some Level q becomes partitioned (loses connectivity) and there is a physical path through a Level 2 area, the L1L2 routers can establish a "healing" link to bandage such a breakdown. In OSPF this functionality is known as a virtual link, where an ABR can establish a healing link throughout a nonzero area. If you have experience with OSPF virtual links you know that they are a sure way to mess up your network, because the flooding topology becomes different than the physical topology. Because of this additional level of complexity their use should generally be avoided.

Most implementers read the keyword "should" in any spec as "can be ignored." So it is with IS-IS. The partition repair functionality is not supported either in JUNOS or in the majority of IS-IS implementations used for routing in the Internet. The pragmatic design rule to follow is:

"Never let your Level 1 area become partitioned."

Pseudonodes and Designated Routers on Broadcast LANs

When IS-IS was designed back in the late 80s the original authors were very cautious about its scalability in large LAN environments. There was some fear that a large number of IS-IS speakers on broadcast LANs could represent too much overhead in the IS-IS database.

If each router were to report all the other routers it sees on a broadcast LAN then the amount of adjacencies to be modeled in the link-state database would grow by $(n*n - 1)/2$. In Figure 11-12 you can see that even on a small LAN many P2P relationships exist. This simple example with six speakers on a LAN results in 15 adjacencies to maintain within the link-state database. Forty IS-IS speakers on the LAN results in 40 $(40 - 1)/2 = 780$ router-to-router relationships. The amount of information that each IS-IS speaker can advertise is limited, and there are some good reasons to avoid that database explosion.

With this scalability problem in mind, the original designers developed the idea that IS-IS speakers on LANs should not report their adjacencies to routers but to their LANs. The problem here is that the LANs are generally dumb, passive devices and cannot speak for themselves, so somebody has to lend the LAN its voice. In IS-IS the router that gives the LAN its voice is the *Designated Intermediate System* (DIS). This LAN that the DIS is speaking for is called the *pseudonode*.

In Figure 11-13 you can see that the DIS on this LAN, Madrid-1, lends its sys-ID to the pseudonode.

In Figure 11-14 you can see how fast the link-state database can grow. At the right end of the diagram are the previously mentioned 40 IS-IS speakers reporting a total amount of 780 adjacencies. The problem of relationship explosion in a full-mesh environment is sometimes called the "N^2 problem."

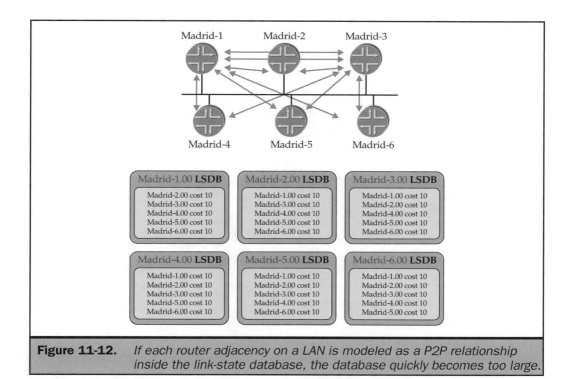

Figure 11-12. *If each router adjacency on a LAN is modeled as a P2P relationship inside the link-state database, the database quickly becomes too large.*

In fact it is not only the pure database size that scared the original authors, but also the associated dynamics that might result. If one node goes down then all (N – 1) speakers must update their LSPs and flood them throughout their area. In a worst-case scenario all routers at the same time detect that there is a problem with one router and flood their LSPs throughout the LAN. These new LSPs are reflooded on all links. Such suboptimal flooding behavior can result in large network-wide churns.

To fix the N^2 problem, link-state protocols use the *pseudonode abstraction*. This results in smaller overall databases (except in the two-speaker case) and in less LSPs to update in case a neighbor goes down.

In general it should also be noted that large numbers of IS-IS speakers on a LAN is in today's designs mostly a corner case. In most network designs there are rarely more than a dozen IS-IS speakers on a single LAN.

There is ongoing work inside the IETF concerning IS-IS behavior on small LANs. draft-shen-isis-ospf-p2p-over-lan-01.txt[5] describes the issues and proposes a fix that

---

[5] "IS-IS Point-to-Point Operation over LAN in Link-State Routing Protocols," draft-shen-isis-ospf-p2p-over-lan-01.txt.

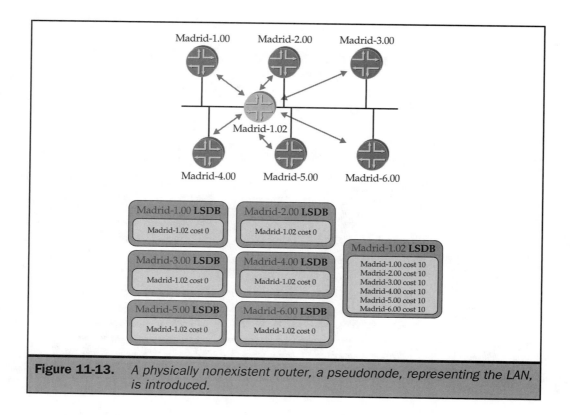

Figure 11-13. *A physically nonexistent router, a pseudonode, representing the LAN, is introduced.*

models P2P Ethernet connections as P2P adjacencies in the link-state database without generation of a pseudonode. Although the savings in CPU cycles are minor (a few microseconds per SPF run, and one less LSP to flood) implementation of this draft will contribute to a more readable link-state database. The only real saving is that an IS-IS router connected with lots of broadcast circuits does not need to allocate a pseudonode-ID per circuit. Pseudonode IDs are limited to 255 per box, because they are only 8 bits wide. Theoretically a pseudonode ID needs to get allocated only once a router becomes DIS on a LAN. This is considered an uninteresting optimization as a router needs to be ready anytime to become DIS on as many as 255 LANs. JUNOS software allocates one pseudonode ID per broadcast circuit, as soon as IS-IS is enabled; thereby not generating the pseudonode is frugal with the limited pseudonode space an IS-IS speaker has.

SPF-Based Route Calculation

IS-IS uses an algorithm called *Dijkstra* (named after the Dutch Mathematician who invented it) to construct loop-free paths. This algorithm is a member of the family of graph algorithms. Its purpose is to find the shortest path between two nodes on a

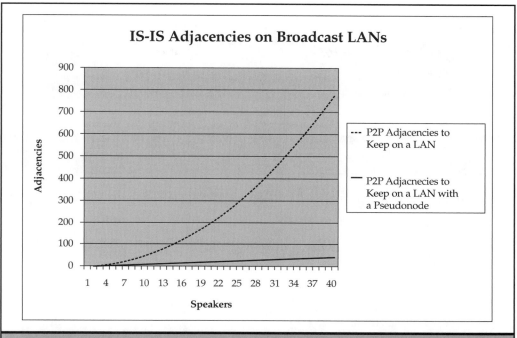

Figure 11-14. *If IS-IS adjacencies were modeled strictly as P2P, the amount of elements in the link-state database would grow exponentially.*

graph and because of that purpose it is also often referred to as a *Shortest Path First* algorithm. As IS-IS and OSPF do share the SPF algorithms for computing routes, see Chapter 9 for a detailed discussion of how an SPF computation works in a step-by-step fashion.

In the preceding sections many similarities between IS-IS and OSPF have been discussed. The following sections focus only on IS-IS.

ISO Addressing

When people begin studying IS-IS, the first pitfall for them is OSI addressing. In time, however, they recognize that IS-IS addressing it is not that complicated, because IS-IS just needs one address per router. Arguably, IP addressing is more complicated because a large core router has many IP addresses to define and to administer. In the subsequent paragraph, only the most common addressing schemes are discussed.

The main difference from IP addressing is that *Network Entity Titles* (NETs), which is the name for OSI subnets, are variable in length.

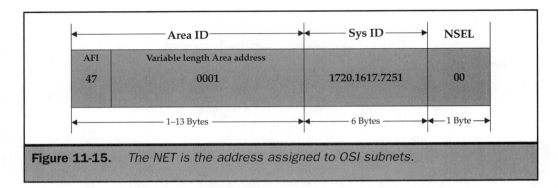

Figure 11-15.   *The NET is the address assigned to OSI subnets.*

Figure 11-15 shows a generalized version of a NET. The NET consists of three parts:

- The area ID
- The system ID
- The NET Selector (NSEL)

Area ID

The area ID is the variable part of the NET and can range from 1 byte to 13 bytes in length. In most deployments area ID sizes of 1, 3, or 5 bytes are used. The content of the first byte tells how to interpret the rest of the area ID. This first byte is called the *Address Family Identifier* (AFI).

The following well-known AFIs are defined:

- 39 DCC (data country code)
- 45 E.164
- 47 ICD (international code designator)
- 49 private-addressing

E.164, DCC, or the ICD addressing schemes are not covered in this chapter because they describe pure delegation schemes either according to a phone-numbering plan (E.164), per country (DCC), or per international organization (ICD). If you want to learn more about AFIs, see the *ATM Forum Addressing User Guide Version 1.0.*[6]

Because selecting an area ID is an AS-local matter, you can pick any of the preceding three or use AFI 49. This AFI has been specially created for purely private addressing. AFI 49 can be thought of as the RFC 1918[7] of OSI addressing. Recall that RFC 1918 delegates the 10/8, 172.16/12, and 192.168/16 prefixes for private use.

---

[6]   ATM Forum Technical Committee, "ATM Forum Addressing: User Guide Version 1.0," AF-RA-0105.000, January 1999, ftp://ftp.atmforum.com/pub/approved-specs/af-ra-0105.000.pdf.

[7]   Y. Rekhter, B. Moskowitz, D. Karrenberg, G. J. de Groot, E. Lear, "Address Allocation for Private Internets," RFC1918, February 1996, http://www.ietf.org/rfc/rfc1918.txt.

System ID

The system ID must be unique in a given area or level. In the IP world there is also demand for uniqueness, such as the router ID that protocols such as BGP and OSPF require for the unique identification of a single router in a network.

One of the oddities of IS-IS is that in ISO 10589 there is support for variable length system IDs; however, no vendor has ever implemented sys-IDs with a length other than 6 bytes. JUNOS software ignores updates from speakers (Hellos and LSPs) with a sys-ID length other than 6 bytes.

It is common practice to encode the 32-bit (4-byte) IP-router-ID into the 48-bit (6-byte) IS-IS system-ID. The encoding scheme is known as *binary coded decimal* (BCD) encoding. Using BCD encoding each decimal digit of an IPv4 address is coded in 4 bits of the IS-IS system ID. In Figure 11-14 you can see the encoding of the 12-digit IP address 172.016.177.251 to an IS-IS system ID of 1720.1617.7251. Note that before doing the conversion, which is simply moving some dots, the second byte (16) is filled up with leading zeros so that each byte is extended to result in three decimal digits.

NSEL

Compared with the IP world, the NSEL is like the protocol field in the IP header, and can further multiplex several subsystems on a given NET. For IS-IS routers the NSEL is always set to zero, meaning "this system."

Examples of ISO Addressing

This section presents four examples of ISO addresses you can use in JUNOS.

```
01.1921.6812.7222.00
```

This first address is the minimalist form of an IS-IS NET, with a total length of 8 bytes. Because the 1-byte NSEL is always 0 and the sys-ID is always 6 bytes, this leaves room for only 1 byte of area-ID, which results in a possible 255 areas. The sys-ID is derived from the IPv4 address 192.168.127.222.

```
49.0001.1921.6824.4192.00
```

This second address is the most commonly deployed format of an ISO NET. It uses the "private" AFI 49 along with a 2-byte area number, which even gives in large IS-IS clouds plenty of room to grow. The sys-ID is derived from the IPv4 address 192.168.244.192.

```
49.0CF8.0001.1720.3120.8001.00
```

If two service providers merge, there might be Level 1 area ID collisions. The second example can be enhanced to make the area ID unique by extending the area ID to 4 bytes and prepending a 2-byte routing domain (ISO speak for AS number) in the form of the 2-byte area number. Note that 0x0cf8 is the hex encoding for ASN 3320. The sys-ID is derived from the IPv4 address 172.31.208.1.

```
47.0005.0000.0000.0000.20ff.0001.0100.5304.4148.00
```

The 20-byte NET is the extreme case of IS-IS addressing. RFC 1237[8] reveals further details about how the space between byte 2 and byte 9 is structured and what the leading 0x0005 represents. Prepended to the system ID is the 2-byte routing domain along with the 2-byte area number. Note that 0x20ff is the hex encoding for ASN 8447. The sys-ID is derived from the IPv4 address 10.53.44.148.

You can configure any of these formats on JUNOS software, by setting the address under the `family iso` statement on *any* interface. Normally the virtual loopback interface lo0 is used.

```
hannes@London> show configuration
[ ...]
interfaces {
    lo0 {
        unit 0 {
            family inet {
                address 172.31.208.1/32;
            }
            family iso {
                address 49.0cf8.0001.1720.3120.8001.00;
            }
        }
    }
}
[ ... ]
```

Fragmentation of Large LSPs

OSPF runs on top of IP, one benefit of which is that if a router has to announce many IP routes and the OSPF packet is bigger than a given medium's *Maximum Transmission Unit* (MTU), and hence needs to be split up, then OSPF simply passes the >MTU byte

---

[8] Richard Colella, Ella Gardner, Ross Callon, "Guidelines for OSI NSAP Allocation in the Internet," RFC 1237, July 1991, http://www.ietf.org/rfc/rfc1237.txt.

packet down the IP stack. OSPF itself does not care about fragmentation because this is a mandatory function built into every IP stack.

For instance if the local OSPF router does generate a 1700-byte packet and it needs to transmit it on an Ethernet circuit having an MTU value of 1500 bytes, the "application" OSPF does not bother as the IP stack itself is handling the fragmentation.

IS-IS runs on top of Layer 2 media such as Ethernet or PPP. At Layer 2 there is no fragmentation and reassembly function, hence IS-IS has to do fragmentation on its own. In IS-IS each LSP has an additional byte to indicate a fragment number, as shown in Figure 11-16.

The fragment IDs are linearly filled up: Fragment 1 is started if fragment 0 is full; fragment 2 is started if fragment 1 is full, and so on. Fragment 0 has a special meaning, as some TLVs (the information carriers in IS-IS), such as the Area TLV #1, are mandatory in fragment 0.

The fragment number is an 8-bit entity and hence 256 fragments are supported, resulting in a "storage-space" of *LSPbuffersize* of 1492*256 = 381,952 bytes of information an individual IS-IS speaker can generate.

This is almost six times the storage space that OSPF offers, although in practice these upper fill-limits are never reached; 42,000–43,000 routes will exhaust the LSP storage space.

The LSPbuffersize is an architectural constant defined in ISO 10589 that makes sure that an IS-IS PDU does not exceed any common media MTU it is running on. To transmit IS-IS packets, JUNOS requires each circuit to have an MTU of at least 1492 bytes.

OSI Model and the IS-IS Stack

Unlike any other IP routing protocol, IS-IS runs natively on its respective link layer. In general there is support for broadcast media and P2P media encapsulation.

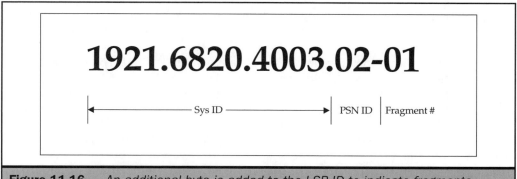

Figure 11-16.   *An additional byte is added to the LSP ID to indicate fragments.*

Broadcast media encapsulation can be one of the following:

- Ethernet
- FDDI*
- Token ring*

Note that the items with an * are not available on Juniper Networks routers.

P2P media encapsulation can be one of the following:

- P2P protocol
- Cisco HDLC
- Frame relay

Unlike OSPF there is no support for Point-to-Multipoint (P2MP) interfaces. If such a topology is desired it has to be modeled using a mesh of P2P links.

For simplicity, only one example is presented for each medium encapsulation type.

IS-IS over Broadcast LAN

The most popular broadcast medium is Ethernet; hence, Ethernet is used to show how an IS-IS packet sits on the network stack.

There are a variety of Ethernet encapsulations. Excluding Novell's proprietary encapsulations there are three common ones:

- 802.3 LLC
- 802.3 Ether type
- 802.3 SNAP

Although there are Ether types for OSI, IS-IS is encapsulated using only 802.3 LLC encapsulation. If an IS-IS implementation from another vendor *would* generate, for example, 802.3 SNAP frames, Juniper Networks routers would drop the update on the incoming interface.

Figure 11-17 shows the Ethernet encapsulation of an IS-IS PDU. You can see that the destination MAC address is either set to the well-known functional address *AllL1ISs* (0180:c200:0014) for Level 1 PDUs and to the well-known functional address *AllL2ISs* (0180:c200:0015) for Level 2 PDUs. ISO 10589 also defines a third well-known functional MAC address called *All-Intermediate-Systems* (0900:2b00:0005), which is not used for router-to-router communication. After the MAC addresses 2 bytes containing the length information of the frame follow. The next 2 bytes are set to 0xFE, the SAP designated for OSI. The 802.2 LLC control field is set to 0x03 indicating that this is unnumbered information. Note that unnumbered information has nothing to do with unnumbered interface addressing. This is just a legacy from the early 802.3 times, when people believed in transport protocols working at the MAC layer. As IS-IS uses

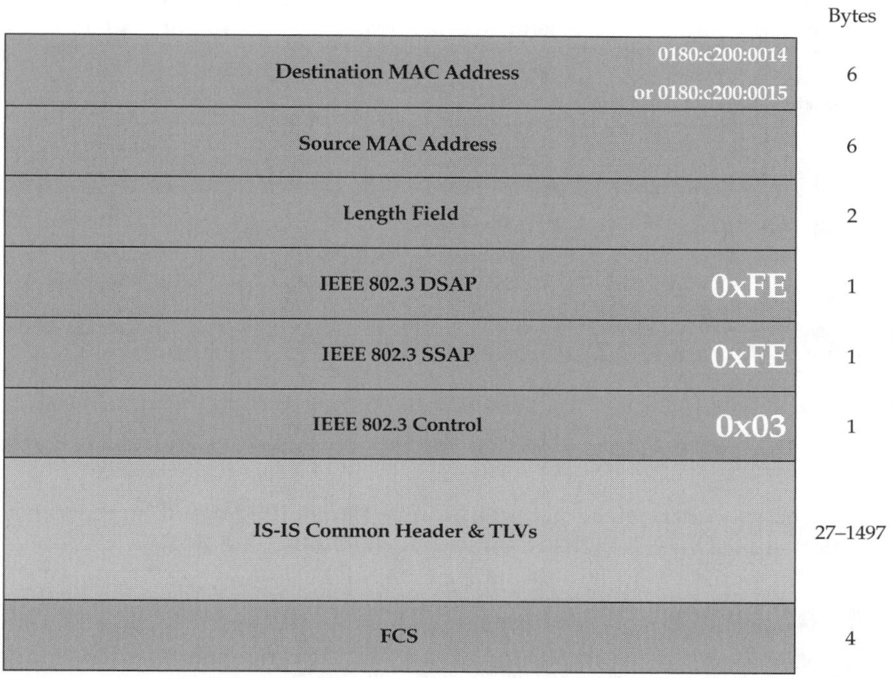

		Bytes
Destination MAC Address	0180:c200:0014 or 0180:c200:0015	6
Source MAC Address		6
Length Field		2
IEEE 802.3 DSAP	0xFE	1
IEEE 802.3 SSAP	0xFE	1
IEEE 802.3 Control	0x03	1
IS-IS Common Header & TLVs		27–1497
FCS		4

Figure 11-17 *IS-IS packets are transmitted over IEEE 802.3 LLC Ethernet.*

CSNPs and PSNPs to reliable transmit routing updates, you do not need an additional transport protocol at the MAC layer, hence setting it to 0x03 turns it off at the MAC layer.

IS-IS over PPP

For each line running the PPP, there is first an exchange of the PPP-LCP (Link Control Protocol, see RFC 1570[9]) that is used for line-specific messages, such as keepalives.

Next, all Layer 2 and Layer 3 protocols (such as IP, IPv6, MPLS, and OSI) that run over PPP first must indicate to the remote end of the P2P link that it is willing to accept frames of the respective network protocol. For each Layer 3 protocol there is a dedicated control protocol to perform that function. These protocols are called *Network Control Protocols* (NCPs). The NCP for OSI is the OSI control protocol over PPP (code point 0x8023) that indicates, once in the *open* state, that both peers are willing to exchange OSI

---

9   W. Simpson, "PPP LCP Extensions," RFC 1570, January 1994, http://www.ietf.org/rfc/rfc1570.txt.

packets. You can check the PPP-LCP and PPP-OSICP state using the `show interface detail` command. In JUNOS CLI output, the term ISO is equivalent to OSI:

```
hannes@Stockholm> show interfaces so-0/0/0 detail
Physical interface: so-0/0/0, Enabled, Physical link is Up
  Interface index: 14, SNMP ifIndex: 23, Generation: 13
  Link-level type: PPP, MTU: 4474, Clocking: Internal, Speed: oc48, Loopback: None, FCS: 32
  Device flags   : Present Running
  Interface flags: Point-To-Point SNMP-Traps
  Link flags     : Keepalives
  Hold-times     : Up 0 ms, Down 0 ms
  Keepalive settings: Interval 10 seconds, Up-count 1, Down-count 3
  Keepalive statistics:
    Input : 43509 (last seen 00:00:02 ago)
    Output: 43508 (last sent 00:00:08 ago)
  LCP state: Opened
  NCP state: inet: Opened, inet6: Not-configured, iso: Opened, mpls: Not-configured
[ ... ]
```

Once the control channel is up, frames can be transmitted based on the structure described in Figure 11-18 with the PPP protocol-ID 0x0023.

IS-IS Packet Types

The most boring part of most networking books is the part containing descriptions of frame formats and packet dumps. Too often the frame formats have been extracted right out of the respective specs and do not add much commentary or illustration for a deeper understanding. Sometimes the reader even gets lost trying to understand where the packet, frame, or message is placed in network stack.

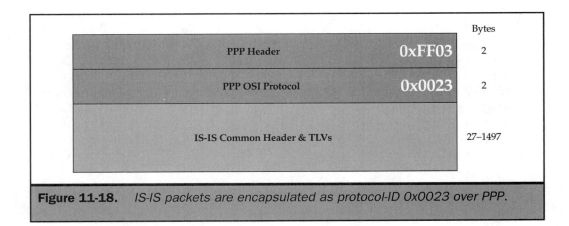

Figure 11-18. *IS-IS packets are encapsulated as protocol-ID 0x0023 over PPP.*

In Figure 11-19 you can see the grayscale that is used throughout this chapter's illustrations. Lighter gray tones indicate a higher-level position inside the IS-IS stack and darker gray tones indicate more proximity towards the Layer 2 protocol.

To keep the decoding engine at the receiver simple, IS-IS shares the common fixed header shown in Figure 11-20 for all its PDUs.

The first field, *Intradomain Routing Protocol Discriminator*, is a constant and is set to 0x83, which tells the OSI stack that IS-IS is inside this packet. Each IS-IS header starts with the first byte set to 0x83; however, looking at the first byte of their network layer can simply identify all packet types found today in ISP backbones:

0x83	IS-IS
0x45-4f	IPv4
0x60-6F	IPv6

Because it is so easy to distinguish between IP and IS-IS packets, there is an Internet draft that proposes skipping the Layer 2 encapsulation entirely. More sophisticated MPLS features of JUNOS such as *LSP as interfaces* make use of this NULL encapsulation, which is described in draft-hsmit-isis-aal5mux-00.txt.[10]

The *Header Length Indicator* is a constant for version 1, set to 8.

Version is a constant, set to 1.

According to the ISO 10589, *ID Length* can be set to a value between 1 and 8. But in all serious implementations for integrated IS-IS this is a constant set to 0, indicating an

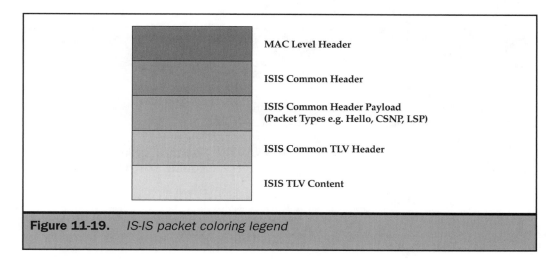

Figure 11-19. *IS-IS packet coloring legend*

---

[10]   H. Smit, draft-hsmit-isis-aal5mux-00.txt, Work in Progress.

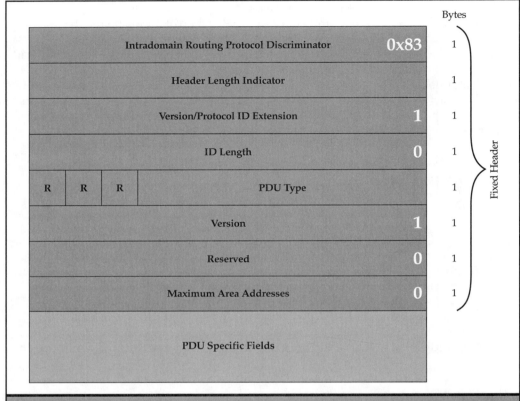

	Bytes
Intradomain Routing Protocol Discriminator **0x83**	1
Header Length Indicator	1
Version/Protocol ID Extension **1**	1
ID Length **0**	1
R R R PDU Type	1
Version **1**	1
Reserved **0**	1
Maximum Area Addresses **0**	1
PDU Specific Fields	

Figure 11-20. *IS-IS fixed header packet format encapsulating nine PDU types*

ID-Length of 6. Making the ID Length 6 bytes (48 bits) makes it handy to derive these IDs from MAC addresses, which are also 6 bytes in size.

PDU Type determines what follows the fixed header. The nine PDU types are defined in Table 11-2. IS-IS would have five general packet types. For most general packet types, however, there exist mutations for Level 1 and Level 2, resulting in 9 PDU types.

IS-IS Hello Packets

IS-IS uses a variety of Hello packet types. There are different Hello packets at each level, because both a Level 1 and a Level 2 adjacency can be formed over a single circuit.

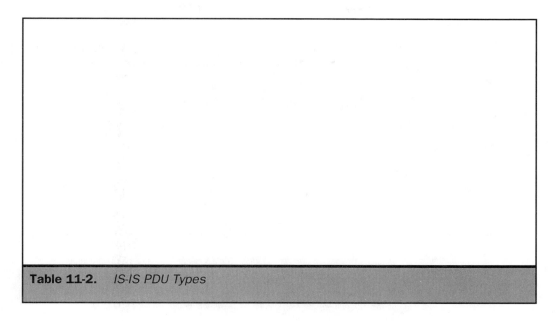

Table 11-2. *IS-IS PDU Types*

Using the `show isis adjacency` command you can see that there is a Level 1 and a Level 2 relationship between Amsterdam and Paris in the sample topology:

```
hannes@Paris> show isis adjacency
IS-IS adjacency database:
Interface         System       L State      Hold (secs) SNPA
so-0/1/0.0        Madrid-2     1 Up                  25
so-6/0/0.0        Frankfurt    2 Up                  18
so-7/0/0.0        Amsterdam    1 Up                   8
so-7/0/0.0        Amsterdam    2 Up                   8
```

Additionally there are different Hello types for LAN, broadcast, and P2P media. If you do the math IS-IS would in theory use 4 different Hello packet types, but this is not the case. The P2P Hellos for Level 1 and Level 2 share the same format, so there are

- LAN Level 2 Hellos
- LAN Level 1 Hellos
- P2P Hellos

The following sections briefly explain these three subtypes.

IS-IS P2P Hellos

Figure 11-21 shows a P2P Hello that is using PDU type #17, prepended by the fixed header.

Circuit Type can be set to one of four bit combinations, shown here in both binary and decimal form:

- 00b/0d, illegal setting—must be discarded
- 01b/1d, Level 1
- 10b/2d, Level 2
- 11b/3d, Levels 1 and 2

Source ID is set to the sys-ID, which is part of the NET.

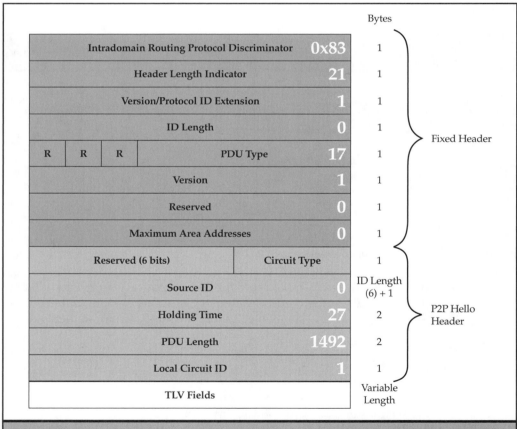

Figure 11-21.   *IS-IS P2P Hello PDU type #17 always has a PDU header length of 21 bytes.*

Holding Time is the time that can pass by before a neighbor is declared down. In JUNOS software the hold time, unless specified otherwise, is 27 seconds for all levels on p2p interfaces.

For LAN interfaces the timer interval depends if the router is the DIS for the LAN or not. JUNOS software does divide the hold timer by 9 to calculate the Hello interval for IIHs. The default value of 27 seconds is divided by 9, resulting in a 3-second Hello timer for the DIS in LAN environments. The dead timer follows a similar scheme. The non-DIS dead-timer is divided by 3, which is 9 seconds. This results in faster detection if the DIS goes down. Although IS-IS has no backup-DIS the re-election is much faster than with OSPF.

Interestingly, in IS-IS, routers on a common LAN may have different timer settings. The concept of individual hold times is much more powerful than a shared dead timer such as OSPF uses. The power is in the flexibility that each IS has to tell its neighbor how long to wait before declaring it dead. Each message (IIH, LSP, SNP) that is received from that IS resets the hold timer to its maximum value. The hold timer starts to count down again until it has reached 0, which ultimately declares the associated neighboring IS as down. OSPF, in contrast, requires all dead timers to be the same on all interfaces and only OSPF-HELLO messages reset the dead-timer.

To detect MTU mismatches, the length of an IS-IS P2P Hello is always 1497 bytes for the first few packets. If a link, such as a SONET DCC subband channel (512 bytes), does not support this MTU, adjacencies simply do not come up because the Hello never gets through. To fill up the 1492 bytes with TLVs there is a special *padding TLV (type 8)*, as shown in Figure 11-22. JUNOS software does *smart padding*, which means all IIHs are padded until an adjacency is up on both sides. Once the adjacency is up, JUNOS software no longer pads IIHs to the full MTU size.

Because the Type and Length fields of the general TLV format are 8-bit entities, the maximum length of the TLV is 255 bytes; therefore an IS-IS router has to place multiple Padding TLVs to fill up to the full MTV (1497 bytes), as shown in Figure 11-23.

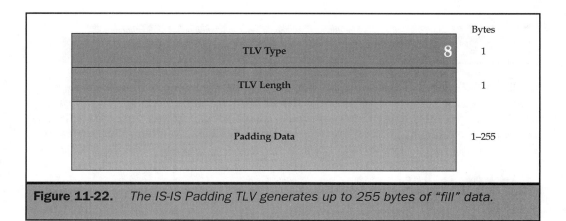

Figure 11-22.   *The IS-IS Padding TLV generates up to 255 bytes of "fill" data.*

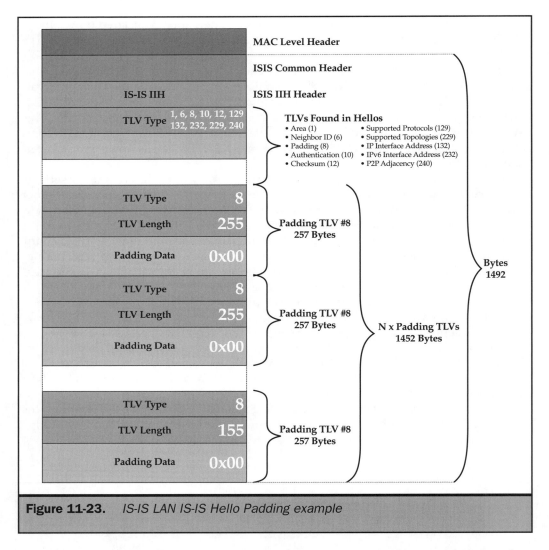

Figure 11-23. *IS-IS LAN IS-IS Hello Padding example*

ISO 10589 says that the local circuit ID is set to a unique number among the sending router's interfaces. These numbers do not need to match between neighboring routers. The local circuit ID has no practical meaning except for debugging purposes. As it has only link-local meaning and no practical purpose, the JUNOS software implementers chose to hard-code it to 0x01.

IS-IS LAN Hellos

LAN Level 1 Hellos are identified in the fixed header as PDU type 15 and are sent to the MAC Level multicast address "AllL1ISs" (01-80-C2-00-00-14). LAN Level 2

Hellos are PDU type 16 and are sent to the MAC Level multicast address "AllL2ISs" (01-80-C2-00-00-15). LAN Hellos are shown in Figure 11-24.

The holding time depends on whether a system is a DIS or not. If the router sending the Hello is not a DIS then the holding time is 27 seconds unless specified otherwise. If the router sending the Hello has been elected as the DIS on a LAN then the holding time is 9 seconds unless specified otherwise. In JUNOS software the correlation between Hellos and DIS Hellos is determined by a constant divisor set to 3 (27s/3 = 9s).

Priority is a 7-bit entity expressing preference for becoming the DIS. The speaker with the highest priority becomes the DIS. In case there are two or more speakers having equal priority the SNPA (MAC address) becomes the tiebreaker. In JUNOS software a priority of 64 is used unless specified otherwise.

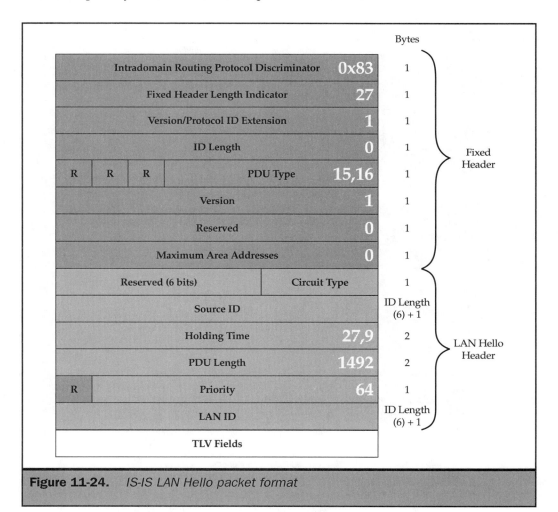

Figure 11-24.   *IS-IS LAN Hello packet format*

The length of the LAN ID is commonly 7 bytes. It is a combination of the sys-ID and the Circuit ID obtained from the LANs DIS for the respective level.

All Ethernet interfaces support an MTU of at least 1500 bytes, which is more than the minimum IS-IS requirement of 1492 bytes (maxLSPbuffersize); therefore, padding on LAN circuits makes no sense at all.

IS-IS Link State PDU

Figure 11-25 shows the LSP header format. Level 1 Link State PDUs use PDU type 18 and are sent to the MAC Level multicast address "AllL1ISs" (01-80-C2-00-00-14). Level 2 Link State PDUs use PDU type 20 and are sent to the MAC Level multicast address "AllL2ISs" (01-80-C2-00-00-15).

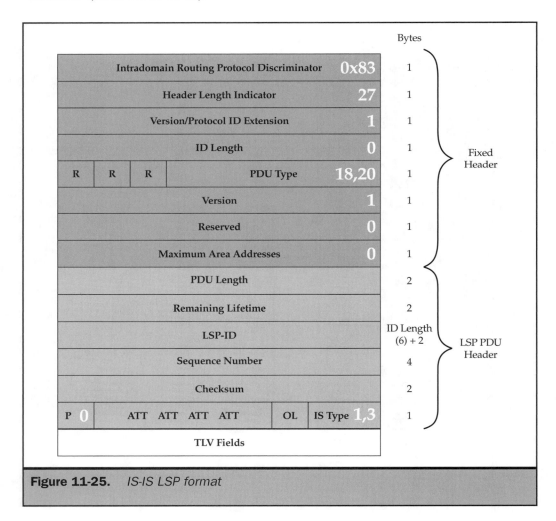

Figure 11-25. *IS-IS LSP format*

PDU length is the length of the entire packet.

Remaining Lifetime is the field that holds the aging mechanism in IS-IS. Initially this is set to 1200 seconds. In JUNOS software you can increase that default up to 65535 seconds using the `protocols isis lsp-lifetime` statement. Doing so causes the router to refresh its LSPs more infrequently and thus reduces the background refresh noise in large networks.

```
hannes@Munich-2> show configuration
[ ... ]
protocols {
    isis {
        level 2 disable;
        lsp-lifetime 65535;
        interface so-0/0/0.0;
        interface ge-0/1/0.0;
    }
[ ... ]
```

LSP ID uniquely identifies the LSP in its respective level. Figure 11-26 shows the structure of the LSP ID. The first 6 bytes identify the System ID of the router originating that LSP. The penultimate byte is called the *Pseudonode ID.* It is set to 0 for nonpseudonodes, and to nonzero for pseudonodes. *Fragment Number* describes which chunk of a fragmented LSP this piece represents. LSPs are fragmented only if all the TLVs do not fit into a single LSPbuffersize (1492 bytes) packet. The dense packaging of TLVs inside an LSP is a JUNOS optimization that ISO10589 does suggest, but does not make mandatory. In modern implementations of Link-state protocols reducing the amount of flooding load is key to scalability. By generating the least fragments possible, JUNOS software thereby does reduce the flooding load.

Sequence Number contains the "version number" of an LSP. Initially this is set to 1 and incremented on subsequent adjacency changes.

Checksum contains a checksum of all the data after the Remaining Lifetime field, computed according to the ITU-T X.233 ("Fletcher checksum") algorithm.

The *Partition Repair* bit is set to 0 on most implementations of IS-IS.

The *ATTach bits* indicate if a system is connected to other areas. It is set separately for all the metric types IS-IS supports; 4 bits are used, expressing if the issuing IS is "attached" to other areas using

- Bit 7, the error metric
- Bit 6, the expense metric
- Bit 5, the delay metric
- Bit 4, the default metric

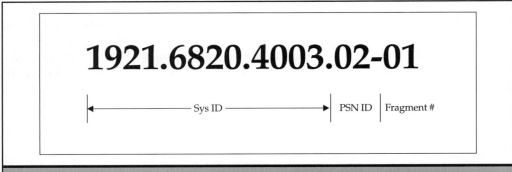

Figure 11-26.   *LSP-ID structure consisting of the sysID, pseudonode number, and fragment number*

Most implementations (including JUNOS) support only the Default metric; therefore, bits 5, 6, and 7 are set to 0. You can verify if the ATT bit is set, using the show isis database command:

```
hannes@Munich-1> show isis database
IS-IS level 1 link-state database:
LSP ID                      Sequence Checksum Lifetime Attributes
Munich-1.00-00                 0x429   0xeb83      832 L1
Munich-2.00-00                 0x428   0x342d     1178 L1
Frankfurt.00-00                0x324   0xfe14      916 L1 L2 Attached
Stockholm.00-00                 0x98   0x80a       438 L1 L2 Attached
  3 LSPs
```

A pure Level 1 router will install a default route towards the closest L1L2 router that has the ATT bit set. This is the default behavior that ISO 10589 and RFC 1195 dictate. In JUNOS software you can turn off this behavior using a configuration knob called ignore-attached-bit, which suppresses installation of the 0/0 (default) route in a given Level 1 router:

```
hannes@Amsterdam> show configuration
[ ... ]
protocols {
    isis {
        ignore-attached-bit;
    [ ... ]
    }
}
```

The *Overload* (OL) bit indicates that the issuing system is facing a temporary overload situation and does not want to be used in any path calculation. The overload could be caused by

■ A memory shortage, in which it cannot hold the entire LSP database and might compute incorrect paths

■ The system running out of fragments

■ An administrative setting

Memory shortage was a concern in the early days of the Internet where CPU horsepower and memory for routers were small. Modern routers are loaded with hundreds of megabytes of memory and have sufficient CPU horsepower (hundreds of MIPS) to afford the storage space even for large IS-IS domains.

A system running out of fragments happens by accident when an administrator unintentionally, due to lack of understanding of routing policy processing, exports a full Internet routing table into IS-IS. IS-IS has in its 256×1492-byte fragments storage for only 42,000–43,000 routes. Once this boundary is crossed and it runs out of fragments it sets the overload bit and hopefully attracts the attention of network administrators that there is something wrong.

Being able to administratively set the OL bit is a nifty feature of IS-IS, which allows an administrator to safely remove a node from the router mesh for doing maintenance tasks. By setting the OL bit in an updated LSP other routers disregard the "administratively overloaded" router for forwarding traffic. If there are other paths this is nondisruptive to your traffic.

Note that disregarding the router applies only for transit traffic. The directly connected subnets are still reachable. This is important, because you must still be able to connect to an overloaded router via SSH or Telnet.

You can verify if one of your routers is out of service by issuing the following command:

```
hannes@Stockholm> show isis database
IS-IS level 1 link-state database:
LSP ID                    Sequence Checksum Lifetime Attributes
Munich-1.00-00               0x429   0xeb83      832 L1 Overload
Munich-2.00-00               0x428   0x342d     1178 L1
Frankfurt.00-00              0x324   0xfe14      916 L1 L2 Attached
Stockholm.00-00               0x98   0x80a       438 L1 L2 Attached
   3 LSPs
```

The overload bit on Munich-1 is set, which means the router may be accessed using Telnet or SSH, and all local segments can be reached, but nonlocal transit traffic avoids the router:

```
hannes@Stockholm> ping 192.168.1.7
PING 192.168.1.7 (192.168.1.7): 56 data bytes
64 bytes from 192.168.1.7: icmp_seq=0 ttl=255 time=0.234 ms
64 bytes from 192.168.1.7: icmp_seq=1 ttl=255 time=0.221 ms
64 bytes from 192.168.1.7: icmp_seq=2 ttl=255 time=0.243 ms
^C
--- 172.16.2.9 ping statistics ---
3 packets transmitted, 3 packets received, 0% packet loss
round-trip min/avg/max/stddev = 0.221/0.232/0.243/0.031 ms
```

IS Type is a 2-bit-wide field that holds two valid values, listed here in both binary and decimal format:

- 00b/0d, unused value
- 01b/1d, Level 1 IS
- 10b/2d, unused value
- 11b/3d, Level 2 IS

Level 2 LSPs are using PDU type 20. IS-IS Level 1 LSPs are sent to the MAC Level multicast address "AllL2ISs" (01-80-C2-00-00-15).

IS-IS PSNP

Figure 11-27 shows the PSNP format. PSNP Level 1 PDUs are using PDU type 26 and sent to the MAC level multicast address "AllL1ISs" (01-80-C2-00-00-14). PSNP Level 2 PDUs are using PDU type 27 and sent to the MAC Level multicast address "AllL2ISs" (01-80-C2-00-00-15).

By sending PSNPs, routers do one of two things:

- Request a more recent LSP
- Acknowledge the receipt of an LSP on P2P circuits

Source ID is set to the system ID of the sender emitting this PDU.

Both PSNPs and CSNPs contain the LSP TLV #9 in its variable length part as shown in Figure 11-28.

The LSP TLV contains one or more LSP entries, each 16 bytes in size. Each LSP contains

- LSP ID
- Sequence number

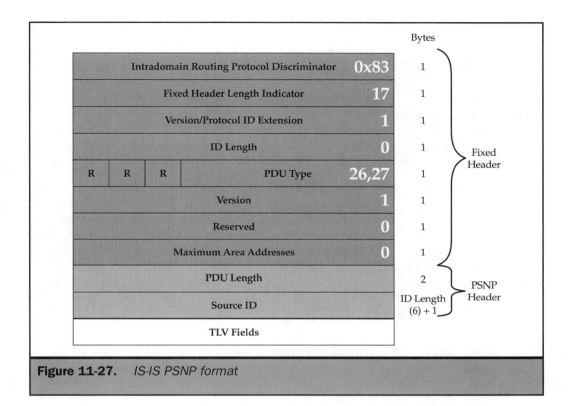

Figure 11-27.   *IS-IS PSNP format*

- Checksum
- Remaining lifetime

TLV #9 is the universal transport container packaging all the LSPs at a given level. Virtually all subsystems of IS-IS make use of TLV #9. The LSP TLV #9 is used in LSPs, PSNPs and CSNPs.

You can easily verify the contents of this TLV by issuing a show isis database command.

```
hannes@Amsterdam> show isis database
[ ... ]
IS-IS level 2 link-state database:
LSP ID                    Sequence Checksum Lifetime Attributes
1921.6800.1005.00-00      0x7b     0x85fe       815 L1 L2
1921.6800.1003.00-00      0x7a     0x5c23      1120 L1 L2
[ ... ]
```

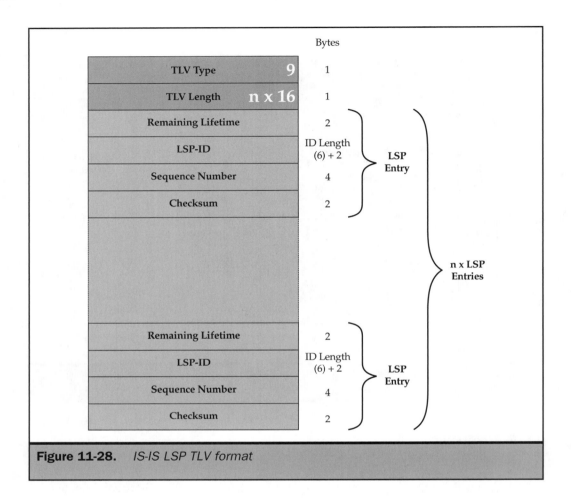

Figure 11-28.   *IS-IS LSP TLV format*

In this example, if a neighboring system of Amsterdam requests LSP ID 1921.6800.1005.00-00, Amsterdam responds with the data found in the corresponding level 2 LSP and generates a PSNP based on that data.

IS-IS Complete Sequence Numbers PDU

Figure 11-29 shows the format of the CSNP. CSNP Level 1 PDUs use PDU type 24 and are sent to the MAC level multicast address "AllL1ISs" (01-80-C2-00-00-14). CSNP Level 2 PDUs use PDU type 25 and are sent to the MAC level multicast address "AllL2ISs" (01-80-C2-00-00-15).

PDU Length is set to the length of the entire packet including the headers.

Source ID is set to the system ID of the router transmitting the CSNP. The Circuit field (byte 7) is always set to zero.

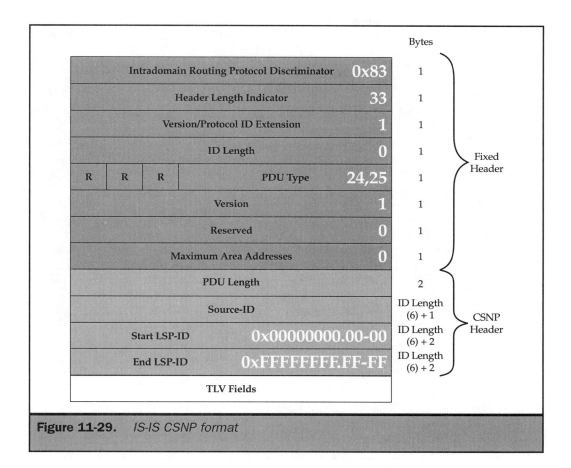

Figure 11-29. *IS-IS CSNP format*

The IS-IS protocol designers wanted to optimize the search process for LSPs once they are mentioned in CSNPs. To speed that operation up they specified that the lowest LSP ID and the highest LSP ID are to be reported in the CSNP header. Today, however, implementers consider this an uninteresting optimization. In JUNOS software, therefore, the Start-LSP-ID is always set to 0, and the end-LSP-ID is always set to 0xFFFFFFFF.

IS-IS TLV Types

IS-IS was prepared from day one for extension; therefore, all the content transported on the previously described nine packet types are TLV encoded.

TLV encoding means that information is stored in the form of triplets, which are

- Type (1 byte)
- Length (1 byte)
- Value (variable length between 1 and 255 bytes)

Type indicates what the following information is about. *Length* indicates the length of the data to follow (length of value), and *value* contains the data itself.

TLV encoding makes it very easy for the receiver of a given PDU to parse that packet. Even if it does not understand a given TLV type the receiver can easily calculate the position of the next TLV in the packet, by looking at the Length field. The consequent TLV encoding is the reason why IS-IS is so easily extensible and downward compatible. Unlike OSPF, there is no fixed rule about the exact byte position of an LSP inside an IS-IS PDU.

Figure 11-30 shows the basic TLV structure that IS-IS uses. The Type field is 1 octet, which leaves room for 255 TLV types. The Length field is also 1 octet, which also gives a maximum of 255 bytes that can be transported in a single TLV. If a router needs to send more information it repeats the TLV with various contents. There can be more than a single TLV of each type per PDU.

TLV encoding is friendly to the developers because they do not need to touch stable areas of their code to add an extension. "Developer friendliness" results in more stable implementations because the likelihood of inserting bugs decreases. BGP is another example of a protocol that is easily extended due to the use of TLV encoding.

JUNOS software recognizes and makes use of the TLVs listed in Table 11-3. Today there are many extensions to the basic IS-IS protocol mentioned in ISO 10589. The column "*source*" shows a pointer to the spec describing this extension or new TLV. The right columns show in which of the nine packet types each TLV is used.

Area Address TLV

Figure 11-31 shows the structure of the Area Address TLV. This TLV can hold more than one area address. The maximum number of areas that a router in one level can be in, as indicated in the common header, is three.

In JUNOS software the area information is adopted from the configuration of an address statement under the ISO family of any interface in the system. Preferably this is

	Bytes
TLV Type **1-255**	1
TLV Length **1-255**	1
TLV Value	1–255

Figure 11-30. *Basic IS-IS TLV structure, using 1-octet Type and Length fields*

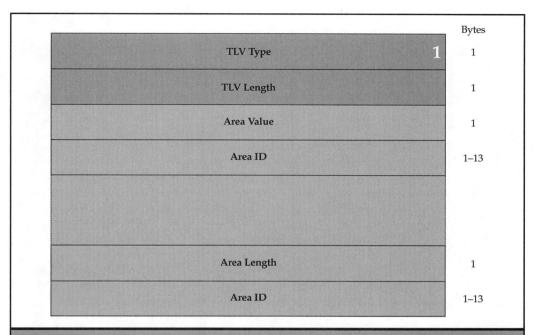

Figure 11-31.   *Area Address TLV showing an area "49.0001" having an area length of 3 bytes*

the loopback interface (lo0) because the loopback interface is virtual interfaces, which have the nice property of never going down. In the following snippet you can see the configuration that generated the content for Figure 11-31:

```
[edit]
hannes@Amsterdam# show interfaces
interfaces {
    lo0 {
        unit 0 {
            family iso {
                address 49.0001.1921.6800.1001.00;
            }
        }
    }
}
```

TLV #	Source	15 LAN Hello L1	16 L2	17 P2P Hello	18 LSP L1	20 L2	24 CSNP L1	25 L2	26 PSNP L1	27 L2	Representive Figure
Area Address	1	ISO10589	X	X	X	X	X					Figure 11-20
IS Reachability	2	ISO10589				X	X					Figure 11-32
IS Neighbors	6	ISO10589	X	X								Figure 11-21
Padding	8	ISO10589	X	X	X							Figure 11-18
LSP Entry	9	ISO10589						X	X	X	X	Figure 11-14
Authentication	10	ISO10589, draft-ietf-isis-hmac-03.txt	X	X	X	X	X	X	X	X	X	Figure 11-22
Checksum	12	draft-ietf-isis-wg-snp-checksum-03.txt	X	X	X			X	X	X	X	Figure 11-23
Extended IS Reachability	22	draft-ietf-isis-traffic-02.txt				X	X					Figure 11-25
IP Internal Reachability	128	RFC1195, RFC 2966				X	X					Figure 11-34
Protocols Supported	129	RFC1195	X	X	X	X	X					Figure 11-37
IP External Reachability	130	RFC1195, RFC 2966 (*)				X(*)	X					Figure 11-38

Table 11-3. *IS-IS TLVs*

| | | | 15 | 16 | 17 | 18 | 20 | 24 | 25 | 26 | 27 | |
| | | | LAN Hello | | P2P Hello | LSP | | CSNP | | PSNP | | |
	TLV #	Source	L1	L2		L1	L2	L1	L2	L1	L2	Representive Figure
IP Interface Address	132	RFC1195	X	X	X	X	X					Figure 11-35
TE Router ID	134	draft-ietf-isis-traffic-02.txt				X	X					Figure 11-24
Extended IP Reachability	135	draft-ietf-isis-traffic-02.txt				X	X					Figure 11-30
Dynamic Hostname	137	RFC2763				X	X					Figure 11-26
Multi-Topology IS Reachability	222	draft-ietf-isis-wg-multi-topology-00.txt				X	X					Figure 11-27
Multi-Topologies Supported	229	draft-ietf-isis-wg-multi-topology-00.txt	X	X	X	X	X					Figure 11-28
IPv6 Interface Address	232	draft-ietf-isis-ipv6-02.txt	X	X	X	X	X					Figure 11-36
Multi-Topology IP Reachability	235	draft-ietf-isis-wg-multi-topology-00.txt				X	X					Figure 11-31
IPv6 Reachability	236	draft-ietf-isis-ipv6-02.txt				X	X					Figure 11-33
P2P Adjacency State	240	draft-ietf-isis-3way-04.txt			X							Figure 11-29

Table 11-3. *IS-IS TLVs* (continued)

IS Reachability TLV

The IS Reachability TLV, shown in Figure 11-32, is used to express a bidirectional link between two Intermediate Systems. Depending on the topology there can be some repetitions of the basic structure containing the Neighbor ID plus a bunch of 6-bit metrics.

A basic IS reachability block in the TLV takes about 12 octets, which means that 21 IS adjacencies fit into a single TLV. If more than 21 IS adjacencies are needed, then a second TLV is generated.

In JUNOS all the TOS Routing fields are depreciated and hence the respective S bit is set to one.

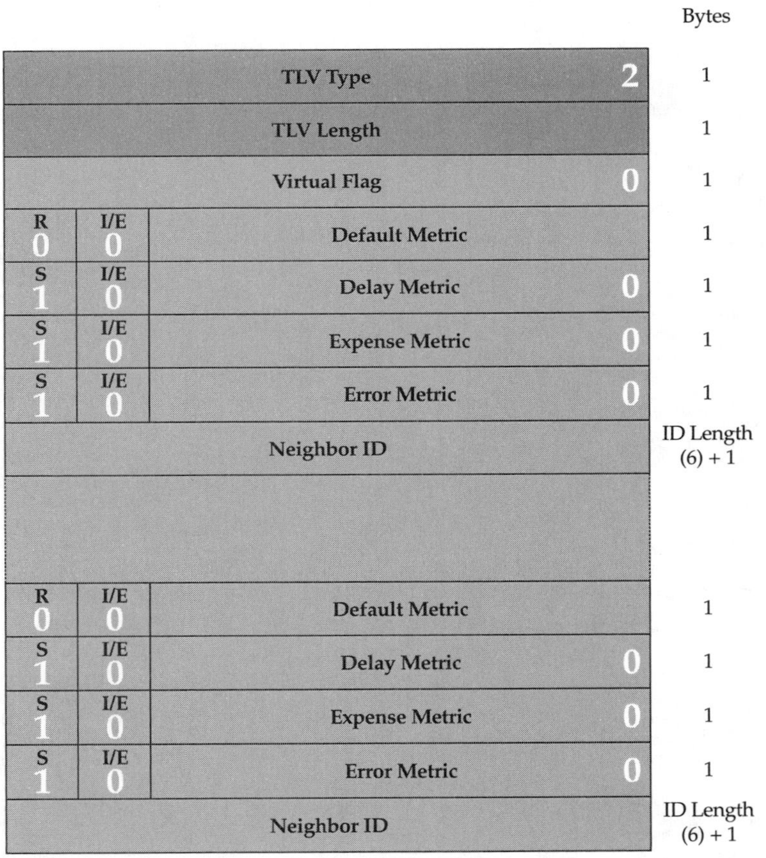

			Bytes
	TLV Type	2	1
	TLV Length		1
	Virtual Flag	0	1
R 0 / I/E 0	Default Metric		1
S 1 / I/E 0	Delay Metric	0	1
S 1 / I/E 0	Expense Metric	0	1
S 1 / I/E 0	Error Metric	0	1
	Neighbor ID		ID Length (6) + 1
R 0 / I/E 0	Default Metric		1
S 1 / I/E 0	Delay Metric	0	1
S 1 / I/E 0	Expense Metric	0	1
S 1 / I/E 0	Error Metric	0	1
	Neighbor ID		ID Length (6) + 1

Figure 11-32.   *The IS Reachability TLV in JUNOS uses only the default metric; all other metrics are set to zero.*

If the virtual flag is set, it indicates that the link is a Level 2 path to fix a broken area. For Level 1 the virtual flag is always set to zero. Because partition repair is not supported in JUNOS software this octet is always set to zero.

IS Extended Reachability TLV

Over time the IS-IS community did not feel comfortable with the limited possibilities of the 6-bit metric space that the IS Reachability TLV offered. The main problem with small metric fields is that they become almost the same if there is a big disparity between the lowest bandwidth and the highest bandwidth at a given area or level.

To illustrate this dilemma imagine a regional link in a network running at E3 (34 Mbps) speed. The fastest link in the backbone is OC-48, so the reference point is OC-48 with a metric of one. The metric calculation results in 2488 Mpbs/34 Mbps = 73. In IS-IS, however, all metrics get capped to the maximum value that can be expressed using 6 bits, which is 63; therefore, a single E3 segment has a metric of 63.

Next, imagine another regional link in the network, but running at T1 rather than E1. The metric calculation is 2488 Mpbs/1.544 Mbps = 1611. This metric also is capped to a 6-bit metric space, which is again, 63.

So an E3 line is indistinguishable from a T1 line in this scenario.

Figure 11-33 shows the basic TLV structure.

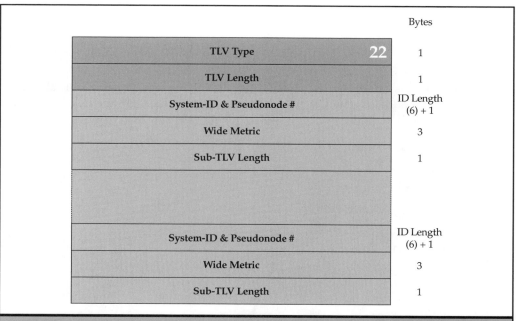

Figure 11-33. *The extended reachability TLV #22 has support for 24-bit (3-octet) metrics and is extensible through the use of sub TLVs.*

The Extended Reachability spec was the second line of extensions for IS-IS to support IP. Based on the experience from RFC 1195 the metric has changed to 24 bits for accommodating a maximum 256 hops with max-metric fitting into a 32-bit entity, without generating an overflow using 32-bit integer arithmetic. A 24-bit (3-byte) metric space leaves ample room for even big disparities between the highest and the lowest bandwidth link in the network. Here a network with a 16-hop diameter in which the slowest link is an E1 and the fastest link is an OC-12288 link could theoretically be realized.

It is very convenient to specify a reference-bandwidth that the system uses to automatically calculate the IS-IS metric for a given interface. As a common design practice the reference-bandwidth is being set to 1 terabit (1000 gigabits). Think 1 terabit is too high? Ten years ago people believed a reference bandwidth of 100 megabits that had been hard-coded in the OSPF specification was a barrier that would *never* be crossed. You can set the `reference-bandwidth` at the `protocols isis` level of the configuration.

```
[edit]
hannes@Stockholm# show
[ ... ]
protocols {
    isis {
        reference-bandwidth 1000g;
        [ ... ]
        }
    }
}
```

For traffic engineering purposes it is desired to know as much as possible about the current reservation state in the network. The extended reachability TLV has seven optional sub TLVs:

- Administrative group (color)
- IPv4 interface address
- IPv4 neighbor address
- Maximum link bandwidth
- Reservable link bandwidth
- Unreserved bandwidth
- TE 1default metric

You can display these settings for a given link by looking at the link-state database:

```
hannes@Paris> show isis database extensive
[ ... ]
```

```
TLVs:
  Area address: 49.0001 (3)
  Speaks: IP
  IP router id: 192.168.1.1
  IP address: 192.168.1.1
  Hostname: Paris
  IS neighbor: Frankfurt.00, Metric: default 1
    IP address: 192.168.21.6
    Traffic engineering metric: 3000
    Current reservable bandwidth:
      Priority 0 : 9952Mbps
      Priority 1 : 9952Mbps
      Priority 2 : 9952Mbps
      Priority 3 : 9952Mbps
      Priority 4 : 9952Mbps
      Priority 5 : 9952Mbps
      Priority 6 : 9952Mbps
      Priority 7 : 9952Mbps
    Maximum reservable bandwidth: 9952Mbps
    Maximum bandwidth: 9952bps
    Administrative groups:  0  <none>
  IP prefix: 192.168.1.1/32 metric 0 up
  IP prefix: 192.168.21.4/30 metric 10 up
 No queued transmissions
[ ... ]
```

JUNOS software by default does not generate these sub TLVs. As soon as you turn on RSVP and MPLS on an interface the IS-IS router transmits the optional traffic-engineering sub TLVs as part of its Extended IS Reachability TLV #22.

```
hannes@Paris> show configuration
protocols {
    rsvp {
        interface so-0/0/0.0;
    }
    mpls {
        interface so-0/0/0.0;
    }
[ ... ]
}
```

If you want your Juniper Networks routers to generate only new-style TLV #22 information, you can suppress generation of TLV #2 by setting the `protocols isis level 1|2 wide-metrics-only` configuration option:

```
hannes@Frankfurt> show configuration
[ ... ]
protocols {
    isis {
        level 2 {
            wide-metrics-only;
[ ... ]
        }
    }
}
[ ... ]
```

If you want revert back to the old-style TLVs you can suppress generation of TLV #22 by disabling `traffic-engineering` at the `protocols isis` level. Unfortunately, suppressing TLV #22 is available only on a per-box/instance basis, not a per-level basis.

```
hannes@Frankfurt> show configuration
[ ... ]
protocols {
    isis {
        traffic-engineering disable;
[ ... ]
        }
    }
}
[ ... ]
```

IS Neighbors TLV

This TLV is used only in Level 1 and Level 2 LAN Hellos to confirm two-way connectivity.

Looking at the sample topology, Madrid-1 receives a LAN Hello from Madrid-2. Madrid-1 includes Madrid-2's SNPA (=MAC Address) in its Hello packets to confirm back to Madrid-2 "I have heard you." Figure 11-34 shows the simple structure of this TLV, which is a list of seen Neighboring SNPAs (MAC addresses).

In ISO speak, the term *SNPA* is often used. Sub Network Point of Attachment is the ISO term for a Layer 2 address. JUNOS software uses the MAC address of the outgoing

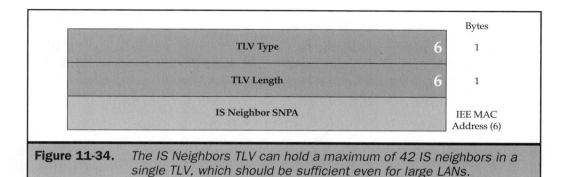

	Bytes
TLV Type	**6**	1
TLV Length	**6**	1
IS Neighbor SNPA	IEE MAC Address (6)

Figure 11-34.   *The IS Neighbors TLV can hold a maximum of 42 IS neighbors in a single TLV, which should be sufficient even for large LANs.*

Fast Ethernet or Gigabit Ethernet interface. You can display the MAC address using the show interface command:

```
hannes@Madrid-1> show interfaces ge-0/1/0
Physical interface: ge-0/1/0, Enabled, Physical link is Up
  Interface index: 13, SNMP ifIndex: 13
  Link-level type: Ethernet, MTU: 1514, Source filtering: Disabled
  Speed: 1000mbps, Loopback: Disabled, Flow control: Enabled
  Device flags   : Present Running
  Interface flags: SNMP-Traps
  Link flags     : None
  Current address: 00:90:69:d1:e0:1f, Hardware address: 00:90:69:d1:e0:1f
  Input rate     : 22538304 bps (6364 pps), Output rate: 17139888 bps (5681 pps)
  Active alarms  : None
  Active defects : None
  [ … ]
```

Authentication TLV

The Authentication TLV is used to protect the integrity of both Hellos and LSP Updates. JUNOS software supports two authentication types:

- Clear text passwords
- MD5 passwords

MD5 passwords are recommended, because today it is very easy to eavesdrop on broadcast media and the protocols that run on them. IS-IS makes heavy use of MAC-level multicast. All ports, even in a switched environment, receive the Hello, making it easy by attaching a protocol analyzer to a SPAN port of LAN switch to sniff the passwords.

Figure 11-35 shows the structure of TLV #10 if the authentication type is set to MD5. JUNOS software offers per-interface authentication and per-level authentication.

You can configure per-level authentication using the protocol isis level x authentication-key and protocol isis level x authentication-type statements:

```
hannes@Paris> show configuration
[ ... ]
protocols {
    isis {
        level 2 {
            authentication-key "$9$-tbwgq.5Qz6bsi.Pfn6"; # SECRET-DATA
            authentication-type md5;
        }
        interface so-6/0/0.0 {
            level 1 disable;
        }
        interface so-7/0/0.0 {
            level 1 disable;
        }
        interface lo0.0;
        [ ... ]
    }
}
[ ... ]
```

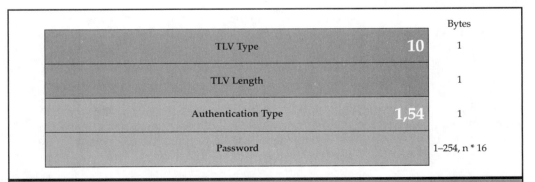

	Bytes
TLV Type **10**	1
TLV Length	1
Authentication Type **1,54**	1
Password	1–254, n * 16

Figure 11-35. *Using MD5 authentication, including the authentication type descriptor, this TLV always has a length of 17 octets.*

JUNOS software per-level authentication authenticates all three IS-IS packet types (LSPs, SNPs, *and* IIHs). This authentication is in contrast to Cisco Systems' IOS implementation of IS-IS, which authenticates only LSPs and SNPs, not IIHs. The only way to make this work is to make the Cisco routers send authenticated IIHs as well. You do this by adding a per-interface authentication on the Cisco side using the `interface xyz isis password` command. In Cisco Systems IOS Implementation of IS-IS there is a domain and an area password. The domain password is being used for authenticating Level 2 LSPs, SNPs and the area password is being used for authenticating Level 1 LSPs plus SNPs.

Here is a quick overview:

For Level 1   Cisco IOS area password must match JUNOS Level 1 password; additional Cisco IOS interface password must match Cisco IOS area password

For Level 2   Cisco IOS domain password must match JUNOS Level 2 password; additional Cisco IOS interface password must match Cisco IOS domain password

The Cisco Systems IOS implementation of IS-IS as per 12.2 supports only simple-text authentication, which means that all passwords travel clear-text over the line. This modest level of security protects against only unintentional misconfiguration. While MD5 authentication protects the shared password confidentiality, it is no general panacea for securing routing updates. Plain MD5 has no cryptographic checksum for protecting against replay attacks. There is ongoing work in the IETF about these issues; please see draft-zinin-isis-auth-anti-replay-00.txt[11] for details. Cisco Systems incorporated MD5 authentication in IOS 12.2S. Cisco IOS does not authenticate CSNPs and PSNPs per default. To make it authenticating the two PDU types you have to provide the `authenticate snp` keyword after the `domain & area password`, which makes the Cisco router to send the CSNPs and PSNPs proper authenticated. The option `send-only` makes the IS sending the CSNP and PSNP; however, it does not check if a PSNP and CSNP are properly authenticated. This is for downward compatibility with older software releases on other interfaces.

The following Cisco IOS configuration illustrates this.

```
Brussels#show running-config
Building configuration...
[ ... ]
```

---

[11] "Protecting ISIS from Replay Attacks," draft-zinin-isis-auth-anti-replay-00.txt, Work in Progress.

```
interface FastEthernet0/0
 ip address 172.16.2.1 255.255.255.0
 ip router isis
 isis password darthvader level-1
 isis password hansolo level-2
 !
router isis
 net 49.0012.1921.6800.1009.00
 domain-password hansolo authenticate snp send-only
 area-password darthvader authenticate snp send-only
 [ ... ]
```

The domain password is hansolo and the area password is darthvader. For seamless interoperation with JUNOS additionally the *same* set of passwords has been configured on the link (=Fast Ethernet) between the router running JUNOS (=Amsterdam) and the router running IOS (=Brussels).

```
hannes@Amsterdam> show configuration
[ ... ]
protocols {
    isis {
        /* this is the equivalent to IOS' domain password */
        level 2 {
            authentication-key "$9$JkUi.QF/0BEP5BEcyW8ZUj"; # SECRET-DATA
            authentication-type simple;
        }
        /* this is the equivalent to IOS' area password */
        level 1 {
            authentication-key "$9$roQvMXY2aUi.WLaU"; # SECRET-DATA
            authentication-type simple;
        }
        interface ge-0/0/1.0 {
        interface lo0.0;
    }
}
[ ... ]
```

To interoperate in between IOS and JUNOS all you have to make sure is to use simple text authentication on *Brussels*.

Unfortunately previous versions of IOS 12.2 and IOS 12.0.18(5ST) do not support authentication of SNP packets. The only way to interoperate between IOS and JUNOS software is to turn off authentication checking. Turning off authentication checking effectively sends authenticated PDUs but does accept any unauthenticated or bogus-authenticated PDU.

You can activate this behavior using the `protocols isis no-authentication-check` command. This is useful for migration purposes.

```
hannes@Amsterdam> show configuration
[ ... ]
protocols {
    isis {
        no-authentication-check;
[ ... ]
    }
}
```

There is sometimes confusion about the *two* authentication TLVs #10 and #133. RFC 1195 mentions a dedicated TLV #133 for IP prefix authentication. Today, TLV #133 is depreciated as no vendor ever has implemented TLV #133. JUNOS is always using TLV #10 for authentication purposes.

Checksum TLV

Historically there have been cases where IS-IS CSNPs and PSNPs and IIHs can be corrupted by faulty implementations of Layer 2 hardware or lack of check summing on a specific network technology. Because authentication can never replace proper check summing, <draft-ietf-isis-hmac-03.txt> describes an extension to IS-IS to optionally generate and honor checksums for IIHs, PSNPs, and CSNPs.

Figure 11-36 shows the optional checksum TLV #12, which has a fixed length of 2 octets holding one 16-bit standard X.233 Fletcher checksum. It is generated once per LSP fragment.

Checksum generation can be turned on in the `protocols isis interface` section:

```
hannes@Stockholm> show configuration
[ ... ]
protocols {
    isis {
      [ ... ]
        }
        interface so-7/2/0.0 {
            checksum;
        }
    }
}
[ ...]
```

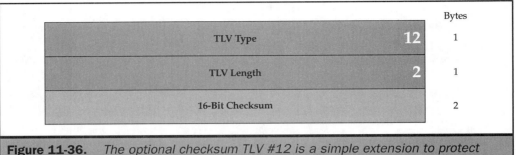

Figure 11-36.   *The optional checksum TLV #12 is a simple extension to protect packet integrity for IIHs, PSNPs, and CSNPs.*

Protocols Supported NLPID TLV

The Protocols Supported TLV makes IS-IS a true multiprotocol routing protocol. For each protocol an IS-IS router speaks, it announces a separate NLPID. NLPIDs are the OSI equivalent for Ether types, but are only 8 bits wide.

JUNOS software generates the following NLPIDs:

- IPv4 (0xCC)
- IPv6 (0x8E)

In Figure 11-37 you can see the simple structure of the Protocols Supported TLV, which is a simple array of NLPIDs. The Protocols Supported TLV is present in both IIHs and LSPs.

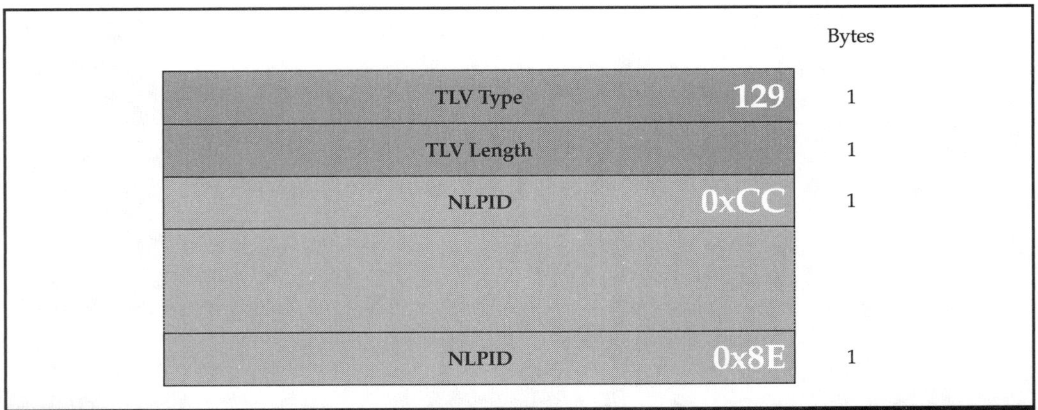

Figure 11-37.   *The Protocols Supported TLV typically holds 1–3 NLPIDs.*

You can find out what protocols any IS-IS router can speak by looking at the link-state database using the `show isis database extensive` command:

```
hannes@Paris> show isis database extensive Stockholm
[ ... ]
  TLVs:
    Area address: 49.0001 (3)
    Speaks: IP
    Speaks: IPv6
    IP router id: 192.168.1.10
    IP address: 192.168.1.10
    Hostname: Stockholm
    IS neighbor: Frankfurt.00, Metric: default 1
      IP address: 172.16.3.17
[ ... ]
```

You can find out what protocols your neighboring IS-IS routers speak by looking at your adjacencies using the `show isis adjacency detail` command:

```
hannes@Paris> show isis adjacency detail
Amsterdam
  Interface: so-6/0/0.0, Level: 2, State: Up, Expires in 26 secs
  Priority: 0, Up/Down transitions: 3, Last transition: 02:05:11 ago
  Circuit type: 2, Speaks: IP, IPv6
  IP addresses: 172.16.3.31
[ ... ]
```

IP Interface Address TLV

The IP Interface Address TLV is used both in IIHs and LSPs. In IIHs it informs the receiving node about the IP addresses configured on the originating router's interface. Looking at Figure 11-38, you might notice that the LSP structure permits more than one IP address to be sent. This makes it possible to send the primary address and the secondary addresses of a given interface. In the case of unnumbered interfaces JUNOS sends the IP address of its primary address configured on the lo0.0 interface.

The IP Interface Address TLV #132 is sent in LSP updates as well, indicating the router ID of the announcing router. For each IS-IS router speaking IP there must be at least one occurrence of TLV #132.

This TLV is useful for initial debugging, if IS-IS adjacencies are up but IP connectivity is down. You can display TLV #132 by issuing the command:

```
hannes@London> show isis adjacency detail
IS-IS adjacency database:
```

```
Amsterdam
  Interface: so-7/0/0.0, Level: 2, State: Up, Expires in 20 secs
  Priority: 0, Up/Down transitions: 3, Last transition: 1w3d 02:03:12 ago
  Circuit type: 2, Speaks: IP, IPv6
  IP addresses: 172.16.3.77
```

If you want to find out the IP router ID of an IS-IS speaker look at the link-state database:

```
hannes@Paris> show isis database extensive Stockholm
[ ... ]
  TLVs:
    Area address: 49.0001 (3)
    Speaks: IP
    Speaks: IPv6
    IP router id: 192.168.1.10
    IP address: 192.168.1.10
    Hostname: Stockholm
    IS neighbor: Frankfurt.00, Metric: default 1
      IP address: 172.16.3.17
[ ... ]
```

Note that the line beginning with "IP router ID" does *not* display the contents of TLV #132. This is TLV #134, which is discussed in the next section. In most environments both TLVs transport the same IP address.

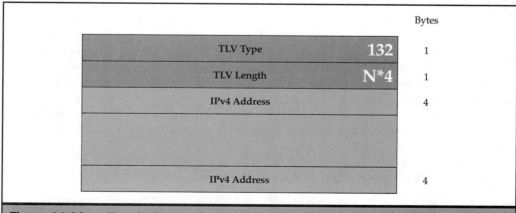

Figure 11-38.   *The IP Interface Address TLV has space for 63 IP addresses.*

TE Router ID TLV

The Traffic Engineering Router ID is used to uniquely identify a given router for computing the Traffic Engineering Database. Because this information is provided both in the OPSF TE extensions and IS-IS TE extensions, mappings for both the OSPF and IS-IS topologies can be computed.

As you can see in Figure 11-39 the TE router ID TLV has a length of 4 bytes.

If you want to find the TE router ID of an IS-IS speaker look at the link-state database:

```
hannes@Paris> show isis database extensive Stockholm
[ ... ]
  TLVs:
    Area address: 49.0001 (3)
    Speaks: IP
    Spekas: IPv6
    IP router id: 192.168.1.10
    IP address: 192.168.1.10
    Hostname: Stockholm
    IS neighbor: Frankfurt.00, Metric: default 1
      IP address: 192.168.41.5
[ ... ]
```

The IP Reachability TLVs #128, #130, #135

For people new to the IS-IS protocol it is hard to understand initially why there are three different TLVs used to carry IP prefixes. A lot of the reasoning for this can be found by looking at the protocol's history.

RFC 1195 first mentions the IP Internal Reachability TLV #128 (Figure 11-40) and the IP external Reachability TLV #130 (Figure 11-41).

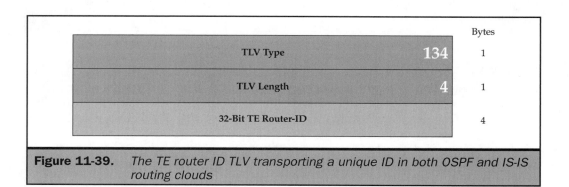

	Bytes
TLV Type **134**	1
TLV Length **4**	1
32-Bit TE Router-ID	4

Figure 11-39. *The TE router ID TLV transporting a unique ID in both OSPF and IS-IS routing clouds*

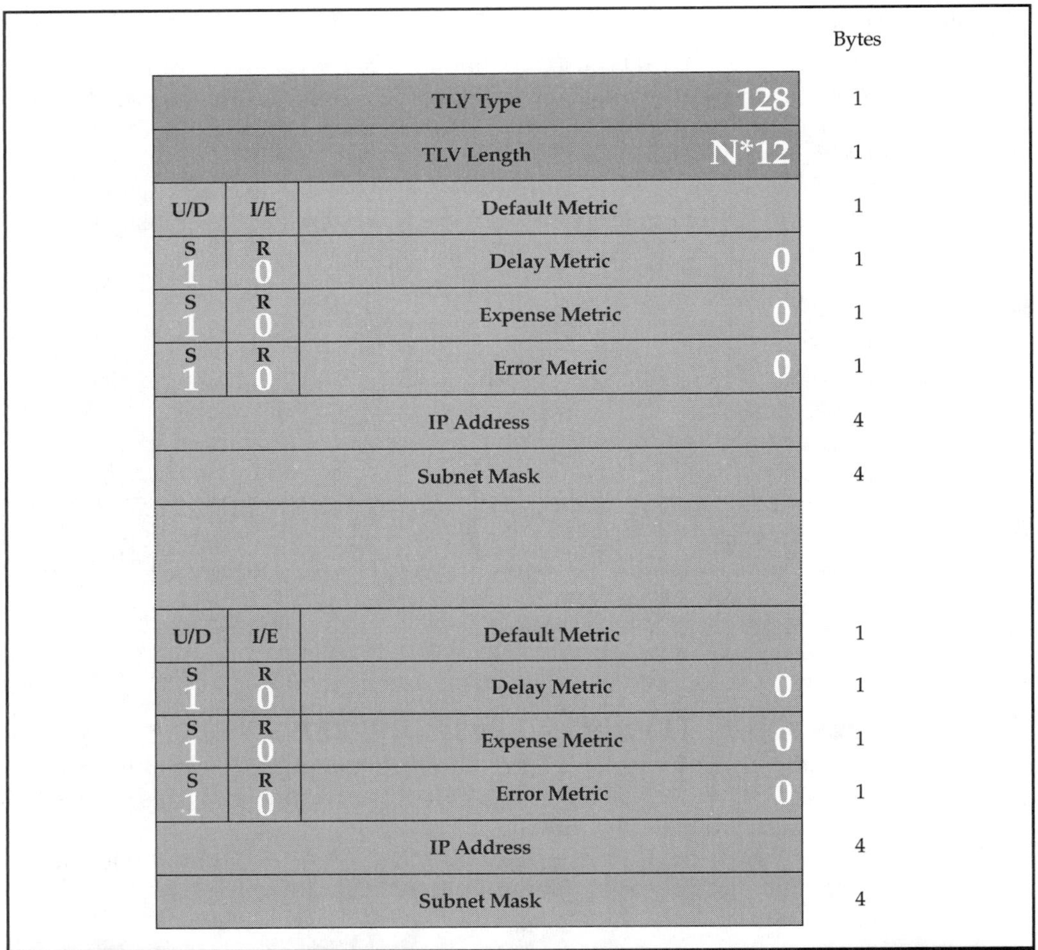

				Bytes
		TLV Type	**128**	1
		TLV Length	**N*12**	1
U/D	I/E	Default Metric		1
S **1**	R **0**	Delay Metric	**0**	1
S **1**	R **0**	Expense Metric	**0**	1
S **1**	R **0**	Error Metric	**0**	1
		IP Address		4
		Subnet Mask		4
U/D	I/E	Default Metric		1
S **1**	R **0**	Delay Metric	**0**	1
S **1**	R **0**	Expense Metric	**0**	1
S **1**	R **0**	Error Metric	**0**	1
		IP Address		4
		Subnet Mask		4

Figure 11-40.   *The IP Reachability TLV #128*

The I/E Bit   For virtually all routing protocols, users want to be able to inject routes from other sources. During the transfer of a route from one protocol to the other each transferred route gets a metric and an indicator bit concerning the metric's nature. This 1 bit indicates metrics that are either directly comparable with the metrics used by IS-IS or not comparable with the metrics used by IS-IS.

The I/E bit was defined as a mechanism for distinguishing between these two types, with the comparable metrics being identified as "internal metric type," and the noncomparable metrics being identified as "external metric type."

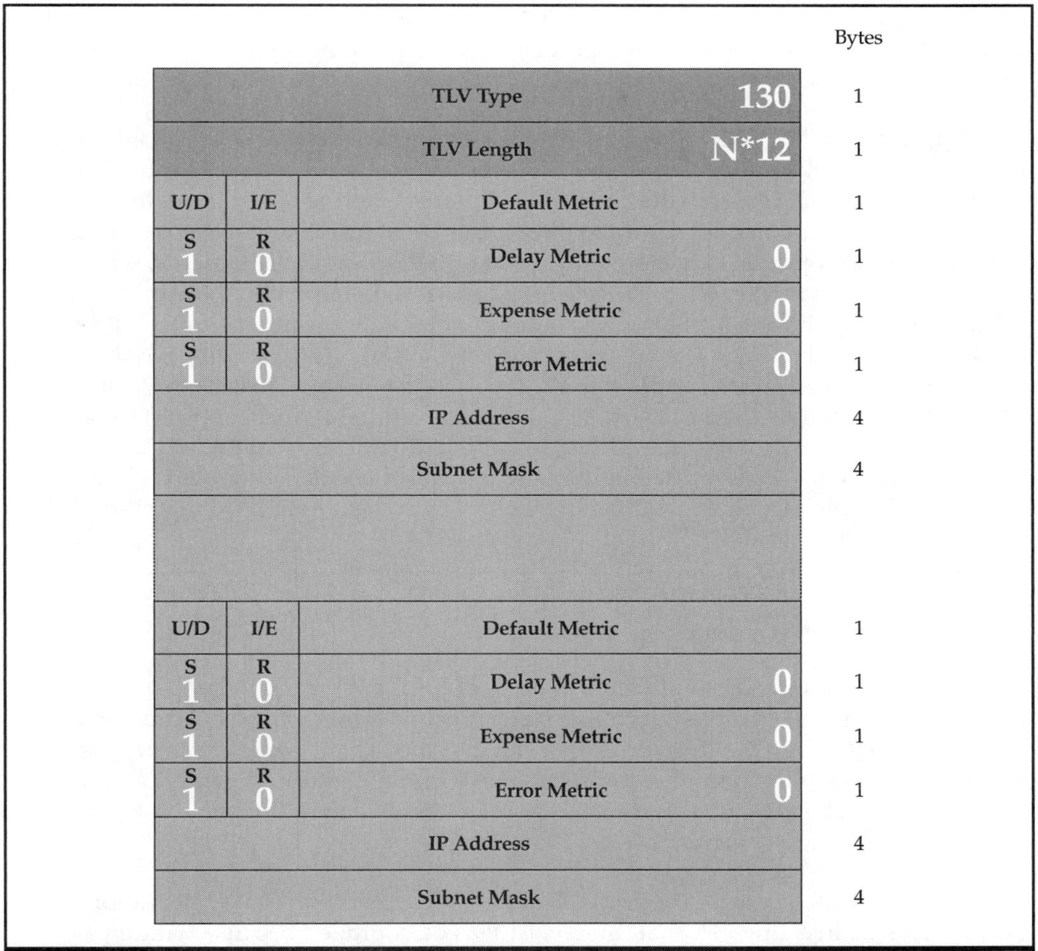

				Bytes
	TLV Type		130	1
	TLV Length		N*12	1
U/D	I/E	Default Metric		1
S 1	R 0	Delay Metric	0	1
S 1	R 0	Expense Metric	0	1
S 1	R 0	Error Metric	0	1
		IP Address		4
		Subnet Mask		4
U/D	I/E	Default Metric		1
S 1	R 0	Delay Metric	0	1
S 1	R 0	Expense Metric	0	1
S 1	R 0	Error Metric	0	1
		IP Address		4
		Subnet Mask		4

Figure 11-41.   *The IP External Reachability TLV #130*

Only the *internal* metric type is valid for IP Internal Reachability TLV #128 information. Both the internal or external metric type is valid for IP External Reachability information. IP External Reachability info using the internal metric type is treated similarly to Internal Reachability info, but IP External Reachability info is less preferred than if it used external metric type instead.

Then something happened that is typical for implementations of IP Routing Protocols: In the first successful deployment of Cisco Systems' IOS IS-IS code the I/E bit was accidentally masked wrong. No customer complained about it, and thus it became the actual standard to treat the I/E bit as an "invisible" seventh bit of the metric. Figure 11-40 and 11-41 show the 6 metric bits after the I/E bit; therefore, prefixes with the I/E bit being set always are by a metric of 128 worse than if the I/E would be clear.

The Up/Down Bit   RFC 1195 has some nice scaling properties. Level 1 routes can be passed up to Level 2 but never vice versa. To get connectivity, a Level 1 router installs a default route (0/0) towards the closest L1L2 router with the ATT bit set. In some ISP scenarios, however, you might want to have a few Level 2 prefixes "leaked" into Level 1. This is useful for optimal exit routing or proper BGP MED advertisements, where the MED is derived from the IGP cost. RFC 2966 describes in more detail the motivations behind changing the leftmost bit in the default metric to indicate if a prefix has been leaked down. If it has been leaked down, to avoid routing loops it will never be passed up again. JUNOS software supports the U/D bit in its internal IP reachability TLV #128, external IP reachability TLV #130 and in its extended IP reachability TLV #135.

To be downward compatible with systems that do not support the RFC2966 semantics, JUNOS software versions prior to 5.1 do *not* use the suggested leftmost (MSB) bit. For the internal IP reachability TLV #128 and external IP reachability TLV #130, JUNOS instead sets the I/E bit once you leak

■ Internal Level 2 routes down to Level 1

■ External Level 1 routes up to Level 2

Setting the I/E bit instead of the U/D bit in TLV #128, #130 is compatible with Cisco IOS of honoring the I/E bit as part of the metric and has proven to be interoperable.

Starting with JUNOS 5.1, *both* the U/D bit and the I/E bit are set once prefixes are leaked. There is a transition plan to get back to documented use of the U/D bit until JUNOS 5.4. For the extended IP reachability TLV there is no notion of an I/E bit so the bit serving as the up/down indicator is "at the right place."

External Routes   Per RFC 1195 the IP External Reachability TLV #130 is supported only at Level 2. Injecting externals at Level 1 was discouraged because without a supplemental bit this could result in routing loops.

Figure 11-42 shows the flow and content of the IP Reachability TLVs #128 and #135 if an internal route is injected into the IS-IS domain. Level 2 prefixes must be manually leaked down to Level 1 through the use of a policy that marks the route by setting the I/E bit to *external*. Recall that by default JUNOS software generates both old-style TLVs (#2, #128, and #130) and new-style TLVs (#22 and #135).

Internal IP reachability information is stored in TLV #128 (old-style) and TLV #135 (new-style).

Madrid-1 and Madrid-2 are both announcing their local Gigabit Ethernet subnet 10/8 as part of their Level 1 LSP. They use both TLV #128 and TLV #135 to carry the prefix. The initial metric is 10 and the Up/Down bit is clear (Up), which means this prefix may be distributed only to Level 2.

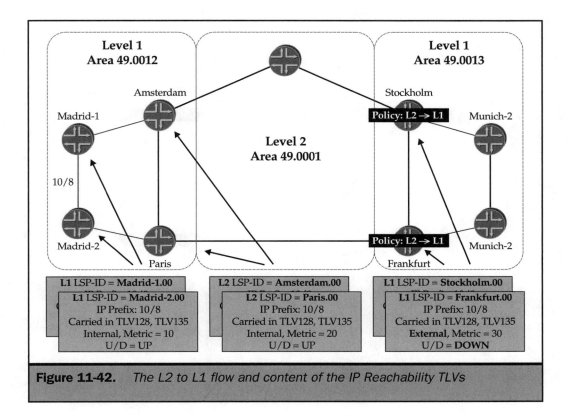

Figure 11-42. *The L2 to L1 flow and content of the IP Reachability TLVs*

IS-IS by default leaks all internal IP reachability information from Level 1 up to Level 2, so 10/8 is announced automatically in Amsterdam and Paris's Level 2 LSP. The metric field changes according to Amsterdam and Paris's perspective. Both routers are one hop away from the subnet 10/8. In JUNOS the default metric on a link is 10. The original cost of 10 plus the links metric of 10 to the originating routers Madrid-1 and Madrid-2 makes Amsterdam and Paris reannounce the prefix with metric 20.

IS-IS by default does not leak internal Level 2 information down to Level 1. You have to enforce that through the use of a policy. The policy implicitly marks the 10/8 prefix as having an external metric-type by setting the I/E bit. This is done to ensure that prefixes leaked by policy are depreferred over original Level 1 routing information. The Up/Down bit gets set (Down) during policy processing, marking the route so that it never gets passed up again.

Figure 11-43 shows the flow and content of the IP reachability TLVs #130 and #135 if an external route is injected into the IS-IS domain. Level 1 external prefixes have to be manually leaked up to Level 2 through the use of a policy that marks the route by setting the I/E bit to *external*.

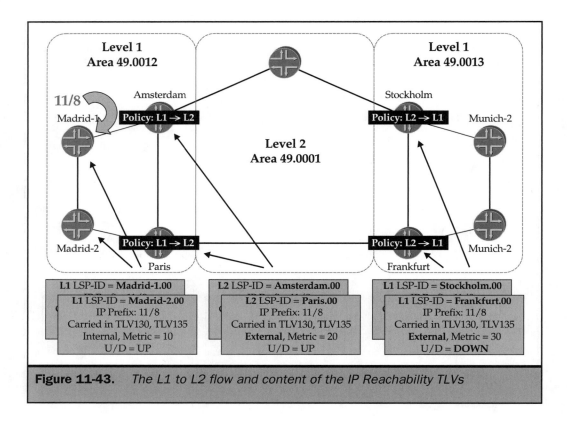

Figure 11-43. *The L1 to L2 flow and content of the IP Reachability TLVs*

Madrid-1 is injecting the route 11/8 from an external source such as static, RIP, OSPF, or BGP into its Level 1 LSP. Madrid-1 uses both TLV #130 and TLV #135 to carry that information. The I/E bit is clear (internal metric-type) and the Up/Down bit is clear (Up) as well. The initial metric is 10.

JUNOS software by default does not leak external IP reachability information from Level 1 to Level 2. You have to enforce that through the use of a policy. Once the prefix is processed through the first policy the I/E bit gets set. The Up/Down bit remains clear.

IS-IS by default does not leak external Level 2 information down to Level 1. You have to enforce that through the use of a second policy. The policy implicitly marks the 11/8 prefix as having an external metric-type by setting the I/E bit. This is done to ensure that prefixes leaked by policy are depreferred over original Level 1 routing information. The Up/Down bit gets set (Down) during policy processing, marking the route so that it never gets passed up again.

Extended IP Reachability TLV

To overcome the small 6-bit metric space, to clean up the mess around the usage of TLV #128 and TLV #130, and to be able to inject external routes anywhere in the network the IS-IS Working Group in the IETF decided to create a new IP Reachability TLV that addresses all these needs together in a single TLV.

Figure 11-44 shows the outcome of these efforts, the extended IP Reachability TLV #135. As you can see, TLV #135 does not use the fixed size packaging of TLV #128 or TLV #130, in which each prefix needs 12 bytes. Coding the prefix length directly instead of using a netmask saves 3 bytes. Depending on prefix length, variable packaging results in an average 65 percent better use of TLV space.

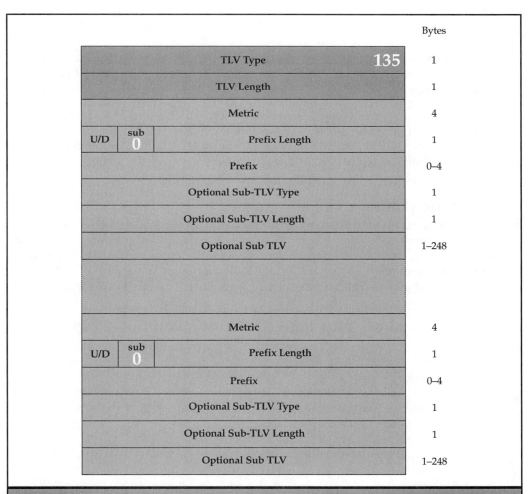

Figure 11-44. *JUNOS does not use sub TLVs in the Extended IP Reachability TLV #135.*

Variable packaging means that for prefixes 1 to 8 bytes long, only the first byte of the prefix is stored. This is okay because the remaining part would be all zeroes. Prefixes 9 to 16 bytes long store 2 bytes, and so on.

For example, the prefix 172.16/12 consumes 7 bytes of storage space using TLV #135. In contrast, encoding it in TLV #128 or TLV #130 would consume 12 bytes.

The metric field has been extended to 32 bits to allow the import of routes from all routing sources without the need for crippling or translating the metric during the import.

You might ask why the designers of TLV #135 decided to use 6 bits for the prefix length. Because an IP address is a 32-bit entity, in theory that could have been coded in 5 bits. Recall that a default route can also be carried, so in fact there are 33 distinct prefix lengths and hence 6 bits are necessary.

The authors of TLV #135 doubted the usefulness of the Internal/External bit. Henk Smit, one of the authors of draft-ietf-isis-traffic-04.txt[12] noted once on a posting to the ISIS-WG mailing list:

> "I have never really understood the need for both TLV128 and TLV130. This was also one of the reasons why we decided to not carry the I/E metric bit semantics forward into TLV135 (the new IP prefix TLV defined in the IS-IS TE extensions draft). The most important reason was of course the fact that we had no bits left, and did not want to spend another byte per prefix."

Dynamic Host Name TLV

IS-IS uses a 48-bit number, represented in most router CLIs as a 12-digit hexadecimal number, to represent nodes in a network. It is obvious that for management and operation reasons it would be easier to remember a symbolic name rather than 12 hexadecimal digits.

Implementations sometimes have a static table that maps symbolic names to 12-hexadecimal-digit sys-IDs. You can manually store static name to sys-ID mappings using the `system static-host-mapping` configuration option:

```
hannes@Stockholm> show configuration
system {
[ ... ]
    static-host-mapping {
        Stockholm sysid 1921.6800.1001;
        Frankfurt sysid 1921.6800.1002;
        Paris sysid 1921.6800.1003;
        Amsterdam sysid 1921.6800.1004;
        London sysid 1921.6800.1005;
    }
```

---

[12]   H. Smit et al, draft-ietf-isis-traffic-04.txt, Work in Progress.

```
}
[ ... ]
```

As networks began to grow it was very awkward to distribute mapping information each time a router was added to the network. Dynamic mappings relying on an external server such as the DNS are not a viable choice either, because in standard DNS software there is no support for OSI sys-IDs. Also relying on an external server for troubleshooting a network might not be a good idea because connectivity to the server providing the translation service itself might get disrupted.

RFC 2763[13] describes a mechanism to advertise hostnames along with a routers LSP to distribute a name to sys-ID mapping information throughout a given level, using the Dynamic Host Name TLV (Figure 11-45). JUNOS implements RFC 2763 by always sending the hostname specified under the `system host-name` statement in the TLV:

```
hannes@Stockholm> show configuration
system {
    host-name Stockholm;
[ ... ]
}
```

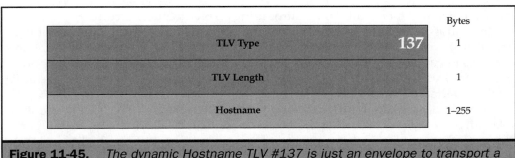

Figure 11-45. *The dynamic Hostname TLV #137 is just an envelope to transport a simple ASCII string.*

13 N. Shen, H. Smit, "Dynamic Hostname Exchange Mechanism for IS-IS," RFC 2763, February 2000, http://www.ietf.org/rfc/rfc2763.txt.

You can verify if the dynamic Host Name TLV is present by looking at the link-state database:

```
hannes@Paris> show isis database extensive
[ ... ]
  TLVs:
    Area address: 49.0001 (3)
    Speaks: IP, IPv6
    IP router id: 192.168.1.10
    IP address: 192.168.1.10
    Hostname: Stockholm
    IS neighbor: Frankfurt.00, Metric: default 1
      IP address: 172.16.3.45
[ ... ]
```

P2P Adjacency TLV

In the base ISO 10589 spec, on a P2P interface an IS-IS speaker can never be sure if true bidirectional connectivity exists. An IS can see the remote router Hellos, but it does not know if the remote router sees its Hellos. draft-ietf-isis-3way-04.txt describes a backward-compatible three-way handshake that insures that bidirectional connectivity is in place before an adjacency is declared up. A three-way handshake means to send a "Hello I have seen you" message, similar to the IS-reachability TLV #6. The three-way handshaking is accomplished using P2P Adjacency TLVs, shown is Figure 11-46. It also overcomes the limitation of 8-bit circuit IDs by introducing 32-bit extended circuit IDs.

In contrast to the base spec ISO 10589, implementers think that unique circuit IDs are needed only for Designated ISs on a LAN and not for P2P links due to the link-local meaning of circuit IDs on P2P links. Previous versions to JUNOS 5.1 do not support either the extended local circuit ID or the two following fields. JUNOS sets the circuit-ID on P2P interfaces always to 0x01.

JUNOS software up through 5.0 supports the P2P Adjacency TLV #240, but only at a length of 1 byte, just indicating the Adjacency state. JUNOS 5.1 and higher support the full 15-byte version, including support for extended circuits IDs on both sides. The extended circuit-ID fields are filled with the interface index (ifindex) of the P2P interface.

Troubleshooting IS-IS

In the process of explaining the structure and function of the various IS-IS data entities, the previous sections have also shown you examples of IS-IS configurations. Coupled with the general protocol configuration steps you have learned from Chapters 8 and 9, you now have all the information you need to create the most common IS-IS configurations using JUNOS software. This section begins demonstrating troubleshooting techniques through the presentation of case studies.

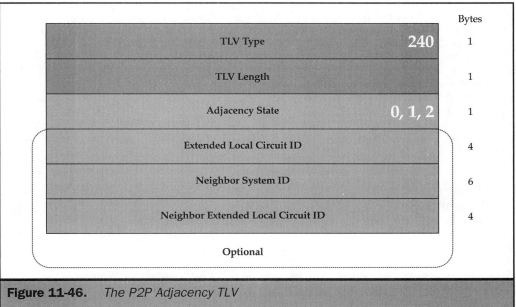

	Bytes
TLV Type **240**	1
TLV Length	1
Adjacency State **0, 1, 2**	1
Extended Local Circuit ID	4
Neighbor System ID	6
Neighbor Extended Local Circuit ID	4
Optional	

Figure 11-46. *The P2P Adjacency TLV*

Case Study: Broken IS-IS Adjacency

Referring back to the example topology in Figure 11-1, you can see that the two routers Munich-1 and Munich-2 should have a Level 1 adjacency inside Area 49.0013 to each other and to their respective neighbors Stockholm and Frankfurt.

In this case study, the three adjacencies

- ■ (Munich-2, Stockholm)
- ■ (Munich-1, Munich-2)
- ■ (Munich-1, Frankfurt)

are all down. The physical interface configuration has been checked, and is correct. Layer 2 communication is possible because the show interfaces xyz detail command shows that the PPP IP-CP and PPP OSI-CP are in the Opened state:

```
hannes@Stockholm> show interfaces so-0/0/0 detail
Physical interface: so-0/0/0, Enabled, Physical link is Up
  Interface index: 14, SNMP ifIndex: 23
  Link-level type: PPP, MTU: 4474, Clocking: Internal, Speed: oc48, Loopback: None,
CRC: 16  Device flags   : Present Running
```

```
Interface flags: Point-To-Point SNMP-Traps
Link flags      : Keepalives
Keepalive settings: Interval 10 seconds, Up-count 1, Down-count 3
Keepalive Input: 126 (00:00:07 ago), Output: 126 (00:00:01 ago)
LCP state: Opened
NCP state: inet: Opened, iso: Opened, mpls: Not-configured
Input rate      : 32 bps (0 pps)
Output rate     : 168 bps (0 pps)
Active alarms   : None
Active defects  : None
[ ... ]
```

Given these facts, the next step is to perform IS-IS adjacency troubleshooting in a pair-by-pair fashion.

First the Munich-2 to Stockholm configuration is examined:

```
hannes@Stockholm> show configuration
[ ... ]
interfaces {
    so-0/0/0 {
      description "oc48_to_Munich-2_wan"
        unit 0 {
            family inet {
                address 172.16.2.1/30;
            }
          family iso;
        }
    }
    so-6/0/0 {
      description "oc192_to_London_wan"
        unit 0 {
            family inet {
                address 172.16.2.18/30;
            }
          family iso;
        }
    }
    so-7/0/0 {
      description "oc192_to_Frankfurt_wan"
        unit 0 {
            family inet {
```

```
                    address 172.16.2.13/30;
            }
        family iso;
        }
    }
    lo0 {
        unit 0 {
            family inet {
                address 192.168.1.1/32;
            }
            family iso {
                address 49.0013.1921.6800.1001.00;
            }
        }
    }
}
[ ... ]
protocols {
    isis {
        interface so-0/0/0.0 {
            level 2 disable;
        }
        interface so-6/0/0.0 {
            level 1 disable;
        }
        interface so-7/0/0.0 {
            level 1 disable;
        }
    interface lo0;
    }
}
[ ... ]
```

The Stockholm configuration seems to be correct:

■ `family iso` is configured on all interfaces.

■ There is an `iso address` on the `lo0` interface and has the same Area number as Munich-2 (a must for L1 adjacencies).

■ Under the `protocols isis` section, all WAN interfaces are listed.

The Munich-2 configuration seems to be correct as well:

```
hannes@Munich-2> show configuration
[ ... ]
interfaces {
    so-0/0/0 {
       description "oc48_to_Stockholm_wan"
         unit 0 {
             family inet {
                 address 172.16.2.2/30;
             }
           family iso;
         }
     }
    ge-0/1/0 {
       description "ge_to_munich-1_lan"
         unit 0 {
             family inet {
                 address 172.16.2.5/30;
             }
             family iso;
         }
     }
    lo0 {
         unit 0 {
             family inet {
                 address 192.168.1.6/32;
             }
             family iso {
                 address 49.0013.1921.6800.1006.00;
             }
         }
     }
}
[ ... ]
protocols {
    isis {
         level 2 disable;
         interface so-0/0/0.0;
         interface ge-0/1/0.0;
     }
}
[ ... ]
```

After the configurations are verified, check all the interfaces that are actively speaking IS-IS. One could argue that this has been checked by viewing the configuration, but keep in mind that in JUNOS software if something is accepted by the parser it still might be silently discarded by the routing protocols. To check if the IS-IS subsystem has all the interfaces from the parser, issue a `show isis interface` command:

```
hannes@Stockholm> show isis interface
IS-IS interface database:
Interface       L CirID Level 1 DR       Level 2 DR       L1/L2 Metric
so-0/0/0.0      1   0x1 Point to Point    Disabled            4/4
so-6/0/0.0      2   0x1 Disabled          Point to Point      1/1
so-7/0/0.0      2   0x1 Disabled          Point to Point      1/1
lo0.0           0   0x1 Passive           Disabled            0/0
```

On Stockholm IS-IS is sending out Hello messages on all the configured interfaces, but on Munich-2 the same command reveals that the loopback interface is disabled on both levels:

```
hannes@Munich-2> show isis interface
IS-IS interface database:
Interface       L CirID Level 1 DR       Level 2 DR       L1/L2 Metric
so-0/0/0.0      1   0x1 Point to Point    Disabled            4/4
ge-0/1/0        1   0x2 Munich-2.02       Disabled          10/10
lo0.0           0   0x1 Disabled          Disabled            0/0
```

To gather further evidence the debugger under the `protocols isis traceoptions` branch is enabled. On "error, general, and normal" conditions specific to the IS-IS routing protocol the debug log is written into a file named "isis-troubleshoot" on the local hard drive:

```
hannes@Munich-2> show configuration
 [ ... ]
protocols {
    isis {
        traceoptions {
            file isis-troubleshoot;
            flag error;
            flag general;
            flag normal;
        }
        level 2 disable;
        interface so-0/0/0.0;
        interface ge-0/1/0.0;
```

```
      }
}
[ ... ]
```

The next step is to watch the log. You do that using the `monitor start` command, which displays the most recent lines written to a file on your screen:

```
hannes@Munich-2> monitor start isis-troubleshoot
hannes@Munich-2>
*** isis-troubleshoot ***
Aug 10 07:30:34 ERROR: received IIH but have no local sysid
Aug 10 07:30:34 ERROR: received IIH but have no local sysid
Aug 10 07:30:41 ERROR: received IIH but have no local sysid
Aug 10 07:30:43 ERROR: received IIH but have no local sysid
Aug 10 07:30:48 ERROR: received IIH but have no local sysid
```

This output tells you that Munich-2 is complaining that it cannot respond to a Hello because it does not have a valid sys-ID.

Before analyzing the output, turn off the monitoring.

```
hannes@Munich-2> monitor stop isis-troubleshoot
```

So what does the output mean? Recall that in IS-IS you need to have at least one interface that contains a valid NET (the sys-ID is part of the NET). On both Stockholm and Munich-2 NETs are configured on the lo0.0 interface. The only difference between Stockholm and Munich-2 is that on Stockholm's configuration the lo0.0 interface is listed under `protocols isis` and on Munich-2 it is not.

The way IS-IS works on JUNOS software is to scan all configured interfaces for a valid NET. If one interface contains a valid NET then it extracts the area portion and the sys-ID NET and thus acquires an "identity." If the interface containing the NET is omitted from the IS-IS protocol configuration, the router never gets an identity and hence refuses to talk.

The `traceoptions` are removed and the lo0.0 interface is added at the `protocols isis` level:

```
hannes@Munich-2> show configuration
  [ ... ]
protocols {
    isis {
        level 2 disable;
        interface so-0/0/0.0;
        interface ge-0/1/0.0;
```

```
        interface lo0.0;
    }
}
[ ... ]
```

After committing the change you can check the adjacency state using the show
isis adjacency command:

```
hannes@Munich-2> show isis adjacency
IS-IS adjacency database:
Interface         System          L State          Hold (secs) SNPA
so-0/0/0.0        Stockholm       1 Up                      24
```

The adjacency to Stockholm is now up, but the adjacency to Munich-1 is missing.
First check the configuration of Munich-1:

```
hannes@Munich-1> show configuration
[ ... ]
interfaces {
    so-0/0/0 {
        description "oc48_to_Frankfurt_wan"
          unit 0 {
              family inet {
                  address 172.16.2.10/30;
              }
            family iso;
          }
      }
    ge-0/1/0 {
        description "ge_to_munich-2_lan"
          unit 0 {
              family inet {
                  address 172.16.2.6/30;
              }
          }
      }
    lo0 {
        unit 0 {
              family inet {
                  address 192.168.1.7/32;
              }
              family iso {
                  address 49.0023.1921.6800.1007.00;
```

```
            }
        }
    }
}
[ ... ]
protocols {
    isis {
        level 2 disable;
        interface so-0/0/0.0;
        interface ge-0/1/0.0;
        interface lo0.0;
    }
}
[ ... ]
```

Notice that the `family iso` statement is missing on the interface definition. The inbound I/O manager ASIC discards all protocols that it does not know on a specific interface. You can see using the `show interfaces extensive` command if a packet was discarded due to being an unknown protocol:

```
hannes@Munich-1> show interface ge-0/1/0 extensive
Physical interface: ge-0/1/0, Enabled, Physical link is Up
  Interface index: 13, SNMP ifIndex: 13
  Link-level type: Ethernet, MTU: 1514, Source filtering: Disabled
  Speed: 1000mbps, Loopback: Disabled, Flow control: Enabled
  Device flags   : Present Running
  Interface flags: SNMP-Traps
  Link flags     : None
  Current address: 00:90:69:e4:a0:3f, Hardware address: 00:90:69:e4:a0:3f
  Statistics last cleared: Never
  Traffic statistics:
   Input  bytes  :                5563                  456 bps
   Output bytes  :               61006                  510 bps
   Input  packets:                  65                    0 pps
   Output packets:                  96                    1 pps
  Input errors:
    Errors: 0, Drops: 0, Framing errors: 0, Runts: 0, Policed discards: 27
    L3 incompletes: 0, L2 channel errors: 0, L2 mismatch timeouts: 0
    FIFO errors: 0
  Output errors:
    Carrier transitions: 7, Errors: 0, Collisions: 0, Drops: 0, Aged packets: 0
    HS link CRC errors: 0, FIFO errors: 0
  Active alarms  : None
  Active defects : None
[ ... ]
```

The counter `policed discards` is increasing every 9–10 seconds, which is roughly the IS-IS hello timer on LAN interfaces.

To fix this, the `family iso` statement is added to the interface ge-0/1/0. In this example the policed discards stop increasing, but the adjacency to Munich-2 is still missing:

```
hannes@Munich-1> show isis adjacency

hannes@Munich-1>
```

The next step is to again use tracing to see what is going on:

```
hannes@Munich-1> show configuration
 [ ... ]
protocols {
    isis {
        traceoptions {
            file isis-troubleshoot;
            flag error;
            flag general;
            flag normal;
        }
        level 2 disable;
        interface so-0/0/0.0;
        interface ge-0/1/0.0;
    }
}
[ ... ]
```

Monitoring the log file reveals interesting news:

```
hannes@Munich-1> monitor start isis-troubleshoot
hannes@Munich-1>
*** isis-troubleshoot ***
Aug 10 11:12:04 ERROR: IIH from Munich-2 with no matching areas, interface ge-
0/1/0.0, our area 49.0023
Aug 10 11:12:06 ERROR: IIH from Munich-2 with no matching areas, interface ge-
0/1/0.0, our area 49.0023
Aug 10 11:12:13 ERROR: IIH from Munich-2 with no matching areas, interface ge-
0/1/0.0, our area 49.0023
```

Munich-1 is rejecting Hellos from Munich-2 because of nonmatching areas. It is insisting that its configured area is area 49.0023. Take another look at Munich-1s lo0.0

configuration shown previously, and you will find a typo. The NET should begin with 49.0013, but instead it starts with 49.0023. After correcting that error all the adjacencies are up on Munich-1:

```
hannes@Munich-1> show isis adjacency
IS-IS adjacency database:
Interface        System        L State      Hold (secs) SNPA
ge-0/1/0.0       Munich-2      1 Up                  26 00:90:69:b8:70:3f
so-0/0/0.0       Frankfurt   1 Up             23
```

One of the nice things about IS-IS is that it runs on top of layer-2, so you can use it to troubleshoot IP addressing problems. For instance, if you cannot PING from Munich-1 to Frankfurt but the adjacency is up, there is a high probability that something is wrong with the IP addressing:

```
hannes@Munich-1> ping 172.16.2.9
PING ping 172.16.2.9 (ping 172.16.2.9): 56 data bytes
^C
--- ping 172.16.2.9 ping statistics ---
4 packets transmitted, 0 packets received, 100% packet loss
hannes@Munich-1>
```

On all IP enabled interfaces in IS-IS there must be a copy of the IP interface Address TLV #132 present in the Hello PDUs. The remote router's IP address can be displayed using the `show isis adjacencies detail` command:

```
hannes@Munich-1> show isis adjacency detail
IS-IS adjacency database:

Frankfurt
  Interface: so-0/0/0.0, Level: 1, State: Up, Expires in 25 secs
  Priority: 0, Up/Down transitions: 1, Last transition: 00:02:43 ago
  Circuit type: 3, Speaks: IP
  IP addresses: 172.162.10
[ ... ]
```

This output shows that Frankfurt has the same IP address as Munich-1, which is an illegal configuration. Once the IP address on Frankfurt is changed to 172.16.2.9, the PING succeeds:

```
hannes@Munich-1> ping 172.16.2.9
PING 172.16.2.9 (172.16.2.9): 56 data bytes
```

```
64 bytes from 172.16.2.9: icmp_seq=0 ttl=255 time=0.164 ms
64 bytes from 172.16.2.9: icmp_seq=1 ttl=255 time=0.171 ms
64 bytes from 172.16.2.9: icmp_seq=2 ttl=255 time=0.183 ms
^C
--- 172.16.2.9 ping statistics ---
3 packets transmitted, 3 packets received, 0% packet loss
round-trip min/avg/max/stddev = 0.164/0.172/0.182/0.035 ms
```

Case Study: Unintentionally Injecting 100,000 Prefixes into IS-IS

There have been many documented cases of the entire Internet routing table being accidentally injected into IS-IS or OSPF. This case study demonstrates the results of such a mistake happening at Munich-2 in the example network.

When you look at the link-state database of any peering router in the German area 49.0013, notice that one specific router has set the overload bit set:

```
hannes@Stockholm> show isis database
IS-IS level 1 link-state database:
LSP ID                    Sequence Checksum Lifetime Attributes
Munich-2.00-00                0x11    0xc935    1161 L1 Overload
Munich-2.00-01                0x6     0            0 L1
Munich-2.00-02                0x6     0            0 L1
Munich-2.00-03                0x6     0            0 L1
Munich-2.00-04                0x6     0            0 L1
Munich-2.00-05                0x6     0            0 L1
Munich-2.00-06                0x6     0            0 L1
Munich-2.00-07                0x6     0            0 L1
Munich-2.00-08                0x6     0            0 L1
Munich-2.00-09                0x6     0            0 L1
Munich-2.00-0a                0x6     0            0 L1
Munich-2.00-0b                0x6     0            0 L1
Munich-2.00-0c                0x6     0            0 L1
Munich-2.00-0d                0x5     0            0 L1
Munich-2.00-0e                0x5     0            0 L1
Munich-2.00-0f                0x5     0            0 L1

[ ... ]

Munich-2.00-f8                0x1     0            0 L1
Munich-2.00-f9                0x1     0            0 L1
```

```
Munich-2.00-fa                  0x1        0          0 L1
Munich-2.00-fb                  0x1        0          0 L1
Munich-2.00-fc                  0x1        0          0 L1
Munich-2.00-fd                  0x1        0          0 L1
Munich-2.00-fe                  0x1        0          0 L1
Munich-2.00-ff                  0x1        0          0 L1
Munich-1.00-00                  0x4      0x3f52      581 L1
Stockholm.00-00                 0xf      0xe45e      898 L1
Frankfurt.00-00                 0x11     0x1286     1001 L1
    259 LSPs

[ ... ]
```

Additionally, you can check the log files on the router that has the overload bit set:

```
hannes@Munich-2> show log messages
[ ... ]
Aug 28 15:14:51 Munich-2 rpd[344]: RPD_ISIS_OVERLOAD: IS-IS database overload
Aug 28 15:24:52 Munich-2 rpd[344]: RPD_ISIS_OVERLOAD: IS-IS database overload
Aug 28 15:34:53 Munich-2 rpd[344]: RPD_ISIS_OVERLOAD: IS-IS database overload
Aug 28 15:44:54 Munich-2 rpd[344]: RPD_ISIS_OVERLOAD: IS-IS database overload
Aug 28 15:54:55 Munich-2 rpd[344]: RPD_ISIS_OVERLOAD: IS-IS database overload
[ ... ]
```

What has happened is that routing information exceeding the 256*1492 bytes link-state database capacity has been injected to IS-IS. As Munich-2 ran out of fragments it put itself out of the game by setting the overload bit.

The root cause for this massive amount of routing information being injected into IS-IS is revealed by examining the IS-IS export policies:

```
hannes@ Munich-2> show configuration
[ ... ]
protocols {
    isis {
        export direct_to_isis;
    [ ... ]
    }
}
```

You see that there is just one policy named "direct_to_isis." The configuration of that policy is:

```
hannes@Munich-2> show configuration
[ ... ]
policy-statement direct_to_isis {
    term reject_management {
        from {
            route-filter 10.0.0.0/8 orlonger;
        }
        then reject;
    }
    term direct_connected {
        from protocol direct;
    }
    then accept;
}
```

At first sight this policy looks good; however, a closer view reveals that the `then accept` statement is not part of the term "direct_connected." Worse, it is part of the main clause, which is lacking a `from` statement. So what this policy does is run through the terms "reject_management" and "direct_connected," and then at the end of the policy it unconditionally accepts everything that is in the inet.0 routing table.

To fix the problem the `then accept` statement is moved into the term `direct_connected`:

```
hannes@Munich-2> show configuration
[ ... ]
policy-statement direct_to_isis {
    term reject_management {
        from {
            route-filter 10.0.0.0/8 orlonger;
        }
        then reject;
    }
    term direct_connected {
        from protocol direct;
        then accept;
    }
}
```

After committing the change you will still see all those stale fragments in the database. After 10 minutes they are removed automatically. If you want to clean the database manually, issue the `clear isis database` command and watch the database:

```
hannes@Munich-2> clear isis database
hannes@Munich-2>

hannes@Stockholm> show isis database
IS-IS level 1 link-state database:
LSP ID                        Sequence Checksum Lifetime Attributes
Munich-2.00-00                    0x12   0x2a3b     1198 L1
Munich-1.00-00                     0x4   0x3f52      532 L1
Stockholm.00-00                    0xf   0xe45e      711 L1
Frankfurt.00-00                   0x11   0x1286      933 L1
   4 LSPs
[ ... ]
```

The database looks normal again, and the overload bet has automatically been removed.

Case Study: Leaking Level 2 Prefixes into Level 1

One of the Madrid routers in the example network, Madrid-1, is connected to the espanIX national peering point. Munich-1 is in turn connected to INXS. To determine for the Level 1 routers in the network the best exit point, and for peering autonomous systems (ASs) to determine the most optimal entrance point, you want to make those two routers' loopback IP addresses available in the other IS-IS areas.

For BGP, which is detailed in Chapters 12 and 13, the IGP cost is part of the route decision process. In JUNOS software the route decision process is, in order:

1. Prefer higher BGP LOCAL_PREF

2. Prefer shorter AS_PATH

3. Prefer lower origin code

4. igp

5. egp

6. Incomplete

7. Prefer lower MED on neighboring ASs (on all ASs if there is *always-compare-MED* configured)

8. Prefer route type

9. Internal routes (originated within your AS)

10. External routes received on an EBGP connection

11. External routes received on an IBGP connection

12. Prefer routes with lower IGP cost to the BGP_NEXT_HOP

13. Prefer routes having higher table ID *(inet.3 over inet.0)* pointing to the BGP_NEXT_HOP

14. Prefer routes having more equal cost paths to the BGP_NEXT_HOP

15. Prefer routes having a shorter CLUSTER_LIST

16. Prefer routes with higher BGP router-ID

17. Prefer routes with higher BGP update-source address

18. Prefer router with the numerical lower BGP_NEXT_HOP

For each received BGP route JUNOS software considers the IGP cost to the router in the BGP_NEXT_HOP field. By modifying the IGP cost you can influence the route decision process.

Figure 11-47 shows what is happening in the IS-IS Level 1 areas of the example network. No prefixes get leaked from the Level 2 to the Level 1. The L1L2 routers Stockholm, Frankfurt, Amsterdam, and Paris set the ATT bit to indicate that they are attached to another area. Pure Level 1 routers such as Madrid1-3 and Munich1-2 install a default route pointing to the closest L1L2 router with the ATT bit being set. You can

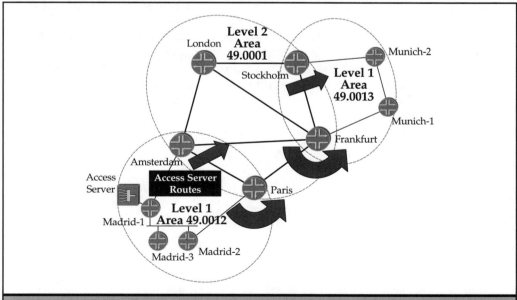

Figure 11-47. *To select the optimal exit point, Munich-1's loopback IP address is leaked into area 49.0012, and Madrid-3's into area 49.0013.*

check if a default route has been installed, and to what L1L2 router it is forwarding traffic to, using the show isis route command:

```
hannes@madrid-1> show isis route
 IS-IS routing table                    Current version: L1: 234 L2: 1
Prefix              L Version Metric Type Interface    Via
0.0.0.0/0           1     5      10 int  so-0/0/0.0   Amsterdam
[ ... ]
```

You can check if the default route has been installed in the main routing table (inet.0) using the show route command:

```
hannes@madrid-1> show route

inet.0: 105623 destinations, 105623 (105623 active, 0 holddown, 0 hidden)
+ = Active Route, - = Last Active, * = Both

0.0.0.0/0             *[IS-IS/18] 00:04:57, metric 10, tag 1
                      > to 172.16.3.139 via so-0/0/0.0
[ ... ]
```

Madrid-3 considers Amsterdam as its best exit point; however, the forwarding of all traffic from Madrid-1 to Amsterdam results in suboptimal routing for some destinations. For example, for traffic coming from Madrid-3 and going to Munich-1, Paris is the most optimal exit point. Munich-1's loopback IP address, 192.168.1.7/32, needs to be leaked into area 49.0012. For the return traffic Madrid-3's loopback IP address, 192.168.1.10/32, must be leaked into area 49.0013 to make sure that traffic going to Madrid-3 always takes Frankfurt as its exit point.

JUNOS software's default policy is to not leak IS-IS Level 2 routes into Level 1. You can override this default policy by writing an export policy:

```
hannes@Paris> show configuration
[ ... ]
protocols {
    isis {
        export leak-l2-to-l1 ;
        [ ... ]
    }
}
```

```
policy-options {
    policy-statement leak-l2-to-l1 {
        from {
            protocol isis;
            level 2;
            route-filter 192.168.1.7/32 exact;
        }
        to {
            protocol isis;
            level 1;
        }
        then accept;
    }
}
[ ... ]
```

The policy on Paris, named "leak-l2-to-l1," is evaluated like an if/then program. It reads as follows:

If there is an *active* route
learned via IS-IS, *and*
coming from Level 2, *and*
matching exactly the 32-bit prefix 192.168.1.7, *and*
being redistributed to IS-IS, *and*
going to Level 1,
then accept the route and install it in the main (inet.0) routing table.

You might wonder why you need to specify the `to` statement. As you know from Chapter 7, all the routing protocols use a hidden default policy. Although you cannot display the default policy, if you could it would look like the following:

```
policy-options {
    policy-statement default {
        from {
            protocol isis;
            level 2;
        }
        to {
            protocol isis;
```

```
            level 1;
        }
        then reject;
    }
}
```

By setting the `export leak-l2-to-l1` statement in the `protocols isis` section you override this default behavior with a custom policy.

After applying the policy on both Amsterdam and Paris, you can verify that Munich-1's address 192.168.1.7 has been leaked into Madrid-3's Level 1 area:

```
hannes@madrid-3> show isis route
 IS-IS routing table                       Current version: L1: 234 L2: 1
Prefix              L Version Metric Type Interface   Via
0.0.0.0/0           1      5      4 int  ge-0/0/0.0  Madrid-1
192.168.1.7/32      1     17     19 int  ge-0/0/0.0  Madrid-2
[ ... ]
```

You can also check to see if BGP is now using the Madrid-2-to-Paris path when traffic exits area 49.0012 using the `show route` command. For example, suppose you know that one of the peering partners on the INXS peering point is advertising the prefix 47.11/16. Examining the entry for that prefix, you find the following:

```
hannes@madrid-3> show route 47.11/16

inet.0: 105623 destinations, 105623 (105623 active, 0 holddown, 0 hidden)
+ = Active Route, - = Last Active, * = Both

47.11.0.0/16 (1 entry, 1 announced)
        *BGP    Preference: 170/-101
                Source: 192.168.1.7
                Nexthop: 172.16.3.122 via ge-0/0/0.0, selected
                Protocol Nexthop: 192.168.1.7
                Indirect nexthop: 84d36e8 21
                State: <Active Int Ext>
                Local AS:  3320 Peer AS:  3320
                Age: 7:27       Metric2: 30
                Task: BGP_100.192.168.1.4+1039
                Announcement bits (2): 0-KRT 4-Resolve inet.0
                AS path: 702 701 I
                Localpref: 100
                Router ID: 192.168.1.7
```

You can see that the route goes to BGP_NEXT_HOP (Protocol Nexthop) 192.168.1.7, which in turn is reached via Madrid-2's interface address 172.16.3.122. Madrid-2 subsequently forwards traffic to Paris. So the policy "leak-l2-to-l1" gives the Level 1 area a hint about what L1L2 router to take for traffic between Madrid-3 and Munich-1.

Case Study: Leaking External Level 1 Prefixes into Level 2

In Figure 11-48, an access server is deployed in the Spanish area 49.0012. Unfortunately it does not speak IS-IS, but can speak OSPF; therefore, OSPF is set up locally on the private Ethernet link between the access server and the router Madrid-1, using area 22. Madrid-1's OSPF configuration is

```
hannes@Madrid-1> show configuration
protocols {
  [ ... ]
    ospf {
        area 0.0.0.22 {
            interface fe-0/0/1.0;
        }
    }
}
```

With OSPF up and running, three routes are learned from the access server:

```
hannes@Madrid-1> show ospf route
Prefix               Route/Path/NextHop Type  Metric  Next hop i/f  NH addr/Label
192.168.1.11/32      Intra  Router      IP    100     fe-0/0/1.0
47.12/16             Ext2   Network     IP    100     fe-0/0/1.0
47.13/16             Ext2   Network     IP    100     fe-0/0/1.0
```

The intra-area route is the server's loopback IP address and the two external routes are the ones to be injected into IS-IS. A policy named "access-server-ospf-to-isis" is configured on Madrid-1 to accept all routes learned via OSPF:

```
hannes@Madrid-1> show configuration
policy-options {
    policy-statement access-server-ospf-to-isis {
        from {
            protocol ospf;
        }
        then accept;
    }
}
```

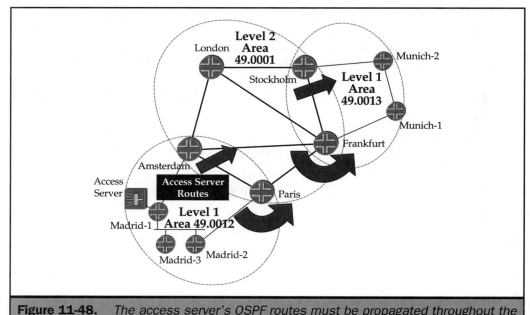

Figure 11-48. *The access server's OSPF routes must be propagated throughout the network, but IS-IS by default does not leak external information from Level 1 to Level 2.*

That policy is then applied under the `protocols isis export` section of the configuration:

```
hannes@ Madrid-1> show configuration
[ ... ]
protocols {
    isis {
        export access-server-ospf-to-isis;
    [ ... ]
    }
}
```

Make sure that the IS-IS router is advertising the prefixes as part of its LSP, by using the `show isis database detail` command to check what TLV the route is packaged in:

```
hannes@Madrid-1> show isis database Madrid-1 detail
IS-IS level 1 link-state database:
[ ... ]
  Packet: LSP id: Madrid-1.00-00, Length: 225 bytes, Lifetime : 1022 secs
    Checksum: 0xc89d, Sequence: 0x63, Attributes: 0xb <L1>
    NLPID: 0x83, Fixed length: 27 bytes, Version: 1, Sysid length: 0 bytes
    Packet type: 18, Packet version: 1, Max area: 0

  TLVs:
    Area address: 49.0012 (3)
    Speaks: IP
    IP router id: 192.168.1.9
    IP address: 192.168.1.9
    Hostname: Madrid-1
    IS neighbor: Amsterdam.00, Internal, Metric: default 4
    IP prefix: 192.168.1.9/32, Internal, Metric: default 0
    IP prefix: 172.16.3.121/30 metric 10 up
    IP prefix: 192.168.1.2/32 metric 0 up
    IP external prefix: 192.168.1.11/32, Internal, Metric: default 0
    IP external prefix: 47.12.0.0/16, Internal, Metric: default 0
    IP external prefix: 47.13.0.0/16, Internal, Metric: default 0
    IP prefix: 192.168.1.11/32 metric 0 up
    IP prefix: 47.12.0.0/16 metric 0 up
    IP prefix: 47.13.0.0/16 metric 0 up
[ ... ]
```

The prefix is correctly announced as part of the IP External Reachability TLV #130 (shown in the output as *IP external prefix*) and the extended IP reachability TLV #135 *(IP prefix)*. JUNOS software's default behavior is to announce external prefixes using both the old-style TLVs and the new-style TLVs. You can see that all three routes coming from the access server are properly announced as part of Madrid-1's Level 1 LSP.

The three routes are propagated throughout the Level 1 area 49.00012; however, a look at Frankfurt's routing table shows that the default IS-IS behavior is preventing the routes from being propagated to the Level 2 area:

```
hannes@Frankfurt> show route 47.12/16

hannes@Frankfurt>
```

If you could see the default policy, it would look like this:

```
policy-options {
    policy-statement default {
        from {
            protocol isis;
            level 1;
            external;
        }
        to {
            protocol isis;
            level 2;
        }
        then reject;
    }
}
```

All you have to do is write a policy that overrules the default policy:

```
hannes@Frankfurt> show configuration
[ ... ]
policy-options {
    policy-statement leak-l1-external-to-l2 {
        from {
            protocol isis;
            level 1;
            external;
            route-filter 47/8 orlonger;
        }
        to {
            protocol isis;
            level 2;
        }
        then accept;
    }
}
```

Just the action (the then portion) of the policy is changed, and a route-filter statement is added to limit the exportable routes from the access server. Recall from Chapter 7 that all elements in the from portion of a policy are ANDed together, so the routes in this example must match four properties.

The policy is applied on all L1L2 routers for area 49.0012 (Amsterdam and Paris) at the `protocols isis export` level:

```
hannes@Amsterdam> show configuration
[ ... ]
protocols {
    isis {
        leak-l1-external-to-l2 ;
    [ ... ]
    }
}
```

You can verify Amsterdam's Level 2 LSP using `show isis database extensive` to see if the access server's prefixes are properly announced:

```
hannes@Amsterdam> show isis database Amsterdam detail
IS-IS level 2 link-state database:
[ ... ]
  Packet: LSP id: Amsterdam.00-00, Length: 335 bytes, Lifetime : 933 secs
    Checksum: 0x48fd, Sequence: 0x10f, Attributes: 0xb <L1 L2 Attached>
    NLPID: 0x83, Fixed length: 27 bytes, Version: 1, Sysid length: 0 bytes
    Packet type: 19, Packet version: 1, Max area: 0

  TLVs:
    Area address: 49.0001 (3)
    Speaks: IP
    IP router id: 192.168.1.1
    IP address: 192.168.1.1
    Hostname: Amsterdam
    IS neighbor: London.00, Internal, Metric: default 1
[ ... ]
    IP prefix: 192.168.1.9/32, Internal, Metric: default 0
    IP prefix: 172.16.3.177/30 metric 10 up
    IP prefix: 192.168.1.9/32 metric 0 up
    IP external prefix: 192.168.1.11/32, External, Metric: default 0
    IP external prefix: 47.12.0.0/16, External, Metric: default 0
    IP external prefix: 47.13.0.0/16, External, Metric: default 0
    IP prefix: 192.168.1.11/32 metric 0 up
    IP prefix: 47.12.0.0/16 metric 0 up
    IP prefix: 47.13.0.0/16 metric 0 up
[ ... ]
```

All the access server's prefixes appear in the Level 2 link-state database. Note that the metric type has been changed from internal to external, which is always the case for IS-IS once a route is processed through a nondefault policy.

The access server routes are now seen in the Spanish area 49.0012 at Level 1 as well as in area 49.0001 at Level 2; however, the three routes are not seen in Area 49.0013 at Level 1 because IS-IS default behavior does not pass routes from Level 2 down to Level 1. If you want to pass these routes down to the German area 49.0013, you must write a policy similar to the one in the previous case study and apply it to Stockholm and Frankfurt:

```
hannes@Stockholm> show configuration
[ ... ]
protocols {
    isis {
        export leak-12-external-to-l1 ;
        [ ... ]
    }
}
policy-options {
    policy-statement leak-12-to-l1 {
        from {
            protocol isis;
            level 2;
            external;
            route-filter 47/8 orlonger;
        }
        to {
            protocol isis;
            level 1;
        }
        then accept;
    }
}
[ ... ]
```

The Complete Reference

Chapter 12

Interdomain Routing Theory

by E. Gary Hauser Jr. and Peter J. Moyer

This chapter will cover Interdomain Routing and the Border Gateway Protocol, otherwise known as BGP. BGP is used extensively in the Internet and has been for some time. Knowledge of BGP is required for all IP engineers in the ISP industry. This chapter will cover the theory of how BGP works and will also cover the JUNOS software configuration for BGP.

BGP Overview

Interdomain routing was developed in the 1980s as a means of connecting multiple routing domains homogeneously. A routing domain or *Autonomous System* (AS), as defined at that time, was a set of *gateways* operating under a single administration. A gateway was a device with the purpose of routing IP datagrams to their destination networks. This sounds a lot like a router. The gateway implementation was originally done by BBN and was written in macro-11 assembly language and ran on a Digital Equipment Corporation (DEC) PDP-11 or LSI-11 16-bit processor.

Prior to this time, there was really no concept of a domain, as the same authoritative group (the ARPANET) operated each of the gateways. Thus, this internetwork was considered to be a single routing domain; however, it became evident to the early operators of this internet that there would be a time when they would need to begin to think of the internet as a set of routing domains or ASs. The ARPANET was to be considered the core of that internet and responsible for transporting IP datagrams between the so-called *stub domains.* Taking that thought a step further, it became evident that the internet would eventually consist of a number of coequal domains, or ASs, whereby many of these domains might be used to transport IP datagrams between other domains. This is when internet transit networks would be born.

Today, an AS is defined as a set of routers under a single technical administration, using one or more *Interior Gateway Protocols* (IGPs) to route datagrams to internal destinations, and using an *Exterior Gateway Protocol* (EGP) to route datagrams to external destinations. This AS should have a single coherent interior routing plan and it should present a consistent picture of what destinations are reachable through it.

It is interesting to note that the classic definition of an AS has actually changed a bit over time. Originally, the definition in the applicable RFCs mentioned the use of a single IGP using common metrics. Today, an AS can have many IGPs or use no IGP at all; however, no one is advocating designing a network with no IGP.

Border Gateway Protocol (BGP) version 4 is the current exterior routing protocol that is used to "glue" the Internet together. Each *Internet Service Provider* (ISP) uses BGP to logically connect to other ISPs. Some enterprises, particularly the larger ones, use BGP to logically connect to one or more ISPs for access to and from the Internet. Also, these large enterprises often use BGP as the protocol of choice to connect their internal corporate domains together. BGP passes the required routing information between routing domains, and this routing information is what routers use to determine where to send IP datagrams.

Although somewhat jarring at this point in the chapter, a still-valid summary of BGP is in RFC 1267, dated October 1991, an excerpt of which is given here.

"Two systems form a transport protocol connection between one another. They exchange messages to open and confirm the connection parameters. The initial data flow is the entire BGP routing table. Incremental updates are sent as the routing tables change. BGP does not require periodic refresh of the entire BGP routing table. Therefore, a BGP speaker must retain the current version of the entire BGP routing tables of all of its peers for the duration of the connection. *Keepalive* messages are sent periodically to ensure the liveness of the connection. Notification messages are sent in response to errors or special conditions. If a connection encounters an error condition, a notification message is sent and the connection is closed."

Now that you have been exposed to the "BGP in 10 seconds" explanation, it is time to delve into each aspect of BGP in detail.

History of BGP

BGP v4 has been used extensively in the Internet since roughly 1995. Prior to that, BGP v3 was used. Before that, there was EGP. Even prior to that, there was *Gateway-to-Gateway Protocol* (GGP). As you can see, there has been an evolution that eventually led to BGP v4 as the standard exterior routing protocol to be used in the Internet today. BGP v4 provides many benefits over earlier versions, most notably the support for routing information aggregation and reduction based on the architecture of *classless interdomain routing* (CIDR) (RFC 1817). CIDR is needed to scale the Internet, due to the large growth of routing prefixes that have been experienced. As of this writing, there are more than 100,000 active prefixes that each default-free Internet backbone router must store and route to. If not for CIDR, this number would be much higher. There are some large ISPs that have more than 200,000 active prefixes in their core BGP routing tables. This is because they are also carrying all their internal destinations, in a nonaggregated fashion.

Storing this many prefixes poses a memory and processor burden on the Internet backbone routers. This is one of the reasons why Internet backbone routers must be purposely built to solve the many scaling problems relating to growing the Internet infrastructure.

When the Internet was being transformed from a U.S. government–funded research network to a more open IP infrastructure, the *exterior gateway protocols* in use were also being transformed. GGP, as mentioned previously, was the first protocol used to tie the gateways together. The gateways used GGP to determine connectivity to networks and neighboring gateways. They also used GGP to perform a dynamic, shortest-path routing algorithm. This was called the minimum distance vector and it used hop count to create a list of neighbor gateways through which to send traffic to each network. The entry for each network contained one of the neighbors that is the minimum distance away from that network. GGP had the basic exterior routing protocol requirements implemented, such as, neighbor discovery, exchanging of routing information, computing routes, adding and removing networks, and neighbor maintenance. Neighbor maintenance consisted of sending GGP echo messages every 15 seconds to each neighbor to verify connectivity and declaring a neighbor "down" if three of four echo messages were not replied to. Remember that at the time that GGP was implemented, there was considered to be only a single routing domain, so minimum distance vector did not count domain hops or AS hops, but only gateway hops. Around 1982, EGP was implemented to allow other gateways and gateway systems (called *stub* gateways) to pass routing information to the ARPANET internet gateways. The ARPANET gateways were considered to be the core of this newly emerging Internet. The use of EGP allowed the ARPANET core to be used as a transport media for traffic originating in some other AS and destined for yet another AS, while allowing the user to view all the networks and gateways as part of one total Internet communications system. EGP was first documented in RFC 827, dated October 1982, and authored by BBN. It was also at this time that the AS identifier came into use, which is a 16-bit number (excluding the use of all zeros).

EGP was not a routing algorithm. It enabled exterior neighbors to exchange routing information, which is used as input to a routing algorithm, such as GGP. GGP was still used in the core of the Internet, that being the ARPANET. So, GGP was now considered to be an IGP! Imagine a network using GGP as the interior routing protocol, and using EGP to pass routing information to other routing domains. These other routing domains could also be using GGP as their interior routing protocol, or they could have implemented any other IGP.

EGP, like GGP, did not have any mechanism for loop detection. The topology of ASs needed to be engineered to be loop-free. It was intended that the ASs would be connected in a tree structure, with no *cycles,* a cycle being a circular topology that would naturally loop. Since the Internet was not anything close to the Internet of today, this engineering feat was somewhat achievable for a short while.

EGP had three major processes: Neighbor Acquisition Protocol, Neighbor Reachability Protocol, and Network Reachability determination. All EGP messages were defined to travel a single hop, with the *Time to Live* (TTL) field set to a very small value. A more formal specification for EGP came later, in RFC 904, dated April 1984. This RFC specified in detail how to encode the different message types and their uses.

EGP was used as the exterior routing protocol throughout the 1980s, as more and more networks were connected to the ARPANET, and soon several backbones became peers of the ARPANET. Most notably, a new NFSNET backbone was created, which used a shortest path first (SPF)–based interior routing protocol adapted from the IS-IS protocol submitted by ANSI for standardization to the ISO. The ANSI IS-IS was based on work done at DEC and was adapted to the Internet environment. EGP was used as the exterior routing protocol until the first version of BGP was implemented and subsequently documented in RFC 1105, dated June 1989.

BGP v1 was a natural follow-on to EGP, with some major improvements. Most importantly, BGP was developed to be loop-free. It included the AS numbers in the update messages, so a receiving BGP speaker can create a graph of AS connectivity and prune this graph to be loop-free. This AS matrix of sorts also allowed routing policy to be implemented on received routes and routing decisions to be influenced. Another very important improvement from EGP was the use of TCP as the transport protocol for BGP, and the introduction of incremental updates for BGP. Using TCP as the transport protocol allowed reliable delivery of BGP messages. The notion of incremental updates, rather than sending the entire BGP routing table led to benefits such as:

- BGP consuming less bandwidth than EGP
- BGP consuming less CPU cycles than EGP

These benefits were confirmed by measurements at the interconnection points between the CA*NET and the T1 NSFNET during this time period.

When BGP v2 came along, one of the additions and advantages over BGP v1 was the implementation of more advanced path selection criteria. One of the complications of interdomain routing was the lack of any universally agreed-on metric that can be used to evaluate which path, among a set of paths, is the best path to use and re-advertise to neighbors. In traditional routing protocols, such as RIP, there was an easy metric (for example, hop-count) that was used to evaluate paths. BGP v2 introduced several new path attributes that can be evaluated by the protocol itself, or the configured routing policy, to influence path selection. Some of these attributes were: AS count, path origin, link dynamics, and the presence or absence of a certain AS in the path. BGP v2 was documented in RFC 1163, dated June 1990.

Roughly another year of operational experience went by before BGP was again modified. In October 1991, RFC 1267 was drafted, specifying BGP v3; however, unlike the upgrade from v1 to v2, there were no major changes in v3. The changes mostly dealt with a few of the BGP attributes and also specified the sending of BGP messages with special precedence settings to indicate priority over other IP traffic. At that time, there was some concern that using TCP might be causing slow convergence in the presence of congestion. It was realized that BGP messages were lost due to link congestion. After investigation, however, it became evident that the congestion was not caused by BGP, but rather BGP was the victim of the congestion. It was at this time that there were several recommendations to avoid BGP messages being dropped during times of congestion. This led to the setting of precedence bits in the BGP messages to indicate priority over other IP traffic.

It is interesting to note the size of the Internet at this time, for historical perspective. In an informational Internet draft dated October 1991, it was stated that:

- Link speeds ranged from 56 Kbps to 45 Mbps.
- There were a total of 56 border routers running BGP, spanning seven ASs.
- The size of the Internet routing table consisted of more than 2000 networks.

It is also interesting to note that during this time period it was acceptable to let the IGP carry the external routing information that was received by BGP, and there was no hard requirement to use BGP on all the routers. This is often referred to today as *redistributing BGP into the IGP.* This was possible at that time due to the minimal number of BGP routes that were carried in the Internet. Today, the practice of letting the IGP carry the full Internet routing table is avoided at all costs.

In March 1995, RFC 1771 and 1772 were drafted, specifying BGP v4. Even today, BGP v4 is by no means finished. There are many new features that continually need to be supported by BGP. There are also many Internet drafts that have modified BGP v4 to support these new features and applications. Some of these new features have to do with scalability of BGP and some deal with new ways of using BGP. Just a few examples are dynamic route refresh, dynamic capability detection, soft reconfiguration, and multiprotocol BGP. ISPs are continually upgrading their networks to support new applications, thus the routing protocols need to be frequently enhanced.

When speaking with up and coming network engineers it appears that most feel BGP to be the most complex routing protocol to learn, understand, and master. If you know BGP intimately, you should have no problem finding a senior network-engineering position with an established ISP or router vendor. But is BGP really that complex a protocol to learn and master? Or is it that only a small community of network engineers gets the exposure needed to master this protocol? The answer is the latter. BGP, as you will see in this chapter, is not such a difficult protocol to master. It is the lack of exposure to most network engineers, particularly in the enterprise world, that makes BGP appear to be difficult.

In the enterprise world, network engineers rarely get to experience BGP in a production environment. Typically, the only BGP that an enterprise will run is some simple peering to their ISP, or possibly multiple peerings to different ISPs for redundancy (multihoming). Some very large enterprises have implemented BGP inside their network to control routing between their many regional networks or domains. These large enterprises will also use BGP to pass their internal routing information to their ISP and often to select which of several exits to take for optimal routing. In today's global Internet, practically every ISP uses BGP inside their network; however, there might be some smaller ISPs that still exist today that use only BGP to connect to other ISPs. These small ISPs use a default route (0.0.0.0/0) to reach external destinations, and therefore, resemble the connectivity from an enterprise. Although this solution is simple to implement, it does not provide optimal routing decisions from within their network. If an ISP were small enough such that it needed only a single external connection, then a default route would suffice; however, most ISPs today have multiple external connections to many different ISPs. They must, therefore, use BGP to pass their internal routing information to these ISPs. They must also use BGP to pass external routing information that they receive from the ISPs to each of their internal BGP routers. These internal BGP routers are not considered border routers. These internal BGP routers exist so that from anywhere within their network they can make an intelligent decision as to which border router they should send traffic. This is explained better with a picture, so please see Figure 12-1.

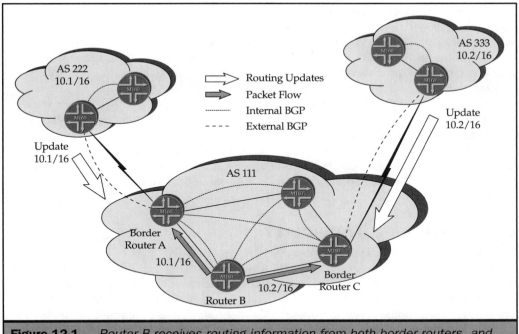

Figure 12-1.   *Router B receives routing information from both border routers, and chooses the appropriate border router as the exit point.*

As you can see in Figure 12-1, the internal BGP routers receive routing information about the external networks that exist in the Internet. They then decide which border router to forward traffic to, to reach those external destinations. These decisions can be made purely by the default nature of BGP itself, or can be influenced by configuration. The ISP can decide, and in doing so override the default BGP decision, which border router to forward traffic to. This decision can be made based on cost, bandwidth, or any number of factors. In its simplest form, this is the nature of routing policy.

What Is Different About BGP v4?

"The purpose of the Exterior Gateway Protocol (EGP) is to enable one or more autonomous systems to be used as transport media for traffic originating in some other autonomous system and destined for yet another, while allowing the end-user to see the composite of all the ASs as a single internet, with a flat, uniform address space." (RFC 827) The basic use of BGP v4 is really not much different from that original explanation of the purpose of EGP. That was written in 1982!

As was mentioned earlier, in EGP there was no dynamic capability to detect routing loops. The network had to be an engineered spanning tree structure and it was up to the network operators to ensure that the topology had no loops.

For path selection, GGP and EGP use strict hop count. They count the number of gateways, or hops, much like RIP does today. In that sense, GGP and EGP are very similar to distance-vector routing protocols.

BGP introduced the ability to detect routing loops based on the AS_PATH attribute and also to base path selection on this attribute, rather than gateway hops. This was a great improvement over EGP.

When BGP v4 was introduced, with it came the ability to aggregate routes and the notion of CIDR. CIDR support in BGP is another example of a considerable improvement over the previous exterior routing protocol. This enhancement is mainly for scalability reasons.

Why Use TCP as a Transport?

BGP uses TCP port 179 as its transport mechanism. The developers of BGP realized that if they used the connection-oriented TCP for transport, they would not need to reinvent the wheel by adding all the features of TCP to BGP, such as fragmentation, retransmission, acknowledgment, and sequencing. Needless to say, if two routers cannot establish a reliable TCP session between them, then BGP peering will never come up. Just because you can PING a neighboring router does not mean you can establish a BGP peering between them. This is because PING does not use TCP for delivery.

Another important implication of using TCP is that it is a reliable and proven point-to-point protocol; therefore, there must be (intentionally) separate point-to-point BGP peering sessions between neighbors, and neighbors must be manually configured. The benefit of this becomes evident in the next section.

Peering

BGP requires that all peerings must be configured explicitly. This is not a vendor-specific implementation detail, but the nature of the beast. The developers chose to explicitly configure all BGP peerings and not give BGP the ability to perform automatic neighbor discovery. An IGP should perform automatic neighbor discovery because the network should discover the routed topology quickly and reliably. The nature of IGPs in use today requires that each router know the routed topology and also quickly discover when the topology changes. Because BGP is the critical protocol that makes the Internet work, it would be dangerous and unscalable to allow the routers to automatically discover neighbors in the Internet at large. Instead of the thousands (or is it tens of thousands?) of routers today that have their BGP neighbors manually configured, imagine that they can dynamically discover all direct neighbors. Suppose that there were no boundaries to this discovery process, other than the discovery protocol itself. The first interesting question would be, How long would this process take? To fully populate a database consisting of all the Internet routers would take an enormously long time. What would be the size of this imaginary database? Consider the memory and processor constraints this would have on all the routers. Besides that, how would an ISP distinguish itself from its competitors? All the routers would automatically discover each other and propagate all routing information freely. There would be little or no boundaries between ISPs and the concept of routing domains would be nearly meaningless. Without such a competitive environment, innovation and differentiation among the many ISPs would disappear and the growth and progression of the Internet would suffocate. As you can see, forcing explicit configuration of peerings is a required necessity for scalability and security reasons.

There are at least two types of BGP peerings, *Internal* (IBGP) and *External* (EBGP). (Actually, there are three types of BGP peerings, the third being Confederation BGP, which is discussed in the "Confederations" section later in this chapter.) For the time being, consider only these two peerings. There are distinct differences between how the protocol behaves if configuring IBGP or EBGP. If two routers are peering and they both are in the same AS, then they are using IBGP. If the two routers are in different ASs, then they are using EBGP. It is almost that simple. There are some minor differences in the configuration, but there are major differences in the behavior of some key BGP attributes. Think back to the discussion of path attribute in the "History of BGP" section. Path attributes are used to identify characteristics of a route, or prefix, and are regularly used to implement routing policy. Routing policy could be used to influence which path, among a set of paths, to use to forward traffic on. The BGP protocol itself has the ability to select the best path to use, but network operators often need to influence this behavior. Full explanation of all BGP attributes will come later, but for now let us briefly mention two key ones, AS_PATH and NEXT_HOP.

By default, IBGP peers do not modify the AS_PATH or the NEXT_HOP attribute. BGP keeps these two attributes unchanged when passing a received routing update to an IBGP neighbor. The AS_PATH is the list of ASs that the route has propagated through. As each BGP border router sends an update to its EBGP neighbor, it will prepend, or add, its own AS number to this AS_PATH attribute. The AS number is prepended to the front, or leftmost position, of the AS_PATH, enabling you to distinguish from which AS the routing update originated. Since the AS numbers are prepended to the leftmost position, the rightmost AS number represents the originating AS.

Remember, this is necessary for routing loop detection and avoidance. EGP did not use this attribute, and the result was the Internet was very prone to routing loops with EGP. With BGP, when a router receives a routing update, one of the first things the router will do is look in the AS_PATH. If the locally configured AS number is already present in the AS_PATH, then the prefix must have already propagated through the local AS. This means the prefix has looped, so the router will drop the prefix as shown in Figure 12-2. Now imagine what would happen if a BGP border router prepended its own AS number to an update as it passed this update to its IBGP neighbor. As mentioned, this is the default behavior for EBGP. In the case of IBGP, when the receiving internal router receives this update it looks in the AS_PATH. The router would see its own AS number and would drop the update. This would prevent all routing information from entering the internal portions of the network. So, it is absolutely necessary that when passing routing updates to IBGP neighbors, the border router must not prepend its AS number to the AS_PATH attribute.

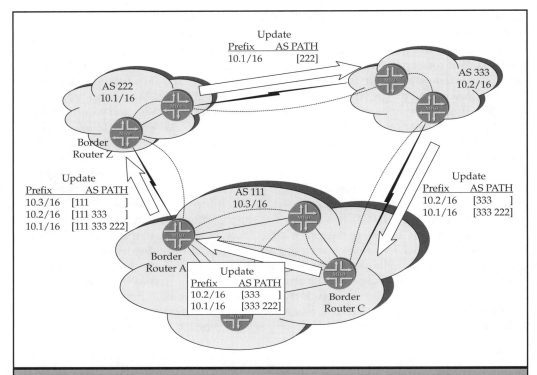

Figure 12-2.   *Border router Z receives the EBGP update containing prefixes 10.1/16, 10.2/16, and 10.3/16 from border router A. Border router Z drops prefix 10.1/16 due to AS_PATH loop detection.*

The second use of the AS_PATH attribute is for path selection. This is discussed in detail in the "BGP Decision Process" section later in this chapter.

BGP also will not, by default, modify the NEXT_HOP attribute when passing routing updates to IBGP peers. The NEXT_HOP attribute is used to tell the routers where they must forward traffic to reach a particular external destination. This NEXT_HOP is, by default, the EBGP routers' external interface IP address in the neighboring AS, as shown in Figure 12-3.

So, all internal routers in AS 111 know that to reach network 10.2/16 in AS 333, they must forward traffic to border router N who owns 192.168.2.2. This address, 192.68.2.2, is resolved from the IGP. Border router C will not modify this NEXT_HOP attribute when sending routing updates to its IBGP peers. Only when the routing update reaches the other side of AS 111 and is propagated to AS 222 will the BGP NEXT_HOP attribute change. Referring back to Figure 12-3, border router A will change the NEXT_HOP to reflect its IP address. Routers in AS 222 now know that they must send traffic for 10.2/16 to border router A. Follow the NEXT_HOP address of 10.2/16 from border router Y in AS 222 to see where it gets changed.

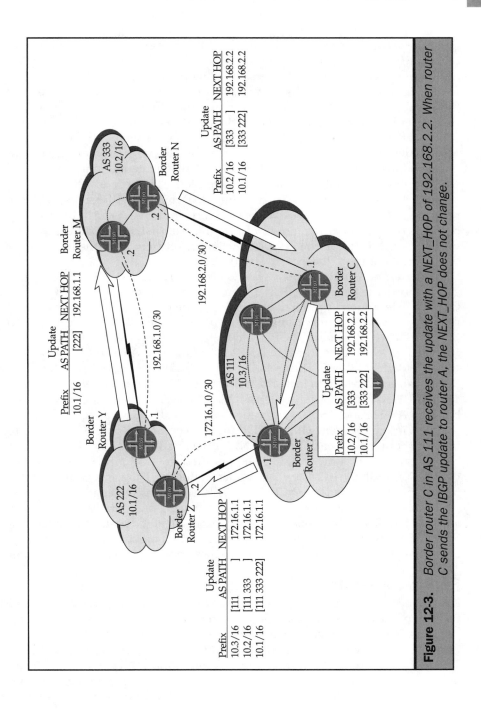

Figure 12-3.   *Border router C in AS 111 receives the update with a NEXT_HOP of 192.168.2.2. When router C sends the IBGP update to router A, the NEXT_HOP does not change.*

A not-so-obvious question that might follow this explanation is, Why do IBGP peers not modify the NEXT_HOP attribute by default? The answer is partly related to the desire to prevent possible suboptimal routing paths inside a network and partly related to historical BGP designs. Historically, not all routers inside an ISP used BGP. Today there is this concept of a full IBGP mesh, meaning that every router in the AS must be IBGP peered to every other router inside the AS. Reasons for this come in later sections. Historically, however, not all the routers inside an AS were fully IBGP peered to every other router. In such a scenario, the best forwarding path to an external network might not even traverse the BGP routers because not all the internal routers used BGP. In other words, there might not be a 1-to-1 correspondence between the BGP speaking routers and other routers within the AS. If all the IBGP routers modified the NEXT_HOP to reflect their IP address, the best or shortest forwarding path can be affected suboptimally because routers that are sending traffic to this external network must then forward the traffic toward the IBGP router. It is much more efficient to let the IGP figure out what the shortest path is to the external border router.

In Figure 12-4, only routers A, B, and G in AS 111 are peering using IBGP. The white arrow shows the path of the BGP update. The other routers in AS 111 are using only OSPF. Border router A receives an EBGP update for prefix 10.2/16 from AS 222. Border router A passes this prefix using IBGP to border router B and G without modifying the BGP NEXT_HOP (default IBGP behavior). So, the BGP NEXT_HOP for 10.2/16 is 192.168.1.1, which is router Z in AS 222. Internally to AS 111, the 10.2/16 prefix is redistributed into OSPF. This is so the other internal routers can reach this destination. Border router G needs to forward traffic to 10.2.1.1. The BGP NEXT_HOP will be 192.168.1.1, which is border router Z in AS 222, which shares the multi-access segment between AS 222 and AS 111 with routers A and F. Router F advertises this multi-access segment into OSPF, since it is the DR for this segment. Router G needs to forward traffic to router F to reach the BGP NEXT_HOP address of 192.168.1.1. Everything works as expected; however, if IBGP modified the BGP NEXT_HOP by default, the BGP NEXT_HOP for 10.2/16 will be router A. Router G now forwards traffic to router A, instead of to router F, to reach 10.2/16. This is a suboptimal path.

Although this seems like an extreme corner case, particularly with only routers A, B, and G using IBGP, this scenario was very probable in the past. Remember, not all routers in the AS used BGP in the past and it was common practice to redistribute BGP routes into the IGP. Today, of course, neither of these practices is considered a good idea.

Passive Peering

Passive peering can be configured when you do not want your router to initiate the peering process by sending a BGP Open message. BGP Open messages bring up BGP peerings. Your router will accept valid Open messages, and will respond with its own Open message to complete the FSM, but your router will not initiate the peering process. This feature can be useful during network migrations. Consider that you are bringing online many new IBGP peers. Prior to the actual bringing up of the new IBGP peers, you can configure your existing IBGP routers with the new peer IP addresses. If you

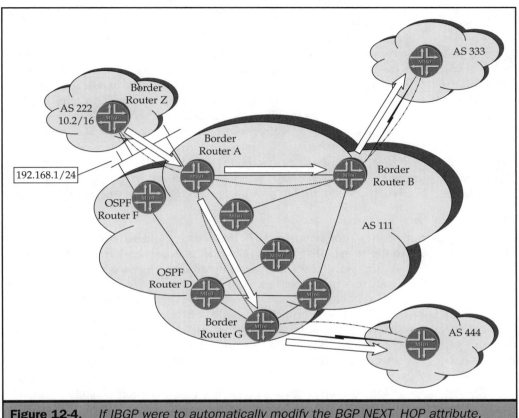

Figure 12-4.   *If IBGP were to automatically modify the BGP NEXT_HOP attribute,
suboptimal routing can occur.*

configure these new peers as "passive," then the local BGP speaker will not constantly
send Open messages to the new IBGP peers in an attempt to bring up the peering session.
That way, the logs of the new IBGP peers will not fill with Open and Notification
messages. When you bring up the new IBGP peers and configure them with the peering
addresses of your existing peers, they will then start the FSM and initiate the peering
session by sending Open messages. Your passive peers will respond and the peering
session will come up. You can configure this feature with the following command:

```
user@hostname# set protocols bgp group group-name neighbor address passive
```

This feature can be applied at the neighbor level, as stated in the previous command. It
can also be applied at the BGP group level, or globally in BGP for all configured neighbors.

BGP Message Types

There are four message types in BGP: Open, Update, Notification, and Keepalive. Each of these messages serves a specific function, and together they enable BGP to accomplish its job of routing in the Internet. In BGP, the maximum message size is 4096 bytes and the minimum is 19 bytes. Each message has a fixed-sized header, consisting of 19 bytes. You will see that the smallest BGP message is the sending of the header alone, and this serves a specific purpose. If three of these messages are examined and discussed first, then it becomes clear how simple BGP really is. Open starts or opens the BGP peering session, Update transfers all the necessary routing information between peers during the session, and Notification stops or closes the BGP peering session. The remaining message type, Keepalive, keeps the session active so that the established peers know that each other is still alive. It is that simple. Now each message will be discussed in detail.

Open

After a transport connection (for example, TCP) has been established, the Open message is sent by the BGP router to establish or open the BGP peering session. Either router of a peering session can initiate the session by sending an Open message. This message is sent unicast to the IP address that is configured as the peer or neighbor. If both routers simultaneously attempt to open a BGP session by sending Open messages to each other, then only one of the BGP sessions should be established. Such an occurrence is called a BGP connection collision. A syslog message will typically be seen when this happens, assuming syslog is configured. One of the sessions must be terminated so that there are not two peering sessions opened between the peers. RFC 1267, BGP v3, originally specified this scenario and also how implementations should behave to ensure that only a single BGP session is opened in such a scenario. Inside the Open message there is significant information regarding the peering session (see Figure 12-5). Some of the information in the Open message is nonnegotiable, meaning that it must match what is configured on the router. For instance, if a router is configured to peer to neighbor 192.168.1.1 in AS 65200, but receives an Open message from 192.168.1.1 with AS 65201, it will not accept this Open message. There is a mismatch of AS numbers, which is likely a configuration problem. What happens in such a situation will be discussed later when error handling in BGP is explained.

- **Version** This 1-octet unsigned integer indicates the protocol version number of the message. The current BGP version number is 4.

- **My Autonomous System** This 2-octet unsigned integer indicates the AS number of the sender.

- **Holdtime** This 2-octet unsigned integer indicates the number of seconds that the sender proposes for the value of the holdtimer. On receipt of an Open message, a BGP speaker must calculate the value of the holdtimer by using the smaller of its configured holdtime and the holdtime received in the Open message. The calculated value indicates the maximum number of seconds that might elapse between the receipt of successive Keepalive and/or Update messages by the sender. The holdtime must be at least 6 seconds in JUNOS software. An implementation can choose to reject the peering connection based on the holdtime.

- **BGP Identifier**   This 4-octet unsigned integer indicates the BGP identifier of the sender. A given BGP speaker sets the value of its BGP identifier to an IP address assigned to that BGP speaker. The value of the BGP identifier is determined on startup and is typically the router's loopback IP address, unless configured otherwise. The BGP identifier is also referred to as the router ID.

- **Optional Parameters Length**   This 1-octet unsigned integer indicates the total length of the Optional Parameters field in octets. If the value of this field is zero, no optional parameters are present.

- **Optional Parameters**   Each parameter in this field is encoded as a <Parameter Type, Parameter Length, Parameter Value> triplet. Parameter Type is a 1-octet field that unambiguously identifies individual parameters. Parameter Length is a 1-octet field that contains the length of the Parameter Value field in octets. Parameter Value is a variable length field that is interpreted according to the value of the Parameter Type field.

  Examples of optional parameters are Optional Parameters Type 1, which represents authentication of the Open message, and Type 2, which represents capabilities advertisement.

To fully discuss the Open message, there is a need to introduce one of the enhancements to BGP v4, that is the capabilities advertisement. Capabilities advertisement is described in RFC 2842 and was introduced into BGP v4 in May 2000.

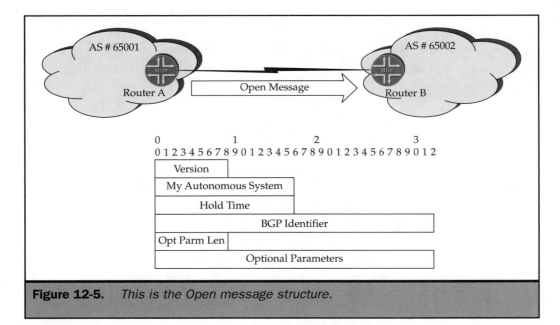

Figure 12-5.   *This is the Open message structure.*

It uses the Optional Parameter Type 2 in the Open message. Its purpose is to facilitate new features into BGP v4 so that the protocol can continue to evolve seamlessly. As was mentioned earlier, BGP v4 is not finished. It must continually evolve to support new features and applications that are needed to scale and grow the Internet infrastructure. The capabilities advertisement allows two BGP peers to negotiate which of the many new features they will mutually support, such as shown in Figure 12-6. So, one of the peers can be from a router vendor that implemented one of the new enhancements to BGP v4 and the other peer can be a router from another vendor that has not yet implemented this new enhancement. Through capabilities negotiation they will agree to not use the specific feature, since they both do not support it. Prior to this enhancement there was no way to introduce a new feature to BGP v4. There is a detailed description of this capability in the "Capabilities Advertisement" section later in this chapter.

Update

The Update message is responsible for disseminating all the necessary routing information between BGP speakers. This single message type will contain all the active prefixes (and their related attributes) that a BGP router needs to export or advertise to its peer. There will be numerous Update messages exchanged between peers to propagate all the routing information that is required in the Internet today.

The process of passing all the required Update messages necessary to propagate the current Internet routing table can take from several seconds to several minutes and depends on vendor implementation and other processes the routers are busy doing.

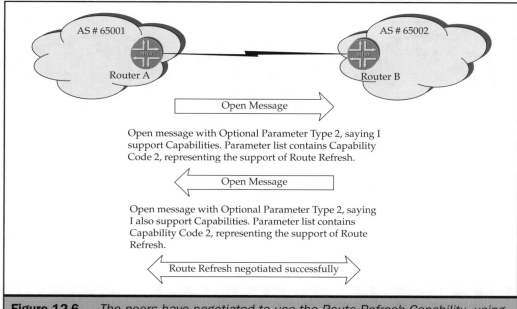

Figure 12-6. *The peers have negotiated to use the Route Refresh Capability, using Capability Code 2.*

Along with the required 19-byte header, each Update message can contain feasible routes, withdrawn routes, path attributes, and appropriate *Network Layer Reachability Information* (NLRI). Note that it is possible to pack multiple IP prefixes sharing common attributes into the NLRI fields of a single Update message. This allows for more efficient processing of Update messages by the receiving systems.

This packing of prefixes is actually recommended in modern BGP implementations for efficiency reasons. Imagine if a BGP implementation were to advertise a unique Update message per IP prefix. The overhead associated with doing this would be quite large. JUNOS software does implement the more efficient implementation of packing prefixes in Update messages, whenever possible.

Figure 12-7 shows the structure and format of the update message.

- **Unfeasible Routes Length**   This 2-octet unsigned integer indicates the total length of the Withdrawn Routes field in octets. A value of 0 indicates that no routes are being withdrawn from service, and that the Withdrawn Routes field is not present in this Update message.

- **Withdrawn Routes**   This is a variable length field that contains a list of IP prefixes for the routes that are being withdrawn from service.

- **Total Path Attribute Length**   This 2-octet unsigned integer indicates the total length of the Path Attributes field in octets. A value of 0 indicates that no Network Layer Reachability Information field is present in this Update message.

- **Path Attributes**   A variable length sequence of path attributes is present in every Update. Each path attribute is a triple <attribute type, attribute length, attribute value> of variable length. The Attribute Type field contains the code of the path attribute.

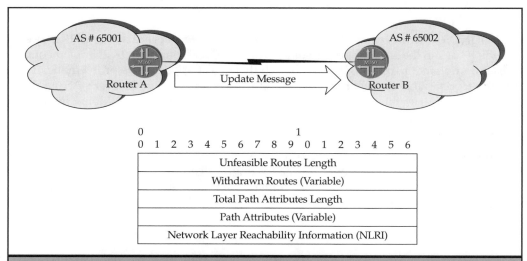

Figure 12-7.   *This is the structure of the Update message.*

Currently defined attributes are listed in the following table:

Type Code	Attribute
1	ORIGIN
2	AS_PATH
3	NEXT_HOP
4	MED
5	LOCAL_PREF
6	ATOMIC_AGGREGATE
7	AGGREGATOR
8	COMMUNITY
9	ORIGINATOR ID
10	CLUSTER_LIST
11	DPA
12	ADVERTISER
13	RCID_PATH / CLUSTER_ID
14	MP_REACH_NLRI
15	MP_UNREACH_NLRI
16	EXTENDED COMMUNITY

In JUNOS software, valid Updates received from EBGP peers are sent to all BGP peers, including back to the sending peer. In other words, JUNOS software's BGP implementation does not implement split-horizon. Although this might appear to be problematic, it is not. The Updates that are sent back to the sending peer will contain the peer's AS number in the AS_PATH, so they will be dropped. This behavior is valuable if doing inter-AS multicast with MSDP.

As stated in RFC 1771:

"For the benefit of future support of inter-AS multicast capabilities, a BGP speaker that participates in inter-AS multicast routing shall advertise a route it receives from one of its external peers and if it installs it in its Loc-RIB, it shall advertise it back to the peer from which the route was received."

Update messages are also responsible for withdrawing routing information. A list of IP prefixes for the routes that are being withdrawn from service will be listed in the Withdrawn Routes field. The global Internet is a dynamic and highly complex conglomerate of routing systems. It is constantly changing to accommodate new routing information and to remove old routing information that is withdrawn for various reasons.

Network engineers are always improving their network by replacing routers with higher performing routers and upgrading circuits to larger bandwidths. They are also improving their existing routers by upgrading software or changing the routers' configuration, and this inevitably leads to a certain amount of human or process error. When these failures or errors happen, more likely than not, a withdrawal of routing information then follows.

There was an interesting dialogue on the North American Network Operators' Group (NANOG) mailing list attempting to determine the percentages of each type of failure in the Internet, and the impact of such failures. Although no official conclusive study was done, there was a small consensus that the majority of these failures were related to software. This was due to either upgrading software on the existing router base, or software bugs. More recently, however, router software is more stable than in the past. This is partly due to the increasing importance and visibility of the Internet, which compels router vendors to produce more stable code. Keep in mind that whenever prefixes are withdrawn from the Internet routing table, this is a CPU-intensive effort and often affects the ability of legacy routers to forward traffic. Legacy routers are defined as those routers that are not designed and built to perform in today's Internet. These routers still exist in the Internet because of budget, operational, or political constraints.

In the past, the result of a single error or failure resulted in additional outages due to the poor performance of legacy routers or unstable router code. *Damping*, which is discussed later, is an effort to reduce the impact of constantly withdrawn routes on these legacy routers. During the exchange of NANOG mail on this topic, it was said that the second-highest failure affecting the Internet was probably due to human error.

Notification

The Notification message is typically sent when a BGP router experiences an error condition that is fatal enough to warrant a termination of the peering session. The error notification mechanism used in BGP assumes that the transport protocol supports a "graceful" close, that is, that all outstanding data will be delivered before the connection is closed (RFC 1267).

Another common situation of sending the Notification message is during the Open message exchange. If, during the exchange of Open messages, there is a problem with some piece of information contained in the Open message, the sensing BGP router will send a Notification message to its peer describing the error condition it has experienced. This error condition notification is useful in debugging peering problems. When using JUNOS software BGP traceoptions, there is usually a clear text description accompanying the notification codes that explains the error condition. The Notification messages will contain a code related to the high-level error condition that was detected. There will also be a subcode that specifies in more detail what the error was.

When a Notification is sent, the sending BGP peer will then gracefully terminate the peering and transport connection. All resources for the connection are released and the IP prefixes associated with the remote peer are marked as invalid. Update messages are sent to all remaining peers withdrawing the now invalid IP prefixes. (See Figure 12-8.)

- **Error Code**   This 1-octet unsigned integer indicates the type of Notification.

- **Error Subcode**   This 1-octet unsigned integer provides more specific information about the nature of the reported error. Each error code might have one or more error subcodes associated with it. If no appropriate error subcode is defined, then a zero value is used for the error subcode field.

- **Data**   This variable-length field is used to diagnose the reason for the Notification. The contents of the Data field depend on the error code and error subcode.

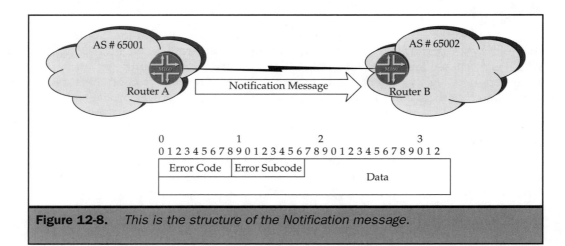

Figure 12-8.   *This is the structure of the Notification message.*

The current Notification messages are listed in the following table:

Error Code	Error Subcode	Data (Description)
1		Message Header Error
	1	Connection Not Synchronized
	2	Bad Message Length
	3	Bad Message Type
2		Open Message Error
	1	Unsupported Version Number
	2	Bad Peer AS
	3	Bad BGP Identifier
	4	Unsupported Optional Parameter
	5	Authentication Failure
	6	Unacceptable Holdtime
	7	Unsupported Capability
3		Update Message Error
	1	Malformed Attribute List
	2	Unrecognized Well-known Attribute
	3	Missing Well-known Attribute
	4	Attribute Flags Error
	5	Attribute Length Error
	6	Invalid ORIGIN Attribute
	7	AS Routing Loop
	8	Invalid NEXT_HOP Attribute
	9	Optional Attribute Error
	10	Invalid Network Field
	11	Malformed AS_PATH
4		Holdtimer Expired
5		Finite-State Machine Error
6		Cease

Keepalive

The Keepalive message, as its name designates, keeps the BGP peering session alive. In the absence of Update messages, this Keepalive message must be exchanged between peers often enough so that the peers do not terminate the session. There is a timer associated with this Keepalive message called the holdtime. If the holdtime is exceeded, the router will send a Notification message and terminate the peering session. JUNOS Internet software defaults to a holdtime of 90 seconds. This is a configurable parameter, but typically it is not adjusted. If a BGP peer does not receive a message, either Update or Keepalive, within 90 seconds it will send a Notification message and terminate the BGP session. This holdtime is one of the parameters that are negotiated during the exchange of Open messages. This was one of the many changes with BGP v4. If two peers have mismatched holdtime values, either due to manual configuration or different vendor implementation defaults, both peers should agree to use the lower holdtime value. JUNOS software supports a holdtime of 6 seconds or higher.

The Keepalive message is the 19-byte BGP header and is sent one-third the holdtime value. In JUNOS Internet software, with the default holdtime of 90 seconds, Keepalives are exchanged every 30 seconds. Keep in mind that changing the holdtime on an existing peering session will result in the peering session being dropped and renegotiated. This is because the holdtime field is in the Open message.

Some of the known reasons for the holdtime expiring have been link congestion resulting in dropped packets, routing instability resulting in lost or looped packets, and overloaded routers. Routers that are not purposely built for the strains of the Internet environment have been known to drop BGP messages or have been unable to generate BGP Keepalives due to processor overload. Although it seems tempting to lower the holdtime to a lower value than 90 seconds in an effort to detect these errors sooner and speed convergence, this is not recommended. Too short a timer will result in peers dropping more often, which leads to Notification messages and Update messages withdrawing the appropriate prefixes. This flooding of additional information in the network can exacerbate the congestion or the condition that led to the Keepalives being dropped in the first place. In an effort to avoid the BGP messages being dropped during times of congestion, most modern BGP implementations code all BGP messages with an IP Precedence value of 110, which signifies Internetwork Control. Routers should prioritize these messages, such that in times of bandwidth congestion, best effort IP datagrams are dropped before BGP messages. (See Figure 12-9).

■ **Marker** This 16-octet field contains a value that the receiver of the message can predict. If the Type of the message is Open, or if the Open message carries no authentication information (as an Optional Parameter), then the marker must be all 1's. Otherwise, the value of the marker can be predicted by some other computation specified as part of the authentication mechanism (which is specified as part of the authentication information) used. The marker can be used to detect loss of synchronization between a pair of BGP peers, and to authenticate incoming BGP messages.

- **Length**   This 2-octet unsigned integer indicates the total length of the message, including the header, in octets. Thus, it allows you to locate in the transport-level stream the (Marker field of the) next message. The value of the Length field must always be at least 19 and no greater than 4096, and might be further constrained, depending on the message type. No "padding" of extra data after the message is allowed, so the Length field must have the smallest value required given the rest of the message.

- **Type**   This 1-octet unsigned integer indicates the type code of the message. The type codes are defined in the following table.

Type Code	Message Type
1	OPEN
2	UPDATE
3	NOTIFICATION
4	KEEPALIVE

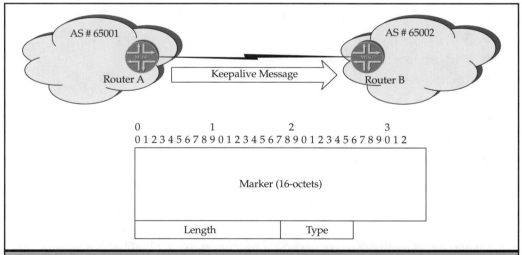

Figure 12-9.   *This is the structure of the Keepalive message, which is the standard 19-byte BGP header that accompanies every BGP message.*

Finite-State Machine

The idea of a *finite-state machine* (FSM) comes from a branch of mathematics called formal language theory. The concept is basically that with a specific and known input, there is a finite number of possible outputs, or states. It is a mathematical way of describing the possible states that BGP can progress through, as the protocol attempts to establish a valid BGP connection.

There are six BGP states:

- Idle
- Connect
- Active
- Open-sent
- Open-confirm
- Established

There are 13 BGP events, which either trigger a state change or are the result of a state change:

- BGP start
- BGP stop
- BGP transport connection open
- BGP transport connection closed
- BGP transport connection open failed
- BGP transport fatal error
- Connect-retry timer expired
- Holdtimer expired
- Keepalive timer expired
- Receive Open message
- Receive Keepalive message
- Receive Update message
- Receive Notification message

Initially, BGP is in the *idle* state. In this state, there is no attempt to establish a session and all incoming BGP connections are refused. Basically, BGP has not started for this specific peer. Note that each peering session goes through its own FSM. If you have configured your BGP peer but the peer does not progress out of the idle state, there is most likely a problem with your configuration that is preventing a BGP start event. A BGP start event will trigger the start of the FSM. A start event is usually triggered by manual configuration of BGP peering by an operator. With a start event, the router will start a connect-retry timer, initiate a TCP connection to the specified peer, simultaneously listen for a TCP connection attempt from that peer, and then will transition to the *connect* state.

Remember that each peer can initiate the peering session. In the event that the attempts are simultaneous and parallel, then there will be a connection collision and one of the connections will be torn down.

Once in the connect state, the router is now waiting for the TCP connection to be completed. Once the TCP connection is successful, the router clears the connect-retry timer, sends an Open message to the peer, and transitions to the *open-sent* state. As you can see, the state descriptions are very revealing. Open-sent means that the router has sent an Open message.

From the connect state, the router can actually transition to several different states depending on the event. If the TCP connection fails (for example, retransmission timeout), the router restarts the connect-retry timer, continues to listen for a TCP connection attempt from the peer, and transitions to the *active* state.

If the connect-retry timer were to expire, the router would restart the timer and again attempt to establish a TCP connection to the peer. It would remain in the connect state while doing this. The connect-retry timer is left to vendor implementation; however, it should be sufficiently large enough to allow TCP initialization.

If the router were to receive an error at this time, it would change its state back to idle.

Watching closely as the peer transitions through these states, the astute engineer can determine what is happening and begin to make assumptions on possible outcomes. For example, if you have configured the peer and watched as the peer transitions to connect, only to see it transition to active within a few seconds, you can assume that the initial TCP connection attempt has failed. This would imply that there is a problem with basic TCP connectivity to the remote peer. An attempt to PING the peer to validate basic reachability might reveal more information to aid in troubleshooting at this point. Of course, it can also have been a transient problem that has since cleared.

If in active state, the peer is again attempting to create a successful TCP connection. If the TCP connection is successful this time, the router clears the connect-retry timer, sends an Open message to the peer, and changes to open-sent.

If the connect-retry timer were to expire, the router would restart the timer and again attempt to establish a TCP connection to the peer. It would transition to the connect state while doing this.

If the router were to receive an error at this time, it would change its state back to idle.

In the open-sent state, the router is waiting for an Open message from its peer. The router has successfully completed its required work up to this point and is waiting for its peer to do the same. When an Open message is received, the router checks all the fields in the message for correctness. If an error is detected, a Notification is sent to the peer with the appropriate code and subcode, the TCP connection is dropped, and the router transitions back to idle.

If there are no errors detected in the received Open message, the router will send its first Keepalive message to this peer. The holdtime is set to the negotiated value, that being the lower of either the locally configured value or the value in the Open message from its peer. The router then starts a Keepalive timer, which is one-third the holdtime. The router then transitions to open-confirm. Note that the router is smart enough to look at the AS field in the Open message to determine whether this BGP connection is either internal or external. If the AS number is the same as the locally configured value, it is an internal peering session.

If the holdtime expires at this time, or the router receives or experiences another event that signifies an error condition, the router will send a Notification message with the appropriate error code, drop the TCP connection, and transition back to idle.

In the open-confirm state, the router is waiting for a Keepalive message from its peer. Once a Keepalive is received, the router will transition to *established* and the peering session is considered up.

If the holdtime expires at this time, or the router receives or experiences another event that signifies an error condition, the router will send a Notification message with the appropriate error code, drop the TCP connection, and transition back to idle.

In the established state, the router can exchange Keepalive and Update messages with its peer. This is where the exchange of Update messages will happen and each router will initially send its peer the entire active Internet routing table. Once the entire routing table is exchanged, only incremental updates will happen after that. Each router will keep the routing table it has received indefinitely. Unlike IGP routes, BGP routes do not timeout by themselves. The route will change only if the router were to receive an Update message changing some attribute of that route or withdrawing that route entirely; however, the router can receive the same IP prefix from another peer and decide that the newly received path is better. In that case, the currently active path will be demoted to inactive and the newly received better path will be marked as active. Only active routes are eligible for exporting to neighbors.

If the holdtime expires at this time, or the router receives or experiences another event that signifies an error condition, the router will send a Notification message with the appropriate error code, drop the BGP peering session, and transition back to idle.

To summarize the FSM, if you ever see "active" in the peering process, you can assume that there is a problem; however, the problem might be transient and might clear itself so no immediate action should be required. If the peer states toggle between active and connect for more than several minutes, then perhaps the condition that is preventing the TCP connection from succeeding is not transient and action might be required. Use tools such as PING and traceroute to the peer IP address to see if you can discover additional information regarding the problem.

Routing Information Bases (RIBs)

RIBs, in their simplest definition, are unique memory blocks where BGP routing tables are held for storage; or you can think of them as unique routing tables. There are three primary RIBs that interact with BGP: adj-rib-in, local-rib, and adj-rib-out. This does not imply, however, that there is a single adj-rib-in and a single adj-rib-out. There are actually many adj-ribs-in and adj-ribs-out. Typically, there is a unique adj-rib-in for each BGP peer, and previously in JUNOS software, there was a unique adj-rib-out for each EBGP peer. JUNOS software R4.4 and later is more efficient and will create adj-ribs-out by grouping peers that have common routing policies.

RIBs are named in JUNOS software by specifying the protocol family followed by a nonnegative integer. An example is *inet.0,* which is the primary unicast IP v4 RIB. When a route is learned, it is imported into one or more RIBs. Import policies might filter the route, in which case it might not be installed in the primary RIB. Routes in RIBs might be exported to other protocols or the same protocol on another interface. JUNOS software exports routes from a RIB to a protocol.

adj-rib-in

Valid routes that are learned from BGP Update messages are stored in the adj-rib-in. By default, JUNOS software stores all valid, nonlooped received routes in the adj-rib-in, even if there is an input routing policy in place that discards a specific received route. This is because the adj-rib-in contains BGP routes BEFORE the input policy has been applied to them. This allows JUNOS software to implement, by default, what is often referred to as *soft reconfiguration.* Soft reconfiguration refers to the act of updating a local routing policy, without the need to disruptively close and reopen the peering session. For example, if a router were configured to discard a specific received prefix with a configured import routing policy, this prefix will still remain in the adj-rib-in. It will not, however, be installed in the local-rib, which is where all valid and accepted routes are stored. The local-rib can be considered the primary IP v4 unicast routing table, or *inet.0* in JUNOS software. If this import policy was later changed to now allow the specific prefix to be accepted into the local-rib, and thus eligible to be exported out, JUNOS software is able to accomplish this without notifying the sending neighbor to resend this specific prefix. This is because the discarded prefix is actually kept in the adj-rib-in. Legacy BGP code in some vendors used to force a clearing of the BGP session to again receive a set of prefixes that were previously discarded due to policy. This obviously had very detrimental effects on the global Internet; however, there is a downside to keeping all routes in the adj-rib-in. Nothing is free! Additional memory is needed in the router to store all these extra prefixes. The benefit of doing this, however, is deemed worth the tradeoff. The result is a more stable routing infrastructure, due to the dynamic capability of updating routing policy nondisruptively.

To view a route in the adj-rib-in, use this command:

```
user@hostname> show route receive-protocol bgp bgp-neighbor-address
```

This command will show you the valid received routes that have passed the BGP sanity check. Looped and hidden routes will not be displayed.

If you want to keep all received routes in the adj-rib-in, even the routes that have a looped AS_PATH, use this command.

```
user@hostname# set protocols bgp keep all
```

Keep in mind that this will likely require the use of more memory on the router to store all the additional routes.

local-rib

As mentioned, the local-rib is the primary routing table, or *inet.0* in JUNOS software. *inet.0* stores all IP v4 prefixes, not just the ones learned via BGP. These are routes that have passed the configured input routing policies. There is no separate BGP routing table in JUNOS software. To view a route in the local-rib, use this command:

```
user@hostname> show route ip-prefix-address
```

To parse the output to show only a specific BGP route, use this command:

```
user@hostname> show route protocol bgp ip-prefix-address
```

adj-rib-out

The adj-rib-out is the routing table AFTER export routing policy has been applied. In other words, this is the table that stores all the BGP routes that are advertised in Update messages to peers. To view these BGP routes, use this command:

```
user@hostname> show route advertising-protocol bgp bgp-neighbor-address
```

In Figure 12-10, you see two EBGP peers and the execution of two commands, which imply by their syntax that you should be seeing the exact same information with each command. In reality, however, you will not see the exact same set of information with these commands. This is because the user@hostname> show route advertising-protocol bgp *bgp-neighbor-address* does not actually show you the route exactly as it appears in the Update message that the router is sending. For instance, notice that the AS_PATH does not show the local AS that will be prepended when the route is actually exported to the EBGP peer. Using this command, JUNOS software is showing you the adj-rib-out that BGP has stored for the specified neighbor. JUNOS software will prepend the local AS on the fly as it creates the Update message.

There are two additional cases worth mentioning in which you will not see the exact output as what is in the Update message. When using private ASs and stripping them with

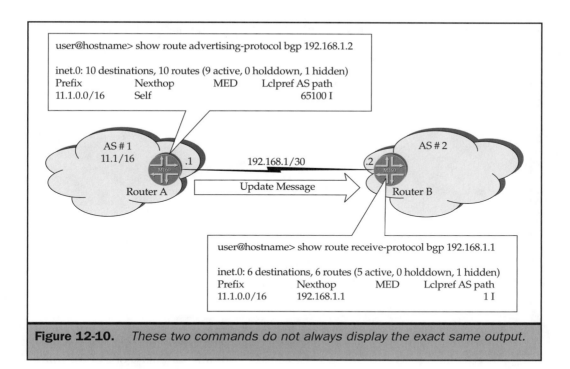

Figure 12-10.   *These two commands do not always display the exact same output.*

the `user@hostname# set protocols bgp group` *group-name* `remove-private` command, you will not see the private ASs being stripped with the `user@hostname> show route advertising-protocol bgp` *bgp-neighbor-address* command. This is due to the same reason as with the first case mentioned, in that JUNOS software will remove the private ASs on the fly while creating the Update message. This is for memory efficiency reasons. Also, when using this command on a route reflector, you will see routes that are being sent to its client. If this client is the originator of one of the routes, that route will not be reflected back to the originating client. This command, however, will show you the route. Again, this is because the Update message is created on-the-fly.

IBGP and EBGP Basics

When configuring BGP in JUNOS software, there is little difference between internal BGP and external BGP. Both IBGP and EBGP need the same type of information to successfully negotiate a peering session. The required information is actually very minimal. The local AS number, the remote AS number and the peer IP address are all that is really required. With IBGP, you might also need to specify the local IP address, depending on the BGP design. In the following code snippet, notice that the configuration is simple and minimal.

```
routing-options {
    autonomous-system 111;
}
protocols {
    bgp {
        group ibgp {
            peer-as 111;
            local-address 100.100.1.3;
            neighbor 100.100.1.1;
        }
        group ebgp {
            peer-as 333;
            neighbor 200.200.20.2;
        }
    }
}
```

There are a few things to note in the previous snippet. In the internal group named `ibgp`, there is the `local-address 100.100.1.3` command. This is one of the things that is typically used with IBGP peering that is not usually required with EBGP peering. This is because most BGP designs today use the routers loopback interface IP address as the peering address. The loopback interface is a logical software interface only and will never go down. So long as there is at least one physical IP interface working on the router, the loopback interface is active. Why would you peer to the loopback interface rather than the physical interface of a neighbor? For one, if you peered to a physical interface of a neighbor and that interface were to fail, the IBGP peering session would also fail. Remember that BGP peerings are point-to-point TCP connections and if one end point of this connection were to fail, the connection will subsequently fail. Peering to the loopback interface will allow the BGP peering session to be rerouted in case a physical interface were to fail. This way, the IBGP peering session will not fail so long as there is at least one IP interface on the neighbor working and this IP address and the loopback IP address are reachable via the IGP. Redundancy is the keyword here.

With EBGP peering, you will note that the `local-address ip-address` command is missing. Typically with EBGP peerings, the two neighbors are directly connected over a physical link, be it copper or fiber. This link can span a large distance with a physical circuit, such as DS3 or OC3, but the neighbors are directly connected nonetheless.

Also, there is no IGP or routing protocol running between these neighbors prior to configuring BGP. So, in this situation you cannot peer to the neighbor's loopback interface because the local router does not know how to reach that remote interface.

You would require a routing protocol to advertise that IP address to you, but there is none. Plus, since the two neighbors are directly connected over a single piece of wire in most cases, there is no capability to reroute if the neighbors' physical interface were to fail. The circuit between the neighbors would also fail. So, there is no additional redundancy achieved, unlike with IBGP peerings. So it is common practice to peer to the neighbor's directly connected physical interface IP address when configuring EBGP. The local router knows how to reach this IP address since the subnet, most likely a /30 subnet, is directly connected.

When TCP attempts a connection to the neighbor IP address, it will use the outgoing interface IP address as the source of this connection. This is automatic and requires no additional configuration. This is why you do not need to specify the `local-address` `ip-address` with EBGP peering. The TCP connection, and thus the BGP connection, will automatically use the outgoing interface IP address as the source or local address.

The other thing worth noting at this time in the BGP code snippet is that there is no command telling the router whether the peers are internal or external. A command, such as `type [internal|external]`, can be configured to specify this but it is not required. So, how does the router know what type of peering this is? The answer to that question lies in the *[routing-options]* portion of the configuration. Here is where you specify the local AS number for the router, using the `local-as autonomous-system-number` command. This bit of information, combined with the `peer-as autonomous-system-number` command in the BGP peer group, tells the router whether the peering is internal or external. If the peer AS number is the same as the local AS number, then the peering must be IBGP. In previous versions of JUNOS software, the `type [internal|external]` was required, but it no longer is. The software is now intelligent enough to figure this out.

Advantages of Peer Group Configurations

BGP peer groups are a method of grouping BGP peers together that have some property in common, such as having the same routing policies applied or being members of the same remote AS. This makes the router configuration more efficient and much easier to read. It also makes the BGP protocol more efficient in terms of memory use. Previous to JUNOS software R4.4, each EBGP peer maintained a separate adj-rib-out. From R4.4 onward, if the peers in a peer group have the same set of routing policies applied, these peers will share an adj-rib-out. This change was done for scalability reasons. Peer groups can be configured for internal or external peers. Peer groups are required in JUNOS software, however, the decision of which peers to group together is flexible. It makes sense to group all full-mesh IBGP peers into a common peer group. It also makes sense to group all external peers belonging to the same remote AS in the same peer group. It is unlikely that both internal and external peers will receive the same set of routing policies, so grouping them into a common peer group does not make sense. When configuring route reflection, the route reflector clients should all be in the same peer group. A commonly used strategy for grouping peers is shown here for reference.

```
protocols {
    bgp {
        group ibgp-mesh {
            peer-as 111;
            export nexthop-self;
            local-address 100.100.1.3;
            neighbor 100.100.1.1;
            neighbor 100.100.1.2;
            neighbor 100.100.1.4;
        }
        group rr-cluster {
            peer-as 111;
            cluster 100.100.1.3;
            export nexthop-self;
            local-address 100.100.1.3;
            neighbor 100.100.1.11;
            neighbor 100.100.1.12;
        }
        group private-peer-222 {
            peer-as 222;
            export [ no-bogons send-agg send-customers ];
            import [ no-bogons-or-default private-peer-in ];
            neighbor 200.200.20.2;
        }
        group private-peer-333 {
            peer-as 333;
            export [ no-bogons send-agg send-transit send-customers ];
            import [ no-bogons-or-default private-peer-in ];
            neighbor 212.212.212.2;
        }
        group private-peer-444 {
            peer-as 444;
            export [ no-bogons send-agg send-customers ];
            import [ no-bogons-or-default private-peer-in ];
            neighbor 211.211.10.1;
        }
    }
}
```

Note that in the displayed BGP configuration, there are separate peer groups for the internal IBGP mesh, the route reflector clients, and for each remote neighbor AS. In JUNOS software, when EBGP peers share the same set of export routing policies, they will share the same adj-rib-out. This is for resource efficiency reasons. In the preceding configuration, peer 200.200.20.2 in AS 222 and peer 211.211.10.1 in AS 444 will share the same adj-rib-out because they share the same set of export policies. This is regardless of whether they are in the same peer group. Grouping peers in the same remote AS in the same peer group is still a good practice, as that makes the configuration easier to read and understand.

Protocol Differences

Although there is little basic configuration difference between IBGP and EBGP peerings, there are protocol differences.

AS_PATH

Although there is little basic configuration difference between IBGP and EBGP peerings, there are protocol differences, those differences being how IBGP and EBGP natively treat the AS_PATH and NEXT_HOP attribute differently. To cover those differences in more detail, remember that the AS_PATH is used by BGP for loop detection. Each EBGP router will prepend its local AS number to this attribute when it advertises routing updates in the update message. Additionally, when a BGP speaker receives an update message with a list of prefixes and their associated path attributes, one of the first things the router does is to look into the AS_PATH to see if its local AS number is present. If it is, there is likely a routing loop and the prefix is dropped. With IBGP peering, the router cannot prepend its local AS number to this path as it sends Updates to IBGP peers, for if it did, the remote IBGP peer would end up dropping the prefix due to loop detection.

Although not related to IBGP or EBGP peering, it is possible to relax the AS_PATH loop detection. This feature is useful in certain MPLS VPN environments, which is beyond the scope of this book. The command to accomplish this is shown here.

```
user@hostname# set routing-options autonomous-system 1 loops 1
```

The command shown is for a router in AS 1 and this command has allowed the router to accept an AS_PATH loop of 1.

NEXT_HOP

Regarding the NEXT_HOP attribute, by default when an EBGP router advertises prefixes in Update messages, the NEXT_HOP field is populated with the outgoing interface IP address. This is considered the BGP NEXT_HOP address to the remote EBGP peer. This is also the same IP address used as the endpoint to the point-to-point TCP connection. The receiving EBGP peer then completes a sanity check on this BGP NEXT_HOP IP address by doing a recursive lookup in the IP routing table. The router must know how to reach the BGP NEXT_HOP IP address, or the BGP prefixes that it has received would be useless. This recursive lookup is done quickly and automatically.

If the router can resolve the BGP NEXT_HOP IP address via the routing table, then the router will then initiate the BGP Decision Process on the prefix. This recursive lookup in the routing table could be resolved by the IGP, static routes, or directly connected routes. The BGP Decision Process explanation comes in the "BGP Decision Process" section later in this chapter. For now, just consider that the router will install the received prefix in the routing table *inet.0* and mark this prefix as active. If the router were to now receive datagrams destined to this BGP prefix, the router will forward them to the BGP NEXT_HOP address.

For IBGP, the advertising BGP router will not modify the NEXT_HOP attribute by default.

That is a fundamental difference between IBGP and EBGP. As a matter of fact, the IBGP router sending Update messages will not modify the NEXT_HOP attribute at all unless the router is told to do so with routing policy. Assuming no routing policy is modifying this attribute, the IBGP router will leave the original IP address in the NEXT_HOP field and pass the Update message along. This was depicted in Figure 12-3 earlier in the chapter.

Typically within ISP networks, network operators create a policy to modify the NEXT_HOP attribute when exporting external prefixes to IBGP peers. When a border router re-advertises the EBGP learned prefixes to all its IBGP peers, this routing policy will change the BGP NEXT_HOP address to be the border routers loopback IP address. Again, this is better visualized with a picture. Please see Figure 12-11.

The routing policy in place on border router C that accomplishes the NEXT_HOP change is shown following this paragraph. Note that specifying "self" as the next-hop IP address translates to putting its loopback IP address as the BGP NEXT_HOP IP

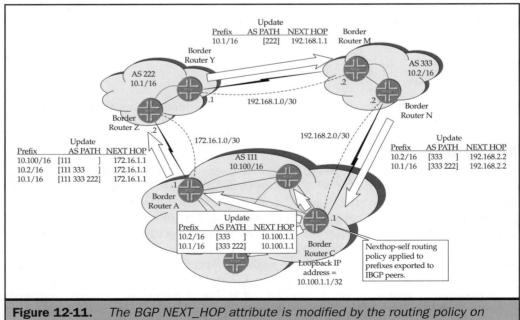

Figure 12-11.   *The BGP NEXT_HOP attribute is modified by the routing policy on border router C.*

address. The routers loopback IP address is advertised in the IGP and all internal routers can reach this address. This is shown in the Update that router C is sending its IBGP peers. Note the NEXT_HOP is 10.100.1.1, rather than 192.168.2.2.

```
interfaces {
    lo0 {
        unit 0 {
            family inet {
                address 10.100.1.1/32;
            }
        }
    }
}
protocols {
    bgp {
        group ibgp-mesh {
            peer-as 111;
            export nexthop-self;
            local-address 10.100.1.1;
            neighbor 10.100.1.2;
            neighbor 10.100.1.3;
            neighbor 10.100.1.4;
        }
policy-options {
    policy-statement nexthop-self {
            from protocol bgp;
            then {
                next-hop self;
            }
        }
    }
}
```

As mentioned, this is a very common policy in ISP networks today. The reason is that typically the IP subnet between EBGP peers might not be part of the local ISP's address space. That specific subnet is considered external and might not be advertised into the IGP. So, the internal routers might not know about this subnet and they cannot route to this subnet. If border router C does not change the BGP NEXT_HOP to "self," then the internal BGP speakers will not be able to use any of the BGP prefixes they received from router C. When the internal BGP routers perform the automatic recursive lookup to verify reachability to the NEXT_HOP, this lookup would fail and the learned BGP prefixes from router C would be marked as unusable. In JUNOS software, these unusable routes would also be marked as "hidden" and you would need to use the hidden option to view these routes. This is shown from router A.

```
user@A> show route 10.2/16

inet.0: 9 destinations, 9 routes (7 active, 0 holddown, 1 hidden)
+ = Active Route, - = Last Active, * = Both

user@A> show route 10.2/16 hidden

inet.0: 9 destinations, 9 routes (7 active, 0 holddown, 1 hidden)
+ = Active Route, - = Last Active, * = Both

10.2.0.0/16          [BGP/170] 00:02:13, localpref 100, from 10.100.1.1
                       AS path: 333 I
                     Unusable
```

Notice that the unusable route is hidden and without using the hidden option, you cannot view this route. When using the hidden plus the extensive option as shown following this paragraph, note that the route is marked as unusable and the reason given is the next-hop is unusable.

```
user@A> show route 10.2/16 hidden extensive

inet.0: 9 destinations, 9 routes (7 active, 0 holddown, 1 hidden)
+ = Active Route, - = Last Active, * = Both

10.2.0.0/16 (1 entry, 0 announced)
TSI:

        BGP     Preference: 170/-101
                Next hop type: Unusable
                State: <Hidden Int Ext>
                Local AS:    111 Peer AS:    111
                Age: 4:17
                Task: BGP_111.10.100.1.1+1476
                AS path: 333 I
                Localpref: 100
                Router ID: 10.100.1.1
```

Now, let us look at this same route after the next-hop-self policy is applied to router C.

```
user@A> show route 10.2/16 extensive

inet.0: 9 destinations, 9 routes (8 active, 0 holddown, 0 hidden)
+ = Active Route, - = Last Active, * = Both

10.2.0.0/16 (1 entry, 1 announced)
TSI:
KRT in-kernel 10.2.0.0/16 -> {indirect(39)}

        *BGP      Preference: 170/-101
                  Source: 10.100.1.1
                  Nexthop: via so-0/2/0.0, selected
                  Protocol Nexthop: 10.100.1.1 Indirect nexthop: 84d34c8 39
                  State: <Active Int Ext>
                  Local AS:    111 Peer AS:    111
                  Age: 8:17       Metric2: 1
                  Task: BGP_111.10.100.1.1+1476
                  Announcement bits (2): 0-KRT 4-Resolve inet.0
                  AS path: 333 I
                  Localpref: 100
                  Router ID: 10.100.1.1
                  Indirect nexthops: 1
                          Protocol nexthop: 10.100.1.1 Metric: 1 Indirect
nexthop: 84d34c8 39
                          Indirect path forwarding nexthops: 1
                                  Nexthop: via so-0/2/0.0
```

Notice that the NEXT_HOP IP address is the loopback IP address of router C, which is 10.100.1.1.

It is worth noting that the `policy-statement nexthop-self` is applied as an export policy in the IBGP peer group. It is a somewhat common mistake to apply this policy as an import policy in the EBGP peer group. The result in doing this is that all received EBGP routes will be installed in the routing table with the local router as the BGP NEXT_HOP. These routes are now unusable and will be hidden.

While on this topic, it is worth discussing another common way of resolving the unusable route issue. As mentioned earlier, often the external IP subnet is not included in the IGP. Due to this, the border router must modify the NEXT_HOP attribute to make the BGP routes usable to its IBGP peers; however, if the border router did add this external IP subnet to the IGP, then the next-hop-self policy is not required. To add the external IP subnet to the IGP requires that you add the external interface to the IGP portion of the configuration. When doing this, you should always mark this external interface as "passive" to prevent an IGP adjacency from being formed over this connection. If you did not mark this external interface as passive, then the router will send IGP Hellos out this interface in an attempt to discover IGP neighbors. If the remote ISP did the same configuration (by mistake) on its border router and was using the same IGP, you might create an IGP adjacency between the ASs. If that were to happen, all your internal IGP routes would be now sent to the neighboring ISP and all its internal IGP routes would be received by your routers. The routing domains have just been connected into a single domain. This is obviously not a good thing.

So, adding the external interface to the IGP configuration as passive allows this external IP subnet to be advertised inside your IGP. In our scenario, the IBGP routers receive BGP routes from border router C but the BGP NEXT_HOP is not router C but remains the remote AS border router N. See Figure 12-12.

Now, look at a route from AS 333 from border router C's perspective.

```
user@C> show route 10.2/16 extensive

inet.0: 10 destinations, 10 routes (9 active, 0 holddown, 0 hidden)
+ = Active Route, - = Last Active, * = Both

10.2.0.0/16 (1 entry, 1 announced)
TSI:
KRT in-kernel 10.2.0.0/16 -> {indirect(39)}

        *BGP    Preference: 170/-101
                Source: 10.100.1.1
                Nexthop: via so-0/2/0.0, selected
                Protocol Nexthop: 192.168.2.2 Indirect nexthop: 84d34c8 39
                State: <Active Int Ext>
                Local AS:    111 Peer AS:    111
                Age: 11:22      Metric2: 2
                Task: BGP_111.10.100.1.1+1476
                Announcement bits (2): 0-KRT 4-Resolve inet.0
                AS path: 333 I
                Localpref: 100
                Router ID: 10.100.1.1
                Indirect nexthops: 1
                        Protocol nexthop: 192.168.2.2 Metric: 2 Indirect
nexthop: 84d34c8 39
                        Indirect path forwarding nexthops: 1
                                Nexthop: via so-0/2/0.0
```

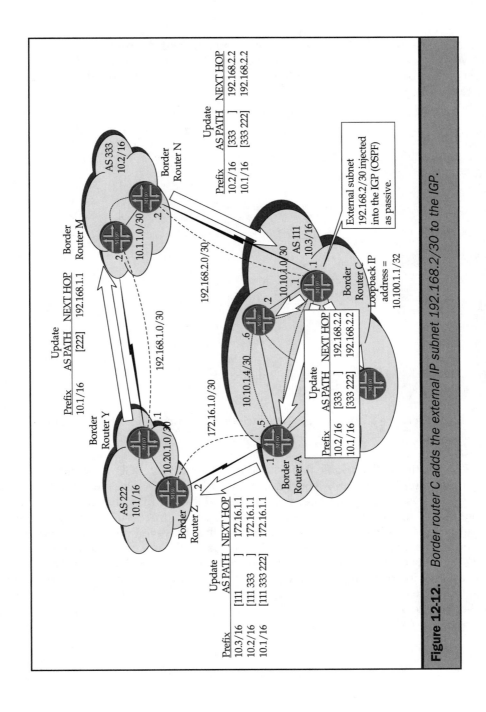

Figure 12-12.   *Border router C adds the external IP subnet 192.168.2/30 to the IGP.*

Note that the BGP NEXT_HOP address remains border router N, not border router C. When router A receives the BGP prefixes 10.2/16, it performs a recursive lookup to resolve the BGP NEXT_HOP address. Router A finds that this IP address, 192.168.2.2, is reachable via OSPF.

```
user@A> show route 192.168.2.2 extensive

inet.0: 10 destinations, 10 routes (9 active, 0 holddown, 0 hidden)
+ = Active Route, - = Last Active, * = Both

192.168.2.0/30 (1 entry, 1 announced)
TSI:
KRT in-kernel 192.168.2.0/30 -> {so-0/2/0.0}

        *OSPF    Preference:  10
                 Nexthop: via so-0/2/0.0, selected
                 State: <Active Int>
                 Local AS:    111
                 Age: 1:29       Metric: 2
                 Area: 0.0.0.0
                 Task: OSPF
                 Announcement bits (2): 0-KRT 4-Resolve inet.0
                 AS path: I
```

This is because border router C has included the external interface in OSPF as passive.

MED

MED is another path attribute that is handled differently by IBGP than with EBGP. MED, or multi-exit discriminator, is used as a metric in the BGP Decision Process for path selection. It is typically used between AS boundaries. If an AS has two connections to another AS and wants to influence the path-selection process of the neighboring AS, it might use MEDs in an attempt to accomplish this; however, there is no guarantee the remote AS will honor the use of MEDs. Typically, the use of MEDs between ASs is negotiated between ISPs in peering agreements; however, an AS can send MED values at any time in an attempt to influence their neighbors' path selection process. If you consider the name, multi-exit discriminator, in this context then the name actually describes the intended purpose of this attribute. It is a metric used to try to discriminate an ASs exit decision, assuming the AS has multiple exits. The lower the MED value, the more preferred the path is.

As stated, MED is typically used between ASs to influence the BGP path selection process. When an IBGP peer re-advertises an EBGP learned prefix into the IBGP mesh, the MED is carried with the prefix. This might influence the IBGP peers path selection, in that, if they receive the same prefix from two border routers, they might decide to prefer the prefix from the border router that advertised a lower MED value. In this case, the MED value has successfully discriminated on which of multiple exit points to use. If MEDs are not used, both prefixes would have their MED values default to zero and no distinction would be made between the prefixes based on MED. In other words, the prefixes would be equal from a MED perspective.

When a border router advertises a prefix to a remote AS, by default the MED value is reset to zero. So, MEDs are not carried with the prefix as it is advertised across an AS boundary. By default, the MED value is reset to zero at each AS boundary. This is the difference in behavior between IBGP and EBGP peers. EBGP peers will, by default, reset the MED value to zero. IBGP peers will, by default, leave the MED value intact. In JUNOS software, if a received route has no MED value, it is treated as a MED value of zero.

LOCAL_PREF

The LOCAL_PREF path attribute is used only internally in an AS to affect path selection. The default value is 100, and the higher the value, the more preferred the path is. LOCAL_PREF is passed only between IBGP peers, never between EBGP peers. It is used locally to influence the path selection process inside an AS, whereas MED is used by the remote AS to influence the path selection process between ASs.

LOCAL_PREF is a very powerful attribute and is very commonly used by ISPs for path selection. There are many ways to use LOCAL_PREF, too many to list them all here; however, let's cover one of the more common scenarios for using LOCAL_PREF. Please take a look at Figure 12-13.

In Figure 12-13, border router C has a routing policy to change the LOCAL_PREF value for prefix 10.1/16 to a value of 200. The default LOCAL_PREF value is 100. This forces internal routers in AS 111 to prefer border router C for prefix 10.1/16. Note that the AS_PATH length for prefix 10.1/16 is shorter on the update received from border router A. This would usually be the path selection tie-breaker when deciding which border router to use to reach this prefix; however, the routing policy on border router C changing the LOCAL_PREF value forces all routers in AS 111 to use it as the exit point, rather than border router A, for this specific prefix. Note that even border router A will

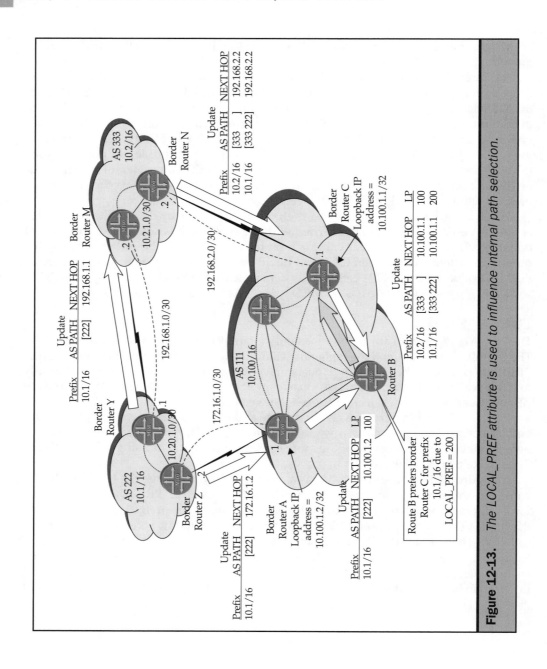

Figure 12-13. The LOCAL_PREF attribute is used to influence internal path selection.

use border router C as the exit point for prefix 10.1/16, even though this router is directly connected to AS 222, where this prefix originates.

This routing policy is shown.

```
protocols {
bgp {
        group ibgp {
            local-address 10.100.1.1;
            peer-as 111;
            export nexthop-self;
            neighbor 10.100.1.2;
        }
        group ebgp {
            peer-as 333;
            import local-pref-200;
            neighbor 192.168.2.2;
        }
    }
ospf {
    area 0.0.0.0 {
        interface so-0/2/0.0;
                            }
        }
    }
}
policy-options {
    policy-statement nexthop-self {
        from protocol bgp;
        then {
            next-hop self;
        }
    }
    policy-statement local-pref-200 {
        from {
            route-filter 10.1.0.0/16 exact;
        }
        then {
            local-preference 200;
        }
    }
}
```

In the previous configuration snippet, the bgp per group "ebgp" has an import policy by which the LOCAL_PREF gets set to 200 for prefix 10.1/16. When router C sends this prefix to its IBGP peers, the LOCAL_PREF value is included in the Update.

Realize that the LOCAL_PREF attribute is used solely inside the AS. This attribute is not passed to EBGP peers.

IBGP Rule

There is one last difference between IBGP and EBGP, and this difference has a large impact on BGP routing domains and designs. This is not a path attribute, but is a special rule of IBGP. This rule states that a prefix that was learned via IBGP cannot be passed to other IBGP peers. Said another way, if a local BGP peer learns a prefix from a remote IBGP peer, the local IBGP peer cannot forward this prefix to any other IBGP peers. Each IBGP peer in the AS must learn this prefix directly from the remote IBGP speaker. Examining a picture always helps. Please see Figure 12-14.

Border router C is receiving IP prefix 10.2/16 from its EBGP neighbor, border router N. Router C passes this prefix to routers A and B, but not to D. Although A and B have this prefix in their routing and forwarding tables, and are IBGP peered directly with router D,

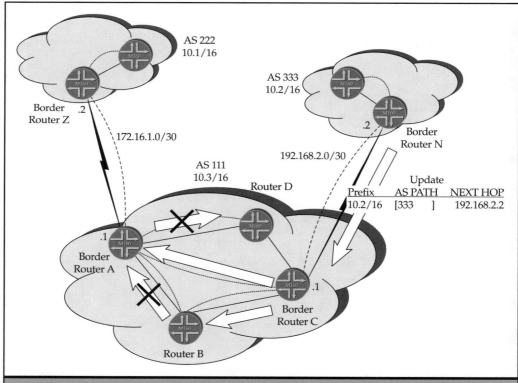

Figure 12-14.   *Border router C sends the IP prefix from AS 333 to its IBGP peers, routers A and B.*

they cannot advertise this prefix to router D. So, router D does not receive this prefix. If router D is in the forwarding path to this destination, then the traffic will be black-holed in router D. For example, border router A forwards packets to router D in an attempt to reach 10.2/16. This might be due to the combined IGP metric to router C (path A-D-C) being lower when going through router D than it is when going through router B (path A-B-C). Router D will receive the packets but will not know about destination 10.2/16 and will, therefore, drop them in the bit-bucket.

Why is this special IBGP rule needed? To fully explain this, one must go back to the discussion of how IBGP treats the AS_PATH attribute differently than EBGP. Remember that an IBGP peer will not prepend its local AS number to the AS_PATH as it advertises routes. If it did, the receiving IBGP peer would drop the route due to loop detection. Since the AS_PATH attribute is used to prevent routing loops in BGP and the Internet at large, but it is not used for IBGP, how are BGP routing loops prevented inside an AS?

BGP routing loops inside an AS are prevented by this special IBGP rule. If a BGP router were to re-advertise a prefix learned via IBGP to another IBGP peer, the receiving peer would accept the route and re-advertise it to its IBGP peers and eventually you will have a loop formed. Take a look at Figure 12-15.

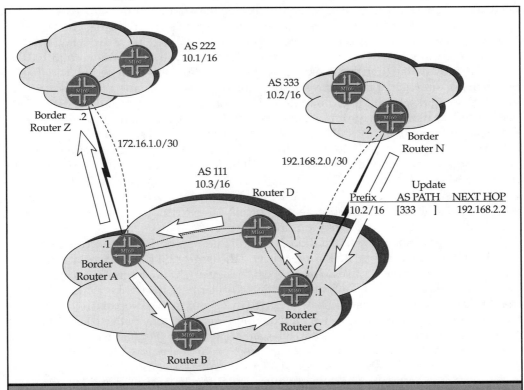

Figure 12-15.   *If not for the special IBGP rule, IBGP routers would loop prefixes.*

In Figure 12-15, if router D were to send this prefix to its IBGP peer, router A, then router A would send it to router B, which would loop the prefix back to router C. The AS_PATH attribute has no involvement inside AS 111 for loop prevention.

So, this rule is absolutely required in IBGP to prevent loops. There is a special configuration called Route Reflection that relaxes this rule, and that is discussed in the "Route Reflection" section later in this chapter.

Along with this IBGP rule comes the requirement for a full IBGP mesh. If a network intends to have consistent routing capability across all routers, then every router needs to IBGP peer to every other router. Not abiding by this full-mesh rule can cause black holes. This is seen in Figure 12.15. Router A was not peering to router C, so did not receive prefix 10.2/16. Router A is a black hole for this prefix. To correct this problem, configure an IBGP peering session between router C and A.

BGP Decision Process

The BGP decision process is the act of selecting the best BGP path to a given destination prefix, among a set of BGP paths. Often this is referred to as the BGP path selection process. In the Internet today, BGP routers will typically learn of multiple paths to a specific destination network. The BGP speaker will receive these paths from many other BGP speakers. Each BGP speaker will send only its best path to this given destination network, however, there are many ASs that an ISP is peering with, hence there are many EBGP peers for a given ISP network. In today's full Internet table, there are more than 100,000 active prefixes. By the time this book has reached your desk, this number will very likely be much higher. Each of these active and unique prefixes represents a network, or a group of networks. With the proliferation of CIDR and route aggregation, most of the active prefixes represent a group of networks but there are still many /24 prefixes in the global Internet table, most likely representing a single LAN segment.

So, it is the job of the BGP router to decide which path to a given destination network is the best path, and only these best paths will be installed in the router's *Forwarding Information Base* (FIB) and eligible for re-advertisement to its peers. No BGP speaker will advertise or export its full routing table. Only the best paths, called the active paths, are eligible for re-advertisement. Typically, the RIB storing all these alternate paths will consist of hundreds of thousands of paths.

It might be worth noting that although the full Internet routing table consists of more than 100,000 active prefixes, BGP routers inside the largest ISPs in the world will often have many more active prefixes. This is because they might not aggregate customer networks inside their AS, but only at the borders to other ISPs. It would not be surprising that the largest ISPs can possibly have more than 200,000 active prefixes in their BGP routing tables. Of these 200,00 active prefixes, there can be several paths to each of these.

For further clarification on RIBs and FIBs, although the RIB (*inet.0*) can have hundreds of thousands of paths, the FIB is where the active prefixes are stored for forwarding purposes. The FIB consists of high-speed SRAM memory because route lookup speeds are important in an Internet backbone router. The RIB is lower-speed and lower-cost

DRAM memory. Juniper Networks routers have been proven to store more than 2,000,000 prefixes in the RIB and more than 600,000 in the FIB. These numbers are bound to change over time, so are not critically important to memorize.

When evaluating best paths, the BGP attributes associated with a path are used as the input to the decision process. The exact ordering of which of these attributes are more important in path selection, thus which should be evaluated first, is not a hard fast rule in the BGP RFCs. There are some things a BGP speaker must do when executing the decision process, but the output of this algorithm is flexible enough that there are discrepancies between vendor implementations. What is important for this book is how the decision process is done in JUNOS software.

The decision process is broken into three phases:

- Calculating the best path to a destination from EBGP peers and advertising that best path to IBGP peers. Said another way, examining all the external peer adj-ribs-in and picking the best path.

- Having selected the best path to a given destination, the process should now mark this best path as active in the local-rib. Note that BGP has nothing to do with populating the FIB. That is handled elsewhere.

- Having populated the RIB, the process should now advertise active prefixes to all EBGP peers. Said another way, take the active prefixes in the local-rib and copy them to the adj-ribs-out.

Although at a high level, this process might seem simple, in reality there is much more going on. Although not spelled out in Phase 1, this is where the many path attributes of a prefix are examined in a specific order to decide the best path. This is also where vendor implementations can differ.

Here is the JUNOS software path selection decision tree, as it relates to BGP routes:

- Prefer the path with higher local preference value. The default local preference value is 100. Local preference is a metric that is set internally to the AS by local routing policy. External BGP neighbors cannot set local preference in routes, as the local preference value is not passed between AS boundaries.

- Prefer the route with a shorter AS_PATH. Confederation sequences are considered to have an AS_PATH length of 0, and AS and confederation sets are considered to have an AS_PATH length of 1.

- Prefer the route with the lower ORIGIN code. Routes learned from an IGP have an ORIGIN code of *I*, which is lower than those learned from an EGP, which have an ORIGIN code of *E*. Both of these have lower ORIGIN codes than incomplete routes, which have an ORIGIN code of *?*. Incomplete codes are for routes whose origins are unknown. Some BGP implementations set the ORIGIN code to *?*, if those routes are redistributed into BGP from another protocol. JUNOS software sets the ORIGIN code to 1 when redistributing routes from one protocol into BGP.

■ For paths with the same neighboring AS numbers at the front of the AS_PATH, prefer the path with the lowest MED value–in other words, for paths that come from the same neighboring AS. Confederation AS numbers are not considered when deciding what the neighbor AS number is. The default MED value is 0 and a missing MED value is treated as if it were 0.

■ If always comparing MEDs, whether or not the peer ASs of the compared routes are the same, prefer the path with the lowest MED value. This would apply if `path-selection always-compare-med` is configured in BGP.

■ Prefer strictly external (EBGP) paths over external paths learned through internal sessions (IBGP).

■ Prefer the path for which BGP NEXT_HOP is resolved through the IGP route with the lowest metric.

■ Prefer the path with the shortest CLUSTER_LIST length. This is similar in nature to comparing paths with a shorter AS_PATH length.

■ Prefer the path with the lowest IP address value for the BGP router ID. If no router ID is explicitly set on the router, it will inherit the loopback IP address as the router ID.

Keep in mind that this list applies only to BGP routes. This is a subset of a larger decision tree on how the active route is selected in JUNOS software. Since there are many IP networks today that are multivendor, it would be helpful to compare the JUNOS software BGP path selection to the IOS BGP path selection.

In general, the JUNOS software and IOS software path selection rules result in the choice of the same best route; however, they do differ. Where they differ is at the step of shortest CLUSTER_LIST length in the JUNOS software path-selection tree. At this point, IOS will prefer the route with the lowest IP address value for the BGP router ID. If the path contains route reflector attributes, IOS then substitutes the originator ID for the BGP router ID. Then, shortest cluster list comes after that step in IOS. So, basically swap these steps in IOS, remove the substitution of originator ID for router ID, and then JUNOS software and IOS will behave the same. This difference in path selection is the basis for a case study in Chapter 13. The case study will examine whether this difference is significant enough to cause a routing loop.

There is another difference in behavior between JUNOS software and IOS, in regards to route selection. This is the preference value given to each specific protocol. In JUNOS software, IGP routes are more preferred over BGP routes. For example, assume a BGP speaker learns of the same exact prefix from OSPF and from BGP. In JUNOS software, the router will prefer the OSPF route since its protocol preference is 10 and the BGP protocol preference is 170. In other words, a JUNOS router will believe and use the route learned from its internal network protocol before it believes or uses a route learned from an external network protocol. The result of this, however, is that the received BGP prefix is not marked as active. The OSPF route is the active route in *inet.0*, with the BGP route being an alternate route in case the OSPF route were to disappear. Since the BGP route is not marked as active, it is not eligible for export or advertisement. There is a command to export or advertise this inactive BGP route called `advertise-inactive`. This command will advertise only the best BGP routes that are inactive, not all the alternate BGP routes. The BGP route is marked as inactive because there is another exactly matching prefix marked as active in the routing table and this prefix is received from a protocol with a lower preference than BGP. This could be a prefix learned from an IGP, static, or directly connected. In IOS, the EBGP learned prefix would be preferred over the OSPF prefix, due to the default protocol preferences assigned in IOS.

BGP Basics

This section covers basic, yet critical, topics in BGP. Concepts surrounding BGP attributes, aggregation, and load balancing using multihop or multipath are covered.

Attributes

The goal of any routing protocol, be it an IGP or an EGP, is to evaluate all feasible paths to a prefix and to choose the best one to submit as a candidate for active route selection. Information that is carried with a prefix and describes its features is generically called the path's *attributes.* Metric, along with the NEXT_HOP address, are examples of path attributes. For IGPs, these two attributes are enough to make a valid active route selection; but for BGP, there are many more attributes that can be used for active path selection. These attributes are discussed in the following sections.

As mentioned previously, BGP is often considered to be a difficult protocol to master. It does not have to be. The primary difficulty is related to the fact that nothing is automatic in BGP. The most accurate analogy, since they are both distance/path vector protocols, likens RIP to an automatic riding lawnmower and BGP to a high performance motorcycle. They are both forms of transportation (or routing protocols, as the case might be) but without ever driving either, it is evident that the high performance motorcycle takes significantly more skill to drive.

One of the easiest ways to describe BGP is to think of each AS in the Internet as one giant virtual router with each EBGP peer as an exit interface attached to the router. Traversing the Internet from a high-level perspective really is no different than a packet traversing a series of local networks. The packet is processed in a router-by-router fashion each hop along the way. From BGP's point of view, a packet is processed AS by AS, as if each AS were a hop. (See Figure 12-16.)

Simply put, viewing an AS as a virtual router emphasizes the point that BGP is responsible only for entering and exiting the AS, and something else (for example, OSPF, IS-IS, RIP, STATIC) is responsible for getting you from the entrance to the exit. Attributes enable the ability to influence which entry or exit point to take.

For BGP there are many attributes that describe each prefix. The path vector algorithm to select BGP's best path to a given destination uses some of these attributes. The attributes have various weights to their values. To control this value, an 8-bit field in the BGP header is reserved to describe which of the four attribute classes each attribute belongs to.

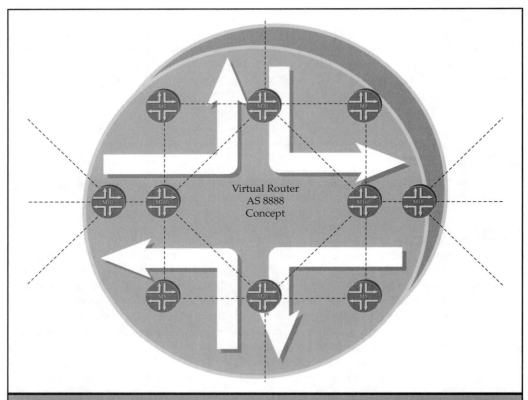

Figure 12-16. *An AS can be represented as a virtual router with each exit interface associated with an EBGP peer.*

Attribute Classes

The attribute classes, well-known mandatory, well-known discretionary, optional transitive, and optional nontransitive are described in RFC 1771. Well-known mandatory attributes must be supported by all BGP implementations and are included in every BGP update. Well-known discretionary attributes must be supported by all BGP implementations and be included in one or more BGP updates, but are not required to be included in every update. Optional transitive attributes should be accepted and passed to other peers unchanged but are not required to be supported by every BGP implementation. Lastly, optional nontransitive attributes that are not recognized by a BGP peer are to be ignored and not passed to other BGP peers.

AS_PATH Attribute

AS_PATH is a well-known mandatory attribute. This attribute describes the path of ASs that were traversed to announce the prefix to the local AS. This attribute can be represented in two formats: AS_SEQUENCE, which describes the ordered path of ASs that a packet must travel to reach the destination network, and AS_SET, which is an unordered set of ASs that a packet must travel to reach the destination network. In the AS_PATH, the rightmost AS number shows the origin AS of the prefix, and the leftmost AS number is the directly connected neighbor.

Many people mistakenly believe that the AS_PATH attribute is primarily used for shortest path selection. Returning to the example of the virtual router, assume for a moment that all virtual routers are equal; then, perhaps, this would be true. The reality of the situation is that AS 19000 might contain two routers or 2000 routers. It is not the job of BGP to attempt to describe the size or topology of an AS. The true purpose of the AS_PATH attribute is loop avoidance. That point is so important that it needs to be said again, loop avoidance! If prefix 19.0.0.0/8 is announced to AS 19000 and this prefix contains the AS_PATH [10 210 701 19000 2 888], the fact that this prefix includes the local AS number of 19000 suggests a routing loop. The local BGP router will drop this prefix due to the AS_PATH routing loop.

LOCAL_PREF Attribute

Using the virtual router analogy, LOCAL_PREF is a well-known discretionary attribute that is used by the IBGP router to determine which exit (if there is more than one) a packet should take. (See Figure 12-17.)

This attribute is considered the most powerful BGP attribute that you can manipulate on a Juniper Networks router. The most common way in which you configure this attribute depends (as do most things in BGP) on policy. For a less controlled approach to setting LOCAL_PREF, you can use the following:

```
user@hostname# set local-preference <0-4294967295>
```

The default value is 100. This command can be executed at the neighbor, group, or global level. This attribute should be manipulated and passed to an IBGP peer only, as it has no purposeful effect on an EBGP neighbor. On a Juniper Networks router, the code is designed to limit this behavior to follow the rules, even if the engineer configuring the box does not! LOCAL_PREF allows control over which exit to use to leave an AS. This does not imply that this attribute can control the path of a packet once it leaves the local domain.

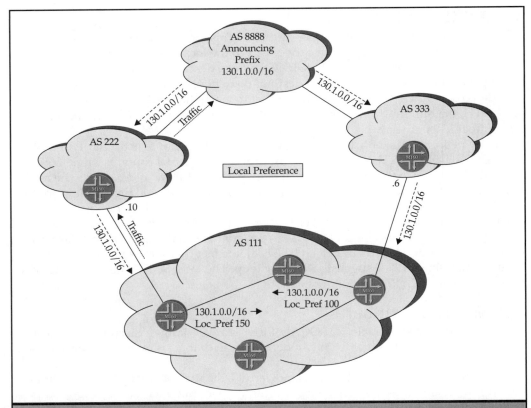

Figure 12-17.   *The LOCAL_PREF attribute influences the outbound path selection of the local AS.*

MED Attribute

The *multi-exit discriminator* (MED) attribute is an optional nontransitive attribute that receives limited usage, compared to LOCAL_PREF. The idea sounds great. How would you like to be able to control the EBGP entrance to your AS that your neighbor AS uses? That is the idea. The MED attribute is the closest thing to a typical IGP metric that BGP has to offer. In fact in BGP-3 this attribute was called the intra-AS metric. The only problem is that MED is very low on the active path selection tree so functionally it is very weak. It is primarily used between two ASs that have two or more EBGP connections between them. By default, only MEDs between the same ASs will be compared when selecting the best path. As in IGP metrics, in which two prefixes are compared, the one with the lower MED or metric is selected as active. It makes sense in a peering arrangement in which two ISPs share common policies and service-level agreements. Effectively, if routing policy is designed to allow the MED attribute to be the tie-breaking element in best path selection, then you have theoretically extended the IGP across the AS boundaries for selective prefixes. The possible values for the MED attribute are in the range of 0 to 4,294,967,295 with 0 or lack of metric being the most likely to be selected. By default all routes that are not set with a MED value have the value of 0. If you manipulate the MED value, you should either manipulate the value on all exit points or manipulate the value only on the less-preferred entrance, allowing the preferred entrance to advertise the prefix with the default MED of 0. (See Figure 12-18.)

In addition to the default behavior of comparing only MEDs from the same AS, if multiple ASs have a peering agreement to honor MED than the behavior can be modified by including the `always-compare-med` command under protocols BGP as shown in the following example:

```
user@hostname# set protocols bgp path-selection always-compare-med
```

The MED attribute can be set directly under protocols BGP or by the use of routing policy. Setting MED directly can be done at the global level, the group level, and the

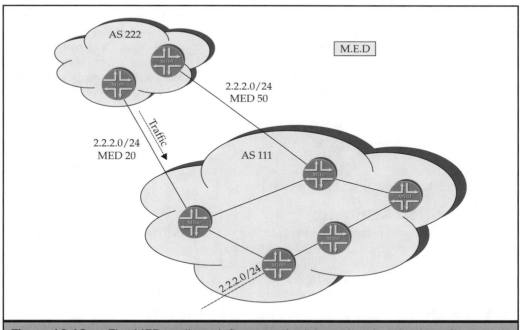

Figure 12-18. *The MED attribute influences the inbound path selection of neighboring ASs.*

neighbor level, with the neighbor level superseding the other levels in preference. The command to set MED directly is `metric-out`. This command has three argument options as shown:

```
user@hostname# set protocols bgp metric-out (metric | minimum-igp | igp)
```

Use of the argument `metric` allows the ability to set a value in the range of 0 to 4,294,967,295. Use of the option `minimum-igp` sets the outbound MED value to the minimum metric value calculated by the IGP to reach the internal BGP NEXT_HOP. Even if the IGP metric increases (due to route fluctuation and subsequent reconvergence) the MED value remains unchanged. This is desirable as any change in a BGP prefix's attributes can cause an update to flap throughout the Internet. If the IGP recomputes a lower metric this change is propagated to the BGP peers. The third value, IGP, sets the value to the most current IGP metric value and changes the value when an increase or decrease in the IGP metric occurs.

ORIGIN Attribute

The ORIGIN attribute gives a slight clue about where a prefix originated. There are three possible sources of routing-information origination; IGP, EGP, and incomplete. The best source of information is one learned from an IGP. The second best source of information can be had from the EGP, and if neither of those sources is known, the ORIGIN will be marked as coming from a source of incomplete. An example of an incomplete routing source would be an aggregate route that loses information in the aggregation process. On a Juniper Networks router, all sources of information whether it is IGP or a static or aggregate route, are advertised with an ORIGIN code of IGP by default. These sources are learned from the routing table and advertised into BGP via policy, which is also the only way to change the ORIGIN code of a Juniper Networks-originated prefix. The ORIGIN codes main use is for route selection. On a Juniper Networks router, to view the ORIGIN information source, use the `show route detail` operational command. This attribute code is shown at the end of the AS_PATH as either an I for IGP, E for EGP, or ? for incomplete.

BGP Next-Hop Attribute

"This is a well-known mandatory attribute that defines the IP address of the border router that should be used as the next-hop to the destinations listed in the Network Layer Reachability field of the UPDATE message." (RFC 1771)

Without a valid entry in this field a prefix cannot be advertised to any EBGP neighbors. Why? To answer that question, examination of the forwarding process of a general-purpose router is required. When a packet arrives on a routed interface and is decapsulated, the routing table is searched based on the destination IP address. The result of the longest match lookup is selected for forwarding. It does not end there.

The selected route has a next-hop IP address associated with it. The routing table is searched again to find the exit interface associated with the directly connected subnet of the next-hop IP address. The same general goals apply with BGP. When an IBGP speaker receives an Update including a new prefix, it attempts to install the route as an active route in the routing table. There are many criteria for route selection but the next-hop must be able to be resolved by the local router to even consider the other criteria. Like any generic router, the local IBGP speaker attempts to resolve the BGP NEXT_HOP by looking for a longest match in the local routing table. A local IGP route, or some other routing information source, then resolves the BGP NEXT_HOP IP address.

There are many ways to resolve the BGP NEXT_HOP IP address. Several variations are covered in the "Resolving BGP Next-Hop Addresses" section later in the chapter.

COMMUNITY Attribute

The COMMUNITY attribute is one of the most heavily used attributes by the Internet service provider community. This optional transitive attribute was not an original part of BGP v4 as described by RFC 1771. One of the primary design goals of BGP is to flexibly control the announcement of reachable networks. Prior to the COMMUNITY attribute described in RFCs 1997 and 1998, there were only two ways to filter and control the announcement of networks: IP prefix filtering (the scalpel approach) and AS_PATH filtering (the sledge-hammer approach). It is important to use the right tool for the right job; neither of these tools gives an engineer the flexibility to create effective routing policies in all cases. So, necessity being mother of invention, the Internet community created a tool to fit those situations that fall in between. The COMMUNITY attribute is a 4-byte field with an undetermined length. In English that means you can add them, subtract them, delete them, and filter them based on any combination of their values, as long as each value is four-bytes in length. In other words, it is a route tag that can be matched on to simplify routing policies. In JUNOS policy language, a named community alias must be created first, and then a value or string of values can be associated to the named community. This is accomplished in JUNOS software under the policy-options hierarchy, as shown here.

```
[edit policy-options]
community name members [as-number :community-value as-number :community-
value ...];
```

The generally accepted format for Community IDs is 16 bits describing the AS number which tagged the route followed by a colon and an ID number that is determined by the user to have an arbitrary policy value. For example, a Community ID of 222:6666 might mean routes tagged in AS 222 are not to be sent to external peers due to lack of a transit peering agreement with the origin AS, whereas a Community ID of 222:8888 might mean routes tagged in AS 222 are valid for transit routing and should be sent to EBGP peers. (See Figure 12-19.)

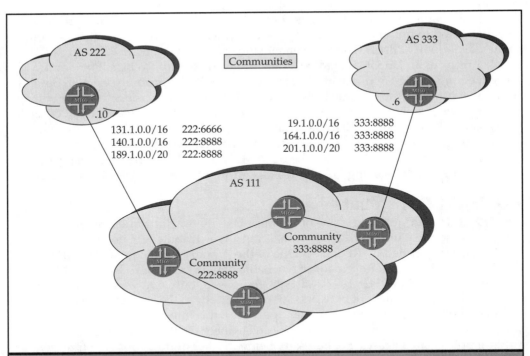

Figure 12-19. The COMMUNITY attribute is used to identify communities of interest by grouping prefixes via AS number and a unique community ID value.

Communities can be added, removed, or set (replaced) in JUNOS software policy based on AS_PATH, neighbor, protocol, other Community IDs, next-hop value, and other matching criteria.

In JUNOS software, there are four predefined or well-known communities. The first three are standards based on well-known communities that all BGP speakers should recognize by their hexadecimal values. The fourth is JUNOS software–specific.

- **NO_EXPORT (0xFFFFFF01)** Routes with this associated attribute must not be advertised outside of an AS boundary.

- **NO_ADVERTISE (0xFFFFFF02)** Routes with this associated attribute must not be advertised to other BGP neighbors.

- **NO_EXPORT_SUBCONFED (0xFFFFFF03)** Routes with this associated attribute must not be advertised to other CBGP neighbors outside of a BGP subconfederation.

- **NONE** Explicitly exclude BGP community information with a static route. Include this option when configuring an individual route in the route portion to override a community option specified in the defaults portion.

AGGREGATOR Attribute

The AGGREGATOR attribute is an Optional Transitive attribute that is closely related to the ATOMIC_AGGREGATE attribute. This attribute contains the AS number and router ID of the router that originates the aggregate route. To avoid inconsistent AS_PATH information sourced from multiple routers inside an AS, include the `no-aggregator-id` command in the policy for aggregate route propagation from redundant but nonprimary information sources.

ATOMIC_AGGREGATE Attribute

The ATOMIC_AGGREGATE attribute is a well-known discretionary attribute. If a prefix or set of prefixes is a subset of a less specific route, and that route is selected as the active prefix to be announced to a BGP peer, then the advertising BGP peer attaches the ATOMIC_AGGREGATE attribute to the prefix. This attribute informs the downstream neighbors that the AS_PATH information might be incomplete and/or in a nonordered set. Due to this lack of complete accurate information, a downstream BGP peer should not remove or modify this information except in such cases where further aggregation is performed. In JUNOS software, aggregate routes are considered a separate protocol information source that must be exported via policy for propagation to neighbors. The aggregate route is configured under the routing-options hierarchy.

```
[edit routing-options]
aggregate { defaults { aggregate-options; }  route destination-prefix {
policy policy-name; aggregate-options; }
```

Although loss of information might seem at first like a bad thing, it goes a long way towards controlling route churn in the Internet. Implementing effective aggregation policies can be a complex task and is covered in greater detail in the "Aggregation" section.

CLUSTER_LIST

The CLUSTER_LIST attribute described in RFC 1966 is a new optional nontransitive BGP attribute. It consists of the sequence of route reflector identifiers that represent the path a prefix has taken through the AS. A unique 32-bit number called the CLUSTER_ID represents the route reflector identifier. Route Reflector concepts and design issues are covered in detail in the "Route Reflection" section and in Chapter 13. The primary purpose of this attribute is to provide a multi route reflector loop avoidance algorithm inside of the AS much as the way the AS_PATH attribute does for EBGP path vector loop avoidance.

ORIGINATOR_ID

The ORIGINATOR_ID attribute is another new optional nontransitive BGP attribute that relates to route reflection. The purpose of this attribute is to identify the originator of the route that is reflected by a route reflector. Copying the router ID from the source router into the ORIGINATOR_ID field accomplishes this. The route reflector will create this attribute and enter the appropriate ORIGINATOR_ID. When a router receives a route that has its own router ID in the ORIGINATOR_ID field, then the router knows the route has looped and it will ignore the route. When a route reflector receives a route and appends the ORIGINATOR_ID attribute to it, the route reflector knows not to send the information back to the source.

Multihop

The default behavior for EBGP is to set the TTL of the IP packet carrying BGP messages to 1. This is because there is an assumption that your external neighbor is directly connected to you, thus is one hop away. IBGP does not impose such limitations because IBGP peers are very commonly more than one hop away. For EBGP peerings there are several network designs in which this default behavior would cause a failure to connect. In an Internet exchange point, for instance, the neighbors might be connected to a Layer 3 switch that does not act as a BGP peer but as a pass-through Layer 3 connection. The actual BGP neighbors are now two hops away. Another design involves using the IP layer to load balance packets across multiple connections between EBGP peers. This load balancing design will be discussed in a detailed example in Chapter 13, but briefly, the BGP session is moved from the physical interface to the loopback interface of each peer. Moving the session to any other interface except the directly connected physical interface will increase the hop count beyond 1. Yet another design that involves this issue is BGP connectivity between sub-ASs in a confederation. The typical design of BGP peering inside an AS involves using the loopback IP addresses as peering addresses. This is for redundancy reasons. Now, the BGP peering is more than one hop away. The solution to all these problems is the use of the `multihop` command. It might be specified at the BGP global, peer group, or neighbor level. If it is used without any argument, it sets the TTL to 255. You can limit the scope of EBGP reachability by specifying the keyword `ttl` and a TTL count after the command.

```
[edit protocols bgp]
      group external-peers {
          type external;
          multihop ttl 2;
          peer-as 32;
          neighbor 10.32.0.1;
```

This configuration shows the use of multihop in the EBGP peer group, and it sets the TTL to 2. Using multihop to obtain EBGP load balancing functionality will be explained in detail in Chapter 13.

Multipath

BGP load balancing is a topic that is high on the list of items that most ISP and large Internet connected enterprise network engineers need to know. There are two basic designs for this: BGP load balancing using the `multipath` command, and BGP load balancing using the `multihop` command. The multipath command alters the BGP default of selecting only one next-hop to eight equal-cost next-hops on an IP1 equipped Juniper Networks router, and 16 equal-cost next-hops on an IP2 equipped router. As stated earlier, the BGP path selection algorithm will select only a single best path to a given prefix. So, there is a single BGP NEXT_HOP associated with each BGP prefix. If there are multiple equal-cost IGP paths to the selected BGP NEXT_HOP, then JUNOS software will distribute the BGP prefixes across the multiple equal-cost paths, allowing for a per-prefix-based load balancing scheme. If a given BGP prefix is received from more than one BGP peer, and all path selection decisions are equal up to the final tie-break decision of which BGP peer has a lower router ID, then multipath can be used to enable the use of more than a single BGP peer. Normally, the path selection algorithm will choose only one of the peers and the duplicate prefixes received from the other peers are not installed in the FIB. They will act as backup paths, in the event the primary path fails. This will also be explained in detail in Chapter 13.

The multipath command can be specified at the BGP global, peer group, or neighbor level.

```
[edit protocols bgp]
        group external-peers {
            type external;
            multipath;
            peer-as 32;
            neighbor 10.32.0.1;
            neighbor 10.32.1.1;
```

This configuration uses multipath in the EBGP peer group.

Aggregation

Roughly in 1993, the Internet community realized that the growth in the size of the default-free Internet routing table required new ways of advertising routes. Studies were done base-lining the past and current growth rates of the Internet routing table, and extrapolated from that were future growth rates. It was clearly evident that route aggregation needed to be implemented in all BGP-speaking routers to continue to scale the Internet. The growth of routing tables in Internet routers was growing beyond the ability of current software, hardware, and people to effectively manage.

Route aggregation is simply defined as a way of grouping more specific prefixes into a less specific single route advertisement. There are some requirements for this to work:

- The more specific prefixes must be *aggregatable,* meaning the IP prefixes must be aligned in such a way that they are able to be represented by a single, less specific IP prefix.

- Classless routing capabilities must exist in BGP routers.

There were practices put in place to solve both these requirements. The first was the deployment of a new IP address plan. The InterNIC, being the central authority in assigning IP address blocks to service providers and companies, would allocate IP addresses to service providers in blocks. Service providers would then hierarchically assign IP address blocks to their customers, and these blocks would come from their assigned address space. The service-provider customers could be other service providers or enterprises. So the assignment of IP address space in blocks would start at the core of the Internet where the so-called Tier-1 providers exist. This would allow for natural hierarchical route aggregation, and each level of this hierarchy could aggregate their assigned address space more efficiently. Take a look at Figure 12-20.

In Figure 12-20, the enterprise using private AS 65001 advertises its assigned address space toward its ISP. The ISP in AS 111, in turn, advertises its larger address block to its upstream provider. The upstream provider, a Tier-1 ISP in AS 222 in this case, advertises

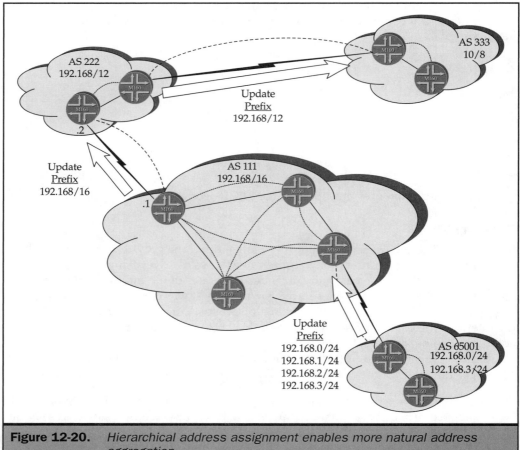

Figure 12-20. *Hierarchical address assignment enables more natural address aggregation.*

its assigned address block to its peer. Note that each layer of this hierarchy is dealing within the same IP address block.

Along with this address and aggregation plan, CIDR protocols needed to be implemented. BGP v4 solved this problem, being the first interdomain routing protocol to support CIDR. Classless routing refers to the concept of *variable-length subnet masks* (VLSMs) and the elimination of classes of IP address numbers (A, B, and C). So, a network prefix such as 172.16.1/24 is no longer considered a Class B network. This created the terms *supernet* and *CIDR block*. These terms refer to an address prefix and its corresponding prefix length, of which the prefix length is shorter than the original classful structure. For example, 172.16/12 can be considered a supernet instead of a legacy Class B address.

One other advantage to aggregation is that routing flaps are often hidden. This is because the more specific routes are being aggregated into a less specific route. The less specific route will not flap each time one of its more specific routes flap. In other words, assume you have two routes in your network such as 172.9.109.16/28 and 172.9.109.32/28. You can aggregate these into 172.9.109/24 and advertise only this less-specific route to peers, which results in hiding the more specific /28 routes. If 172.9.109.16/28 were to flap, the aggregate 172.9.109/24 would not flap. The upstream peers receiving this aggregate would not need to be bothered about the 172.9.109.16/28 flapping route. This adds stability to Internet routing. This hiding of more specific routing information is generally good for stability, but can also have a certain downside. For example, the AS_PATH attribute can also be affected by aggregation.

Aggregation also "hides" the original AS numbers from the more specific prefixes. Suppose a local network in AS 222 sends a /21 prefix to its upstream provider. The upstream provider might aggregate the /21 prefix into a less-specific prefix, say, a /20. Suppose this is due to a human configuration error in the upstream provider's border router. AS 222 is now not included in the AS_PATH of the upstream's aggregate announcement. It is possible that this /20 aggregate is imported back into the local AS 222 from another provider. Since the local AS 222 is not included in the AS_PATH of the /20 aggregate, the aggregate is accepted. This can lead to a routing loop.

A framework for interdomain route aggregation is documented in RFC 2519, written in February 1999.

The JUNOS Software Way of Aggregation

In JUNOS software, creating a route called `aggregate` under the `[routing-options]` hierarchy of the configuration installs the aggregate route in *inet.0*. There are a few snippets of this aggregate worth explaining.

```
routing-options {
    aggregate {
        route 10.100.0.0/16 community 65535:65281;
    }
}
```

```
      autonomous-system 111;
}

user@C> show route 10.100/16 extensive

inet.0: 13 destinations, 13 routes (13 active, 0 holddown, 0 hidden)
+ = Active Route, - = Last Active, * = Both

10.100.0.0/16 (1 entry, 1 announced)
TSI:

KRT in-kernel 10.100.0.0/16 -> {}

       *Aggregate       Preference: 130
              Next hop type: Reject
              State: <Active Int Ext>
              Age: 3:38
              Task: Aggregate
              Announcement bits (2): 0-KRT 5-Resolve inet.0
              AS path: I
              Communities: no-export
              Flags:  Depth: 0        Active
              AS path list:
                    AS path: I Refcount: 2
              Contributing Routes (2):
                    10.100.1.1/32        proto Direct
                    10.100.1.2/32        proto OSPF
```

First, note in the show route command the aggregate has a protocol preference of 130 and is installed as active in *inet.0*. Also, note that there are contributing, or more specific, routes in *inet.0*. These happen to be a directly connected and an OSPF route, and these contributing routes are required by default for the aggregate to be considered an active route. A contributing route need not be an OSPF route. Any route that is active in *inet.0* and more specific to the aggregate will suffice; however, if these contributing routes were to disappear, the aggregate would no longer be active. So, in this case the aggregate would flap when all the contributing routes disappeared. You must have at least one contributing route for the aggregate to remain active. If you want to keep the aggregate active, even with no contributing routes, then you can mark the aggregate with the passive option, as shown here.

```
user@hostname# set routing-options aggregate route 10.100/16 passive
```

This is often referred to as "nailing up the aggregate." This adds stability to the aggregate and is a recommended best practice on border routers. This way, the aggregate is always active and exported and the remote AS will always receive this route, so long as BGP peering is working. This prevents the aggregate from flapping if all the contributing routes flap. The remote AS will appreciate this behavior, as they will not be affected by local network instabilities.

Notice in the previous display that the aggregate has a next-hop of "reject." This is the default and expected behavior, although this seems to confuse a few engineers the first time they see this. The reject next-hop is there for this reason:

- A packet arrives at the local border router that is exporting the aggregate.

- The destination of this packet is a more specific prefix that is part of the aggregate.

- The more specific destination network, however, is not currently active due to a failure somewhere in the local network infrastructure.

- The local border router will reject (bit-bucket) the packet and send an ICMP unreachable message to the source.

This is the preferred behavior. If the destination network is not active, the local border router should drop the packet. The more specific prefix is not active in the local border routers FIB, so the router has no choice but to discard the packet. As mentioned earlier, if the more specific destination network is not active due to a failure in the local network infrastructure, the border router should not propagate this failure to the Internet. This would cause all Internet routers to withdraw this network prefix from their routing tables, which causes instability in the Internet. It is much better to keep the instabilities local to the network.

One additional note about the aggregate route configuration. In the configuration shown previously, the aggregate is tagged with a community of 65535:65281. This value is the hex representation of the "no-export" community. This can be verified when viewing the output of the `show route 10.100/16 extensive` command. Notice the Communities field contains `no-export`.

Synchronization

Synchronization refers to the mode in which a BGP speaker will not install a BGP route into the forwarding table unless the IGP also has this route. In other words, if a BGP speaker received prefix 172.16/16 but the IGP does not have knowledge of this prefix, it will not be installed in the FIB nor exported to BGP peers. This is a legacy mode of Cisco IOS. JUNOS software does not have this mode of operation. There is no knob in JUNOS software to enable or disable synchronization. The reason for this is that synchronization does not apply in ISP routing environments.

The original reason for synchronization is when router A does not want to export a prefix to router B in BGP if router B cannot reach this prefix via the IGP. In this mode, the IGP and BGP are synchronized. If router B is synchronized, when it receives the BGP prefix it will look into its routing table to verify reachability to this prefix. If the prefix is reachable via the routing table, then the IGP has converged on this prefix, and the BGP prefix will be installed. If not, the BGP prefix will not be installed. This mode is typically disabled in Cisco IOS routers in the ISP community. That is because in most ISP networks, all routers are BGP speakers. Since JUNOS software is specifically built to operate in ISP environments where all routers are running BGP, this mode is not needed or warranted. So, in JUNOS software, synchronization is disabled by default.

Capabilities Advertisement

Capabilities advertisement, specified in RFC 2842, dated May 2000, allows a BGP peer to advertise which of the BGP capabilities it can support. This capability is included in the Open message, specifically the Optional Parameter field. This field lists the capabilities supported by the peer. The receiving peer will look at the list of capabilities and decide which ones it is capable of supporting. If the receiving peer does not support capabilities advertisement, it will send a Notification message with the error subcode set to Unsupported Optional Parameter and terminate the session. The originating peer should then attempt to re-establish the session by sending another Open message without the Capabilities Optional Parameter.

In the Optional Parameter field, the capability code will represent which capability the peer supports. An example of this is the Capability Code 2. This code represents the Route Refresh capability. If a BGP peer receives an Open message with this capability code, it will know that the sending peer supports Route Refresh and is attempting to negotiate the use of this capability. If the receiving peer does not support this specific capability, it will send a Notification message and terminate the session. The sending peer will then send another Open message without this capability code and hopefully the session will become established. The function of the Route Refresh capability is covered in the "Route Refresh" section later in this chapter. To view which capabilities have been successfully negotiated between peers in JUNOS software, use the command user@hostname> show bgp neighbor *neighbor-address* and look at the field labeled Peer Supports. The number listed in parentheses is the capability code. An example output is listed.

```
user@hostname> show bgp neighbor 192.168.1.2
Peer: 192.168.1.2+179 AS 2      Local: 192.168.1.1+1454 AS 1
  Type: External     State: Established     Flags: <>
  Last State: OpenConfirm    Last Event: RecvKeepAlive
  Last Error: None
  Export: [ send-statics ]
  Options: <Preference HoldTime RemovePrivateAS PeerAS Refresh>
  Holdtime: 90 Preference: 170
  Number of flaps: 0
  Peer ID: 10.255.254.3     Local ID: 10.1.1.1          Active Holdtime: 90
  Keepalive Interval: 30
  NLRI advertised by peer: inet-unicast
```

```
    NLRI for this session: inet-unicast
    Peer supports Refresh capability (2)
    Table inet.0 Bit: 10000
      Send state: in sync
      Active prefixes: 0
      Received prefixes: 0
      Suppressed due to damping: 0
    Last traffic (seconds): Received 5      Sent 5      Checked 5
    Input messages:  Total 169     Updates 1        Refreshes 0      Octets 3238
    Output messages: Total 171     Updates 1        Refreshes 0      Octets 3300
    Output Queue[0]: 0

user@hostname>
```

Without this feature, it is difficult to introduce new capabilities into BGP v4. RFC 1771 stated that if, during the Open message exchange, there is a feature specified that the router does not understand or support, the router should terminate the peering session and no attempt will be made to re-establish it. Following this RFC, introducing new features in BGP required that both routers of a peering session needed their software upgraded simultaneously or the peering session would never be established. Imagine how difficult this would be in the global Internet today. Two ISPs would need to agree to upgrade the software on their peering routers simultaneously, and actually in most cases this would require more than two ISPs to be involved. This is because in most cases today, a peering router peers to multiple ISPs.

RFC 2842 states that the Internet Assigned Numbers Authority (IANA) is responsible for assigning the capability codes. Capability Code 0 is reserved. Codes 1 through 63 are to be assigned by IANA using the IETF Consensus policy. This policy is defined in RFC 2434 and states that new values are assigned through the IETF consensus process. This is typically done via new RFCs. Codes 64 through 127 are assigned by IANA on a first-come, first-served basis. Codes 128 through 255 are reserved for private use, typically meaning they are vendor-specific.

Scaling BGP

This section focuses on internal BGP design issues. As networks grow larger and contain more and more IBGP routers, the design of the IBGP mesh becomes very critical.

The IBGP Full-Mesh Problem

One of the fundamental aspects of BGP is the concept of a full mesh for IBGP. The reason in summary is simple. IBGP has no built-in way to perform routing loop detection. So all IBGP neighbors in the same AS must be connected to each other in a n*(n – 1)/2 fashion. The problem: scaling this in an AS of say 200 or more routers begins to be painful. Consider 200*(200 – 1)/2 = 19900. That is a lot of BGP peer statements, not to mention the overhead of all those stateful TCP connections. Although the full IBGP mesh design is not absolutely required for all topologies, the concept is generally implemented in most if not all ISPs today. It can be possible to have a topology such that the full IBGP mesh is not required and there would be no impact on routing capability, however, it is not a good idea to do this. Your topology would then be very restricted and as you grew your network you would invariably run into routing inconsistencies and black holes. It is interesting to note the terminology in the more recent RFCs and Internet drafts when talking about the full IBGP mesh rule. If you take a look at an old RFC, it mentioned this full-mesh concept but not in such a way that the reader felt this was a requirement. In the more recent RFCs and drafts, this rule is now listed as a hard requirement, based on lessons learned or scar tissue, I presume.

There are two common solutions to overcome this full-mesh scaling problem: route reflection and confederations.

Route Reflection

Route reflection involves relaxing that special rule of IBGP stating that a BGP speaker that receives a route via IBGP cannot pass that route to another IBGP speaker. This rule is required to avoid routing loops inside an AS. This rule also leads to the requirement for the full IBGP mesh. As has been discussed, the full IBGP mesh leads to scaling issues inside the AS. So, here is where route reflection comes in, to alleviate the full IBGP mesh scaling issue by relaxing the rule that led to the scaling issue in the first place!

The basic idea of route reflection is very simple. Figure 12-21 depicts this in a simple route reflection environment.

In Figure 12-21, router C is where the route reflection (RR) configuration and implementation happens. This router is the RR server, and routers E and F are its RR clients. Routers E and F are not aware they are RR clients and there is no additional configuration needed on these routers to implement this. Only the RR server requires additional configuration. In Figure 12-21, border router A advertises the external prefix 10.2/16 using IBGP to its internal peers, routers B, C, and D. These routers are part of the IBGP full-mesh, as all these routers are IBGP peering to each other; however, note that routers E and F are IBGP peering only to router C. These two routers are not participating in the full IBGP mesh. Prior to configuring router C as the RR server, routers E and F will not receive the BGP prefix 10.2/16 from AS 333. As explained earlier, router C will not export the IBGP learned prefix 10.2/16 to routers E and F. If it did and the new attributes associated with route reflection are not used, this can cause a routing loop. The special rule of IBGP that was discussed earlier prevents this from happening.

Once route reflection is configured on router C, the special rule of IBGP is relaxed and this router then exports the 10.2/16 prefix to routers E and F. Before router C reflects the route, however, there are a few things it must do. Router C will add to the path attributes two new attributes, CLUSTER_LIST and ORIGINATOR_ID. As discussed in the "Route Reflection" section, these attributes apply only to RR environments. They are needed to prevent routing loops inside the AS when using route reflection. Remember,

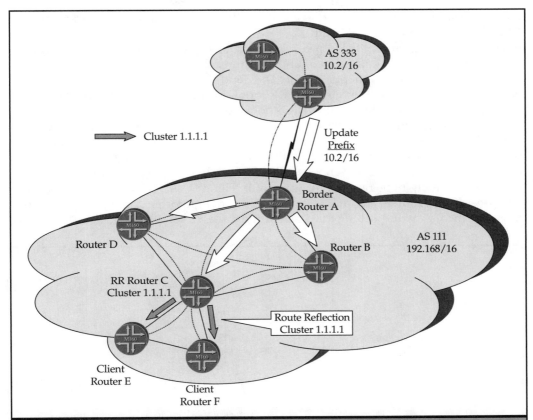

Figure 12-21. *Router C is a route reflector and it reflects routes to its clients, routers E and F. The reverse happens as well, that is, routes from the clients get reflected by the route reflector to its IBGP peers.*

the special IBGP rule that route reflection relaxes is there to prevent routing loops inside an AS. If that rule is relaxed, some other mechanism must exist to prevent routing loops from occurring. Router C adds its configured cluster ID to the CLUSTER_LIST. It also adds the ORIGINATOR_ID attribute, which is the router ID of router A in this case, to the path attributes. Router A originated the route into the AS, so its router ID is used as the ORIGINATOR_ID. In this scenario, the RR cluster consists of routers C, E, and F. The cluster ID is a configured value on the RR server. This value is typically the router ID of the RR server, which is typically the routers loopback IP address. There are no requirements that you use the loopback address as the cluster ID and in some cases you will not use this address, but in a simple RR environment this is commonly done.

The use of the CLUSTER_LIST and ORIGINATOR_ID to prevent loops is better explained with a drawing. Although Figure 12-22 might not represent a typical route reflector environment, it serves a good purpose in explaining the need for the CLUSTER_LIST and ORIGINATOR_ID.

In Figure 12-22, three of the four core IBGP routers are configured as route reflectors. Border router A is not configured as an RR. Router B is the RR for its client, router C. Router C is the RR for its clients, routers D, E, and F. Router D is the RR for its client, border router A. Although having this RR topology might seem somewhat strange, having an RR be a client for another RR is not so strange. This is referred to as "nested route reflection," and is not only a valid configuration but is deployed in many ISP networks. The nested RR solution is used to further scale the IBGP peering mesh. A network might have a large number of IBGP routers and the topology might be such that a single level of route reflection is not sufficient. In that case, multiple levels of route reflection might be required or wanted. In Figure 12-22, RR router C still has its previous clients, routers E and F. These clients are not important right now, so ignore those for the moment. Assume that each of the three RRs has the same cluster ID

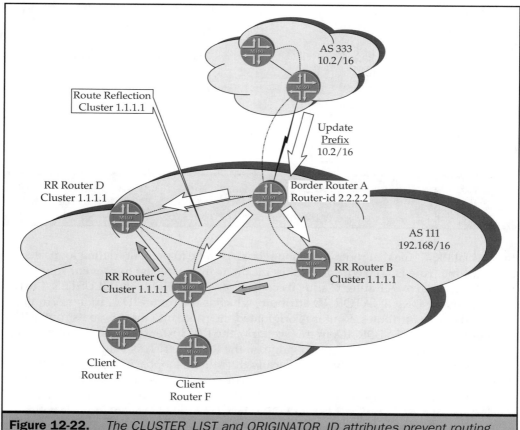

Figure 12-22.   *The CLUSTER_LIST and ORIGINATOR_ID attributes prevent routing loops in route reflection environments.*

configured, that is, they are all using cluster ID 1.1.1.1. Thus, it can be said that the RR cluster is Cluster 1.1.1.1. Examine the use of the CLUSTER_LIST and ORIGINATOR_ID.

- Prefix 10.2/16 enters the network from border router A.

- Router A exports this prefix to all its IBGP peers, routers B, C, and D.

- RR router B exports this same prefix to its RR client, router C. This is where route reflection begins to happen. Router B creates a CLUSTER_LIST and adds its cluster ID 1.1.1.1 to this list. Router B also creates an ORIGINATOR_ID and inputs the router ID of the router originating this prefix into the AS, that being border router As router ID of 2.2.2.2. If router B were not an RR, it would not export the IBGP learned prefix to its IBGP peer.

- Router C has received two copies of this prefix at this point. The first copy was received directly from border router A, and this prefix is accepted and installed. The second copy is received from its RR, router B. This prefix contains a CLUSTER_LIST of 1.1.1.1 and an ORIGINATOR_ID of 2.2.2.2. Router C, being a RR itself, immediately checks the CLUSTER_LIST to verify the cluster IDs in this list are not the same as its own cluster ID. In this case, the cluster ID is the same so router C will drop this prefix from router B.

- Router C, being the RR for router D, exports the prefix to router D. This is, again, a case of route reflection so router C will create a CLUSTER_LIST and add its cluster ID of 1.1.1.1 to this list. Router C will also create an ORIGINATOR_ID and use the router ID of router A for this value.

- Router D, much like router C, has received two copies of this prefix at this point. The first copy was received directly from border router A, and this prefix is accepted and installed. The second copy is received from its RR, router C. This prefix contains a CLUSTER_LIST of 1.1.1.1 and an ORIGINATOR_ID of 2.2.2.2. Router D, being an RR itself, immediately checks the CLUSTER_LIST to verify the cluster IDs in this list are not the same as its own cluster ID. In this case, the cluster ID is the same so router D will drop this prefix from router C.

- Router D's behavior is exactly like router C's behavior, in that they both accept the prefix received directly from border router A, but drop the reflected prefix from their RR to avoid loops. This is the value of the CLUSTER_LIST attribute.

- To take this a step further, router D is also an RR for border router A. Router D, thus, should reflect this prefix to its client, border router A; however, in JUNOS software an RR never reflects a prefix to the originator of the route. In this case, border router A is the originator of this prefix, 10.2/16. Another potential loop is now avoided.

- If border router A did receive the 10.2/16 prefix it had originated into the cluster, it still would not be a loop. Border router A would realize that the ORIGINATOR_ID of 2.2.2.2 is the same as its router ID and would drop the prefix to avoid a loop. This is the purpose of the ORIGINATOR_ID.

It should be noted that although route reflection alleviates a network from the required IBGP full-mesh rule, it does not eliminate IBGP meshing entirely. Typically, there is still a set of routers that are fully IBGP meshed, forming a smaller and more manageable core IBGP mesh. In our scenario, these are routers A, B, C, and D; however, the clients of the RRs peer only to their respective RR. This is where the benefit of route reflection comes from, in that the clients do not need to IBGP peer to every other BGP speaker in the AS. In Figure 12-22, there are a total of eight IBGP peering sessions. If all routers were fully IBGP meshed with no route reflection, there would be a total of 15 IBGP peering sessions.

There are special rules that all BGP implementations that support route reflection must follow. When an RR receives a route from an IBGP peer, it selects the best path based on its path selection process. After it has selected the best path, it will mark this as active and the route will get installed in the FIB. The RR must then meet these additional rules:

- If the route came from a nonclient IBGP peer, the RR will reflect this to all its clients.

- If the route came from a client peer, the RR will reflect this route to all nonclient IBGP peers and to all other clients.

- When reflecting a route, by default the RR should not modify any of these BGP attributes: NEXT_HOP, AS_PATH, LOCAL_PREF, and MED.

- If the route came from an EBGP peer, do not add the CLUSTER_LIST or ORIGINATOR_ID. This route is not a reflected route.

The JUNOS software implementation meets these rules, with a few enhancements. Referring to the second rule, when a JUNOS software RR reflects routes received from a client peer, it will not reflect the route back to the originating client peer; however, doing so would not cause harm, as the originating client peer would see its router ID as the ORIGINATOR_ID and would drop the update due to loop detection. Referring to the third rule, due to the strong capability of the JUNOS software Routing Policy language, you can modify the mentioned path attributes when reflecting routes. By default, the RR will not modify these attributes but the default behavior can be overridden with routing policy. There is a case study showing such a scenario in Chapter 13.

Another benefit of route reflection that adds to large BGP network scalability is the fact that an RR reflects only its best path. Clients receive a summarized view of the BGP network. They do not receive every alternate path that the core IBGP meshed routers receive. So, the client peers do not need to maintain very large RIBs, unlike the core IBGP meshed routers. In certain cases, however, this summarized view of the BGP network can result in suboptimal routing paths. Remember, an RR reflects only its best path to its clients; however, it can be possible depending on topology or other attributes that have influence in the BGP path selection process, that the client would have selected a different best path than the RR has selected. The client, however, is given only the best path from the RR's perspective. The client does not receive the full set of BGP paths. Having said that, you can see that this summarizing of routes can have both good and bad results.

Cluster ID

To configure an RR, you simply add a single command to the BGP configuration, as shown here.

```
user@hostname# set protocols bgp group group-name cluster number
```

The value to use as the cluster ID is somewhat arbitrary; however, it must be unique per route reflector cluster. As mentioned, often this is the RR's loopback IP address. This makes debugging and troubleshooting easier, as, if you see this cluster ID anywhere in the network you can ascertain which RR this came from.

Remember, the cluster ID is the value in the CLUSTER_LIST that prevents loops between route reflectors. Such an example was discussed in Figure 12-22.

Something worth pointing out is the cluster ID implementation difference between JUNOS software and IOS. In JUNOS software, the cluster ID is an IP address. It need not be a routable IP address, but the structure is like an IP address having 4 bytes, each separated by a period. In IOS, the cluster ID is a 4-byte integer. If you want to convert the IOS 4-byte integer to the JUNOS software syntax, there is a formula to use. For example, to convert the IOS cluster ID of 123456 to the JUNOS software syntax, divide the 123456 by 256 and the result is 482 with a remainder of 64. The remainder value of 64 becomes the fourth octet. Divide the 482 by 256 and the result is 1 with a remainder of 226. The remainder of 226 is the third octet. Divide 1 by 256 and the result is 0 with a remainder of 1. The remainder of 1 is the second octet.

$$123456/256 = 482 \text{ with remainder of } 64$$
$$482/256 = 1 \text{ with remainder of } 226$$
$$1/256 = 0 \text{ with remainder of } 1$$

So, the IOS cluster ID of 123456 converts to a JUNOS software cluster ID of 0.1.226.64.

It is worth noting that the route reflector must be configured with a cluster ID in JUNOS software. The clients need no additional configuration.

Originator ID

When reflecting routes, the RR populates the Originator ID field automatically. This field will contain the router ID of the router that originated the update into the AS. This is a border router somewhere in the local network. As explained earlier, the Originator ID is also used for loop prevention when using route reflection. This requires no configuration.

Redundancy

If you have a need for additional resiliency, you can configure redundant route reflectors. In other words, you can have clients being served by two route reflectors. This gives you redundancy, in that one of the route reflectors can fail and the clients will not become isolated from the core IBGP mesh. If using redundant route reflectors, then there are additional considerations for determining the cluster ID.

Before getting into a discussion of what cluster ID value to use with redundant route reflectors, examine a simple redundant route reflector environment.

In Figure 12-23, notice that client routers E and F are now attached and IBGP peered to both routers B and C. Routers B and C are now route reflectors for this cluster. If either router B or C were to fail, the clients would continue to receive updates from the other route reflector.

There is some debate when using redundant route reflectors as to the value of the cluster IDs. Either you configure both of the route reflectors with the same cluster ID, or you configure each of the redundant route reflectors with a unique cluster ID, such as using their loopback IP addresses.

Is one of these options preferred, and if so, why?

Although both options are valid, and both options are used in today's RR environments, this topic has often resulted in debate. It is similar to the OSPF versus IS-IS debate, or the RR versus confederations debate. There two sides to each of these debates, but often the answer is one of personal preference rather than technical superiority.

It can be said that using unique cluster IDs on each RR can result in additional resiliency. The downside, however, is duplication of paths and the additional memory and processor overhead associated with duplicate paths in the RRs.

In Figure 12-24, both RRs are using the same cluster ID of 2.2.2.2. If the IBGP peering session between routers B and F were to fail, external prefixes that are exported into AS 111

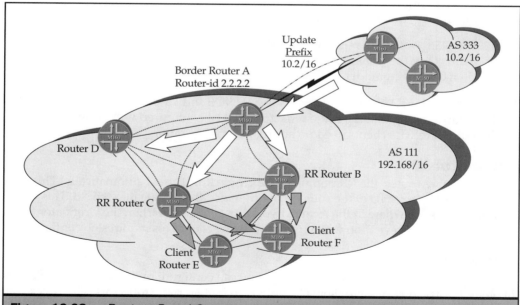

Figure 12-23. *Routers B and C serve as redundant route reflectors.*

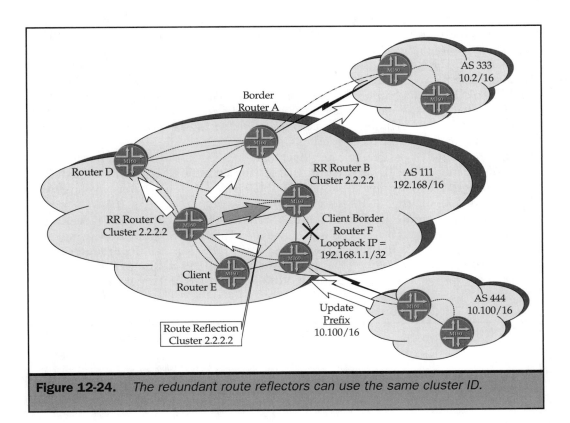

Figure 12-24. *The redundant route reflectors can use the same cluster ID.*

router F would never get to router B. If router B were to fail entirely, this would not be a problem as router C would reflect for the cluster; however, if the IBGP peering session only between routers B and F were to fail, there could be a black hole. If router B were in the forwarding path for prefix 10.100/16 and router B were to receive packets destined for this prefix, it would not know about this destination and it would drop these packets.

For example:

- AS 333 is sending packets to 10.100/16. The packets get sent to border router A.

- Router A has the BGP prefix 10.100/16 as active and the BGP NEXT_HOP is 192.168.1.1, which is router F's loopback IP address. Router F is doing next-hop self.

- Router A does an IGP lookup on 192.168.1.1 and finds that router B is the physical next-hop. Router A forwards the packets to router B.

- Router B does not know how to reach destination 10.100/16 and drops the packets in the bit bucket.

So, why does router B not learn about 10.100/16?

Although router F also sends 10.100/16 to router C, which in turn sends it to all its IBGP peers including router B, router B will drop it due to detecting its cluster ID in the CLUSTER_LIST. Router C, when reflecting the prefix, will add its configured cluster ID of 2.2.2.2 to the CLUSTER_LIST. Router B will see 2.2.2.2 in the CLUSTER_LIST and would think this prefix has looped. Remember, in this scenario both routers B and C are configured with the same cluster ID of 2.2.2.2. The end result is router B will not receive prefix 10.100/16 if the IBGP peering session to router F were to fail. Although it is not very likely that the IBGP peering session would fail unless one of the routers failed, it is remotely possible. For instance, this can happen due to human error (misconfiguration or accidental clearing this session with the CLI). Even during a link failure, the IGP is usually able to reroute the IBGP peering session before the holdtime expires, thus keeping the IBGP session up.

Take a look at Figure 12-25 and the same scenario, that is, with the IBGP peering session between routers B and F failing. However, routers B and C are now using different cluster IDs. As in the last case, router F sends the same prefix to router C, which in turn sends it to all its IBGP peers, including router B. Router B will, in this case, accept this prefix because it contains a different cluster ID than what router B is configured for. Remember, the RR adds its cluster ID to the update when reflecting

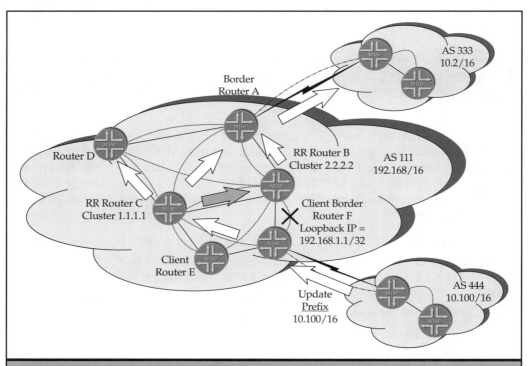

Figure 12-25. *The redundant route reflectors can also use different cluster IDs.*

routes. Router B will see router C's cluster ID of 1.1.1.1 in the CLUSTER_LIST, but since it is not the same as 2.2.2.2, there is no potential loop and the prefix is accepted. If router A now forwards packets to router B for 10.100/16, router B will forward the packets to border router F. This is the added resiliency that using different cluster IDs can buy you.

So, why not always configure redundant route reflectors with different cluster IDs? Also, is the potential black-hole issue not experienced with any IBGP peering? In other words, if any IBGP peering session were to fail, each peer of this failed session would not receive prefixes from the other peer. The result is the same potential black hole as described in Figure 12-24. So, this issue is not anything new or different than with plain IBGP peering. It is the nature of IBGP.

Back to our scenario using different cluster IDs on the RRs. When all peerings are working, router B receives the prefixes twice. It receives them directly from router F, and it also receives them from router C. Router B will make a path selection decision on which is the best path and will usually prefer the paths learned directly from router F due to IGP cost. The duplicate paths from router C will be stored in the RIB. This duplicate set of paths consumes additional memory in router B. Is this trade-off worth the added resiliency? Quite a few engineers think so. The other downside to this solution is that from a network design perspective, you kind of lose the concept of a cluster. In Figure 12-25, where is the cluster boundary? The client routers E and F are part of two different clusters. In Figure 12-24, it is easy to distinguish the cluster, which consists of the RRs using the same cluster ID, plus their clients. Although this difference has little technical merit, it is cleaner from a design perspective. These two reasons are why not everyone chooses to use different cluster IDs on redundant route reflectors.

Design Considerations

When implementing route reflection there are some additional things to keep in mind, particularly from a design perspective. You must consider more factors than what to use for the cluster IDs when selecting route reflection as your solution to the IBGP mesh problem.

In general, it is required that the route reflectors themselves be fully IBGP meshed together. In essence, you still abide by the IBGP full-mesh rule, but on a smaller scale. This ensures that every RR receives all the available BGP paths in the network, directly from every other RR.

The route reflection logical topology should always follow the physical topology. At a minimum, not abiding by this rule will make the route reflection design more complicated than it need be. This leads to complexity from a support perspective. This can also cause routing problems in certain scenarios.

Another design guideline is to always configure redundant RRs, if possible. If your RR clusters contain more than a few clients, it is not prudent to risk isolating all these clients with a single point of failure, which would be the RR itself.

It is also possible that an RR client can be an RR for another cluster. This is referred to as "nested RR." For very large BGP networks, this might be the preferred design. There can be multiple layers of route reflection, as depicted in Figure 12-26.

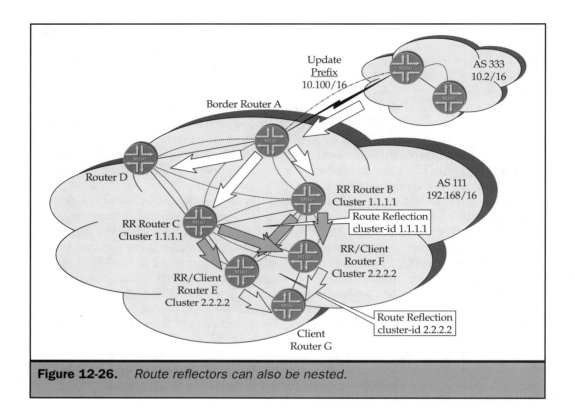

Figure 12-26. *Route reflectors can also be nested.*

In Figure 12-26, routers A, B, C and D are fully IBGP meshed. Routers B and C are the first level of route reflection. Their clients are routers E and F and these four routers represent cluster 1.1.1.1. Routers E and F are also route reflectors themselves, for client router G. These three routers represent cluster 2.2.2.2 and they are the second level of route reflection.

Another option with route reflection is to fully mesh the clients. If the client routers are located next to each other or connected over a direct physical link, it might make sense to IBGP peer them together. This would alleviate some of the reflection that the RR needs to perform. As shown in Figure 12-27, client F is IBGP peered to its redundant route reflectors, routers B and C, as usual. It is also IBGP peered to the other client in this cluster, router E.

This option alleviates the RRs from reflecting intracluster routes. That is, routes from one of the clients do not need to be reflected to the other clients. The client receives prefixes from the other client directly. The RR needs to reflect only the client routes into the core IBGP mesh, and the IBGP mesh routes down into the cluster. In Figure 12-27, client router E receives prefix 10.100/16 directly from client router F.

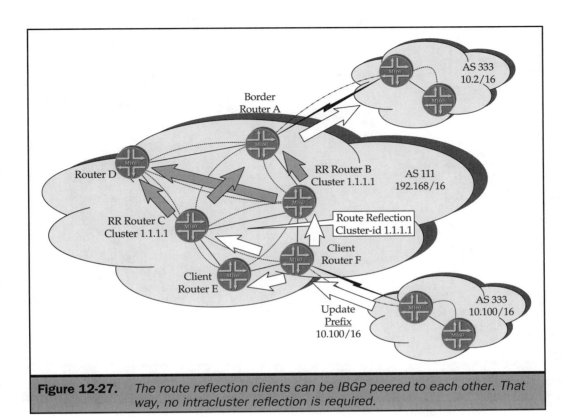

Figure 12-27. *The route reflection clients can be IBGP peered to each other. That way, no intracluster reflection is required.*

If not for this knob, RRs B and C would have reflected the prefix down to client router E. To enable this solution, peer the clients together and add this command to the RRs:

```
user@hostname# set protocols bgp group group-name no-client-reflect
```

This command tells the RR not to reflect intracluster routes. The clients in the cluster will receive the routes directly from other clients.

When the no-client-reflect knob is used, it is important to remember to peer the clients together. If not, there is the potential of a black hole. Take another look at Figure 12-27. If clients E and F are not directly IBGP peered, router E will not receive prefix 10.100/16. The RRs, routers B and C, are configured to not reflect intracluster routes so they will not send prefix 10.100/16 down to client E. If RR router C is sending packets to 10.100/16 and uses router E as the physical next-hop, router E will drop the packets.

In JUNOS software, it is possible to have a route reflector serve two different clusters. That is, the RR can have multiple unique cluster IDs configured. This is very useful in certain topologies when doing redundant route reflectors. Look at Figure 12-28.

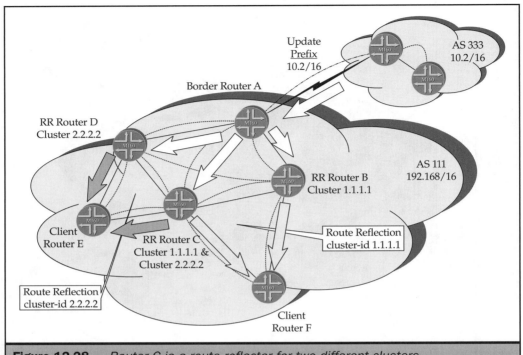

Figure 12-28.   *Router C is a route reflector for two different clusters.*

In Figure 12-28, RR router C is serving two RR clusters. RR cluster 1.1.1.1 has router F as the client and routers B and C as the RRs. RR cluster 2.2.2.2 has router G as the client and routers C and D as the RRs. This is possible because in JUNOS software, the cluster ID is configured at the peer group level. Router C has three peer groups in this scenario.

- Peer group ibgp-mesh has routers A, B, and D as neighbors.
- Peer group cluster-1.1.1.1 has router F as a neighbor and cluster ID 1.1.1.1 configured.
- Peer group cluster-2.2.2.2 has router G as a neighbor and cluster ID 2.2.2.2 configured.

```
protocols {
    bgp {
        group ibgp-mesh {
            peer-as 111;
```

```
        export nexthop-self;
        local-address 100.100.1.1;
        neighbor 100.100.1.2;
        neighbor 100.100.1.3;
        neighbor 100.100.1.4;
  }
   group rr-cluster {
        peer-as 111;
        cluster 1.1.1.1;
        export nexthop-self;
        local-address 100.100.1.1;
        neighbor 100.100.1.10;
    }
   group rr-cluster {
        peer-as 111;
        cluster 2.2.2.2;
        export nexthop-self;
        local-address 100.100.1.1;
        neighbor 100.100.1.11;
    }
```

One last important note about route reflection before confederations are discussed. There is a known issue with certain route reflection designs that can result in a condition known as Persistent Route Oscillation. This is covered in Chapter 13, and is important to understand so that you can design around this condition.

Confederations

Many engineers over the years have groaned when confederations are mentioned. They are not so difficult! The idea is to take a large AS and divide it into two or more smaller ones. The net result is an exponential decrease in the amount of IBGP peer connections. Simply splitting an AS into two, in and of itself, would cause significant grief to the surrounding ISP communities as the new resulting longer AS_PATH can cause the results of their path selection to change. In addition the increased size of the AS_PATH attribute would result in more memory consumption for the entire Internet community. In general more information is better, but additional knowledge of the internal topology of a now split larger AS has little probable benefit. (See Figure 12-29.)

The *Confederation BGP* solution allows the benefits of subdividing larger ASs into smaller ones, while hiding the new Sub-ASs from the outside world. To do this, a few new modifications to the Border Gateway Protocol described in RFC 1771 had to be made. These new terms or modifications are described in the most current RFC on Confederation BGP, RFC 3065. The first new term, *AS confederation identifier,* is the external AS number

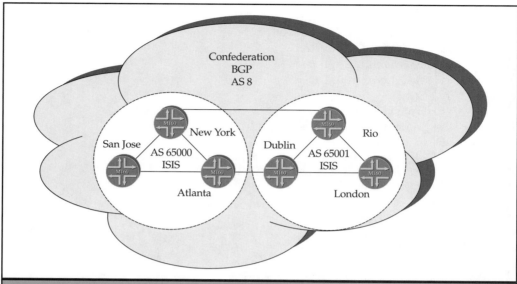

Figure 12-29. *BGP confederation designs allow for greater control of IGPs and path selection inside an AS and for reducing the number of peerings required for the IBGP full-mesh.*

that describes the confederation and is leaked to the outside world. The next term, *member AS number,* is an AS number assigned to a Sub-AS within a confederation and is not to be leaked to the outside world. To complete the modifications, the behavior of some of the standard BGP attributes needs to be changed. The AS_PATH attribute is enhanced to include the AS_CONFED_SET path segment type and the AS_CONFED_SEQUENCE path segment type. These new types describe unordered sets or ordered sequences of Member-AS numbers within the confederation. The ways in which an AS_PATH attribute can be updated by a BGP speaker are listed in section 6.1c of RFC 3065, as quoted here.

- 6.1. AS_PATH Modification Rules

    - c) When a given BGP speaker advertises the route to a BGP speaker located in a neighboring AS that is not a member of the current AS confederation, the advertising speaker shall update the AS_PATH attribute as follows:

        - if the first path segment of the AS_PATH is of type AS_CONFED_SEQUENCE, that segment and any immediately following segments of the type AS_CONFED_SET or AS_CONFED_SEQUENCE are removed from the AS_PATH attribute, leaving the sanitized AS_PATH attribute to be operated on by steps 2 or 3.

- if the first path segment of the remaining AS_PATH is of type AS_SEQUENCE, the local system shall prepend its own confederation ID as the last element of the sequence (put it in the leftmost position).

- if there are no path segments following the removal of the first AS_CONFED_SET/AS_CONFED_SEQUENCE segments, or if the first path segment of the remaining AS_PATH is of type AS_SET the local system shall prepend a new path segment of type AS_SEQUENCE to the AS_PATH, including its own confederation ID in that segment.

Fundamentally, the rules in the previously quoted section of the RFC describe ways in which Member-AS numbers for a confederation are removed from the AS_PATH prior to the update leaving the encompassing confederation AS. The Member-AS numbers are replaced with the confederation ID when sending an update to a nonconfederation EBGP speaker.

Since most Confederation BGP-based ASs are managed by a single group sharing the same administrative control (such as an ISP), a few other BGP attribute behaviors can be relaxed. The NEXT_HOP attribute for instance is not required to be updated when leaving a Confederation BGP peer connection. This requires that the provider retain end-to-end reachability within its confederation AS. This allows NEXT_HOP resolution policies to stay consistent on the AS's external boundaries. The LOCAL_PREF attribute behavior, which is normally useful only when advertised to IBGP peers to influence which exit a packet will take from an AS, can now be sent across subconfederation boundaries unchanged. Finally the MED attribute can be used to prevent route oscillation inside your AS by influencing how other Sub-ASs forward packets through the confederation.

Private ASs

When creating a Confederation BGP network design it is recommended that you assign the Subautonomous Systems Member_IDs from the Private Autonomous Numbers range. These numbers, in the range of 64,512 to 65,535, have multiple advantages. First, because they are reserved for private usage they do not require additional registrations with the regional Internet authority, thus conserving the rapidly depleting available AS number supply. Secondly, although RFC 3065 states that all subconfederation member_IDs should be removed from the AS_PATH attribute when communicating with an external AS, there are always buggy protocol implementations that might leak these Member_IDs. Can you imagine the havoc that would occur if a confederation AS is using a previously registered AS number inside its confederation and that path leaked unfiltered into the global Internet? Previously valid paths might become unusable due to falsely detected routing loops.

Private ASs have other uses besides Sub-AS assignment in confederations. If an AS is multihomed to the same service provider in different POPs there is no need to use a registered AS number. Some ISPs that are running Confederation BGP might feel that adding customers into their confederation is not appropriate. The disadvantage of private AS usage outside of Confederation BGP is that attributes and policy control do not flow in the private AS as they would in a subconfederation. The second and more important issue with the use of private AS numbers is that connectivity to the Internet will be allowed only through providers that strip private ASs for transit announcements but allow them within their own AS. To do this on a Juniper Networks M-series router you must include the `remove-private` command at the BGP global, group, or neighbor level on the transit routers with connectivity to public ASs. (See Figure 12-30.)

Confederation BGP-Based AS Design Considerations

When designing a Confederation BGP-based AS, there are three general philosophies. The first and simplest design involves splitting a large AS into two Sub-ASs. The primary concerns involved in this scenario involve redundancy for the Confederation BGP connections between the subconfederations, and using attributes such as MED to control traffic flow through the now subdivided AS to avoid suboptimal paths for

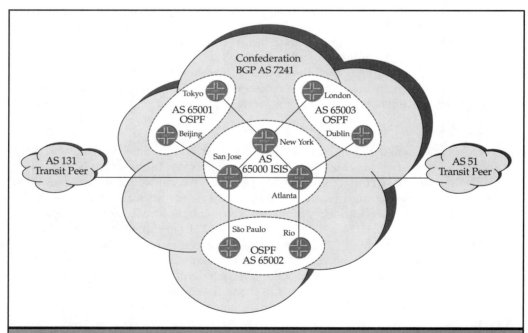

Figure 12-30.   *The central sub-AS design concept allows for stricter control of transit routing with all transit ASs being interconnected into the central AS.*

traffic flow. The second design that seems to be employed involves creating a core Sub-AS that has all major external transit peerings flowing through it, and several smaller Sub-ASs that have regional customer connectivity. This design, as do all Confederation BGP designs, suffers from the same problems that the first design incurs as well. The advantage to this design which logically resembles an OSPF two-layer hierarchy, is that a more selective and effective set of customer-specific policies can be placed on the subconfederations. The third approach is a noncore-oriented regional or geographical approach. The major advantage here comes into play with global providers and allows for regional administration and control of Sub-ASs.

Resolving BGP Next-Hop Addresses

Just to stay true to the virtual router theme, imagine a big virtual router called an AS. The idea here is simple. "How does a packet get into and out of a router, or in this case an AS?" If thinking in terms of each EBGP peering being an entrance/exit to our virtual router, and that for a real router to forward packets it must

- First find a longest match in the routing table,
- Look at the associated next-hop,
- Then resolve that next-hop to a directly connected interface.

Then the only difference between a real router and the (AS) virtual router is how to get from an entrance interface to an exit interface inside of the AS. Now that this concept is established, look at the similarities and differences between AS forwarding and single router forwarding. To begin, there is still a longest match lookup on the entrance router. If the route's longest match is a BGP-advertised prefix, then look at the associated next-hop (by default, the IP address for the remote advertising peer on which the exit subnet of the AS virtual router resides). Then, once again, search the local routing table for a local path to reach that exit subnet. (The additional step!) Finally, search the routing table(s) for an exit interface associated with the local next-hop. There are many ways to make sure that the exit subnet is reachable by all the IBGP neighbors, but there are four best-practice methods to achieve this goal. Listed in accepted order of preference, they are next-hop self, IGP passive, static routing, and redistribute direct networks.

Next-Hop Self Policy

There is an advantage to using a *next-hop-self* to solve the BGP NEXT_HOP address to a local next-hop address and outgoing interface. Namely, the network(s) between EBGP peers (often called DMZ networks), which might not be under your administration, does not need to be advertised or reachable by other routers inside the local AS. The net result of setting next-hop self is that the prefix advertisement's BGP NEXT_HOP field is overwritten with the router's router ID, which is generally the router's loopback IP address, before advertising the prefixes to IBGP peers. Setting next-hop self on a Juniper Networks router involves the use of routing policy. There is no next-hop self knob. The sample policy is applied as an export policy in your IBGP peer group(s).

```
policy-statement nhs {
    from {
        protocol bgp;
        neighbor [ 122.16.30.18 182.16.40.14 ];
    }
    then {
        next-hop self;
    }
}
```

Care should be taken to avoid having a next-hop self policy that is applied to a Route Reflector peer group. The next-hop rewrite function of a policy will rewrite the BGP NEXT_HOP on prefixes received from clients as well, if not designed selectively enough. This is covered in detail in a case study in Chapter 13. The best practice is to apply the "nhs" policy as an export policy to the neighbors in your IBGP peer group. In other words, as the local BGP speaker exports external prefixes to its IBGP peers, it will rewrite the BGP NEXT_HOP address to itself.

Passive Interface

Passive interface is a routing protocol independent feature that most vendors support in some form or another. The rule states that with a passively configured interface, a speaker will listen to protocol traffic from neighbors on the interface but will not send any protocol traffic out of the interface. This behavior affects the various IGPs differently. For link-state routing protocols such as OSPF and IS-IS this feature prevents protocol hello traffic from being sent. If hellos are not sent no adjacencies can be formed with other speakers and the link from an OSPF or IS-IS point of view becomes a stub network. The subnet that matches the interface is then injected into the IGP. When this feature is configured on an interface that corresponds to an EBGP link the subnet is advertised into the IGP without the possibility of another AS running the same routing protocol and becoming adjacent from an IGP perspective. Now that the DMZ link(s) are reachable, IBGP speakers can perform normal route resolution to solve the BGP NEXT_HOP to a local next-hop address. The following example illustrates a passively configured EBGP interface running OSPF as the IGP. Interface `so-0/0/0.120` is configured as the passive IGP interface.

```
Ospf {
      Area 0.0.0.0 {
            interface lo0.0
            interface fe-0/0/0.0
            interface so-0/0/0.120 {
                  Passive;
            }
      }
}
```

Static Routes

The use of static routes to solve the BGP NEXT_HOP issue is probably the oldest solution to the problem. The disadvantage of static routes is obvious. They lack any dynamic capabilities to detect and/or reroute around network failures. There have been many attempts to create static route designs with solutions to the nondynamic behavior problem, such as the concept of "floating static routes." If going through this much trouble, why not just run an internal routing protocol?

Export Direct

The last solution involves using routing policy to match on directly connected interface routes in the routing table and injecting them into the IGP for forwarding. This approach nets the same result as IGP passive with significantly more effort. There is also one other large disadvantage to this approach in that all interface routes are injected into the IGP, not just the one for the DMZ network. This results in additional interfaces in the IGP database. For instance if using OSPF, additional external LSAs are generated, one per interface. This adds overhead to the calculation of SPF, the database, and the routing table. Creating a route filtering policy to achieve the desired result can modify this behavior, in effect, limiting which subnets are injected into the IGP with the use of route filters. Again, this involves significantly more effort.

Hot-Potato Routing

Hot-potato routing is a common phrase used by ISP engineers. It refers to the paradigm of interdomain route selection in the Internet, where the routing policies that are put in place result in the selection of the nearest egress router as the exit point of the network.

This is also called *closest-exit routing*. Basically, the packets are considered "hot potatoes" and passed as quickly as possible to the closest egress router. This alleviates the ISP from carrying these packets across the local network any longer than it has to, which results in less traffic on the local network, which should correlate to a more efficient infrastructure. Basically, the local network uses less resources than might have otherwise been required, had it attempted to carry the packets as close to the real destination as possible. The downside of this paradigm is that the closest egress router on the local network might not, in fact, be on the shortest path to the destination. Figure 12-31 shows this in more detail.

In Figure 12-31, with no routing policy applied on the routers in AS 111, router C will choose to exit the AS by sending packets toward router B. This is because when router C does its best path selection, all attributes are equal up to the MED decision. Since the two paths to prefix 10.1.1/24 are from the same neighboring AS, then MED is evaluated by default. The path from border router B has a MED of 50, while the path from border router A has a MED of 100. The lower MED value wins, so router C will install the path to router B as the best. AS 444 has local routing policies configured to intentionally set the MED to these values, because the segment 10.1.1/24 is closer to border router B in AS 111. This makes sense to the engineers operating the network in AS 444.

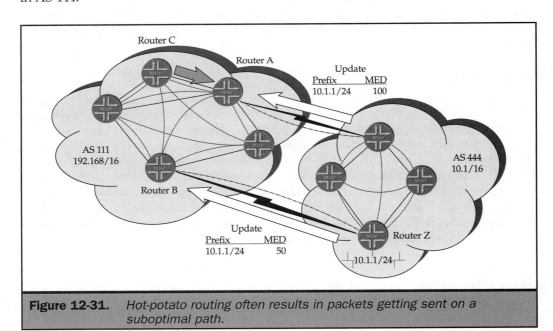

Figure 12-31.   *Hot-potato routing often results in packets getting sent on a suboptimal path.*

The engineers operating network AS 111, however, do not want to carry the traffic to 10.1.1/24 across their local backbone any more than necessary. They would like to have router C forward traffic to 10.1.1/24 to border router A because that border router is closer to router C. This makes sense to them. So, routing policies are configured on border routers A and B to reset all received MED values to 0. When router C now receives these two paths, all attributes are equal including MED. The next path selection decision that is not equal in this case is IGP metric. Router C has a lower IGP metric to border router A than to border router B. Router C will now install the path to border router A as the best path. Hot-potato routing has now been accomplished.

The alternative to this is often referred to as *best-exit routing*. This typically requires less work on the routing policy side as the default BGP path selection algorithms commonly result in this outcome. Best-exit routing can also be referred to as *cold-potato routing*. As one engineer wrote on a NANOG mailing list regarding this topic, "In the real world, with aggregation and the like, cold-potato routing typically resembles something more akin to 'mashed-potato routing,' and is usually given thrust by service-provider marketing folks."

Damping

Route damping (RFC 2439), often referred to as route dampening, is a feature that was created to protect the CPU use of legacy routers. It also adds to the general stability of the Internet. When a prefix gets withdrawn from the global Internet, for any number of reasons, each BGP speaker needs to be informed. They will then withdraw the specific prefix from their forwarding table. When a BGP speaker receives an Update with a list of withdrawn routes, the local CPU must process that message and perform the removal of the specified prefixes from the FIB. When those prefixes are again re-announced, the local BGP speaker must then reinstall those prefixes into the RIB, perform its path selection process, and then copy the prefix into the FIB. If the local BGP speaker receives constant withdrawals and re-announcements for the same set of prefixes, it spends more processing power handling this "route churn." Damping is basically a penalty system, whereby the local BGP speaker penalizes the flapping prefixes by not reinstalling them immediately after they are re-announced.

This reduces the route update load, without limiting convergence time for well-behaved prefixes. Route damping is applied to EBGP peers, not IBGP peers, however, it can also be used on confederation boundaries. There is specific terminology for the parameters associated with damping and specific default JUNOS software values. Note that the default values for other BGP implementations might differ. This is important if you have a multivendor BGP network and you want consistent damping parameters across your network. You must modify the parameters so that they match, if that is the case.

Figure of Merit

The figure of merit is the penalty value. Its default is zero, meaning there is no penalty applied to the prefix. There is a figure of merit associated with each prefix, if damping is enabled. In JUNOS software, the prefix figure of merit increases by 1000 with each withdrawal. It again increases by 1000 when the offending prefix is re-announced. For any path attribute change for a prefix, a figure of merit of 500 is added.

Suppress Threshold

The suppress threshold is the ceiling that, once the figure of merit is exceeded, causes the prefix to become damped. While in a damped state, the prefix is not active in the FIB and is not re-advertised to peers. It is basically unusable. The default suppress threshold in JUNOS software is 3000. So, when a prefix's figure of merit goes over 3000, the prefix is suppressed.

Half-Life for Exponential Decay

There is an exponential decaying algorithm applied to the figure of merit value. This results in the figure of merit being reduced while the prefix is stable. Basically, after a configurable time period, called the half-life, expires and the prefix has been stable over that time period, the figure of merit is reduced by half (50 percent); however, this reduction of the figure of merit does not happen at once. It is reduced gradually over the half-life time period. So, the result is that if a prefix has a figure of merit of 2000, after the half-life default of 15 minutes, the figure of merit is reduced to 1000. This assumes, of course, that the flapping prefix has been stable for these 15 minutes.

Reuse Threshold

The reuse threshold is the threshold that allows a damped prefix to once again be used. As the exponential decaying algorithm reduces the figure of merit, once the figure of merit goes below the reuse threshold, the prefix is once again marked as active, installed in the FIB and exported to peers. The default JUNOS software reuse threshold is 750.

Maximum Suppress

There are situations in which a prefix can flap many, many times in a very short time period. If that were to happen, the figure of merit would continually increase to a very high number. The figure of merit can increase such that, over several or many half-lives, the figure of merit would still not go below the reuse threshold and would remain damped for an extended period. There is a maximum suppression time period of 60 minutes in JUNOS software. This is also configurable, as are the other parameters discussed so far. The result of this default suppression value is that a prefix that has stabilized can be damped only for a maximum of 60 minutes.

Keep in mind that while a prefix is damped, the local router cannot forward packets to that destination. The destination is unusable and unreachable, as far as the local router is concerned. The prefix to that destination can have been re-announced and remains stable, but due to the damping penalty, the destination remains unusable until the reuse threshold is reached. This damping penalty system to protect router resources seems to be counter-productive to Internet reachability, to some observers.

You can apply damping to all prefixes, specific prefixes, or to specific neighbors. You can also apply different sets of damping parameters to different sets of prefixes. There is a damping approach referred to as "flat and gentle," in which all prefixes are treated equally from a damping perspective. Although this is the easiest approach, it is not the most useful. Prefixes that are aggregated should be damped less than unaggregated prefixes. Aggregated prefixes are typically more stable anyway, due to the nature of aggregation. Another approach to damping, referred to as "progressive," is more typically implemented. This approach penalizes longer prefixes more than shorter (aggregated) prefixes. Also, it should be noted that there are some prefixes in the global Internet that should never or rarely be damped. These are referred to as "golden prefixes," and are the root name servers.

In the following example, the local router will damp some prefixes more aggressively than other prefixes, based on the configured route filters. Prefixes matching the first route filter of 11/8 will be damped with the parameters specified in the damping profile called "high." The prefixes matching the second route filter of 15/8 will be damped with the parameters specified in the damping profile called "medium." The rest of the received BGP prefixes that fall through these two route filters will match the third router filter of 0/0 up to /24, so long as their prefix length is /24 or shorter, and they will not be damped at all. In this example, there is another policy not listed here that catches those prefixes that have a prefix length longer then /24 and rejects them.

```
policy-options {
        policy-statement damp {
            from {
                route-filter 11/8 exact damping high;
                route-filter 15/8 exact damping medium;
                route-filter 0/0 upto /24 damping none;
            }
            then accept;
        }
        damping high {
            half-life 15;
            suppress 3000;
```

```
              reuse 2500;
              max-suppress 50;
        }
        damping medium {
              half-life 3;
              max-suppress 4;
        }
        damping none {
              disable;
```

There are several commands to use to examine routes that are affected by damping. A very useful command that shows a quick snapshot of the BGP peers, the BGP routes and whether any of the routes are damped is shown here.

```
user@hostname> show bgp summary
Groups: 1 Peers: 1 Down peers: 0
Table          Tot Paths  Act Paths Suppressed     History Damp State     Pending
inet.0                 2          1          1           0          1           0
inet.2                 0          0          0           0          0           0
Peer          AS   InPkt   OutPkt    OutQ   Flaps Last Up/Dwn
State|#Active/Received/Damped
192.168.1.2   2       15       15       0       0         5:17 1/2/1
```

In the preceding output, you can see that the BGP peer 192.168.1.2 in AS 2 is established by looking at the State fields. When the peer is transitioning through the FSM, you can see what state the peer is in by using this command. The states you see here are the ones described earlier in this chapter in the "Finite-State Machine" section. When the peer is up and established, engineers often expect to see "established" as the state. Rather than merely tell the user that the peer is established, this command will show you how many prefixes are received from that peer, how many of those prefixes are active in the FIB, and how many prefixes are damped. The numbers 1/2/1 in the preceding display mean that two prefixes have been received, of which one is active. The other prefix is currently suppressed due to damping. 1/2/1 correlates to active/received/damped.

To examine more information about the suppressed prefix, use this command.

```
user@hostname> show route damping suppressed detail

inet.0: 7 destinations, 7 routes (5 active, 0 holddown, 2 hidden)
+ = Active Route, - = Last Active, * = Both
```

```
10.1.0.0/16 (1 entry, 0 announced)
        BGP     Preference: /-101
                Source: 192.168.1.2
                Nexthop: 192.168.1.2 via so-0/2/0.0, selected
                State: <Hidden Ext>
                Local AS:     1 Peer AS:     2
                Age: 5:09
                Task: BGP_2.192.168.1.2+179
                AS path: 2 I
                Localpref: 100
                Router ID: 192.168.50.3
                Merit (last update/now): 3511/2786
                Default damping parameters used
                Last update:        00:05:09
                First update:       00:21:08
                Flaps: 6
                Suppressed.   Reusable in:        00:28:40
                Preference will be: 170
```

Prefix 10.1/16 is suppressed. While suppressed, this prefix is not active in the FIB and is not exported to any peers. The character next to the protocol that distinguishes whether the prefix is active is an asterisk. The asterisk is not present next to BGP in this output, verifying that this prefix is not active. This command also shows the figure of merit, which is 2786, and that default damping parameters are being used. This prefix is reusable in 28 minutes, 40 seconds.

Internal BGP Timers

BGP timers, such as Keepalive and Holdtime, are well-known timers. BGP also employs internal timers that facilitate proper operation and convergence.

BGP employs five internal timers: ConnectRetry, Holdtime, KeepAlive, Minimum ASOriginationInterval, and MinimumRouteAdvertisementInterval. RFC 1772 suggests specific values for these timers, although it is left to the vendor implementation to decide to use these suggested values or not.

The suggested value for the ConnectRetry timer is 120 seconds. The ConnectRetry timer is used during the Finite State Machine, that is when BGP peering is being established. The timer marks the time period elapsed while waiting for a TCP connection to be completed. Once the TCP connection is completed, the BGP peering session can be established. JUNOS software uses a minimum ConnectRetry of 32 seconds.

The suggested value for the HoldTime is 90 seconds. The Holdtime is a timer that marks the elapsed time period when no Keepalive or Update messages are received. If the HoldTime is expired, the BGP peering session is terminated. When either a Keepalive or an Update message is received, the HoldTime is restarted. JUNOS software defaults to a HoldTime of 90 seconds.

The suggested value for the KeepAlive timer is 30 seconds. This value is one-third the HoldTime. This is the time period between successive Keepalive messages. JUNOS software defaults to a Keepalive time of 30 seconds. If the HoldTime is changed in JUNOS software, the Keepalive will also be changed, as it is always one-third the HoldTime.

The suggested value for the MinASOriginationInterval is 15 seconds. This timer marks the minimum amount of time that must elapse between successive advertisements of Update messages that report changes within the advertising BGP speaker's own AS. JUNOS software defaults to a MinASOriginationInterval of 1 second.

The suggested value for the MinRouteAdvertisementInterval is 30 seconds. This timer marks the time period between successive Update packets. It is important to send the Update packets as quickly as possible for convergence purposes, however, sending too quickly can have a possible impact to stability. If you send Updates too quickly, it is possible to overload the receiving BGP peer. JUNOS software defaults to a MinRouteAdvertisementInterval of 1 second.

New BGP v4 Knobs and Features

This section briefly covers some of the new features that have been added to BGP v4. Although there are many more features being added or considered for BGP v4, not all are discussed here.

Multiprotocol Extensions for BGP v4

Multiprotocol BGP, also known as BGP-MP or MBGP, are extensions to BGP v4 that allow BGP to carry routing information for multiple network-layer protocols and additional addressing families, other than IP v4. Originally, BGP was created to carry only IP v4 reachability information, but now BGP can carry numerous other addressing families, such as IP v6, IPX, and even MPLS VPN labels.

As with the other extensions, this feature is optional and is negotiated with the capabilities advertisement, using code 1. When enabled, the router will use a new nontransitive attribute called MP_REACH_NLRI for carrying multiprotocol BGP information.

Multicast

MBGP can be used to create a dedicated routing table used for *Reverse Path Forwarding* (RPF) checks. MBGP might not be required for multicast routing, depending on whether the unicast NEXT_HOP is the same as the multicast NEXT_HOP used for RPF checks. If the NEXT_HOPs are not the same, then MBGP is required.

Essentially, MBGP is used to provide two sets of routing information. One set is for unicast routing and is stored in *inet.0.* The other set is for multicast routing and is stored in *inet.2*. This allows the RPF checks to use *inet.2*. This allows a single prefix to have two forwarding paths, one for unicast routing using *inet.0* and one for multicast forwarding using *inet.2*.

To enable BGP to carry multicast *Network Layer Reachability Information* (NLRI), you would use this command.

```
user@hostname# set protocols bgp family inet multicast
```

This command can be applied at the global bgp level, the bgp group level, or the bgp neighbor level. By default, `family inet unicast` is enabled. You can enable both unicast and multicast by specifying `family inet any`, rather than `family inet multicast`.

MPLS VPNs

If using MPLS VPNs, MBGP can carry the VPN information in the MP_REACH_NLRI attribute. This would consist of the VPN-IP v4 route, plus the MPLS label. Although not a topic of this chapter, the VPN-IP v4 field consists of the IP v4 address and a route distinguisher (RD). The RD is needed to provide unambiguous address space, due to the large potential for overlapping private IP address space when offering VPN services to multiple customers. RFC 1918 address space is commonly used inside enterprises to conserve limited publicly registered address space. For instance, two companies can both be using the 10/8 address space and a service provider can still offer both of these companies a VPN service over a common IP infrastructure. Tagging the two separate 10/8s with unique RDs allows them to be identified uniquely within the common IP service provider network.

Extended Communities

As discussed earlier in this chapter, BGP v4 is not done. There seems to be constant work in the IETF to extend this interdomain routing protocol to support the new functions and applications needed in today's Internet. One of these extensions is support for Extended Communities.

Extended communities, currently a work in progress in the IETF, adds additional capabilities to the community attribute discussed earlier. The primary enhancements are

- It provides an extended range for community values, from a 4-octet value to an 8-octet value. This allows communities to be used more extensively, without fear of overlapping values. This is similar in reasoning for moving from IP v4 addressing to IP v6 addressing.

- It provides a Type field in the attribute, which delivers more structure for the community space. This allows for easier grouping of community values. For instance, you can match on a specific community Type rather than explicitly identifying all the community values for a routing policy to match on.

This new attribute is a transitive optional attribute. There are three predefined extended communities:

- **Route Target Community** This identifies the destination the route is going to. Said another way, it identifies the set of routers that might receive the route.

- **Route Origin Community** This identifies the source of the route. Said another way, it identifies the router, or set of routers, that originate the route into BGP.

- **Link Bandwidth Community** This identifies the external link speed in bytes per second that connects the local network to a network in another AS. Said another way, the link speed of the physical link that the local EBGP router is using to connect to its EBGP peer in another AS.

Of these three predefined extended communities, in practice only the Route Target and Route Origin are currently used. These are typically used in networks that deploy RFC 2547bis, or MPLS Layer 3 VPNs, and are used to control VPN route distribution.

The Route Target community identifies the set of routers that are part of a VPN and should receive the VPN routes. Other routers that are not part of the particular VPN will not receive the VPN routes. The extended community and associated routing policy to accomplish this route filtering is manually configured on the VPN provider edge (PE) routers.

The Route Origin community identifies the router or set of routers that are part of a VPN and originated a route into the VPN. Again, it is useful for route filtering purposes to avoid routes from VPN A going to VPN B.

When using extended communities, the values used in the Community fields are also different than those used in standard communities. There are two options with extended communities for these values.

When the high-order octet of the Type field contains 0x00, the Value field contains a registered AS number and a community number that has meaning to the local network engineering staff, such as:

```
user@hostname# set policy-options community name members [target:11111:99];
```

In the previous example, the local AS number of 11111 and the community number of 99 are in the community Value field, which has some significant meaning to the internal engineering staff. The Type field of this extended community contains a Route Target.

When the high-order octet of the Type field contains 0x01, the Value field contains a registered IP v4 address and a community number that has meaning to the local network engineering staff, such as:

```
user@hostname# set policy-options community name members [origin:1.1.1.1:99];
```

In the previous example, the community Value field contains the IP address 1.1.1.1 and the community number of 99, which has some significant meaning to the internal engineering staff. The Type field of this extended community contains a Route Origin. In this case, the IP address of 1.1.1.1 is probably the router ID of the BGP speaker that is originating the update into the VPN.

If a BGP implementation supports Extended Communities, there should be no issue with carrying updates containing both standard community attributes and extended community attribute.

Route Refresh

Route refresh is a new extension to BGP v4. It is a new capability that is advertised in the Open message using capabilities advertisement code 2. This capability allows for the dynamic exchange of route refresh requests between BGP speakers and the subsequent re-advertisement of the respective adj-ribs-out.

Prior to this capability, there was no mechanism in BGP v4 to dynamically request a re-advertisement of the updates previously sent by a peer. When the inbound routing policy for a BGP speaker changes, all prefixes from its peers must be somehow re-evaluated against this new policy. If the local BGP speaker did not store a complete set of prefixes from its peers, then a command to re-advertise those prefixes had to be initiated on the local router. JUNOS software does, by default, store a complete set of prefixes from each peer in the adj-ribs-in. This feature of storing the complete set of prefixes from each peer is often referred to as *soft reconfiguration*. Other BGP implementations from other vendors might not be capable of this, or this might not be their default behavior; however, if the option `keep none` were configured on the local JUNOS software router to save memory, the local router would then not store the complete set of prefixes sent by each peer.

The route refresh feature is particularly useful in BGP environments using MPLS VPNS (RFC 2547bis). This is due to the extensive filtering policies needed in such an environment and the fact that VPN membership might be subject to common adds, moves, and deletes. When an inbound filter is changed, the local router can dynamically send its peers a route refresh message to request they resend their prefixes. With the expected greater concern for memory efficiency in MPLS VPN environments, this capability adds great value. Also, with the larger memory requirements of MPLS VPNs, it is more likely that the option of `keep none` is enabled on VPN routers.

A BGP speaker can send a peer this route refresh message only if the peer supports this feature, as advertised in the capabilities advertisement during their exchange of Open messages.

Cooperative Route-Filtering Capability

Another new extension to BGP v4 is cooperative route-filtering capability, otherwise known as *outbound route filter* (ORF). ORF is also a work in progress in the IETF. It enables a local BGP speaker to send a message to its remote peer to enable that peer to implement new outbound route filters toward the local peer. This allows for dynamic notification of route filtering lists.

It is common for a BGP speaker to have an inbound route filter policy in place to filter out unwanted prefixes. If both peers supported ORF, the local BGP peer would never receive the unwanted prefixes in the first place. The local peer would send a set of ORFs to the remote peer, which would apply these outbound filters in addition to its locally configured outbound filters, to suppress the sending of unwanted prefixes to the local peer. This saves the remote peer from the unneeded formation and transmission of prefixes that the local peer would reject anyway.

As of this writing, this capability is not supported in JUNOS software; however, by the time this book reaches your desk that is subject to change.

Graceful Restart Mechanism for BGP

BGP graceful restart is a mechanism that helps minimize the negative effects on routing caused by a BGP restart. A BGP restart is when the BGP software on a BGP router crashes and restarts. This graceful restart mechanism is currently defined in an Internet draft and is a work in progress.

A new BGP capability, termed *graceful restart capability,* is defined in this draft as capability code 64. This new BGP capability can be used by a BGP speaker to inform its peers of its ability to preserve its forwarding state during a BGP restart event. Preserving forwarding state while BGP restarts is the essence of this draft. This way, the router continues to forward packets while the BGP software restarts.

This new capability is negotiated in the Open message, as are other BGP capabilities. Once negotiated, an Update message with an empty withdrawn NLRI field signals an end-of-rib marker. This marker is used to signify that the peer has completed its initial routing table update, after the BGP peering session is established.

When BGP restarts on this peer, the peer will maintain its current forwarding state for BGP routes but will mark them as stale. While marked as stale, they are still used to forward packets, however, they are not exported to any peers. So, during the restart time the router continues to forward packets based on its previous forwarding table. When the BGP peering session is re-established, the restarting peer will receive BGP Updates normally; however, it will defer route selection until it has received the end-of-rib marker from all its eligible peers. It should be noted that until the end-of-rib marker is received, the local peer has no routes to advertise to its peers and no routes to update the forwarding table.

Once the end-of-rib marker is received from all eligible peers, the local peer will perform its normal route selection algorithm. The RIB and FIB will then be updated and all routes previously marked as stale will be removed. The local peer can then export its best BGP routes, as it normally would. Once it completes its advertisement, it will generate its own end-of-rib marker, signifying to its peers that is has sent all its best BGP routes.

This mechanism is needed in the Internet to minimize the effects and instability caused by software crashes. Although, like the ORF feature, it is not supported in JUNOS software at the time of this writing, that is subject to change by the time this book hits your desk.

The Complete Reference

## Chapter 13

Interdomain Routing Case Studies

by E. Gary Hauser Jr. and Peter J. Moyer

713

BGP is used to exchange routing information among routers in different autonomous systems. The best way to learn to use BGP is via hands-on experience. However, because most ISPs are not going to allow you to play with their core network to learn BGP, we will take the second-best approach in this chapter to help you learn by example. The next few sections display several common ISP configurations, a few not so common ISP configurations, and one large enterprise configuration. When possible, best practices will be used. In addition, some common configuration mistakes in the configuration of BGP on Juniper Networks routers will be highlighted.

Basic BGP Configuration and Best Practices

The following examples, based on the basic BGP configuration design shown in Figure 13-1, use various `show` commands on both an IBGP peer and EBGP peer to demonstrate best-practice configuration principles.

Each example begins by explaining the configuration statements for each type of BGP speaker, followed by analyses of the most common commands used in troubleshooting. The output of the troubleshooting commands displays what would be expected in a fully functional configuration.

The configuration of BGP on a Juniper Networks router assumes the use of *peer groups*. The peer group name can be anything that makes sense; however, it is best practice to use a name that is self documenting. In the following code snippet, the

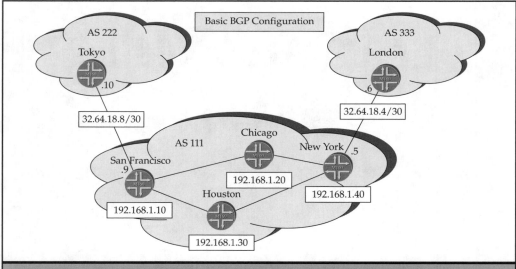

Figure 13-1. *A multi-AS topology demonstrating the basics of BGP configuration*

name `IBGP` was chosen to describe and document that this peer group includes IBGP peers.

```
lab@Chicago> show configuration

routing-options {
    router-id 192.168.1.20;
    autonomous-system 111;
}
protocols {
    bgp {
        group IBGP {
            type internal;
            local-address 192.168.1.20;
            neighbor 192.168.1.30;
            neighbor 192.168.1.40;
            neighbor 192.168.1.10;
        }
    }
}
```

Now take a look at some of the key pieces of the IBGP peer group. The command `type Internal` tells the BGP process that the neighbors listed in this group are in the same local AS. This command is required because the `peer-as` command is not used.

The command `local-address 192.168.1.20` changes the source of BGP messages from the outgoing interface IP address to the specified IP address, which is 192.168.1.20 in this example. The typical use of the `local-address` command is to specify the loopback IP address. If the outgoing interface fails, but the underlying IGP has a path to reach the loopback IP address of this router, the TCP connection to the BGP peer will stay up. Otherwise, if the source address of the BGP peer connection is the outgoing interface IP address and this interface fails, the BGP peering session will also fail. This design is used predominantly with IBGP and only in special configurations with EBGP. The issue with using this command with EBGP lies in the default TTL value of 1 for EBGP messages. Because the loopback interface is always +1 hop away from the physical interface, the `multihop` command must be used in conjunction with this command for EBGP. Also, with EBGP peering, it is typical that no routing protocol runs between the peers other than BGP. If the outgoing interface fails, the remote peer cannot reroute on another link to reach the local loopback IP address. So, the `multihop` command gains you nothing with EBGP except in special circumstances such as load balancing.

The local autonomous system number is configured under a different hierarchy called `routing-options` using the command `autonomous-system 111`. The last command from this section of the preceding code is optional but is again a best practice. The `router-id 192.168.1.20` command sets the router-id (RID) for both BGP and

OSPF. If not explicitly set, the RID is set to be the loopback interface IP address. If no loopback interface has been configured, the first interface IP address to come up will be used as the RID.

To illustrate the basic configuration of an EBGP router using JUNOS software commands, take a look at the following code snippet from router New York:

```
lab@NewYork> show configuration

routing-options {
    router-id 192.168.1.40;
    autonomous-system 111;
}
protocols {
    bgp {
        group EBGP-AS333 {
            type external;
            peer-as 333;
            neighbor 32.64.18.6;
        }
        group IBGP {
            type internal;
            local-address 192.168.1.40;
            export Next-hop-self-policy;
            neighbor 192.168.1.20;
            neighbor 192.168.1.30;
            neighbor 192.168.1.10;
        }
    }
}
```

This configuration has two BGP peer groups. The peer group labeled EBGP-AS333 is of type external and requires that you specify a peer-as 333 at either the group level as shown, or specify the peer-as 333 statement, which can appear beneath the individual neighbor statements. To differentiate EBGP connections to various autonomous systems in a single peer group, you can configure the peer-as beneath the neighbor statement. Also notice that an export policy has been applied to the IBGP group. The Next-hop-self-policy is a best-practices policy and is part of a larger policy or group of policies to manage an autonomous system.

The policy called Next-hop-self-policy, shown in the following snippet, is only one of several ways you can solve the problem of internal BGP routers resolving the BGP NEXT_HOP. The from section of the policy specifies not only routes tagged with the source protocol BGP, but specifically routes from EBGP neighbor 32.64.18.6:

```
policy-options {
    policy-statement Next-hop-self-policy {
        term NHS {
            from {
                protocol bgp;
                neighbor 32.64.18.6;
            }
            then {
                next-hop self;
            }
        }
    }
}
```

While not always necessary, writing policy in such a specific way protects you from unintentionally overwriting the *NEXT_HOP* attribute of other prefixes. This strict behavior becomes important when used on BGP peers that are also configured as route reflectors. This problem is discussed in greater detail in the section, "Issues with Route Reflection and Next-hop-self." The most often used show command for troubleshooting BGP is show bgp summary, as shown in Listing 13-1:

isting 13-1
The *show*
p summary
command
llows quick
isibility into
the routers
BGP
onnectivity.

```
lab@NewYork> show bgp summary
Groups: 1 Peers: 2 Down peers: 0
Table           Tot Paths  Act Paths Suppressed    History Damp State    Pending
inet.0                  0          0          0          0          0
inet.2                  0          0          0          0          0
Peer           AS     InPkt    OutPkt  OutQ  Flaps Last Up/Dwn   State|#Active/Received/Damped
32.64.18.6     333   14409     14405     0      0  5d 0:03:05    2/2/0
192.168.1.20   111    3285      9125     0      1  4d 23:54:53   0/0/0
```

This listing gives you a quick, one-line per peer summary of the remote AS, the state of the BGP peer, the uptime or downtime, the number of active routes, the number of received routes, and the number of damped routes. Several variations of this command exist.

For example, the show bgp neighbor 192.168.1.40 command, shown in Listing 13-2, is a useful troubleshooting command that provides detailed information about the state of the peer connection.

isting 13-2
The show
gp neighbor
command
outputs
detailed
atus for the
IBGP peer.

```
lab@Chicago> show bgp neighbor 192.168.1.40
Peer: 192.168.1.40+179 AS 111    Local: 192.168.1.20+2486 AS 111
  Type: Internal     State: Established     Flags: <>
  Last State: OpenConfirm   Last Event: RecvKeepAlive
  Last Error: None
  Options: <Preference LocalAddress HoldTime Refresh>
  Local Address: 192.168.1.20 Holdtime: 90 Preference: 170
```

```
Number of flaps: 0
Peer ID: 192.168.1.40     Local ID: 192.168.1.20     Active Holdtime: 90
Keepalive Interval: 30
NLRI advertised by peer: inet-unicast
NLRI for this session: inet-unicast
Peer supports Refresh capability (2)
Table inet.0 Bit: 10000
  Send state: in sync
  Active prefixes: 2
  Received prefixes: 2
  Suppressed due to damping: 0
Last traffic (seconds): Received 29    Sent 29    Checked 29
Input messages:  Total 8      Updates 1      Refreshes 0      Octets 189
Output messages: Total 9      Updates 0      Refreshes 0      Octets 197
Output Queue[0]: 0
```

The second line of Listing 13-2 shows the remote peers' IP address, TCP port number, and AS number. The *+179* that appears after the IP address of *192.168.1.40* shows that the remote peer is using port 179 for this TCP connection. This means that the remote peer opened the TCP connection by sending data to this port number, which is the defined TCP port number for BGP. On the same line, the local peer IP address, TCP port number, and AS number are shown. The *+2486* is the randomly chosen TCP port number for this connection. This number is from the range 1024 to 65535.

The third line, `Type: Internal`, signifies that this is an IBGP, or internal, peer. This could also have been determined from the second line, in which the Peer and Local AS numbers are both *AS 111*. The next field in the third line, `State: Established`, says that this BGP connection is up and passing routing information. The state is taken from the BGP finite state machine, which is described in Chapter 12.

The sixth line from the bottom of Listing 13-2, `Received prefixes: 2`, shows that two prefixes have been received from this neighbor, and the line above shows that they are both active (`Active prefixes: 2`). Later in the chapter, these two received prefixes will be examined using a different `show` command.

The same command displayed on an EBGP neighbor, shown in Listing 13-3, shows the peer information on the second line.

Listing 13-3
The *show bgp neighbor* command outputs detailed status for the EBGP peer.

```
lab@NewYork> show bgp neighbor
Peer: 32.64.18.6+179  AS 333    Local: 32.64.18.5+2381 AS 111
  Type: External     State: Established     Flags: <>
  Last State: OpenConfirm    Last Event: RecvKeepAlive
  Last Error: None
  Options: <Preference HoldTime PeerAS Refresh>
  Holdtime: 90 Preference: 170
  Number of flaps: 0
  Peer ID: 172.31.5.1      Local ID: 172.31.12.1      Active Holdtime: 90
```

```
Keepalive Interval: 30
NLRI advertised by peer: inet-unicast
NLRI for this session: inet-unicast
Peer supports Refresh capability (2)
Table inet.0 Bit: 10000
  Send state: in sync
  Active prefixes: 2
  Received prefixes: 2
  Suppressed due to damping: 0
Last traffic (seconds): Received 3    Sent 3    Checked 3
Input messages:  Total 49      Updates 1      Refreshes 0      Octets 961
Output messages: Total 52      Updates 2      Refreshes 0      Octets 1078
Output Queue[0]: 0
```

The `Type` field on the third line confirms that this is an EBGP connection with `Type:` `External` and shows that the connection is established.

Listing 13-4 shows the IPv4 unicast routing table called `inet.0`.

```
lab@Chicago> show route protocol bgp detail

inet.0: 11 destinations, 11 routes (11 active, 0 holddown, 0 hidden)
+ = Active Route, - = Last Active, * = Both

111.111.111.0/24 (1 entry, 1 announced)
        *BGP    Preference: 170/-101
                Source: 192.168.1.40
                Nexthop: 10.32.1.2 via fe-0/0/0.0, selected
                State: <Active Int Ext>
                Local AS:    111 Peer AS:    111
                Age: 1:16        Metric2: 1
                Task: BGP_111.192.168.1.40+179
                Announcement bits (2): 0-KRT 4-BGP_Sync_Any
                AS path: 333 I
                BGP next hop: 192.168.1.40
                Localpref: 100
                Router ID: 192.168.1.40


 222.222.222.0/24 (1 entry, 1 announced)
        *BGP    Preference: 170/-101
                Source: 192.168.1.40
                Nexthop: 10.32.1.2 via fe-0/0/0.0, selected
                State: <Active Int Ext>
                Local AS:    111 Peer AS:    111
                Age: 1:16        Metric2: 1
                Task: BGP_111.192.168.1.40+179
```

```
Announcement bits (2): 0-KRT 4-BGP_Sync_Any
AS path: 333 I
BGP next hop: 192.168.1.40
Localpref: 100
Router ID: 192.168.1.40
```

The routing table shown in Listing 13-4 stores entries from the populated areas of the forwarding table, or Forwarding Information Base (FIB). The `show route protocol bgp detail` command shows the routing table as it looks after import policies have been applied. `BGP Preference: 170/-101` is the protocol preference value assigned to both IBGP and EBGP in JUNOS software. In JUNOS software, no distinction in preference values exists for IBGP verses EBGP learned routes. EBGP routes are preferred in the route selection process over IBGP routes, as strictly external (EBGP) paths are preferred over external paths learned through interior sessions (IBGP).

Use of the modifier `detail` in this command shows all populated BGP attribute fields. Notice in Listing 13-4 that no Communities field is displayed. This is because no communities have been set for these two displayed prefixes.

In Listing 13-5, the `show route receive-protocol bgp <neighbor> (detail)` command shows all prefixes that have been sent from the 32.64.18.6 neighbor, with all modified attributes. This is a great way to see the native NEXT_HOP before modification by import routing policy.

Listing 13-5
The *show route receive-protocol bgp 32.64.18.6 detail* command allows you to view the routing information base (RIB-in) for this EBGP neighbor.

```
lab@NewYork> show route receive-protocol bgp 32.64.18.6 detail

inet.0: 13 destinations, 13 routes (13 active, 0 holddown, 0 hidden)
Prefix              Nexthop           MED    Lclpref AS path
111.111.111.0/24 (1 entry, 1 announced)
      Nexthop: 32.64.18.6
      AS path: 333 I
222.222.222.0/24 (1 entry, 1 announced)
      Nexthop: 32.64.18.6
      AS path: 333 I
```

The routing table shown is the *inbound routing information base-in,* or *adj-RIB-in* for short. An adj-RIB-in is included for each BGP peer that you are configured to listen to.

In Listing 13-6, the `show route advertise-protocol bgp <neighbor> (detail)` command shows all prefixes that are being exported to neighbor 192.168.1.20. From this view, it is evident that a next-hop self policy has been applied to this neighbor in the *outbound* or *export* fashion, as the modified *NEXT_HOP* attribute displays `self`.

```
lab@NewYork> show route advertising-protocol bgp 192.168.1.20 detail


inet.0: 13 destinations, 13 routes (13 active, 0 holddown, 0 hidden)
Prefix              Nexthop              MED    Lclpref AS path
111.111.111.0/24 (1 entry, 1 announced)
 BGP group IBGP type Internal
     Nexthop: Self
     Localpref: 100
     AS path: 333 I
222.222.222.0/24 (1 entry, 1 announced)
 BGP group IBGP type Internal
     Nexthop: Self
     Localpref: 100
     AS path: 333 I
```

Also notice in Listing 13-6 that, in accordance with the default rules for the *LOCAL_PREF* attribute, the default value of *100* has been added to these prefixes. By default, the *AS_PATH* attribute has not been modified because this is an IBGP peer. The routing table that this is showing is called the *routing information base-out,* or *adj-RIB-out* for short.

The last show route receive-protocol <neighbor> (detail), shown in Listing 13-7, shows the adj-RIB-in for the next-hop IBGP neighbor in this path. Notice that the *NEXT_HOP* attribute now displays *192.168.1.40.* This is the RID of the advertising router in Listing 13-6.

```
lab@Chicago> show route receive-protocol bgp 192.168.1.40 detail

inet.0: 11 destinations, 11 routes (11 active, 0 holddown, 0 hidden)
Prefix              Nexthop              MED    Lclpref AS path
111.111.111.0/24 (1 entry, 1 announced)
     Nexthop: 192.168.1.40
     Localpref: 100
     AS path: 333 I
222.222.222.0/24 (1 entry, 1 announced)
     Nexthop: 192.168.1.40
     Localpref: 100
     AS path: 333 I
```

ISP Design Using Routing Policy for BGP Control

BGP itself is not too complex, as you've seen in the last chapter. However, when you add in all the routing policies that need to be implemented in ISP networks, you can end up with some very complex configurations.

This section will focus on typical and best-practice routing policies that are often implemented in ISP networks. Although a common set of routing policies are usually implemented, each ISP has its own unique routing requirements, so no two ISPs use the exact same policies.

Routing policies are driven by technical, political, and monetary factors. Most are technically driven. Routing policies are often implemented during the initial configuration of the network. These policies should not change too frequently, as doing so adds operational issues and tends to lead to frequent human error. Policies do change sometimes, however, and modification of routing policies is a daily occurrence on some system somewhere in the Internet.

Some of the new features of BGP v4, such as Route Refresh and Outbound Route Filter, help reduce the impact of changing routing policies. Vendor BGP implementations that support rich policy language are appealing to ISP engineers. JUNOS software is one such implementation. JUNOS software includes a routing policy test feature that allows some routing policies to be tested for accurate behavior prior to deployment. This reduces potential human error and adds stability to the Internet during deployment of the policies, because debugging can occur prior to activation.

Take a look at a typical ISP network shown in Figure 13-2. In this case study, our focus will be on examining routing policies that impact traffic patterns. Best-practice routing policies that are deployed for security and stability reasons will also be covered. The Internet is a scary place, and although peering agreements are made between ISPs, it is not prudent to leave your network open to false or possibly malicious routing information.

Figure 13-2 shows five ASs. The local AS 111 is the focus. Peering to this AS are two customer ASs: AS 222 and AS 555. Customer AS 222 is multihomed to two service providers. AS 333 is a private peer, and AS 444 is the transit provider. This case study will focus on the routing policies on routers A, E, C, and F. These are the border routers of AS 111, where routing policies are usually configured.

Exporting Routes

First let's look at what the local ISP is exporting to its peers and customers.

Aggregate Routes

The local AS has an aggregate route configured on two routers, representing the IP address space of the ISP. Routers A and C anchor the aggregate, and other BGP speakers in AS 111 will receive the aggregate from these two border routers. The

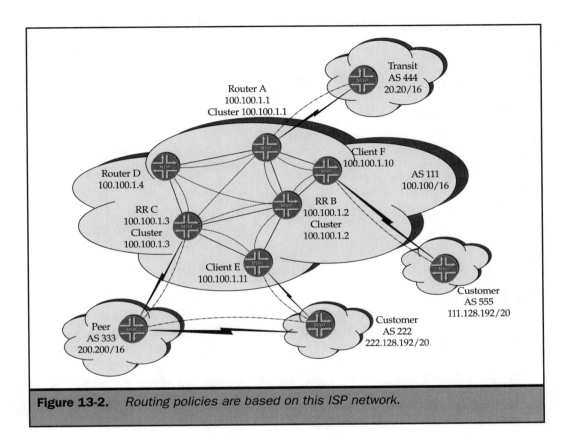

Figure 13-2.   *Routing policies are based on this ISP network.*

aggregate is configured as *passive*, so that it will always be present, regardless of whether contributing routes are present. This configuration scheme is often referred to as *nailing up the aggregate*. This is in contrast to a *conditional* aggregate. A conditional aggregate must have at least one contributing route active in the routing table. If not, the aggregate route will not be active. This contributing route must be more specific— that is, have a longer prefix length than the aggregate and must be part of the aggregate address space. Aggregates are configured under the routing-options hierarchy in the configuration file.

A policy statement called *send-agg* exports this aggregate. The second term of this policy is needed to explicitly suppress the more specific prefixes of the aggregate.

```
routing-options {
    aggregate {
        route 100.100.0.0/16 passive;
```

```
        }
    autonomous-system 111;
}
policy-options {
    policy-statement send-agg {
        term agg {
            from route-filter 100.100/16 exact;
            then accept;
        }
        term suppress-specifics {
            from route-filter 100.100/16 longer;
            then reject;
        }
    }
}
```

Martian Routes

A martian route should never be routed in the Internet. (You could say that it's from another planet so it's not a valid route on the planet called the Internet.) These routes are specified in RFC 1918 and are often used by enterprise networks. Some ISPs also use these routes internally. They serve a critical purpose, in that they are private IP addresses, and many enterprises and ISPs can use the same private IP address range. Using martian routes allows you to conserve the publicly registered IP address space. However, they must never be routed in the Internet since many enterprises and ISPs use the same private address space internally.

Still, parts of AS 111 use private addresses out of the RFC 1918 10/8 block. A martian route filter called *no-bogons* prevents any RFC 1918 routes from being exported out of AS 111. This is a courtesy policy to all the neighbor ASs—a form of Internet *netiquette*, as some engineers call it.

The martian route filter is configured as a separate policy statement and is called from a BGP export statement. All border routers have this policy to ensure that the private IP addresses are not leaked to any peer.

```
policy-statement no-bogons {
    term one {
        from {
            route-filter 10.0.0.0/8 orlonger;
            route-filter 127.0.0.0/8 orlonger;
            route-filter 169.254.0.0/16 orlonger;
            route-filter 172.16.0.0/12 orlonger;
            route-filter 192.0.2.0/24 orlonger;
```

```
                route-filter 192.168.0.0/16 orlonger;
                route-filter 224.0.0.0/3 orlonger;
        }
        then reject;
    }
```

JUNOS software includes a default martian route table. This route table contains addresses for which all routing information is ignored.

```
user@hostname> show route martians table inet.0

inet.0:
        0.0.0.0/0  -- allowed
        0.0.0.0/8 orlonger -- disallowed
        127.0.0.0/8 orlonger -- disallowed
        128.0.0.0/16 orlonger -- disallowed
        191.255.0.0/16 orlonger -- disallowed
        192.0.0.0/24 orlonger -- disallowed
        223.255.255.0/24 orlonger -- disallowed
        240.0.0.0/4 orlonger -- disallowed
```

Juniper Networks routers will not route the address ranges that are disallowed in this table. It is possible to install additional addresses to and remove addresses from this route table. Although you can add RFC 1918 routes to this table, rather than having a *no-bogons* martian route filter, doing this is not advised, as it will prevent the local router from routing these address ranges, and it is too easy to forget that these addresses are installed in the martian route table. If, in the future, the local router has an interface that is configured with one of these addresses, or is sent a routing *Update* with one of these addresses, the router will not route the packet or accept the *Update*. The network operations group maintaining the local router may not realize that this failure to route is due to having the address in the martian route table, and such a situation could take some time to troubleshoot and correct. Having a martian route filter is the preferred method of blocking RFC 1918 routes, as this setup is easily viewable in the configuration file of the router.

Transit Peer Routes

The nailed-up aggregate is exported to the transit provider. All customer routes from AS 222 and AS 555, and the customer routes of peer AS 333, are also exported to the transit provider. Policies that match on a community value are used on router A to ensure that only these routes are exported.

In the next example, customer routes that enter the local network directly or through the private peer are matched and accepted. This example shows the use of communities rather than direct-route filters. This is the preferred method, as it is easier to support.

```
policy-statement send-customers {
    term customers {
        from community [ CUSTOMERS PRIVATE-PEER-CUSTOMERS ];
        then accept;
    }
    term reject-rest {
        then reject;
```

Private Peer Routes

Only direct customer routes and the aggregate route are exported to the private peer. No transit routes are exported. The same policy `send-customers` is used, as the explicit `then reject` will ensure that transit routes are not exported to the private peer.

Customer Routes

Both customers receive the aggregate route, other customer routes, and a BGP default route. The default route exported to customer AS 222 has a MED of 50. Per the agreement with this customer, the local AS will be used for transit only as a backup path.

Private peer AS 333 provides the customer's primary path. Private peer AS 333 is sending the customer a default route with a MED value less than 50. Remember that the lower the MED value the more preferred the route. The customer needs to ensure that their BGP routers compare MEDs from different ASs, as this is not the default behavior for BGP. To accomplish this feature in JUNOS software, you use the command `user@hostname# set protocols bgp path-selection always-compare-med`.

The configuration snippet for router E is shown here.

```
routing-options {
    static {
        route 0.0.0.0/0 {
    metric 50;
    reject;
        }
    }
    autonomous-system 111;
}
policy-options {
    policy-statement send-customers {
        term customers {
```

```
                    from community [ CUSTOMERS ];
                    then accept;
            }
        }
    policy-statement send-default {
        term one {
            from {
                route-filter 0.0.0.0/0 exact;
            }
            then accept;
        }
        term two {
            then reject;
        }
    }
}
```

Importing Routes

More policy is involved when importing routes due to the desire to affect internal BGP decisions and traffic patterns and the need to protect the local AS from false or malicious routing information.

Martian Routes

A martian route filter is used in the import policies to ensure that the peers do not accidentally export a martian route to the local AS. In addition to the martian routes is a route filter in the import policy that denies any prefix beginning with *0.0.0.0* from entering the local network, regardless of its prefix length. This serves to prevent not only the traditional default route, *0/0*, from entering the network, but it prevents any route that has *0.0.0.0* as its prefix from entering. It is possible to send a malicious (or accidental) default route with a prefix length longer than */0* in an attempt to slip by route filters that are matching only on *0/0*.

The route filter qualifier `through` is used in this policy. This qualifier is rarely used in practice, because it matches on only an exclusive set of routes.

```
policy-statement no-bogons-or-default {
        term one {
            from {
                route-filter 0.0.0.0/0 through 0.0.0.0/32;
                route-filter 10.0.0.0/8 orlonger;
                route-filter 127.0.0.0/8 orlonger;
```

```
        route-filter 169.254.0.0/16 orlonger;
        route-filter 172.16.0.0/12 orlonger;
        route-filter 192.0.2.0/24 orlonger;
        route-filter 192.168.0.0/16 orlonger;
        route-filter 224.0.0.0/3 orlonger;
    }
    then reject;
}
```

Prefix Length

It is common for ISPs to have filters in place to prevent prefix lengths longer than a specific value to be imported into the local network in an effort to reduce the size of the default free Internet routing tables. The specific prefix length depends on the ISP; however, prefixes longer than /24 are regularly not allowed. Some engineers believe a global filtering policy should be enforced by all ISPs. For instance, they suggest denial of prefixes longer than /20 or /21. This practice is also an attempt to convince ISPs to perform more aggregation of routes, which is also a good thing.

```
policy-statement prefix-length-24 {
    term one {
        from {
            route-filter 0.0.0.0/0 upto /24;
        }
        then next policy;
    }
    term two {
        then reject;
    }
}
```

The preceding route filter will match any prefix with a prefix length of /24 or shorter. These prefixes will be processed by the next policy and the remaining prefixes with a longer prefix length will be rejected. This is applied at all peering points. If the prefixes that matched the *from* clause were explicitly accepted rather than sent to the next policy, they would not be processed by any remaining policies. Once they are accepted, they are bounced out of any further policy processing.

Prefix Limits

On all peering points, the border router has a configured prefix limit that is not configured in a policy, but is part of the BGP configuration. This prevents a neighbor AS from accidentally sending an excessive number of prefixes to the local AS. The prefix limit is set on per-peer basis using agreed-upon prefix limits. On the private and transit border routers, the prefix limit is set high enough to allow flexibility in the number of prefixes that will be accepted. On the customer border router, the prefix limit is set without much headroom for error.

In the following example at the peering point to customer AS 222, the prefix limit is set to 5. All the prefix limits are set to start a syslog warning when the number of prefixes has reached 90 percent of the limit specified. This prefix limit is configured so that the BGP session will be torn down if the limit is exceeded. The default behavior ensures that a syslog warning is issued only when the limit is reached. In JUNOS software, the session will remain down for a configurable time limit.

```
protocols {
    bgp {
        group customer-222 {
            peer-as 222;
            neighbor 100.100.20.2 {
                family inet {
                    unicast {
                        prefix-limit {
                            maximum 5;
                            teardown 90;
                        }
                    }
                }
            }
        }
    }
}
```

Local Preference

The local AS is configured to set the *LOCAL_PREF* to 200 on customer routes. Customer routes of private peer AS 333 are set to a *LOCAL_PREF* of 170. *LOCAL_PREF* is examined early in the BGP decision process to ensure that the local AS forwards traffic directly to these customers. These import policies are applied on the border routers that are peering to the customers and the private peer. For example, router C has an import policy setting the *LOCAL_PREF* of peer AS 333's customer routes to 170. This is accomplished with an *AS_PATH* filter, because it would be difficult to continually match on all of the customer routes of AS 333.

Peer routes internal to AS 333 are set with a *LOCAL_PREF* of 150. This is also configured on router C.

Transit routes are set with a *LOCAL_PREF* of 130. This is configured as an import policy on router A.

Here is the local preference routing policy configuration from router C:

```
policy-options {
    policy-statement private-peer-in {
        term local-pref-150 {
            from as-path PEER-333;
            then }
                local-preference 150;
                community set PRIVATE-PEER;
                accept;
            }
        }
    term local-pref-170 {
            from as-path PEER-333-CUSTOMERS;
            then }
                local-preference 170;
                community set PRIVATE-PEER-CUSTOMERS;
                accept;
            }
        }
    term reject-rest {
            then reject;
        }
    }
    community PRIVATE-PEER members 111:1200;
    community PRIVATE-PEER-CUSTOMERS members 111:1100;
    as-path PEER-333 "333";
    as-path PEER-333-CUSTOMERS "333 .";
}
```

Here is the local preference policy for router E:

```
policy-options {
    policy-statement customer-222-in {
        term local-pref-200 {
            from route-filter 222.128.192/20 exact;
            then }
                local-preference 200;
                community set CUSTOMERS;
                accept;
            }
        }
```

```
    term reject-rest {
        then reject;
    }
  }
  community CUSTOMERS members 111:1000;
}
```

Note that the policy used here allows only the customer aggregate route, and then sets the *LOCAL_PREF* to 200 and tags the route with community CUSTOMERS. The route filter is an additional security measure that prevents routes that are not expected from the customer from entering the local network.

Communities

Communities are heavily used in ISP routing policies. Communities are popular because of their flexibility and because they allow easy "grouping" of routes. Communities are typically set in routes on the inbound direction with an import policy. Tagging routes with community values that are meaningful to the local network allows the local network staff to use routing policies that match on the community value and execute a policy change. Communities also aid in troubleshooting and give the network staff more visibility into the local routing environment. On any router in the local network, CLI commands can be issued to examine routes and the associated community values. The community value can tell the operator where this route entered the network and to whom it belongs.

In this case study, the local network staff is identifying all customer routes with a specific community of 111:1000. The private peers' customer routes are identified with a community value of 111:1100, and the private peer internal routes are tagged with 111:1200. In the term that sets the local preference and community value, notice that the then community clause is tagging the route with a set keyword rather than an add keyword. These keywords have different results. If you wish to retain existing communities with the prefix and merely add a new community to the community string, you would use add. If you wish to remove all existing communities and add only the new community, you would use set. Our examples use the set community string with a new community value, and any existing community values are removed.

No Export Community

Router A's import policy for the transit peer has a term that tags all transit routes with a community of no-export, along with the locally meaningful community. The no-export community is one of the well-known community values that ensures that the local AS does not export these routes outside the local AS.

```
policy-options {
```

```
policy-statement transit-in {
    term local-pref-130 {
        from as-path TRANSIT-444;
        then }
            local-preference 130;
            community set [TRANSIT NO-EXPORT];
            accept;
        }
    }
}
community TRANSIT members 111:1300;
community NO-EXPORT members no-export;
as-path TRANSIT-444 "444 .*";
}
```

Notice in this `transit-in` policy that the *from* clause is matching on a specific *AS_PATH*. The *AS_PATH* that is being matched is *any AS_PATH* that shows the transit AS number in the leftmost position. This is another form of security. Updates can be sent accidentally or maliciously with invalid *AS_PATHs*. Although not all of the invalid *AS_PATHs* will be caught with this policy, the extra protection to the local AS is a good thing.

Some BGP implementations may perform a sanity check on received BGP *Updates* to verify that the leftmost AS number is the same as that configured for the remote peer. This will accomplish the same goal as the `transit-in` policy. However, if the local peer is peering to a route server, this sanity check will prevent the local router from accepting *any Updates* from the route server. The route server is designed to be transparent to forwarding decisions and provides routing information only. A route server is another method of reducing the need for full BGP meshing.

In EBGP scenarios, the *Updates* from the route server do not show the route server's AS number in the leftmost position of the *AS_PATH*. The route server does not desire to influence *AS_PATH* decisions. For example, assume the route server is configured with AS 3. It will send *Updates* from AS 1 to AS 2, and the leftmost AS number in those *Updates* will be AS 1 (not its local AS 3). Some BGP implementations will not accept these *Updates* due to sanity checking. JUNOS software *will* accept these *Updates*, however, as the sanity check was relaxed for this exact requirement.

Local Address Filter

Another common route filter is designed to prevent the local network from accepting prefixes that are part of its address space—a best-practice policy that is used for security reasons. A peering partner can accidentally send a specific prefix that is part of the local network's address space. If the local network accepts this prefix, it is possible that traffic sent toward the peering partner is really destined for somewhere in the local network. The local address filter is applied as an import filter at all peering points.

In the following snippet, the local network is using 100.100/16, so this policy will reject any prefixes from being imported into the local network from that address space.

```
policy-options {
    policy-statement prevent-local-addresses {
        term deny-local {
            from {
                route-filter 100.100/16 orlonger;
            }
            then reject;
        }
    }
}
```

The router configurations that are pertinent to the discussed policies are shown in the following sections.

Router A

```
routing-options {
    aggregate {
        route 100.100/16 passive;
    }
    autonomous-system 111;
}
protocols {
    bgp {
        group ibgp-mesh {
            peer-as 111;
            export nexthop-self;
            local-address 100.100.1.1;
            neighbor 100.100.1.2;
            neighbor 100.100.1.3;
            neighbor 100.100.1.4;
        }
        group rr-cluster {
            peer-as 111;
            cluster 100.100.1.1;
            export nexthop-self;
            local-address 100.100.1.1;
            neighbor 100.100.1.10;
        }
        group transit-444 {
            peer-as 444;
            export [ no-bogons send-agg send-customers ];
            import [ no-bogons-or-default prevent-local-addresses prefix-
            length-24 transit-in ];
            neighbor 20.20.20.2;
        }
    }
}
policy-options {
    policy-statement no-bogons {
```

```
        term one {
            from {
                route-filter 10.0.0.0/8 orlonger;
                route-filter 127.0.0.0/8 orlonger;
                route-filter 169.254.0.0/16 orlonger;
                route-filter 172.16.0.0/12 orlonger;
                route-filter 192.0.2.0/24 orlonger;
                route-filter 192.168.0.0/16 orlonger;
                route-filter 224.0.0.0/3 orlonger;
            }
            then reject;
        }
    }
    policy-statement send-agg {
      term agg {
            from route-filter 100.100/16 exact;
            then accept;
        }
      term suppress-specifics {
            from route-filter 100.100/16 longer;
            then reject;
    }
    }
    policy-statement send-customers {
        term customers {
            from community [ CUSTOMERS PRIVATE-PEER-CUSTOMERS ];
            then accept;
        }
      term reject-rest {
            then reject;
    }
    }
    policy-statement no-bogons-or-default {
        term one {
            from {
                route-filter 0.0.0.0/0 through 0.0.0.0/32;
                route-filter 10.0.0.0/8 orlonger;
                route-filter 127.0.0.0/8 orlonger;
                route-filter 169.254.0.0/16 orlonger;
                route-filter 172.16.0.0/12 orlonger;
                route-filter 192.0.2.0/24 orlonger;
                route-filter 192.168.0.0/16 orlonger;
                route-filter 224.0.0.0/3 orlonger;
            }
            then reject;
        }
    }
    policy-statement prefix-length-24 {
        term one {
          from {
              route-filter 0.0.0.0/0 upto /24;
          }
          then next policy;
        }
        term two {
         then reject;
        }
    }
```

```
    policy-statement transit-in {
        term local-pref-130 {
            from as-path TRANSIT-444;
            then }
                local-preference 130;
                community set [TRANSIT NO-EXPORT];
                accept;
            }
        }
    }
    policy-statement nexthop-self {
      term match-community
          from {
            protocol bgp;
            community TRANSIT;
                }
          then {
              next-hop self;
          }
    }
    policy-statement prevent-local-addresses {
        term deny-local {
            from {
                route-filter 100.100/16 orlonger;
            }
            then reject;
        }
    }
    community CUSTOMERS members 111:1000;
    community NO-EXPORT members no-export;
    community PRIVATE-PEER-CUSTOMERS members 111:1100;
    community TRANSIT members 111:1300;
    as-path TRANSIT-444 "444 .*";
}
```

Router C

```
routing-options {
    aggregate {
        route 100.100/16 passive;
    }
    autonomous-system 111;
}
protocols {
    bgp {
        group ibgp-mesh {
          peer-as 111;
          export nexthop-self;
          local-address 100.100.1.3;
          neighbor 100.100.1.1;
          neighbor 100.100.1.2;
          neighbor 100.100.1.4;
        }
        group rr-cluster {
            peer-as 111;
            cluster 100.100.1.3;
            export nexthop-self;
            local-address 100.100.1.3;
            neighbor 100.100.1.11;
        }
        group private-peer-333 {
            peer-as 333;
            export [ no-bogons send-agg send-customers ];
            import [ no-bogons-or-default prevent-local-addresses prefix-length-24 private-peer-in ];
```

```
                neighbor 200.200.20.2;
            }
        }
    }
policy-options {
    policy-statement no-bogons {
        term one {
            from {
                route-filter 10.0.0.0/8 orlonger;
                route-filter 127.0.0.0/8 orlonger;
                route-filter 169.254.0.0/16 orlonger;
                route-filter 172.16.0.0/12 orlonger;
                route-filter 192.0.2.0/24 orlonger;
                route-filter 192.168.0.0/16 orlonger;
                route-filter 224.0.0.0/3 orlonger;
            }
            then reject;
        }
    }
    policy-statement send-agg {
        term agg {
            from route-filter 100.100/16 exact;
            then accept;
        }
        term suppress-specifics {
            from route-filter 100.100/16 longer;
            then reject;
        }
    }
    policy-statement send-customers {
        term customers {
            from community [ CUSTOMERS ];
            then accept;
        }
        term reject-rest {
            then reject;
        }
    }
    policy-statement no-bogons-or-default {
        term one {
            from {
                route-filter 0.0.0.0/0 through 0.0.0.0/32;
                route-filter 10.0.0.0/8 orlonger;
                route-filter 127.0.0.0/8 orlonger;
                route-filter 169.254.0.0/16 orlonger;
                route-filter 172.16.0.0/12 orlonger;
                route-filter 192.0.2.0/24 orlonger;
                route-filter 192.168.0.0/16 orlonger;
                route-filter 224.0.0.0/3 orlonger;
            }
            then reject;
        }
    }
    policy-statement prefix-length-24 {
        term one {
            from {
                route-filter 0.0.0.0/0 upto /24;
            }
            then next policy;
        }
        term two {
            then reject;
        }
    }
    policy-statement nexthop-self {
        term match-community
            from {
                protocol bgp;
                community PRIVATE-PEER;
            }
            then {
                next-hop self;
```

```
            }
    }
    policy-statement prevent-local-addresses {
        term deny-local {
            from {
                route-filter 100.100/16 orlonger;
            }
            then reject;
        }
    }
    policy-statement private-peer-in {
        term local-pref-150 {
            from as-path PEER-333;
            then {
                local-preference 150;
                community set PRIVATE-PEER;
                accept;
            }
        }
      term local-pref-170 {
            from as-path PEER-333-CUSTOMERS;
            then {
                local-preference 170;
                community set PRIVATE-PEER-CUSTOMERS;
                accept;
            }
        }
      term reject-rest {
            then reject;
      }
    }
    community PRIVATE-PEER members 111:1200;
    community PRIVATE-PEER-CUSTOMERS members 111:1100;
    community CUSTOMERS members 111:1000;
    as-path PEER-333 "333";
    as-path PEER-333-CUSTOMERS "333 .";
}
```

Router E

```
routing-options {
    static {
        route 0.0.0.0/0 {
            metric 50;
            reject;
        }
    }
    autonomous-system 111;
}
protocols {
    bgp {
        group ibgp-rr {
          peer-as 111;
          export nexthop-self;
          local-address 100.100.1.11;
          neighbor 100.100.1.2;
          neighbor 100.100.1.3;
        }
        group customer-222 {
            peer-as 222;
            export [ no-bogons send-agg send-customers send-default ];
            import [ no-bogons-or-default prevent-local-addresses prefix-length-24 customer-222-in ];
                neighbor 100.100.20.2 {
                family inet {
                    unicast {
                        prefix-limit {
                            maximum 5;
                            teardown 90;
                        }
                    }
                }
            }
        }
```

```
            }
        }
    }
policy-options {
    policy-statement no-bogons {
        term one {
            from {
                route-filter 10.0.0.0/8 orlonger;
                route-filter 127.0.0.0/8 orlonger;
                route-filter 169.254.0.0/16 orlonger;
                route-filter 172.16.0.0/12 orlonger;
                route-filter 192.0.2.0/24 orlonger;
                route-filter 192.168.0.0/16 orlonger;
                route-filter 224.0.0.0/3 orlonger;
            }
            then reject;
        }
    }
    policy-statement send-agg {
      term agg {
            from route-filter 100.100/16 exact;
            then accept;
      }
      term suppress-specifics {
            from route-filter 100.100/16 longer;
            then reject;
      }
    }
    policy-statement send-customers {
      term customers {
            from community [ CUSTOMERS ];
            then accept;
      }
    }
    policy-statement no-bogons-or-default {
        term one {
            from {
                route-filter 0.0.0.0/0 through 0.0.0.0/32;
                route-filter 10.0.0.0/8 orlonger;
                route-filter 127.0.0.0/8 orlonger;
                route-filter 169.254.0.0/16 orlonger;
                route-filter 172.16.0.0/12 orlonger;
                route-filter 192.0.2.0/24 orlonger;
                route-filter 192.168.0.0/16 orlonger;
                route-filter 224.0.0.0/3 orlonger;
            }
            then reject;
        }
    }
    policy-statement prefix-length-24 {
     term one {
            from {
                route-filter 0.0.0.0/0 upto /24;
            }
            then next policy;
        }
     term two {
            then reject;
      }
    }
    policy-statement nexthop-self {
      term match-community {
            from {
              protocol bgp;
              community CUSTOMERS;
            }
            then {
                next-hop self;
            }
      }
    }
    policy-statement prevent-local-addresses {
        term deny-local {
```

```
        from {
            route-filter 100.100/16 orlonger;
        }
        then reject;
    }
}
policy-statement customer-222-in {
    term local-pref-200 {
        from route-filter 222.128.192/20 exact;
            then {
            local-preference 200;
            community set CUSTOMERS;
            accept;
        }
    }
    term reject-rest {
        then reject;
    }
}
policy-statement send-default {
    term one {
        from {
            route-filter 0.0.0.0/0 exact;
        }
        then accept;
    }
    term two {
        then reject;
    }
}
community PRIVATE-PEER-CUSTOMERS members 111:1100;
community CUSTOMERS members 111:1000;
}
```

Router F   The configuration for router F is similar to that of router E. The one exception is the static default route, *0/0*, does not have a metric set. It will assume the default metric of *0*.

If you examine router E's `routing-options` configuration, you will notice that the static default route is configured as `reject`. Two options are available for the next-hop when configuring a static default route. Configuring the static default route with `reject` will enable the sending of ICMP unreachables to the source when the local router does not have an active route in the FIB that matches the destination address. Configuring the static default route with `discard` will not enable the sending of ICMP unreachables to the source. The packets will be discarded silently.

This concludes this case study on BGP best-practice routing policy.

Load Balancing with BGP

Load balancing, or load sharing, can be obtained in BGP and is gaining popularity, but it is important that you keep in mind that when the protocol was being developed, load balancing was not one of the design goals.

The default BGP load-balancing functionality in JUNOS software is on a per-prefix basis. If multiple equal-cost IGP paths to the BGP NEXT_HOP address are present, JUNOS software will distribute the BGP prefixes over those equal-cost paths in a psuedo-random fashion. The more prefixes, the better the distribution. If per-packet load balancing is configured on an Internet Processor I (IP1)–equipped Juniper

Networks router, the router will spread the packets over a maximum of 8 equal-cost paths. If per-packet load balancing is configured on an Internet Processor II (IP2)–equipped Juniper Networks router, the router will spread the prefixes over a maximum of 16 equal-cost paths.

Two enhanced forms of BGP load balancing are used: BGP multipath and BGP multihop. For each form of load balancing there are two ways of load distribution: per-prefix and per-packet.

Load Balancing with EBGP Using Multipath

The EBGP multipath software feature allows EBGP to load balance on up to 16 equal-cost next-hops with an IP2-equipped router. Figure 13-3 shows load balancing using multipath in three locations: San Francisco, Tokyo, and Beijing.

```
protocols {
    bgp {
        group load-balance {
            type external;
            peer-as 222;
            multipath;
            neighbor 100.1.1.1;
            neighbor 100.1.2.1;
            neighbor 100.1.3.1;
            neighbor 100.1.4.1;
            neighbor 100.1.5.1;
            neighbor 100.1.6.1;
            neighbor 100.1.7.1;
            neighbor 100.1.8.1;
        }
    }
}
```

These code statements display the peer group configuration for the router in AS 111 in the BGP multipath scenario shown in Figure 13-3. The Juniper Networks M-series router platform offers two different levels of performance for this feature. On M-series routers equipped with an IP1 ASIC, the multipath configuration in Figure 13-3 allows for load balancing on up to 8 equal-cost next-hops. On an M-series router with an IP2 ASIC, multipath allows load balancing on up to 16 equal-cost next-hops.

Without the multipath option configured, the San Francisco router in AS 111 will select either the Tokyo router or the Beijing router, based on the BGP path selection algorithm. It will then install the paths from that selected router as the best paths. If San Francisco selects Tokyo based on its having a lower router-id, the San Francisco router will not actively use paths received from Beijing, assuming all received paths

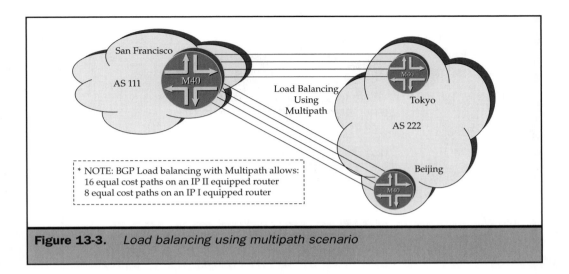

Figure 13-3.   *Load balancing using multipath scenario*

are equal in nature up to the lower RID decision. The Beijing paths will be used only if the paths from Tokyo disappear. If AS 111 wants to utilize both routers Tokyo and Beijing simultaneously, multipath can be configured on San Francisco. San Francisco will then distribute received prefixes between Tokyo and Beijing. This is because multipath actually ignores the tie-break lower RID path selection decision in the BGP decision process. If paths are equal up to that point and the paths are received from more than a single EBGP peer, both peers will be used.

Listing 13-8 shows the output of the `show route` command, which displays eight equal-cost next-hops.

Listing 13-8 *The output of the show route command displays eight equal-cost next-hops as a result of the multipath configuration.*

```
lab@Sanfran> show route


inet.0: 28 destinations, 28 routes (28 active, 0 holddown, 0 hidden)
+ = Active Route, - = Last Active, * = Both

1.1.1.0/24          *[BGP/170] 00:22:56, localpref 100, from 100.1.1.1
                      AS path: 222 I
                      to 100.1.1.1 via fe-0/0/0.1
                      to 100.1.2.1 via fe-0/0/0.2
                      to 100.1.3.1 via fe-0/0/0.3
                      to 100.1.4.1 via fe-0/0/0.4
                      to 100.1.5.1 via fe-0/0/0.5
                      to 100.1.6.1 via fe-0/0/0.6
                      to 100.1.7.1 via fe-0/0/0.7
                    > to 100.1.8.1 via fe-0/0/0.8
```

```
             [BGP/170] 00:22:53, localpref 100
               AS path: 222 I
             > to 100.1.2.1 via fe-0/0/0.2
             [BGP/170] 00:22:49, localpref 100
               AS path: 222 I
             > to 100.1.3.1 via fe-0/0/0.3
             [BGP/170] 00:22:45, localpref 100
               AS path: 222 I
             > to 100.1.4.1 via fe-0/0/0.4
             [BGP/170] 00:22:41, localpref 100
               AS path: 222 I
             > to 100.1.5.1 via fe-0/0/0.5
             [BGP/170] 00:22:36, localpref 100
               AS path: 222 I
             > to 100.1.6.1 via fe-0/0/0.6
             [BGP/170] 00:22:56, localpref 100
               AS path: 222 I
             > to 100.1.7.1 via fe-0/0/0.7
             [BGP/170] 00:22:52, localpref 100
               AS path: 222 I
             > to 100.1.8.1 via fe-0/0/0/8
```

The routing table in Listing 13-8 shows that for prefix 1.1.1.0/24, the Network Layer Reachability Information (NLRI) is reachable via eight different sources. The default distribution method is for per-prefix load balancing. For prefix 1.1.1.0/24, the psuedo-random hashing algorithm has chosen 100.1.8.1 as the next-hop for this prefix. This is evident from the display because the greater-than character (>) appears to the left of that next-hop. With per-prefix load balancing, the total number of prefixes learned from a neighboring autonomous system is pseudo-randomly hashed against the number of equal-cost paths being considered by the multipath configuration. The distribution, as shown in Listing 13-9, is not quite even. Eight prefixes are advertised and only five of the valid next-hops have routes associated with them.

Listing 13-9

The show route forwarding-table detail command shows the next-hop(s) that a packet will take to reach the prefix listed.

```
lab@Sanfran> show route forwarding-table detail
Routing table:: inet
Internet:
Destination      Type   RtRef  InIf   Flags   Nexthop      Type   Index  NhRef  Netif
default          perm   0      0      0x10                 rjct   10     1
1.1.1.0/24       user   0      0      0x10    100.1.8.1    ucst   48     3      fe-0/0/0.8
2.2.2.0/24       user   0      0      0x10    100.1.4.1    ucst   49     4      fe-0/0/0.4
3.3.3.0/24       user   0      0      0x10    100.1.5.1    ucst   43     5      fe-0/0/0.5
4.4.4.0/24       user   0      0      0x10    100.1.6.1    ucst   46     9      fe-0/0/0.6
5.5.5.0/24       user   0      0      0x10    100.1.7.1    ucst   45     2      fe-0/0/0.7
6.6.6.0/24       user   0      0      0x10    100.1.5.1    ucst   43     5      fe-0/0/0.5
7.7.7.0/24       user   0      0      0x10    100.1.7.1    ucst   45     2      fe-0/0/0.7
8.8.8.0/24       user   0      0      0x10    100.1.4.1    ucst   49     4      fe-0/0/0.4
```

You might expect a one-to-one correlation between next-hop and prefix distribution. Although not shown in Listing 13-9, in larger BGP routing tables such as the 100,000-plus core ISP routing tables of today, the load distribution averages out more closely to a 12 percent load distribution per next-hop in an 8 equal-cost next-hop design, or an approximate 6 percent load distribution per next-hop in a 16 equal-cost next-hop design. In other words, the more prefixes that are load balanced, the better the distribution because the algorithm is optimized for large Internet forwarding tables.

Rather than using per-prefix load distribution, you can use a per-packet load balancing policy, as shown here:

```
policy-options {
    policy-statement load-balance {
        from protocol bgp;
        then {
            load-balance per-packet;
        }
    }
}
```

The syntax of `load-balance per-packet` would suggest that all packets are sent equally across all available equal-cost next-hops. This is not exactly the case, though, as a pseudo-random hashing algorithm distributes the packets. Note that with the IP1, load balancing will occur pseudo-randomly over 8 equal-cost next-hops. With IP2, load balancing will occur pseudo-randomly over 16 equal-cost next-hops. The configuration statement syntax does not change, but the behavior does change on an IP2-equipped router.

The per-packet load distribution algorithm in an IP2-equipped router examines four fields:

- Layer 3 source IP address
- Layer 3 destination IP address
- Layer 4 protocol number
- The interface through which the packet entered the router

These fields form a unique signature that identifies a single application conversation, otherwise known as a *flow*. Each identified flow is then assigned to a valid next-hop, and all subsequent packets for this unique flow will exit the same interface to avoid TCP out-of-order sequencing problems.

It is also possible to add the source and destination port numbers to this algorithm by adding this command:

```
user@hostname# set forwarding-options hash-key family inet layer-4
```

This command will add two fields to the load-balancing algorithm. So the final algorithm will be based on six fields, as shown here:

```
routing-options {
    autonomous-system 111;
    forwarding-table {
        export load-balance;
    }
}
```

This `load-balance` policy is applied as an export policy to the forwarding table under the `routing-options` hierarchy in the JUNOS software configuration. This is necessary to enable the per-packet (with IP1) or per-flow (with IP2) load-balancing algorithm.

The `show route detail` command output is shown in Listing 13-10 to view the equal-cost next-hops for this prefix.

Listing 13-10
The *show route detail* command output

```
lab@SanFran> show route detail

inet.0: 28 destinations, 28 routes (28 active, 0 holddown, 0 hidden)
+ = Active Route, - = Last Active, * = Both

1.1.1.0/24 (8 entries, 1 announced)
        *BGP    Preference: 170/-101
                Source: 100.1.1.1
                Nexthop: 100.1.1.1 via fe-0/0/0.1
                Nexthop: 100.1.2.1 via fe-0/0/0.2
                Nexthop: 100.1.3.1 via fe-0/0/0.3
                Nexthop: 100.1.4.1 via fe-0/0/0.4
                Nexthop: 100.1.5.1 via fe-0/0/0.5
                Nexthop: 100.1.6.1 via fe-0/0/0.6
                Nexthop: 100.1.7.1 via fe-0/0/0.7
                Nexthop: 100.1.8.1 via fe-0/0/0.8, selected
                State: <Active Ext>
                Local AS:    111 Peer AS:    222
                Age: 8:23:15
                Task: BGP_222.100.1.1.1+179
                Announcement bits (2): 0-KRT 3-BGP.0.0.0.0+179
                AS path: 222 I
                Localpref: 100
                Router ID: 192.168.8.1
```

After the per-packet load-balancing policy is applied and the routing table is examined, it appears as though nothing has changed in table *inet.0*. This is to be expected. The policy is applied to the forwarding table, not a routing protocol.

Now look at the forwarding table again to see what effect the policy has had. Listing 13-11 shows the `ulst` next-hop object in the output of the `show route forwarding-table` detail command.

```
lab@Sanfran> show route forwarding-table detail
Routing table:: inet
Internet:
Destination     Type  RtRef  InIf  Flags   Nexthop     Type   Index   NhRef   Netif
    default     perm    0      0    0x10                rjct   10      1
    1.1.1.0/24  user    0      0    0x10                ulst   67      11
                                            100.1.1.1   ucst   46      2       fe-0/0/0.1
                                            100.1.3.1   ucst   47      2       fe-0/0/0.3
                                            100.1.7.1   ucst   48      2       fe-0/0/0.7
                                            100.1.2.1   ucst   49      2       fe-0/0/0.2
                                            100.1.4.1   ucst   50      2       fe-0/0/0.4
                                            100.1.8.1   ucst   51      2       fe-0/0/0.8
                                            100.1.5.1   ucst   64      2       fe-0/0/0.5
                                            100.1.6.1   ucst   65      2       fe-0/0/0.6
```

One of the first things you should notice about the new forwarding table is that the prefix has no next-hop listed in the Nexthop field. Also noticeably different is that the route family type is `ulst`. Normally, `ucst` (for unicast list) is shown here or `rjct` (for reject) appears. The `ulst` is a next-hop pointer that allows the data structures to point to a list of unicast next-hops and distribute the load among them. This form of load balancing is not random at all. Unlike the preceding example of per-prefix form of load balancing shown in Listing 13-9, this forwarding table shows that all eight next-hops are considered.

Load Balancing with IBGP Using Multipath

Before IBGP multipath, the only way that IBGP load balancing could be achieved is through the IGP. If the underlying IGP had multiple equal-cost routes to the IBGP peer, per-prefix route distribution would occur. IBGP multipath is a fairly recent enhancement to BGP implementations that changed this paradigm. EBGP multipath support has been around for some time, so the multipath load balancing concept is not new. However, it was previously defined for use only between ASs. With IBGP multipath, BGP load balancing can now be enabled inside the AS. Also, confederation BGP would benefit significantly from a multipath feature.

This feature works basically the same as the EBGP multipath feature: If two or more paths exist to the BGP *NEXT_HOP*, the path selection algorithm will by default result in only one of those paths being selected as the best path. This best path is then installed in the FIB. The additional alternative paths are installed in the RIB as backup paths, in case the best path fails. If multipath is enabled and the path-selection algorithm reaches the final tie-break decision of lower RID, this decision is ignored and all the equal-cost next-hops are then installed. Because IBGP multipath is best explained with an illustration, Figure 13-4 should make the concept a little clearer.

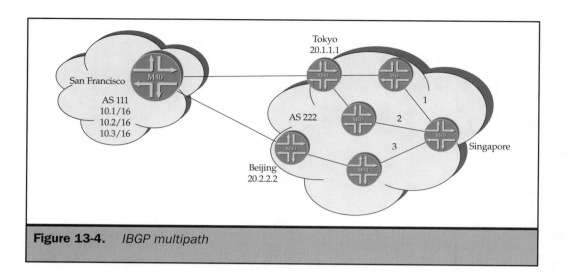

Figure 13-4. *IBGP multipath*

In Figure 13-4, router Singapore is IBGP peering to all routers in AS 222 and is receiving prefixes from AS 111 from Tokyo and Beijing. Without multipath, Singapore will run its path selection algorithm and will select Tokyo because of its lower RID (20.1.1.1 versus 20.2.2.2). All internal metrics to Tokyo and Beijing are equal, so the tie-break decision is based on lower RID. If no RID is explicitly configured on routers Tokyo and Beijing, the router with the lowest IP address on its loopback interface is chosen as best. This is because, by default, the loopback IP address is used as the BGP RID. Singapore selects Tokyo and installs the AS 111 prefixes with 20.1.1.1 as the BGP *NEXT_HOP*. Singapore does a recursive lookup on 20.1.1.1 and finds that the IGP has two equal-cost paths to this address. Singapore will psuedo-randomly distribute the prefixes from AS 111 over these two equal-cost paths. These paths are marked as numbers 1 and 2 in the figure. This is the default per-prefix load balancing behavior in JUNOS software.

With multipath enabled in the IBGP peer group configuration of Singapore, all of the equal-cost paths to prefixes in AS 111 are now used to forward traffic. Singapore no longer bases its best path decision on lower RID. This step in the path selection algorithm is ignored, and both Tokyo and Beijing are used to forward traffic to AS 111. In other words, Singapore will install both 20.1.1.1 and 20.2.2.2 as valid *NEXT_HOPs* for prefixes to AS 111. Now all three paths, marked 1, 2, and 3, are used to forward traffic to AS 111.

Load Balancing with BGP Using Multihop

The multihop form of load balancing relies upon IP to do its work. The per-prefix distribution of a load is applied to local next-hops and not to the BGP *NEXT_HOP*. In Figure 13-5, an EBGP peering session extends between two routers in different ASs. This EBGP peering session is between the routers' loopback addresses, rather than

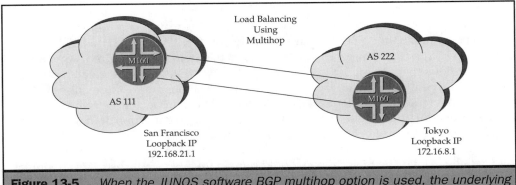

Figure 13-5.   *When the JUNOS software BGP multihop option is used, the underlying IGP is relied upon for load balancing.*

between the external interface IP addresses. Since no IGP is running between these two routers, the loopback IP address is not reachable before a BGP adjacency is established. To enable EBGP to peer to the remote loopback IP address, static routes are configured. On each router are two static routes to the remote peers' loopback IP address. One static route points to one data link, and the other static route points to the other data link. This enables IP to load balance to the remote peers' loopback address.

Connecting these routers together are two equal-cost data links. Each data link has a unique IP subnet. The remote BGP peers' loopback address shows up in the local routing table as having two valid equal-cost next-hops, due to the static route configuration. The prefixes learned from the remote BGP peer will have only one valid BGP *NEXT_HOP*, which is the remote peers' loopback address. During the recursive BGP *NEXT_HOP* lookup, the router will realize that two statically routed paths exist to this address. IP will distribute prefixes across both of these links—in effect, enabling EBGP load balancing.

A few specific items need to be configured under BGP to make this work. The following configuration statements from the San Francisco router display an EBGP multihop configuration:

```
protocols {
    bgp {
        group multihop-loadbalance {
            type external;
            multihop ttl 2;
            local-address 192.168.12.1;
            peer-as 222;
            neighbor 172.16.8.1;
        }
    }
}
```

The key statement here is `multihop ttl 2`. The TTL value can be any number in the range 1 to 255, but it makes sense to use a value of 2 or greater. This allows the BGP peer to be more than the EBGP default of one hop away. To establish this BGP peering session, the `local-address 192.168.12.1` statement is also required. As explained in the previous chapter, the `local-address X.X.X.X` statement is used to modify the local endpoint IP address for the BGP session. The neighbor statement now also reflects the remote peers' loopback IP address, rather than one of the remote peers' data-link IP addresses. These commands enable the TCP connection, and thus the BGP peering session, to exist between the loopback IP addresses.

An additional benefit of this multihop configuration is redundancy. If one of the two data links fails, the BGP session would remain up and established. This is similar in functionality to configuring IBGP peerings between loopback IP addresses, rather than physical interface IP addresses.

As you're viewing routing table *inet.0* after this load-balancing configuration (shown in Listing 13-12), notice that it looks similar to the multipath output. In fact, the only major difference is that the source of the route is now the remote peers' loopback address instead of one of the next-hops listed. The hashing algorithm is going to pseudo-randomly assign all prefixes from this peer to one of the valid local next-hops. Listing 13-12 shows eight active next-hops that the routing protocol has selected.

Listing 13-12
The *show route detail* command is used to view the active next-hop that the routing protocol has selected.

```
lab@Sanfran> show route detail

inet.0: 30 destinations, 30 routes (30 active, 0 holddown, 0 hidden)
+ = Active Route, - = Last Active, * = Both

1.1.1.0/24 (1 entry, 1 announced)
        *BGP    Preference: 170/-101
                Source: 172.16.8.1
                Nexthop: 100.1.7.1 via fe-0/0/0.7, selected
                Nexthop: 100.1.8.1 via fe-0/0/0.8
                State: <Active Ext>
                Local AS:   111 Peer AS:   222
                Age: 1:13     Metric2: 1
                Task: BGP_222.172.16.8.1+179
                Announcement bits (3): 0-KRT 3-BGP.0.0.0.0+179 4-BGP_Sync_Any
                AS path: 222 I
                BGP next hop: 172.16.8.1
                Localpref: 100
                Router ID: 172.16.8.1
```

In Listing 13-13, you can see that only the best source for each prefix is chosen in the routing table *inet.0*. The resulting best choices are then used to populate the forwarding table.

```
lab@Sanfran> show route forwarding-table detail
Routing table:: inet
Internet:
Destination    Type    tRef   InIf    Flags   Nexthop    Type    Index  NhRef  Netif
default        perm    0      0       0x10               rjct    10     1
1.1.1.0/24     user    0      0       0x10    100.1.7.1  ucst    48     2      fe-0/0/0.7
2.2.2.0/24     user    0      0       0x10    100.1.8.1  ucst    51     3      fe-0/0/0.8
3.3.3.0/24     user    0      0       0x10    100.1.8.1  ucst    47     3      fe-0/0/0.8
4.4.4.0/24     user    0      0       0x10    100.1.7.1  ucst    47     2      fe-0/0/0.7
5.5.5.0/24     user    0      0       0x10    100.1.7.1  ucst    50     2      fe-0/0/0.7
6.6.6.0/24     user    0      0       0x10    100.1.8.1  ucst    51     3      fe-0/0/0.8
7.7.7.0/24     user    0      0       0x10    100.1.7.1  ucst    64     2      fe-0/0/0.7
8.8.8.0/24     user    0      0       0x10    100.1.7.1  ucst    50     2      fe-0/0/0.7
```

Eight prefixes are being advertised, yet the distribution is not four prefixes to 100.1.7.1 and four prefixes to 100.1.8.1, which would be a 50/50 distribution. Again, in a larger BGP forwarding table, the load distribution averages out more closely to an even load. A per-packet or per-flow configuration may be applied in conjunction with this form of load balancing as well.

Route Reflection and Path Selection in a Multi-Vendor Network

As discussed in Chapter 12, simple *route reflection* is one of the preferred methods of alleviating the stress of the full-IBGP mesh. In this case study, rather than discuss a simple route reflection scenario, a not-so-straightforward design using route reflection will be discussed. This case study includes a multi-vendor route reflection environment with an interesting scenario with BGP path selection.

Because the Internet is a partial mesh of hundreds of IP networks, with multiple router vendors supplying the IP routing equipment, vendor BGP implementation differences are often a topic of discussion and debate among ISP engineers. This case study will reinforce the details of route reflection and at the same time point out some vendor differences that at first glance appear to result in routing issues.

As stated in Chapter 12, not everything in BGP is specified in the RFC documentation. Some areas are left open to vendor implementation and interpretation. In general, this is a good philosophy because it allows vendors to solve problems in different and vendor-specific ways. If the RFC specified every detail of a BGP implementation, the RFC would be enormous! Nevertheless, the RFC should be complete enough so that vendor implementations can interoperate.

One of the most important requirements of a BGP implementation is the *path-selection process*. It is interesting to note that the path-selection process is not dictated by the RFC, so different router vendors have implemented slightly different path-selection algorithms. Although this diversity of path-selection rules might appear to be risky to have on the Internet, it is not likely to cause problems. Of course, in a lab environment, it is possible to create a scenario in which the different path-selection rules can create a routing loop. In the lab, though, you can create a scenario to prove almost any point—so remember that a lab environment is not the same as the real-world Internet.

Figure 13-6 depicts a multi-vendor route-reflection network. Juniper Networks routers, along with another vendor's routers, are used in this network. The other vendor router is called *Router A*.

Three route reflection clusters appear in Figure 13-6: cluster 1.1.1.1, cluster 2.2.2.2, and cluster 3.3.3.3. Routers D and E are the route reflectors (RRs) for cluster 1.1.1.1. Routers C and D are the RRs for cluster 2.2.2.2. Notice that RR D is used for two different clusters. This is easily accomplished in JUNOS software by adding Client I in a peer group configured with cluster 1.1.1.1, and Clients G and F in a peer group configured with cluster 2.2.2.2. Routers F and G are the RRs for cluster 3.3.3.3. This is a second level of route reflection, referred to as *multi-level* or *nested* route reflection. In JUNOS software, the shorter *CLUSTER_LIST* length is a tie-break path-selection decision that's made prior to the final tie-breaker route, which is the lower RID. At the *CLUSTER_LIST* decision point, the path with the shortest *CLUSTER_LIST* is selected as

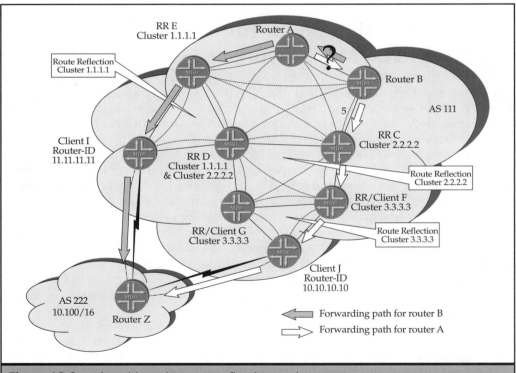

Figure 13-6. *A multi-vendor route-reflection environment*

the best path. In the other vendors' path-selection algorithm, the shortest *CLUSTER_LIST* length comes after a tie-break decision of lower originator-id. It is not likely, in the other vendor's implementation, that the path selection will still be undecided after the lower originator-id step. In other words, it is likely that the lower originator-id is the final tie-break decision, with *CLUSTER_LIST* length rarely being evaluated. It appears, then, that because the JUNOS software evaluates shorter *CLUSTER_LIST* length while another implementation will rarely evaluate this same decision, the result is a potential for a routing loop in a multi-level, multi-vendor route-reflection environment. This case study will focus on this anomaly in BGP path selection.

In Figure 13-6, Router A is another vendor's router and the rest are Juniper Networks routers. Local AS 111 is peering to AS 222 at two peering points. Each peering router is a RR client router. Router I is a client of RR cluster 1.1.1.1. Router J is a client of RR cluster 3.3.3.3. The same prefix, *10.100/16*, is exported from AS 222 to the local AS at each peering point. The internal IBGP routers receive two paths to this prefix. They must make a tie-break decision as to which path they consider the best. Ignoring IGP metrics for a moment, from Router B's perspective it appears that the path with the shorter *CLUSTER_LIST* length will be selected as the best. The arrow going to the left in Figure 13-6 shows the forwarding path of Router B toward 10.100/16. Since the other vendor router, Router A, tie-breaks on lower originator-id, in our example it selects the path pointing to the right in Figure 13-6. Although this path has a longer *CLUSTER_LIST* length, the *CLUSTER_LIST* length is not evaluated because the lower originator-id is the tie-break decision for Router A. The path to the right of Router A in Figure 13-6 has a *CLUSTER_LIST* length of [2.2.2.2 3.3.3.3], while the path to the left in Figure 13-6 has a *CLUSTER_LIST* length of [1.1.1.1].

Client Router I has a router-id of 11.11.11.11. This becomes the originator-id for the prefix that Router I originates into AS 111. Client Router J has a router-id of 10.10.10.10. This becomes the originator-id for the prefix that it originates into AS 111. Note that as the route reflectors reflect this prefix, the *CLUSTER_LIST* is created, and this list lengthens as the route is reflected by additional RRs.

Here are the steps for advertising 10.100/16 into AS 111:

1. Border Router Z in AS 222 exports 10.100/16 to border Router J in AS 111.

2. Router J sends the prefix to Routers F and G as it is IBGP peering to only these two routers. Before exporting this prefix to its IBGP peers, Router J changes the BGP *NEXT_HOP* to 10.10.10.10. This is done because Router J has a "next-hop self" routing policy applied as an export policy in its IBGP peer group.

3. Router F creates a *CLUSTER_LIST* attribute and inserts cluster-id 3.3.3.3. Router F also creates an *ORIGINATOR_ID* attribute and inserts 10.10.10.10. It then reflects this prefix to its IBGP peers, Routers C, D, and G. Router F does not reflect this prefix back to Router J, as it knows that Router J is the originator of this prefix.

4. Router G receives this prefix from Router F in step 3. Router G looks in the *CLUSTER_LIST* and sees its configured cluster-id of 3.3.3.3 in the list and drops

this prefix. It believes the prefix has looped. However, this is not a problem, because Router G has also received this prefix directly from Router J, the originator of the prefix.

5. Router C receives this prefix from Router F and looks in the *CLUSTER_LIST*. Because cluster-id 2.2.2.2, which Router C is configured to use, is not in the *CLUSTER_LIST*, this prefix is not looped. It examines the *ORIGINATOR_ID* of 10.10.10.10 and because this is not its configured router-id, it also does not constitute a loop and Router C accepts the prefix. It adds cluster-id 2.2.2.2 to the existing *CLUSTER_LIST* and reflects this prefix to its IBGP peers, Routers A, B, D, and E. Router C does not reflect this prefix to client Router G. This is because Router C is configured with the `no-client-reflect` knob. Because client Routers F and G are IBGP peering to each other, there is no need to reflect this prefix back down into cluster 2.2.2.2. Remember, client Router G receives this prefix directly from Router J in step 4.

6. Router B receives the prefix from Router C. Router B does not have another path to 10.100/16 at this point. The BGP *Update* tells Router B that the BGP *NEXT_HOP* address for 10.100/16 is 10.10.10.10. Router B does a recursive lookup in its routing table for 10.10.10.10 and the IGP tells it that Router C is the next-hop router to 10.10.10.10. It installs this prefix as active with Router C as the next-hop router.

7. Router A also receives this prefix from Router C and performs the same actions as Router B. The one exception is that the recursive lookup for 10.10.10.10 in Router A reveals that Router B is the next-hop router. It installs this prefix as active with Router B as the next-hop router.
To detail the other path to 10.100/16, border Router Z also exports 10.100/16 to border Router I.

8. Router I sends the prefix to Routers D and E. Router I is IBGP peering only to these two routers. Before exporting this prefix to its IBGP peers, Router I changes the BGP *NEXT_HOP* to 11.11.11.11. This is done because Router I has a "next-hop self" routing policy applied as an export policy in its IBGP peer group.

9. Router E receives this prefix and creates a *CLUSTER_LIST* attribute and inserts cluster-id 1.1.1.1. Router E also creates an *ORIGINATOR_ID* attribute and inserts 11.11.11.11. Router E then reflects this prefix to its IBGP peers, Routers A, B, C, and D. Router E does not reflect this prefix back to Router I, as it knows that Router I is the originator of this prefix.

10. Router A receives this prefix from Router E. Router A already has an active path to 10.100/16 in its FIB. This is the path it received earlier from Router C. Router A compares this new path against the existing active path by running the BGP path selection algorithm. Ignoring IGP metrics for now, Router A will prefer the existing active path because it has a lower originator-id of 10.10.10.10.

Remember that in this router's BGP implementation, it replaces the lower router-id check with the lower originator-id check. Router A installs the new path as an alternate path in the routing table because it did not win this decision. In effect, nothing has changed in Router A except that it now has an alternate path to 10.100/16, which is via Router E.

11. Router B also receives the prefix from Router E and performs the same actions as Router A. The one exception is that the BGP path selection for Router B tie-breaks on a shorter *CLUSTER_LIST* length. It selects this new path from Router E as the best path because its *CLUSTER_LIST* is shorter and installs it as the active path. It keeps the original path as an alternative path to 10.100/16. In effect, Router B has installed the path from Router E and has demoted the path from Router C.

12. Router B does a recursive lookup on the BGP *NEXT_HOP* for the best path to 10.100/16, which is now 11.11.11.11, and finds that the IGP tells it to use Router A as the next-hop router to 11.11.11.11.

The result of this exercise is that Router B forwards traffic to 10.100/16 toward Router A, while Router A forwards traffic to 10.100/16 toward Router B.

It appears that this anomaly in path selection, as it relates to *CLUSTER_LIST* length, causes a routing loop. Router B will send packets with a destination of 10.100/16 to Router A. Router A will send packets with a destination of 10.100/16 to Router B. However, if the links are configured with appropriate IGP metrics, it becomes clear that it is not possible for Router A to have equal cost paths to Routers I and J *at the same time* that Router B has equal cost paths to Routers I and J. Regardless of which values are used as the IGP metrics on the associated links, this equal-cost path scenario will not happen simultaneously for both Routers A and B. In other words, if the path A-E-I is equal from an IGP metric perspective to path A-B-C-F-J, it is not possible that path B-A-E-I is equal to path B-C-F-J at the same time—that is, so long as the IGP metrics have been configured on each router in a consistent manner. The link between Routers A and B must be configured the same on both routers. It is possible to have Router A use one metric value, while Router B is using a different metric value for this same physical link. But that is possible only if the metrics have been configured erroneously on one of the routers.

So, one of the routers, either Router A or Router B, will tie-break on lower cumulative IGP metric. This will prevent the potential loop that was originally thought possible. That is because one of the routers, either A or B, will tie-break during the IGP metric path selection point, before reaching the point in path selection that is being discussed.

A few additional points are worth discussing with this scenario. Take another look at Figure 13-6. After all the internal routers in AS 111 have converged on prefix 10.100/16, what path does Router D select and why? Figure this out before reading on, as the answer is given next.

The answer is the path that has a lower IGP metric. All earlier path selection decisions are equal in this scenario. So, Router D examines the IGP metric to Router I and to Router J. They are the BGP *NEXT_HOPs* for this prefix. Router D will select the path with the lower IGP metric. But, assume that the IGP metrics are equal to both Router I and Router J. Which path is now selected as best?

The path from Router I is selected as the best path because of the shorter *CLUSTER_LIST* length decision. The path to Router I has no *CLUSTER_LIST* attribute, as it has not been reflected yet. The path to Router J has a *CLUSTER_LIST* of [3.3.3.3].

Here are the decisions of Router D.

1. Router D receives the prefix 10.100/16 from Router G. This prefix already contains the *CLUSTER_LIST* and *ORIGINATOR_ID* that Router G created. In the *CLUSTER_LIST* is cluster 3.3.3.3. In the *ORIGINATOR_ID* is 10.10.10.10.

2. Router D also receives this prefix from Router F. It contains the same *CLUSTER_LIST* and *ORIGINATOR_ID*. Router D runs its BGP path selection and selects the path from the router with the lower router-id. It installs this path as the best in the FIB.

3. Router D now adds cluster 2.2.2.2 to the *CLUSTER_LIST* and reflects this path to its IBGP peers, Routers A, B, C, and E.

4. Router D also receives the prefix from Router I. This path does not contain a *CLUSTER_LIST* or *ORIGINATOR_ID*, as this path has not been reflected. Router D runs the path selection algorithm again and will likely select this new path as best due to lower IGP metric. Router D has a decision as to which of the paths has a lower IGP metric to the BGP *NEXT_HOP*. These *NEXT_HOPs* are 10.l0.10.10 (Router J) and 11.11.11.11 (Router I). It is likely that in this topology, the path to 11.11.11.11 (Router I) has a lower IGP metric. So, the result is that when the network has converged from a BGP perspective, the path from Router I will be installed as the active path in Router D's FIB.

5. Router D sends an *Update* message to its IBGP peers, Routers A, B, C, and E, withdrawing the previous path it advertised. That path is no longer the best path from Router D's perspective.

6. Router D creates a *CLUSTER_LIST* and adds cluster 1.1.1.1 to the new best path received from Router I. It also creates an *ORIGINATOR_ID* and adds 11.11.11.11 to this attribute. It then advertises this best path to its IBGP peers, Routers A, B, C, and E.

Now, to delve deeper into this scenario, assume that the IGP metrics to the BGP *NEXT_HOPs* are equal and IBGP multipath is configured on Router D. Does this affect Router D's path selection? And which path does Router D now reflect to its IBGP peers? Or does multipath enable router D to reflect both paths?

IBGP multipath removes the final tie-break decision in the BGP decision tree. In JUNOS software, this is the lower RID decision. If all earlier decisions are equal, multipath will enable Router D to install the 10.100/16 prefix with two valid next-hops, that being, to Router I and Router J. This would enable some load sharing capability to 10.100/16 and other routes from AS 222 for Router D. In this scenario, the shorter *CLUSTER_LIST* length is still the tie-breaker, so multipath does nothing for Router D. If the *CLUSTER_LIST* length is equal and multipath is enabled, this would affect the local path selection decision of Router D only and would not affect which path Router D reflects to its IBGP peers. Router D would still reflect the best path based on the lower RID decision, ignoring the ability that multipath enabled. No route reflector can reflect more than a single best path to a destination at a time. If a better path becomes known to the route reflector, it will withdraw its previously announced best path and announce the new best path, but the rule remains that only a single best path can be announced at a time.

This case study focuses on path selection and route reflection, with the added twist of a multi-vendor network environment. Although the route reflection environment is not overly complex, route reflection concepts have been reinforced, along with concepts in BGP path selection.

Issues with Route Reflection and next-hop-self

One of the features with route reflection that is worth pointing out is the ability, in JUNOS software, to change the BGP *NEXT_HOP* attribute on the route reflector when reflecting routes. In Chapter 12, you learned that the RFC states that when reflecting routes, the route reflector should not modify the *NEXT_HOP, AS_PATH, LOCAL_PREF* or *MED* attributes. This is to prevent possible routing loops. In JUNOS software, the powerful policy language can permit the route reflector to change these attributes. In other words, there is "a lot of rope" in the JUNOS software policy language.

Why might it be useful to modify the *NEXT_HOP* attribute when reflecting routes? In most cases, doing this is not desired, due to the potential for loops. Figure 13-7 shows how modifying the *NEXT_HOP* when reflecting routes might cause a routing loop.

In Figure 13-7, client Router G is receiving 10.100/16 from its EBGP peering session to AS 222 [1]. This client router passes the *Update* to its RR, Router C [2]. The client Router G has a policy called *next-hop-self* to change the *NEXT_HOP* to its loopback IP address before exporting this prefix to RR Router C. This is normal and causes no problem. Without this policy, routers in AS 111 cannot resolve the BGP *NEXT_HOP* for prefix 10.100/16.

RR Router C reflects the prefix into its IBGP mesh [3]. Prior to reflecting, Router C changes the *NEXT_HOP* to its loopback IP address. This is not required to resolve this prefix, yet this does not cause any problems, either. If Router A, B, or D needs to forward packets to 10.100/16, it will send them toward RR Router C. No routing loop or issues yet.

RR Router C also reflects the prefix down to its other clients in cluster 2.2.2.2 [4]. These are Routers F and H. The same policy on RR Router C that changes the BGP *NEXT_HOP* to self when exporting the prefix to its IBGP mesh changes the *NEXT_HOP*

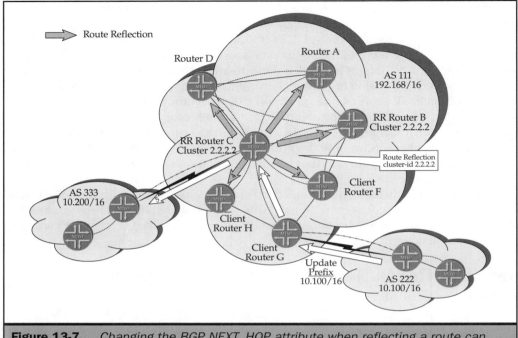

Figure 13-7. *Changing the BGP NEXT_HOP attribute when reflecting a route can cause a routing loop.*

on prefixes reflected down into the cluster. This is where the problem starts. Client Router F has received 10.100/16 from its RR, Router C. The BGP NEXT_HOP is Router C's loopback IP address. Here is what happens:

1. Router A in AS 111 needs to forward traffic to 10.100/16 in AS 222. It has this prefix in its FIB, with Router C as the BGP *NEXT_HOP*. Recursive lookup on this *NEXT_HOP* reveals that Router B is the physical next-hop router. It forwards the packets to Router B.

2. Router B has 10.100/16 in its FIB with Router C as the BGP *NEXT_HOP*. Recursive lookup on the BGP *NEXT_HOP* address reveals that Router C is also the physical next-hop router. It forwards the packets to Router C.

3. Router C has 10.100/16 in its FIB with Router G as the BGP *NEXT_HOP*. Recursive lookup on the BGP *NEXT_HOP* address reveals that Router F is the physical next-hop router. It forwards the packets to Router F.

4. Router F has 10.100/16 in its FIB with Router C as the BGP *NEXT_HOP*. Recursive lookup on the BGP *NEXT_HOP* address reveals that Router C is also the physical next-hop router. It forwards the packets back to Router C.

A routing loop has been formed.

This scenario is more interesting than it appears at first glance. There are at least three solutions to prevent this routing loop.

- Modify the next-hop-self policy on Router C so that it does not change the BGP *NEXT_HOP* to self when reflecting the prefix. However, it still needs to change the BGP *NEXT_HOP* for routes received from its EBGP peer in AS 333. If this is done, all internal routers that receive prefix 10.100/16 will have Router G as the BGP *NEXT_HOP* and forwarding works as expected.

- Nested route reflection can also solve this problem. If Routers F and H were configured as route reflectors for Router G, the routing loop would not happen. They would be configured with a different cluster-id than what is configured on Router C. Routers F and H would then receive the 10.100/16 prefix directly from Router G. When Router F receives packets destined for 10.100/16, it would not have Router C as the BGP *NEXT_HOP*. This would also prevent the routing loop.

- Configure RR Routers B and C for `no-client-reflect` and IBGP peer F, H, and G to each other. Routers F and H will receive the 10.100/16 prefix directly from Router G. This would also prevent the routing loop.

In summary, any of the three alternate solutions will prevent this routing loop, but from a design perspective, it would be recommended to implement both of the first two alternate solutions. This is because a contributing issue that led to the routing loop is that the route reflection topology did not map to the physical topology. This broke one of the golden rules of route reflection. Router G should not be a client of Router C, but it should really be a client of Routers F and H.

It should be noted that deploying a solution where the RR changes the *NEXT_HOP* to self is not the more common case; however, this solution is deployed in certain topologies. The ability of JUNOS software to do this can be useful in certain scenarios. Figure 13-8 shows one such scenario.

In Figure 13-8, notice that in this scenario, nested route reflection is deployed. RR Router C is configured for cluster-id 2.2.2.2 and Routers F and H are its clients in that cluster. Routers F and H are also route reflectors for Router G. They have cluster-id 3.3.3.3 configured to form this second level cluster.

Router C has a policy to change the BGP *NEXT_HOP* to *self* when exporting routes into its full IBGP mesh. Although this is typically not the case with route reflectors, in this topology this accomplishes a useful result. Prefix 10.5/16 from AS 444 is exported from Router C into the IBGP mesh, and is also exported down into its 2.2.2.2 cluster. The external IP subnet connecting Routers C and Z is not advertised into the IGP. Unless Router C changed the BGP *NEXT_HOP* to *self*, all the internal IBGP routers in AS 111 would not be able to resolve the BGP *NEXT_HOP* and the 10.5/16 would be unusable from their perspective.

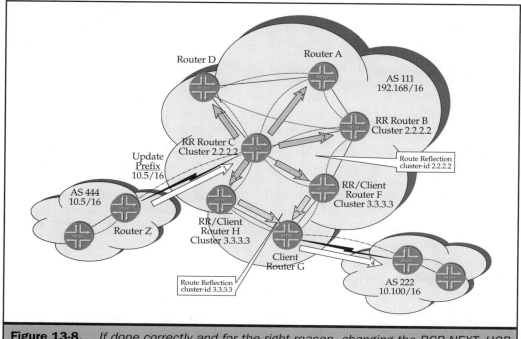

Figure 13-8.   *If done correctly and for the right reason, changing the BGP NEXT_HOP attribute when reflecting a route can be useful.*

There is one more thing worth pointing out in this case study. In the next-hop-self policy on Router C, notice the *from* clause contains `from protocol bgp`. Is this really required?

```
policy-options {
    policy-statement nexthop-self {
        term one {
            from protocol bgp;
            then {
                next-hop self;
            }
        }
    }
}
```

Since this policy is applied as an export statement in BGP, the policy gets applied only to active BGP routes anyway. Since that is the default case, the `from protocol` `bgp` appears redundant. Actually, it is unnecessary from a technical perspective; however, this *from* clause can prevent a common configuration mistake. Notice the `then next-hop self` does not contain a `then accept`. The default policy in BGP is to accept and export active BGP routes, so the `then accept` is not needed. However, it can be a careless mistake to add `then accept` to a routing policy, even when this extra statement is the default action and not required. Imagine writing this policy in a slightly different way, as shown here:

```
policy-options {
    policy-statement nexthop-self {
        term one {
            then {
                next-hop self;
                accept;
            }
        }
    }
}
```

What is the result of this policy being applied as an export statement in BGP?

The result is that because there is no *from* clause, this gets applied to all active routes in inet.0. This normally would not cause a problem, because only active BGP routes are by default exported to BGP peers. But the `then accept` changes this default behavior. This policy accepts all active routes in inet.0 and the result is that the entire inet.0 table is now exported to BGP!

It is a good best practice to use `from protocol bgp` when configuring a next-hop-self policy, to override and compensate for an accidental addition of `then accept`.

This case study has shown where it is valuable to change the BGP *NEXT_HOP* to self on route reflectors. However, it is also pointed out that changing the *NEXT_HOP* on routes received from clients may not be desired. To avoid changing the *NEXT_HOP* on client routes, an additional *from* clause must be implemented in the next-hop-self policy. Take a look at the following configuration from Router A in the Routing Policy case study and compare that to Figure 13-2. Router A in Figure 13-2 is a route reflector. In this scenario, it is necessary to change the *NEXT_HOP* to self on routes that it has received from its EBGP peer. However, it is not desired in this scenario to rewrite the *NEXT_HOP* on routes it receives from its client, Router F. The next-hop-self policy of Router A shows how this can be accomplished.

```
policy-options {
    policy-statement nexthop-self {
```

```
term match-community
    from {
    protocol bgp;
    community TRANSIT;
    }
    then {
       next-hop self;
    }
}
}
```

Matching on `community TRANSIT` ensures that only those routes get their BGP *NEXT_HOP* changed to *self*, and the reflected routes will not.

Persistent Route Oscillation with Route Reflection

In certain route-reflection topologies, a corner case called *persistent route oscillation* can occur. Such an occurrence is documented in an informational draft written in late 2000. An interesting aspect of this issue is that the Internet community discovered this fairly recently, although this condition has been possible since the introduction of BGP v4. This shows that Interdomain Routing is a constantly evolving and learning environment.

Persistent route oscillation refers to a scenario in which BGP routers thrash in their path selection process. In other words, a BGP router will select a best path from among a set of feasible paths, and then advertise this best path to its peers. This is normal behavior. One or more of its peers will then select its best path from among a set of feasible paths and advertise those best paths to its peers. The local BGP speaker receives this additional *Update*, which causes it to select a different best path than it previously selected. This new best path is again advertised to its peers. One or more of the local BGP speaker's peers then selects a new best path from its perspective and advertises this new best path. The local BGP speaker again selects a new best path and so on. This condition continues indefinitely.

The problem is inherent in the way BGP works. That is, locally defined policies may conflict globally and this conflict can result in persistent route oscillation, or *route churn*. This scenario manifests itself only in certain route reflection and confederation topologies using a MED for path selection tie-break decisions. This case study will focus on the route reflection scenario only.

As stated in Chapter 12, by default, MED is comparable only when paths are received from the same neighboring AS. If paths are received from two different neighboring ASs, MED is not considered in the path selection algorithm—that is, so long as the BGP knob `path-selection always-compare-med` is not configured.

Chapter 12 also discussed how route reflection can result in suboptimal routing due to the client not having full visibility to all the BGP paths in the AS. The route reflector will select its best path and reflect only that best path to its clients. As a result, the clients do not receive the full view of available paths. This is both good and bad. It is good because the client does not need to maintain state for all the available paths in its RIB. It is bad in that this can result in a suboptimal path from the clients' perspective. A client may have selected a different best path if all the available paths had been visible.

In certain route-reflection topologies, the clients' partial view of the available paths may result in an inconsistent best path selection decision, because the clients do not have all the relevant path information. If this inconsistency is inflicted on more than one BGP router in the AS, it can result in persistent route oscillation.

This undesirable condition is deterministic but can be avoided with appropriate network design principles. The reason for discussing this condition as a case study here is to avoid this condition from happening in your network.

Figure 13-9 shows AS 111 with two route reflectors, RR A and RR B. They are configured with different cluster-ids. RR A has Routers C and D as clients. RR B has Router E as a client. Peering to AS 111 is AS 555 and AS 444. AS 555 has two connections to the local AS 111. AS 444 has a single connection to the local AS. Downstream from the neighbor ASs is AS 333. Both AS 444 and AS 555 are peered to AS 333. AS 333 owns 10.5/16, and this is the only prefix that will be discussed in this case study.

In AS 111, each link has a value adjacent to it, which is the IGP metric of that link. This metric is configured on both routers attached to that link. For example, the IGP metric between RR A and RR B is 1. On the external EBGP connections into AS 111, a value is adjacent to the link. This is the MED value that the neighbor AS is sending with the *Update*. For example, AS 555 is sending prefix 10.5/16 to Router D with a MED value of 1. It is sending prefix 10.5/16 to Router E with a MED value of 0.

First Update

RR A receives two paths for 10.5/16—one from each client. It selects the path in the table that is marked with an asterisk (*). The previously selected active path will be marked with a minus sign or hyphen (–), and any new paths that have been received will be marked with a plus sign (+).

Router		AS_PATH	MED	IGP Metric
A	*	555 333	1	4
A		444 333	10	5

Router A selects the path based on a lower IGP metric. The MED values are not comparable, as the paths are from two different neighbor ASs. RR A sends an *Update* to its IBGP peer, RR B, with the selected best path.

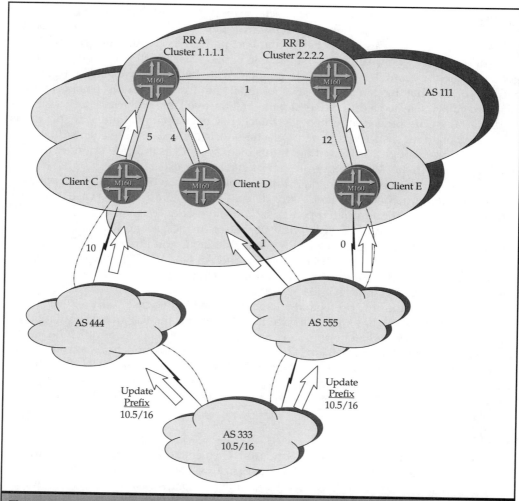

Figure 13-9. *The physical and logical network connectivity for this case study*

Second Update

RR B receives the path from RR A. It also receives a path from Client E. It now has two paths to choose from and selects the best path based on the lower MED value. These two paths are from the same neighboring AS, so the MED values are comparable. The lower MED value wins.

Router		AS_PATH	MED	IGP Metric
B	*	555 333	0	12
B		555 333	1	5

Notice that the IGP metric on the path received from RR A has changed to 5. This is due to the additive IGP metric calculation. RR B receives a path with an IGP metric of 4. It computes the cumulative IGP metric value to reach the BGP *NEXT_HOP*. The BGP *NET_HOP* is Router D. This results in a cumulative IGP metric of 5.

RR B sends an *Update* to RR A notifying it of its best path selection.

Third Update

RR A receives the *Update* from RR B. Its RIB now looks like this:

Router		AS_PATH	MED	IGP Metric
A	+	555 333	0	13
A	−	555 333	1	4
A	*	444 333	10	5

The first path beats the second path based on lower MED. Both paths are from the same neighbor AS 555, so the MED values are comparable. However, the third path beats the first path due to lower IGP metric. The third path is selected as best and an *Update* is sent to RR B.

Since MED is earlier in the BGP decision process, paths with comparable MEDs are compared first. So, the current active path is compared against the new path, which results in the new path winning due to lower MED. This is how BGP works in all deployed vendor implementations. Once a new best path is selected, the software compares this new path to any remaining paths and the result in this scenario is that the third path is selected due to lower IGP metric of 5 versus 13.

RR A sends an *Update* to RR B notifying it of its new best path.

Fourth Update

RR B receives the *Update* and its RIB now looks like this:

Router		AS_PATH	MED	IGP Metric
B	*+	444 333	10	6
B	−	555 333	0	12
B		555 333	1	5

RR B compares its current active path to the new path. These paths are not from the same neighbor AS, so their MED values are not comparable. The new path wins the selection based on a lower IGP metric of 6 versus 12. The IGP metric value of 6 is the cumulative metric to the BGP *NEXT_HOP*. The BGP *NEXT_HOP* in this path is Router C. RR B sends an *Update* to RR A notifying it of its new best path selection.

Fifth Update

RR A receives the *Update* and its RIB now looks like this:

Router		AS_PATH	MED	IGP Metric
A	*	555 333	1	4
A	–	444 333	10	5

In the *Update* message, RR B also issues a withdrawal for its previously announced best path. This happens in each of the previous steps as well. It's only important to point out here because it results in a previous path in RR A's RIB being withdrawn. That path is shown here:

A	555 333	0	13

This is why RR A now has in its RIB only the two paths in the first table. Since MEDs are not comparable, RR A compares the IGP metrics and selects the first path as best. RR A then sends an *Update* to RR B notifying it of its new best path selection.

If you compare the first table shown in this section with the one in the "First Update" section, it is evident that the scenario has come full circle. RR A now sends an *Update* to RR B with its new best path selection, and the oscillation starts over again. This will continue indefinitely, until some intervening event happens to interrupt this cycle.

Now that this persistent route oscillation is explained, what can be done to avoid this from happening? It appears that it is due to the natural path selection algorithm in BGP. Although BGP protocol changes can possibly avoid this oscillation, network design changes can also prevent this.

Prevention of Persistent Route Oscillation

Several changes to the network design can prevent such oscillation. Not all of them are appealing, but each will be discussed.

■ *If the IGP metric on the inter-cluster link is higher than the metric of intra-cluster links, the persistent oscillation is prevented.* For example, if the link between RR A and RR B is 8 rather than 1, the oscillation will be prevented.
Look back at the "Fourth Update," where the lower inter-cluster link metric of 1

causes RR B to select the path from RR A. The cumulative IGP metric of the path from RR A is 6. When RR B compares the path with an IGP metric of 6 to the path from its client Router E, with an IGP metric of 12, the path with the lower IGP metric is selected as the best. If the inter-cluster link metric is 8 or higher, the fourth *Update* would have a cumulative IGP metric of 13 (8 + 5). This will not change the active path selection in RR B and the oscillation will be prevented.

Although some engineers prefer this solution over the others, it appears counter-intuitive to some existing design principles. Typically, the IGP metric is used to reflect the bandwidth of the link. It seems probable that the backbone links connecting route reflectors, which is the inter-cluster link in this example, have a higher capacity than the links to the exit points of the AS. The intra-cluster links are closer to the edge of the local network. The backbone links usually have a higher capacity than edge links, so this recommended link metric change appears counter-intuitive.

- *Implement routing polices so that BGP attributes earlier in the BGP decision process affect the path selection process.* In other words, do not let the path selection process reach the decision to compare MEDs. For instance, use *LOCAL_PREF* to affect path selection.

- *If AS 111 did not accept MEDs from its neighbors, the persistent oscillation will be prevented.* This option may not be feasible, however, as the AS may need to accept MEDs for other reasons.

- *Enable the BGP knob that allows the internal BGP speakers to always compare MEDs, regardless of whether they are received from the same neighbor AS.* This knob is `path-selection always-compare-med`. This is probably a bad idea, as the local AS has little influence on the MED values they will receive from each neighbor AS. In practice, this is not usually recommended.

- *Use a full IBGP mesh.* This option is the least appealing and may not be possible if the local AS has a large number of IBGP routers.

The persistent route oscillation problem is also possible in confederation designs. It is not specific to route reflection. The conditions and results are similar, so it will not be discussed in a separate case study.

Using Confederations for BGP Scalability

Confederation BGP is a scaling function intended to allow the growth of an autonomous system to large sizes by reducing the required IBGP mesh, while controlling the size of IGP implementations inside the AS. This case study will concentrate on the necessary implementation configuration statements and show commands that are used to successfully deploy a confederation design.

In Figure 13-10, AS 222 has been subdivided into five subautonomous systems represented by five private autonomous system numbers. The subdivision separates the core sub-AS 65000 from the customer access sub-ASs. All transit traffic to and from AS 333 or AS 111 will pass through the core sub-AS 65000. Each customer can be tagged with a separate community value, such as *6500X:YYY*, representing and classifying traffic by sub-AS number. For instance, routes from customer F can be tagged with community 65004:111. The 65004: designates which sub-AS these routes entered from and the :111 value is some other locally meaningful value.

The topological design displayed in the figure allows the use of separate IGPs inside each sub-AS. It also allows core routers with larger capacities to be centralized in the core sub-AS where transit traffic will produce the greatest load. In the following sections, configurations from internal and external routers will be examined.

```
root@NewYork# show routing-options
router-id 10.200.13.4;
autonomous-system 65000;
confederation 222 members [ 65000 65001 65002 65003 65004 ];

root@NewYork# show protocols
bgp {
    log-updown;
    group IBGP {
        type internal;
        local-address 10.200.13.4;
        neighbor 10.200.13.3;
        neighbor 10.200.13.1;
    }
    group CBGP-65001 {
        type external;
        multihop;
        local-address 10.200.13.4;
        peer-as 65001;
        neighbor 10.200.14.2;
    }
    group CBGP-65004 {
        type external;
        multihop;
        local-address 10.200.13.4;
        peer-as 65004;
        neighbor 10.200.15.2;
    }
}
```

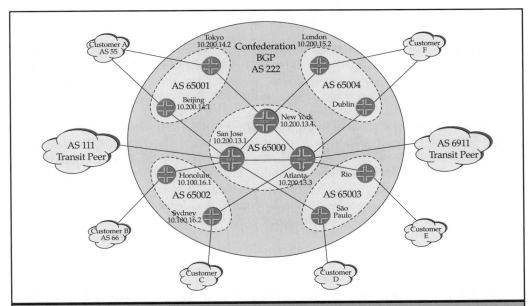

Figure 13-10. *The use of a BGP confederation design allows a single autonomous system to be subdivided into smaller, more manageable administrative sub-ASs.*

The first major difference between a single AS configuration and a confederation AS configuration is the addition of the *confederation* statement under *routing-options*. The `confederation 222 members [ 65000 65001 65002 65003 65004 ]` statement defines the globally viewed AS number 222 as a confederation AS. It also designates which sub-ASs are part of this confederation—in this case, AS numbers 65000, 65001, 65002, 65003, and 65004. All sub-ASs must be listed as members of the confederation. The external Internet continues to view this network as registered AS 222, with no view into the confederation. This is because the private AS numbers that are used as sub-ASs are automatically removed from the *AS_PATH* when routing updates are sent to EBGP peers.

The `autonomous-system 65000` statement defines the local sub-AS number that this router is part of. This sub-AS number must also be listed in the confederation members list. The internal group IBGP is not fundamentally different than any other BGP internal group configuration. The only change in requirements for this group is that you must have a full mesh inside each sub-AS instead of for the entire AS. This is the IBGP scaling benefit of using confederations. If this network is configured in a full IBGP mesh, it would require 55 IBGP peering sessions. This is called the "*N*-squared IBGP scaling problem." To figure out the number of IBGP sessions required in a full IBGP mesh, use this formula:

$N \times (N-1) / 2$
N = number of IBGP peers

With this confederation design, only 15 BGP peering sessions are required inside AS 222.

Some networks are so large that inside each sub-AS, route reflection is configured. In these largest of ISP networks, there are still too many IBGP peers inside the sub-ASs, and the *N*-squared IBGP scaling problem still manifests itself. For instance, in Figure 13-10, if there were too many IBGP peers inside sub-AS 65000, route reflection could be configured to overcome that scaling limitation.

There is a familiar statement in the BGP configuration in the peer groups called CBGP-65001 and CBGP-65004. The connection between AS 65000 and 65001 is an external connection between sub-ASs and, as such, is subject to the "TTL of 1 limitation" imposed by default on all EBGP configurations. Therefore, multihop is also needed in this configuration since the Confederation BGP peering endpoints are between loopback IP addresses. A confederation design may optionally decide to use the outgoing interface IP addresses as Confederation BGP peering endpoints. If this is the case, both the `multihop` and `local-address 10.200.13.4` statements are not needed.

This basically boils down to a question of redundancy. If the network is designed and physically meshed such that a failure in the direct link between router Tokyo and router New York allows the Confederation BGP peering session to reroute and remain established, using the loopback IP addresses as peering endpoints is preferred. Otherwise, if the direct link between these two routers fails, the Confederation BGP peering session will also fail. This is because, by default, the Confederation BGP peering session will use the outgoing interface IP address as the endpoint of the session.

A *show route detail* tells the story of what changes occur in the way a prefix is represented in a confederation topology. The first route in Listing 13-14, 222.222/16, exhibits the default behavior that is expected from a typical IBGP advertisement.

Listing 13-14
The *show route detail* command allows you to view the BGP attributes that are affected by confederation configuration.

```
root@NewYork> show route  detail

inet.0: 123363 destinations, 123363 routes (123362 active, 0 holddown, 0 hidden)
+ = Active Route, - = Last Active, * = Both

222.222.0.0/16 (1 entry, 1 announced)
        *BGP    Preference: 170/-51
                Source: 10.200.13.3
                Nexthop: 10.200.12.14 via so-0/2/3.0, selected
                State: <Active Int Ext>
                Local AS: 65000 Peer AS: 65000
                Age: 13:17:59   Metric2: 10
                Task: BGP_65000.10.200.13.3+179
                Announcement bits (3): 0-KRT 1-BGP.0.0.0.0+179 2-BGP_Sync_Any
                AS path: 6911 I
                Communities: 222:300
                BGP next hop: 10.200.13.3
                Localpref: 50
                Router ID: 10.200.13.3
                ...............
205.205.0.0/16 (1 entry, 1 announced)
```

```
*BGP     Preference: 170/-151
         Source: 10.200.14.2
         Nexthop: 10.200.17.33 via at-0/0/1.105, selected
         State: <Active Int Ext>
         Local AS: 65000 Peer AS: 65001
         Age: 11:55:23   Metric2: 10
         Task: BGP_65001.10.200.14.2+1027
         Announcement bits (3): 0-KRT 1-BGP.0.0.0.0+179 2-BGP_Sync_Any
         AS path: (65001) 55 I
         Communities: 222:100
         BGP next hop: 10.200.14.2
         Localpref: 150
         Router ID: 10.200.14.
```

The local and remote autonomous systems are both 65000 and the advertised prefix originates in external AS 6911. This prefix originates in Transit AS 6911 and is readvertised into AS 222 from router Atlanta. The second prefix, 205.205/16, is learned from sub-AS 65001 in this confederation. This is evident from the local AS of 65000 and the remote AS of 65001. This prefix originated in Customer AS 55, but notice that the *AS_PATH* has an additional value in it. From the screen capture, AS path: (65001) 55 I, the AS number in parentheses is one of the AS numbers listed in the members statement under *routing-options* and is a confederation member. Therefore, this sub-AS number is wrapped in parentheses, designating it for local use only and not to be exported to ASs external to AS 222. This sub-AS is part of a confederation sequence *AS_PATH* and will be stripped automatically when this prefix is exported outside of AS 222.

In the show route receive-protocol bgp 10.200.14.2 detail command shown in Listing 13-15, notice that although the *AS_PATH* has been prepended with the marked sub-AS number, the BGP *NEXT_HOP* attribute has not been updated. These prefixes originated in AS 55 and passed through sub-AS 65001 before reaching the core sub-AS 65000. The BGP *NEXT_HOP* is actually the loopback address of router Tokyo in sub-AS 65001. This implies that there is a common IGP running between all member ASs in the confederation.

ing 13-15
The *show*
e receive-
tocol bgp
200.14.2
detail
command
ws you to
view the
adj-RIB-in
for this
ederation
neighbor.

```
root@NewYork> show route receive-protocol bgp 10.200.14.2 detail
199.199.0.0/16 (1 entry, 1 announced)
      Nexthop: 10.200.14.2
      Localpref: 150
      AS path: (65001) 55 I
      Communities: 222:100
199.199.0.0/24 (1 entry, 1 announced)
      Nexthop: 10.200.14.2
      Localpref: 150
      AS path: (65001) 55 I
      Communities: 222:100
```

```
199.199.1.0/24 (1 entry, 1 announced)
     Nexthop: 10.200.14.2
     Localpref: 150
     AS path: (65001) 55 I
     Communities: 222:100
199.199.2.0/24 (1 entry, 1 announced)
     Nexthop: 10.200.14.2
     Localpref: 150
     AS path: (65001) 55 I
     Communities: 222:100
```

The fact that the BGP *NEXT_HOP* is 10.200.14.2 signifies that this IP address is reachable from all BGP speakers in AS 222. Otherwise the prefixes from AS 55 are not reachable. Since the BGP *NEXT_HOP* is the loopback IP address of router Tokyo, this address must be advertised in the local IGP to all BGP speakers in AS 222.

If you want to take advantage of a confederation scaling benefit of running different IGPs inside each sub-AS, care must be taken on selecting which address to use as the BGP *NEXT_HOP* when exporting prefixes into the AS. Running different IGPs inside each sub-AS can help scale a very large network. This allows the IGP to be broken into multiple instances or domains. For instance, in Figure 13-10, a different IGP domain could reside inside each sub-AS. These IGPs would not talk to each other. All reachability information between sub-ASs would be from Confederation BGP. This allows each sub-AS to grow very large in size. The network in Figure 13-10 does not use this design because there is no need to break the IGP into multiple domains. This network, as depicted, is not large enough to warrant that kind of segmentation. With one exception, a single IGP is running in AS 222, and this IGP is unaware of the BGP confederation topology. They are "ships passing in the night," so to speak.

The one exception is sub-AS 65002. This sub-AS network is a recent acquisition of AS 222, and rather than merging the IGPs together, it was decided to allow this sub-AS to maintain its own IGP. This decision was based almost purely on speed of integration, as it is easier to allow this sub-AS to maintain its own IGP and use Confederation BGP as the glue connecting this sub-AS to the rest of AS 222 rather than engineering a solution whereby the IGP in sub-AS 65002 becomes part of the larger IGP in AS 222.

The following code listing from router Honolulu displays a confederation IBGP and Confederation BGP configuration and a normal EBGP code set for an external connection. As stated earlier, this sub-AS is using a separate IGP from the other sub-ASs. This requires a few changes from the previous confederation configuration.

```
root@Honolulu# show routing-options
router-id 10.100.16.1;
autonomous-system 65002;
```

```
confederation 222 members [ 65000 65001 65002 65003 65004 ];
[edit]

root@Honolulu# show protocols
bgp {
    log-updown;
    group EBGP-66 {
        type external;
        export ebgp-export;
        local-address 142.16.50.29;
        peer-as 66;
        neighbor 142.16.50.30;
    }
    group IBGP {
        type internal;
        local-address 10.100.16.1;
        export nhs;
        neighbor 10.100.16.2;
    }
    group CBGP-65000 {
        type external;
        export update-source;
        local-address 10.200.100.1;
        peer-as 65000;
        neighbor 10.200.100.2;
    }
}

root@Honolulu#  show policy-options
prefix-list loopbacks {
    10.100.16.1;
    10.100.16.2;
}
policy-statement update-source {
    from {
        prefix-list loopbacks;
    }
    then {
        community add no-export;
        accept;
    }
}
community no-export members no-export;
```

First, a new policy is required to inject the loopback IP addresses from this sub-AS into Confederation BGP. These loopback IP addresses are going to be the next-hop-self addresses for prefixes received from external customers B and C. When advertised to the rest of AS 222, these external prefixes will have the BGP *NEXT_HOP* reset to *self* with an export policy on routers Sydney and Honolulu. These loopback IP addresses need to be reachable from the rest of AS 222. Because the IGP in this sub-AS is not part of the larger IGP in AS 222, these loopback IP addresses are not advertised into the larger IGP in AS 222. In this case, a prefix list to match the loopback IP addresses is used. The policy `update-source` is then used to redistribute the loopback IP addresses into Confederation BGP.

The second change from the previous confederation configuration is that the Confederation BGP peering endpoints are the physical interface IP addresses. In the configuration for router Honolulu, notice that the neighbor in group CBGP-65000 is 10.200.100.2. This is the directly connected interface address of router San Jose. The `local-address 10.200.100.1` in this same CBGP-65000 group is not required but is included for clarity. When router Honolulu sends BGP messages to its Confederation BGP peer router San Jose, it will send those messages to IP address 10.200.100.2 and the source of those messages will be the outgoing interface IP address, which is 10.200.100.1. This is the default nature of BGP, as explained in Chapter 12. Since no IGP is running between sub-AS 65002 and sub-AS 65000, peering between loopback IP addresses does not provide any additional redundancy.

The `show route advertising-protocol bgp` command displayed in the top half of Listing 13-16 shows two sample routes that are sent to customer B from router Honolulu.

Listing13-16
The *show route advertise- protocol bgp 142.16.50.30 detail* and *show route receive- protocol bgp 142.17.50.29* commands allow you to view the adj-RIB-out and adj-RIB-in for this external peer.

```
root@Honolulu> show route advertising-protocol bgp 142.16.50.30 detail

inet.0: 123182 destinations, 123182 routes (123178 active, 0 holddown, 0 hidden)
Prefix              Nexthop           MED     Lclpref AS path
12.0.0.0/8 (2 entries, 1 announced)
 BGP 142.16.50.30 (External AS 66)
      Nexthop: Self
      AS path: (65002 65000) 6911 65222 10458 14203 701 7018 I
      Communities: 222:300
12.0.48.0/20 (2 entries, 1 announced)
 BGP 142.16.50.26 (External AS 66)
      Nexthop: Self
      AS path: (65002 65000) 6911 65222 10458 14203 701 209 1742 I
      Communities: 222:300
```

```
root@CustomerB> show route receive-protocol bgp 142.16.50.29 detail

inet.0: 123077 destinations, 123077 routes (123077 active, 0 holddown, 0 hidden)
Prefix              Nexthop           MED     Lclpref AS path
12.0.0.0/8 (1 entry, 1 announced)
```

```
      Nexthop: 142.16.50.29
      AS path: 222 6911 65222 10458 14203 701 7018 I
      Communities: 222:300
12.0.48.0/20 (1 entry, 1 announced)
      Nexthop: 142.16.50.29
      AS path: 222 6911 65222 10458 14203 701 209 1742 I
      Communities: 222:300
```

These routes are 12/8 and 12.0.48/20. Customer B is in AS 66 and is an EBGP peer and views the local confederation as AS 222. The output from the `show route advertising-protocol bgp` command might lead you to believe that the BGP advertisement contains an *AS_PATH* with the private sub-AS numbers of `AS path:` `(65002 65000)` and the private AS number of 65222. First, it is important to point out that private AS numbers, in and of themselves, are not automatically stripped from the *AS_PATH*. Only AS numbers, both public and private, that are listed in the *members* section of the `routing-options` configuration statement will be stripped from the *AS_PATH* and replaced with the confederation ID. To verify that the private sub-AS numbers are being removed and replaced with the confederation ID, a `show route receive-protocol bgp` command on the external customer B router is used. The lower half of Listing 13-16 displays this. It shows that prefix 12/8 has an *AS_PATH* value of 222 6911 65222 10458 14203 701 7018. The leftmost AS number in the *AS_PATH* is the AS number that is prepended by router Honolulu when the prefix is exported to external peers. This clearly shows the replacement of the private sub-ASs (65002 65000) with the confederation ID of 222. It also clearly proves the other point, that just because an AS is in the private range of 64512–65535 does not mean that it will be removed. If you want to remove all private AS numbers, you need to add the command `remove-private` in the BGP configuration. This command will strip out the AS 65222 from the *AS_PATH* before exporting prefixes to BGP peers. Having this private AS number in any *AS_PATH* is obviously a bad thing in the global Internet. It exists in this *AS_PATH* for education purposes only.

Many designs for confederation BGP are available for use. Although they may differ in size and topology, the basic requirements can be met with the configurations presented in this section.

BGP in the Enterprise

In Chapter 12, you read that BGP is also used in large enterprise networks. Although BGP is the glue that holds the Internet together, it can also be used in the large IP networks that enterprises are building or that they have built. These large enterprises are finding that the requirements of their current and future IP data networks resemble the requirements of a large service provider's IP data network. The network architectural differences between large enterprise networks and service provider networks are becoming less distinguishable, due in part to the rapid acceptance of IP as the de-facto network protocol. As enterprise managers migrate their legacy applications to IP-based applications, they may find that BGP can serve a similar purpose in their networks as BGP serves in service provider networks. One obvious difference is that an enterprise will not use BGP to allow Internet transit traffic to pass through their IP infrastructures. In that sense, these large enterprise IP networks are similar to the stub autonomous systems of yesteryear.

The final case study will examine how BGP is used in a large enterprise IP data network.

Existing Network Connectivity

The existing particulars for this network are as follows:

- IP is the network protocol used in a newly created backbone.
- If legacy network protocols, such as IPX and SNA, are in use, they are tunneled in IP across the backbone.
- This large enterprise has nine regional wide area networks (WANs) across the United States Each WAN has between 50 and 100 routers.
- Different IGPs are in use in each regional WAN. OSPF is the dominant choice, but RIP is also used in some of the smaller regional WANs. This is because each WAN is operated by a different engineering and operations group.
- The regional WANs are currently connected together in an ad-hoc fashion.
- IGP mutual redistribution is used at the interconnecting routers to connect the WANs. Complex route filter lists are in place at each redistribution point in an effort to prevent routing loops.
- End-to-end IP connectivity is possible in most cases. Maintaining this connectivity is difficult and often results in suboptimal routing.
- Three registered AS numbers are assigned to three of the larger regional WANs, which are multihomed to different service providers for Internet connectivity and use BGP for this connectivity.
- The remaining WANs are each connected to a single service provider and do not use BGP for their connectivity.
- Several registered CIDR blocks are in use in this enterprise.
- Region-to-region connectivity is becoming a hard requirement for supporting new applications that the enterprise intends to deploy across the United States.

With those requirements in mind, a decision is made to build a common backbone infrastructure. Each regional WAN will connect to this new backbone in two locations, for redundancy. BGP is chosen as the routing protocol to tie the regional WANs together. IGP mutual redistribution will no longer be used, as it is complex and prone to routing loops and suboptimal routing paths.

Figure 13-11 depicts the enterprise network before this new IP backbone is built. Notice in Figure 13-11 that the connectivity between the 10 distinct IP networks is ad-hoc and the topology is prone to routing loops and suboptimal routing paths. This network grew over time, with each regional WAN operating independently from the other regions. Acquisitions also added to the ad-hoc connectivity.

New Network Design

BGP is chosen to connect these networks. A new backbone infrastructure will be deployed to support this new connectivity. Goals of this new design are as follows:

- Allow any-to-any IP connectivity in a redundant, reliable, and stable fashion.
- Eliminate routing loops and suboptimal routing paths.
- Eliminate the need for IGP mutual redistribution and the complex route filters at the current interconnect points.
- Allow each region to maintain its internal IP infrastructure and IGP.
- Allow flexibility and control on which IP network blocks are advertised from each region.

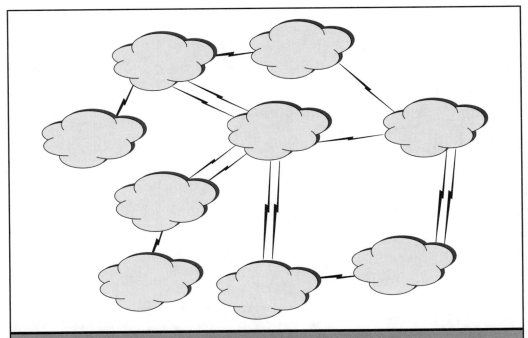

Figure 13-11.   *The large enterprise network currently looks like this.*

Figure 13-12 shows the logical topology of the new infrastructure connectivity.

In Figure 13-12, a new AS is created that serves as a transit AS. All of the region-to-region IP connectivity goes through this transit AS. This transit AS consists of 10 routers that are connected in a partial mesh of links. Logically, these transit routers represent a single AS; however, the transit routers reside physically in the regions. Each region has one transit router and two border routers. The transit router connects to other transit routers in a partial mesh of circuits but a full mesh of IBGP peering.

The border routers are in two different physical locations, or hubs, in the regions. These border routers are connected and EBGP peering to a neighboring AS border router. If the transit router connectivity fails due to equipment or circuit failure, one of the border routers will provide the path out of the AS. Suboptimal routing may occur in such a failure scenario, which is deemed acceptable until the failure is corrected.

The physical topology is shown in Figure 13-13. Due to high expense, there is no full mesh of circuits between all 10 transit routers. Each transit router is connected to

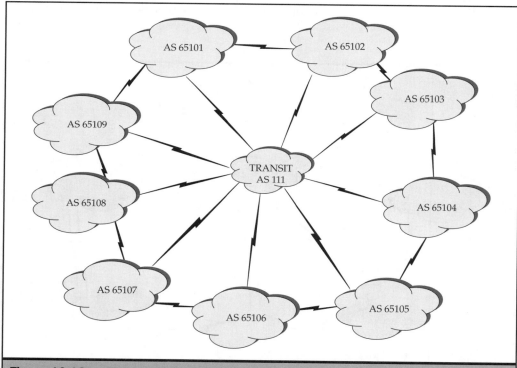

Figure 13-12.   *The logical topology of the new IP infrastructure*

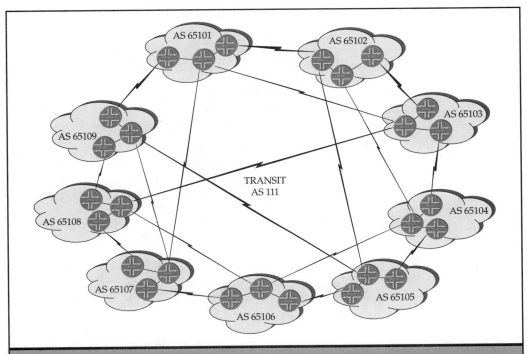

Figure 13-13.   *The physical topology of the new IP infrastructure*

two other transit routers. The core mesh appears random, however, it is structured so that the OSPF Area 0 domain in the core does not become partitioned.

Figure 13-14 shows the connectivity inside one of the regions. The IBGP peering between the AS 65106 border routers is shown. These border routers use EBGP to peer to the neighbor AS border routers and EBGP to peer to the local AS 111 transit router. All the AS 111 transit routers are configured in a full IBGP mesh. OSPF is the IGP in this AS, and all internal routers are participating in the local OSPF domain, except the transit router. The transit AS is also running OSPF to carry the IBGP peering addresses, which are the loopback IP addresses of the transit routers. The transit AS OSPF domain is not connected to any regional OSPF domain. Private AS numbers are used in the regions.

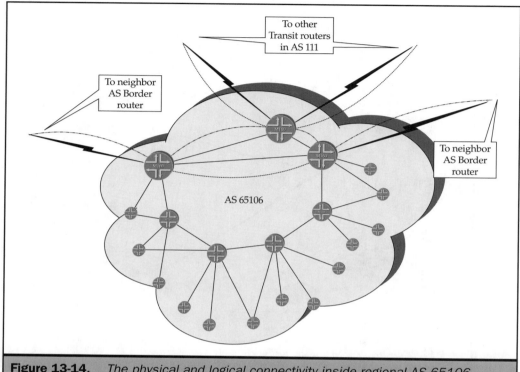

Figure 13-14.   *The physical and logical connectivity inside regional AS 65106*

Figure 13-15 shows the logical connectivity between three regions. (Only three regions are shown in this diagram to keep it simple.) Notice that although the transit routers are physically located in the region, they are logically in AS 111. The transit routers are physically distributed throughout the regions for redundancy purposes. Because AS 111 is the registered AS the enterprise will use to peer to service providers, Internet connectivity will come from the transit AS. These transit routers will advertise only the CIDR blocks assigned to the enterprise to the service providers. This will prevent the transit AS from being used as an Internet transit AS, which obviously is to be avoided at all costs.

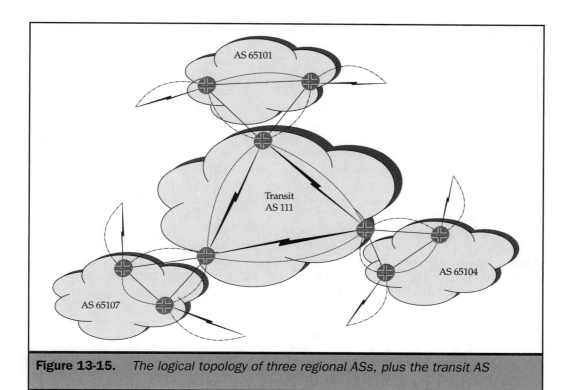

Figure 13-15.   *The logical topology of three regional ASs, plus the transit AS*

As stated, the transit routers are EBGP peering to their respective border routers. From these border routers, the transit routers receive the IP address blocks that have been assigned to each region. These IP address blocks come out of the assigned CIDR blocks. The two border routers in each region are IBGP peered to each other and EBGP peered to neighbor AS border routers. It is possible that a region can use another region for transit, although this path is not the primary path. Each region's border routers receive the neighboring regions' IP address blocks directly from the neighboring AS border routers. The transit routers also advertise the regional IP address blocks down to their respective border routers.

Figure 13-16 shows the 111.200/20 *Updates* being sent from AS 65104. It also shows the transit router advertising the 111.200/16 to the service provider. Notice that the transit routers pass the 111.200/20 into each regional AS border router. The border routers also receive the 111.200/20 from their neighbor AS border router.

Take a look at border router A in AS 65107. This router receives 111.200/20 from its transit router and also from its neighbor AS border router. A longest match route lookup will result in these prefixes being equal for path selection purposes, so another attribute must be used to force border router A to prefer the transit AS path rather than its neighbor AS path. *LOCAL_PREF* is used in this case. Border routers A and B have an import policy that changes the *LOCAL_PREF* value to 150 on all prefixes received from the transit router, except for the prefixes received from its directly connected regional AS. The prefixes received from neighbor AS border routers use the default *LOCAL_PREF* value of 100. This forces border router A to prefer the transit AS path and mark that path as the active path and install it in the FIB. The neighbor AS path is installed in the RIB as a backup path. The exception to this policy is the regions that are directly adjacent. Because there is no need to forward traffic to the transit AS if the destination is the adjacent regional AS, *LOCAL_PREF* is set to 150 on all routes received from the transit AS except for the routes originating from the adjacent regional ASs. In

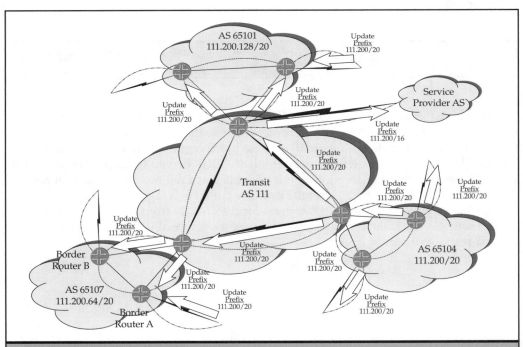

Figure 13-16.   *The routing updates emanating from regional AS 65104 are passed to the other ASs.*

that case, *AS_PATH* would be the deciding factor, and the local regional AS would forward traffic directly to its adjacent regional AS, without using the transit AS.

Default Routes

The transit routers that are peered to service providers inject a conditional default route into the IBGP mesh. This default is conditional in that if the peering to the service provider fails, the default route will disappear. This is best accomplished by having the service provider send the default route, *0/0*, in BGP to the enterprise transit routers. This default is then passed to all the border routers, which export this default into their respective IGP domains. All the internal regional routers will follow the IGP default route, *0/0*, to the nearest border router to reach destinations external to the region.

The Complete Reference

Chapter 14

Introduction to MPLS

by Julian K. Lucek and Tony Hill

Multi-Protocol Label Switching (MPLS) had its beginnings in the mid-1990s, a time of rapid growth in Internet traffic. Although it was created to fill the need for higher packet-forwarding rates through network equipment, it was soon realized that MPLS provided other benefits, which led to the development of powerful applications such as traffic engineering and virtual private networks (VPNs) that are used in service providers' networks today.

This chapter introduces the Juniper Networks implementation of MPLS. It describes the signaling protocols used by MPLS, how traffic is mapped to MPLS paths, and the use of traffic engineering and traffic protection mechanisms in MPLS. Chapter 15 provides an introduction to MPLS VPNs.

History of MPLS

In the mid-1990s, service providers were concerned that the current routers would be unable to scale to meet increasing traffic demands. The IP lookup function within those routers was performed by software running on a general-purpose CPU. In contrast, ATM switches performed forwarding function in hardware. This hardware-based forwarding was possible because the VPI/VCI translation function carried out by an ATM switch was a simpler process than the longest-match prefix lookup carried out by a router. As a result, the throughput of ATM switches of the time was at least an order of magnitude higher than that of routers. Some network equipment vendors began to devise ways of using the switching capability of an ATM switch in conjunction with an IP router to give higher throughput to IP packets.

Cell Switch Router and IP Switch

Two proposals for incorporating IP forwarding into ATM switches emerged at approximately the same time. Toshiba proposed the Cell Switch Router[1] (CSR), and Ipsilon proposed the IP Switch. Both of these devices consisted of an IP processor connected to an ATM switch. The idea was that at any one time, only a small proportion of the traffic would need to pass through the IP processor section of the device. Instead, the bulk of the traffic would pass straight through the ATM switch section. This was achieved by identifying "flows" of traffic and creating a means for identified flows to "cut through" transit devices at the ATM layer rather than being handled on an IP hop-by-hop basis. The following paragraph describes the operation of an IP Switch, but the CSR's principle of operation was similar.

The IP Switch consisted of an IP processor attached to one of the ports of an ATM switch fabric. By default, traffic arrived at the ATM switch ports on a default virtual circuit and was passed to the IP processor. The IP processor, as well as having the usual

---

[1] Y. Katsube, K. Nagami, and H. Esaki, "Toshiba's Router Architecture Extensions for ATM: Overview," RFC 2098, February 1997.

IP lookup and forwarding capabilities, could be set to identify flows. For example, packets having the same source and destination IP address could be defined as belonging to a flow, and the arrival of a certain number of packets within a defined period of time could trigger the recognition of that flow. This resulted in the IP processor signaling, using a proprietary protocol,[2] to the upstream IP Switch so that subsequent traffic belonging to that flow arrived on a VC dedicated exclusively to that flow. The adjacent downstream IP Switch, as a result of its also detecting the flow, would signal the IP processor. This would result in a dedicated VC being used on the outbound port as well. By binding the inbound and outbound VCs in the ATM switch table, subsequent traffic was directly switched by the ATM hardware without passing through the IP processor. Once the process was complete, data from that flow passed through the transit devices at the ATM level so each of those devices was simply carrying out an ATM label-swapping operation and did not need to carry out an IP lookup. The flow state was maintained by the use of periodic refresh messages sent in the upstream direction.

An issue with this flow-driven model is the processing and memory overhead associated with identifying each flow and maintaining its state. In addition, there is a time lag between the detection of a flow and the creation of the dedicated VC. As a result, service providers questioned the suitability of such a model within Internet backbones with large numbers of simultaneous flows, many of which are only a few seconds in duration. In the end, this issue and the fact that hardware-based IP routers were on the horizon meant that no significant deployments occurred. Nevertheless, these schemes introduced the concept of mapping IP traffic to a label and using that label for the forwarding operation.

ARIS

Aggregate Route-Based IP Switching (ARIS) was proposed by IBM. In common with IP Switching and the CSR, ARIS proposed the use of hybrid ATM/IP devices and allowed IP packets to be mapped to ATM VCs to cut through transit devices within a network. An important difference between ARIS and IP Switching/CSR, however, was that rather than being flow-driven, the creation of the switched paths was driven by routing protocol information in such a way that packets destined to a particular egress router from a particular ingress router followed the same switched path. ARIS was the first instance of a "control-driven" approach; control-driven approaches are regarded as more scalable than flow-driven approaches because less signaling and state are required. This philosophy has been carried through to MPLS and is a key contribution to the flexibility of the MPLS architecture.

---

[2]   P. Newman, W. L. Edwards, R. Hinden, E. Hoffman, F. Ching Liaw, T. Lyon, and G. Minshall, "Ipsilon Flow Management Protocol Specification for IPv4 Version 1.0," RFC 1953, May 1996.

Tag Switching

In 1997, *tag switching* was proposed by Cisco Systems in the form of an informational RFC.[3] By analogy with the action of the hybrid ATM/IP devices already discussed, in which an incoming VCI is swapped for an outgoing one, the forwarding action of a tag switch is to swap an incoming tag (label) for an outgoing one by reference to a tag information base. The tag could either have the form of a "shim" placed between the Layer 2 and Layer 3 header, or in the case of ATM interfaces, it could be part of the Layer 2 header itself.

Tag switches were implemented by modifying the software of existing routers and ATM switches. Like ARIS, tag switching improved on the previous schemes by being control-driven rather than flow-driven. That is to say, the mapping of packets to a particular tag could be determined by routing so that, for example, packets destined for a particular egress point in the network would share the same tag. A signaling protocol called Tag Distribution Protocol (TDP) was defined, which is one of the precursors to the Label Distribution Protocol (LDP) that has since been defined for MPLS. The tag switching scheme allowed for a hierarchy by accommodating the use of label stacking, so that multiple inner labels could be mapped to a single outer label. This label-stacking concept has been inherited by MPLS and underpins the operation of Layer 3 and Layer 2 MPLS VPNs.

MPLS

In 1996, an IETF working group called "mpls" was formed to create standards based on the schemes described earlier in this section. RFC 3031[4] sets the MPLS architectural framework. It introduces the concept of labels and defines the manner in which they are distributed, but without specifying the signaling protocol to be used. It also describes the label hierarchy and label operations. The group has also worked on signaling protocols, including the definition of Label Distribution Protocol (LDP)[5] and of extensions to Resource Reservation Setup Protocol (RSVP)[6] for MPLS signaling. (RSVP and LDP are discussed in detail later in this chapter in "RSVP Protocol" and "The Label Distribution Protocol," respectively.) At the time of writing, MPLS-related work is also being carried out in other working groups such as ccamp (Common Control and Measurement Plane), tewg (Internet Traffic Engineering), and ppvpn (Provider Provisioned Virtual Private Networks).

---

[3]   Y. Rekhter, B. Davie, D. Katz, E. Rosen, and G. Swallow, "Cisco Systems' Tag Switching Architecture Overview," RFC 2105, February 1997.

[4]   E. Rosen, A. Viswanathan, R. Callon, "Multiprotocol Label Switching Architecture," RFC 3031, January 2001.

[5]   L. Andersson, P. Doolan, N. Feldman, A. Fredette, B. Thomas, "LDP Specification," RFC 3036, January 2001.

[6]   Daniel O. Awduche, Lou Berger, Der-Hwa Gan, Tony Li, Vijay Srinivasan, George Swallow, "RSVP-TE: Extensions to RSVP for LSP Tunnels," Work in Progress.

One of the main premises behind the precursors to MPLS, the need to improve forwarding performance, is no longer relevant with the advent of hardware-based routers such as the Juniper Networks M-series, which can forward IP packets at wire-rate. However, other powerful applications that make use of the MPLS architecture have become apparent. Applications that have been deployed by service providers and are in use in production networks today include traffic engineering, traffic protection, and VPNs. These applications are made possible because MPLS provides a separation between control and forwarding, so that packets can be mapped to labels on the basis of different criteria, depending on the application. At the time of this writing, much MPLS-related activity resides within the IETF. For example, work is being carried out on Generalized MPLS[7] (GMPLS), which allows MPLS to be used as the control plane of a greater range of network devices, such as optical cross-connects, than previously.

JUNOS Software and MPLS

From the outset, MPLS has been a key component of the JUNOS software feature set. Features such as traffic engineering, traffic protection, and Circuit Cross-Connect (CCC) have been available since 1999. LDP and LDP over RSVP tunnels followed soon after in 2000, and Layer 3 and Layer 2 MPLS VPNs became available in 2001. Juniper Networks has played a leading part in the formulation of MPLS standards and will remain at the forefront of the implementation of new MPLS features in the future.

Overview of MPLS

This section describes the MPLS terminology, label structure, label distribution mechanisms, and operations that are performed on the labels themselves. Numerous RFCs and Internet drafts on MPLS are an invaluable source of information on its workings and current developments; you are encouraged to read them, if possible. Much of the information in this section is based on the RFCs and Internet drafts listed in Table 14-1.

Multi-Protocol Label Switching Terminology

When you are embarking on the study of a new technology, an important first step is to know and understand the terminology that is used to describe the components of that technology. Fortunately, most of the terms and abbreviations used in MPLS are relatively intuitive.

---

[7]   Peter Ashwood-Smith, et al., "Generalized MPLS: Signaling Functional Description,"
     Work in Progress.

Title/Description	RFC Number
MPLS Label Switching Architecture[1]	3031
MPLS Label Stack Encoding[2]	3032
LDP Specification[3]	3036
Carrying Label Information in BGP4[4]	3107
MPLS Using LDP and ATM VC Switching[5]	3035
BGP/MPLS VPNs[6]	2547. See also E. Rosen et al., "BGP/MPLS VPNs" (work in progress, 2547bis).
Multiprotocol Extensions for BGP4[7]	2858
MPLS Based Layer 2 VPNS[8]	K. Kompella et al., "MPLS based Layer 2 VPNs" (work in progress).

[1] E. Rosen, A. Viswanathan, R. Callon, "Multiprotocol Label Switching Architecture", RFC 3031, January 2001.

[2] E. Rosen, D. Tappan, G. Fedorkow, Y. Rekhter, D. Farinacci, T. Li, and A. Conta, "MPLS Label Stack Encoding," RFC 3032, January 2001.

[3] L. Andersson, P. Doolan, N. Feldman, A. Fredette, B. Thomas, "LDP Specification," RFC 3036, January 2001.

[4] Y. Rekhter and E. Rosen, "Carrying Label Information in BGP-4," RFC 3107, May 2001.

[5] B. Davie, J. Lawrence, K. McCloghrie, E. Rosen, G. Swallow, Y. Rekhter, and P. Doolan, "MPLS using LDP and ATM VC Switching," RFC 3035, January 2001.

[6] E. Rosen and Y. Rekhter, "BGP/MPLS VPNs," RFC 2547, March 1999.

[7] T. Bates, Y. Rekhter, R. Chandra, and D. Katz, "Multiprotocol Extensions for BGP-4," RFC 2858, June 2000.

[8] K. Kompella et al., "MPLS-based Layer 2 VPNs" (work in progress).

Table 14-1.   *Useful RFCs and Internet Drafts*

Following are the most widely used label switching terms:

- **MPLS**   Stands for Multi-Protocol Label Switching, which implies that it is used for many protocols, not just IP. However, to date it is used throughout the industry almost exclusively for IP, even though its mechanisms and techniques can be applied to other protocols.

- **Label Switching Router (LSR)**   Any router or device that supports MPLS. This is a generic term that describes any device that is capable of performing label-switching operations and that understands MPLS control protocols.

It can run one or more Layer 3 routing protocols and may perform native Layer 3 forwarding. This term is often used interchangeably with *MPLS node*. The distinction is that an LSR is an MPLS node that performs native Layer 3 forwarding, such as any one of the Juniper Networks range of routers.

- **MPLS Domain** A group of contiguous MPLS nodes that operate MPLS forwarding and control mechanisms within a single routing or administrative domain.

- **Label Edge Router (LER)** An MPLS node that is situated at the edge of an MPLS domain and that connects the domain to an external device that is outside the domain, either because the external device does not run MPLS or because it belongs to another MPLS domain. This term is often used interchangeably with *MPLS edge node*.

- **MPLS ingress node** An MPLS edge node or LER that receives packets from outside an MPLS domain, assigns labels to them, and forwards them into an MPLS domain.

- **MPLS egress node** An MPLS edge node or LER that receives labeled packets as they leave an MPLS domain and forwards them outside of the domain, possibly using conventional Layer 3 forwarding techniques.

- **Label swapping** The process of looking up a label within an incoming packet, determining the outgoing label for that packet, and forwarding it out of the specified interface, with the appropriate encapsulation, to the next hop MPLS node.

- **Forwarding Equivalence Class (FEC)** The classification of packets that have common forwarding criteria so that they are forwarded in the same manner and with the same treatment. FECs are discussed in more detail in the next section.

- **Label Switched Path (LSP)** The path that packets containing labels and that belong to a particular FEC take across all or a subset of the MPLS nodes within the MPLS domain.

- **Label stack** A series of one or more labels encoded into a packet before it is forwarded to the next hop MPLS node. An MPLS node always forwards a packet based on the top, or outermost, label if more than one label is on the label stack of a packet. Label stacks provide a mechanism for scaling and hierarchical forwarding within an MPLS domain.

- **Label Distribution** The process used by MPLS nodes to advertise labels to their MPLS-capable neighbors. Several mechanisms can be used for advertising and assigning labels. This chapter concentrates on the two most widely used methods, the Label Distribution Protocol (LDP) and the Resource Reservation Protocol (RSVP). Both methods are discussed in more detail later in this section.

- **Label binding** The process used by an MPLS node to associate a label, advertised by its MPLS neighbor, to a particular FEC.

Forwarding Equivalence Class

One of the most important terms found in the RFCs and other documents describing MPLS is the FEC.

In conventional forwarding, the router examines the IP header of each incoming packet on a hop-by-hop basis to determine which interface to use to send the packet out toward its next hop. The forwarding decision is based on a comparison between the destination address in the IP header of each packet and an IP network entry in the router's RIB (routing information base)—that is, its routing table. The criterion used for making the forwarding decision is based on a longest match between the two.

All packets for which the same forwarding decision is made are said to belong to the same FEC, irrespective of whether the information in their IP headers is different. For example, an entry in the router's RIB for network 192.168.0.0 may direct packets to outgoing interface X, next hop Y. Two IP packets with destination IP addresses of 192.168.1.1 and 192.168.2.1 are destined for different networks, but they both belong to the same FEC because they both match the same network entry in the router's RIB. Both packets will, therefore, be sent out of interface X toward next hop Y.

MPLS relies on another table, rather than the RIB, to make forwarding decisions. This table is called the *Forwarding Information Base* (FIB). The FIB, much like the RIB, holds information about which outgoing interface packets should be forwarded out of. It also contains information on the outgoing label to use, the interface encapsulation type, and the next hop Layer 2 rewrite information. The FIB is built during the label binding process when advertised labels and their corresponding FECs (IP network prefixes) are received from neighboring MPLS nodes during label distribution. The FIB is the key to the switching operation of MPLS.

The FIB and the RIB complement each other in MPLS. The RIB, built using an IGP, contains the network reachability information for the FECs, and the FIB provides the label forwarding information for those FECs. In Juniper Networks routers, two RIBs are used to hold information on network prefixes that are advertised to the local router. The inet.0 RIB contains prefixes that are advertised by the IGP, and the inet.3 RIB contains prefixes that are advertised by the label distribution protocol. These and other routing and forwarding tables are described in more detail in the section, "Route Resolution."

The output below from a Juniper Networks router shows a sample of the inet.0 RIB that is populated with IS-IS derived routes, followed by the inet.3 RIB that is populated with LDP derived routes.

```
root@R1> show route
inet.0: 11 destinations, 11 routes (10 active, 0 holddown, 1 hidden)
+ = Active Route, - = Last Active, * = Both
.

.
192.168.1.2/32     *[IS-IS/18] 01:07:36, metric 10, tag 2
                    > to 10.1.1.2 via fe-0/3/2.0
```

```
192.168.1.3/32        *[IS-IS/18] 00:46:29, metric 20, tag 2
                       > to 10.1.1.2 via fe-0/3/2.0
192.168.1.4/32        *[IS-IS/18] 00:41:44, metric 30, tag 2
                         to 10.1.1.2 via fe-0/3/2.0
.
.
.
inet.3: 3 destinations, 3 routes (3 active, 0 holddown, 0 hidden)
+ = Active Route, - = Last Active, * = Both
192.168.1.2/32        *[LDP/9] 01:07:33, metric 1
                       > to 10.1.1.2 via fe-0/3/2.0
192.168.1.3/32        *[LDP/9] 00:35:33, metric 1
                       > to 10.1.1.2 via fe-0/3/2.0, Push 100007
192.168.1.4/32        *[LDP/9] 00:35:02, metric 1
                       > to 10.1.1.2 via fe-0/3/2.0, Push 100008
```

A third table, called the mpls.0 table, holds the labels that are received and used by the local router to label switch packets to the next hop router.

```
mpls.0: 6 destinations, 6 routes (6 active, 0 holddown, 0 hidden)
+ = Active Route, - = Last Active, * = Both
0                     *[MPLS/0] 01:20:40, metric 1
                        Receive
1                     *[MPLS/0] 01:20:40, metric 1
                        Receive
100007                *[LDP/9] 01:07:33, metric 1
                       > to 10.1.1.2 via fe-0/3/2.0, Pop
100007(S=0)           *[LDP/9] 01:07:33, metric 1
                       > to 10.1.1.2 via fe-0/3/2.0, Pop
100008                *[LDP/9] 00:35:33, metric 1
                       > to 10.1.1.2 via fe-0/3/2.0, Swap 100007
100009                *[LDP/9] 00:35:02, metric 1
                       > to 10.1.1.2 via fe-0/3/2.0, Swap 100008
```

The significance of label values 0 and 1 in this mpls.0 switching table is described later in the "Structure of the MPLS Label" section.

The FIB is constructed from information in the preceding tables. A sample is shown in the following output:

```
root@R1> show route forwarding-table detail
Routing table:: inet
Internet:
Destination       Type RtRef  InIf Flags Nexthop         Type Index NhRef Netif
.
.
.
192.168.1.1/32    intf    0      0  0x10 192.168.1.1     locl   26    1
192.168.1.2/32    user    1      0  0x10 10.1.1.2        ucst   31   11 fe-0/3/2.0
192.168.1.3/32    user    0      0  0x10 10.1.1.2        ucst   31   11 fe-0/3/2.0
```

```
192.168.1.4/32     user    0     0  0x10 10.1.1.2        ucst   31    11 fe-0/3/2.0
.
.
MPLS:
Interface.Label    Type RtRef  InIf Flags Nexthop        Type Index NhRef Netif
default            perm    0     0  0x10                  dscd    3     1
0                  user    0     0  0x10                  recv    5     2
1                  user    0     0  0x10                  recv    5     2
100007             user    0     0  0x10 10.1.1.2         Pop              fe-0/3/2.0
100007(S=0)        user    0     0  0x10 10.1.1.2         Pop              fe-0/3/2.0
100008             user    0     0  0x10 10.1.1.2         Swap 100007      fe-0/3/2.0
100009             user    0     0  0x10 10.1.1.2         Swap 100008      fe-0/3/2.0
```

The end-to-end path taken by a packet as it traverses the MPLS network, having undergone a series of hop-by-hop label swaps, is called the *Label Switched Path* (LSP). An LSP is unidirectional. One LSP is required for packets to be label switched toward a specific destination across the network, and another LSP is required for the packets to return. The FECs are associated with specific LSPs after the LSPs have been built end-to-end by the label distribution process.

The assignment of packets to a particular FEC is done once only, at the entry (ingress) point of the LSP. The FEC to which each packet belongs is encoded using a small, fixed-length label within each packet. The label is used at each hop as an index into the FIB, which specifies the next hop, and a new label. The old label is replaced with the new label and the packet is forwarded to its next hop. The label that is used at each hop is either locally significant to the LSR as a whole or locally significant to the interface from which it is being forwarded. This is discussed later in "LDP Label Space."

No further analysis of the IP header is carried out on the packets after they are assigned to a FEC, and the label is used for all subsequent forwarding decisions as the packets traverse the LSP toward the exit (egress) point. Much greater forwarding flexibility results from this ability to divorce the forwarding of packets from any IP header analysis. Some of the advantages of this approach are listed here:

- Devices that are not capable of performing IP header analysis can forward packets.

- Packets can be placed into FECs and forwarded based on information that does not exist in an IP header. For example, packets that arrive on different interfaces can be assigned to separate FECs, as can packets that need to be forwarded based on a particular class of service.

- Packets can be forwarded based on predetermined paths (LSPs) across the MPLS network, rather than following the route that is determined dynamically by a routing protocol.

Structure of the MPLS Label

The RFC definition of an MPLS label is "a short, fixed length, locally significant identifier that is used to identify a FEC." The format of label encoding across the ATM link layer is different from that used for non-ATM media. This is described in more detail later on in the section "Cell Mode MPLS."

Frame Mode MPLS

In Frame Mode MPLS, the structure of the Layer 3 packet does not change in any way as it traverses the network. The framing does change, of course, as the packet traverses different types of media, but complete frames are always transmitted between neighboring devices.

With ATM, the label encoding and swapping mechanism is different, as described later in the section "Cell Mode MPLS."

The structure of an MPLS header used for non-ATM media is shown in Figure 14-1.

The MPLS label is always positioned between the Layer 2 and Layer 3 headers of a packet. More than one label may be encoded within a packet; this is known as a *label stack*. Each label within a stack consists of four octets called a *label stack entry*. The top label is closest to the Layer 2 header of the packet. The Layer 3 header follows immediately after the label that has the *S* (Bottom of Stack) bit set.

Figure 14-2 illustrates the positioning of the label header in different types of non-ATM link Layer encapsulations. The Ethernet frame in Figure 14-2 contains a label stack rather than an individual label so the S bit is used to denote which are the top (outer) and bottom (inner) labels in the stack. The S bit is set to 1 to indicate the bottom label.

The label header shown in Figure 14-1 is broken down into the following fields:

- **Label value**   The actual 20-bit value of the label.

- **EXP Bits**   These bits are reserved for experimental use. However, they are often used to reflect the IP precedence of a packet as it enters the MPLS domain by copying the three IP precedence bits from the Type of Service byte into this field as the label is encoded.

- **Bottom of Stack (S bit)**   This bit is set to *1* in the label that is closest to the Layer 3 header of the packet (the bottom label in the stack). It is set to *0* in all other labels in the stack.

- **TTL**   The Time to Live value of the label. The TTL value from the IP packet can be copied into this field as it enters the MPLS domain, at the discretion of the domain's administrator. The IP packet's TTL value is not copied if the domain administrator wishes the LSP across the MPLS domain to appear as a single hop to the outside world.

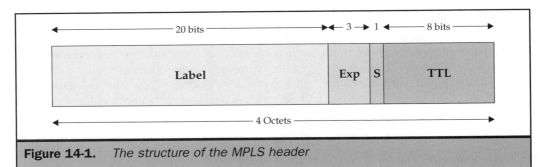

Figure 14-1.   *The structure of the MPLS header*

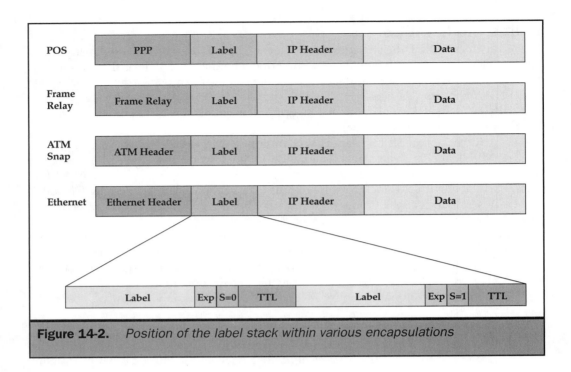

Figure 14-2.   *Position of the label stack within various encapsulations*

When an MPLS node receives a labeled packet, it looks up the value of the label at the top of the stack. The results of the lookup tell the MPLS node

■ The operation that should be performed on the label stack before forwarding the packet. This operation could be replacing the top label stack entry with another label (*swapping*), extracting (*popping*) the top label from the stack, or replacing the top label and putting (*pushing*) one or more additional labels onto the stack.

■ The next hop to which the label is to be forwarded.

Once the next hop is determined and the label stack is processed accordingly, the packet is forwarded to the relevant outgoing interface and the appropriate link layer encapsulation for that interface is applied.

The operation that is carried out on the label stack is determined by several reserved label values of 0 to 15. Presently, only values 0 through 3 have significance.

A label value of 0 represents the "IPv4 Explicit Null Label." This value is legal only at the bottom of the label stack. When an LSR receives a packet with a bottom label value of 0, it must "pop" the entire label stack and forward the packet based on its IPv4 header.

A label value of 1 represents the "Router Alert Label." This value is legal anywhere in the stack, *except* at the bottom. When an LSR receives a packet containing a label with this value at the top of the stack, it is delivered to a local software module for further processing. The label beneath this one in the stack determines where to forward the packet after processing of the packet's contents is complete. The Router Alert Label is pushed back onto the top of the stack before the packet is forwarded to the downstream LSR, if the downstream LSR is required to carry out further processing of the packet's contents.

The Router Alert Label is analogous to the Router Alert Option in IP packets. The Router Alert Option informs a receiving router to intercept and "examine this packet more closely," even though the packet is not addressed to the receiving router itself. The IP Router Alert mechanism is used in RSVP to tell each router along an RSVP path to intercept an RSVP packet when it arrives and to process it before forwarding it to the next hop. For example, the protocol stack in a router intercepts arriving RSVP PATH messages and passes them to the RSVP software component so that the sequence of RSVP objects within the message can be parsed and some kind of action carried out before the packet is forwarded to the next hop router.

Although the Router Alert Label is defined as part of the MPLS standard and must be supported by the protocol stack, it is not currently used in MPLS.

A label value of 2 represents the "IPv6 Explicit Null Label." This value is legal only at the bottom of the label stack. It indicates that the label stack must be "popped" and the packet forwarded based on its IPv6 header.

A label value of 3 represents the "Implicit Null Label." This label may be assigned and distributed by an LSR using LDP or RSVP, but it is never actually encoded in the label stack itself. The Implicit Null Label is used only at the edge of an MPLS domain. For example, in Figure 14-3, an LSR at the edge of the MPLS domain connects to an upstream MPLS node within the MPLS domain on interface X and a non-MPLS node on interface Y.

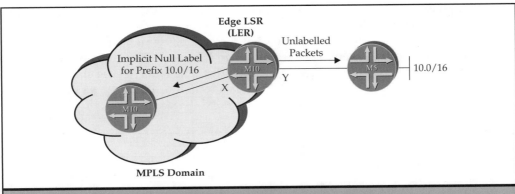

Figure 14-3. *Using the Implicit Null label*

The edge LSR receives labeled packets through interface X within the MPLS domain, removes the labels, and forwards the packets using conventional IP forwarding out of interface Y. The edge LSR must remove the labels because the device it connects to over interface Y is not MPLS capable.

This entails two operations: examining and popping the label stack, and then forwarding the unlabeled packets out of interface Y.

The edge LSR can overcome this inefficiency by informing its upstream LSR neighbor that it should pop the label stack before sending packets to it over interface X so that they are received without any labels whatsoever. The edge LSR does this by advertising the Implicit Null label to its upstream neighbor for those IP prefixes that it can reach over interface Y.

The LSR immediately upstream of the egress LSR is called the *penultimate* LSR, and the procedure of popping the label at the penultimate LSR is called *Penultimate Hop Popping* (PHP).

Cell Mode MPLS

Juniper Networks does not manufacture ATM switches, so a detailed description of Cell Mode MPLS is not within the scope of this chapter. However, the distinction between Frame Mode and Cell Mode MPLS is an important one and is described briefly in this section.

With ATM, devices at the edge of the network apply the frame encapsulation (AAL5 SNAP for example), and the frame is divided into small, 53-byte fixed-length cells by the Segmentation and Reassembly (SAR) function for transmission across the ATM switches. The cells that constitute the frame are switched across the network individually, based on their VPI/VCI values, to their destination. Once the destination device receives all the cells, they are reassembled into the original frame and the Layer 3 packet is extracted and processed accordingly.

As far as the edge devices are concerned, they are still running Frame Mode MPLS, even though they are connected to ATM switches. So any of the Juniper range of LSRs, for example, connected to an ATM switch simply creates an AAL5 SNAP frame, encodes the label header into the payload of the frame, segments the frame, and transmits it into the ATM network normally. The ATM switches in the network are unaware that the payload contains a MPLS header. The label header in the SNAP payload is sometimes referred to as a "shim" header. Figure 14-4 shows the format of a SNAP frame with the shim label header encoded.

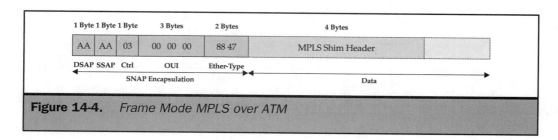

Figure 14-4.   *Frame Mode MPLS over ATM*

An LSR that receives a frame with EtherType 0x8847 knows that it is an MPLS frame rather than one that contains a native IP packet.

But the MPLS standards also define mechanisms for the switches within the ATM network itself to support MPLS (RFC 3035), known as Cell Mode MPLS.

Following are the three main obstacles to be overcome for an ATM switch to support MPLS:

- There is no scope to change the format or structure of an ATM cell to incorporate a label stack.

- A native ATM switch is not capable of performing Layer 3 RIB or label FIB lookups, let alone label distribution and processing.

- The structure of the Layer 3 packet is changed across the network because it is chopped into 53-byte cells rather than being forwarded within a complete frame.

The first obstacle can be overcome relatively easily, in theory at least, in that ATM already uses small, fixed-length values (VPI/VCIs) to switch cells across the network. The VPI/VCI value within each cell effectively becomes the label for that cell.

The second obstacle is much more difficult to overcome. One approach to providing MPLS support on a native ATM switch is to "graft" an external MPLS-capable device onto it. The external device effectively controls the label distribution and binding process on behalf of the switch and runs a routing protocol to create the RIB and FIB forwarding tables for the switch. It then tells the switch which labels (VPI/VCIs) to use to forward the cells, allowing the switch to move on with simple cell forwarding. This hybrid switch is called an *ATM-LSR*. The device that controls the ATM switch is called a Label Switch Controller, or LC-ATM. Another and much more elegant solution is to build an ATM-LSR from scratch with all the necessary functionality included in one box.

The third obstacle presents some interesting problems related to the label allocation, advertisement, and binding processes. In Figure 14-5, the links between LSR A, LSR B, and LSR C are using Frame Mode MPLS—they are not ATM connections. Edge LSR C on the right can reach two IP prefixes that are outside the MPLS domain. It uses LDP to advertise label 20 for prefix 20.0.0.0 and label 30 for prefix 30.0.0.0 to LSR B inside the MPLS domain. LSR B considers the prefixes to be in the same FEC, assuming that the desired forwarding behavior is the same for both of the prefixes, and advertises a single label, label 10, to LSR A for both prefixes.

When LSR A forwards data frames destined for either of the two prefixes to LSR B using label 10, LSR B has no trouble distinguishing between the frames as they arrive (because they are separate entities) and takes the appropriate label-switching steps to forward them to LSR C. This label-sharing capability is efficient and is one of the many benefits of MPLS.

However, if LSR A, LSR B, and LSR C are ATM-LSRs and the links between them are using Cell Mode MPLS, label sharing becomes problematic. In Figure 14-6, if ATM-LSR B advertises the same label (VPI/VCI) 100/10 to ATM-LSR A for both of the

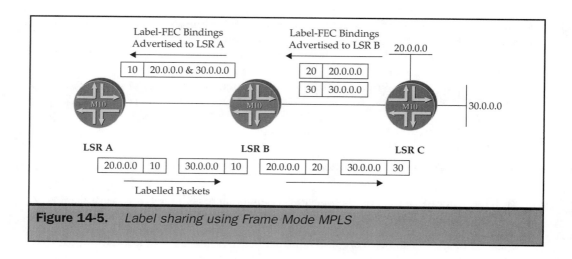

Figure 14-5.   *Label sharing using Frame Mode MPLS*

prefixes reachable via ATM-LSR C, it has no way to tell which cells belong to which frames as they arrive from ATM-LSR A. This is because the cells from each frame may be interleaved.

There are two solutions to this problem. The first solution is to carry on sharing the same label (VPI/VCI) for both prefixes but to adopt a mechanism known as *VC Merge*. VC Merge means that ATM-LSR A has to buffer all the cells that it receives from an upstream ATM-LSR destined for each of the prefixes on ATM-LSR C and to send all the cells that belong to one frame first, followed by all the cells that belong to the next frame. In other words, no cell interleaving between frames takes place between ATM-LSR A and ATM-LSR B. The time penalties for this are relatively small but this negates somewhat the benefits of independent cell switching.

The second solution is not to use a shared label at all and for ATM-LSR B to advertise two distinct labels (VPI/VCIs) to ATM-LSR A for each of the prefixes. In actual fact, ATM-LSR A would have to request these separate labels from ATM-LSR B using *downstream-on-demand* label distribution, rather than just letting ATM-LSR B advertise them using the more usual *downstream unsolicited* label distribution method. This is the more pernicious of the two solutions because it effectively means that each and every FEC requires a separate VC between the ATM-LSRs. This could result in a proliferation of VCs in some networks, which would deplete resources in the ATM switches significantly.

Distribution of Labels

Three methods of label allocation and distribution in MPLS are discussed in this chapter: manual configuration, RSVP, and LDP. The MPLS Architecture RFC (RFC 3031) contains

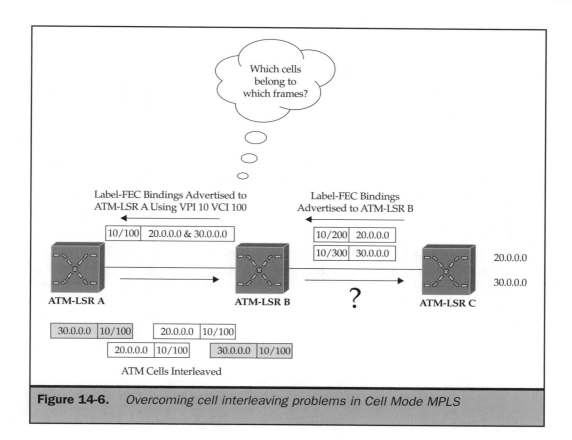

Figure 14-6.   *Overcoming cell interleaving problems in Cell Mode MPLS*

a reminder that a number of different protocols are in the process of being, or have already been, standardized for this purpose. Some existing protocols have been extended so that label distribution can be piggybacked onto them, such as MPLS-BGP and RSVP.

An example of how to configure static LSPs on Juniper LSRs by assigning labels manually is shown in the section "Static LSPs." The specific messages used by RSVP and how RSVP is used to distribute labels between Juniper LSRs are described in the section "RSVP Protocol."

The terms *upstream* and *downstream* appear frequently in discussions about label distribution. Given two LSRs, one of them is referred to as being upstream with respect to the other if the former is forwarding labelled packets in the direction of the latter. The LSR that is receiving the labelled packets is downstream of the one that is forwarding them. In Figure 14-7, LSR A is considered to be upstream of LSR B.

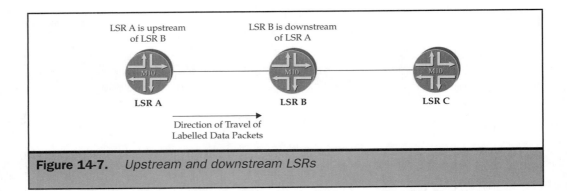

Figure 14-7. *Upstream and downstream LSRs*

Static LSPs

This section introduces JUNOS software MPLS configuration by showing how a static LSP is set up on Juniper Networks routers. In practice, the static method of setting up an LSP is not used because of the configurational effort required. However, discussing it here serves to highlight the label-swapping paradigm used within the MPLS forwarding path. Figure 14-8 shows an example network in which setting up an LSP between routers Lister and Kryten via routers Cat and Holly is required.

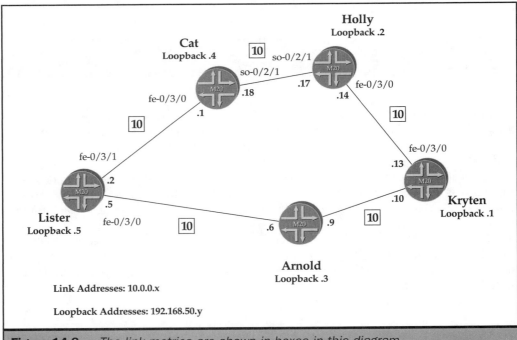

Figure 14-8. *The link metrics are shown in boxes in this diagram.*

The steps required to set up the LSP are as follows:

1. On each router, enable the MPLS protocol family on each interface required for MPLS forwarding. Also, list the interfaces to be used for MPLS under the MPLS protocol section of the configuration.

2. On the ingress router, Lister, configure the static LSP with the egress point (the loopback address of Kryten), the next-hop (the address of the interface of Cat that is connected to Lister), and the value of the label to push onto the IP packet.

3. On each transit router, configure the incoming interface, the incoming label, the label value to swap, and the address of the next-hop.

This is the configuration for the ingress router, Lister:

```
interfaces {
    fe-0/3/0 {
        unit 0 {
            family inet {
                address 10.0.0.5/30;
            }
            family mpls;
        }
    }
    fe-0/3/1 {
        unit 0 {
            family inet {
                address 10.0.0.2/30;
            }
            family mpls;
        }
    }
    fxp0 {
        unit 0 {
            family inet {
                address 10.255.254.5/24;
            }
        }
    }
    lo0 {
        unit 0 {
            family inet {
                address 127.0.0.1/32;
                address 192.168.50.5/32;
            }
        }
    }
```

```
        }
    }
routing-options {
    router-id 192.168.50.5;
}
protocols {
    mpls {
        static-path inet {
            192.168.50.1/32 {
                next-hop 10.0.0.1;
                push 424;
            }
        }
        interface fe-0/3/1.0;
        interface fe-0/3/0.0;
    }
    ospf {
        area 0.0.0.0 {
            interface fe-0/3/0.0 {
                metric 10;
            }
            interface fe-0/3/1.0 {
                metric 10;
            }
            interface lo0.0;
        }
    }
}
```

The interface configurations for the transit routers Cat and Holly are similar to that of Lister, so in the following configurations of the transit routers, only the MPLS sections are shown. The configuration of router Cat is as follows. Note that the configuration must include the incoming interface, the incoming label, the address of the next-hop, and the outgoing label:

```
mpls {
        interface so-0/2/1.0;
        interface fe-0/3/0.0 {
            label-map 424 {
                next-hop 10.0.0.17;
                swap 533;
```

```
                }
            }
        }
```

The configuration of Holly is as follows. Note that an outgoing label value of 3 is set. As already described in the section entitled "Overview of MPLS," label value 3 represents the Implicit Null Label, meaning that Holly pops the incoming label and forwards the packet to the specified next-hop (the egress router) as a plain IP packet. Although configuring static LSPs in this way is not obligatory, this Penultimate Hop Popping action is the mode of operation used with signaled LSPs:

```
mpls {
        interface so-0/2/1.0 {
            label-map 533 {
                next-hop 10.0.0.13;
                swap 3;
            }
        }
        interface fe-0/3/0.0;
    }
```

As a result of the PHP action carried out by Holly, Kryten does not require any configuration related to the static LSP.

Examination of the routing table on the ingress router, Lister, shows a static route to the loopback address of the egress router pointing to the LSP. Note the label value of 424 to be pushed onto the packet, and that there is also an OSPF route to that destination, but the static route is preferred due to its lower (more favorable) preference value:

```
root@Lister > show route 192.168.50.1
192.168.50.1/32     *[Static/5] 00:00:38
                    > to 10.0.0.1 via fe-0/3/1.0, Push      424
                    [OSPF/10] 00:00:37, metric 20
                    > to 10.0.0.6 via fe-0/3/0.0
```

When MPLS is configured on a Juniper Networks router, an MPLS table called mpls.0 is created. The table shows the action to be taken on each incoming label—for example, a label swap or a pop operation. The MPLS table on each transit router can be examined to confirm that the label swap operation occurs as expected. Table mpls.0 of transit router Cat is as follows. Note how the incoming label is mapped to the outgoing label value and next-hop that are configured in the mpls section of the configuration.

```
show route table mpls.0
mpls.0: 3 destinations, 3 routes (3 active, 0 holddown, 0 hidden)
+ = Active Route, - = Last Active, * = Both

0                      *[MPLS/0] 01:02:50, metric 1
                         Receive
1                      *[MPLS/0] 01:02:50, metric 1
                         Receive
424                    *[Static/5] 00:18:19
                       > to 10.0.0.17 via so-0/2/1.0, Swap      533
```

Table mpls.0 of transit router Holly is shown below. Note the pop action:

```
mpls.0: 3 destinations, 3 routes (3 active, 0 holddown, 0 hidden)
+ = Active Route, - = Last Active, * = Both

0                      *[MPLS/0] 00:32:17, metric 1
                         Receive
1                      *[MPLS/0] 00:32:17, metric 1
                         Receive
533                    *[Static/5] 00:18:36
                       > to 10.0.0.13 via fe-0/3/0.0, Pop
```

The operational state of the LSP can be confirmed by carrying out a traceroute to the egress loopback address from the ingress router. Note the label values shown in the replies:

```
root@Lister> traceroute 192.168.50.1
traceroute to 192.168.50.1 (192.168.50.1), 30 hops max, 40 byte packets
 1  10.0.0.1 (10.0.0.1)  0.871 ms  0.703 ms  0.665 ms
    MPLS Label=424 CoS=0 TTL=1 S=1
 2  10.0.0.17 (10.0.0.17)  9.950 ms  0.697 ms  0.673 ms
    MPLS Label=533 CoS=0 TTL=1 S=1
 3  192.168.50.1 (192.168.50.1)  0.767 ms  0.690 ms  0.673 ms
```

As already indicated, static LSPs are not used in practice because of the amount of configurational effort required: Each router apart from the egress router requires explicit configuration related to each LSP. Also the potential for errors increases when configuring the label values. From the operational point of view, there is little visibility of the state of the LSP apart from the traceroute tool and no automatic mechanism to repair an LSP if, for example, a link fails. As a result, in practice, signaled LSPs are used.

Signaled LSPs

The previous section described how to set up static LSPs. As discussed, in practice such LSPs are not used because of the configurational effort required and difficulty of troubleshooting. Furthermore, features such as traffic protection and CCC are not available with static LSPs.

For practical purposes, it is better to use signaling protocols for the creation and maintenance of MPLS LSPs. These protocols offer the advantages of automatic label assignment and the ability to take account of changes in network topology. Also, in the case of RSVP, there is good visibility of the state of the LSPs. The MPLS architecture document does not stipulate the use of any particular signaling protocol, but, by specifying the properties of MPLS LSPs, it implicitly sets down some of the requirements that an MPLS signaling protocol must meet. JUNOS software supports both RSVP and LDP as MPLS signaling protocols.

RSVP-signaled LSPs are a key component of traffic-engineering and traffic protection. Traffic engineering is the process of controlling the paths along which data travels through a network. The use of MPLS traffic engineering allows for the more efficient use of network resources by directing traffic along paths in a way that would be impossible using the IGP alone. For example, in Figure 14-9, if the path followed by traffic is determined by the IGP alone, it would be impossible for all traffic from A to F to follow the path A–C–D–F while at the same time all traffic from B to F follows the path B–C–E–F. This is because once the traffic arrives at C, the forwarding decision cannot take account of the origin of the traffic.

In MPLS-based traffic engineering, this is possible through the use of RSVP-signaled LSPs. There are extensions to RSVP that allow the creation of LSPs along any prescribed path, which may differ from the path dictated by the IGP. In the example shown in Figure 14-9, two LSPs could be created—one that follows the path A-C-D-F and the other that follows the path B–C–E–F. Applications of traffic engineering include diverting certain traffic from congested nodes or links in the network and enforcing load balancing across links in complicated scenarios.

LDP creates LSPs whose path is dictated by the IGP. Therefore, LDP cannot be used for traffic engineering. However, LDP requires little effort to deploy, both in terms of initial configuration of a network and the incremental change required when adding routers to the network. Like RSVP LSPs, LDP LSPs can be used as a carrier of Layer 3 and Layer 2 VPN traffic. An extended form of LDP called Constraint Based Routing LDP (CR-LDP) has been defined by the IETF. CR-LDP allows for traffic-engineering by offering mechanisms similar to those offered by RSVP to specify particular transit nodes that must be traversed by an LSP. However, very few implementations of CR-LDP exist due to lack of demand, and CR-LDP is not available in JUNOS software.

Both RSVP and LDP in principle allow MPLS networks to be built in which the core routers do not need any external routing information. That is to say, the core routers do not need to run BGP. In practice, one way of achieving this that uses the properties of RSVP and LDP signaled LSPs to their best advantage is to have an RSVP-based core and an LDP-based edge.

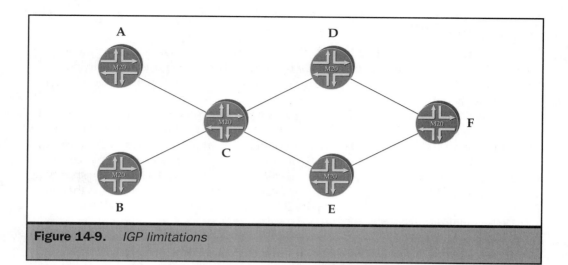

Figure 14-9. *IGP limitations*

RSVP Protocol

RSVP predates MPLS. Originally, RSVP was intended as a protocol for creating bandwidth reservations for traffic flows—for example, individual application flows between hosts. However, it was realized that the protocol can be extended so that it can be used to set up an MPLS LSP along a particular path, reserve bandwidth resources for that LSP, and assign and distribute labels for the LSP. This was preferable to reinventing the wheel and designing a brand-new signaling protocol. In JUNOS software, RSVP is used solely for the creation and maintenance of MPLS LSPs.

The main RSVP message types of interest are as follows:

- Path
- Resv
- PathTear
- ResvTear
- PathErr
- ResvErr

To create an RSVP-signaled LSP, the ingress router sends a Path message to the egress router. The egress router responds with a Resv message. The flow of Path and Resv messages is illustrated in Figure 14-10. As described in more detail in the following sections, the Path and Resv messages contain the necessary information to partly or fully specify the path to be taken by the LSP, the resources required by the LSP, and the label values to be used. RSVP is a *soft-state protocol*. That is, the reservation must be refreshed by the use of periodic Path and Resv messages. By default, these are sent every 45 seconds. If the messages are not received, the reservation times out and it is assumed that the LSP is no longer required.

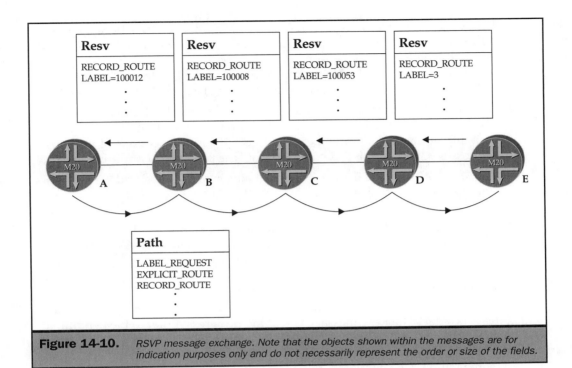

Figure 14-10. *RSVP message exchange. Note that the objects shown within the messages are for indication purposes only and do not necessarily represent the order or size of the fields.*

Path Message

The Path message is sent by the ingress router and is addressed to the egress router. The address of the egress router is known to the ingress router through configuration. The Router Alert option is set so that transit routers can inspect and modify the contents of the message. A Path message includes the following objects:

- **LABEL_REQUEST**   This object indicates that a label binding for the path is requested, triggering each transit router and the egress router to allocate the local label value to be used for the LSP. The value of the label chosen is communicated within the Resv message as described in the next section.

- **EXPLICIT_ROUTE**   The Explicit Route Object (ERO) specifies a list of routers that the LSP must pass through. Naming a particular router as a *strict hop* implies that it must be directly attached to the ingress router (if it is the first one named) or to the router that precedes it in the list of hops. Naming a particular router as a *loose hop* means that there may be other routers between it and the previous router in the list. For example, in Figure 14-11, suppose you wish to create an LSP from A to G. If you wish the LSP pass through E, but do not otherwise mind which path the LSP follows, this can be achieved by setting "E loose" within the ERO. Note that an ERO containing "E strict" alone would be illegal as E is not directly connected to A. Alternatively, if you wish the LSP to follow the path ABE on its way to G, this can be achieved by setting the ERO to "B strict, E strict." In this scenario, from E the LSP may go straight to G or may follow the path E-F-G depending on the values of the IGP metrics since the egress router is an implicit loose hop. If you wish the LSP to go directly from E to G, this can be achieved by setting the ERO to "B strict, E strict, G strict."

- **RECORD_ROUTE**   This object requests that the actual path followed by the LSP be recorded as a list of router addresses. RECORD_ROUTE provides visibility of the actual path taken by an LSP. If a router sees one of its own addresses in this object, this could indicate the presence of a routing loop.

- **SESSION_ATTRIBUTE**   This object contains parameters related to preemption, priority, and protection and also identifies the session by carrying the LSP name as a character string.

- **Sender TSPEC**   This object carries information that defines the characteristics of the data flow that the sender (the ingress router) will send. As an example, it requests the desired bandwidth for the LSP.

Resv Message

When the egress router of the LSP to be created receives a Path message, it responds with a Resv message. The Resv message is sent by the egress router to the penultimate router, which in turn sends a Resv message to the next upstream transit router, and so on. If the Resv message were addressed directly to the ingress router by the egress router, there would be the danger that due to potential asymmetric routing, it might not follow the reverse of the path used by the Path message.

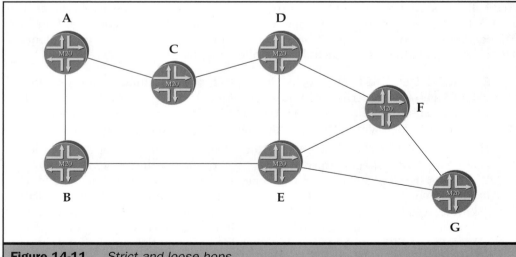

Figure 14-11.   *Strict and loose hops*

The Resv message includes the following objects:

- **RECORD_ROUTE**   As in Path messages, this object provides visibility of the LSP path and can be used to detect routing loops.

- **LABEL**   The Resv message is sent hop-by-hop from the egress router to the ingress router. It is the Resv message that carries out the bandwidth reservation for the LSP and allocates the label values to be used for the LSP. The LABEL object is changed on a hop-by-hop basis. For example, when the penultimate router receives the Resv message from the egress router, it stores the LABEL value received. It replaces the LABEL value in the Resv message with one that it allocates, and forwards the Resv message to its upstream neighbor. In this way, a set of label bindings is created that defines the forwarding state of the LSP. This mode of label allocation is referred to as *downstream label allocation*. Referring back to Figure 14-10, the egress router E sends a label value of 3 to transit router D. D stores this value and chooses to send a label value of 100053 to C. C in turn stores the value and sends a label value of 100008 to B. In this way, when an MPLS packet arrives at C having a label of 100008, it knows to swap this label for 100053 and send the packet to D.

PathTear Message

This message is sent toward the egress router and is used to remove the path state. If the LSP is cleared by the ingress router—for example due to a reoptimization of the LSP path—the ingress router sends this message. This message would also be sent in the case of an outage such as a link failure.

ResvTear Message

This message is sent toward the ingress router (that is, in the opposite direction of the PathTear message) and removes the reservation state (for example following the time out of the reservation state at a node). Following an outage such as a link failure, the node that detects the failure sends a message of this type.

PathErr Message

This message is sent toward the ingress router to report errors in incoming Path messages. For example, a routing loop may be detected, or the Explicit Route Object within the Path message may contain a strict hop that is not attached to the transit router that generated the error message.

ResvErr Message

This message is sent toward the egress router to report errors in Resv messages.

Hello Extension

An optional hello extension is available to provide node failure detection. Hello messages are sent between directly connected RSVP neighbors with a TTL of one.

In JUNOS software, the default hello interval is 3 seconds. An associated parameter is the *keep-multiplier*, *k*. If *2k+1* consecutive hellos are missed, the neighbor is considered to be down. The default value of *k* is 3, so it will take approximately 21 seconds for the hello mechanism to detect that the neighbor is down. Note that when a point-to-point link such as SONET/SDH fails, the system detects the failure immediately in any case. However, the hello mechanism is useful for detecting the failure of a neighbor's routing process or the failure of a neighbor's interface on a broadcast or point-to-multipoint system.

RSVP Signaled LSPs

There are two methods of setting up RSVP-signaled LSPs. The default method involves the use of an algorithm called *Constrained Shortest Path First* (CSPF). This algorithm is used at the ingress router to compute the complete path for the LSP, taking into account constraints set by the network administrator. The computed path is input to the RSVP ERO as a series of strict hops. The other method of setting up an RSVP signaled LSP is to disable CSPF. In this case, the path of the LSP is determined hop-by-hop by the IGP but can be influenced by manually specifying strict or loose nodes to be input into the ERO.

In either case, a bandwidth reservation can be requested for the LSP. Note that, at the time of writing, this does not mean that the actual traffic traveling along the LSP is limited to that value. Rather, the bandwidth parameter is used as form of admission control. Each RSVP interface in the network has an associated maximum reservable bandwidth, which by default is 100 percent of the link speed. The sum of the reservations of all LSPs (whether ingress or transit) exiting an interface cannot exceed the maximum reservable bandwidth.

In most cases, the default (CSPF) method of setting up RSVP signaled LSPs is used because it provides more flexible methods for influencing the path of an LSP, such as the use of link *colors*. However, as will be explained in the section "RSVP Signaled LSPs with CSPF," the complete path of such an LSP must lie within a single IGP area. RSVP signaled LSPs without CSPF are therefore useful for situations in which an LSP is required to cross IGP boundaries.

RSVP-Signaled LSPs Without CSPF

Returning to the example network shown in Figure 14-8, this section demonstrates how to set up an RSVP-signaled LSP between Lister and Kryten, instead of using the static LSP demonstrated previously. If the LSP is configured without specifying any transit nodes, it follows the path dictated by the IGP, namely Lister-Arnold-Kryten. However, specifying one or more strict or loose hops influences the placement of the LSP. If you want the LSP to follow the path Lister-Cat-Holly-Kryten, this can be accomplished, for example, by specifying Holly as a loose hop.

These are the steps required to configure this LSP:

1. As in the static LSP case described previously, enable the MPLS protocol family on each interface required for MPLS forwarding and list the interfaces to be used for MPLS under the MPLS protocol section of the configuration.

2. Enable RSVP on the required interfaces.

3. On the ingress router, Lister, configure the LSP in the MPLS protocol section of the configuration with a name; the address of the egress point, Kryten; and the address of router Holly as a loose hop. Optionally, a bandwidth reservation can be configured if required.

The protocols section of the configuration on the ingress router, Lister, is as follows. Note that the egress address of the LSP "LtoK" is set to the loopback address of Kryten. The no-cspf statement is used to disable the default CSPF mode of operation. Optionally, a bandwidth reservation can be requested for the LSP, a value of 15 Mbps is chosen in the example:

```
protocols {
    rsvp {
        traceoptions {
            file rsvp;
            flag packets detail;
        }
        interface fe-0/3/1.0 {
            hello-interval 3;
        }
        interface fe-0/3/0.0;
    }
    mpls {
        label-switched-path LtoK {
            to 192.168.50.1;
            primary LtoK-primary;
            bandwidth 15m;
            no-cspf;
        }
        path LtoK-primary {
            192.168.50.2 loose;
        }
        interface fe-0/3/1.0;
        interface fe-0/3/0.0;
```

```
        }
        ospf {
            area 0.0.0.0 {
                interface fe-0/3/0.0 {
                    metric 10;
                }
                interface fe-0/3/1.0 {
                    metric 10;
                }
                interface lo0.0;
            }
        }
    }
```

The protocols section of the configuration of transit router Cat is as follows. Note that a bandwidth limit of 70 Mbps has been set on interface so-0/2/1. This means that the sum of the bandwidth reservations of all the LSPs (whether ingress or transit) that go out of that interface cannot exceed that limit. No bandwidth limit is explicitly configured for interface fe-0/3/0 so the limit for this interface defaults to the link speed (100 Mbps):

```
protocols {
    rsvp {
        interface so-0/2/1.0 {
            bandwidth 70m;
        }
        interface fe-0/3/0.0;
    }
    mpls {
        interface so-0/2/1.0;
        interface fe-0/3/0.0;
    }
    ospf {
        area 0.0.0.0 {
            interface fe-0/3/0.0 {
                metric 10;
            }
            interface so-0/2/1.0 {
                metric 10;
            }
            interface lo0.0;
        }
    }
}
```

The example illustrates that once RSVP and MPLS are enabled on all routers, to set up a particular LSP, only the ingress router needs to be configured with the LSP parameters. This is in contrast to the static LSP example shown earlier in the chapter, where transit nodes also required some configuration.

For networks with a large number of LSPs, it is useful to set the `aggregate` option under the appropriate interfaces in the RSVP section of the configuration. This improves efficiency by bundling RSVP messages together rather than sending them individually.

Note that the hello interval is explicitly set within one of the configurations discussed. This is merely to show where it would appear in the configurations if a nondefault value were required. However, in practice for most cases, the default value is suitable, and hence the parameter does not need to be explicitly set.

RSVP traceoptions can be activated to monitor RSVP traffic. Here is an example of a Path message sent by Lister. Note that the name configured for the LSP is used as the RSVP session name. The configured bandwidth reservation of 15 Mbps can be seen in the Tspec field. Note the configured loose hop of 192.168.50.2 in the SrcRoute field:

```
Jun 20 11:07:59 RSVP send Path 192.168.50.5->192.168.50.1 Len=192 fe-0/3/1.0
Jun 20 11:07:59    Session7 Len 16 192.168.50.1(port/tunnel ID 23) Proto 0
Jun 20 11:07:59    Hop      Len 12 10.0.0.2/0x003351c4
Jun 20 11:07:59    Time     Len  8 30000 ms
Jun 20 11:07:59    Name     Len 12 Prio (7,0) flag 0x0 "LtoK"
Jun 20 11:07:59    Sender7  Len 12 192.168.50.5(port/lsp ID  1)
Jun 20 11:07:59    Tspec    Len 36 rate 15Mbps size 15Mbps peak Infbps m 20 M 1500
Jun 20 11:07:59    ADspec   Len 48
Jun 20 11:07:59    SrcRoute Len 20  10.0.0.1 S 192.168.50.2 L
Jun 20 11:07:59    LabelReq Len  8 EtherType 0x800
Jun 20 11:07:59    RecRoute Len 12  10.0.0.2 S
```

Here is the Resv message received in response to the above Path message. Note that the Resv message contains the MPLS label value (in this case 100000) assigned by the downstream router. Also note the RecRoute field which shows the contents of the RSVP RECORD_ROUTE object:

```
Jun 20 11:07:59 RSVP recv Resv 10.0.0.1->10.0.0.2 Len=136 fe-0/3/1.0
Jun 20 11:07:59    Session7 Len 16 192.168.50.1(port/tunnel ID 23) Proto 0
Jun 20 11:07:59    Hop      Len 12 10.0.0.1/0x003351c4
Jun 20 11:07:59    Time     Len  8 30000 ms
Jun 20 11:07:59    Style    Len  8 FF
Jun 20 11:07:59    Flow     Len 36 rate 15Mbps size 15Mbps peak Infbps m 20 M 1500
Jun 20 11:07:59    Filter7  Len 12 192.168.50.5(port/lsp ID  1)
Jun 20 11:07:59    Label    Len  8  100000
Jun 20 11:07:59    RecRoute Len 28  10.0.0.1 S 10.0.0.17 S 10.0.0.13 S
```

Useful CLI commands are provided to monitor the state of LSPs and the RSVP sessions that under-pin them.

The show mpls lsp command shows the names and states of all LSPs (whether ingress, egress, or transit) on the router. The show mpls lsp extensive version of the command shows the most detail, including the path taken by each LSP, the bandwidth of each LSP, and the history of each LSP, which might include changes to the path over time due to link failures:

```
root@Lister> show mpls lsp extensive
Ingress LSP: 1 sessions

192.168.50.1
  From: 192.168.50.5, State: Up, ActiveRoute: 0, LSPname: LtoK
  ActivePath: LtoK-primary (primary)
  LoadBalance: Random
 *Primary    LtoK-primary     State: Up
    Bandwidth: 15Mbps
    4 Jun 20 11:06:23  Selected as active path
    3 Jun 20 11:06:23  Record Route:  10.0.0.1 S 10.0.0.17 S 10.0.0.13 S
    2 Jun 20 11:06:23  Up
    1 Jun 20 11:06:23  Originate Call
   Created: Wed Jun 20 11:06:23 2001
Total 1 displayed, Up 1, Down 0

Egress LSP: 0 sessions
Total 0 displayed, Up 0, Down 0

Transit LSP: 0 sessions
Total 0 displayed, Up 0, Down 0
```

The show rsvp interfaces command shows details of the bandwidth reservations associated with each interface. The example shown is from Cat. The data associated with interface so-0/2/1.0 shows that the maximum reservable bandwidth is 70 Mbps and that the sum of the current reservations is 15 Mbps. Hence, there is 55 Mbps of available bandwidth. The highwater mark shows the maximum reservation level that has occurred on this interface:

```
root@Cat> show rsvp interface
RSVP interface: 2 active
                    Active                Static     Available    Reserved    Highwater
Interface   State   resv   Subscription   BW         BW           BW          mark
fe-0/3/0.0  Up         0   100%           100Mbps    100Mbps      0bps        0bps
so-0/2/1.0  Up         1   100%           70Mbps     55Mbps       15Mbps      15Mbps
```

The show rsvp statistics command shows how many RSVP messages of each type (hello, Path, Resv, etc.) have been sent and received:

```
root@Kryten> show rsvp statistics
   PacketType              Total                Last 5 seconds
                     Sent      Received      Sent      Received
   Path                 0          20           0           0
   PathErr              0           0           0           0
   PathTear             0           0           0           0
   Resv FF             19           0           0           0
   Resv WF              0           0           0           0
   Resv SE              0           0           0           0
   ResvErr              0           0           0           0
   ResvTear             0           0           0           0
   ResvConf             0           0           0           0
   Hello              251         251           2           2

   Errors                        Total        Last 5 seconds
   Rcv pkt bad length              0                 0
   Rcv pkt unknown type            0                 0
   Rcv pkt bad version             0                 0
   Rcv pkt auth fail               0                 0
   Rcv pkt bad checksum            0                 0
   Rcv pkt bad format              0                 0
   Memory allocation fail          0                 0
   No path information             0                 0
   Resv style conflict             0                 0
   Port conflict                   0                 0
   Resv no interface               0                 0
   PathErr to client               0                 0
   ResvErr to client               0                 0
   Path timeout                    0                 0
```

Shown next is the output of the show RSVP neighbor command. Note that a neighbor is not listed in the output until a corresponding RSVP session occurs, at which point the neighbor is learned. The output of this command from Cat is shown. As can be seen, only neighbor 10.0.0.14 is listed, as this is the only neighbor with which there is, or has been, an RSVP session:

```
root@Cat> show rsvp neighbor
RSVP neighbor: 1 learned
  Address          Idle Up/Dn LastChange HelloInt HelloTx/Rx MsgRcvd MsgType
  10.0.0.14           0  3/2    1:49:24        3   2224/2205     161 Path
```

> **Note**   *At the time of writing, RSVP-signaled LSPs are unidirectional, whether computed using CSPF or not. Therefore, a separate LSP must be configured if one is required in the reverse direction.*

In summary, this section has shown how RSVP-signaled LSPs are set up without the use of CSPF. Compared to static LSPs, the configurational effort is much less and there is more visibility of the state of the LSP. As already discussed, in practice in the majority of cases, RSVP-signaled LSPs are generated with the aid of CSPF. This is described later in more detail in the section entitled "RSVP Signaled LSPs with CSPF."

Route Resolution

Once an LSP has been created, it potentially can be used to forward traffic. This section describes the route resolution process—that is, the process by which an LSP becomes the next-hop for particular routes in the routing table.

Juniper Networks routers, by default, store unicast routes in the inet.0 routing table. However, MPLS routes are stored in a separate table called inet.3. In inet.3, the egress address of each LSP is listed with the LSP itself as the next-hop. By default, only the BGP can make use of the routes listed in inet.3.

As Chapters 12 and 13 describe, the BGP routing process involves identifying the BGP next-hop for a particular route and then identifying the IGP route required to reach the BGP next-hop. If there is an LSP whose egress address is the BGP next-hop, as part of this recursive lookup process, BGP sees that route in inet.3 and uses it in preference to any IGP route in inet.0. This is because, by default, RSVP routes have a lower preference number (are more favored) than IGP routes. In the case that a route in inet.0 has the same preference as a route in inet.3, the tie-breaker rule is that the route in inet.3 wins. As a result, when BGP installs its route in inet.0, it lists the LSP as the next-hop for that route. Therefore, the LSP is used to forward traffic whose BGP next-hop is the egress address of the LSP. In other words, the FEC associated with the LSP is the set of routes whose BGP next-hop is the egress address of the LSP. The relationship between the routing tables and the routing/signaling protocols is illustrated in Figure 14-12.

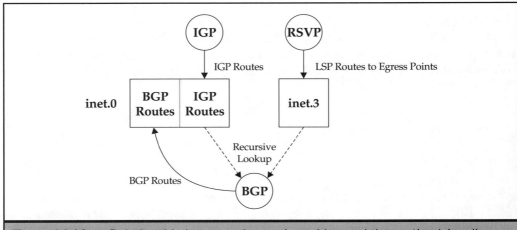

Figure 14-12.   *Relationship between the routing tables and the routing/signaling protocols*

The example network and LSP described in the previous section can be used to illustrate the route resolution process. Figure 14-13 shows an addition to the network in which Kryten has an EBGP peering with router Starbug. Starbug announces the route 10.100.0.0/16 to Kryten. Kryten, in turn, announces the route to Lister over the IBGP peering, setting the BGP next-hop to its own loopback address 192.168.50.1.

Examination of inet.3 on Lister shows the loopback address of Kryten with the LSP as the next-hop. Note the preference value of 7 associated with the route:

```
root@Lister> show route 192.168.50.1 table inet.3

inet.3: 1 destinations, 1 routes (1 active, 0 holddown, 0 hidden)
+ = Active Route, - = Last Active, * = Both

192.168.50.1/32    *[RSVP/7] 01:54:43, metric 20, metric2 0
                    > to 10.0.0.1 via fe-0/3/1.0, label-switched-path LtoK
```

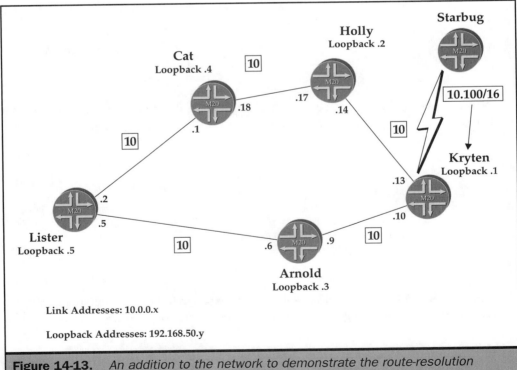

Figure 14-13. *An addition to the network to demonstrate the route-resolution process*

Examination of inet.0 on the same router shows the loopback address of Kryten listed as a plain OSPF route. Note the preference value of *10* associated with the route.

```
root@Lister> show route 192.168.50.1 table inet.0

inet.0: 17 destinations, 17 routes (16 active, 0 holddown, 1 hidden)
+ = Active Route, - = Last Active, * = Both

192.168.50.1/32    *[OSPF/10] 00:10:13, metric 20
                   > via fe-0/3/0.0
```

When the BGP process on Lister carries out the recursive lookup for the route 10.100.0.0, it selects the route to the BGP next-hop 192.168.50.1 in inet.3 rather than the one in inet.0, because the one in inet.3 has the lower (more favorable) preference value. As a result, the LSP appears against the route entry for 10.100.0.0 installed by BGP in inet.0:

```
root@Lister> show route 10.100

inet.0: 17 destinations, 17 routes (16 active, 0 holddown, 1 hidden)
+ = Active Route, - = Last Active, * = Both

10.100.0.0/16      *[BGP/170] 00:20:37, localpref 100, from 192.168.50.1
                     AS path: 65001 I
                   > to 10.0.0.1 via fe-0/3/1.0, label-switched-path LtoK
```

A traceroute can be used to confirm that traffic to destinations encompassed by that route uses the LSP:

```
root@Lister> traceroute 10.100.0.1
traceroute to 10.100.0.1 (10.100.0.1), 30 hops max, 40 byte packets
 1  10.0.0.1 (10.0.0.1)  0.915 ms  0.722 ms  0.655 ms
     MPLS Label=100000 CoS=0 TTL=1 S=1
 2  10.0.0.17 (10.0.0.17)  0.754 ms  0.681 ms  0.666 ms
     MPLS Label=100003 CoS=0 TTL=1 S=1
 3  10.0.0.13 (10.0.0.13)  0.584 ms  0.536 ms  0.538 ms
etc
```

Note that if a network operator deliberately wishes to hide the topology of an MPLS network, the following command can be set on each desired LSP:

```
root@Lister# set label-switched-path <LSP name> no-decrement-ttl
```

This command works only if all the routers in the path are Juniper Networks routers. Alternatively, the following interoperable command can be invoked at the global MPLS level on each router in the path:

```
root@Lister# set protocols mpls no-propagate-ttl
```

To summarize this section, the default route-resolution behavior is that only BGP traffic can make use of an LSP, and the LSP is used only if the egress address is the *same* as the BGP next-hop address. Note that if an LSP goes only part way to the BGP next-hop, traffic to that next-hop will not use the LSP. This means that if Kryten had not set the BGP next-hop for the route 10.100/16 to self, the LSP from Lister to Kryten would not have been used to reach that destination. However, there are ways of modifying this default route resolution behavior. These will be described later in the section entitled "Advanced Route Resolution."

RSVP Signaled LSPs with CSPF

This section describes how RSVP-signaled LSPs are set up with the aid of CSPF, which is the default mode of operation for RSVP-signaled LSPs. CSPF is an algorithm that calculates the full path of an LSP at the ingress router based on *constraints* set by the user and knowledge of the state of the links within the domain and their current attributes.

A constraint is a parameter that influences the placement of an LSP. An example is the bandwidth reservation required by the LSP. CSPF calculates a path that includes only links that have the required bandwidth available to reserve. As will be shown in this section, the use of CSPF provides additional methods for influencing the path to be taken by an LSP.

Knowledge of the state of links in the network and their current attributes is provided by traffic engineering extensions to OSPF[8] or IS-IS.[9] These extensions carry information about link coloring and available and maximum bandwidth. The information allows each router in the domain to build up a database (the *traffic engineering database,* or *TED*) that contains the traffic engineering (TE) information pertaining to each link in the network. This information allows the CSPF process on the ingress router to calculate the path to be taken by the LSP. The result of the CSPF calculation is a path vector that that specifies the entire path to be followed by the LSP. This path vector is input to the ERO of the RSVP path message as a series of strict hops.

The relationship among CSPF, the extended IGP, the TED, and RSVP is illustrated in Figure 14-14. The following sections describe the IGP extensions and the CSPF algorithm in more detail.

---

[8] Dave Katz, Derek Yeung, and Kireeti Kompella, "Traffic Engineering Extensions to OSPF," Work in Progress.

[9] Tony Li and Henk Smit, "IS-IS Extensions for Traffic Engineering," Work in Progress.

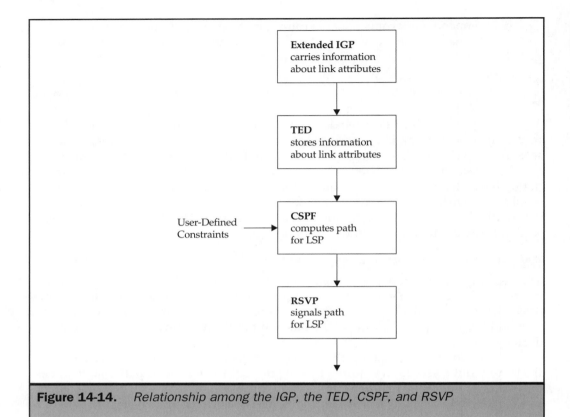

Figure 14-14.   *Relationship among the IGP, the TED, CSPF, and RSVP*

Traffic Engineering Extensions for the IGP   As described in previous chapters, the purpose of the IGPs, namely OSPF and IS-IS, is to allow each router to acquire knowledge of the topology of the area(s) of which it is a member and the metrics of all the links within the area. The capabilities of OSPF and IS-IS could be extended to allow them to carry information about traffic engineering-related attributes. In OSPF, this is provided by an opaque LSA, the type 10 LSA. In IS-IS, this is provided by an extended IS reachability TLV type 22. In either case, there is a sub-TLV for each of the following attributes:

- **Local interface IP address (4 octets)**
- **Remote interface IP address (4 octets)**
- **Traffic engineering metric**
- **Maximum bandwidth (4 octets)**   The actual bandwidth of the link.
- **Maximum reservable bandwidth (4 octets)**   The maximum total bandwidth that can be reserved on the link. The value can be greater than the maximum bandwidth parameter if oversubscription is in use.

- **Unreserved bandwidth (32 octets)** The amount of bandwidth available for reservation at each of the eight different *priority levels* (discussed in the following section, "Constrained Shortest Path First").

- **Administrative group (color) (4 octets)** An interface can belong to any combination or none of the 32 administrative groups (colors). The membership is expressed in the form of a bit vector.

Each router that participates in traffic engineering stores the information received in the TED, which is separate from the normal IGP database. It may be the case that the topology described in the TED differs from that in the normal IGP database because traffic engineering may not be activated on all routers and links.

Note that with both IS-IS and OSPF, the scope of the traffic-engineering extensions is within one IS-IS or OSPF area. Because CSPF needs knowledge of the link attributes to calculate a path for an LSP, the LSP must be contained entirely within a single IS-IS or OSPF area. A router belonging to multiple IGP areas has a separate TED for each area and can create LSPs in each area as long as they do not cross the area boundary.

Constrained Shortest Path First   CSPF is the algorithm that enables the ingress router to calculate the path to be taken by an LSP, taking into account constraints determined by the network administration. It is a modified form of the Shortest Path First (SPF) algorithm used by the normal link state IGPs.

The constraints that can be applied to an LSP are

- Bandwidth
- Maximum hop count
- Strict and/or loose hops
- Administrative group (color)

The bandwidth is reserved for the LSP on all links that it traverses. Note that, at the time of writing, this does not mean that the actual traffic traveling along the LSP is limited to that value. Rather, the bandwidth parameter is used as a form of admission control when it comes to the placement of LSPs, because the CSPF algorithm will discount links that it knows (from the TED) have insufficient bandwidth for the LSP in question. For example, the bandwidth of each LSP can be set to one tenth of the bandwidth of the link speed used in the network, so that not more than 10 LSPs share a particular link.

Another example is shown in Figure 14-15. Suppose that all the links in the network have a maximum reservable bandwidth of 2.5 Gbps, all LSPs have the same priority, and LSPs X and Y already exist as shown, each with a reservation of 1 Gbps. If you want to set up a new LSP, LSP Z, between nodes A and F, having a bandwidth of 1 Gbps, CSPF knows from the TED that link C–E cannot be used, so it calculates a path that avoids that link. This behavior is different from the `no-cspf` case. In the `no-cspf` case, if the path of an LSP, as determined hop-by-hop by the IGP and any configured strict and loose hops, passes over a link with insufficient bandwidth, the LSP fails.

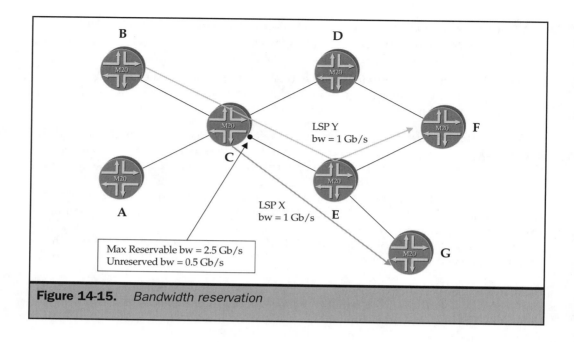

Figure 14-15. *Bandwidth reservation*

Bandwidth can be reserved at one of eight priority levels, 0 being the highest and 7 the lowest. Note that the discussion in the preceding paragraph assumed that all LSPs have the same priority. An LSP has a setup priority and a hold priority. If a bandwidth reservation associated with a new LSP causes an interface in the network to exceed the maximum reservable bandwidth for the interface, the reservation associated with the new LSP can *preempt* existing reservations if those reservations' hold-priority is lower than the set-up priority of the new LSP. As a result, LSP(s) having the lower priority are torn down as required to accommodate the higher priority reservation.

Returning to Figure 14-15, if the newly created LSP Z has a higher setup priority than the hold priority of LSP X or LSP Y, one of the latter LSPs would be torn down to accommodate LSP Z. The hold priority must be greater than or equal to the setup priority to avoid preemption loops. Note that the default setup and hold priorities are such that preemption can never occur.

Maximum hop count is the maximum number of hops that the network administration wishes the LSP to have. This is useful for situations in which it is preferred that the LSP setup fail, rather than have the LSP follow a circuitous path.

Strict and/or *loose hops* specify the transit routers through which an LSP can pass. These have the same meaning as in the non-CSPF case. Naming a particular router as a strict hop implies that it must be directly attached to the ingress router (if it is the first one named) or it must be attached to the router that precedes it in the list of hops. Naming a particular router as a loose hop means that other routers may be located between it and the previous router in the list.

An LSP can be configured such that it uses only links that have a particular color or at least one of a specified set of colors; this is called the *administrative group (color)*. An LSP can also be configured never to use links that have particular colors associated with them. Colors are a key component of traffic engineering as they allow control of LSP placement in a generic way without having to name specific transit routers within the path. For example, links within the network that tend to suffer from congestion can be assigned a particular color, and some LSPs can be configured to avoid those links. Figure 14-16 shows an example network and assigned link colors. An LSP might be requested from A to G with the constraint that it should exclude red links, in which case it would follow the path A-C-D-E-G. Alternatively, it might be configured to use only links that are colored blue or green, in which case it would follow the path A-C-D-F-G.

Note that it is the ingress router that calculates the entire path to be taken by the LSP. Only the ingress router has knowledge of the constraints set by the network administrator (through configuration), and it has all the information it requires about the state of the links in the domain through the traffic engineering database. This is unlike the case when CSPF is not used, in which the path is determined on a hop-by-hop basis by the IGP.

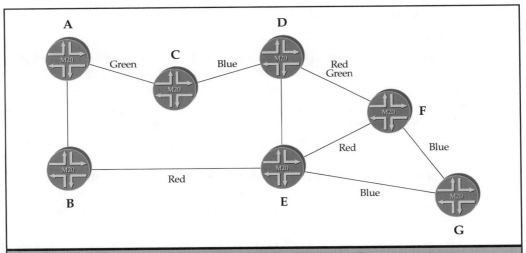

Figure 14-16.   *Network showing assigned administrative groups (colors)*

The CSPF algorithm works as follows:

1. If the LSP has an associated bandwidth requirement, the TED is pruned of all links that have insufficient reservable bandwidth at that priority level.

2. If the LSP is required to include links having a particular color(s), the TED is pruned of all links that do not have at least one of those colors. This means that links having no color are also pruned, so in Figure 14-16 the path A–C–D–E–G would not be valid if the LSP is required to include blue or green.

3. If the LSP is required to exclude links having a particular color(s), the TED is pruned of all links having at least one of those colors (links having no color are not pruned).

4. The shortest path to the egress point that uses the remaining links is found. If the LSP has strict or loose nodes specified, separate shortest path calculations are carried out between the nodes.

Figure 14-17 shows an example network in which an LSP is required from Rome to Ipswich such that it avoids the link London-Ipswich, which is congested. One way of achieving this is to apply a particular administrative group (color) to the interfaces on that link and to configure the LSP to exclude links having that color. The following configurational steps are required to achieve this:

1. Enable the MPLS protocol family on each interface required for MPLS forwarding, and list the interfaces to be used for MPLS under the MPLS protocol section of the configuration.

2. Enable RSVP on the required interfaces.

3. Activate traffic-engineering extensions for the IGP on each router. In the IS-IS case, these are enabled by default. In the OSPF case, these must be explicitly activated using the traffic-engineering option under the protocols ospf section.

4. On each router, define the administrative groups (colors) that are in use in the network and apply administrative groups to interfaces as required. In the example, the interfaces on the link between Ipswich and London are given the color red.

5. On the ingress router, Rome, configure the LSP in the protocols mpls section of the configuration with a name and the address of the egress point, Ipswich. Optionally, a bandwidth reservation can be configured if required. The LSP is configured to exclude links with the color red.

The protocols section of the configuration of router Rome follows, assuming a bandwidth reservation of 50 Mbps for the LSP. Optionally, the priority for the LSP can be set. The first number in the priority entry is the setup priority. This controls the order in which LSPs having their ingress at this router are set up and the likelihood of this LSP preempting existing LSPs if required. The second number is the hold priority,

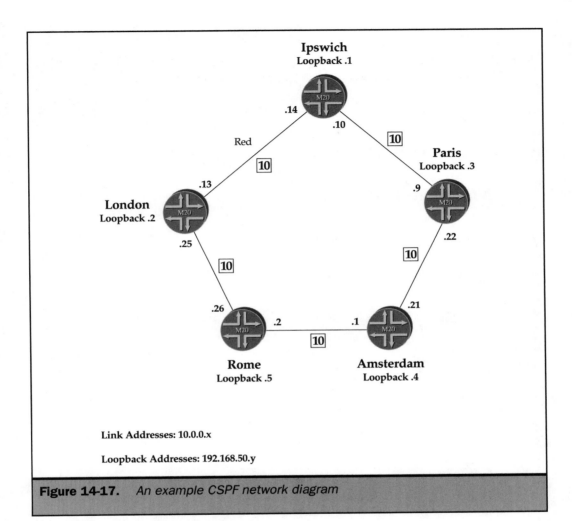

Ipswich
Loopback .1

.14

.10

Red

London
Loopback .2

.13

.25

Paris
Loopback .3

.9

.22

.26

.2   .1

.21

Rome
Loopback .5

Amsterdam
Loopback .4

Link Addresses: 10.0.0.x

Loopback Addresses: 192.168.50.y

Figure 14-17.   *An example CSPF network diagram*

which determines the priority level at which the bandwidth reservation is made and hence determines the likelihood of the reservation being preempted. Both the setup and the hold priority are set to a medium level of 3 in the example. In the admin-groups section, each required admin-group (color) is given a name and mapped to a number between 0 and 31:

```
protocols {
    rsvp {
        interface fe-0/3/1.0;
```

```
            interface so-0/2/0.0;
        }
    mpls {
        admin-groups {
            red 0;
        }
        label-switched-path Ro-Ip {
            to 192.168.50.1;
            bandwidth 50m;
            priority 3 3;
            admin-group {
                exclude red;
            }
        }
        interface fe-0/3/1.0;
        interface so-0/2/0.0;
    }
    ospf {
        traffic-engineering;
        area 0.0.0.0 {
            interface so-0/2/0.0 {
                metric 10;
            }
            interface fe-0/3/1.0 {
                metric 10;
            }
            interface lo0.0;
        }
    }
}
```

The protocols section of the configuration of router London is as follows. Note that interface fe-0/3/0.0 is configured as a member of admin-group red, which means that the LSP configured on router Rome cannot exit that interface:

```
rsvp {
    interface so-0/2/2.0 {
        bandwidth 80m;
    }
    interface fe-0/3/0.0;
}
```

```
mpls {
    admin-groups {
        red 0;
    }
    interface so-0/2/2.0;
    interface fe-0/3/0.0 {
        admin-group red;
    }
}
ospf {
    traffic-engineering;
    area 0.0.0.0 {
        interface fe-0/3/0.0 {
            metric 10;
        }
        interface so-0/2/2.0 {
            metric 10;
        }
        interface lo0.0;
    }
}
```

The show mpls lsp extensive command can be used to examine the state of the LSP and its history. Note that the ERO computed by CSPF is shown. As expected, the record route field confirms that this is the actual path taken by the LSP:

```
root@Rome> show mpls lsp extensive
Ingress LSP: 1 sessions

192.168.50.1
  From: 192.168.50.5, State: Up, ActiveRoute: 1, LSPname: Ro-Ip
  ActivePath:  (primary)
  LoadBalance: Random
  Exclude: red
 *Primary                    State: Up
    Priorities: 3 3
    Bandwidth: 50Mbps
    Computed ERO (S [L] denotes strict [loose] hops): (CSPF metric: 30)
             10.0.0.1 S        10.0.0.22 S        10.0.0.10 S
    5 Jul  5 13:25:14  Selected as active path
    4 Jul  5 13:25:14  Record Route:  10.0.0.1 S 10.0.0.22 S 10.0.0.10 S
    3 Jul  5 13:25:14  Up
    2 Jul  5 13:25:14  Originate Call
```

```
    1 Jul  5 13:25:14  CSPF: computation result accepted
    Created: Thu Jul  5 13:25:14 2001
Total 1 displayed, Up 1, Down 0

Egress LSP: 0 sessions
Total 0 displayed, Up 0, Down 0

Transit LSP: 0 sessions
Total 0 displayed, Up 0, Down 0
```

The show ospf database command shows the opaque LSAs that are generated by each router. An opaque LSA is generated for each OSPF interface:

```
root@Rome> show ospf database

    OSPF link state database, area 0.0.0.0
  Type        ID               Adv Rtr          Seq         Age   Opt  Cksum   Len
  Router      192.168.50.1     192.168.50.1     0x80000013  1278  0x2  0x77b8   72
  Router      192.168.50.2     192.168.50.2     0x80000016   770  0x2  0xe81f   72
  Router      192.168.50.3     192.168.50.3     0x80000017  1039  0x2  0x79e9   84
  Router      192.168.50.4     192.168.50.4     0x8000001d    73  0x2  0x2cf0   72
  Router     *192.168.50.5     192.168.50.5     0x8000001f   696  0x2  0x917d   72
  Network    *10.0.0.2         192.168.50.5     0x80000009   996  0x2  0xb4b3   32
  Network     10.0.0.13        192.168.50.1     0x80000009    78  0x2  0x1a4d   32
  OpaqArea 1.0.0.1             192.168.50.1     0x80000003   978  0x2  0xf023   28
  OpaqArea 1.0.0.1             192.168.50.2     0x80000004   470  0x2  0xf21e   28
  OpaqArea 1.0.0.1             192.168.50.3     0x80000005   739  0x2  0xf419   28
  OpaqArea 1.0.0.1             192.168.50.4     0x80000004   973  0x2  0xfa12   28
  OpaqArea*1.0.0.1             192.168.50.5     0x80000009   396  0x2  0xf411   28
  OpaqArea 1.0.0.2             192.168.50.1     0x80000004   678  0x2  0x9e9b  124
  OpaqArea 1.0.0.2             192.168.50.2     0x80000005   170  0x2  0xc273  124
  OpaqArea 1.0.0.2             192.168.50.3     0x80000007   439  0x2  0x72e1  124
  OpaqArea 1.0.0.2             192.168.50.4     0x80000006   373  0x2  0x1940  124
  OpaqArea*1.0.0.2             192.168.50.5     0x80000010    96  0x2  0x537b  124
  OpaqArea 1.0.0.3             192.168.50.1     0x80000004   378  0x2  0xfad   124
  OpaqArea 1.0.0.3             192.168.50.2     0x80000004  1070  0x2  0xb003  124
  OpaqArea 1.0.0.3             192.168.50.3     0x80000006   139  0x2  0x911b  124
  OpaqArea 1.0.0.3             192.168.50.4     0x80000007   673  0x2  0xcf67  124
  OpaqArea*1.0.0.3             192.168.50.5     0x8000000e  1572  0x2  0x7624  124
```

Here is the detailed version of the opaque LSA generated by router London corresponding to interface fe-0/3/0. Note the value of *1* against the color entry. Membership of administrative groups is expressed as a bit vector having bits numbered from 0 to 31, and the color entry expresses that value in decimals. The interface is configured with the admin-group red, which was mapped to bit 0 in the configurations, hence the value of *1* is seen:

```
OpaqArea 1.0.0.2            192.168.50.2      0x80000005   204  0x2  0xc273 124
   Area-opaque TE LSA
   Link (2), length 100:
     Linktype (1), length 1:
       2
     LinkID (2), length 4:
       10.0.0.13
     LocIfAdr (3), length 4:
       10.0.0.14
     RemIfAdr (4), length 4:
       0.0.0.0
     TEMetric (5), length 4:
       10
     MaxBW (6), length 4:
       100Mbps
     MaxRsvBW (7), length 4:
       100Mbps
     UnRsvBW (8), length 32:
         Priority 0, 100Mbps
         Priority 1, 100Mbps
         Priority 2, 100Mbps
         Priority 3, 100Mbps
         Priority 4, 100Mbps
         Priority 5, 100Mbps
         Priority 6, 100Mbps
         Priority 7, 100Mbps
     Color (9), length 4:
       1
```

This is the opaque LSA corresponding to interface so-0/2/0 on router Paris. Note that as a result of the LSP crossing that interface, the bandwidth at the corresponding hold-priority level (3) and below has been decremented, because 50 Mbps of bandwidth is now unavailable for reservation by LSPs having a priority number of 3 or more. Because each router has a copy of this LSA, all routers are aware of the current bandwidth availability at this interface:

```
OpaqArea 1.0.0.2            192.168.50.3      0x80000007   473  0x2  0x72e1 124
   Area-opaque TE LSA
   Link (2), length 100:
     Linktype (1), length 1:
       1
     LinkID (2), length 4:
       192.168.50.1
     LocIfAdr (3), length 4:
       10.0.0.9
     RemIfAdr (4), length 4:
```

```
      10.0.0.10
    TEMetric (5), length 4:
      10
    MaxBW (6), length 4:
      155Mbps
    MaxRsvBW (7), length 4:
      155Mbps
    UnRsvBW (8), length 32:
        Priority 0, 155Mbps
        Priority 1, 155Mbps
        Priority 2, 155Mbps
        Priority 3, 105Mbps
        Priority 4, 105Mbps
        Priority 5, 105Mbps
        Priority 6, 105Mbps
        Priority 7, 105Mbps
    Color (9), length 4:
      0
```

As discussed, the information carried by the opaque LSAs is used to populate the TED. Here are the contents of the TED as displayed by router Rome. The TED is easier to read than the opaque LSAs themselves because colors are referred to by name rather than by number:

```
root@Rome> show ted database extensive

TED database: 0 ISIS nodes 7 INET nodes
NodeID: 192.168.50.1
  Type: Rtr, Age: 4378 secs, LinkIn: 2, LinkOut: 2
  Protocol: OSPF(0.0.0.0)
    To: 10.0.0.13-1, Local: 10.0.0.13, Remote: 0.0.0.0
      Color: 0x1 red
      Metric: 10
      Static BW: 100Mbps
      Reservable BW: 100Mbps
      Available BW [priority] bps:
        [0] 100Mbps     [1] 100Mbps     [2] 100Mbps     [3] 100Mbps
        [4] 100Mbps     [5] 100Mbps     [6] 100Mbps     [7] 100Mbps
    To: 192.168.50.3, Local: 10.0.0.10, Remote: 10.0.0.9
      Color: 0 <none>
      Metric: 10
      Static BW: 155Mbps
      Reservable BW: 155Mbps
      Available BW [priority] bps:
        [0] 155Mbps     [1] 155Mbps     [2] 155Mbps     [3] 155Mbps
        [4] 155Mbps     [5] 155Mbps     [6] 155Mbps     [7] 155Mbps
```

```
NodeID: 10.0.0.2-1
  Type: Net, Age: 4378 secs, LinkIn: 2, LinkOut: 2
  Protocol: OSPF(0.0.0.0)
    To: 192.168.50.5, Local: 0.0.0.0, Remote: 0.0.0.0
      Metric: 0
    To: 192.168.50.4, Local: 0.0.0.0, Remote: 0.0.0.0
      Metric: 0
NodeID: 192.168.50.2
  Type: Rtr, Age: 103 secs, LinkIn: 2, LinkOut: 2
  Protocol: OSPF(0.0.0.0)
    To: 192.168.50.5, Local: 10.0.0.25, Remote: 10.0.0.26
      Color: 0 <none>
      Metric: 10
      Static BW: 155Mbps
      Reservable BW: 80Mbps
      Available BW [priority] bps:
        [0] 80Mbps      [1] 80Mbps      [2] 80Mbps      [3] 80Mbps
        [4] 80Mbps      [5] 80Mbps      [6] 80Mbps      [7] 80Mbps
    To: 10.0.0.13-1, Local: 10.0.0.14, Remote: 0.0.0.0
      Color: 0x1 red
      Metric: 10
      Static BW: 100Mbps
      Reservable BW: 100Mbps
      Available BW [priority] bps:
        [0] 100Mbps     [1] 100Mbps     [2] 100Mbps     [3] 100Mbps
        [4] 100Mbps     [5] 100Mbps     [6] 100Mbps     [7] 100Mbps
NodeID: 192.168.50.3
  Type: Rtr, Age: 2470 secs, LinkIn: 2, LinkOut: 2
  Protocol: OSPF(0.0.0.0)
    To: 192.168.50.4, Local: 10.0.0.22, Remote: 10.0.0.21
      Color: 0 <none>
      Metric: 10
      Static BW: 155Mbps
      Reservable BW: 155Mbps
      Available BW [priority] bps:
        [0] 155Mbps     [1] 155Mbps     [2] 155Mbps     [3] 155Mbps
        [4] 155Mbps     [5] 155Mbps     [6] 155Mbps     [7] 155Mbps
    To: 192.168.50.1, Local: 10.0.0.9, Remote: 10.0.0.10
      Color: 0 <none>
      Metric: 10
      Static BW: 155Mbps
      Reservable BW: 155Mbps
      Available BW [priority] bps:
        [0] 155Mbps     [1] 155Mbps     [2] 155Mbps     [3] 105Mbps
        [4] 105Mbps     [5] 105Mbps     [6] 105Mbps     [7] 105Mbps
NodeID: 192.168.50.4
  Type: Rtr, Age: 2472 secs, LinkIn: 2, LinkOut: 2
```

```
  Protocol: OSPF(0.0.0.0)
    To: 10.0.0.2-1, Local: 10.0.0.1, Remote: 0.0.0.0
      Color: 0 <none>
      Metric: 10
      Static BW: 100Mbps
      Reservable BW: 100Mbps
      Available BW [priority] bps:
        [0] 100Mbps     [1] 100Mbps     [2] 100Mbps     [3] 100Mbps
        [4] 100Mbps     [5] 100Mbps     [6] 100Mbps     [7] 100Mbps
    To: 192.168.50.3, Local: 10.0.0.21, Remote: 10.0.0.22
      Color: 0 <none>
      Metric: 10
      Static BW: 155Mbps
      Reservable BW: 155Mbps
      Available BW [priority] bps:
        [0] 155Mbps     [1] 155Mbps     [2] 155Mbps     [3] 105Mbps
        [4] 105Mbps     [5] 105Mbps     [6] 105Mbps     [7] 105Mbps
NodeID: 192.168.50.5
  Type: Rtr, Age: 2475 secs, LinkIn: 2, LinkOut: 2
  Protocol: OSPF(0.0.0.0)
    To: 10.0.0.2-1, Local: 10.0.0.2, Remote: 0.0.0.0
      Color: 0 <none>
      Metric: 10
      Static BW: 100Mbps
      Reservable BW: 100Mbps
      Available BW [priority] bps:
        [0] 100Mbps     [1] 100Mbps     [2] 100Mbps     [3] 50Mbps
        [4] 50Mbps      [5] 50Mbps      [6] 50Mbps      [7] 50Mbps
    To: 192.168.50.2, Local: 10.0.0.26, Remote: 10.0.0.25
      Color: 0 <none>
      Metric: 10
      Static BW: 155Mbps
      Reservable BW: 155Mbps
      Available BW [priority] bps:
        [0] 155Mbps     [1] 155Mbps     [2] 155Mbps     [3] 155Mbps
        [4] 155Mbps     [5] 155Mbps     [6] 155Mbps     [7] 155Mbps
NodeID: 10.0.0.13-1
  Type: Net, Age: 4378 secs, LinkIn: 2, LinkOut: 2
  Protocol: OSPF(0.0.0.0)
    To: 192.168.50.1, Local: 0.0.0.0, Remote: 0.0.0.0
      Metric: 0
    To: 192.168.50.2, Local: 0.0.0.0, Remote: 0.0.0.0
      Metric: 0
```

In addition to these commands, the RSVP diagnostic and tracing commands demonstrated in the section entitled "RSVP Signaled LSPs without CSPF" can be used.

Optimization   Note that, by default, once an LSP whose path has been calculated using CSPF is up, its path does not change unless an event such as a link failure along the path triggers a recalculation. Returning to the example shown in Figure 14-17, this means that if a new link were to come into service directly between A and D having a lower IGP metric than the sum of the metrics via B and C, the LSP would not automatically move to the new link. However, there are two ways of forcing a CSPF recalculation so as to optimize the path of the LSP. The first is to request a one-off recalculation from the command line for the LSP in question using the following command:

```
root@Rome> clear mpls lsp name Ro-Ip optimize
```

The second way is to permanently configure the `optimize` option on the LSP. This causes a CSPF recalculation to occur at intervals defined by the optimization timer. In the example below, the timer is set to 3600 seconds:

```
label-switched-path Ro-Ip {
    to 192.168.50.1;
    primary Ro-Ip-primary {
        admin-group {
            exclude red;
        }
    }
    secondary Ro-Ip-secondary {
        standby;
    }
    bandwidth 50m;
    optimize-timer 3600;
    priority 3 3;
}
```

The choice of optimization interval is a trade-off between having the potential for excessive "churn" in the placement of LSPs if the interval is too short and the network topology is changing and not being able to take timely advantage of a more optimal path if the interval is too long. In many cases, an interval of several hours is a good compromise.

Traffic Protection

Two mechanisms are available to protect traffic on an LSP if the LSP should fail while in use, for example due to the failure of a transmission link. The two mechanisms are *fast reroute* and *secondary paths*.

Several events occur when these traffic protection mechanisms are not in use.

1. When an RSVP-signaled LSP fails due to a link failure, the ingress router receives an RSVP error message, such as a ResvTear message.

2. As a result, the ingress router attempts to calculate a new path for the LSP, taking into account any constraints that are configured for the LSP.

3. If it is not possible to calculate a new path, due to a lack of available links that fulfill the constraints, further attempts are made to calculate a path at intervals of time governed by the retry timer, the default value of which is 30 seconds.

4. It is also possible to configure a retry limit. Once the number of attempts reaches that limit, no further attempts are made to reestablish the path.

5. A failed LSP is removed from the routing table so that traffic does not use it.

6. In that case, in the absence of any other LSPs that could be valid next-hops for the traffic, normal IP forwarding occurs and the traffic follows the path dictated by the IGP.

Two complimentary approaches to traffic protection are available in JUNOS software to increase the likelihood of an LSP recovering from a network failure. The first approach is to allow alternative (secondary) paths from ingress to egress to be preconfigured for an LSP. One of these can potentially take over if the main (primary) path fails. The second approach is to provide a mechanism called *fast reroute* for a temporary local detour to be created around the point of failure in the path of an LSP. The two mechanisms can be configured on the same LSP or each can be used separately if required. The following sections describe these mechanisms in more detail.

Primary and Secondary Paths

An RSVP-signaled LSP can be configured with multiple paths. The primary path is the preferred path and is used whenever possible, given the constraints associated with the path and the current state of the links within the network. One or more secondary paths can be configured for the LSP. If the primary path fails, one of the secondary paths can be used instead. If multiple secondary paths exist, these are tried in the order that they appear in the configuration. A secondary path can be configured with different constraints to the primary. The network administrator may choose to configure the secondary with a more relaxed set of constraints than the primary to increase the probability of it succeeding when the primary fails. The discussion that follows assumes that there is one secondary path in addition to the primary path.

For a secondary path to be useful, it should, as far as possible, avoid links and transit routers used by the primary path. In the case of paths computed using CSPF, this is achieved automatically (where possible, given the topology) by a modification to the CSPF algorithm when computing the secondary path. In the computation, links that are used by the primary path are given an artificially high metric when the secondary path is computed so that the secondary path tends to avoid them. Note, however, that when the primary path is calculated, no account is taken of the fact that a secondary is required, so for certain network topologies and link metrics, it may be the case that the secondary cannot completely avoid the primary.

This is illustrated in Figure 14-18. An LSP having primary and secondary paths is required between A and D. Given the metrics shown, CSPF calculates a path A–F–C–D for the primary path. As a result, when the secondary path is calculated, it cannot avoid partially overlapping the primary path. In this situation, it may be advisable to rethink the link metrics or to use appropriate constraints to make it less likely that primary and secondary paths coincide. For cases in which CSPF is not used, it is necessary to ensure that the primary and secondary follow different paths through appropriate configuration, for example by configuring different strict or loose hops for each.

A secondary path can be used in two ways. By default, the ingress router signals for the secondary path to be set up only when the primary path fails. This means an inevitable delay occurs before the secondary can be used, which corresponds to the period of time taken for the RSVP signaling process to occur. Alternatively, the secondary path can be configured in a hot-standby mode. In this case, the secondary path is signaled even when the primary is up. This means that the ingress router can begin to make use of the secondary path as soon as it is aware that the primary path has failed. Although extra signaling overhead is associated with maintaining the path state when using the standby mode, it is sometimes considered worthwhile to use because of the faster fail-over advantages.

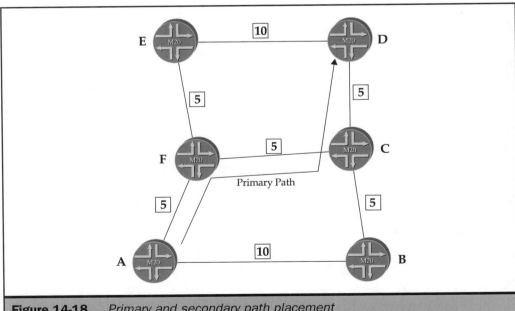

Figure 14-18. *Primary and secondary path placement*

While the secondary path is in use, the ingress router attempts to re-establish the primary at intervals defined by the retry timer. If successful, after a period of time, the primary is used for traffic again. Note that the path taken by the primary may not necessarily be the same as the original path (for example, if the original failure has not been rectified) and could in fact be the same as the path taken by the secondary, subject to the configured constraints. Even if subsequently the original failure is repaired and the optimum path for the primary is through the failure point, the primary does not reroute through that point if it has already become established via some other path, unless the optimize option if configured on the LSP or if a one-off optimization is requested from the CLI.

The network shown in Figure 14-17 illustrates the use of primary and secondary paths. Assume that, as before, the network administrator wishes to create an LSP between Rome and Ipswich that avoids the link between Ipswich and London. However, the administrator is prepared to allow the LSP to use that link if it is the only way to reach Ipswich as a result of link failures elsewhere. This can be accomplished by defining a primary path for the LSP with the constraint that it must avoid links belonging to the red administrative group and defining a secondary LSP that has no constraints.

The MPLS section of the configuration on router Rome required to achieve this follows. Note that under the LSP part of the configuration, primary and secondary paths are defined, each of which can have different constraints. Note that the standby option is used on the secondary path:

```
mpls {
    admin-groups {
        red 0;
    }
    label-switched-path Ro-Ip {
        to 192.168.50.1;
        primary Ro-Ip-primary {
            admin-group {
                exclude red;
            }
        }
        secondary Ro-Ip-secondary {
            standby;
        }
        bandwidth 50m;
        priority 3 3;
    }
    path Ro-Ip-primary;
    path Ro-Ip-secondary;
    interface fe-0/3/1.0;
    interface so-0/2/0.0;
}
```

The output below shows the state of the LSP when all the links shown in Figure 14-17 are up. Note that both primary and secondary paths are shown. You can see that the primary path follows the path Rome–Amsterdam–Paris–Ipswich and that the secondary path follows the path Rome–London–Ipswich. The primary path is named in the ActivePath section, and the asterisk (*) symbol shows that the primary path is the active path.

```
root@Rome> show mpls lsp extensive
Ingress LSP: 1 sessions

192.168.50.1
  From: 192.168.50.5, State: Up, ActiveRoute: 1, LSPname: Ro-Ip
  ActivePath: Ro-Ip-primary (primary)
  LoadBalance: Random
 *Primary    Ro-Ip-primary    State: Up
    Priorities: 3 3
    Bandwidth: 50Mbps
    Exclude: red
    Computed ERO (S [L] denotes strict [loose] hops): (CSPF metric: 30)
            10.0.0.1 S        10.0.0.22 S        10.0.0.10 S
  Standby    Ro-Ip-secondary  State: Up
    Priorities: 3 3
    Bandwidth: 50Mbps
    Computed ERO (S [L] denotes strict [loose] hops): (CSPF metric: 20)
            10.0.0.25 S       10.0.0.13 S
    Created: Fri Jul  6 11:44:42 2001
Total 1 displayed, Up 1, Down 0
```

The following shows an excerpt from the RSVP log on Rome when the link between Paris and Ipswich goes down. As you can see, a ResvTear message (originating at Paris) arrives at Rome:

```
Jul  6 13:36:37 RSVP recv ResvTear 10.0.0.1->10.0.0.2 Len=56 fe-0/3/1.0
```

As a result, the primary path is declared down and the secondary path takes over as the active path, as shown by this excerpt from the MPLS log on Rome:

```
root@Rome> show log mpls
Jul  6 13:36:37 mpls lsp Ro-Ip primary Down
Jul  6 13:36:37 mpls lsp Ro-Ip primary Deselected as active
Jul  6 13:36:37 mpls lsp Ro-Ip secondary Ro-Ip-secondary Selected as active path
Jul  6 13:36:37 MPLS lsp Ro-Ip switch from primary(Ro-Ip-primary) to secondary(Ro-Ip-secondary),
 Route  10.0.0.25 S 10.0.0.13 S
```

Examination of the LSP information shows that the secondary is now the active path and that the primary is down. Note the entry stating that the primary is enqueued for recomputation in 27 seconds. CSPF attempts to compute a path for the primary at intervals defined by the retry period, which by default is 30 seconds:

```
root@Rome> show mpls lsp detail
Ingress LSP: 1 sessions

192.168.50.1
  From: 192.168.50.5, State: Up, ActiveRoute: 1, LSPname: Ro-Ip
  ActivePath: Ro-Ip-secondary (secondary)
  LoadBalance: Random
  Primary    Ro-Ip-primary      State: Dn
    Priorities: 3 3
    Bandwidth: 50Mbps
    Exclude: red
    Will be enqueued for recomputation in 27 second(s).
   83 Jul  6 13:37:03  CSPF failed: no route toward 192.168.50.1
  *Standby   Ro-Ip-secondary  State: Up
    Priorities: 3 3
    Bandwidth: 50Mbps
    Computed ERO (S [L] denotes strict [loose] hops): (CSPF metric: 20)
            10.0.0.25 S          10.0.0.13 S
Total 1 displayed, Up 1, Down 0

Egress LSP: 0 sessions
Total 0 displayed, Up 0, Down 0

Transit LSP: 0 sessions
Total 0 displayed, Up 0, Down 0
```

Fast Reroute

Fast reroute is an optional mechanism that provides a rapid temporary repair of an LSP that has failed due to a link or router failure. Fast reroute is configured on the LSP's ingress router. The ingress router uses RSVP to signal to the downstream routers that fast reroute is required for the LSP in question. At the time that the LSP is first set up, the ingress router and the transit routers each compute a detour path for the LSP that avoids the downstream neighbor router and that arrives at the router that is immediately downstream from that neighbor router. (The penultimate router computes a detour that avoids the outgoing link to the egress point and that arrives at the egress point via some other route.) If it is impossible to compute a detour path to that router, attempts are made to compute detours to routers progressively further downstream.

If, while the LSP is up, a router detects that an outgoing link or its downstream neighbor has failed, the traffic is moved to the detour path and an RSVP error message is sent upstream toward the ingress router so that it can take appropriate action. Appropriate action includes computing a new path for the primary and moving traffic to a secondary path, if one is configured. The fast-reroute detour is used only as a temporary measure, because the path taken by the LSP with the detour may be circuitous compared to the new primary path calculated by the ingress router, or compared to the secondary path if one is configured.

The fast-reroute process can be illustrated with the network topology shown in Figure 14-19. Again, suppose that the network administrator wishes to run an LSP between Rome and Ipswich, avoiding links belonging to admin-group red. Because the topology is richer than in the example shown in Figure 14-17, fast reroute can be used. In the absence of link failures, the LSP follows the path Rome–Amsterdam–Paris–Ipswich because that is the lowest metric path that fulfills the constraints. Each router computes a detour that avoids the outgoing link and the downstream neighbor. For example, Amsterdam computes a detour Amsterdam–Brussels–Ipswich.

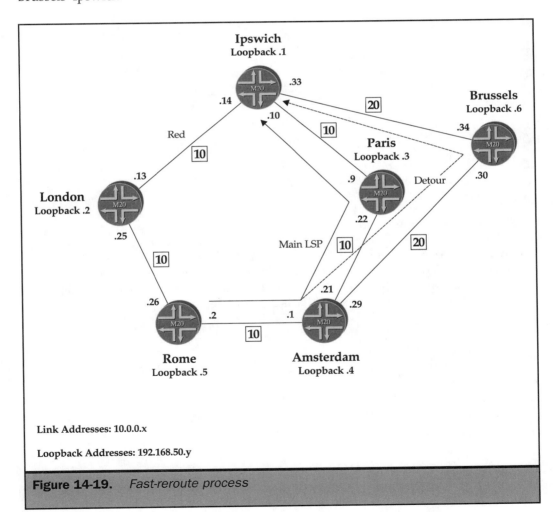

Figure 14-19. *Fast-reroute process*

Here is the MPLS section of the configuration of Ipswich. Note the `fast-reroute` option set under the LSP. This is all that is required to set up fast reroute, because the ingress router signals to the transit routers that fast reroute is required within the RSVP Path messages:

```
mpls {
        traceoptions {
            file mpls;
            flag state;
            flag error;
        }
        admin-groups {
            red 0;
        }
        label-switched-path Ro-Ip {
            to 192.168.50.1;
            bandwidth 50m;
            fast-reroute;
            admin-group {
                exclude red;
            }
        }
        interface fe-0/3/1.0;
        interface so-0/2/0.0;
    }
```

The following shows information related to the LSP on transit router Amsterdam. The path of the main LSP is shown, followed by details of computed detours. A detour computed by Amsterdam that follows the path Amsterdam–Brussels–Ipswich is shown. Also shown is a detour computed by Paris that follows the path Paris–Amsterdam–Brussels–Ipswich. The effect of this latter detour, therefore, is to double-back along the link between Paris and Amsterdam:

```
root@AMSTERDAM> show mpls lsp extensive
Ingress LSP: 0 sessions
Total 0 displayed, Up 0, Down 0

Egress LSP: 0 sessions
Total 0 displayed, Up 0, Down 0

Transit LSP: 1 sessions, 1 detours

192.168.50.1
```

```
From: 192.168.50.5, LSPstate: Up, ActiveRoute: 1, LSPname: Ro-Ip
Resv style: 1 FF, Label in: 100018, Label out: 100019
Time left:  142,  Since: Fri Jul  6 13:49:56 2001
Tspec: rate 0bps size 0bps peak Infbps m 20 M 1500
Port number: sender 1 receiver 58 protocol 0
FastReroute
PATH rcvfrom: 10.0.0.2  (fe-0/3/0.0) 2 pkts
PATH sentto: 10.0.0.22 (so-0/2/2.0) 2 pkts
RESV rcvfrom: 10.0.0.22  (so-0/2/2.0) 3 pkts
Explct route: 10.0.0.22  10.0.0.10
Record route: 10.0.0.2  <self>  10.0.0.22  10.0.0.10
  Detour is Up
  Detour PATH sentto: 10.0.0.30 (fe-0/3/1.0) 1 pkts
  Detour RESV rcvfrom: 10.0.0.30  (fe-0/3/1.0) 2 pkts
  Detour Explct route: 10.0.0.30  10.0.0.33
  Detour Record route: 10.0.0.2  <self>  10.0.0.30  10.0.0.33
 Detour branch from 10.0.0.22, to skip 192.168.50.1, Up
  PATH rcvfrom: 10.0.0.22  (so-0/2/2.0) 1 pkts
  PATH sentto: 10.0.0.30 (fe-0/3/1.0) 0 pkts
  RESV rcvfrom: 10.0.0.30  (fe-0/3/1.0) 0 pkts
  Explct route: 10.0.0.30  10.0.0.33
  Record route: 10.0.0.2  10.0.0.21  10.0.0.22  <self>  10.0.0.30
  10.0.0.33
Total 1 displayed, Up 1, Down 0
```

It is also interesting to see the RSVP Path messages associated with the LSP. This is the Path message related to the main LSP, as received by router Ipswich. Notice that the last line contains the constraints to be used by transit routers to compute detours for fast reroute, such as link coloring requirements. If fast reroute were not configured, these constraints would not be carried within the Path message because only the ingress router would need to know this information:

```
Jul  6 14:07:45 RSVP recv Path 192.168.50.5->192.168.50.1 Len=224 so-0/2/0.0
Jul  6 14:07:45   Session7 Len 16 192.168.50.1(port/tunnel ID 58) Proto 0
Jul  6 14:07:45   Hop      Len 12 10.0.0.9/0x00302388
Jul  6 14:07:45   Time     Len  8 30000 ms
Jul  6 14:07:45   Name     Len 16 Prio (7,0) flag 0x0 "Ro-Ip"
Jul  6 14:07:45   Sender7  Len 12 192.168.50.5(port/lsp ID  2)
Jul  6 14:07:45   Tspec    Len 36 rate 50Mbps size 50Mbps peak Infbps m 20 M 1500
Jul  6 14:07:45   ADspec   Len 48
Jul  6 14:07:45   SrcRoute Len 12  10.0.0.10 S
Jul  6 14:07:45   LabelReq Len  8 EtherType 0x800
Jul  6 14:07:45   RecRoute Len 28  10.0.0.9 S 10.0.0.21 S 10.0.0.2 S
Jul  6 14:07:45   FastReroute Len 20 Prio(7,0) Hop 6 BW 0bps Include 0x00000000 Exclude 0x00000001
```

Shown below is a Path message received by Ipswich related to a detour path. The last line shows that this is related to the detour computed by Amsterdam to avoid Paris.

```
Jul  6 14:07:06 RSVP recv Path 192.168.50.5->192.168.50.1 Len=216 fe-0/3/1.0
Jul  6 14:07:06   Session7 Len 16 192.168.50.1(port/tunnel ID 58) Proto 0
Jul  6 14:07:06   Hop      Len 12 10.0.0.34/0x002ff1c4
Jul  6 14:07:06   Time     Len  8 30000 ms
Jul  6 14:07:06   Name     Len 16 Prio (7,0) flag 0x0 "Ro-Ip"
Jul  6 14:07:06   Sender7  Len 12 192.168.50.5(port/lsp ID  2)
Jul  6 14:07:06   Tspec    Len 36 rate 0bps size 0bps peak Infbps m 20 M 1500
Jul  6 14:07:06   ADspec   Len 48
Jul  6 14:07:06   SrcRoute Len 12  10.0.0.33 S
Jul  6 14:07:06   LabelReq Len  8 EtherType 0x800
Jul  6 14:07:06   RecRoute Len 28  10.0.0.34 S 10.0.0.29 S 10.0.0.2 S
Jul  6 14:07:06   Detour   Len 12 branch from 10.0.0.29 to avoid 192.168.50.3
```

It is instructive to examine the MPLS table on Amsterdam, using the `show route table mpls.0 detail` command. Shown below is one of the entries from that table. Note that at this stage, no link failure has occurred. You can see two entries for the incoming label 100020. The first entry is active and shows that the outgoing interface is `so-0/2/2`. This entry relates to the main LSP path. The fact that the outgoing label is the same as the incoming one is simply coincidence. The second entry is inactive and relates to the detour path from Amsterdam via Brussels to Ipswich—note that the outgoing interface is `fe-0/3/1.0` and that the outgoing label is 100006.

```
100020 (2 entries, 1 announced)
        *RSVP    Preference:   7
                 Nexthop: via so-0/2/2.0, selected
                 label-switched-path Ro-Ip
                 Swap  100020
                 State: <Active Int>
                 Age: 19:13      Metric: 1
                 Task: RSVP
                 Announcement bits (1): 0-KRT
                 AS path: I

         RSVP    Preference:   7
                 Nexthop: 10.0.0.30 via fe-0/3/1.0, selected
                 label-switched-path Ro-Ip
                 Swap  100006
                 State: <NotBest Int>
                 Inactive reason: Not Best in its group
                 Age: 18:56      Metric: 255
                 Task: RSVP
                 AS path: I
```

The output below shows the MPLS table on router Amsterdam just after the failure of the link between Paris and Ipswich. Note that the precomputed detour shown previously has now become the active path. The fast-reroute process is fast because router Amsterdam has all the information it requires to install the detour into the forwarding table as soon as it detects the link failure:

```
100020 (1 entry, 1 announced)
        *RSVP    Preference:    7
                 Nexthop: 10.0.0.30 via fe-0/3/1.0, selected
                 label-switched-path Ro-Ip
                 Swap  100006
                 State: <Active Int>
                 Age: 23:29        Metric: 255
                 Task: RSVP
                 Announcement bits (1): 0-KRT
                 AS path: I
```

Note that the fast-reroute detour is used only as a temporary measure. Once the ingress router is aware (through RSVP messages) that the link failure occurred, it computes a new path for the LSP, as shown next. The history log shows the original path computed for the LSP. It also shows that the main path of the LSP went down and shows the new path calculated for the LSP as a result. In this example, it so happens that the new path computed for the LSP is the same as the detour path that was temporarily used, but this would not necessarily be the case for all topologies:

```
root@Rome> show mpls lsp extensive
Ingress LSP: 1 sessions

192.168.50.1
  From: 192.168.50.5, State: Up, ActiveRoute: 1, LSPname: Ro-Ip
  ActivePath:  (primary)
  FastReroute
  LoadBalance: Random
  Exclude: red
  *Primary                   State: Up
    Bandwidth: 50Mbps
    Computed ERO (S [L] denotes strict [loose] hops): (CSPF metric: 50)
              10.0.0.1 S        10.0.0.30 S        10.0.0.33 S
    12 Jul  6 14:32:29  Record Route:  10.0.0.1 S 10.0.0.30 S 10.0.0.33 S
    11 Jul  6 14:32:29  Up
    10 Jul  6 14:32:29  CSPF: computation result accepted
     9 Jul  6 14:32:29  CSPF: link down/deleted
     8 Jul  6 14:08:53  Record Route:  10.0.0.1 S 10.0.0.22 S 10.0.0.10 S
     7 Jul  6 14:08:53  Up
     6 Jul  6 14:08:52  CSPF: computation result accepted
```

If the link between Paris and Ipswich comes back into service, the LSP would not change its path to Rome–Amsterdam–Paris–Ipswich because the `optimize` option is not configured on the LSP.

Advanced Route Resolution

As illustrated earlier, the default behavior is that an LSP can be used only for BGP traffic, and only if the egress address of the LSP is the same as the BGP next-hop address. This section describes two ways in which the route resolution process can be modified so that an LSP can also be used by traffic other than that whose BGP next-hop is the egress point of the LSP. The `traffic-engineering shortcuts` option allows an LSP to be used for traffic whose next-hop is beyond the egress point of an LSP. The `traffic-engineering bgp-igp` option allows an LSP to be used by non-BGP traffic.

IGP Shortcuts

The example earlier in the "Route Resolution" section showed that, by default, traffic uses an LSP only if the BGP next-hop address is the egress address of the LSP. This default behavior in itself is often not useful in practice, because usually the BGP next-hop is an access/border router, since by definition it is this type of router that announces routes from other ASs. This means that to be usable by BGP traffic, the egress points of the LSPs would have to be access routers. However, in reality, one only wishes to traffic engineer within the core of the network, since typically within Point of Presence (POP) sites, access routers are symmetrically placed with respect to the core routers, and the internal links are usually oversized compared to the expected traffic. Therefore, it would be useful if LSPs had to be built only within the core of the network yet still be usable by traffic whose BGP next-hop is beyond the egress point of an LSP. For a case in which a full mesh of LSPs exists, this would result in a reduction in the number of LSPs from order N^2 to order n^2 where N is the number of access routers and n is the number of core routers. This is a significant reduction, given that the ratio of the number of access routers to the number of core routers may be 5 or 10. Furthermore, the access routers and core routers may be located in different IGP areas, in which case it is not possible to have CSPF-computed LSPs end-to-end anyway. IGP shortcuts provide a means for LSPs between core routers to be used when resolving routes whose next-hop is an access router.

IGP shortcuts is an option that, when configured on a router, applies globally to all ingress RSVP signaled LSPs on that router. When configured alone, it allows BGP traffic having a BGP next-hop beyond the egress point of an LSP to potentially use that LSP. The definition of *beyond* is that the egress point of the LSP must lie on the branch of shortest-path tree calculated by the IGP that leads to the BGP next-hop.

This is illustrated in Figure 14-20, in which a network is shown with its IGP metrics. The shortest-path tree calculated by the IGP on router Rome is shown in Figure 14-21. Consider BGP traffic arriving at Rome whose BGP next-hop is the loopback address of router Oslo. If there is an LSP from Rome to Ipswich, it can be used to forward the traffic toward Oslo, because the egress point of the LSP is on the branch of the shortest-path tree that leads to Oslo. If, instead, an LSP was located between Rome and Paris,

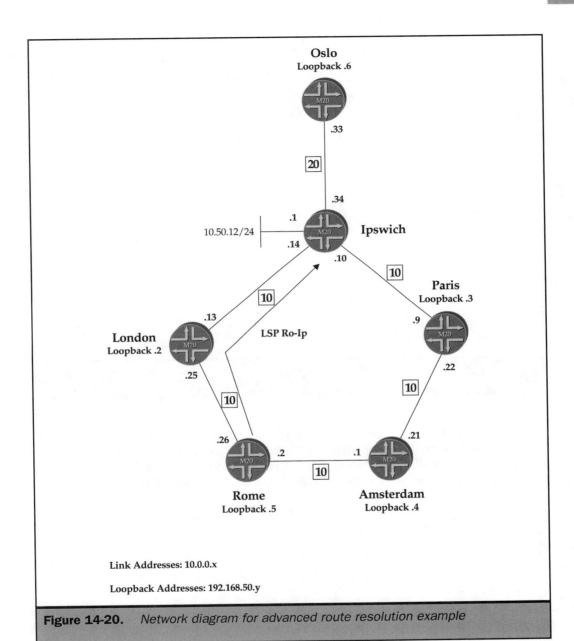

Oslo
Loopback .6

.33

20

.34

.1
10.50.12/24

.14

Ipswich

.10

10

Paris
Loopback .3

.9

LSP Ro-Ip

10

.13

London
Loopback .2

.25

.22

10

10

.26

.2   .1

.21

10

Rome
Loopback .5

Amsterdam
Loopback .4

Link Addresses: 10.0.0.x

Loopback Addresses: 192.168.50.y

Figure 14-20.   *Network diagram for advanced route resolution example*

this would not be used for traffic to Oslo even though the egress point is closer to Oslo than the ingress point. This because the egress point of the LSP, Paris, does not lie along the branch of the shortest-path tree that leads to Oslo.

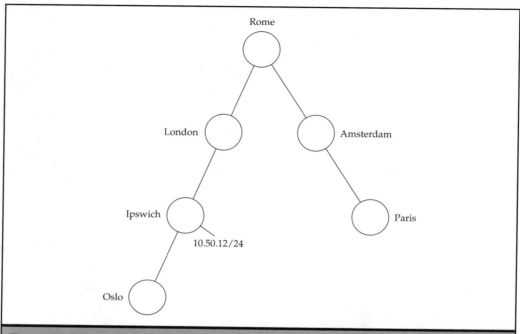

Figure 14-21.   *Schematic shortest-path tree from the point of view of router Rome*

Suppose that Oslo announces the route 10.200.0.0/16 that it learns from an EBGP peer into the domain shown in Figure 14-21. Rome is the ingress to an LSP whose egress is Ipswich. Without IGP shortcuts enabled, the route 10.200.0.0/16 on Rome is as shown here. It can be seen that the LSP is *not* used to resolve the route:

```
10.200.0.0/16        *[BGP/170] 00:06:07, localpref 100, from 192.168.50.6
                        AS path: 65002 I
                     > via so-0/2/0.0
```

Table inet.3 follows. Note that the only entry is the loopback address of the egress point of the LSP:

```
inet.3: 1 destinations, 1 routes (1 active, 0 holddown, 0 hidden)
+ = Active Route, - = Last Active, * = Both

192.168.50.1/32      *[RSVP/7] 00:00:16, metric 20, metric2 0
                        > via so-0/2/0.0, label-switched-path Ro-Ip
```

To activate IGP shortcuts, the following command is entered on router Rome (IS-IS would be substituted for OSPF in the command shown if IS-IS were the IGP in use):

```
ps@Rome# set protocols ospf traffic-engineering shortcuts
```

Note that as a result of this change, networks beyond the egress point of the LSP are now installed in inet.3:

```
inet.3: 5 destinations, 5 routes (5 active, 0 holddown, 0 hidden)
+ = Active Route, - = Last Active, * = Both

10.0.0.8/30          *[OSPF/10] 00:05:23, metric 30
                        > via so-0/2/0.0, label-switched-path Ro-Ip
10.0.0.32/30         *[OSPF/10] 00:05:23, metric 40
                        > via so-0/2/0.0, label-switched-path Ro-Ip
10.50.12.0/24        *[OSPF/10] 00:05:23, metric 21
                        > via so-0/2/0.0, label-switched-path Ro-Ip
192.168.50.1/32      *[RSVP/7] 00:05:23, metric 20, metric2 0
                        > via so-0/2/0.0, label-switched-path Ro-Ip
                     [OSPF/10] 00:05:23, metric 20
                        > via so-0/2/0.0, label-switched-path Ro-Ip
192.168.50.6/32      *[OSPF/10] 00:05:23, metric 40
                        > via so-0/2/0.0, label-switched-path Ro-Ip
```

Note that the BGP next-hop for the route 10.200.0.0/16 is 192.168.50.6, the loopback address of Oslo. This loopback address is now in inet.3 and points to the LSP. Hence, when the BGP process installs the route 10.200.0.0/16, it points it to the LSP:

```
10.200.0.0/16        *[BGP/170] 00:00:04, localpref 100, from 192.168.50.6
                        AS path: 65002 I
                     > via so-0/2/0.0, label-switched-path Ro-Ip
```

As a result, traffic entering Rome having a BGP next-hop of Oslo uses the LSP. Note that this would still be the case if Ipswich and Oslo were in different IGP areas and Ipswich were an OSPF ABR or an IS-IS L2/L1 router joining the two areas.

The traffic-engineering bgp-igp Option

By default, only BGP traffic whose BGP next-hop is the egress point of an LSP can use that LSP. This is because, as described earlier, routes that point to an LSP are stored in the inet.3 routing table, and only BGP can make use of the routes in that table. To allow IGP traffic to also use the LSP, the `traffic-engineering bgp-igp` option is provided. This global command has the action of placing routes that point to an LSP into inet.0. As a result, protocols other than BGP can make use of those routes.

As an example, refer again to the network shown in Figure 14-20 with an LSP between Rome and Ipswich. The `traffic-engineering bgp-igp` option is invoked as follows:

```
ps@Rome# set protocols mpls traffic-engineering bgp-igp
```

This results in the following routing table on Rome (note that IGP shortcuts are not configured at this point). It can be seen that inet.3 table is empty and that the route to the egress of the LSP appears in inet.0:

```
ps@Rome> show route

inet.0: 20 destinations, 20 routes (19 active, 0 holddown, 1 hidden)
+ = Active Route, - = Last Active, * = Both

10.0.0.0/30          *[Direct/0] 1d 03:57:37
                      > via fe-0/3/1.0
10.0.0.2/32          *[Local/0] 1d 03:57:37
                       Local
10.0.0.8/30          *[OSPF/10] 00:00:08, metric 30
                      > to 10.0.0.1 via fe-0/3/1.0
                        via so-0/2/0.0
10.0.0.12/30         *[OSPF/10] 00:00:08, metric 20
                      > via so-0/2/0.0
10.0.0.20/30         *[OSPF/10] 00:00:08, metric 20
                      > to 10.0.0.1 via fe-0/3/1.0
10.0.0.24/30         *[Direct/0] 02:44:06
                      > via so-0/2/0.0
                       [OSPF/10] 00:00:08, metric 10
                      > via so-0/2/0.0
10.0.0.26/32         *[Local/0] 1d 03:54:17
                       Local
10.0.0.32/30         *[OSPF/10] 00:00:08, metric 40
                      > via so-0/2/0.0
10.50.12.0/24        *[OSPF/10] 00:00:08, metric 21
                      > via so-0/2/0.0
10.200.0.0/16        *[BGP/170] 00:00:08, localpref 100, from 192.168.50.6
                       AS path: 65002 I
                      > via so-0/2/0.0
10.255.254.0/24      *[Direct/0] 1w4d 23:21:31
                      > via fxp0.0
10.255.254.5/32      *[Local/0] 1w4d 23:21:31
                       Local
192.168.50.1/32      *[RSVP/7] 00:00:09, metric 20, metric2 0
                      > via so-0/2/0.0, label-switched-path Ro-Ip
                       [OSPF/10] 00:00:08, metric 20
```

```
                          > via so-0/2/0.0
192.168.50.2/32          *[OSPF/10] 00:00:08, metric 10
                          > via so-0/2/0.0
192.168.50.3/32          *[OSPF/10] 00:00:08, metric 20
                          > to 10.0.0.1 via fe-0/3/1.0
192.168.50.4/32          *[OSPF/10] 00:00:08, metric 10
                          > to 10.0.0.1 via fe-0/3/1.0
192.168.50.5/32          *[Direct/0] 1d 03:57:37
                          > via lo0.0
192.168.50.6/32          *[OSPF/10] 00:00:08, metric 40
                          > via so-0/2/0.0
224.0.0.5/32             *[OSPF/10] 1d 03:57:37, metric 1

mpls.0: 2 destinations, 2 routes (2 active, 0 holddown, 0 hidden)
+ = Active Route, - = Last Active, * = Both

0                        *[MPLS/0] 1d 03:57:37, metric 1
                          Receive
1                        *[MPLS/0] 1d 03:57:37, metric 1
                          Receive
```

The result is that all traffic, including IGP traffic, having a destination address of 192.168.50.1 uses the LSP. In practice, little traffic would have a destination of the loopback address of a router. However, suppose there is a server farm attached to the network 10.50.12.0/24 on Ipswich. The network administrator wishes IGP traffic passing through Rome destined to the server farm to use the LSP between Rome and Ipswich. This can be achieved by activating IGP shortcuts in addition to the `traffic-engineering bgp-igp` option. These options in combination mean that IGP traffic to destinations at or beyond the end of the LSP (including the server farm subnet) can use the LSP. The resulting routing table is shown here:

```
ps@Rome> show route

inet.0: 20 destinations, 20 routes (19 active, 0 holddown, 1 hidden)
+ = Active Route, - = Last Active, * = Both

10.0.0.0/30              *[Direct/0] 1d 04:15:33
                          > via fe-0/3/1.0
10.0.0.2/32              *[Local/0] 1d 04:15:33
                          Local
10.0.0.8/30              *[OSPF/10] 00:00:04, metric 30
                          > via so-0/2/0.0, label-switched-path Ro-Ip
10.0.0.12/30             *[OSPF/10] 00:03:50, metric 20
                          > via so-0/2/0.0
10.0.0.20/30             *[OSPF/10] 00:03:50, metric 20
```

```
                              > to 10.0.0.1 via fe-0/3/1.0
   10.0.0.24/30               *[Direct/0] 03:02:02
                              > via so-0/2/0.0
                              [OSPF/10] 00:00:04, metric 10
                              > via so-0/2/0.0
   10.0.0.26/32              *[Local/0] 1d 04:12:13
                              Local
   10.0.0.32/30              *[OSPF/10] 00:00:04, metric 40
                              > via so-0/2/0.0, label-switched-path Ro-Ip
   10.50.12.0/24             *[OSPF/10] 00:00:04, metric 21
                              > via so-0/2/0.0, label-switched-path Ro-Ip
   10.200.0.0/16             *[BGP/170] 00:03:50, localpref 100, from 192.168.50.6
                               AS path: 65002 I
                              > via so-0/2/0.0, label-switched-path Ro-Ip
   10.255.254.0/24           *[Direct/0] 1w4d 23:39:27
                              > via fxp0.0
   10.255.254.5/32           *[Local/0] 1w4d 23:39:27
                               Local
   192.168.50.1/32           *[RSVP/7] 00:18:05, metric 20, metric2 0
                              > via so-0/2/0.0, label-switched-path Ro-Ip
                              [OSPF/10] 00:00:04, metric 20
                              > via so-0/2/0.0, label-switched-path Ro-Ip
   192.168.50.2/32           *[OSPF/10] 00:03:50, metric 10
                              > via so-0/2/0.0
   192.168.50.3/32           *[OSPF/10] 00:03:50, metric 20
                              > to 10.0.0.1 via fe-0/3/1.0
   192.168.50.4/32           *[OSPF/10] 00:03:50, metric 10
                              > to 10.0.0.1 via fe-0/3/1.0
   192.168.50.5/32           *[Direct/0] 1d 04:15:33
                              > via lo0.0
   192.168.50.6/32           *[OSPF/10] 00:00:04, metric 40
                              > via so-0/2/0.0, label-switched-path Ro-Ip
   224.0.0.5/32              *[OSPF/10] 1d 04:15:33, metric 1

mpls.0: 2 destinations, 2 routes (2 active, 0 holddown, 0 hidden)
+ = Active Route, - = Last Active, * = Both

0                            *[MPLS/0] 1d 04:15:33, metric 1
                              Receive
1                            *[MPLS/0] 1d 04:15:33, metric 1
                              Receive
```

Table 14-2 summarizes which types of traffic are mapped to an LSP, depending on which options are invoked.

	No Options	IGP Shortcuts Only	TE bgp-igp Only	Both IGP Shortcuts *and* TE bgp-igp
BGP traffic (nexthop=LSP egress)	√	√	√	√
BGP traffic (nexthop beyond LSP egress)		√		√
IGP traffic (destination=LSP egress)			√	√
IGP traffic (destination beyond LSP egress)				√

Table 14-2.   *Effect of Route-Resolution Options*

Advertise LSP

An alternative approach to the mechanisms described in the preceding section is to use a newer feature that allows an LSP to be advertised in the IGP as a point-to-point link between the ingress and the egress. A detailed discussion of this is beyond the scope of this chapter. However, in brief, the advertise LSP feature allows the "sphere of influence" of an LSP to be extended to routers upstream from an LSP ingress as well as routers downstream from the LSP egress, because all routers take the LSP link and associated metric into account in their SPF computation. Note that in contrast, IGP shortcuts affect routing decisions only on the router on which they are configured and hence cannot affect traffic upstream from the LSP ingress.

MPLS Load Balancing

MPLS traffic engineering can be used to achieve load balancing of traffic in complicated situations. Figure 14-22 shows a section of a core network in which three links exist between routers A, B and routers C, D. These three links are expensive (they might be transoceanic links or long-haul terrestrial links) so it is required that you achieve the maximum utilization from the links and avoid a situation in which one link is saturated and the others are underused. The traffic volume entering A is X and the traffic volume entering B is Y. By arranging for each link to carry $(X + Y)/3$, the probability of any one link becoming saturated as $(X + Y)$ increases over time is minimized. This can be achieved through the use of multiple RSVP-signaled LSPs. On each router, an LSP is configured per long-haul link to each of the two routers on the far side. For example, A would have three LSPs to C, each using a different long-haul link and similarly would have three LSPs to D. These LSPs are shown in Figure 14-22. This scheme is valid if the extra latency associated with not taking a direct path is small compared to the propagation delay of the long-haul links and if the local links A–B and C–D are oversized compared to the long-haul links. Traffic automatically load-balances across the LSPs and automatically rebalances if one of the long-haul circuits fails.

The easiest way of implementing this scheme is to assign each long-haul link to a different administrative group (color) and to constrain each LSP to use only one of the links. The assigned colors are shown by line type in Figure 14-22.

The MPLS section of the configuration of router A is shown next. Note that in addition to the configuration shown, `traffic-engineering shortcuts` should be configured in the IGP section of the configuration if the BGP next-hop of some of the traffic is beyond C and D, which is likely to be the case if A, B, C, and D are core routers:

```
mpls {
        admin-groups {
            common 0;
            circuit1 1;
            circuit2 2;
            circuit3 3;
        }
        label-switched-path AtoC-circuit1 {
            to 192.168.50.4;
            admin-group {
                include [ circuit1 common ];
            }
        }
        label-switched-path AtoC-circuit2 {
            to 192.168.50.4;
            admin-group {
                include [ circuit2 common ];
            }
        }
        label-switched-path AtoC-circuit3 {
            to 192.168.50.4;
            admin-group {
                include [ circuit3 common ];
            }
        }
        label-switched-path AtoD-circuit1 {
```

```
            to 192.168.50.2;
            admin-group {
                include [ circuit1 common ];
            }
        }
        label-switched-path AtoD-circuit2 {
            to 192.168.50.2;
            admin-group {
                include circuit2;
            }
        }
        label-switched-path AtoD-circuit3 {
            to 192.168.50.2;
            admin-group {
                include circuit3;
            }
        }
        interface so-0/2/0.0 {
            admin-group common;
        }
        interface so-0/3/2.0 {
            admin-group circuit2;
        }
        interface so-0/3/0.0 {
            admin-group circuit3;
        }
    }
```

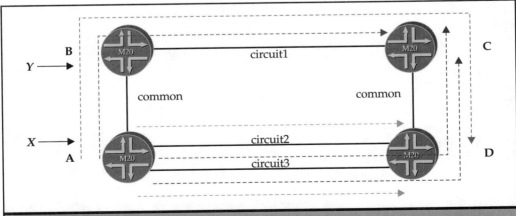

Figure 14-22.   *MPLS load-balancing example showing LSPs originating at A (dotted lines) and assigned administrative groups (colors)*

Note that an administrative group called "common" has been assigned to the links AB and CD. If these links were left uncolored, it would not be possible to create LSPs such as AtoC-circuit1 in this example, because uncolored links are not considered valid by CSPF once a color is configured on the LSP in question. When the colors "common" and "circuit1" are configured on that LSP, CSPF considers links having either of those colors (or both) as valid.

To invoke the hash-based load-balancing feature of the Internet Processor II, the following additions are required in the policy-options and routing-options sections of the configuration:

```
routing-options {
    forwarding-table {
        export pplb;
    }
}
policy-options {
    policy-statement pplb {
        then {
            load-balance per-packet;
        }
    }
}
```

Following is part of the routing table of router A. Each route has three next-hops corresponding to each of the three LSPs that lead toward the destination in question. For example, 3.0.0.0/8 is reachable via router C, and so all three LSPs from A to C, each corresponding to a different long-haul circuit, are installed in the routing table:

```
3.0.0.0/8          *[BGP/170] 00:06:09, localpref 100, from 192.168.50.4
                      AS path: I
                    > via so-0/2/0.0, label-switched-path AtoC-circuit1
                      via so-0/3/0.0, label-switched-path AtoC-circuit3
                      via so-0/3/2.0, label-switched-path AtoC-circuit2
4.0.0.0/8          *[BGP/170] 00:01:49, localpref 100, from 192.168.50.2
                      AS path: I
                    > via so-0/2/0.0, label-switched-path AtoD-circuit1
                      via so-0/3/0.0, label-switched-path AtoD-circuit3
                      via so-0/3/2.0, label-switched-path AtoD-circuit2
6.0.0.0/8          *[BGP/170] 00:06:09, localpref 100, from 192.168.50.4
                      AS path: I
                    > via so-0/2/0.0, label-switched-path AtoC-circuit1
                      via so-0/3/0.0, label-switched-path AtoC-circuit3
                      via so-0/3/2.0, label-switched-path AtoC-circuit2
```

```
9.2.0.0/16            *[BGP/170] 00:06:09, localpref 100, from 192.168.50.4
                         AS path: I
                       > via so-0/2/0.0, label-switched-path AtoC-circuit1
                         via so-0/3/0.0, label-switched-path AtoC-circuit3
                         via so-0/3/2.0, label-switched-path AtoC-circuit2
9.20.0.0/17           *[BGP/170] 00:01:49, localpref 100, from 192.168.50.2
                         AS path: I
                         via so-0/2/0.0, label-switched-path AtoD-circuit1
                       > via so-0/3/0.0, label-switched-path AtoD-circuit3
                         via so-0/3/2.0, label-switched-path AtoD-circuit2
```

The forwarding table on router A can be examined to verify that three nexthops are present for each route. The example below shows the output for the route 3.0.0.0/8:

```
3.0.0.0/8             user      0              indr    34     4
                                               ulst    42     1
                                               Push  100003   so-0/2/0.0
                                               Push  100007   so-0/3/0.0
                                               Push  100006   so-0/3/2.0
```

The Label Distribution Protocol

LSRs use MPLS-LDP to distribute labels in a number of ways. The LDP concepts are relatively straightforward and knowledge of it is a good way for you to get to know other label distribution mechanisms and to understand the principal aim of all label distribution methods—which is to bind labels to FECs so as to create LSPs across a network.

LDP Messages

LDP is a set of procedures and messages used by LSRs to keep each other informed of their label to FEC bindings, which are used to establish one or more LSPs across a network. Two LSRs that exchange LDP messages over an LDP session are called *LDP peers*. Only one bidirectional LDP session is required between a pair of LSRs for a given label space.

There are four categories of LDP messages:

- Discovery messages
- Session messages
- Advertisement messages
- Notification messages

Discovery Messages   Discovery messages are essentially hello messages that are periodically sent out by each of the LSRs to allow them to discover each other. There are two types of LDP discovery: basic and extended.

The basic LDP discovery mechanism is used by LSRs that are directly connected at the link level and the hello messages are addressed to the All Routers on this Subnet multicast address (224.0.0.2) using UDP packets with well-known port number 646. The basic discovery mechanism is by far the most widely used of the two methods and is the default method used by JUNOS software.

The extended LDP discovery mechanism is used by LSRs that are not directly connected to establish a LDP session with each other across intermediate hops. The extended LDP hello message is targeted at the destination LSR using a specific IP address and UDP packets with well-known port number 646. The IP address of the target LSR is configured manually.

The extended discovery mechanism was developed primarily to allow LDP to be used across intermediate hops that do not support LDP. For example, LSR A is directly connected to both LSR B and LSR C, and LSR B and LSR C are connected, in turn, to LSR D, which is two hops away from LSR A. LSR B supports LDP but LSR C does not. LSR A has established a LDP session with directly connected LSR B using the basic discovery method and a second LDP session direct with LSR D, via LSR C, using the "targeted" extended discovery method. Labeled packets arriving at LSR A for one particular FEC may be label switched via LSR B towards LSR D while labeled packets for another FEC may be label switched direct from LSR A to LSR D across LSR C.

In Juniper Networks routers, the extended discovery mechanism is used to provide LDP tunneling capabilities across RSVP-signaled LSPs.

Session Initialization and Maintenance Methods   Upon receipt of a hello message, using either the basic or extended discovery methods, an LSR may begin an LDP session initialization procedure with a peer LSR using session messages.

The LDP session initialization steps are as follows:

1. The LSR with the highest IP address becomes the active LSR for a session and the other becomes the passive LSR.

2. The active LSR initiates the session with session messages addressed to TCP port 646.

3. The following information is exchanged between LSRs once the session is initialized: the LDP protocol version, the label distribution method, the label space being used (Label Space ID), timer values and VPI/VCI ranges on ATM, or DLCI ranges on frame relay.

Hello messages continue to be used for checking and maintaining LDP link integrity between LSRs even after the LDP session has been established. If there are multiple links between LSRs, hellos are sent on each link every 5 seconds. The same label space ID (discussed in the section "LDP Label Space") is used on all of the parallel links.

Each LSR also keeps track of its session adjacencies using session *keepalive* packets. If the last keepalive from a specific peer exceeds a predefined time-out value, the LDP adjacency is deleted. The keepalive interval is 10 seconds and the time-out value is 30 seconds.

Advertisement Messages   Advertisement messages are used to advertise the label-FEC bindings themselves to the peer LSR(s) using a structured TLV encoding scheme. The different methods used to advertise the label bindings are discussed in the section "LDP Distribution Methods."

Notification Messages   Notification messages are used to inform peers of the status of the LDP session itself and to report session or other errors to the peer LSR(s).

TCP is used as the transport for session, advertisement, and notification messages because the exchange of messages must be in sequence and reliable. The TCP well-known port number 646 is used for these message types.

LDP and Label-Switched Paths

So how do LSPs relate to the labels that have been advertised on a hop-by-hop basis between the peers, and how do the LSPs get built, end-to-end, across the network?

Each LDP advertisement message sent by an LSR to a peer contains, among other things, a label TLV and an FEC TLV. These TLVs together are the binding between the label(s) being advertised and the FEC(s) to which they belong. This binding is crucial at the ingress point, or *head-end*, of the LSP because it tells the LSR which LSP to forward labeled packets into toward the destination prefix, or prefixes. Once the packets have been labelled and forwarded into the LSP at the ingress point, they are label swapped and forwarded by the next-hop downstream LSRs until they emerge from the LSP at the egress point.

In Figure 14-23, LSR C on the right is advertising two prefixes for networks 30.0.0.0 and 40.0.0.0 to LSR B over an LDP session. In this example, an LSP is built between LSR A and LSR C. LSR C advertises one label because the desired forwarding treatment of all the packets toward both networks across the LSP is the same.

LSR B receives the advertisement with a Label TLV containing the value 30 together with an FEC TLV containing the values 30.0.0.0 and 40.0.0.0. LSR B associates the label (value 30) received from LSR C to the FEC containing the prefixes for both the networks and creates an entry in its FIB. LSR B now advertises its own label (value 100) to LSR A and creates a mapping between Label 100 and Label 30.

LSR A is the ingress of the LSP and has no upstream LDP sessions itself because it is at the edge of the MPLS domain. Therefore, it has no need to advertise the label-FEC binding further once it receives the advertisement from LSR B. All it does is associate the label (value 100) received from LSR B with the FEC for networks 30.0.0.0 and 40.0.0.0 and create an entry for the FEC in its FIB.

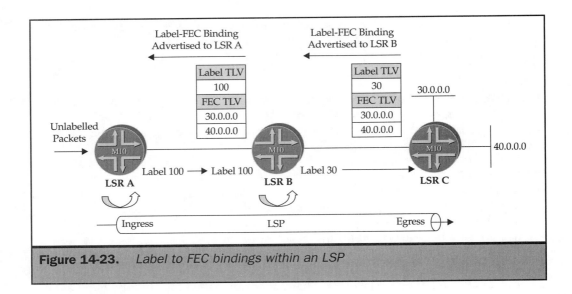

Figure 14-23.   *Label to FEC bindings within an LSP*

When LSR A receives an unlabeled IP packet destined for one of the prefixes in this FEC, it consults its FIB and determines which label to use to forward the packet and the next-hop to forward it to. In this case, the label is 100 and the next-hop is LSR B. The packet is forwarded into the LSP toward next-hop LSR B. LSR B receives the labelled packet, consults its FIB, and discovers that it has a mapping between label 100 and label 30 and that the next-hop is LSR C. It swaps label 100 with label 30 and forwards it to LSR C. LSR C is at the edge of the MPLS domain because it connects to networks 30.0.0.0 and 40.0.0.0 directly. As it can forward only unlabelled IP packets onto these subnets, it removes the label header and forwards the packet as a native IP packet to the appropriate destination subnet.

This example illustrates the hop-by-hop approach taken by each of the MPLS nodes in a simple network to advertise labels and to forward packets across the LSP. It is also worth noting that LSR B could receive unlabelled packets via one of its own directly connected interfaces and could, itself, become the ingress point of another LSP. This is why the label-FEC binding is carried in all advertisements and stored at every hop.

Also, recall from the earlier discussion about Penultimate Hop Popping (PHP) that, in practice, LSR C can advertise label value 3 for the FEC to LSR B to inform LSR B that it should "pop" the label stack before forwarding the packet to LSR C.

Different forwarding behavior can be achieved in the preceding example by binding different labels to each of the prefixes separately. In other words, label 100 could be used for FEC 30.0.0.0 and label 101 for FEC 40.0.0.0. In this case, it would be possible for LSR A to be the ingress point of two LSPs, each of which use different precedence criteria or even paths through the network to the egress point.

To summarize, each individual LSR makes a simple, local forwarding decision on a hop-by-hop basis. But from the end-to-end perspective, the packet is traversing an LSP based on the advertised label-FEC bindings. These bindings determine not only the label and next-hop to use, but also the path the packet takes across the network and possibly even the packets' priority.

LDP LSPs and JUNOS Software   In the current versions of JUNOS software, the default behavior is for LDP not to advertise all the IP prefixes as label FECs, and only those prefixes that have a /32 mask are advertised. The loopback address of a router is typically configured with an IP prefix that has a /32 mask. Therefore, LDP LSPs can be built only to the loopback IP address of remote routers within the MPLS domain, with the loopback IP address being the egress point of each LSP. It is no coincidence that the loopback address is also typically used to define the IBGP peer routers within the domain.

An entry for each of the /32 LSP egress IP addresses is installed in the inet.3 table with an associated label FEC. Equivalent entries for the egress points are also installed in the inet.0 RIB by the IGP. This is shown here for the prefixes 192.168.1.3/31 and 192.168.1.4/32:

```
ps@R2# run show route

inet.0: 9 destinations, 9 routes (9 active, 0 holddown, 0 hidden)
+ = Active Route, - = Last Active, * = Both

10.1.1.4/30        *[Direct/0] 03:40:02
                    > via so-0/2/0.0
10.1.1.8/30        *[IS-IS/18] 03:14:40, metric 20, tag 2
                    > to 10.1.1.6 via so-0/2/0.0
10.255.254.0/24    *[Direct/0] 22:39:35
                    > via fxp0.0
.
.
.
.
192.168.1.3/32     *[IS-IS/18] 03:14:40, metric 10, tag 2
                    > to 10.1.1.6 via so-0/2/0.0
192.168.1.4/32     *[IS-IS/18] 03:05:38, metric 20, tag 2
                    > to 10.1.1.6 via so-0/2/0.0

inet.3: 2 destinations, 2 routes (2 active, 0 holddown, 0 hidden)
+ = Active Route, - = Last Active, * = Both

192.168.1.3/32     *[LDP/9] 02:44:28, metric 1
                    > via so-0/2/0.0, Push  100000
192.168.1.4/32     *[LDP/9] 02:40:14, metric 1
                    > via so-0/2/0.0, Push  100001
```

The path "preference" [LDP/9] and metric of the LSP entries for prefixes 192.168.1.3/32 and 192.168.1.4/32 in the inet.3 table is less than that of the equivalent entries in the inet.0 RIB, which means that the LDP LSPs to both prefixes are preferred over the paths determined by the IGP. In addition, only BGP is capable of consulting the inet.3 table, as described previously. Therefore, only destinations that have BGP next-hops that resolve to entries in the inet.3 table are reachable across the LDP LSPs. Traffic that is destined for all other IP prefixes in the inet.0 RIB continues to follow the path determined by the IGP.

In the output, labels 100000 and 100001 are used to label switch packets onto each of the LSPs that have the egress IP addresses of 192.168.1.3/32 and 192.168.1.4/32, respectively.

Further LDP Command Output   The following outputs show samples of LDP information from a Juniper Networks router called R1 that is the first of four routers (R1 to R4) that are all connected in series. In other words, R1 connects to R2, which connects to R3, which connects to R4. The loopback IP addresses of each of the routers are 192.168.1.1, 192.168.1.2, 192.168.1.3, and 192.168.1.4, respectively. The basic LDP discovery method is used between each of the routers.

The show ldp interface, show ldp session and show ldp neighbor commands on R1 below show that R1 has one LDP session adjacency with R2. R1's Loopback address is 192.168.1.1, and R2's Loopback address is 192.168.1.2. The LDP session adjacency is formed on interface fe-0/3/2 over IP subnet 10.1.1.0/30. The local label space ID on R1 is 192.168.1.1:0 and the label space ID from R2 is 192.168.1.2:0.

```
root@R1> show ldp interface
Interface               Label space ID          Nbr count     Next hello
lo0.0                   192.168.1.1:0               0             0
fe-0/3/2.0              192.168.1.1:0               1             3

root@R1> show ldp session
  Address               State          Connection     Hold time
192.168.1.2             Operational    Open              21

root@R1> show ldp neighbor extensive
Address               Interface          Label space ID          Hold time
10.1.1.2              fe-0/3/2.0          192.168.1.2:0              12
   Transport address: 192.168.1.2, Configuration sequence: 4
   Up for 01:13:41
   Reference Count: 1, Hold Time: 15
```

In the next script example, the show ldp database command on R1 shows the labels that it receives from R2 for the loopback IP addresses of routers R2 to R4 in the Input Label Database. The labels that R1 allocates and advertises to other routers for the prefixes that it knows about are shown in the Output Label Database. The loopback IP address of R2 in the Input Label Database is associated with a label value of 3 so that R1 knows that it has to perform a Penultimate Hop Popping and use native-IP forwarding when sending packets addressed to R2's loopback interface. But R1 will advertise a label value of 100007 to other routers that need to reach IP address 192.168.1.2 through it. R1 also allocates a label value of 3 to its own loopback interface IP address.

```
root@R1> show ldp database extensive
Input label database, 192.168.1.1:0-192.168.1.2:0
   Label       Prefix
       3       192.168.1.2/32
               State: Active
   100007      192.168.1.3/32
               State: Active
   100006      192.168.1.1/32
               State: Active
   100008      192.168.1.4/32
               State: Active

Output label database, 192.168.1.1:0-192.168.1.2:0
   Label       Prefix
   100007      192.168.1.2/32
               State: Active
   100008      192.168.1.3/32
               State: Active
   100009      192.168.1.4/32
               State: Active
       3       192.168.1.1/32
               State: Active
```

The show ldp path command on R1 in the following code reflects the label allocations shown in the preceding output. But it also shows that R1 is the egress point of the LSP that terminates on its own loopback IP address (denoted by the line "Attached route: 192.168.1.1"). R1 advertises label value 3 to other LDP peers so that they know they should perform a Penultimate Hop Popping when sending packets to this prefix.

The output also shows that R1 is the ingress point of the LSPs to all of the other prefixes.

```
root@R1> show ldp path extensive
Output Session (label)          Input Session (label)
```

```
192.168.1.2:0(3)                            (egress)
  Attached route:   192.168.1.1/32
  Refcount: 3, Global label: 3
192.168.1.2:0(100007)             192.168.1.2:0(3)
  Attached route:   192.168.1.2/32, Ingress route
  Refcount: 2, Transit route, Global label: 100007
192.168.1.2:0(100008)             192.168.1.2:0(100007)
  Attached route:   192.168.1.3/32, Ingress route
  Refcount: 2, Transit route, Global label: 100008
192.168.1.2:0(100009)             192.168.1.2:0(100008)
  Attached route:   192.168.1.4/32, Ingress route
  Refcount: 2, Transit route, Global label: 100009
```

The `show ldp route` command on R1 next shows the next-hop interface that is used to reach other prefixes on routers R2, R3, and R4. As discussed previously, labels are associated only with the loopback /32 IP addresses of the other routers.

```
root@R1> show ldp route extensive
Destination           Next-hop intf/lsp            Next-hop address
  10.1.1.0/30         fe-0/3/2.0
  10.1.1.4/30         fe-0/3/2.0                    10.1.1.2
  10.1.1.8/30         fe-0/3/2.0                    10.1.1.2
  192.168.1.1/32      lo0.0
    Bound to outgoing label 3, Topology entry: 0x84c2fd0
  192.168.1.2/32      fe-0/3/2.0                    10.1.1.2
    Session 192.168.1.1:0--192.168.1.2:0
    Bound to outgoing label 100007, Topology entry: 0x84e5268
  192.168.1.3/32      fe-0/3/2.0                    10.1.1.2
    Session 192.168.1.1:0--192.168.1.2:0
    Bound to outgoing label 100008, Topology entry: 0x84e5370
  192.168.1.4/32      fe-0/3/2.0                    10.1.1.2
    Session 192.168.1.1:0--192.168.1.2:0
    Bound to outgoing label 100009, Topology entry: 0x84e53f4
```

LDP Label Space

Two types of label spaces are used: *per interface* and *per platform*. Per-interface label space is used for ATM or frame relay interfaces where VCIs and DLCIs, respectively, are used as labels. This means that each per-interface label space has local significance and the label spaces can be the same or even overlap. Per-platform label space means that the labels must be unique and have local significance with respect to the platform as a whole. Juniper Networks routers employ per-platform label space.

The label space that is supported and managed by an LSR is indicated to a peer LSR using a six-octet label space identifier. The label space identifier consists of a four-octet globally unique value (a router ID, for example) followed by a two-octet value identifying the label space itself. The label space identifier is embedded in the LDP hello messages that are sent to a peer periodically.

A single LSR can manage multiple label spaces. This situation arises if an ATM-LSR has two physical ATM links to the same ATM-LSR peer. A separate LDP session is established over each of the links to the peer, one for each label space. A separate label space identifier is sent to the ATM-LSR peer over each interface, because the labels for each link are interface specific.

Another situation in which more than one LDP session is established between peers is when different interface types are used to connect those peers. For example, two LSRs that are directly attached to each other using both an ATM interface and an Ethernet interface require two LDP sessions. A per-platform label space identifier is sent for the Ethernet interface and a per-interface identifier for the ATM interface. However, two LSRs connected by more than one Ethernet interface require only one LDP session between them.

LDP Distribution Methods

LDP uses two main types of label distribution: *downstream unsolicited* and *downstream on demand*. Both of these methods may be used in the same network at the same time provided that two adjacent LDP peers know which method the other is using, thus avoiding the situation in which the downstream peer is advertising label bindings and the upstream peer is requesting them at the same time.

In downstream unsolicited label distribution, the downstream LSR advertises its label-FEC bindings to its upstream peer even though the upstream peer has not requested them.

In downstream on demand distribution, the downstream peer does not advertise its label-FEC bindings until the upstream LSR requests them.

Use of the latter method is described earlier in the discussion about Cell Mode MPLS, where the upstream ATM-LSR requested a separate label for each of the prefixes from its downstream peer to avoid a cell-interleaving problem. Juniper Networks LSRs use only the downstream-unsolicited method because they operate using Frame Mode MPLS and are not subject to a cell-interleaving problem.

LDP Distribution Control Methods

Two methods can be used to control the way that LSPs are set up across the MPLS network: *independent* and *ordered* LSP control.

With independent LSP control, each LSR may advertise its label bindings at any time. For example, an LSR using downstream-unsolicited label distribution may advertise a label-FEC binding to its upstream peer before it has received a label binding for the same FEC from its downstream peer. A consequence of this is that the LSP is built toward its ingress point before label bindings from the downstream LSRs at the LSP egress point have been received.

With ordered LSP control, each LSR must wait for a label-FEC binding to be received from the downstream LSRs at the egress point of the LSP before it can advertise label-FEC bindings upstream toward the ingress point of the LSP. In other words, the LSP is built in an orderly fashion from the egress point all the way across the network to the ingress point. Juniper Networks LSRs use the ordered LSP control method.

Having exchanged label-FEC bindings and built LSPs across a network, another important consideration is what happens to those bindings if, for example, the network is disrupted by link or node failures. An upstream LSR that has received label bindings from its downstream LDP peers (via on demand or unsolicited label distribution) suddenly discovers that one of its downstream peers has become unavailable. The upstream LSR has two choices: one is to retain the label bindings from the failed peer, and the other is to discard them.

LDP Retention Methods

With *liberal retention mode* the upstream LSR retains and keeps track of all of the label-FEC bindings received from all its peers, including the failed peer. This allows the LSR to reuse those bindings as soon as the downstream peer becomes available again. With *conservative retention mode* the upstream LSR discards the label-FEC bindings completely and they have to be reacquired, by whatever method, once the peer becomes available again.

Liberal retention mode allows for faster adaptation to state and routing changes in the network but requires that all label-FEC bindings be retained, whereas conservative retention mode means that the LSR need hold fewer labels at any given time.

As a rule of thumb, a non-ATM-LSR uses liberal retention mode in conjunction with unsolicited downstream label distribution. An ATM-LSR uses conservative retention mode in conjunction with downstream on demand label distribution. Conservative retention mode allows an ATM-LSR to minimize the number of labels (VPI/VCIs) that it must maintain at any given moment in time thereby optimizing resources, and the downstream on demand label distribution allows it to overcome the problem of cell-interleave.

The Complete Reference

Chapter 15

Introduction to MPLS Virtual Private Networks

by Tony Hill and Julian K. Lucek

The generic definition of a virtual private network (VPN) is "the use of a shared infrastructure to provide connections between multiple sites belonging to the same user community such that communication between those sites is as independent and secure as it would be with a dedicated, private network."

You can accomplish the type of connectivity required for a VPN in many ways. The use of ATM by service providers to interconnect several different customer sites over a shared physical network of ATM switches is perhaps one of the most common examples of a VPN used in the 1990s. This is often referred to as the *overlay model*—that is, the Virtual Path Identifier/Virtual Circuit Identifier (VPI/VCI) logical connections within each customer community are overlaid on a network of physical trunks that interconnect the ATM switches. Similar functionality can be provided by a number of different Layer 2 technologies, including X.25, frame relay, and SMDS. The main advantage of the Layer 2 overlay VPN model is its simplicity. A circuit-orientated approach is well suited to networks that have well-defined connection requirements and traffic profiles that do not change regularly, such as branch offices that connect to a central head office for communication to it, and through it connect with each other. This is known as a *hub and spoke* topology. The main disadvantage of the overlay model occurs when the customer traffic flows dictate that a higher degree of meshing among the branch offices is necessary for any-to-any connectivity. The proliferation of point-to-point circuits becomes more difficult to maintain, especially if the circuit capacities between each of the sites need to change regularly.

Another approach to providing VPNs is to use Layer 3 rather than Layer 2 functionality. In the traditional Layer 3 approach, the customer premises' equipment connects to a service provider network that consists of routers, rather than just Layer 2 switches. The service provider network acts purely as a transport for IP packets, and the VPN functionality is provided via tunneling. IP in IP, IPSec, Layer 2 Forwarding (L2F), Layer 2 Tunneling Protocol (L2TP), and Point-to-Point Tunneling Protocol (PPTP) are all examples of tunneling mechanisms that are used to provide segregation of traffic and security for multiple user communities sharing a Layer 3 infrastructure.

The main advantage of a Layer 3 VPN is that the routing protocols within the service provider network provide optimum paths for the traffic that moves between customer sites. It is not necessary to provision and maintain hundreds of point-to-point circuits, and hub and spoke and any-to-any topologies are supported equally well. The main disadvantage of a Layer 3 VPN is that it is difficult to continue to provide optimum routing if the user communities around the network grow disproportionately. In addition, tuning the routing protocol metrics adequately to balance the traffic load within the core can become a complex task. Buying additional bandwidth to fix the problem is an expensive option. Traffic engineering and quality of service mechanisms can be used to relieve some of these pressures, at the expense of increased complexity within the network. The JUNOS software offers three methods for providing VPN functionality that make use of the best aspects of both the Layer 2 overlay and the Layer 3 models across a service provider's core network. These are 2547bis (Layer 3) MPLS VPNs, Layer 2 circuit cross-connect (CCC) and Layer 2 MPLS VPNs. These are all described in the following sections.

2547bis MPLS Virtual Private Networks

The label switching router (LSR) was defined in Chapter 14 as an MPLS node that is capable of performing both label (Layer 2) switching and Layer 3 forwarding. The marriage of these two capabilities in one device means that MPLS lends itself extremely well to the VPN environment, offering the benefits of both the Layer 2 overlay and the Layer 3 VPN models.

The label forwarding paradigm is analogous to the Layer 2 switching employed in the overlay model. The label stacking capability provides the mechanism by which traffic belonging to different VPNs is tunneled across a shared infrastructure, providing both traffic segregation between VPNs and excellent security. The use of routing protocols to advertise reachability information for the Forwarding Equivalence Classes (FECs) provides the default optimum routing behavior required for any-to-any connectivity, while the label switch paths (LSPs), especially those built using RSVP, offer a considerable amount of control over the paths that traffic takes throughout the service provider network.

2547bis MPLS VPN Components

Figure 15-1 shows an example of a simple service provider network that provides intersite connectivity for two customers, Frieda's Frozen Foods and Doug's Delicious Donuts.

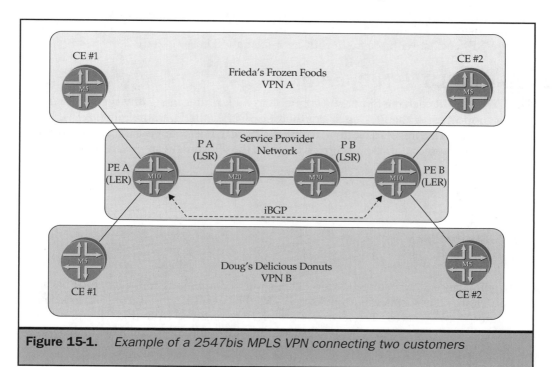

Figure 15-1. *Example of a 2547bis MPLS VPN connecting two customers*

The routers belonging to the two customers are not MPLS-capable devices; they operate using conventional IP routing and forwarding between the customer network and the service provider network. These are referred to as *customer edge* (CE) routers, which are situated at the customer premises. The CEs connect to the service provider network via *provider edge* (PE) routers, which in turn connect to the service provider core routers. These are called simply *provider* (P) routers. The PE and P routers are MPLS-capable devices, which means that the PE routers are label edge routers (LERs) and the P routers are LSRs.

The PE and P routers within the service provider's core network are typically configured to use an IGP, such as OSPF or IS-IS. An IBGP connection is configured between the PE routers and MPLS is enabled on all the interfaces between the PE and P routers. LDP or RSVP is used to set up LSPs between the PE routers' loopback addresses. Two LSPs are set up, one in each direction.

This hierarchy using CE, PE, and P routers is a standard model for providing 2547bis MPLS VPNs, and the terminology is encountered frequently when discussing this topic.

Customer route prefixes advertised from the CE routers towards the PE routers are placed into per-VPN routing tables called Virtual Routing Forwarding (VRF) tables. Each PE has a separate VRF to hold the route prefixes for each of the VPNs that it is servicing; this mechanism (together with route distinguishers and route targets, described in the following section) provides the routing segregation that is required for the operation of separate VPNs. In Figure 15-1, PE A and PE B each have two VRF tables, one for customer Frieda (VPN A) and the other for customer Doug's Donuts (VPN B). These VRFs coexist with the main routing information base (inet.0).

2547bis MPLS VPN Operation

The CE router at each customer site connects to a PE router using any type of interface that is supported by the PE—such as Ethernet, SONET/SDH, frame relay, ATM, E1, etc. The routing protocols that are currently supported between the CE and PE routers for the advertisement of route prefixes to/from the CE routers are listed below:

- EBGP
- OSPF
- RIP
- Static routing
- IS-IS

The interfaces that connect different CE routers that belong to the same VPN to the PE router are all associated with the same VRF. For example, in Figure 15-2, Frieda's CE router #1 connects to PE A so any route prefixes received from this CE will placed into VRF A on PE A. Route prefixes received from Doug's CE router #1, which also connects to PE A, will be held separately in VRF B.

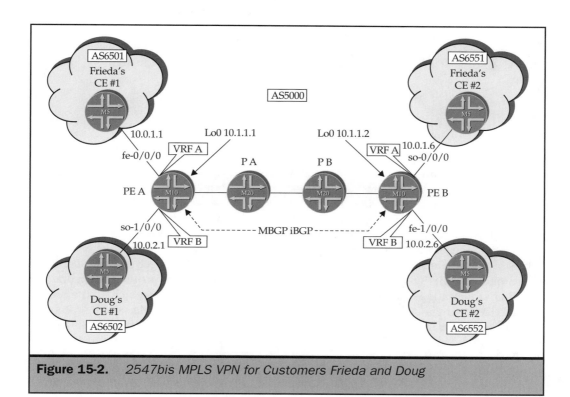

Figure 15-2. *2547bis MPLS VPN for Customers Frieda and Doug*

Each VRF is given a name when it is configured on the PE router. The following sample shows the configuration for the VRFs for VPNs A and B on PE router A, called *vpna* and *vpnb*, respectively. The VRFs are configured under the routing instances configuration hierarchy and are set to instance type VRF.

Here's the configuration for PE A:

```
routing-instances {
    vpna {
        instance-type vrf;
        interface fe-0/0/0.0;
            .
            .
            .
    }

    vpnb {
```

```
            instance-type vrf;
            interface so-1/0/0.0;
            .

            .

            .

    }
}
```

Frieda's CE router is connected to PE A via interface `fe-0/0/0`, and Doug's CE router is connected via interface `so-1/0/0`, so each of the interfaces is configured under the VRF that it belongs to.

The per-VPN routing tables, or VRF tables to be more precise, that are created on the PE router as a result of the above configuration are called *vpna.inet.0* and *vpnb.inet.0*. These coexist with, and are in addition to, the main *inet.0* RIB. The VRF tables are populated with prefixes that are received from their directly connected CE routers and via BGP from other PE routers within the service provider network. Another table, called *bgp.l3vpn.0 RIB*, is a kind of holding area into which all the routes that are received via BGP advertisements from other PE routers are placed. The received routes in the *bgp.l3vpn.0* RIB are processed and moved into the appropriate VRF table based upon the import policy for each VPN on the PE router.

Each customer prefix that is advertised by a CE router into its corresponding VRF on the PE router is "tagged" by the PE router with an eight-octet field called the *route distinguisher* (RD). The RD allows different customers to use overlapping IP address spaces across the service provider's core, because it disambiguates the prefixes. The RD that is prepended to two identical prefixes distinguishes them when they are advertised across the service provider network and placed in the *bgp.l3vpn.0* holding area.

The format of the RD used in the sample configurations in this section is a two-octet Type field, a four-octet Administrator field, plus a two-octet Assigned Number field. Only the Administrator and Assigned Number fields are configured. The 4-byte loopback address of the PEs is used for the Administrator field, so an example RD might be 10.1.1.1:100.

The corresponding configuration on PE B at the other side of the network places Frieda's CE router #2 into VPN A and Doug's CE router #2 into VPN B.

Here's the configuration on PE B:

```
routing-instances {
    vpna {
        instance-type vrf;
        interface so-0/0/0.0;
        .

        .

        .
```

```
    }

    vpnb {
        instance-type vrf;
        interface fe-1/0/0.0;
        .
        .
        .

    }
}
```

For the PE routers to receive the route prefixes from each of the CE routers into their corresponding VRF tables, you must configure a routing protocol between the CE and PE routers on each of the interfaces. This is shown in the configuration for PE routers A and B that follows. EBGP is used in this example, but any one of the currently supported protocols mentioned earlier in this chapter can also be used.

Here's the configuration on PE A:

```
routing-options {
    autonomous-system 5000;
}
.
.
routing-instances {
    vpna {
        instance-type vrf;
        interface fe-0/0/0.0;
        .
        .
        .

        protocols {
          bgp {
              group ce-frieda {
                  type external;
                  peer-as 6501;
                  neighbor 10.0.1.1;
              }
          }
        }
    }

    vpnb {
        instance-type vrf;
```

```
        interface so-1/0/0.0;
      .
      .
      .

      protocols {
        bgp {
          group ce-doug {
              type external;
              peer-as 6502;
              neighbor 10.0.2.1
          }
        }
      }
    }
  }
```

Here's the configuration on PE B:

```
routing-options {
    autonomous-system 5000;
}
.
.
.
routing-instances {
    vpna {
        instance-type vrf;
        interface so-0/0/0.0;
        .
        .
        .

        protocols {
          bgp {
            group ce-frieda {
                type external;
                peer-as 6551;
                neighbor 10.0.1.6;
            }
          }
        }
    }
}

    vpnb {
```

```
            instance-type vrf;
            interface fe-1/0/0.0;
          .


          .


          .

     protocols {
        bgp {
           group ce-doug {
              type external;
              peer-as 6552;
              neighbor 10.0.2.6
           }
        }
     }
  }
}
```

The above configurations allow route prefixes from Frieda's CE router in AS number 6501 to be advertised into VRF A on PE A, and route prefixes from Doug's CE router in AS number 6502 to be advertised into VRF B on PE A. On the other side of the network, route prefixes from Frieda's CE router in AS number 6551 are advertised into VRF A on PE B, and route prefixes from Doug's CE router in AS 6552 are advertised into VRF B on PE B. The AS number of the service providers network is set to 5000, which is configured under the routing options hierarchy level on PE A and PE B.

Having received the route prefixes on each of the PE routers, the missing piece of the puzzle is advertising them between the PE routers so that they end up in the right VRFs at either side of the network. This must be achieved while keeping the routing information from each VPN distinct as well as advertising a label for the prefixes so that label switching can take place across the core.

This is accomplished using a combination of multi-protocol BGP (MBGP) and BGP extended communities called *route targets*, or RTs. RFC 2858 describes how a special address family has been defined to carry enhanced BGP Network Layer Reachability Information (NLRI) in routing updates between BGP peers. This enhancement allows the RD, RT, Label, and corresponding route prefix to be carried across an MBGP, IBGP connection between the PE routers in a MPLS VPN.

The RTs are defined as extended communities that are added to the routing updates when a prefix is "exported" from a VRF by a PE. When the PE at the other side of the network receives the routing update via IBGP, it examines the RTs in each of the updates and "imports" only those prefixes that have RTs that match the import policy for the VRF.

The BGP sample trace here shows the information contained in a MBGP NLRI update for prefix 163.1.1.0/30 received by PE router B.

```
Oct 31 00:49:51 BGP RECV 10.1.1.1+1555 -> 10.1.1.2+179
Oct 31 00:49:51 BGP RECV message type 2 (Update) length 92
```

```
Oct 31 00:49:51 BGP RECV flags 0x40 code Origin(1): IGP
Oct 31 00:49:51 BGP RECV flags 0x40 code ASPath(2): <null>
Oct 31 00:49:51 BGP RECV flags 0x40 code NextHop(3): 10.1.1.1
Oct 31 00:49:51 BGP RECV flags 0x40 code LocalPref(5): 100
Oct 31 00:49:51 BGP RECV flags 0xc0 code Extended Communities(16): 2:1000:1
Oct 31 00:49:51 BGP RECV flags 0x80 code MP_reach(14): AFI/SAFI 1/128
Oct 31 00:49:51 BGP RECV        nhop 10.1.1.1 len 12
Oct 31 00:49:51 BGP RECV        10.1.1.1:2:163.1.1.0/30 (label 100002)
Oct 31 00:49:51 bgp_read_v4_update: done with 10.1.1.1 (Internal AS 5000) received 92 octets 1 update 1 route
```

The update contains an extended community (or RT) of 2:1000:1, the prefix 163.1.1.0/30 being advertised, and the RD of 10.1.1.1:2 that has been prepended to it. The update contains additional information provided by the MBGP NLRI enhancements, which are denoted by the Address Family Identifier (AFI) of 1 and Sub Address Family Identifier (SAFI) of 128. The update contains an extended community (or RT) of 2:1000:1, the prefix 163.1.1.0/30 being advertised and the RD of 10.1.1.1 that has been prepended to it. The update also contains the label value (100002) that will be used as the inner label to forward traffic toward prefix 163.1.1.0/30 once it arrives at PE A.

The mechanism described here is shown in Figure 15-3. Router PE A receives a route prefix of 192.168.1.0 via EBGP from CE #1 in Doug's VPN. The route is received

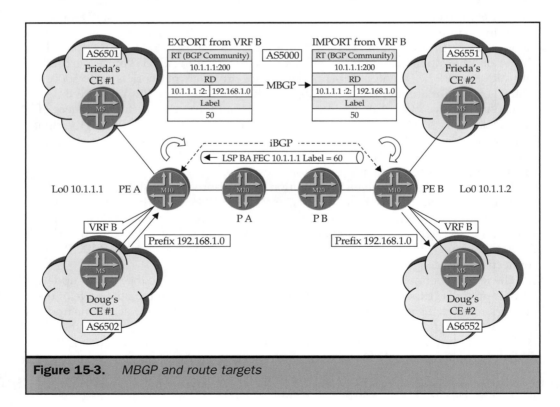

Figure 15-3. *MBGP and route targets*

into VRF B and the RD that is configured for VRF B is prepended to the prefix and a label is allocated to it. The VRF B export policy adds an RT (BGP extended community equal to 10.1.1.1:200) to the update and advertises it to PE B using the MP_REACH_NLRI attributes. When PE B receives the routing update, it examines the RT derived from the community field in the BGP update message and compares it with its VRF import policies. It finds that VRF B has an import policy that matches the BGP extended community of 10.1.1.1:200, so it imports the prefix into VRF B. The import policy for VRF A uses a different RT so the prefix is not imported into VRF A. All other updates that do not have matching RTs for either VRF A or B are not considered for import.

After the prefix has been imported successfully into VRF B, PE B resolves the BGP next-hop, which is the egress point of the LDP or RSVP LSP on the PE router from which the update was received. The label that resolves to the BGP next-hop becomes the outer label, and the label that was received in the MBGP NLRI update becomes the inner label. Next-hop resolution is performed using the *inet.3* RIB, which is discussed in Chapter 14.

The configurations that enable VPN processing for PE A and PE B are shown in the following. Only the parts that are relevant to the VPN functionality are shown; the interface and IGP configuration have been left out for clarity.

Here's the configuration on PE A:

```
routing-options {
    autonomous-system 5000;
}
protocols {
    bgp {
        group IBGP {
            type internal;
            local-address 10.1.1.1;
            neighbor 10.1.1.2 {
                family inet {
                    unicast;
                }
                family inet-vpn {
                    unicast;
                }
            }
        }
    }
}
policy-options {
    policy-statement vpna-import {
        term 1 {
```

```
                from {
                    protocol bgp;
                    community vpna;
                }
                then accept;
            }
            term 2 {
                then reject;
            }
        }
        policy-statement vpna-export {
            term 1 {
                then {
                    community add vpna;
                    accept;
                }
            }
            term 2 {
                then reject;
            }
        }
        policy-statement vpnb-import {
            term 1 {
                from {
                    protocol bgp;
                    community vpnb;
                }
                then accept;
            }
            term 2 {
                then reject;
            }
        }
        policy-statement vpnb-export {
            term 1 {
                then {
                    community add vpnb;
                    accept;
                }
            }
            term 2 {
                then reject;
```

```
            }
        }
    community vpna members target:10.1.1.1:100;
    community vpnb members target:10.1.1.1:200;
}
.
.
.
routing-instances {
    vpna {
        instance-type vrf;
        interface fe-0/0/0.0;
        route-distinguisher 10.1.1.1:1;
        vrf-import vpna-import;
        vrf-export vpna-export;
        protocols {
            bgp {
                group ce-frieda {
                    type external;
                    peer-as 6501;
                    neighbor 10.0.1.1;
                }
            }
        }
    }
    vpnb {
        instance-type vrf;
        interface so-1/0/0.0;
        route-distinguisher 10.1.1.1:2;
        vrf-import vpnb-import;
        vrf-export vpnb-export;
        protocols {
            bgp {
                group ce-doug {
                    type external;
                    peer-as 6502;
                    neighbor 10.0.2.1
                }
            }
        }
    }
}
```

Here's the configuration on PE B:

```
routing-options {
    autonomous-system 5000;
}
protocols {
    bgp {
        group IBGP {
            type internal;
            local-address 10.1.1.2;
            neighbor 10.1.1.1 {
                family inet {
                    unicast;
                }
                family inet-vpn {
                    unicast;
                }
            }
        }
    }
}
policy-options {
    policy-statement vpna-import {
        term 1 {
            from {
                protocol bgp;
                community vpna;
            }
            then accept;
        }
        term 2 {
            then reject;
        }
    }
    policy-statement vpna-export {
        term 1 {
            then {
                community add vpna;
                accept;
            }
        }
        term 2 {
```

```
                    then reject;
            }
    }
    policy-statement vpnb-import {
        term 1 {
            from {
                protocol bgp;
                community vpnb;
            }
            then accept;
        }
        term 2 {
            then reject;
        }
    }
    policy-statement vpnb-export {
        term 1 {
            then {
                community add vpnb;
                accept;
            }
        }
        term 2 {
            then reject;
        }
    }
    community vpna members target:10.1.1.1:100;
    community vpnb members target:10.1.1.1:200;
}
.
.
.
routing-instances {
    vpna {
        instance-type vrf;
        interface so-0/0/0.0;
        route-distinguisher 10.1.1.2:1;
        vrf-import vpna-import;
        vrf-export vpna-export;
        protocols {
            bgp {
                group ce-frieda {
                    type external;
```

```
                        peer-as 6551;
                        neighbor 10.0.1.6;
                    }
                }
            }
        }
        vpnb {
            instance-type vrf;
            interface fe-1/0/0.0;
            route-distinguisher 10.1.1.2:2;
            vrf-import vpnb-import;
            vrf-export vpnb-export;
            protocols {
                bgp {
                    group ce-doug {
                        type external;
                        peer-as 6552;
                        neighbor 10.0.2.6
                    }
                }
            }
        }
    }
```

These configurations and mechanisms provide the means by which customer route prefixes are advertised across the service provider's network and stored on the PE routers. The integrity of the Frieda and Doug VPNs is preserved in that each route prefix is identified securely with its corresponding VPN, and strict import and export policies control the allocation of prefixes to the appropriate VRF tables on the PE routers.

The following sample output on PE B shows the information for prefix 192.168.1.0 that is received from PE A. Both the *vpnb.inet.0* and *bgp.l3vpn.0* tables are displayed to show how the information in both tables correlates:

```
root@peb# run show route protocol bgp extensive
 .
 .
 .
vpnb.inet.0: 1 destinations, 1 routes (1 active, 0 holddown, 0 hidden)
+ = Active Route, - = Last Active, * = Both
192.168.1.0/24 (1 entry, 1 announced)
TSI:
```

```
KRT in-kernel 192.168.1.0/24 -> {so-0/2/0.0}
        *BGP       Preference: 170/-101
                   Route Distinguisher: 10.1.1.1:2
                   Source: 10.1.1.1
                   Nexthop: via so-0/2/0.0, selected
                   Push 100050, Push 100060(top)
                   State: <Secondary Active Int Ext>
                   Local AS:  5000 Peer AS:  5000
                   Age: 22:50:09   Metric2: 1
                   Task: BGP_5000.10.1.1.1+1030
                   Announcement bits (1): 1-KRT
                   AS path: I
                   Communities: target:10.1.1.1:200
                   BGP next hop: 10.1.1.1
                   Localpref: 100
                   Router ID: 10.1.1.1
                   Primary Routing Table bgp.l3vpn.0
  .
  .
  .
  .
bgp.l3vpn.0: 1 destinations, 1 routes (1 active, 0 holddown, 0 hidden)
+ = Active Route, - = Last Active, * = Both
10.1.1.1:1:192.168.1.0/24 (1 entry, 0 announced)
TSI:
        *BGP       Preference: 170/-101
                   Route Distinguisher: 10.1.1.1:2
                   Source: 10.1.1.1
                   Nexthop: via so-0/2/0.0, selected
                   Push 100050, Push 100060(top)
                   State: <Active Int Ext>
                   Local AS:  5000 Peer AS:  5000
                   Age: 17:56       Metric2: 1
                   Task: BGP_5000.10.1.1.1+1030
                   AS path: I
                   Communities: target:10.1.1.1:200
                   BGP next hop: 10.1.1.1
                   Localpref: 100
                   Router ID: 10.1.1.1
                   Secondary tables: vpnb.inet.0
```

This output clearly shows that the update belongs to Doug's VPN B because the RT extended community of 10.1.1.1:200 is allocated for VPN B by PE A. The inner label is

100050 and the outer (top) label is 100060. The last line of each table entry informs us that the primary table for the prefix is the *bgp.l3vpn.0* table and the secondary table is the *vpnb.inet.0* table. This is because the prefix is received into the *bgp.l3vpn.0* table first, as mentioned earlier, before being evaluated by the import policy for VPN B and being inserted into the *vpnB.inet.0 table* by PE B.

Having received the route prefix advertisement for network 192.168.1.0 from PE A, PE B advertises it to Doug's CE #2 using EBGP. When a member of Doug's VPN, attached to CE #2, sends traffic destined for network 192.168.1.0 into the service provider's network, the packet is received as an unlabelled packet on PE B. PE B knows the inner and outer labels it should use to forward the packet toward PE A because it received the inner label with the MBGP NLRI update and resolved the outer label to the BGP next-hop of PE A.

Figure 15-4 shows how a data packet is processed as it is sent from PE B to PE A.

PE B inserts a label header onto the packet and pushes the label received from PE A onto the label stack. This is known as the *inner label*. However, as mentioned earlier, two LSPs have already been established between PE A and PE B, one in each direction. LSP BA has its ingress point on PE B and the FEC associated with it is the loopback address of PE A. PE B pushes the label associated with the LSP BA onto the label stack;

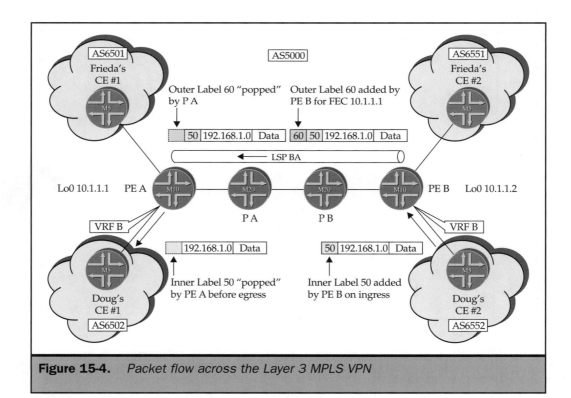

Figure 15-4.   *Packet flow across the Layer 3 MPLS VPN*

this is known as the *outer label*. The packet now has two labels in the stack. PE B forwards the packet to the LSP next-hop LSR P B using the outer label. LSR P B performs a label swap and forwards the packet to LSR P A also using the new outer label. When LSR P A receives the packet, it "pops" the top label from the stack because it received the label-FEC binding for PE A's loopback address with a label value of 3. It then forwards the packet to PE A using the inner label. This is the Penultimate Hop Popping process that was discussed in Chapter 14. PE A allocated this label in the first place, so when it receives the packet it knows that the single label remaining on the stack is associated with VRF B, and that the packet should be forwarded out of interface *so-1/0/0* toward the next-hop CE #1 in Doug's VPN. PE A removes the label header from the packet and forwards it toward it destination using conventional IP forwarding.

Additional Notes on 2547bis MPLS VPN

The example in the previous section shows a relatively straightforward MPLS VPN setup, in which the customer CE routers are all configured to use different AS numbers. In a real-life scenario it may be that the customers' AS numbers are not configured so conveniently. Detailed descriptions of how to circumvent all the potential problems are beyond the scope of this chapter. However, three possible problem scenarios and how to overcome them are described in the following paragraphs.

It may be possible that two or more of the customer's CE routers are configured with the same AS number but are connected at different points to the core. This would result in BGP dropping updates as they are sent from one CE router to the other because the CE routers would detect that their own AS number is present in the AS path. In such a case, you would need to configure the PEs to use the AS override function to replace the entire AS path from the CEs with the AS number that is used within the core. Another option is to use the AS *loop N feature*, which allows a router to receive BGP updates with its own AS number appearing N times in the AS path. But both of these options must be used with care to ensure that routing integrity is maintained and that routing loops are avoided.

In another scenario, consider a situation in which two customer CE routers with different AS numbers are connected directly to each other, as well as to the MPLS VPN, at different points. The customer may want routing between these two CE routers to take place across the direct connection between them rather than across the MPLS VPN. In this case, it is possible to configure a BGP site of origin (SOO) community on the PE routers and add it to the route prefixes when they are received from each of the CE routers and advertised across the VPN. Any prefixes containing this community that are received by the PE routers are dropped instead of being imported into the VRF tables, thus ensuring that no routes are available across the VPN, only across the direct connection between the CE routers.

The third scenario occurs when two customers want their VPNs to remain distinct, for the most part, but they want certain route prefixes to be available between the VPNs. In this case, the RTs, along with specific route filters, can be used judiciously to import and export certain prefixes between the VPNs into the relevant VRFs. However, if this "route leaking" is desired between CE routers that attach to the same PE router, it is necessary to configure RIB groups on the PE router they attach to. The use of rib-groups allows routes to be exchanged between the respective VRF tables. (Bear in mind that the *bgp.13vpn.0* table mentioned earlier is used only for MBGP updates received from remote PE routers and cannot be used to exchange routes between VRFs on the same PE).

The following sample shows how this is configured for two different CEs belonging to VPNs A and B respectively that attach to the same PE router. The configuration allows only prefix 192.168.1.0/24 to be imported from VRF B into VRF A.

Here's the configuration on the PE for CE A and CE B:

```
policy-options {
    policy-statement vpna-import {
        term 1 {
            from {
                protocol bgp;
                route-filter 192.168.1.0/24 exact;
                community vpna;
            }
            then accept;
        }
        term 2 {
            then reject;
        }
    }
    policy-statement vpna-export {
        term 1 {
            then {
                community add vpna;
                accept;
            }
        }
        term 2 {
            then reject;
        }
    }
    policy-statement vpnb-import {
        term 1 {
            from {
                protocol bgp;
```

```
                    community vpnb;
            }
            then accept;
        }
        term 2 {
            then reject;
        }
    }
    policy-statement vpnb-export {
        term 1 {
            then {
                community add vpnb;
                accept;
            }
        }
        term 2 {
            then reject;
        }
    }
    community vpna members target:10.1.1.1:100;
    community vpnb members target:10.1.1.1:200;
}
.
.
routing-options {
    rib-groups {
        vpna-vpnb {
            import-rib [ vpna.inet.0 vpnb.inet.0 ];
        }
        vpnb-vpna {
            import-rib [ vpnb.inet.0 vpna.inet.0 ];
        }
    }
    autonomous-system 5000;
}
routing-instances {
    vpna {
        instance-type vrf;
        interface so-0/0/0.0;
        route-distinguisher 10.1.1.2:1;
        vrf-import vpna-import;
        vrf-export vpna-export;
```

```
            routing-options {
                interface-routes {
                    rib-group inet vpna-vpnb;
                }
            }
            protocols {
                bgp {
                    group ce-a {
                        type external;
                        .

                        .
                        family inet {
                            unicast {
                            rib-group vpna-vpnb;
                            }
                        }
                    }
                }
            }
        }
        vpnb {
            instance-type vrf;
            interface fe-1/0/0.0;
            route-distinguisher 10.1.1.2:2;
            vrf-import vpnb-import;
            vrf-export vpnb-export;
            routing-options {
                interface-routes {
                    rib-group inet vpnb-vpna;
                }
            }
            protocols {
                bgp {
                    group ce-b {
                        type external;
                        .

                        .
                        family inet {
                            unicast {
                            rib-group vpnb-vpna;
                            }
                        }
                    }
```

```
                    }
                }
            }
        }
```

Circuit Cross-Connect

CCC allows the creation of transparent connections between two "circuits." These circuits could be, for example, Ethernet VLANs, frame relay DLCIs, ATM VCs, or MPLS LSPs.

There are three types of CCC:

- **Layer 2 switching cross-connect**   Allows a connection between a pair of like Layer 2 circuits on the same router. This does not involve MPLS so it is not discussed further in this chapter.

- **MPLS tunnel cross-connect**   Allows a connection between a pair of like Layer 2 circuits, each member of the pair being on a separate router. A dedicated LSP in each direction is used to carry the traffic between the routers.

- **LSP stitching cross-connect**   Allows two LSPs to be joined together so that traffic from one automatically flows into the other.

MPLS Tunnel Cross-Connect

A connection can be created between two like Layer 2 circuits—ATM adaptation layer 5 (AAL5), frame relay, HDLC, PPP, or VLAN—on separate routers. Traffic arriving on a circuit is mapped to a dedicated LSP by pushing the appropriate MPLS header onto the Layer 2 frame. On arrival at the remote router, the MPLS header is popped and the Layer 2 frame is sent out on the corresponding Layer 2 circuit. The feature provides the means to create a virtual private circuit between a pair of customer sites. No IP lookup is carried out on the ingress, transit, or egress routers of the LSP, so the customer can use private IP addresses or can even use the service for non-IP traffic.

Figure 15-5 shows a cross-section through a network that provides a CCC service. Routers C1 and C2 are customer routers having Ethernet connections to the SP's routers SP1 and SP2, respectively.

Here are the steps required to set up the required CCC connection:

1. Activate RSVP and family MPLS on the required interfaces—that is the SP1 and SP2 interfaces that face into the SP network. Create an RSVP-signaled LSP from SP1 to SP2 and another from SP2 to SP1.

2. On the customer-facing interfaces on SP1 and SP2, configure CCC encapsulation. Note that in the case of *vlan-ccc*, the VLAN IDs must be the same on SP1 and SP2. The VLAN ID must lie in the range 512 to 4095.

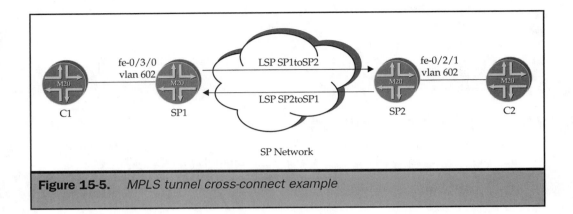

Figure 15-5. *MPLS tunnel cross-connect example*

3. In the connections section under the protocols part of the configuration, name the CCC connection and bind it to the customer-facing interface and the incoming and outgoing LSPs.

Here are the interfaces and protocols sections of the configuration of router SP1. Note that the customer-facing interface (*fe-0/3/0*) does not have `family inet` configured since SP1 does not route packets that arrive on this interface:

```
interfaces {
    so-0/2/2 {
        unit 0 {
            family inet {
                address 10.0.0.21/30;
            }
            family mpls;
        }
    }
    fe-0/3/0 {
        vlan-tagging;
        encapsulation vlan-ccc;
        unit 602 {
            encapsulation vlan-ccc;
            vlan-id 602;
        }
    }
    fxp0 {
        unit 0 {
            family inet {
```

```
                        address 10.255.254.4/24;
                }
            }
        }
        lo0 {
            unit 0 {
                family inet {
                    address 127.0.0.1/32;
                    address 192.168.50.4/32;
                }
            }
        }
    }
}
routing-options {
    router-id 192.168.50.4;
}
protocols {
    rsvp {
        interface so-0/2/2.0;
    }
    mpls {
        label-switched-path SP1toSP2 {
            to 192.168.50.1;
        }
        interface so-0/2/2.0;
    }
    ospf {
        traffic-engineering;
        area 0.0.0.0 {
            interface so-0/2/2.0 {
                metric 10;
            }
            interface lo0.0;
        }
    }
    connections {
        remote-interface-switch BigCorp {
            interface fe-0/3/0.602;
            transmit-lsp SP1toSP2;
            receive-lsp SP2toSP1;
        }
    }
}
```

The following command can be used to verify that the connection is up:

```
lab@SP1> show connections
CCC connections
   Legend for status (St)                Legend for connection types
   UN -- uninitialized                   if-sw:  interface switching
   NP -- not present                     rmt-if: remote interface switching
   WE -- wrong encapsulation             lsp-sw: LSP switching
   DS -- disabled
   Dn -- down                            Legend for circuit types
   -> -- only outbound conn is up        intf -- interface
   <- -- only inbound  conn is up        tlsp -- transmit LSP
   Up -- operational                     rlsp -- receive LSP


Connection/Circuit                     Type    St  Time last up         # Up trans
BigCorp                                rmt-if  Up  Aug  3 12:58:56              1
   fe-0/3/0.602                        intf  Up
   SP1toSP2                            tlsp  Up
   SP2toSP1                            rlsp  Up
```

It is interesting to examine the MPLS section of the forwarding table on SP1. Notice that Penultimate Hop Popping is *not* used in the case of LSPs that are used for CCC connections. This is because the egress router needs to use the incoming label as an index into the forwarding table to find the appropriate outbound interface.

In the following example, packets having a label of 100000 are popped and sent to the CCC interface `fe-0/3/0.602`:

```
Routing table:: mpls
MPLS:
Interface.Label    Type RtRef Nexthop        Type Index NhRef Netif
default            perm    0                 dscd    1     1
0                  user    0                 recv    3     2
1                  user    0                 recv    3     2
100000             user    0                 ucst   27     1 fe-0/3/0.602
fe-0/3/0. (CCC)    user    0                 Push 100016   so-0/2/2.0
```

Note that when an LSP is used for a CCC connection of this type, it is dedicated to that CCC connection. As a result, the LSP does not appear in the routing table and cannot be used by other traffic:

```
lab@SP1> show route table inet.3
lab@SP1>
```

Using CCC connections of this type, it is possible to create a small-scale Layer 2 VPN. For large-scale Layer 2 VPNs, it is recommended that you use the MPLS Layer 2 VPN functionality described in the section "Layer 2 MPLS Virtual Private Networks." This uses CCC as the underlying mechanism but with the added advantage of auto-provisioning capabilities.

When deploying CCC, note that it is important to ensure that the maximum transmission unit (MTU) of the links carrying the LSPs are sufficiently large to accommodate the maximum size packet that the client can send, taking into account the MPLS encapsulation overhead.

LSP Stitching Cross-Connect

This type of CCC connection allows two LSPs to be joined together, which is useful in situations where MPLS forwarding is required across IGP area boundaries. In this case, it is not possible to create a single (CSPF-based) LSP, because the scope of this type of LSP is within a single IGP area. Referring to Figure 15-6, if LSP X and LSP Y are stitched at router B, traffic exiting LSP X at that router is automatically sent into LSP Y. Note that the ingress router, A, of LSP X does not "know" that LSPs are stitched. Therefore, the traffic that enters LSP X is the same as if there were no stitching. In practice, this means that the traffic engineering shortcuts option need to be activated on router A for the LSP to be useful, so that router A uses the LSP X for traffic having a BGP next-hop of router C.

This is the configuration required to stitch the two LSPs at router B, assuming that LSPs X and Y have been configured on routers A and B, respectively:

```
connections {
        lsp-switch stitchXtoY {
            transmit-lsp Y;
            receive-lsp X;
        }
    }
```

An alternative to using stitching would be to configure an LSP from end-to-end with CSPF deactivated. However, this could be disadvantageous because some features available with CSPF, such as administrative groups, could not be used to constrain the placement of the LSP.

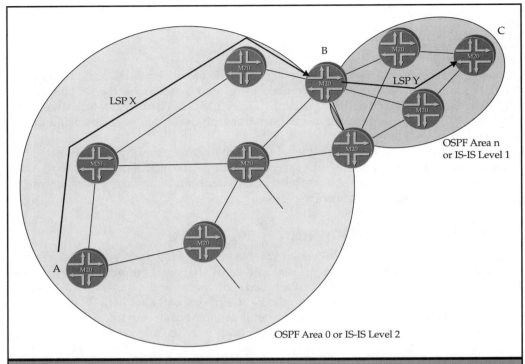

Figure 15-6. *LSP X and LSP Y are stitched at router B.*

Layer 2 MPLS Virtual Private Networks

A Layer 2 MPLS VPN is a collection of customer sites that attach to a service provider's network using Layer 2 protocols. The sites are cross-connected across the service provider's network using MPLS LSPs. From the customers' point of view, the sites appear to be connected to a large, virtual Layer 2 switch. The security and privacy of an MPLS Layer 2 VPN is the same as that of an overlay VPN based on ATM or frame relay switches.

The main difference between a Layer 2 MPLS VPN and a 2547bis Layer 3 MPLS VPN is that in a Layer 2 VPN, the customer's CE routers do not exchange Layer 3 routing information with the service provider's core network routers. The customers are responsible for configuring and managing their own routing protocols and policies. The service provider has only to ensure that designated customer sites are connected to each other using reliable, point-to-point circuits that are capable of transporting Layer 2 PDUs between the sites. In other words, the customer's routing protocols and policies are transparent to the service provider.

Currently, two emerging work-in-progress drafts for Layer 2 MPLS VPNs exist: the *Kompella L2 Draft* and the *Martini L2 Circuit Drafts*. These drafts describe how the Layer 2 interface information for each CE to PE router connection is bound to labels and advertised (signaled) across a service provider's MPLS network. These connection-to-label bindings allow label-switched, point-to-point LSP circuits to be set up between designated sites within a VPN. The drafts also describe the method used to encapsulate and transport Layer 2 PDUs across the point-to-point LSP circuits once they have been established. The Kompella and Martini drafts specify different label distribution and Layer 2 PDU encapsulation methods and are not interoperable.

> **Note** *There are actually two Martini Drafts: draft-martini-l2circuit-trans-mpls and draft-martini-l2circuit-encap-mpls. The former describes the label signaling and distribution method, and the latter describes the Layer 2 circuit PDU encapsulations that are supported. Both Martini drafts will become informational RFCs.*

The Juniper Networks range of routers use the Kompella draft approach for signaling and provisioning Layer 2 VPNs. All the functionality available with the Martini draft approach is available with the Kompella draft Layer 2 VPN, including PDU sequencing. In addition, JUNOS software supports both the Kompella and Martini encapsulation methods and future versions of JUNOS software will support the Martini signaling method. The main reason for choosing to adopt the Kompella approach for signaling and provisioning is that MBGP is used to advertise label bindings across the MPLS network, whereas the Martini approach uses LDP for advertising label bindings. The use of BGP has significant advantages because it is already deployed widely and most service providers have a good working knowledge of it. Also, the configuration of L2 VPNs is similar to that of 2547bis Layer 3 VPNs when MBGP is used. Another reason is that BGP provides a mechanism for inter-provider Layer 2 VPN communication, whereas the Martini draft approach currently caters only to intra-VPN communication.

The following sections describe the Kompella draft Layer 2 VPN and MBGP approach in more detail.

Layer 2 MPLS VPN Components

The basic structure and components of a Layer 2 MPLS network are similar to those in a 2547bis Layer 3 MPLS network. That is, the service provider's network consists of P and PE routers in the core with the customer CE routers attaching to the PE routers at the edge. The service provider network typically uses an IGP, such as OSPF or ISIS, within the core to provide reachability information for the LDP or RSVP LSPs to be set up between the PE routers. Multi-protocol IBGP is used between the PE routers to advertise the labels that identify each CE to PE router Layer 2 connection within the VPNs. As with 2547bis MPLS VPNs, the LSP labels are the outer labels and the Layer 2 connection labels are the inner, or VPN, labels. Each CE to PE router Layer 2 connection is identified uniquely within a VPN using a 16-bit site identifier, also referred to as the CE ID.

EBGP communities, or RTs, are associated with specific NLRIs in the same way that they are in 2547bis Layer 3 MPLS networks. The RTs allow the PE routers to export and import the Layer 2 VPN connection information that is carried by multi-protocol IBGP across the network.

Layer 2 VPN Signaling

The FECs in a Layer 2 MPLS VPN network are the inner labels that are bound to the Layer 2 connections configured on the PE routers, rather than IP prefixes that are used in a 2547bis Layer 3 MPLS network. A new multi-protocol BGP NLRI element is defined to carry the L2 VPN CE router connection information between PE routers. This is shown in Figure 15-7.

The Length field denotes the total length of the Layer 2 VPN NLRI element in octets. The other fields are described in the following sections.

Encapsulation Type   The Encapsulation Type field identifies one of the following encapsulations for the CE to PE router connections:

- Frame relay
- ATM AAL5 PDUs
- ATM cell relay
- PPP
- Cisco-HDLC
- Ethernet VLAN

The encapsulation type of all the interfaces within a Layer 2 VPN must be the same throughout that VPN. For example, all of the interfaces in VPN Red can be frame relay

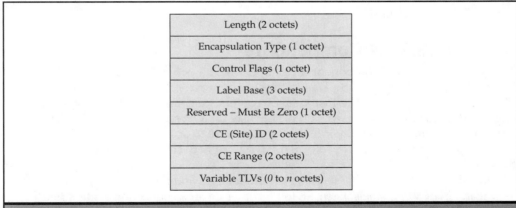

Figure 15-7.   *Layer 2 VPN NLRI information*

and all of the interfaces in VPN Blue can be ATM. The CE and PE router interfaces are configured with the same physical encapsulation types and logical interface identifiers—VPI/VCIs or DLCIs for example. The following sample shows the configurations for a CE and PE router that use two frame relay DLCI connections (DLCIs 700 and 701) to connect to each other.

```
CE Router (Frame Relay)
so-0/1/0 {
        encapsulation frame-relay;
        unit 1 {
            dlci 700;
            family inet {
                address 10.0.1.250/30;
            }
        }
        unit 2 {
            dlci 701;
            family inet {
                address 10.0.1.245/30;
            }
        }
}
```

```
PE Router (Frame Relay)
so-0/1/3 {
        dce;
        encapsulation frame-relay-ccc;
        unit 1 {
            encapsulation frame-relay-ccc;
            dlci 700;
        }
        unit 2 {
            encapsulation frame-relay-ccc;
            dlci 701;
        }
}
```

For frame relay connections, it is possible to use one set of DLCI numbers between an ingress CE to PE router connection on one side of the network and a different set of DLCI numbers on an egress PE to CE connection at the other side of the network. In other words, the DLCI numbering must follow the same rules followed for conventional frame relay switching, because the DLCIs have local significance within the service provider network. The same applies to ATM VPI/VCI connections using AAL5 PDU encapsulation because the AAL5 PDUs are transported intact across the MPLS VPN network. When the PDUs arrive at the egress PE router, they are segmented into cells, allocated a new (or the same) VPI/VCI number, and forwarded to the relevant outgoing PE-to-CE router interface.

However, for cell relay, the service provider's network treats the point-to-point LSP circuit between sites as a transport for a stream of individual cells rather than AAL5 PDUs. In this case, the same VPI/VCI numbering must be used on both sides of the network; otherwise the cells with nonmatching VPI/VCIs are dropped at the egress PE router.

Here is a sample ATM AAL5 PDU connection for VPI 0 VCI 32 in the CE to PE router configurations:

```
CE Router (ATM)
at-0/3/0 {
        atm-options {
            vpi 0 maximum-vcs 2000;
        }
        unit 32 {
            vci 32;
            family inet {
                address 10.0.2.9/30;
            }
        }
}

PE Router (ATM)
at-1/0/0 {
        dce;
        encapsulation atm-ccc-vc-mux;
        atm-options {
            vpi 0 maximum-vcs 1000;
        }
        unit 32 {
            encapsulation atm-ccc-vc-mux;
            vci 0.32;
        }
}
```

Control Flags The Control Flags field is a single octet that is used to specify whether sequenced delivery of Layer 2 PDUs is required across the point-to-point LSP circuits between sites. If bit 7 (the S bit) is set, it signals to the PE routers that they have to enforce a PDU sequencing algorithm. The remaining six bits are reserved for future use.

Label Base   The PE router uses the Label Base field to advertise the *first* of a contiguous set of labels (the label block) to remote PE routers, and the Label Range field specifies how many labels are in the label block. The labels in the label block are the inner labels used by CE sites attached to remote PE routers to connect to the advertising PE router's CE sites.

CE (Site) ID   The CE (Site) ID is a 16-bit number that identifies a CE site uniquely within a VPN. The CE site IDs are configured on the PE routers to establish the total number of sites within the VPN for the label block allocation and to specify which sites are connected to each other across the MPLS network.

CE Range   The CE Range field denotes the number of labels in the label block. The advertising PE router sets the CE Range field in its advertisements based on the number of CE sites to which it has been configured to connect. The label assignment works as follows. If PE1 has a site CE1 attached to it, and PE1 is configured to connect to sites CE7 and CE8 attached to remote PE2, PE1 advertises a label-base of x in the Label Base field and a CE range of *8* in the CE Range field. So if PE1 advertises a label-base of $x = 32768$ for its attached site CE1, it knows that packets destined for CE1 from remote site CE7 attached to PE2 will use a label of 32774, and those from site 8 will use a label of 32775.

To summarize, if a site with site identifier y is attached to a remote PE router, the remote PE router uses the following inner label to forward traffic from site y to site x attached to the local PE router:

(Label Base of Site x) + y − 1

Sub-TLVs   The Sub-TLV fields, as the name implies, are TLVs imbedded in other TLVs. Sub-TLVs are used to provide extensibility for the signaling mechanism if new TLVs need to be added in the future.

Layer 2 VPN Frame Format

The format of each layer PDU that is transported across the point-to-point LSP circuits between sites is described for all the encapsulation types in following sections and in Figure 15-8.

Frame Encapsulation	Outer Label	Inner Label	Sequence Number	Modified Layer 2 Frame

Figure 15-8.   *Layer 2 VPN PDU format*

The outer label is used to transport the PDUs to the PE that is attached to the destination CE across the service provider's LDP or RSVP LSPs, much as it is in MPLS Layer 3 VPNs. In fact, Layer 2 and Layer 3 VPNs, as well as regular non-VPN LSPs within the service provider network, may use the outer label simultaneously.

The inner label is used by the destination PE to determine to which CE router connection to send the packet. In other words, this is the label that is mapped to a specific logical interface. The label itself is 20 bits. The experimental bits are named N (Notification), C (Control), and L (Loss), as shown in Figure 15-9.

The sequence number is an optional two-octet unsigned number (that wraps back to zero) that is used to ensure in-sequence delivery of L2 PDUs. The Sequence Number field is included only if its use is indicated by the Control Flags field in the MBGP NLRI element. For each Layer 2 connection, the sequence number field is set to 0 for the first PDU transmitted and incremented by 1 for each subsequent PDU sent on the same Layer 2 connection. When an out-of-sequence PDU arrives at the receiving PE router, it may be buffered or discarded, depending on how out-of-sequence packet handling is implemented on the PE router.

The Layer 2 frames are modified so that they can be transported across the point-to-point LSP circuits within the MPLS Layer 2 PDUs. The modification depends on the Layer 2 type. The following sections describe the modification for each protocol type and other per-protocol information.

Frame Relay

The DLCI octets are removed from the frame relay frames by the ingress PE router as they arrive from a CE router. The "non-address" bits in the DLCI, namely the Forward and Backward Explicit Congestion Notification (FECN and BECN), the Command/Response (C/R) bit and the Discard Eligible (DE) bit, are copied into the experimental bits as follows: BECN to the N bit, C/R bit to the C bit, and DE to the L bit. If the Layer 2 VPN implementation does not honor these nonaddress bits, the experimental bits are all set to 0.

The rest of the frame, including the Layer 3 payload, is transported across the MPLS LSP to the egress PE router inside the MPLS Layer 2 PDU. Upon receipt of the frame relay PDU, the egress PE router copies the N bit to BECN of the outgoing DLCI,

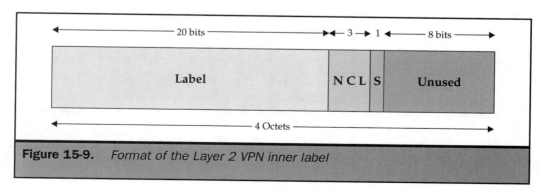

Figure 15-9. *Format of the Layer 2 VPN inner label*

the C bit to C/R, and the L bit to DE. A new DLCI is added at the egress PE router, and the fully formed frame relay frame is sent to the destination CE router.

This mechanism allows the DE bit setting to be honored within the MPLS network. For example, a Layer 2 frame relay PDU with the L bit set could be label switched across a separate, less preferred LSP than PDUs that do not have the L bit set.

ATM AAL5

ATM cells that constitute a complete frame are received from a CE router by the ingress PE router, and an ATM ALL5 PDU is constructed. The AAL5 PDU is transported across the MPLS network without any VPI/VCI information. The AAL5 PDU is segmented into cells at the egress PE router, a cell header with the correct VPI/VCI is added to each cell, and the cells are sent to the destination CE router.

The ingress PE router sets the L bit in the AAl5 PDU if any of the cells that constitute the PDU have the CLP bit set when they are received by the ingress PE router. The egress PE router sets the CLP bit in each cell when segmenting the AAL5 PDU if the L bit is set in the inner label of the PDU when it arrives at the egress PE router.

The ingress PE router may give preferential treatment to the ATM PDU based on whether any cell has the CLP bit set or all cells have their CLP bits clear.

ATM Cells

For ATM cell VPNs, the cells (including the five-octet header) are received by the ingress PE router from a CE router and transported across the point-to-point LSP circuits individually. The cells are sent by the egress PE router to the destination CE router. The experimental bits of the inner label are set to zero at the ingress PE router and are ignored by the egress PE router.

PPP, Cisco HDLC, and Ethernet

For PPP, Cisco HDLC, and nonswitched Ethernet VLAN VPNs, the Layer 2 frames are transported whole, without any modification, inside the MPLS Layer 2 PDUs. The Layer 2 frames do not include HLDC flags, an Ethernet preamble, or the Ethernet cyclic redundancy checksum. The frames are sent to the destination CE router by the egress PE router.

The experimental bits of the inner label are set to zero at the ingress PE router and ignored by the egress PE router.

Layer 2 MPLS VPN Operation

Figure 15-10 shows a Layer 2 MPLS VPN that connects four CE routers from two different customers—Frieda's Frozen Foods Ltd. and Doug's Delicious Donuts. Frieda has two sites in VPN Blue, and Doug has three sites in VPN Red that are fully meshed. Both companies share the CE router at the top right-hand side of the network because it is situated at an ACME site that has struck a deal to supply goods to both companies.

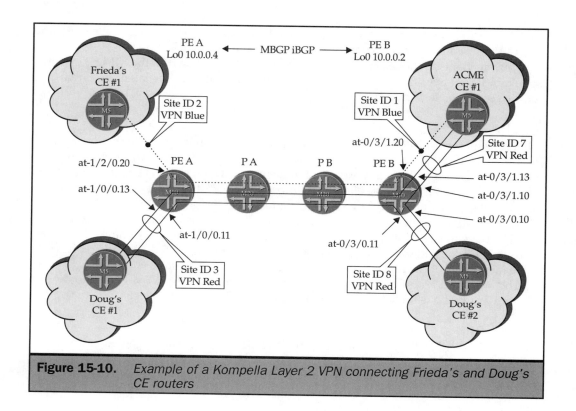

Figure 15-10. *Example of a Kompella Layer 2 VPN connecting Frieda's and Doug's CE routers*

Frieda's connection across the Layer 2 MPLS VPN is a simple point-to-point ATM AAL5 virtual circuit that connects logical interface `at-1/2/0.20` in Site ID 2 on Frieda's CE #1 to interface `at-0/3/1.20` in Site ID 1 on ACME's CE #1. Doug's VPN connections are a little more complicated because they are a three-way full mesh with the following connections:

Site Owner	Source Site ID	Source Interface	Site Owner	Destination Site ID	Destination Interface
Doug	3	at-1/0/0.13	ACME	7	at-0/3/1.13
Doug	3	at-1/0/0.11	Doug	8	at-0/3/0.11
Doug	8	at-0/3/0.10	ACME	7	at-0/3/1.10

The configurations for PE A in Figure 15-10 for Frieda's connections in VPN Blue and Doug's connections in VPN Red are shown below. All the connections are configured using ATM AAl5 circuits across the MPLS network.

```
system {
    host-name PEA;
}
.
.
.
interfaces {
    .
    .
    .
    at-1/0/0 {
         encapsulation atm-ccc-vc-mux;
        atm-options {
            vpi 0 maximum-vcs 1000;
        }
        unit 11 {
            description "Connection to Doug CE #1, VCI 11, Site ID 3, VPN Red";
            encapsulation atm-ccc-vc-mux;
            vci 0.11;
        }
        unit 13 {
            description "Connection to Doug CE #1, VCI 13, Site ID 3, VPN Red";
            encapsulation atm-ccc-vc-mux;
            vci 0.13;
        }
    }
    at-1/2/0 {
         encapsulation atm-ccc-vc-mux;
        atm-options {
            vpi 0 maximum-vcs 1000;
        }
        unit 20 {
            description "Connection to Frieda CE #1, VCI 20, Site ID 2, VPN Blue";
            encapsulation atm-ccc-vc-mux;
            vci 0.20;
        }
    }
    lo0 {
        unit 0 {
            family inet {
                address 10.0.0.4/32;
            }
        }
    }
}
routing-options {
    autonomous-system 2;
}
```

```
protocols {
    mpls {
        interface all;
    }
    bgp {
        group IBGP {
            type internal;
            local-address 10.0.0.4;
            neighbor 10.0.0.2 {
                family inet {
                    unicast;
                }
                family l2-vpn {
                    unicast;
                }
            }
        }
    }
    ldp {
        interface all;
    }
}
.
.
.
policy-options {
    policy-statement imp-red {
        term 1 {
            from {
                protocol bgp;
                community red;
            }
            then accept;
        }
        then reject;
    }
    policy-statement exp-red {
        term 1 {
            then {
                community add red;
                accept;
            }
        }
        then reject;
    }
    policy-statement imp-blue {
        term 1 {
```

```
            from {
                protocol bgp;
                community blue;
            }
            then accept;
        }
        term 2 {
            then reject;
        }
    }
    policy-statement exp-blue {
        term 1 {
            then {
                community add blue;
                accept;
            }
        }
    }
    community red members target:2:100;
    community blue members target:2:999;
}
routing-instances {
    red {
        instance-type l2vpn;
        interface at-1/0/0.11;
        interface at-1/0/0.13;
        route-distinguisher 10.0.0.4:1;
        vrf-import imp-red;
        vrf-export exp-red;
        protocols {
            l2vpn {
                encapsulation-type atm-aal5;
                site doug3 {
                    site-identifier 3;
                    interface at-1/0/0.11 {
                        remote-site-id 8;
                    }
                    interface at-1/0/0.13 {
                        remote-site-id 7;
                    }
                }
            }
        }
    }
    blue {
        instance-type l2vpn;
        interface at-1/2/0.20;
```

```
        route-distinguisher 10.0.0.4:2;
        vrf-import imp-blue;
        vrf-export exp-blue;
        protocols {
            l2vpn {
                encapsulation-type atm-aal5;
                site frieda2 {
                    site-identifier 2;
                    interface at-1/2/0.20 {
                        remote-site-id 1;
                    }
                }
            }
        }
    }
}
```

The `l2-vpn unicast` family configuration command under the bgp protocols hierarchy level enables multi-protocol IBGP between PE A and PE B so that the Layer 2 VPN label to Site ID bindings can be exchanged using the new multi-protocol IBGP NLRI element between the PE routers.

The full configuration for PE B in Figure 15-10 for Frieda's connections in VPN Blue and Doug's connections in VPN Red is shown below. All the connections are configured using ATM AAl5 circuits across the MPLS network.

```
system {
    host-name PEB;
}
.
.
.
interfaces {
    .
    .
    .
    at-0/3/0 {
        encapsulation atm-ccc-vc-mux;
        atm-options {
            vpi 0 maximum-vcs 1000;
        }
        unit 10 {
            description "Connection to Doug CE #2, VCI 10, Site ID 8, VPN Red";
            encapsulation atm-ccc-vc-mux;
            vci 0.10;
        }
```

```
        unit 11 {
            description "Connection to Doug CE #2, VCI 11, Site ID 8, VPN Red";
            encapsulation atm-ccc-vc-mux;
            vci 0.11;
        }
    }
    at-0/3/1 {
        encapsulation atm-ccc-vc-mux;
        atm-options {
            vpi 0 maximum-vcs 1000;
        }
        unit 10 {
            description "Connection to ACME CE #1, VCI 10, Site ID 7, VPN Red";
            encapsulation atm-ccc-vc-mux;
            vci 0.10;
        }
        unit 13 {
            description "Connection to ACME CE #1, VCI 13, Site ID 7, VPN Red";
            encapsulation atm-ccc-vc-mux;
            vci 0.13;
        }
        unit 20 {
            description "Connection to ACME CE #1, VCI 20, Site ID 1, VPN Blue";
            encapsulation atm-ccc-vc-mux;
            vci 0.20;
        }
    }
    lo0 {
        unit 0 {
            family inet {
                address 10.0.0.2/32;
            }
        }
    }
}
routing-options {
    autonomous-system 2;
}
protocols {
    mpls {
        interface all;
    }
    bgp {
        group IBGP {
            type internal;
            local-address 10.0.0.2;
            neighbor 10.0.0.4 {
```

```
                    family inet {
                        unicast;
                    }
                    family l2-vpn {
                        unicast;
                    }
                }
            }
        }
        ldp {
            interface all;
        }
    }
    policy-options {
        policy-statement imp-red {
            term 1 {
                from {
                    protocol bgp;
                    community red;
                }
                then accept;
            }
            then reject;
        }
        policy-statement exp-red {
            term 1 {
                then {
                    community add red;
                    accept;
                }
            }
            then reject;
        }
        policy-statement imp-blue {
            term 1 {
                from {
                    protocol bgp;
                    community blue;
                }
                then accept;
            }
            then reject;
        }
        policy-statement exp-blue {
            term 1 {
                then {
                    community add blue;
```

```
                    accept;
                }
            }
        then reject;
    }
    community red members target:2:100;
    community blue members target:2:999;
}
routing-instances {
    red {
        instance-type l2vpn;
        interface at-0/3/0.10;
        interface at-0/3/0.11;
        interface at-0/3/1.10;
        interface at-0/3/1.13;
        route-distinguisher 10.0.0.2:1;
        vrf-import imp-red;
        vrf-export exp-red;
        protocols {
            l2vpn {
                encapsulation-type atm-aal5;
                site doug8 {
                    site-identifier 8;
                    interface at-0/3/0.10 {
                        remote-site-id 7;
                    }
                    interface at-0/3/0.11 {
                        remote-site-id 3;
                    }
                }
                site acme {
                    site-identifier 7;
                    interface at-0/3/1.13 {
                        remote-site-id 3;
                    }
                    interface at-0/3/1.10 {
                        remote-site-id 8;
                    }
                }
            }
        }
    }
    blue {
        instance-type l2vpn;
        interface at-0/3/1.20;
        route-distinguisher 10.0.0.2:2;
        vrf-import imp-blue;
```

```
        vrf-export exp-blue;
        protocols {
            l2vpn {
                encapsulation-type atm-aal5;
                site acme {
                    site-identifier 1;
                    interface at-0/3/1.20 {
                        remote-site-id 2;
                    }
                }
            }
        }
    }
}
```

The two configurations for PE A and PE B clearly show the mappings between the different Site IDs within VPN Blue and VPN Red. Each PE router generates a label base and specifies a label range for the remote sites that have been configured to connect to its local sites. A `show l2vpn connections` command on PE A shows the label base and label range that it advertises to PE B for the sites on remote router Doug CE 2 to connect to the local sites on local router Doug CE 1.

The output of this command may vary slightly on future implementations of JUNOS.

```
lab@pea> show l2vpn connections
L2VPN Connections :
Instance : red
Local site: doug3
offset: 1, range: 8, label-base: 32768
    connection-site        Type   St   Time last up            # Up trans
    7                       rmt    Up   Jun 17 09:53:5 2001              1
       Local circuit: at-1/0/0.13, Status: Up
       Remote  PE: 10.0.0.2
       Incoming label:32774, Outgoing label: 32770
    8                       rmt    Up   Jun 17 09:53:54 2001             1
       Local circuit: at-1/0/0.11, Status: Up
       Remote PE: 10.0.0.2
       Incoming label: 32775, Outgoing label: 32778
```

This output shows that the local site, doug3, is configured in VPN Instance *red*. The local site includes the two subinterfaces *at-1/0/0.13* and *at-1/0/0.11*.

Router PE A advertises label base 32768 to router PE B with a label range of *8* because this is the highest remote site ID that has been configured to connect to PE A. Remote site 7 falls within this range and label 32774 is used by router PE B for all

Layer 2 PDUs that should be forwarded to subinterface `at-1/0/0.13`. Router PE B uses label 32775 for remote site 8, which is associated with subinterface `at-1/0/0.11`. These are shown as the incoming labels in the preceding output. Router PE B uses these labels as the inner labels for Layer 2 PDUs that it sends to router PE A across the service provider's network. The labels advertised to router PE B for remote sites 7 and 8 are calculated by Router PE B as follows:

Label for remote site 7 = 32768 + 7 − 1 = 32774
Label for remote site 8 = 32768 + 8 − 1 = 32775

Remote sites 1, 2, 4, 5, and 6 also fall within this label range and can connect to local site 3 if they are configured on the local, or remote, PE routers in the future. In other words, there are sufficient labels in the label block to support all remote sites starting with an offset of 1 all the way up to 8. A separate label block is created if an additional site outside this range is configured to connect to router PE A. You should plan the number of sites if contiguous labels and label blocks are required in a Layer 2 VPN implementation. This is not mandatory because the PE routers will allocate labels as they are needed, but contiguous labels and label blocks could help to identify specific sites and VPNs for troubleshooting purposes.

The outgoing labels are derived from the label base that is advertised by router PE B. Router PE A uses these outgoing labels as the inner labels to connect to remote sites attached to router PE B. Router PE B's loopback address (10.0.0.2) is displayed next to sites 7 and 8, confirming that these outgoing labels have been received from router PE B.

Chapter 16

Internet Processor II and Firewall Filters

by Harry Reynolds

I t could be convincingly argued that the Internet Processor is the heart and soul of a Juniper Network's backbone Internet router. In March 2000 Juniper released the second generation of Internet Processor, known as the *Internet Processor II* (IP2), which began shipping with the M160 platform. While early M40 and M20 routers may need field upgrades to obtain IP2 functionality, all M-series routers now ship with the IP2.

This chapter examines various IP2 application case studies and gives examples of the corresponding configuration, along with analysis of the screen dumps that result from firewall and IP2-related operational commands.

This chapter provides a detailed discussion of the following IP2 features:

- Firewall filters
- Counting
- Packet classification for queuing and loss probability
- Rate limiting
- Filter Based Forwarding (FBF)
- Logging and sampling
- Denial of Service (DoS) tracking

Overview of IP2 Features and Capabilities

Before getting into the "nuts and bolts" of IP2 applications and configuration, it would be wise to spend a few moments describing the general features and abilities of the IP2.

The benefits of Juniper Networks centralized router design is clearly demonstrated by the fact that migration to the new Internet Processor II ASIC (application specific integrated circuit), with all of its associated features, does not require any modifications to your current Flexible PIC Concentrators (FPCs), Physical Interface Cards (PICs), or Routing Engine (RE).

"Performance Without Compromise"

"Performance without compromise" is the Juniper Networks mantra, and the IP2 ASIC is certainly no exception to this philosophy. The IP2's ability to provide industry leading forwarding rates while simultaneously supporting complex firewall, sampling, and rate limiting features opens a new realm of opportunities to service providers and end users alike.

In the past, service providers were faced with the difficult decision of maximizing routing performance *or* enabling services; the generalized design of legacy routing platforms, often coupled with the need for software interaction when supporting valued added services, simply would not allow for high-speed operation while concurrently supporting advanced packet filtering operations. The IP2 heralds a new era in that service providers can now deploy enhanced features with the assurance that enabling these services will not significantly impact the router's forwarding rate and latency.

Typical IP2 Test Results

The wide range of features supported by the IP2, coupled with the various ways in which these features can be implemented and combined, make definitive statements about performance a somewhat intractable question. By way of example, a user with a 1800-term filter that makes heavy use of counting operations will see performance that is only slightly diminished when compared to a similar filter that does not employ counting operations.

When undergoing stress testing, IP2 forwarding performance is rarely observed to fall below 80 percent of line rate. Most complex IP2 filters have no problem achieving 100 percent line rate operation when presented with a realistic Internet traffic mix, however. When one considers that legacy platforms often have trouble hitting 80 percent of line rate in the absence of any services, this "worst-case" number falls into perspective.

Figure 16-1 displays typical stress-test performance results for an IP2-equipped M20 with four OC-48c interfaces. Note that during this test, all four ports have filters applied in both directions, and that each of the 2800 prefixes in the firewall filter are active and carrying traffic. During this test, the M20 carried a total of 60,000 active routes, with each interface contributing 15,000 routes to the table. As shown in the figure, the IP2 is able to maintain line rate forwarding for virtually all packet sizes, despite the extreme nature of this stress test.

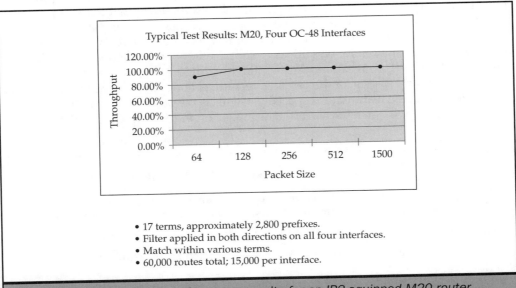

Figure 16-1. *Stress-test performance results for an IP2-equipped M20 router*

Forwarding performance is certainly a critical measurement, but latency and jitter measurements are important performance metrics that must also be taken into account when evaluating the impact of enhanced services on a routing platform. In recent backbone router testing conducted by Light Reading, the provisioning of enhanced IP2 services produced negligible increases in observed latency and jitter. Table 16-1 provides a summary of test results for the baseline Internet Processor forwarding tests (no IP2 features) and the ingress/egress accept/deny firewall filtering tests.

Both tests incorporated 12 OC-48c ports driven at 99.8 percent of line rate using 40-byte Internet Protocol (IP) packets. While several filtering tests were conducted, the results shown in the table represent the most demanding test in that filters making use of both deny and accept actions were applied in both directions, and on all ports. The "0.0" value for observed jitter indicates results that were less than the 100 nanosecond threshold of the SmartBits test set. The "All" in the test name column indicates the aggregate results for all streams being sent over all 12 ports used in the test.

 *You can visit the Light Reading Web site at **http://www.lightreading.com/testing/** to learn more about the test methodology and to view the complete test results.*

Overview of IP2 Firewall Features

The IP2 ASIC supports a rich variety of Layers 3 and 4 packet-matching conditions using a human-friendly syntax that is similar to the JUNOS Policy Language. Deploying a functional firewall is a two-step process in JUNOS software in that the user must define and apply a firewall filter before it becomes operational. While the user will be able to commit a configuration in which a filter has been defined but not applied to an interface, the opposite cannot be said, as the application of an undefined firewall filter will prevent the user from committing candidate configuration.

JUNOS software allows for the copying, renaming, and resequencing of terms within a firewall filter. These features are especially useful, as the order in which firewall filter terms are applied will often have a dramatic impact on the overall operation of the filter.

Baseline Performance Results (No IP2 Services)			
Test Name	**Minimum Latency (microseconds)**	**Maximum Latency (microseconds)**	**Average Latency (microseconds)**	**Jitter (microseconds)**
All	13.2	21.0	15.0	0.0
Preformance Results with IP2 Ingress and Egress Filtering			
All	13.9	21.3	15.0	0.0

Table 16-1. *Effects of IP2 Services on Latency and Jitter*

Routing Engine vs. Transit Filtering

There is an important distinction between filters that are intended to protect the router's own Routing Engine (RE) and filters that are intended to act upon traffic that is transiting the router's Packet Forwarding Engine (PFE).

When RE protection is desired, the firewall filter should be applied to the router's *Loopback 0 (lo0)* interface. Such a filter will have no impact on forwarded traffic, but it will, based on filter directionality, affect traffic that is originated by or destined to the local RE. When the goal is to filter traffic that is transiting the router—for example to support an outsourced firewall service—the filters are applied to transit interfaces within the PFE complex. Figure 16-2 illustrates the differences in firewall filter application.

The RE maintains copies of all filters applied to PFE ports, with the result being that traffic originated by the RE will be subject to a given firewall filter just as transit traffic would. As an example, assume that an ICMP (Internet Control Message Protocol) blocking filter is applied to *fe-0/0/1* in the output direction. The copy kept in the RE will prevent locally generated ICMP traffic from leaving on the *fe-0/0/1* interface. It should be reiterated that the same filter applied to the RE's *lo0* interface would prevent ICMP traffic from ever leaving the chassis!

> **Note**   *cflowd and statistical sampling is covered later in this chapter. For now, it is enough to simply note that sampling and cflowd export is only supported for transit interfaces on IP2-equipped router platforms.*

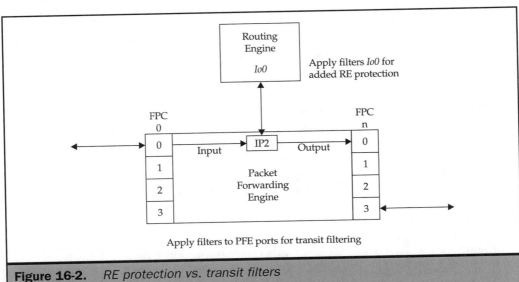

Figure 16-2.   *RE protection vs. transit filters*

Since the original Internet Processor (the IP1) did not support transit filtering, the same filtering effect was achieved when filters were applied to the router's *lo0* or transit interfaces—that is, only traffic destined to or originating from the local RE was affected. However, filter applications such as this will be problematic when the router is upgraded to the IP2 ASIC, as the filters that were originally protecting the RE will now begin taking actions upon transit traffic.

While the application of "pre-IP2" filters to numerous transit interfaces (as opposed to the single *lo0* interface) should be somewhat rare, the existence of such filters on an IP1-equipped router must be considered before attempting to upgrade the platform to the IP2.

Packet Classification via Firewall Filters

In addition to conventional packet filtering, the IP2 is also capable of performing packet classification functions that can be used to affect queue selection and Packet Loss Priority (PLP). Such packet classification can be brought to bear with granularity that ranges from interface level all the way to specific Layer 4 flows.

IP2-based packet classification at the edge, used in conjunction with Juniper Networks' support of hardware based Weighted Round Robin (WRR) queuing and Random Early Detection (RED) in the core provides the functionality needed to enable high-performance, differentiated service offerings.

Firewall Counters

The IP2 supports 64-bit byte counters and 32-bit packet counters that can be incremented based on match conditions. Since the hardware-based counters are maintained in the PFE hardware and are made available to the RE upon command-line interface (CLI) request, excessive counting can impact forwarding rates due to PFE hardware interrupts, so it is recommended that you use interface-based counters when the goal is to count large volumes of traffic on high-speed interfaces.

Rate Limiting with the IP2

The IP2 provides a mechanism by which the speed of an interface, or a specific Layer 3/4 flow, can be rate limited using a token bucket policing algorithm. This provides functions that are similar to those associated with the support of a Committed Access Rate (CAR) with the exception that an excess burst capability is currently not supported.

Prior to the introduction of the IP2, some router interfaces supported rate-limiting functions while others did not—that is, SONET and DS3 interfaces supported leaky bucket policers, while Ethernet type interfaces supported no limiting mechanisms at all. (In addition to leaky bucket policing, some router interfaces are capable of operating at sub-rate speeds, which also limits the amount of traffic supported by a given interface. Examples of such interfaces would include the DS3, E3, DS1, and channelized OC 12.) It is important to note that the IP2 can rate limit any interface type and IP-related traffic flow using a common approach and configuration syntax that can simplify network operations.

Filter Based Forwarding

Filter Based Forwarding is an IP2 feature that provides policy-based routing control by resolving the next-hops of matching packets through specially populated routing tables. On a hop-by-hop basis, these routing instances can force matching packets along a path that differs from the "normal" forwarding path contained in the main routing instance (*inet.0*). An FBF application might force all Web traffic onto a set of links reserved for this purpose, for example.

Logging and Statistical Sampling

The IP2 also supports sophisticated logging and statistical sampling functions. These are extremely useful tools that are often deployed to test the operation of a firewall filter or when conducting capacity planning and DoS tracking.

Logging

IP2 logging functions cause the key data from the notification cell to be written into a cache maintained by the JUNOS kernel. This cache displays entries starting with the most recent and can hold about 100 entries before it "wraps" and begins overwriting the oldest entries. At present, there is no command to clear the logging cache, and the cache entries are lost if the router is powered down or rebooted.

Statistical Sampling

The IP2's logging functions are typically used for tactical reasons—that is, for determining the nature of a DoS attack—while its statistical sampling abilities are often used for the strategic planning of backbone capacity and the optimization of peering relationships. A key difference between logging and sampling is the ability to statistically sample matching packets with ratios that range from 1:1 at the high end to 1:65,535 at the low end. Low sampling rates should be deployed on high-speed interfaces to prevent congesting the *fxp1* link and the excessive consumption of RE compute cycles.

The samples taken by the IP2 can be stored locally as an ASCII text file on the router's rotating storage, or the sampled data can be exported to a remote host running one of several available NetFlow analysis packages, where additional analysis and processing can be performed on the flow records. Juniper routers currently support NetFlow versions 5 and 8 export formats.

The IP2 and Non–Internet Protocols

Currently, the various IP2 services discussed in this chapter (firewall filtering, rate limiting, sampling, logging, and so on) are supported only for the *inet* family of protocols. As a result, Intermediate System to Intermediate System (IS-IS) protocol data units and Multi-Protocol Label Switching (MPLS)-labeled packets are immune to the presence of firewall filters. Presently, the IP2 does not offer support of statistical sampling or rate limiting for traffic that is part of a MPLS label switched path (LSP). The IP2 can sample and rate limit traffic at the ingress node before it has been labeled and placed into an MPLS LSP, however.

IP1 vs. IP2: Features Summary

Table 16-2 summarizes the key differences in feature support between the IP1 and IP2 ASICS.

The additional 4MB of static RAM (SRAM) on the IP2 is used for storing compiled firewall filter code, counters, and various other data structures. Both Internet Processors support a forwarding table that is at least 4MB and can support more than 420,000 active routes.

Determining Whether Your Router Is IP2 Equipped

By now you are no doubt ready to dive into the guts of this chapter and begin configuring various IP2 services in earnest, but one question remains: "Does your router have an IP2 processor?" Fortunately, this is a question that is easily answered. First, if you own an M160 or M5/M10 backbone router, the answer is an automatic "yes," as these platforms always ship equipped with an IP2. The M40's System Control Board (SCB) and the M20's System Switching Board (SSB) should be labeled with "Internet Processor II" when they are so equipped, so a simple visual inspection may suffice.

Feature	IP1	IP2
Firewall filters	RE protection only	RE and transit
Rate limiting	Not supported	Supported
Packet classification	Not supported	Supported
Sampling/logging	Not supported	Supported
Load balancing	8 next-hops, per prefix (default) or per packet	16 next-hops, per prefix (default) or per Layer 4 flow
Filter Based Forwarding	Not supported	Supported
L2 and L3 VPNs (PE functionality)	Not supported	Supported
SRAM	4MB	8MB

Table 16-2. *IP vs. IP2 Feature Comparison*

You can also use the CLI `show chassis hardware` command on all platforms to display the Internet Processor version. The `show chassis (FEB|SSB|SCB)` command is platform specific and also displays the Internet Processor version. Below is the result of a `show chassis hardware` command issued on an IP2-equipped M20 platform:

```
user@router> show chassis hardware
Hardware inventory:
Item              Version  Part number  Serial number     Description
Chassis                                 20208             M20
Backplane         REV 07   710-001517   AB5929
Power supply B    Rev 02   740-001465   000259            AC
Maxicab
Minicab
Display           REV 04   710-001519   AD1914
Host 0                                  2a000006175d8501  Present
SSB slot 0        REV 01   710-001951   AF8732            Internet Processor II
SSB slot 1        N/A      N/A          N/A               backup
FPC 0             REV 01   710-001292   AC5299
  PIC 2           REV 03   750-000612   AD4909            2x OC-3 ATM, MM
FPC 2             REV 01   710-001292   AC2321
  PIC 0           REV 03   750-000612   AD4838            2x OC-3 ATM, MM
  PIC 2           REV 03   750-000611   AC1551            4x OC-3 SONET, MM
```

Because the IP2 ASIC is surface mounted onto the system's control board, an upgrade to the IP2 requires a control board swap. For the M40 and M20 platforms, this equates to a field upgrade of the SCB and SSB, respectively. Hot swapping the control board will force a reboot of the PFE, so this operation should be performed during a maintenance window when possible.

JUNOS software will allow an IP2-related configuration to commit on a non-IP2 equipped router, so the ability to commit a candidate configuration does not offer proof that your router contains an IP2 ASIC. (This is in keeping with the Juniper philosophy of allowing the user to configure interfaces that are not currently present, etc. In this case, it is better to allow the commit and put as much of the configuration into effect in the case that a spare non-IP2 SCB/SSB has to be used or a future IP2 upgrade is planned.) Since all Juniper routers support RE-based firewall protection, you will also be able to issue firewall-related commands on routers containing an IP1.

Firewall Filter Syntax and Operation

We will now explore the actual syntax and operation of JUNOS firewall filters, beginning with a brief review of key IP-related protocols to the extent necessary for the discussion of security and packet filtering in general.

Several filtering case studies will be presented along the way; each will be associated with a JUNOS software configuration that meets the scenario's requirements.

Stateful Inspection vs. Packet Filtering

Simply put, firewalls fall into two main categories—stateful inspection and packet filtering. The IP2 is not capable of stateful inspection, so this section will focus on packet filtering concepts and techniques.

A packet filter firewall is able to look into the bits of various protocol layers when making a decision as to whether the packet is allowed. Such a firewall has no "memory," in the sense that it cannot base a current forwarding decision on previous protocol exchanges. For example, it is impossible to make a packet filter accept incoming Domain Name System (DNS) replies on the condition that a corresponding DNS query was recently observed. Stateful inspection firewalls maintain protocol state tables that allow them to understand the context of a packet as well as its binary makeup. Generally speaking, a stateful firewall can perform packet-based filtering, but the opposite is not true—a packet filtering firewall cannot perform stateful inspection.

While stateful inspection allows for stronger rule sets and therefore better security and control, there is a downside. They can be expensive, are often application specific, and are generally not capable of operating anywhere near wire speed on a single OC-192 interface, let alone concurrent operation on eight such interfaces!

IP, TCP, and UDP Structural and Operational Review

While it is assumed that you have a good understanding of TCP/IP operation, a brief review of some key elements that are applicable to packet filtering and protocol security are discussed here.

The IP Protocol

Figure 16-3 illustrates the IP V4 header. The IP2 is able to match on virtually all bit fields contained in the standard 20-byte header, including the fragmentation and options fields.

Address Fields   The IP source and destination address fields can be matched on using a *x.x.x.x/y* notation, with all address matches having a "don't care" function for prefix bits that fall outside the specified mask length. Therefore, a filter configured to block 192.168/16, for example, will block any packet with an address containing 192.168 in the high order address bits.

JUNOS matching syntax supports keywords such as `source-address`, `destination-address`, and `address`. JUNOS also supports prefix lists that can be called from within a firewall filter term; these lists are typically populated with commonly used addresses groupings such as "admin," "net-ops," or "engineering."

When multiple addresses are listed under a single `from` condition they are treated as a logical OR with the longest match being preferred. This is a notable exception to the logical AND that is normally applied when multiple conditions are listed under a `from` statement.

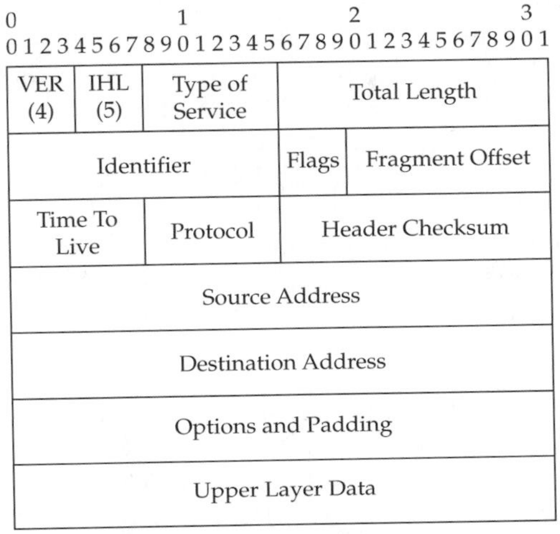

Figure 16-3.   *The IP V4 header format*

Type Of Service (TOS) Field   The IP header contains an 8-bit Type Of Service (TOS) field that is used to indicate the packet's relative drop priority and the metric that matters most to this particular application—that is, delay, throughput, or reliability. RFC 2474 "Definition of the Differentiated Services Field (DS Field) in the IPv4 and IPv6 Headers" redefines the IP TOS byte to convey a 6-bit Differentiated Services Code Point (DSCP) that can code up to 63 different forwarding classes, but many of these code points are reserved for backward compatibility.

The IP2 is capable of matching on the three precedence bits or on the entire DSCP field, which encompasses the precedence and the type of service indication bits. The IP2 can match on the 12 Assured Forwarding classes and the Expedited Forwarding class using readable keywords such as `af11` or `ef`. These capabilities make it easy to classify and properly queue packets using firewall filters.

Total Length Field   The Total Length field indicates the size of the IP datagram including the header. The IP2 can match upon a specific packet size or a range of packet sizes using the `packet-length` keyword.

Identifier, Flags, and Fragment Offset Fields   These fields are used to accommodate IP fragmentation. The IP2 can match on the fragment offset and flags field using keywords such as `is-fragment`, `last-fragment`, `first-fragment`,

`fragment-offset`, and `fragment-flags`. Some keywords actually summarize various bit settings. For example, the `first-fragment` keyword looks for packets with the *more fragments* bit set and an offset value of 0. Bit fields can usually be specified with either a number or a symbolic name. So the term `from fragment-flags 0x4000` is equivalent to specifying `from fragment-flags don't-fragment`.

The capability to match on fragmented packets is useful when one considers the large number of exploits that involve malformed or illegally formatted fragmentation fields. For example, the teardrop attack makes use of overlapping fragments, while the "Ping of death" exploit causes a machine to try to reassemble a datagram that is larger than the 65,535-byte maximum; both have been known to cause the dreaded "blue screen of death."

Protocol Field   The Protocol field is used to identify the upper layer protocol being carried in the IP datagram's payload. JUNOS firewall syntax supports keywords for common protocols but also allows the numeric specification of a protocol value. Thus, using `from protocol icmp` will achieve the same results as specifying `from protocol 1`. Common protocol numbers would include TCP (6), UDP (17), OSPF (89), BGP4 (179), and RSVP (46).

Using the `protocol` keyword, an operator can easily create a filter that allows TCP while denying another protocol such as ICMP.

Options Field   The Options field is used to convey options such as source route and record route. By using the keyword `ip-options` followed by either a numeric or symbolic representation of the option, the operator can easily create firewalls that reject or accept certain options. IP options with text keywords include `router-alert`, `strict-source-route`, `loose-source-route`, `record-route`, and `timestamp`.

The ICMP Protocol

The ICMP protocol is often used to report reachability problems such as unreachable destinations, but it is also the force behind the popular PING utility. Some implementations of the traceroute utility may also make use of the ICMP protocol. ICMP messages are carried directly within IP datagrams and use a protocol identifier of 1. Figure 16-4 illustrates the ICMP header format.

Type Field   The Type field is used to indicate the ICMP message type. The most common message types are shown in Table 16-3. JUNOS firewall filter syntax supports ICMP-based matches using keywords such as `icmp-type redirect`.

Code Field   The Code field varies by message type and is used to provide additional information. Table 16-4 lists common code values associated with the "destination unreachable" message type.

The IP2 allows matching on 24 different ICMP codes using keywords such as `destination-host-unknown` and `protocol-unreachable`.

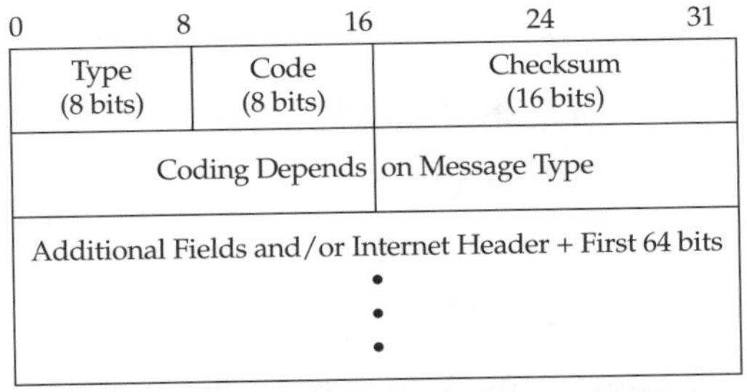

Type (8 bits)	Code (8 bits)	Checksum (16 bits)
Coding Depends on Message Type		
Additional Fields and/or Internet Header + First 64 bits • • •		

0   8   16   24   31

Figure 16-4.   *The ICMP header format*

The UDP Protocol

The UDP protocol provides a best-effort, connectionless transport service. It is often used for transaction-based applications (such as DNS queries) or for the transport of real-time media. Both types of applications benefit from the computationally simple, low overhead nature of the UDP protocol.

In essence, UDP adds two things to the services provided by IP: payload error detection and the indication of which applications are involved through the use of *ports* (sometimes called *sockets*). It can be said that IP accommodates the routing of data *to* the host, while transport layer ports facilitate the routing of application data *within* the host.

Figure 16-5 illustrates the UDP header format.

ICMP Type	Purpose
0/8	Echo reply/request
3	Destination unreachable
5	Redirect
4	Source quench
11	Time exceeded
13/14	Timestamp request/reply
17/18	Address mask request/reply

Table 16-3.   *Common ICMP Message Types*

ICMP Code	Meaning
0	Network unreachable
1	Host unreachable
2	Protocol unreachable
3	Port unreachable
4	Fragmentation required; do not fragment bit set
13	Communications administratively prohibited

Table 16-4. *ICMP Codes Associated with the "Destination Unreachable" Message Type*

Source and Destination Port Fields

Source and Destination Port Fields   The UDP Source and Destination Port fields are used to identify the application processes that are communicating. Generally speaking, port numbers below 512 are reserved for well-known server processes, and ports between 512 and 1023 are considered privileged in that they are normally reserved for system-level functions. Client processes dynamically select ports in the range of 1024 to 65,535.

Figure 16-6 illustrates the relationship between source and destination ports from both the server and client perspectives. Here it can be seen that the client contacts the sever process using a well-known destination port, while choosing a source port greater than 1023. The source and destination port values are reversed on the server's replies.

JUNOS firewall filters support port-related keywords such as `from port`, `from destination-port`, and `from source-port`. The first option will match on either the source or destination port fields, while the last two options match on specific source or destination ports respectively.

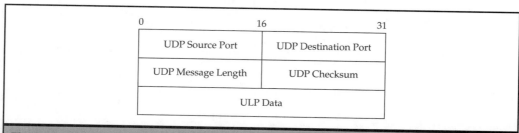

Figure 16-5.   *The UDP header format*

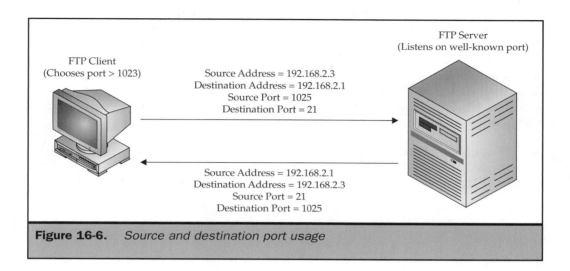

Figure 16-6.   *Source and destination port usage*

The TCP Protocol

The TCP protocol operates in a connection-oriented manner, providing reliable delivery services to the applications that ride over it. The TCP header structure is shown in Figure 16-7.

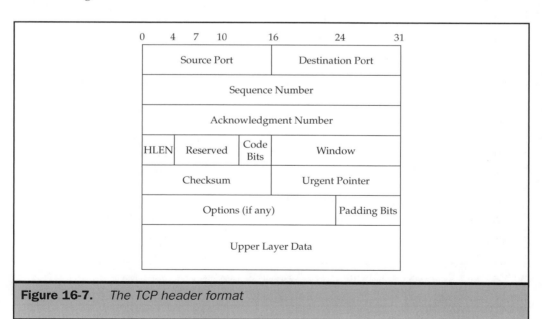

Figure 16-7.   *The TCP header format*

Source and Destination Port Fields   The TCP Source and Destination Port fields are used to identify the application processes in the manner described previously for UDP.

Where possible, both UDP and TCP use the same port numbers, as the difference in the protocol identified is sufficient to disambiguate which applications and processes are actually involved. Table 16-5 lists common port assignments for both protocols. For a definitive listing of protocol and port assignments, you can consult the latest assigned numbers RFC, which can always be found as *STD0002*.

TCP Flags (Code Bits) Field   The TCP Code Bits field indicates the context and meaning of a particular segment, so an understanding of its structure is critical to the successful deployment of firewalls. Figure 16-8 shows the structure of the Code Bits field.

■ **The Urgent bit**   Signals that the segment payload carries data that is to be processed out of sequence.

Port Number	Protocol	Application
7	TCP/UDP	Echo
15	TCP	Netstat
20, 21	TCP	FTP data and control
22	TCP	SSH
23	TCP	Telnet
25	TCP	SMTP
53	TCP/UDP	Domain Name Service
67, 68	TCP/UDP	BOOTP Server and client
70	TCP	Gopher
80	TCP	WWW
110	TCP	POP3
123	TCP/UDP	NTP
161, 162	UDP	SNMP, SNMP trap
179	TCP	BGP4

Table 16-5.   *Popular TCP and UDP Port Assignments*

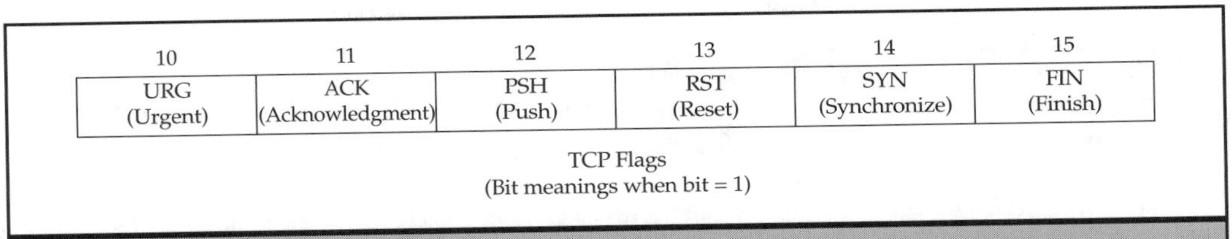

10	11	12	13	14	15
URG (Urgent)	ACK (Acknowledgment)	PSH (Push)	RST (Reset)	SYN (Synchronize)	FIN (Finish)

TCP Flags
(Bit meanings when bit = 1)

Figure 16-8. *The TCP Code Bits (flags) field*

- **The Acknowledgment bit**   Indicates that the segment's acknowledgment field is valid and that it should be accepted and acted upon. The ACK bit is never set in the segment that initiates the TCP connection, but all other segments will normally have the ACK bit set. The setting of the ACK bit provides important clues to a packet filter regarding which end initiated the TCP connection. This information can be used to build filters that will allow or deny TCP connections based on the direction of connection establishment. JUNOS software supports these match types using the `tcp-initial` and `tcp-established` keywords.

- **The Push (PSH) bit**   Indicates to the receiving TCP that the payload should be delivered to the application as soon as possible. It is common to see the PSH bit set on Telnet traffic due to its delay sensitivity and small payloads.

- **The Reset (RST) bit**   Used when rejecting or abruptly terminating a connection. The latter may be caused by manual actions such as the rebooting of a server, or by protocol errors.

- **The Synchronize (SYN) bit**   Used in the three-way connection handshake to indicate that the remote TCP should initialize its receive sequence number to the value indicated in this segment's sequence number field. From a packet filter's perspective, a SYN segment is an indication that a connection is being formed. The combination of a reset ACK bit and set SYN bit is the mechanism by which firewalls differentiate the first of the three packets exchanged during TCP connection establishment. The `tcp-initial` keyword detects these flag combinations to allow or deny a connection request based on its direction.

- **The Finish (FIN) bit**   Used in the graceful closure of a TCP connection. Receipt of a FIN segment indicates that the sender has completed its transfer; the receiving TCP may still send data but will normally follow with its own FIN segment. Once each end has sent a FIN segment and received acknowledgment, the connection is closed.

The TCP Connection Ladder

The following diagram shows the three-way TCP connection handshake, data sequencing, and a typical four-way graceful closure exchange.

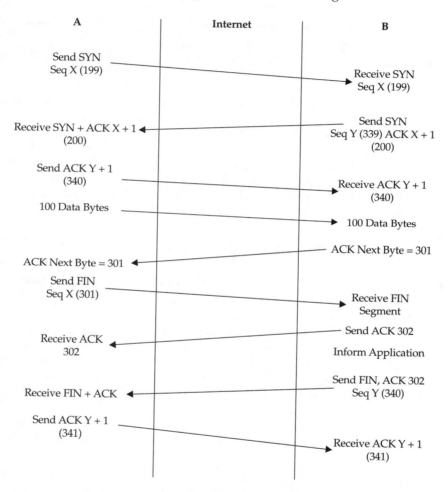

1. *A* initiates a TCP connection to *B* by sending a TCP segment with the ACK bit cleared and the SYN bit set. In this example, *A* has chosen 199 as its initial sequence number.

2. *B* responds to this request by sending its own SYN segment, in this case with the ACK bit set and 200 in the Acknowledgment field. In this example, *B* has chosen 339 as its starting sequence number.

3. The connection is complete when *A* acknowledges *B*'s SYN segment by returning a TCP segment with the ACK bit set, indicating receipt of *B*'s segment with an acknowledgment field of 340.

4. To gracefully disconnect, either end can send a FIN segment. In this example, *A* sends a FIN segment with a sequence number of 301. *B* acknowledges this segment with an acknowledgment field of 302 and sends its own FIN segment to *B*. The connection is officially closed when *A* acknowledges B's FIN segment.

JUNOS Firewall Syntax and Processing Rules

Firewall filters are created at the *[edit firewall]* portion of the JUNOS configuration hierarchy. JUNOS software requires named filters, but the filter name can include (or be entirely composed of) numeric values. Quotes are required when the name contains white space or control characters such as a pipe (|).

Generic Firewall Syntax

The generic syntax of a JUNOS firewall filter is shown here:

```
[edit firewall]
filter foo {
    term term-name {
        from {
            match-condition;
        }
        then {
            action;
            action-modifier;
        }
    }
    term default-rule {
        then discard;
    }
}
```

If you are familiar with JUNOS policy language, you will immediately see the many similarities between firewall and policy syntax. It should be emphasized that while policy deals with the filtering and manipulation of routes, firewall filters deal with the filtering of packets.

The generic syntax for a firewall filter consists of a named filter, one or more named terms, and ends with an implicit term (shown explicitly in the example above) that denies all remaining traffic. Unlike policy language, firewall filter syntax mandates the creation of a term, even when creating a single term filter.

JUNOS Firewall Processing

The preceding syntax shows a firewall named "foo" that is made up of multiple terms. Each term requires a name and will normally consist of one or more matching criteria in the form of a `from` condition, along with the action to be performed when a match occurs. When multiple conditions are specified under the `from` condition, a logical AND is performed such that a match is declared only when all conditions test true.

 It its worth stressing the point that all JUNOS firewall filters end with an implicit "deny all" term that denies all traffic not accepted by previous terms. This deny all term is not displayed when viewing firewall filters.

Order of Term Processing

A given packet is compared against each term in the order in which the terms are listed; if a packet does not match a given term, it is then compared to the next term in the appropriate sequence. When a packet matches a term that results in a termination action—accept, `discard`, `reject`, etc.—no additional terms will be evaluated. It should be obvious, then, that the sequence of terms in a firewall is extremely important.

JUNOS software supports the reordering of firewall terms using the `insert` command, which is useful when modifications are being made to a filter as new terms are added to the end of the existing filter by default.

As an example, consider this filter, where the sequencing of terms is causing allowed packets to be rejected:

```
[edit firewall]
user@router# show
filter foo {
    term 1 {
        from {
            address {
                0.0.0.0/0;
            }
        }
        then {
            reject;
        }
    }
    term 2 {
        from {
            address {
```

```
                    10.0.1.10/32;
                }
            }
        then accept;
        }
    }
```

In this case, the `from address 0.0.0.0/0` term causes all packets to be rejected, meaning that no packet ever sees term 2 and its `from address 10.0.3.2/32` match condition. Using the `insert` command to place term 2 before term 1 would resolve this problem. The JUNOS `rename` command can now be used to rename the terms so that their names correctly convey the order of their processing.

The Implicit "Discard All"   Unlike the various default routing policies, all JUNOS firewall filters end with an implicit "discard all" functionality. This is a critical point, as any packet that has not been explicitly accepted by previous terms will be silently discarded when it hits the end of your filter.

 Failing to keep this point in mind can cause serious problems when you apply your filter, only to realize that you have inadvertently denied valid traffic, and as a result, find that you have locked yourself out of the router in the process!

The Need for Multiple Terms in a Firewall Filter

Another significant difference between firewall filters and JUNOS routing policies is the fact that only one filter can be applied on a particular logical unit (LU) in a particular direction. In other words, you cannot chain together firewall filters, nor can you perform Boolean grouping as can be done with routing policy.

The result is that a firewall filter will always consist of multiple terms, as you cannot combine the functionality of two separate filters on the same LU in a given direction. In fact, if you remember that a firewall filter requires at least one explicit term and always ends with the implicit deny all term, it could be accurately stated that a firewall filter always will, at a minimum, consist of at least two terms—one explicitly specified by the operator and the other automatically added by JUNOS software in an implicit fashion.

The JUNOS Firewall from Statement

Generally speaking, each term in a filter will begin with a set of match conditions that are specified with the `from` keyword under a specific term name. The `from` condition is optional, but it must be stressed that all packets are considered to match a term when no `from` condition has been specified. It is common to see users add an explicit "discard all" for all previously unmatched traffic as the last term in a filter. This is a classic example of appropriately configuring a term with no `from` condition.

The following screen dump shows the results of a `set from ?` command issued at the *[edit firewall filter foo term 1]* portion of the configuration hierarchy:

```
[edit firewall filter foo term 1]
user@router# set from ?
Possible completions:
> address                 Match IP source or destination address
+ apply-groups            Groups from which to inherit configuration data
> destination-address     Match IP destination address
+ destination-port        Match TCP/UDP destination port
+ destination-port-except Don't match TCP/UDP destination port
> destination-prefix-list Match IP destination prefix-list
+ dscp                    Match diffserv codepoint
+ dscp-except             Don't match diffserv codepoint
  first-fragment          Match if packet is the first fragment
  fragment-flags          Match fragment flags
+ fragment-offset         Match fragment offset
+ fragment-offset-except  Don't match fragment offset
+ icmp-code               Match ICMP message code
+ icmp-code-except        Don't match ICMP message code
+ icmp-type               Match ICMP message type
+ icmp-type-except        Don't match ICMP message type
+ interface-group         Match interface group
+ interface-group-except  Don't match interface group
  ip-options              Match IP options
  is-fragment             Match if packet is a fragment
+ packet-length           Match packet length
+ packet-length-except    Don't match packet length
+ port                    Match TCP/UDP source or destination port
+ port-except             Don't match TCP/UDP source or destination port
+ precedence              Match IP precedence value
+ precedence-except       Don't match IP precedence value
> prefix-list             Match IP source or destination prefix-list
+ protocol                Match IP protocol type
+ protocol-except         Don't match IP protocol type
> source-address          Match IP source address
+ source-port             Match TCP/UDP source port
+ source-port-except      Don't match TCP/UDP source port
> source-prefix-list      Match IP source prefix-list
  tcp-established         Match packet of an established TCP connection
  tcp-flags               Match TCP flags
  tcp-initial             Match initial packet of a TCP connection
[edit firewall filter foo term 1]
```

Based on the discussion that has led to this point, the majority of these match conditions should already be familiar to you. The following focuses on the remaining match options and the logic rules that govern firewall term evaluation.

Logic Rules for JUNOS Firewalls

When multiple conditions are specified under a `from` condition, the result may be a logical AND, a logical OR, or both, as determined by the following rules.

Single Keyword, Multiple Values   When multiple values are specified under a common keyword, the result is treated as a logical OR:

```
[edit firewall]
user@router# show
filter foo {
    term 1 {
        from {
            protocol [ tcp udp ospf ];
        }
        then discard;
    }
}
```

In this example, a match occurs when the packet contains the TCP, UDP, or OSPF protocol; JUNOS software always treats parameters enclosed in brackets as a logical OR.

When entering multiple values under a common keyword, you can simply enter multiple `set` commands, in which case JUNOS software will add the brackets for you. Alternatively, you can opt to enter a single `set` command containing a group of variables enclosed by the [and] delimiters.

Multiple Keywords, Single Value   When multiple keywords are specified in a `from` condition, the result is treated as a logical AND. In this example, a match will occur only when both the TCP protocol and port 21 are present in a given packet:

```
[edit firewall]
user@router# show
filter foo {
    term 1 {
        from {
            protocol tcp;
            port 21;
        }
        then discard;
```

```
        }
}

[edit firewall]
```

Multiple Keywords, Multiple Values   When multiple keywords are specified under a `from` condition and multiple variables have been configured under a common keyword, the result is a logical AND for values specified with different keywords and a logical OR for values configured under a common keyword. In this example you see both Boolean operations in action. Here, a match will occur only when the packet has port 7 and is carrying the UDP or TCP protocol:

```
[edit firewall]
user@router# show
filter foo {
    term 1 {
        from {
            protocol [ tcp udp ];
            port 7;
        }
        then discard;
    }
}
```

The except Keyword   Many match conditions also have an `except` counterpart; `except` can also be added to variables such as IP addresses. Using `except` essentially inverts the state of a positive match, thereby causing a mismatch to be declared. A common use of `except` is to exempt a particular address, port, or protocol in a term that would normally match. An example of such a technique can be seen in this filter example:

```
[edit firewall]
user@router# show
filter foo {
    term 1 {
        from {
            address {
                0.0.0.0/0;
                10.0.1.10/32 except;
            }
        }
```

```
        then accept;
    }
}
```

The `from address 0.0.0.0/0` statement will match on every possible source and destination IP address that does not find a more specific match in the term. Since multiple addresses in a `from` statement are treated as a longest match logical OR, any packet with 10.0.1.10 as either a source or destination address will explicitly not match this term and be discarded; all other addresses will be allowed to pass. (You did remember the implicit deny all at the end of this filter, right?) This is an example of a permissive filter in that the operator is permitting all addresses except those explicitly listed.

Prefix Lists   Prefix lists allow you to reference a predefined list of addresses from within a firewall; their use can reduce your workload while keeping your configurations nice and tidy. JUNOS software supports `prefix-list`, `source-prefix-list`, and `destination-prefix-list`. If you wanted to define all your internal addresses just once and then match on them whenever they are used as the source address of a packet, you would use the `source-prefix-list` keyword followed by the name you used when creating the prefix list.

Prefix lists are defined under the *[edit policy-options]* portion of the configuration. The structure of a prefix list is as follows:

```
[edit]
user@router# show policy-options
prefix-list my-internal-addresses {
    10.0.1.0/24;
    200.0.0.1/32;
}
```

You would apply this prefix list in a firewall filter, as shown:

```
from {
    source-prefix-list {
        my-internal-addresses;
    }
}
then accept;
```

Interface Groups   Interface groups allow JUNOS firewall filters to match packets based upon the ingress interface. A common use of this feature is to group interfaces that have a particular purpose and then allow or deny packets the use of those interfaces based on the packet's interface group.

By way of example, consider a service provider that has decided to offer a Voice-over IP (VoIP) service. This provider may decide to dedicate a subset of its interfaces to be used strictly for the carriage of voice packets. By assigning all VoIP interfaces to a common interface group, say group 10, and then placing firewall filters on VoIP interfaces that allow packets only from group 10, the provider is able to ensure that only VoIP packets will be allowed to use a VoIP interface.

Caution *Port matches do not imply protocols!*

A casual observer would likely find nothing amiss with the following filter syntax:

```
[edit firewall]
user@router# show
filter mistake {
    term 1 {
        from {
            port telnet;
        }
        then accept;
    }
}
```

The problem, however, is that the IP2 does not make assumptions regarding the relationship of applications or ports to a corresponding transport protocol. While you are undoubtedly aware that Telnet makes use of TCP, the IP2 will, by design, not draw the same conclusion. Therefore, the filter above will pass any packet that has a decimal 23 (the TCP port value associated with the Telnet application) in what would normally be the source and destination port fields of the TCP and UDP protocols (the first 32 bits of the IP packet's payload).

To ensure that this filter does not mistakenly accept other applications or protocols, you need to make sure that the IP2 is testing whether or not the IP packet is carrying TCP in its payload. Testing for both protocol 6 (TCP) and a decimal value of 23 for the TCP port will ensure that arbitrary bit patterns in the IP payload will not cause inadvertent matches.

Here is an example of a properly written Telnet filter:

```
[edit firewall]
user@router# show
filter no-mistake {
    term 1 {
        from {
            protocol tcp;
```

```
            port ssh;
        }
        then accept;
    }
}
```

The JUNOS Firewall then Statement

When a match condition tests true in a firewall filter term, the corresponding then action is performed. JUNOS software allows the association of multiple then actions within a single term.

The options available for then actions in JUNOS software are shown here:

```
[edit firewall]
user@router# set filter A term 1 then ?
Possible completions:
  accept                Accept the packet
+ apply-groups          Groups from which to inherit configuration data
  count                 Count the packet in the named counter
  discard               Discard the packet
  forwarding-class      Classify packet to forwarding class
  log                   Log the packet
  loss-priority         Classify packet to loss-priority
  policer               Police the packet using the named policer
> reject                Reject the packet
  routing-instance      Provide routing instance
  sample                Sample the packet
  syslog                Syslog information about the packet
```

Action Types: Terminating and Modifier

The accept, reject, routing-instance, and discard actions are considered "terminating" in that a packet that encounters one of these actions will not be subject to further firewall processing. Actions modifiers allow you take some form of action on a packet without immediately accepting, rejecting, or discarding it. Examples of action modifiers include the sample, log, and count actions.

The Effects of Omitting a Termination Action   Specifying a then action without an explicit terminating action results in an implied accept action. Similarly, a default accept action is associated with any term that has no then action specified.

Based on these rules, the following two JUNOS filters are functionally equivalent, even though filter *B* does not include an explicit `accept` action:

```
[edit firewall]
user@router# show
filter A {
    term 1 {
        from {
            protocol tcp;
        }
        then {
            log;
            accept;
        }
    }
}
filter B {
    term 1 {
        from {
            protocol tcp;
        }
        then log;
    }
}
```

The JUNOS policy language allows the modification of a route's attributes without actually accepting or rejecting the route; in these cases the route will be subject to additional policy processing until it meets with an `accept` or `reject` action in the default policy if need be. Currently, JUNOS software does not support the concept of `then next term` for firewall filters. It is therefore recommended that the user always include a terminating action when using an action modifier to avoid the ambiguity that can be caused by the implicit `accept` that will otherwise occur when an action such as `count` is specified.

Description of JUNOS Firewall Actions

The success or failure of a firewall is dependent upon both the accuracy of the match criteria and the actions that occur when matches are declared. This section describes the JUNOS firewall actions.

accept   The `accept` action causes a matching packet to be accepted and forwarded. The `accept` action causes the packet to break out of additional firewall processing; once a packet is accepted, it can never be rejected by a subsequent term in the firewall filter.

reject   The `reject` action causes a matching packet to be rejected with a user specified ICMP error message. Like `accept`, `reject` will cause the packet to break out of additional firewall processing in that it is a terminating action. The use of `reject` can assist troubleshooting, but it may provide an attacker with additional information in the form of the resulting error message, so its use is not recommended when security is paramount or when the traffic being filtered is likely to have a "spoofed" source address. (Generating ICMP `reject` messages based on packets with forged source addresses will effectively cause the rightful owners of the addresses to be "smurfed" with error messages they do not deserve.)

When the `reject` action is used in a firewall filter, the user has the option of specifying what type of ICMP error message should be sent to the packet's originator. When no message type is specified, the default action is to generate a destination unreachable-administratively prohibited message.

Other JUNOS `reject` options include these:

```
[edit firewall]
user@router# set filter A term 1 then reject ?
Possible completions:
  <[Enter]>              Execute this command
  administratively-prohibited  Send ICMP Administratively Prohibited message
  bad-host-tos           Send ICMP Bad Host TOS message
  bad-network-tos        Send ICMP Bad Network TOS message
  host-prohibited        Send ICMP Host Prohibited message
  host-unknown           Send ICMP Host Unknown message
  host-unreachable       Send ICMP Host Unreachable message
  network-prohibited     Send ICMP Network Prohibited message
  network-unknown        Send ICMP Network Unknown message
  network-unreachable    Send ICMP Network Unreachable message
  port-unreachable       Send ICMP Port Unreachable message
  precedence-cutoff      Send ICMP Precedence Cutoff message
  precedence-violation   Send ICMP Precedence Violation message
  protocol-unreachable   Send ICMP Protocol Unreachable message
  source-host-isolated   Send ICMP Source Host Isolated message
  source-route-failed    Send ICMP Source Route Failed message
  tcp-reset              Send TCP Reset message
```

The use of `tcp-reset` will reset (abruptly close) a TCP session; this option returns nothing for non-TCP protocols such as UDP.

discard   The `discard` action causes a matching packet to be silently discarded. This option is generally preferred to `reject` for both security and performance reasons. Generally, security is enhanced by not providing any information as opposed to an error message of some type. The fact that error messages no longer have to be produced and then routed towards the packet's source address can have significant performance impacts—especially in the face of a massive *Distributed Denial of Service* (D-DoS) attack.

Using `discard` can make troubleshooting difficult as many networking problems produce "black holes" and technicians may forget to look for firewall-related causes.

syslog   The `syslog` action modifier causes the RE to log firewall matches to the syslog. Since syslog entries are written to the local hard drive and can also be sent to a remote syslog host, the use of `syslog` has many advantages of the `log` action modifier.

Syslog entries cased by the `syslog` action modifier in firewall filters take the following form:

```
user@router> show log messages | match jfw
Mar  3 00:27:59 router tnp_scb JFW: fe-0/0/0.0   A icmp 10.0.2.2 192.168.2.1   0    0 (2 packets)
Mar  3 00:28:04 router tnp_scb JFW: fe-0/0/0.0   A icmp 10.0.2.2 192.168.2.1   0    0 (5 packets)
```

Here, the operator has passed the results of a `show log messages` command through the `match` function, with the match criteria being *JFW*, an acronym that stands for *Juniper Firewall Filter*.

Here we can see that *fe-0/0/0* was the ingress interface for the packet; knowledge of ingress interfaces can greatly simplify the job of backtracking toward the source of a spoofed DoS attack. The *A* indicates that the action associated with this match was to accept the packet. *D* and *R* would indicate the discard and reject actions, respectively.

You can also see that the protocol is ICMP and that the source address in the packet is 10.0.2.2. The destination address of 192.168.2.1 is also listed. The count values indicate that the corresponding message was repeated *n* times. The ability to indicate repetitive messages in this fashion improves performance when dealing with high packet rates, as the RE does not have to write each individual entry into the syslog.

count <name>   The `count` action modifier causes the IP2 to increment a named 64-bit byte counter and 32-bit packet counter for each matching packet. The *<name>* argument specified after the `count` action will be used to reference the counter. The IP2 associates each firewall filter with zero or more named counters. Therefore, using the same counter name in two independent firewall filters will result in two unrelated counters that happen to have the same name.

Excessive use of counting should be avoided, as forwarding performance may be impacted if an operator tries to count every packet on a highly utilized OC-192c interface using a firewall filter. (This could result in the need to count over 24 million packets per second!). You would be better served by using the `show interface <name> detail` or the `monitor interface <name>` commands to display an interface's byte and packet counters for this type of application.

While it is possible for many independent firewall terms to point to a common counter, it is recommended that you use multiple counters for maximum performance. The counter results can be externally summed to obtain a total packet count if needed.

Firewall counter results can be displayed with the `show firewall <name>` command. When no name is specified, all firewall counters are shown. The counters can be cleared with the `clear firewall <all|name>` command.

Here is an example of a JUNOS firewall filter that will count ICMP traffic using a counter called "icmp." All other protocol traffic will be counted with a counter called "other":

```
[edit]
user@router# show firewall
filter foo {
    term 1 {
        from {
            protocol icmp;
        }
        then {
            count icmp;
            log;
            accept;
        }
    }
    term 2 {
        then {
            count other;
            accept;
        }
    }
}
```

To display firewall counter results, the user would enter the `show firewall <name>` operational mode command, as shown here:

```
user@router> show firewall
Filter/Counter                 Packet count           Byte count
foo
   icmp                                   5                  420
   other                                 72                 4976
faa
```

Here you can see that two firewall filters have been defined. The "foo" filter has two counters defined (icmp and other). In contrast, the "faa" filter is not associated with any counter operations.

In this example, the author generated five 64-byte PINGs. The total packet size was brought to 84 bytes with the addition of the 20-byte IP header; the byte count value of 420 reflects this fact nicely. Since JUNOS firewall counters do not count link level encapsulation overhead, the count values will only indicate Layer 3 packet and byte counts.

The `clear firewall < all|name>` command is used to reset firewall counters:

```
user@router> clear firewall all
user@router> show firewall
Filter/Counter                          Packet count              Byte count
foo
   icmp                                           0                        0
   other                                          0                        0
faa
```

log   The `log` action modifier causes the PFE to send the packet's key data to a memory cache maintained by the kernel. These log messages will be made available to the RE at the user's request. The log is currently kept in system RAM on the PFE, and it cannot be cleared except by reboot. The cache will hold 100 entries before it wraps around and begins to overwrite entries. You can view the firewall log with the command `show firewall log`. Firewall log entries take the following form:

```
user@router> show firewall log
Time      Filter     A Interface       Pro Source address   Destination address
02:36:01 foo         A fe-0/0/0.0      ICM 10.0.2.2         192.168.5.1:19533
02:36:00 foo         A fe-0/0/0.0      ICM 10.0.2.2         192.168.5.1:13151
02:35:50 pfe         A fe-0/0/0.0      ICM 10.0.2.2         192.168.2.1:45072
02:35:49 pfe         A fe-0/0/0.0      ICM 10.0.2.2         192.168.2.1:48951
```

The log is ordered with the most recent entries listed first; you can use the JUNOS search function to locate specific entries easily.

The fields in the log display are similar to those described for the `syslog` option— the ingress interface, protocol, source and destination addresses are listed. The log displays protocol type with a three-letter acronym—ICM for ICMP, RSV for RSVP, and so on. It should be noted that even though the same filter is involved for all the log entries shown, the name of the filter may or may not be displayed, based on where the filter action is performed. In the case of the first two entries, the 192.168.5.1 target is the address of the local RE, while the 192.168.2.1 target shown in the last two entries is a remote router. When the filter action is performed in the PFE hardware, as is the case for transit traffic, the filter name is replaced with the letters *pfe* as the PFE hardware does not maintain the data structures necessary to know the name of a given filter. When the filter action occurs in the RE, the filter name is displayed.

Log entries are lost if the router is powered down or rebooted. To preserve the contents, you can manually write log entries to a file by piping the output to the CLI's `save` function.

It is critical to note that all packets matching a term with a corresponding logging action will be logged—that is, there is a 1:1 ratio between matching packets and the logging action. Therefore, statistical sampling is a better choice when dealing with high-speed interfaces.

Because high logging rates will cause the firewall log to wrap around quickly, entries may be lost if the log is not analyzed in a timely manner. For this reason the `syslog` option is generally preferred as these entries are written to the hard disk where they can be analyzed at your leisure.

output-queue   The `output-queue` action modifier causes the packet to be placed into a particular WRR queue on the egress interface. JUNOS software currently supports four queues (numbered 0–3) per PIC port. JUNOS support of Class of Service (CoS) features such as WRR queuing, transmit buffer depths, and RED profiles allow service providers to offer differentiated service classes across their backbones.

Packet classification via firewall filters provides significant advantages when compared to the rather coarse approach of queuing based on the IP precedence field alone. As discussed earlier, IP2 firewall filters provide improved granularity for packet classification using criteria such as IP precedence, upper-layer protocols, application ports, and so on.

Firewall-based classification will override ingress-based precedence mappings. This is because IIIP2-based queuing decisions occur *after* any ingress-based classifications have been made. In other words, if an input precedence map says the packet should be placed into queue 2, but an IP2 firewall filter wants it to go into queue 3, the packet will be placed into queue 3.

Packet Loss Priority   The Packet Loss Priority (PLP) action modifier allows the packet's notification data to be tagged with a PLP value of either 0 (reset) or 1 (set). The PLP bit operates in conjunction with RED profiles to determine the loss probability of a given packet based on current queue depth. Generally speaking, packets with a set PLP bit will have a higher loss probability then those that have a cleared PLP bit. In many ways, you can analogize the PLP bit to the functionality provided by frame relay's Discard Eligibility (DE) or ATM's Cell Loss Priority (CLP) indications.

The PLP bit is internal to Juniper routers. The JUNOS `precedence-rewrite` function can be used to convey the setting of this bit between chassis using the least significant bit of the IP precedence field.

policer   The `policer` action modifier causes the packet to be subjected to a token bucket policer defined in the same firewall filter. IP2-based rate limiting is discussed in detail in the "IP2 Rate Limiting" section below.

sample   The `sample` action modifier causes the packet's key data to be sent to the RE where it can be written to disk in an ASCII file format or exported to a remote host using the *cflowd* format. IP2 sampling is covered in detail in the "Sampling Configuration" section.

routing-instance   Newer versions of JUNOS software support a feature called Filter Based Forwarding (FBF). FBF provides the ability to perform policy based routing by resolving the next-hop for matching packets through a particular routing instance and the corresponding route table.

By way of example, the following configuration stanzas create a routing instance called *www* that contains a default route pointing to a particular IP next-hop address. Packets that match the firewall filter (HTTP server responses) will be resolved against the *www* routing instance, causing them to be forwarded to 10.0.0.1:

```
[edit]
lab@host# show firewall
filter test {
    term 1 {
        from {
            protocol tcp;
            source-port http;
        }
        then routing-instance www;
    }
    term 2 {
        then accept;
    }
}
[edit]
lab@host# show routing-instances
www {
    instance-type forwarding;
    routing-options {
        static {
            route 0.0.0.0/0 next-hop 10.0.0.1;
        }
    }
}
[edit]
lab@host# show routing-options
interface-routes {
    rib-group inet www-ifg;
}
rib-groups {
    www-ifg {
        import-rib [ inet.0 www.inet.0 ];
    }
}
```

The `routing-options` stanza creates an interface RIB group called *www-ifg*, which functions to install the directly connected interface routes into both the main routing instance (*inet.0*) and the *www* instance (*www.inet.0*).

It should be noted that FBF classification functions only when the related firewall filter is applied as an input filter.

Resequencing and Deleting Firewall Terms

The ability to rearrange the ordering of terms within a firewall filter is an invaluable tool. In many cases, the difference between a successful filter and one that fails horribly comes down to a matter of term sequencing.

The insert Command

The ability to rearrange the ordering of terms within a firewall filter is an important skill. Despite its name, the `insert` command's primary purpose is to resequence terms that have already been added to a filter using the `set` command. The `insert` command can also be used to add parameters to an existing `from` or `then` statement.

By way of example, the `insert` command is used in the following to correct the term sequencing problems in this filter:

```
[edit firewall]
user@router# show
filter foo {
    term 1 {
        from {
            address {
                0.0.0.0/0;
            }
        }
        then {
            reject;
        }
    }
    term 2 {
        from {
            address {
                10.0.1.10/32;
            }
        }
        then accept;
    }
}
```

Since packets to or from address 10.0.1.10 should be allowed, you must move term 2 so that it is processed before term 1. To accomplish this goal, the `insert` command is used, as shown:

```
[edit firewall filter foo]
user@router# insert term 2 ?
Possible completions:
  after                  Insert after given data element
+ apply-groups           Groups from which to inherit configuration data
  before                 Insert before given data element
> from                   Define match criteria
> then                   Action to take if the 'from' condition is matched
[edit firewall filter foo]
user@router# insert term 2 before term 1
```

In this example, the operator has requested context-sensitive help for the `insert` command, and you can see that it will accept the arguments `after` or `before`.

To see the results of the resequencing, you can display the modified filter:

```
[edit firewall filter foo]
user@router# show
term 2 {
    from {
        address {
            10.0.1.10/32;
        }
    }
    then accept;
}
term 1 {
    from {
        address {
            0.0.0.0/0;
        }
    }
    then {
        reject;
    }
}
```

The fact that term 2 is now being processed before term 1 may seem objectionable. To fix this, you can use the JUNOS `rename` command, as shown here:

```
[edit firewall filter foo]
user@router# rename term 2 to term tmp
[edit firewall filter foo]
user@router# rename term 1 to term 2
[edit firewall filter foo]
user@router# rename term tmp to term 1
[edit firewall filter foo]
user@router# show
term 1 {
    from {
        address {
            10.0.1.10/32;
        }
    }
    then accept;
}
term 2 {
    from {
        address {
            0.0.0.0/0;
        }
    }
    then {
        reject;
    }
}
[edit firewall filter foo]
```

This example first renamed one of the terms to a temporary value (*tmp*), as JUNOS software will not permit duplicate term names in a firewall filter. The results of the show command should now make even the most discriminating Network Operations Center (NOC) engineer proud.

Deleting Filters, Terms, and Attributes

The JUNOS delete command is used to remove entire filters, terms within a filter, or entries associated with the from and then statements within a given term. To illustrate the use of delete, consider the following filter:

```
[edit firewall]
user@router# show
filter foo {
    term 1 {
```

```
        from {
            protocol [ tcp icmp ];
        }
        then accept;
    }
}
[edit firewall]
```

In this case, term 1 has been set to match on both the TCP and ICMP protocols.

The `delete` command will now be used to remove the ICMP match condition in term 1:

```
[edit firewall]
user@router# delete filter foo term 1 from protocol icmp
[edit firewall]
user@router# show filter foo
term 1 {
    from {
        protocol tcp;
    }
    then accept;
}
[edit firewall]
```

Copying Filters and Terms

The JUNOS `copy` command can be used to copy a complete filter or individual terms within a single filter. The copied filter or term can then be modified with the `insert`, `set`, and `delete` commands as necessary.

Applying JUNOS Firewall Filters

Based on the material covered to this point, you have no doubt already configured your first JUNOS firewall. So, why doesn't it seem to be working? One likely reason is that the filter has not yet been applied to an interface, which means it has not been put into effect.

RE vs. Transit Filtering

As previously mentioned, a filter is applied to the router's *lo0* interface when local RE protection is required; such a filter application will have no effect on transit traffic. Filters that are applied to a PFE interface will affect both transit and local RE traffic as the RE brings to bear local copies of the PFE filters when originating or receiving traffic.

Filter Directionality

A JUNOS firewall filter is applied to an interface after a directional keyword that indicates whether the filter will act upon *input* or *output* traffic. If desired, the same filter can be applied as both an input and output filter, but this rarely makes sense because a filter will often contain terms that have directionally specific aspects.

Since virtually all protocols require bidirectional traffic flow, blocking either the protocol requests or the resulting responses is normally sufficient to prevent communications. It is therefore somewhat rare to see the application of bidirectional filters that are intended to block the same application or protocols. Using a filter in one direction for accounting and a filter in the opposite direction for security is a common use of a bidirectional filter application.

Blocking requests normally involves input filtering and has the advantage of filtering packets close to their ingress so that network bandwidth and host resources are not wasted. Blocking responses normally makes use of output filters and may have the drawback of wasted resources, as requests for unauthorized services are routed across the Internet only to have the resulting responses filtered near the source of the service request. One advantage to output filtering is that network operations during the course of a DoS attack can be simplified. Once the attack is reported, an existing output filter can easily be modified to both minimize the effects of the attack and help track its source.

Applying Filters

JUNOS filters are always applied under the *family inet* portion of an interface's configuration as IP2 functionality is currently supported only for the IP family of protocols.

Under a given logical unit, a maximum of two filters may be applied: one in the input direction and the other in the output direction. Interfaces that support a single logical unit can support two filters at a maximum. Multi-point interfaces such as frame relay or ATM support multiple logical units and may therefore support the application of multiple input and output filters. For example, JUNOS currently supports a maximum of 1024 VLANs on Ethernet interfaces. With a maximum of two filters per LU, this means you could apply as many as 2048 filters to a single Ethernet interface!

In this example, a filter named "f00" is applied as an input filter to the router's *lo0* interface:

```
user@router#
[edit interfaces lo0]
user@router# set unit 0 family inet filter input f00
[edit interfaces lo0]
```

The `show` command verifies the filter's application as an input filter:

```
[edit interfaces lo0]
user@router# show
unit 0 {
    family inet {
        filter {
            input f00;
        }
        address 192.168.5.1/32;
    }
}
[edit interfaces lo0]
```

However, the candidate configuration will not commit due to the following error:

```
[edit interfaces lo0]
user@router# commit
[edit interfaces lo0 unit 0 family inet filter]
  'input "f00"'
    Referenced filter not defined
error: configuration check-out failed
[edit interfaces lo0]
```

The problem is that there is no firewall filter named "f00," so the configuration will not pass the commit check. While you can commit a configuration with filters that have been defined but not applied, the opposite is not true. If a filter is applied to an interface but not defined, the commit check will not allow your candidate to become the active configuration.

You can fix this problem by renaming the filter currently named "foo" to "f00":

```
[edit]
user@router# rename firewall filter foo to filter f00
[edit]
user@router# commit
commit complete
[edit]
```

At present, the operator must look at the configuration to determine whether filters have been applied to a given interface, as no CLI operational mode command exists for this purpose.

Interface Groups

Interface group associations are made by applying the *group* statement under the *filter* portion of an interface's configuration hierarchy, as shown in this example:

```
[edit interfaces]
user@router# set fe-0/0/0 unit 0 family inet filter group 10
[edit interfaces]
user@router# show fe-0/0/0
unit 0 {
    family inet {
        filter {
            input foo;
            group 10;
        }
        address 10.0.2.1/24;
    }
}
```

By adding the *group* statement, packets entering the router on the *fe-0/0/0.0* interface will be tagged with an interface group value of "10." The *group* tag is purely internal to the Juniper router, so no evidence of interface groups will be seen outside of this chassis. Interface groups are often deployed when the goal is to partition interfaces based on application type. As an example, a service provider may allocate certain interfaces to an application such as VoIP; interface groups provide a way of enforcing this policy as they allow the operator to limit the set of interfaces that a packet can use for egress.

The *group* tag added by an ingress filter may then be used as one of your match conditions in an egress filter:

```
[edit firewall]
user@router# show
filter foo {
    term 1 {
        from {
            interface-group 10;
        }
        then {
            reject;
        }
    }
    term 2 {
        then accept;
    }
}
```

The deployment of interface groups should be carefully considered, because their use can cause connectivity problems. In the preceding example, what will happen to all the non-VoIP packets when the interface normally used to transmit them fails and the only interface left has a VoIP group specific output filter applied?

In practice, the VoIP interfaces will often have their IGP metrics set so high that the IGP would never even want to use them. MPLS Label Switched Paths (LSPs) are then established to transport the voice packets with constraints that force them to use the reserved interfaces. Combining this technique with interface group output filters will ensure that your voice-oriented service-level agreements are not violated in the event of circuit or interface failures.

Case Study 1: Routing Engine Protection

Now that you understand the operation, syntax, and application of JUNOS firewall filters, it is time to put your knowledge to use by creating real-world filters that meet specific filtering criteria. This first case study will provide an example of firewall filter RE protection.

Security Models: Permissive vs. Prudent

It could be said that there are four distinct security philosophies—namely promiscuous, permissive, prudent, and paranoid. The promiscuous and paranoid models will not be considered in these case studies as they represent two philosophical extremes, with the former involving no security at all while the latter represents a machine that is no longer even networked!

Permissive Security Model

A permissive security model sets out to block what is specifically considered "bad" while allowing everything else by default. This type of filter has the advantage of configuration simplicity, but it offers poor security due to the rapid pace at which Internet protocols evolve and the fact that computer criminals are not prone to sending e-mail to system administrators when they have gained unauthorized access to a machine or resource. Generally, a permissive filter is deployed when guarding against specific threats that are known about in advance.

When a user makes a mistake with a permissive filter, the result will likely be compromised security.

Prudent Security Model

A prudent security model sets out to allow what is considered "good" while blocking everything else by default. A prudent filter requires significantly more initial effort to configure and maintain, but it offers improved security in that new protocols and applications have to be specifically allowed before they will operate.

Mistakes made with a prudent filter will normally result in the denial of valid services. As end users are normally more than willing to complain about such things, the problem will be quickly brought to the system administrator's attention for corrective action.

JUNOS filters are inherently prudent due to the implicit "discard all" term present at the end of every filter. The addition of an explicit term that accepts everything causes the filter to operate in a permissive manner.

What Should Be Allowed?

With a prudent filtering model, one of the first questions you must ask yourself is "What do I want to allow?" The answer depends on many variables and will normally vary to the extent that the ability to use a common filter on numerous interfaces is precluded.

Since this case study involves the protection of the local RE, you must now ask yourself "What should be allowed into and out of, the RE?" Figure 16-9 sheds light on this question as it illustrates the operational environment of your router. Of the three routers shown, you will be working on the center router, R2. Routers R1 and R3 are present to produce traffic and demonstrate connectivity (or the lack thereof, as the situation develops). (Note that you are attached to R1 and have established a Telnet session to R2 for this work order.)

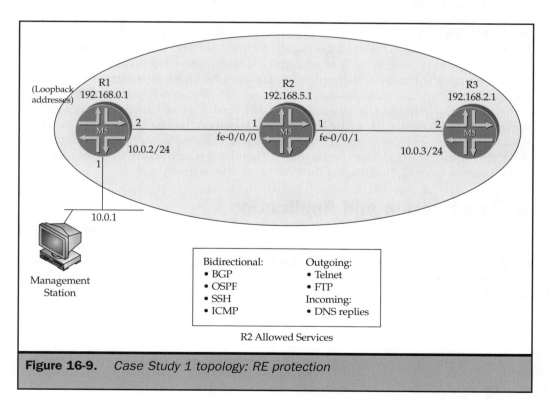

Figure 16-9. *Case Study 1 topology: RE protection*

Based on this figure, you can conclude that the following protocols and applications should be allowed:

- Bidirectional ICMP echo request and replies
- OSPF
- Bidirectional BGP4
- Bidirectional SSH from internal addresses only
- Outgoing FTP only
- Outgoing Telnet only
- Incoming DNS replies

Since you are building a prudent filter, all other protocols and applications will be denied. An explicit "reject all" term will be added at the end of the filter so as to enable the logging and counting of unauthorized traffic.

Filter Direction

Since you want to protect the local RE, an input filter is mandatory; only blocking responses via an output filter would not shield the RE from the barrage induced by a massive DoS attack. Whether or not an output filter should be applied is a matter of some debate. You can achieve all the requirements listed previously with a single inbound filter. However, the lack of an outbound filter means that unauthorized traffic would be permitted to leave the router. On the other hand, a single filter is easier to configure and maintain when compared to a pair of filters, and hence the debate.

In the end, choosing to deploy unidirectional versus bidirectional filters is a tactical decision that will have to be made by each user based on the needs and risks involved with a particular security scenario. In this case, you will employ only in-bound filtering since you "trust" the operators of the router. Besides, the inbound filtering of responses should curtail most of the mischief they could otherwise get into.

Filter Construction and Application

You will now build and apply your RE protection filter based on the requirements stated previously. First you'll walk through the configuration of the first term; subsequent terms will be shown and described. The filter in this example will be called *local-re*.

Before starting work on R2, the operator issues the following commands on R2 to verify that all is well:

```
user@r2> show ospf neighbor
  Address         Interface        State    ID              Pri  Dead
  10.0.2.2        fe-0/0/0.0       Full     192.168.0.1     128  34
  10.0.3.2        fe-0/0/1.0       Full     192.168.2.1     128  33
```

```
user@r2> show bgp summary
Groups: 1 Peers: 2 Down peers: 0
Table          Tot Paths  Act Paths Suppressed    History Damp State   Pending
inet.0                 0          0          0          0      0          0
inet.2                 0          0          0          0      0          0
Peer              AS     InPkt     OutPkt     OutQ    Flaps Last Up/Dwn State|#Active/Received/Damped...
192.168.0.1    65321       196        198        0        0    1:37:59 0/0/0                0/0/0
192.168.2.1    65321         2          3        0        0         29 0/0/0                0/0/0
```

Here you can see that R2 has functional OSPF adjacencies and IBGP sessions to both R1 and R3.

Term 1: Allow Bidirectional ICMP Echoes and Responses

The operator has already parked at the *[edit firewall filter local-re]* portion of the configuration hierarchy. If the filter named *local-re* did not already exist, JUNOS will have automatically created it. The following commands are entered to create term 1 (allow ICMP echoes):

```
[edit firewall filter local-re]
user@r2# set term 1 from protocol icmp icmp-type echo-request
[edit firewall filter local-re]
user@r2# set term 1 from protocol icmp icmp-type echo-reply
[edit firewall filter local-re]
user@r2# set term 1 then accept
[edit firewall filter local-re]
```

Now to check our work so far:

```
[edit firewall filter local-re]
user@r2# show
term 1 {
    from {
        protocol icmp;
        icmp-type [ echo-request echo-reply ];
    }
    then accept;
}
[edit firewall filter local-re]
user@r2#
```

Being that you are somewhat new to the JUNOS firewall environment, it has been decided that the partial filter will be applied and committed so that its functionality can be confirmed before any additional terms are added.

Applying the RE Protection Filter

The *local-re* filter will now be applied as an input filter on the router's *lo0* interface and the candidate configuration committed:

```
user@r2> configure
Entering configuration mode
[edit]
user@r2# set interfaces lo0 unit 0 family inet filter input local-re
```

Now confirm the filter's application:

```
[edit]
user@r2# show interfaces lo0
unit 0 {
    family inet {
        filter {
            input local-re;
        }
        address 192.168.5.1/32;
    }
}
[edit]
```

Now for the commit:

```
[edit]
user@r2# commit
commit complete
[edit]
user@r2#
```

At this point, your Telnet session "hangs" and has to be aborted by pressing the CONTROL-] key sequence:

```
telnet> quit
Connection closed.
lab@r1>
```

A look at the OSPF and BGP connection status on R1 is enough to make even a hardened NOC engineer more then a little queasy:

```
lab@r1> show ospf neighbor
  Address          Interface        State      ID              Pri  Dead
10.0.2.1           fxp0.0           Init      192.168.5.1      128   36
lab@r1> show bgp summary
Groups: 1 Peers: 2 Down peers: 2
Table           Tot Paths  Act Paths Suppressed    History Damp State   Pending
inet.0                  0          0          0          0        0           0
inet.2                  0          0          0          0        0           0
Peer             AS      InPkt     OutPkt    OutQ   Flaps Last Up/Dwn
State|#Active/Received/Damped...
192.168.2.1     65321        39         44       0       1     6:55 Active
192.168.5.1     65321       234        238       0       1     6:51 Active
lab@r1>
```

Oddly, the operator notices that PINGs are still successful from R1 to the directly connected interface on R2:

```
lab@r1> ping 10.0.2.1
PING 10.0.2.1 (10.0.2.1): 56 data bytes
64 bytes from 10.0.2.1: icmp_seq=0 ttl=255 time=0.951 ms
64 bytes from 10.0.2.1: icmp_seq=1 ttl=255 time=0.448 ms
^C
--- 10.0.2.1 ping statistics ---
2 packets transmitted, 2 packets received, 0% packet loss
round-trip min/avg/max/stddev = 0.448/0.700/0.951/0.252 ms
lab@r1>
```

Failure Analysis: A Case for Commit Confirmed   So what happened? How could such an innocuous looking filter bring down OSPF adjacencies, break IBGP sessions, and sever remote access all at the same time?

The answer, of course, lies in the implicit "discard all" at the end of a JUNOS firewall filter. Looking back on the filter you just committed, it is easy (in hindsight) to realize that your filter permits ICMP echoes and nothing else!

Now that you have brought down a functional router and locked yourselves out of remote access at the same time, there is not much you can do except gain console access to R2 so that you may issue a `rollback 1` command. Had the operator thought things through, the `commit confirmed` option would no doubt have been used so that your current inability to recommit would trigger an automatic rollback to the previously committed (and functional) configuration.

After seeing this example, the significance of the implicit "deny all" term and the utility of the `commit confirmed` option should be forever imprinted in your mind.

Term 2: Allow OSPF

The operator has regained connectivity to R2 and has rebuilt term 1 to allow ICMP echoes (in this example, the `rollback 1` command results in the loss of the filter and the *lo0* filter reference). The second term, which allows OSPF, has now been added:

```
[edit firewall filter local-re]
user@r2# show term 2
from {
    protocol ospf;
}
then accept;

[edit firewall filter local-re]
```

Term 3: Allow BGP

The next term in your filter permits BGP connections, regardless of which end initiates them:

```
[edit firewall filter local-re]
user@r2# show term 3
from {
    protocol tcp;
    port bgp;
}
then accept;

[edit firewall filter local-re]
```

It is important to note that this term requires the presence of the TCP protocol and a source or destination port of 179 for a match to occur; remember that specification of a port alone will not automatically cause a test for the corresponding protocol.

Term 4: Bidirectional ssh from Internal Addresses

The next term in our filter permits ssh connection initiation and termination, but only when the source address matches an entry in the prefix list called "internal":

```
[edit firewall filter local-re]
user@r2# show term 4
from {
    source-prefix-list {
```

```
        internal;
    }
    protocol tcp;
    port ssh;

then accept;
[edit firewall filter local-re]
```

The prefix list "internal" is defined under the *[policy-options]* portion of the hierarchy and will contain all trusted (internal) addresses in this case:

```
[edit firewall filter local-re]
user@r2# top
[edit]
user@r2# show policy-options
prefix-list internal {
    10.0.1.2;
    10.0.2.1;
    10.0.2.2;
    10.0.3.1;
    10.0.3.2;
    192.168.0.0/21;
}
[edit]
user@r2#
```

The prefix list contains the addresses from all internal interfaces as it is difficult to predict what interface a given router will use when sourcing an ssh connection. (Note that some versions of JUNOS software do not support the sourcing of Telnet or ssh connections from the *lo0* address, as can be done with PINGs and traceroutes.) Loopback addresses are listed here to support instances where the ssh connection is initiated to a remote router's *lo0* address, as this will result in ssh responses that originate from the remote router's *lo0* address.

Terms 5 and 5a: Outgoing FTP Control, Bidirectional FTP Data

The next two terms in your filter permit FTP control connections that originate from the local RE and allow the establishment of FTP data connections in either direction. The use of the `tcp-established` keyword in conjunction with the `source-port ftp` clause prevent the acceptance of incoming FTP control connections. (The `tcp-established` keyword should be sufficient to prevent incoming connections; the inclusion of a `source-port = 21` provides additional assurance as an incoming FTP control connection should have a source port greater than 1023 and a destination port of 21.) Both ports 21 (ftp) and 20 (ftp-data) have been specified to allow normal and passive FTP operations:

```
[edit]
user@r2# edit firewall filter local-re
[edit firewall filter local-re]
user@r2# show term 5
from {
    protocol tcp;
    source-port ftp;
    tcp-established;
}
then accept;
[edit firewall filter local-re]
user@r2# show term 5a
from {
    protocol tcp;
    port ftp-data;
}
then accept;
[edit firewall filter local-re]
```

Term 6: Outgoing Telnet

The next term in your filter permits Telnet connections that originate from the local RE. The use of the `tcp-established` keyword prevents the acceptance of incoming Telnet connections. The source port specification provides additional security as incoming Telnet connections will normally have a source port greater than 1023:

```
[edit firewall filter local-re]
user@r2# show term 6
from {
    protocol tcp;
    source-port telnet;
    tcp-established;
}
then accept;
[edit filter local-re]
```

Term 7: Incoming DNS Replies

Term 7 allows UDP packets with a source port of 53. Since some JUNOS versions lack a keyword for the DNS application, the operator has numerically specified the port in this example:

```
[edit firewall filter local-re]
user@r2# show term 7
from {
    protocol udp;
    source-port 53;
}
then accept;
```

Term Else: Reject Everything Else

Term *else* is an explicit reject all else term that has been added to permit the counting and logging of unauthorized traffic:

```
[edit firewall filter local-re]
user@r2# show term else
then {
    count disallowed;
    log;
    reject;
}
```

Filter Verification

The proper operation of the RE protection filter will now be verified from the perspectives of R1 and R2.

Filter Verification: R1

The proper operation of the RE protection filter will now be tested by generating various types of traffic from R1:

```
lab@r1> ping count 1 192.168.5.1
PING 192.168.5.1 (192.168.5.1): 56 data bytes
64 bytes from 192.168.5.1: icmp_seq=0 ttl=255 time=0.503 ms
--- 192.168.5.1 ping statistics ---
1 packets transmitted, 1 packets received, 0% packet loss
round-trip min/avg/max/stddev = 0.503/0.503/0.503/0.000 ms
```

PINGs to R2 are working properly.

```
lab@r1> ssh 192.168.5.1
lab@192.168.5.1's password:
--- JUNOS 4.3R2 built 2001-02-22 03:24:10 UTC
lab@r2> quit
Connection to 192.168.5.1 closed.
```

ssh connections to R2 are working properly.

```
lab@r1> telnet 192.168.5.1
Trying 192.168.5.1...
^C
lab@r1> ftp 192.168.5.1
^C
lab@r1>
```

Telnet and FTP connections to R2 fail as per the filter's design.

```
lab@r1> ftp 192.168.2.1
Connected to 192.168.2.1.
220 r3 FTP server (Version 6.00) ready.
Name (192.168.2.1:lab): lab
331 Password required for lab.
Password:
230 User lab logged in.
Remote system type is UNIX.
Using binary mode to transfer files.
ftp> quit
221 Goodbye.
lab@r1>
```

FTP connections through R2 work normally as the *lo0* filter has no effect on transit traffic.

Filter Verification: R2

Now verify proper filter functionality from the perspective of R2:

```
user@r2> show firewall
Filter/Counter                   Packet count           Byte count
local-re
  disallowed                          8                    472
user@r2> show firewall log
Time      Filter    A Interface     Pro Source address   Destination address
00:59:20  pfe       R fe-0/0/0.0    TCP 10.0.2.2          192.168.5.1:21
00:59:17  pfe       R fe-0/0/0.0    TCP 10.0.2.2          192.168.5.1:21
00:59:07  pfe       R fe-0/0/0.0    TCP 10.0.2.2          192.168.5.1:23
00:59:05  pfe       R fe-0/0/0.0    TCP 10.0.2.2          192.168.5.1:23
```

You can see from this display that eight packets have been rejected and counted by the last term in your filter. From the log you see that the source of these packets was 10.0.2.2 (R1), and that the destination ports involved were 21 and 23 (FTP control and Telnet). You can also glean from the log that these rejected packets entered the router on the router's *fe-0/0/0* interface. The fact that the filter is actually applied to R2's *lo0* interface is not apparent in the display.

So far, all seems good with your RE protection filter. Now to test outgoing Telnet:

```
user@r2> telnet 192.168.0.1
Trying 192.168.0.1...
Connected to 192.168.0.1.
Escape character is '^]'.
r1 (ttyp1)
login: lab
Password:
Last login: Tue Mar  6 10:50:50 from 10.0.1.100
--- JUNOS 4.3R1.4 built 2001-01-19 07:26:27 UTC
lab@r1> quit
Connection closed by foreign host.
```

Good. Outgoing Telnet sessions can be established as per the filter's design. Now test outgoing FTP:

```
user@r2> ftp 192.168.0.1
Connected to 192.168.0.1.
220 r1 FTP server (Version 6.00) ready.
Name (192.168.0.1:user): lab
331 Password required for lab.
Password:
230 User lab logged in.
Remote system type is UNIX.
Using binary mode to transfer files.
ftp> quit
221 Goodbye.
user@r2>
```

Outgoing FTP sessions can be established as per the scenario's requirements. The ability to FTP from R1 to R3 indicates that OSPF adjacencies have been correctly established and the IBGP sessions from R2 to R1 and R3 have been reestablished.

Based on these results, you can conclude that your filter is operating as per its design. Congratulations!

Case Study 2: Transit Filtering

This case study will look at how the IP2 can be used for transit filtering in the support of a firewall service as offered by an Internet Service Provider (ISP). As shown in Figure 16-10, R1 now represents a customer access router with a relatively low bandwidth access link. R2 is an IP2-equipped edge router that will implement the firewall service. As before, the firewall related terms "input" and "output" will be used from the perspective of the IP2 processor. The figure shows that the customer has implemented a Demilitarized Zone (DMZ) with a bastion host used to protect its internal network with application proxy services. A "sacrificial" Web server is attached to the DMZ and must be reachable from the Internet.

Even though the access router may be applying its own set of firewall filter rules, outsourcing a second set of filters to a service provider has many advantages:

■ Two sets of expertise are brought to bear on the problem; mistakes are less likely to cause compromised security.

■ Even with firewall rules in the access router, a DoS attack can still effectively remove the customer from the Internet due to a lack of access link bandwidth;

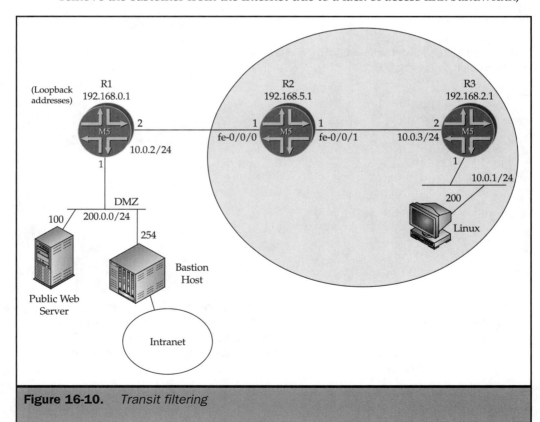

Figure 16-10. *Transit filtering*

filtering at the customer location is good for security, but it's "too late" for bandwidth preservation.

- The access router will often have to implement firewall rules in software, so complex rule sets may have undesirable performance ramifications.

- Rate limiting and DoS tracking services are easily added once the initial outsourced firewall filter is in place

- The potential for added costs and provisioning delays when modifications have to be made to the filter are some of the principal drawbacks to an outsourced firewall service.

Firewall Requirements

The customer has requested that incoming connection requests to the public Web server be limited to HTTP (port 80) only. While this machine is running additional services (I know it's not the best security practice, but the customer is always right, right?), only the TCP based World Wide Web (WWW) service is to be reachable from the Internet. The bastion host provides additional security functions in support of its web, e-mail, FTP, and other applications, and it should be reachable via the Internet with one exception— the Web-based management interface on the bastion host uses SSL over TCP port 8089. Access to this port from the Internet is to be limited to a specific set of IP addresses. All remaining ports on the bastion host should be accessible by any address on the Internet.

In this case study, the service provider is also implementing a source address verification policy to prevent the origination of address spoofing from within its network. To enforce this policy, an input filter will be applied to validate the address of all packets entering the router from the customer site.

Filter Analysis and Verification

Now examine two filters that meet the requirements of this case study. The flexibility of JUNOS firewall filter syntax virtually guarantees that other solutions to the same criteria are possible. In this case, the author has sought to implement a filter with the minimum number of terms possible.

Spoof Prevention

The first filter serves to prevent the customer from generating packets with invalid source addresses.

Spoof Prevention Filter Syntax   The *fe-0/0/0-in* filter has been created to stop packets with invalid or forged source addresses from entering the Internet:

```
[edit firewall filter fe-0/0/0-in]
user@r2# show
term 1 {
```

```
        from {
            source-address {
                200.0.0.0/24;
                10.0.2.2/32;
            }
        }
        then accept;
    }
    term 2 {
        then {
            count spoofs;
            syslog;
            discard;
        }
    }
```

The first term of this filter explicitly accepts packets with source addresses of 200.0.0/24 and 10.0.2.2/32. The latter prefix was added to facilitate diagnostic and maintenance work on the access router, as packets that originate from this router will carry a source address of 10.0.2.2 by default.

All packets not accepted by the first term will be discarded, counted, and logged to R2's syslog via the `syslog` action modifier. Term 2 matches all remaining traffic as no `from` condition has been specified. The reject action should not be deployed when spoofed addresses are suspected, as the resulting error ICMP messages will be sent to the rightful owner of the forged address, which only serves to compound the problem.

The filter name of *fe-0/0/0-in* was chosen to represent the associated interface and the directionality of the filter's application—that is, the filter will be applied in the input direction.

DMZ Security Filter

The second filter serves to protect the public Web server and bastion host on the customer's DMZ.

Web Server and Bastion Host Filter Syntax   The filter named *fe-0/0/0-out* enforces the security requirements of the customer's DMZ:

```
[edit firewall filter fe-0/0/0-out]
user@r2# show
term 1 {
    from {
        destination-address {
```

```
                    200.0.0.100/32;
            }
            protocol [ tcp icmp udp ];
            destination-port [ 1-79 81-65535 ];
        }
        then discard;
    }
    term 2 {
        from {
            source-address {
                192.168.0.0/21 except;
                0.0.0.0/0;
            }
            destination-address {
                200.0.0.254/32;
            }
            protocol tcp;
            destination-port 8089;
        }
        then {
            syslog;
            reject;
        }
    }
    term else {
        then accept;
    }
```

Term 1 ensures that all traffic from all protocols in the port ranges of 1–79 and 81–65,535 is discarded when the packet's destination is 200.0.0.100 (the Web server). The result is that only TCP/UDP packets that have a destination port of 80 (HTTP) can be sent to the public Web server. In this case, all ICMP packets will be dropped as the concept of ports does not apply to ICMP. In other words, ICMP-related port matches always test true.

The astute reader will note that term 1 permits UDP segments with a destination port of 80. This should not be a problem as the UDP is normally not associated with the HTTP protocol so the server has no UDP process listening on this port. Additional terms could easily be added to prevent this traffic if it was a concern.

Term 2 controls access to the bastion host (200.0.0.254) by matching on TCP packets with a destination port of 8089 from all sources except those that are encompassed by the 192.168.0/21 range. Packets with a source address in the range of 192.168.0-7.x do not match this term due to the use of the except keyword and will therefore be evaluated by the next term. Packets matching term 2 will cause syslog entries and will be rejected. The syslog option is being used in term 2, as matches here indicate unauthorized attempts to access the bastion host's Web-based management port; a definite security concern.

Term *else* accepts all traffic that has not already been discarded or rejected by terms 1 and 2.

Filter Application

Two filters have been applied to the *fe-0/0/0* interface on R2 with the proper directionality:

```
[edit]
user@r2# show interfaces fe-0/0/0
unit 0 {
    family inet {
        filter {
            input fe-0/0/0-in;
            output fe-0/0/0-out;
        }
        address 10.0.2.1/24;
    }
}
```

Filter Verification

The proper operation of the spoof prevention and DMZ security filters will now be verified.

Spoof Prevention Filter Verification   The proper operation of the spoof prevention filter will be verified by generating PINGs with different source addresses from R1:

```
lab@r1> ping count 2 192.168.5.1
PING 192.168.5.1 (192.168.5.1): 56 data bytes
64 bytes from 192.168.5.1: icmp_seq=0 ttl=255 time=21.708 ms
64 bytes from 192.168.5.1: icmp_seq=1 ttl=255 time=0.418 ms

--- 192.168.5.1 ping statistics ---
2 packets transmitted, 2 packets received, 0% packet loss
round-trip min/avg/max/stddev = 0.418/11.063/21.708/10.645 ms

lab@r1> ping local 200.0.1.1 count 2 192.168.5.1
PING 192.168.5.1 (192.168.5.1): 56 data bytes
```

```
64 bytes from 192.168.5.1: icmp_seq=0 ttl=255 time=0.450 ms
64 bytes from 192.168.5.1: icmp_seq=1 ttl=255 time=0.420 ms

--- 192.168.5.1 ping statistics ---
2 packets transmitted, 2 packets received, 0% packet loss
round-trip min/avg/max/stddev = 0.420/0.435/0.450/0.015 ms

lab@r1> ping local 192.168.0.1 count 2 192.168.5.1
PING 192.168.5.1 (192.168.5.1): 56 data bytes

--- 192.168.5.1 ping statistics ---
2 packets transmitted, 0 packets received, 100% packet loss
```

You can see that packets with a source address of 200.0.0/24 or 10.0.2.2/32 are successful, while those sourced from the 192.168.0.1 *lo0* address of R1 fail.

Examination of the log file on R2 shows that the following packets arrived on *fe-0/0/0* and are met with a discard action:

```
[edit]
user@r2# run show firewall log
Time      Filter    A Interface      Pro Source address   Destination address
20:15:54 pfe        D fe-0/0/0.0     TCP 192.168.0.1      192.168.5.1:1142
20:15:54 pfe        D fe-0/0/0.0     TCP 192.168.0.1      192.168.5.1:1142
```

The firewall counter named "spoofs," which is associated with the *fe-0/0/0-in* filter, is also incrementing:

```
[edit]
user@r2# run show firewall
Filter/Counter                 Packet count          Byte count
fe-0/0/0-out
local-re
  disallowed                              0                   0
fe-0/0/0-in
  spoofs                               1377               78388
[edit]
```

Based on these results, you can conclude that all is well with the operation of the source address verification filter.

DMZ Security Filter Verification The proper operation of the DMZ security filter will be verified using a variety of techniques, beginning with a port scan directed at the public Web server before application of the DMZ filter:

```
[root@linux-box scanners-etc]# ./nmap -O -PI 200.0.0.100
Starting nmap V. 2.54BETA2 ( www.insecure.org/nmap/ )
Interesting ports on  (200.0.0.100):
(The 1513 ports scanned but not shown below are in state: closed)
Port        State        Service
7/tcp       open         echo
9/tcp       open         discard
13/tcp      open         daytime
17/tcp      open         qotd
19/tcp      open         chargen
21/tcp      open         ftp
23/tcp      open         telnet
25/tcp      open         smtp
42/tcp      open         nameserver
80/tcp      open         http
135/tcp     open         loc-srv
139/tcp     open         netbios-ssn
443/tcp     open         https
1025/tcp    open         listen
1031/tcp    open         iad2
6666/tcp    open         irc-serv
7007/tcp    open         afs3-bos

TCP Sequence Prediction: Class=random positive increments
                         Difficulty=17354 (Worthy challenge)
Remote operating system guess: Windows 2000 RC1 through final release
Nmap run completed -- 1 IP address (1 host up) scanned in 2 seconds
```

Wow, talk about a hackers delight! From these results you can conclude that the access router's DMZ security filters are either nonexistent, or poorly written at best!

This situation provides a good argument for using two sets of filters in the hope that at least one of the filters will be implemented correctly. In case you are curious, the -O option on the nmap command line enables remote operating system fingerprinting while the PI option instructs nmap to scan only hosts that respond to ICMP echoes.

After applying our DMZ filter in R2, another port scan is performed:

```
[root@linux-box mgen]# ~/scanners-etc/nmap -O -PI 200.0.0.100

Starting nmap V. 2.54BETA2 ( www.insecure.org/nmap/ )
```

```
Note: Host seems down. If it is really up, but blocking our ping probes,
try -P0
Nmap run completed -- 1 IP address (0 hosts up) scanned in 60 seconds
[root@linux-box mgen]#
```

The presence of our DMZ filter has caused nmap to feel the host is down due to its inability to PING 200.0.0.100. You must now tell nmap not to base port scanning on the ability to PING the target host. This is accomplished with the P0 flag on the nmap command line:

```
[root@linux-box scanners-etc]# ./nmap -O -P0 -p 1-1024 200.0.0.100
Starting nmap V. 2.54BETA2 ( www.insecure.org/nmap/ )
Interesting ports on  (200.0.0.100):
(The 1023 ports scanned but not shown below are in state: filtered)
Port        State        Service
80/tcp      open         http
TCP Sequence Prediction: Class=random positive increments
                         Difficulty=12931 (Worthy challenge)
Remote OS guesses: FreeBSD 3.2-STABLE, Windows 2000 RC1 through final
release
Nmap run completed -- 1 IP address (1 host up) scanned in 365 seconds
[root@linux-box scanners-etc]#
```

The results of this scan would indicate that only TCP port 80 is reachable on the public Web server.

You will now do a host scan on the 200.0.0/24 subnet to see if the bastion host can respond to PINGs:

```
[root@linux-box mgen]# ~/scanners-etc/nmap -sP -PI 200.0.0.0-254

Starting nmap V. 2.54BETA2 ( www.insecure.org/nmap/ )

Host  (200.0.0.1) appears to be up.
Host  (200.0.0.254) appears to be up.
Nmap run completed -- 256 IP addresses (2 hosts up) scanned in 45 seconds
[root@linux-box mgen]#
```

Notice that the DMZ filter has successfully "hidden" the public server from ICMP-based scans; the access router and bastion host are allowed to respond to PINGs so they have been detected by the scan.

Now you will verify that only authorized hosts can attempt to connect to the bastion host's management port, which listens on TCP port 8089:

```
[root@linux-box mgen]# telnet 200.0.0.1 8089
Trying 200.0.0.1...
telnet: Unable to connect to remote host: Connection refused
```

In this case, the access router has rejected the connection request, as there is no process listening on this port.

```
[root@linux-box mgen]# telnet 200.0.0.254 8089
Trying 200.0.0.254...
telnet: Unable to connect to remote host: No route to host
[root@linux-box mgen]#
```

Identical connection requests to the bastion host result in an ICMP destination unreachable error message, as the protocol capture in Figure 16-11 shows.

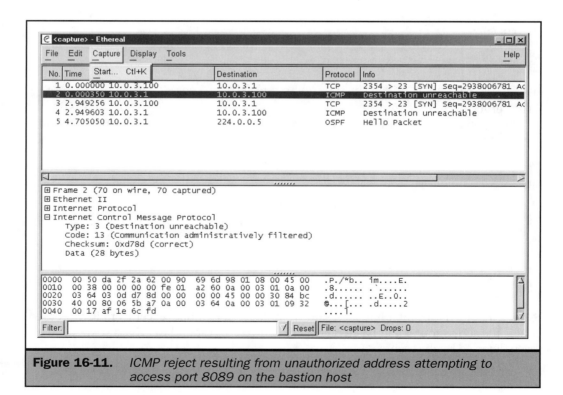

Figure 16-11.   *ICMP reject resulting from unauthorized address attempting to access port 8089 on the bastion host*

The source address of the ICMP destination unreachable message is 10.0.3.1, which is the egress interface associated with the 10.0.1/24 subnet on R2.

Finally, view R2's syslog to view the results of the `syslog` action modifier in term 2.

```
user@r2# run show log messages | match JFW | match 200.0.0.254
Mar  7 21:37:54 r2 tnp_scb JFW: fe-0/0/1.0   R  tcp 10.0.1.200 200.0.0.254  2454  8089 (1 packets)
```

Here we can see that a packet from 10.0.1.200, destined to 200.0.0.254 port 8089, entered the router on the *fe-0/0/1* interface and was rejected. Note the fancy use of double-command output piping!

The results of the testing confirm that both firewall filters are operating as per the requirements of the case study.

IP2 Rate Limiting

As discussed in the introduction, the IP2 is able to rate limit interfaces and protocol flows via a token bucket-based policer. IP2-based rate limiting is more flexible than interfaced-based leaky buckets, and it can be deployed on any interface type or Layer 3/4 flow.

Shaping vs. Policing

Before describing IP2 rate limiting specifics, it may be beneficial to understand the difference between shaping and policing, as IP2 rate limiting is achieved through policing.

Shapers

Figure 16-12 illustrates both macro and micro views of a shaper at work. You can see that the shaper uses a scheduling algorithm to place packets onto the transmission link, such that n packets will cross a given point in a specific unit of time. The packets leaving the shaper will have a minimum interpacket gap that varies inversely with the shaper's output rate. The device at the remote end of the transmission link should not require significant buffering, as packet clumping does not occur with a shaper.

The shaper's tolerance to bursts is determined by the size of the shaper queue. Traffic that exceeds the shaper queue is discarded.

A key aspect of shaping is that unused scheduler slots do not amount to credit buildup; failing to send a packet during a given window does not allow two packets to be sent in the next available window.

Policers

Figure 16-13 provides the same macro and micro views of a policer in operation. The policer attempts to empty its queue as quickly as possible so that, from a micro view, the packets appear to cross a given point with widely varying packet gaps. The effective rate of the policer is determined by the speed at which credit is added to the buffer. Discards occur when the packet arrival rate exceeds the rate of credit allocation.

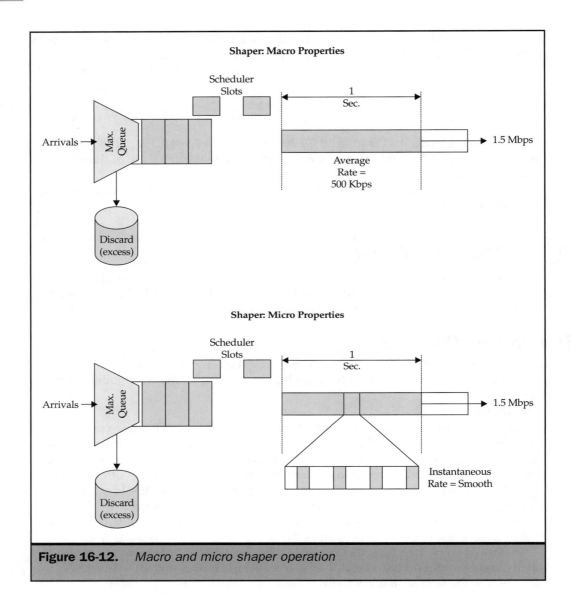

Figure 16-12. *Macro and micro shaper operation*

In contrast to a shaper, a policer allows credits to accumulate when bits are not being presented to the policer's input. This results in the policer's ability to send packet bursts.

The Net Effect

When both devices are analyzed from a macro view, you can see that, to a large degree, their operation is identical in that the same number of bits end up being sent—or

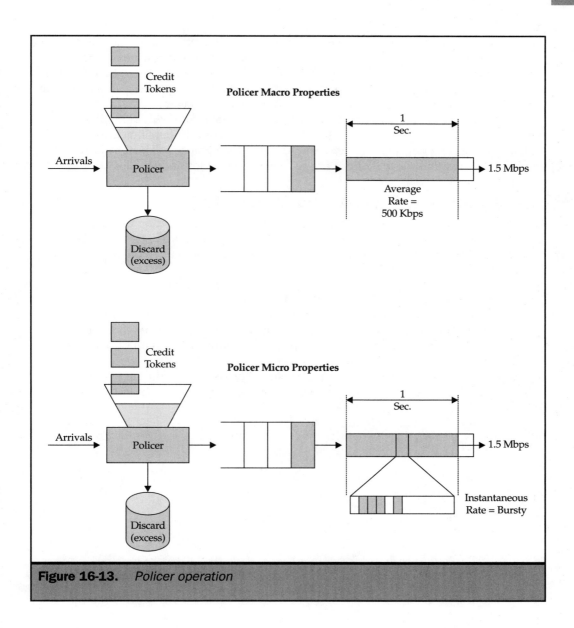

Figure 16-13. *Policer operation*

discarded for that matter—regardless of which technique is being used. In a nutshell, policers allow bursting while shapers provide smoothing by delaying the transmission of packets.

From the micro view, you can see that the device at the other end of the transmission link will need to deploy larger buffers to accommodate the bursty nature of a policer if data loss is to be avoided. Lack of buffer space can always be a problem, but it should not be aggravated by the choice of policer versus shaper because they both generate the same amount of traffic over time frames of a few milliseconds or longer.

A properly designed network should generally be operating with a significant margin of free buffer space anyway. Instead of adding value, buffers that are chronically full actually act as a detriment to network performance, because full buffers lead to increased latency and the loss of protection against congestion-induced losses.

IP2 Rate Limiting Syntax and Processing

IP2 policers are defined within firewall filters. Terms within the filter can point to a given policer when a match occurs. Although multiple policers can be defined in a single filter, currently a given packet may be subjected only to one policing action before being either accepted or discarded.

Traffic presented to a policer is said to be in profile when it does not exceed the policer's bandwidth and burst size limits. In-profile traffic is not affected by the policer and will be handed back to the calling term for final processing—that is, after being policed, the traffic can be sampled, logged, counted, and soon. Traffic that is out of profile can be discarded or placed into a specific transmit queue, with or without modification of its PLP bit setting.

JUNOS policers automatically count packet discards with a counter listed under the policer's name. You can display these counts using the `show firewall <name>` command.

A typical JUNOS policer is shown here:

```
firewall {
    filter foo {
        policer p1 {
            if-exceeding {
                bandwidth-limit 200m;
                burst-size-limit 45k;
            }
            then discard;
        }
        term 1 {
    from {
        protocol tcp;
        port 80;
    }
    then {
```

```
        policer p1;
        count accepted;
        accept;
    }
}
```

Here you see that the filter named "foo" has a single policer named "p1" defined. The operator has specified the bandwidth and burst size limits as arguments to the `if-exceeding` keyword in the policer definition. Traffic that is within the policer limits will be handed back to the calling term, where it will increment a counter named "accepted." Traffic in excess of the policer's limits will be discarded. Since matches in term 1 will evoke the policer, this example demonstrates how HTTP traffic can be rate limited.

Policer Bandwidth-Limit

`bandwidth-limit` represents the rate of token bucket credit renewal, as measured over the course of 1 second.

There is no absolute minimum value for `bandwidth-limit`, but any value below 61,040 bps results in an effective rate of 32,000 bps. The maximum `bandwidth-limit` value is 3.2 Gbps.

Policer Burst-Limit

`burst-limit` specifies the size of the policer's token bucket and places a limit on how much credit can be earned. Burst size is measured in bytes and has a maximum value of 100 million. The burst size should never be set smaller than the maximum size of the IP packets being policed, as physical and link layer protocols require the line rate transmission of complete protocol data units (PDUs). For optimal performance, it is recommended that you set the burst-size parameter based on a bandwidth-delay product using the following formula:

Interface bandwidth (bps) × small delay (1–5 msec) / 8

Using this formula on an OC3c interface, you would arrive at a minimum recommended `burst-limit` setting in the range of 19.3 to 96.8KB.

155 Mbps × (1–5 msec) / 8 = 19.3KB to 96.8KB

When specifying the values for the bandwidth and burst-limit parameters, the operator can use suffixes like *k* for kilo, *m* for meg, and *g* for gig. Thus, entering a `bandwidth-limit` of 1000000 is equivalent to entering *1m*.

Case Study 3: Rate Limiting

Figure 16-14 provides the topology for this IP2 rate limiting case study. In this example, a tier 3 service provider owning AS 65010 has arranged to buy transit peering from the tier 1 provider who owns AS 65021. The private peering point is based on Fast Ethernet in this example, but the concepts presented here apply equally well to any interface type.

As transit peering can be expensive, the tier 1 provider has offered a "fractional Ethernet" peering option that allows its customers to buy the peering bandwidth they need, regardless of the underlying Network Access Point (NAP) technology.

Policer Requirements

The peering arrangement negotiated in this example allows no more than 15 Mbps of IP layer throughput. The maximum burst (or token bucket) size has been established at 65,000 bytes.

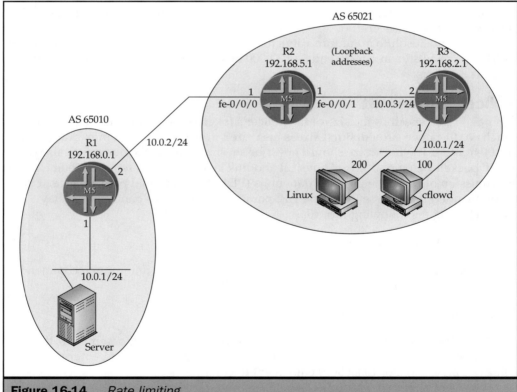

Figure 16-14. *Rate limiting*

Policer Configuration and Verification

A JUNOS firewall policer that meets these requirements will now be configured, starting with the policer itself:

```
[edit firewall filter police]
user@r2# set policer p1 if-exceeding bandwidth-limit 15m
[edit firewall filter police]
user@r2# set policer p1 if-exceeding burst-size-limit 65k
[edit firewall filter police]
user@r2# set policer p1 then ?
Possible completions:
+ apply-groups        Groups from which to inherit configuration data
  discard             Discard the packet
  output-queue        Set output queue for packet (0..3)
  plp                 Mark the packet (0..1)
[edit firewall filter police]
user@r2# set policer p1 then discard
```

In this example, a policer called "p1" has been configured to allow a maximum burst credit of 65,000 bytes with a sustained throughput of 15 Mbps. A question mark (?) was used when setting the policer's then action to display the actions the policer can take on out-of-profile traffic. In this case, the policer action has been set to discard.

Now complete the rate limiting firewall by adding a term to indicate what traffic should be subjected to the policer's wrath. Since this case study is demonstrating interface-based rate limiting, create a match-all term:

```
[edit firewall filter police]
user@r2# set term 1 then policer p1
[edit firewall filter police]
```

The resulting rate limiting filter looks like this:

```
[edit firewall filter police]
user@r2# show
policer p1 {
    if-exceeding {
        bandwidth-limit 15m;
        burst-size-limit 65k;
    }
    then discard;
```

```
    }
term 1 {
    then policer p1;
}
```

Since everything matches term 1 in the filter, all traffic associated with the LU to which this filter is applied will be rate limited. Traffic that is in profile will be handed back to term 1, where it will be accepted. (It bears restating that the accept action is performed for any firewall term that does not have an explicit discard or reject action.) Out-of-profile traffic is counted and discarded by the policer.

To verify the functionality of your rate-limiting filter, generate a packet stream at a known rate, while observing the resulting traffic loads both before and after the filter's application. To generate traffic, you will produce 500-byte packets at a rate of 8049 packets per second using the *mgen* utility on a Linux box. With the 28 bytes of IP and UDP headers factored in, the total packet size is brought to 528 bytes. The resulting traffic stream will represent approximately 34 Mbps ($528 \times 8 \times 8,048 = 33.99$ Mbps). The packets are addressed to the 200.0.0/24 subnet that is owned by the tier 3 provider.

To see the traffic loads before the filter is applied, issue the monitor interface fe-0/0/0 command. The results, shown in Listing 16-1, clearly show the *fe-0/0/0* interface is outputting 34 Mbps of traffic.

Listing 16-1
Traffic load prior to the application of the rate-limiting filter

```
r2                              Seconds: 592                      Time: 02:14:02
                                                                  Delay: 1/1/2

Interface: fe-0/0/0, Enabled, Link is up
Encapsulation: Ethernet, Speed: 100mbps
Traffic statistics:                                              Current delta
  Input bytes:            970184646 (0 bps)                         [12129]
  Output bytes:          4896728299 (34017864 bps)             [2499837256]
  Input packets:            183907 (0 pps)                            [163]
  Output packets:          9275739 (8053 pps)                     [4734680]
Error statistics:
  input errors:                  0                                      [0]
  Input drops:                   0                                      [0]
  Input framing errors:          0                                      [0]
  Policed discards:              0                                      [0]
  L3 incompletes:                0                                      [0]
  L2 channel errors:             0                                      [0]
  Packet error count:            0                                      [0]




Next='n', Quit='q' or ESC, Freeze='f', Thaw='t', Clear='c', Interface='i'
```

Now you'll apply the filter with a policing action to the *fe-0/0/0* interface in both directions. If desired, an interface can be *asymmetrically* limited, or limited in one direction only. It is important to note that because the filter is being applied at the LU level, it is possible to have multiple input and output policers applied to the same physical interface. This means that a provider can set up VLANs at a Gigabit Ethernet–based NAP and offer various levels of throughput over the same interface.

```
user@r2> configure
Entering configuration mode
[edit]
user@r2# edit interfaces fe-0/0/0
[edit interfaces fe-0/0/0]
user@r2# set unit 0 family inet filter output police
[edit interfaces fe-0/0/0]
user@r2# set unit 0 family inet filter input police
[edit interfaces fe-0/0/0]
user@r2# commit and-quit
commit complete
Exiting configuration mode
```

To verify that this is working correctly, once again monitor the *fe-0/0/0* interface with the results shown in Listing 16-2. You can clearly see that the interface load has fallen from 34 Mbps to 14.6 Mbps, which is near the 15 Mbps configured in the policer. Based on the crudeness of the author's test bed, it would appear that the policer is performing to specification.

Listing 16-2
Traffic load after application of the rate-limiting filter

```
r2                             Seconds: 43              Time: 02:40:09
                                                        Delay: 2/1/2

Interface: fe-0/0/0, Enabled, Link is up
Encapsulation: Ethernet, Speed: 100mbps
Traffic statistics:                                     Current delta
  Input bytes:           2200817122 (0 bps)                    [892]
  Output bytes:         12101991451 (14648832 bps)        [76943242]
  Input packets:           4170341 (0 pps)                      [14]
  Output packets:         22922645 (3468 pps)               [145739]
Error statistics:
  input errors:                    0                             [0]
  Input drops:                     0                             [0]
  Input framing errors:            0                             [0]
  Policed discards:                0                             [0]
  L3 incompletes:                  0                             [0]
  L2 channel errors:               0                             [0]
```

```
Packet error count:                 0                          [0]




Next='n', Quit='q' or ESC, Freeze='f', Thaw='t', Clear='c', Interface='i'
```

Now examine the firewall counters to confirm that traffic in excess of the policer's profile is being discarded:

```
user@r2> show firewall
Filter/Counter                    Packet count              Byte count
fe-0/0/0-in
  spoofs                                    0                         0
fe-0/0/0-out
local-re
  disallowed                                0                         0
police
  p1                                   337756                        NA
```

And approximately 5 seconds later, issue the same command. (To gain some measure of accuracy, the following command chain was entered at the JUNOS shell: cli -c "show firewall"; sleep 5; cli -c "show firewall";).

```
user@r2> show firewall
Filter/Counter                    Packet count              Byte count
fe-0/0/0-in
  spoofs                                    0                         0
fe-0/0/0-out
local-re
  disallowed                                0                         0
police
  p1                                   361630                        NA
```

Based on the counts associated with policer "p1," you can see that 23,874 packets have been discarded in approximately 5 seconds. This equates to roughly 20 Mbps that has been discarded by the policer, a number that once again closely approximates the difference between the offered load (34 Mbps) and the policer's configuration (15 Mbps): 34 − 15 = 19.

IP2 Statistical Sampling

As mentioned in the chapter introduction, the IP2 ASIC supports the statistical sampling of transit traffic. Traffic samples can be stored on the RE's hard drive or exported to a remote host running cflowd using NetFlow export packet formats. Sampling can be used for the tracking of DoS attacks and for the strategic analysis of traffic patterns. The first feature can help you provide a valuable service to your customers, while the latter one can help you optimize your BGP peering relationships or the design of your backbone.

The Need for Statistical Sampling

Trying to sample every packet on high-speed interfaces is just not possible, especially on production routers. Frankly, the need to sample every packet should be extremely rare, as statistical sampling, if implemented over a reasonable period of time, will provide similar accuracy with far less strain on the sampling platform. The actual sampling rate on a Juniper router is determined by the interrelationship of the following factors:

- The configured sampling rate (0–65,535)
- The configured run length (0–20)
- The level of discrimination used in the firewall filter terms that evoke the sampling action
- Interface speed and packet size distribution
- The number of sampling filters in use

Since the interplay between these factors is complex, and therefore difficult to predict, the support of a `max-packets-per-second` knob ensures that the RE can be protected from oversampling, regardless of how the sampling features have been configured and applied.

To prevent problems with routing protocol convergence, especially when large route flaps are possible, it is recommended that the user keep the total sampling rate to less then 1000 packets per second. This is the default setting for the `max-packets-per-second` option.

Sampling Configuration

Before the sampling action modifier can be successfully used in a firewall filter, the user must first configure sampling under the *[edit forwarding-options sampling]* portion of the configuration. This configuration entails the setting of sampling `input` and `output` options.

Configuring Sampling Input

Sampling input parameters are configured under the *[edit forward-options sampling input]* portion of the hierarchy. Sampling `input` parameters are used to specify the protocol family being sampled, as well as the statistical sampling rate and run-length associated with the sampling function. The user must specify the `family inet` under `sampling input` as JUNOS software currently supports sampling functions for IP traffic only.

The options available for sampling input are shown here:

```
[edit forwarding-options sampling input]
user@r2# set family inet ?
Possible completions:
  <[Enter]>                Execute this command
+ apply-groups             Groups from which to inherit configuration data
  max-packets-per-second   Threshold of samples per second before dropping
  rate                     Ratio of packets to be sampled (1 out of N)
  run-length               Number of samples after initial trigger (0..20)
  |                        Pipe through a command
[edit forwarding-options sampling input]
```

The Rate Parameter   The overall sampling rate can be capped by setting the `max-packets-per-second` parameter. By default, this is set to 1000 samples per second. The `rate` parameter controls the ratio of packets that are sampled. The default sampling rate is 0, so sampling cannot occur until this parameter is modified. The `rate` keyword takes as an argument a number in the range of 1 to 65,535, inclusive. A setting of 1 indicates that every matching packet should be sampled, while 65,536 indicates that, on average, 1 packet will actually be sampled for every 65,536 instances of a firewall filter evoking the sampling action.

By way of example, assume that a "match-all" sampling firewall filter has been applied to an OC-192c interface. Setting the rate to 1 would be a real problem here, as an OC-192c interface is capable of generating some 24 million 40-byte packets per second! However, setting the rate to its minimum ratio of 1/65,535 would result in a total sampling load of only 366.2 samples per second—a rate that is well within the recommended 1000 samples per second threshold.

It is important to note that JUNOS software incorporates a randomness function into the decision to sample a packet. The effect is that a sampling rate of 10 will not result in the sampling of every tenth matching packet. Such a setting will, however, result in an average sampling rate of 1 out of every 10 matching packets. The presence of this dithering component in the sampling process is necessary to ensure the statistical validity of the sampled data.

The run-length Parameter   The `run-length` parameter is used to determine whether the next *n* matching packets should be sampled for context. A setting of 5 indicates that once a sample is taken, the next five matching packets will also be sampled independent of the configured sampling rate and randomizing factor. By default the `run-length` parameter is set to 0 with valid options ranging from 0 to 20, inclusive.

Configuring Sampling Output

Sampling output functions are configured under the *[edit forward-options sampling output]* portion of the hierarchy. Sampling output parameters are used to specify the destination of sampled data. Generally speaking, the operator has two choices here: the sampled packets can be written to the RE's hard disk in the form of an ASCII file, or they can be converted to NetFlow export and sent to a remote host for collection and analysis.

Local ASCII Storage   Configuring file related options under *[edit forward-options sampling output]* enables the local storage of samples on the RE's hard drive. The configuration options for local storage are shown here:

```
user@r2# set file ?
Possible completions:
  filename           Name of file to contain sampled packet dumps
  files              Maximum number of sampled packet dump files
  no-stamp           Don't timestamp every packet in the dump
  no-world-readable  Don't allow any user to read the sampled dump
  size               Maximum sample dump file size
  stamp              Timestamp every packet in the dump
  world-readable     Allow any user to read the sampled dump
[edit forwarding-options sampling output]
```

The `filename` parameter is used to indicate the name of the file to which sampled packets should be written. The file will be created in the /var/tmp directory, so you will need to include the path when using the `show log` command as the default directory for log files is /var/log.

The `files` keyword specifies how many maximum-sized sample files should be archived before older files are overwritten with new sample data. When the sample file is full, it will be renamed to "filename.0" while the previous "filename.0" file becomes "filename.1," and so on, to the number of files specified. The argument range for `files` is 2–100, inclusive, with 5 being the default. The size parameter limits the maximum size of each sample file. The arguments are specified in bytes, with the default being 1MB for sampling files.

The `no-stamp` and `stamp` options determine whether timestamps are written into the sample log periodically or with each sample written. The `no-stamp` mode of operation is enabled by default. The `world-readable` and `no-world-readable` knobs are used to control access to the sample file itself. By default, only root and members of the "wheel" group—that is, superusers—are allowed to view the file's contents.

As an example, here is an operator configuring the local storage of samples to a file called foo. The system is also being told to keep 10 archived copies of foo (foo.0 through foo.9), and that each entry should be individually time stamped:

```
[edit forwarding-options sampling output]
user@r2# set file filename foo files 10 size 10m stamp
```

A complete sampling configuration for local ASCII storage is shown here:

```
[edit forwarding-options sampling]
user@r2# show
input {
    family inet {
        rate 100;
    }
}
output {
    file filename foo files 10 size 10m stamp;
}

[edit forwarding-options sampling]
```

This stanza configures the sampling of 1 out of every 100 candidate packets, with storage to a series of files called foo in the /var/tmp directory on the local hard drive.

cflowd Export   Configuring cflowd options under *[edit forward-options sampling output]* enables the export of sampled packets in a format NetFlow-compatible format for use with tools such as cflowd. The exported flow records enable the collection of various byte and packets counts for the sampled flows passing through the router. The generic configuration syntax for cflowd export takes the following form:

```
cflowd host-name {
        aggregation {
        autonomous-system;
        destination-prefix;
        protocol-port;
        source-destination-prefix;
        source-prefix;
    }
    autonomous-system-type (origin | peer);
    (local-dump | no-local-dump);
    port port-number;
    version format;
    }
```

The `hostname` field is set to the domain name or IP address of the remote host running the cflowd process. The cflowd collector (*cflowdcollect*) process is responsible for periodically polling one or more cflowd hosts to consolidate all NetFlow records onto a single machine for post-collection analysis. The `aggregation` knob enables local RE-based aggregation of matching cflowd records to minimize network bandwidth requirements and cflowd host processing loads.

When aggregation is enabled, the local RE caches matching NetFlow records, processes them locally, and then sends the summary results to the cflowd host. Without aggregation, all record types are exported. Aggregation is available only when using NetFlow version 8.

The `autonomous-system-type` option determines whether the originating or peer's Autonomous System (AS) number is included in the exported records. By default, the origin AS number is sent in the exported records. The `local-dump` option writes copies of exported cflowd records to the log file on the local hard drive. This option is intended to assist the debugging of cflowd problems during initial activation. Because `local-dump` increases the workload placed on the RE, it should be used only when actively troubleshooting. It should be noted that `local-dump` writes copies of flow records to the /var/tmp/sampled.pkts file by default, even though a different filename may be configured for the local storage of ASCII-formatted sampled data. If desired, the user can configure `traceoptions` at the *[forwarding-options sampling]* portion of the hierarchy to configure a different file for locally dumped cflowd records. The file specified under `traceoptions` will be created in the /var/log directory. As a result, you will be able to view the file's contents without having to specify a path as the `show log` command looks in /var/log by default.

The UDP port being used by the remote cflowd host is configured with the `port` keyword. The argument to the `port` keyword can be any valid port on the remote host. There is no JUNOS default for this parameter; by default the cflowd process listens on UDP port 2055. The `version` command determines whether version 5 or 8 records are sent, with the default being version 5.

Note   *You can visit the CAIDA Web site at **http://www.caida.org** for more information on the cflowd package and the availability of post-processing tools for traffic visualization. You can also look at **http://www.switch.ch/tf-tant/floma/software.html** for a listing of currently available NetFlow analysis tools.*

Case Study 4: Statistical Sampling

In this case study, you will configure and verify the operation of statistical sampling both with local file storage and cflowd export. The topology for this case study is shown in Figure 16-15.

In this scenario, the operator of AS 65021 has decided to conduct statistical sampling at its peering points to evaluate transit traffic patterns. Once these patterns are known,

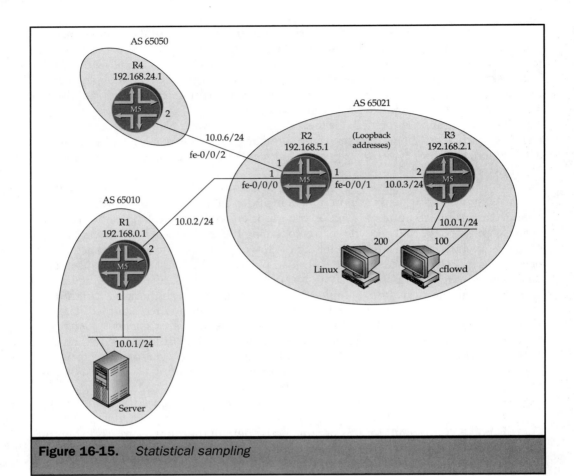

Figure 16-15. *Statistical sampling*

MPLS-based traffic engineering can be brought to bear to maximize the efficiency of the backbone. This study will focus on sampling conducted at the operator's peering point with AS 65010. In this demonstration, AS 65050 is generating Telnet and ICMP traffic flows toward subnet 200.0.0/24 in AS 65010, while AS 65021 is generating FTP UDP traffic to the same destination. To help verify sampling accuracy, the UDP test traffic is produced at a known rate. Though this example does not demonstrate a true Internet mix, the results accurately represent the current capabilities of JUNOS software and IP2 sampling.

The Sampling Filter

The following firewall filter with a sampling action is applied as an output filter on R2's *fe-0/0/0* interface:

```
[edit firewall]
user@r2# show filter sample
term 1 {
    from {
        protocol udp;
        port 5000;
    }
    then {
        count udp-test;
        sample;
        accept;
    }
}
term 2 {
    then {
        sample;
        accept;
    }
}
```

Term 1 has been added so that UDP test traffic can be introduced to validate the sampling process. This traffic will originate within AS 65021 from host 10.0.1.200.

Forwarding Options

The *[forwarding-options]* portion of the configuration has been set to support local ASCII storage with a sampling rate of .01 (1/100):

```
[edit forwarding-options]
user@r2# show
sampling {
    input {
        family inet {
            rate 100;
```

```
            run-length 0;
        }
    }
    output {
        file filename sample files 3 size 20m stamp;
    }
}
```

The *input* portion of the stanza configures an average sampling rate of 1 percent for the packets that are marked by the filter as candidates for sampling. This is a high sampling rate, considering that it can produce as many as 1.7 thousand samples if it is assumed that the Fast Ethernet link is fully loaded with 64-byte frames. While the default `max-packets-per-second` setting of 1000 will ensure that the RE is not overburdened with sample processing, lower sampling rates are recommended on production networks to avoid the loss of samples. While the RE can handle sampling rates higher than 1000 samples per second, other processes in the RE may exhibit diminished performance due to processor contention with higher sampling rates.

The sample output will be written to a file called "sample" in the /var/tmp directory. JUNOS has been told to create three 20MB archived copies before beginning to overwrite the oldest file, and to include timestamps for each sample entry written to the file.

Sampling Verification and Analysis

The sampling configuration has been committed and will now be verified using various CLI commands.

Viewing the Firewall Counter

Since you are sampling 1 percent of all traffic being sent from AS 65021 to AS 65010, the sampling file should already be populated with samples. To verify, issue the following commands:

```
user@r2>
user@r2> show firewall
Filter/Counter                      Packet count              Byte count
local-re
  disallowed                                   0                       0
sample
  udp-test                                     0                       0
```

Viewing the Sampling File

Based on the counter results, you can see that either the generation of UDP test traffic has not yet commenced or sampling is broken. You can quickly resolve this question by examining the contents of the sampling file:

```
user@r2> show log /var/tmp/sample
# Mar 10 19:17:32
#          Time            Dest          Src  Dest  Src Proto  TOS   Pkt  Intf    IP    TCP
#                          addr          addr port  port            len   num  frag  flags
# Mar 13 17:34:33      200.0.0.1   192.168.12.1    0     0    1  0x0    84    5  0x0    0x0
# Mar 13 17:34:33      200.0.0.1   192.168.12.1   23  1042    6  0x10   52    5  0x4000 0x10
# Mar 13 17:34:33      200.0.0.1   192.168.12.1    0     0    1  0x0    84    5  0x0    0x0
```

The sampling file's contents confirm that timestamped entries are being written and that both ICMP and Telnet protocols are present at the AS 65010 peering point, so all seems to be well with your sampling process.

 Sampling problems can be caused by faulty firewall filter construction, incorrect firewall application, or a lack of matching traffic. While rare, malfunctions in the sampling daemon can occur. If needed, the operator can restart the sampling daemon from the CLI with the `restart sampling` *operational mode command. Examining the sampling daemon log using* `show log sampled` *can also assist with fault isolation.*

To save room on the display, the sampling file lists the upper layer protocol numerically—like so: 06 = TCP—while 1 indicates ICMP. The TCP flag field shows the setting of the various TCP flags in a hexadecimal format. The TCP segment in this example has a set an ACK flag, which indicates the packet is part of an established connection. The *intf num* column lists ingress interfaces by their *Interface Logical Index* (IFL) value. These values can be correlated to a physical interface and LU using the following command:

```
user@r2> show interfaces | match "index 5"
  Logical interface fe-0/0/2.0 (Index 5) (SNMP ifIndex 19)
```

Here you can see that the samples have all entered R2's *fe-0/0/2.0* interface, which attaches to R4 in AS 65050. Knowing the ingress interface of a packet, especially those with illegitimate source addresses, is critical when tracking the source of a spoofed attack.

Note *Logical interface indexes are somewhat ephemeral in that they can change after a reboot, especially if hardware has been added or removed. The timely analysis of sampling files is recommended to ensure the validity of the IFLs being used to determine ingress interface.*

Verifying Sampling Accuracy

Test traffic will now be generated to confirm the accuracy of statistical sampling:

```
[root@linux-box mgen]# ./mgen -b 200.0.0.86 -r 200 -d 30
MGEN: Version 3.2a1
MGEN: Loading event queue ...
MGEN: Seeding random number generator ...
MGEN: Beginning packet generation ...
       (Hit <CTRL-C> to stop)                    MGEN: Packets Tx'd: 6000
MGEN: Transmission period:     30.001 seconds.
MGEN: Ave Tx pkt rate   :    199.992 pps.
MGEN: Interface Stats   :       eth0
           Frames Tx'd :        0
               Tx Errors :      0
MGEN: Done.
```

Since the *mgen* test was configured to produce 6000 packets that match term 1 of the firewall filter, you should see a packet count of 6000, and approximately 60 samples (1 percent of the total) for this flow in the sample log:

```
user@r2> show firewall
Filter/Counter                          Packet count              Byte count
local-re
   disallowed                                      0                       0
sample
   udp-test                                     6000                  552000
```

The *udp-test* counter is spot on. Now to verify the number of samples taken:

```
user@r2> show log /var/tmp/sample | match 200.0.0.86
# Mar 13 17:47:12      200.0.0.86      10.0.1.200  5000  1047    17  0x0    92    4  0x0    0x0
# Mar 13 17:47:12      200.0.0.86      10.0.1.200  5000  1047    17  0x0    92    4  0x0    0x0
...
user@r2> show log /var/tmp/sample |match 200.0.0.86 | count
Count: 55 lines
user@r2>
```

Nominally, you should see 60 samples, but in this case 55 samples were taken of the test flow. In a subsequent test, 65 samples were observed for the same flow, so over time the actual rate of sampled packets should closely track the nominal sampling rate configured.

The Need for Post Processing

So great, you now have a large flat file that contains thousands of sampled packets. What are you supposed to do with all this raw data? For firewall filter verification or the simple tracing of a DoS attack, the information in this file can be used as is; for the complex analysis of protocol flows and transit traffic patterns, the format of this flat file would mandate a large amount of manual labor or the need to write customized post processing tools. Then again, you could just enable cflowd export and leave the post sampling analysis to the readily available off-the-shelf tools that were designed for this purpose.

Tools such as cflowd also offer the significant advantage of centralized data collection and flow-record storage. The use of a flat sampling file on multiple machines places the burden of sample collection on the operator and can result in storage limitations, as the RE has limited disk storage when compared to the storage abilities of a high-end server.

Because the collection and processing of NetFlow records that have been collected by numerous cflowd processes can result in significant processing and storage requirements on the collector host, it is recommended that the operator use a high-performance platform dedicated to the function of data collection and analysis. Such a machine should be equipped with a high-performance and large-capacity file system such as a Small Computer System Interface (SCSI) array to prevent storage bottlenecks. Exported samples should never be placed on a machine's root partition to avoid the risk of crashing the collection host.

Configuring cflowd Export

The *forwarding-options* portion of R2's configuration has been modified to support the export of NetFlow version 5 records. To assist with troubleshooting, the `local-dump` option has been enabled so that copies of the exported records will also be written to the RE's hard drive. This option will be removed after the proper operation of cflowd export has been verified, because using it on a production router is not recommended due to the increased RE processing burden. The modified *forwarding-options* stanza on R2 is displayed next; the `autonomous-system-type` and `version` options have been explicitly set to their default in this example, and the remote cflowd host is 10.0.1.100:

```
[edit forwarding-options sampling]
user@r2# show
input {
    family inet {
        rate 100;
        run-length 0;
    }
```

```
    }
output {
    cflowd 10.0.1.100 {
        port 2055;
        version 5;
        local-dump;
        autonomous-system-type origin;
    }
}
```

Analyzing the local-dump File

Before looking for NetFlow records on the cflowd host, it is a good idea to verify that flow records are being written to the router's hard drive. Locally dumped flow records are placed into /var/log/sampled by default; the operator can use the trace-options knob under *[forwarding-options sampling]* to specify a different filename if desired. Monitoring the "sampled" file confirms that records are being correctly written in this case:

```
user@r2> monitor start sampled
user@r2>
*** /var/log/sampled ***
Mar 13 20:28:25 v5 flow entry
Mar 13 20:28:25     Src addr: 192.168.12.1
Mar 13 20:28:25     Dst addr: 200.0.0.1
Mar 13 20:28:25     Nhop addr: 10.0.2.2
Mar 13 20:28:25     Input interface: 19
Mar 13 20:28:25     Output interface: 17
Mar 13 20:28:25     Pkts in flow: 366
Mar 13 20:28:25     Bytes in flow: 30744
Mar 13 20:28:25     Start time of flow: 17799
Mar 13 20:28:25     End time of flow: 17845
Mar 13 20:28:25     Src port: 0
Mar 13 20:28:25     Dst port: 0
Mar 13 20:28:25     TCP flags: 0x0
Mar 13 20:28:25     IP proto num: 1
Mar 13 20:28:25     TOS: 0x0
Mar 13 20:28:25     Src AS: 65050
Mar 13 20:28:25     Dst AS: 65010
Mar 13 20:28:25     Src netmask len: 32
Mar 13 20:28:25     Dst netmask len: 24
Mar 13 20:28:25 v5 flow entry
```

```
Mar 13 20:28:25      Src addr: 192.168.12.1
Mar 13 20:28:25      Dst addr: 200.0.0.1
Mar 13 20:28:25      Nhop addr: 10.0.2.2
Mar 13 20:28:25      Input interface: 19
Mar 13 20:28:25      Output interface: 17
Mar 13 20:28:25      Pkts in flow: 1
Mar 13 20:28:25      Bytes in flow: 52
Mar 13 20:28:25      Start time of flow: 17786
Mar 13 20:28:25      End time of flow: 17786
Mar 13 20:28:25      Src port: 1042
Mar 13 20:28:25      Dst port: 23
Mar 13 20:28:25      TCP flags: 0x10
Mar 13 20:28:25      IP proto num: 6
Mar 13 20:28:25      TOS: 0x10
Mar 13 20:28:25      Src AS: 65050
Mar 13 20:28:25      Dst AS: 65010
Mar 13 20:28:25      Src netmask len: 32
Mar 13 20:28:25      Dst netmask len: 24
... (third recorded omitted for brevity)
cflowd header:
Mar 13 20:28:25   Num-records: 3
Mar 13 20:28:25   Version: 5
Mar 13 20:28:25   Flow seq num: 0
Mar 13 20:28:25   Engine id: 0
Mar 13 20:28:25   Engine type: 0
Mar 13 20:28:25 Sent v5 flows (0 entries left in tree)
Mar 13 20:28:25 Read 71 bytes; total 829
```

The flows are dumped with the flow records listed first followed by the common cflowd header. Here, two of the three flows, and the corresponding cflowd header, are shown. A *flow* is defined as a unique grouping of source and destinations address, a protocol, and the associated ports, and each flow record displays these values. Here you see that the ICMP traffic is reported in the first flow, while the Telnet session is reported in the second flow record.

You can also see that the flow records contain the source and destination AS numbers, the IP next-hop used to forward the packet, and the coding of the IP TOS and TCP flag fields. It should be obvious that the RE has an added processing burden when exporting flow records, as it must populate the records with values that cannot be derived directly from the sampled packets—that is, the origin/destination AS numbers and the subnet mask fields.

The flow records also indicate the flow's ingress and egress interfaces using the SNMP interface index; this should be contrasted to the IFL index that is used to identify the ingress interface in the locally stored flat sampling file. Like IFL, the SNMP index can change over time, especially when hardware changes have occurred, so prompt analysis is recommended when using this information to track the source of spoofed packets.

The Engine id and Engine type fields are used to identify the source of the flow record when multiple active REs are controlling a single box. Juniper routers do not use these fields, as their design always results in a single RE in control of the entire sampling process. With Juniper routers The *Router ID* (RID) provides sufficient information to disambiguate the source of a particular record; redundant REs should never have the same RID assigned to both the primary and backup RE.

cflowd Analysis

Since the local dump of flow records indicates that all is well on the Juniper router, now cast your attention to the cflowd host to verify that the flow records are being received. A brief demonstration of flow record analysis using several of the utilities included with the cflowd and arts++ packages is provided. During these captures, the *mgen* utility on the Linux machine was configured to send 200 UDP packets per second to port 5000:

```
[root@snafu bin]# ./flowwatch '(protocol == 17)'
FLOW
  index:          0xc7ffff
  router:         10.0.3.1
  src IP:         10.0.1.200
  dst IP:         200.0.0.86
  input ifIndex:  18
  output ifIndex: 17
  src port:       1047
  dst port:       5000
  pkts:           141
  bytes:          12972
  IP nexthop:     10.0.2.2
  start time:     Tue Mar 13 15:07:32 2001
  end time:       Tue Mar 13 15:07:32 2001
  protocol:       17
  tos:            0
  src AS:         65021
  dst AS:         65010
  src masklen:    24
  dst masklen:    24
  TCP flags:      0x0
  engine type:    0
  engine id:      0
```

The output of the cflowd *flowwatch* utility, which has been told to display only UDP flows, confirms that flow records are being received from R2. The raw cflowd dump file can also be analyzed offline with the cflowd *flowdump* utility.

Using the cflowd *cfdases* tool we can see the source and destination AS numbers for the traffic being sampled:

```
[root@snafu bin]# ./cfdases 192.168.5.1
period: 03/13/2001 15:09:46 - 03/13/2001 15:13:46 PST (4 min, 0 sec)
ifIndex: 18 (fe-0/0/1.0 10.0.3.1)
   srcAS  dstAS       packets         bytes       pkts/sec      bits/sec
   -----  -----  ------------  ------------  ------------  ------------
   65021  65010           435         40020             1          1334
   65021  65021           469        687786             1         22926

ifIndex: 19 (fe-0/0/2.0 10.0.6.1)
   srcAS  dstAS       packets         bytes       pkts/sec      bits/sec
   -----  -----  ------------  ------------  ------------  ------------
   65050  65010          1765        148100             7          4936
```

One of the flows indicates that the source and destination AS were both 65021. In reality, this flow represents an FTP transfer from 10.0.1.200 in AS 65021 to 192.168.0.1 (R1's *lo0* address) in AS 65010. The erroneous source AS is the result of a static route on R2 that is preferred over the same prefix being advertised with BGP by R1:

```
user@r2> show route 192.168.0.1
inet.0: 15 destinations, 15 routes (14 active, 0 holddown, 1 hidden)
+ = Active Route, - = Last Active, * = Both
192.168.0.1/32     *[Static/5] 00:00:21
                    > to 10.0.2.2 via fe-0/0/0.0
                    [BGP/170] 08:27:48, localpref 100
                      AS path: 65010 I
                    > to 10.0.2.2 via fe-0/0/0.0
```

This is an important point, as it demonstrates that the RE will populate flow records for a given destination based on information associated with the preferred routing protocol. This anomaly can be fixed through the addition of AS path information under the static route's definition:

```
[edit]
user@r2# show routing-options static
route 192.168.0.1/32 {
    next-hop 10.0.2.2;
```

```
    as-path {
        path 65010;
    }
}
```

The cflowd *cfdportmatrix* tool breaks down flows based on the protocols and ports being used:

```
[root@snafu bin]# ./cfdportmatrix 192.168.5.1
period: 03/13/2001 15:09:46 - 03/13/2001 15:13:46 PST (4 min, 0 sec)
ifIndex: 18 (fe-0/0/1.0 10.0.3.1)
   srcPort  dstPort       packets         bytes      pkts/sec      bits/sec
   -------  -------   -------------  -------------  --------------------------
      2816       20             12          17960             0           598
      2817       20             10          15000             0           500
      2818       20             42          63000             0          2100
      2819       20             35          50516             0          1683
      2820       20             53          78428             0          2614
      2821       20             98         142000             0          4733
      2822       20             45          65476             0          2182
      2823       20             72         107344             0          3578
      2824       20             44          63976             0          2132
      1047     5000            435          40020             1          1334
      2812       21              1             74             0             2
ifIndex: 19 (fe-0/0/2.0 10.0.6.1)
   srcPort  dstPort       packets         bytes      pkts/sec      bits/sec
   -------  -------   -------------  -------------  --------------------------
      1042       23              5            260             0             8
```

The numerous FTP data ports (port 20) listed under the *fe-0/0/1* interface result from an *mput* * transfer with prompting turned off. As each transfer completes, a new data connection is negotiated for the next file to be transferred. You can see from this display that the FTP control port has been sampled (21) and that the UDP test traffic on port 5000 has also made the cut.

It is interesting to note that the *1* that appears under the pkts/sec column represents the 200 packets-per-second flow coming from the *mgen* utility. If you divide the total packet count of 435 by the 4-minute length of the current sampling interval, you arrive at an actual packet-per-second rate of 1.8. This is reasonably close to the expected rate of 2 (1 percent of 200), considering all the other traffic that was flowing during the test.

The tools included with the cflowd package can display statistics only for the current 5-minute sampling interval. For long-term analysis, the raw flow data needs to be collected by the *cfdcollect* entity for storage in an arts++ binary file. Once converted to this binary format, a variety of utilities included in the arts++ package may be used to analyze flow data collected over a 24-hour period:

```
[root@linux-box /root]# artsases
usr/local/arts/data/cflowd/192.168.5.1/arts.20010314
...
router:  192.168.5.1
ifIndex: 19 (fe-0/0/2.0 10.0.6.1)
period:  03/13/2001 22:14:47 - 03/13/2001 22:19:47 PST
  Src AS  Dst AS         Pkts       Pkts/sec        Bytes     Bits/sec
  ------  ------   -------------  -------------  -------------  ------------
   65050   65010             6        0.02             312      8.32
router:  192.168.5.1
ifIndex: 18 (fe-0/0/1.0 10.0.3.1)
period:  03/13/2001 22:19:47 - 03/13/2001 22:24:47 PST
  Src AS  Dst AS         Pkts       Pkts/sec        Bytes     Bits/sec
  ------  ------   -------------  -------------  -------------  ------------
   65021   65010           598        1.99333        315744   8419.84
router:  192.168.5.1
ifIndex: 19 (fe-0/0/2.0 10.0.6.1)
period:  03/13/2001 22:19:47 - 03/13/2001 22:24:47 PST
  Src AS  Dst AS         Pkts       Pkts/sec        Bytes     Bits/sec
  ------  ------   -------------  -------------  -------------  ------------
   65050   65010             7        0.0233333        364      9.70667
...
```

Here, the operator has run the *artsases* utility against a arts++ data file. The file is automatically named according to the exporting router and the day of collection. This screen dump shows the portion of the arts++ file representing the 5-minute collection period that began at 10:19:47 P.M. on March 13. The traffic generated by the *mgen* utility (arriving on *fe-0/0/1*) has been measured at 1.99333 packets per second—a value that falls right in line with the configured 1 percent sampling rate and the 200 packets per second being produced by the traffic generator.

After the FTP transfer completed, another NetFlow analysis tool called the *Extremely Happy NetFlow Tool* (EHNT), was evoked in "top" mode with the results following. Here you can see that autonomous networks 65050 and 65021 are both sending data to AS 65010 and that the bulk of the traffic is being sourced from AS 65050. This knowledge might cause the administrator of AS 65021 to re-evaluate his transit peering agreement with AS 65050:

```
[root@nat ehnt-0.1]# ./ehnt -s localhost:2056 -m top
Starting.
Summary for interval (00:06:52 total) ending Sat Mar 10 14:00:10 2001
 Total          5kbits/s
Rank|-------------Source---------------|  |--------------Dest---------------|
    |----AS Name/Num----|-bw;% of total-|  |----AS Name/Num----|-bw,% of total-|
  1:      <unknown>( 65050)     4 ; 86.93%     <unknown>( 65010)     5 ; 100.00%
  2:      <unknown>( 65021)     1 ; 13.07%     <unknown>(     0)     0 ; 0.00%
  3:      <unknown>(     0)     0 ; 0.00%      <unknown>(     0)     0 ; 0.00%
```

```
 4:     <unknown>(    0)      0 ; 0.00%    <unknown>(    0)      0 ; 0.00%
 5:     <unknown>(    0)      0 ; 0.00%    <unknown>(    0)      0 ; 0.00%
 6:     <unknown>(    0)      0 ; 0.00%    <unknown>(    0)      0 ; 0.00%
 7:     <unknown>(    0)      0 ; 0.00%    <unknown>(    0)      0 ; 0.00%
 8:     <unknown>(    0)      0 ; 0.00%    <unknown>(    0)      0 ; 0.00%
 9:     <unknown>(    0)      0 ; 0.00%    <unknown>(    0)      0 ; 0.00%
10:     <unknown>(    0)      0 ; 0.00%    <unknown>(    0)      0 ; 0.00%
. . . . .
```

The information provided by statistical sampling can provide network operators with invaluable insights into the nature of the traffic that is flowing across their routers. Armed with this information, network administrators can make decisions regarding the need for bandwidth upgrades, MPLS-based traffic engineering, and renegotiated peering relationships. In this rather simple example, the operator of AS 65021 may conclude that a traffic engineered path should be established to AS 65010 due to the volume of FTP traffic flowing into that AS.

Case Study 5: Tracing and Minimizing DoS Attacks

This case study will discuss how a network operator can use IP2-related features and commands to trace the source of a DoS attack while also minimizing its disruption. As the use of forged source addresses is becoming increasingly more common in these types of attacks, the ability to associate a packet with an ingress interface is a powerful feature of the IP2. Since the source address of these packets is forged, ingress interface tracking is the only real means of backtracking towards their source.

You will be happy to hear that no new information is required for this scenario. If you've made it this far, you need only bring to bear the various IP2 features and CLI commands already described in this chapter to solve this case study. The topology for this case study is shown in Figure 16-16.

This scenario begins with a frantic call from a customer at the R1 site who is complaining that their public server keeps crashing and that their Internet access is virtually nonexistent. You log into R2 and issue various interface-related commands to determine whether the access link is operating correctly. PING tests indicate that, while traffic is being lost, basic connectivity is there. You next enter the `monitor interface fe-0/0/0` CLI command and notice that the outgoing packet and bytes counters are nearly pegged at line rate! You think to yourself "Something very odd is happening here," and are thankful that your routers are IP2 equipped.

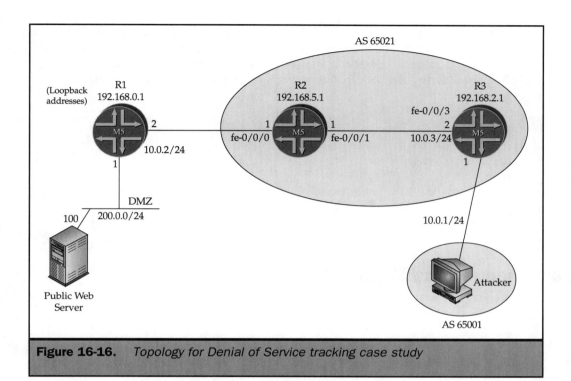

Figure 16-16.   *Topology for Denial of Service tracking case study*

The Initial Filter

You decide to create an "accept-all" filter with a logging action to get a quick idea of the nature of the traffic. You hope that once the specific nature of the traffic is determined, the filter can be modified to discard the suspect traffic to reduce the effects of the DoS attack. To this end, you apply the following filter in the outbound direction of the *fe-0/0/0* interface on R2:

```
[edit]
lab@r2# show firewall
filter dos {
    term 1 {
        then log;
    }
}
```

As you are aware that you will soon be logging every packet that exits *fe-0/0/0,* you decide to leave the filter in place only long enough to capture a snapshot of the traffic heading to the customer. Long-term analysis would be better suited to statistical sampling, considering the nondiscriminating nature of your filter and the high data rates involved.

```
[edit]
lab@r2# commit
commit complete
[edit]
lab@r2# deactivate interfaces fe-0/0/0 unit 0 family inet filter
[edit]
lab@r2# commit
commit complete
```

Log Analysis and Filter Modification

Log analysis makes it clear what you are dealing with:

```
[edit]
lab@r2# run show firewall log
Time      Filter    A Interface       Pro Source address  Destination address
06:13:29 pfe        A fe-0/0/1.0       TCP 172.23.1.69     200.0.0.1:20
06:13:29 pfe        A fe-0/0/1.0       TCP 172.23.1.69     200.0.0.1:20
06:13:29 pfe        A fe-0/0/1.0       TCP 172.23.1.69     200.0.0.1:20
06:13:29 pfe        A fe-0/0/1.0       TCP 172.23.1.69     200.0.0.1:20
06:13:29 pfe        A fe-0/0/1.0       TCP 172.23.1.69     200.0.0.1:20
06:13:29 pfe        A fe-0/0/1.0       TCP 172.23.1.69     200.0.0.1:20
06:13:29 pfe        A fe-0/0/1.0       TCP 172.23.1.69     200.0.0.1:19
06:13:29 pfe        A fe-0/0/1.0       TCP 172.23.1.69     200.0.0.1:19
06:13:29 pfe        A fe-0/0/1.0       TCP 172.23.1.69     200.0.0.1:19
06:13:29 pfe        A fe-0/0/1.0       TCP 172.23.1.69     200.0.0.1:19
```

The vast majority of the packets in the log claim to come from address 172.23.1.69. The presence of a martian address is a sure sign of address spoofing at work. The repeat hits to sequential TCP port numbers makes this look like a TCP SYN flood attack. The use of sampling could easily confirm this theory as sampled packets display the settings of the TCP flag field.

The log entries show that all the traffic is arriving on R2's *fe-0/0/1* interface. This coupled with the single forged address makes it likely that this is not a Distributed Denial of Service (D-DoS) attack. With this information, you now know that you must move your logging filter to R3's *fe-0/0/3* interface to track further back toward the source of the traffic.

Applying this filter to R3 allows you to determine that the traffic is entering your autonomous system from your peering point with AS 65001. You initiate contact with the AS 65001's administrator while also applying an inbound filter to discard all traffic from 172.23.1.69 as it attempts to enter your network.

Equally important, you can now minimize the disruption of the attack by modifying the filter on R2 to discard all suspect traffic. Even if you had to discard all traffic addressed to the sever, such as might be the case when dealing with a large D-DoS attack, your filter would still free up access link bandwidth so the user's other Internet applications can resume normal operation.

Had this have been a distributed SYN attack, you would likely have chosen to block all TCP SYN segments being sent to the server, as the number of remote zombie machines is likely to be high, which makes a source address filter problematic. The following modified filter example below makes use of counting to assist in determining when the SYN flood has subsided:

```
lab@r2# show
term 1 {
    from {
        source-address {
            172.23.1.69/32;
        }
        protocol tcp;
    }
    then {
        count dos-counter;
        discard;
    }
}
term 2 {
    then accept;
}
```

Index

X

Y

INTERNATIONAL CONTACT INFORMATION

AUSTRALIA
McGraw-Hill Book Company Australia Pty. Ltd.
TEL +61-2-9417-9899
FAX +61-2-9417-5687
http://www.mcgraw-hill.com.au
books-it_sydney@mcgraw-hill.com

CANADA
McGraw-Hill Ryerson Ltd.
TEL +905-430-5000
FAX +905-430-5020
http://www.mcgrawhill.ca

**GREECE, MIDDLE EAST,
NORTHERN AFRICA**
McGraw-Hill Hellas
TEL +30-1-656-0990-3-4
FAX +30-1-654-5525

MEXICO (Also serving Latin America)
McGraw-Hill Interamericana Editores S.A. de C.V.
TEL +525-117-1583
FAX +525-117-1589
http://www.mcgraw-hill.com.mx
fernando_castellanos@mcgraw-hill.com

SINGAPORE (Serving Asia)
McGraw-Hill Book Company
TEL +65-863-1580
FAX +65-862-3354
http://www.mcgraw-hill.com.sg
mghasia@mcgraw-hill.com

SOUTH AFRICA
McGraw-Hill South Africa
TEL +27-11-622-7512
FAX +27-11-622-9045
robyn_swanepoel@mcgraw-hill.com

**UNITED KINGDOM & EUROPE
(Excluding Southern Europe)**
McGraw-Hill Education Europe
TEL +44-1-628-502500
FAX +44-1-628-770224
http://www.mcgraw-hill.co.uk
computing_neurope@mcgraw-hill.com

ALL OTHER INQUIRIES Contact:
Osborne/McGraw-Hill
TEL +1-510-549-6600
FAX +1-510-883-7600
http://www.osborne.com
omg_international@mcgraw-hill.com